Second Edition

TERRORISM AND COUNTERTERRORISM

UNDERSTANDING THE NEW SECURITY ENVIRONMENT

READINGS & INTERPRETATIONS

RUSSELL D. HOWARD
BRIGADIER GENERAL USA (RET.)

REID L. SAWYER
MAJOR USA

FOREWORD BY
BARRY R. MCCAFFREY
GENERAL USA (RET.)

McGraw Hill
Contemporary Learning Series

STAFF

Larry Loeppke Managing Editor
Jill Peter Senior Developmental Editor
Nichole Altman Developmental Editor
Lori Church Permissions Coordinator
Beth Kundert Production Manager
Jane Mohr Project Manager
Kari Voss Lead Typesetter
Luke David eContent Coordinator
Maggie Lytle Cover Designer

McGraw Hill **Contemporary Learning Series**

2460 Kerper Blvd., Dubuque, Iowa 52001

Cover: Tom Sperduto

Cover Design Maggie Lytle

The credit section for this book begins on page 602 and is considered an extension of the copyright page.

Library of Congress Control Number 2002106286

ISBN 0-07-352771-8

Printed in the United States of America

10 9 8 7 6 5 4 3 2

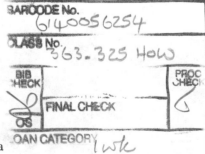

Second Edition

TERRORISM AND COUNTERTERRORISM

Understanding the New Security Environment

Readings & Interpretations

About the Authors

Brigadier General (Retired) Russell D. Howard is the former head of the Department of Social Sciences and the founding director of the Combating Terrorism Center at West Point. As a Special Forces officer, Brigadier General (Retired) Howard served at every level of command including: A Detachment Commander in the 7th Special Forces Group to Group, B Detachment Commander in the 1st Special Forces Group, Battalion Commander in the Special Warfare Center and School, and Commander of the 1st Special Forces Group. In preparation for his academic position, he earned degrees from San Jose State University, the University of Maryland, the Monterey Institute of International Studies, and Harvard University. Presently, he is finishing a Ph.D. in international security studies at the Fletcher School of Law and Diplomacy. During the course of his career, Brigadier General (Retired) Howard has had antiterror and counterterror responsibilities and has taught and published articles on the subject. He is also the co-editor of *Defeating Terrorism and Homeland Security and Terrorism.*

Major Reid Sawyer, a career military intelligence officer, is the former director of Terrorism Studies and a founding member of the Combating Terrorism Center at the United States Military Academy. He is currently a fellow with the Center and an adjunct assistant professor at Columbia University, where he teaches a graduate seminar on terrorism studies. As an intelligence officer, Major Sawyer previously served in counternarcotics and special operations assignments. Major Sawyer earned his undergraduate degree from the United States Military Academy and holds a masters of public administration from Columbia University, where he is currently pursuing his doctorate degree. Major Sawyer has lectured widely on the topic of terrorism and counterterrorism. He is also the co-editor of *Defeating Terrorism.*

Contents in Brief

Contents

Foreword

On September 11, 2001, the United States was confronted with the stark reality of modern terrorism. The brutal murder of thousands of innocent lives stripped away our ability to ignore the threat posed by the emergence of transnational terrorist organizations. The terrorism we witnessed on September 11, 2001 was a giant escalation of an evolving threat. Prior to these tragic attacks, Americans had witnessed a steadily growing series of violent attacks culminating in more than 5,000 casualties in the terrorist bombings of our East African embassies in 1998. The attacks in Madrid and in London unequivocally demonstrate that the terrorist targets are shifting from the Global South to Western Europe and that new members are joining what has become a global movement. The question is not *if* further terrorist attacks will occur in the United States, but *when* and *what* magnitude. One thing is certain, terrorists will continue to try to adapt to the changing counterterror security environment.

Terrorism, at its very roots, centers on fear and targets our liberal democratic values. The fear generated by terrorism speaks to our vulnerabilities and the government's apparent lack of ability to stop further attacks. The current proliferation of lethal technologies, combined with radical ideologies, potentially presents truly horrific scenarios. We will continue to witness new forms of terrorism, be it viruses that selectively attack target populations or suicide bombers attempting to slaughter our children in our nation's schools. It is imperative for all of us to study and learn about these new threats. We will be driven to understand why terrorism occurs and how best to counter terrorism's driving forces. No single solution or sole instrument of national power can hope to resolve these questions alone. Instead, we must search out new and different solutions that challenge our traditional assumptions. The goal of this superb collection of articles is to heighten the reader's awareness of the critical issues related to the threat of terrorism. Although it is impossible for any single work to address the entire breadth of the terrorism field, this volume captures the most salient pieces on the subject.

There are many terrorism experts in academia. However, there are only a handful of individuals who combine impressive academic credentials with extensive special operations combat and training experience. The editors of this compilation, Brigadier General (Retired) Russ Howard and Major Reid Sawyer, are two distinguished scholars who have also spent careers on the cutting edge of U.S. military special operations. Their combined experience of over 40 years in the front lines of the struggle to prevent terrorism provides them with a distinct and uniquely informed perspective on the current war on terrorism. Together, they have gathered and edited the best works of more than fifteen of the leading commentators on terrorism at a critical time in our nation's history.

This superbly researched book also reflects their experience in teaching security-related courses in the Department of Social Sciences at West Point. Brigadier General

(Retired) Howard and Major Sawyer have refined their thinking on the topic by their experimentation with the curriculum in these national security courses. Students of national security polity will find this book to be a unique combination of well-known and astute thinkers who have articulated the current and future policy implications of terrorism. The relevant experience of both Howard and Sawyer as editors places them in the best position to bring together this wide-ranging material.

There is much uncertainty about the future. However, we are sure that only through diligent and creative study can America effectively address this very real asymmetrical threat to our national security. We are challenged to develop a conceptual framework to reevaluate the security environment. Clearly we must craft flexible and effective counterterrorism strategies. The policy solutions to this complex threat of terrorism do not lie solely with our military, or even our government. Instead, we must create cooperative efforts to find a national solution to manage the terrorist threat, which involves a partnership with the international community combined with an integrated and coherent strategy that unites community, state, and federal authorities supported by business, the health professions, and academia. We also cannot allow ourselves to become trapped in overly simplistic views of the threat. Our challenge is to dramatically embrace our domestic security while carefully preserving our precious freedoms guaranteed in the Bill of Rights as well as the safety and dignity of foreigners living among us.

Through the thoughtful study of the definitions, issues, and recommendations provided by these accomplished authors and the editors, we can hopefully move toward a better understanding of terrorism and its causes.

Barry R. McCaffrey

Preface

The haunting image of New York's falling twin towers defined for the world the reality of the "new terrorism." Americans had faced terrorism before September 11. However, terrorism's previous incarnations, were not nearly as organized, deadly, or personal as the attacks inflicted on New York City and Washington, D.C., or on that remote Pennsylvania field.

In 1984 when I first became involved in the antiterrorism and counterterrorism efforts, most international and national terrorism was ideological. It was part of the East versus West, left versus right confrontation—a small but dangerous side-show to the greater, bipolar, Cold War drama. In the past, terrorism was almost always the province of groups of militants that had the backing of political forces and states hostile to American interests. Under the old rules, "terrorists wanted a lot of people watching, not a lot of people dead."[1] They did not want large body counts because they wanted converts. They wanted a seat at the table. Today's terrorists are not particularly concerned about converts and don't want a seat at the table, "They want to destroy the table and everyone sitting at it."[2]

What is new to me and my generation, but not to Reid Sawyer and his, is the emergence of terrorism that is not ideological in a political sense. Instead it is inspired by religious extremism and ethnic-separatist elements, who might be individuals such as the Unabomber, or like-minded people working in cells, small groups, or larger coalitions.[3] They do not answer completely to any government, operate across national borders, and have access to funding and advanced technology.[4] Such groups are not bound by the same constraints or motivated by the same goals as nation-states. And, unlike state-sponsored groups, religious extremists, ethnic separatists, and lone Unabombers are not susceptible to traditional diplomacy or military deterrence. There is no state with which to negotiate or to retaliate against. And, today's terrorists are not concerned about limiting casualties. Religious terrorists, such as al Qaeda in particular, want casualties—lots of them.[5]

The new terrorism is not an ideological ism like communism or capitalism whose value can be debated in the classroom or decided at polls. It is an ancient tactic and instrument of conflict. Terrorism today has a global reach that it did not have before globalization and the information technology revolution. It can ride the back of the Web, use advanced communications to move immense financial sums from Sudan to the Philippines, to Australia, to banks in Florida.[6] And, for $28.50, any Internet surfer can purchase *Bacteriological Warfare: A Major Threat to North America*, which shows how to grow deadly bacteria that could be used in a weapon of mass destruction.

Clearly, the United States and its citizens are favored targets of the new terrorists. Many wonder why. "Why do They Hate Us?" was the banner headline in *Newsweek* and the *Christian Science Monitor* soon after 9/11. Why should Islamic extremists hate us? After all, was it not the United States that saved those who follow the Islamic faith in Kuwait, liberated them in Iraq, and continues to protect them in Bosnia and Kosovo? Is it a Jihad, a war of faiths between Christians and Moslems as some suggest? Or is the United

States a target because of the resentment it has spread through societies demoralized by their recent history. As one knowledgeable journalist put it, "A sense of failure and injustice is rising in the throats of millions," because Arab nations have lost three wars against Israel, their arch-foe and America's ally.[7]

Many also believe that globalization is not only a technological tool for terrorists, but that it is a root cause of terrorism either separately or in conjunction with religious extremism. Extreme Muslim fundamentalists and others who have missed the rewards of globalization worry that unbridled globalization exploits workers and replaces ancient cultures with McDonald's and Mickey Mouse.[8] According to some, globalization is based on the American economic system, and because the United States is the dominant world power, it has succeeded in expanding the reach of its version of globalization to more and more areas of the world. As the gap between the rich and poor has grown wider during the last twenty years of U.S.-led globalization the poor have watched American wealth and hegemony expand, while they, themselves, have received little or no benefit.[9]

There are other theories about rising terrorism and future targets, many of which will be covered in this book. One thing is certain however, America is a target. It has been attacked and will be again unless the attacks can be prevented or preempted. Rudi Giuliani made this very clear to West Point's 2002 graduating class when he was the guest speaker at their final dinner banquet. He theorized that America was attacked for a number of reasons: it prizes political and economic freedom, elects its political leaders, and has lifted people out of poverty; it also has religious freedom, respects human rights as well as the rights of women. America's adversaries do not, and they are threatened by the freedoms we have. "We are right and they are wrong," Giuliani said to thunderous applause. "There is no excuse and no justification for these attacks," he said. The mayor told the cadets that America has already won the war on terrorism. "We still have a lot of battles to win, but we have actually won the war on terrorism because the terrorists tried, but could not break our spirit."

This book, edited at West Point, will address those "battles to win"—how to fight and win them, and why America and the free world are in the dubious position of having to fight the battles in the first place. Why edit the book at West Point? More importantly, why have two career soldiers edit the book? Brigadier General Dan Kaufman, West Point's dean, answered these questions in a Los Angeles Times interview. "Suddenly, now the world is a much more dangerous place," he said. "The nation is at risk again. The notion that the American homeland is vulnerable is new to all of us. Given where West Point sits—fifty miles from ground zero—there is a sense of immediacy here."[10]

Organization

Terrorism and Counterterrorism: Understanding the New Security Environment, 2nd ed., is in two parts. Part I analyzes the philosophical, political, and religious roots of terrorist activities around the world and discusses the national, regional, and global effects of historical and recent terrorist acts. In addition to material on the threats from suicide bombers, as well as from chemical, biological, radiological and nuclear weapons, there are also important contributions analyzing new and growing threats: narcoterrorism, terrorist recruitment on the Internet, and genomic terrorism.

Part I, "Defining the Threat"

Part I contains six chapters. Chapter 1, "Terrorism Defined," consists of articles by Bruce Hoffman, Paul Pillar, and Eqbal Ahmad, who define terrorism and address several specific questions, in some cases from very different perspectives: What is terrorism? What is counterterrorism? Who is a terrorist? And, why do these questions matter? Hoffman's "Defining Terrorism" emphasizes the changing nature of terrorism. He succinctly defines its past and present, explains its evolution, and delineates terrorism from other concepts such as insurgency, criminals, etc. His offering is an important primer that will prepare the reader for the rest of the book. In his article, "The Dimensions of Terrorism and Counterterrorism," Paul Pillar considers what terrorism is and why it is a real problem. As the title suggests, however, Pillar goes further and identifies the necessary elements and limitations of any counterterrorism policy. Pillar, a CIA veteran, believes counterterrorism policy should not stand alone but be part of a broader effort to maintain national security and that it needs to be integrated into all foreign policy decision making. Ahmad's "Terrorism: Theirs & Ours," like Hoffman's article also emphasizes change. "To begin with," writes Ahmad, "terrorists change. The terrorist of yesterday is the hero of today, and the hero of yesterday becomes the terrorist of today." His example is Osama bin Laden, who was once an American ally in the fight against the Soviet Union and is now public enemy number one.

What motivates people to turn to terrorism is examined in Chapter 2, "Why Terrorism?" Articles by professional colleagues Martha Crenshaw and Audrey Kurth Cronin look at more than the traditional psychological, cultural, and socioeconomic reasons for terrorism. Addressing terrorism in a greater globalization context in "The Logic of Terrorism: Terrorist Behavior as a Product of Strategic Choice," Crenshaw shows that terrorism is a perfectly rational and logical choice for some individuals and groups: "The central problem is to determine when extremist organizations find terrorism useful. ... Terrorism is not the only method of working toward radical goals, and thus it must be compared to the alternative strategies available to dissidents."

Audrey Kurth Cronin's "Behind the Curve: Globalization and International Terrorism," argues that terrorism is not only a reaction to globalization but is also facilitated by it, while the U.S. response to the terrorist threat has been reactive and anachronistic. She introduces a theme echoed elsewhere in this volume that while military power is an important tool in this conflict, it can only be a supporting instrument in the campaign against terrorism.

Chapter 3, "The New Terrorism," explores the rise and impact of new terrorism in greater depth and then looks at some of the technological and control mechanisms that make today's terrorists more difficult to detect and defeat than the left-wing terrorists of earlier eras.

I begin this dialogue in "Understanding Al Qaeda's Application of the New Terrorism," by outlining eight ways today's terrorism differs from that of the Cold War. Specifically the new terrorism is more violent and better financed than in the Cold War era. The new terrorists operate globally, are better trained, more difficult to penetrate, and have access to and say they will use weapons of mass destruction. Perhaps most important for all to remember is that victory will be elusive. More than likely there will be no formal surrender by a defeated foe, no armistice ending combat on acceptable terms, no arrest and incarceration of all the members of a terrorist organization. My article discusses the advantages present-day terrorists, particularly al Qaeda, have over their counterparts in the 1960s, 70s, and 80s.

A trio of RAND specialists—John Arquilla, David Ronfeldt, and Michele Zanini—suggest in "Networks, Netwar, and Information-Age Terrorism" that a new type of enemy and warfare will be the product of the information revolution, including the rise of new, more complex forms of terrorism. New systems and organizations and modes of conflict used by modern-day terrorists will inevitably affect the nature and styles of warfare. Using "netwar" and "cyberwar" as weapons, these terrorists will attack modern societies' vulnerabilities. The authors recommend that new organizations, strategies, technologies, and doctrines will be required to defeat this new form of enemy.

An old saying I learned as a child is that "More people have been killed in the name of God than for any other reason." Things have not changed. Indeed the articles in Chapter 4, "Religion and the Intersection with Terrorism," argue that religious terrorism is on the rise and is unprecedented in its militancy and activism. In his article, "Terrorism in the Name of Religion," Ranstorp explores the reasons for the dramatic increase of religiously motivated terrorism. Mark Juergensmeyer's "Logic of Religious Violence" uses the struggle of the Sikhs in India as a case study to suggest why some religions "propel the faithful rather easily into militant confrontation" while others do not. "The pattern of religious violence of the Sikhs could be that of Irish Catholics, or Shi'ite Muslims in Palestine, or fundamentalist Christian bombers of abortion clinics in the United States." He argues that violence associated with religion is not an aberration but arises from the fundamental beliefs of all the world's major religions.

Chapter 5, "Weapons of Mass Destruction," explains why weapons of mass destruction (WMD)—chemical, biological, radiological, and nuclear—are becoming the weapons of choice among terrorist organizations and some governments.

Richard K. Betts in "The New Threat of Mass Destruction" presents the reader with an overview of the threat of weapons of mass destruction that is every bit as relevant today, and perhaps more so, as it was when he wrote this article in 1998. In the article, he cautions the reader that "the interest at the very core—protecting the American homeland from attack— may now often be in conflict with security more broadly conceived and with the interests that mandate promoting American political values, economic interdependence, social Westernization, and stability in regions beyond Western Europe and the Americas." His identification of the very issues that came to clash on 9/11 is equally relevant today when we think about and consider the ramifications of weapons of mass destruction. Betts' examination of concepts such as deterrence and civil defense are valuable in helping the reader sort out the issues at hand.

Adam Dolnik's "All God's Poisons: Reevaluating the Threat of Religious Terrorism," takes issue with the common assertion that religious terrorist groups are more likely to use WMD than their secular counterparts. Unfortunately, writes Dolnik, the logic of the assertion is greatly simplified and inaccurate. In his view, religious terrorists are essentially very similar to other secular terrorists narrow minded—individuals who fail to see alternative perspectives on the issues they are fighting for. Dolnik reaches the conclusion that conducting a "superterrorist" attack with unconventional weapons would be extremely difficult for any terrorist group, religious or secular, and believes the likelihood of a successful mass-casualty attack remains low.

In "The Bioterrorist Threat in the United States," Richard Pilch formalizes the way to assess the current bioterrorism threat to the United States by using a simple formula: Threat = Vulnerability x Capability x Intent. Pilch emphasizes the major technical hurdles involved in acquiring, producing, and delivering a potential biological warfare agent. The article uses a crop-duster scenario for a case study and concludes that while the likelihood of a bioterrorist attack is small, policy makers must take a worst-case scenario seriously.

The intersection of radical ideology and technology presents unparalleled security challenges for the future. Counter-proliferation is an important, but undercovered, topic in the terrorism field. Michael Eastman and Robert Brown assess three potential strategies for keeping WMD out of terrorists' hands in "Security Strategy in the Gray Zone." The two authors discussion of deterrence, prevention, and preemption not only addresses the strengths and weaknesses of each strategy, but the authors conclude that efforts must begin with preventing "hostile" states from acquiring WMD in the first place—the best of "three bad options" for safeguarding the nation against WMD attacks.

"Terrorism in the Genomic Age," by John Ellis paints a frightening picture of the possible misuse of the human genome. Breaking the DNA code has many positive possibilities, writes Ellis, a biological terrorism expert and Pulitzer Prize nominee for his work at the *Boston Globe*. It also has many liabilities. Consider narcotics. Shortly after the attacks on the World Trade Center and the Pentagon, *The New York Times* reported that Osama bin Laden had funded an effort to develop a genetically modified "super heroin." In theory, genetically modified poppy plants could lead to the development of an instantly addictive and wildly potent heroin product that could be introduced to a much broader market segment. If the number of junkies doubles or triples, narcotrafficking becomes seriously destabilizing. Ellis also argues that breaking the DNA code will allow terrorists to develop biological agents that can selectively attack certain racial vulnerabilities and not others.

Chapter 6, "The Threat of Other Forms of Terrorism," identifies nontraditional forms of terrorism and potential terrorist weapons that could be used with deadly results. In "Narcotics, Terrorism, and International Crime: The Convergence Phenomenon," General (Retired) Barry McCaffrey and Major John Basso use case studies from different world regions to illustrate the insidious and debilitating nature of narcoterror. McCaffrey, former drug czar in the Clinton administration, is the ideal person to address this issue and is still passionate about halting the flow of drugs into America and stopping drug production in the less-developed world.

Martha Crenshaw's article earlier in the book defines the "logic of terrorism" in strategic terms. Bruce Hoffman's complimentary piece "The Logic of Suicide Terrorism," in this chapter, describes how the tactics of terrorists, particularly suicide bombing, are also very logical. Written in easily understood, cost-benefit terms, Hoffman explains that "the fundamental characteristics of suicide bombing, and its strong attraction for the terrorist organizations behind it, are universal: Suicide bombings are inexpensive and effective." Hoffman's syntax forces one to rethink modern warfare's technological jargon. According to him, suicide bombers are the ultimate smart bomb. They guarantee media coverage and are less complicated and compromising than other kinds of terrorist operations. Hoffman uses Israel, which has more experience with suicide bombers than any other place, as the case study for his articles. Hoffman notes that Israel is not the United States, but says Americans can take precautions to substantially reduce the threat of suicide bombing in America based on Israel's experience.

Ami Pedahzur's comment on Robert A. Pape's "The Strategic Logic of Suicide Terrorism" and Mia M. Bloom's "Palestinian Suicide Bombing: Public Support, Market Share and Outbidding" presents a concise and powerful model for a theoretical understanding of suicide terrorism. He offers a three-part model, which "has both the capacity to describe and explain the process that begins with a rational strategic decision-making among the organization's elites, and concluded in the explosion of the suicide terrorist." In building his model, Pedahzur assumes a more macro-level approach but does not ignore the individual level of the actor. This comment is an excellent companion to Hoffman's article "The Logic of Suicide Terrorism."

Madeleine Gruen, one of the nation's true experts on the use of the Internet by terrorist organizations, presents a compelling and chilling article written for this edition that outlines the "mastery of the medium [the Internet that] has made it possible for [terrorists] to expand their sphere of influence to include Western Populations." This article is a comprehensive look at the different means of internet usage—from propagation of ideology to recruitment—in which she shows how the "Internet is ... indispensable to political and militant Islamist groups, who rely on it to support and sustain core components of operations." This medium of communication is significant because it allows terrorists to not only communicate with one another but, the Internet allows groups to recruit and build organizations. The implications for counterterror governments are significant—if the governments can find, recognize and take action against an increasingly sophisticated and dangerous mode of communications.

In "The Leaderless Nexus: When Crime and Terror Converge," Chris Dishman argues that the shift from hierarchical to more diverse organizational structures is not only happening within terrorist organizations but also in criminal organizations. The result is that actors on both sides have more flexibility to act independently. Individual criminal entrepreneurship results in what Dishman calls a "leaderless nexus" between criminal networks and terrorist organizations. This new phenomenon not only complicates counterterrorism efforts but creates a much more flexible operating environment of the terrorists to obtain the logistical support needed to conduct terrorist operations.

Part II, "Countering the Terrorist Threat"

Part II of this book deals with past, present, and future national and international responses to terrorism and defenses against it. Organized into three chapters, the essays and articles in Part II analyze and debate the practical, political, ethical, and moral questions raised by military and nonmilitary responses, including preemptive actions outside the context of declared war. In addition, two detailed appendices—"Background Information on Designated Foreign Terrorist Organizations" and "Chronology of Significant Terrorist Incidents, 2002-2004"—are provided at the end of Part II.

Chapter 7, "The Challenges of Terrorism to a Free Society," examines the challenge to states when combating terrorism. Richard Betts asserts that a strategy of terrorism "flows from the coincidence of two conditions: intense political grievance and gross imbalance of power." Says Betts, terrorism "may become instrumentally appealing by default—when one party in conflict lacks other military options." "This is why terrorism is the premier form of 'asymmetric warfare,' the Pentagon buzzword for the type of threats likely to confront the United States in the post-Cold War world."

In his final article in this book, "A Nasty Business," Bruce Hoffman notes the difficulty intelligence organizations in democracies have in collecting intelligence against terrorists: "Gathering 'good intelligence' against terrorists is an inherently brutish enterprise, involving methods a civics class might not condone." Written in 2002, Hoffman was prescient in the questions he asked about the limits of interrogation and the efficacy of torture. Hoffman also advances the question asked by many after September 11: How much of their civil rights, liberties, and freedoms are Americans willing to give up in order to prosecute the war on terrorism? This article is a must-read for any student of this subject.

In "Dilemmas Concerning Media Coverage of Terrorist Attacks," Boaz Ganor frames the media debate in larger terms. He identifies the media's dilemma in covering terrorism—the need to report on the events, otherwise referred to as the "public's right to know," and the benefits terrorists derive from the media coverage. Ganor uses Israel as a case study to explore this dynamic.

Mark Basile examines a different challenge that governments face in combating terrorism—that of terrorist financing. He concludes that "Al Qaeda's sophisticated financial network and informal transfer systems throughout the world make it almost impossible to stop Al Qaeda from moving money." This conclusion paints a picture that is daunting. If we cannot stop the money, then the terrorists will continue to have the means to recruit, arm, and conduct attacks. In his article, Basile outlines three reasons why this is central to any discussion of terrorism financing.

The selections in Chapter 8, "Strategies and Approaches for Combating Terrorism," discuss grand strategies (or the lack thereof) executed by the United States and its opponents in terrorism and counterterrorism warfare. General (Retired) Wayne Downing, like most of the other contributors to this book, agrees that a multinational and multilateral approach is the only way to defeat al Qaeda and other terrorist groups. In his article, the former Deputy National Security Advisor for Combating Terrorism argues that the national strategy must be refocused and must acknowledge the changing nature of the threat. He concludes his article with an important reminder to any strategist—that while terrorism may never be defeated in whole, we should strive to limit the terrorists' scope, lethality, and means such that terrorists no longer present a global threat but are reduced to a local threat to be dealt with by local and national law enforcement agencies.

In "Preemptive Military Doctrine: No Other Choice," I argue that deterrence and containment, the previous foundations of U.S. strategy, are no longer valid when confronting transnational, non-state terrorists. I agree with President Bush that the United States must identify and destroy the terrorist threat before it reaches our borders and, if necessary, act alone and use preemptive force. In my view, the traditional economic, political, diplomatic, and military applications of American power used to leverage and influence states in the past are not effective against non-state actors. Whom do you sanction or embargo? With whom do you negotiate? How do you defend against or deter Osama bin Laden? You don't. The only effective way to influence the bin Ladens of the world is to preempt them before they can act.

In "The Struggle Against Terrorism: Grand Strategy, Strategy, and Tactics," Barry Posen asserts that the United States should pursue a comprehensive strategy of selective engagement to prosecute its campaign against terrorism. Posen introduces the idea that special operations forces are the ideal for executing a selective engagement strategy. "Flexible, fast, and relatively discriminate forces are essential," Posen argues, and "the United States has large special operations well suited to the counterterror mission."

Paul Pillar, a senior CIA official and a noted terrorism scholar, paints a picture of the new al Qaeda—one characterized by decentralization. His exploration of the changing nature of the threat and the implications of that change for governments is one of the first to explore the problems of fighting a decentralized enemy. In other words, we are no longer facing the al Qaeda of 2001—we are instead facing a disparate and dispersed enemy that may come from any corner of the radicalized factions of Sunni Islam. In his article, "Counterterrorism after Al Qaeda," Pillar begins with the challenges that this new form poses for intelligence agencies before moving to a discussion of the international cooperation needed to address the threat. He concludes his article with a call to maintain the commitment to this struggle.

In the final article of this chapter, Steven Simon and Jeff Martini address one of the most critical questions in this fight against al Qaeda—how to deny the organization its popular support. In their article, "Terrorism: Denying Al Qaeda Its Popular Support," the authors explain that "Denying terrorists the support of these constituents is a crucial component in the war on terrorism and requires approaches that go beyond the standard strategies employed in the current campaign." Without such an approach, the terrorists' message will continue to hold sway and gain support from this broader population that provides the recruits, the money, and the legitimacy sought by the terrorists.

Organizing to fight is the topic of Chapter 9, "Organizing to Fight Terrorism." Specifically, which organizations should be charged with fighting the terrorist threat, and how must they adapt for the fight? Although written before 9/11, Martha Crenshaw's "Counterterrorism Policy and the Political Process" describes how difficult it is for any president to implement a coherent counterterrorism policy. "Due to pressures from Congress," says Crenshaw, "the president will not be able to set the agenda for counterterrorism policy with as much freedom as he can in other policy areas." Crenshaw also contends that implementing counterterrorism policy decisions will "also be affected by controversy, due to rivalries among agencies with operational responsibilities." Thus, she correctly predicted before 9/11 that "it will be difficult for any administration to develop a consistent policy based on an objective appraisal of the threat of terrorism to American national interests."

In "The Limits of Military Power," Rob de Wijk states that "the West's armed forces are fundamentally flawed. Conceptually, the focus is still on conventional warfare, but the new wars will be unconventional. . . .The West needs special forces to confront unconventional irregular fighters such as terrorists, and those forces are not available in large quantities." Nevertheless, de Wijk contends that the military, including special forces, cannot win the war on terrorism alone. There must also be a "campaign to win the hearts and minds of the Islamic people."

Richard Shultz, Jr., concludes this book with an interesting look at why the United States never deployed its special operations forces against al Qaeda prior to 9/11. This article is a must-read for any student seeking to understand the bureaucratic nature of policy making in this area. Shultz has spent his career studying terrorism, special operations, and military strategy. In his article "Showstoppers," he brings this vast amount of knowledge to bear in analyzing the interviews he conducted with senior policy makers who were involved in the decisions not to deploy our special operations forces against al Qaeda.

Notes

1. Brian Michael Jenkins, "Will Terrorists Go Nuclear?" RAND Paper P-5541 (1975), p. 4.
2. James Woolsey, 1994.
3. Stephen A. Cambone, *A New Structure for National Security Policy Planning*, Washington D.C.: Government Printing Office, 1996, p. 43.
4. Gideon Rose, "It Could Happen Here—Facing the New Terrorism," *Foreign Affairs*, March-April, 1999, p. 1.
5. Bruce Hoffman, *Inside Terrorism*, New York: Columbia University Press, 1998, p. 205.
6. Paul Mann, "Modern Military Threats: Not All They Might Seem?" *Aviation Week & Space Technology*, April 22, 2002, p. 1. (Gordon Adams quote)

Part I

Defining the Threat

Chapter 1

Terrorism Defined

Chapter 1 introduces the problems inherent in defining a topic as complex as terrorism. In the news everywhere, used to describe events from the Philippines to Central America, from the Middle East to the United States, we "think we know what it is when we see it." But is that enough? Bruce Hoffman does not think so. In his reading "Defining Terrorism" he struggles to come up with a definition of the term that avoids the "promiscuous" and imprecise labeling of a range of acts. He provides dictionary definitions but finds them to be "unsatisfying" because ultimately a society's definition is a reflection of the political and social tenor of the times. Hoffman traces the historical use of the term "terrorism" from the reign of terror that followed the French Revolution; to the communist and fascist movements in Russia, Italy, and Germany; to the narco-terrorism of the 1990s. He concludes with a definition that seeks to distinguish terrorists from guerrillas, ordinary criminals, and assassins.

Paul Pillar, because of his years of experience in the U.S. Army and Central Intelligence Agency, approaches terrorism from a practical, problem-solving vantage point. As such, his primary intention is to provide sound counterterrorism policy. Pillar feels that arguing the semantics of a precise definition is "confusing" and "cumbersome" and that it does not ultimately help one to determine good policy. He begins his study of terrorism and counterterrorism from a working definition used by the U.S. government, "as good a definition as any." The reading that follows examines the effects, both direct and indirect, of terrorism and outlines the four elements of good counterterrorism policy. The selection concludes with Pillar's reflections on the evolving nature of the world order, and the need for policy that adapts to change.

Eqbal Ahmad, in contrast to Paul Pillar, finds the official definition of and approach to terrorism to be an extremely limiting one, which stirs up emotion without "exercising our intelligence." Ahmad maintains that we do need to know what terrorism is before we can determine how to stop it. Most important, we must first study the motives of the terrorists. Throughout his reading, Ahmad uses Osama bin Laden and his transformation from U.S. ally to terrorist as a case study. His reading concludes with three recommendations to the United States for dealing with terrorism, which, although written in 1998, are remarkably prophetic in light of the events of September 11, 2001.

Bruce Hoffman, 1998

Defining Terrorism

What is terrorism? Few words have so insidiously worked their way into our everyday vocabulary. Like 'Internet'—another grossly over-used term that has similarly become an indispensable part of the argot of the late twentieth century—most people have a vague idea or impression of what terrorism is, but lack a more precise, concrete and truly explanatory definition of the word. This imprecision has been abetted partly by the modern media, whose efforts to communicate an often complex and convoluted message in the briefest amount of air-time or print space possible have led to the promiscuous labelling of a range of violent acts as 'terrorism'. Pick up a newspaper or turn on the television and—even within the same broadcast or on the same page—one can find such disparate acts as the bombing of a building, the assassination of a head of state, the massacre of civilians by a military unit, the poisoning of produce on supermarket shelves or the deliberate contamination of over-the-counter medication in a chemist's shop all described as incidents of terrorism. Indeed, virtually any especially abhorrent act of violence that is perceived as directed against society—whether it involves the activities of anti-government dissidents or governments themselves, organized crime syndicates or common criminals, rioting mobs or persons engaged in militant protest, individual psychotics or lone extortionists—is often labelled 'terrorism'.

Dictionary definitions are of little help. The pre-eminent authority on the English language, the much-venerated *Oxford English Dictionary [OED]*, is disappointingly unobliging when it comes to providing edification on this subject, its interpretation at once too literal and too historical to be of much contemporary use:

> **Terrorism:** A system of terror. 1. Government by intimidation as directed and carried out by the party in power in France during the revolution of 1789–94; the system of 'Terror'. 2. *gen.* A policy intended to strike with terror those against whom it is adopted; the employment of methods of intimidation; the fact of terrorizing or condition of being terrorized.

These definitions are wholly unsatisfying. Rather than learning what terrorism is, one instead finds, in the first instance, a somewhat potted historical—and, in respect of the modern accepted usage of the term, a uselessly anachronistic—description. The second definition offered is only slightly more helpful. While accurately communicating the fear-inducing quality of terrorism, the definition is still so broad as to apply to almost any action that scares ('terrorizes') us. Though an integral part of 'terrorism', this definition is still insufficient for the purpose of accurately defining the phenomenon that is today called 'terrorism'.

A slightly more satisfying elucidation may be found in the *OED*'s definition of the perpetrator of the act than in its efforts to come to grips with the act itself. In this respect, a 'terrorist' is defined thus:

> 1. As a political term: a. Applied to the Jacobins and their agents and partisans in the French Revolution, esp. to those connected with the Revolutionary tribunals during the 'Reign of Terror'. b. Any one who attempts to further his views by a system of coercive intimidation; *spec.* applied to members of one of the extreme revolutionary societies in Russia.

This is appreciably more helpful. First, it immediately introduces the reader to the notion of terrorism as a *political* concept. As will be seen, this key characteristic of terrorism is absolutely paramount to understanding its aims, motivations and purposes and critical in distinguishing it from other types of violence.

Terrorism, in the most widely accepted contemporary usage of the term, is fundamentally and inherently political. It is also ineluctably about power: the pursuit of power, the acquisition of power, and the use of power to achieve political change. Terrorism is thus violence—or, equally important, the threat of violence—used and directed in pursuit of, or in service of, a political aim. With this vital point clearly illuminated, one can appreciate the significance of the additional definition of 'terrorist' provided by the *OED*: 'Any one who attempts to further his views by a system of coercive intimidation'. This definition underscores clearly the other fundamental characteristic of terrorism: that it is a planned, calculated, and indeed systematic act.

Given this relatively straightforward elucidation, why, then, is terrorism so difficult to define? The most compelling reason perhaps is because the meaning of the term has changed so frequently over the past two hundred years.

The Changing Meaning of Terrorism

The word 'terrorism' was first popularized during the French Revolution. In contrast to its contemporary usage, at that time terrorism had a decidedly *positive* connotation. The system or *régime de la terreur* of 1793–4—from which the English word came—was adopted as a means to establish order during the transient anarchical period of turmoil and upheaval that followed the uprisings of 1789, as it has followed in the wake of many other revolutions. Hence, unlike terrorism as it is commonly understood today, to mean a *revolutionary* or anti-government activity undertaken by non-state or subnational entities, the *régime de la terreur* was an instrument of governance wielded by the recently established revolutionary *state*. It was designed to consolidate the new government's power by intimidating counter-revolutionaries, subversives and all other dissidents whom the new regime regarded as 'enemies of the people'. The Committee of General Security and the Revolutionary Tribunal ('People's Court' in the modern vernacular) were thus accorded wide powers of arrest and judgement, publicly putting to death by guillotine persons convicted of treasonous (i.e. reactionary) crimes. In this manner, a powerful lesson was conveyed to any and all who might oppose the revolution or grow nostalgic for the *ancien régime.*

Ironically, perhaps, the terrorism in its original context was also closely associated with the ideals of virtue and democracy. The revolutionary leader Maximilien Robespierre firmly believed that virtue was the mainspring of a popular government at peace, but that during the time of revolution must be allied with terror in order for democracy to triumph. He appealed famously to 'virtue, without which terror is evil; terror, without which virtue is helpless', and proclaimed; 'Terror is nothing but justice, prompt, severe and inflexible; it is therefore an emanation of virtue.'

Despite this divergence from its subsequent meaning, the French Revolution's 'terrorism' still shared at least two key characteristics in common with its modern-day variant. First, the *régime de la terreur* was neither random nor indiscriminate, as terrorism is often portrayed today, but was organized, deliberate and systematic. Second, its goal and its very justification—like that of contemporary terrorism—was the creation of a 'new and better society' in place of a fundamentally corrupt and undemocratic political system. Indeed, Robespierre's vague and utopian exegeses of the revolution's central goals are remarkably similar in tone and content to the equally turgid, millenarian manifestos issued by many contemporary revolutionary—primarily left-wing, Marxist-oriented—terrorist organizations. For example, in 1794 Robespierre declared, in language eerily presaging the communiqués issued by groups such as Germany's Red Army Faction and Italy's Red Brigades nearly two centuries later:

> We want an order of things… in which the arts are an adornment to the liberty that ennobles them, and commerce the source of wealth for the public and not of monstrous opulence for a few families… In our country we desire morality instead of selfishness, honesty and not mere 'honor', principle and not mere custom, duty and not mere propriety, the sway of reason rather than the tyranny of fashion, a scorn for vice and not a contempt for the unfortunate…

Like many other revolutions, the French Revolution eventually began to consume itself. On 8 Thermidor, year two of the new calendar adopted by the revolutionaries (26 July 1794), Robespierre announced to the National Convention that he had in his possession a new list of traitors. Fearing that their own names might be on that list, extremists joined forces with moderates to repudiate both Robespierre and his *régime de la terreur*. Robespierre and his closest followers themselves met the same fate that had befallen some 40,000 others: execution by guillotine. The Terror was at an end; thereafter terrorism became a term associated with the abuse of office and power—with overt 'criminal' implications. Within a year of Robespierre's demise, the word had been popularized in English by Edmund Burke who, in his famous polemic against the French Revolution, described the 'Thousands of those Hell hounds called Terrorists… let loose on the people'.

One of the French Revolution's more enduring repercussions was the impetus it gave to anti-monarchial sentiment elsewhere in Europe. Popular subservience to rulers who derived their authority from God through 'divine right of rule', not from their subjects, was increasingly questioned by a politically awakened continent. The advent of nationalism, and with its notions of statehood and citizenship based on the common identity of a people rather than the lineage of a royal family, were resulting in the unification and creation of new nation-states such as Germany and Italy. Meanwhile, the massive socio-economic changes engendered by the industrial revolution were creating new 'universalist' ideologies (such as communism/Marxism), born of the alienation and exploitative conditions of nineteenth-century capitalism. From this milieu a new era of terrorism emerged, in which the concept had gained many of the familiar revolutionary, anti-state connotations of today. Its chief progenitor was arguably the Italian republican extremist, Carlo Pisacane, who had forsaken his birthright as duke of San Giovanni only to perish in 1857 during an ill-fated revolt against Bourbon rule. A passionate advocate of federalism and mutualism, Pisacane is remembered less on this account than for the theory of 'propaganda by deed', which he is credited with defining—an idea that has exerted a compelling influence on rebels and terrorists alike ever since. 'The propaganda of the idea is a chimera,' Pisacane wrote. 'Ideas result from deeds, not the latter from the former, and the people will not be free when they are educated, but educated when they are free.' Violence, he argued, was necessary not only to draw attention to, or generate publicity for, a cause, but to inform, educate and ultimately rally the masses behind the revolution. The didactic purpose of violence, Pisacane argued, could never be effectively replaced by pamphlets, wall posters or assemblies.

Perhaps the first organization to put into practice Pisacane's dictum was the Narodnaya Volya, or People's Will (sometimes translated as People's Freedom), a small group of Russian constitutionalists that had been founded in 1878 to challenge tsarist rule. For the Narodnaya Volya, the apathy and alienation of the Russian masses afforded few alternatives to the resort to daring and dramatic acts of violence designed to attract attention to the group and its cause. However, unlike the many late twentieth-century terrorist organizations who have cited the principle of 'propaganda by deed' to justify the wanton targeting of civilians in order to assure them publicity through the shock and horror produced by wholesale bloodshed, the Narodnaya Volya displayed an almost quixotic attitude to the violence they wrought. To them, 'propaganda by deed' meant the selective targeting of specific individuals whom the group considered the embodiment of the autocratic, oppressive state. Hence their victims—the tsar, leading members of the royal family, senior government officials—were deliberately chosen for their 'symbolic' value as the dynastic heads and subservient agents of a corrupt and tyrannical regime. An intrinsic element in the group's collective beliefs was that 'not one drop of superfluous blood' should be shed in pursuit of aims, however noble or utilitarian they might be. Even having selected their targets with great care and the utmost deliberation, group members still harboured profound regrets about taking the life of a fellow human being. Their unswerving adherence to this principle is perhaps best illustrated by the failed attempt on the life of the Grand Duke Serge Alexandrovich made by a successor organization to the Narodnaya Volya in 1905. As the royal carriage came into view, the terrorist tasked with the assassination saw that the duke was unexpectedly accompanied by his children and therefore aborted his mission rather than risk harming the intended victim's family (the duke was killed in a subsequent attack). By comparison, the mid-air explosion caused by a terrorist bomb on Pan Am flight 103 over Lockerbie, Scotland, December 1988 indiscriminately claimed the lives of all 259 persons on board—innocent men, women and children alike—plus eleven inhabitants of the village where the plane crashed.

Ironically, the Narodnaya Volya's most dramatic accomplishment also led directly to its demise. On 1 March 1881 the group assassinated Tsar Alexander II. The failure of eight previous plots had led the conspirators to take extraordinary measures to ensure the success of this attempt. Four volunteers were given four bombs each and deployed along the alternative routes followed by the tsar's cortege. As two of the bomber-assassins stood in wait on the same street, the sleighs carrying the tsar and his Cossack escort approached the first terrorist, who hurled his bomb at the passing sleigh, missing it by inches. The whole entourage came to a halt as soldiers seized the hapless culprit and the tsar descended from his sleigh to check on a bystander wounded by the explosion. 'Thank God, I am safe,' the tsar reportedly declared—just as the second bomber emerged from the crowd and detonated his weapon, killing both himself and his target. The full weight of the tsarist state now fell on the heads of the Narodnaya Volya. Acting on information provided by the arrested member, the secret police swept down on the group's safe houses and hide-outs, rounding up most of the plotters, who were quickly tried, convicted and hanged. Further information from this group led to subsequent arrests, so that within a year of the assassination only one member of the original executive committee was still at large. She too was finally apprehended in 1883, at which point the first generation of Narodnaya Volya terrorists ceased to exist, although various successor organizations subsequently emerged to carry on the struggle.

At the time, the repercussions of the tsar's assassination could not have been known or appreciated by either the condemned or their comrades languishing in prison or exiled to Siberia. But in addition to precipitating the beginning of the end of tsarist rule, the group also deeply influenced individual revolutionaries and subversive organizations elsewhere. To the nascent anarchist movement, the 'propaganda by deed' strategy championed by the Narodnaya Volya provided a model to be emulated. Within four months of the tsar's murder, a group of radicals in London convened an 'anarchist conference' which publicly applauded the assassination and extolled tyrannicide as a means to achieve revolutionary change. In hopes of encouraging and coordinating worldwide anarchist activities, the conferees decided to establish an 'Anarchist International' (or 'Black International'). Although this idea, like most of their ambitious plans, came to nought, the publicity generated by even a putative 'Anarchist International' was sufficient to create a myth of global revolutionary pretensions and thereby stimulate fears and suspicions disproportionate to its actual impact or political achievements. Disparate and uncoordinated though the anarchists' violence was, the movement's emphasis on individual action or operations carried out by small cells of like-minded radicals made detection and prevention by the police particularly difficult, thus further heightening public fears. For example, following the assassination of US President William McKinley in 1901 (by a young Hungarian refugee, Leon Czolgocz, who, while not a regular member of any anarchist organization, was nonetheless influenced by the philosophy), Congress swiftly enacted legislation barring known anarchists or anyone 'who disbelieves in or is opposed to all organized government' from entering the United States. However, while anarchists were responsible for an impressive string of assassinations of heads of state and a number of particularly notorious bombings from about 1878 until the second decade of the twentieth century, in the final analysis, other than stimulating often exaggerated fears, anarchism made little tangible impact on either the domestic or the international politics of the countries affected. It does, however, offer an interesting historical footnote: much as the 'information revolution' of the late twentieth century is alleged to have made the means and methods of bomb-making and other types of terrorist activity more readily available via the Internet, on CD-ROM, and through ordinary libraries and bookstores, one of anarchism's flourishing 'cottage industries' more than a century earlier was the widespread distribution of similar 'how-to' or DIY-type manuals and publications of violence and mayhem.

On the eve of the First World War, terrorism still retained its revolutionary connotations. By this time, growing unrest and irredentist ferment had already welled up within the decaying Ottoman and Habsburg Empires. In the 1880s and 1890s, for example, militant Armenian nationalist movements in eastern Turkey pursued a terrorist strategy against continued Ottoman rule of a kind that would later be adopted by most of the post–Second

World War ethno-nationalist/separatist movements. The Armenians' objective was simultaneously to strike a blow against the despotic 'alien' regime through repeated attacks on its colonial administration and security forces, in order to rally indigenous support, as well as to attract international attention, sympathy and support. Around the same time, the Inner Macedonian Revolutionary Organization (IMRO) was active in the region overlapping present-day Greece, Bulgaria and Serbia. Although the Macedonians did not go on to suffer the catastrophic fate that befell the Armenians during the First World War (when an estimated one million persons perished in what is considered to be the first officially implemented genocide of the twentieth century), IMRO never came close to achieving its aim of an independent Macedonia and thereafter degenerated into a mostly criminal organization of hired thugs and political assassins.

The events immediately preceding the First World War in Bosnia are of course more familiar because of their subsequent cataclysmic impact on world affairs. There, similar groups of disaffected nationalists—Bosnian Serb intellectuals, university students and even schoolchildren, collectively known as Mlada Bosnia, or Young Bosnians—arose against continued Habsburg suzerainty. While it is perhaps easy to dismiss the movement, as some historians have, as comprised of 'frustrated, poor, dreary and maladjusted' adolescents—much as many contemporary observers similarly denigrate modern-day terrorists as mindless, obsessive and maladjusted—it was a member of Young Bosnia, Gavrilo Princip, who is widely credited with having set in motion the chain of events that began on 28 June 1914, when he assassinated the Habsburg Archduke Franz Ferdinand in Sarajevo, and culminated in the First World War. Whatever its superficially juvenile characteristics, the group was nonetheless passionately dedicated to the attainment of a federal South Slav political entity—united Slovenes, Croats and Serbs—and resolutely committed to assassination as the vehicle with which to achieve that aim. In this respect, the Young Bosnians perhaps had more in common with the radical republicanism of Giuseppe Mazzini, one of the most ardent exponents of Italian unification in the nineteenth century, than with groups such as the Narodnaya Volya—despite a shared conviction in the efficacy of tyrannicide. An even more significant difference, however, was the degree of involvement in, and external support provided to, Young Bosnian activities by various shadowy Serbian nationalist groups. Principal among these was the pan-Serb secret society, the Narodna Obrana ('The People's Defence' or 'National Defence').

The Narodna Obrana had been established in 1908 originally to promote Serb cultural and national activities. It subsequently assumed a more subversive orientation as the movement became increasingly involved with anti-Austrian activities—including terrorism—mostly in neighbouring Bosnia and Hercegovina. Although the Narodna Obrana's exclusionist pan-Serbian aims clashed with the Young Bosnians' less parochial South Slav ideals, its leadership was quite happy to manipulate and exploit the Bosnians' emotive nationalism and youthful zeal for their own purposes. To this end, the Narodna Obrana actively recruited, trained and armed young Bosnians and Hercegovinians from movements such as the Young Bosnians who were then deployed in various seditious activities against the Habsburgs. As early as four years before the archduke's assassination, a Hercegovinian youth, trained by a Serb army officer with close ties to the Narodna Obrana, had attempted to kill the governor of Bosnia. But, while the Narodna Obrana included among its members senior Serbian government officials, it was not an explicitly government-controlled or directly state-supported entity. Whatever hazy government links it maintained were further and deliberately obscured when a radical faction left the Narodna Obrana in 1911 and established the Ujedinjenje ili Smrt, 'The Union of Death' or 'Death or Unification'—more popularly known as the Crna Ruka, or the 'Black Hand'. This more militant and appreciably more clandestine splinter has been described by one historian as combining

> the more unattractive features of the anarchist cells of earlier years—which had been responsible for quite a number of assassinations in Europe and whose methods had a good deal of influence via the writings of Russian anarchists upon Serbian youth—and of the [American] Ku Klux Klan. There were gory rituals and oaths of loyalty, there were murders of backsliding members, there was identification of members by number, there were distributions of guns and bombs. And there was a steady traffic between Bosnia and Serbia.

This group, which continued to maintain close links with its parent body, was largely composed of serving Serbian military officers. It was led by Lieutenant-Colonel Dragutin Dmitrievich (known by his pseudonym, Apis), himself the chief of the Intelligence Department of the Serbian general staff. With this key additional advantage of direct access to military armaments, intelligence and training facilities, the Black Hand effectively took charge of all Serb-backed clandestine operations in Bosnia.

Although there were obviously close links between the Serbian military, the Black Hand and the Young Bosnians, it would be a mistake to regard the relationship as one of direct control, much less outright manipulation. Clearly, the Serbian government was well aware of the Black Hand's objectives and the violent means the group employed in pursuit of them; indeed, the Serbian Crown Prince Alexander was one of the group's benefactors. But this does not mean that the Serbian government was necessarily as committed to war with Austria as the Black Hand's leaders were, or that it was prepared to countenance the group's more extreme plans for fomenting cross-border, anti-Habsburg terrorism. There is some evidence to suggest that the Black Hand may have been trying to force Austria's hand against Serbia and thereby plunge both countries into war by actively abetting the Young Bosnians' plot to assassinate the archduke. Indeed, according to one revisionist account of the events leading up to the murder, even though the pistol used by Princip had been supplied by the Black Hand from a Serb military armoury in Kragujevac, and even though Princip had been trained by the Black Hand in Serbia before being smuggled back across the border for the assassination, at the eleventh hour Dmitrievich had apparently bowed to intense government pressure and tried to stop the assassination. According to this version, Princip and his fellow conspirators would hear nothing of it and stubbornly went ahead with their plans. Contrary to popular assumption, therefore, the archduke's assassination may not have been specifically ordered or even directly sanctioned by the Serbian government. However, the obscure links between high government officials and their senior military commanders and ostensibly independent, transnational terrorist movements, and the tangled web of intrigue, plots, clandestine arms provision and training, intelligence agents and cross-border sanctuary these relationships inevitably involved, provide a pertinent historical parallel to the contemporary phenomenon known as 'state-sponsored' terrorism (that is, the active and often clandestine support, encouragement and assistance provided by a foreign government to a terrorist group), which is discussed below.

By the 1930s, the meaning of 'terrorism' had changed again. It was now used less to refer to revolutionary movements and violence directed against governments and their leaders, and more to describe the practices of mass repression employed by totalitarian states and their dictatorial leaders against their own citizens. Thus the term regained its former connotations of abuse of power by governments, and was applied specifically to the authoritarian regimes that had come to power in Fascist Italy, Nazi Germany and Stalinist Russia. In Germany respectively, the accession to office of Hitler and Mussolini had depended in large measure on the 'street'—the mobilization and deployment of gangs of brown- or black-shirted thugs to harass and intimidate political opponents and root out other scapegoats for public vilification and further victimization. 'Terror? Never,' Mussolini insisted, demurely dismissing such intimidation as 'simply... social hygiene, taking those individuals out of circulation like a doctor would take out a bacillus'. The most sinister dimension of this form of 'terror' was that it became an intrinsic component of Fascist and Nazi governance, executed at the behest of, and in complete subservience to, the ruling political party of the land—which had arrogated to itself complete, total control of the country and its people. A system of government-sanctioned fear and coercion was thus created whereby political brawls, street fights and widespread persecution of Jews, communists and other declared 'enemies of the state' became the means through which complete and submissive compliance was ensured. The totality of party control over, and perversion of, government was perhaps most clearly evinced by a speech given by Hermann Goering, the newly appointed Prussian minister of the interior, in 1933. 'Fellow Germans,' he declared,

> My measures will not be crippled by any judicial thinking. My measures will not be crippled by any bureaucracy. Here I don't have to worry about Justice; my mission is only to destroy and exterminate, nothing more. This struggle will be a struggle against chaos, and such a struggle I shall not conduct with the power of the police. A bourgeois State might have done that. Certainly, I shall use the power of the State and the police to the utmost, my dear Communists, so don't draw any false conclusions; but the struggle to the death, in which my fist will grasp your necks, I shall lead with those there—the Brown Shirts.

The 'Great Terror' that Stalin was shortly to unleash in Russia both resembled and differed from that of the Nazis. On the one hand, drawing inspiration from Hitler's ruthless elimination of his own political opponents, the Russian dictator similarly transformed the political party he led into a servile instrument responsive directly to his personal will, and the state's police and security apparatus into slavish organs of coercion, enforcement and repression. But conditions in the Soviet Union of the 1930s bore little resemblance to the turbulent political, social and economic upheaval afflicting Germany and Italy during that decade and the previous one. On the other hand, therefore, unlike either the Nazis or the Fascists, who had emerged from the political free-for-alls in their own countries to seize power and then had to struggle to consolidate their rule and retain their unchallenged authority, the Russian Communist Party had by the mid-1930s been firmly entrenched in power for more than a decade. Stalin's purges, in contrast to those of the French Revolution, and even to Russia's own recent experience, were not 'launched in time of crisis, or revolution and war... [but] in the coldest of cold blood, when Russia had at last reached a comparatively calm and even moderately prosperous condition'. Thus the political purges ordered by Stalin became, in the words of one of his biographers, a 'conspiracy to seize total power by terrorist action', resulting in the death, exile, imprisonment or forcible impressment of millions.

Certainly, similar forms of state-imposed or state-directed violence and terror against a government's own citizens continue today. The use of so-called 'death squads' (often off-duty or plain-clothes security or police officers) in conjunction with blatant intimidation of political opponents, human rights and aid workers, student groups, labour organizers, journalists and others has been a prominent feature of the right-wing military dictatorships that took power in Argentina, Chile and Greece during the 1970s and even of elected governments in El Salvador, Guatemala, Colombia and Peru since the mid-1980s. But these state-sanctioned or explicitly ordered acts of *internal* political violence directed mostly against domestic populations—that is, rule by violence and intimidation by those *already* in power against their own citizenry—are generally termed 'terror' in order to distinguish that phenomenon from 'terrorism', which is understood to be violence committed by non-state entities.

Following the Second World War, in another swing of the pendulum of meaning, 'terrorism' regained the revolutionary connotations with which is it most commonly associated today. At that time, the term was used primarily in reference to the violent revolts then being prosecuted by the various indigenous nationalist/anti-colonialist groups that emerged in Asia, Africa and the Middle East during the late 1940s and 1950s to oppose continued European rule. Countries as diverse as Israel, Kenya, Cyprus and Algeria, for example, owe their independence at least in part to nationalist political movements that employed terrorism against colonial powers. It was also during this period that the 'politically correct' appellation of 'freedom fighters' came into fashion as a result of the political legitimacy that the international community (whose sympathy and support was actively courted by many of these movements) accorded to struggles for national liberation and self-determination. Many newly independent Third World countries and communist bloc states in particular adopted this vernacular, arguing that anyone or any movement that fought against 'colonial' oppression and/or Western domination should not be described as 'terrorists', but were properly deemed to be 'freedom fighters'. This position was perhaps most famously explained by the Palestine Liberation Organization (PLO) chairman Yassir Arafat, when he addressed the United Nations General Assembly in November 1974. 'The difference between the revolutionary and the terrorist,' Arafat stated, 'lies in the reason for which each fights. For whoever stands by a just cause and fights for the freedom and liberation of his land from the invaders, the settlers and the colonialists, cannot possibly be called terrorist.... '

During the late 1960s and 1970s, terrorism continued to be viewed within a revolutionary context. However, this usage now expanded to include nationalist and ethnic separatists groups outside a colonial or neo-colonial framework as well as radical, entirely ideologically motivated organizations. Disenfranchised or exiled nationalist minorities—such as the PLO, the Quebecois separatist group FLQ (Front de Libération du Québec), the Basque ETA (Euskadi ta Askatasuna, or Freedom for the Basque Homeland) and even a hitherto unknown South Moluccan irredentist group seeking independence from Indonesia—adopted terrorism as a means to draw attention to themselves and their respective causes, in many instances with the specific aim, like their anti-colonial predecessors, of attracting international sympathy and support. Around the same time, various left-wing political extremists—drawn mostly from the radical student organizations and

Marxist/Leninist/Maoist movements in Western Europe, Latin America and the United States—began to form terrorist groups opposing American intervention in Vietnam and what they claimed were the irredeemable social and economic inequalities of the modern capitalist liberal-democratic state.

Although the revolutionary cum ethno-nationalist/separatist and ideological exemplars continue to shape our most basic understanding of the term, in recent years 'terrorism' has been used to denote broader, less distinct phenomena. In the early 1980s, for example, terrorism came to be regarded as a calculated means to destabilize the West as part of a vast global conspiracy. Books like *The Terror Network* by Claire Sterling propagated the notion to a receptive American presidential administration and similarly susceptible governments elsewhere that the seemingly isolated terrorist incidents perpetrated by disparate groups scattered across the globe were in fact linked elements of a massive clandestine plot, orchestrated by the Kremlin and implemented by its Warsaw Pact client states, to destroy the Free World. By the middle of the decade, however, a series of suicide bombings directed mostly against American diplomatic and military targets in the Middle East was focusing attention on the rising threat of state-sponsored terrorism. Consequently, this phenomenon—whereby various renegade foreign governments such as the regimes in Iran, Iraq, Libya and Syria became actively involved in sponsoring or commissioning terrorist acts—replaced communist conspiracy theories as the main context within which terrorism was viewed. Terrorism thus became associated with a type of covert or surrogate warfare whereby weaker states could confront larger, more powerful rivals without the risk of retribution.

In the early 1990s the meaning and usage of the term 'terrorism' were further blurred by the emergence of two new buzzwords: 'narco-terrorism' and the so-called 'gray area phenomenon'. The former term revived the Moscow-orchestrated terrorism conspiracy theories of previous years while introducing the critical new dimension of narcotics trafficking. Thus 'narco-terrorism' was defined by one of the concept's foremost propagators as the 'use of drug trafficking to advance the objectives of certain governments and terrorist organizations'—identified as the 'Marxist-Leninst regimes' of the Soviet Union, Cuba, Bulgaria and Nicaragua, among others. The emphasis of 'narco-terrorism' as the latest manifestation of the communist plot to undermine Western society, however, had the unfortunate effect of diverting official attention away from a bona fide emerging trend. To a greater extent than ever in the past, entirely criminal (that is, violent, *economically* motivated) organizations were now forging strategic alliances with terrorist and guerrilla organizations or themselves employing violence for specifically political ends. The growing power of the Colombian cocaine cartels, their close ties with left-wing terrorist groups in Colombia and Peru, and their repeated attempts to subvert Colombia's electoral process and undermine successive governments constitute perhaps the best-known example of this continuing trend.

Those who drew attention to this 'gray area phenomenon' were concerned less with grand conspiracies than with highlighting the increasingly fluid and variable nature of subnational conflict in the post–Cold War era. Accordingly, in the 1990s terrorism began to be subsumed by some analysts within the 'gray area phenomenon'. Thus the latter term came to be used to denote 'threats to the stability of nation states by non-state actors and non-governmental processes and organizations'; to describe violence affecting 'immense regions or urban areas where control has shifted from legitimate governments to new half-political, half-criminal powers'; or simply to group together in one category the range of conflicts across the world that no longer conformed to traditionally accepted notions of war as fighting between the armed forces of two or more established states, but instead involved irregular forces as one or more of the combatants. Terrorism had shifted its meaning again from an individual phenomenon of subnational violence to one of several elements, or part of a wider pattern, of non-state conflict.

Why Is Terrorism So Difficult to Define?

Not surprisingly, as the meaning and usage of the word have changed over time to accommodate the political vernacular and discourse of each successive era, terrorism has proved increasingly elusive in the face of attempts to construct one consistent definition. At one time, the terrorists themselves were far more cooperative in this endeavour than they are today. The early practitioners didn't mince their words or hide behind the semantic camouflage of more anodyne labels such as 'freedom fighter' or 'urban guerrilla'. The nineteenth-century anarchists, for example, unabashedly proclaimed themselves to be terrorists and frankly proclaimed their tactics to be terrorism. The members of Narodnaya Volya similarly displayed no qualms in using these same words to describe themselves and their deeds. However, such frankness did not last. The Jewish terrorist group of the 1940s known as Lehi (the Hebrew acronym for Lohamei Herut Yisrael, the Freedom Fighters for Israel, more popularly known simply as the Stern Gang after their founder and first leader, Abraham Stern) is thought to be one of the last terrorist groups actually to describe itself publicly as such. It is significant, however, that even Lehi, while it may have been far more candid than its latter-day counterparts, chose as the name of the organization not 'Terrorist Fighters for Israel', but the far less pejorative 'Freedom Fighters for Israel'. Similarly, although more than twenty years later the Brazilian revolutionary Carlos Marighela displayed few compunctions about openly advocating the use of 'terrorist' tactics, he still insisted on depicting himself and his disciples as 'urban guerrillas' rather than 'urban terrorists'. Indeed, it is clear from Marighela's writings that he was well aware of the word's undesirable connotations, and strove to displace them with positive resonances. 'The words "aggressor" and "terrorist"', Marighela wrote in his famous *Handbook of Urban Guerrilla War* (also known as the 'Mini-Manual'), 'no longer mean what they did. Instead of arousing fear or censure, they are a call to action. To be called an aggressor or a terrorist in Brazil is now an honour to any citizen, for it means that he is fighting, with a gun in his hand, against the monstrosity of the present dictatorship and the suffering it causes.'

This trend towards ever more convoluted semantic obfuscations to side-step terrorism's pejorative overtones, has, if anything, become more entrenched in recent decades. Terrorist organizations almost without exception now regularly select names for themselves that consciously eschew the word 'terrorism' in any of its forms. Instead these groups actively seek to evoke images of:

- freedom and liberation (e.g. the National Liberation Front, the Popular Front for the Liberation of Palestine, Freedom for the Basque Homeland, etc.);
- armies or other military organizational structures (e.g. the National Military Organization, the Popular Liberation Army, the Fifth Battalion of the Liberation Army, etc.);

- actual self-defence movements (e.g. the Afrikaner Resistance Movement, the Shankhill Defence Association, the Organization for the Defence of the Free People, the Jewish Defense Organization, etc.);
- righteous vengeance (the Organization for the Oppressed on Earth, the Justice Commandos of the Armenian Genocide, the Palestinian Revenge Organization, etc.);

—or else deliberately choose names that are decidedly neutral and therefore bereft of all but the most innocuous suggestions or associations (e.g. the Shining Path, Front Line, al-Dawa ('The Call'), Alfaro Lives—Damn It!, Kach ('Thus'), al-Gamat al-Islamiya ('The Islamic Organization'), the Lantero Youth Movement, etc.).

What all these examples suggest is that terrorists clearly do not see or regard themselves as others do. 'Above all I am a family man,' the arch-terrorist Carlos, 'The Jackal', described himself to a French newspaper following his capture in 1994. Cast perpetually on the defensive and forced to take up arms to protect themselves and their real or imagined constituents only, terrorists perceive themselves as reluctant warriors, driven by desperation—and lacking any viable alternative—to violence against a repressive state, a predatory rival ethnic or nationalist group, or an unresponsive international order. This perceived characteristic of self-denial also distinguishes the terrorist from other types of political extremists as well as from persons similarly involved in illegal, violent avocations. A communist or a revolutionary, for example, would likely readily accept and admit that he is in fact a communist or a revolutionary. Indeed, many would doubtless take particular pride in claiming either of those appellations for themselves. Similarly, even a person engaged in illegal, wholly disreputable or entirely selfish violence activities, such as robbing banks or carrying out contract killings, would probably admit to being a bank robber or a murderer for hire. The terrorist, by contrast, will *never* acknowledge that he is a terrorist and moreover will go to great lengths to evade and obscure any such inference or connection. Terry Anderson, the American journalist who was held hostage for almost seven years by the Lebanese terrorist organization Hezbollah, relates a telling conversation he had with one of his guards. The guard had objected to a newspaper article that referred to Hezbollah as terrorists. 'We are not terrorists,' he indignantly stated, 'we are fighters.' Anderson replied, 'Hajj, you are a terrorist, look it up in the dictionary. You are a terrorist, you may not like the word and if you do not like the word, do not do it.' The terrorist will always argue that it is society or the government or the socio-economic 'system' and its laws that are the *real* 'terrorists', and moreover that if it were not for this oppression, he would not have felt the need to defend either himself or the population he claims to represent. Another revealing example of this process of obfuscation-projection may be found in the book *Invisible Armies*, written by Sheikh Muhammad Hussein Fadlallah, the spiritual leader of the Lebanese terrorist group responsible for Anderson's kidnapping. 'We don't see ourselves as terrorists,' Fadlallah explains, 'because we don't believe in terrorism. We don't see resisting the occupier as a terrorist action. We see ourselves as *mujihadeen* [holy warriors] who fight a Holy War for the people.'

On one point, at least, everyone agrees: terrorism is a pejorative term. It is a word with intrinsically negative connotations that is generally applied to one's enemies and opponents, or to those with whom one disagrees and would otherwise prefer to ignore. 'What is called terrorism', Brian Jenkins has written, 'thus seems to depend on one's point of view. Use of the term implies a moral judgement; and if one party can successfully attach the label *terrorist* to its opponent, then it has indirectly persuaded others to adopt its moral viewpoint.' Hence the decision to call someone or label some organization 'terrorist' becomes almost unavoidably subjective, depending largely on whether one sympathizes with or opposes the person/group/cause concerned. If one identifies with the victim of the violence, for example, then the act is terrorism. If, however, one identifies with the perpetrator, the violent act is regarded in a more sympathetic, if not positive (or, at the worst, an ambivalent) light; and it is not terrorism.

The implications of this associational logic were perhaps most clearly demonstrated in the exchanges between Western and non-Western member states of the United Nations following the 1972 Munich Olympics massacre, in which eleven Israeli athletes were killed. The debate began with the proposal by the then UN Secretary-General, Kurt Waldheim, that the UN should not remain a 'mute spectator' to the acts of terrorist violence then occurring throughout the world but should take practical steps that might prevent further bloodshed. While a majority of the UN member states supported the Secretary-General, a disputatious minority—including many Arab states and various African and Asian countries—derailed the discussion, arguing (much as Arafat would do two years later in his own address to the General Assembly) that 'people who struggle to liberate themselves from foreign oppression and exploitation have the right to use all methods at their disposal, including force'.

The Third World delegates justified their position with two arguments. First, they claimed that all bona fide liberation movements are invariably decried as 'terrorists' by the regimes against which their struggles for freedom are directed. The Nazis, for example, labelled as terrorists the resistance groups opposing Germany's occupation of their lands, Moulaye el-Hassen, the Mauritanian ambassador, pointed out, just as 'all liberation movements are described as terrorists by those who have reduced them to slavery'. Therefore, by condemning 'terrorism' the UN was endorsing the power of the strong over the weak and of the established entity over its non-established challenger—in effect, acting as the defender of the status quo. According to Chen Chu, the deputy representative of the People's Republic of China, the UN thus was proposing to deprive 'opposed nations and peoples' of the only effective weapon they had with which to oppose 'imperialism, colonialism, neocolonialism, racism and Israeli Zionism'. Second, the Third World delegates argued forcefully that it is not the violence itself that is germane, but its 'underlying causes': that is, the 'misery, frustration, grievance and despair' that produce the violent acts. As the Mauritanian representative again explained, the term 'terrorist' could 'hardly be held to apply to persons who were denied the most elementary human rights, dignity, freedom and independence, and whose countries objected to foreign occupation'. When the issue was again raised the following year, Syria objected on the grounds that 'the international community is under legal and moral obligation to promote the struggle for liberation and to resist any attempt to depict this struggle as synonymous with terrorism and illegitimate violence'. The resultant definitional paralysis subsequently throttled UN efforts to make any substantive progress on international cooperation against terrorism beyond very specific agreements on individual aspects of the problem (concerning, for example, diplomats and civil aviation).

The opposite approach, where identification with the victim determines the classification of a violent act as terrorism, is evident in the conclusions of a parliamentary working group of NATO (an organization comprised of long-established, status quo Western states). The final report of the 1989 North Atlantic Assembly's Subcommittee on Terrorism states: 'Murder, kidnapping, arson and other felonious acts constitute criminal behavior, but many non-Western nations have proved reluctant to condemn as terrorist acts what they consider to be struggles of natural liberation.' In this reasoning, the defining characteristic of terrorism is the act of violence itself, not the motivations or justification for or reasons behind it. This approach has long been espoused by analysts such as Jenkins who argue that terrorism should be defined 'by the nature of the act, not by the identity of the perpetrators or the nature of their cause'. But this is not an entirely satisfactory solution either, since it fails to differentiate clearly between violence perpetrated by states and by non-state entities, such as terrorists. Accordingly, it plays into the hands of terrorists and their apologists who would argue that there is no difference between the 'low-tech' terrorist pipe-bomb placed in the rubbish bin at a crowded market that wantonly and indiscriminately kills or maims everyone within a radius measured in tens of feet and the 'high-tech' precision-guided ordnance dropped by air force fighter-bombers from a height of 20,000 feet or more that achieves the same wanton and indiscriminate effects on the crowded marketplace far below. This rationale thus equates the random violence inflicted on enemy population centres by military forces—such as the Luftwaffe's raids on Warsaw and Coventry, the Allied firebombings of Dresden and Tokyo, and the atomic bombs dropped by the United States on Hiroshima and Nagasaki during the Second World War, and indeed the countervalue strategy of the post-war superpowers' strategic nuclear policy, which deliberately targeted the enemy's civilian population—with the violence committed by substate entities labelled 'terrorists', since both involve the infliction of death and injury on noncombatants. Indeed, this was precisely the point made during the above-mentioned UN debates by the Cuban representative, who argued that 'the methods of combat used by national liberation movements could not be declared illegal while the policy of terrorism unleashed against certain peoples [by the armed forces of established states] was declared legitimate'.

It is a familiar argument. Terrorists, as we have seen, deliberately cloak themselves in the terminology of military jargon. They consciously portray themselves as bona fide (freedom) fighters, if not soldiers, who—though they wear no identifying uniform or insignia—are entitled to treatment as prisoners of war (POWs) if captured and therefore should not be prosecuted as common criminals in ordinary courts of law. Terrorists further argue that, because of their numerical inferiority, far more limited firepower and paucity of resources compared with an established nation-state's massive defence and national security apparatus, they have no choice but to operate clandestinely, emerging from the shadows to carry out dramatic (in other words, bloody and destructive) acts of hit-and-run violence in order to attract attention to, and ensure publicity for, themselves and their cause. The bomb-in-the-rubbish-bin, in their view, is merely a circumstantially imposed 'poor man's air force': the only means with which the terrorist can challenge—and get the attention of—the more powerful state. 'How else can we bring pressure to bear on the world?' one of Arafat's political aides once enquired. 'The deaths are regrettable, but they are a fact of war in which innocents have become involved. They are no more innocent than the Palestinian women and children killed by the Israelis and we are ready to carry the war all over the world.'

But rationalizations such as these ignore the fact that, even while national armed forces have been responsible for far more death and destruction than terrorists might ever aspire to bring about, there nonetheless is a fundamental qualitative difference between the two types of violence. Even in war there are rules and accepted norms of behaviour that prohibit the use of certain types of weapons (for example, hollow-point or 'dum-dum' bullets, CS 'tear' gas, chemical and biological warfare agents), proscribe various tactics and outlaw attacks on specific categories of targets. Accordingly, in theory, if not always in practice, the rules of war—as observed from the early seventeenth century when they were first proposed by the Dutch jurist Hugo Grotius and subsequently codified in the famous Geneva and Hague Conventions on Warfare of the 1860s, 1899, 1907 and 1949—not only grant civilian non-combatants immunity from attack, but also

- prohibit taking civilians as hostages;
- impose regulations governing the treatment of captured or surrendered soldiers (POWs);
- outlaw reprisals against either civilians or POWs;
- recognize neutral territory and the rights of citizens of neutral states; and
- uphold the inviolability of diplomats and other accredited representatives.

Even the most cursory review of terrorist tactics and targets over the past quarter-century reveals that terrorists have violated all these rules. They not infrequently have

- taken hostage civilians, whom in some instances they have then brutally executed (e.g. the former Italian prime minister Aldo Moro and the German industrialist Hans Martin Schleyer, who were respectively taken captive and later murdered by the Red Brigades and the Red Army Faction);
- similarly abused and murdered kidnapped military officers—even when they were serving on UN-sponsored peacekeeping or truce supervisory missions (e.g. the American Marine Lieutenant-Colonel William Higgins, the commander of a UN truce monitoring detachment, who was abducted by Lebanese Shi'a terrorists in 1989 and subsequently hanged);
- undertaken reprisals against wholly innocent civilians, often in countries far removed from the terrorists' ostensible 'theatre of operation', thus disdaining any concept of neutral states or the rights of citizens of neutral countries (e.g. the brutal 1986 machine-gun and hand-grenade attack on Turkish Jewish worshippers at an Istanbul synagogue carried out by the Palestinian Abu Nidal Organization in retaliation for a recent Israeli raid on a guerrilla base in southern Lebanon); and
- repeatedly attacked embassies and other diplomatic installations (e.g. the bombings of the US embassies in Beirut and Kuwait City in 1983 and 1984, and the mass hostage-taking at the Japanese ambassador's residence in Lima, Peru, in 1996–7), as well as deliberately targeting diplomats and other accredited representatives (e.g. the British ambassador to Uruguay, Sir Geoffrey Jackson, who was kidnapped by leftist terrorists in that country in 1971, and the fifty-two American diplomats taken hostage at the Tehran legation in 1979).

Admittedly, the armed forces of established states have also been guilty of violating some of the same rules of war. However, when these transgressions do occur—when civilians are deliberately and wantonly attacked on war or taken hostage and killed by military forces—the term 'war crime' is used to describe such acts and, imperfect and flawed as both international and national judicial remedies may be, steps nonetheless are often taken to hold the perpetrators accountable for these crimes. By comparison, one of the fundamental *raisons d'être* of international terrorism is a refusal to be bound by such rules of warfare and codes of conduct. International terrorism disdains any concept of delimited areas of combat or demarcated battlefields, much less respect of neutral territory. Accordingly, terrorists have repeatedly taken their often parochial struggles to other, sometimes geographically distant, third party countries and there deliberately enmeshed persons completely unconnected with the terrorists' cause or grievances in violent incidents designed to generate attention and publicity.

The reporting of terrorism by the news media, which have been drawn into the semantic debates that divided the UN in the 1970s and continue to influence all discourse on terrorism, has further contributed to the obfuscation of the terrorist/'freedom fighter' debate, enshrining imprecision and implication as the lingua franca of political violence in the name of objectivity and neutrality. In striving to avoid appearing either partisan or judgemental, the American media, for example, resorted to describing terrorists—often in the same report—as variously guerrillas, gunmen, raiders, commandos and even soldiers. A random sample of American newspaper reports of Palestinian terrorist activities between June and December 1973, found in the terrorism archives and database maintained at the University of St. Andrews in Scotland, provided striking illustrations of this practice. Out of eight headlines of articles describing the same incident, six used the word 'guerrillas' and only two 'terrorists' to describe the perpetrators. An interesting pattern was also observed whereby those accounts that immediately followed a particularly horrific or tragic incident—that is, involving the death and injury of innocent persons (in this instance, the attack on a Pan Am airliner at Rome airport, in which thirty-two passengers were killed)—tended to describe the perpetrators as 'terrorists' and their act as 'terrorism' (albeit in one case only in the headline, before reverting to the more neutral terminology of 'commando', 'militants', and 'guerrilla attack' in the text) more frequently than did reports of less serious or non-lethal incidents. One *New York Times* leading article, however, was far less restrained than the stories describing the actual incident, describing it as 'bloody' and 'mindless' and using the words 'terrorists' and 'terrorism' interchangeably with 'guerrillas' and 'extremists'. Only six months previously, however, the same newspaper had run a story about another terrorist attack that completely eschewed the terms 'terrorism' and 'terrorist', preferring 'guerrillas' and 'resistance' (as in 'resistance movement') instead. The *Christian Science Monitor*'s reports of the Rome Pan Am attack similarly avoided 'terrorist' and 'terrorism' in favour of 'guerrillas' and 'extremists'; an Associated Press story in the next day's *Los Angeles Times* also stuck with 'guerrillas', while the two *Washington Post* articles on the same incident opted for the terms 'commandos' and 'guerrillas'.

This slavish devotion in terminological neutrality, which David Rapoport first observed over twenty years ago, is still in evidence today. A recent article appearing in the *International Herald Tribune* (a Paris-based newspaper published in conjunction with the *New York Times* and *Washington Post*) reported an incident in Algeria where thirty persons had been killed by perpetrators who were variously described as 'terrorists' in the article's headline, less judgementally as 'extremists' in the lead paragraph and as the still more ambiguous 'Islamic fundamentalists' in the article's third paragraph. In a country that since 1992 has been afflicted with an unrelenting wave of terrorist violence and bloodshed that has claimed the lives of an estimated 75,000 persons, one might think that the distinctions between 'terrorists', mere 'extremists' and ordinary 'fundamentalists' would be clearer. Equally interesting was the article that appeared on the opposite side of the same page of the newspaper that described the 'decades of sporadic *guerrilla* [my emphasis] warfare by the IRA' in Northern Ireland. Yet fifty years ago the same newspaper apparently had fewer qualms about using the word 'terrorists' to describe the two young Jewish men in pre-independence Israel who, while awaiting execution after having been convicted of attacking British military targets, committed suicide. Other press accounts of the same period in *The Times* of London and the *Palestine Post* similarly had no difficulties, for example, in describing the 1946 bombing by Jewish terrorists of the British military headquarters and government secretariat located in Jerusalem's King David Hotel as a 'terrorist' act perpetrated by 'terrorists'. Similarly, in perhaps the most specific application of the term, the communist terrorists against whom the British fought in Malaya throughout the late 1940s and 1950s were routinely referred to as 'CTs'—for 'Communist terrorists'. As Rapoport warned in the 1970s, 'In attempting to correct the abuse of language for political purposes our journalists may succeed in making language altogether worthless.'

The cumulative effect of this proclivity towards equivocation is that today there is no one widely accepted or agreed definition for terrorism. Different departments or agencies of even the same government will themselves often have very different definitions for terrorism. The US State Department, for example, uses the definition of terrorism contained in Title 22 of the United States Code, Section 2656f(d):

> premeditated, politically motivated violence perpetrated against noncombatant targets by subnational groups or clandestine agents, usually intended to influence an audience,

while the US Federal Bureau of Investigation (FBI) defines terrorism as

> the unlawful use of force or violence against persons or property to intimidate or coerce a Government, the civilian population, or any segment thereof, in furtherance of political or social objectives,

and the US Department of Defense defines it as

> the unlawful use of—or threatened use of—force or violence against individuals or property to coerce or intimidate governments or societies, often to achieve political, religious, or ideological objectives.

Not surprisingly, each of the above definitions reflects the priorities and particular interests of the specific agency involved. The State Department's emphasis is on the premeditated and planned or calculated nature of terrorism in contrast to more spontaneous acts of political violence. Its definition is also the only one of the three to emphasize both the ineluctably political nature of terrorism and the perpetrators' fundamental 'subnational' characteristic. The State Department definition, however, is conspicuously deficient in failing to consider the psychological dimension of terrorism. Terrorism is as much about the threat of violence as the violent act itself and, accordingly, is deliberately conceived to have far-reaching psychological repercussions beyond the actual target of the act among a wider, watching, 'target' audience. As Jenkins succinctly observed two decades ago, 'Terrorism is theatre.'

Given the FBI's mission of investigating and solving crimes—both political (e.g. terrorism) and other—it is not surprising that its definition focuses on different elements. Unlike the State Department, this definition does address the psychological dimensions of the terrorist act described above, laying stress on terrorism's intimidatory and coercive aspects. The FBI definition also identifies a much broader category of terrorist targets than only 'noncombatants', specifying not only governments and their citizens, but also inanimate objects, such as private and public property. The FBI definition further recognizes social alongside political objectives as fundamental terrorist aims—though it offers no clearer elucidation of either.

The Department of Defense definition of terrorism is arguably the most complete of the three. It highlights the terrorist threat as much as the actual act of violence and focuses on terrorism's targeting of whole societies as well as governments. The Defense Department definition further cites the religious and ideological aims of terrorism alongside its fundamental political objectives—but curiously omits the social dimension found in the FBI's definition.

It is not only individual agencies within the same governmental apparatus that cannot agree on a single definition of terrorism. Experts and other long-established scholars in the field are equally incapable of reaching a consensus. In the first edition of his magisterial survey, *Political Terrorism: A Research Guide*, Alex Schmid devoted more than a hundred pages to examining more than a hundred different definitions of terrorism in an effort to discover a broadly acceptable, reasonably comprehensive explication of the word. Four years and a second edition later, Schmid was no closer to the goal of his quest, conceding in the first sentence of the revised volume that the 'search for an adequate definition is still on'. Walter Laqueur despaired of defining terrorism in both editions of his monumental work on the subject, maintaining that it is neither possible to do so nor worthwhile to make the attempt. 'Ten years of debates on typologies and definitions', he responded to a survey of definitions conducted by Schmid, 'have not enhanced our knowledge of the subject to a significant degree.' Laqueur's contention is supported by the twenty-two different word categories occurring in the 109 different definitions that Schmid identified in his survey (see Table 1).

At the end of this exhaustive exercise, Schmid asks 'whether the above list contains all the elements necessary for a good definition. The answer', he suggests, 'is probably "no".' If it is impossible to define terrorism, as Laqueur argues, and fruitless to attempt to cobble together a truly comprehensive definition, as Schmid admits, are we to conclude that terrorism is impervious to precise, much less accurate definition? Not entirely. If we cannot define terrorism, then we can at least usefully distinguish it from other types of violence and identify the characteristics that make terrorism the distinct phenomenon of political violence that it is.

Distinctions as a Path to Definition

Guerrilla warfare is a good place to start. Terrorism is often confused or equated with, or treated as synonymous with, guerrilla warfare. This is not entirely surprising, since guerrillas often employ the same tactics (assassination, kidnapping, bombings of public gathering-places, hostage-taking, etc.) for the same purposes (to intimidate or coerce, thereby affecting behaviour through the arousal of fear) as terrorists. In addition, both terrorists and

Table 1.1

Frequencies of Definitional Elements in 109 Definitions of 'Terrorism'

	Element	Frequency (%)
1	Violence, force	83.5
2	Political	65
3	Fear, terror emphasized	51
4	Threat	47
5	(Psychological) effects and (anticipated) reactions	41.5
6	Victim–target differentiation	37.5
7	Purposive, planned, systematic, organized action	32
8	Method of combat, strategy, tactic	30.5
9	Extranormality, in breach of accepted rules, without humanitarian constraints	30
10	Coercion, extortion, induction of compliance	28
11	Publicity aspect	21.5
12	Arbitrariness; impersonal, random character; indiscrimination	21
13	Civilians, noncombatants, neutrals, outsiders as victims	17.5
14	Intimidation	17
15	Innocence of victims emphasized	15.5
16	Group, movement, organization as perpetrator	14
17	Symbolic aspect, demonstration to others	13.5
18	Incalculability, unpredictability, unexpectedness of occurrence of violence	9
19	Clandestine, covert nature	9
20	Repetitiveness; serial or campaign character of violence	7
21	Criminal	6
22	Demands made on third parties	4

Source: Alex P. Schmid, Albert J. Jongman et al., *Political Terrorism: A New Guide to Actors, Authors, Concepts, Data Bases, Theories, and Literature*. New Brunswick, Transaction Books, 1988, pp. 5-6.

guerrillas wear neither uniform nor identifying insignia and thus are often indistinguishable from noncombatants. However, despite the inclination to lump both terrorists and guerrillas into the same catch-all category of 'irregulars', there are nonetheless fundamental differences between the two. 'Guerrilla', for example, in its most widely accepted usage, is taken to refer to a numerically larger group of armed individuals, who operate as a military unit, attack enemy military forces, and seize and hold territory (even if only ephemerally during daylight hours), while also exercising some form of sovereignty or control over a defined geographical area and its population. Terrorists, however, do not function in the open as armed units, generally do not attempt to seize or hold territory, deliberately avoid engaging enemy military forces in combat and rarely exercise any direct control or sovereignty either over territory or population.

It is also useful to distinguish terrorists from ordinary criminals. Like terrorists, criminals use violence as a means to attaining a specific end. However, while the violent act itself may be similar—kidnapping, shooting, arson, for example—the purpose or motivation clearly is not. Whether the criminal employs violence as a means to obtain money, to acquire material goods, or to kill or injure a specific victim for pay, he is acting primarily for selfish, personal motivations (usually material gain). Moreover, unlike terrorism, the ordinary criminals' violent act is not designed or intended to have consequences or create psychological repercussions beyond the act itself. The criminal may of course use some short-term act of violence to 'terrorize' his victim, such as waving a gun in the face of a bank clerk during a robbery in order to ensure the clerk's expeditious compliance. In these instances, however, the bank robber is conveying no 'message' (political or otherwise) through his act of violence beyond facilitating the rapid handing over of his 'loot'. The criminal's act therefore is not meant to have any effect reaching beyond either the incident itself or the immediate victim. Further, the violence is neither conceived nor intended to convey any message to anyone other than the bank clerk himself, whose rapid cooperation is the robber's only objective. Perhaps most fundamentally, the criminal is not concerned with influencing or affecting public opinion: he simply wants to abscond with his money or accomplish his mercenary task in the quickest and easiest way possible so that he may reap his reward and enjoy the fruits of his labours. By contrast, the fundamental aim of the terrorist's violence is ultimately to change 'the system'—about which the ordinary criminal, of course, couldn't care less.

The terrorist is also very different from the lunatic assassin, who may use identical tactics (e.g. shooting, bombing) and perhaps even seeks the same objective (e.g. the death of a political figure). However, while the tactics and targets of terrorists and lone assassins are often identical, their purpose is not. Whereas the terrorist's goal is again ineluctably *political* (to change or fundamentally alter a political system through his violent act), the lunatic assassin's goal is more often intrinsically idiosyncratic, completely egocentric and deeply personal. John Hinckley, who tried to kill President Reagan in 1981 to impress the actress Jodie Foster, is a case in point. He acted not from political motivation or ideological conviction but to fulfil some profound personal quest (killing the president to impress his screen idol). Such entirely *apolitical* motivations can in no way be compared to the rationalizations used by the Narodnaya Volya to justify its campaign of tyrannicide against the tsar and his minions, nor even to the Irish Republican Army's efforts to assassinate Prime Minister Margaret Thatcher or her successor, John Major, in hopes of dramatically changing British policy towards Northern Ireland. Further, just as one person cannot credibly claim to be a political party, so a lone individual cannot be considered to constitute a terrorist group. In this respect, even though Sirhan Sirhan's assassination of presidential candidate and US Senator Robert Kennedy in 1968 had a political motive (to protest against US support for Israel), it is debatable whether the murder should be defined as a terrorist act since Sirhan belongs to no organized political group and acted entirely on his own, out of deep personal frustration and a profound animus that few others shared. To qualify as terrorism, violence must be perpetrated by some organizational entity with at least some conspiratorial structure and identifiable chain of command beyond a single individual acting on his or her own.

Finally, the point should be emphasized that, unlike the ordinary criminal or the lunatic assassin, the terrorist is not pursuing purely egocentric goals—he is not driven by the wish to line his own pocket or satisfy some personal need or grievance. The terrorist is fundamentally an *altruist*: he believes that he is serving a 'good' cause designed to achieve a greater good for a wider constituency—whether real or imagined—which the terrorist and his organization purport to represent. The criminal, by comparison, serves no cause at all, just his own personal aggrandizement and material satiation. Indeed, a 'terrorist without a cause (at least in his own mind)', Konrad Kellen has argued, 'is not a terrorist'. Yet the possession or identification of a cause is not a sufficient criterion for labelling someone a terrorist. In this key respect, the difference between terrorists and political extremists is clear. Many persons, of course, harbour all sorts of radical and extreme beliefs and opinions, and many of them belong to radical or even illegal or proscribed political organizations. However, if they do not use violence in the pursuance of their beliefs, they cannot be considered terrorists. The terrorist is fundamentally a *violent intellectual*, prepared to use and indeed committed to using force in the attainment of his goals.

By distinguishing terrorists from other types of criminals and terrorism from other forms of crime, we come to appreciate that terrorism is

- ineluctably political in aims and motives;
- violent—or, equally important, threatens violence;
- designed to have far-reaching psychological repercussions beyond the immediate victim or target;
- conducted by an organization with an identifiable chain of command or conspiratorial cell structure (whose members wear no uniform or identifying insignia); and
- perpetrated by a subnational group or non-state entity.

We may therefore now attempt to define terrorism as the deliberate creation and exploitation of fear through violence or the threat of violence in the pursuit of political change. All terrorist acts involve violence or the threat of violence. Terrorism is specifically designed to have far-reaching psychological effects beyond the immediate victim(s) or object of the terrorist attack. It is meant to instil fear within, and thereby intimidate, a wider 'target audience' that might include a rival ethnic or religious group, an entire country, a national government or political party, or public opinion in general. Terrorism is designed to create power where there is none or to consolidate power where there is very little. Through the publicity generated by their violence, terrorists seek to obtain the leverage, influence and power they otherwise lack to effect political change on either a local or an international scale.

Bruce Hoffman is an authoritative analyst of terrorism and a recipient of the U.S. Intelligence Community Seal Medallion, the highest level of commendation given to a nongovernment employee. He is currently the director of the Washington, D.C., office of the RAND Corporation, where he heads the terrorism research unit, and he regularly advises both governments and businesses throughout the world. This reading is a chapter from his book *Inside Terrorism*.

Paul R. Pillar, 2001

The Dimensions of Terrorism and Counterterrorism

Delimiting a subject is the first step in dealing with it intelligently, and this is especially true of terrorism and counterterrorism. Terrorism has often been conceived in intractably broad ways, while the costs of terrorism and the ways to combat it tend to be construed too narrowly.

What Terrorism Is

Efforts to define terrorism have consumed much ink. A recent book on terrorism, for example, devotes an entire chapter to definitions; the chapter documents previous definitional attempts by earlier scholars, some of whom gave up the effort.[1] Many students of terrorism clearly consider its definition an important and unresolved issue.[2] The concern about definitions, besides reflecting any scholar's commendable interest in being precise about one's subject matter, stems from the damage done by the countless twisted and polemical uses through the years of the term "terrorism." The one thing on which every user of the term agrees is that terrorism is bad. So it has been a catch-all pejorative, applied mainly to matters involving force or political authority in some way but sometimes applied even more broadly to just about any disliked action associated with someone else's policy agenda.

The semantic quagmire has been deepened not only by indiscriminate application of the term terrorism but also by politically inspired efforts *not* to apply it. This was most in evidence in the 1970s, when multilateral discussion of the subject in the United Nations General Assembly and elsewhere invariably bogged down amid widespread resistance to any condemnation—and hence any labeling as terrorism—of the actions of groups that had favored status as "national liberation movements" or the like. Variations on this pattern have continued to frustrate efforts to arrive at an internationally accepted definition of terrorism.

Another, less frequent, tendentious approach to defining terrorism is to define it in ways that presuppose particular policy responses. For example, define it as a crime if you want to handle it mainly as a law enforcement matter, define it as war if you intend to rely on military means, and so on. Arguing semantics as a surrogate for arguing about policy is a confusing, cumbersome, and ultimately poor way to arrive at a policy.

A reasonable definition of terrorism would capture the key elements of what those leaders and respondents to opinion polls who have expressed concern about terrorism probably have in mind, without being so broad as to include much else that is not in fact the concern of those whose job descriptions mention terrorism. As good a definition as any, given some clarification and minor modification, is the statutory one that the U.S. government uses in keeping statistics on international terrorism: terrorism, for that purpose, means "premeditated, politically motivated violence perpetrated against noncombatant targets by subnational groups or clandestine agents, usually intended to influence an audience."[3] This definition has four main elements.

The first, premeditation, means there must be an intent and prior decision to commit an act that would qualify as terrorism under the other criteria. An operation may not be executed as intended and may fail altogether, but the intent must still be there. The action is the result of someone's policy, or at least someone's decision. Terrorism is not a matter of momentary rage or impulse. It is also not a matter of accident.

The second element, political motivation, excludes criminal violence motivated by monetary gain or personal vengeance. Admittedly, these latter forms of violence often must be dealt with in the same fashion as terrorism for purposes of law enforcement and physical security. Criminal violence can also have political consequences if it is part of a larger erosion of order (as in Russia). And ordinary crime is part of the world of many terrorists, either because they practice it themselves to get money or because they cooperate with criminal organizations.[4] Terrorism is fundamentally different from these other forms of violence, however, in what gives rise to it and in how it must be countered, beyond simple physical security and police techniques. Terrorists' concerns are macroconcerns about changing a larger order; other violent criminals are focused on the microlevel of pecuniary gain and personal relationships. "Political" in this regard encompasses not just traditional left-right politics but also what are frequently described as religious motivations or social issues. What all terrorists have in common and separates them from other violent criminals is that they claim to be serving some greater good.[5]

The third element, that the targets are noncombatants, means that terrorists attack people who cannot defend themselves with violence in return. Terrorism is different from a combat operation against a military force, which can shoot back. In this regard, "noncombatant" means (and has been so interpreted for the government's statistical purposes) not just civilians but also military personnel who at the time of an incident are unarmed or off duty (as at Khubar Towers or at the U.S. Marine barracks in Beirut).

The fourth element, that the perpetrators are either subnational groups or clandestine agents, is another difference between terrorism and normal military operations. An attack by a government's duly uniformed or otherwise identifiable armed forces is not terrorism; it is war. The requirement that nongovernmental perpetrators be "groups" is one point, however, on which the statutory definition could usefully be modified. A lone individual can commit terrorism. Mir Aimal Kansi's shooting spree outside the Central Intelligence Agency was politically motivated, and the four-year manhunt for him was always rightly regarded as a counterterrorist operation. Because there was no indication that he had acted at anyone else's behest, however, his attack never counted in the government's statistics on terrorism. For the present purposes, Kansi and any others like him may be considered one-person terrorist groups.

There is one other respect in which terrorism must be conceived somewhat more broadly than the statutory definition above. Terrorism as an issue is not just a collection of incidents that have already occurred; it is at least as much a matter of what might occur in the future. The threat of a terrorist attack is itself terrorism. Moreover, the mere possibility of terrorist attacks, even without explicit threats, is a counterterrorist problem. Indeed, one of the most vexing parts of that problem concerns groups that have not yet performed terrorist operations (or maybe have not even yet become groups) but might conduct terrorist attacks in the future. There is no good way to record this potential or to quantify it, and it would be pointless to manipulate formal definitions to try to embrace it. But counterterrorist specialists must worry about it. It is part of the subject at hand.

The conception of terrorism given above excludes some things that have occasionally been labeled as "terrorism" and are themselves significant national security issues—in particular, certain possible uses by hostile regimes of their military forces, such as ballistic missiles fired at civilian populations. To be sure, there are some similarities to terrorism, involving the motivations of the perpetrators, the impact on the target populations, and even the identity of some of the governments involved. These other security issues, however, have their own communities to deal with them, both inside and outside government. The relationships between different security issues must be noted and analyzed, but that does mean expanding the concept of an issue beyond workable limits. Counterterrorist specialists have enough on their plates without, say, weighing into debates on ballistic missile defense.

The concept of terrorism delineated here is not just reflected in a U.S. statute. It is also in the mainstream of what most students of terrorism seem to have in mind, despite their collective definitional angst. Moreover, it also is in the mainstream of what modest international consensus has evolved on the subject, at least the farther one gets from large multilateral debating halls and the closer to rooms where practical cooperation takes place. The latter point is important, given the necessarily heavy U.S. dependence on foreign help for counterterrorism. It is also important that whatever concept of terrorism the United States uses not be capable of being twisted to apply to actions the United States itself may take in pursuit of its security interests.

About the latter point, two distinctions are critical. The first is the one between terrorism and the overt use of military force. As the world's preeminent military power, it is in the United States' interest to keep that distinction clear, but this is not just a unilateral U.S. interest. The distinction has a broader moral and legal basis, as reflected in international humanitarian law on armed conflict and its rules requiring combatants to identify themselves openly.[6] The second key distinction is between actions that are the willful result of decisions taken by governmental or group leaders, and actions that result from accidents or impulsive behavior by lower-ranking individuals. The latter are bound to happen, and have happened, in incidents involving the United States, just because of the number of circumstances in which U.S. personnel find themselves in which it could happen. One's concept of terrorism must distinguish clearly—as the definition above does—between, for example, the alleged bombing by Libyan agents of Pan Am 103 and the accidental shooting down of Iran Air 655 in the Persian Gulf by the U.S. cruiser *Vincennes*. Despite the similarities of these incidents (290 people perished in the downing of the Iranian flight in July 1988; 270 people died in the Pan Am incident in December of the same year), and even though Tehran was still calling the Iran Air incident a "crime" more than a decade later, these were fundamentally different events. One was a government's deliberate use of its agents to murder scores of innocent travelers; the other was a tragic case of mistaken identity by a warship's crew that believed itself to be in a military engagement.

The place of clandestine agents and subnational groups in the definition of terrorism requires a bit more reflection, because the United States has used many of both. Not only that, but such use has sometimes involved lethal force, and some of that force has caused civilian casualties. But the real question is whether the intentional (that is, premeditated) infliction of civilian casualties through agents or sponsored groups—say, to undermine a hostile regime—is an option that the United States can safely forswear. It is. For one thing, the irregular use of lethal force against civilians would likely be counterproductive, by enabling the targeted regime to rally popular support in the face of a presumed external threat. Just as important, such methods are contrary to what the American public would support as being consistent with American values (a key test to be applied to any proposed covert action, even ones never likely to become public knowledge). Recent operations such as air strikes against Yugoslavia or Iraq have shown the great emphasis the United States has come to place on *avoiding* civilian casualties, even as collateral damage in a conventional military campaign.[7]

The conceptual lines between terrorism and other forms of politically driven violence are blurry. They would be blurry under any definition. The definition given above is at least as clear as any other, but it still leaves uncertainty as to whether certain specific incidents are acts of terrorism. The U.S. government has an interagency panel that meets monthly to consider such incidents (for the sake only of keeping accurate statistics, not of determining policy). The panel debates such questions as whether a particular target or intended target should be considered a noncombatant. Split votes are not unusual.

Good policy on terrorism does not, however, require hand-wringing about how exactly to define it. For the great majority of counterterrorist activities, the late Justice Potter Stewart's approach toward pornography will suffice: that it is unnecessary to go to great lengths to define it, because one knows it when one sees it.[8] Even though the U.S. government itself has several other definitions of terrorism written for different purposes, definitional discussions are seldom part of intragovernmental deliberations on the subject, beyond the statistic-keeping panel just mentioned. Lawyers do sometimes have to inject precision about whether certain statutory criteria have been met. This usually revolves around not the meaning of terrorism itself, however, but rather, for example, whether certain conditions (such as U.S. citizenship of the victims) are present that would permit a criminal prosecution. In most situations in which a counterterrorist response may be required, government officials simply recognize terrorism when they see it and do what they need to do. Any uncertainty about whether a given incident is terrorism is due not to semantics but rather to incomplete information.

The blurriness of the definitional lines is a salutary reminder that terrorism is but one form of behavior along a continuum of possible political behaviors of those who strongly oppose the status quo. Alternative forms include other types of violence (such as guerrilla warfare), nonviolent but illegal actions, regular partisan or diplomatic activity, or simple expressions of opinion that never even crystallize into something as specific as a political party, resistance movement, or terrorist group. Sound counterterrorist policy does not focus narrowly only on terrorism itself (however defined) but instead takes into account that terrorists have a menu of other tactics and behaviors from which to choose, and that the conflicts underlying terrorism invariably have other dimensions that also affect U.S. interests.

The distinction between terrorism, as defined here, and other forms of violence by subnational groups is apt to be faint in the eyes of some of the people directly involved. The Muslim fight against Indian control of Kashmir, for example, has been a blend of terrorist attacks against civilians and guerrilla warfare against Indian military forces. At least some of the insurgent leaders recognize the distinction publicly and deny attacking civilians. "We are a legitimate freedom movement," said a leader of one of the larger groups, "and we do not want to be stigmatized with the terrorist label."[9] But attacks in Kashmir against cinemas and parliamentary candidates continue, along with ambushes of Indian army patrols. The course of the conflict in Kashmir, and how each side privately views it, will not depend on the exact proportion of attacks against civilian rather than military targets. Both kinds of attack are unjustified in Indian eyes; both kinds are part of an overall struggle for self-determination, in the eyes of the militants. The selection of targets has probably depended in large part on such tactical factors as the physical vulnerabilities of the targets and the local capabilities of the groups.

For most Americans, however—and for many others—the distinction between terrorism against civilians and warfare (including guerrilla warfare) against an army entails an important moral difference. The warrior who dons a uniform is understood to be assuming certain risks that the civilian does not, and the guerrilla who fires at someone who is armed and can fire back is not regarded as embracing the same evil as one who kills the helpless and the unarmed. While the United States must be cognizant of the tendency of many to gloss over such distinctions, it should not let the distinctions be forgotten. Its message should be that terrorist techniques, in any context, are unacceptable.

Which gets to the most important point to remember about definitions: terrorism is a *method*—a particularly heinous and damaging one—rather than a set of adversaries or the causes they pursue. Terrorism is a problem of what people (or groups, or states) *do*, rather than who they are or what they are trying to achieve. (If Usama bin Ladin, for example, did not use or support terrorist methods, he would be of little concern to the United States—probably receiving only minor notice for his criticism of the Saudi government and his role in the Afghan wars.) Terrorism and our attention to it do not depend on the particular political or social values that terrorists promote or attack.[10] And counterterrorism is not a war against some particular foe; it is an effort to civilize the manner in which any political contest is waged.

Why It Matters

Terrorism has many different costs. The direct physical harm inflicted on people and property is the most obvious, but it is by no means the only, or even the most important, cost. It is the most measurable ones, in that deaths and injuries can be counted and property damage can be assessed. The significance of even these direct physical costs can be a matter of debate, however, involving disagreements over exactly what should be measured and against what standard the measurement should be compared.

Start with the question of whose casualties to count. In any discussion of U.S. policy, U.S. citizens are clearly the primary concern. Six hundred and sixty-six American citizens died from international terrorism in the 1980s and 1990s.[11] During the same period 190 Americans died from domestic terrorism within the United States, for a total of 856 American deaths from terrorism during the past two decades.[12] Going beyond U.S. citizens, however, greatly expands the numbers. Deaths of all nationalities from international terrorist incidents during the same twenty years totaled 7,152. (There were also more than 31,000 wounded.) The scale of death and suffering expands yet another order of magnitude if one takes account of terrorism that is not "international" because it takes place within a single nation's borders and directly involves only that country's nationals. There are no statistics on this type of terrorism worldwide, but consider just one of the bloodier examples:

Algeria. Most published estimates of the number killed in Algeria by the extremist violence that broke out in 1992 are around 100,000. Many of these deaths were not from terrorism, but many others were, including particularly gruesome mass throat-slittings in villages. Even without U.S. citizens being involved, and even without considering the indirect effects that might be more significant for U.S. interests, this scale of bloodshed warrants attention. The death toll has certainly been at least comparable to that of many natural disasters to which the United States has felt obliged to respond. The deaths in Algeria did, in fact, lead the counterterrorism community in the U.S. government to examine ways in which it might help.

Returning to the more direct U.S. concern with American casualties, what is the right frame of reference for assessing their magnitude? To any contention that the victims of terrorism are many—or few—one is entitled to ask, "compared with what?" Against some possible standards of comparison, such as highway deaths (more than 40,000 annually in the United States), the number of victims of terrorism seems tiny. And the number is less than the bathtub drownings, lightning strikes, and some other standards that critics have used. A more appropriate basis for comparison might be other deaths from foreigners committing political violence—that is, warfare. Even there, American fatalities from terrorism are minuscule compared with such major efforts as World War II (291,557 U.S. battle deaths), Korea (33,651) or Vietnam (47,378).[13]

U.S. military activity since Vietnam, however, provides a different perspective. U.S. deaths from nonterrorist hostile action in military operations during the 1980s and 1990s (including the Iranian hostage rescue attempt, peacekeeping in Lebanon, the bombing of Libya, the escorting of Kuwaiti tankers, and Operations Urgent Fury in Grenada, Just Cause in Panama, Desert Storm in the Persian Gulf, Restore Hope in Somalia, and Uphold Democracy in Haiti) totaled 251. Even adding the 263 deaths from nonhostile causes (most of which were incurred in Desert Shield and Desert Storm) yields a total of 514, less than the number of Americans killed by terrorists during the same period. The biggest single inflictor of casualties on the U.S. military during this period was a terrorist attack: the bombing of the U.S. Marine barracks in Beirut in 1983, which killed 241. Besides, some of the other military deaths (the eight who died in the attempt to rescue hostages in Iran in 1980, and the two who were lost during the air strikes against Libya in 1986) were casualties of U.S. responses to terrorism. The nature of the hazard that Americans face in carrying out official duties overseas has evolved over the past quarter century to the point that a commission studying the U.S. overseas presence could state in 1999 that "since the end of the Vietnam War, more ambassadors have lost their lives to hostile actions than generals and admirals from the same cause."[14]

There has been an underlying evolution in how U.S. policymakers view casualties, and this also affects how the consequences of terrorism are likely to be viewed. Since Vietnam, the United States has expended lives, or put them in harm's way, more reluctantly than before. The casualties that the U.S. military suffered in Somalia in 1993 (and their graphic and wrenching coverage in the media) appear to have accentuated this trend. Survey research suggests that policymakers and other civilian and military elites may be overestimating the American public's aversion to casualties in military operations incurred in performance of missions that have at least the potential to be successful.[15] Whether or not that is true, policies and strategies, including warfighting strategies, now place very high priority on minimizing casualties. The remarkable phenomenon of a major military campaign without any U.S. battle casualties—the air war against Yugoslavia in 1999—was the apotheosis of this trend. The trend can only accentuate the significance that Americans will place on whatever American lives are lost to terrorism in the future.

Two other dimensions of what terrorists have been doing lately, or appear poised to do in the future, bear on how to think about the direct physical costs of terrorism. One is that terrorism in recent years has become increasingly lethal. More terrorist attacks than before are designed to inflict high casualties. Deaths from international terrorism more than doubled from the first half of the 1990s to the latter half of the decade, even though the number of incidents declined 19 percent. This trend is associated... with the nature of some of the terrorist groups that have come to the fore during this time, and there is no reason to expect a reversal of the pattern anytime soon.

The other dimension is the much-ballyhooed danger of chemical, biological, radiological, or nuclear (CBRN) terrorism inflicting mass casualties. There are some legitimate reasons for concern about this to be greater now than a few years ago. The just-mentioned increased lethality of international terrorism is one reason; the more that terrorists use conventional means to kill large numbers of people, the less of a conceptual leap it is that they would use unconventional means to try to accomplish the same objective. Related to that is the increased role of small, religiously driven groups like the World Trade Center bombers, who are less likely than many larger groups (or states) to be deterred by the consequences of their own escalating violence—because they have no constituent populations to abhor their methods and no fixed assets to be the target of retaliation. The availability of materials and expertise relevant to CBRN weapons is another basis for concern. The focus has been on what might come out of the former Soviet Union (not just "loose nukes" but also substances related to biological or chemical weapons, as well as the knowledge and skills of displaced Soviet weapons scientists) and on weapons-related information that is now readily available on the Internet. Intelligence that shows some terrorist groups to be interested in CBRN capabilities is another concern. So is the precedent set by Aum Shinrikyo's attempt in 1995 to use sarin in a Tokyo subway to inflict mass casualties. Finally, the enormous public attention given to the danger of CBRN terrorism has itself probably increased the danger by pointing out to terrorists some of the possibilities—not only how such weapons might be used but also how much they frighten people.

Public discussion of CBRN terrorism has tended to stress many of these concerns—and the vulnerabilities of the United States to conceivable mass-casualty CBRN attacks—but given less emphasis to reasons that such attacks may still be unlikely. The General Accounting Office [GAO] has noted this pattern and emphasized the important distinction between conceivable terrorist threats and likely ones. The GAO observes that some of the public statements of U.S. officials about the CBRN threat have omitted important qualifications to the information they have presented.[16] The qualifications can be found not only in the classified material that the GAO reviewed but also in what is now a sizable scholarly literature on CBRN terrorism.[17] Experts who have studied the subject in depth have found numerous reasons to doubt whether CBRN terrorism is as much a wave of the future as is widely perceived.

Some of those reasons involve technical and other difficulties that any terrorist would face in acquiring the capability to inflict mass casualties with CBRN devices or agents. Some of the substances in question (for example, virulent forms of pathogens that would be needed to make biological weapons, as distinct from other forms that might be used in the production of vaccines) are not as easy to obtain as is commonly supposed.[18] Even with raw material in hand, there are formidable challenges in converting it into an effective and deployable device. Some toxic agents are difficult to keep both potent and stable. Dissemination is a major challenge, with both biological and chemical agents. Airborne particles containing anthrax, for example, can easily be either too large or too small to infect people through inhalation. Chemical agents need to be produced in large quantities and dispersed over wide areas to have hope of causing large numbers of casualties. Given such challenges, development of a CBRN capability to cause mass casualties would require a major, sophisticated program that is well beyond the reach of the great majority of terrorist groups. Aum Shinrikyo demonstrated this point. Despite being unusually well endowed in money and technical talent and going to great lengths to develop CBRN capabilities, Aum's biological program failed completely, and its attempt to use sarin to kill hundreds or thousands on the Tokyo subway instead killed only twelve.

Other reasons for doubt involve terrorist intentions. Terrorists have generally been tactically conservative and have favored proven methods. The hazards and uncertain effects of using CBRN materials are not likely to be attractive to many of them, particularly given the proven effectiveness of old-fashioned truck bombs—in places as diverse as Beirut and Oklahoma City—in causing casualties numerous enough to be considered "mass." The fear-inducing aspect of an unseen killer like a biological pathogen may have appeal to some terrorists, but the theatrical aspect of an event that makes a loud explosion is apt to appeal to even more. Moreover, the large and well-organized groups that have the best chance of obtaining a CBRN capability are also the ones that—because they have the most to lose by outraging their constituencies or inviting forceful retaliation—are most likely to be deterred from using such a capability. Aum Shinrikyo was an exception, but what may be most significant (with more than five years having passed since the incident in the Tokyo subway) is that Aum did not start a trend.

The foregoing leads to the following conclusions about CBRN terrorism. First, it is a legitimate cause for concern; it represents one more way in which terrorism can entail major costs, and one more reason to be serious about countering it. Second, the actual threat of CBRN terrorism—which is impossible to gauge with anything approaching precision—has probably risen somewhat over the last few years but is much less than the alarmist treatment of the subject in the United States would lead one to believe. Third, actual CBRN attacks would (as with such attacks in the past) be more likely to cause few, rather than many, casualties. Their impact would be less a matter of the direct physical effects than the indirect psychological effects on the target population. How a government conditions its public to think about such an attack… is thus critical in determining what the impact will be.

A fourth conclusion (bearing in mind the preceding two) is that the specter of CBRN terrorism should not be the main basis for shaping thinking about terrorism overall or for organizing efforts to confront it. It would be a mistake to redefine counterterrorism as a task of dealing with "catastrophic," "grand," or "super" terrorism, when in fact these labels do not represent most of the terrorism that the United States is likely to face or most of the costs that terrorism imposes on U.S. interests. A CBRN incident that causes very many casualties is the sort of high-impact, low-probability event that, because of the high impact, policy must take into account. The potentially high consequences may be reason enough to devote more attention and resources to preparing for such an event. But the low-probability aspect of the scenario should also be remembered, and the scenario should not be allowed to distort or downgrade the attention paid to more probable forms of terrorism.

Similar considerations apply to cyberterrorism, about which high concern is even more recent, and the uncertainties even greater. Some terrorist groups have indeed demonstrated considerable sophistication with computers and computer networks. Presumably some groups that lack the necessary expertise for conducting electronic sabotage could purchase it from venal and adventurous individuals. Electronic attacks to date that have been associated with terrorist groups have been few and simple, such as "spam" attacks in which large numbers of messages overload a government's server. The capability of terrorist groups to conduct electronic attacks more damaging than these incidents, or than the nonterrorist sabotage that has occasionally disabled major web sites, is more questionable. Terrorist intentions regarding cyberterrorism are even more problematic. Linking the objectives of actual terrorist groups to scenarios of electronic sabotage that would serve those objectives is conjecture.

To express such skepticism is not to deny the worth of security measures that would protect against unconventional terrorism, not only because of the potentially high consequences of such terrorism but also because many of those measures would also guard against other dangers. Almost all of the steps being taken to safeguard the nation's electronic infrastructure from terrorist groups, for example, would also help to protect it against attacks from the sources that, based on recent experience, seem to pose the main threat of electronic sabotage: individual hackers, and perhaps others driven by nonterrorist motives. This last point is true as well of some measures to defend against biological terrorism, which might include a strengthening of the public health system (including, perhaps, the additional acquisition of vaccines or antidotes) that would be needed anyway to deal effectively with natural or accidental outbreaks of disease.[19]

Terrorism in general, even when conducted with conventional means, tends to have greater psychological impact relative to the physical harm it causes than do other lethal activities, including warfare. In this regard, the earlier comparisons with casualties from past military operations understate, in a sense, the significance of terrorism. The distinction between the fair fight of an open military engagement and the unfair one of a terrorist attack on helpless victims comes into play. Ask the average American if the life of a soldier who dies in battle is worth the same as the life of a countryman who has died from terrorism, and the answer will be yes. But ask after each type of event how much shock and revulsion that American is feeling, and the reaction will be stronger after the terrorist incident. That the felt impact of terrorism tends to be disproportionate to the material damage has led some to argue that if government (and others who comment on terrorism) would only play down its significance and treat it more like ordinary crime, its actual importance and usefulness to the terrorist would lessen.[20] How government publicly portrays terrorism does indeed matter. But however much one might try to talk down the subject, some of the special shock of a terrorist attack will always be there; it is in the nature of the event.

The indirect costs of terrorism are, overall, significantly greater than the direct physical ones. The indirect costs are many and varied. They start with the fear instilled in individual citizens, and what it leads those citizens to do. The fear itself—the sheer mental discomfort—is a cost. So is the economic effect of fearful citizens not taking trips or not patronizing certain businesses. And so is the social effect of those citizens arming themselves or ostracizing fellow citizens of particular ethnic backgrounds that are associated with terrorism, or doing any of a number of other dysfunctional things that less fearful citizens would not do.

Countermeasures against terrorism are also a major indirect cost. Price tags can be placed on some of them but capture only part of the expense. What was labeled as the terrorism-related portion of the Clinton administration's budget for fiscal year 2000, for example, amounted to about $10 billion, although that is a malleable figure depending on what one includes under the counterterrorist label. To take a single type of expense as a more tractable example, the panel chaired by retired Admiral William Crowe that studied the bombings in East Africa estimated that $14 billion would be required over ten years to implement its recommendations for improving the security of U.S. diplomatic missions.[21] Federal expenditures are only part of the picture, because many security countermeasures against terrorism are expenses of state or local governments or of the private sector. And the cost of many measures cannot realistically be estimated at all, although they have innumerable second- and third-order effects that, aggregating them over the entire nation, are surely huge. Every time someone empties his pockets and takes a detour through a metal detector to gain access to a public building, there are costs—which may include not only inconvenience to an individual but also the time and thus the expense involved in transacting a piece of business.

The expenditures made in responding to a problem beg the question, of course, of how many of those expenditures have been necessary and effective. Most of the success stories about countermeasures against terrorism are fragmentary and anecdotal, and it is impossible to calculate how much trouble would have occurred in their absence. But the very fact that so many resources are consumed—however necessary or unnecessary, effective or ineffective, any particular countermeasure may be—is itself a reason for the subject to command policy attention.

With some antiterrorist programs—including some big, expensive ones—past effectiveness and the future need to spend substantial resources are easier to see. Aviation security is an example. A major success story over the past quarter century has been a drastic reduction in skyjackings. Although some other factors affecting terrorists' choice of methods have been involved, the chief reason for this welcome development has been a comprehensive security system that has made it much harder to bring on board an aircraft the wherewithal to hijack it. This system is costly, including the visible costs of x-ray machines, metal detectors, and the staff to operate them, as well as less visible costs such as lengthening the time required to make business trips. The Federal Aviation Administration is now endeavoring to reduce the vulnerability of civil aviation in the United States to the other terrorist threat it faces—in-flight bombings—by enhancing procedures for screening checked baggage on domestic flights. The FAA estimates that this single change would cost $2.8 billion over ten years.[22]

Finally, the costs of terrorism embrace a host of other political and policy effects. They include the governmental equivalent of fear among individual citizens—that is, the government does not do certain things (which could be anything from a trip by a VIP to the holding of a New Year's celebration), or does them in a more gingerly or less effective manner, than it otherwise would because of fear of terrorist attacks. Costs also include the shaping of the political environment in unfavorable ways. Any challenge to government's monopoly on the use of force (which terrorism and other politically motivated violence necessarily entails) affects citizens' views toward government itself, including the trust they place in it to meet their needs for order and security.[23]

The costs of terrorism also include major effects on U.S. foreign relations and foreign interests, especially the following.

First, the possibility of terrorist attacks inhibits, or at least complicates, a wide range of U.S. activities overseas and the maintenance of an official U.S. presence abroad. This includes the necessary concern that almost any official American working overseas must have with security (and in some places it is a high concern), which means a distraction from that official's primary job. It also includes major security-driven operational decisions having significant impact on other missions. For example, the United States vacated its embassy in Sudan in February 1996 (without formally breaking diplomatic relations) because of terrorism. The specific concerns were not only with the terrorism-related policies of the Sudanese government but also with whether U.S. officials living and working in Khartoum would be safe, given the presence in Sudan of a rogue's gallery of international terrorist groups.[24] The absence of a resident diplomatic mission in Sudan, which has the largest territory of any African country and touches on numerous conflicts in the unstable northeastern and East Africa regions, unavoidably hinders support for U.S. interests in the area. One of the things it has hindered is collection of intelligence, including intelligence on terrorist threats that could materialize elsewhere. (It is worth remembering that most of those arrested in June 1993 for plotting to bomb the Hudson River tunnels and other landmarks in New York City were Sudanese.)

A similar security-driven redeployment was the move, following the bombing of Khubar Towers in 1996, of nearly 4,000 U.S. troops in Saudi Arabia from the urban areas of Dhahran and Riyadh to the isolated (and hence less vulnerable to terrorism) Prince Sultan Air Base. The move itself cost $200 million (which the U.S. and Saudi governments agreed to split). Perhaps more costly was the impact on morale, training, and readiness of the isolation and accompanying changes in deployment policy, including the withdrawal of command sponsorship for dependents and the cutting in half (from ninety days to forty-five) of the tours of the fighter pilots who overfly Iraq.[25]

Besides the impediments to official U.S. activity, there are also security-related complications for the private sector. If a U.S. business decides to brave the risk of terrorism in making a direct investment in a hazardous area, it will have expenses for security that will be an added cost of doing business. If the risk dissuades it from making the investment, then an opportunity for making and repatriating profits, and for enhancing employment in the local economy, will have been lost.

A second cost of terrorism in terms of foreign policy is the undermining of peace processes, including ones in which the United States has invested heavily and which, absent the disruption of fresh terrorist attacks, might otherwise be ripe for progress. The series of suicide bombings in Israel by Hamas and the Palestine Islamic Jihad in early 1996, for example, caused popular support for the Labor Party's peace policies to crumble, paved the way for Benjamin Netanyahu's upset election victory, and retarded progress toward further Arab-Israeli accords. In Northern Ireland, attacks in August 1998 by the republican splinter group calling itself the "Real IRA" (especially a car bomb in Omagh that killed 29 and injured at least 330) led to an unraveling of the Good Friday peace accord to the point that, later in the year, the agreement seemed close to collapse. More recently, it has been the main IRA's retention of its means of terror (the issue of "decommissioning of arms") that has been the principal reason for setbacks in the Northern Ireland peace process, such as the temporary suspension of the provincial government in February 2000.

Third, terrorism risks enflaming other regional conflicts that are already closer to war than to peace. (The spark that ignited World War I—the assassination of Archduke Francis Ferdinand—was a terrorist act.) The hijacking by Kashmiri militants of an Indian airliner in December 1999, for example, led to a new round of recriminations between India and Pakistan and raised the temperature of their dispute. Neither this incident nor most others like it have led to a war, but they at least temporarily increase the danger of one breaking out.

Fourth, the concern of an otherwise friendly government that it will become a target of terrorism may dissuade it from cooperating with the United States. Sometimes it fears being perceived as doing Washington's bidding. Sometimes what Washington asks it to do is unpopular for other reasons. In either case the specific fear is that extreme opponents of the requested cooperation will strike back with violence. The cooperation in question may range from diplomatic support to the hosting of a military deployment.

And fifth, terrorism can destabilize friendly governments. This is much less common than merely influencing the policies of such governments, and terrorism itself seldom topples regimes. It has sometimes caused major damage to the social or economic fabric of important countries, however, and as a result has called regimes' political stamina into question. This was true of Peru at the height of Sendero Luminoso's campaign of violence, and to a lesser degree of Egypt when terrorist attacks devastated that country's economically vital tourist industry in the early 1990s.

None of these costly consequences for U.S. foreign relations results *only* from terrorism. Numerous other political, economic, military, diplomatic, and cultural dimensions of the global environment (or regional environments) also affect them. Many of these dimensions involve the United States directly or are subject to U.S. influence. This is part of why counterterrorist policy must be considered and formulated as an integral part of U.S. foreign policy. Counterterrorism is one means by which to pursue the objectives implied above—stable and cooperative allies, effective regional peace processes, and so forth—and others as well. The means, including counterterrorism, used to pursue these objectives must be employed as part of a consistent, well-integrated strategy. And in the judgment of history, whether these objectives are achieved is likely to be at least important as the means used to achieve them.

Of course, the basic counterterrorist goal of saving lives and property from terrorist attack is a worthy end in its own right and not just a means. Indeed, some of the objectives posited above, such as effective regional peacemaking, could just as appropriately be viewed as means toward, among other things, the end of reducing violence, especially terrorist violence. The permutations of ends and means relationships between counterterrorism and other foreign policy goals are innumerable. That is the point. Counterterrorism is part of a larger, complicated web of foreign policy endeavors and interests, with numerous trade-offs and unintended consequences that should not be ignored.

The Elements of Counterterrorist Policy

No single approach makes an effective counterterrorist policy. The policy must have several elements. In that respect, counterterrorism is similar to many other policy problems, including other ones that involve the physical well-being of the public.

Consider, for example, highway safety. Highway deaths and injuries are a function of the highways themselves, the vehicles that travel them, the traffic laws, the enforcement of those laws, and the drivers. Government can reduce deaths and injuries somewhat through action on each of these fronts (for example, installing guard rails, raising crash resistance standards for cars, lowering speed limits, putting more police on patrol, tightening licensing requirements for drivers). Each type of measure addresses only part of the problem. Each has diminishing returns. Each entails compromises with other interests, such as competing demands for use of tax dollars, ease and efficiency in getting people where they want go, or environmental concerns. So some measures are taken in all of these areas, rather than concentrating safety efforts in only one of them.

The major fronts on which the problem of terrorism can be addressed are the root conditions and issues that give rise to terrorist groups in the first place and motivate individuals to join them; the ability of such groups to conduct terrorist attacks; the intentions of groups regarding whether to launch terrorist attacks; and the defenses erected against such attacks. Each of these corresponds to a phase in the life cycle of terrorism, from simmering discontent to the conduct of an actual terrorist operation. As with the example of highway safety, important and useful work can be done on each front. But also like that example, efforts on any one front are insufficient to manage the problem and are necessarily limited by competing objectives and equities. Effective counterterrorism requires attention to all four areas.

Roots

Cutting the roots of terrorism is not commonly thought of—or officially expressed as—an element of U.S. counterterrorist policy, for a couple of reasons. One is that it is farther removed than any of the other elements from the here-and-now worries of imminent threats, actual attacks, and what to do about them. It is not as pressing a concern as other counterterrorist work, the links between roots and people actually getting killed or maimed are often tenuous and twisted, and cause-and-effect relationships are difficult to prove. The other reason is that doing something about roots involves the management of numerous foreign policy matters that are not primarily the responsibility of people who call themselves counterterrorist officials. In fact, it embraces a huge swath of U.S. foreign policy on such things as regional and local conflicts, political instability within states, and social and economic conditions in countries in which terrorist groups have arisen or could arise.

Just because a cause-and-effect relationship is difficult to measure, however, does not make it nonexistent. Conditions do matter. Terrorists and terrorist groups do not arise randomly, and they are not distributed evenly around the globe. Scholars who have examined the origins of subnational political violence in general have pointed to the need to consider the perceived deprivation and other grievances that provide motives for violence, as well as the calculations and political opportunities of dissident leaders who mobilize such discontent, to understand better when and where violence breaks out.[26]

Two types of antecedent conditions are germane to the emergence of terrorists. One consists of the issues expressed directly by the terrorists and those who sympathize with their cause: political repression, a lack of self-determination, the depravity of their rulers, or whatever. People who are angry over such issues are more likely to resort to extreme measures, including terrorism and other forms of violence, than ones who are not.

Palestinian support for violence against Israeli targets, for example, has to some extent varied inversely with progress in the peace process aimed at realizing Palestinian self-determination. This is true even though most Palestinians realize that Islamist terrorism against Israel has been counter-productive in the sense of retarding the peace process itself, boosting electoral support for harder-line Israeli leaders, undermining the economy of the Occupied Territories, and causing the Palestinian Authority to be preoccupied with security rather than with political development.[27]

The other type of root condition includes the living standards and socioeconomic prospects of populations that are, or may become, the breeding stock for terrorists. Terrorism is a risky, dangerous, and very disagreeable business. Consequently, few people who have a reasonably good life will be inclined to get into that business, regardless of their political viewpoint. Those who have more desolate lives and little hope of improving them will have fewer reservations about getting into it. The majority of terrorists worldwide are young adult males, unemployed or underemployed (except by terrorist groups), with weak social and familial support, and with poor prospects for economic improvement or advancement through legitimate work. To take the Palestinian example, most members of the extremist Palestine Islamic Jihad are of low social origin and live in poverty in the bleak neighborhoods or refugee camps of the Gaza Strip.[28] Hamas also does its most successful recruiting in Gaza.

The connection between lifestyles and proclivity for terrorism has been the basis for a technique that has been used successfully to get low-level members of certain terrorist groups to leave the terrorist business and to stay out of it. Tell the young man that if he cuts all ties with his current organization he will receive assistance in finding a job and a new place to live. Tell him also that the financial assistance he receives will depend partly on his getting married (and, preferably, having children). Settling down into a stable family life with some means of supporting it makes a return to terrorism very unlikely. For such reclamation cases, the principal roots of terrorism have been severed.

Obviously not every terrorist or potential terrorist can be bought off in this way. Policy initiatives on a larger scale do affect the roots of terrorism, however. Peace processes that lead to some measure of self-determination may do so. Political reforms that open up peaceful channels for dissent may do so. And economic development that improves prospects for a better standard of living may do so. The possibilities for snipping away at the roots of terrorism in these and similar ways should be noted and made part of the policy deliberations. But there are three major constraints on what can be done by focusing on roots alone.

The first constraint is the complexity of the relationship between antecedent conditions and the emergence of terrorists. It is not nearly as simple a matter as giving disgruntled people votes or a higher income. No one has produced a good algorithm for the many variables that, in combination, breed terrorists. In the nineteenth century, terrorism frequently emerged in direct response to repression, but the correlation between political grievances and terrorism in more recent times is less obvious.[29] In fact, terrorism today appears more often in free than in unfree societies.[30] Peace processes that realize the aspirations of a majority may, at least in the short term, enflame a minority that opposes a settlement for other reasons. As for economic conditions, one must take account of cases such as the emergence of Islamic terrorist groups in some wealthy Muslim societies like Kuwait but not in some poor ones like Niger.[31] The tearing of traditional social fabrics by economic development may have actually encouraged terrorism in some places.

The second constraint is that counterterrorism can never be the only consideration, or sometimes even the chief one, in determining U.S. policies that affect the economic well-being of certain foreign populations or self-determination for certain ethnic groups. Resource limitations obviously weigh heavily on decisions regarding economic assistance. On the political side, U.S. support for even so long-standing a principle as self-determination has always been limited by a variety of interests and concerns.[32] Some things that an unhappy, potentially terrorist-breeding, population may consider unjust may be viewed by the United States, for politically and ethically sound reasons, as not unjust and in no need of major change. The likely effect on emergent terrorism should be one factor, but only one of many, that is brought to bear on policies that affect these sorts of political and economic conditions overseas.

And third, no matter how much effort is expended on cutting out roots of terrorism, there will always remain a core of incorrigibles—and these will include the terrorists about whom the United States must worry the most. They will remain because for some individuals (even though they are sane and political, not pathological), terrorism also serves personal needs—self-fulfillment, making a big mark, or following some other inner demon—that have little to do with the order of the outside world.[33] They will also remain because the viewpoints of some are simply too extreme to be accommodated. And they will remain because once terrorist groups and terrorist leaders emerge, they develop their own goals and dynamics that go beyond the causes that may have bred them in the first place. The second and third of these factors, and probably the first, apply, for example, to Usama bin Ladin and his inner circle. As former State Department counterterrorism coordinator L. Paul Bremer has put it: "There's no point in addressing the so-called causes of bin Ladin's despair with us. We are the root cause of his terrorism. He doesn't like America. He doesn't like our society. He doesn't like what we stand for. He doesn't like our values. And short of the United States going out of existence, there's no way to deal with the root cause of his terrorism."[34]

Capabilities

Reducing the ability of terrorist groups to conduct attacks—conduct them effectively, or in many different places—is at the heart of U.S. counterterrorist programs (especially in the narrow sense of counterterrorism as offensive efforts against terrorists, as distinct from defensive antiterrorism programs). This work involves a variety of intelligence, legal, and other counterterrorist instruments....

Attacking terrorist capabilities has been an effective way of reducing many brands of terrorism. Most of the successes have been unpublicized, piecemeal acts of disruption—a cell rolled up here, a terrorist operative arrested there. A more visible and dramatic example of how effective even a single blow against a group can be was the Peruvian raid in April 1997 at the Japanese ambassador's residence in Lima, which had been seized four months earlier by the Tupac Amaru Revolutionary Movement (MRTA). The raid not only freed all but one of the seventy-two remaining hostages; it also crippled the MRTA's capability to conduct future terrorism. Several of the group's most able operational leaders died in the raid.

As with the other elements of counterterrorist policy, however, a focus on degrading the capabilities of groups has inherent limitations. One limitation, as the bombing in

Oklahoma City demonstrated, is that even the infliction of mass casualties does not always require much capability. That horror was accomplished with two men, a truck, and homemade fertilizer-based explosives. A prior detention (or just investigation) of Timothy McVeigh and Terry Nichols conceivably could have prevented the bombing, but there was nothing else that authorities could have done before the incident to reduce terrorist capabilities to conduct it. Infrastructures and networks of cells—which are critical to the ability of many foreign terrorist groups to conduct attacks—were not present in the case.

Too little capability for U.S. authorities to go after is one limitation; too much capability is yet another one. A major transnational terrorist group such as Lebanese Hizballah is simply too large and widespread an organization to wipe out with a few well-conceived counterterrorist operations. Using such operations to chip away at Hizballah's capabilities is, and should remain, a priority task for U.S. counterterrorism. Such operations can be effective at least in curtailing the group's ability to strike in certain regions. But such a group is not as vulnerable as a smaller one like the MRTA. It must be assumed that, even in the face of vigorous counterterrorist operations, the group will retain a capability that must be negated through the other elements of counterterrorist policy.

Intentions

There is indeed an enormous amount of terrorist capability around the world, in the hands of groups as well as hostile states, which could inflict major harm on the United States (or others) if those who control that capability decided to do so. This includes not only avowedly anti-American groups such as Lebanese Hizballah (which has not directly carried out a confirmed terrorist attack against a U.S. target since at least 1996) but also highly capable groups (such as Hamas or the Tamil Tigers) that have directed their violence elsewhere. Having less rather than more terrorism is thus a function not only of degrading terrorist capabilities but also of terrorist leaders *choosing*—for whatever reason—not to use what capabilities they have to attack. In short, terrorist intentions matter.

The intentions of terrorist groups (what the leaders of groups that already exist choose to do) raise some of the same motives and issues that are related to terrorism's roots (why terrorist groups arise in the first place and people join them). The status of the Arab-Israeli peace process, for example, affects Palestinian terrorism through its influence on intentions (decisions by Hamas's leadership on whether, when, and against what targets to stage attacks) as well as on roots (the emergence of Hamas and the Palestine Islamic Jihad in the first place and the willingness of young Palestinians to be recruited for suicide missions). Again, the issues involved go well beyond counterterrorism, and policy decisions on them necessarily also reflect other objectives and equities.

Measures that are more commonly regarded as counterterrorism also affect terrorist intentions. Punishing terrorists through prosecution or retaliatory strikes, for example, might have some deterrent effect.... The posture that the United States takes toward the political aspirations of groups it has officially branded as terrorist affects the intentions of those groups. The same could be said of state sponsors of terrorism.

One of the longest standing and most frequently expressed tenets of U.S. counterterrorist policy also has to do with terrorist intentions: that the United States will make no concessions to terrorists. The principle is simple: that not rewarding terrorism will give terrorists less incentive to try using it again. It would be difficult to prove that the principle always works in practice, but some analysis has pointed to past patterns of how terrorists have attempted to coerce different states at different times to suggest it has some validity.[35]

The U.S. part of the record is clouded by the fact that the United States has at times made concessions to terrorism. The most notorious instance was the Iran-Contra affair, in which the United States secretly sold arms to Iran in 1986 as part of an effort to gain release of hostages held by Iranian-backed terrorists in Lebanon. That episode certainly tarnished the U.S. image of steadfastness against terrorism, but in some respects terrorists still have good reason to view the United States as one of their most obdurate opponents. Even Israel—despite being a famously hard-line fighter against terrorism that has refused to make concessions while hostages were held—has struck deals with extremist opponents, including ones in which large numbers of prisoners were released in return for much smaller numbers of Israeli nationals. It is with regard to the classic type of terrorist coercion—holding the target country's citizens hostage to obtain a release of prisoners—that the United States has stood most firm. Even Iran-Contra did not involve opening any U.S. jail cells.

A benefit of that firmness was seen after the MRTA's capture of the Japanese ambassador's residence in Lima. The six U.S. officials who were at the reception when the terrorists struck were among the first to be released. The kidnappers let them go five days after the incident began while keeping 140 other hostages, including many foreign officials as well as Peruvians. The MRTA probably calculated (correctly) that to the extent the United States stayed directly involved, it would counsel a harder line to the Peruvian leadership than would many of the Asian and Latin American governments whose officials the MRTA had also seized.

An obvious limitation to firmness in any hostage incident is the immediate risk to the lives of the hostages. No government, the United States included, can promise itself or anyone else that it would never, under any circumstances, make concessions to save the lives of its citizens. Its management of the incident would have to take into account the magnitude and credibility of the harm being threatened, along with its own longer-term credibility and reputation. Accordingly, the rhetorical emphasis of this aspect of U.S. counterterrorist policy perhaps should be less on "no concessions" and more on the slightly more flexible "terrorism will not be rewarded." A concession made in the face of an immediate threat of great harm need not constitute a reward unless the terrorists were demanding some irreversible act, and there are few of those (even released prisoners can be recaptured).[36] Once the immediate peril is over, the terrorists can be hunted to the ends of the earth and appropriate action taken to ensure that when the books on the incident are closed, it will not count as a reward for terrorism.[37] Certainly no government need feel obliged to observe commitments made under duress. Consider the repatriation of the crew of the USS *Pueblo*, a U.S. Navy ship that North Korea seized in 1968; the United States repudiated the "admission" (of violating territorial waters) demanded by the North Koreans even as it was signing it.

A broader limitation on how much can be expected from this kind of firmness is that the classic hostage-and-specific-demand incident is simply not as big a part of international terrorism as it used to be. Although U.S. citizens have been bit players in a few such incidents in recent years (such as the Lima event and the hijacking of the Air India jet), U.S. crisis managers have not for a long time had to wrestle directly with dramatic, well-publicized, hostage situations in which lives are staked against a need to stay tough on terrorism. The great majority of terrorist attacks today (and most of the best-known recent incidents) involve terrorists going right out and killing people, rather than making specific demands and putting themselves in a position to kill people if the demands are not met. The very U.S. firmness discussed above (and stronger backbones grown by some other governments) probably has had something to do with this, and to that extent it is another endorsement for a policy of firmness....

Terrorists who suddenly detonate a bomb may still be looking for a concession, even though there are no apparent hostages and no explicit negotiations. Hizballah's bombings of the U.S. and French embassies in Beirut in April 1983, for example, and its attacks later that year on the U.S. Marine barracks and a French military base, were aimed largely at expelling from Lebanon the multilateral peacekeeping force of which the U.S. and French contingents were a part. In such circumstances, the United States is in a sort of bargaining relationship with the terrorists, whether or not it wants to be or says it is. It cannot ignore the public demands of the terrorist group, and its own policies regarding the subject matter of those demands are in effect part of the negotiation.[38] So there is yet an opportunity to demonstrate firmness, but one with even more potential problems and complications than in the traditional hostage incident. Refusal to act the way the terrorists want not only risks further attacks along the lines of what has already occurred (which was certainly an implicit threat in Lebanon) but also may mean continuing a policy that is unwise or unsustainable for other reasons. The alternative is to do what the terrorists would wish (which the United States and its allies did in Lebanon, pulling their troops out in early 1984), which—regardless of how the move is billed and the other reasons for it—may be seen as a concession to terrorism.

Other terrorist attacks are conducted without any particular concessions in mind; the destruction is more of an end in itself, motivated by hatred or revenge. With those who would wage this brand of terrorism (exemplified by the bombing of the World Trade Center by Ramzi Yousef's group), there is no way to influence intentions over the long term—whether by being steadfast in not rewarding terrorism, or being forceful in punishing it, or through any other means. The incorrigibility of such people is the main limitation of this element of counterterrorism. An ad hoc terrorist such as Yousef, who was not part of any permanent organization, is particularly unlikely to be deterred for long or to be coaxed on to a less violent path. Yousef was out to kill as many Americans as he could, he and his colleagues did not have fixed assets that could be bombed in retaliation, and he showed no sign of caring about his cohorts being caught and prosecuted.

Defenses

The one way in which the bin Ladins and Yousefs can be deterred is at the short-term, tactical level, by erecting security countermeasures that persuade them that a contemplated attack would fail. Some security measures that the United States has used overseas have had this effect. In at least one recent instance, a plot to attack a U.S. embassy was called off in the planning stage because the terrorists concluded that the security they had observed there could not be overcome. Antiterrorist defenses, therefore, are another way to influence terrorist intentions.

Physical defenses are also an element in their own right in saving lives from terrorism, even where they do not deter. And lives are saved even when attacks are not defeated entirely. The security measures at Khubar Towers, which kept the explosive-laden truck from penetrating the perimeter of the compound, prevented a death toll that would have far exceeded the nineteen U.S. servicemen who were killed. Similarly, in both Nairobi and Dar es Salaam in 1998, physical barriers and the refusal of guards to admit onto embassy grounds the trucks used by the terrorists greatly minimized U.S. casualties. Besides, the bigger the bomb the terrorists have to build, and the larger and more complex their operation has to become to defeat the defenses, the greater the chance that their operation will be compromised and discovered.

Antiterrorist defenses constitute a very large proportion of the U.S. fight against terrorism, certainly in resources but also in leadership attention. At the state and local level and in the private sector defenses are virtually the entire effort. Efforts at the federal level include defensive measures at both home and abroad. The two major overseas defensive programs—protection for U.S. diplomatic and military installations—have each received renewed emphasis in response to attacks in recent years.

On the diplomatic side, the bombings in Nairobi and Dar es Salaam highlighted the failure to meet standards for embassy security that had been established after earlier tragedies in Lebanon (the so-called Inman standards, after Admiral Bobby R. Inman, who chaired an Advisory Panel on Overseas Security in 1985). As of mid-1999, 229 of the 260 U.S. diplomatic posts worldwide still lacked the 100-foot setback (from the compound perimeter) specified in the Inman standards.[39] The funding level that the Crowe panel recommended is unlikely to be reached, but the Clinton administration in its last year budgeted more than $1.1 billion for embassy security in fiscal year 2001 and requested $3.4 billion in advance appropriations for fiscal years 2002 through 2005.[40]

Protection for military forces received a comparable fillip from the attack at Khubar Towers. In September 1996, Secretary of Defense William Perry issued a fresh directive on defending against terrorism (DoD Directive 2000.12) and initiated numerous enhancements to U.S. force protection efforts. A new section, headed by a general officer, within the Joint Staff was given responsibility for coordinating and promoting the military's antiterrorism efforts, promulgating doctrine on the subject, implementing a comprehensive training program, and conducting vulnerability assessments of installations around the world. The annual military antiterrorist budget is now about $3.5 billion.

The cost of defensive measures—particularly in dollars but also in restrictions on freedom of movement—is their main limitation. Comprehensive protection for everything in the terrorists' sights would be prohibitively expensive. As the Crowe panel acknowledged, "We understand that there will never be enough money to do all that should be done. We will have to live with partial solutions and, in turn, a high level of threat and vulnerability for quite some time."[41] A related limitation is that terrorists sometimes respond to security countermeasures by shifting their attention to more vulnerable targets. In some cases this means—given the terrorists' own limitations on where and how they can operate—that no attack occurs. But in others it means that a target with less robust defenses gets hit. The shift can be from one specific target to another (for example, from military bases to private businesses).[42]

Another limitation is that some terrorists are remarkably resourceful in adapting to, and overcoming, antiterrorist defenses. The Irish Republican Army (IRA), for example, has cleverly changed its methods for detonating bombs, using devices ranging from radar guns to photographic flash equipment, to stay ahead of the British use of electronic measures to prevent detonations.[43] Yousef demonstrated comparable operational cleverness with the method he devised for bombing U.S. airliners over the Pacific (and which he successfully tested, with a small amount of explosive, on a Philippine Airlines plane in December 1994). The technique involved bringing on board innocuous-looking items (including a prepared digital watch and a bottle for contact lens solution that really contained a liquid explosive), assembling them in a lavatory, and leaving the assembled device hidden on the aircraft when the terrorist got off at an intermediate stop.

Such ingenuity points to the limitations of using technology to defend against terrorism. It is not as if good minds have not been put on the problem. The federal government has a Technical Support Working Group that oversees a vigorous program of research, development, and rapid prototyping of antiterrorist technologies; the program has grown rapidly in recent years to reach an annual budget of close to $40 million. The Defense Science Board, an advisory body that includes some of the nation's leaders in applying technology to problems of national security, devoted its 1997 summer study to transnational threats, including terrorism, and how to respond to them.[44] The threat itself is not, at bottom, technological. Technology is useful in limited ways in defending against it but is not itself a solution.

All counterterrorist work—regardless of the instruments employed, the particular partners enlisted, or the specific enemies confronted—involves one or more of the elements just described. The limitations of each are patent; the need to address all of them together is strong. But the challenges facing U.S. counterterrorist policy reflect not just the limitations of counterterrorism itself. That policy must be adapted to a real world in which both the terrorist threat and the place of the United States as a terrorist target have evolved in important ways.

A former U.S. Army officer and executive fellow at the Brookings Institution, **Paul R. Pillar** has been a member of the Central Intelligence Agency (CIA) since 1977. In 2000 he was appointed the national intelligence officer for the Near East and South Asia of the National Intelligence Council of the CIA. His particular areas of interest include terrorism, negotiation, and counterterrorist policy. This reading is from his book *Terrorism and U.S. Foreign Policy*.

Notes

1. Bruce Hoffman, *Inside Terrorism* (Columbia University Press, 1998), chap. 1. Another recent chapter-length discussion of definitions is in David Tucker, *Skirmishes at the Edge of Empire: The United States and International Terrorism* (Praeger, 1997), chap. 2, pp. 51–69.
2. See, for example, the several articles on the subject in the autumn 1996 issue of the journal *Terrorism and Political Violence*, particularly Andrew Silke, "Terrorism and the Blind Men's Elephant," vol. 8 (Autumn 1996), pp. 12–28.
3. 22 U.S.C. 2656f (d).
4. For an argument that terrorism and crime should be kept conceptually distinct, see Phil Williams, "Terrorism and Organized Crime: Convergence, Nexus, or Transformation," in Brad Roberts, ed., *Hype or Reality: The "New Terrorism" and Mass Casualty Attacks* (Alexandria, Va.: Chemical and Biological Arms Control Institute, 2000), pp. 117–45. A contrasting view is in Roger Mead and Frank Goldstein, "International Terrorism on the Eve of a New Millennium," *Studies in Conflict and Terrorism*, vol. 20 (July-September 1997), p. 301.
5. Hoffman, *Inside Terrorism*, p. 43.
6. The discussion in chapter 4 on multilateral diplomacy addresses further what these rules, and recent modifications to them, imply for counterterrorism.

7. Assassination as a possible counterterrorist tactic is discussed in chapter 4.
8. Concurring opinion by Justice Stewart in *Jacobellis v. Ohio*, 378 U.S. 184, 197 (1964).
9. Quoted in Pamela Constable, "Kashmiri Rebels Pressure Pakistan," *Washington Post*, October 20, 1999, p. 23.
10. As Brian Jenkins has pointed out, this conception of terrorism does involve one value judgment: that an end does not justify the means. Brian M. Jenkins, "Terrorism: A Contemporary Problem with Age-old Dilemmas," in Lawrence Howard, ed., *Terrorism: Roots, Impact, Responses* (Praeger, 1992), p. 14.
11. International terrorism includes any incident that is terrorism under the statutory definition given above and that involves two or more nationalities when one considers the perpetrators, the victims, and the location of the incident.
12. Statistics are from unpublished FBI data.
13. Statistics on U.S. military casualties are Department of Defense data (web1.wbs.osd.mil/mmid/m01/sms223r.htm (November 2001).
14. Overseas Presence Advisory Panel, *America's Overseas Presence in the 21st Century* (Washington, November 1999), p. 38.
15. Peter D. Fravet and Christopher Gelpi, "How Many Deaths Are Acceptable? A Surprising Answer," *Washington Post*, November 7, 1999, p. B3.
16. General Accounting Office, *Combating Terrorism: Issues in Managing Counterterrorist Programs*, T-NSIAD-00 145 (April 6, 2000), pp. 3–4.
17. The most comprehensive study is Richard A. Falkenrath, Robert D. Newman, and Bradley A. Thayer, *America's Achilles' Heel: Nuclear, Biological, and Chemical Terrorism and Covert Attack* (MIT Press, 1998). Despite the somewhat ominous title, this is a well researched work that lays out arguments both for and against the idea that terrorists are likely to employ unconventional weapons. A useful survey is Roberts, *Hype or Reality*, especially the chapter by Brian Jenkins, which summarizes points on which there appears to be consensus among most specialists. A recent book that touches on diverse aspects of the subject is Jessica Stern, *The Ultimate Terrorists* (Harvard University Press, 1999). Jonathan B. Tucker, ed., *Toxic Terror: Assessing Terrorist Use of Chemical and Biological Weapons* (MIT Press, 2000), examines several past cases of attempted or reported terrorists' use of chemical or biological substances. Reasons to be skeptical about the magnitude of an unconventional terrorist threat are discussed in David C. Rapoport, "Terrorism and Weapons of the Apocalypse," *National Security Studies Quarterly*, vol. 5 (Summer 1999), pp. 49–67; Ehud Sprinzak, "The Great Superterrorism Scare," *Foreign Policy*, no. 112 (Fall 1998), pp. 110–24; Jonathan B. Tucker and Amy Sands, "An Unlikely Threat," *Bulletin of the Atomic Scientists*, vol. 55 (July-August 1999), pp. 46–52; Brian M. Jenkins, "The Limits of Terror: Constraints on the Escalation of Violence, " *Harvard International Review*, vol. 17 (Summer 1995), pp. 44–45, 77–78; Henry Sokolski, "Rethinking Bio-Chemical Dangers," *Orbis*, vol. 44 (Spring 2000), pp. 207–19; the exchange on "WMD Terrorism" in *Survival*, vol. 40 (Winter 1998–99), pp. 168–83; and part 1 of the *First Annual Report of the Advisory Panel to Assess Domestic Response Capabilities for Terrorism Involving Weapons of Mass Destruction*, December 15, 1999.
18. This is all the more true of acquiring a usable nuclear device or the fissile material necessary to make one, both of which—despite the breakdown of many of the controls in the former USSR—are still protected by significant safeguards. Partly for this reason, use of a device producing a nuclear yield is the least likely CBRN terrorist event. Use of radioactive material as a containment to be dispersed by a conventional bomb is more probable.
19. W. Seth Carus, "Biohazard," *New Republic*, vol. 221 (August 2, 1999), pp. 14–16.
20. See, for example, John Mueller and Karl Mueller, "Sanctions of Mass Destruction," *Foreign Affairs*, vol. 78 (May-June 1999), p. 44.
21. *Report of the Accountability Review Boards on the Bombings of the US Embassies in Nairobi, Kenya and Dar es Salaam, Tanzania on August 7, 1998* (January 8, 1999), Key Recommendations, sec. 1.A.12 (www.terrorism.com/state/accountability_report.html [November 2000]).
22. FAA Notice 99-05, "Security of Checked Baggage on Flights Within the United States," *Federal Register*, vol. 64 (April 19, 1999), p. 19230. This cost estimate is a maximum, assuming a combination of profiling of passengers and matching passengers with their bags. Greater use

of explosives detection machines (which are hardly inexpensive themselves) might reduce the cost.

23. Philip B. Heymann, *Terrorism and America: A Commonsense Strategy for a Democratic Society* (MIT Press, 1998), p. 16.
24. Barbara Crossette, "Fearing Terrorism, U.S. Plans to Press Sudan," *New York Times*, February 2, 1996, p. A6.
25. Steven Lee Myers, "At a Saudi Base, U.S. Digs In, Gingerly, for a Longer Stay," *New York Times*, December 29, 1997, p. A1.
26. See, for example, the research on ethnically based conflict reported in Ted Robert Gurr, *Minorities at Risk: A Global View of Ethnopolitical Conflicts* (Washington: U.S. Institute of Peace Press, 1993).
27. Khalil Shikaki, "The Politics of Paralysis II: Peace Now or Hamas Later," *Foreign Affairs*, vol. 77 (July-August 1998), pp. 35–36.
28. Ziad Abu-Amr, *Islamic Fundamentalism in the West Bank and Gaza: Muslim Brotherhood and Islamic Jihad* (Indiana University Press, 1994), p. 96.
29. Walter Laqueur, "Reflections on Terrorism," *Foreign Affairs*, vol. 65 (Fall 1986), p. 91.
30. Leonard B. Weinberg and William L. Bubank, "Terrorism and Democracy: What Recent Events Disclose," *Terrorism and Political Violence*, vol. 10 (Spring 1998), pp. 108–18.
31. Daniel Pipes, "It's Not the Economy, Stupid: What the West Needs to Know about the Rise of Radical Islam," *Washington Post*, July 2, 1995, p. C2.
32. Richard N. Haas, *Conflicts Unending: The United States and Regional Disputes* (Yale University Press, 1990), p. 53.
33. See Martha Crenshaw, "How Terrorists Think: What Psychology Can Contribute to Understanding Terrorism," in Howard, *Terrorism: Roots, Impact, Responses*, pp. 71–93; Jerrold M. Post, "Terrorist Psycho-logic: Terrorist Behavior as a Product of Psychological Forces," in Walter Reith, ed., *Origins of Terrorism: Psychologies, Ideologies, Theologies, States of Mind* (Cambridge University Press, 1990), pp. 25–40; Robert S. Robins and Jerrold M. Post, *Political Paranoia: The Psychopolitics of Hatred* (Yale University Press, 1997), chaps. 4 and 6; and Laqueur, *The New Terrorism*, pp. 93–96.
34. *The NewsHour with Jim Lehrer*, Public Broadcasting System, August 25, 1998.
35. See, for example, Richard Clutterbuck, "Negotiating with Terrorists," in Alex P. Schmid and Ronald D. Crelinsten, eds., *Western Responses to Terrorism* (London: Frank Cass, 1993), p. 285.
36. Thomas C. Schelling, "What Purposes Can 'International Terrorism' Serve?" in R. G. Frey and Christopher W. Morris, eds., *Violence, Terrorism, and Justice* (Cambridge University Press, 1991), pp. 31–32.
37. See Heymann, *Terrorism and America*, pp. 40–46; and Tucker, *Skirmishes at the Edge of Empire*, pp. 74–80.
38. Schelling, "What Purposes Can 'International Terrorism' Serve?" p. 25.
39. Fact Sheet on Funding for Embassy Security, Department of State, August 4, 1999 (www.usinfo.state.gov/topical/pol/terror/99080404.htm [October 2000]).
40. White House Fact Sheet on Embassy Security Funding, February 10, 2000 (www.usinfo.state.gov/topical/pol/terror/00021004.htm [November 2000]).
41. *Report of the Accountability Review Boards*, Introduction.
42. Walter Enders and Todd Sandler in "The Effectiveness of Anti-Terrorism Policies: A Vector-Autoregression-Intervention Analysis," *American Political Science Review*, vol. 87 (December 1993), pp. 829–44, analyze statistics on terrorist incidents to conclude that the fortification of diplomatic installations has reduced attacks on those installations but has led terrorists to conduct more assassinations instead. They reach a similar conclusion about the installation of metal detectors in airports.
43. Hoffman, *Inside Terrorism*, pp. 180–82.
44. Defense Science Board 1997 Summer Study Task Force, *DoD Responses to Transnational Threats*, volume 1: Final Report (October 1997).

Eqbal Ahmad, 1998

Terrorism: Theirs & Ours

Eqbal Ahmad was one of the major activist scholars of this era. He was born in India probably in 1934. He was never quite sure. He left with his brothers for the newly created state of Pakistan in 1947. In 1996, the BBC did a powerful and moving TV documentary chronicling Ahmad's trek in a refugee caravan from his village in Bihar to Pakistan. The film, not shown on PBS in the U.S., is remarkable not just as an historical document but also for providing insight into the dangers of sectarian nationalism. Ahmad's secular thinking was surely shaped by the wrenching communal and political violence he experienced as a youngster. Even before the subcontinent was engulfed in the homicidal convulsions of 1947, Ahmad witnessed his own father murdered before him.

Ahmad came to the United States in the 1950s to study at Princeton. Later he went to Algeria. It was there that his ideas about national liberation and anti-imperialism crystallized. He worked with Frantz Fanon, author of The Wretched of the Earth, *during the revolt against the French. Returning to the U.S., he became active in the civil rights and anti-Vietnam War movements. It was during his involvement in the latter that I first heard his name. He was accused of plotting to kidnap Henry Kissinger. The trumped-up charges were dismissed.*

I did my first interview with him in the early 1980s in his apartment on New York's Upper West Side. It was memorable. I had just gotten a new tape recorder. I returned home thinking, Wow, I've got a great interview. I hit play and discovered the tape was blank. I had failed to turn the machine on. With considerable embarrassment I explained to him what happened. He said, "No problem." He invited me over the next day and we did another interview. This time, I pressed the right buttons. Whenever I tell that story, his friends would nod and say, "That's Eqbal."

Ahmad's radical politics and outspoken positions made him a pariah in academic circles. After years of being an intellectual migrant worker, Hampshire College in Amherst, Massachusetts, hired him in the early 1980s as a professor. He taught there until his retirement in 1997. He spent most of his final years in Islamabad where he wrote a weekly column for Dawn, *Pakistan's oldest English-language newspaper. His political work consisted chiefly of trying to bridge differences with India on the issues of Kashmir and nuclear weapons. He was also speaking out against the rise of Islamic fundamentalism and was concerned about the possible Talibanization of Pakistan.*

Eqbal Ahmad died in Islamabad, Pakistan, on May 11, 1999. His close friend Edward Said wrote, "He was perhaps the shrewdest and most original anti-imperialist analyst of the postwar world, particularly of the dynamics between the West and postcolonial Asia and Africa; a man of enormous charisma, dazzling eloquence, incorruptible ideals, unfailing generosity and sympathy.... Whether on the conflict between Israelis and Palestinians or

India and Pakistan, he was a force for a just struggle but also for a just reconciliation.... Humanity and genuine secularism... had no finer champion."

"Terrorism: Theirs & Ours" was one of Eqbal Ahmad's last public talks in the United States. He spoke at the University of Colorado at Boulder in October 1998. It was broadcast nationally and internationally on my weekly Alternative Radio program. Eqbal Ahmad's near prophetic sense is stunning. After the September 11 terrorist attacks, I aired the speech again. Listeners called in great numbers requesting copies. They almost all believed that the talk had just been recorded.

—David Barsamian

Until the 1930s and early 1940s, the Jewish underground in Palestine was described as "terrorist." Then something happened: around 1942, as news of the Holocaust was spreading, a certain liberal sympathy with the Jewish people began to emerge in the Western world. By 1944, the terrorists of Palestine, who were Zionists, suddenly began being described as "freedom fighters." If you look in history books you can find at least two Israeli prime ministers, including Menachem Begin,[1] appearing in "Wanted" posters saying, TERRORISTS, REWARD [THIS MUCH]. The highest reward I have seen offered was 100,000 British pounds for the head of Menachem Begin, the terrorist.

From 1969 to 1990, the Palestine Liberation Organization (PLO) occupied center state as a terrorist organization. Yasir Arafat has been repeatedly described as the "chief of terrorism" by the great sage of American journalism, William Safire of *The New York Times*. On September 29, 1998, I was rather amused to notice a picture of Yasir Arafat and Israeli prime minister Benjamin Netanyahu standing on either side of President Bill Clinton. Clinton was looking toward Arafat, who looked meek as a mouse. Just a few years earlier, Arafat would appear in photos with a very menacing look, a gun holstered to his belt. That's Yasir Arafat. You remember those pictures, and you'll remember the next one.

In 1985, President Ronald Reagan received a group of ferocious-looking, turban-wearing men who looked like they came from another century. I had been writing about the very same men for *The New Yorker*. After receiving them in the White House, Reagan spoke to the press, referring to his foreign guests as "freedom fighters." These were the Afghan mujahideen. They were at the time, guns in hand, battling the "Evil Empire." For Reagan, they were the moral equivalent of our Founding Fathers.

In August 1998, another American president ordered missile strikes to kill Osama bin Laden and his men in Afghanistan-based camps. Mr. bin Laden, at whom fifteen American missiles were fired to hit in Afghanistan, was only a few years earlier the moral equivalent of George Washington and Thomas Jefferson. I'll return to the subject of bin Laden later.

I am recalling these stories to point out that the official approach to terrorism is rather complicated, but not without characteristics. To begin with, terrorists change. The terrorist of yesterday is the hero of today, and the hero of yesterday becomes the terrorist of today. In a constantly changing world of images, we have to keep our heads straight to know what terrorism is and what it is not. Even more importantly, we need to know what causes terrorism and how to stop it.

Secondly, the official approach to terrorism is a posture of inconsistency, one which evades definition. I have examined at least twenty official documents on terrorism. Not one offers a definition. All of them explain it polemically in order to arouse our emotions, rather than exercise our intelligence. I'll give you an example which is representative. On October 25, 1984, Secretary of State George Shultz gave a long speech on terrorism at the Park Avenue Synagogue in New York City. In the State Department Bulletin of seven single-spaced pages, there is not a single clear definition of terrorism. What we get instead are the following statements. Number one: "Terrorism is a modern barbarism that we call terrorism." Number two is even more brilliant; "Terrorism is a form of political violence." Number three: "Terrorism is a menace to Western moral values." Do these accomplish anything other than arouse emotions? This is typical.

Officials don't define terrorism because definitions involve a commitment to analysis, comprehension, and adherence to some norms of consistency. That's the second characteristic of the official approach to terrorism. The third characteristic is that the absence of definition does not prevent officials from being globalistic. They may not define terrorism, but they can call it a menace to good order, a menace to the moral values of Western civilization, a menace to humankind. Therefore, they can call for it to be stamped out worldwide. Antiterrorist policies therefore, must be global. In the same speech he gave in New York City, George Shultz also said: "There is no question about our ability to use force where and when it is needed to counter terrorism." There is no geographical limit. On the same day, U.S. missiles struck Afghanistan and Sudan. Those two countries are 2,300 miles apart, and they were hit by missiles belonging to a country roughly 8,000 miles away. Reach is global.

A fourth characteristic is that the official approach to terrorism claims not only global reach, but also a certain omniscient knowledge. They claim to know where terrorists are, and therefore, where to hit. To quote George Shultz again, "We know the difference between terrorists and freedom fighters and as we look around, we have no trouble telling one from the other." Only Osama bin Laden doesn't know that he was an ally one day and an enemy another. That's very confusing for Osama bin Laden. I'll come back to him toward the end; it's a real story.

Fifth, the official approach eschews causation. They don't look at why people resort to terrorism. Cause? What cause? Another example: on December 18, 1985, *The New York Times* reported that the foreign minister of Yugoslavia—you remember the days when there was a Yugoslavia—requested the secretary of state of the U.S. to consider the causes of Palestinian terrorism. The secretary of state, George Shultz, and I'm quoting from *The New York Times*, "went a bit red in the face. He pounded the table and told the visiting foreign minister, "There is no connection with any cause. Period." Why look for causes?

A sixth characteristic of the official approach to terrorism is the need for the moral revulsion we feel against terror to be selective. We are to denounce the terror of those groups which are officially disapproved. But we are to applaud the terror of those groups of whom officials do approve. Hence, President Reagan's statement, "I am a contra." We know that the contras of Nicaragua were by any definition terrorists, but the media heed the dominant view.

More importantly to me, the dominant approach also excludes from consideration the terrorism of friendly governments. Thus, the United States excused, among others, the terrorism of Pinochet, who killed one of my closest friends, Orlando Letelier, one of Chilean President Salvador Allende's top diplomats, killed in a car bombing in Washington, DC in 1976. And it excused the terror of Zia ul-Haq, the military dictator of Pakistan, who killed many of my friends there. All I want to tell you is that according to my ignorant calculations, the ratio of people killed by the state terror of Zia ul-Haq, Pinochet, Argentinian, Brazilian, Indonesian type, versus the killing of the PLO and other organizations is literally, conservatively 1,000 to 1. That's the ratio.

History unfortunately recognizes and accords visibility to power, not to weakness. Therefore, visibility has been accorded historically to dominant groups. Our time—the time that begins with Columbus—has been one of extraordinary unrecorded holocausts. Great civilizations have been wiped out. The Mayas, the Incas, the Aztecs, the American Indians, the Canadian Indians were all wiped out. Their voices have not been heard, even to this day. They are heard, yes, but only when the dominant power suffers, only when resistance has a semblance of costing, of exacting a price, when a Custer is killed or when a Gordon is besieged. That's when you know that there were Indians or Arabs fighting and dying.

My last point on this subject is that during the Cold War period, the United States sponsored terrorist regimes like Somoza in Nicaragua and Batista in Cuba, one after another. All kinds of tyrants have been America's friends. In Nicaragua it was the contra, in Afghanistan, the mujahideen.

Now, what about the other side? What is terrorism? Our first job should be to define the damn thing, name it, give it a description other than "moral equivalent of founding fathers" or "a moral outrage to Western civilization." This is what *Webster's Collegiate Dictionary* says: "Terror is an intense, overpowering fear." Terrorism is "the use of terrorizing methods of governing or resisting a government." This simple definition has one great virtue: it's fair. It focuses on the use of violence that is used illegally, extra-constitutionally, to coerce. And this definition is correct because it treats terror for what it is, whether a government or private group commits it.

Have you noticed something? Motivation is omitted. We're not talking about whether the cause is just or unjust. We're talking about consensus, consent, absence of consent, legality, absence of legality, constitutionality, absence of constitutionality. Why do we keep motives out? Because motives make no difference. In the course of my work I have identified five types of terrorism; state terrorism, religious terrorism (Catholics killing Protestants, Sunnis killing Shiites, Shiites killing Sunnis), criminal terrorism, political terrorism, and oppositional terrorism. Sometimes these five can converge and overlap. Oppositional protest terrorism can become pathological criminal terrorism. State terror can take the form of private terror. For example, we're all familiar with the death squads in Latin America or in Pakistan where the government has employed private people to kill its opponents. It's not quite official. It's privatized. In Afghanistan, Central America, and Southeast Asia, the CIA employed in its covert operations drug pushers. Drugs and guns often go together. The categories often overlap.

Of the five types of terror, the official approach is to focus on only one form—political terrorism—which claims the least in terms of loss of human lives and property. The form that exacts the highest loss is state terrorism. The second highest loss is created by religious terrorism, although religious terror has, relatively speaking, declined. If you are looking historically, however, religious terrorism has caused massive loss. The next highest loss is caused by criminal terrorism. A Rand Corporation study by Brian Jenkins examining a ten-year period (1978 to 1988) showed fifty percent of terrorism was committed without any political cause. No politics. Simply crime and pathology. So the focus is on only one, the political terrorist, the PLO, the bin Laden, whoever you want to take.

Why do they do it? What makes terrorists tick?

I would like to knock out some quick answers. First, the need to be heard. Remember, we are dealing with a minority group, the political, private terrorist. Normally, and there are exceptions, there is an effort to be heard, to get their grievances recognized and addressed by people. The Palestinians, for example, the superterrorists of our time, were dispossessed in 1948. From 1948 to 1968 they went to every court in the world. They knocked on every door. They had been completely deprived of their land, their country, and nobody was listening. In desperation, they invented a new form of terror: the airplane hijacking. Between 1968 and 1975 they pulled the world up by its ears. That kind of terror is a violent way of expressing long-felt grievances. It makes the world hear. It's normally undertaken by small, helpless groupings that feel powerless. We still haven't done the Palestinians justice, but at least we all know they exist. Now, even the Israelis acknowledge. Remember what Golda Meir, prime minister of Israel, said in 1970: There are no Palestinians. They do not exist.

They damn well exist now.

Secondly, terrorism is an expression of anger, of feeling helpless, angry, alone. You feel like you have to hit back. Wrong has been done to you, so you do it. During the hijacking of the TWA jet in Beirut, Judy Brown of Belmar, New Jersey, said that she kept hearing them yell, "New Jersey, New Jersey." What did they have in mind? She thought that they were going after her. Later on it turned out that the terrorists were referring to the U.S. battleship New Jersey, which had heavily shelled the Lebanese civilian population in 1983.

Another factor is a sense of betrayal, which is connected to that tribal ethic of revenge. It comes into the picture in the case of people like bin Laden. Here is a man who was an ally of the United States, who saw America as a friend; then he sees his country being occupied by the United States and feels betrayal. Whether there is a sense of right and wrong is not what I'm saying. I'm describing what's behind this kind of extreme violence.

Sometimes it's the fact that you have experienced violence at other people's hands. Victims of violent abuse often become violent people. The only time when Jews produced terrorists in organized fashion was during and after the Holocaust. It is rather remarkable that Jewish terrorists hit largely innocent people or U.N. peacemakers like Count Bernadotte of Sweden, whose country had a better record on the Holocaust. The men of Irgun, the Stern Gang, and the Hagannah terrorist groups came in the wake of the Holocaust. The experience of victimhood itself produces a violent reaction.

In modern times, with modern technology and means of communications, the targets have been globalized. Therefore, globalization of violence is an aspect of what we call globalization of the economy and culture in the world as a whole. We can't expect everything else to be globalized and violence not to be. We do have visible targets. Airplane hijacking is something new because international travel is relatively new, too. Everybody now is in your gunsight. Therefore the globe is within the gunsight. That has globalized terror.

Finally, the absence of revolutionary ideology has been central to the spread of terror in our time. One of the points in the big debate between Marxism and anarchism in the nineteenth century was the use of terror. The Marxists argued that the true revolutionary does not assassinate. You do not solve social problems by individual acts of violence. Social problems require social and political mobilization, and thus wars of liberation are to be distinguished from terrorist organizations. The revolutionaries didn't reject violence, but they rejected terror as a viable tactic of revolution. That revolutionary ideology has gone out at the moment.

In the 1980s and 1990s, revolutionary ideology receded, giving in to the globalized individual. In general terms, these are among the many forces that are behind modern terrorism.

To this challenge rulers from one country after another have been responding with traditional methods. The traditional method of shooting it out, whether it's with missiles or some other means. The Israelis are very proud of it. The Americans are very proud of it. The French became very proud of it. Now the Pakistanis are very proud of it. The Pakistanis say, Our commandoes are the best. Frankly, it won't work. A central problem of our time: political minds rooted in the past at odds with modern times, producing new realities.

Let's turn back for a moment to Osama bin Laden. *Jihad*, which has been translated a thousand times as "holy war," is not quite that. *Jihad* in Arabic means "to struggle." It could be struggle by violence or struggle by non-violent means. There are two forms, the small *jihad* and the big *jihad*. The small *jihad* involves external violence. The big *jihad* involves a struggle within oneself. Those are the concepts. The reason I mention it is that in Islamic history, *jihad* as an international violent phenomenon had for all practical purposes disappeared in the last four hundred years. It was revived suddenly with American help in the 1980s. When the Soviet Union intervened in Afghanistan, which borders Pakistan, Zia ul-Haq saw an opportunity and launched a *jihad* there against godless communism. The U.S. saw a God-sent opportunity to mobilize one billion Muslims against what Reagan called the Evil Empire. Money started pouring in. CIA agents starting going all over the Muslim world recruiting people to fight in the great *jihad*. Bin Laden was one of the early prize recruits. He was not only an Arab, he was a Saudi multimillionaire willing to put his own money into the matter. Bin Laden went around recruiting people for the *jihad* against communism.

I first met Osama bin Laden in 1986. He was recommended to me by an American official who may have been an agent. I was talking to the American and asked him who were the Arabs there that would be very interesting to talk with. By *there* I meant in Afghanistan and Pakistan. The American official told me, "You must meet Osama." I went to see Osama. There he was, rich, bringing in recruits from Algeria, from Sudan, from Egypt, just like Sheikh Abdul Rahman, an Egyptian cleric who was among those convicted for the 1993 World Trade Center bombing. At that moment, Osama bin Laden was a U.S. ally. He remained an ally. He turned at a particular moment. In 1990 the U.S. went into Saudi Arabia with military forces. Saudi Arabia is the holy place of Muslims, home of Mecca and Medina. There had never been foreign troops there. In 1990, during the build-up to the Gulf War, they went in in the name of helping Saudi Arabia defend itself. Osama bin Laden remained quiet. Saddam was defeated, but the American foreign troops stayed on in the land of the kaba (the sacred site of Islam in Mecca). Bin Laden wrote letter after letter saying, Why are you here? Get out! You came to help but you have stayed on. Finally he started a *jihad* against the other occupiers. His mission is to get American troops out of Saudi Arabia. His earlier mission was to get Russian troops out of Afghanistan.

A second point to be made about him is that he comes from a tribal people. Being a millionaire doesn't matter. His code of ethics is tribal. The tribal code of ethics consists of two words: loyalty and revenge. You are my friend. You keep your word. I am loyal to you. You break your word, I go on my path of revenge. For him, America has broken its word. The loyal friend has betrayed him. Now they're going to go for you. They're going to do a lot more. These are the chickens of the Afghanistan war coming home to roost.

What is my recommendation to America?

First, avoid extremes of double standards. If you're going to practice double standards, you will be paid with double standards. Don't use it. Don't condone Israeli terror, Pakistani terror, Nicaraguan terror, El Salvadoran terror, on the one hand, and then complain about Afghan terror or Palestinian terror. It doesn't work. Try to be even-handed. A superpower cannot promote terror in one place and reasonably expect to discourage terrorism in another place. It won't work in this shrunken world.

Do not condone the terror of your allies. Condemn them. Fight them. Punish them. Avoid covert operations and low-intensity warfare. These are breeding grounds for terrorism and drugs. In the Australian documentary about covert operations, *Dealing with the Demon*, I say that wherever covert operations have been, there is a drug problem. Because the structure of covert operations, Afghanistan, Vietnam, Nicaragua, Central America, etcetera, have been very hospitable to the drug trade. Avoid covert operations. It doesn't help.

Also, focus on causes and help ameliorate them. Try to look at causes and solve problems. Avoid military solutions. Terrorism is a political problem. Seek political solutions. Diplomacy works. Take the example of President Clinton's attack on bin Laden. Did they know what they were attacking? They say they know, but they don't know. At another point, they were trying to kill Qadaffi. Instead, they killed his young daughter. The poor child hadn't done anything. Qadaffi is still alive. They tried to kill Saddam Hussein. Instead they killed Laila bin Attar, a prominent artist, an innocent woman. They tried to kill bin Laden and his men. Twenty-five other people died. They tried to destroy a chemical factory in Sudan. Now they are admitting that they destroyed a pharmaceutical plant that produced half the medicine for Sudan.

Four of the missiles intended for Afghanistan fell in Pakistan. One was slightly damaged, two were totally damaged, one was totally intact. For ten years the American government has kept an embargo on Pakistan because Pakistan was trying, stupidly, to build nuclear weapons and missiles. So the U.S. has a technology embargo on my country. One of the missiles was intact. What do you think the Pakistani official told the *Washington Post*? He said it was a gift from Allah. Pakistan wanted U.S. technology. Now they have the technology, and Pakistan's scientists are examining this missile very carefully. It fell into the wrong hands. Look for political solutions. Military solutions cause more problems than they solve.

Finally, please help reinforce and strengthen the framework of international law. There was a criminal court in Rome. Why didn't the U.S. go there first to get a warrant against bin Laden, if they have some evidence? Enforce the United Nations. Enforce the International Court of Justice. Get a warrant, then go after him internationally.

Eqbal Ahmad was born in India but moved to the newly created state of Pakistan in 1947. His theories about national liberation and anti-imperialism developed over years of involvement in radical causes worldwide. Ahmad spent the last years of his life addressing the conflict between India and Pakistan regarding Kashmir and speaking out against the rise of Islamic fundamentalism and the influence of the Taliban in Pakistan. This reading is a transcript of a public talk he gave at the University of Colorado in October 1998. Ahmad died in 1999.

Note

1. Yitzhak Shamir is the other.

Chapter 2

Why Terrorism?

The psychology behind the motivation and behavior of terrorists has been examined extensively, but the public, as well as many specialists, have often been content to write-off terrorists as irrational fanatics. Rather than see terrorism as an unintended outcome or the last resort of pathological individuals, Martha Crenshaw examines the use of terrorism as a deliberate strategy. She describes a framework of rational decision making, examining the calculations of cost versus benefit that go into the choice of terrorism as a weapon. Crenshaw concludes that neither the psychological nor the strategic explanation alone is adequate for examining terrorist behavior, but offers the strategic choice framework as an "antidote" to the persistent psychological stereotypes that she believes are nonproductive and fairly pervasive.

In the second article, Audrey Kurth Cronin argues that the current wave of international terrorism is characterized by unpredictable and unprecedented threats from nonstate actors. According to Dr. Cronin, terrorism is not only a reaction to globalization but is facilitated by it, while the U.S. response to the terrorist threat has been reactive and anachronistic. Furthermore, she explains, the combined focus of the United States on state-centric threats and its attempt to cast twenty-first century terrorism into familiar strategic terms avoids and often undermines effective response to the current nonstate terrorist phenomena. Military power, writes Cronin, is an important but supporting instrument in the campaign against terrorism. More effective, however, will be nonmilitary instruments such as intelligence, public diplomacy, and cooperation with allies.

Martha Crenshaw, 1998

The Logic of Terrorism: Terrorist Behavior as a Product of Strategic Choice

This [selection] examines the ways in which terrorism can be understood as an expression of political strategy. It attempts to show that terrorism may follow logical processes that can be discovered and explained. For the purpose of presenting this source of terrorist behavior, rather than the psychological one, it interprets the resort to violence as a willful choice made by an organization for political and strategic reasons, rather than as the unintended outcome of psychological or social factors.[1]

In the terms of this analytical approach, terrorism is assumed to display a collective rationality. A radical political organization is seen as the central actor in the terrorist drama. The group possesses collective preferences or values and selects terrorism as a course of action from a range of perceived alternatives. Efficacy is the primary standard by which terrorism is compared with other methods of achieving political goals. Reasonably regularized decision-making procedures are employed to make an intentional choice, in conscious anticipation of the consequences of various courses of action or inaction. Organizations arrive at collective judgments about the relative effectiveness of different strategies of opposition on the basis of abstract strategic conceptions derived from ideological assumptions. This approach thus allows for the incorporation of theories of social learning.

Conventional rational-choice theories of individual participation in rebellion, extended to include terrorist activities, have usually been considered inappropriate because of the "free rider" problem. That is, the benefits of a successful terrorist campaign would presumably be shared by all individual supporters of the group's goals, regardless of the extent of their active participation. In this case, why should a rational person become a terrorist, given the high costs associated with violent resistance and the expectation that everyone who supports the cause will benefit, whether he or she participates or not? One answer is that the benefits of participation are psychological....

A different answer, however, supports a strategic analysis. On the basis of surveys conducted in New York and West Germany, political scientists suggest that individuals can be *collectively* rational.[2] People realize that their participation is important because group size and cohesion matter. They are sensitive to the implications of free-riding and perceive their personal influence on the provision of public goods to be high. The authors argue that "average citizens may adopt a collectivist conception of rationality because they recognize that what is individually rational is collectively irrational."[3] Selective incentives are deemed largely irrelevant.

One of the advantages of approaching terrorism as a collectively rational strategic choice is that it permits the construction of a standard from which deviations can be measured. For example, the central question about the rationality of some terrorist organizations, such as the West German groups of the 1970s or the Weather Underground in the United States, is whether or not they had a sufficient grasp of reality—some approximation, to whatever degree imperfect—to calculate the likely consequences of the courses of action they chose. Perfect knowledge of available alternatives and the consequences of each is not possible, and miscalculations are inevitable. The Popular Front for the Liberation of Palestine (PFLP), for example, planned the hijacking of a TWA flight from Rome in August 1969 to coincide with a scheduled address by President Nixon to a meeting of the Zionist Organization of America, but he sent a letter instead.[4]

Yet not all errors of decision are miscalculations. There are varied degrees of limited rationality. Are some organizations so low on the scale of rationality as to be in a different category from more strategically minded groups? To what degree is strategic reasoning modified by psychological and other constraints? The strategic choice framework provides criteria on which to base these distinctions. It also leads one to ask what conditions promote or discourage rationality in violent underground organizations.

The use of this theoretical approach is also advantageous in that it suggests important questions about the preferences or goals of terrorist organizations. For example, is the decision to seize hostages in order to bargain with governments dictated by strategic considerations or by other, less instrumental motives?

The strategic choice approach is also a useful interpretation of reality. Since the French Revolution, a strategy of terrorism has gradually evolved as a means of bringing about political change opposed by established governments. Analysis of the historical development of terrorism reveals similarities in calculation of ends and means. The strategy has changed over time to adapt to new circumstances that offer different possibilities for dissident action—for example, hostage taking. Yet terrorist activity considered in its entirety shows a fundamental unity of purpose and conception. Although this analysis remains largely on an abstract level, the historical evolution of the strategy of terrorism can be sketched in its terms.[5]

A last argument in support of this approach takes the form of a warning. The wide range of terrorist activity cannot be dismissed as "irrational" and thus pathological, unreasonable, or inexplicable. The resort to terrorism need not be an aberration. It may be a reasonable and calculated response to circumstances. To say that the reasoning that leads to the choice of terrorism may be logical is not an argument about moral justifiability. It does suggest, however, that the belief that terrorism is expedient is one means by which moral inhibitions are overcome....

The Conditions for Terrorism

The central problem is to determine when extremist organizations find terrorism useful. Extremists seek either a radical change in the status quo, which would confer a new advantage, or the defense of privileges they perceive to be threatened. Their dissatisfaction with the policies of the government is extreme, and their demands usually involve the displacement of existing political elites.[6] Terrorism is not the only method of working toward radical goals, and thus it must be compared to the alternative strategies available to dissidents. Why is terrorism attractive to some opponents of the state, but unattractive to others?

The practitioners of terrorism often claim that they had no choice but terrorism, and it is indeed true that terrorism often follows the failure of other methods. In nineteenth-century Russia, for example, the failure of nonviolent movements contributed to the rise of terrorism. In Ireland, terrorism followed the failure of Parnell's constitutionalism. In the Palestinian-Israeli struggle, terrorism followed the failure of Arab efforts at conventional warfare against Israel. In general, the "nonstate" or "substate" users of terrorism—that is, groups in opposition to the government, as opposed to government itself—are constrained in their options by the lack of active mass support and by the superior power arrayed against them (an imbalance that has grown with the development of the modern centralized and bureaucratic nation-state). But these constraints have not prevented oppositions from considering and rejecting methods other than terrorism. Perhaps because groups are slow to recognize the extent of the limits to action, terrorism is often the last in a sequence of choices. It represents the outcome of a learning process. Experience in opposition provides radicals with information about the potential consequences of their choices. Terrorism is likely to be a reasonably informed choice among available alternatives, some tried unsuccessfully. Terrorists also learn from the experiences of others, usually communicated to them via the news media. Hence the existence of patterns of contagion in terrorist incidents.[7]

Thus the existence of extremism or rebellious potential is necessary to the resort to terrorism but does not in itself explain it, because many revolutionary and nationalist organizations have explicitly disavowed terrorism. The Russian Marxists argued for years against the use of terrorism.[8] Generally, small organizations resort to violence to compensate for what they lack in numbers.[9] The imbalance between the resources terrorists are able to mobilize and the power of the incumbent regime is a decisive consideration in their decision making.

More important than the observation that terrorism is the weapon of the weak, who lack numbers or conventional military power, is the explanation for weakness. Particularly, why does an organization lack the potential to attract enough followers to change government policy or overthrow it?

One possibility is that the majority of the population does not share the ideological views of the resisters, who occupy a political position so extreme that their appeal is inherently limited. This incompatibility of preferences may be purely political, concerning, for example, whether or not one prefers socialism to capitalism. The majority of West Germans found the Red Army Faction's promises for the future not only excessively vague but distasteful. Nor did most Italians support aims of the neofascist groups that initiated the "strategy of tension" in 1969. Other extremist groups, such as the *Euzkadi ta Akatasuna* (ETA) in Spain or the Provisional Irish Republican Army (PIRA) in Northern Ireland, may appeal exclusively to ethnic, religious, or other minorities. In such cases, a potential constituency of like-minded and dedicated individuals exists, but its boundaries are fixed and limited. Despite the intensity of the preferences of a minority, its numbers will never be sufficient for success.

A second explanation for the weakness of the type of organization likely to turn to terrorism lies in a failure to mobilize support. Its members may be unwilling or unable to expend the time and effort required for mass organizational work. Activists may not possess the requisite skills or patience, or may not expect returns commensurate with their endeavors. No matter how acute or widespread popular dissatisfaction may be, the masses do not rise spontaneously; mobilization is required.[10] The organization's leaders, recognizing the advantages of numbers, may combine mass organization with conspiratorial activities. But resources are limited and organizational work is difficult and slow even under favorable circumstances. Moreover, rewards are not immediate. These difficulties are compounded in an authoritarian state, where the organization of independent opposition is sure to incur high costs. Combining violent provocation with nonviolent organizing efforts may only work to the detriment of the latter.

For example, the debate over whether to use an exclusively violent underground strategy that is isolated from the masses (as terrorism inevitably is) or to work with the people in propaganda and organizational efforts divided the Italian left-wing groups, with the Red Brigades choosing the clandestine path and Prima Linea preferring to maintain contact with the wider protest movement. In prerevolutionary Russia the Socialist-Revolutionary party combined the activities of a legal political party with the terrorist campaign of the secret Combat Organization. The IRA has a legal counterpart in Sinn Fein.

A third reason for the weakness of dissident organizations is specific to repressive states. It is important to remember that terrorism is by no means restricted to liberal democracies, although some authors refuse to define resistance to authoritarianism as terrorism.[11] People may not support a resistance organization because they are afraid of negative sanctions from the regime or because censorship of the press prevents them from learning of the possibility of rebellion. In this situation a radical organization may believe that supporters exist but cannot reveal themselves. The depth of this latent support cannot be measured or activists mobilized until the state is overthrown.

Such conditions are frustrating, because the likelihood of popular dissatisfaction grows as the likelihood of its active expression is diminished. Frustration may also encourage unrealistic expectations among the regime's challengers, who are not able to test their popularity. Rational expectations may be undermined by fantastic assumptions about the role of the masses. Yet such fantasies can also prevail among radical undergrounds in Western democracies. The misperception of conditions can lead to unrealistic expectations.

In addition to small numbers, time constraints contribute to the decision to use terrorism. Terrorists are impatient for action. This impatience may, of course, be due to external factors, such as psychological or organizational pressures. The personalities of leaders, demands from followers, or competition from rivals often constitute impediments to strategic thinking. But it is not necessary to explain the felt urgency of some radical organizations by citing reasons external to an instrumental framework. Impatience and eagerness for action can be rooted in calculations of ends and means. For example, the organization may perceive an immediate opportunity to compensate for its inferiority vis-à-vis the government. A change in the structure of the situation may temporarily alter the balance of resources available to the two sides, thus changing the ratio of strength between government and challenger.

Such a change in the radical organization's outlook—the combination of optimism and urgency—may occur when the regime suddenly appears vulnerable to challenge. This vulnerability may be of two sorts. First, the regime's ability to respond effectively, its capacity for efficient repression of dissent, or its ability to protect its citizens and property may weaken. Its armed forces may be committed elsewhere, for example, as British forces were during World War I when the IRA first rose to challenge British rule, or its coercive resources may be otherwise overextended. Inadequate security at embassies, airports, or military installations may become obvious. The poorly protected U.S. Marine barracks in Beirut were, for example, a tempting target. Government strategy may be ill-adapted to responding to terrorism.

Second, the regime may make itself morally or politically vulnerable by increasing the likelihood that the terrorists will attract popular support. Government repressiveness is thought to have contradictory effects; it both deters dissent and provokes a moral backlash.[12] Perceptions of the regime as unjust motivate opposition. If government actions make average citizens willing to suffer punishment for supporting antigovernment causes, or lend credence to the claims of radical opponents, the extremist organization may be tempted to exploit this temporary upsurge of popular indignation. A groundswell of popular disapproval may make liberal governments less willing (as opposed to less able) to use coercion against violent dissent.

Political discomfort may also be internationally generated. If the climate of international opinion changes so as to reduce the legitimacy of a targeted regime, rebels may feel encouraged to risk a repression that they hope will be limited by outside disapproval. In such circumstances the regime's brutality may be expected to win supporters to the cause of its challengers. The current situation in South Africa furnishes an example. Thus a heightened sensitivity to injustice may be produced either by government actions or by changing public attitudes.

The other fundamental way in which the situation changes to the advantage of challengers is through acquiring new resources. New means of financial support are an obvious asset, which may accrue through a foreign alliance with a sympathetic government or another, richer revolutionary group, or through criminal means such as bank robberies or kidnapping for ransom. Although terrorism is an extremely economical method of violence, funds are essential for the support of full-time activists, weapons purchases, transportation, and logistics.

Technological advances in weapons, explosives, transportation, and communications also may enhance the disruptive potential of terrorism. The invention of dynamite was thought by nineteenth-century revolutionaries and anarchists to equalize the relationship between government and challenger, for example. In 1885, Johann Most published a pamphlet titled *Revolutionary War Science*, which explicitly advocated terrorism. According to Paul Avrich, the anarchists saw dynamite "as a great equalizing force, enabling ordinary workmen to stand up against armies, militias, and police, to say nothing of the hired gunmen of the employers."[13] In providing such a powerful but easily concealed weapon, science was thought to have given a decisive advantage to revolutionary forces.

Strategic innovation is another important way in which a challenging organization acquires new resources. The organization may borrow or adapt a technique in order to exploit a vulnerability ignored by the government. In August 1972, for example, the Provisional IRA introduced the effective tactic of the one-shot sniper. IRA Chief of Staff Sean MacStiofain claims to have originated the idea: "It seemed to me that prolonged sniping from a static position had no more in common with guerrilla theory than mass confrontations."[14] The best marksmen were trained to fire a single shot and escape before their position could be located. The creation of surprise is naturally one of the key advantages of an offensive strategy. So, too, is the willingness to violate social norms pertaining to restraints on violence. The history of terrorism reveals a series of innovations, as terrorists deliberately selected targets considered taboo and locales where violence was unexpected.

These innovations were then rapidly diffused, especially in the modern era of instantaneous and global communications.

It is especially interesting that, in 1968, two of the most important terrorist tactics of the modern era appeared—diplomatic kidnappings in Latin America and hijackings in the Middle East. Both were significant innovations because they involved the use of extortion or blackmail. Although the nineteenth-century Fenians had talked about kidnapping the prince of Wales, the People's Will (Narodnaya Volya) in nineteenth-century Russia had offered to halt its terrorist campaign if a constitution were granted, and [although] American Marines were kidnapped by Castro forces in 1959, hostage taking as a systematic and lethal form of coercive bargaining was essentially new....

Terrorism has so far been presented as the response by an opposition movement to an opportunity. This approach is compatible with the findings of Harvey Waterman, who sees collective political action as determined by the calculations of resources and opportunities.[15] Yet other theorists—James Q. Wilson, for example—argue that political organizations originate in response to a threat to a group's values.[16] Terrorism can certainly be defensive as well as opportunistic. It may be a response to a sudden downturn in a dissident organization's fortunes. The fear of appearing weak may provoke an underground organization into acting in order to show its strength. The PIRA used terrorism to offset an impression of weakness, even at the cost of alienating public opinion: in the 1970s periods of negotiations with the British were punctuated by outbursts of terrorism because the PIRA did want people to think that they were negotiating from strength.[17] Right-wing organizations frequently resort to violence in response to what they see as a threat to the status quo from the left. Beginning in 1969, for example, the right in Italy promoted a "strategy of tension," which involved urban bombings with high numbers of civilian casualties, in order to keep the Italian government and electorate from moving to the left.

Calculation of Cost and Benefit

An organization or a faction of an organization may choose terrorism because other methods are not expected to work or are considered too time-consuming, given the urgency of the situation and the government's superior resources. Why would an extremist organization expect that terrorism will be effective? What are the costs and benefits of such a choice, compared with other alternatives? What is the nature of the debate over terrorism? Whether or not to use terrorism is one of the most divisive issues resistance groups confront, and numerous revolutionary movements have split on the question of means even after agreeing on common political ends.[18]

The costs of terrorism. The costs of terrorism are high. As a domestic strategy, it invariably invites a punitive government reaction, although the organization may believe that the government reaction will not be efficient enough to pose a serious threat. This cost can be offset by the advance preparation of building a secure underground. *Sendero Luminoso* (Shining Path) in Peru, for example, spent ten years creating a clandestine organizational structure before launching a campaign of violence in 1980. Furthermore, radicals may look to the future and calculate that present sacrifice will not be in vain if it inspires future resistance. Conceptions of interest are thus long term.

Another potential cost of terrorism is loss of popular support. Unless terrorism is carefully controlled and discriminate, it claims innocent victims. In a liberal state, indiscriminate violence may appear excessive and unjustified and alienate a citizenry predisposed to loyalty to the government. If it provokes generalized government repression, fear may diminish enthusiasm for resistance. This potential cost of popular alienation is probably least in ethnically divided societies, where victims can be clearly identified as the enemy and where the government of the majority appears illegal to the minority. Terrorists try to compensate by justifying their actions as the result of the absence of choice or the need to respond to government violence. In addition, they may make their strategy highly discriminate, attacking only unpopular targets.

Terrorism may be unattractive because it is elitist. Although relying only on terrorism may spare the general population from costly involvement in the struggle for freedom, such isolation may violate the ideological beliefs of revolutionaries who insist that the people must participate in their liberation. The few who choose terrorism are willing to forgo or postpone the participation of the many, but revolutionaries who oppose terrorism insist that it prevents the people from taking responsibility for their own destiny. The possibility of vicarious popular identification with symbolic acts of terrorism may satisfy some revolutionaries, but others will find terrorism a harmful substitute for mass participation.

The advantages of terrorism. Terrorism has an extremely useful agenda-setting function. If the reasons behind violence are skillfully articulated, terrorism can put the issue of political change on the public agenda. By attracting attention it makes the claims of the resistance a salient issue in the public mind. The government can reject but not ignore an opposition's demands. In 1974 the Palestinian Black September organization, for example, was willing to sacrifice a base in Khartoum, alienate the Sudanese government, and create ambivalence in the Arab world by seizing the Saudi Arabian embassy and killing American and Belgian diplomats. These costs were apparently weighed against the message to the world "to take us seriously." Mainstream Fatah leader Salah Khalef (Abu Iyad) explained: "We are planting the seed. Others will harvest it.... It is enough for us now to learn, for example, in reading the *Jerusalem Post*, that Mrs. Meir had to make her will before visiting Paris, or that Mr. Abba Eban had to travel with a false passport."[19] George Habash of the PFLP noted in 1970 that "we force people to ask what is going on."[20] In these statements, contemporary extremists echo the nineteenth-century anarchists, who coined the idea of propaganda of the deed, a term used as early as 1877 to refer to an act of insurrection as "a powerful means of arousing popular conscience" and the materialization of an idea through actions.[21]

Terrorism may be intended to create revolutionary conditions. It can prepare the ground for active mass revolt by undermining the government's authority and demoralizing its administrative cadres—its courts, police, and military. By spreading insecurity—at the extreme, making the country ungovernable—the organization hopes to pressure the regime into concessions or relaxation of coercive controls. With the rule of law disrupted, the people will be free to join the opposition. Spectacular humiliation of the government demonstrates strength and will and maintains the morale and enthusiasm of adherents and sympathizers. The first wave of Russian revolutionaries claimed that the aims of terrorism were to exhaust the enemy, render the government's position untenable, and wound the government's prestige by delivering a moral, not a physical, blow. Terrorists hoped to paralyze the government by their presence merely by showing signs of life from time to time. The hesitation, irresolution, and tension they would produce would undermine the processes of government and make the Czar a prisoner in his own palace.[22] As Brazilian revolutionary Carlos Marighela explained: "Revolutionary terrorism's great weapon is initiative, which guarantees its survival and continued activity. The more committed terrorists and revolutionaries devoted to anti-dictatorship terrorism and sabotage there are, the more military power will be worn down, the more time it will lose following false trails, and the more fear and tension it will suffer through not knowing where the next attack will be launched and what the next target will be."[23]

These statements illustrate a corollary advantage to terrorism in what might be called its excitational function: it inspires resistance by example. As propaganda of the deed, terrorism demonstrates that the regime can be challenged and that illegal opposition is possible. It acts as a catalyst, not substitute, for mass revolt. All the tedious and time-consuming organizational work of mobilizing the people can be avoided. Terrorism is a shortcut to revolution. As the Russian revolutionary Vera Figner described its purpose, terrorism was "a means of agitation to draw people from their torpor," not a sign of loss of belief in the people.[24]

A more problematic benefit lies in provoking government repression. Terrorists often think that by provoking indiscriminate repression against the population, terrorism will heighten popular disaffection, demonstrate the justice of terrorist claims, and enhance the attractiveness of the political alternative the terrorists represent. Thus, the West German Red Army Faction sought (in vain) to make fascism "visible" in West Germany.[25] In Brazil, Marighela unsuccessfully aimed to "transform the country's political situation into a military one. Then discontent will spread to all social groups and the military will be held exclusively responsible for failures."[26]

But profiting from government repression depends on the lengths to which the government is willing to go in order to contain disorder, and on the population's tolerance for both insecurity and repression. A liberal state may be limited in its capacity for quelling violence, but at the same time it may be difficult to provoke to excess. However, the government's reaction to terrorism may reinforce the symbolic value of violence even if it avoids repression. Extensive security precautions, for example, may only make the terrorists appear powerful.

Summary. To summarize, the choice of terrorism involves considerations of timing and of the popular contribution to revolt, as well as of the relationship between government and opponents. Radicals choose terrorism when they want immediate action, think that only violence can build organizations and mobilize supporters, and accept the risks of challenging the government in particularly provocative way. Challengers who think that organizational infrastructure must precede action, that rebellion without the masses is misguided, and that premature conflict with the regime can only lead to disaster favor gradualist strategies. They prefer methods such as rural guerrilla warfare, because terrorism can jeopardize painfully achieved gains or preclude eventual compromise with the government.

The resistance organization has before it a set of alternatives defined by the situation and by the objectives and resources of the group. The reasoning behind terrorism takes into account the balance of power between challengers and authorities, a balance that depends on the amount of popular support the resistance can mobilize. The proponents of terrorism understand this constraint and possess reasonable expectations about the likely results of action or inaction. They may be wrong about the alternatives that are open to them, or miscalculate the consequences of their actions, but their decisions are based on logical processes. Furthermore, organizations learn from their mistakes and from those of others, resulting in strategic continuity and progress toward the development of more efficient and sophisticated tactics. Future choices are modified by the consequences of present actions.

Hostage Taking as Bargaining

Hostage taking can be analyzed as a form of coercive bargaining. More than twenty years ago, Thomas Schelling wrote that "hostages represent the power to hurt in its purest form."[27] From this perspective, terrorists choose to take hostages because in bargaining situations the government's greater strength and resources are not an advantage. The extensive resort to this form of terrorism after 1968, a year that marks the major advent of diplomatic kidnappings and airline hijackings, was a predictable response to the growth of state power. Kidnappings, hijackings, and barricade-type seizures of embassies or public buildings are attempts to manipulate a government's political decisions.

Strategic analysis of bargaining terrorism is based on the assumption that hostage takers genuinely seek the concessions they demand. It assumes that they prefer government compliance to resistance. This analysis does not allow for deception or for the possibility that seizing hostages may be an end in itself because it yields the benefit of publicity. Because these limiting assumptions may reduce the utility of the theory, it is important to recognize them.

Terrorist bargaining is essentially a form of blackmail or extortion.[28] Terrorists seize hostages in order to affect a government's choices, which are controlled both by expectations of outcome (what the terrorists are likely to do, given the government reaction) and preferences (such as humanitarian values). The outcome threatened by the terrorist—the death of the hostages—must be worse for the government than compliance with terrorist demands. The terrorist has two options, neither of which necessarily excludes the other: to make the threat both more horrible and more credible or to reward compliance, a factor that strategic theorists often ignore.[29] That is, the cost to the government of complying with the terrorists' demands may be lowered or the cost of resisting raised.

The threat to kill the hostages must be believable and painful to the government. Here hostage takers are faced with a paradox. How can the credibility of this threat be assured when hostage takers recognize that governments know that the terrorists' control over the situation depends on live hostages? One way of establishing credibility is to divide the threat, making it sequential by killing one hostage at a time. Such tactics also aid terrorists in the process of incurring and demonstrating a commitment to carrying out their threat. Once the terrorists have murdered, though, their incentive to surrender voluntarily is substantially reduced. The terrorists have increased their own costs of yielding in order to persuade the government that their intention to kill all the hostages is real.

Another important way of binding oneself in a terrorist strategy is to undertake a barricade rather than a kidnapping operation. Terrorists who are trapped with the hostages find it more difficult to back down (because the government controls the escape routes) and, by virtue of this commitment, influence the government's choices. When terrorists join the hostages in a barricade situation, they create the visible and irrevocable commitment that Schelling sees as a necessary bond in bargaining. The government must expect desperate behavior, because the terrorists have increased their potential loss in order to demonstrate the firmness of their intentions. Furthermore, barricades are technically easier than kidnappings.

The terrorists also attempt to force the "last clear chance" of avoiding disaster onto the government, which must accept the responsibility for noncompliance that leads to the deaths of hostages. The seizure of hostages is the first move in the game, leaving the next move—which determines the fate of the hostages—completely up to the government. Uncertain communications may facilitate this strategy.[30] The terrorists can pretend not to receive government messages that might affect their demonstrated commitment. Hostage takers can also bind themselves by insisting that they are merely agents, empowered to ask only for the most extreme demands. Terrorists may deliberately appear irrational, either through inconsistent and erratic behavior or unrealistic expectations and preferences, in order to convince the government that they will carry out a threat that entails self-destruction.

Hostage seizures are a type of iterated game, which explains some aspects of terrorist behavior that otherwise seem to violate strategic principles. In terms of a single episode, terrorists can be expected to find killing hostages painful, because they will not achieve their demands and the government's desire to punish will be intensified. However, from a long-range perspective, killing hostages reinforces the credibility of the threat in the next terrorist incident, even if the killers then cannot escape. Each terrorist episode is actually a round in a series of games between government and terrorists.

Hostage takers may influence the government's decision by promising rewards for compliance. Recalling that terrorism represents an iterative game, the release of hostages unharmed when ransom is paid underwrites a promise in the future. Sequential release of selected hostages makes promises credible. Maintaining secrecy about a government's concessions is an additional reward for compliance. France, for example, can if necessary deny making concessions to Lebanese kidnappers because the details of arrangements have not been publicized.

Terrorists may try to make their demands appear legitimate so that governments may seem to satisfy popular grievances rather than the whims of terrorists. Thus, terrorists may ask that food be distributed to the poor. Such demands were a favored tactic of the *Ejercito Revolucionario del Pueblo (ERP)* in Argentina in the 1970s.

A problem for hostage takers is that rewarding compliance is not easy to reconcile with making threats credible. For example, if terrorists use publicity to emphasize their threat to kill hostages (which they frequently do), they may also increase the costs of compliance for the government because of the attention drawn to the incident.

In any calculation of the payoffs for each side, the costs associated with the bargaining process must be taken into account.[31] Prolonging the hostage crisis increases the costs to both sides. The question is who loses most and thus is more likely to concede. Each party presumably wishes to make the delay more costly to the other. Seizing multiple hostages appears to be advantageous to terrorists, who are thus in a position to make threats credible by killing hostages individually. Conversely, the greater the number of hostages, the greater the cost of holding them. In hijacking or barricade situations, stress and fatigue for the captors increase waiting costs for them as well. Kidnapping poses fewer such costs. Yet the terrorists can reasonably expect that the costs to governments in terms of public or international pressures may be higher when developments are visible.

Furthermore, kidnappers can maintain suspense and interest by publishing communications from their victims.

Identifying the obstacles to effective bargaining in hostage seizures is critical. Most important, bargaining depends on the existence of a common interest between two parties. It is unclear whether the lives of hostages are a sufficient common interest to ensure a compromise outcome that is preferable to no agreement for both sides. Furthermore, most theories of bargaining assume that the preferences of each side remain stable during negotiations. In reality, the nature and intensity of preferences may change during a hostage-taking episode. For example, embarrassment over the Iran-*contra* scandal may have reduced the American interest in securing the release of hostages in Lebanon.

Bargaining theory is also predicated on the assumption that the game is two-party. When terrorists seize the nationals of one government in order to influence the choices of a third, the situation is seriously complicated. The hostages themselves may sometimes become intermediaries and participants. In Lebanon, Terry Waite, formerly an intermediary and negotiator, became a hostage. Such developments are not anticipated by bargaining theories based on normal political relationships. Furthermore, bargaining is not possible if a government is willing to accept the maximum cost the terrorists can bring to bear rather than concede. And the government's options are not restricted to resistance or compliance; armed rescue attempts represent an attempt to break the bargaining stalemate. In attempting to make their threats credible—for example, by sequential killing of hostages—terrorists may provoke military intervention. There may be limits, then, to the pain terrorists can inflict and still remain in the game.

Conclusions

This essay has attempted to demonstrate that even the most extreme and unusual forms of political behavior can follow an internal, strategic logic. If there are consistent patterns in terrorist behavior, rather than random idiosyncrasies, a strategic analysis may reveal them. Prediction of future terrorism can only be based on theories that explain past patterns.

Terrorism can be considered a reasonable way of pursuing extreme interests in the political arena. It is one among the many alternatives that radical organizations can choose. Strategic conceptions, based on ideas of how best to take advantage of the possibilities of a given situation, are an important determinant of oppositional terrorism, as they are of the government response. However, no single explanation for terrorist behavior is satisfactory. Strategic calculation is only one factor in the decision-making process leading to terrorism. But it is critical to include strategic reasoning as a possible motivation, at a minimum as an antidote to stereotypes of "terrorists" as irrational fanatics. Such stereotypes are a dangerous underestimation of the capabilities of extremist groups. Nor does stereotyping serve to educate the public—or, indeed, specialists—about the complexities of terrorist motivations and behaviors.

Martha Crenshaw is the John Andrus professor of government at Wesleyan University, where she has taught international politics since 1974. She is the editor, with John Pimlott, of the *International Encyclopedia of Terrorism* and the author of countless articles and texts on the subject of political terrorism.

Crenshaw currently serves on a task force concerning foreign policy toward the Islamic world at the Brookings Institution.

Notes

1. For a similar perspective (based on a different methodology) see James DeNardo, *Power in Numbers: The Political Strategy of Protest and Rebellion* (Princeton, N.J.: Princeton University Press, 1985). See also Harvey Waterman, "Insecure 'Ins' and Opportune 'Outs': Sources of Collective Political Activity," *Journal of Political and Military Sociology* 8 (1980): 107–12, and "Reasons and Reason: Collective Political Activity in Comparative and Historical Perspective," *World Politics* 33 (1981): 554–89. A useful review of rational choice theories is found in James G. March, "Theories of Choice and Making Decisions," *Society* 20 (1982): 29–39.
2. Edward N. Muller and Karl-Dieter Opp, "Rational Choice and Rebellious Collective Action," *American Political Science Review* 80 (1986): 471–87.
3. Ibid., 484. The authors also present another puzzling question that may be answered in terms of either psychology or collective rationality. People who expected their rebellious behavior to be punished were more likely to be potential rebels. This propensity could be explained either by a martyr syndrome (or an expectation of hostility from authority figures) or intensity of preference—the calculation that the regime was highly repressive and thus deserved all the more to be destroyed. See pp. 482 and 484.
4. Leila Khaled, *My People Shall Live: The Autobiography of a Revolutionary* (London: Hodder and Stoughton, 1973), 128–31.
5. See Martha Crenshaw, "The Strategic Development of Terrorism," paper presented to the 1985 Annual Meeting of the American Political Science Association, New Orleans.
6. William A. Gamson, *The Strategy of Social Protest* (Homewood, Illinois: Dorsey Press, 1975).
7. Manus I. Midlarksy, Martha Crenshaw, and Fumihiko Yoshida, "Why Violence Spreads: The Contagion of International Terrorism," *International Studies Quarterly* 24 (1980): 262–98.
8. See the study by David A. Newell, *The Russian Marxist Response to Terrorism: 1878–1917* (Ph.D. dissertation, Stanford University, University Microfilms, 1981).
9. The tension between violence and numbers is a fundamental proposition in DeNardo's analysis; see *Power in Numbers*, chapters 9–11.
10. The work of Charles Tilly emphasizes the political basis of collective violence. See Charles Tilly, Louise Tilly, and Richard Tilly, *The Rebellious Century 1830–1930* (Cambridge: Harvard University Press, 1975), and Charles Tilly, *From Mobilization to Revolution* (Reading, Mass.: Addison-Wesley, 1978).
11. See Conor Cruise O'Brien, "Terrorism under Democratic conditions: The Case of the IRA," in *Terrorism, Legitimacy, and Power: The Consequences of Political Violence,* edited by Martha Crenshaw (Middletown, Conn.: Wesleyan University Press, 1983).
12. For example, DeNardo, in *Power in Numbers*, argues that "the movement derives moral sympathy from the government's excesses" (p. 207).
13. Paul Avrich, *The Haymarket Tragedy* (Princeton: Princeton University Press, 1984), 166.
14. Sean MacStiofain, *Memoirs of a Revolutionary* (N.p.: Gordon Cremonisi, 1975), 301.
15. Waterman, "Insecure 'Ins' and Opportune 'Outs'" and "Reasons and Reason."
16. *Political Organizations* (New York: Basic Books, 1973).
17. Maria McGuire, *To Take Arms: My Year with the IRA Provisionals* (New York: Viking, 1973), 110–11, 118, 129–31, 115, and 161–62.
18. DeNardo concurs; see *Power in Numbers*, chapter 11.
19. See Jim Hoagland, "A Community of Terror," *Washington Post*, 15 March 1973, pp. 1 and 13; also *New York Times*, 4 March 1973, p. 28. Black September is widely regarded as a subsidiary of Fatah, the major Palestinian organization headed by Yasir Arafat.
20. John Amos, *Palestinian Resistance: Organization of a Nationalist Movement* (New York: Pergamon, 1980), 193; quoting George Habash, interviewed in *Life Magazine*, 12 June 1970, 33.

21. Jean Maitron, *Histoire du mouvement anarchiste en France (1880–1914)*, 2d ed. (Paris: Société universitaire d'éditions et de librairie, 1955), 74–5.
22. "Stepniak" (pseud. for Sergei Kravshinsky), *Underground Russia: Revolutionary Profiles and Sketches from Life* (London: Smith, Elder, 1883), 278–80.
23. Carlos Marighela, *For the Liberation of Brazil* (Harmondsworth: Penguin, 1971), 113.
24. Vera Figner, *Mémoires d'une révolutionnaire* (Paris: Gallimard, 1930), 206.
25. *Textes des prisonniers de la "fraction armée rouge" et dernières lettres d'Ulrike Meinhof* (Paris: Maspéro, 1977), 64.
26. Marighela, *For the Liberation of Brazil*, 46.
27. Schelling, *Arms and Influence* (New Haven, Conn.: Yale University Press, 1966), 6.
28. Daniel Ellsburg, *The Theory and Practice of Blackmail* (Santa Monica: Rand Corporation, 1968).
29. David A. Baldwin, "Bargaining with Airline Hijackers," in *The 50% Solution*, edited by William I. Zartman, 404–29 (Garden City, N.Y.: Doubleday, 1976), argues that promises have not been sufficiently stressed. Analysts tend to emphasize threats instead, surely because of the latent violence implicit in hostage taking regardless of outcome.
30. See Roberta Wohlstetter's case study of Castro's seizure of American Marines in Cuba: "Kidnapping to Win Friends and Influence People," *Survey* 20 (1974): 1–40.
31. Scott E. Atkinson, Todd Sandler, and John Tschirhart, "Terrorism in a Bargaining Framework," *Journal of Law and Economics* 30 (1987): 1–21.

Audrey Kurth Cronin, 2002

Behind the Curve

Globalization and International Terrorism

The coincidence between the evolving changes of globalization, the inherent weaknesses of the Arab region, and the inadequate American response to both ensures that terrorism will continue to be the most serious threat to U.S. and Western interests in the twenty-first century. There has been little creative thinking, however, about how to confront the growing terrorist backlash that has been unleashed. Terrorism is a complicated, eclectic phenomenon, requiring a sophisticated strategy oriented toward influencing its means and ends over the long term. Few members of the U.S. policymaking and academic communities, however, have the political capital, intellectual background, or inclination to work together to forge an effective, sustained response. Instead, the tendency has been to fall back on established bureaucratic mind-sets and prevailing theoretical paradigms that have little relevance for the changes in international security that became obvious after the terrorist attacks in New York and Washington on September 11, 2001.

The current wave of international terrorism, characterized by unpredictable and unprecedented threats from nonstate actors, not only is a reaction to globalization but is facilitated by it; the U.S. response to this reality has been reactive and anachronistic. The combined focus of the United States on state-centric threats and its attempt to cast twenty-first-century terrorism into familiar strategic terms avoids and often undermines effective responses to this nonstate phenomenon. The increasing threat of globalized terrorism must be met with flexible, multifaceted responses that deliberately and effectively exploit avenues of globalization in return; this, however, is not happening.

As the primary terrorist target, the United Sates should take the lead in fashioning a forward-looking strategy. As the world's predominant military, economic, and political power, it has been able to pursue its interests throughout the globe with unprecedented freedom since the breakup of the Soviet Union more than a decade ago. Even in the wake of the September 11 terrorist attacks on the World Trade Center and the Pentagon, and especially after the U.S. military action in Afghanistan, the threat of terrorism, mostly consisting of underfunded and ad hoc cells motivated by radical fringe ideas, has seemed unimportant by comparison. U.S. strategic culture has a long tradition of downplaying such atypical concerns in favor of a focus on more conventional state-based military power.[1] On the whole, this has been an effective approach: As was dramatically demonstrated in Afghanistan, the U.S. military knows how to destroy state governments and their armed forces, and the American political leadership and public have a natural bias toward using power to achieve the quickest results. Sometimes it is important to show resolve and respond forcefully.

The United States has been far less impressive, however, in its use of more subtle tools of domestic and international statecraft, such as intelligence, law enforcement, economic sanctions, educational training, financial controls, public diplomacy, coalition building, international law, and foreign aid. In an ironic twist, it is these tools that have become central to the security of the United States and its allies since September 11. In an era of globalized terrorism, the familiar state-centric threats have not disappeared; instead they have been joined by new (or newly threatening) competing political, ideological, economic, and cultural concerns that are only superficially understood, particularly in the West. An examination of the recent evolution of terrorism and a projection of future developments suggest that, in the age of globalized terrorism, old attitudes are not just anachronistic; they are dangerous.

Terrorism as a phenomenon is not new, but for reasons explained below, the threat it now poses is greater than ever before. The current terrorist backlash is manifested in the extremely violent asymmetrical response directed at the United States and other leading powers by terrorist groups associated with or inspired by al-Qaeda. This backlash has the potential to fundamentally threaten the international system. Thus it is not just an American problem. Unless the United States and its allies formulate a more comprehensive response to terrorism, better balanced across the range of policy instruments, the results will be increasing international instability and long-term failure.

The article proceeds in five main sections. First, it provides a discussion of the definition, history, causes, and types of terrorism, placing the events of September 11, 2001, in their modern context. Second, it briefly describes key trends in modern terrorism, explaining how the phenomenon appears to be evolving. Third, it analyzes the implications of these trends for the stability and security of the international community generally, and the United States and its allies more specifically. Fourth, the article outlines the prospects of these trends. It concludes with a range of policy recommendations suggested by the analysis.

Definition, Origins, Motivations, and Types of Modern Terrorism

The terrorist phenomenon has a long and varied history, punctuated by lively debates over the meaning of the term. By ignoring this history, the United States runs the risk of repeating the plethora of mistakes made by other major powers that faced similar threats in the past. This section begins with an explanation of the definition of terrorism, then proceeds to an examination of terrorism's origins, major motivations, and predominant types.

Definition of Terrorism

Terrorism is notoriously difficult to define, in part because the term has evolved and in part because it is associated with an activity that is designed to be subjective. Generally speaking, the targets of a terrorist episode are not the victims who are killed or maimed in the attack, but rather the governments, publics, or constituents among whom the terrorists hope to engender a reaction—such as fear, repulsion, intimidation, overreaction, or radicalization. Specialists in the area of terrorism studies have devoted hundreds of pages toward trying to develop an unassailable definition of the term, only to realize the fruitlessness of their efforts: Terrorism is intended to be a matter of perception and is thus seen differently by different observers.[2]

Although individuals can disagree over whether particular actions constitute terrorism, there are certain aspects of the concept that are fundamental. First, terrorism always has a political nature. It involves the commission of outrageous acts designed to precipitate political change.[3] At its root, terrorism is about justice, or at least someone's perception of it, whether man-made or divine. Second, although many other uses of violence are inherently political, including conventional war among states, terrorism is distinguished by its nonstate character—even when terrorists receive military, political, economic, and other means of support from state sources. States obviously employ force for political ends: When state force is used internationally, it is considered an act of war; when it is used domestically, it is called various things, including law enforcement, state terror, oppression, or civil war. Although states can terrorize, they cannot by definition be terrorists. Third, terrorism deliberately targets the innocent, which also distinguishes it from state uses of force that inadvertently kill innocent bystanders. In any given example, the latter may or may not be seen as justified; but again, this use of force is different from terrorism. Hence the fact that precision-guided missiles sometimes go astray and kill innocent civilians is a tragic use of force, but it is not terrorism. Finally, state use of force is subject to international norms and conventions that may be invoked or at least consulted; terrorists do not abide by international laws or norms and, to maximize the psychological effect of an attack, their activities have a deliberately unpredictable quality.[4]

Thus, at a minimum, terrorism has the following characteristics: a fundamentally political nature, the surprise use of violence against seemingly random targets, and the targeting of the innocent by nonstate actors.[5] All of these attributes are illustrated by recent examples of terrorism—from the April 2000 kidnapping of tourists by the Abu Sayyaf group of the Philippines to the various incidents allegedly committed by al-Qaeda, including the 1998 bombings of the U.S. embassies in Kenya and Tanzania and the September 11 attacks. For the purposes of this discussion, the shorthand (and admittedly imperfect) definition of terrorism is the threat or use of seemingly random violence against innocents for political ends by a nonstate actor.

Origins of Terrorism

Terrorism is as old as human history. One of the first reliably documented instances of terrorism, however, occurred in the first century B.C.E. The Zealots-Sicarri, Jewish terrorists dedicated to inciting a revolt against Roman rule in Judea, murdered their victims with daggers in broad daylight in the heart of Jerusalem, eventually creating such anxiety among the population that they generated a mass insurrection.[6] Other early terrorists include the Hindu Thugs and the Muslim Assassins. Modern terrorism, however, is generally considered to have originated with the French Revolution.[7]

The term "terror" was first employed in 1795, when it was coined to refer to a policy systemically used to protect the fledgling French republic government against counter-revolutionaries. Robespierre's practice of using revolutionary tribunals as a means of publicizing a prisoner's fate for broader effect within the population (apart from questions of legal guilt or innocence) can be seen as a nascent example of the much more highly developed, blatant manipulation of media attention by terrorist groups in the mid- to late twentieth century.[8] Modern terrorism is a dynamic concept, from the outset dependent to some degree on the political and historical context within which it has been employed.

Decolonization and Antiglobalization: Drivers of Terrorism?

Although individual terrorist groups have unique characteristics and arise in specific local contexts, an examination of broad historical patterns reveals that the international system within which such groups are spawned does influence their nature and motivations. A distinguishing feature of modern terrorism has been the connection between sweeping political or ideological concepts and increasing levels of terrorist activity internationally. The broad political aim has been against (1) empires, (2) colonial powers, and (3) the U.S.-led international system marked by globalization. Thus it is important to understand the general history of modern terrorism and where the current threat fits within an international context.

David Rapoport has described modern terrorism such as that perpetuated by al-Qaeda as part of a religiously inspired "fourth wave." This wave follows three earlier historical phases in which terrorism was tied to the breakup of empires, decolonization, and leftist anti-Westernism.[9] Rapoport argues that terrorism occurs in consecutive if somewhat overlapping waves. The argument here, however, is that modern terrorism has been a power struggle along a continuum: central power versus local power, big power versus small power, modern power versus traditional power. The key variable is a widespread perception of opportunity, combined with a shift in a particular political or ideological paradigm. Thus, even though the newest international terrorist threat, emanating largely from Muslim countries, has more than a modicum of religious inspiration, it is more accurate to see it as part of a larger phenomenon of antiglobalization and tension between the have and have-not nations, as well as between the elite and underprivileged within those nations. In an era where reforms occur at a pace much slower than is desired, terrorists today, like those before them, aim to exploit the frustrations of the common people (especially in the Arab world).

In the nineteenth century, the unleashing of concepts such as universal suffrage and popular empowerment raised the hopes of people throughout the western world, indirectly resulting in the first phase of modern terrorism. Originating in Russia, as Rapoport argues, it was stimulated not by state repression but by the efforts of the czars to placate demands for economic and political reforms, and the inevitable disappointment of popular expectations that were raised as a result. The goal of terrorists was to engage in attacks on symbolic targets to get the attention of the common people and thus provoke a popular response that would ultimately overturn the prevailing political order. This type of modern terrorism was reflected in the activities of groups such as the Russian Narodnaya Volya (People's Will) and later in the development of a series of movements in the United States and Europe, especially in territories of the former Ottoman Empire.

The dissolution of empires and the search for a new distribution of political power provided an opportunity for terrorism in the nineteenth and twentieth centuries. It climaxed in the assassination of Archduke Franz Ferdinand on June 28, 1914, an event that catalyzed the major powers into taking violent action, not because of the significance of the man himself but because of the suspicion of rival state involvement in the sponsorship of the killing. World War I, the convulsive systemic cataclysm that resulted, ended the first era of modern terrorism, according to Rapoport.[10] But terrorism tied to popular movements seeking greater democratic representation and political power from coercive empires has not ceased. Consider, for example, the Balkans after the downfall of the former state of Yugoslavia. The struggle for power among various Balkan ethnic groups can be seen as the final devolution of power from the former Ottoman Empire. This postimperial scramble is also in evidence elsewhere— for example, in Aceh, Chechnya, and Xinjiang, to mention just a few of the trouble spots within vast (former) empires. The presentation of a target of opportunity, such as a liberalizing state or regime, frequently evokes outrageous terrorist acts.

According to Rapoport, a second, related phase of modern terrorism associated with the concept of national self-determination developed its greatest predominance after World War I. It also continues to the present day. These struggles for power are another facet of terrorism against larger political powers and are specifically designed to win political independence or autonomy. The mid–twentieth-century era of rapid decolonization spawned national movements in territories as diverse as Algeria, Israel, South Africa, and Vietnam.[11] An important by-product was ambivalence toward the phenomenon in the international community, with haggling over the definition of terrorism reaching a fever pitch in the United Nations by the 1970s.

The question of political motivation became important in determining international attitudes toward terrorist attacks, as the post–World War II backlash against the colonial powers and the attractiveness of national independence movements led to the creation of a plethora of new states often born from violence. Arguments over the justice of international causes and the designation of terrorist struggles as "wars of national liberation" predominated, with consequentialist philosophies excusing the killing of innocent people if the cause in the long run was "just." Rapoport sees the U.S. intervention in Vietnam, and especially the subsequent American defeat by the Vietcong, as having catalyzed a "third wave" of modern terrorism; however, the relationship between the Vietnam conflict and other decolonization movements might just as easily be considered part of the same phase. In any case, the victory of the Vietcong excited the imaginations of revolutionaries throughout the world and, according to Rapoport, helped lead to a resurgence in terrorist violence. The Soviet Union underwrote the nationalist and leftist terrorist agendas of some groups, depicting the United States as the new colonial power—an easy task following the Vietnam intervention—and furthering an ideological agenda oriented toward achieving a postcapitalist, international communist utopia. Other groups, especially in Western Europe, rejected both the Soviet and capitalist models and looked admiringly toward nationalist revolutionaries in the developing world.[12] Leftist groups no longer predominate, but the enduring search for national self-determination continues, not only in the areas mentioned above but also in other hot spots such as the Basque region, East Timor, Sri Lanka, and Sudan.

Terrorism achieved a firmly international character during the 1970s and 1980s,[13] evolving in part as a result of technological advances and partly in reaction to the dramatic explosion of international media influence. International links were not new, but their centrality was. Individual, scattered national causes began to develop into international organizations with links and activities increasingly across borders and among differing causes. This development was greatly facilitated by the covert sponsorship of states such as Iran, Libya, and North Korea, and of course the Soviet Union, which found the underwriting of terrorist organizations an attractive tool for accomplishing clandestine goals while avoiding potential retaliation for the terrorist attacks.

The 1970s and 1980s represented the height of state-sponsored terrorism. Sometimes the lowest common denominator among the groups was the concept against which they were reacting—for example, "Western imperialism"—rather than the specific goals they sought. The most important innovation, however, was the increasing commonality of international connections among the groups. After the 1972 Munich Olympics massacre of eleven Israeli athletes, for example, the Palestinian Liberation Organization (PLO) and its associated groups captured the imaginations of young radicals around the world. In Lebanon and elsewhere, the PLO also provided training in the preferred techniques of twentieth-century terrorism such as airline hijacking, hostage taking, and bombing.

Since the September 11 attacks, the world has witnessed the maturation of a new phase of terrorist activity, the jihad era, spawned by the Iranian Revolution of 1979 as well as the Soviet defeat in Afghanistan shortly thereafter. The powerful attraction of religious and spiritual movements has overshadowed the nationalist or leftist revolutionary ethos of earlier terrorist phases (though many of those struggles continue), and it has become the central characteristic of a growing international trend. It is perhaps ironic that, as Rapoport observes, the forces of history seem to be driving international terrorism back to a much earlier time, with echoes of the behavior of "sacred" terrorists such as the Zealots-Sicarii clearly apparent in the terrorist activities of organizations such as al-Qaeda and its associated groups. Religious terrorism is not new; rather it is a continuation of an ongoing modern power struggle between those with power and those without it. Internationally, the main targets of these terrorists are the United States and the U.S.-led global system.

Like other eras of modern terrorism, this latest phase has deep roots. And given the historical patterns, it is likely to last at least a generation, if not longer. The jihad era is animated by widespread alienation combined with elements of religious identity and doctrine—a dangerous mix of forces that resonate deep in the human psyche.

What is different about this phase is the urgent requirement for solutions that deal both with the religious fanatics who are the terrorists and the far more politically motivated states, entities, and people who would support them because they feel powerless and left behind in a globalizing world. Thus if there is a trend in terrorism, it is the existence of a two-level challenge: the hyperreligious motivation of small groups of terrorists and the much broader enabling environment of bad governance, nonexistent social services, and poverty that punctuates much of the developing world. Al-Qaeda, a band driven by religious extremism, is able to do so much harm because of the secondary support and sanctuary it receives in vast areas that have not experienced the political and economic benefits of globalization. Therefore, the prescription for dealing with Osama bin Laden and his followers is not just eradicating a relatively small number of terrorists, but also changing the conditions that allow them to acquire so much power. Leaving aside for the moment the enabling environment, it is useful to focus on the chief motivations of the terrorists themselves, especially the contrasting secular and spiritual motivations of terrorism.

Leftist, Rightist, Ethnonationalist/Separatist, and "Sacred" Terrorism

There are four types of terrorist organizations currently operating around the world, categorized mainly by their source of motivation: left-wing terrorists, right-wing terrorists, ethnonationalist/separatist terrorists, and religious or "sacred" terrorists. All four types have enjoyed periods of relative prominence in the modern era, with left-wing terrorism intertwined with the Communist movement,[14] right-wing terrorism drawing its inspiration from Fascism,[15] and the bulk of ethnonationalist/separatist terrorism accompanying the wave of decolonization especially in the immediate post–WorldWar II years. Currently, "sacred" terrorism is becoming more significant.[16] Although groups in all categories continue to exist today, left-wing and right-wing terrorist groups were more numerous in earlier decades. Of course, these categories are not perfect, as many groups have a mix of motivating ideologies—some ethnonationalist groups, for example, have religious characteristics or agendas[17]—but usually one ideology or motivation dominates.

Categories are useful not simply because classifying the groups gives scholars a more orderly field to study (admittedly an advantage), but also because different motivations have sometimes led to differing styles and modes of behavior. Understanding the type of terrorist group involved can provide insight into the likeliest manifestations of its violence and the most typical patterns of its development. At the risk of generalizing, left-wing terrorist organizations, driven by liberal or idealist political concepts, tend to prefer revolutionary, antiauthoritarian, antimaterialistic agendas. (Here it is useful to distinguish between the idealism of individual terrorists and the frequently contradictory motivations of their sponsors.) In line with these preferences, left-wing organizations often engage in brutal criminal-type behavior such as kidnapping, murder, bombing, and arson, often directed at elite targets that symbolize authority. They have difficulty, however, agreeing on their long-term objectives.[18] Most left-wing organizations in twentieth-century Western Europe, for example, were brutal but relatively ephemeral. Of course, right-wing terrorists can be ruthless, but in their most recent manifestations they have tended to be less cohesive and more impetuous in their violence than leftist terrorist groups. Their targets are often chosen according to race but also ethnicity, religion, or immigrant status, and in recent decades at least, have been more opportunistic than calculated.[19] This makes them potentially explosive but difficult to track.[20] Ethnonationalist/separatist terrorists are the most conventional, usually having a clear political or territorial aim that is rational and potentially negotiable, if not always justifiable in any given case. They can be astoundingly violent, over lengthy periods. At the same time, it can be difficult to distinguish between goals based on ethnic identity and those rooted in the control of a piece of land. With their focus on gains to be made in the traditional state-oriented international system, ethnonationalist/separatist terrorists often transition in and out of more traditional paramilitary structures, depending on how the cause is going. In addition, they typically have sources of support among the local populace of the same ethnicity with whom their separatist goals (or appeals to blood links) may resonate. That broader popular support is usually the key to the greater average longevity of ethnonationalist/ separatist groups in the modern era.[21]

All four types of terrorist organizations are capable of egregious acts of barbarism. But religious terrorists may be especially dangerous to international security for at least five reasons.

First, religious terrorists often feel engaged in a Manichaean struggle of good against evil, implying an open-ended set of human targets: Anyone who is not a member of their religion or religious sect may be "evil" and thus fair game. Although indiscriminate attacks are not unique to religious terrorists, the exclusivity of their faith may lead them to dehumanize their victims even more than most terrorist groups do, because they consider nonmembers to be infidels or apostates—as perhaps, for instance, al-Qaeda operatives may have viewed Muslims killed in the World Trade Center.

Second, religious terrorists engage in violent behavior directly or indirectly to please the perceived commands of a deity. This has a number of worrisome implications: The whims of the deity may be less than obvious to those who are not members of the religion, so the actions of violent religious organizations can be especially unpredictable. Moreover, religious terrorists may not be as constrained in their behavior by concerns about the reactions of their human constituents. (Their audience lies elsewhere.)

Third, religious terrorists consider themselves to be unconstrained by secular values or laws. Indeed the very target of the attacks may be the law-based secular society that is embodied in most modern states. The driving motivation, therefore, is to overturn the current post-Westphalian state system—a much more fundamental threat than is, say, ethnonationalist terrorism purporting to carve out a new secular state or autonomous territory.

Fourth, and related, religious terrorists often display a complete sense of alienation from the existing social system. They are not trying to correct the system, making it more just, more perfect, and more egalitarian. Rather they are trying to replace it. In some groups, apocalyptic images of destruction are seen as a necessity—even a purifying regimen—and this makes them uniquely dangerous, as was painfully learned on September 11.[22]

Fifth, religious terrorism is especially worrisome because of its dispersed popular support in civil society. On the one hand, for example, groups such as al-Qaeda are able to find support from some Muslim nongovernmental foundations throughout the world,[23] making it truly a global network. On the other hand, in the process of trying to distinguish between the relatively few providers of serious support from the majority of genuinely philanthropic groups, there is the real risk of igniting the very holy war that the terrorists may be seeking in the first instance.

In sum, there are both enduring and new aspects to modern terrorism. The enduring features center on the common political struggles that have characterized major acts of international terrorism. The newest and perhaps most alarming aspect is the increasingly religious nature of modern terrorist groups. Against this historical background, the unique elements in the patterns of terrorist activity surrounding September 11 appear starkly.

Key Trends in Modern Terrorism

By the late 1990s, four trends in modern terrorism were becoming apparent: an increase in the incidence of religiously motivated attacks, a decrease in the overall number of attacks, an increase in the lethality per attack, and the growing targeting of Americans.

Statistics show that, even before the September 11 attacks, religiously motivated terrorist organizations were becoming more common. The acceleration of this trend has been dramatic: According to the RAND–St. Andrews University Chronology of International Terrorism,[24] in 1968 none of the identified international terrorist organizations could be classified as "religious"; in 1980, in the aftermath of the Iranian Revolution, there were 2 (out of 64), and that number had expanded to 25 (out of 58) by 1995.[25]

Careful analysis of terrorism data compiled by the U.S. Department of State reveals other important trends regarding the frequency and lethality of terrorist attacks. The good news was that there were fewer such attacks in the 1990s than in the 1980s: Internationally, the number of terrorist attacks in the 1990s averaged 382 per year, whereas in the 1980s the number per year averaged 543.[26] But even before September 11, the absolute number of casualties of international terrorism had increased, from a low of 344 in 1991 to a high of 6,693 in 1998.[27] The jump in deaths and injuries can be partly explained by a few high-profile incidents, including the bombing of the U.S. embassies in Nairobi and Dar-es-Salaam in 1998;[28] but it is significant that more people became victims of terrorism as the decade proceeded. More worrisome, the number of people killed per incident rose significantly, from 102 killed in 565 incidents in 1991 to 741 killed in 274 incidents in 1998.[29] Thus, even though the number of terrorist attacks declined in the 1990s, the number of people killed in each one increased.

Another important trend relates to terrorist attacks involving U.S. targets. The number of such attacks increased in the 1990s, from a low of 66 in 1994 to a high of 200 in the year 2000.[30] This is a long-established problem: U.S. nationals consistently have been the most targeted since 1968.[31] But the percentage of international attacks against U.S. targets or U.S. citizens rose dramatically over the 1990s, from about 20 percent in 1993–95 to almost 50 percent in 2000.[32] This is perhaps a consequence of the increased role and profile of the United States in the world, but the degree of increase is nonetheless troubling.

The increasing lethality of terrorist attacks was already being noticed in the late 1990s, with many terrorism experts arguing that the tendency toward more casualties per incident had important implications. First it meant that, as had been feared, religious or "sacred" terrorism was apparently more dangerous than the types of terrorism that had predominated earlier in the twentieth century. The world was facing the resurgence of a far more malignant type of terrorism, whose lethality was borne out in the larger death toll from incidents that increasingly involved a religious motivation.[33] Second, with an apparent premium now apparently placed on causing more casualties per incident, the incentives for terrorist organizations to use chemical, biological, nuclear, or radiological (CBNR) weapons would multiply. The breakup of the Soviet Union and the resulting increased availability of Soviet chemical, biological, and nuclear weapons caused experts to argue that terrorist groups, seeking more dramatic and deadly results, would be more drawn to these weapons.[34] The 1995 sarin gas attack by the Japanese cult Aum Shinrikyo in the Tokyo subway system seemed to confirm that worry. More recently, an examination of evidence taken from Afghanistan and Pakistan reveals al-Qaeda's interest in chemical, biological, and nuclear weapons.[35]

In addition to the evolving motivation and character of terrorist attacks, there has been a notable dispersal in the geography of terrorist acts—a trend that is likely to continue. Although the Middle East continues to be the locus of most terrorist activity, Central and South Asia, the Balkans, and the Transcaucasus have been growing in significance over the past decade. International connections themselves are not new: International terrorist organizations inspired by common revolutionary principles date to the early nineteenth century; clandestine state use of foreign terrorist organizations occurred as early as the 1920s (e.g., the Mussolini government in Italy aided the Croat Ustasha); and complex mazes of funding, arms, and other state support for international terrorist organizations were in place especially in the 1970s and 1980s.[36] During the Cold War, terrorism was seen as a form of surrogate warfare and seemed almost palatable to some, at least compared to the potential prospect of major war or nuclear cataclysm.[37] What has changed is the self-generating nature of international terrorism, with its diverse economic means of support allowing terrorists to carry out attacks sometimes far from the organization's base. As a result, there is an important and growing distinction between where a terrorist organization is spawned and where an attack is launched, making the attacks difficult to trace to their source.

Reflecting all of these trends, al-Qaeda and its associated groups[38] (and individuals) are harbingers of a new type of terrorist organization. Even if al-Qaeda ceases to exist (which is unlikely), the dramatic attacks of September 2001, and their political and economic effects, will continue to inspire similarly motivated groups—particularly if the United States and its allies fail to develop broad-based, effective counterterrorist policies over the long term. Moreover, there is significant evidence that the global links and activities that al-Qaeda and its associated groups perpetuated are not short term or anomalous. Indeed they are changing the nature of the terrorist threat as we move further into the twenty-first century. The resulting intersection between the United States, globalization, and international terrorism will define the major challenges to international security.

The United States, Globalization, and International Terrorism

Whether deliberately intending to or not, the United States is projecting uncoordinated economic, social, and political power even more sweepingly than it is in military terms. Globalization,[39] in forms including Westernization, secularization, democratization, consumerism, and the growth of market capitalism, represents an onslaught to less privileged people in conservative cultures repelled by the fundamental changes that these forces are bringing—or angered by the distortions and uneven distributions of benefits that result.[40] This is especially true of the Arab world. Yet the current U.S. approach to this growing repulsion is colored by a kind of cultural naïveté, an unwillingness to recognize —let alone appreciate or take responsibility for—the influence of U.S. power except in its military dimension. Even doing nothing in the economic, social, and political policy realms is still doing something, because the United States is blamed by disadvantaged and alienated populations for the powerful Western-led forces of globalization that are proceeding apace, despite the absence of a focused, coordinated U.S. policy. And those penetrating mechanisms of globalization, such as the internet, the media, and the increasing flows of goods and peoples, are exploited in return. Both the means and ends of terrorism are being reformulated in the current environment.

The Means

Important changes in terrorist methods are apparent in the use of new technologies, the movement of terrorist groups across international boundaries, and changes in sources of support. Like globalization itself, these phenomena are all intertwined and overlapping but, for ease of argument, they are dealt with consecutively here.

First, the use of information technologies such as the internet, mobile phones, and instant messaging has extended the global reach of many terrorist groups. Increased access to these technologies has so far not resulted in their widely feared use in a major cyberterrorist attack: In Dorothy Denning's words, terrorists "still prefer bombs to bytes."[41] Activists and terrorist groups have increasingly turned to "hacktivism"—attacks on internet sites, including web defacements, hijackings of websites, web sit-ins, denial-of-service attacks, and automated email "bombings"—attacks that may not kill anyone but do attract media attention, provide a means of operating anonymously, and are easy to coordinate internationally.[42] So far, however, these types of attacks are more an expense and a nuisance than an existential threat.

Instead the tools of the global information age have led to enhanced efficiency in many terrorist-related activities, including administrative tasks, coordination of operations, recruitment of potential members, communication among adherents, and attraction of sympathizers.[43] Before the September 11 attacks, for example, members of al-Qaeda communicated through Yahoo email; Mohammed Atta, the presumed leader of the attacks, made his reservations online; and cell members went online to do research on subjects such as the chemical-dispersing powers of crop dusters. Although not as dramatic as shutting down a power grid or taking over an air traffic control system, this practical use of technology has significantly contributed to the effectiveness of terrorist groups and the expansion of their range.[44] Consider, for example, the lethal impact of the synchronized attacks on the U.S. embassies in 1998 and on New York andWashington in 2001, neither of which would have been possible without the revolution in information technology. When he was arrested in 1995, Ramzi Yousef, mastermind of the 1993 World Trade Center attack, was planning the simultaneous destruction of eleven airliners.[45]

The internet has become an important tool for perpetuating terrorist groups, both openly and clandestinely. Many of them employ elaborate list serves, collect money from witting or unwitting donors, and distribute savvy political messages to a broad audience online.[46] Groups as diverse as Aum Shinrikyo, Israel's Kahane Chai, the Popular Front for the Liberation of Palestine, the Kurdistan Workers' Party, and Peru's Shining Path maintain user-friendly official or unofficial websites, and almost all are accessible in English.[47] Clandestine methods include passing encrypted messages, embedding invisible graphic codes using steganography,[48] employing the internet to send death threats, and hiring hackers to collect intelligence such as the names and addresses of law enforcement officers from online databases.[49] All of these measures help to expand and perpetuate trends in terrorism that have already been observed: For example, higher casualties are brought about by simultaneous attacks, a diffusion in terrorist locations is made possible by internet communications, and extremist religious ideologies are spread through websites and videotapes accessible throughout the world.

More ominous, globalization makes CBNR weapons increasingly available to terrorist groups.[50] Information needed to build these weapons has become ubiquitous, especially through the internet. Among the groups interested in acquiring CBNR (besides al-Qaeda) are the PLO, the Red Army Faction, Hezbollah, the Kurdistan Workers' Party, German neo-Nazis, and the Chechens.[51]

Second, globalization has enabled terrorist organizations to reach across international borders, in the same way (and often through the same channels) that commerce and business interests are linked. The dropping of barriers through the North American Free Trade Area and the European Union, for instance, has facilitated the smooth flow of many things, good and bad, among countries. This has allowed terrorist organizations as diverse as Hezbollah, al- Qaeda, and the Egyptian al-Gama'at al-Islamiyya to move about freely and establish cells around the world.[52] Movement across borders can obviously enable terrorists to carry out attacks and potentially evade capture, but it also complicates prosecution if they are apprehended, with a complex maze of extradition laws varying greatly from state to state. The increased permeability of the international system has also enhanced the ability of nonstate terrorist organizations to collect intelligence (not to mention evade it); states are not the only actors interested in collecting, disseminating, and/or acting on such information. In a sense, then, terrorism is in many ways becoming like any other international enterprise—an ominous development indeed.

Third, terrorist organizations are broadening their reach in gathering financial resources to fund their operations. This is not just an al-Qaeda phenomenon, although bin Laden's organization—especially its numerous business interests—figures prominently among the most innovative and wealthy pseudocorporations in the international terrorist network. The list of groups with global financing networks is long and includes most of the groups identified by the U.S. government as foreign terrorist organizations, notably Aum Shinrikyo, Hamas, Hezbollah, and the Tamil Tigers. Sources of financing include legal enterprises such as nonprofit organizations and charities (whose illicit activities may be a small or large proportion of overall finances, known or unknown to donors); legitimate companies that divert profits to illegal activities (such as bin Laden's large network of construction companies); and illegal enterprises such as drug smuggling and production (e.g., the Revolutionary Armed Forces of Colombia—FARC), bank robbery, fraud, extortion, and kidnapping (e.g., the Abu Sayyaf group, Colombia's National Liberation Army, and FARC).[53] Websites are also important vehicles for raising funds. Although no comprehensive data are publicly available on how lucrative this avenue is, the proliferation of terrorist websites with links or addresses for contributions is at least circumstantial evidence of their usefulness.

The fluid movement of terrorists' financial resources demonstrates the growing informal connections that are countering the local fragmentation caused elsewhere by globalization. The transit of bars of gold and bundles of dollars across the border between Afghanistan and Pakistan as U.S. and allied forces were closing in on the Taliban's major strongholds is a perfect example. Collected by shopkeepers and small businessmen, the money was moved by operatives across the border to Karachi, where it was transferred in the millions of dollars through the informal *hawala* or *hundi* banking system to the United Arab Emirates.[54] There it was converted into gold bullion and scattered around the world before any government could intervene. In this way, al-Qaeda preserved and dispersed a proportion of its financial resources.[55] In addition to gold, money was transferred into other commodities—such as diamonds in Sierra Leone and the Democratic Republic of Congo, and tanzanite from Tanzania —all while hiding the assets and often making a profit,[56] and all without interference from the sovereign governments that at the time were at war with al-Qaeda and the Taliban.[57]

As this example illustrates, globalization does not necessarily require the use of high technology: It often takes the form of traditional practices used in innovative ways across increasingly permeable physical and commercial borders. Terrorist groups, whose assets comparatively represent only a small fraction of the amount of money that is moved by organized crime groups and are thus much more difficult to track, use everything from direct currency transport (by couriers) to reliance on traditional banks, Islamic banks, money changers (using accounts at legitimate institutions), and informal exchange (the *hawala* or *hundi* system).

This is by no means a comprehensive presentation of global interpenetration of terrorist means, and some of the connections described above have existed for some time and in other contexts. The broad strategic picture, however, is of an increasing ability of terrorist organizations to exploit the same avenues of communication, coordination, and cooperation as other international actors, including states, multinational corporations, non-governmental organizations, and even individuals. It would be naïve to assume that what is good for international commerce and international communication is not also good for international terrorists[58]—who are increasingly becoming opportunistic entrepreneurs whose "product" (often quite consciously "sold") is violence against innocent targets for a political end.

The Ends

The objectives of international terrorism have also changed as a result of globalization. Foreign intrusions and growing awareness of shrinking global space have created incentives to use the ideal asymmetrical weapon, terrorism, for more ambitious purposes.

The political incentives to attack major targets such as the United States with powerful weapons have greatly increased. The perceived corruption of indigenous customs, religions, languages, economies, and so on, are blamed on an international system often unconsciously molded by American behavior. The accompanying distortions in local communities as a result of exposure to the global marketplace of goods and ideas are increasingly blamed on U.S.-sponsored modernization and those who support it. The advancement of technology, however, is not the driving force behind the terrorist threat to the United States and its allies, despite what some have assumed.[59] Instead, at the heart of this threat are frustrated populations and international movements that are increasingly inclined to lash out against U.S.-led globalization.

As Christopher Coker observes, globalization is reducing tendencies toward instrumental violence (i.e., violence between states and even between communities), but it is enhancing incentives for expressive violence (or violence that is ritualistic, symbolic, and communicative).[60] The new international terrorism is increasingly engendered by a need to assert identity or meaning against forces of homogeneity, especially on the part of cultures that are threatened by, or left behind by, the secular future that Western-led globalization brings.

According to a report recently published by the United Nations Development Programme, the region of greatest deficit in measures of human development—the Arab world—is also the heart of the most threatening religiously inspired terrorism.[61] Much more work needs to be done on the significance of this correlation, but increasingly sources of political discontent are arising from disenfranchised areas in the Arab world that feel left behind by the promise of globalization and its assurances of broader freedom, prosperity, and access to knowledge. The results are dashed expectations, heightened resentment of the perceived U.S.-led hegemonic system, and a shift of focus away from more proximate targets within the region.

Of course, the motivations behind this threat should not be oversimplified: Anti-American terrorism is spurred in part by a desire to change U.S. policy in the Middle East and Persian Gulf regions as well as by growing antipathy in the developing world vis-à-vis the forces of globalization. It is also crucial to distinguish between the motivations of leaders such as Osama bin Laden and their followers. The former seem to be more driven by calculated strategic decisions to shift the locus of attack away from repressive indigenous governments to the more attractive and media-rich target of the United States.

The latter appear to be more driven by religious concepts cleverly distorted to arouse anger and passion in societies full of pent-up frustration. To some degree, terrorism is directed against the United States because of its engagement and policies in various regions.[62] Anti-Americanism is closely related to antiglobalization, because (intentionally or not) the primary driver of the powerful forces resulting in globalization is the United States.

Analyzing terrorism as something separate from globalization is misleading and potentially dangerous. Indeed globalization and terrorism are intricately intertwined forces characterizing international security in the twenty-first century. The main question is whether terrorism will succeed in disrupting the promise of improved livelihoods for millions of people on Earth. Globalization is not an inevitable, linear development, and it can be disrupted by such unconventional means as international terrorism. Conversely, modern international terrorism is especially dangerous because of the power that it potentially derives from globalization—whether through access to CBNR weapons, global media outreach, or a diverse network of financial and information resources.

Prospects for the Future

Long after the focus on Osama bin Laden has receded and U.S. troops have quit their mission in Afghanistan, terrorism will be a serious threat to the world community and especially to the United States. The relative preponderance of U.S. military power virtually guarantees an impulse to respond asymmetrically. The lagging of the Arab region behind the rest of the world is impelling a violent redirection of antiglobalization and antimodernization forces toward available targets, particularly the United States, whose scope and policies are engendering rage. Al-Qaeda will eventually be replaced or redefined, but its successors' reach may continue to grow via the same globalized channels and to direct their attacks against U.S. and Western targets. The current trajectory is discouraging, because as things currently stand, the wellspring of terrorism's means and ends is likely to be renewed: Arab governments will probably not reform peacefully, and existing Western governments and their supporting academic and professional institutions are disinclined to understand or analyze in depth the sources, patterns, and history of terrorism.

Terrorism is a by-product of broader historical shifts in the international distribution of power in all of its forms—political, economic, military, ideological, and cultural. These are the same forms of power that characterize the forces of Western-led globalization. At times of dramatic international change, human beings (especially those not benefiting from the change—or not benefiting as much or as rapidly from the change) grasp for alternative means to control and understand their environments. If current trends continue, widening global disparities, coupled with burgeoning information and connectivity, are likely to accelerate—unless the terrorist backlash, which is increasingly taking its inspiration from misoneistic religious or pseudoreligious concepts, successfully counters these trends. Because of globalization, terrorists have access to more powerful technologies, more targets, more territory, more means of recruitment, and more exploitable sources of rage than ever before. The West's twentieth-century approach to terrorism is highly unlikely to mitigate any of these long-term trends.

From a Manichean perspective, the ad hoc and purportedly benign intentions of the preponderant, secular West do not seem benign at all to those ill served by globalization. To frustrated people in the Arab and Muslim world, adherence to radical religious philosophies and practices may seem a rational response to the perceived assault, especially when no feasible alternative for progress is offered by their own governments. This is not to suggest that terrorists should be excused because of environmental factors or conditions. Instead, Western governments must recognize that the tiny proportion of the population that ends up in terrorist cells cannot exist without the availability of broader sources of active or passive sympathy, resources, and support. Those avenues of sustenance are where the center of gravity for an effective response to the terrorist threat must reside. The response to transnational terrorism must deal with the question of whether the broader enabling environment will increase or decrease over time, and the answer will be strongly influenced by the policy choices that the United States and its allies make in the near future.

Conclusions and Policy Prescriptions

The characteristics and causes of the current threat can only be analyzed within the context of the deadly collision occurring between U.S. power, globalization, and the evolution of international terrorism. The U.S. government is still thinking in outdated terms, little changed since the end of the Cold War. It continues to look at terrorism as a peripheral threat, with the focus remaining on states that in many cases are not the greatest threat. The means and the ends of terrorism are changing in fundamental, important ways; but the means and the ends of the strategy being crafted in response are not.

Terrorism that threatens international stability, and particularly U.S. global leadership, is centered on power-based political causes that are enduring: the weak against the strong, the disenfranchised against the establishment, and the revolutionary against the status quo. Oversimplified generalizations about poverty and terrorism, or any other single variable, are caricatures of a serious argument.[63] The rise in political and material expectations as a result of the information revolution is not necessarily helpful to stability, in the same way that rising expectations led terrorists to take up arms against the czar in Russia a century ago. Indeed the fact that so many people in so many nations are being left behind has given new ammunition to terrorist groups; produced more sympathy for those willing to take on the United States; and spurred Islamic radical movements to recruit, propagandize, and support terrorism throughout many parts of the Muslim world. The al-Qaeda network is an extremist religious terrorist organization, its Taliban puppet regime was filled with religious zealots, and its suicide recruits were convinced that they were waging a just holy war. But the driving forces of twenty-first-century terrorism are power and frustration, not the pursuit of religious principle. To dismiss the broad enabling environment would be to focus more on the symptoms than the causes of modern terrorism.

The prescriptions for countering and preventing terrorism should be twofold: First, the United States and other members of the international community concerned about this threat need to use a balanced assortment of instruments to address the immediate challenges of the terrorists themselves. Terrorism is a complex phenomenon; it must be met with short-term military action, informed by in-depth, long-term, sophisticated analysis. Thus far, the response has been virtually all the former and little of the latter. Second, the United States and its counterterrorist allies must employ a much broader array of longer-term policy tools to reshape the international environment, which enables terrorist networks to breed and become robust. The mechanisms of globalization need to be exploited to thwart the globalization of terrorism.

In the short term, the United States must continue to rely on capable military forces that can sustain punishing air strikes against terrorists and those who harbor them with an even greater capacity for special operations on the ground. This requires not only improved stealthy, long-range power projection capabilities but also agile, highly trained, and lethal ground forces, backed up with greater intelligence, including human intelligence supported by individuals with language skills and cultural training. The use of military force continues to be important as one means of responding to terrorist violence against the West, and there is no question that it effectively preempts and disrupts some international terrorist activity, especially in the short term.[64]

Over time, however, the more effective instruments of policy are likely to remain the nonmilitary ones. Indeed the United States needs to expand and deepen its nonmilitary instruments of power such as intelligence, public diplomacy, cooperation with allies, international legal instruments, and economic assistance and sanctions. George Kennan, in his 1947 description of containment, put forth the same fundamental argument, albeit against an extremely different enemy.[65] The strongest response that the United States can muster to a serious threat has to include political, economic, and military capabilities—in that order; yet, the U.S. government consistently structures its policies and devotes its resources in the reverse sequence.

The economic and political roots of terrorism are complex, increasingly worrisome, and demanding of as much breadth and subtlety in response as they display in their genesis. The United States must therefore be strategic in its response: An effective grand strategy against terrorism involves planning a global campaign with the most effective means available, not just the most measurable, obvious, or gratifying. It must also include plans for shaping the global environment after the so-called war on terrorism has ended—or after the current political momentum has subsided.

The United States, working with other major donor nations, needs to create an effective incentive structure that rewards "good performers"—those countries with good governance, inclusive education programs, and adequate social programs—and works around "bad performers" and intervenes to assist so-called failed states. Also for the longer term, the United States and its allies need to project a vision of sustainable development—of economic growth, equal access to basic social needs such as education and health, and good governance—for the developing world. This is particularly true in mostly Muslim countries whose populations are angry with the United States over a perceived double standard regarding its long-standing support for Israel at the expense of Palestinians, policies against the regime of Saddam Hussein at the expense of some Iraqi people, and a general abundance of American power, including the U.S. military presence throughout the Middle East. Whether these policies are right or wrong is irrelevant here; the point is that just as the definition of terrorism can be subjective and value laden, so too can the response to terrorism take into account perceptions of reality. In an attempt to craft an immediate military response, the U.S. government is failing to put into place an effective long-term grand strategy.

This is not just a problem for the U.S. government. The inability to develop a strategy with a deep-rooted, intellectually grounded understanding of the history, patterns, motivations, and types of terrorism is reflective of the paucity of understanding of the terrorist phenomenon in the academic community. Terrorism is considered too policy-oriented an area of research in political science,[66] and it operates in an uncomfortable intersection between disciplines unaccustomed to working together, including psychology, sociology, theology, economics, anthropology, history, law, political science, and international relations. In political science, terrorism does not fit neatly into either the realist or liberal paradigms, so it has been largely ignored.[67] There are a few outstanding, well-established senior scholars in the terrorism studies community— people such as Martha Crenshaw, David Rapoport, and Paul Wilkinson—but in the United States, most of the publicly available work is being done in policy-oriented research institutes or think tanks that are sometimes limited by the narrow interests and short time frames of the government contracts on which they depend. Some of that research is quite good,[68] but it is not widely known within the academy. The situation for graduate students who wish to study terrorism is worse: A principal interest in terrorism virtually guarantees exclusion from consideration for most academic positions. This would not necessarily be a problem if the bureaucracy were more flexible and creative than the academy is, but as we know from the analysis of the behavior of U.S. agencies shortly before September 11, it is not. In the United States, academe is no more strategic in its understanding of terrorism than is the U.S. government.

The globalization of terrorism is perhaps the leading threat to long-term stability in the twenty-first century. But the benefit of globalization is that the international response to terrorist networks has also begun to be increasingly global, with international cooperation on law enforcement, intelligence, and especially financial controls being areas of notable recent innovation.[69] If globalization is to continue—and there is nothing foreordained that it will—then the tools of globalization, including especially international norms, the rule of law, and international economic power, must be fully employed against the terrorist backlash. There must be a deliberate effort to move beyond the current episodic interest in this phenomenon: Superficial arguments and short attention spans will continue to result in event-driven policies and ultimately more attacks. Terrorism is an unprecedented, powerful nonstate threat to the international system that no single state, regardless of how powerful it may be in traditional terms, can defeat alone, especially in the absence of long-term, serious scholarship engaged in by its most creative minds.

Audrey Kurth Cronin is specialist in international terrorism at the Congressional Research Service at the Library of Congress. The article was written when she was visiting associate professor at the Edmund A. Walsh School of Foreign Service and a research fellow at the Center for Peace and Security Studies, Georgetown University.

Notes

1. The issue of U.S. strategic culture and its importance in the response to international terrorism is explored in more depth in Audrey Kurth Cronin, "Rethinking Sovereignty: American Strategy in the Age of Terror," *Survival*, Vol. 44, No. 2 (Summer 2002), pp. 119–139.
2. On the difficulty of defining terrorism, see, for example, Omar Malik, *Enough of the Definition of Terrorism!* Royal Institute of International Affairs (London: RIIA, 2001); and Alex P. Schmid, *Political Terrorism: A Research Guide* (New Brunswick, N.J.: Transaction Books, 1984). Schmid spends more than 100 pages grappling with the question of a definition, only to conclude that none is universally accepted.
3. Saying that terrorism is a political act is not the same as arguing that the political ends toward which it is directed are necessarily negotiable. If violent acts do not have a political aim, then they are by definition criminal acts.

4. The diabolical nature of terrorism has given resonance to Robert Kaplan's view that the world is a "grim landscape" littered with "evildoers" and requiring Western leaders to adopt a "pagan ethos." But such conclusions deserve more scrutiny than space allows here. See Steven Mufson, "The Way Bush Sees the World," *Washington Post*, Outlook section, February 17, 2002, p. B1.
5. R.G. Frey and Christopher W. Morris, "Violence, Terrorism, and Justice," in Frey and Morris, eds., *Violence, Terrorism, and Justice* (Cambridge: Cambridge University Press, 1991), p. 3.
6. Walter Laqueur, *Terrorism* (London: Weidenfeld and Nicolson, 1977, reprinted in 1978), pp. 7–8; and David C. Rapoport, "Fear and Trembling: Terrorism in Three Religious Traditions," *American Political Science Review*, Vol. 78, No. 3 (September 1984), pp. 658–677.
7. David C. Rapoport, "The Fourth Wave: September 11 in the History of Terrorism," *Current History*, December 2001, pp. 419–424; and David C. Rapoport, "Terrorism," *Encyclopedia of Violence, Peace, and Conflict* (New York: Academic Press, 1999).
8. Ironically, Robespierre's tactics during the Reign of Terror would not be included in this article's definition of terrorism, because it was state terror.
9. Rapoport, "The Fourth Wave."
10. Ibid., pp. 419–420.
11. Ibid., p. 420.
12. Adrian Gulke, *The Age of Terrorism and the International Political System* (London: I.B. Tauris, 1995), pp. 56–63.
13. This is not to imply that terrorism lacked international links before the 1970s. There were important international ties between anarchist groups of the late nineteenth century, for example. See David C. Rapoport, "The Four Waves of Modern Terrorism," in Audrey Kurth Cronin and James Ludes, eds., *The Campaign against International Terrorism* (Washington, D.C.: Georgetown University Press, forthcoming).
14. Groups such as the Second of June Movement, the Baader-Meinhof Gang, the Red Brigades, the Weathermen, and the Symbionese Liberation Army belong in this category.
15. Among right-wing groups would be other neo-Nazi organizations (in the United States and Europe) and some members of American militia movements such as the Christian Patriots and the Ku Klux Klan.
16. The list here would be extremely long, including groups as different as the Tamil Tigers of Sri Lanka, the Basque separatist party, the PLO, and the Irish Republican Army (IRA) and its various splinter groups.
17. Bruce Hoffman notes that secular terrorist groups that have a strong religious element include the Provisional IRA, Armenian factions, and perhaps the PLO; however, the political/separatist aspect is the predominant characteristic of these groups. Hoffman, "Terrorist Targeting: Tactics, Trends, and Potentialities," *Technology and Terrorism* (London: Frank Cass, 1993), p. 25.
18. An interesting example is France's Action Directe, which revised its raison d'être several times, often altering it to reflect domestic issues in France—anarchism and Maoism, dissatisfaction with NATO and the Americanization of Europe, and general anticapitalism. See Michael Dartnell, "France's Action Directe: Terrorists in Search of a Revolution," *Terrorism and Political Violence*, Vol. 2, No. 4 (Winter 1990), pp. 457–488.
19. For example, in the 1990s Germany and several other European countries experienced a rash of random arson attacks against guest houses and offices that provided services to immigrants, many of whom were Middle Eastern in origin. Other examples include the violence associated with groups such as Europe's "football hooligans." A possible American example of the opportunistic nature of right-wing terrorism may be the anthrax letter campaign conducted in October 2001. See Susan Schmidt, "Anthrax Letter Suspect Profiled: FBI Says Author Likely Is Male Loner; Ties to Bin Laden Are Doubted," *Washington Post*, November 11, 2001, p. A1; and Steve Fainaru, "Officials Continue to Doubt Hijackers' Link to Anthrax: Fla. Doctor Says He Treated One for Skin Form of Disease," *Washington Post*, March 24, 2002, p. A23.
20. It is interesting to note that, according to Christopher C. Harmon, in Germany, 1991 was the first year that the number of indigenous rightist radicals exceeded that of leftists. Harmon, *Terrorism Today* (London: Frank Cass, 2000), p. 3.

21. For example, in discussing the longevity of terrorist groups, Martha Crenshaw notes only three significant terrorist groups with ethnonationalist ideologies that ceased to exist within ten years of their formation (one of these, EOKA, disbanded because its goal—the liberation of Cyprus—was attained). By contrast, a majority of the terrorist groups she lists as having existed for ten years or longer have recognizable ethnonationalist ideologies, including the IRA (in its many forms), Sikh separatist groups, Euskadi Ta Askatasuna, the various Palestinian nationalist groups, and the Corsican National Liberation Front. See Crenshaw, "How Terrorism Declines," *Terrorism and Political Violence*, Vol. 3, No. 1 (Spring 1991), pp. 69–87.
22. On the characteristics of modern religious terrorist groups, see Bruce Hoffman, *Inside Terrorism* (New York: Columbia University Press, 1998), especially pp. 94–95; and Bruce Hoffman, "Terrorism Trends and Prospects," in Ian O. Lesser, Bruce Hoffman, John Arguilla, Michelle Zanini, and David Ronfeldt, eds., *Countering the New Terrorism* (Santa Monica, Calif.: RAND, 1999), especially pp. 19–20. On the peculiar twists of one apocalyptic vision, see Robert Jay Lifton, *Destroying the World to Save It: Aum Shinrikyo, Apocalyptic Violence, and the New Global Terrorism* (New York: Henry Holt, 1999).
23. There is a long list of people and organizations sanctioned under Executive Order 13224, signed on September 23, 2001. Designated charitable organizations include the Benevolence International Foundation and the Global Relief Foundation. The list is available at http://www.treas.gov/offices/enforcement/ofac/sanctions/t11ter.pdf (accessed November 26, 2002).
24. The RAND–St. Andrews University Chronology of International Terrorism is a databank of terrorist incidents that begins in 1968 and has been maintained since 1972 at St. Andrews University, Scotland, and the RAND Corporation, Santa Monica, California.
25. Hoffman, *Inside Terrorism*, pp. 90–91; and Nadine Gurr and Benjamin Cole, *The New Face of Terrorism: Threats from Weapons of Mass Destruction* (London: I.B. Tauris, 2000), pp. 28–29.
26. Statistics compiled from data in U.S. Department of State, *Patterns of Global Terrorism*, published annually by the Office of the Coordinator for Counterterrorism, U.S. Department of State.
27. Ibid. For a graphical depiction of this information, created on the basis of annual data from *Patterns of Global Terrorism*, see Cronin, "Rethinking Sovereignty," p. 126.
28. In the 1998 embassy bombings alone, for example, 224 people were killed (with 12 Americans among them), and 4,574 were injured (including 15 Americans). U.S. Department of State, *Patterns of Global Terrorism, 1998*.
29. Ibid. For a graphical depiction of deaths per incident, created on the basis of annual data from *Patterns of Global Terrorism*, see Cronin, "Rethinking Sovereignty," p. 128.
30. Ibid.
31. Hoffman, "Terrorist Targeting," p. 24.
32. U.S. Department of State, *Patterns of Global Terrorism*, various years.
33. Examples include Bruce Hoffman, *"Holy Terror": The Implications of Terrorism Motivated by a Religious Imperative*, RAND Paper P-7834 (Santa Monica, Calif.: RAND, 1993); and Mark Juergensmeyer, "Terror Mandated by God," *Terrorism and Political Violence*, Vol. 9, No. 2 (Summer 1997), pp. 16–23.
34. See, for example, Steven Simon and Daniel Benjamin, "America and the New Terrorism," *Survival*, Vol. 42, No. 1 (Spring 2000), pp. 59–75, as well as the responses in the subsequent issue, "America and the New Terrorism: An Exchange," *Survival*, Vol. 42, No. 2 (Summer 2000), pp. 156– 172; and Hoffman, "Terrorism Trends and Prospects," pp. 7–38.
35. See Peter Finn and Sarah Delaney, "Al-Qaeda's Tracks Deepen in Europe," *Washington Post*, October 22, 2001, p. A1; Kamran Khan and Molly Moore, "2 Nuclear Experts Briefed Bin Laden, Pakistanis Say," *Washington Post*, December, 12, 2001, p. A1; James Risen and Judith Miller, "A Nation Challenged: Chemical Weapons—Al Qaeda Sites Point to Tests of Chemicals," *New York Times*, November 11, 2001, p. B1; Douglas Frantz and David Rohde, "A Nation Challenged: Biological Terror—2 Pakistanis Linked to Papers on Anthrax Weapons," *New York Times*, November 28, 2001; and David Rohde, "A Nation Challenged: The Evidence—Germ Weapons Plans Found at a Scientist's House in Kabul," *New York Times*, December 1, 2001.
36. Laqueur, *Terrorism*, pp. 112–116.

37. Ibid., pp. 115–116.
38. Groups with known or alleged connections to al-Qaeda include Jemaah Islamiyah (Indonesia, Malaysia, and Singapore), the Abu Sayyaf group (Philippines), al-Gama'a al-Islamiyya (Egypt), Harakat ul-Mujahidin (Pakistan), the Islamic Movement of Uzbekistan (Central Asia), Jaish-e-Mohammed (India and Pakistan), and al-Jihad (Egypt).
39. For the purposes of this article, globalization is a gradually expanding process of interpenetration in the economic, political, social, and security realms, uncontrolled by (or apart from) traditional notions of state sovereignty. Victor D. Cha, "Globalization and the Study of International Security," *Journal of Peace Research*, Vol. 37, No. 3 (March 2000), pp. 391–393.
40. With respect to the Islamic world, there are numerous books and articles that point to the phenomenon of antipathy with the Western world, either because of broad cultural incompatibility or a specific conflict between Western consumerism and religious fundamentalism. Among the earliest and most notable are Samuel P. Huntington, "The Clash of Civilizations?" *Foreign Affairs*, Vol. 72, No. 3 (Summer 1993); Benjamin R. Barber, *Jihad vs. McWorld: Terrorism's Challenge to Democracy* (New York: Random House, 1995); and Samuel P. Huntington, *The Clash of Civilizations and the Remaking of World Order* (New York: Simon and Schuster, 1996).
41. For more on cyberterrorism, see Dorothy Denning, "Activism, Hacktivism, and Cyberterrorism: The Internet as a Tool for Influencing Foreign Policy," paper presented at Internet and International Systems: Information Technology and American Foreign Policy Decision-making Workshop at Georgetown University, http://www.nautilus.org/info-policy/workshop/papers/denning.html (accessed January 5, 2003); Dorothy Denning, "Cyberterrorism," testimony before the U.S. House Committee on Armed Services, Special Oversight Panel on Terrorism, 107th Cong., 1st sess., May 23, 2001, available on the Terrorism Research Center website, http://www.cs.georgetown.edu/?denning/infosec/cyberterror.html (accessed January 5, 2003); Jerold Post, Kevin Ruby, and Eric Shaw, "From Car Bombs to Logic Bombs: The Growing Threat of Information Terrorism," *Terrorism and Political Violence*, Vol. 12, No. 2 (Summer 2000), pp. 97–122; and Tom Regan, "When Terrorists Turn to the Internet," *Christian Science Monitor*, July 1, 1999, http://www.csmonitor.com (accessed January 5, 2003).
42. Ibid. Dorothy Denning cites numerous examples, among them: In 1989, hackers released a computer worm into the NASA Space Physics Analysis Network in an attempt to stop a shuttle launch; during Palestinian riots in October 2000, pro-Israeli hackers defaced the Hezbollah website; and in 1999, following the mistaken U.S. bombing of the Chinese embassy in Belgrade during the war in Kosovo, Chinese hackers attacked the websites of the U.S. Department of the Interior, showing images of the three journalists killed during the bombing.
43. Paul R. Pillar, *Terrorism and U.S. Foreign Policy* (Washington, D.C.: Brookings, 2001), p. 47.
44. Ibid.
45. Simon Reeve, *The New Jackals: Ramzi Yousef, Osama bin Laden, and the Future of Terrorism* (Boston: Northeastern University Press, 1999), p. 260.
46. Dorothy Denning, "Cyberwarriors: Activists and Terrorists Turn to Cyberspace," *Harvard International Review*, Vol. 23, No. 2 (Summer 2001), pp. 70–75. See also Brian J. Miller, "Terror.org: An Assessment of Terrorist Internet Sites," Georgetown University, December 6, 2000.
47. Miller, "Terror.org," pp. 9, 12.
48. Steganography is the embedding of messages usually in pictures, where the messages are disguised so that they cannot be seen with the naked eye. See Denning, "Cyberwarriors."
49. I am indebted to Dorothy Denning for all of this information. The Provisional IRA hired contract hackers to find the addresses of British intelligence and law enforcement officers. See Denning, "Cyberterrorism"; and Denning, "Cyberwarriors."
50. There are many recent sources on CBNR. Among the best are Jonathan B. Tucker, ed., *Toxic Terror: Assessing Terrorist Use of Chemical and Biological Weapons* (Cambridge, Mass.: MIT Press, 2000); Joshua Lederberg, *Biological Weapons: Limiting the Threat* (Cambridge, Mass.: MIT Press, 1999); Richard A. Falkenrath, Robert D. Newman, and Bradley A. Thayer, *America's Achilles' Heel: Nuclear, Biological, and Chemical Terrorism and Covert Attack* (Cambridge, Mass.: MIT Press, 1998); Gurr and Cole, *The New Face of Terrorism*; Jessica

Stern, *The Ultimate Terrorists* (Cambridge, Mass.: Harvard University Press, 1999); and Brad Roberts, ed., *Terrorism with Chemical and Biological Weapons: Calibrating Risks and Responses* (Alexandria, Va.: Chemical and Biological Arms Control Institute, 1997).

51. See Falkenrath, Newman, and Thayer, *America's Achilles' Heel*, pp. 31–46.
52. A clear example of this phenomenon was the uncovering in December 2001 of a multinational plot in Singapore by the international terrorist group Jemaah Islamiyah to blow up several Western targets, including the U.S. embassy. A videotape of the intended targets (including a description of the plans in Arabic) was discovered in Afghanistan after al Qaeda members fled. Thus there are clear connections between these organizations, as well as evidence of cooperation and coordination of attacks. See, for example, Dan Murphy, "'Activated' Asian Terror Web Busted," *Christian Science Monitor*, January 23, 2002, http://www.csmonitor.com (accessed January 23, 2002); and Rajiv Chandrasekaran, "Al Qaeda's Southeast Asian Reach," *Washington Post*, February 3, 2002, p. A1.
53. Rensselaer Lee and Raphael Perl, "Terrorism, the Future, and U.S. Foreign Policy," issue brief for Congress, received through the Congressional Research Service website, order code IB95112, Congressional Research Service, Library of Congress, July 10, 2002, p. CRS-6.
54. Roger G. Weiner, "The Financing of International Terrorism," Terrorism and Violence Crime Section, Criminal Division, U.S. Department of Justice, October 2001, p. 3. According to Weiner, the *hawala* (or *hundi*) system "relies entirely on trust that currency left with a particular service provider or merchant will be paid from bank accounts he controls overseas to the recipient specified by the party originating the transfer." Ibid. See also Douglas Frantz, "Ancient Secret System Moves Money Globally," *New York Times*, October 3, 2001, http://www.nytimes.com (accessed October 3, 2001).
55. International efforts to freeze bank accounts and block transactions between suspected terrorists have hindered, at least to some degree, al-Qaeda's ability to finance attacks; however, a proportion remains unaccounted for. "Cash Moves a Sign Al-Qaeda Is Regrouping," *Straits Times*, March 18, 2002, http://www.straitstimes.asia1.com.sg (accessed March 18, 2002).
56. U.S. Department of State, *Patterns of Global Terrorism, 2001*. According to the U.S. Department of State, Hezbollah also may have transferred resources by selling millions of dollars' worth of Congolese diamonds to finance operations in the Middle East.
57. Douglas Farah, "Al Qaeda's Road Paved with Gold," *Washington Post*, February 17, 2002, pp. A1, A32.
58. Pillar, *Terrorism and U.S. Foreign Policy*, p. 48.
59. Many in the United States focus on the technologies of terrorism, with a much less developed interest in the motivations of terrorists. Brian M. Jenkins, "Understanding the Link between Motives and Methods," in Roberts, *Terrorism with Chemical and Biological Weapons*, pp. 43–51. An example of a study that focuses on weapons and not motives is Sidney D. Drell, Abraham D. Sofaer, and George W. Wilson, eds., *The New Terror: Facing the Threat of Biological and Chemical Weapons* (Stanford, Calif.: Hoover Institution, 1999).
60. Christopher Coker, *Globalisation and Insecurity in the Twenty-first Century: NATO and the Management of Risk*, Adelphi Paper 345 (London: International Institute for Strategic Studies, June 2002), p. 40.
61. The indicators studied included respect for human rights and human freedoms, the empowerment of women, and broad access to and utilization of knowledge. See United Nations Development Programme, Arab Fund for Economic and Social Development, *Arab Human Development Report, 2002: Creating Opportunities for Future Generations* (New York: United Nations Development Programme, 2002).
62. Martha Crenshaw, "Why America? The Globalization of Civil War," *Current History*, December 2001, pp. 425–432.
63. A number of recent arguments have been put forth about the relationship between poverty and terrorism. See, for example, Anatol Lieven, "The Roots of Terrorism, and a Strategy against It," Prospect (London), October 2001, http://www.ceip.org/files/Publications/lieventerrorism.asp? from=pubdate (accessed November 17, 2002); and Daniel Pipes, "God and Mammon: Does Poverty Cause Militant Islam?" *National Interest*, No. 66 (Winter 2001/02), pp. 14–21. This is an extremely complex question, however, and much work remains to be done. On the

origins of the new religious terrorism, see Hoffman, *Inside Terrorism*; and Mark Juergensmeyer, *Terror in the Mind of God: The Global Rise of Religious Violence* (Berkeley: University of California Press, 2000). Important earlier studies on the sources of terrorism include Martha Crenshaw, "The Causes of Terrorism," *Comparative Politics*, July 1981, pp. 379–399; Martha Crenshaw, *Terrorism in Context* (University Park: Pennsylvania State University Press, 1995); and Walter Reich, ed., *Origins of Terrorism: Psychologies, Ideologies, Theologies, States of Mind*, 2d ed. (Washington, D.C.: Woodrow Wilson Center for International Scholars, 1998).

64. For more discussion on the traditional elements of U.S. grand strategy, especially military strategy, see Barry R. Posen, "The Struggle against Terrorism: Grand Strategy, Strategy, and Tactics," *International Security*, Vol. 26, No. 3 (Winter 2001/02), pp. 39–55.
65. George F. Kennan, "The Sources of Soviet Conduct," *Foreign Affairs*, Vol. 25, No. 4 (July 1947), pp. 575–576.
66. See the extremely insightful article by Bruce W. Jentleson, "The Need for Praxis: Bringing Policy Relevance Back In," *International Security*, Vol. 26, No. 4 (Spring 2002), pp. 169–183.
67. I am indebted to Fiona Adamson for this observation.
68. Important terrorism scholars in the think tank community include Walter Laqueur (Center for Strategic and International Studies), Brian Jenkins (RAND), Bruce Hoffman (RAND) and, from the intelligence community, Paul Pillar. This list is illustrative, not comprehensive.
69. On these issues, see Cronin and Ludes, T*he Campaign against International Terrorism.*

I am grateful for helpful comments and criticisms on previous drafts from Robert Art, Patrick Cronin, Timothy Hoyt, James Ludes, and an anonymous reviewer. I have been greatly influenced by conversations and other communications with Martha Crenshaw, to whom I owe a huge debt. None of these people necessarily agrees with everything here. Also beneficial was a research grant from the School of Foreign Service at Georgetown University. My thanks to research assistants Christopher Connell, William Josiger, and Sara Skahill and to the members of my graduate courses on political violence and terrorism. Portions of this article will be published as "Transnational Terrorism and Security: The Terrorist Threat to Globalization," in Michael E. Brown, ed., *Grave New World: Global Dangers in the Twenty-First Century* (Washington, D.C.: Georgetown University Press, forthcoming).

Chapter 3

The New Terrorism

Brigadier General (Retired) Russell Howard presents a framework for understanding the new terrorism. This framework distinguishes between the old politically motivated terrorist and the new transnational religiously motivated terrorist. He argues that terrorism is more violent, groups operate globally; they are better financed, better trained, and more difficult to penetrate; and the potential future use of weapons of mass destruction completely changes the calculus of today's terrorists. The nexus of these elements creates an enemy that is difficult to find, difficult to defeat, and very dangerous. In thinking about this more dangerous world, it is important to understand how terrorism has changed so that we can move to a better understanding of how to address the problem in a comprehensive manner. Howard's framework is the starting point for any such analysis.

John Arquilla, David Ronfeldt, and Michele Zanini examine changes in terrorism in the information age. The classic motivation and rationales will not change, but conduct and operational characteristics of terrorism will change. The authors explore—often in what they outline as a deliberately speculative manner—organizational changes that allow for less hierarchical structures and flatter networks of power with dense communications; they look at changes in strategy and technology and the manner in which terrorism is evolving toward what they label as *netwar*.

The third article, "The Post-Madrid Face of Al Qaeda" by Rohan Gunaratna, examines the shift in al Qaeda from a group to that of an ideology. He argues that al Qaeda's role as a terrorist group is complete—that the group has inspired other groups, individuals, and a rising generation of militants to join the fight. The Madrid attacks symbolizes the changing nature of the battlefield from the Global South—places such as Bali, Casablanca, and Saudi Arabia—to the Global North. He argues that a singular focus on al Qaeda as a group will preclude intelligence and law enforcement agencies from comprehending the changing nature of the threat. To be truly effective in this conflict, counterterror governments must focus their attention not only on the established groups but also on their support cells and ideologues.

Finally, Matthew Levitt presents an argument that counterterrorism efforts should be thought of in terms of shaping, defining, and ultimately constricting terrorists' support environments. In his article, Levitt demonstrates that the numerous groups share a "network of interlocking logistical support groups."

The logistical and support intersections present unique opportunities to interdict and disrupt terrorist group plans and operations. Many times, policy makers and intelligence specialists look to "pigeonhole" terrorists as members of one group or another. Levitt argues that this myopic approach to terrorism analysis is problematic and misses the true nature of the terrorist environment today. Failing to identify and understand these connections undercuts the existing counterterror programs.

Brigadier General Russell D. Howard, 2005

Understanding Al Qaeda's Application of the New Terrorism—The Key to Victory in the Current Campaign

Bruce Hoffman, head of terrorism research at the Rand Corporation and arguably one of the world's leading experts, put it this way: "I don't mean to sound perverse, but there is maybe a certain nostalgia for the old style of terrorism, where there wasn't the threat of loss of life on a massive scale. It's a real commentary on how much the world has changed."[1] In much the same way that many Cold Warriors miss the predictability and transparency of the U.S.-Soviet confrontation, many intelligence professionals, military operators, pundits, and academics miss the familiar type of terrorism that, although quite dangerous, was in the end merely a nasty sideshow to the greater East-West conflict.[2] Much of this "Cold War" terrorism was inspired by Marxist-Leninist ideology; its perpetrators sought to draw attention to their cause and to gain political concessions. They were motivated by secular rather than apocalyptic ends and were quick to claim responsibility for their attacks.[3] The commando-style terrorism waged by the likes of Andreas Baader and Ulrike Meinhof of the German extreme left Rote Armee Fraction or by Abu Nidal of the Fatah National Council (who was killed in Baghdad in 2002) was ruthless. But it was not nearly as deadly as the threat the world faces today.[4] Now the old, predominantly state-sponsored terrorism has been supplanted by a religiously and ethnically motivated terrorism that "neither relies on the support of sovereign states nor is constrained by the limits on violence that state sponsors observed themselves or placed on their proxies."[5]

American security experts and intelligence analysts have not yet come to terms with the nature of al Qaeda and like-minded groups or with how they differ from the terrorist groups I was familiar with during the Cold War. One difference is the alleged objective. While Cold War terrorist groups had goals that were theoretically attainable and mostly political in nature, "al Qaeda goes beyond the political into what Ralph Peters, military strategist and author, calls the transcendental—a vision formed by religion."[6]

Many terrorist motives are also new. Terrorist groups such as al Qaeda have international objectives, and globalization has enabled and facilitated terrorists' worldwide goals. "Rather than using terrorism to create change within a single society or focus on a specific government, terrorism has gone international to support global causes, and the U.S. and the West have become primary targets."[7] Terrorist attacks have become increasingly sophisticated and designed to achieve mass casualties, and this is likely to continue. However, the difference is more than the increasing magnitude of deliberate mass-casualty attacks against civilians and non-combatants. These attacks are targeted against societies ever more vulnerable since they depend on openness and globalization for their existence. [8]

This new terrorism has a much greater potential to cause harm to America, the West, and all secular countries, including those in the Muslim world. Led by al Qaeda and Osama bin Laden, it "is built around loosely linked cells that do not rely on a single leader or state sponsor." It is transnational, borderless, and prosecuted by non-state actors, and it is very, very dangerous.[9] The old and new styles of terrorism are distinguishable in at least eight different ways:

1. The September 11 attacks effectively shattered the illusion of an invulnerable U.S. homeland, protected by two oceans and bordered by friendly or weak neighbors. In the past, the nation was not vulnerable to terrorists, except for the homegrown, mostly right-wing variety such as the Oklahoma City bomber. Now, the American homeland is very much at risk. "When, not if" is how many terrorism experts regard the likelihood of another 9/11 type attack.
2. The new terrorism is more violent. Under the old paradigm, terrorists wanted attention, not mass casualties. Now they want both.
3. Unlike their Cold War counterparts, who were usually sub-state actors trying to effect change in local politics, today's terrorists are transnational, non-state actors who operate globally and want to destroy the West and all Islamic secular states.
4. The new terrorists are much better financed than their predecessors, who relied mainly on crime or the largess of state sponsors. Today's terrorists have income streams from legal and illegal sources, and are not accountable to state sponsors—or anybody else.
5. Today's terrorists are better trained. We know this from the materials captured in al Qaeda's training camps in Afghanistan and from the similar training materials of other Muslim extremist groups found in Europe and Central Asia.
6. This generation's terrorists are more difficult to penetrate than terrorists of previous generations. The networked, cellular structure used by al Qaeda and its allies is especially difficult to penetrate for a hierarchical security apparatus like that of the United States. Bribes and sex traps could catch terrorists for prosecution and information in the old days; it is difficult to "turn" religious extremists with these methods. The $50 million reward on Osama bin Laden has yet to be collected, and it is unclear how successful other methods have been in getting bin Laden's followers to talk.
7. Most insidious is the availability of weapons of mass destruction (WMD). In the 1980s, when I first became engaged in counterterrorism, we were concerned about small arms, explosives (particularly plastique), rocket-propelled grenades, and the occasional shoulder-fired anti-aircraft missile. Today, the concern is about nuclear, radiological, chemical, and biological weapons—all potentially catastrophic, with massive killing potential.
8. Victory will be elusive. More than likely there will be no formal surrender by a defeated foe, no armistice ending combat on acceptable terms, no arrest and incarceration of all the members of a terrorist organization. There will be no victory parade. At best, the U.S. and the West can probably return to a life of inconvenience with infrequent incidents. However, free societies will have to remain permanently on alert.

This article discusses these eight distinguishing characteristics of the new terrorism and argues that they must be understood and addressed if the United States hopes to prevail. Osama bin Laden's al Qaeda is my case study because his ideology, organization, surrogates, and followers epitomize the new terrorism and are the number-one threat to America's security.

America at Risk

September 11 shattered the illusion that Americans are safe from troubles originating beyond our shores, traditionally protected by geography and by weak or friendly neighbors. The attacks forced American citizens and policymakers to learn how to fight a new kind of war. Some have compared September 11, 2001, to December 7, 1941, the only other occasion since the War of 1812 that American territory has been attacked.[10] There are many similarities. Both were surprise attacks, were predictable and possibly avoidable, were extraordinarily costly in life and national treasure, and were defining points in American history. However, as David Halberstam notes in *War in a Time of Peace,* there are also many differences. According to Halberstam, the historical demarcation point that the United States crossed on September 11 is even greater than the one it crossed with the bombing of Pearl Harbor.[11] The post–Pearl Harbor war was easily understood. The enemy was a state, and interstate warfare was more traditional, definable, and susceptible to American's industrial and technological advantages. Today's enemy is not a state but a transnational, nonstate actor. Its method of warfare is not traditional: It is more elusive, operates in the shadows, often at a great distance but sometimes right among us with secret cells and aliases, and it exploits America's industrial and technological advantages.[12]

Different, too, seems the resolve of the American people to wage war. Throughout our history, Americans have traditionally displayed an extraordinary degree of resourcefulness and self-sacrifice in times of war.[13] The best example of that tradition is World War II, when the war effort became an immediate extension of America's national will and purpose.[14] Today, says Stephen Flynn, "we are breaking with that tradition. Our nation faces grave peril, but we seem unwilling to mobilize at home to confront the threat before us."[15] Why are the American people unwilling to mobilize at home? Two reasons come to mind. First, they understand conventional war but not the war on terror. Second, they fail to realize the security implications of globalization and information technology.

The war on terror is not like engaging an enemy massed on a foreign battlefield. Destroying or confiscating the enemy's battlefield capabilities and dispersing its troops will not insure victory.[16] Today, as Halberstam explains, "the more visible the enemy is, the further he is from the magnetic field of our intelligence operations and any potential military strike."[17]

> It is not that America, as it enters a very different kind of battle, lacks weaponry; it is that the particular kind of weaponry we specialize in lacks targets. This will be a difficult military-intelligence-security challenge: What we do best, they are not vulnerable to. What we do least well, they are vulnerable to. What they do best, we are—to a considerable degree—vulnerable to.[18]

Combating terrorism, particularly the al Qaeda variety, is as much about fighting an international idea as an organized military force maneuvering within defined geographical boundaries. The danger posed by al Qaeda, its followers, and its surrogates cannot be managed by relying primarily on military campaigns overseas. "There are no fronts in the war on terrorism."[19]

> The 9/11 attacks highlighted the fact that our borders offer no effective barrier to terrorists intent on bringing their war to our soil. Nor do their weapons have to be imported, since they have proven how easy it is to exploit the modern systems we rely upon in our daily lives and use them against us.[20]

These modern systems are the sophisticated networks that move people, goods, energy, money, and information at higher volumes and greater velocities[21]—the very systems that ensure America's competitive edge in the age of globalization. For years, our growing dependence on these networks has not been matched by a parallel focus on securing them.[22]

> The architects of these networks have made efficiency and diminishing costs their highest priority. Security considerations have been widely perceived as annoying speed bumps in achieving their goals. As a result, the systems that underpin our prosperity are soft targets for those bent on challenging U.S. power.[23]

The attacks on the World Trade Center and the Pentagon ended a unique historical span for the United States as a great power. For nearly a century, America has been a major player in the world; but until 9/11, the homeland had escaped the ravages of modern warfare and weaponry because of its unique geographical position and unparalleled industrial technological base. When confronted with threats, the United States dealt with them on our adversaries' or allies' turf. Except for the occasional disaster or heinous crime, life in America had been terror-free. It has taken a group of rebels without a country—a ghost nation as it were—to pose a threat to America and our way of life.[24]

More Violent

In the past, "terrorists wanted a lot of people watching, not a lot of people dead."[25] Unlike the terrorists of the 1960s to the 1990s, who generally avoided high-casualty attacks for fear of the negative publicity they would generate, al Qaeda is not in the least worried about that.[26] Terrorists in past decades did not want large body counts because they wanted converts; they also wanted a seat at the table. Today's terrorists are not particularly concerned about converts, and rather than wanting a seat at the table, "they want to destroy the table and everyone sitting at it."[27] Religious terrorists, al Qaeda, in particular, want casualties—lots of them.[28]

In the past, civilians usually became victims of terrorist operations either because they were captives of hostage-taking events or because they happened to be in the wrong place at the wrong time. Terrorists took hostages for three reasons: to gain attention for their cause, the release of imprisoned comrades, or ransom. The odds were—96 percent of the time in the 1980s—that hostages would survive the event. Victims were generally casualties because they happened to be in the proximity of an explosion, ambush, or bank robbery. However, the motive was to get attention or money, not cause the deaths of civilians. Today, however, mass casualties are a primary aspect of bin Laden's strategy:

> By causing mass casualties on a regular basis [bin Laden] could hope to persuade the Americans to keep clear of overseas conflicts. There was also a retributive element to the strategy ... the militants of al-Qaeda and like-minded groups clearly wanted to pun-

> ish the Americans for a whole range of policies, particularly for those it pursued in the Middle East, as well as for what they saw as its irreligious decadence.[29]

For example, nine months after the attack on New York, Osama bin Laden forwarded a chilling announcement on a now defunct al Qaeda-affiliated Web site, www.alneda.com, stating: "We have the right to kill four million Americans—two million of them children—and to exile twice as many and wound and cripple hundreds of thousands."[30]

Despite successes against al Qaeda by coalition military forces in Afghanistan and police agencies around the world, some predict that the "frequency and reach of al-Qaeda's attacks will continue to increase, even though their lethality may decrease slightly."[31]

Truly Global: Conducted by Transnational, Non-State Actors

In the 1970s and 1980s, terrorism was mostly local. The terrorists were sub-state actors intent on overturning a state's political and/or economic system. Today, there has been a shift from localized terrorist groups, supported by state sponsors, to loosely organized global networks. Today, the new terrorists have global motives and capabilities. They are backed by like-minded organizations throughout the world and in many respects have achieved *de facto* sovereign status by acquiring the means to conduct war—and have in fact declared war—posing significant military and security policy challenges for which the United States and the West had no preplanned response.[32] This parallels a change from primarily politically motivated terrorism to a more religiously motivated variety.[33]

Al Qaeda's global network consists of independently operating permanent or semi-permanent cells of trained militants in more than 76 countries.[34] In fact, since September 11, more than 4,300 al Qaeda operatives, hailing from 49 countries, have been arrested in 97 countries.[35] Moreover, the concept of global terrorism applies not just to al Qaeda but collectively to many terrorist organizations throughout the world. These organizations operate through an interconnected network that often provides mutual aid and support, making it difficult to isolate a particular group or faction.[36] There is also growing evidence that al Qaeda is now subcontracting work to like-minded terrorists. According to Jessica Stern:

> Bin Laden's organization has also nurtured ties with a variety of other groups around the world, including: Ansar al Islam, based mainly in Iraq and Europe, Jemaah Islamiah in Southeast Asia, Abus Sayyaf and the Moro Islamic Liberation Front in the Philippines, and many Pakistani jihadi groups.[37]

These affiliated or like-minded groups have the capacity to carry out attacks and inflict pain on the United States under al Qaeda's banner, says Bruce Hoffman. In fact, new revelations about the emerging al Qaeda network—the depth of its ranks and its ties to "franchise" terrorists in up to 70 countries—shows that the intent to attack America, the West, and secular states around the world has not diminished.[38] According to some, successes against al Qaeda in Afghanistan and elsewhere may have made defeating the organization more difficult. Since al Qaeda lost its sanctuary in Afghanistan, Jason Burke believes "there is no longer a central hub for Islamic militancy."[39] Instead, the al Qaeda worldview, or "al Qaedaism," is what sustains acts of terrorism against the West and the United States.[40]

> This radical internationalist ideology—sustained by anti-Western, anti-Zionist, and anti-Semitic rhetoric—has adherents among many individuals and groups, few of whom

> are currently linked in any substantial way to bin Laden or those around him. They merely follow his precepts, models, and methods. They act in the style of al Qaeda, but they are only part of al Qaeda in the very loosest sense.[41]

Perhaps most troubling is recent evidence that al Qaeda—a Sunni organization—is now cooperating with Hezbollah, a Shiite group considered by many to be the most sophisticated terrorist organization in the world.[42] "Hezbollah, which enjoys backing from Syria and Iran, is based in southern Lebanon and in the lawless 'tri-border' region of South America, where Paraguay, Brazil, and Argentina meet."[43]

Al Qaeda's targeting is global, which is also different from the local, tactical focus of earlier terrorist groups. Now, not only are targets selected to cause casualties without limit, they are selected to undermine the global economy. "They might be called strategic acts of destruction, rather than the tactical terrorist acts of the past."[44] According to Air Marshall Sir Timothy Garden, "it may have been possible for the international community to live with occasional acts of local terrorism around the world; it is much more difficult to live with non-state actors who have a mission to destroy a large part of the global system."[45]

In summary, we have seen the emergence of terrorism that is not ideological in a political sense but is inspired by religious extremists working in cells, small groups, and larger coalitions.[46] They do not answer completely to any government; they operate across national borders; and they have access to funding and advanced technology.[47] Such groups are not bound by the same constraints or motivated by the same goals as nation-states. And unlike state-sponsored groups, religious extremists such as al Qaeda are not susceptible to traditional diplomacy or military deterrence. There is no state with which to negotiate or against which to retaliate.

Well-Financed

Al Qaeda learned from the failings of previous terrorist groups, such as the Baeder Meinhof, Red Brigades, and the Abu Nidal group, all of which were perennially under-capitalized. According to Bruce Hoffman, al Qaeda under Osama bin Laden saw the need to be much more flexible and to maintain a steady supply of money, which is crucial to lubricate the wheels of terrorism.[48]

Estimates of Osama bin Laden's personal wealth range from $18 million to as high as $200 million, but "it is most commonly agreed that bin Laden inherited approximately $57 million at age sixteen." [49] Bin Laden has been able to leverage his millions into a global financial empire by investing in legitimate businesses, taking advantage of the globalized financial system, abusing the Islamic banking (*hawala*) system, and coercing an entire network of Islamic philanthropic and charitable institutions. The total net worth of the al Qaeda financial empire is unclear—I would put it in the hundreds of millions. Between September 11, 2001, and October 2002, more than 165 countries enacted blocking actions against terrorist assets, and approximately $112 million of these assets have been frozen worldwide ($34 million in the United States and $78 million overseas).[50] According to at least one report, international efforts to curtail terrorists' fund-raising, money-laundering, and financing activities have resulted in a 90 percent reduction in al Qaeda's income, compared with before 11 September.[51] However, most experts disagree and believe that al Qaeda and like-minded terrorist groups have moved out of normal channels into other sources of revenue that sustain operations at near pre-9/11 levels. For example, in a dissertation recently completed for RAND, Steven Kiser concluded that al Qaeda's financial infrastructure has shown an impressive ability to adapt to adverse conditions, quickly take advantage of available opportunities, pursue creative, non-traditional, and unorthodox methods of money management, and geographically move operations to areas where laws are lax or non-existent. As Kiser explains, "this amoeba-like ability—to form oneself in whatever shape is necessary and still function effectively—has proven exceptionally useful."[52]

In fact, Osama bin Laden's entrepreneurial skills are legendary. During his five-year stint in Sudan, he cornered the market on gum Arabic, the basic ingredient in fruit juices produced in the United States.[53] "He also started an Islamic Bank, built a tannery, created an export company, launched construction projects and developed agricultural schemes."[54] Other business ventures included a trading company in Kenya and a ceramic plant, publishing outlet, and appliance firm in Yemen.[55]

Al Qaeda's misuse of the ancient *hawala* underground banking system, which allows money transfers without actual money movement, is particularly instructive. Seemingly custom-made for al-Qaeda, the *hawala* is an ancient system that originated in South Asia and is still used worldwide to conduct legitimate business as well as for money laundering. The components of *hawala* that distinguish it from other parallel remittance systems are trust and the extensive use of connections, such as family relationships or regional affiliations. Unlike traditional banking, *hawala* makes minimal use of any sort of negotiable instruments or documentation. Transfers of money take place based on communications between members of a network of *hawaladars,* or *hawala* dealers.[56] A recent Council on Foreign Relations study illustrates how the *hawala* system works:

> Customers in one city hand their local *hawaladar* some money. That individual then contacts his counterpart across the world, who in turn distributes money out of his own resources to the intended recipient. The volume of transactions flowing through the system in both directions is such that the two *hawaladars* rarely have to worry about settlement.[57]

Hawaladars charge their customers a nominal cash transaction fee for the service. They are willing to carry each other's debts for long periods of time because they are often related through familial, clan, or ethnic associations.[58]

Al Qaeda also uses other methods to move funds. Cash smuggling is one; moving assets in the form of precious metals and gemstones is another. The gold trade and the *hawala* are especially symbiotic: They flourish in the same locales and offer complementary services to those moving assets across borders. Al Qaeda also uses traditional smuggling routes and methods favored by international drug traffickers, arms dealers, and other organized criminal groups.[59]

Charities and philanthropic organizations have also been sources of al Qaeda funding. "Since December 2001, the assets of more than a dozen Islamic charities worldwide have been frozen, three of them based in the United States."[60] For example, U.S. authorities have designated the U.S.-based Benevolence International Foundation (BIF) a terrorist financier with links to the al Qaeda network, and its assets have been frozen in the United States, Canada, and Bosnia. But the bin Laden network is not the only terrorist group skimming funds from U.S.-based charities.[61] In fact, the U.S. Treasury Department found overwhelming evidence that the Holy Land Foundation for Relief and Development, the self-proclaimed largest Muslim charity in the United States, was an arm of Hamas, a radical Islamic organization that operates in the West Bank and Gaza strip.[62]

Al Qaeda–trained cells choose from a variety of methods to obtain local funding. "Credit card fraud, car theft and document forgery are popular among Algerian cells in Europe.[63] In North America, terrorist financiers practice cigarette smuggling and coupon scams, both of which provide large profits but result in minor penalties if apprehended."[64]

More recently, there is evidence that financial operations are taking place between Islamist organizations—notably al Qaeda and affiliates—and criminal organizations. According to Steven Kiser:

> Al Qaeda appears to have a cooperative but limited relationship with some organized criminal networks, using these organizations to acquire materials they require for terrorist attacks, as well as aiding in the laundering money. The biggest links are with rebel groups that also served as diamond smuggling networks in western Africa. Al Qaeda's affiliates also are beginning to cooperate with organized crime. For example, Abu Sayyaf now raises funds through kidnapping ransoms, piracy and gunrunning.[65]

Additionally, the terrorists responsible for the 11 March 2004 bombings in Madrid are believed to have funded their operation at least partially through the sale of narcotics.[66]

Well-Trained

Formalized terrorist training during the Cold War was generally conducted by the states sponsoring terrorist groups. It is known, for instance, that the former Soviet Union ran terrorism training camps at Simferpol in the Crimea, Ostrova in Czechoslovakia, and Pankow in East Germany. Captured PLO terrorist Adnan Jaber has given a comprehensive account of his Soviet training:

> He did a six-month course there, during which Russian military and civilian instructors covered propaganda methods, political affairs, tactics and weapons. Other such courses dealt with advanced explosives work, bomb-making, and training in biological and chemical warfare.[67]

However, it would be incorrect to assume that most terrorists during the Cold War years went through such formal training. More than likely, many went into action without such instruction and simply learned by doing.[68]

This is not at all the case today. In fact, graduating from training camp is the common denominator and rite of passage for al Qaeda operatives and their allies. The camps have trained both formal al Qaeda members and members of allied Islamist organizations.[69]

Al Qaeda manuals and records captured in Afghanistan training camps portray a comprehensive program that emphasizes paramilitary training, Islamic studies, and current politics. Common to all members of al Qaeda and its associated groups are the following personality traits and qualifications, which are required before one can become an Islamist military operative:

> Knowledge of Islam, ideological commitment, maturity, self-sacrifice, discipline, secrecy and concealment of information, good health, patience, unflappability, intelligence and insight, caution and prudence, truthfulness and wisdom, and the ability to observe and analyze, and the ability to act.[70]

Aspiring operatives are also taught forgery, assassination techniques, and the conducting of maritime or vehicle suicide attacks.[71] As a means of avoiding sophisticated National Security Administration signal intelligence capabilities, al Qaeda teaches its operatives how to use couriers and sophisticated telecommunications, the Internet, and encryption technologies to try to outfox U.S. surveillance.[72]

An al Qaeda manual, *Military Studies in the Jihad Against the Tyrants,* which was seized in Manchester, England, at the home of a bin Laden follower, is a condensed version of thousands of pages of al Qaeda training materials seized in Afghanistan. An English translation of the 180-page Arabic document was placed in evidence during the recent Kenya and Tanzania bombing trials in New York City. The manual is extraordinarily comprehensive and instructs terrorist operatives in an array of techniques, including Jihad (Holy War); military organization; financial precautions and forged documents; security measures in public transportation; special operations and weapons; guidelines for beating and killing hostages; how to assassinate with poisons, spoiled food, and feces; and methods of physical and psychological torture.[73]

Al Qaeda's training is very eclectic and comprehensive; its tacticians and trainers have taken much from the special operations forces of several nations, including the United States, United Kingdom, and Russia. Indeed, al Qaeda fighters are as well or better trained than those of many national armies (as was the case in Afghanistan). What is even more startling is its intelligence and "black operations" acumen. "Unlike the rag-tag terrorist groups of the Cold War period," says Rohan Gunaratna, "sophisticated terrorist groups of the post-Cold War period, such as al Qaeda, have developed intelligence wings comparable to government intelligence agencies."[74]

Difficult to Penetrate

Another difference between old and new terrorism is that the latter has adopted a networked and less hierarchical form. "Both the anti-capitalist and national liberation terrorist groups of the 1970s and 1980s mostly had hierarchical forms and chains of command."[75] But in response to improvements in counterterror capabilities and increased cooperation among governments, groups like al Qaeda have adopted networked structural models instead of hierarchical structures. Rapid advances in digital communication have also increased the viability of these networks, though they are not totally dependent on the latest information technology. "While information technology has made networks more effective, low-tech means such as couriers and landline telephones can enable networks in certain circumstances."[76]

Strict adherence to a flat, diffused, cellular, networked structure has allowed al Qaeda to maintain a high degree of secrecy and security. "These cells are independent of other local groups al Qaeda may be aligned with and range in size from two to fifteen members."[77] Using code, targets are announced in the general media, and individuals or independent cells are expected to use initiative, stealth, and flexibility to destroy them.

The network will obviously be more likely to achieve long-term effectiveness if its members share a unifying ideology, common goals, and mutual interests, as is the case with al Qaeda.[78] Networks are most effective when they distribute the responsibility for operations and provide redundancies for key functions. "Operating cells need not contact or coordinate with other cells except for those essential to a particular operation or function."[79]

Avoiding unnecessary coordination or approval provides deniability to terrorist leaders and enhances the security of terrorist operations.

Washington's predilection for technical means of intelligence collection at the expense of covert and clandestine operations with human sources, compounded by an acute lack of culturally attuned operatives, analysts, and linguists, has contribute greatly to the inability for U.S. operators to penetrate tightly knit cells of al Qaeda and other militant Islamic groups.[80]

Al Qaeda's loss of sanctuary in Afghanistan has forced it to disperse and go underground, thus making it more difficult to penetrate. Also, like-minded terrorist organizations operating on their own in loosely affiliated groups have increased. "In particular, Islamic terrorist groups tend to be loosely organized, recruit their members from many different countries, and obtain support from an informal international network of like-minded extremists."[81] The new terrorism resembles a virus that morphs as its environment changes. Individual cells and nodes evolve their own strategy, and if hit, will adapt, regroup, generate new leadership, shift locations, adjust tactics, and evolve into a new set of cells and networks capable of reconstitution, dispersal, and innovation.[82] The resulting transnational and decentralized structure facilitates terrorists avoiding detection and penetration.[83]

Though weakened by the disruption of its finances and communications, its base destroyed, and its leaders in flight, al Qaeda is still dangerous and very difficult to penetrate.[84] Though they may share a common militant Islamic ideology, they have become a loose and "ever-shifting alliance of like-minded groups."[85] Instead of large, well-orchestrated attacks like those of September 11, al Qaeda operations are now smaller and less ambitious. They remain extremely dangerous, however, and their "killer cells" seem to be growing and spawning imitations around the world.[86]

Access to Weapons of Mass Destruction

The seventh way the new terrorists differ from old is the most worrisome: They are determined to obtain and use nuclear, radiological, chemical, and biological weapons of mass destruction (WMDs). According to Graham Allison's recent book *Nuclear Terrorism,* polls taken in 2003 found that four out of every 10 Americans worry about the chances of nuclear attack.[87] In the judgment of many experts, these fears are not exaggerated. For example, a study conducted in 2000 by Howard Baker and Lloyd Cutler determined that the most urgent unmet national security threat to the United States today is the danger that WMDs or weapons-usable material in Russian could be stolen, sold to terrorists, and used against Americans abroad or at home.[88]

With a single act, terrorists using a WMD can cause the deaths of thousands, even millions.[89] Acquiring WMD has been made easier thanks to Information Age technologies and the availability of suppliers;[90] recent discoveries in Afghanistan have confirmed that al Qaeda and other terrorist groups are actively pursuing biological agents for use against the United States and its allies.[91] According to David Kay, this should not be a surprise:

> Only a blind, deaf and dumb terrorist group could have survived the last five years and not been exposed at least to the possibility of the use of WMD, while the more discerning terrorists would have found some tactically brilliant possibilities already laid out on the public record.[92]

"We must be prepared for new types of attacks; anything could happen," says Koichi Oizumi, an international relations professor at Nihon University in Tokyo, the city where the Aum Shinrikio used saran nerve gas to kill 12 and injure 250 in the first major use of chemical agent in a terrorist attack.[93]

Steven Miller, director of the International Security Program at Harvard's Kennedy School, says that policy-makers should be particularly concerned about terrorist access to nuclear weapons. "Opportunities for well-organized and well-financed terrorists to infiltrate a Russian nuclear storage facility are greater than ever."[94] Miller believes that there have been more than two dozen thefts of weapons-usable materials in the former Soviet Union in recent years. Although "several suspects have been arrested in undercover sting operations," he wonders about those who may have gotten away.[95] These thefts go back to at least 1994, "when 350 grams of plutonium were smuggled on board a Lufthansa flight from Moscow to Munich. Fortunately, SWAT teams confiscated the material as soon as it arrived."[96]

In the past, any state that allowed a terrorist group it sponsored to use WMD against the United States knew it would be committing suicide, and the fear of nuclear retaliation was ample motivation for sponsors to keep the lid on. Today any terrorist group with a known base of operations, even if it does not have a state sponsor, would similarly risk annihilation for waging a WMD terrorist attack. But al Qaeda has no state sponsor and is a loosely organized global network, which makes retaliation much more problematic.

Defining Victory and Defeat

Much has been written about winning the war on terrorism, defeating al Qaeda, and ending terrorism. In the last presidential campaign, both candidates implied that the war on terror may not be winnable, and were criticized for saying so. In my opinion, however, they were correct. Victory and defeat are ellusive terms in a war on terrorism. Unlike World Wars I and II and the first Gulf War, when victory was sealed with an agreement, and the Vietnam War, when defeat was understood when Saigon fell, the war on terror will have no such defining moments. I believe the war against terrorism will never be over, at least in my lifetime. "There will always be a threat that someone will blow up an airplane or a building or a container ship."[97] The fact is, "one cannot defeat terrorism. Terrorism in one form or another has been around for centuries and will be around for many more."[98] Counterterrorism is not about defeating terrorism; it is about defeating terrorists, such as al Qaeda. The measures of success in a war against terror are different too. Instead of body counts and casualty rates, success in the war on terror may be measured in numbers voting, schools opened, and women in the workforce.[99] Success against al Qaeda and like-minded terrorist groups will come when their operational, logistical, and financial activities are difficult to conduct and their freedom of movement to conduct operations is severely restricted.[100] The best we may be able to achieve is to understand that we live in danger, without living in fear.

Conclusion

To recap, eight key factors differentiate the al Qaeda terrorist network from the terrorist organizations of more recent generations. First, al Qaeda attacked the United States homeland, seriously undermining American's sense of security and well-being. The attack raised serious questions about the ability of the United States to respond to radically different threats and to meet "the paramount responsibility of any government—assuring the security of all persons, citizens or not, who legally reside within its sovereign territory."[101] Second, terrorism today is more violent. It has been responsible for the most lethal terrorist attack in history and has achieved the highest ever rate of lethality per attack.[102]

Third, while earlier terrorist organizations had local aspirations, al Qaeda has global reach and strategic objectives. Its operators are transnational, non-state actors whose allegiance is to a cause, not a state. This is problematic because the traditional forms of state interaction—diplomatic, economic, and military—to solve differences prior to conflict are difficult to apply with a non-state actor. When things get testy, with whom do you negotiate, whom do you sanction, and whom do you threaten with force? And if a transnational, non-state actor like bin Laden uses a WMD against you, whom do you nuke?

Fourth, al Qaeda is a wealthy multinational organization with several income streams. It has investments and concealed accounts worldwide, many in the Western societies bin Laden most despises.[103] He and his followers will use their wealth to continue to leverage (i.e., coerce) governments for access and safe haven, just as they have done in the Sudan and Afghanistan. They will also pay to subcontract and franchise the services of like-minded terrorist organizations, all for the purpose of killing Americans.

Fifth, as Rohan Gunaratna says, al Qaeda is not a ragtag outfit. Al Qaeda operatives are well-trained in military, special operations, and intelligence functions. Notwithstanding the coalition's victory in Afghanistan, the allies learned what made the al Qaeda global terrorist network a daunting foe: "a relatively sophisticated, well-trained, and well-financed organization that drew on ongoing grass-roots support and a fanatical willingness to fight to the death."[104]

Sixth, strict adherence to its networked, cellular structure makes penetrating al Qaeda extremely difficult. Composed of many cells whose members do not know one another, never assemble in one place together, and use strict communication discipline, the al Qaeda model is more than a match for Western intelligence agencies that rely mainly on technical means of intelligence collection.[105] "America's new enemies can't be bought, bribed, or even blackmailed."[106] They want to kill Americans and will do so at any cost.

Seventh and most worrisome is al Qaeda's determination to acquire nuclear, radiological, chemical, and biological WMDs. The potential for acquiring these weapons is greater because of globalization, information technology, and the availability of shady suppliers. Indeed, the new terrorism has an unprecedented global reach. It can ride the back of the Web, using advanced communications to move immense financial flows from Sudan to the Philippines or from Australia to banks in Florida.[107] And for $28.50, any Internet surfer can purchase *Bacteriological Warfare: A Major Threat to North America,* which teaches how to grow deadly bacteria. Shady suppliers come from many countries, particularly Russia, which cannot offer employment to many ex-Soviet scientists and weaponeers. In fact, there are reports of plutonium for sale across Eastern Europe and of Russian scientists who once worked in Soviet labs linked to germ warfare now selling their services in the Middle East for hefty fees.[108]

Eighth and most frustrating is that we will not know when or whether we have achieved victory or if the enemy is defeated. More than likely, victory in the traditional warfare sense will never be achieved in our lifetime. At a minimum, reducing the risks from terrorism so that an atmosphere of pre-9/11 security exists will define victory. In the long-run, al Qaeda and like-minded terrorist groups will go the way of the Baedar Meinhof, the Red Brigades, and the Japanese Red Army. However, terrorism in some form will continue to exist.

As envisioned by al Qaeda, the "perfect new warfare" would entail multiple attacks against America designed to produce the greatest number of casualties. For maximum effect, these attacks would take place nearly simultaneously and at several locations, much like the attacks of September 11 in New York City and Washington D.C.[109]

One might say that America's war against the new terrorism is far colder than the Cold War— "cold" as in the cold-blooded murder of September 11. At least with the Soviets, we always knew who was in charge and that we couldn't be attacked without his orders. In fact, the U.S. president had a direct line to Soviet leaders and could work through difficult moments with them personally. By contrast, on September 11, 2001, we lost thousands of people; but although we know Osama bin Laden ordered the killing, we have no direct line to him or anyone else in his leadership. We also know that he and his followers will continue to hit the United States, its allies, and secular Islamic states again and again until he and his network are stopped.

It has been said that generals always make the mistake of preparing for the last war instead of the next one. This article has emphasized changes in the terrorist threat from the Cold War decades so that today's generals and their civilian masters can understand how to fight and win the current war, and so that having won it, we will never have to fight a war like this again.

NOTES

1. "Terror Cells of Today Hard to Combat" (August 20, 2002), *The New York Times,* http://www.nytimes.com/aponline/international/AP-Evolution-of-Terror.html.
2. John Mearsheimer (August 1990), "Why We Will Soon Miss the Cold War," *Atlantic Monthly.* See also, Glenn Sacks (October 2, 2001), "Why I Miss the Cold War," http://www.glennsacks.com.
3. Brian H. Hook, Margaret J. A. Peterlin, and Peter L. Welsh (December 2001), "Intelligence and the New Threat: The USA PATRIOT Act and Information Sharing Between the Intelligence and Law Enforcement Communities," *Federalist Society for Law and Public Policy Studies,* p. 3.
4. Brian Murphy (August 21, 2002), "The Shape of Terrorism Changes," *Fayetteville Observer,* p. 9A.
5. Steven Simon and Daniel Benjamin (Spring 2000), "America and the New Terrorism," *Survival,* vol. 42, no. 1, p. 69.
6. Sebestyen L. v. Gorka (January 13, 2005), "Al Qaeda's Rhetoric and Its Implications," *Jane's Terrorism and Security Monitor,* p. 1.
7. "Combating Terrorism and Its Implications for Intelligence" (June 2004), DCAF Internal Paper, p. 8.
8. Ibid.
9. Ibid.
10. Some in the Southwest may include Pancho Villa's excursion into New Mexico as an attack.
11. David Halberstam (2001), *War in Time of Peace* (New York: Simon and Schuster), p. 498.
12. Ibid., pp. 496-497.
13. Stephen Flynn (2004), *America the Vulnerable* (New York: HarperCollins), p. x.
14. Halberstam, p. 496.
15. Flynn, p. x.
16. Hook, et al., p. 3.
17. Halberstam, p. 497.
18. Ibid.
19. Flynn, p. x.
20. Ibid.
21. Ibid., p. 5.

22. Ibid.
23. Ibid., p. 5
24. Halberstam, p. 498.
25. Quote attributed to Brian Jenkins in 1974. See Jessica Stern (June 19, 1996), "Loose Nukes, Poisons, and Terrorism: The New Threats to International Security."
26. Rohan Gunaratna (May 2002), *Inside Al Qaeda-Global Network of Terror* (New York: Columbia University Press), p. 91.
27. Quote attributed to James Woolsey, 1994.
28. Bruce Hoffman (1998), *Inside Terrorism* (New York: Columbia University Press), p. 205.
29. Lawrence Freeman, "Out of Nowhere—Bin Laden's Grievances," BBC Online, http://www.bbc.co.uk/history/war/sept_11/build_up_05.shtml.
30. Graham Allison (2004), *Nuclear Terrorism* (New York: Times Books), p. 13.
31. Bruce Newsome (June 13, 2003), "Executive Summary," *Mass-Casualty Terrorism: Second Quarterly Forecast by the University of Reading Terrorism Forecasting Group,* p. 3, http://www.rdg.ac.uk/GSEIS/University_of_Reading_Terrorism_Forecast_2003Q2.pdf.
32. "Combating Terrorism and Its Implications for Intelligence," p. 8.
33. Michael Whine, "The New Terrorism," http://www.ict.org.il/articles/articledet.cfm?articleid=427.
34. Jerrold M. Post (2002), "Killing in the Name of God: Osama Bin Laden and Al Qaeda." In *Know Thy Enemy: Profiles of Adversary Leaders and Their Strategic Cultures,* Barry R. Schneider and Jerrold M. Post, eds. (Maxwell Air Force Base: USAF Counterproliferation Center), p. 33.
35. Conversation with Dr. Rohan Gunaratna, November 15, 2002, in Garmisch, Germany.
36. Ibid., p. 9.
37. Jessica Stern (July–August, 2003), "The Protean Enemy," *Foreign Affairs,* p. 33.
38. Ann Tyson (June 24, 2002), "Al Qaeda Broken, but Dangerous," *Christian Science Monitor,* http://www.csmonitor.com/2002/0624/p01s02-usgn.htm.
39. Jason Burke (May/June 2004), "Al Qaeda," *Foreign Policy,* p. 18.
40. Ibid.
41. Ibid.
42. Jessica Stern (July–August, 2003), "The Protean Enemy (Al Qaeda)," *Foreign Affairs,* p. 31.
43. Ibid., p. 32.
44. Ibid.
45. Timothy Garden, "Security and the War Against Terrorism," *Foreign and Security Policy by Tim Garden,* http://www.tgarden.demon.co.uk/writings/articles/2002/020320riia.html
46. Stephen A. Cambone (1996), *A New Structure for National Security Policy Planning* (Washington, D.C.: Government Printing Office), p. 43.
47. Gideon Rose (March–April, 1999), "It Could Happen Here—Facing the New Terrorism," *Foreign Affairs,* p. 1.
48. Discussion with Bruce Hoffman.
49. Multiple conversations with John Dorschner. Also, see John Dorschner (September 24, 2001), "A Shadowy Empire of Hate Was Born of a War in Afghanistan," Knight Ridder Newspapers.
50. "CDI Primer: Terrorist Finances" (October 25, 2002), http://www.cdi.org/terrorism/finance_primer-pr.cfm.
51. Martin Rudner, p. 222. See also, "Al Qaeda Income Cut, Says Foreign Office" (April 7, 2003), *Daily Telegraph,* London.
52. Steve Kiser (March 2005), "Al Qaeda's Financial Empire," unpublished dissertation for RAND, p. 45.
53. Robin Wright (2001), *Sacred Rage* (New York: Simon and Schuster), p. 252.
54. Ibid.
55. Ibid.
56. Patrick M. Yost and Harjit Singh Sandhu (January 2002), "The *Hawala* Alternative Remittance System and Its Role in Money Laundering," Interpol General Secretariat, http://www.interpol.int/Public/FinancialCrime/MoneyLaundering/hawala/default.asp.
57. Maurice Greenberg (2002), "Terrorist Financing," Council on Foreign Relations Report, p. 11.
58. Ibid.

59. Ibid.
60. Neil A. Lewis (June 21, 2003), "The Money Trail—Court Upholds Freeze on Assets of Muslim Group Based in U.S.," *New York Times,* p. A11.
61. "US Accuses Charity of Financing Terror" (November 20, 2002), *BBC Online.*
62. Lewis, p. A11.
63. Steve Kiser (March 2005), "Al Qaeda's Financial Empire," unpublished dissertation, RAND, p.16.
64. Ibid., p. 16.
65. Ibid., p. 19.
66. Ibid.
67. Christopher Dobson and Ronald Payne (1982), *The Terrorists, Their Weapons, Leaders and Tactics* (New York: Facts on File), p. 80.
68. Ibid.
69. Post, p. 35.
70. Gunaratna, p. 73.
71. Ibid.
72. Rudner, p. 203. See also Robert Fisk (December 6, 2002), "With Runners and Whispers, al Qaeda Outfoxes U.S. Forces," *The Independent*, London.
73. Abdullah Ali Al-Salama, *Military Espionage in Islam,* http://www.skfriends.com/bin-laden-terrorist-manual.htm.
74. Gunaratna, p. 76.
75. Michael Whine, "The New Terrorism," http://www.ict.org.il/articles/articledet.cfm?articleid=427.
76. *A Military Guide to Terrorism in the Twenty-First Century* (May 13, 2003), Version 1.0, p. 40.
77. Ibid., p. 33.
78. John Arqilla and David Ronfeldt, eds. (2001), *Networks and Netwars* (Santa Monica: RAND, 2001), p. 9.
79. *A Military Guide to Terrorism in the the Twenty-First Century,* p. 40.
80. Rudner, p. 216.
81. "Combating Terrorism and Its Implications for Intelligence." p. 9.
82. Ibid.
83. Ibid.
84. "Al-Qaeda, An Ever-Shifting Web" (October 19–25, 2002), *The Economist,* p. 26.
85. Ibid.
86. Ibid.
87. Allison, p. 8.
88. Ibid., p. 9.
89. Richard B. Myers (August 19, 2002), "Fighting Terrorism in an Information Age," U.S. Department of State, International Information Programs, p. 2, http://usinfo.state.gov/regional/nea/sasia/text/0819info.htm.
90. Ibid.
91. Judith Miller (September 14, 2002), "Lab Suggests Qaeda Planned to Build Arms, Officials Say," *New York Times,* p. 1.
92. David Kay (2001), "WMD Terrorism: Hype or Reality." In James M. Smith and William C. Thomas, eds., *The Terrorism Threat and US Government Response: Operational and Organizational Factors* (US Air Force Academy: INSS Book Series), p. 12.
93. "Terror Cells of Today Hard to Combat" (August 20, 2002).
94. Doug Gavel (Autumn 2002), "Can Nuclear Weapons Be Put Beyond the Reach of Terrorists," *Kennedy School of Government Bulletin,* p. 43.
95. Ibid., p. 45.
96. Ibid., p. 48.
97. James Fallows (January–February, 2005), "Success Without Victory," *The Atlantic Monthly.*
98. Matthew Levitt (Winter–Spring 2004), "Untangling the Terror Web: Identifying and Counteracting the Phenomenon of Crossover Between Terrorist Groups," *SAIS Review,* vol. 24, no. 1, p. 35.

99. Rowan Scarborough (April 5, 2005), "Metrics Help Guide the Pentagon," *Washington Times,* p. 3.
100. Ibid., p. 35
101. Richard H. Ullman (2002 Edition), "9/11 a New Day for Counterterrorism?" *Great Decisions,* p. 5.
102. Newsome, p. 3.
103. Wright, p. 253.
104. Ann Tyson (March 7, 2002), "Al Qaeda, Resilient and Organized," *Christian Science Monitor,* p. 1.
105. Gunaratna, p. 76.
106. Sacks, p. 1.
107. Paul Mann (April 22, 2002), "Modern Military Threats: Not All They Might Seem?" *Aviation Week & Space Technology,* p. 1.
108. For example, see the 1997 National Academies Press report, "Proliferation Concerns: Assessing U.S. Efforts to Help Contain Nuclear and Other Dangerous Materials and Technologies in the Former Soviet Union."
109. "A Military Assessment of the al Qaeda Training Tapes," (June 28, 2003), http://www.strategypage.com/articles/tapes/5.asp.

John Arquilla, David Ronfeldt, and Michele Zanini, 1999

Networks, Netwar, and Information-Age Terrorism

The rise of network forms of organization is a key consequence of the ongoing information revolution. Business organizations are being newly energized by networking, and many professional militaries are experimenting with flatter forms of organization. In this [selection], we explore the impact of networks on terrorist capabilities, and consider how this development may be associated with a move away from emphasis on traditional, episodic efforts at coercion to a new view of terror as a form of protracted warfare. Seen in this light, the recent bombings of U.S. embassies in East Africa, along with the retaliatory American missile strikes, may prove to be the opening shots of a war between a leading state and a terror network. We consider both the likely context and the conduct of such a war, and offer some insights that might inform policies aimed at defending against and countering terrorism.

A New Terrorism (With Old Roots)

The age-old phenomenon of terrorism continues to appeal to its perpetrators for three principal reasons. First, it appeals as a weapon of the weak—a shadowy way to wage war by attacking asymmetrically to harm and try to defeat an ostensibly superior force. This has had particular appeal to ethnonationalists, racist militias, religious fundamentalists, and other minorities who cannot match the military formations and firepower of their "oppressors"—the case, for example, with some radical Middle Eastern Islamist groups vis-à-vis Israel, and, until recently, the Provisional Irish Republican Army (PIRA) vis-à-vis Great Britain.

Second, terrorism has appealed as a way to assert identity and command attention—rather like proclaiming, "I bomb, therefore I am." Terrorism enables a perpetrator to publicize his identity, project it explosively, and touch the nerves of powerful distant leaders. This kind of attraction to violence transcends its instrumental utility. Mainstream revolutionary writings may view violence as a means of struggle, but terrorists often regard violence as an end in itself that generates identity or damages the enemy's identity.

Third, terrorism has sometimes appealed as a way to achieve a new future order by willfully wrecking the present. This is manifest in the religious fervor of some radical Islamists, but examples also lie among millenarian and apocalyptic groups, like Aum Shinrikyo in Japan, who aim to wreak havoc and rend a system asunder so that something new may emerge from the cracks. The substance of the future vision may be only vaguely defined, but its moral worth is clear and appealing to the terrorist.

In the first and second of these motivations or rationales, terrorism may involve retaliation and retribution for past wrongs, whereas the third is also about revelation and rebirth, the coming of a new age. The first is largely strategic; it has a practical tone, and the objectives may be limited and specific. In contrast, the third may engage a transcendental, unconstrained view of how to change the world through terrorism.

Such contrasts do not mean the three are necessarily at odds; blends often occur. Presumptions of weakness (the first rationale) and of willfulness (in the second and third) can lead to peculiar synergies. For example, Aum's members may have known it was weak in a conventional sense, but they believed that they had special knowledge, a unique leader, invincible willpower, and secret ways to strike out.

These classic motivations or rationales will endure in the information age. However, terrorism is not a fixed phenomenon; its perpetrators adapt it to suit their times and situations. What changes is the conduct of terrorism—the operational characteristics built around the motivations and rationales.

This [selection] addresses, often in a deliberately speculative manner, changes in organization, doctrine, strategy, and technology that, taken together, speak to the emergence of a "new terrorism" attuned to the information age. Our principal hypotheses are as follows:

- **Organization.** Terrorists will continue moving from hierarchical toward information-age network designs. Within groups, "great man" leaderships will give way to flatter decentralized designs. More effort will go into building arrays of transnationally internetted groups than into building stand-alone groups.
- **Doctrine and strategy.** Terrorists will likely gain new capabilities for lethal acts. Some terrorist groups are likely to move to a "war paradigm" that focuses on attacking U.S. military forces and assets. But where terrorists suppose that "information operations" may be as useful as traditional commando-style operations for achieving their goals, systemic *disruption* may become as much an objective as target *destruction*. Difficulties in coping with the new terrorism will mount if terrorists move beyond isolated acts toward a new approach to doctrine and strategy that emphasizes campaigns based on swarming.
- **Technology.** Terrorists are likely to increasingly use advanced information technologies for offensive and defensive purposes, as well as to support their organizational structures. Despite widespread speculation about terrorists using cyberspace warfare techniques to take "the Net" down, they may often have stronger reasons for wanting to keep it up (e.g., to spread their message and communicate with one another).

In short, terrorism is evolving in a direction we call *netwar*. Thus, after briefly reviewing terrorist trends, we outline the concept of netwar and its relevance for understanding information-age terrorism. In particular, we elaborate on the above points about organization, doctrine, and strategy, and briefly discuss how recent developments in the nature and behavior of Middle Eastern terrorist groups can be interpreted as early signs of a move toward netwar-type terrorism.

Given the prospect of a netwar-oriented shift in which some terrorists pursue a war paradigm, we then focus on the implications such a development may have for the U.S. military. We use these insights to consider defensive antiterrorist measures, as well as proactive counterterrorist strategies. We propose that a key to coping with information-age terrorism will be the creation of interorganizational networks within the U.S. military and government, partly on the grounds that it takes networks to fight networks.

Recent Views About Terrorism

Terrorism remains a distinct phenomenon while reflecting broader trends in irregular warfare. The latter has been on the rise around the world since before the end of the Cold War. Ethnic and religious conflicts, recently in evidence in areas of Africa, the Balkans, and the Caucasus, for awhile in Central America, and seemingly forever in the Middle East, attest to the brutality that increasingly attends this kind of warfare. These are not conflicts between regular, professional armed forces dedicated to warrior creeds and Geneva Conventions. Instead, even where regular forces play roles, these conflicts often revolve around the strategies and tactics of thuggish paramilitary gangs and local warlords. Some leaders may have some professional training; but the foot soldiers are often people who, for one reason or another, get caught in a fray and learn on the job. Adolescents and children with high-powered weaponry are taking part in growing numbers. In many of these conflicts, savage acts are increasingly committed without anyone taking credit—it may not even be clear which side is responsible. The press releases of the protagonists sound high-minded and self-legitimizing, but the reality at the local level is often about clan rivalries and criminal ventures (e.g., looting, smuggling, or protection rackets).[1]

Thus, irregular warfare has become endemic and vicious around the world. A decade or so ago, terrorism was a rather distinct entry on the spectrum of conflict, with its own unique attributes. Today, it seems increasingly connected with these broader trends in irregular warfare, especially as waged by nonstate actors. As Martin Van Creveld warns:

> In today's world, the main threat to many states, including specifically the U.S., no longer comes from other states. Instead, it comes from small groups and other organizations which are not states. Either we make the necessary changes and face them today, or what is commonly known as the modern world will lose all sense of security and will dwell in perpetual fear.[2]

Meanwhile, for the past several years, terrorism experts have broadly concurred that this phenomenon will persist, if not get worse. General agreement that terrorism may worsen parses into different scenarios. For example, Walter Laqueur warns that religious motivations could lead to "superviolence," with millenarian visions of a coming apocalypse driving "postmodern" terrorism. Fred Iklé worries that increased violence may be used by terrorists to usher in a new totalitarian age based on Leninist ideals. Bruce Hoffman raises the prospect that religiously-motivated terrorists may escalate their violence in order to wreak sufficient havoc to undermine the world political system and replace it with a chaos that is particularly detrimental to the United States—a basically nihilist strategy.[3]

The preponderance of U.S. conventional power may continue to motivate some state and nonstate adversaries to opt for terror as an asymmetric response. Technological advances and underground trafficking may make weapons of mass destruction (WMD—nuclear, chemical, biological weapons) ever easier for terrorists to acquire.[4] Terrorists' shifts toward looser, less hierarchical organizational structures, and their growing use of advanced communications technologies for command, control, and coordination, may further empower small terrorist groups and individuals who want to mount operations from a distance.

There is also agreement about an emergence of two tiers of terror: one characterized by hard-core professionals, the other by amateur cut-outs.[5] The deniability gained by terrorists operating through willing amateurs, coupled with the increasing accessibility of ever more destructive weaponry, has also led many experts to concur that terrorists will be attracted to engaging in more lethal destruction, with increased targeting of information and communications infrastructures.[6]

Some specialists also suggest that "information" will become a key target—both the conduits of information infrastructures and the content of information, particularly the media.[7] While these target-sets may involve little lethal activity, they offer additional theaters of operations for terrorists. Laqueur in particular foresees that, "If the new terrorism directs its energies toward information warfare, its destructive power will be exponentially greater than any it wielded in the past—greater even than it would be with biological and chemical weapons."[8] New planning and scenario-building is needed to help think through how to defend against this form of terrorism.[9]

Such dire predictions have galvanized a variety of responses, which range from urging the creation of international control regimes over the tools of terror (such as WMD materials and advanced encryption capabilities), to the use of coercive diplomacy against state sponsors of terror. Increasingly, the liberal use of military force against terrorists has also been recommended. Caleb Carr in particular espoused this theme, sparking a heated debate.[10] Today, many leading works on combating terrorism blend notions of control mechanisms, international regimes, and the use of force.[11]

Against this background, experts have begun to recognize the growing role of networks—of networked organizational designs and related doctrines, strategies, and technologies—among the practitioners of terrorism. The growth of these networks is related to the spread of advanced information technologies that allow dispersed groups, and individuals, to conspire and coordinate across considerable distances. Recent U.S. efforts to investigate and attack the bin Laden network (named for the central influence of Osama bin Laden) attest to this. The rise of networks is likely to reshape terrorism in the information age, and lead to the adoption of netwar—a kind of information-age conflict that will be waged principally by nonstate actors. Our contribution... is to present the concept of netwar and show how terrorism is being affected by it.

The Advent of Netwar—Analytical Background[12]

The information revolution is altering the nature of conflict across the spectrum. Of the many reasons for this, we call attention to two in particular. First, the information revolution is favoring and strengthening network forms of organization, often giving them an advantage over hierarchical forms. The rise of networks means that power is migrating to nonstate actors, who are able to organize into sprawling multi-organizational networks (especially all-channel networks, in which every node is connected to every other node) more readily than can traditional, hierarchical, state actors. Nonstate-actor networks are thought to be more flexible and responsive than hierarchies in reacting to outside developments, and to be better than hierarchies at using information to improve decisionmaking.[13]

Second, as the information revolution deepens, conflicts will increasingly depend on information and communications matters. More than ever before, conflicts will revolve around "knowledge" and the use of "soft power."[14] Adversaries will emphasize "information operations" and "perception management"—that is, media-oriented measures that aim to attract rather than coerce, and that affect how secure a society, a military, or other actor feels about its knowledge of itself and of its adversaries. Psychological disruption may become as important a goal as physical destruction.

Thus, major transformations are coming in the nature of adversaries, in the type of threats they may pose, and in how conflicts can be waged. Information-age threats are likely to be more diffuse, dispersed, multidimensional, and ambiguous than more traditional threats. Metaphorically, future conflicts may resemble the Oriental game of *Go* more than the Western game of chess. The conflict spectrum will be molded from end to end by these dynamics:

- *Cyberwar*—a concept that refers to information-oriented military warfare—is becoming an important entry at the military end of the spectrum, where the language has normally been about high-intensity conflicts (HICs).
- *Netwar* figures increasingly at the societal end of the spectrum, where the language has normally been about low-intensity conflict (LIC), operations other than war (OOTW), and nonmilitary modes of conflict and crime.[15]

Whereas cyberwar usually pits formal military forces against each other, netwar is more likely to involve nonstate, paramilitary, and irregular forces—as in the case of terrorism. Both concepts are consistent with the views of analysts such as Van Creveld, who believe that a "transformation of war" is under way.[16] Neither concept is just about technology; both refer to comprehensive approaches to conflict—comprehensive in that they mix organizational, doctrinal, strategic, tactical, and technological innovations, for offense and defense.

Definition of Netwar

To be more precise, netwar refers to an emerging mode of conflict and crime at societal levels, involving measures short of traditional war, in which the protagonists use network forms of organization and related doctrines, strategies, and technologies attuned to the information age. These protagonists are likely to consist of dispersed small groups who communicate, coordinate, and conduct their campaigns in an internetted manner, without a precise central command. Thus, information-age netwar differs from modes of conflict and crime in which the protagonists prefer formal, stand-alone, hierarchical organizations, doctrines, and strategies, as in past efforts, for example, to build centralized movements along Marxist lines.

The term is meant to call attention to the prospect that network-based conflict and crime will become major phenomena in the decades ahead. Various actors across the spectrum of conflict and crime are already evolving in this direction. To give a string of examples, netwar is about the Middle East's Hamas more than the Palestine Liberation Organization (PLO), Mexico's Zapatistas more than Cuba's Fidelistas, and the American Christian Patriot movement more than the Ku Klux Klan. It is also about the Asian Triads more than the Sicilian Mafia, and Chicago's Gangsta Disciples more than the Al Capone Gang.

This spectrum includes familiar adversaries who are modifying their structures and strategies to take advantage of networked designs, such as transnational terrorist groups, black-market proliferators of WMD, transnational crime syndicates, fundamentalist and ethno-nationalist movements, intellectual property and high-sea pirates, and smugglers of black-market goods or migrants. Some urban gangs, back-country militias, and militant single-issue groups in the United States are also developing netwar-like attributes. In addition, there is a new generation of radicals and activists who are just beginning to create information-age ideologies, in which identities and loyalties may shift from the nation-state to the transnational level of global civil society. New kinds of actors, such as anarchistic and nihilistic leagues of computer-hacking "cyboteurs," may also partake of netwar.

Many—if not most—netwar actors will be nonstate. Some may be agents of a state, but others may try to turn states into *their* agents. Moreover, a netwar actor may be both subnational and transnational in scope. Odd hybrids and symbioses are likely. Furthermore, some actors (e.g., violent terrorist and criminal organizations) may threaten U.S. and other nations' interests, but other netwar actors (e.g., peaceful social activists) may not. Some may aim at destruction, others at disruption. Again, many variations are possible.

The full spectrum of netwar proponents may thus seem broad and odd at first glance. But there is an underlying pattern that cuts across all variations: the use of network forms of organization, doctrine, strategy, and technology attuned to the information age.

More About Organizational Design

The notion of an organizational structure qualitatively different from traditional hierarchical designs is not recent; for example, in the early 1960s Burns and Stalker referred to the organic form as "a network structure of control, authority, and communication," with "lateral rather than vertical direction of communication." In organic structure,[17]

> omniscience [is] no longer imputed to the head of the concern; knowledge about the technical or commercial nature of the here and now task may be located anywhere in the network; [with] this location becoming the ad hoc centre of control authority and communication.

In the business world, virtual or networked organizations are being heralded as effective alternatives to bureaucracies—as in the case of Eastman Chemical Company and the Shell-Sarnia Plant—because of their inherent flexibility, adaptiveness, and ability to capitalize on the talents of all members of the organization.[18]

What has long been emerging in the business world is now becoming apparent in the organizational structures of netwar actors. In an archetypal netwar, the protagonists are likely to amount to a set of diverse, dispersed "nodes" who share a set of ideas and interests and who are arrayed to act in a fully internetted "all-channel" manner. Networks come in basically three types (or topologies) (see Figure 1):[19]

- The *chain* network, as in a smuggling chain where people, goods, or information move along a line of separated contacts, and where end-to-end communication must travel through the intermediate nodes.
- The *star*, hub, or wheel network, as in a franchise or a cartel structure where a set of actors is tied to a central node or actor, and must go through that node to communicate and coordinate.
- The *all-channel network*, as in a collaborative network of militant small groups where every group is connected to every other.

Each node in the diagrams of Figure 1 may be to an individual, a group, an institution, part of a group or institution, or even a state. The nodes may be large or small, tightly or loosely coupled, and inclusive or exclusive in membership. They may be segmentary or specialized—that is, they may look alike and engage in similar activities, or they may undertake a division of labor based on specialization. The boundaries of the network may be well defined, or blurred and porous in relation to the outside environment. All such variations are possible.

Figure 1

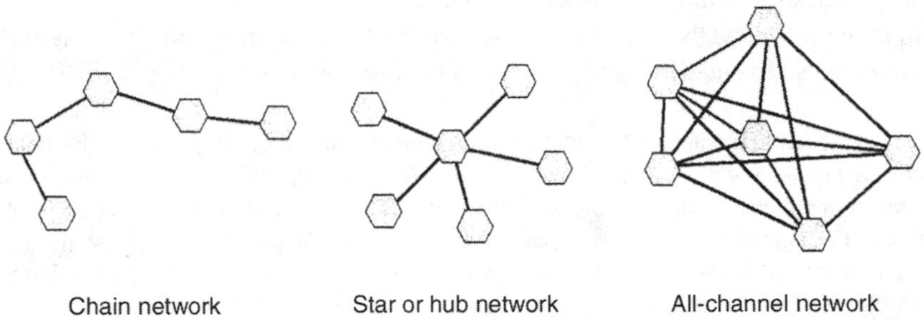

Each type may be suited to different conditions and purposes, and all three may be found among netwar-related adversaries—e.g., the chain in smuggling operations, the star at the core of terrorist and criminal syndicates, and the all-channel type among militant groups that are highly internetted and decentralized. There may also be hybrids. For example, a netwar actor may have an all-channel council at its core, but use stars and chains for tactical operations. There may also be hybrids of network and hierarchical forms of organization, and hierarchies may exist inside particular nodes in a network. Some actors may have a hierarchical organization overall, but use networks for tactical operations; other actors may have an all-channel network design, but use hierarchical teams for tactical operations. Again, many configurations are possible, and it may be difficult for an analyst to discern exactly what type of networking characterizes a particular actor.

Of the three network types, the all-channel has been the most difficult to organize and sustain historically, partly because it may require dense communications. However, it gives the network form the most potential for collaborative undertakings, and it is the type that is gaining strength from the information revolution. Pictorially, an all-channel netwar actor resembles a geodesic "Bucky ball" (named for Buckminster Fuller); it does not resemble a pyramid. The design is flat. Ideally, there is no single, central leadership, command, or headquarters—no precise heart or head that can be targeted. The network as a whole (but not necessarily each node) has little to no hierarchy, and there may be multiple leaders. Decision-making and operations are decentralized, allowing for local initiative and autonomy. Thus the design may sometimes appear acephalous (headless), and at other times polycephalous (Hydra-headed).[20]

The capacity of this design for effective performance over time may depend on the presence of shared principles, interests, and goals—at best, an overarching doctrine or ideology—that spans all nodes and to which the members wholeheartedly subscribe. Such a set of principles, shaped through mutual consultation and consensus-building, can enable them to be "all of one mind," even though they are dispersed and devoted to different tasks. It can provide a central ideational, strategic, and operational coherence that allows for tactical decentralization. It can set boundaries and provide guidelines for decisions and actions so that the members do not have to resort to a hierarchy—"they know what they have to do."[21]

The network design may depend on having an infrastructure for the dense communication of functional information. All nodes are not necessarily in constant communication, which may not make sense for a secretive, conspiratorial actor. But when communication is needed, the network's members must be able to disseminate information promptly and as broadly as desired within the network and to outside audiences.

In many respects, then, the archetypal netwar design corresponds to what earlier analysts called a "segmented, polycentric, ideologically integrated network" (SPIN):[22]

> By segmentary I mean that it is cellular, composed of many different groups.... By polycentric I mean that it has many different leaders or centers of direction.... By networked I mean that the segments and the leaders are integrated into reticulated systems or networks through various structural, personal, and ideological ties. Networks are usually unbounded and expanding.... This acronym [SPIN] helps us picture this organization as a fluid, dynamic, expanding one, spinning out into mainstream society.

Caveats About the Role of Technology

To realize its potential, a fully interconnected network requires a capacity for constant, dense information and communications flows, more so than do other forms of organization (e.g., hierarchies). This capacity is afforded by the latest information and communications technologies—cellular telephones, fax machines, electronic mail (e-mail), World Wide Web (WWW) sites, and computer conferencing. Moreover, netwar agents are poised to benefit from future increases in the speed of communication, dramatic reductions in the costs of communication, increases in bandwidth, vastly expanded connectivity, and integration of communication with computing technologies.[23] Such technologies are highly advantageous for a netwar actor whose constituents are geographically dispersed.

However, caveats are in order. First, the new technologies, however enabling for organizational networking, may not be the only crucial technologies for a netwar actor. Old means of communications such as human couriers, and mixes of old and new systems, may suffice. Second, netwar is not simply a function of the Internet; it does not take place only in cyberspace or the infosphere. Some key battles may occur there, but a war's overall conduct and outcome will normally depend mostly on what happens in the real world. Even in information-age conflicts, what happens in the real world is generally more important than what happens in the virtual worlds of cyberspace or the infosphere.[24] Netwar is not Internet war.

Swarming, and the Blurring of Offense and Defense

This distinctive, often ad-hoc design has unusual strengths, for both offense and defense. On the offense, networks are known for being adaptable, flexible, and versatile vis-à-vis opportunities and challenges. This may be particularly the case where a set of actors can engage in *swarming*. Little analytic attention has been given to swarming, yet it may be a key mode of conflict in the information age. The cutting edge for this possibility is found among netwar protagonists.[25]

Swarming occurs when the dispersed nodes of a network of small (and perhaps some large) forces converge on a target from multiple directions. The overall aim is the *sustainable pulsing* of force or fire. Once in motion, swarm networks must be able to coalesce rapidly and stealthily on a target, then dissever and redisperse, immediately ready to recombine for a new pulse. In other words, information-age attacks may come in "swarms" rather than the more traditional "waves."

In terms of defensive potential, well-constructed networks tend to be redundant and diverse, making them robust and resilient in the face of adversity. Where they have a capacity for interoperability and shun centralized command and control, network designs can be difficult to crack and defeat as a whole. In particular, they may defy counterleadership targeting—attackers can find and confront only portions of the network. Moreover, the deniability built into a network may allow it to simply absorb a number of attacks on distributed nodes, leading the attacker to believe the network has been harmed when, in fact, it remains viable, and is seeking new opportunities for tactical surprise.

The difficulties of dealing with netwar actors deepen when the lines between offense and defense are blurred, or blended. When *blurring* is the case, it may be difficult to distinguish between attacking and defending actions, particularly when an actor goes on the offense in the name of self-defense. The *blending* of offense and defense will often mix the strategic and tactical levels of operations. For example, guerrillas on the defensive strategically may go on the offense tactically; the war of the *mujahideen* in Afghanistan provides a modern example.

The blurring of offense and defense reflects another feature of netwar: it tends to defy and cut across standard boundaries, jurisdictions, and distinctions between state and society, public and private, war and peace, war and crime, civilian and military, police and military, and legal and illegal. A government has difficulty assigning responsibility to a single agency—military, police, or intelligence—to respond.

Thus, the spread of netwar adds to the challenges facing the nation-state in the information age. Nation-state ideals of sovereignty and authority are traditionally linked to a bureaucratic rationality in which issues and problems can be neatly divided, and specific offices can be charged with taking care of specific problems. In netwar, things are rarely so clear. A protagonist is likely to operate in the cracks and gray areas of society, striking where lines of authority crisscross and the operational paradigms of politicians, officials, soldiers, police officers, and related actors get fuzzy and clash.

Networks Versus Hierarchies: Challenges for Counternetwar

Against this background, we are led to a set of three policy-oriented propositions about the information revolution and its implications for netwar and counternetwar.[26]

Hierarchies have a difficult time fighting networks. There are examples across the conflict spectrum. Some of the best are found in the failings of governments to defeat transnational criminal cartels engaged in drug smuggling, as in Colombia. The persistence of religious revivalist movements, as in Algeria, in the face of unremitting state opposition, shows the robustness of the network form. The Zapatista movement in Mexico, with its legions of supporters and sympathizers among local and transnational nongovernmental organizations (NGOs), shows that social netwar can put a democratizing autocracy on the defensive and pressure it to continue adopting reforms.

It takes networks to fight networks. Governments that would defend against netwar may have to adopt organizational designs and strategies like those of their adversaries. This does not mean mirroring the adversary, but rather learning to draw on the same design principles of network forms in the information age. These principles depend to some extent upon technological innovation, but mainly on a willingness to innovate organizationally and doctrinally, and by building new mechanisms for interagency and multijurisdictional cooperation.

Whoever masters the network form first and best will gain major advantages. In these early decades of the information age, adversaries who have adopted networking (be they criminals, terrorists, or peaceful social activists) are enjoying an increase in their power relative to state agencies.

Counternetwar may thus require effective interagency approaches, which by their nature involve networked structures. The challenge will be to blend hierarchies and networks skillfully, while retaining enough core authority to encourage and enforce adherence to networked processes. By creating effective hybrids, governments may better confront the new threats and challenges emerging in the information age, whether generated by terrorists, militias, criminals, or other actors.[27] The U.S. Counterterrorist Center, based at the Central Intelligence Agency (CIA), is a good example of a promising effort to establish a functional interagency network,[28] although its success may depend increasingly on the strength of links with the military services and other institutions that fall outside the realm of the intelligence community.

Middle Eastern Terrorism and Netwar

Terrorism seems to be evolving in the direction of violent netwar. Islamic fundamentalist organizations like Hamas and the bin Laden network consist of groups organized in loosely interconnected, semi-independent cells that have no single commanding hierarchy.[29] Hamas exemplifies the shift away from a hierarchically oriented movement based on a "great leader" (like the PLO and Yasser Arafat).[30]

The netwar concept is consistent with patterns and trends in the Middle East, where the newer and more active terrorist groups appear to be adopting decentralized, flexible network structures. The rise of networked arrangements in terrorist organizations is part of a wider move away from formally organized, state-sponsored groups to privately financed, loose networks of individuals and subgroups that may have strategic guidance but enjoy tactical independence. Related to these shifts is the fact that terrorist groups are taking advantage of information technology to coordinate the activities of dispersed members. Such technology may be employed by terrorists not only to wage information warfare [IW], but also to support their own networked organizations.[31]

While a comprehensive empirical analysis of the relationship between (a) the structure of terrorist organizations and (b) group activity or strength is beyond the scope of this paper,[32] a cursory examination of such a relationship among Middle Eastern groups offers some evidence to support the claim that terrorists are preparing to wage netwar. The Middle East was selected for analysis mainly because terrorist groups based in this region have been active in targeting U.S. government facilities and interests, as in the bombings of the Khobar Towers, and..., the American embassies in Kenya and Tanzania.

Middle Eastern Terrorist Groups: Structure and Actions

Terrorist groups in the Middle East have diverse origins, ideologies, and organizational structures, but can be roughly categorized into traditional and new-generation groups. Traditional groups date back to the late 1960s and early 1970s, and the majority of these were (and some still are) formally or informally linked to the PLO. Typically, they are also relatively bureaucratic and maintain a nationalist or Marxist agenda. In contrast, most new-generation groups arose in the 1980s and 1990s, have more fluid organizational forms, and rely on Islam as a basis for their radical ideology.

The traditional, more-bureaucratic groups have survived to this day partly through support from states such as Syria, Libya, and Iran. The groups retain an ability to train and prepare for terrorist missions; however, their involvement in actual operations has been limited in recent years, partly because of successful counterterrorism campaigns by Israeli and Western agencies. In contrast, the newer and less hierarchical groups, such as Hamas, the Palestinian Islamic Jihad (PIJ), Hizbullah, Algeria's Armed Islamic Group (GIA), the Egyptian Islamic Group (IG), and Osama bin Laden's Arab Afghans, have become the most active organizations in and around the Middle East.

The traditional groups. Traditional terrorist groups in the Middle East include the Abu Nidal Organization (ANO), the Popular Front for the Liberation of Palestine (PFLP), and three PFLP-related splinters—the PFLP-General Command (PFLP-GC), the Palestine Liberation Front (PLF), and the Democratic Front for the Liberation of Palestine (DFLP).

The ANO was an integral part of the PLO until it became independent in 1974. It has a bureaucratic structure composed of various functional committees.[33] The activism it displayed in the 1970s and 1980s has lessened considerably, owing to a lessening of support from state sponsors and to effective counterterrorist campaigns by Israeli and Western intelligence services.[34] The very existence of the organization has recently been put into question, given uncertainty as to the whereabouts and fate of Abu Nidal, the leader of the group.[35]

The PFLP was founded in 1967 by George Habash as a PLO-affiliated organization. It has traditionally embraced a Marxist ideology, and remains an important PLO faction. However, in recent years it has suffered considerable losses from Israeli counterterrorist strikes.[36] The PFLP-General Command split from the PFLP in 1968, and in turn experienced a schism in the mid-1970s. This splinter group, which called itself the PLF, is composed of three subgroups, and has not been involved in high-profile acts since the 1985 hijacking of the Italian cruise ship *Achille Lauro*.[37] The PFLP was subjected to another split in 1969, which resulted in the Democratic Front for the Liberation of Palestine. The DFLP resembles a small army more than a terrorist group—its operatives are organized in battalions, backed by intelligence and special forces.[38] DFLP strikes have become less frequent since the 1970s, and since the late 1980s it has limited its attacks to Israeli targets near borders.[39]

What seems evident here is that this old generation of traditional, hierarchical, bureaucratic groups is on the wane. The reasons are varied, but the point remains—their way of waging terrorism is not likely to make a comeback, and is being superseded by a new way that is more attuned to the organizational, doctrinal, and technological imperatives of the information age.

The most active groups and their organization. The new generation of Middle Eastern groups has been active both in and outside the region in recent years. In Israel and the occupied territories, Hamas, and to a lesser extent the Palestinian Islamic Jihad, have shown their strength over the last four years with a series of suicide bombings that have killed more than one hundred people and injured several more.[40] Exploiting a strong presence in Lebanon, the Shi'ite Hizbullah organization has also staged a number of attacks against Israeli Defense Forces troops and Israeli cities in Galilee.[41]

The al-Gama'a al-Islamiya, or Islamic Group (IG), is the most active Islamic extremist group in Egypt. In November 1997 IG carried out an attack on Hatshepsut's Temple in Luxor, killing 58 tourists and 4 Egyptians. The Group has also claimed responsibility for the bombing of the Egyptian embassy in Islamabad, Pakistan, which left 16 dead and 60 injured.[42] In Algeria, the Armed Islamic Group (GIA) has been behind the most violent, lethal attacks in Algeria's protracted civil war. Approximately 70,000 Algerians have lost their lives since the domestic terrorist campaign began in 1992.[43]

Recently, the loosely organized group of Arab Afghans—radical Islamic fighters from several North African and Middle Eastern countries who forged ties while resisting the Soviet occupation of Afghanistan[44]—has come to the fore as an active terrorist outfit. One of the leaders and founders of the Arab Afghan movement, Osama bin Laden, a Saudi entrepreneur who bases his activities in Afghanistan,[45] is suspected of sending operatives to Yemen to bomb a hotel used by U.S. soldiers on their way to Somalia in 1992, plotting to assassinate President Clinton in the Philippines in 1994 and Egyptian President Hosni Mubarak in 1995, and of having a role in the Riyadh and Khobar blasts in Saudi Arabia that resulted in the deaths of 24 Americans in 1995 and 1996.[46] U.S. officials have pointed to bin Laden as the mastermind behind the U.S. embassy bombings in Kenya and Tanzania, which claimed the lives of more than 260 people, including 12 Americans.[47]

To varying degrees, these groups share the principles of the net-worked organization—relatively flat hierarchies, decentralization and delegation of decisionmaking authority, and loose lateral ties among dispersed groups and individuals.[48] For instance, Hamas is loosely structured, with some elements working openly through mosques and social service institutions to recruit members, raise funds, organize activities, and distribute propaganda. Palestinian security sources indicate that there are ten or more Hamas splinter groups and factions with no centralized operational leadership.[49] The Palestine Islamic Jihad is a series of loosely affiliated factions, rather than a cohesive group.[50] The pro-Iranian Hizbullah acts as an umbrella organization of radical Shiite groups, and in many respects is a hybrid of hierarchical and network arrangements; although the formal structure is highly bureaucratic, interactions among members are volatile and do not follow rigid lines of control.[51] According to the U.S. Department of State, Egypt's Islamic Group is a decentralized organization that operates without a single operational leader,[52] while the GIA is notorious for the lack of centralized authority.[53]

Unlike traditional terrorist organizations, Arab Afghans are part of a complex network of relatively autonomous groups that are financed from private sources forming "a kind of international terrorists' Internet."[54] The most notorious element of the network is Osama bin Laden, who uses his wealth and organizational skills to support and direct a multinational alliance of Islamic extremists. At the heart of this alliance is his own inner core group, known as Al-Qaeda ("The Base"), which sometimes conducts missions on its own, but more often in conjunction with other groups or elements in the alliance. The goal of the alliance is opposition on a global scale to perceived threats to Islam, as indicated by bin Laden's 1996 declaration of a holy war against the United States and the West. In the document, bin Laden specifies that such a holy war will be fought by irregular, light, highly mobile forces using guerrilla tactics.[55]

Even though bin Laden finances Arab Afghan activities and directs some operations, he apparently does not play a direct command and control role over all operatives. Rather, he is a key figure in the coordination and support of several dispersed activities.[56] For instance, bin Laden founded the "World Islamic Front for Jihad Against Jews and Crusaders."[57] And yet most of the groups that participate in this front (including Egypt's Islamic Group) remain independent, although the organizational barriers between them are fluid.[58]

From a netwar perspective, an interesting feature of bin Laden's Arab Afghan movement is its ability to relocate operations swiftly from one geographic area to another in response to changing circumstances and needs. Arab Afghans have participated in operations conducted by Algeria's GIA and Egypt's IG. Reports in 1997 also indicated that Arab Afghans transferred training operations to Somalia, where they joined the Islamic Liberation Party (ILP).[59] The same reports suggest that the Arab Afghan movement has considered sending fighters to Sinkiang Uighur province in western China, to wage a holy war against the Chinese regime.[60] This group's ability to move and act quickly (and, to some extent, to swarm) once opportunities emerge hampers counterterrorist efforts to predict its actions and monitor its activities. The fact that Arab Afghan operatives were able to strike the U.S. embassies in Kenya and Tanzania substantiates the claim that members of this network have the mobility and speed to operate over considerable distances.

Although the organizational arrangements in these groups do not match all the basic features of the network ideal,[61] they stand in contrast to more traditional groups. Another feature that distinguishes the newer generation of terrorist groups is their adoption of information technology.

Middle Eastern Terrorist Groups and the Use of Information Technology

Information technology (IT) is an enabling factor for networked groups; terrorists aiming to wage netwar may adopt it not only as a weapon, but also to help coordinate and support their activities. Before exploring how Middle Eastern terrorist groups have embraced the new technology, we posit three hypotheses that relate the rise of IT to organization for netwar:

- The greater the degree of organizational networking in a terrorist group, the higher the likelihood that IT is used to support the network's decisionmaking.
- Recent advances in IT facilitate networked terrorist organizations because information flows are becoming quicker, cheaper, more secure, and more versatile.
- As terrorist groups learn to use IT for decisionmaking and other organizational purposes, they will be likely to use the same technology as an offensive weapon to destroy or disrupt.

Middle Eastern terrorist groups provide examples of information technology being used for a wide variety of purposes. As discussed below, there is some evidence to support the claim that the most active groups—and therefore the most decentralized groups—have embraced information technology to coordinate activities and disseminate propaganda and ideology.[62] At the same time, the technical assets and know-how gained by terrorist groups as they seek to form into multi-organizational networks can be used for offensive purposes—an Internet connection can be used for both coordination and disruption. The anecdotes provided here are consistent with the rise in the Middle East of what has been termed *techno-terrorism*, or the use by terrorists of satellite communications, e-mail, and the World Wide Web.[63]

Arab Afghans appear to have widely adopted information technology. According to reporters who visited bin Laden's headquarters in a remote mountainous area of Afghanistan, the terrorist financier has computers, communications equipment, and a large number of disks for data storage.[64] Egyptian "Afghan" computer experts are said to have helped devise a communication network that relies on the World Wide Web, e-mail, and electronic bulletin boards so that the extremists can exchange information without running a major risk of being intercepted by counterterrorism officials.[65]

Hamas is another major group that uses the Internet to share operational information. Hamas activists in the United States use chat rooms to plan operations and activities.[66] Operatives use e-mail to coordinate activities across Gaza, the West Bank, and Lebanon. Hamas has realized that information can be passed securely over the Internet because it is next to impossible for counterterrorism intelligence to monitor accurately the flow and content of Internet traffic. Israeli security officials have difficulty in tracing Hamas messages and decoding their content.[67]

During a recent counterterrorist operation, several GIA bases in Italy were uncovered, and each was found to include computers and diskettes with instructions for the construction of bombs.[68] It has been reported that the GIA uses floppy disks and computers to store and process instructions and other information for its members, who are dispersed in Algeria and Europe.[69] Furthermore, the Internet is used as a propaganda tool by Hizbullah, which manages three World Wide Web sites—one for the central press office (at www.hizbollah.org), another to describe its attacks on Israeli targets (at www.moqawama.org), and the last for news and information (at www.almanar. com.lb).[70]

The presence of Middle Eastern terrorist organizations on the Internet is suspected in the case of the Islamic Gateway, a World Wide Web site that contains information on a number of Islamic activist organizations based in the United Kingdom. British Islamic activists use the World Wide Web to broadcast their news and attract funding; they are also turning to the Internet as an organizational and communication tool.[71] While the vast majority of Islamic activist groups represented in the Islamic Gateway are legitimate, one group—the Global Jihad Fund—makes no secret of its militant goals.[72] The appeal of the Islamic Gateway for militant groups may be enhanced by a representative's claim, in an Internet Newsnet article in August 1996, that the Gateway's Internet Service Provider (ISP) can give "CIA-proof" protection against electronic surveillance.[73]

Summary Comment

This review of patterns and trends in the Middle East substantiates our speculations that the new terrorism is evolving in the direction of netwar, along the following lines:[74]

- An increasing number of terrorist groups are adopting networked forms of organization and relying on information technology to support such structures.
- Newer groups (those established in the 1980s and 1990s) are more networked than traditional groups.
- A positive correlation is emerging between the degree of activity of a group and the degree to which it adopts a networked structure.[75]
- Information technology is as likely to be used for organizational support as for offensive warfare.
- The likelihood that young recruits will be familiar with information technology implies that terrorist groups will be increasingly networked and more computer-friendly in the future than they are today.

Terrorist Doctrines—The Rise of a "War Paradigm"

The evolution of terrorism in the direction of netwar will create new difficulties for counterterrorism. The types of challenges, and their severity, will depend on the kinds of doctrines that terrorists develop and employ. Some doctrinal effects will occur at the operational level, as in the relative emphasis placed on disruptive information operations as distinct from destructive combat operations. However, at a deeper level, the direction in which terrorist netwar evolves will depend upon the choices terrorists make as to the overall doctrinal paradigms that shape their goals and strategies.

At least three terrorist paradigms are worth considering: terror as coercive diplomacy, terror as war, and terror as the harbinger of a "new world." These three engage, in varying ways, distinct rationales for terrorism—as a weapon of the weak, as a way to assert identity, and as a way to break through to a new world—discussed earlier in this [selection]. While there has been much debate about the overall success or failure of terrorism,[76] the paradigm under which a terrorist operates may have a great deal to do with the likelihood of success. Coercion, for example, implies distinctive threats or uses of force, whereas norms of "war" often imply maximizing destruction.

The Coercive-Diplomacy Paradigm

The first paradigm is that of coercive diplomacy. From its earliest days, terrorism has often sought to persuade others, by means of symbolic violence, either to do something, stop doing something, or undo what has been done. These are the basic forms of coercive diplomacy,[77] and they appear in terrorism as far back as the Jewish Sicarii Zealots who sought independence from Rome in the first century AD, up through the Palestinians' often violent acts in pursuit of their independence today.

The fact that terrorist coercion includes violent acts does not make it a form of war—the violence is exemplary, designed to encourage what Alexander George calls "forceful persuasion," or "coercive diplomacy as an alternative to war."[78] In this light, terrorism may be viewed as designed to achieve specific goals, and the level of violence is limited, or proportional, to the ends being pursued. Under this paradigm, terrorism was once thought to lack a "demand" for WMD, as such tools would provide means vastly disproportionate to the ends of terror. This view was first elucidated over twenty years ago by Brian Jenkins—though there was some dissent expressed by scholars such as Thomas Schelling—and continued to hold sway until a few years ago.[79]

The War Paradigm

Caleb Carr, surveying the history of the failures of coercive terrorism and the recent trends toward increasing destructiveness and deniability, has elucidated what we call a "war paradigm."[80] This paradigm, which builds on ideas first considered by Jenkins,[81] holds that terrorist acts arise when weaker parties cannot challenge an adversary directly and thus turn to asymmetric methods. A war paradigm implies taking a strategic, campaign-oriented view of violence that makes no specific call for concessions from, or other demands upon, the opponent. Instead, the strategic aim is to inflict damage, in the context of what the terrorists view as an ongoing war. In theory, this paradigm, unlike the coercive diplomacy one, does not seek a proportional relationship between the level of force employed and the aims sought. When the goal is to inflict damage generally, and the terrorist group has no desire or need to claim credit, there is an attenuation of the need for proportionality—the worse the damage, the better. Thus, the use of WMD can be far more easily contemplated than in a frame of reference governed by notions of coercive diplomacy.

A terrorist war paradigm may be undertaken by terrorists acting on their own behalf or in service to a nation-state. In the future, as the information age brings the further empowerment of nonstate and transnational actors, "stateless" versions of the terrorist war paradigm may spread. At the same time, however, states will remain important players in the war paradigm; they may cultivate their own terrorist-style commandos, or seek cut-outs and proxies from among nonstate terrorist groups.

Ambiguity regarding a sponsor's identity may prove a key element of the war paradigm. While the use of proxies provides an insulating layer between a state sponsor and its target, these proxies, if captured, may prove more susceptible to interrogation and investigative techniques designed to winkle out the identity of the sponsor. On the other hand, while home-grown commando-style terrorists may be less forthcoming with information if caught, their own identities, which may be hard to conceal, may provide undeniable evidence of state sponsorship. These risks for states who think about engaging in or supporting terrorism may provide yet more reason for the war paradigm to increasingly become the province of nonstate terrorists—or those with only the most tenuous linkages to particular states.

Exemplars of the war paradigm today are the wealthy Saudi jihadist, Osama bin Laden, and the Arab Afghans that he associates with. As previously mentioned, bin Laden has explicitly called for war-like terrorism against the United States, and especially against U.S. military forces stationed in Saudi Arabia. President Clinton's statement that American retaliation for the U.S. embassy bombings in East Africa represented the first shots in a protracted war on terrorism suggests that the notion of adopting a war paradigm to counter terror has gained currency.

The New-World Paradigm

A third terrorist paradigm aims at achieving the birth of what might be called a "new world." It may be driven by religious mania, a desire for totalitarian control, or an impulse toward ultimate chaos.[82] Aum Shinrikyo would be a recent example. The paradigm harks back to the dynamics of millennialist movements that arose in past epochs of social upheaval, when prophetae attracted adherents from the margins of other social movements and led small groups to pursue salvation by seeking a final, violent cataclysm.[83]

This paradigm is likely to seek the vast disruption of political, social, and economic order. Accomplishing this goal may involve lethal destruction, even a heightened willingness to use WMD. Religious terrorists may desire destruction for its own sake, or for some form of "cleansing." But the ultimate aim is not so much the destruction of society as a rebirth after a period of chaotic disruption.

The Paradigms and Netwar

All three paradigms offer room for netwar. Moreover, all three paradigms allow the rise of "cybotage"—acts of disruption and destruction against information infrastructures by terrorists who learn the skills of cyberterror, as well as by disaffected individuals with technical skills who are drawn into the terrorist milieu. However, we note that terrorist netwar may also be a battle of ideas—and to wage this form of conflict some terrorists may want the Net *up*, not down.

Many experts argue that terrorism is moving toward ever more lethal, destructive acts. Our netwar perspective accepts this, but also holds that some terrorist netwars will stress disruption over destruction. Networked terrorists will no doubt continue to destroy things and kill people, but their principal strategy may move toward the nonlethal end of the spectrum, where command and control nodes and vulnerable information infrastructures provide rich sets of targets.

Indeed, terrorism has long been about "information"—from the fact that trainees for suicide bombings are kept from listening to international media, through the ways that terrorists seek to create disasters that will consume the front pages, to the related debates about countermeasures that would limit freedom of the press, increase public surveillance and intelligence gathering, and heighten security over information and communications systems. Terrorist tactics focus attention on the importance of information and communications for the functioning of democratic institutions; debates about how terrorist threats undermine democratic practices may revolve around freedom of information issues.

While netwar may be waged by terrorist groups operating with any of the three paradigms, the rise of networked groups whose objective is to wage war may be the one most relevant to and dangerous from the standpoint of the military. Indeed, if terrorists perceive themselves as warriors, they may be inclined to target enemy military assets or interests....

[Conclusion] Targeting Terrorists in the Information Age

The transition from hierarchical to networked terrorist groups is likely to be uneven and gradual. The netwar perspective suggests that, for the foreseeable future, various networked forms will emerge, coexisting with and influencing traditional organizations. Such organizational diversity implies the need for a counterterrorism strategy that recognizes the differences among organizational designs and seeks to target the weaknesses associated with each.

Counterleadership strategies or retaliation directed at state sponsors may be effective for groups led by a charismatic leader who enjoys the backing of sympathetic governments, but are likely to fail if used against an organization with multiple, dispersed leaders and private sources of funding. Networked organizations rely on information flows to function, and disruption of the flows cripples their ability to coordinate actions. It is no coincidence, for instance, that while the separation between Hamas political and military branches is well documented, this terrorist group jealously guards information on the connections and degree of coordination between the two.[84]

At the same time, the two-way nature of connectivity for information networks such as the Internet implies that the dangers posed by information warfare are often symmetric—the degree to which a terrorist organization uses information infrastructure for offensive purposes may determine its exposure to similar attacks by countering forces. While it is true that terrorist organizations will often enjoy the benefit of surprise, the IW tactics available to them can also be adopted by counterterrorists.

The key task for counterterrorism, then, is the identification of organizational and technological terrorist networks. Once such structures are identified, it may be possible to insert and disseminate false information, overload systems, misdirect message traffic, preclude access, and engage in other destructive and disruptive activities to hamper and prevent terrorist operations.

John Arquilla is a RAND Corporation consultant and an associate professor of defense analysis at the United States Naval Postgraduate School in Monterey, California.

David Ronfeldt is a senior social scientist at RAND whose research focuses on issues such as information revolution, netwar, and the rise of transnational networks of nongovernmental organizations.

Michele Zanini is a researcher at RAND. These experts are all contributors to the book *Countering the New Terrorism* (1999).

Notes

1. For an illuminating take on irregular warfare that emphasizes the challenges to the Red Cross, see Michael Ignatieff, "Unarmed Warriors," *The New Yorker*, March 24, 1997, pp. 56–71.
2. Martin Van Creveld, "In Wake of Terrorism, Modern Armies Prove to Be Dinosaurs of Defense," *New Perspectives Quarterly*, Vol. 13, No. 4, Fall 1996, p. 58.
3. See Walter Laqueur, "Postmodern Terrorism," *Foreign Affairs*, Vol. 75, No. 5, September/October 1996, pp. 24–36; Fred Iklé, "The Problem of the Next Lenin," *The National Interest*, Vol. 47, Spring 1997, pp. 9–19; Bruce Hoffman, *Responding to Terrorism Across the Technological Spectrum*, RAND, P-7874, 1994; Bruce Hoffman, *Inside Terrorism*, Columbia University Press, New York, 1998; Robert Kaplan, "The Coming Anarchy," *Atlantic Monthly*, February 1994, pp. 44–76.
4. See J. Kenneth Campbell, "Weapon of Mass Destruction Terrorism," Master's thesis, Naval Postgraduate School, Monterey, California, 1996.
5. Bruce Hoffman and Caleb Carr, "Terrorism: Who Is Fighting Whom?" *World Policy Journal*, Vol. 14, No. 1, Spring 1997, pp. 97–104.
6. For instance, Martin Shubik, "Terrorism, Technology, and the Socioeconomics of Death," *Comparative Strategy*, Vol. 16, No. 4, October–December 1997, pp. 399–414; as well as Hoffman, 1998.
7. See Matthew Littleton, "Information Age Terrorism," MA thesis, U.S. Naval Postgraduate School, 1995, and Brigitte Nacos, *Terrorism and the Media*, Columbia University Press, New York, 1994.

8. Laqueur, 1996, p. 35.
9. For more on this issue, see Roger Molander, Andrew Riddile, and Peter Wilson, *Strategic Information Warfare: A New Face of War*, RAND, MR-661-OSD, 1996; Roger Molander, Peter Wilson, David Mussington, and Richard Mesic, *Strategic Information Warfare Rising*, RAND, 1998.
10. Caleb Carr, "Terrorism as Warfare," *World Policy Journal*, Vol. 13, No. 4, Winter 1996–1997, pp. 1–12. This theme was advocated early by Gayle Rivers, *The War Against the Terrorists: How to Fight and Win*, Stein and Day, New York, 1986. For more on the debate, see Hoffman and Carr, 1997.
11. See, for instance, Benjamin Netanyahu, *Winning the War Against Terrorism*, Simon and Schuster, New York, 1996, and John Kerry (Senator), *The New War*, Simon & Schuster, New York, 1997.
12. This analytical background is drawn from John Arquilla and David Ronfeldt, *The Advent of Netwar*, RAND, MR-678-OSD, 1996, and David Ronfeldt, John Arquilla, Graham Fuller, and Melissa Fuller, *The Zapatista "Social Netwar" in Mexico*, RAND, MR-994-A, forthcoming. Also see John Arquilla and David Ronfeldt (eds.), *In Athena's Camp: Preparing for Conflict in the Information Age*, RAND, MR-880-OSD/RC, 1997.
13. For background on this issue, see Charles Heckscher, "Defining the Post-Bureaucratic Type," in Charles Heckscher and Anne Donnelon (eds.), *The Post-Bureaucratic Organization*, Sage, Thousand Oaks, California, 1995, pp. 50–52.
14. The concept of soft power was introduced by Joseph S. Nye in *Bound to Lead: The Changing Nature of American Power*, Basic Books, New York, 1990, and further elaborated in Joseph S. Nye and William A. Owens, "America's Information Edge," *Foreign Affairs*, Vol. 75, No. 2, March/April 1996.
15. For more on information-age conflict, netwar, and cyberwar, see John Arquilla and David Ronfeldt, "Cyberwar is Coming!" *Comparative Strategy*, Vol. 12, No. 2, Summer 1993, pp. 141–165, and Arquilla and Ronfeldt, 1996 and 1997.
16. Martin Van Creveld, *The Transformation of War*, Free Press, New York, 1991.
17. T. Burns and G. M. Stalker, *The Management of Innovation*, Tavistock, London, 1961, p. 121.
18. See, for instance, Jessica Lipnack and Jeffrey Stamps, *The Age of the Network*, Wiley & Sons, New York, 1994, pp. 51–78, and Heckscher, "Defining the Post-Bureaucratic Type," p. 45.
19. Adapted from William M. Evan, "An Organization-Set Model of Interorganizational Relations," in Matthew Tuite, Roger Chisholm, and Michael Radnor (eds.), *Interorganizational Decisionmaking*, Aldine Publishing Company, Chicago, 1972.
20. The structure may also be cellular, although the presence of cells does not necessarily mean a network exists. A hierarchy can also be cellular, as is the case with some subversive organizations. A key difference between cells and nodes is that the former are designed to minimize information flows for security reasons (usually only the head of the cell reports to the leadership), while nodes in principle can easily establish connections with other parts of the network (so that communications and coordination can occur horizontally).
21. The quotation is from a doctrinal statement by Louis Beam about "leaderless resistance," which has strongly influenced right-wing white-power groups in the United States. See *The Seditionist*, Issue 12, February 1992.
22. See Luther P. Gerlach, "Protest Movements and the Construction of Risk," in B. B. Johnson and V. T. Covello (eds.), *The Social and Cultural Construction of Risk*, D. Reidel Publishing Co., Boston, Massachusetts, 1987, p. 115, based on Luther P. Gerlach and Virginia Hine, *People, Power, Change: Movements of Social Transformation*, The Bobbs-Merrill Co., New York, 1970. This SPIN concept, a precursor of the netwar concept, was proposed by Luther Gerlach and Virginia Hine in the 1960s to depict U.S. social movements. It anticipates many points about network forms of organization that are now coming into focus in the analysis not only of social movements but also some terrorist, criminal, ethno-nationalist, and fundamentalist organizations.
23. See Wolf V. Heydenbrand, "New Organizational Forms," *Work and Occupations*, No. 3, Vol. 16, August 1989, pp. 323–357.

24. See Paul Kneisel, "Netwar: The Battle Over Rec.Music.White-Power," *ANTIFA INFOBULLETIN*, Research Supplement, June 12, 1996, unpaginated ASCII text available on the Internet. Kneisel analyzes the largest vote ever taken about the creation of a new Usenet newsgroup—a vote to prevent the creation of a group that was ostensibly about white-power music. He concludes that "The *war* against contemporary fascism will be won in the 'real world' off the net; but *battles* against fascist netwar are fought and won on the Internet." His title is testimony to the spreading usage of the term netwar.
25. Swarm networks are discussed by Kevin Kelly, *Out of Control: The Rise of Neo-Biological Civilization*, A William Patrick Book, Addison-Wesley Publishing Company, New York, 1994. Also see Arquilla and Ronfeldt, 1997.
26. Also see Alexander Berger, "Organizational Innovation and Redesign in the Information Age: The Drug War, Netwar, and Other Low-End Conflict," Master's Thesis, Naval Postgraduate School, Monterey, California, 1998, for additional thinking and analysis about such propositions.
27. For elaboration, see Arquilla and Ronfeldt, 1997, Chapter 19.
28. Vernon Loeb, "Where the CIA Wages Its New World War," *Washington Post*, September 9, 1998. For a broader discussion of interagency cooperation in countering terrorism, see Ashton Carter, John Deutch, and Philip Zelikow, "Catastrophic Terrorism," *Foreign Affairs*, Vol. 77, No. 6, November/December 1998, pp. 80–94.
29. Analogously, right-wing militias and extremist groups in the United States also rely on a doctrine of "leaderless resistance" propounded by Aryan nationalist Louis Beam. See Beam, 1992; and Kenneth Stern, *A Force Upon the Plain: The American Militia Movement and the Politics of Hate*, Simon and Schuster, New York, 1996. Meanwhile, as part of a broader trend toward netwar, transnational criminal organizations (TCOs) have been shifting away from centralized "Dons" to more networked structures. See Phil Williams, "Transnational Criminal Organizations and International Security," *Survival*, Vol. 36, No. 1, Spring 1994, pp. 96–113; and Phil Williams, "The Nature of Drug-Trafficking Networks," *Current History*, April 1998, pp. 154–159. As noted earlier, social activist movements long ago began to evolve "segmented, polycephalous, integrated networks." For a discussion of a social netwar in which human-rights and other peaceful activist groups supported an insurgent group in Mexico, see David Ronfeldt and Armando Martinez, "A Comment on the Zapatista 'Netwar'," in John Arquilla and David Ronfeldt, 1997, pp. 369–391.
30. It is important to differentiate our notions of information-age networking from earlier ideas about terror as consisting of a network in which all nodes revolved around a Soviet core (Claire Sterling, *The Terror Network*, Holt, Rinehart & Winston, New York, 1981). This view has generally been regarded as unsupported by available evidence (see Cindy C. Combs, *Terrorism in the Twenty-First Century*, Prentice-Hall, New York, 1997, pp. 99–119). However, there were a few early studies that did give credit to the possibility of the rise of terror networks that were bound more by loose ties to general strategic goals than by Soviet control (see especially Thomas L. Friedman, "Loose-Linked Network of Terror: Separate Acts, Ideological Bonds," *Terrorism*, Vol. 8, No. 1, Winter 1985, pp. 36–49).
31. For good general background, see Michael Whine, "Islamist Organisations on the Internet," draft circulated on the Internet, April 1998 (*www.ict.org.il/articles*).
32. We assume that group activity is a proxy for group strength. Group activity can be measured more easily than group strength, and is expected to be significantly correlated with strength. The relationship may not be perfect, but it is deemed to be sufficiently strong for our purposes.
33. Office of the Coordinator for Counterterrorism, *Patterns of Global Terrorism*, 1996, U.S. Department of State, Publication 10433, April 1997.
34. Loeb, 1998; and John Murray and Richard H. Ward (eds.), *Extremist Groups*, Office of International Criminal Justice, University of Illinois, Chicago, 1996.
35. Youssef M. Ibrahim, "Egyptians Hold Terrorist Chief, Official Asserts," *New York Times*, August 26, 1998.
36. Murray and Ward, 1996.
37. *Patterns of Global Terrorism*, 1996, and Murray and Ward, 1996.
38. Murray and Ward, 1996.

39. *Patterns of Global Terrorism*, 1995, 1996, 1997.
40. For instance, in 1997 Hamas operatives set off three suicide bombs in crowded public places in Tel Aviv and Jerusalem. On March 21, a Hamas satchel bomb exploded at a Tel Aviv café, killing three persons and injuring 48; on July 30, two Hamas suicide bombers blew themselves up in a Jerusalem market, killing 16 persons and wounding 178; on September 4, three suicide bombers attacked a Jerusalem pedestrian mall, killing at least five persons (in addition to the suicide bombers), and injuring at least 181. The Palestinian Islamic Jihad has claimed responsibility (along with Hamas) for a bomb that killed 20 and injured 75 others in March 1996, and in 1995 it carried out five bombings that killed 29 persons and wounded 107. See *Patterns of Global Terrorism*, 1995, 1996, 1997.
41. See "Hizbullah," Israeli Foreign Ministry, April 11, 1996. Available on the Internet at *http://www.israel-mfa.gov.il*.
42. See *Patterns of Global Terrorism*, 1995, 1996, 1997.
43. *Patterns of Global Terrorism*, 1997.
44. "Arab Afghans Said to Launch Worldwide Terrorist War," *Paris al-Watan al-'Arabi*, FBIS-TOT-96-010-L, December 1, 1995, pp. 22–24.
45. William Gertz, "Saudi Financier Tied to Attacks," *Washington Times*, October 23, 1996.
46. Tim Weiner, "U.S. Sees bin Laden as Ringleader of Terrorist Network," *New York Times*, August 21, 1998; M. J. Zuckerman, "Bin Laden Indicted for Bid to Kill Clinton," *USA Today*, August 26, 1998.
47. Pamela Constable, "Bin Laden 'Is Our Guest, So We Must Protect Him'," *Washington Post*, August 21, 1998.
48. We distinguish between deliberate and factional decentralization. Factional decentralization—prevalent in older groups—occurs when subgroups separate themselves from the central leadership because of differences in tactics or approach. Deliberate or operational decentralization is what distinguishes netwar agents from others, since delegation of authority in this case occurs because of the distinct advantages this organizational arrangement brings, and not because of lack of consensus. We expect both influences on decentralization to continue, but newer groups will tend to decentralize authority even in the absence of political disagreements.
49. "Gaza Strip, West Bank: Dahlan on Relations with Israel, Terrorism," *Tel Aviv Yedi'ot Aharonot*, FBIS-TOT-97-022-L, February 28, 1997, p. 18.
50. The leader of the PIJ's most powerful faction, Fathi Shaqaqi, was assassinated in October 1995 in Malta, allegedly by the Israeli Mossad. Shaqaqi's killing followed the assassination of Hani Abed, another PIJ leader killed in 1994 in Gaza. Reports that the group has been considerably weakened as a result of Israeli counterleadership operations are balanced by the strength demonstrated by the PIJ in its recent terrorist activity. See "Islamic Group Vows Revenge for Slaying of Its Leader," *New York Times*, October 30, 1995, p. 9.
51. Magnus Ranstorp, "Hizbullah's Command Leadership: Its Structure, Decision-Making and Relationship with Iranian Clergy and Institutions," *Terrorism and Political Violence*, Vol. 6, No. 3, Autumn 1994, p. 304.
52. *Patterns of Global Terrorism*, 1996.
53. "Algeria: Infighting Among Proliferating 'Wings' of Armed Groups," *London al-Sharq al-Aswat*, FBIS-TOT-97-021-L, February 24, 1997, p. 4.
54. David B. Ottaway, "US Considers Slugging It Out With International Terrorism," *Washington Post*, October 17, 1996, p. 25.
55. "Saudi Arabia: Bin-Laden Calls for 'Guerrilla Warfare' Against US Forces," *Beirut Al-Diyar*, FBIS-NES-96-180, September 12, 1996.
56. It is important to avoid equating the bin Laden network solely with bin Laden. He represents a key node in the Arab Afghan terror network, but there should be no illusions about the likely effect on the network of actions taken to neutralize him. The network conducts many operations without his involvement, leadership, or financing—and will continue to be able to do so should he be killed or captured.
57. "Militants Say There Will Be More Attacks Against U.S.," *European Stars and Stripes*, August 20, 1998.

58. For instance, there have been reports of a recent inflow of Arab Afghans into Egypt's Islamic Group to reinforce the latter's operations. See Murray and Ward, 1996, and "The CIA on Bin Laden," *Foreign Report*, No. 2510, August 27, 1998, pp. 2–3.
59. This move was also influenced by the Taliban's decision to curb Arab Afghan activities in the territory under its control as a result of U.S. pressure. See "Arab Afghans Reportedly Transfer Operations to Somalia," *Cairo al-Arabi*, FBIS-TOT-97-073, March 10, 1997, p. 1.
60. "Afghanistan, China: Report on Bin-Laden Possibly Moving to China," *Paris al-Watan al-'Arabi*, FBIS-NES-97-102, May 23, 1997, pp. 19–20.
61. While it is possible to discern a general trend toward an organizational structure that displays several features of a network, we expect to observe substantial differences (and many hierarchy/network hybrids) in how organizations make their specific design choices. Different network designs depend on contingent factors, such as personalities, organizational history, operational requirements, and other influences such as state sponsorship and ideology.
62. Assessing the strength of the relationship between organizational structure and use of information technology is difficult to establish. Alternative explanations may exist as to why newer groups would embrace information technology, such as age of the group (one could speculate that newer terrorist groups have on average younger members, who are more familiar with computers), or the amount of funding (a richer group could afford more electronic gadgetry). While it is empirically impossible to refute these points, much in organization theory supports our hypothesis that there is a direct relationship between a higher need for information technology and the use of network structures.
63. "Saudi Arabia: French Analysis of Islamic Threat," *Paris al-Watan al-'Arabi*, FBIS-NES- 97-082, April 11, 1997, pp. 4–8.
64. "Afghanistan, Saudi Arabia: Editor's Journey to Meet Bin-Laden Described," *London al-Quds al-'Arabi*, FBIS-TOT-97-003-L, November 27, 1996, p. 4.
65. "Arab Afghans Said to Launch Worldwide Terrorist War," 1995.
66. "Israel: U.S. Hamas Activists Use Internet to Send Attack Threats," *Tel Aviv IDF Radio*, FBIS-TOT-97-001-L, 0500 GMT October 13, 1996.
67. "Israel: Hamas Using Internet to Relay Operational Messages," *Tel Aviv Ha'aretz*, FBIS-TOT-98-034, February 3, 1998, p. 1.
68. "Italy: Security Alters Following Algerian Extremists' Arrests," *Milan Il Giornale*, FBIS-TOT-97-002-L, November 12, 1996, p. 10.
69. "Italy, Vatican City: Daily Claims GIA 'Strategist' Based in Milan," *Milan Corriere della Sera*, FBIS-TOT-97-004-L, December 5, 1996, p. 9.
70. "Hizbullah TV Summary 18 February 1998," *Al-Manar Television World Wide Webcast*, FBIS-NES-98-050, February 19, 1998. Also see "Developments in Mideast Media: January–May 1998," Foreign Broadcast Information Service (FBIS), May 11, 1998.
71. "Islamists on Internet," FBIS Foreign Media Note-065EP96, September 9, 1996.
72. "Islamic Activism Online," FBIS Foreign Media Note-02JAN97, January 3, 1997.
73. The Muslim Parliament has recently added an Internet Relay Chat (IRC) link and a "Muslims only" List-Serve (automatic e-mail delivery service). See "Islamic Activism Online," FBIS Foreign Media Note-02JAN97, January 3, 1997.
74. Similar propositions may apply to varieties of netwar other than the new terrorism.
75. We make a qualification here. There appears to be a significant positive association between the degree to which a group is active and the degree to which a group is decentralized and networked. But we cannot be confident about the causality of this relationship or its direction (i.e., whether activity and strength affect networking, or vice-versa). A host of confounding factors may affect both the way groups decide to organize and their relative success at operations. For instance, the age of a group may be an important predictor of a group's success—newer groups are likely to be more popular; popular groups are more likely to enlist new operatives; and groups that have a large number of operatives are likely to be more active, regardless of organizational structure. Another important caveat is related to the fact that it is difficult to rank groups precisely in terms of the degree to which they are networked, because no terrorist organization is thought to represent either a hierarchical or network ideal-type. While the conceptual division between newer-generation and traditional groups is appropriate for our scope

here, an analytical "degree of networking" scale would have to be devised for more empirical research.

76. See, for instance, William Gutteridge (ed.), *Contemporary Terrorism*, Facts on File, Oxford, England, 1986; Hoffman and Carr, 1997; and Combs, 1997.
77. See Alexander George and William Simons, *The Limits of Coercive Diplomacy*, Westview Press, Boulder, 1994.
78. Alexander George, *Forceful Persuasion: Coercive Diplomacy as an Alternative to War*, United States Institute of Peace Press, Washington, DC, 1991.
79. Brian Jenkins, *The Potential for Nuclear Terrorism*, RAND, P-5876, 1977; Thomas Schelling, "Thinking about Nuclear Terrorism," *International Security*, Vol. 6, No. 4, Spring 1982, pp. 68–75; and Patrick Garrity and Steven Maaranen, *Nuclear Weapons in a Changing World*, Plenum Press, New York, 1992.
80. Carr, 1996.
81. Brian Jenkins, *International Terrorism: A New Kind of Warfare*, RAND, P-5261, 1974.
82. For a discussion of these motives, see Laqueur, 1996; Iklé, 1997; and Hoffman, 1998, respectively.
83. See, for instance, Michael Barkun, *Disaster and the Millennium*, Yale University Press, New Haven, 1974; and Norman Cohn, *The Pursuit of the Millennium: Revolutionary Messianism in Medieval and Reformation Europe and Its Bearing on Modern Totalitarian Movements*, Harper Torch Books, New York, 1961.
84. Bluma Zuckerbrot-Finkelstein, "A Guide to Hamas," *Internet Jewish Post*, available at *http://www.jewishpost.com/jewishpost/jp0203/jpn0303.htm*.

Rohan Gunaratna, 2004

The Post-Madrid Face of Al Qaeda

For two-and-a-half years after the September 11, 2001, attacks on the United States' most iconic landmarks, Al Qaeda and its associated groups struck Western targets only in the global South, in places such as Bali, Casablanca, Saudi Arabia, Pakistan, Turkey, Chechnya, and Tunisia. Despite the September 11 attacks and the continuing threat, Europe remained an active center for terrorist support activity—propaganda, recruitment, fundraising, and procurement. As support cells were enmeshed in the socioeconomic, cultural, and political fabric of migrant and diaspora Muslims, European law enforcement, security, and intelligence services targeted only the operational cells that appeared on their radar screen. It was considered politically incorrect to revise the legislative framework to target several hundred terrorist support cells active on European soil. Some Europeans even believed that Al Qaeda had spared the continent because of its policy tolerating terrorist support infrastructure.

Although successive attacks against Jewish and British targets in Istanbul in November 2003 demonstrated Al Qaeda's intentions, capabilities, and opportunities for attack on the continent, European law enforcement, intelligence, and security services did not take the threat seriously. Although the Turkish case clearly demonstrated that terrorists planning to strike could survive undetected for years, there was neither a proper appreciation of the threat nor an appreciable effort to increase the quality of intelligence by penetrating the politicized and radicalized segments of Europe's diaspora and migrant communities. Even the fact that three of the four September 11 suicide pilots were recruited from the heart of Europe did not generate the same sense of urgency in Europe that prevailed in the United States. Without becoming a victim of a major terrorist attack on its soil, European leaders refused to do what was necessary to protect Europe. Like many countries around the world, European countries unfortunately needed their own wake-up call.

Al Qaeda as an organization has learned and adapted its structure and strategy to combat measures implemented to destroy it after the September 11 attacks. First, having lost their own state-of-the-art training and operational infrastructure in Afghanistan, Al Qaeda members had to rely on the organization's associated groups for survival. As the most-hunted terrorist group in history, Al Qaeda began to operate through these associated groups. Although the threat shifted, European security and intelligence services have continued to focus on Al Qaeda. Furthermore, the terrorist cells in Europe knew the risk of being monitored by European security and intelligence agencies. To evade technical methods of monitoring, they developed greater discipline and operational security.

As human sources were sparse within the security services—the guardians of Europe—there was no way of knowing what was happening in radical pockets within the diaspora and migrant communities. Preemptive arrests were an anathema in Europe. The only methodology available for detecting terrorist planning and preparation was investment in human source penetration, a capability that could not be developed in the short term. The United States' unilateral invasion of Iraq, the adaptation of the terrorist network in Europe, and the unwillingness of Europeans to change their way of life to deal with terrorists steadfastly escalated the threat to, and increased the vulnerability of, Europe to terrorist attack. The March 11, 2004, Al Qaeda attacks in Madrid clearly revealed Europe's false sense of security and reaffirmed that the West remains the primary target of Al Qaeda and its associated groups.

Al Qaeda since September 11

Three overarching developments mark the post-September 11 attacks trajectory of Al Qaeda and its associated groups, helping to explain the status of the terrorist threat today. First, Al Qaeda, with Osama bin Laden as its leader, has evolved into a movement of two dozen groups. In its founding charter authored by Palestinian-Jordanian Abdullah Azzam in 1988, Al Qaeda was to play the role of a pioneering vanguard of the Islamic movements. Every attack by Al Qaeda, including the group's watershed 2001 attacks on the World Trade Center and the Pentagon, was intended to inspire and instigate its associated groups to take the fight against both near enemies (apostate regimes and rulers) and distant enemies (infidels) of Islam.

By ideologically inciting local and regional Islamist groups to fight not only corrupt Muslim regimes and false Muslim rulers such as those in Algeria, Egypt, Jordan, Saudi Arabia, Morocco, Kuwait, Indonesia, and Pakistan but also those governments' patrons, the United States and its allies, Al Qaeda has achieved its goal. Al Qaeda itself has not been responsible for the bulk of terrorist attacks since September 11, 2001. Rather, they have been carried out by its associated groups with origins in the Middle East, East Africa, Asia, and the Caucuses, such as the Al Zarkawi group, Al Ansar Al Islami, Al Ansar Mujahidin, Jemmah Islamiyah, Salafi Jehadiya, the Salafi Group for Call and Combat, and the Abu Sayyaf Group. Even as the international intelligence community continues to focus on Al Qaeda, the threat has shifted to Al Qaeda's associated groups.

Since the September 11 attacks, Al Qaeda's strength shrank from about 4,000 members to a few hundred members, and nearly 80 percent of Al Qaeda's operational leadership and membership in 102 countries has been killed or captured. Al Qaeda adapted, however, instilling its mission and vision in associated groups and transferring its capabilities to them. The U.S. focus on Iraq, Al Qaeda, and eliminating the Al Qaeda leadership limited the ability for U.S. officials to understand and respond better to the changing threat.

Second, despite all efforts and resources applied to the U.S.-led war on terrorism, the terrorist threat has escalated several-fold since September 11, 2001. Although Al Qaeda itself has conducted an average of only one terrorist attack a year since that time, four times that number, or an average of one attack every three months, has been mounted by its associated groups. The drastic increase in the terrorist threat has been a result of Al Qaeda's transformation from a group into a movement. Al Qaeda has demonstrated its ability to coordinate operations despite the loss of its traditional sanctuary, the death or capture of leaders and members, the seizure of resources, and the disruption to the network. During the past two-and-a-half years, law enforcement authorities worldwide have detected, disrupted, or deterred more than 100 terrorist attacks in the planning, preparation, and execution phases. In the United States alone, the government has disrupted more than 40 attacks.

Despite enhanced law enforcement and detection capabilities in the worldwide hunt for members and supporters of Al Qaeda, the incidents of terrorism has increased. Although the ability of terrorist groups to mount attacks, especially against well-defended facilities or hard targets such as diplomatic missions, military bases, and other government targets, has declined, terrorists remain just as intent to attack. The terrorist threat has instead shifted from hard targets to soft ones such as commercial infrastructure and population centers, making mass fatalities and casualties inevitable. Such vulnerable targets are too numerous to protect. Considering the sustained terrorist drive to attack, the West is not likely to stop suffering periodic terrorist attacks any time soon.

Third, Al Qaeda has adapted its organization significantly during the past two-and-a-half years, increasing the terrorist threat worldwide. Although the heightened security environment has forced some terrorist cells to abort operations, others have merely postponed their operations so that the threat has been delayed rather than defeated. Al Qaeda believes it can, and has shown the ability to, mount operations even in the now-heightened security environment. According to a Central Intelligence Agency debriefing of the mastermind of the September 11 attacks, Khalid Sheikh Mohammed (alias Mokhtar, "The Brain"), Al Qaeda was planning an operation to attack London's Heathrow airport, even in the current security environment. As the coordinated simultaneous attacks in Turkey and Madrid demonstrated, Al Qaeda and its associated groups will continue to mount operations amid government security measures and countermeasures, even in Western countries.

The Reformulated Threat

Immediately after the September 11 attacks, arrests in the United Kingdom, France, Germany, Spain, the Netherlands, and Italy, among other countries, damaged Al Qaeda cells in Europe. Nevertheless, European Islamists that currently subscribe to Al Qaeda's ideology have learned rapidly from the past mistakes of Al Qaeda and its associated cells. Current dedicated operational cells of Al Qaeda and its associated groups are now familiar with and can easily circumvent governmental measures, making the cells difficult to detect, particularly using technical methods such as phone monitoring.

U.S. and European counterterrorist strategies differ markedly. After suffering the greatest terrorist attack in world history, Americans changed their strategy of fighting terrorism from a reactive to a proactive one. Prior to September 11, 2001, the Federal Bureau of Investigation waited for a lead to start an investigation. Highly trained terrorist operatives left no leads or traces. After September 11, 2001, it became a matter of survival to target cells at home proactively and strike them overseas preemptively. One way of understanding this shift is to think of it as a shift from fishing to hunting. When fishing, a fisherman waits until fish attacks the bait; a hunter, conversely, requires initiative and creativity to target its prey proactively. Even after the September 11 attacks, however, European countries continued to behave like fishermen.

One particular flaw of the European counterterrorism approach that might have increased Europe's vulnerability to attack has been its tendency to target operational (attack/combat) cells and overlook support cells that disseminate propaganda, recruit members, procure supplies, maintain transport, forge false and adapted identities, facilitate travel, and organize safe houses. Operating through front, cover, and sympathetic organizations, Al Qaeda and its associate groups established charities, human rights groups, humanitarian organizations, community centers, and religious associations to raise funds and recruit youth. Traditionally, financial support generated and members recruited in Europe, the United States, Canada, Australia, and New Zealand have gone to terrorist groups active in Chechnya, Algeria, Yemen, Kashmir, Afghanistan, and the Philippines. As Al Qaeda preferred operatives with Western passports, Muslim converts and those from the European cradle were treated equally, warmly received, ideologically as well as physically trained, and dispatched back to the West. Those introduced back to the migrant and diaspora communities were in no hurry to commence operations. Although they reintegrated back into their Western communities, they maintained contact with their comrades, trainers, and handlers. Taking advantage of freedoms enshrined in the liberal democracies of the West, such as the freedom of movement, association, and dissent, Al Qaeda and its associated groups slowly and steadily built a robust network of members, collaborators, supporters, and sympathizers in the West.

Host enforcement and intelligence services tolerated these support cells in the United States until September 11, 2001, and in Europe until March 11, 2004, because those support activities seemed to pose no immediate and direct threat to host countries. When regimes in the global South asked Western governments to detain or deport some of the terrorist ideologues or fundraisers, they were told that Western criminal justice and prison systems were incompatible with Third World standards. The governments of the global South essentially were told that Western governments did not find these support networks all that great a threat. To evade the issue, some governments such as those of Canada and the United States spoke of human rights while others such as Switzerland and Germany spoke of political asylum throughout the 1980s and 1990s. Some Europeans opposed targeting charities and other Islamic institutions in Europe used by terrorists for fundraising or as cover for reasons of political correctness. They turned a blind eye to the terrorist infiltration of Muslim migrant and diaspora communities, permitting terrorists and extremists to take control of Muslim institutions including mosques, schools, and charities.

Under the cover of human rights, humanitarian, socioeconomic, cultural, political, educational, welfare, and religious organizations, terrorist ideologues and operatives built state-of-the-art support networks that raised millions of U.S. dollars throughout the European continent and in the United States. Western neglect created the conditions for terrorist support cells to grow in size and strength within the socioeconomic, political, and religious fabric of Muslim communities. Even if European law enforcement had made good faith efforts to detect and eliminate terrorist contingencies, disabling them became politically, legislatively, and operationally difficult. With bin Laden's constant call to jihad as the duty of every good Muslim after September 11, 2001, these support cells began to mutate into operational cells.

For example, the north London cell that authorities discovered in January 2003 that had manufactured ricin was originally an Algerian support cell. Throughout Europe, Algerian terrorist support cells had generated propaganda, funds, and supplies for their campaign to replace the military government in Algeria with an Islamic state. Except for the French, who suffered from Algerian terrorism, the rest of Europe was soft on the Algerian support cells until recently. Historically, terrorist groups in the Middle East, Asia, and Africa have looked toward Europe for support and sanctuary. For example, Al Ansar Al Islami and the Abu Musab Al Zrakawi group, the most active groups in Iraq, have established cells in Europe to generate support as well as to recruit fighters, including suicide terrorists.

The Effects of Iraq and Afghanistan

As the conflict in Iraq worsens, Muslims living in Europe will grieve. Muslim anger and resolve will create the conditions for terrorist support and operational cells to spawn and function more easily in Europe. Just as European Muslims had gone to train and fight in Afghanistan, Bosnia, and Chechnya, while a small percentage had participated directly in terrorist operations back in Europe, the continuing conditions bred by European laxity in counterterrorism will tacitly draw terrorists from the new breeding grounds in Iraq to Europe.

For the foreseeable future, Iraq and Afghanistan will remain the land of jihad. After the training infrastructure was destroyed by Operation Enduring Freedom in the fall of 2001, Al Qaeda decentralized its operations. In the Middle East, Asia, Africa, and the Caucuses, Al Qaeda began to work with the associated groups it financed, armed, trained, and indoctrinated. After Al Qaeda lost its Afghanistan base, it desperately needed another land of jihad in which to train and fight. Iraq has provided such a place. The United States' unilateral actions in Iraq unified and enraged the wrath of the Muslim community. The very imams in Egypt that condemned the September 11 attacks as un-Islamic are now encouraging Muslim youth to go to Iraq and fight the invaders.

A terrorist group can sustain itself and conduct operations on the support it is able to generate. As a result of the highly successful U.S.-led global coalition against terrorism, several terrorist groups have suffered, especially Al Qaeda. Nonetheless, the U.S. invasion of Iraq increased the worldwide threat of terrorism many times over. Even moderate Muslims are angry about the invasion and postinvasion developments. This animosity toward the United States makes it easier for terrorist and extremist groups to continue to generate recruits and support from the suffering and grieving Muslims of Iraq. Because of perceived injustices attributed to the West in general, particularly in Pakistan and Iraq, there will be significant support for the new generation of mujahideen in Iraq. Groups that were dying are making a comeback, and several new groups have emerged in Iraq, Indonesia, Pakistan, and even in Europe.

Considering the significance Al Qaeda and its associated groups attach to Iraq, one can expect them to continue to focus on Iraq's political developments in coming years. Before Saudi security forces killed Al Qaeda ideological mastermind Yousef Al Aiyyeri in early June 2003, he defined the stakes for the war, or the insurgency against the U.S. occupation, in Iraq. Previously, he had been a bodyguard to bin Laden, an instructor in the Al Farooq training camp in Afghanistan, and the webmaster of Al Qaeda's main Web site. He stated that the establishment of democracy in Iraq would be the death knell for Islam. According to him, democracy is man-made law, and Muslims should only respect Islamic law, or God's law. Gradually, Muslims from the Levant and the Persian Gulf region, from North Africa and the European cradle, and converted Muslims will gravitate to Iraq. It is seen as a land of symbolic value. Iraq is likely to provide the same experience to radicalized Muslims in this decade as Afghanistan and Bosnia did in the 1980s and 1990s.

Even more than those of the United States, Europe's long-term strategic interests demand that it play an active role in Iraq, given that country's location on the doorstep of Europe. Although the U.S.-led invasion of Iraq was a fatal mistake, withdrawing from Iraq would be an even greater one. U.S. withdrawal from Iraq and turning responsibility over to the United Nations would only strengthen terrorist capabilities in general and Al Qaeda more specifically. Europe must remain engaged in Iraq because an Iraq in conflict holds adverse implications for European security. It is only a matter of time until Al Ansar Al Islami, founded by Mullah Krekar, now living in Norway, and other groups active in Iraq will expand their theater of operations into Europe. Failure to stabilize Iraq will increase the threat of terrorism to Europe and beyond.

What Now?

With the terrorist threat moving beyond the star of Al Qaeda into the galaxy of violent Islamist groups, the international security and intelligence communities will have to expand the range of their focus. With Al Qaeda's strength now estimated by the U.S. intelligence community to be less than 1,000 members, better understanding and targeting of its associated and equally committed and skilled groups is necessary. As the target moves, intelligence must evolve to reflect the new reality. If the agencies of Western governments had focused only on Al Qaeda, they never would have detected the Salafi Group for Call and Combat in the United States, Al Tawhid in Germany, Takfir Wal Hijra in the United Kingdom, or the Moroccan Islamist terrorists in Spain.

Overemphasis on Al Qaeda will be detrimental to Western governments. Accomplishing a transformation in Western enforcement and intelligence services from a single focus on Al Qaeda to a broader focus will require specialists on various terrorist groups. Traditionally, most governments provide cross training and produce generalists to work both on a policy and a strategic level. They had no incentive to specialize on a group or country. With the dispersal of the terrorist threat and sophistication of these groups, producing specialists who can work at tactical and operational levels is essential.

There are early indications that the terrorist threat is further shifting from small groups to motivated and resourceful individuals. To emphasize the evolving nature of the threat beyond various groups to individuals, for example, Al Musab Al Zarkawi, the Palestinian-Jordanian who is responsible for coordinating the largest number of suicide and non-suicide attacks in Iraq, works with a dozen groups, serving to amplify the threat. Although he trained with Al Qaeda in the Herat camp and even lost a leg in combat, he works not only with Al Qaeda but also with Al Ansar Al Islami in Iraq and Al Tawhid in Europe. Thus, as much as groups are important, tracking individuals of concern is becoming more important as well. In the post-Iraq war environment, violent Islamists will use any group to advance their objectives or the greater objective of jihad.

Unless Western law enforcement, security, and intelligence services develop the ability to penetrate Islamist organizations with human sources, Al Qaeda and its associated cells will remain invisible to them. As Islamist terrorist groups develop in sophistication, leads in the planning and preparation phases of attack operations will become scarcer. Thus, counterterrorism operations must not be dependent only on intelligence to attack operational cells but also develop intelligence-led operations to target support and operational cells proactively. The West, and Europe in particular, has recognized that it is not immune from the terrorist threat. Unless European authorities and agencies develop a proactive mindset to target both support and operational cells, Al Qaeda will survive in Europe and another attack will be inevitable. Furthermore, Al Qaeda could once again use Europe as a staging area from which to infiltrate the United States and conduct another terrorist attack.

Today, the terrorist threat has moved beyond the individual and the group to an ideology. Even if bin Laden and his principal strategist Ayman Al Zawahiri are killed or captured, the terrorist threat will not diminish. Even if Al Qaeda is completely destroyed, the terrorist threat will continue. In many ways, Al Qaeda has completed its mission of being the vanguard or spearhead of Islamic movements, envisioned by Azzam. Before it dies, it will have inspired a generation of existing groups and shown the way for an emerging generation of them.

It is therefore crucial to develop a truly multipronged strategy to fight the multidimensional character of violent Islamists. Instead of only tactically targeting identifiable terrorist cells, it is essential to prevent the creation of terrorists strategically. The bloc of nations with staying power in the West must work with the Muslim countries—their governments and nongovernmental organizations—to target the ideology that is producing the terrorist. It is necessary to send the message that Al Qaeda and its associated groups are not Koranic organizations and that they are presenting a corrupt version of Islam by misinterpreting and misrepresenting the Koran and other texts. Only by countering the belief that it is the duty of every good Muslim to wage jihad can the extant and emerging terrorist threat be reduced. As Al Qaeda is constantly adapting to the changing security environment and morphing its structure, the key to defeating Al Qaeda and reducing the terrorist threat is to develop a multi-agency, multijuristic, and multinational strategy to combat this ideology.

Rohan Gunaratna is head of the International Centre for Political Violence and Terrorism Research at the Institute of Defence and Strategic Studies in Singapore.

Matthew Levitt, 2004

Untangling the Terror Web: Identifying and Counteracting the Phenomenon of Crossover Between Terrorist Groups

Counterterrorism should be seen not as an effort to rid the world of terrorism, but as an ongoing struggle to constrict the operating environment in which terrorists raise funds, procure documents, engage in support activities, and conduct attacks. One of the most effective ways to constrict the operating environment and crack down on terrorist financing is to target the network of interlocking logistical support groups. Many of these groups are not particular to a single terrorist organization. In fact, militant Islamist organizations from the al Qaeda to Hamas intertact and support one another in the international matrix of logistical, financial, and sometimes operational terrorist activity. This matrix of relationships is what makes the threat of international terrorism so dangerous. Prosecuting the war on terror, whether on the battlefield or in the courtroom, demands greater attention to the web of interaction among these various groups and state sponsors. Indeed, as this paper suggests, concerted action against terrorist financing is one of the best ways to advance not only the war on terror, but other national security priorities such as pursuing the Roadmap to Israeli-Palestinian peace, and the stabilization of Iraq.

Pundits and politicians alike tend to think of the war on terror against al Qaeda as a completely disparate phenomenon from the battle against other terrorist groups. This is, in part, a logical supposition as groups like Hamas and Hezbollah do not belong to the more tightly knit family of al Qaeda-associated terrorist groups. Hezbollah and Palestinian terrorist groups do not conduct joint operational activity with al Qaeda, and despite some ad hoc cooperation and personal relationships, they have no official or institutional links. Nonetheless, these groups are no less benign for their independence from al Qaeda.

Indeed, the overall strength and effectiveness of the war on terror is undermined by the failure to appreciate these overarching connections. The interconnectivity between radical Islamist terrorist groups, including those that do not plan and implement attacks together, demands a more coordinated and comprehensive counterterrorism strategy than simply trying to target each of these groups individually, one at a time. Though historically this proved effective in the battle against leftist European groups in the 1970s and 1980s, the links between radical Islamist groups are qualitatively different than the informal links that existed between leftist European terrorist organizations.

Networks and relationships best describe the current state of international terrorism. This matrix of relationships between terrorists who belong to one or another group is what makes the threat of international terrorism so dangerous today. For example, while there are no known headquarter-to-headquarter links between al Qaeda and Hezbollah, the two groups are known to have held senior level meetings over the past decade and to maintain ad hoc, person-to-person ties in the areas of training and logistical support activities. As recent attacks in Casablanca and Istanbul reemphasized, these relationships—not particular group affiliations—are the driving force behind al Qaeda's continued ability to conduct devastating terrorist attacks, even after two and half years of the war on terror.

Too often people insist on pigeonholing terrorists as members of one group or another, as if such operatives carry membership cards in their wallets. In reality, much of the "network of networks" that characterizes today's terrorist threat is informal and unstructured. Not every al Qaeda operative has pledged an oath of allegiance (a *bayat*) to Osama bin Laden, while many terrorists maintain affiliations with members of other terrorist groups and facilitate one another's activities. This analysis applies to Palestinian terrorist groups as well. Groups like Hamas have no concrete connections to the al Qaeda "network of networks." However, in the area of terrorist financing and logistical support there is significant overlap and cooperation between these and other terrorist groups.

Between "Operatives" and "Supporters"

September 11 drove home the central role logistical and financial support networks play in international terrorist operations. Clearly, individuals who provide such support must be recognized as terrorists of the same caliber as those who use that support to execute attacks. To be sure, taken together the plethora of individuals, organizations and other fronts that provided logistical and financial support to the 9-11 plotters combine to form the single most significant enabling factor behind the September 11 attacks. Indeed, prior to September 11, officials frequently made the mistake of distinguishing between terrorist "operatives" and terrorist "supporters." Several of the September 11 plotters were identified as terrorist "supporters" prior to the attacks, but were not apprehended because they were not considered terrorist "operatives."

By now it should be clear to investigators, intelligence officers and decision makers alike that the logistical and financial supporters of terrorism warrant increased attention, not only because they facilitate acts of terror and radicalize and recruit future terrorists, but because distinguishing between "supporters" and "operatives" assures that the plotters of the next terrorist attack—today's "supporters"—will only be identified after they conduct whatever attack they are now planning—and are thus transformed into "operatives." In particular, any serious effort to crack down on terrorist financing, so critical to disrupt terrorist activity, demands paying special attention to these support networks.

Key Nodes in the Matrix of Terror Financing

A close examination of these networks reveals there are key nodes in this matrix that have become the preferred conduits used by terrorists from multiple terrorist groups to fund and facilitate attacks. Shutting down these organizations, front companies and charities will go a long way toward curtailing logistical support and stemming the flow of funds to and among terrorist groups.

Many critics of the economic war on terrorism mistakenly suggest that because the amount of money that has been frozen internationally is in the low millions, very little has actually been accomplished. The dollar amount frozen, however, is a poor litmus test. Terrorist groups will always find other sources of funding. A more telling yardstick that the amount of money frozen and put into an escrow account is whether authorities have shut down the key nodes through which terrorists raise, launder and transfer funds.

Indeed, similarly unrealistic litmus tests are applied to the war on terrorism itself. Too often people talk about winning the war on terrorism, defeating al Qaeda, or ending terrorism. But the fact is, one cannot defeat terrorism. Terrorism in one form or another has been around for centuries and will be around for many more. It has not, however, always presented as critical a national security challenge as it does today—nor will it necessarily continue to do so. Bringing the phenomenon of terrorism back down to tolerable levels is a very attainable goal.[1] Counterterrorism, therefore, is not about defeating terrorism, it is about constricting the operating environment—making it harder for terrorists to operate at every level, such as conducting operations, procuring and transferring false documents, ferrying fugitives from one place to another, and financing, laundering, and transferring funds. Authorities need to make it more difficult for terrorists to conduct their operational, logistical and financial activities, and to deny them the freedom of movement to conduct these activities. In fact, one can so constrict a terrorist group's operating environment that it will eventually suffocate. In its day, the Abu Nidal organization was the al Qaeda of its time, and it no longer exists. A time will come when the primary international terrorist threat will no longer be posed by al Qaeda, but by other nascent groups.

If, therefore, we are serious about constricting terrorists' operating environment and cracking down on terrorist financing, then we need to look at key nodes in the network of terrorists' logistical support groups.

Many of these organizations are not particular to one terrorist group. Militant Islamist groups from al Qaeda to Hamas interact and support one another in an international matrix of logistical, financial, and sometimes operational terrorist activity. As former National Security Council terrorism czar Richard Clarke recently testified, "al Qaeda is a small part of the overall challenge we face from radical terrorist groups which associate themselves with Islam. Autonomous cells, regional affiliate groups, radical Palestinian organizations, and groups sponsored by Iran's Revolutionary Guards are engaged in mutual support arrangements, including funding."[2]

In short, inattention to any one part of the web of militant Islamist terror undermines the effectiveness of measures taken against other parts of that web.

Links between Terror Groups: The Network of Relationships

September 11 produced a political will, markedly absent after previous attacks, to take concrete action to counter and disrupt the terrorist threat to America and its allies. These efforts, however, tend to focus on al Qaeda to the exclusion of other groups. Al Qaeda and these other groups, however, maintain logistical and financial links that reveal a matrix of illicit activity on an international scale. Indeed, if authorities are serious about cracking down on terrorist financing, they must not only prevent the purportedly political or social-welfare wings of terrorist groups from flourishing; they must take concrete steps to disrupt their activities. Accomplishing this requires an appreciation of the network of relationships that exists between various terrorists groups.

Consider the following examples of the terror web:

- In November 2001, the U.S. government designated the al-Taqwa banking system as a terrorist entity for "provid[ing] cash transfer mechanisms for Al Qaida."[3] But al-Taqwa also financed the activities of several other terrorist organizations, including Hamas. In fact, not only was al-Taqwa originally established in 1988 with seed money from the Egyptian Muslim Brotherhood, but Hamas members and individuals tied to al Qaeda feature prominently among its shareholdcrs.[4] According to the February 2002 testimony of Deputy Assistant Secretary of the Treasury Juan C. Zarate, "$60 million collected annually for Hamas was moved to accounts with Bank al-Taqwa."[5] Six years earlier, a 1996 report by Italian intelligence had already linked al-Taqwa to Hamas and other Palestinian groups, as well as to the Algerian Armed Islamic Group and the Egyptian al-Gama'a al-Islamiyya.[6]
- According to court documents, two men played central roles in radicalizing, training and funding the cell of American Muslims in Portland that tried to enter Afghanistan via China and Hong Kong to fight alongside al Qaeda and the Taliban against U.S. forces. In another sign of the crossover between terrorist elements, one of these men is associated with Palestinian terrorism, the other with al Qaeda. According to court documents, Ali Khaled Steitiye, a Hamas supporter who underwent terrorist training in South Lebanon and an unindicted coconspirator in the Portland case, engaged in weapons training with members of the Portland cell. Steitiye possessed several weapons, "which were used by members of the conspiracy to engage in weapons training to prepare the conspirators to assist the forces in the territory of Afghanistan controlled by the Taliban, including those associated with al-Qaeda, against the United States and its allies."[7]

  Steitiye's collaborator was Sheikh Mohammed Abdirahman Kariye, a cofounder of the designated al Qaeda front organization Global Relief Foundation. According to an FBI affidavit, cell members were secretly recorded describing how Kariye, the Imam of the local mosque, instructed his followers to fight with their fellow Muslims against Americans in Afghanistan. Kariye provided $2,000 to cover the travel costs of the cell members, money he acquired from members of the mosque. According to the affidavit, one cell member, Jeffrey Battle, explained that in the wake of Stietiye's arrest in October 2001, "Kariye directed the group of jihadists to return to the United States if they were unable to enter Afghanistan."[8]
- In May 2003, several individual European countries joined the United States in freezing the assets of the al Aqsa International Foundation, a Hamas front organization funding "Palestinian fighters" while recording its disbursements as "contributions for charitable projects."[9] Significantly, al Aqsa's representative in Yemen, Mohammed Ali Hasan al-Moayad, was arrested not only for funding Hamas, but also for providing money, arms, communication gear and recruits to al Qaeda.[10] According to an Israeli report on Hezbollah's global activity, the head of the al Aqsa International Foundation office in the Netherlands indicated the office raised funds for Hezbollah in coordination with the group's main office in Germany.[11]

The Matrix of International Terror in Context: the War on Terror, Israeli-Palestinian Conflict, and War in Iraq

Three critical and interrelated national security priorities currently dominate the U.S. foreign policy agenda: the war on terror, the war in Iraq, and the Israeli-Palestinian conflict. Indeed, each is made that much more difficult to navigate by the complicating factor of the dizzying matrix of relationships between various terrorist groups, fronts, and individual members that define international terrorism today.

Again, consider a few examples:

War on Terror: Working Through Organizational Crossover

Hamas funding comes from sources closely tied to other groups, especially al Qaeda. Take for example Muhammad Zouaydi, a senior al Qaeda financier in Madrid whose home and offices were searched. Spanish investigators found a five-page fax dated October 24, 2001, revealing Zouaydi was not only financing the Hamburg cell responsible for the September 11 attacks, but also Hamas. In the fax, which Zouaydi kept for his records, the Hebron Muslim Youth Association solicited funds from the Islamic Association of Spain. According to Spanish prosecutors, "the Hebron Muslim Youth Association is an organization known to belong to the Palestinian terrorist organization Hamas which is financed by activists of said organization living abroad." Spanish police also say Zouaydi gave $6,600 to Sheikh Helal Jamal, a Palestinian religious figure in Madrid tied to Hamas.[36]

U.S. authorities detained Abdurahman Muhammad Alamoudi, head of the American Muslim Foundation, on charges he was engaging in financial transactions with Libya, a state sponsor of terror subject to U.S. sanctions. According to court documents, $340,000 in cash was seized from Alamoudi on August 16, 2003, as he attempted to board a plane in London bound for Damascus. An unidentified Libyan delivered the cash to Alamoudi in his hotel room the previous night. According to the Bureau of Immigration and Customs Enforcement (ICE), the money may have been "intended for delivery in Damascus to one or more of the terrorists or terrorist organizations in Syria." Alamoudi has publicly lauded Hezbollah and Hamas, expressed his preference for attacks that "hit a Zionist target in America or Europe or elsewhere but not like what happened at the Embassy in Kenya," and was an officer of charities in Northern Virginia tied to Hamas and al Qaeda.[37] Alluding to Hamas, Assistant U.S. Attorney Steve Ward added that "in addition to dealing with Libya, [Alamoudi] has a more direct connection with terrorist organizations designated by the United States government."[38]

According to an affidavit prepared for his bail hearing, Alamoudi laundered and transferred hundreds of thousands of dollars through charities he ran to terrorist groups, including al Qaeda and Hamas.[39] In 2000, for example, a group that received $160,000 from a charity run by Alamoudi was subsequently implicated in the millennial plot foiled that December.[40] In 2002, two of Alamoudi's other organizations, the Success Foundation and the Happy Hearts Trust, sent $95,000 to Hamas front organizations in Jordan and Israel, including the Humanitarian Relief Association and Human Appeal International.[41] Beyond this, court documents assert that tens of thousands of dollars more went through other organizations run by Alamoudi to Hamas.[42]

Similar crossover between funding for Hamas and al Qaeda was recently exposed in the case of Soliman Biheiri, another individual at the center of the massive terror financing investigation in Northern Virginia. Biheiri, described by U.S. officials as "the U.S. banker for the Muslim Brotherhood," headed a since defunct investment company called BMI Inc. in New Jersey[43] The original investors in the company, suspected of financing Hamas, al Qaeda and perhaps other designated terrorist groups, include Yassin al Qadi and Hamas leader Mousa Abu Marzook (both listed as Specially Designated Global Terrorists by the

Networks of Relationships Case Study: Abu Musab al Zarqawi

The case of Abu Musab al Zarqawi (aka Fadel Nazzal Khalayleh) offers a particular insightful perspective on the scope of the informal links, personal relationships, and organizational crossover between disparate terrorist operatives and groups. As the Zarqawi case makes abundantly clear, such networks of relationships are both geographically and organizationally diverse.

Following Secretary of State Colin Powell's February 6 address to the United Nations Security Council, some questioned his description of the "sinister nexus between Iraq and the al Qaeda terrorist network."[12] In fact, the relationship between Baghdad and terrorism mirrors the way in which today's international terrorist groups function: not as tightly structured hierarchies, but rather as shadowy networks that, when necessary, strike ad hoc tactical alliances, bridging religious and ideological schisms. Osama bin Laden's calls on Muslims to come to Iraq's defense, even as he derided the "infidel" regime in Baghdad, are a case in point.[13]

One of the more active terrorist networks in recent years has been that of Abu Musab al-Zarqawi. At least 116 terrorist operatives from Zarqawi's global network have been arrested, including members in France, Italy, Spain, Britain, Germany, Turkey, Jordan, and Saudi Arabia.[14] For example:

Turkey: On February 15, 2002, Turkish police intercepted two Palestinians and a Jordanian who entered Turkey illegally from Iran on their way to conduct bombing attacks in Israel. Zarqawi had dispatched the three men, reportedly members of Beyyiat al-Imam (a group linked to al Qaeda) who fought for the Taliban and received terrorist training in Afghanistan, while he was in Iran.[15] More recently, Abdelatif Mourafik (alias Malek the Andalusian, or Malek the North African), a Moroccan Zarqawi associate wanted for his role in the May 2003 Casablanca suicide bombings, was arrested in Turkey in the fall of 2003.[16] Indeed, according to early assessments by Turkish officials, Zarqawi was the planner behind the two sets of double suicide bombings in Istanbul in November 2003.[17]

Germany: Although the al-Tawhid terrorist cell apprehended in Germany in April 2002 has been tied to Abu Qatada in Britain, Zarqawi controlled its activities. Eight men were arrested, and raids yielded hundreds of forged passports from Iran, Iraq, Jordan, Denmark, and other countries. According to German prosecutors, the group facilitated the escape of terrorist fugitives from Afghanistan to Europe and planned to attack U.S. or Israeli interests in Germany.[18]

Jordan: While in Syria, Zarqawi planned and facilitated the October 2002 assassination of U.S. Agency for International Development official Lawrence Foley in Amman.[19] Jordanian prime minister Abu Ragheb Ali announced that the Libyan and Jordanian suspects arrested in December in connection with the attack received funding and instructions from Zarqawi and had intended to conduct further attacks against "foreign embassies, Jordanian officials, some diplomatic personnel, especially Americans and Israelis."[20] Moreover, during his UN address, Powell revealed that after the murder, an associate of the assassin "left Jordan to go to Iraq to obtain weapons and explosives for further operations."[21] In addition, a key Zarqawi deputy called Foley's assassins on a satellite phone to congratulate them while he was driving out of Iraq toward Turkey, a mistake that led to his capture and confirmation that an al Qaeda cell was operating out of Iraq.[22]

Poison plots: Powell also disclosed that Abuwatia, a detainee who graduated from Zarqawi's terrorist camp in Afghanistan, admitted to dispatching at least nine North African extremists to Europe to conduct poison and explosive attacks.[23] European officials mainrain Zarqawi is the al Qaeda coordinator for attacks there, where chemical attacks were thwarted in Britain, France and Italy.[24] Similarly, Director of Central Intelligence George Tenet has stated that the Zarqawi network was behind poison plots in Europe this year.[25]

Although Zarqawi's active role in organizing terrorist operations suggests that he himself is a major terrorist leader, it is useful to clarify his links to other groups so as to better understand how international terrorism works. There is no precise organizational or command structure to the assemblage of groups that fall under al Qaeda's umbrella or that cooperate with the organization. Hence, whether Zarqawi swore allegiance (*bayat*), to bin Laden makes little difference in whether the two would work together at promoting a common agenda.

The range of actors who have given Zarqawi safe haven and support clearly illustrate the current modus operandi of terrorist networks. Consider his movements since he first surfaced as a terrorist suspect in 1999, when he led Jund al-Shams, an Islamic extremist group and al Qaeda affiliate operating primarily in Syria and Jordan.[26]

Jordan: Zarqawi has been a fugitive since 1999 when Jordanian authorities first tied him to radical Islamic activity leading Jund al-Shams. In 2000, a Jordanian court sentenced him in absentia to fifteen years of hard labor for his role in the al Qaeda millennial terror plot targeting Western interests in Jordan.[27]

Taliban-ruled Afghanistan: In 2000, Zarqawi traveled to Afghanistan, where he oversaw an al Qaeda training camp and worked on chemical and biological weapons.[28] Such camps served as open universities, educating terrorists from a wide array of local and international groups. These students in turn established relationships and networks, like the anti-Soviet mujahedin before them. With every success in the war on terrorism, such networks become increasingly essential to al Qaeda, providing a new cadre of terrorist operatives.

Iran and Iraq: In early 2002, Zarqawi was wounded in the leg while fighting against U.S.-led coalition forces in Afghanistan. He escaped to Iran, then traveled to Iraq in May 2002, where his wounded leg was amputated and replaced with a prosthetic device. According to Secretary Powell, Zarqawi then spent two months recovering in Baghdad, during which time "nearly two dozen extremists converged on Baghdad and established a base of operations there. These al Qaeda affiliates, based in Baghdad, now coordinate the movement of people, money, and supplies into and throughout Iraq for his network, and they've now been operating freely in the capital for more than eight months."[29] Prior to the war in Iraq, Zarqawi had returned to the Ansar al-Islam camp in northern Iraq run by his Jund al-Shams lieutenants. There, he enjoyed safe haven and free passage into and out of Ansar-held areas:[30] Zarqawi is now said to be back in Iran, where he continues to operate with the full knowledge of the regime in Tehran.[31]

Syria and Lebanon: From Baghdad, Zarqawi traveled to Syria and possibly Lebanon.[32] U.S. intelligence officials have definitively linked Zaraqawi to Hezbollah, magnifying their concerns about the ad hoc tactical relationship brewing between Iran's Shi'i proxy and the loosely affiliated al Qaeda network.

In September, when U.S. authorities designated Zarqawi and several of his associates as "Specially Designated Global Terrorist" entities, they revealed that Zarqawi not only has "ties" to Hezbollah, but that plans were in place for his deputies to meet with both Hezbollah and Asbat al Ansar (a Lebanese Sunni terrorist group tied to al Qaeda) "and any other group that would enable them to smuggle mujaheddin into Palestine" in an effort "to smuggle operatives into Israel to conduct operations."[33] Zarqawi received "more than $35,000" in mid-2001 "for work in Palestine," which included "finding a mechanism that would enable more suicide martyrs to enter Israel" as well as "to provide training on explosives, poisons, and remote controlled devices."[34]

At the same time, the Zarqawi network was planning attacks on Jewish or Israeli targets in Europe. According to the Treasury Department, Zarqawi met an associate named Mohamed Abu Dhess in Iran in early September 2001 "and instructed him to commit terrorist attacks against Jewish or Israeli facilities in Germany with 'his [Zarqawi's] people'."[35]

U.S. government), as well as Abdullah Awad bin Laden (Osama Bin Laden's nephew and the former head of the U.S. offices of suspected al Qaeda front the World Assembly of Muslim Youth, WAMY).[44]

Such links are not a new phenomenon. The leader of a Pakistani jihadi organization openly admitted to having "person-to-person contacts" with other groups, adding, "sometimes fighters from Hamas and Hezbollah help us." Asked where his group meets groups like Hamas and Hezbollah," the Pakistani answered, "a good place to meet is in Iran." Offering insight into the importance of interpersonal relationships between members of disparate terrorist groups, he added, "We don't involve other organizations. Just individuals."[45]

Another such link was revealed when U.S. immigration officials briefly detained Muhammad Jamal Khalifa, bin Laden's brother-in-law and a senior IIRO official and al Qaeda financier, in San Francisco in December 1994. Among the material found in his belongings "were extensive discussions of assassination, the use of explosives, military training and jihad as well as details of Islamist movements such as Hamas and Palestinian Islamic Jihad." Khalifa maintained relations with Hamas members working for the IIRO in the Philippines even after he left the organization to open a branch of the Muwafaq Foundation there.[46]

Iraq: Foreign Jihadists and Domestic Baathists Teaming Up to Attack Americans

Even as coalition forces try to plant the seeds of a pluralistic society in Iraq, these trends are being uprooted by swarms of radicals from across the Muslim world who enter Iraq—primarily from Syria and Iran but also from Saudi Arabia—to take advantage of Iraq's newfound status as a failing state. Iraq has now become a magnet for Baathists, Sunni terrorists, Shia radicals and others opposed to the development of a peaceful, pluralistic society in Iraq, much like Afghanistan, Somalia, parts of Yemen, Georgia's Pankisi Gorge, Chechnya and other undergoverned territories.

These destabilizing forces include individual radicals and terrorist groups, but also neighboring states, such as Syria and Iran, both of which allow terrorist elements to cross their borders into Iraq. U.S administrator Paul Bremer, also a noted authority on international terrorism, recently told CNN, "We've certainly seen foreign fighters who sort of fit the al Qaeda profile—people traveling on documents from Syria, Yemen, Sudan, in some cases Saudi Arabia, some of the terrorist groups we've attacked in the west of the country."[47]

According to press reports, coalition intelligence agencies intercepted conversations between radical Islamists from Saudi Arabia and Iraqi Baathists. Officials were reportedly surprised by this, noting the conservative fundamentalist ideology of Saudi extremists, while Baathists are more often moderate if not secular Muslims.[48]

But such cooperation borne of opportunism and a narrow mutual interest in targeting coalition forces should be no surprise. Almost as soon as coalition forces crossed into Iraq, reports leaked out of thousands of Arab irregular forces—some volunteers, some members of terrorist groups like Palestinian Islamic Jihad, Hezbollah and Fatah splinter groups—crossing the Syrian border into Iraq to battle coalition forces. Coalition commanders commonly referred to these irregulars as "Syrians" because so many of them were Syrian, and many carried Syrian travel documents, in some cases specifically marked "reason for entry: Jihad. Length of stay: Indefinite."[49] In one case, U.S. military forces captured a large group of Syrians and confiscated seventy suicide jackets—each filled with twenty-two pounds of military grade C4 explosives, and mercury detonators.[50] In another case, soldiers found several hundred thousands dollars on a bus that came from Syria, together with "leaflets suggesting that Iraqis would be rewarded if they killed Americans."[51] Syrian Foreign Minister Farouq al Shara explained his country's facilitating terrorists' travel to Iraq by asserting quite plainly, "Syria's interest is to see the invaders defeated in Iraq."[52] In case some planners were still unclear on the developing trend, Osama Bin Laden issued a tape-recorded message to the "mujahideen brothers in Iraq" in February stressing "the importance of the martyrdom operations against the enemy."[53] Most recently, Sunni clerics meeting in Stockholm in mid-July at a conference of the European Council for Fatwa and Research approved the use of suicide attacks in Iraq (and Palestine and Kashmir).[54]

Israeli-Palestinian Conflict: Likely Cross-group Cooperation in Gaza Bombing

The recent bombing of a U.S. convoy in Gaza on October 15, 2003, which killed three American contract employees of the U.S. embassy in Tel Aviv and injured a fourth, was neither unprecedented nor unexpected. Indeed, U.S. embassy employees narrowly escaped injury in a similar attack last June, when unknown assailants detonated two bombs near their vehicle.[55] No group has claimed responsibility for the October 15 attack. But Palestinian security officials quickly arrested several members of the Popular Resistance Committee (PRC), a conglomeration of former and current members of Fatah, Islamic Jihad, Hamas and the various Palestinian security forces. Whether the PRC is responsible is unclear. But such a strike would certainly be in keeping with its methods: The group's most daring and successful attack was a February 14, 2002 roadside bombing that demolished an Israeli armored tank. Indeed, that attack was executed with the assistance of a Hezbollah agent who infiltrated Palestinian territory to provide the PRC with technical and operational advice.[56]

Although Hezbollah has not killed Americans recently, it does target them, as CIA Director George Tenet testified in February 2002.[57] Indeed, throughout the 1990's Hezbollah operatives were especially active surveiling American and other interests throughout Southeast Asia.[58] Moreover, according to statements by captured operatives and other information made public by Israeli intelligence, Hezbollah and Lebanon-based operatives from Iran's Islamic Revolutionary Guard Corps have recruited a network of rogue Fatah cells to serve as Hezbollah's West Bank cadres.[59] Hezbollah is particularly well known for its skill at manufacturing and placing sophisticated roadside bombs, a skill the group has now transferred to the West Bank and Gaza. Aside from Hezbollah's role in the aforementioned 2002 tank bombing, in mid-2002 Israeli authorities discovered a type of mine in Hebron that had previously been used only by Hezbollah in Lebanon. Israeli authorities conducting a search in Hebron during that same month arrested Fawzi Ayub, a Hezbollah operative who had entered the territories by sea using his own Canadian passport.[60]

Authorities are also concerned al Qaeda operatives could link up with Palestinian militias and terrorist groups to target Israeli and American interests there. Recently released information indicates that the Mombassa attacks were no aberration, and that al Qaeda is intent on entering the Israeli-Palestinian arena. In August, Israel submitted a report to the UN stating that it had thwarted several attempts by al Qaeda operatives carrying foreign passports to enter Israel in order to gather intelligence and conduct attacks.[61] Israel also noted that it had captured Palestinians recruited by al Qaeda abroad to conduct attacks in Israel. Moreover, pamphlets signed by the "Bin Laden Brigades of Palestine" have been found in Palestinian areas encouraging Palestinians to continue "in the footsteps of Osama bin Laden."[62] Last month, such reports found support in the United States: The U.S. Treasury Department highlighted al Qaeda plans and funding for attacks in Israel, including "training on explosives… and remote controlled devices" such as the one employed on October 15 in Gaza.[63]

Regardless of who bombed the U.S. convoy in Gaza, the attack highlights the increasingly international nature of the Israeli-Palestinian conflict and the devastating cost of failing to identify and confront the increasingly common crossover between otherwise disparate terrorist groups.

The Terror Matrix as an Impediment to Fighting the War on Terror

To be sure, failure to understand the crossover and cooperation between international terrorist groups has already undermined efforts to prosecute the war on terror, both on the global battlefield and in the courtroom.

For example, this lack of understanding has frustrated efforts to curb the flow of funds to al Qaeda and other terrorists. A senior delegation of U.S. Treasury officials traveled to Europe in November 2002 to solicit European cooperation in a trans-Atlantic effort to block the international assets of about a dozen of the most egregious terror financiers. The effort failed however, because European officials were unsatisfied with the fact that the majority of evidence the Americans presented to support their request focused on these financiers' support of groups like Hamas. Material pointing to their financing of al Qaeda activities was limited out of fear of exposing sensitive sources and methods behind such intelligence, while evidence of their funding of Hamas was more readily available. The Americans were told they would have to produce evidence these financiers were funding more than just Hamas (i.e., al Qaeda) if they expected European cooperation.[64]

Similarly, the EU has yet to designate the al Aqsa International Foundation as a terrorist entity, despite its known ties to Hamas, al Qaeda and possibly Hezbollah.

Myopic perspectives such as this, blind to the crossover between terror networks, have also undermined criminal prosecutions of terrorists, including several cases in the United States.

As the myriad of companies, charities, and other suspected terrorist front organizations now under investigation in Northern Virginia highlight, there is a critical need to break away from the tendency to adhere to a strict compartmentalization of terrorist groups in investigating terrorism cases. Investigating the family of organizations in Northern Virginia—including the Safa Group, SAAR Foundation, Success Foundation and many more—strictly as a Hamas, Palestinian Islamic Jihad (PIJ), or al Qaeda cases—clearly did not work. Indeed, the tentacles of this entrenched network are suspected of providing tremendous logistical and financial support to a variety of international terrorist groups.

Tracing these financial trails, however, proved immensely difficult given the various groups' proactive efforts to layer their transactions and obfuscate the terrorist intentions of their many transactions. More than anything, the links between various personalities tied to these organizations on the one hand and to a laundry list of terrorist groups, fronts and operatives on the other, keyed investigators into the network's terror financing and support activities.

Progress on this complex web of front organizations appears to have developed only with the passage of the USA Patriot Act, which facilitated the sharing of intelligence among prosecutors and permitted cross-referencing of information across previously compartmentalized terrorism investigations.

Conclusion

Money has not been a constraint on the activities of al Qaeda, Palestinian terrorist groups, or the jihadists and Ba'athists fighting coalition forces in Iraq. This will continue to be the case until more serious action is taken toward restricting the financing of terrorism, which is indeed one of the most effective ways to advance the war on terror, the Roadmap to Israeli Palestinian peace, and the stabilization of Iraq.

The principal terrorist threat today stems from the web of shadowy relationships between loosely affiliated groups. The sponsors of such groups further complicate the web, be they states or substate actors. Indeed, there is no precise organizational or command structure to the assemblage of groups that cooperate with al Qaeda or fall under the organization's umbrella. Given the multifarious links between international terrorist groups and their relationships with state sponsors of terrorism such as Iran and Syria, the war on terror will be most effective if it has a strategic focus on the full matrix of international terrorism rather than a tactical focus on al Qaeda. Prosecuting the war on terror, whether on the battlefield or in the courtroom, demands greater attention to the web of interaction among these various groups and state sponsors.

Matthew Levitt, a former FBI counterterrorism analyst, is a Senior Fellow in Terrorism Studies at The Washington Institute for Near East Policy and an Adjunct Professor at the Paul H. Nitze School of Advanced International Studies (SAIS) at Johns Hopkins University.

Notes

1. Without trying to quantify current and tolerable levels of terrorism, one can safely assert that reducing the threat of radical Islamic terrorism, the source of the vast majority of terrorist threats today, would significantly reduce the threat level from one in which each day brings

several new terror threats to one in which such threats, while perhaps no less dangerous, are far less frequent.

2. Richard A. Clarke, "Statement before the United States Senate Banking Committee," 22 October 2003, (www.senate.gov/banking/files/clarke.pdf).
3. John B. Taylor, "Statement from the US Department of the Treasury," 7 November 2001, (www.treas.gov/press/releases/po771.htm).
4. "The United States and Italy Designate Twenty-Five New Financiers of Terror," Department of the Treasury Office of Public Affairs, PO-3380, 29 August 2002, (www.ustreas.gov/press/releases/po3380.htm) and Lucy Komisar, "Shareholders in the Bank of Terror?" Salon.com, 15 March 2002; and Mark Hosenball, "Terror's Cash Flow," *Newsweek,* 25 March 2002, 28, 29.
5. Testimony of Juan C. Zarate, Deputy Assistant Secretary, Terrorism and Violent Crime, U.S. Department of the Treasury, House Financial Subcommittee Oversight and Investigations, 12 February 2002.
6. Ibid.
7. United States of America v. Jeffrey Leon Battle et al., United States District Court for the District of Oregon, No. CR 02-399 HA, 2 October 2003.
8. Les Zaitz, "FBI Affidavit Alleges Imam Bankrolled Plot," *The Oregonian,* 23 August 2003, A01.
9. "Treasury Designates Al-Aqsa International Foundation as Financier of Terror: Charity Linked to Funding of the Hamas Terrorist Organization," Department of the Treasury, Office of Public Affairs, 29 May 2003, (www.treas.gov/pres/releases/js439.htm).
10. USA v. Mohammed Ali Hasan Al-Moayad, Affidavit in Support of Arrest Warrant, Eastern District of New York, 5 January 2003.
11. "Hezbollah: Profile of the Lebanese Shiite Terrorist Organization of Global Reach Sponsored by Iran and Supported by Syria," Intelligence and Terrorism Information Center, The Center for Special Studies, Special Information Paper, June 2003, (www.intelligence.org.il/eng/bu/hizbullah/hezbollah.htm).
12. Secretary of State Colin Powell, "Remarks to the United Nations Security Council," 5 February 2003, (www.state.gov/secretary/rm/2003/17300.htm).
13. Audio Message by Osama bin Laden, Al-Jazeera Television, 11February 2003. See BBC transcript, (www.news.bbc.co.uk/2/hi/middle_east/2751019.htm).
14. Secretary of State Colin Powell, "Remarks to the United Nations Security Council" 5 February 2003, (www.state.gov/secretary/rm/2003/17300.htm).
15. Douglas Frantz and James Risen, "A Secret Iran-Arafat Connection is Seen Fueling the Mideast Fire," *The New York Times,* 24 March 2002, A1; and David Kaplan, "Run and Gun: Al Qaeda Arrests and Intelligence Hauls Bring New Energy to the War on Terrorism," *U.S. News and World Report,* 30 September 2002, 36-38, 41.
16. Sebastian Rotella and Richard C. Paddock, "Experts See Major Shift in Al Qaeda's Strategy," *Los Angeles Times,* 19 November 2003, AI.
17. "Istanbul's attacks mastermind identified, consul's window makes appeal," Agence France Presse, 27 November 2003.
18. Philipp Jaklin and Hugh Williamson, "Terror Suspects Detained in Germany," *Financial Times,* 24 April 2002, 6; Edmund L. Andrews, "German Officials Find More Terrorist Groups, and Some Disturbing Parallels," *The New York Times,* 26 April 2002, A12.
19. Secretary of State Colin Powell, "Remarks to the United Nations Security Council," 5 February 2003, <www.state.gov/secretary/rm/2003/17300.htm> and "Treasury Designates Six Al Qaeda Terrorists," U.S. Department of the Treasury press release (JS-757), 24 September 2003, (www.treasury.gov/press/release/js757.htm).
20. "Al Qaeda man behind murder of US diplomat hiding in northern Iraq: Jordan," *Agence France Presse,* 18 December 2002.
21. Secretary of State Colin Powell, "Remarks to the United Nations Security Council," 5 February 2003, (www.state.gov/secretary/rm/2003/17300.htm).
22. Ibid.
23. Ibid.

24. Elaine Sciolino and Desmond Butler, "Europeans Fear That the Threat From Radical Islamists Is Increasing," *The New York Times,* 8 December 2002, A32.
25. George J. Tenet, "Worldwide Threat—Converging Dangers in a Post-9/11 World: Testimony of Director of Central Intelligence George J. Tenet before the Senate Select Committee on Intelligence," 6 February 2002, (http://www.cia.gov/cia/public_affiars/speeches/2002/dci_speech_02062002.html).
26. "Treasury Designates Six Al Qaeda Terrorists," US Department of the Treasury press release (JS-757), 24 September 2003, (http://www.treasury.gov/press/releases/js757.htm).
27. "Al Qaeda man behind murder of US diplomat hiding in northern Iraq: Jordan," *Agency France Press,* 18 December 2002.
28. Secretary of State Colin Powell, "Remarks to the United Security Council," 5 February 2003, (www.state.gov/secretary/rm/2003/17300.htm).
29. Ibid.
30. Ibid.
31. *Al-Sharq al-Awsat,* 1 June 2003; A European intelligence official subsequently confirmed this report in an interview with the author, September 2003.
32. David E. Kaplan, Angie Cannon, Mark Mazzetti, Douglas Pasternak, Kevin Whitelaw, Aamir Latif, "Run and Gun," *U.S. News and World Report,* 30 September 2002, 36.
33. "Treasury Designates Six Al Qaeda Terrorists," US Department of the Treasury press release (JS-757), 24 September 2003, (http://www.treasury.gov/press/releases/js757.htm).
34. Ibid.
35. Ibid.
36. Central Trial Court No. 5, Spanish National High Court (*Audiencia Nacional*), CASE 35/2002 (ordinary procedure), Don Baltasar Garzon Real, Magistrado Juez del Juzgado Central de Instrucción 19 July 2002.
37. Declaration in Support of Detention, USA v. Abdurahman Muhammad Alamoudi, case No 03-1009M, Alexandria Division, Eastern District of Virginia, 30 September 2003.
38. Douglas Farah, "US Says Activist Funded Terrosists; Leader of Muslim Groups Denied Bail," *The Washington Post,* 1 October 2003, A6.
39. Douglas Farah, "US Indicts Prominent Muslim, Affidavit: Alamoudi Funded Terrorists," *The Washington Post,* 24 October 2003. A1.
40. Ibid.
41. Ibid, and Glenn R. Simpson, "Unraveling Terror's Finances," *Wall Street Journal,* 24 October 2003, A2.
42. Ibid.
43. Glenn R. Simpson, "The U.S. Provides Details of Terror-Financing Web Defunct Investment Firm In New Jersey Is the Hub; Suspect to Stay in Custody," *The Wall Street Journal,* 15 September 2003.
44. Ibid.; For information on WAMY's ties to terrorism see "Combating Terrorist Financing, Despite the Saudis," Policywatch #673, The Washington Institute for Near East Policy, 1 November 2002, (www.washingtoninstitute.org/watch/Policywatch/policywatch2002/673.htm).
45. Jessica Stern, *Terror in the Name of God: Why Religious Militants Kill* (New York: Harper Collins, 2003), 211.
46. Rohan Gunaratna, *Inside Al Qaeda: Global Network of Terror* (New York: Columbia University Press, 2002), 114, 145.
47. "Bremer says Hundreds of international terrorists in Iraq," *Agence France Presse,* 24 August 2003.
48. Raymond Bonner, "The Struggle for Iraq: Weapons; Iraqi Arms Catches Cited in Attacks," *The New York Times,* 14 October 2003, A1.
49. Luke Hunt, "Evidence of Iraq's 'terrorist ties' mounts, but bin Laden link elusive," *Agence France Presse,* 16 April 2003.
50. Ibid.
51. Bernard Weinraub, "Fighters from Syria Among Iraqi Prisoners in an American Camp." *The New York Times,* 20 April 2003, B4.

52. "Syria Hits Back at U.S. Says It Supports "Iraqi People" Against Invaders," Agence France Presse, March 31, 2003.
53. Audio Message by Osama bin Laden, Al-Jazeera Television, 11February 2003. See BBC transcript, (news.bbc.co.uk/2/hi/middle_east/2751019,htm).
54. Arnaud de Borchgrave, "Clerics OK suicide-bombers," *United Press International,* 15 August 2003.
55. Margot Dudkevitch, "IDF thwarts two suicide bombings," *Jerusalem Post,* 29 June 2003.
56. James Bennett, "Israeli Killed As His Commandos Demolish West Bank House," *The New York Times,* 16 February 2002, A4.
57. George J. Tenet, "Worldwide Threat—Converging Dangers in a Post-9/11 World: Testimony of Director of Central Intelligence George J. Tenet before the Senate Select Committee on Intelligence," 6 February 2002, (http://www.cia.gov/cia/public_affairs/speeches/2002/dci_speech_02062002.html).
58. Maria Ressa, *Seeds of Terror: An Eyewitness Account of al Qaeda's Newest Center of Operations in Southeast Asia* (New York; Free Press, 2003), Pp.129-132; see also Matthew Levitt, "From the Beqa'a Valley to the Blue Ridge Mountains: Hezbollah's Global Presence and Operations", Lecture presented at The International Policy Institute for Counter-Terrorism (ICT), Third Annual Conference, "Post Modern Terrorism: Trends Scenarios, and Future Threats," 7-10 September 2003, Herzliya, Israel.
59. Matthew Levitt, "Hezbollah's West Bank Foothold," *Peacewatch* #429, The Washington Institute for Near East Policy, 20 August 2003, (www.washingtoninstitute.org/watch/Peacewatch/peacewatch2003/429.htm).
60. "Hezbollah (part 1): Profile of the Lebanese Shiite Terrorist Organization of Global Reach Sponsored by Iran and Supported by Syria," Intelligence and Terrorism Information Center at the Center for Special Studies, Israel, June 2003; and author interview with intelligence sources, July 2003, available at (www.intelligence.org.il/eng/bu/hizbullah/hezbollah.htm).
61. Anna Driver, "Israel Says al Qaeda Active in Palestinian Areas," *Reuters,* 5 August 2003.
62. Ibid.
63. "Treasury Designates Six Al Qaeda Terrorists," US Department of the Treasury press release (JS-757), 24 September 2003, (www.treasury.gov/press/release/js757.htm).
64. Testimony of Jimmy Gurule, Under Secretary for Enforcement, U.S. Department of the Treasury, Before the U.S. Senaté Judiciary Committee, November 20, 2002. (www.ustreas.gov/press/releases/po3635.htm) and Douglas Farah, "U.S. Pinpoints Top Al Qaeda Financiers, Treasury Official Heads to Europe to Seek Help in Freezing Backers' Assets," *The Washington Post,* 18 October 2002. A26.

Chapter 4

Religion and the Intersection with Terrorism

The 1993 bombings of Manhattan's World Trade Center, Aum Shinrikyo's release of sarin nerve gas in the Tokyo underground, and the bombing of the U.S. federal building in Oklahoma City were acts of terrorism carried out by players with vastly different origins, doctrines, and practices, writes Magnus Ranstorp. Yet Ranstorp recognizes one common thread among these terrorist acts: The perpetrators believed "their actions were divinely sanctioned, even mandated by God." Ranstorp charts the rise in terrorism for religious motives and reports that between the mid-1960s and mid-1990s the number of fundamentalist movements of all religious affiliations tripled. Nearly a quarter of all terrorist groups active in the world today are primarily motivated by religious concerns, yet these groups are also driven by practical political considerations—and it is difficult for observers to distinguish the political from the religious in the terrorist acts these groups commit. Ranstorp explores the motives, the "serious sense of crisis in their environment," which nearly all these groups experience and that fuels an escalation in their activities; the threats of secularization from foreign sources these group identify and rail against; the hierarchy of power that emanates from a dynamic so-called leader; the role religious symbolism plays in selecting their targets; and the sense of home and change for vengeance these groups offer to followers who suffer under a history of grievances. Contrary to popular opinion, Ranstorp concludes, "[r]eligious terrorism is anything but disorganized or random, but rather driven by an inner logic common among diverse groups and faiths who use political violence to further their sacred causes."

Mark Juergensmeyer looks at the complex relationship between religion and violence, particularly in the context of the militant Sikhs of India and the violence that seized the Punjab region in the 1980s. Juergensmeyer portrays the Sikhs as a group in crisis, "their separate identity within the Indian family is in danger.... Sikhs fear they could be reabsorbed into the amorphous cultural mass that is Hinduism and disappear as a distinct religious community," he writes. The author examines how the words and rhetoric of a charismatic militant leader can inspire a movement, and how everyday, political issues can be mingled with a struggle for spiritual survival to create a cosmic struggle that sanctifies violent means for religious and political ends.

Mark Sedgwick approaches the intersection of religion and terrorism through the case of al Qaeda. He argues that a distinction exists between the "ultimate aims and the immediate objectives of 'religious' terrorists" in that while the ultimate aims may be articulated in religious terms, the immediate objectives are largely political in nature. In building his argument, he draws parallels to pre-modern terrorists such as the Assassins and Zealots. This framework is very powerful in helping us understand the true nature of the threat despite the associated rhetoric and images. Al Qaeda followed a time-tested pattern with the 9/11 attacks—they were hoping to provoke a repressive and harsh response from the United States that would galvanize other radicals around the world. Sedgwick demonstrates the skill of the al Qaeda leadership in crafting a master narrative that appeals to different audiences through the use of historical and contemporary religious concepts.

Quintan Wiktorowicz's article is a very significant and important contribution to the field. "A Genealogy of Radical Islam" traces the development of radical jihadi thought. Central to his argument is the concept that al Qaeda is not a "theological outlier" but instead part of a larger global community of Salafists. In the article, Wiktorowicz identifies what he terms as the "key points of divergence" among the Salfi community. He concludes by noting that the "development of jihadi thought is characterized by the erosion of critical constraints used to limit warfare and violence in classical Islam." The expansion of al Qaeda's targets from military or political to civilian targets is indicative of the future path toward targeting wider groups of people.

Magnus Ranstorp, 1996

Terrorism in the Name of Religion

Introduction

On 25 February 1994, the day of the second Muslim sabbath during Islam's holy month of Ramadan, a Zionist settler from the orthodox settlement of Qiryat Arba entered the crowded Ibrahim (Abraham's) Mosque, located in the biblical town of Hebron on the West Bank. He emptied three 30-shot magazines with his automatic Glilon assault-rifle into the congregation of 800 Palestinian Muslim worshippers, killing 29 and wounding 150, before being beaten to death. A longstanding follower of the radical Jewish fundamentalist group, the Kach movement,[1] Baruch Goldstein was motivated by a complex mixture of seemingly inseparable political and religious desiderata, fuelled by zealotry and a grave sense of betrayal as his prime minister was "leading the Jewish state out of its God-given patrimony and into mortal danger."[2] Both the location and the timing of the Hebron massacre were heavily infused with religious symbolism. Hebron was the site of the massacre of 69 Jews in 1929. Also, the fact that it occured during the Jewish festival of Purim symbolically cast Goldstein in the role of Mordechai in the Purim story, meting out awesome revenge against the enemies of the Jews.[3] Israeli Prime Minister Yithzak Rabin, speaking for the great mass of Israelis, expressed revulsion and profound sadness over the act committed by a "deranged fanatic." However, a large segment of militant and orthodox Jewish settlers in West Bank and Gaza settlements portrayed Goldstein as a righteous man and hailed him as a martyr.[4] During his funeral, these orthodox settlers also voiced religious fervor in uncompromising and militant terms directed not only against the Arabs, but also against the Israeli government, which they believed had betrayed the Jewish People and the Jewish state.

Israeli leaders and the Jewish community tried to deny or ignore the danger of Jewish extremism by dismissing Goldstein as belonging, at most, to "the fringe of a fringe"[5] within Israeli society. Sadly, any doubts of the mortal dangers of religious zealotry from within were abruptly silenced with the assassination of prime minister Yitzhak Rabin by a young Jewish student, Yigal Amir, who claimed he had acted on orders of God. He had been influenced by militant rabbis and their *halalic* rulings, which he interpreted to mean that the "pursuer's decree" was to be applied against Israel's leader.[6] Most Israelis may be astonished by the notion of a Jew killing another Jew, but Rabin was ultimately the victim of a broader force which has become one of the most vibrant, dangerous and pervasive trends in the post–Cold War world: religiously motivated terrorism.

Far afield from the traditionally violent Middle East, where religion and terrorism share a long history,[7] a surge of religious fanaticism has manifested itself in spectacular acts of terrorism across the globe. This wave of violence is unprecedented, not only in its scope and the selection of targets, but also in its lethality and indiscriminate character. Examples of these incidents abound: in an effort to hasten in the new millenium, the Japanese religious cult Aum Shinrikyo released sarin nerve gas on the Tokyo underground in June last year;[8] the followers of Sheikh 'Abd al-Rahman's al-Jama'a al-Islamiyya[9] caused mayhem and destruction with the bombing of Manhattan's World Trade Center and had further plans to blow up major landmarks in the New York City area; and two American white supremacists carried out the bombing of a U.S. Federal building in Oklahoma City.[10] All are united in the belief by the perpetrators that their actions were divinely sanctioned, even mandated, by God. Despite having vastly different origins, doctrines, institutions, and practices, these religious extremists are unified in their justification for employing sacred violence, whether in efforts to defend, extend or revenge their own communities, or for millenarian or messianic reasons.[11] This article seeks to explore these reasons for the contemporary rise in terrorism for religious motives and to identify the triggering mechanisms that bring about violence out of religious belief in both established and newly formed terrorist groups.

The Wider Trend of Religious Terrorism

Between the mid-1960s and the mid-1990s, the number of fundamentalist movements of all religious affiliations tripled worldwide. Simultaneously, as observed by Bruce Hoffman, there has been a virtual explosion of identifiable religious terrorist groups from none in 1968 to today's level, where nearly a quarter of all terrorist groups active throughout the world are predominantly motivated by religious concerns.[12] Unlike their secular counterparts, religious terrorists are, by their very nature, largely motivated by religion, but they are also driven by day-to-day practical political considerations within their context-specific environment. This makes it difficult for the general observer to separate and distinguish between the political and the religious sphere of these terrorist groups.

Nowhere is this more clear than in Muslim terrorist groups, as religion and politics cannot be separated in Islam. For example, Hizb'allah or Hamas operate within the framework of religious ideology, which they combine with practical and precise political action in Lebanon and Palestine. As such, these groups embrace simultaneously short-term objectives, such as the release of imprisoned members, and long-term objectives, such as continuing to resist Israeli occupation of their homelands and liberating all "believers." This is further complicated with the issue of state-sponsorship of terrorism: Religious terrorist groups become cheap and effective tools for specific states in the advancement of their foreign policy political agendas. They may also contain a nationalist-separatist agenda, in which the religious component is often entangled with a complex mixture of cultural, political, and linguistic factors. The proliferation of religious extremist movements has also been accompanied by a sharp increase in the total number of acts of terrorism since 1988, accounting for over half of the 64,319 recorded incidents between 1970 and July 1995.[13] This escalation by the religious terrorists is hardly surprising given the fact that most of today's active groups worldwide came into existence very recently. They appeared with a distinct and full-fledged organizational apparatus. They range from the Sikh Dal Khalsa and the Dashmesh organizations, formed in 1978 and 1982 respectively[14] and the foundation of the Shi'ite Hizb'allah movement in Lebanon in 1982; to the initial emergence of the militant Sunni organizations, known as Hamas and Islamic Jihad, in conjunction with the 1987 outbreak of the Palestinian Intifada as well as the establishment of the Aum Shinrikyo in the same year.

The growth of religious terrorism is also indicative of the transformation of contemporary terrorism into a method of warfare and the evolution of the tactics and techniques used by various groups, as a reaction to vast changes within the local, regional and global environment over the last three decades. These changes can be seen in numerous incidents, from the spate of hijackings by secular Palestinian terrorists and the mayhem of destruction caused by left- and right-wing domestic terrorists throughout Europe, to today's unprecedented global scope and level of religious extremism.

The evolution of today's religious terrorism neither has occurred in a vacuum nor represents a particularly new phenomenon. It has, however, been propelled to the forefront in the post–Cold war world, as it has been exacerbated by the explosion of ethnic-religious conflicts and the rapidly approaching new millenium.[15] The accelerated dissolution of traditional links of social and cultural cohesion within and between societies with the current globalization process, combined with the historical legacy and current conditions of political repression, economic inequality and social upheaval common among disparate religious extremist movements, have all lead to an increased sense of fragility, instability and unpredictability for the present and the future.[16] The current scale and scope of religious terrorism, unprecedented in militancy and activism, is indicative of this perception that their respective faiths and communities stand at a critical historical juncture: Not only do the terrorists feel the need to preserve their religious identity, they also see this time as an opportunity to fundamentally shape the future.[17] There are a number of overlapping factors that have contributed to the revival of religious terrorism in its modern and lethal form at the end of the millennium. At the same time, it is also possible to discern a number of features which are found in all religious terrorist groups across different regions and faiths. These features serve not only to define the cause and the enemy, but also fundamentally shape the means, methods and the timing of the use of the violence itself.

The Causes and the Enemies of Religious Terrorists

A survey of the major religious terrorist groups in existence worldwide in the 1990s would reveal that almost all experience a serious sense of crisis in their environment, which has led to an increase in the number of groups recently formed and caused an escalation in their activities. This crisis mentality in the religious terrorist's milieu is multifaceted, at once in the social, political, economic, cultural, psychological and spiritual sphere. At the same time, it has been greatly exacerbated by the political, economic and social tumult, resulting in a sense of spiritual fragmentation and radicalization of society experienced worldwide in the wake of the end of the Cold War and the extremist's "fear of the forced march toward 'one worldism.'"[18] Yet, this sense of crisis, as a perceived threat to their identity and survival, has been present to varying degrees throughout history. It has led to recurring phases of resurgence in most faiths. In these revivals, the believers use the religion in a variety of ways: they take refuge in the religion, which provides centuries-old ideals by which to determine goals; they find physical or psychological sanctuary against repression; or they may use it as a major instrument for activism or political action. Thus, religious terrorists perceive their actions as defensive and reactive in character and justify them in this way.[19] Islam's *jihad*, for example, is essentially a defensive doctrine, religiously sanctioned by leading Muslim theologians, and fought against perceived aggressors, tyrants, and "wayward Muslims." In its most violent form, it is justified as a means of last resort to prevent the extinction of the distinctive identity of the Islamic community against the forces of secularism and modernism. As outlined by Sheikh Fadlallah, the chief ideologue of

Hizb'allah: "When Islam fights a war, it fights like any other power in the world, defending itself in order to preserve its existence and its liberty, forced to undertake preventive operations when it is in danger."[20] This is echoed by Sikh extremists, who advocate that, while violence is not condoned, when all peaceful means are exhausted, "you should put your hand on the sword."[21] The defensive character of protecting one's faith through religious violence is also evident in the Sikh's fear of losing their distinct identity in the sea of Hindus and Muslims.[22] In the United States, the paranoid outlook of white supremacist movements is driven by a mixture of racism and anti-Semitism, as well as mistrust of government and all central authority.[23] This sense of persecution is also visible among the Shi'ites as an historically dominant theme for 13 centuries, manifest in the annual Ashura processions by the Lebanese Hizb'allah, commemorating the martyrdom of Imam Husayn. This event and mourning period have been used as justification and as a driving force behind its own practice of martyrdom through suicide attacks.[24]

Other than a few strictly millenarian or messianic groups (such as Aum Shinrikyo or some Christian white supremacist movements), almost all the contemporary terrorist groups with a distinct religious imperative are either offshoots or on the fringe of broader movements. As such, the militant extremists' decisions to organize, break away or remain on the fringe are, to a large extent, conditioned by the political context within which they operate. Their decisions are shaped by doctrinal differences, tactical and local issues, and the degree of threat that they perceive secularization poses to their cause. This threat of secularization may come either from within the movements themselves and the environment within which they come into contact, or from outside influences. If the threat is external, it may amplify their sense of marginality within, and acute alienation from, society. It may also fuel the need to compensate for personal sufferings through the radical transformation of the ruling order.[25] The internal threat of secularization is often manifest in a vociferous and virulent rejection of the corrupt political parties, the legitimacy of the regime, and also the lackluster and inhibited character of the existing religious establishment. Thus, religious terrorism serves as the only effective vehicle for violent political opposition.[26] As explained by Kach's leader, Baruch Marzel, "(w)e feel God gave us in the six-day war, with a miracle, this country. We are taking this present from God and tossing it away. They are breaking every holy thing in this country, the Government, in a very brutal way."[27] Similarly, as voiced by the late Palestinian Islamic Jihad's leader, Fathi al-Shaqaqi, with reference to the Gaza-Jericho agreement between the PLO [Palestine Liberation Organization] and Israel: "Arafat has sold his soul for the sake of his body and is trying to sell the Palestinian people's soul in return for their remaining alive politically."[28] The religious terrorist groups' perception of a threat of secularization from within the same society is also manifest in the symbolism used in the selection of their names, indicating that they have an absolute monopoly of the revealed truth by God. It is, therefore, not surprising that some of the most violent terrorist groups over the last decade have also adopted names accordingly: Hizb'allah (Party of God), Aum Shinrikyo (The Supreme Truth) and Jund al-Haqq (Soldiers of Truth). These names also endow them with religious legitimacy, historical authenticity, and justification for their actions in the eyes of their followers and potential new recruits. They also provide valuable insight into their unity of purpose, direction and degree of militancy, with names like Jundallah (Soldiers of God), Hamas (Zeal), Eyal (Jewish Fighting Organization) and Le Groupe Islamique du Armé (Armed Islamic Group, GIA) which promises unabated struggle and sacrifice.

The threat of secularization from foreign sources is also the catalyst for springing religious terrorists into action. Intrusion of secular values into the extremist's own environment and the visible presence of secular foreign interference provoke self-defensive aggressiveness and hostility against the sources of these evils. This is especially true against colonialism and neo-colonialism by western civilizations or against other militant religious faiths. These defensive sentiments are often combined with the visible emergence and presence of militant clerical leaders. Such leaders have more activist and militant ideologies than the mainstream movement from which they have emerged as either clandestine instruments or breakaway groups. It is often the case that these clerical ideologues and personalities act as a centrifugal force in attracting support, strengthening the organizational mechanisms and in redefining the methods and means through terrorism. At the same time, they provide theological justification, which enables their followers to pursue the sacred causes more effectively and rapidly. The so-called spiritual guides, who ultimately overlook most political and military activities while blessing acts of terrorism, can be found in almost all religious terrorist groups: Examples include Hizb'allah's Sheikh Fadlallah and Hamas' Sheikh Yassin, the militant Sikh leader Sant Bhindranwale and Aum Shinrikyo's leader, Shoko Ashara.

Most active terrorist groups with a religious imperative were actually propelled into existence in reaction to key events. These events either served as a catalyst or inspirational model for the organization or gravely escalated the perception of the threat of foreign secularization, or for messianic or millenarian groups, a heightened sense that time was running out. The latter is evident in the growth and increased activism of doomsday cults, awaiting the imminent apocalypse, whose self-prophetic visions about the future have triggered them to hasten the new millennium.[29] This messianic anticipation, for example, was clearly evident in the attack on the Grand Mosque of Mecca in 1979 (the Islamic year 1400) by armed Muslim militants from al-Ikhwan, who expected the return of their Madhi.[30] The formation of Lebanese Hizb'allah can be attributed to the context of the civil war environment and the inspiring example of Ayatollah Khomeini's Islamic revolution in Iran. However, it was Israel's invasion of Lebanon in 1982 and the subsequent foreign intrusion in the form of the western-led Multinational Forces (MNF) that served as a catalyst for Hizb'allah's actual organizational formation and which to this day has continued to fuel its militancy and religious ideology. Similarly, the 1984 desecration by the Indian army of the Golden Temple in Amritsar, Sikhism's holiest shrine, led not only to the assassination of Prime Minister Indira Gandhi in revenge, but also to a cycle of endless violence between the warring faiths, which hitherto has claimed over 20,000 lives.[31]

In many ways, religious terrorists embrace a total ideological vision of an all-out struggle to resist secularization from within as well as from without. They pursue this vision in totally uncompromising holy terms in literal battles between good and evil. Ironically, there is a great degree of similarity between the stands of the Jewish Kach and Islamic Hamas organizations: Both share a vision of a religious state between the Jordan River and the Mediterranean Sea; a xenophobia against everything alien or secular which must be removed from the entire land, and a vehement rejection of western culture. This distinction between the faithful and those standing outside the group is reinforced in the daily discourse of the clerics of these terrorist groups. The clerics' language and phraseology shapes the followers' reality, reinforcing the loyalty and social obligation of the members to the group and reminding them of the sacrifices already made, as well as the direction of the struggle.[32] In this task, many religious terrorist groups draw heavily upon religious symbolism and rituals to reinforce the sense of collectiveness. Examples of this emphasis on collectivity include the local reputation of the fighters of the underground military wing of Hamas, famous for never surrendering to arrest,[33] the growth of Hamas martyrology, which lionizes martyrs with songs, poems and shrines,[34] and the frequent symbolic burning and desecration of Israeli and American flags by several Islamic groups across the Middle East. This collectiveness is also reinforced by the fact that any deviation or compromise amounts to treachery and a surrender of the principles of the religious faith is often punishable by death.

The sense of totality of the struggle for these religious warriors is one purely defined in dialectic and cosmic terms as believers against unbelievers, order against chaos, and justice against injustice, which is mirrored in the totality and uncompromising nature of their cause, whether that cause entails the establishment of Eretz Israel, an Islamic state based on *sharia* law or an independent Khalistan ("Land of the Pure"). As such, the religious terrorists perceive their struggle as all-out war against their enemies. This perception, in turn, is often used to justify the level and intensity of the violence. For example, this theme of war is continuously detectable in the writings and statements by the terrorists, as exemplified by Yigal Amir's justification for assassinating Rabin;[35] or by Article 8 of Hamas' manifesto justifying that *jihad* is its path and that "[d]eath for the sake of Allah is its most sublime belief."

This totality of the struggle naturally appeals to its acutely disenfranchized, oppressed, and alienated communities with the promises of change and the provision of constructive alternatives. Unlike their recent historical predecessors, like the fringe al-Jihad organization which assassinated the Egyptian President Anwar Sadat in 1981,[36] many of the existing religious terrorist cells are different in that they can often complement their violence with realistic alternatives to secular submission. This is especially true at the grassroots level, due to the penchant for organization inherent in religion and the backing of a vast network of resources and facilities.[37] This has meant that some religious terrorist groups are not solely relying on violence, but also have gradually built an impressive constituency through a strategy of "re-Islamization or re-Judaization from below."[38] The political dimension is complemented with terrorism in confrontation with the enemy or in defense of the sacred cause. This is a process which began in the early 1970s and culminated in the 1990s with a visible shift in strategy among groups, from relying on terrorism while re-Islamizing their environment to complementing terrorism with the use of the electoral process to advance their sacred causes.

Religious terrorism also offers its increasingly suffering and impatient constituents more hope and a greater chance of vengeance against the sources of their historical grievances than they would otherwise have. This is most effectively illustrated by the 1985 Sikh inflight bombing of an Air India airliner, causing 328 deaths, as well as by Hizb'allah's twin suicide-bombings of the U.S. Marine barracks and the French MNF headquarters in Beirut in 1983, killing 241 and 56 soldiers respectively. Violent acts give these groups a sense of power that is disproportionate to their size. The basis for this feeling of power is enhanced by a strategy of anonymity by the religious terrorist which confuses the enemy. In other words, the covernames are used according to where the religious terrorists have come from and where they are heading. Terrorists of the Muslim faith, particularly Shi'ite groups, employ a wide variety of covernames (in the Shi'ite case rooted in history with the notion of *taqiyyah*, or dissimulation) in efforts to protect their communities against repression or retaliation by the enemy after terrorist acts.[39] Yet, these covernames reveal significantly the currents or directions within movements in alignment with their struggles.[40] As such, the religious terrorists tend to "execute their terrorist acts for no audience but themselves."[41] Although the act of violence in and of itself is executed primarily for the terrorists own community as a sign of strength, it naturally embodies wider elements of fear in their actual or potential enemy targets. The perpetrators adeptly exploit this fear by invoking religious symbolism, such as the release of videotaped images of an endless pool of suicide bombers, ready to be dispatched against new targets.

While the religious extremists uniformly strike at the symbols of tyranny, they are relatively unconstrained in the lethality and the indiscriminate nature of violence used, as it is conducted and justified in defence of the faith and the community. Reflecting the dialectic nature of the struggle itself, various religious terrorist groups also refer to their alien or secular enemies in de-humanizing terms which may loosen the moral constraints for them in their employment of particularly destructive acts of terrorism.[42] As explained by an extremist rabbi in conjunction with the funeral of Baruch Goldstein: "There is a great difference in the punishment becoming a person who hurts a Jew and a person who hurts a gentile.... [t]he life of a Jew is worth much more than the lives of many gentiles." This moral self-purification points to the belief that the perpetrators view themselves as divinely "chosen people," who not only possess religious legitimacy and justification for their propensity for violence, but also often act out of the belief that the violence occurs in a divinely sanctioned juncture in history. For example, the Japanese cult leader Shoko Ashara and his followers believed the world would end in 1997 and launched a sarin nerve gas attack on Tokyo's subway system to hasten the new millennium.[43]

In fact, the lack of any moral constraints in the use of violence cannot only be attributed to the totality of the struggle itself but also to the preponderance of recruits of young, educated and newly-urbanized men (often with very radical, dogmatic, and intolerant worldviews), in contemporary religious terrorist organizations.[44] This increased militancy of a younger generation of religious terrorists can be explained by both the fragmentation of groups into rival splinter factions and also the killing or imprisonment of key founding leaders and ideologues.[45] Apart from removing the older generation of terrorist leadership, the experience of persecution and imprisonment has led to the radicalization of younger recruits into the organizations.[46] Also there seems to be an inverse relationship between size and militancy.[47] The Shi'ite terrorist groups are more prone to martyrdom than their Sunni counterparts, due to their different historical legacies and to the more powerful role of Shi'ite clergymen in directly interceding between man and God. However, some Sunni groups have recently broken the mold, as evident in the unprecedented series of 13 Hamas suicide-attacks inside Israel (which killed 136 people between 6 April 1994 and 4 March 1996) after the Hebron massacre and, to a lesser extent, the foiled plan by the GIA to explode its hijacked Air France plane over metropolitan Paris in December 1994. However, as explained by Sheikh Fadlallah: "There is no difference between dying with a gun in your hand or exploding yourself. In a situation of struggle or holy war you have to find the best means to achieve your goals."[48]

While the resort to martyrdom by certain groups can be explained by the heightened sense of threat to the groups and their causes within their own environment, it can also be explained by an increasing level of internationalization between groups both in terms of contact, similarity of causes and as examples of strategies. This is particularly evident among Muslim terrorist groups. For example, many Algerian, Egyptian and Palestinian Muslim extremists have participated alongside the Mujahadin fighters in the Afghanistan conflict. They trained with these Afghan fighters and supported them both physically and ideologically in a war "as much about the forging of a new and revolutionary social order as about national liberation."[49] As a significant example of a revolutionary cause within a Sunni context, as opposed to the more narrow Shi'ite example of the Iranian revolution, the Afghan conflict served as a training ground for their own struggles during the 1980s: Following the collapse of communism, these fighters returned to their respective countries to radicalize the Islamic struggle at home, resorting to increasing violence in the process, either within existing movements or as splinter groups.

Yet, the mechanisms of unleashing acts of religious terrorism, in terms of intensity, methods and timing, are tightly controlled by the apex of the clerical hierarchy and most often dependent on their blessing. This was clearly demonstrated in the 1984 Gush Emunim plot to blow up the Temple Mount (or Dome of the Rock), Islam's third holiest site, in part for messianic reasons (to cause a cataclysmic war between Jews and Muslims to hasten the coming of the Messiah) and in part to foil the return of Jewish sacred land to Arabs in return for peace under the Camp David accord. This act of terrorism never materialized due to the lack of rabbinical backing.[50] Similarly, the role of the spiritual leaders within Islamic terrorist organizations is equally pivotal, as displayed by the central role of Sheikh Omar 'Abd al-Rahman of the Egyptian al-Jama'a al-Islamiyya in issuing the directive, or *fatwa*, for both the 1981 assassination of Anwar Sadat and the 1993 bombing of New York's World Trade Center.[51] As such, in most cases the strictly hierarchical nature of religious terrorist groups with a highly disciplined structure and obedient cadres means not only that the main clerical leaders command full control over the political as well as military activities of the organization but also that the strategies of terrorism are unleashed in accordance with general political directives and agendas.[52]

Yet, the use and sanctioning of religious violence requires clearly defined enemies. The newly-formed religious terrorist groups today do not appear in a vacuum nor are their members naturally born into extremism. The identity of the enemy and the decision to use religious violence against them are dependent on, and shaped by, the heightened degree of the sense of crisis threatening their faiths and communities. This, in turn, is influenced by the historical legacy of political repression, economic inequality or social upheaval, and may be exacerbated by ethnic and military disputes. This sense of grievance is uniquely experienced between the faiths and the individual groups, as well as in alignment with the political strategies and tactics adopted to confront them according to local, regional and international contexts. Internally, this militancy may be directed against the corruption or injustices of the political system, or against other religious communities; externally, it may be focused against foreign influences, which represent a cultural, economic, or political threat to the respective religious communities. The West, particularly the United States as well as Israel, tends to be the favourite target of this militancy, especially by terrorists of the Muslim faith.[53]

Anti-western sentiments and intense hostility towards Israel for the Muslim terrorist is the result of the historical legacy of political oppression and socio-economic marginalization within the Arab world. These hostilities are combined with the discrediting of secular ideologies and the illegitimacy of current political and economic elites, especially after the 1967 defeat of the Arabs by Israel.[54] This sense of crisis has been exacerbated by the Arab-Israeli conflict which served to reinforce a Muslim inferiority complex due to the inability of either Arab regimes or secular Palestinians to defeat Israel. Simultaneously, the West is perceived to be practising neocolonialism through its Israeli surrogate and its unqualified support for existing "un-Islamic" and "illegitimate" regimes across the Arab world. As such, the Islamist movements and their respective armed "terrorist" wings have gradually propelled themselves to the forefront of politics as the true defender of the oppressed and dispossessed and as the only effective spearhead against Israel's continued existence in the heart of Muslim territory and against the West's presence and interference in the region. Apart from the obvious religious dimensions of the loss of Palestine to Zionism, Muslim militants draw heavily on the symbolism of the historical legacy of the Crusades, pitting Christendom against Islam, to explain their current condition of oppression and disinheritance, and to provide workable solutions and defences against the threat of western encirclement and secularization.[55] The Muslim terrorists rework these historic religious symbols to fit present-day conditions as a vehicle to inspire political action and revolutionary violence against its enemies.

While the identity of the enemy is deeply rooted in both distant and recent history, the turn towards, and the direction of, terrorism by militant Muslim movements against foreign enemies have been following distinct phases according to changes in the political and ideological context in the region. These phases are directly influenced by the Iranian revolution in 1979, the Muslim resistance struggle led by the Mujahadin against the Soviets in Afghanistan, the electoral victory of the Front Islamique du Salut (FIS) in Algeria (1990 to 1991), and the signing of the Israeli-Palestinian Declaration of Principles in September 1993. The Iranian revolution provided a revolutionary model of Islam and inspired Islamic movements to seriously challenge existing regimes at home. Additionally, the internationalization of Muslim terrorist violence against the West and Israel during the 1980s supported Iran's efforts to export the revolution abroad and was a cost-effective instrument to change the foreign policies of western states hostile towards the Islamic Republic.[56] The Lebanese Hizb'allah movement in particular, was very useful to the Iranian regime in achieving these ends. It also provided Iran with the opportunity to participate, both indirectly and militarily, in the Arab-Israeli conflict.[57] Additionally, Muslim fighters in Afghanistan during the 1980s forged important networks between various groups and individuals which accelerated the activism among Muslim groups on the homefront when these fighters returned home. The FIS electoral victory in Algeria demonstrated to Muslim terrorist groups that they could use the ballotbox rather than relying solely on bullets in efforts to come to power in various Arab states. The election's subsequent nullification by the Algerian military junta led to radicalization of the Islamists and their turn towards terrorism against the state itself and the French government for extending support.

Simultaneously, the gradual resolution of the Israeli-Palestinian conflict threatens the pan-Islamic goal of militant Islamic movements of liberating Jerusalem. This threat has led to accelerated co-ordination between Islamic terrorist groups in efforts to sabotage the peace process and an increased militancy and confrontation against the West, Israel, and supportive Arab regimes. At the same time, the political wings of these terrorist groups seek to continue and extend the process of re-Islamization of society from below. The confluence of these factors over the last two decades has accelerated the militancy of the Muslim terrorist while it clearly demonstrates that they are closely attuned to changes in the local, regional, and international environment, as well as very adept to reformulating their strategies for political and military action accordingly in efforts to protect, extend or avenge their religious communities.

The Means, Methods, and Timing of the Religious Terrorist

In comparison to their secular counterparts, the religious terrorists have not been particularly inventive when it comes to using new types of weaponry in their arsenals, instead relying on the traditional bombs and bullets.[58] Yet the religious terrorists have demonstrated a great deal of ingenuity in terms of the tactics used in the selection of means, methods and timing of violence to cause maximum effect. They have utilized the notion of martyrdom and self-sacrifice through suicide bombings as a means of last resort against their conventionally more powerful enemies. The first time this tactic was employed by the Hizb'allah was against the American, French and later Israeli military contingents present in Lebanon in 1983. It was emulating the actions of the shock troops of the Iranian Revolutionary Guards in their war with Iraq. While the Hizb'allah clerics gradually encountered theological dilemmas in continuing the sanctioning of this method, as suicide is generally forbidden in Islam except for under exceptional circumstances, the Hamas movement felt compelled to adopt suicide bombings in 1994 as a means of last resort in order to sabotage the Israeli-Palestinian peace process.[59] They believed that its actual implemention on the ground would severely threaten Hamas' revolutionary existence. The tactic of suicide bombing was also used to take revenge against its "Zionist enemy" for the Hebron attack. While few terrorist groups adopt large-scale campaigns of suicide missions, the religious terrorist utilizes the traditional methods of assassination, kidnappings, hijackings, and bombings in a skillful combination in alignment with the current political context on the local, regional, and international level. Despite the growth and array of religious terrorist groups with diverse demands and grievances, they are all united not only in the level and intensity of violence used, but also in the role played by religious symbolism in selecting the targets and the timing of the violence itself.

Many of these terrorist groups are compelled to undertake operations with a distinct political agenda for organizational reasons to release imprisoned members or eliminating opponents. Nonetheless, the targets are almost always symbolic and carefully selected to cause maximum psychological trauma to the enemy and to boost the religious credentials of the terrorist group among their own followers. This is clearly evident from the selection by Muslim terrorists of western embassies, airlines, diplomats and tourists abroad as symbolically striking at the heart of their oppressors. This was evident in the selection of major New York City landmarks by Sheikh Rahman's followers or the multiple attacks by the Hizb'allah against U.S. diplomatic and military facilities.[60] In many instances, these groups have adopted a multi-pronged approach of using terrorism. For example, in Algeria the FIS has targeted foreign tourists, businessmen and diplomats, as well as Algerian officials and other Algerians who engage in un-Islamic behaviour (e.g unveiled women or any form of western culture). At the same time, it engages in the re-Islamization of society from below and simultaneously wages a war of attrition on French soil against symbolic civilian and official targets. In other cases, religious terrorists have used powerful symbolism to provoke deliberate reactions by the enemy, such as Dal Khalsa's severing of cows' heads outside two Hindu temples in Amritsar, which provoked massive disturbances between the

Sikhs and the Hindus in April 1982.[61] This type of symbolism is also seen in the 1969 arson attack on the al-Aqsa mosque in East Jerusalem by a Jewish extremist and the 1982 plan by Jewish fanatics to blow up Temple Mount in order to spark a cataclysmic war between Muslims and Jews.[62]

Finally, the timing of the violence by religious terrorists is carefully selected to coincide with their own theological requirements or to desecrate their enemies' religious holidays and sacred moments. For example, the 1995 bombing of the Alfred P. Murrah Federal Building in Oklahoma by white supremacists was reportedly scripted after *The Turner Diaries*, but also timed to "commemorate the second anniversary of FBI's assault on the Branch Davidian's Waco, Texas compound; [and] to mark the date 220 years before when the American revolution began at Lexington and Concord."[63] Similarly, the symbolism of the timing of religious violence was also evident in the Algerian GIA's decision to hijacking an Air France plane during Christmas after the killing of two Catholic priests, or the cycle of violence by Hamas' suicide bombings against Israel, occurring in February 1996, on the second commemoration of the Hebron massacre.

Conclusions

This article has sought to demonstrate that, contrary to popular belief, the nature and scope of religious terrorism is anything but disorganised or random but rather driven by an inner logic common among diverse groups and faiths who use political violence to further their sacred causes. The resort to terrorism by religious imperative is also not a new phenomenon, but rather deeply embedded in the history and evolution of the faiths. Religions have gradually served to define the causes and the enemies as well as the means, methods and timing of the violence itself. As such, the virtual explosion of religious terrorism in recent times is part and parcel of a gradual process of what can be likened to neo-colonial liberation struggles. This process has trapped religious faiths within meaningless geographical and political boundaries and constraints, and has been accelerated by grand shifts in the global political, economic, military and socio-cultural setting, compounded by difficult local indigenous conditions for the believers. The uncertainty and unpredictability in the present environment as the world searches for a new world order, amidst an increasingly complex global environment with ethnic and nationalist conflicts, provide many religious terrorist groups with the opportunity and the ammunition to shape history according to their divine duty, cause, and mandate while it indicates for others that the end of time itself is near. As such, it is imperative to move away from treating this new religious force in global politics as a monolithic entity but rather seek to understand the inner logic of these individual groups and the mechanisms that produce terrorism in order to undermine their breeding ground and strength, as they are here to stay. At present it is doubtful that the United States or any western government is adequately prepared to meet this challenge.

An internationally recognized expert on terrorism, **Magnus Ranstorp** is a lecturer in international relations at the University of St. Andrews (Scotland) and deputy director of the University's Centre for the Study of Terrorism and Political Violence, where he specialized in the behavior of militant Islamic movements in the Middle East and North Africa. Author of *Hizballah in Lebanon: The Politics of the*

Western Hostage Crisis (1996), he gives lectures and briefings on Middle Eastern terrorism to academic, government, and military audiences around the world.

Notes

1. The Kach movement was founded in 1971 by the ultra-orthodox American Rabbi Meir Kahane when he emigrated to Israel. The group calls for the establishment of a theocratic state in Eretz (Greater) Israel and the forced expulsion of Arabs. For a useful overview see Raphael Cohen-Almagor, "Vigilant Jewish Fundamentalism: From the JDL to Kach (or 'Shalom Jews, Shalom Dogs'), *Terrorism and Political Violence*, 4, No.1 (Spring 1992): pp.44–66; and Ehud Sprintzak, *The Ascendance of Israel's Radical Right* (New York: Oxford University Press, 1991).
2. "The Impossible Decision," *The Economist*, 11–17 November 1995, p.25.
3. For a discussion of Goldstein's decision to carry out the attack during Purim, see Sue Fiskhoff, "Gentle, Kind and Full of Religious Fervor," *Jerusalem Post*, 27 February 1994; and Chris Hedges and Joel Greenberg, "West Bank Massacre: Before Killing, a Final Prayer and a Final Taunt," *New York Times*, 28 February 1994, p. A1.
4. One of Goldstein's rabbinical mentors, Rabbi Dov Li'or, described him in compassionate terms as a man "who could no longer take the humiliation and the disgrace. Everything he did was in honor of Israel and for the glory of God," in *Yediot Aharanot*, 18 March 1994. Also see: Richard Z. Chesnoff, "It Is a Struggle for Survival," *U.S. News & World Report*, 14 March 1994.
5. Charles Krauthammer, "Deathly Double Standard," *Jerusalem Post*, 6 March 1994.
6. Prior to Rabin's assassination, Yigal Amir had tried two previous times. For a very useful biography of the assassin, see John Kifner, "A Son of Israel: Rabin's Assassin," *New York Times*, 19 November 1995; *idem.*, "Israelis Investigate Far Right; May Crack Down on Speech," *New York Times*, 8 November 1995. One of these traditional exemptions for killing is Din Rodef, or Law of the Pursuer. The rule was first set forth in the 12th century by the great Moses Maimonides, a Spanish Jewish scholar. Going beyond the principle of self-defense, it states that even a witness to the act of someone's trying to kill another is allowed to kill the potential assassin. For Yigal Amir's use of the principle as a defense for killing Rabin, see Raine Marcus, "Amir: I Wanted to Murder Rabin," *Jerusalem Post*, 16 March 1996.
7. As aptly observed by David C. Rapoport in his seminal work, the words "zealot," "assassin" and "thug" all derive from historic fanatic movements within, respectively, Judaism, Islam and Hinduism, respectively. See Bruce Hoffman, *"Holy Terror": The Implications of Terrorism Motivated by a Religious Imperative* (Santa Monica: RAND, 1993) pp. 1–2; and David C. Rapoport, "Fear and Trembling: Terrorism in Three Religious Traditions," *American Political Science Review*, 78, no. 3 (September 1984) pp. 668–72. For a useful historical overview, see David C. Rapoport, "Why Does Religious Messianism Produce Terror?" in *Contemporary Research on Terrorism*, ed. Paul Wilkinson and A.M. Stewart, (Aberdeen: Aberdeen University Press, 1987) pp. 72–88.
8. The attack on the Tokyo subway was the first recorded instance of a terrorist group committing mass murder with a weapon of mass destruction. The Aum Shinrikyou religious cult was established in 1987 by Shoko Ashara, a nearly blind acupuncturist and yoga master, and is composed of a synthesized mixture of Buddhist and Hindu theology. For a useful brief biographical sketch of Ashara, see James Walsh, "Shoko Asahara: The Making of a Messiah," *Time*, 3 April 1995. The sarin nerve gas attack on Tokyo's subway killed 8 and injured over 5,500. Also see Martin Wollacott, "The Whiff of Terror," *The Guardian*, 21 March 1995.
9. For a useful overview of al-Jama'a al-Islamiyya and its activities in Egypt, see Barry Rubin, *Islamic Fundamentalism in Egyptian Politics* (London: Macmillan 1990).
10. See Stephen Robinson, "The American Fundamentalist," *Daily Telegraph*, 24 April 1995.
11. For a very comprehensive discussion, see Mark Juergensmeyer, ed. "Violence and the Sacred in the Modern World," *Terrorism and Political Violence*, 3, no. 3 (Autumn 1991).
12. Bruce Hoffman (1993), p. 2. The year 1968 is widely recognized as the point of origin for modern international terrorism. It was the beginning of an explosion of hijackings from Cuba to the United States, as well as attacks against Israeli and Western airlines by various Palestinian

groups. Also see Barry James, "Religious Fanaticism Fuels Terrorism," *International Herald Tribune*, 31 October 1995, p. 3.

13. See Professor Yonah Alexander, "Algerian Terrorism: Some National, Regional and Global Perspectives," Prepared statement before the House Committee on International Relations, Subcommittee on Africa, *Federal News Service*, 11 October 1995. This figure should be compared with 8,339 acts of international terrorism during the period 1970 to 1994 with 3,105 incidents occurring after 1988, see RAND-St. Andrews, *Chronology of International Terrorism* (St. Andrews: Centre for the Study of Terrorism and Political Violence, University of St. Andrews, March 1996).
14. The Dashmesh (meaning "10th") organization was named after the Sikhs' last guru, Gobind Singh, who, in the eighteenth century, transformed the Sikh community into a warrior class by justifying force when necessary. Both the Dashmesh and the Sikh Dal Khalsa advocate the establishment of an independent Khalistan.
15. The emergence of ethnic-religious conflict over conventional inter-state warfare was illuminated by a 1994 report by the United Nations Development Programme in which only 3 out of a total of 82 conflicts worldwide were between states. See Roger Williamson, "The Contemporary Face of Conflict—Class, Colour, Culture and Confession," in *Jane's Intelligence Review Yearbook—The World in Conflict 94/95* (London: Jane's Information Group, 1995) pp. 8–10. Also see Julia Preston, "Boutros Ghali: 'Ethnic Conflict' Imperils Security," *Washington Post*, 9 November 1993, p. 13. Also see Hans Binnendijk & Patrick Clawson, eds., *Strategic Assessment 1995: U.S. Security Challenges in Transition* (Washington: National Defense University Press, 1995); and Martin Kramer, "Islam & the West (including Manhattan)," *Commentary* (October 1993) pp. 33–37.
16. For the wider debate of the religious resurgence, see Scott Thomas, "The Global Resurgence of Religion and the Study of World Politics," *Millenium*, 24, no. 2 (Summer 1995) and Peter Beyer, *Religion and Globalization* (London: Sage, 1994).
17. As observed: At a time when no one knows precisely what form the future may take, the strength of fundamentalism lies in its ability to promise radical change without having to specify its outlines—since God is claimed as its guarantor," in Mahmoud Hussein, "Behind the Veil of Fundamentalism," *UNESCO Courier*, December 1994, p. 25. Also as stated by an ideologue of Jewish extremist group, Kahane Chai: "We are accountable only to our Creator, to He who chose us for our mission in history," in Amir Taheri, "Comentary: The Ideology of Jewish Extremism," *Arab News*, 12 March 1994.
18. Robin Wright, "Global Upheaval Seen as Engine for Radical Groups," *Los Angeles Times*, 6 November 1995.
19. "Fundamentalism Unlimited," *The Economist*, 27 March 1993, p. 67; and Hussein, p. 25.
20. Muhammad Hussein Fadlallah, "To Avoid a World War of Terror," *Washington Post*, 4 June 1986. As reiterated by Sheikh Fadallah: "We are not preachers of violence. Jihad in Islam is a defensive movement against those who impose violence." Laura Marlowe, "A Fiery Cleric's Defense of Jihad," *Time*, 15 January 1996. For further elaboration on this by Sheikh Fadlallah, see *al-Majallah*, 1–7 October 1986.
21. This is often seen in the Sikh slogan: "The Panth [religion] is in danger." See Paul Wallace, "The Sikhs as a 'Minority' in a Sikh Majority State in India," *Asian Survey*, 26, no. 3 (March 1986) p. 363.
22. Laurent Belsie, "At a Sikh Temple, Opinions Reflect Conflicting Religious Traditions," *Christian Science Monitor*, 11 November 1984. For a detailed discussion of the use of violence, see Sohan Singh Sahota, *The Destiny of the Sikhs* (Chandigarh: Modern Publishers, 1970).
23. Bruce Hoffman, "American Right-Wing Terrorism," *Jane's Intelligence Review*, 7, no. 7 (July 1995) pp. 329–30.
24. See John Kifner, "Shiite Radicals: Rising Wrath Jars the Mideast," *New York Times*, 22 March 1987.
25. This theme is developed by David Rapoport, "Comparing Militant Fundamentalist Movements," in *Fundamentalism and the State*, ed. Martin E. Marty and R. Scott Appleby (Chicago: The University of Chicago Press, 1993).

26. See Maha Azzam, "Islamism, the Peace Process and Regional Security," *RUSI Journal* (October 1995) pp. 13–16.
27. Kifner, 19 November 1995.
28. *Al-Hayah*, 4 May 1994. Similarly, according to Hamas' manifesto: "Palestine is a Holy Muslim asset to the end of time, so that no man has the right to negotiate about her or to relinquish [any part of] her," in Amos Oz, "Israel's Far Right Collaborates With Hamas in Thwarting Peace," *The Times*, 11 April 1995.
29. For a useful insight into the dynamics of cults, see Richardo Delgado, "Limits to Proselytizing," *Society* (March/April 1980) pp. 25–33; Margaret Thaler Singer, "Coming of the Cults," *Psychology Today* (January 1979) pp. 73–82.
30. See Robin Wright, "U.S. Struggles to Deal With Global Islamic Resurgence," *Los Angeles Times*, 26 January 1992.
31. For a useful overview, see Pranay Gupte, "The Punjab: Torn by Terror," *New York Times*, 9 August 1985; Vijah Singh, "Les Sikhs, une Secte Traditionnelle Saisié par la Terrorisme," *Liberation*, 1 November 1984.
32. For example, this uncompromising position is clearly evident by Hamas' own charter in Article 11: "The land of Palestine is an Islamic trust (*waqf*) to be maintained by succeeding generations of Muslims until the Day of Judgement. In this responsibility, or any part of it, no negligence will be tolerated, and no surrender." *Mithaq Harakat al-Muqawamah al-Islamiyah* (Hamas, 1988).
33. See Michael Kelly, "In Gaza, Peace Meets Pathology," *New York Times*, 29 November 1994, p. 56.
34. See Michael Parks, "Ready to Kill, Ready to Die, Hamas Zealots Thwart Peace," *Los Angeles Times*, 25 October 1994, p. A10. For interesting insight into mentality of suicide bombers, see Joel Greenberg, "Palestinian 'Martyrs,' All Too Willing," *New York Times*, 25 January 1995; and *Ma'ariv*, 30 December 1994, p. 8. For an example of this martyrology with an extensive list of Izzeldin al-Qassem martyrs since 1990, see *Filastin al'Muslimah*, November 1994, p. 14.
35. In a statement in Israeli court, Amir provided the justification: "When you kill in war, it is an act that is allowed," in Russell Watson, "Blame Time," *Newsweek*, 20 November 1995. As explained by Amir, "I did not commit the act to stop the peace process because there is no concept as the peace process, it is a process of war," *Mideast Mirror*, 6 November 1995.
36. For a useful overview of the incident, see Jihad B. Khazen, *The Sadat Assassination: Background and Implications* (Washington: Georgetown University's Center for Contemporary Arab Studies, 1981); and Dilip Hiro, "Faces of Fundamentalism," *The Middle East*, May 1988, pp. 11–12.
37. See Robert Fisk, "'Party of God' Develops Its Own Political Style," *Irish Times*, 9 February 1995.
38. For a very interesting discussion of this phenomenon, see Gilles Keppel, *The Revenge of God: The Resurgence of Islam, Christianity and Judaism in the Modern World* (London: Polity Press, 1995).
39. For a useful exposition of concealment in Shi'ism, refer to lecture by Prof. Etan Kohlberg, Hebrew University, delivered at the Tel Aviv University (Tel Aviv, Israel: 23 May 1993).
40. See Maskit Burgin, A. Merari, and A Kurz, eds., *Foreign Hostages in Lebanon*, JCSS Memorandum, no. 25, August 1988 (Tel Aviv: Tel Aviv University, 1988).
41. Bruce Hoffman (1993), p. 3.
42. See Bruce Hoffman, "'Holy Terror': The Implications of Terrorism Motivated by a Religious Imperative," in *The First International Workshop on Low Intensity Conflict*, ed. A. Woodcock et al. (Stockholm: Royal Society of Naval Sciences, 1995) p. 43.
43. See Andrew Pollack, "Cult's Prophesy of Disaster Draws Precautions in Tokyo," *New York Times*, 15 April 1995; and Andrew Brown, "Waiting for the End of the World," *The Independent*, 24 March 1995.
44. For example, a survey of imprisoned members of the Egyptian group al-Takfir wal-Hijra (Repentance and Holy Flight) revealed that the average member was in his 20s or early 30s, a university student or recent graduate; had better than average marks in school work; felt intensely about causes but was intolerant of conflicting opinions; and a willingness to employ violence

if necessary. See Ray Vicker, "Islam on the March," *Wall Street Journal*, 12 February 1980. For a similar profile of Sikh terrorists, see Carl H. Haeger, "Sikh Terrorism in the Struggle for Khalistan," *Terrorism*, 14 (1991) p. 227. Also see Hala Mustafa, "The Islamic Movements Under Mubarak," in *The Islamist Dilemma: The Political Role of Islamic Movements in the Contemporary Arab World*, ed. Laura Guazzone (Reading: Ithaca Press, 1995) p. 173.

45. For example, see Paul Wilkinson, "Hamas: An Assessment," *Jane's Intelligence Review* (July 1993) pp. 313–14; and Ziad Abu-Amr, *Islamic Fundamentalism in the West Bank and Gaza* (Indianapolis: Indiana University Press, 1994).
46. As demonstrated in the case of Egypt, "Jihad and other movements were born in [former Presidents] Nasser's and Sadat's prisons," see Robin Wright, "Holy Wars': The Ominous Side of Religion in Politics," *Christian Science Monitor*, 12 November 1987, p. 21. Also see Mustafa, p. 174.
47. Richard Hrair Dekmeijan, *Islam in Revolution: Fundamentalism in the Arab World* (Syracuse: Syracuse University Press, 1985) p. 61–62.
48. George Nader, *Middle East Insight* (June-July 1985).
49. See Anthony Davis, "Foreign Combatants in Afghanistan," *Jane's Intelligence Review* (July 1994) p. 327. Also see Raymond Whitaker, "Afghani Veterans Fan Out to Spread the Word—and Terror," *The Independent*, 16 April 1995.
50. For a detailed discussion of this plan, see Ehud Sprinzak, "Three Models of Religious Violence: The Case of Jewish Fundamentalism in Israel," in Marty and Appleby (1993), pp. 475–76. As stated by Sprinzak: "There has been no act by the Jewish underground which did not have a rabbinical backing." *Yediot Aharanot*, 18 March 1994.
51. See Youssef M. Ibrahim, "Muslim Edicts Take on New Force," *New York Times*, 12 February 1995; and Philip Jacobson, "Muhammad's Ally," *The Times Magazine*, 4 December 1993.
52. For example, see *Ma'ariv*, 28 February 1996; Ze'ev Chafets, "Israel's Quiet Anger," *New York Times*, 7 November 1995.
53. As revealed by Hizb'allah manifesto in 1985, "Imam Khomeini, the leader, has repeatedly stressed that America is the reason for all our catastrophes and the source of all malice. By fighting it, we are only exercising our legitimate right to defend our Islam and the dignity of our nation." See Hizb'allah's manifesto reprinted in Augustus Richard Norton, *Amal and the Shi'a: Struggle for the Soul of Lebanon* (Austin: University of Texas Press, 1987) pp. 167–87. See also Martin Kramer, "The Jihad Against the Jews," *Commentary* (October 1994) pp. 38–42.
54. For example, see David Wurmser, "The Rise and Fall of the Arab World," *Strategic Review* (Summer 1993) pp. 33–46.
55. See Fred Halliday, *Islam and the Myth of Confrontation* (London: I.B. Tauris, 1995).
56. For example see Alvin H. Bernstein, "Iran's Low-Intensity War Against the United States," *Orbis*, 30 (Spring 1986) pp. 149–67; and Sean K. Anderson, "Iran: Terrorism and Islamic Fundamentalism," in *Low-Intensity Conflict: Old Threats in a New World*, ed. Edwin G. Corr and Stephen Sloan (Oxford: Westview Press, 1992) pp. 173–95.
57. See Magnus Ranstorp, *Hizballah in Lebanon: The Politics of the Western Hostage-Crisis* (London: Macmillan, 1996).
58. See Bruce Hoffman (1993).
59. See Martin Kramer, "The Moral Logic of Hizbollah," in *Origins of Terrorism: Psychologies, Ideologies, Theologies, States of Mind*, ed. Walter Reich (Cambridge: Cambridge University Press, 1990) pp. 131–57.
60. See Robert M. Jenkins, "The Islamic Connection," *Security Management* (July 1993) pp. 25–30.
61. See Guy Arnold et al, eds., *Revolutionary & Dissident Movements: An International Guide* (Harlow: Longman Group, 1991) p. 141.
62. See Mir Zohair Husain, *Global Islamic Politics* (New York: Harper Collins, 1995) pp. 186–200.
63. Bruce Hoffman, "Intelligence and Terrorism: Emerging Threats and New Security Challenges in the Post–Cold War Era," *Intelligence and National Security*, 11, no. 3 (April 1996) p. 214. For a broader discussion of millenarian terrorism, see Michael Barkun, ed. *Millennialism and Violence* (London: Frank Cass, 1996).

Mark Juergensmeyer, 1988

The Logic of Religious Violence

When the struggle reaches the decisive phase may I die fighting in its midst.

—Jamail Singh Bhindranwale

In the mid-1970s, when militant young Sikhs first began to attack the Nirankaris—members of a small religious community perceived as being anti-Sikh—few observers could have predicted that that violence would escalate into the savagery that seized the Punjab in the 1980s. The Sikhs as a community were too well off economically, too well educated, it seemed, to be a party to random acts of terror. Yet it is true that militant encounters have often played a part in Sikh history, and in the mid-1960s a radical movement very much like that of the 1980s stormed through the Punjab. The charismatic leader at that time was Sant Fateh Singh, who went on a well-publicized fast and threatened to immolate himself on the roof of the Golden Temple's Akali Takht unless the government made concessions that would lead to the establishment of a Sikh-majority state. The Indian government, captained by Prime Minister Indira Gandhi, conceded, and the old Punjab state was carved in two to produce a Hindu-majority Haryana and a new Punjab. It was smaller than the previous one, and contained enough Sikh-dominated areas to give it a slim Sikh majority.

The violence of this decade, however, seems very different from what one saw in the 1960s.[1] For one thing, the attacks themselves have been more vicious. Often they have involved Sikhs and Hindus indiscriminately, and many innocent bystanders have been targeted along with politically active persons. The new Sikh leader, Jamail Singh Bhindranwale, was stranger—more intense and more strident—than Fateh Singh was, and the goals of Bhindranwale and his allies were more diffuse. Government officials who were trying to negotiate a settlement were never quite certain what their demands were. In fact there was no clear consensus among the activists themselves as to what they wanted, and the items on their lists of demands would shift from time to time. In 1984, shortly before she gave the command for the Indian Army to invade the Golden Temple, an exasperated Indira Gandhi itemized everything she had done to meet the Sikh demands and asked, 'What more can any government do?'[2]

It was a question that frustrated many observers outside the government as well, a good many moderate Sikhs among them. But frustration led to action, and those actions made things worse. The Indian army's brutal assault on the Golden Temple in June 1984, and the heartless massacre of Sikhs by Hindus in Delhi and elsewhere after the assassination of Mrs. Gandhi in November of that year caused the violence to escalate. Still, it is fair to say that quite a bit of bloodshed originated on the Sikh side of the ledger, and within the Sikh community anti-government violence achieved a religious respectability that begs to be explained.

The Rational Explanations

The explanations one hears most frequently place the blame for Sikh violence on political, economic and social factors, and each of these approaches is compelling. The political explanation, for instance, focuses on the weakness of the Sikh political party, the Akali Dal, and its inability to secure a consistent plurality in the Punjab legislature. This is no wonder, since the Sikhs command a bare 51 per cent majority of the post-1966 Punjab. Moreover, the Muslims, who comprised the Punjab's other non-Hindu religious community before 1948, were awarded a nation of their own at the time of India's independence, so it is understandable that many Sikhs would continue to long for greater political power, and even yearn for their own Pakistan.[3]

The economic explanation for Sikh unrest is largely a matter of seeing the achievements of the Sikhs in relation to what they feel their efforts should warrant, rather than to what others in India have received. Compared with almost every other region of India, the Punjab is fairly well-to-do. Yet Sikhs complain, with some justification, that for that very reason they have been deprived of their fair share: resources from the Punjab have been siphoned off to other parts of the nation.[4] Agricultural prices, for example, are held stable in India in part because the government maintains a ceiling on the prices that farmers in rich agricultural areas like the Punjab are permitted to exact. In addition some Sikhs claim that industrial growth has been hampered in the Punjab as the government has encouraged growth in other parts of India, and that the Punjab's agricultural lifeblood—water for irrigation from Punjabi rivers—has been diverted to farming areas in other states.

The social explanation for Sikh discontent is just as straightforward: the Sikhs are a minority community in India, and their separate identity within the Indian family is in danger. Since the religious ideas on which Sikhism is based grew out of the nexus of medieval Hinduism, Sikhs fear they could be reabsorbed into the amorphous cultural mass that is Hinduism and disappear as a distinct religious community.[5] The possibility is real: Sikhism almost vanished in the latter part of the nineteenth century. But in this century secularism is as much a threat as Hinduism, and like fundamentalist movements in many other parts of the world, Sikh traditionalists have seen the secular government as the perpetrator of a dangerous anti-religious ideology that threatens the existence of such traditional religious communities as their own. In the perception of some Sikhs, these two threats—the religious and the secular—have recently combined forces as the Hindu right has exercised increasing political power and Mrs Gandhi's Congress Party has allegedly pandered to its interests.[6]

There is nothing wrong with these political, economic and social explanations of Sikh unrest. Each is persuasive in its own sphere, and together they help us understand why the Sikhs as a community have been unhappy. But they do not help us understand the piety with which a few Sikhs have justified their bloody acts or the passion with which so many of them have condoned them—even the random acts of destruction associated with terrorism. Nor are they the sort of explanations one hears from Sikhs who are most closely involved in the struggle. The socioeconomic and political explanations usually come from observers outside the Sikh community or from those inside it who are least sympathetic to the militant protesters. The point of view of the activists is different. Their frame of reference is more grand: their explanations of the conflict and its causes achieve almost mythical dimensions. To understand this point of view we have to turn to their own words and see what they reveal about the radicals' perception of the world about them.

The Religious Rhetoric of Sikh Violence

To understand the militant Sikh position, I have chosen to focus on the speeches of Jamail Singh Bhindranwale, the man who was without dispute the most visible and charismatic of this generation's militant leaders.[7] He was also the most revered—or despised, depending on one's point of view. During his lifetime he was called a *sant*, a holy man, and a few Sikhs have been bold enough to proclaim him the eleventh *guru*, and thus challenge the traditional Sikh belief that the line of ten gurus ended with Gobind Singh in the early eighteenth century.

Jamail Singh was born in 1947 at the village Rodey near the town of Moga. He was the youngest son in a poor family of farmers from the Jat caste, and when he was 18 years old his father handed him over for religious training to the head of a Sikh center known as the Damdani Taksal. The leader came from the village Bhindran and was therefore known as Bhindranwale, and after his death, when the mantle of leadership fell on young Jamail Singh, he assumed his mentor's name. The young leader took his duties seriously and gained a certain amount of fame as a preacher. He was a stern one at that: Jamail became famous for castigating the easy-living, easy-drinking customs of Sikh villagers, especially those who clipped their beards and adopted modern ways. He carried weapons, and on 13 April 1978, in a bloody confrontation in Amritsar with members of the renegade Nirankaris religious movement, he showed that he was not afraid to use them. This episode was followed by an attack from Nirankaris that killed a number of Bhindranwale's followers, and further counter-attacks ensued.[8] Thus began the bloody career of a man who was trained to live a calm and spiritual life of religious devotion.

Although he was initially at the fringes of Sikh leadership, during the late 1970s Bhindranwale began to be taken seriously within Akali circles because of his growing popularity among the masses.[9] He seemed to have been fixated on the Nirankaris: his fiery sermons condemned them as evil. He regarded them as a demonic force that endangered the very basis of the Sikh community, especially its commitment to the authority of the Sikh gurus. And in time he expanded his characterization of their demonic power to include those who protected them, including the secular government of Indira Gandhi.

Much of what Bhindranwale has to say in sermons of this period, however, might be heard in the sermons of methodist pastors in Iowa or in the homilies of clergies belonging to any religious tradition, anywhere on the globe. He calls for faith—faith in a time of trial—and for the spiritual discipline that accompanies it. In one sermon he rebukes the press and others who call him an extremist, and explains what sort of an extremist he is:

> One who takes the vows of faith and helps others take it; who reads the scriptures and helps others to do the same; who avoids liquor and drugs and helps others do likewise; who urges unity and cooperation; who preaches Hindu-Sikh unity and coexistence... who says: 'respect your scriptures, unite under the flag, stoutly support the community, and be attached to your Lord's throne and home'.[10]

Like many Protestant ministers, Bhindranwale prescribes piety as the answer to every need. 'You can't have courage without reading [the Sikh scriptures]', he admonishes his followers: 'Only the [scripture]-readers can suffer torture and be capable of feats of strength'.[11] He is especially harsh on backsliders in the faith. Those who cut their beards are targets of his wrath: 'Do you think you resemble the image of Guru Gobind Singh?' he asks them.[12] But then he reassures the bulk of his followers. Because of their persistence in the faith, he tells them, 'the Guru will give you strength', adding that 'righteousness is with you'.[13] They will need all the strength and courage they can get, Bhindranwale explains, because their faith is under attack.[14]

Lying only slightly beneath the surface of this language is the notion of a great struggle that Bhindranwale thinks is taking place. On the personal level it is the tension between faith and the lack of faith; on the cosmic level it is the battle between truth and evil. Often his rhetoric is vague about who the enemy really is. 'In order to destroy religion', Bhindranwale informs his congregation, 'on all sides and in many forms mean tactics have been initiated'.[15] But rather than wasting effort in explaining who these forces are and why they would want to destroy religion, Bhindranwale dwells instead on what should be the response: a willingness to fight and defend the faith—if necessary, to the end.

> Unless you are prepared to die, sacrificing your own life, you cannot be a free people.... If you start thinking in terms of service to your community then you will be on the right path and you will readily sacrifice yourself. If you have faith in the Guru no power on earth can enslave you. The Sikh faith is to pray to God, take one's vows before the Guru Granth Sahib [scriptures] and then act careless of consequences to oneself.[16]

At other times Bhindranwale cites what appear to be specific attacks on Sikhism, but again the perpetrators are not sharply defined; they remain a vague, shadowy force of evil. 'The Guru Granth [scripture] has been buried in cowdung and thrown on the roadside', Bhindranwale informs his followers. 'That is your Father, your Guru, that they treat so.'[17] On another occasion he urges his followers to 'seek justice against those who have dishonored our sisters, drunk the blood of innocent persons, and insulted Satguru Granth Sahib'.[18] But the 'they' and the 'those' are not identified.

Occasionally, however, the enemy is more clearly specified: they are 'Hindus', 'the government', 'the press', the Prime Minister—whom he calls that 'lady born to a house of Brahmins'[19]—and perhaps most frequently Sikhs themselves who have fallen from the path. This somewhat rambling passage indicates these diverse enemies and the passionate hatred that Bhindranwale feels towards them:

> I cannot really understand how it is that, in the presence of Sikhs, Hindus are able to insult the [scriptures]. I don't know how these Sikhs were born to mothers and why they were not born to animals: to cats and to bitches.... Whoever insults the Guru Granth Sahib should be killed then and there.... Some youths complain that if they do such deeds then nobody harbours them. Well, no place is holier than this one [the Golden Temple].... I will take care of the man who comes to me after lynching the murderer of the Guru Granth Sahib; I'll fight for his case. What else do you want? That things have come to such a pass is in any event all your own weakness.... The man whose sister is molested and does nothing about it, whose Guru is insulted and who keeps on talking and doing nothing, has he got any right to be known as the son of the Guru? Just think for yourselves![20]

And in a similar vein:

> Talk is not enough against injustice. We have to act. Here you raise your swords but tomorrow you may wipe the dust from the sandals of sister Indira.... We have the right to be Sikhs.... The dearest thing to any Sikh should be the honor of the Guru.... Those

foes—the government and Hindus—are not dangerous. Rather one has to be wary of those who profess Sikhism yet do not behave as Sikhs.[21]

As important as Bhindranwale feels the immediate struggle is, he reminds his followers that the Sikh tradition has always been filled with conflict, and that the current battles are simply the most recent chapters in a long ongoing war with the enemies of the faith. The foes of today are connected with those from the legendary past. Indira Gandhi, for instance, is implicitly compared with the Moghul emperors: 'The rulers [the Congress party leaders] should keep in mind that in the past many like them did try in vain to annihilate the Gurus.'[22] In other speeches, Bhindranwale frequently looks to the past for guidance in dealing with current situations. When Sikhs who had sided with government policies come to him for forgiveness, for instance, he refuses. 'I asked that man', explains Bhindranwale, 'had he ever read a page of our history? Was the man who tortured Guru Arjun pardoned?'[23]

Occasionally Bhindranwale refers to some of the specific political, economic and social demands made by more moderate Sikh leaders. He supports these demands, but they are not his primary concern. In fact, the targets of these demands are often characterized simply as 'injustices', illustrations of the fact that the Sikh community is abused and under attack.[24] Since the larger struggle is the more important matter, these specific difficulties are of no great concern to Bhindranwale; they change from time to time. And it is of no use to win on one or two points and fail on others. Compromise is impossible; only complete victory will signal that the tide has turned. For that reason Bhindranwale scolds the Akali leaders for seeking a compromise settlement of the political demands made by Sikh leaders at Anandpur Sahib in 1973. 'Either full implementation of the Anandpur Sahib resolution', Bhindranwale demands, 'or their heads'.[25]

In a sense, then, Bhindranwale feels that individual Sikh demands can never really be met, because the ultimate struggle of which they are a part is much greater than the contestation between political parties and factional points of view. It is a vast cosmic struggle, and only such an awesome encounter is capable of giving profound meaning to the motivations of those who fight for Sikh causes. Such people are not just fighting for water rights and political boundaries, they are fighting for truth itself.

Clearly the religious language of Sikh militants like Bhindranwale is the language of ultimate struggle. But two related matters are not so obvious: why is this language attached to the more mundane issues of human politics and economics? And why is it linked with violent acts?

A Pause for Definitions: Violence and Religion

Before we turn to these questions, however, it might be useful to pause for a moment for definitions. Since I want to look at issues having to do with the general relation between violence and religion, not merely those that affect the Sikhs, it might be useful if I describe what I mean by these terms.

I will restrict my use of the word violence to actions that are aimed at taking human life—that intend to, and do, kill. Moreover, I mean especially abnormal, illegal, shocking acts of destruction. All acts of killing are violent, of course, but warfare and capital punishment have an aura of normalcy and do not violate our sensibilities in the same way as actions that seem deliberately designed to elicit feelings of revulsion and anger from those who witness them.[26] By speaking of violence in this restricted way, I mean to highlight the characteristics that we usually associate with terrorist acts.

The term religion is more difficult to define. I have been impressed with the recent attempts of several sociologists to find a definition that is not specific to any cultural region or historical period, and is appropriate for thinking about the phenomenon in modern as well as traditional societies. Clifford Geertz, for instance, sees religion as the effort to integrate everyday reality into a pattern of coherence that takes shape on a deeper level.[27] Robert Bellah also thinks of religion as the attempt to reach beyond ordinary reality in the 'risk of faith' that allows people to act 'in the face of uncertainty and unpredictability'.[28] Peter Berger specifies that such faith is an affirmation of the sacred, which acts as a doorway to a different kind of reality.[29] Louis Dupré prefers to avoid the term 'sacred', but integrates elements of both Berger's and Bellah's definition in his description of religion as 'a commitment to the transcendent as to *another* reality'.[30]

What all of these definitions have in common is their emphasis on a certain kind of experience that people share with others in particular communities. It is an experience of another reality, or of a deeper stratum of the reality that we know in everyday life. As [Emile] Durkheim, whose thought is fundamental to each of these thinkers, was adamant in observing, religion has a more encompassing force than can be suggested by any dichotomization of the sacred and the profane. To Durkheim, the religious point of view includes both the notion that there is such a dichotomy, and that the sacred aspects of it will always, ultimately, reign supreme.[31] Summarizing Durkheim's and the others' definitions of religion, I think it might be described as the perception that there is a tension between reality as it appears and as it really is (or has been, or will be).

This definition helps us think of religion as the subjective experience of those who use religious language, and in fact it is easier with this definition to speak of religious language, or a religious way of looking at the world, than to speak of religion in a more reified sense.[32] When we talk of the various 'religions', then, we mean the communities that have a tradition of sharing a particular religious point of view, a world view in which there is an essential conflict between appearance and a deeper reality. There is the hint, in this definition, that the deeper reality holds a degree of permanence and order quite unobtainable by ordinary means, as religious people affirm. The conflict between the two is what religion is about: religious language contains images both of grave disorder and tranquil order, and often holds out the hope that despite appearances to the contrary, order eventually will triumph, and disorder will be contained.

Why Does Religion Need Violence?

There is nothing in this definition that requires religion to be violent, but it does lead one to expect religious language to make sense of violence and to incorporate it in some way into the world view it expresses. Violence, after all, shocks one's sense of order and has the potential for causing the ultimate disorder in any person's life: physical destruction and death. Since religious language is about the tension between order and disorder, it is frequently about violence.

The symbols and mythology of Sikhism, for instance, are full of violence. The most common visual symbol of Sikhism is the two-edged sword (*khanda*), supported by two scabbards and surrounded by a circle. Sikhs often interpret the two edges of this sword as symbolizing spiritual and worldly foes,[33] and they say that a battle sword (*kirpan*) is included among the five objects that Sikhs are supposed to wear at all times to symbolize an awareness of these same enemies.[34] Unlike the Bible, the sacred scriptures of the Sikhs—known collectively as the *Guru Granth Sahib*—do not contain accounts of wars and savage acts, but the stories of the Sikhs' historical past are bloody indeed. In fact, these stories have taken on a canonical character within Sikhism, and they more vividly capture the imagination than the devotional and theological sentiments of the scriptures themselves. The calendar art so prominent in most Sikh homes portrays a mystical Guru Nanak, of course, but alongside him there are pictures of Sikh military heroes and scenes from great battles. Bloody images also leap from brightly-colored oil paintings in the Sikh Museum housed in the Golden Temple. There are as many depictions of martyrs in their wretched final moments as of victors radiant in conquest.

Because the violence is so prominent in Sikh art and legend, and because many symbols of the faith are martial, one might think that Sikhs as a people are more violent than their counterparts in other areas of India. But if one leaves aside the unrest of the past several years, I do not think this can be demonstrated. It would be convenient to say that the prestige of violent symbols in the Sikh religion has increased Sikhs' propensity for violent action, or that the Sikh religion is violent because Sikhs as a people are violent, but I do not think either of these arguments can be made very convincingly.

The fact is that the symbols and mythology of most religious traditions are filled with violent images, and their histories leave trails of blood. One wonders that familiarity can prevent Christians from being repulsed by the violent images portrayed by hymns such as 'Onward Christian Soldiers', 'The Old Rugged Cross', 'Washed in the Blood of the Lamb', and 'There is a Fountain Flowing with Blood'. Or perhaps familiarity is not the issue at all. The central symbol of Christianity is an execution device—a cross—from which, at least in the Roman tradition, the dying body still hangs. From a non-Christian point of view, the most sacred of Christian rituals, the eucharist, looks like ritual cannabalism, where the devout eat the flesh and drink the blood of their departed leader. At a certain level, in fact, this interpretation is accurate; yet few would argue that the violent acts perpetrated by Christians over the centuries are the result of their being subjected to such messages.

The ubiquity of violent images in religion and the fact that some of the most ancient religious practices involve the sacrificial slaughter of animals have led to speculation about why religion and violence are so intimately bound together. Some of these speculators are among the best known modern theorists, Karl Marx, for instance, saw religious symbols as the expression of real social oppression, and religious wars as the result of tension among economic classes.[35] Sigmund Freud saw in religious rituals vestiges of a primal oedipal act that when ritually reenacted provide a symbolic resolution of feelings of sexual and physical aggression.[36] More recently, Rene Girard has revived the Freudian thesis but given it a social rather than psychological coloration. Girard sees the violent images of religion as a symbolic displacement of violence from one's own communal fellowship to a scapegoat foe.[37]

What these thinkers have in common is that they see religious violence as a symptom of and symbol for something else: social hostility, in the case of Marx; sexual and physical aggression, in the case of Freud; social competition, in the case of Girard. They may be right: religion and other cultural forms may have been generated out of basic personal and social needs. Yet it seems to me that even without these explanations the internal logic of religion requires that religious symbols and myths express violent meanings.

Religion deals with the ultimate tension between order and disorder, and disorder is inherently violent, so it is understandable that the chaotic, dangerous character of life is represented in religious images. Of course, the religious promise is that order conquers chaos; so it is also understandable that the violence religion portrays is in some way limited or tamed. In Christianity, for example, the very normalcy with which the blood-filled hymns are sung and the eucharist is eaten indicates their domestication. In ritual, violence is symbolically transferred. The blood of the eucharistic wine is ingested by the supplicant and becomes part of living tissue; it brings new life. In song a similarly calming transformation occurs. For, as Christian theology explains, in Christ violence has been corralled. Christ died in order for death to be defeated, and his blood is that of the sacrificial lamb who atones for our sins so that we will not have to undergo a punishment as gruesome as his.

In the Sikh tradition violent images are also domesticated. The symbol of the two-edged sword has become an emblem to be worn on lockets and proudly emblazened on shops and garden gates. It is at the forefront of the worship center in Sikh *gurudwaras* where it is treated as reverently as Christians treat their own emblem of destruction, the cross. And the gory wounds of the martyrs bleed on in calendar art. As I have suggested, Sikh theologians and writers are no more hesitant to allegorize the meaning of such symbols and stories than their Christian counterparts. They point toward the war between good and evil that rages in each person's soul.

The symbols of violence in religion, therefore, are symbols of a violence conquered, or at least put in place, by the larger framework of order that religious language provides. But one must ask how these symbolic presentations of violence are related to real violence. One might think that they should prevent violent acts by allowing violent feelings to be channelled into the harmless dramas of ritual, yet we know that the opposite is sometimes the case. The violence of religion can be savagely real.

Why Does Violence Need Religion?

A reason often given to explain why religious symbols are associated with acts of real violence is that religion is exploited by violent people. This explanation, making religion the pure and innocent victim of the darker forces of human nature, is undoubtedly too easy; yet it contains some truth. Religion in fact is sometimes exploited, and it is important to understand why people who are engaged in potentially violent struggles do at times turn to the language of religion. In the case of the Sikhs, this means asking why the sort of people who were exercised over the economic, political and social issues explored at the beginning of this article turned to preachers like Bhindranwale for leadership.

One answer is that by sacralizing these concerns the political activists gave them an aura of legitimacy that they did not previously possess. The problem with this answer is that most of the concerns we mentioned—the inadequacy of Sikh political representation, for instance, and the inequity of agricultural prices—were perfectly legitimate, and did not need the additional moral weight of religion to give them respectability. And in fact, the people who were primarily occupied with these issues—Sikh businessmen and political leaders—were not early supporters of Bhindranwale. Even when they became drawn into his campaign, their relation with him remained ambivalent at best.

There was one political demand, however, that desperately needed all the legitimization that it could get. This was the demand for Khalistan, a separate Sikh nation. Separatist leaders such as Jagjit Singh Chauhan were greatly buoyed by such words of Bhindranwale as these:

> We are religiously separate. But why do we have to emphasize this? It is only because we are losing our identity. Out of selfish interests our Sikh leaders who have only the success of their farms and their industries at heart have started saying that there is no difference between Sikh and Hindu. Hence the danger of assimilation has increased.[38]

> When they say the Sikhs are not separate we'll demand separate identity—even if it demands sacrifice.[39]

Bhindranwale himself, interestingly, never came out in support of Khalistan. 'We are not in favor of Khalistan nor are we against it', he said, adding that 'we wish to live in India', but would settle for a separate state if the Sikhs did not receive what he regarded as their just respect.[40] Whatever his own reservations about the Khalistan issue, however, his appeal to sacrifice made his rhetoric attractive to the separatists. It also raised another, potentially more powerful aspect of the sacralization of political demands: the prospect that religion could give moral sanction to violence.

By identifying a temporal social struggle with the cosmic struggle of order and disorder, truth and evil, political actors are able to avail themselves of a way of thinking that justifies the use of violent means. Ordinarily only the state has the moral right to take life—for purposes either of military defense, police protection or punishment—and the codes of ethics established by religious traditions support this position. Virtually every religious tradition, including the Sikhs', applauds non-violence and proscribes the taking of human life.[41] The only exception to this rule is the one we have given: most ethical codes allow the state to kill for reasons of punishment and protection.[42]

Those who want moral sanction for their use of violence, and who do not have the approval of an officially recognized government, find it helpful to have access to a higher source: the meta-morality that religion provides. By elevating a temporal struggle to the level of the cosmic, they can bypass the usual moral restrictions on killing. If a battle of the spirit is thought to exist, then it is not ordinary morality but the rules of war that apply. It is interesting that the best-known incidents of religious violence throughout the contemporary world have occurred in places where there is difficulty in defining the character of a nation state. Palestine and Ireland are the most obvious examples, but the revolution in Iran also concerned itself with what the state should be like, and what elements of society should lead it. Religion provided the basis for a new national consensus and a new kind of leadership.

There are some aspects of social revolution in the Punjab situation as well. It is not the established leaders of the Akali party who have resorted to violence, but a second level of leadership—a younger, more marginal group for whom the use of violence is enormously empowering. The power that comes from the barrel of a gun, as Mao [Tse-tung] is said to have remarked, has a very direct effect. But there is a psychological dimension to this power that may be even more effective. As Frantz Fanon argued in the context of the Algerian revolution some years ago even a small display of violence can have immense symbolic power: the power to jolt the masses into an awareness of their potency.[43]

It can be debated whether or not the masses in the Punjab have been jolted into an awareness of their own capabilities, but the violent actions of the militants among them have certainly made the masses more aware of the militants' powers. They have attained a status of authority rivalling what police and other government officials possess. One of the problems in the Punjab today is the unwillingness of many villagers in the so-called terrorist zones around Batala and Taran Tarn to report terrorist activities to the authorities. The radical youth are even said to have established an alternative government.

By being dangerous the young Sikh radicals have gained a certain notoriety, and by clothing their actions in the moral garb of religion they have given their actions legitimacy. Because their actions are morally sanctioned by religion, they are fundamentally political actions: they break the state's monopoly on morally-sanctioned killing. By putting the right to kill in their own hands, the perpetrators of religious violence are also making a daring claim of political independence.

Even though Bhindranwale was not an outspoken supporter of Khalistan, he often spoke of the Sikhs' separate identity as that of a religious community with national characteristics. The term he used for religious community, *quam*, is an Urdu term that has overtones of nationhood. It is the term the Muslims used earlier in this century in defending their right to have a separate nation, and it is the term that Untouchables used in the Punjab in the 1920s when they attempted to be recognized as a separate social and political entity.[44] Another term that is important to Bhindranwale is *miri-piri*, the notion that spiritual and temporal power are linked.[45] It is this concept that is symbolically represented by the two-edged sword and that justified Sikh support for an independent political party. Young Sikh activists are buttressed in their own aspirations to leadership by the belief that acts that they conceive as being heroic and sacrificial—even those that involve taking the lives of others—have both spiritual and political significance. They are risking their lives for God and the Sikh community.

Not all of the Sikh community appreciates their efforts, however, and the speeches of Bhindranwale make clear that disagreements and rivalries within the community were one of his major concerns. Some of Bhindranwale's harshest words were reserved for Sikhs who he felt showed weakness and a tendency to make easy compromises. In one speech, after quoting a great martyr in Sikh history as having said, 'even if I have to give my head, may I never lose my love for the Sikh Faith', Bhindranwale railed against Sikh bureaucrats and modernized youth who could not make that sacrifice, and ended with a little joke:

> I am sorry to note that many people who hanker after a government position say instead, 'even if I lose my Faith, may I never lose my position'. And our younger generation has started saying this: 'even if I lose my Faith, may a beard never grow on my face'.... If you find the beard too heavy, pray to God saying... 'we do not like this Sikhism and manhood. Have mercy on us. Make us into women....'[46]

But most Sikhs in Bhindranwale's audience, including the youth, were not the sort who would be tempted to cut their hair; and few, especially in the villages where Bhindranwale had been popular, were in a position to 'hanker after a governmental position'. People, such as the Akali leaders whom Bhindranwale castigated for making compromises for the sake of personal gain, were no doubt objects of contempt in the villages long before Bhindranwale came along, and by singling them out, Bhindranwale identified familiar objects of derision—scapegoats—that humbled those who had succeeded in worldly affairs and heightened the sense of unity among those who had not.

Bhindranwale made a great plea for unity. 'Our misfortune is disunity', he told his audiences. 'We try to throw mud at each other. Why don't we give up thinking of mud and in close embrace with each other work with determination to attain our goals.'[47] Those who eventually opposed him, including the more moderate Akali leader, Sant Harchand Singh Longowal, regarded Bhindranwale as a prime obstacle to the very unity he preached. During the dark days immediately preceding Operation Bluestar in June 1984, the two set up rival camps in the Golden Temple and allegedly killed each other's lieutenants. It is no wonder that many of Bhindranwale's followers, convinced the Indian army had a collaborator inside the Golden Temple, were suspicious when Bhindranwale was murdered in the raid and Longowal was led off safely under arrest. No wonder also that many regarded Longowal's assassination a year later as revenge for Bhindranwale's.

While he was alive, Bhindranwale continued to preach unity, but it was clear that what he wanted was everyone else to unite around him. He and his supporters wished to give the impression that they were at the center, following the norm of Sikh belief and behavior, and that the community should therefore group around them. This message had a particular appeal to those who were socially marginal to the Sikh community, including lower-caste people and Sikhs who had taken up residence abroad. Some of the most fanatical of Bhindranwale's followers, including Beant Singh, the assassin of Indira Gandhi, came from the Untouchable castes (Beant Singh was from the lowest caste of Untouchables, the Sweepers), and a considerable amount of money and moral support for the Punjab militants came from Sikhs living in such faraway places as London, Houston, and Yuba City, California.

These groups gained from their identification with Bhindranwale a sense of belonging, and the large Sikh communities in England, Canada and America were especially sensitive to his message that the Sikhs needed to be strong, united and defensive of their tradition. Many of Bhindranwale's supporters in the Punjab, however, received a more tangible benefit from associating with his cause: politically active village youth and small-time clergy were able to gain support from many who were not politically mobilized before. In that sense Bhindranwale was fomenting something of a political revolution, and the constituency was not unlike the one the Ayatollah Khomeini was able to gather in Iran. In so far as Bhindranwale's message was taken as an endorsement of the killings that some of these fundamentalist youth committed, the instrument of religious violence gave power to those who had little power before.

When Does Cosmic Struggle Lead to Real Violence?

The pattern of religious violence of the Sikhs could be that of Irish Catholics, or Shi'ite Muslims in Palestine, or fundamentalist Christian bombers of abortion clinics in the United States. There are a great many communities in which the language of cosmic struggle justifies acts of violence. But those who are engaged in them, including the Sikhs, would be offended if we concluded from the above discussion that their actions were purely for social or political gain. They argue that they act out of religious conviction, and surely they are to some degree right. Destruction is a part of the logic of religion, and virtually every religious tradition carries with it images of chaos and terror. But symbolic violence does not lead in every instance to real bloodshed, and even the eagerness of political actors to exploit religious symbols is not in all cases sufficient to turn religion towards a violent end. Yet some forms of religion do seem to propel the faithful rather easily into militant confrontation: which ones, and why?

The current resurgence of religious violence around the world has given an urgency to attempts to answer these questions, and to identify which characteristics of religion are conducive to violence. The efforts of social scientists have been directed primarily to the social and political aspects of the problem, but at least a few of them have tried to trace the patterns in religion's own logic. David C. Rapoport, for instance, has identified several features of messianic movements that he believes lead to violence, most of which are characterized by a desire for an antinomian liberation from oppression.[48]

My own list of characteristics comes directly from our discussion of the religious language of cosmic struggle. It is informed by my understanding of what has happened in the Sikh tradition, but it seems to me that the following tenets of religious commitment are found whenever acts of religious violence occur.

1. The Cosmic Struggle Is Played Out in History

To begin with, it seems to me that if religion is to lead to violence it is essential for the devout to believe that the cosmic struggle is realizable in human terms. If the war between good and evil, order and chaos, is conceived as taking place in historical time, in a real geographical location, and among actual social contestants, it is more likely that those who are prone to violent acts will associate religion with their struggles. This may seem to be an obvious point, yet we have some evidence that it is not always true.

In the Hindu tradition, for instance, the mythical battles in the Mahabharata and Ramayana epics are as frequently used as metaphors for present-day struggles as are the actual battles in Sikh and Islamic history and in biblical Judaism and Christianity. Like members of these traditions, Hindus characterize their worldly foes by associating them with the enemies of the good in their legendary battles. The main difference between the Hindus and the others is that their enemies are mythical—that is, they seem mythical to us. To many pious Hindus, however, the stories in the epics are no less real than those recorded in the Bible or in the Sikh legends. A believing Hindu will be able to show you where the great war of the Mahabharata was actually fought, and where the gods actually lived. Moreover, the Hindu cycles of time allow for a cosmic destruction to take place in this world, at the end of the present dark age. So the Hindu tradition is not as devoid of images of divine intervention in worldly struggles as outsiders sometimes assume.[49]

The major tradition that appears to lack the notion that the cosmic struggle is played out on a social plane is Buddhism. But this is an exception that proves the rule, for it is a tradition that is characteristically devoid of religiously sanctioned violence. There are instances in Thai history that provide Buddhist justifications for warfare, but these are rare for the tradition as a whole. In general, Buddhism has no need for actual battles in which the pious can prove their mettle.

2. Believers Identify Personally With the Struggle

The Buddhist tradition does affirm that there is a spiritual conflict, however: it is the clash between the perception that this imperfect and illusory world is real and a higher consciousness that surmounts worldly perception altogether. And in a sense, the struggle takes place in this world, in that it takes place in the minds of worldly persons. This kind of internalization of the cosmic struggle does not in itself lead to violence, and Buddhists are not ordinarily prone to violent deeds. Nor are Sufis, the Islamic mystics who have reconceived the Muslim notion of *jihad.* To many Sufis, the greater *jihad* is not the one involving worldly warfare, but the one within: the conflict between good and evil within one's own soul.[50]

This talk about the cosmic struggle as something inside the self would seem to be easily distinguishable from external violence, but in Sikh theology, including the rhetoric of Bhindranwale, they go hand in hand. 'The weakness is in us', Bhindranwale was fond of telling his followers. 'We are the sinners of this house of our Guru.'[51] Militant Shi'ite Muslims are similarly racked with a sense of personal responsibility for the moral decadence of the world, and once again their tendency toward internalization does not necessarily shield them from acts of external violence. The key to the connection, it seems to me, is that at the same time that the cosmic struggle is understood to impinge about the inner recesses of an individual person, it must be understood as occurring on a worldly, social plane. Neither of these notions is by itself sufficient to motivate a person to religious violence. If one believes that the cosmic struggle is largely a matter of large continuing social forces, one is not likely to become personally identified with the struggle; and if one is convinced that the struggle is solely interior there is not reason to look for it outside. But when the two ideas coexist, they are a volatile concoction.

Thus when Bhindranwale spoke about the warfare in the soul his listeners knew that however burdensome that conflict is, they need not bear it alone. They may band together with their comrades and continue the struggle in the external arena, where the foes are more vulnerable, and victories more tangible. And their own internal struggles impel them to become involved in the worldly conflict: their identification with the overall struggle makes them morally responsible, in part, for its outcome. 'We ourselves are ruining Sikhism', Bhindranwale once told his congregation.[52] On another occasion he told the story of how, when Guru Gobind Singh asked an army of 80,000 to sacrifice their heads for the faith, only five assented. Bhindranwale implied that the opportunity was still at hand to make the choice of whether they were to be one of the five or the 79,995.[53] He reminded them that even though the cosmic war was still being waged, and that the evil within them and outside them had not yet been purged, their choice could still make a difference.

Sikhism is not the only tradition in which this link is forged between the external and internal arenas of the cosmic struggle. Shi'ite Muslims bear a great weight of communal guilt for not having defended one of the founders of their tradition, Husain, when he was attacked and martyred by the vicious Yazid. During the Iranian revolution some of them relived that conflict by identifying specific foes—the Shah and President Jimmy Carter—as Yazids returned. There was no doubt that such people should be attacked. Radical Shi'ites in Iran were not about to compound their guilt and miss an historical opportunity of righting an ancient wrong.

The same sort of logic has propelled many Christians into a vicious anti-Semitism. It is a mark of good Christian piety for individuals to bear the responsibility for the crucifixion of Jesus: the theme of Christians taking part in the denial and betrayal of Jesus is the stuff of many a hymn and sermon. Some Christians believe that the foes to whom they allowed Jesus to be delivered were the Jews. Attacks on the present-day Jewish community, therefore, help to lighten their sense of culpability.

3. The Cosmic Struggle Continues in the Present

What makes these actions of Sikhs, Shi'ites and anti-Semitic Christians spiritually defensible is the conviction that the sacred struggle has not ended in some earlier period, but that it continues in some form today. It is a conviction that also excites the members of the Gush Emunim, a militant movement in present-day Israel, who have taken Israel's victory in the Six Day War as a sign that the age of messianic redemption has finally begun.[54]

Not all Israelis respond to this sign with the same enthusiasm, however, just as not all Christians or Shi'ite Muslims are convinced that the apocalyptic conflict prophesied by their tradition is really at hand. Many of the faithful assent to the notion that the struggle exists within, for what person of faith has not felt the internal tension between belief and disbelief, affirmation and denial, order and chaos? But they often have to be persuaded that the conflict currently rages on a social plane, especially if the social world seems orderly and benign.

Bhindranwale took this challenge as one of the primary tasks of his ministry. He said that one of his main missions was to alert his people that they were oppressed, even if they did not know it. He ended one of his sermons with this fervent plea: 'I implore all of you in this congregation. Go to the villages and make every child, every mother, every Singh realise we are slaves and we have to shake off this slavery in order to survive.'[55]

In Bhindranwale's mind the appearances of normal social order simply illustrated how successful the forces of evil had become in hiding their demonic agenda. His logic compelled him to believe that Punjabi society was racked in a great struggle, even if it showed no indication of it. Long before the Punjab was torn apart by its most recent round of violence, Bhindranwale claimed that an even fiercer form of violence reigned: the appearance of normal order was merely a demonic deception. Bhindranwale hated the veil of calm that seemed to cover his community and recognized that his own followers were often perplexed about what he said: 'Many of our brothers, fresh from the villages, ask, "Sant Ji, we don't know about enslavement." For that reason, I have to tell you why you are slaves.'[56]

The evidence that Bhindranwale gave for the oppression of Sikhs was largely limited to examples of police hostility that arose after the spiral of violence in the Punjab began to grow. Some of his allegations, such as the account he gave of the treatment meted out to followers who hijacked Indian airplanes, have a peculiar ring:

> If a Sikh protests in behalf of his Guru by hijacking a plane, he is put to death.... None of the Sikhs in these three hijackings attacked any passenger nor did they damage the planes. But the rule is that for a fellow with a turban, there is the bullet.... For a person who says 'Hare Krishna, Hare Krishna, Hare Rama', there is a government appointment. Sikh brothers, this is a sign of slavery.[57]

Those who attempted to combat Bhindranwale could not win against such logic. If they responded to Sikh violence they would be seen as oppressors. If they did not respond, the violence would escalate. And even if there was neither violence nor repression, the absence of the overt signs of conflict would be an indication to Bhindranwale of a demonical calm.

4. The Struggle Is at a Point of Crisis

On a number of occasions, in referring to the immediacy of the struggle, Bhindranwale seemed to indicate that the outcome was in doubt. His perception of the enormity of the evil he faced and of the torpor of the Sikh response made his prognosis a dismal one. Sometimes he felt that the best efforts of a few faithful Sikhs were doomed: 'today', he darkly proclaimed, 'the Sikh community is under threat'.[58] But on other occasions he seemed to hold out a measure of hope. Things were coming to a head, he implied, and the struggle was about to enter 'the decisive phase'.[59]

What is interesting about this apocalyptic rhetoric is its uncertainty. If the outcome were less in doubt there would be little reason for violent action. If one knew that the foe would win, there would be no reason to want to fight back. Weston LaBarre describes the terrible circumstances surrounding the advent of the Ghost Dance religion of the Plains Indians: knowing that they faced overwhelming odds and almost certain defeat, the tribe diverted their concerns from worldly conflict to spiritual conflict, and entertained the notion that a ritual dance would conjure up sufficient spiritual force to destroy the alien cavalry.[60]

LaBarre concludes that sheer desperation caused them to turn to religion and away from efforts to defend themselves. But by the same token, if they knew that the battle could be won without a struggle, there also would be little reason for engagement. The passive pacifism of what William James calles 'healthy-souled religion'—mainstream Protestant churches, for example, that regard social progress as inevitable—comes from just such optimism.[61] Other pacifist movements, however, have been directly engaged in conflict. Menno Simons, the Anabaptist for whom the Mennonite church is named, and Mohandas Gandhi are examples of pacifist leaders who at times narrowly skirted the edges of violence, propelled by a conviction that without human effort the outcome they desired could not be won. In that sense Gandhi and Bhindranwale were more alike than one might suspect. Both saw the world in terms of cosmic struggle, both regarded their cause as being poised on a delicate balance between oppression and opportunity, and both believed that human action could tip the scales. The issue that divided them, of course, was violence.

5. Acts of Violence Have a Cosmic Meaning

The human action in the Sikh case is certainly not pacifist, for Bhindranwale held that there would be 'no deliverance without weapons.'[62] He was careful, however, to let the world know that these weapons were not be used indiscriminantly: 'It is a sin for a Sikh to keep weapons to hurt an innocent person, to rob anyone's home, to dishonor anyone or to oppress anyone. But there is no greater sin for a Sikh than keeping weapons and not using them to protect his faith.'[63] Contrariwise, there is no greater valor for a Sikh than to use weapons in defense of the faith. Bhindranwale himself was armed to the teeth, and although he never publically admitted to any of the killings that were pinned on him personally, Bhindranwale expressed his desire to 'die fighting', a wish that was fulfilled within months of being uttered.[64]

According to Bhindranwale, those who committed acts of religiously sanctioned violence were to be regarded as heroes and more. Although he usually referred to himself as a 'humble servant, and an 'uneducated fallible person',[65] Bhindranwale would occasionally identify himself with one of the legendary Sikh saints, Baba Deep Singh, who continued to battle with Moghul foes even after his head had been severed from his body. He carried it manfully under his arm.[66] In Bhindranwale's mind, he too seemed destined for martyrdom.

To many Sikhs today, that is precisely what Bhindranwale achieved. Whatever excesses he may have committed during his lifetime are excused, as one would excuse a lethal but heroic soldier in a glorious war. Even Beant Singh, the bodyguard of Indira Gandhi who turned on her, is held to be a saintly hero. Perhaps this has to be: if Indira was such a demonic foe, her assassin must be similarly exalted.

Even those who value the sense of order that religion provides sometimes cheer those who throw themselves into the arena of religious violence. Such people are, after all, struggling for good, and for that reason their actions are seen as ultimately producing order. But until such recognition of their mission can be achieved among the more conservative rank and file, such activists are forced, as prophets and agents of a higher order of truth, to engage in deeds that necessarily startle. Their purpose is to awaken good folk, mobilize their community, insult the evil forces, and perhaps even to demonstrate dramatically to God himself that there are those who are willing to fight and die on his side, and to deliver his judgement of death. The great promise of cosmic struggle is that order will prevail over chaos; the great irony is that many must die in order for certain visions of that victory to prevail and their awful dramas be brought to an end.

Mark Juergensmeyer is a professor at the University of California, Santa Barbara, and also serves as director of the Global & International Studies Program and chair of the Global Peace & Security Program. He was a Fulbright fellow (India), a senior researcher at the American Institute of Indian Studies (India), and a fellow at the Woodrow Wilson International Center for Scholars (Smithsonian Institution). He is the author of *The New Cold War? Religious Nationalism Confronts the Secular State* (1993) and *Terror in the Mind of God: The Global Rise of Religious Violence* (2001).

Notes

1. For general background on the Punjab crisis in the 1980s and a chronicle of events leading up to it, see Mark Tully and Satish Jacob, *Amritsar: Mrs Gandhi's Last Battle* (London: Cape, 1985), Amarjit Kaur, *et al., The Punjab Story* (New Delhi: Roli Books International, 1984), and Kuldip Nayar and Khushwant Singh, *Tragedy of Punjab: Operation Bluestar and After* (New Delhi: Vision Books, 1984).
2. Indira Gandhi, 'Don't Shed Blood, Shed Hatred', All India Radio, 2 June 1984, reprinted in V. D. Chopra, R. K. Mishra and Nirmal Singh, *Agony of Punjab* (New Delhi: Patriot Publishers, 1984), p. 189. Indian government officials seemed to be genuinely caught off-guard by the Sikh militancy. I remember once in the summer of 1984 when the Indian Consul General in San Francisco turned to me after we had been on a radio talk show and said, 'I haven't a clue; can you tell me why in the devil the Sikhs are behaving like this?'
3. The demand for a Khalistan—a Sikh state similar to Pakistan—was raised by a small number of Sikh militants, including a former cabinet minister of the Punjab, Jagjit Singh Chauhan, who set up a movement in exile in London. It was not, however, a significant or strongly supported demand among Sikhs in the Punjab until after Operation Bluestar in June 1984. The Indian government's account of Chauhan's movement is detailed in a report prepared by the Home Ministry, 'Sikh Agitation for Khalistan', reprinted in Nayar and Singh, *Tragedy of Punjab*, pp. 142–55.
4. The Anandpur Resolution supported by leaders of the Akali Dal focused primarily on economic issues. For an analysis of the Punjab crisis from an economic perspective, see Chopra, Mishra and Singh, *Agony of Punjab.*

5. The fear of the absorption of Sikhism into Hinduism is the frequent refrain of Khushwant Singh; see, for instance, the final chapter of his *History of the Sikhs*, Vol. 2 (Princeton, NJ: Princeton University Press, 1966). He attributes the cause of many of the problems in the Punjab in the mid-1980s to this fear as well; see his *Tragedy of Punjab*, pp. 19–21.
6. For an interesting analysis of the general pattern of religious fundamentalism in South Asia of which the Hindu and Sikh movements are a part, see Robert Eric Frykenberg, 'Revivalism and Fundamentalism: Some Critical Observations with Special Reference to Politics in South Asia', in James W. Bjorkman (ed.), *Fundamentalism, Revivalists and Violence in South Asia* (Riverdale, MD: Riverdale, 1986).
7. I am grateful to Professor Ranbir Singh Sandhu, Department of Civil Engineering, Ohio State University, for providing me with several hours of tape-recorded speeches of Sant Jamail Singh Bhindranwale. Professor Sandhu has translated some of these speeches, and I appreciate his sharing these translations with me. For this article I am relying primarily on the words of Bhindranwale. They are found in the following sources: 'Sant Jamail Bhindranwale's Address to the Sikh Congregation', a transcript of a sermon given in the Golden Temple in November 1983, translated by Ranbir Singh Sandhu, April 1985, and distributed by the Sikh Religious and Educational Trust, Columbus, Ohio; excerpts of Bhindranwale's speeches, translated into English, that appear in Joyce Pettigrew, 'In Search of a New Kingdom of Lahore', *Pacific Affairs*, Vol. 60, No. 1 (Spring 1987) (forthcoming), and interviews with Bhindranwale found in various issues of *India Today* and other publications.
8. The spiritual leader of the Nirankaris, Baba Gurbachan Singh, was assassinated at his home in Delhi on 24 May 1980. Bhindranwale was implicated in the murder, but was never brought to trial. Kuldip Nayar claims that Zail Singh, who became President of India, came to Bhindranwale's defense at that time (Nayar and Singh, *Tragedy of Punjab,* p. 37).
9. It is said that Bhindranwale was first brought into the political arena in 1977 by Mrs Gandhi's son, Sanjay, who hoped that Bhindranwale's popularity would undercut the political support of the Akali party (Nayar and Singh, *Tragedy of Punjab*, p. 31, and Tully, *Amritsar*, p. 57–61).
10. Bhindranwale, 'Address to the Sikh Congregation', pp. 10–11.
11. Bhindranwale, excerpt from a speech, in Pettigrew.
12. Ibid., p. 15.
13. Ibid.
14. Bhindranwale, 'Address to the Sikh Congregation', p. 1.
15. Ibid.
16. Bhindranwale, excerpt from a speech, in Pettigrew.
17. Ibid.
18. Bhindranwale, 'Address to the Sikh Congregation', p. 10.
19. Ibid., p. 2.
20. Bhindranwale, excerpt from a speech, in Pettigrew.
21. Ibid.
22. Ibid.
23. Ibid.
24. Bhindranwale, 'Address to the Sikh Congregation', pp. 1–5, and ibid., p. 14.
25. Bhindranwale, excerpt from a speech, in Pettigrew.
26. For an interesting discussion of the definition of violence and terror in political contexts see Thomas Perry Thornton, 'Terrorism as a Weapon of Political Agitation', in Harry Eckstein (ed.), *Internal War: Problems and Approaches* (New York: The Free Press, 1964); and David C. Rapoport, 'The Politics of Atrocity', in Y. Alexander and S. Finger (eds.), *Terrorism: Interdisciplinary Perspectives* (New York: John Jay, 1977).
27. Clifford Geertz defines religion as 'a system of symbols which acts to establish powerful, pervasive and long-lasting moods and motivations in men by formulating conceptions of a general order of existence and clothing these conceptions with such an aura of factuality that the moods and motivations seem uniquely realistic' ('Religion as a Cultural System', reprinted in William A. Lessa and Evon Z. Vogt, (eds.), *Reader in Comparative Religion: An Anthropological Approach* (New York: Harper & Row, 3rd ed., 1972), p. 168).

28. Robert Bellah, 'Transcendence in Contemporary Piety', in Donald R. Cutler, *The Religious Situation: 1969* (Boston: Beacon Press, 1969), p. 907.
29. Peter Berger, *The Heretical Imperative* (New York: Doubleday, 1980), p. 38. See also his *Sacred Canopy: Elements of a Sociological Theory of Religion* (Garden City, NY: Doubleday, 1967).
30. Louis Dupré, *Transcendent Selfhood: The Loss and Re-discovery of the Inner Life* (New York: Seabury Press, 1976), p. 26. For a discussion of Berger and Dupré's definitions, see Mary Douglas, 'The Effects of Modernization on Religious Change', *Daedalus*, Vol. III, No. 1 (Winter 1982), pp. 1–19.
31. Durkheim describes the dichotomy of sacred and profane in religion in the following way: 'In all the history of human thought there exists no other example of two categories of things so profoundly differentiated or so radically opposed to one another.... The sacred and the profane have always and everywhere been conceived by the human mind as two distinct classes, as two worlds between which there is nothing in common.... In different religions, this opposition has been conceived in different ways'. Emile Durkheim, *The Elementary Forms of the Religious Life*, trans. by Joseph Ward Swain (London: George Allen & Unwin, 1976) (originally published in 1915), pp. 38–9. Durkheim goes on to talk about the sacred things that religions encompass; but the first thing he says about the religious view is the perception that there is this dichotomy. From a theological perspective it seems to me that Paul Tillich is saying something of the same thing in arguing for the necessary connection between faith and doubt (see, for example, the first chapter of his *Dynamics of Faith*).
32. On this point I am in agreement with Wilfred Cantwell Smith who suggested some years ago that the noun 'religion' might well be banished from our vocabulary, and that we restrict ourselves to using the adjective 'religious' (*The Meaning and End of Religion: A New Approach to the Religious Traditions of Mankind* (New York: Macmillan, 1962), pp. 119–53).
33. For the significance of the two-edged sword symbol and its links with the Devi cult revered by people, such as Jats, who have traditionally inhabited the foothills of the Himalayas adjacent to the Punjab, see W. H. McLeod, *The Evolution of the Sikh Community* (Oxford: Clarendon Press, 1976), p. 13.
34. Ibid, pp. 15–17, 51–2. These five objects are known as the five K's, since the name for each of them in Punjabi begins with the letter 'k'. The other four are uncut hair, a wooden comb, a metal bangle and cotton breeches. See also W. Owen Cole and Piara Singh Sambhi, *The Sikhs: Their Religious Beliefs and Practices* (London: Routledge & Kegan Paul, 1978), p. 36.
35. Karl Marx, 'Contribution to the Critique of Hegel's Philosophy of Right', reprinted in Karl Marx and Friedrich Engels, *On Religion* (New York: Schocken Books), p. 42; see also Engels' class analysis of a religious revolt, 'The Peasant War in Germany' in the same volume, pp. 97–118.
36. Sigmund Freud, *Totem and Taboo*, trans. by James Strachey (New York: W. W. Norton, 1950).
37. Rene Girard, *Violence and the Sacred*, trans. by Patrick Gregory (Baltimore and London; Johns Hopkins University Press, 1977); see especially Chapters 7 and 8. What is not clear in this book is how symbolic violence leads to real acts of violence; this link is made in a subsequent study of Girard's, *Scapegoat*, trans. by Patrick Gregory (Baltimore and London: Johns Hopkins University Press, 1986).
38. Bhindranwale, excerpt from a speech, in Pettigrew.
39. Ibid.
40. Bhindranwale, 'Address to the Sikh Congregation', p. 9.
41. See my article, 'Nonviolence', in Mircea Eliade (ed.), *The Encyclopedia of Religion* (New York: Macmillan, 1987). For the ethic of non-violence in Sikhism see Cole and Sambhi, *The Sikhs*, p. 138. For Sikh ethical attitudes in general see Avtar Singh, *Ethics of the Sikhs* (Patiala, India: Punjabi University Press); and S. S. Kohli, *Sikh Ethics* (New Delhi: Munshiram Manoharlal, 1975).
42. An excellent anthology of statements of Christian theologians on the ethical justification for war is Albert Marrin (ed.), *War and the Christian Conscience: From Augustine to Martin Luther King, Jr.* (Chicago: Henry Regnery, 1971). On the development of the just war doctrine in Christianity, with its secular parallels, see James Turner Johnson, *Ideology, Reason, and the*

Limitation of War: Religious and Secular Concepts, 1200–1740 (Princeton: Princeton University Press, 1975).

43. Frantz Fanon, *The Wretched of the Earth* (New York: Grove Press, 1963).
44. For a discussion of the term *qaum* in the Untouchable movements, see my *Religion as Social Vision* (Berkeley and London: University of California Press, 1982), p. 45.
45. Joyce Pettigrew argues that the *miri-piri* concept 'gave legitimacy to the political action organized from within the Golden Temple' (Pettigrew, op. cit.). This 'political action' was the establishment of an armed camp of which Bhindranwale was the commander; it was to rout this camp that the Indian army entered the Golden Temple on 5 June 1984, in Operation Bluestar.
46. Bhindranwale, 'Address to the Sikh Congregation', p. 13.
47. Ibid., p. 8.
48. David C. Rapoport, 'Why does Messianism Produce Terror?' paper delivered at the 81st Annual Meeting of the American Political Science Association, New Orleans, 27 August–1 September 1985. Although I find Rapoport's conclusions helpful, and in many ways compatible with my own, his emphasis on messianic movements seems unnecessary. The notion of messianism is largely alien to the Asian religious traditions, and much of what he says about it could be said of religion in general. See also his 'Fear and Trembling: Terrorism in Three Religious Traditions', *American Political Science Review* 78:3 (Sept. 1984), pp. 658–77, which includes case studies of the Thugs, Assassins and Zealots and the essays in David C. Rapoport and Y. Alexander (eds.), *The Morality of Terrorism: Religious and Secular Justifications* (New York: Pergamon, 1982).
49. There are also examples in other cultures where mythic battles are thought to have had a historical effect. At a recent presentation at the Wilson Center, for instance, Professor Billie Jean Isbell described the influence of the notion of cosmic cycles of order and chaos in traditional Andean cosmology on the propensity for violence of the Sendero Luminoso tribal people of Peru ('The Faces and Voices of Terrorism', Politics and Religion Seminar, Wilson Center, 8 May 1986).
50. The term *jihad* is derived from the word for striving for something, and implies 'the struggle against one's bad inclinations' as well as what it has come to mean in the popular Western mind, holy war (Rudolph Peters. *Islam and Colonialism: The Doctrine of Jihad in Modern History*, The Hague: Mouton Publishers, 1979, p. 188).
51. Bhindranwale, 'Address to the Sikh Congregation', p. 7.
52. Bhindranwale, excerpt from a speech, in Pettigrew.
53. Bhindranwale, 'Address to the Sikh congregation', p. 13.
54. For an interesting analysis of the Gush Emunim, see Ehud Sprinzak's essay in this volume.
55. Bhindranwale, 'Address to the Sikh congregation', p. 8.
56. Ibid., p. 2.
57. Ibid., p. 3.
58. Bhindranwale, excerpt from a speech, in Pettigrew.
59. Ibid.
60. Weston LaBarre, *The Ghost Dance: Origins of Religion* (London: Allen & Unwin, 1972).
61. William James, *The Varieties of Religious Experience* (Cambridge, MA: Harvard University Press, 1985) (originally published in 1902), pp. 71–108.
62. Bhindranwale, 'Address to the Sikh Congregation', p. 10.
63. Ibid., p. 10.
64. Bhindranwale, excerpt from a speech, in Pettigrew.
65. Bhindranwale, 'Address to the Sikh Congregation', p. 14.
66. Bhindranwale, excerpt from a speech, in Pettigrew.

Mark Sedgwick, 2004

Al-Qaeda and the Nature of Religious Terrorism

This article examines the nature of religious terrorism, principally with reference to al-Qaeda. It argues that a distinction must be made between the ultimate aims and the immediate objectives of 'religious' terrorists, and that while the ultimate aims will be religiously formulated, the immediate objectives will often be found to be almost purely political. This distinction is illustrated with reference to such premodern religious terrorists as the Assassins and Zealots. Immediate objectives are for many purposes more important than ultimate aims.

Although the immediate objectives of al-Qaeda on 9/11 cannot be established with certainty, it is highly probably that the intention was to provoke a response from the US that would have a radicalizing impact on al-Qaeda's constituency. Reference to public opinion in the Middle East, especially in Egypt, shows that this is indeed what has happened. Such an impact is a purely political objective, familiar to historians of terrorism from at least the time of Errico Malatesta and the 'propaganda of the deed' in the 1870s. While no direct link between Malatesta and al-Qaeda exists, al-Qaeda was certainly in contact with contemporary theories that Malatesta would have recognized, and seems to have applied them.

Even though its immediate objectives are political rather than religious, al-Qaeda is a distinctively Islamic group. Not only is its chosen constituency a confessional one, but al-Qaeda also uses—and when necessary adapts—well-known Islamic religious concepts to motivate its operatives, ranging from conceptions of duty to conceptions of ascetic devotion. This is demonstrated with reference to the 'Last Night' document of 9/11. The conclusion is that terrorism which can be understood in political terms is susceptible to political remedies.

Al-Qaeda is the most famous recent example of an older phenomenon: 'religious terrorism', sometimes called 'sacred terrorism'.[2] The question which this article addresses is whether organizations such as al-Qaeda are best understood in terms of the sacred or in terms of the terrorism. The article argues that while the sacred element in al-Qaeda matters, an understanding of the nature and history of terrorism matters more. Al-Qaeda is more easily explained in terms of classic theories of terrorism as developed by nineteenth-century Italian anarchists than in terms of the religion in the name of which it acts, and with which it is generally identified.[3]

Religion defines several important aspects of al-Qaeda: its ultimate aim (a state or states ruled by its favored form of Islam), the constituency to which it seeks to appeal (the world's Muslims), and the well-known religious concepts which it uses to motivate its operatives (duty, ascetic devotion, and piety). Its immediate objectives, however, are almost certainly political rather than religious, just as are those of any other terrorist group.

This article uses David C. Rapoport's 'wave' theory to place al-Qaeda within the contemporary wave of religious terrorism. After making a distinction between the religious and political aspects of Islam, it refers to three instances of premodern religious terrorism to establish the difference between ultimate aims and immediate objectives, arguing that while the ultimate aims of religious terrorists are invariably religious, immediate objectives may well be purely political.

The article then considers four possible explanations of what al-Qaeda was hoping to achieve on 9/11. Some explanations would mean that al-Qaeda's immediate objectives, as well as its ultimate aims, were purely religious. The article argues that the most likely explanation, however, is that al-Qaeda hoped to provoke the US reaction that it did, in fact, provoke, with the radicalizing consequences for its primary constituency that did in fact follow. It may be rash to argue that the actual consequences of any action were those originally intended, but there is some evidence that al-Qaeda did intend these consequences. While it might be objected that the theory of provocation is the heritage of Western radicalism, not of Islamic groups such as al-Qaeda, this article shows how al-Qaeda must have been exposed to such theories.

Once the political objectives of al-Qaeda have been established, the article ends with a discussion of in what ways al-Qaeda is distinctively Islamic.

Religious Terrorism: The Fourth Wave

A useful starting point for the analysis of al-Qaeda is provided by David C. Rapoport,[4] who groups modern terrorism into four 'waves', a term he prefers to 'cycles' because he sees the waves as slowly building up and then decaying.[5] Rapoport developed his wave theory before 9/11, but al-Qaeda is clearly part of the fourth wave that he already identified as that of religious terrorism. Since this article will later compare al-Qaeda with groups and individuals from Rapoport's first wave, a brief presentation of his theory is in order.

According to Rapoport, 'a different energy drives each wave' of terrorism. His first wave starts in the 1880s in Russia with Narodnya Volya, and encompasses the 'golden age' of international terrorism in the 1890s,[6] when anarchist terrorists assassinated many high profile targets, including the French president, the Spanish prime minister, the empress of Austria, the king of Italy, and finally the US president.[7] It is to this first wave that I will return for the classic theory of terrorism. His second wave is the anti-colonial terrorism of the 1940s, 1950s, and 1960s.[8] His third wave is the leftist terrorism of the 1970s and 1980s, the wave with which people of my own generation grew up and see as quintessential terrorism. As has been said, his fourth wave is contemporary religious terrorism, including al-Qaeda.

This schema is clearly right in its essentials. Each wave does indeed last about one human generation,[9] and has its own characteristic technique—the first wave was distinguished by assassination, the second wave by military targeting, and the third wave by hostage-taking. The current, fourth wave is distinguished by 'suicide bombing'.[10] Each wave does indeed start with a political event 'which excite[s] the hopes of potential terrorists and increase[s] the vulnerability of society to their claims',[11] though Rapoport's identification of the political events at the start of more recent waves might be disputed.[12]

Rapoport dates the fourth wave from three almost simultaneous events: the Iranian Islamic Revolution in 1979, the start of the fifteenth century in the Islamic *hijri* calendar, and the Soviet invasion of Afghanistan—when the violence really started. Of these, I would dismiss the start of the fifteenth *hijri* century, which was important for the armed occupation of the Kaaba in Mecca by a Saudi group about which little is known, but was irrelevant elsewhere. Similarly, while the Iranian Revolution was significant, it was more significant in America than in the Middle East. It was the Iranian Revolution that alerted the television viewers of America to the resurgence of Islam, but the resurgence of Islam in the Arab world is generally agreed to date not from 1979 but from 1967.[13] It was the shockingly sudden and complete defeat of the Arab armies by Israel in that year that began the shattering of the Arab nationalist dream incarnated in Egypt's President Nasser, a process completed by President Sadat's concessions at Camp David in 1979. Just as European radicals had to turn away from Communism after the 1968 invasion of Czechoslovakia, so Arab radicals had to turn elsewhere after 1967. And they did: it was after 1967 that the re-Islamization of Egyptian society started. The Arabs who went to fight for Islam in Afghanistan were in the middle of a wave, not at the start of it.[14] The fourth wave, then, started not in Iran or Afghanistan, but in Palestine and Israel, in almost the same year that the third wave started in Europe and—to a lesser extent—in America.

Religious Terrorism and Political Events

Before proceeding, it is necessary to confront the oft-repeated but misleading maxim that in Islam politics and religion are inseparable.[15] The conventional wisdom is that 'Islam has always been preeminently dedicated to delivering a moral message aimed at transforming social existence in this world'.[16] It is true that Islam has never generally embraced the formal separation of church and state,[17] perhaps because church and state were never in conflict in the way that they were for much of Europe's history.[18] This does not mean, however, that church[19] and state in Islam have never been separate in practice. There have been countless religious groups in Islamic history that have taken no interest whatsoever in politics and countless political groups that have taken no real interest in religion. Certainly, most political groups have in one way or another used religion in their construction of legitimacy and few political groups have ever explicitly denied the authority of religious norms,[20] but this does not mean that politics and religion are one. The idea that politics and religion are inseparable in Islam has been promoted by groups that believe that they *should* be inseparable, and has been accepted by some scholars (especially in the past), but that does not mean that they actually *are* inseparable.

Religious and political factors should be distinguished in the analysis of al-Qaeda, then, as in the analysis of other religious terrorist groups. This requires making a further distinction, between ultimate aims and immediate objectives. Ultimate aims are often intangible, and are generally defined by religion or ideology. For Stalin, the establishment of world communism was an ultimate aim. Immediate objectives are generally more concrete. For Stalin, the installation of a people's republic in Poland (for example) was an immediate objective. In Stalin's case, the ultimate aim was ideological, while the immediate objective in Poland was political.

Before returning to al-Qaeda, this article will explore the distinction between ultimate aims and immediate objectives in the case of three groups of religious terrorists discussed by Rapoport in an article published in 1984: the Kali-worshiping Thugs, the Nizari-Ismaili 'Assassins', and the Sicarii 'Zealots'.[21] Rapoport himself did not make a distinction between ultimate aims and immediate objectives in his 1984 article,[22] but a comparison between these three groups gives a good basis for making this distinction, and so for distinguishing between the religious and the political in 'religious' terrorism in general.

Of these three groups, the Thugs are the most clearly religious. An offshoot of a wider movement devoted to the Hindu goddess Kali, the Thugs waylaid travelers, strangling them to offer their blood to Kali, believing that in so doing they were transmitting the energies that allowed Kali to keep the universe in balance. Their victims' terror was deliberately prolonged for the benefit of the goddess. Both their immediate objectives and their ultimate aims, then, were entirely other-worldly, and the Thugs thus illustrate one variety of religious terrorism, that in which—in Rapoport's words—'the primary audience is the deity'[23] Other scholars also refer to this audience in their examinations of religious terrorism. Bruce Hoffman writes that 'whereas secular terrorists attempt to appeal to actual and potential sympathizers, religious terrorists appeal to no other constituency than themselves'.[24] For Audrey Cronin, religious terrorists act 'directly or indirectly to please the perceived commands of a deity'.[25] This is why, for Hoffman and Cronin, religious terrorism is uniquely destructive and uniquely dangerous.[26] In Cronin's words, 'The whims of the deity may be less than obvious to those who are not members of the religion'.[27] The Thugs, then, might be the archetype of religious terrorism—except that there is a question whether the Thugs can really be considered terrorists in the first place.[28] I would suggest that the Thugs may make more sense as a religious movement practicing human sacrifice than as a terrorist group.

The second group, the Assassins, flourished in what is today Syria during the twelfth century. They assassinated many of their leading opponents, thus both eliminating their most vocal critics and discouraging others from replacing them. The authority that they hoped and failed to establish by these (and other) means was that of their form of Islam,[29] which in practice meant their own political authority. In this objective they differ little from the Fatimids or the Abbasids, or indeed from the Soviet Union in Poland. That ultimate aims are religiously defined—or in the case of the Soviet Union ideologically defined—does not mean that immediate objectives are not political. The immediate objectives of the Soviet Union, the Fatimids and the Assassins ultimately differed little in kind from those of most other states.[30] Unlike the Soviet Union, however, the Assassins, cannot be understood without reference to religion, since their operatives actively sought martyrdom, martyrdom being highly prized in the Shi'i branch of Islam from which the Assassins derived.

The third group, the Zealots, was also a religious group in the same way that the Assassins were, using assassination as part of a broader strategy and welcoming martyrdom. Religion was probably more important to the Zealots than to the Assassins, however. Although the immediate objectives of the Zealots were generally political, on at least one occasion these objectives became as religious as their ultimate aims. During one of their final actions—defending besieged Jerusalem against the Roman army—they deliberately burnt their own food supplies, evidently hoping by this means to hasten divine intervention and the millennium. At this point, the Zealots' immediate objective was not political or military but other-worldly,[31] just like the Thugs' immediate objectives.

Of these three groups, the Thugs emerge as purely religious (but perhaps not as terrorists), the Zealots emerge as religious and political, and the Assassins emerge as political and religious. Although the immediate motivation of *individual* Assassins seeking martyrdom was religious, and although the ultimate aims of the Assassins as a whole were religiously defined, their immediate objectives always remained firmly this-worldly and political. Of the three groups, the closest to al-Qaeda is the Assassins, which may be no coincidence given that both al-Qaeda and the Assassins are Islamic. Like the Assassins, al-Qaeda's ultimate aim is religiously defined— the establishment of one or more states ruled by al-Qaeda's favored form of Islam. Like the Assassins, it will now be argued, al-Qaeda's immediate objectives are political rather than religious, even though its operatives welcome martyrdom, just as those of the Assassins did. A major difference is as Rapoport indicates that the Assassins read the Islamic tradition to mean that only one sort of weapon, the dagger, could be used against Muslims.

Al-Qaeda's Objectives

This article will not examine al-Qaeda's ultimate aims in detail,[32] but will focus on immediate objectives. In examining these, it will move from theory to speculation, a move made necessary by the lack of reliable information on al-Qaeda.[33] This lack of information partly reflects the priorities and organization of academia,[34] but also reflects the nature of al-Qaeda as an activist rather than a theoretical group. None of its members has written much, and none have made any significant contributions to theory. Al-Qaeda has been a consumer of theory, not a producer.

A question which many people—scholars and members of the public—asked themselves after 9/11 is this: what did al-Qaeda think it was going to achieve by destroying the World Trade Center and other targets with such appalling loss of life? Four plausible theories have emerged to answer this question, none of which can at present be properly tested, though there is growing evidence to support the conclusion this article comes to. In considering these theories, it must be recognized that the intentions of the operatives involved may have been different from those of the operation's planners and financiers.

All four explanations assume that America is the enemy of Islam. This is not a view that I myself hold, but it is a view that has been firmly established in the Middle East for decades. Quite how America came to be seen as the enemy of Islam is a question that falls beyond the scope of this article, and involves factors that have nothing to do with America, but it also involves Palestine and Israel. For complex reasons, Israel—or rather, 'the Jews'—are seen as the number one enemy of the Muslims, and America is seen as the number one supporter of the Jews. Ayman al-Zawahiri (b. 1951), the Egyptian physician who may have been an even more important figure in al-Qaeda than Bin Laden himself, wrote in 1998 that 'America is now controlled by the Jews completely, as are its news, its elections, its economics, and its politics'.[35] Many would read this as crude anti-Semitic propaganda, and deny that it was possible that a well-traveled physician from a family of physicians, university professors, and lawyers could possibly believe it. Similar views, however, are held—entirely seriously—by most Egyptians of al-Zawahiri's background.[36] That their analysis would not get much of a grade in a political science class does not mean that it does not have to be taken very seriously.

The first plausible explanation of what the perpetrators of 9/11 thought they were going to achieve is that they all believed that they were fighting the final battle of the last days, at the end of time. This would mean that al-Qaeda is a millenarian movement. There is no direct evidence to support this conclusion, but neither is there any direct evidence to disprove it. Many Arab Muslims of all classes are today convinced that they are living in the last days, since the weakness of Islam and the corruption and decay they see all around them can easily be explained in eschatological terms.[37] If al-Qaeda (or any of its sections) is a millenarian movement, it is more similar to the Zealots than the Assassins, and more religious than religiopolitical.

The second plausible explanation is that the perpetrators of 9/11 were simply not thinking very hard. Many of 9/11's operatives and some of the planners doubtless supposed they were 'fighting for Islam', without asking any more questions, rather as soldiers in World War II might have fought for France or Germany against an enemy about whom they knew little, asking no difficult questions about political systems or international relations. 9/11's perpetrators may have stumbled into an attack on America without much thought for its consequences, through an escalating series of actions, starting with domestic political targets in Egypt, moving through US military targets in Saudi Arabia to US civilian targets abroad, and finally coming to US civilian targets in America.[38] Though not impossible, this explanation is unlikely. The logic of events can sometimes overtake strategy, but it seems unlikely that none of the people involved in planning 9/11 could think strategically. If the planners of 9/11 believed themselves to be in the last days, of course, the time for strategy would have been past, but outside al-Qaeda even the least strategically skilled Arabs realized that an attack on America was not a wise move. I will never forget watching the twin towers burn on an Arabized version of CNN—the CNN transmission had been hastily patched onto Egyptian state television with extempore commentary in Arabic—among a crowd that had gathered around a television in a car showroom in Cairo. The prevalent mood seemed to be one of amazement tinged with fear. 'What would happen now?' was the question on every Cairene's lips over the following weeks. Some form of retaliation was expected, and feared. It was not expected that 9/11 would in any way benefit the Muslim community.

The third plausible explanation accepts strategic thinking on the part of 9/11's planners, but supposes a misreading of America. Having observed that a suicide bomb in Beirut could send the US army home from Lebanon,[39] that the destruction of two helicopters in Mogadishu could send the US army home from Somalia, and that a series of such attacks could send the Israeli army home from South Lebanon, it might have been possible to suppose that a series of events like 9/11 would send US military, diplomatic, and commercial and cultural interests and influence home from the whole of the Middle East, rather as the March 2004 subway bombs in Madrid caused Spain to falter in its commitment to US policy in Iraq.

The fourth and most likely plausible explanation is provocation, the 'propaganda of the deed'. Many readers of this journal will already be familiar with the logic of provocation, but for the sake of those who are not, this article will review this logic, returning to the first wave of international terrorism, to the Italian anarchists of the nineteenth century. In summary, the fourth explanation would be that al-Qaeda was guided by a strategy that has been well known in certain circles for over a century, and that the primary objective of the 'deed' of 9/11 was not its direct impact on America but rather its indirect propaganda impact on al-Qaeda's potential supporters. A secondary objective would have been to 'provoke' America into actions that would alienate al-Qaeda's potential supporters from America, thus turning more of them into actual supporters.

Provocation and Irregular Warfare

Unlike al-Qaeda, late nineteenth-century Italian anarchists were theorists as well as activists. To understand their contributions to theory, we need to take one further step backwards, and think not in terms of terrorism but of 'irregular warfare', sometimes termed 'small war' or 'war in the shadows',[40] the sort of conflict that the Afghan mujahidin waged against the Soviet Union. My intention here is not to engage in a sterile debate about 'freedom fighters' versus 'terrorists', but to place terrorism within its larger theoretical context.

There is nothing new about irregular warfare, which one historian found the Hittite King Mursilis complaining about in the fifteenth century BC.[41] It had been recognized since the time of Sextus Julius Frontinus (d. 104), author of the earliest known Western work on irregular warfare,[42] that the support of the local population was necessary for the success of any guerrilla campaign, and that relations between guerrillas and local civilians therefore mattered enormously.[43] In this sense, politics has always been more important to irregular warfare than it has been to regular warfare.

What is comparatively recent is the combination of irregular warfare with political theory. During the Italian nationalist struggle, the Risorgimento (1831–61), the political aspect of irregular warfare became not a means to an end, but an end in itself. For Giuseppe Mazzini, guerrillas were 'the precursors of the nation, which they would rouse to insurrection'.[44] This understanding was taken up by anarchists, among them Errico Malatesta (1853–1932), who is credited with inventing the description of terrorist actions as the *propaganda dei fatti,* 'propaganda of the deed'[45] (though Kropotkin is also credited with the phrase).

How the 'propaganda of the deed'—the act of provocation—is meant to work can be understood through one of Malatesta's first attempts at using it, in 1877. Malatesta had been involved in planning an unsuccessful socialist insurrection in 1874, but he and others were arrested by the police before the insurrection had even started. Three years later, he and a colleague, Andrea Costa (1851-1911), tried again. The two men—both in their mid-twenties—arrived in a remote mountain village, Letino (some sixty miles north of Naples), and announced the deposition of King Victor Emmanuel II by the Socialist Revolution. Presenting themselves as the agents of the Revolution, they required the local mayor to hand over to them the funds under his control, which he did, against a receipt they signed in the name of the Revolution. Malatesta and Costa distributed the funds they had taken to the inhabitants of the village, and destroyed the local tax records. They then spread the revolution to the neighboring village, Gallo, again distributing sequestered funds and destroying tax records. At this point, troops arrived.[46]

In theory, the villagers should have been convinced by the 'deed' they had previously witnessed that the government's authority was vulnerable, and should have been further alienated by the troops' repression. They should have resisted the troops, so starting an insurrection that would perhaps have ended with the overthrow of the monarchy. In practice, none of this happened. Though the village priest had made what Malatesta called 'a nice speech' welcoming them to Letino after they had taken over there in the name of the Revolution, no general resistance to the troops was forthcoming. Nineteen peasants followed Malatesta and Costa into the mountains, but after a few days the small band was betrayed and arrested, cold and hungry, their powder wet and their weapons useless.[47]

Even though this operation ended in failure, the principle behind it was accepted. The consequence for the anarchists of this and similar disappointments was not the abandonment of the idea of the propaganda of the deed, but the abandonment of the idea of *rural* insurrection. Especially during the 1880s and 1890s, deeds designed to demonstrate the vulnerability of authority were carried out in urban and higher-profile contexts. The targets of these deeds were sometimes individuals, and sometimes groups of individuals associated with the structures of power. The anarchist movement of which Malatesta was a part was responsible for an unprecedented wave of global terrorism between 1884 and 1905. In 1884, the German Kaiser Wilhelm survived a bomb attack against him, but in 1886 eight policemen were killed and 76 injured by a bomb thrown by an anarchist during a demonstration in Haymarket Square, Chicago.[48] In 1892, a Spanish anarchist threw a bomb into Barcelona's smart Liceo theater, killing twenty bourgeois men and women and injuring many more.[49] In 1894, French President Sadi Carnot was killed by one Santo Caseiro, in response to the execution of a colleague of Caseiro's who had thrown a bomb into the chamber of the French parliament two years before. In 1897, Spanish Prime Minister Antonio Cánovas was killed, and in 1898 the Empress Elizabeth of Austria. In 1900, King Umberto I of Italy was shot dead by an Italian anarchist from New Jersey, Gaetano Bresci. Finally, in 1901, US President William McKinley was shot dead in Buffalo, New York by Leon Czolgosz, the anarchist son of Polish immigrants in Detroit.[50] Then, in 1914, Archduke Franz Ferdinand of Austria was killed in Sarajevo—not by an anarchist but by a Serb nationalist who subscribed to theories similar to those of Malatesta. This deed famously started not an insurrection but a world war.

World War I put a temporary end to the propaganda of the deed. The anarchists had concluded that the technique was ineffective. In the words of a contemporary anarchist, 'it led to the public associating violence with the ideals of anarchism. People had difficulty relating to someone they viewed as a murderous fanatic'.[51] The anarchist movement was anyhow eclipsed by the success of its rivals, the Bolsheviks, who had a low opinion of the usefulness of insurrection in general,[52] and reserved the use of terror for internal purposes.

Irregular warfare on Malatesta's model, however, did not disappear. The propaganda of the deed—provocation—is found in all subsequent waves of terrorism, as is the emphasis on political gain rather than on destroying enemy forces. The Irish Easter Rising of 1916 became the classic demonstration of the fact that military defeat may still bring political triumph, i.e., that the resulting propaganda is more important than the deed itself. The actions of the British in defeating the rising created so many republicans that the British loss of Ireland was thereafter almost a foregone conclusion.[53]

The Easter Rising, of course, was not a 'terrorist' enterprise: the Irish fought in uniform and obeyed the rules of war. In this they were close to Malatesta's relatively innocuous activities in the Italian mountains. Twentieth-century terrorists in contrast developed their own version of the doctrine of 'shock and awe'. Human societies evolve 'conventions or boundaries … to regulate coercion'.[54] Principally, these norms govern the use of violence by states or their agents, but they also govern the use of violence by non-state agents. Everyone has a rough idea of how much violence is appropriate for a regular grocery-store hold-up. It became characteristic of later terrorists, however, that the violence used would exceed all conventions and transgress all boundaries.[55]

After 9/11

The consequences of 9/11 have so far been much as Malatesta would have wished.[56] For Malatesta, and so perhaps also for al-Qaeda, 'deeds' such as 9/11 have two audiences, neither of them the deity: the group attacked, and the potential opponents of the group attacked. Of these two audiences, the potential opponents of the group attacked is the most important one, since it contains the potential supporters of the insurrection, and it is to them that the propaganda is primarily addressed. The potential supporters of al-Qaeda's desired insurrection (against regimes such as the Saudi one and against the United States)[57] are, of course, the world's Muslims, or at least the world's Arabs. To the world's Arabs, 9/11 certainly demonstrated the vulnerability of the United States in the most dramatic fashion. By its responses in Afghanistan and—especially—in Iraq, the United States then alienated al-Qaeda's target audience from the United States, just as Malatesta would have hoped. There were many justifications for those responses, but their impact on the Arab world has been reminiscent of the impact of British policy on Ireland in the aftermath of the Easter Rising. To the average Arab, the toppling of the Taliban in Afghanistan appeared as an act of revenge on the people of Afghanistan, and the invasion of Iraq appeared as an unprovoked attack on a long-suffering people whose only crime was to be Arab and Muslim.[58]

I am not suggesting that these views were either accurate or justified.[59] What matters is not what was actually happening, but what most Arabs perceived to be happening. It was as a result of these perceptions that during 2003 volunteers crossed the Syrian border to help their Iraqi 'cousins'. In Egypt, a country where Saddam had had almost no supporters at the time of his invasion of Kuwait, the Iraqi resistance to the invasion of 2003 became a general source of pride—could Arab soldiers, after so many defeats and humiliations, really be holding their own against America?

It turned out that Arab soldiers had not been holding their own. A shocked silence fell over Cairo on 7–8 April 2003, as the television showed pictures of Saddam's statue being pulled down in Baghdad. Egyptians immediately began to search for excuses to justify those Iraqis' behavior. They were not *real* Iraqis, or if they were, they were hungry. Perhaps Saddam had been betrayed by senior commanders who had made a secret deal with the Americans. Despite all the excuses, however, there was a sad awareness that the insurrection had failed, and that—though no-one quite put it in these terms—the Iraqi people had failed, had failed Saddam. This was an astonishing reversal of logic, given that the general line in Egypt during the run-up to the invasion had been that while no-one cared for Saddam, everyone sympathized with the long-suffering Iraqi people.

In general, it is a dangerous fallacy to suppose that people intend the consequences of their actions. This is not always the case: clearly, it was never the intention of the US administration to foment near insurrection in the Middle East. That the consequences of 9/11 came close to fomenting insurrection, then, does not mean that this has to have been the intention of al-Qaeda, and there is no direct evidence that it was the intention of Khalid Shaykh Muhammad, the former mujahid identified by the *9/11 Commission Report* as the key planner of 9/11.[60] It is, however, the most plausible explanation of al-Qaeda's objective, especially since it is much the explanation given by Bin Laden himself for an earlier operation, the 1995 bombings in Riyadh. Asked about the consequences of this attack by a sympathetic interviewer in 1996, Bin Laden said:

> Most important among them [the consequences] is people's awareness of the significance of the American occupation of the land of the two sacred mosques [Saudi Arabia], and that the decrees of the regime are a reflection of the wishes of the American occupiers. People became aware that their main problems were caused by the American occupiers and their puppets in the Saudi regime, both from the religious point of view and from other points of view in their daily lives. People's sympathies … led people to support the General Rectification Movement, which is led by scholars and Callers to Islam [i.e. the religious opposition to the Saudi regime].[61]

Bin Laden's somewhat hopeful description of the impact of those bombings can certainly be taken as evidence of what he had hoped would be their impact.

From Europe to Peshawar

One objection to this explanation of the intentions of al-Qaeda on 9/11 is that al-Qaeda is an Islamic movement that has nothing to do with European radicalism, an objection that will now be addressed.

The Arab world is often supposed to have been untouched by globalization. This is true economically for many Arab countries during the current round of globalization, but was not true during the nineteenth century, when the Middle East was drawn into the expanding world system. It was not true that the Arab world was untouched by globalization intellectually during the nineteenth century, nor is it true today. Since the 1840s, all the major global political movements have been echoed in the Arab world—from constitutionalism and nationalism through socialism, communism and fascism—though often with a delay of one or two decades, and sometimes in distinctive forms. One difficulty in the Middle East has always been how to define the 'national' community. A territorial definition similar to that adopted in France and America was tried, and ultimately became established in Turkey. Elsewhere it failed. A linguistic-ethnic definition similar to that adopted in Italy and Germany underlies the pan-Arab nationalism that was defeated in 1967. A third possible definition of the community, never tried in Europe,[62] is a religious or confessional definition. In these terms, it might be argued that today's radical Islamism is no more than a further attempt at adapting nineteenth-century nationalism to Middle Eastern conditions—nationalism with a confessional definition of community.

Unlike the Assassins and other premodern instances of religious terror, al-Qaeda is not a product of the premodern world but of today's interconnected world. Many of its operatives had personal experience of the wider world;[63] Khalid Shaykh Muhammad, for example, was a graduate of the North Carolina Agricultural and Technical State University.[64] Al-Qaeda itself came into being in Peshawar during the Afghan war against the Soviet army. Peshawar was then a city overflowing with radicals, opportunists, soldiers, and intelligence operatives. I have no direct evidence of what the Arabic-speakers among them were reading and discussing, but certain influences must have been present. For the future leaders and operatives of al-Qaeda, Saudi Wahhabism and the theories of the Egyptian Islamist Sayyid Qutb must have been of greatest importance, and certainly defined their ultimate aim, which was and is religiously defined (so-called 'Sharia' states).[65] Neither Wahhabism nor Qutb have much to say about ways of achieving this aim, however, beyond recommending *hijra* [withdrawal] to a place from which Muslims can return to restore—by force if necessary—a pure Islamic order. The model is the *hijra* of the Prophet Muhammad to Medina, in advance of the return of the Muslims in triumph to Mecca. Afghanistan itself must have seemed to many to be a new Medina. For more detailed objectives and strategy, however, one has to look to other sources.

During the Afghan war, the *mujahidin* were assisted by members of the intelligence agencies and militaries of both Pakistan and America, who were necessarily familiar with the theories of irregular warfare—including later developments since Malatesta—as this was the technique in which they were training the *mujahidin*. Other routes for the transmission of theories of irregular warfare to al-Qaeda in Peshawar pass through Palestine and

Egypt. Bin Laden first worked in Peshawar with Abdullah Azzam (1941–89), a former PLO activist,[66] as did Khalid Shaykh Muhammad.[67] Azzam was not a major intellectual, but was more of an intellectual than Bin Laden,[68] and senior to Khalid Shaykh Muhammad. It is not clear in what faction of the PLO Azzam had belonged, but he can be assumed to have been familiar with the theories then current in PLO circles.[69]

After Afghanistan, Bin Laden worked with Ayman al-Zawahiri, again not a major intellectual, but more of an intellectual than Bin Laden.[70] Al-Zawahiri had an established interest in fomenting insurrection, which had been the objective of the first Islamist group to which he had belonged. In the late 1970 s, this group had planned a small-scale military coup in Cairo, which was expected to be followed by popular insurrection.[71] Khalid Shaykh Muhammad, in turn, worked with the group that planned the first attempt on the World Trade Center in 1993,[72] a group that received training from a former instructor at Fort Bragg, Ali Muhammad (subsequently a leading member of the team that planned al-Qaeda's 1998 Nairobi operation).[73] Ali Muhammad and men like him must have been familiar with theories of irregular warfare. Any number of networks similar to these might have connected Khalid Shaykh Muhammad and Bin Laden to European radicalism and so to theories derived ultimately from Malatesta.

The Islamic Nature of Al-Qaeda

That al-Qaeda's objectives were almost certainly political rather than religious and owe more to European radicalism than to Islam does not mean that Islam is of no importance in explaining al-Qaeda. Al-Qaeda is clearly marked by Islam, and not only in its ultimate aims. Al-Qaeda's potential constituency is the world's Muslims, and the means it uses to mobilize support in this constituency are derived from Islam.

Many political movements have to create their constituency. One of the major tasks of a nationalist or leftist movement is to encourage national or class consciousness (as the case may be), since it is only when a movement's chosen constituency recognizes that it exists that a movement can begin attracting support and recruits from it. An Islamic movement can skip this stage, since its chosen constituency—Muslims—is already very conscious of its existence; it only needs to be made into a *political* constituency.

Secondly, a nationalist or leftist movement has to teach its constituency new concepts and vocabulary, whether 'national character' or 'class war'. An Islamic movement has an easier task, since it can use concepts that are already very well known,[74] adapting them where necessary to its own purposes. Every Muslim knows of the Prophet Muhammad's *hijra* from Mecca to Medina, and his return in strength through *jihad.* To replace Mecca with 'corrupt Jewish-Crusader puppet Arab regimes' and Medina with Afghanistan is easier than explaining social justice to the semiliterate.

When it comes to mobilizing support from within its constituency, mainstream Islamic concepts of duty, ascetic devotion, and piety may be used to political ends. Every Muslim knows that there are two sorts of duty, the individual and the communal. Every individual has the duty of praying, while every community has the duty of keeping alive the scholarly skills required for Quranic exegesis. It is widely agreed, if not universally known, that when the community fails in its duty, that duty passes to every capable individual. If I am a Muslim computer scientist, and there is almost no-one left in the community equipped to do Quranic exegesis, I am personally duty-bound to shift from computer science to Quranic exegesis. In 1998, Bin Laden, al-Zawahiri and others argued that since the community was failing in its duty of *jihad* against the Zionists and the Americans, *jihad* had become a personal duty of all capable Muslims.[75] A nationalist may argue that a patriot should fight for independence, and a leftist may argue that a proletarian should fight for class justice, but both have a harder task in formulating that argument. Of Muslims worldwide, 95 per cent were and are unaware of Bin Laden's argument, and 95 per cent of those who are aware of it are probably unconvinced by it. With a potential constituency of one billion, however, even 5 per cent of 5 per cent gives a pool of 2,500,000— say one million young men as potential recruits.

Suicide bombing also makes use of an established Islamic concept, that of martyrdom. Many religions honor martyrs, but none have as well established a concept of martyrdom as Islam does. Every Sunni Muslim knows that a martyr who falls fighting for Islam is automatically rewarded with a place in heaven. Every Shi'i Muslim knows the stories of the great Shi'i martyrs, retold and even reenacted annually at Ashura. There is a subtle difference, since the great Shi'i martyrs were usually murdered while the classic Sunni martyrs fell in battle, and since the emphasis on participation in martyrdom is greatest in Shi'i Islam. Shi'i Islam first developed the systematic application of martyrdom to modern conflict, adding to its own emphasis on participation in martyrdom a quasi-Sunni definition. After the Iranian Revolution, the Revolutionary Guards encouraged mass martyrdom during the Iran-Iraq war. Self-sacrificing heroism is to some degree encouraged in all armies, but it proved far easier to send thousands of young Iranian soldiers to die for Islam than to die for Iran or for the revolution. This new application of the concept of martyrdom seems to have passed from Iranian Shi'is to Lebanese Shi'is during the Lebanese Civil War. Iranian Revolutionary Guards went to Lebanon to train the Hezbollah militia, and it was the Hezbollah militia that carried out the first suicide bombing attacks in the Arab world.[76]

These attacks were spectacularly successful. When American and French troops entered the Lebanon on peacekeeping missions, Hezbollah wanted them to leave so that it could finish off its enemies. And leave they did: one single suicide bombing operation got rid of the French, and another single such operation got rid of the Americans. These spectacular successes encouraged the adoption of the same technique by Sunni groups in the Lebanon, then next door in Palestine, and finally across the Sunni world. The Sunni groups in question quickly adopted the emphasis on martyrdom that had previously been found mostly in Shi'i Islam, adding this to the pre-existing Sunni definition.

The subtlest use of mainstream Islamic concepts by al-Qaeda is visible in the handwritten document of which copies were found in the luggage of Muhammad Atta and in the wreckage of flight UA 93 in Pennsylvania after 9/11, sometimes called the 'Last Night' document. This is a startling document, mixing the devotional and ascetic with the technical and operational, but with an emphasis on the former. I have never been a soldier, and I have no idea what it takes to approach an enemy machine-gun nest with a grenade in one's hand. It must be even harder to walk down an ordinary shopping street and pull the detonation cord on an explosive waistcoat. To fly an airplane full of people into a building must be even more difficult—an act any human being might be expected instinctively to shy away from. How, then, to prepare oneself mentally for such an act, how to keep on target until the last seconds? By using the established spiritual and mental tools of Islam, tested and improved over millennia.

Islam has an ascetic tradition, commonly identified with Sufism. Mainstream Islam has fasting, which is itself an ascetic exercise. Sufis sometimes fast on alternate days (a lot harder than fasting every day), stay awake all night, live in voluntary destitution, or—in rare cases—stick knives into themselves. All these are also acts that the human mind shies away from. Mastering the ego—as Sufis would put it—sufficiently to perform the easier ascetic acts prepares one to attempt the more difficult, and also opens one to God: the space that the ego vacates can be filled with divine grace. The soul can be strengthened in its struggle with the ego not only by prior experience of spiritual combat, but by prayers and ritual. There is nothing sinister about this, all of which has been in the mainstream of Sufi spirituality for millennia, and has produced countless saints. These concepts and techniques, however, were put to most sinister use on 9/11.

In the 'Last Night' document, the operatives of 9/11 were instructed to concentrate on their intentions, to shave, and to make the ablutions required for a state of ritual purity before leaving for the airport. This is approximately the ritual preparation for a major act of worship such as the pilgrimage. Having thus so-to-speak crossed the threshold into ritual space and time, the operatives were then instructed to make supplications at various points, and 'always be remembering God' [*dhikr*], a standard technique of the Sufis. Much emphasis was put on *sabr* [steadfastness or patience], a major Islamic virtue. Even toward the end, purity of intention was required: 'Do not seek revenge for yourself. Strike for God's sake', admonishes the document, following this admonition with an exemplary tale involving Ali ibn Abi Talib.[77] In short, the whole 9/11 operation was ritualized to the greatest extent possible, and the operatives did not shy away from their task. They kept on target until the last moment.

This application of mainstream Islamic concepts is, to many, shocking. Juan Cole correctly noted with perplexity the Sufi nature of the 'Last Night' document, wondering at it given the historical animosity between Sufism and the Salafi and Wahhabi interpretations of Islam that al-Qaeda follows.[78] To my mind, the sudden Salafi adoption of Sufi methods was as utilitarian as the Sunni adoption of the Shi'i emphasis on martyrdom. Muslim observers reported, almost with shudders, the way in which the document is inspirational as one reads it: the formula used have their impact on any even slightly pious Muslim, despite their context.[79] To find oneself inspired by a text that has been a means of mass murder cannot be a pleasant experience.

Conclusions

Al-Qaeda's ultimate aims are defined religiously. Al-Qaeda is also a distinctively Islamic—or rather, a distinctively religious—movement in that it addresses and recruits from a ready-made, self-conscious constituency, and does not need to create one. Al-Qaeda is also distinctively religious in that its potential constituency is vast, as is that of any major world religion. Finally, al-Qaeda is distinctively religious in that it makes use of well-established, mainstream religious concepts.

Despite these religious elements, however, al-Qaeda's immediate objectives are as much political as are those of any other terrorist group. It follows that its activities are neither irrational nor incomprehensible. This is good news for those working against terrorism, since it is necessary to understand one's enemy, and it is hard to understand the incomprehensible. If religious terrorism has political objectives (and roots) just like any other variety of terrorism, it is probably as susceptible to political solutions as is any other variety of terrorism. Just as religious terrorism turns out to have important political elements, 'secular' terrorism also has important religious elements. Many nationalists have spoken of their cause as 'sacred', and it is not hard to conceive of a leftist speaking of the 'sacred cause of the oppressed masses'. A Russian terrorist of the first wave wrote of terrorism as 'uniting the two sublimities of human nature, the martyr and the hero'.[80]

Many of the most alarming characteristics of religious terrorism identified by counter-terrorism experts are in fact characteristic of terrorism and radical politics as a whole, not just of religious terrorism. Religious terrorists, according to Cronin, 'feel engaged in a Manichaean struggle of good against evil'.[81] This may also be true of many nonreligious terrorists. Similarly, though religious terrorists 'seek to eliminate broadly defined categories of enemies',[82] 'an open-ended set of human targets',[83] so did the nineteenth-century anarchist who threw a bomb into a smart theater in Barcelona, and so did the Nazi and Soviet regimes in the middle of the twentieth century.

Hoffman suggests that 'whereas secular terrorists regard violence as a way to instigate a flaw in a system that is basically good, religious terrorists see themselves … as outsiders seeking fundamental changes in the existing order'.[84] The distinction being made here is not so much one between secularism and religion as one between reformism and revolutionary radicalism, at least as the distinction was understood by the nineteenth-century Spanish philosopher José Ortega y Gasset. In the words of Octavio Paz, the reformer 'respects the structure of the system, and never descends to the roots … the revolutionary is always radical, by which I mean that he does not yearn to correct abuses, but [to change] the uses themselves. [The criticisms of reformers] leave social or cultural structures intact, and aim only to limit or perfect this or that procedure'.[85] All those who use the propaganda of the deed, surely, are radicals rather than reformers. Similarly, it is not only religious terrorists who 'consider themselves to be unconstrained by secular values or laws',[86] and are 'undeterred by political, moral or practical constraints'[87] For Malatesta as well as al-Qaeda, the illegitimacy of the values and laws of the society to be overturned was the central point of the whole enterprise. Neither Malatesta nor Bin Laden were prepared to accept many constraints. The problem is not with religion, I would suggest, but with radicalism.

Audrey Cronin concludes her article on 'Globalization and International Terrorism' in *International Security* with the following observation: 'The strongest response that the United States can muster to a serious threat has to include political, economic, and military capabilities—in that order; yet the U.S. government consistently structures its policies and devotes its resources in the reverse sequence'.[88] Cronin's 'consistently' may be unduly harsh,[89] and it made a lot of sense to take military action in Afghanistan.[90] Military action, however, is not enough, as was recognized in the *9/11 Commission Report*.[91] As the Easter Rising in Ireland showed, the military defeat of an insurgent group may, under some circumstances, contribute directly to its political success. Mao Zedong emphasized that the most important element in the success of any insurgency is remembering the political objective—that the local population must be mobilized as supporters, rather than alienated. Even if mobilizing support is not possible, alienation must be avoided at all costs. In a textbook insurgency, whoever alienates the local population most will lose.

Insurgents, too, can alienate a population, however, as the Anarchists ultimately did. For every one person who could give even the most basic explanation of what the anarchist political philosophy actually was, thousands can summon up mental pictures of a man in a black cloak carrying a round bomb. This is what started to happen to al-Qaeda in May 2003, when five suicide attacks in Casablanca killed thirty one bystanders and injured more than one hundred others. Demonstrations in Casablanca and Rabat attracted over 100,000 protestors. These welcomed representatives of Morocco's Jewish community, and rejected the participation of Morocco's Islamist groups.[92] In Rabat, according to one report, Islamists were pelted with tomatoes by protestors.[93] Malatesta would not have approved.[94]

Notes

1. This article is based on a paper, 'Al-Qaeda, Islam and Italian Anarchism', originally delivered to the Eastern International Region annual meeting of the American Academy of Religion, Cornell University, Ithaca, New York, 30 April-1 May 2004.
2. See for example Bruce Hoffman, *Inside Terrorism* (New York: Columbia University Press, 1998) pp.90-5, and Hoffman, 'Old Madness, New Methods: Revival of Religious Terrorism Begs for Broader U.S. Policy', *Rand Review* 22, no. 2 (Winter 1998/99) p.12. See also Magnus Ranstorp, 'Terrorism in the Name of Religion', *Columbia International Affairs Online* working paper (1996), available http://www.ciaonet.org/wps/ram01/. I refer to 'al-Qaeda' rather than to Qa'idat al-jihad, as it should now properly be known, because the distinction is immaterial for the purposes of this article, and because a failure to use the established term would appear excessively pedantic.
3. This is a point made explicitly by John Gray, *Al-Qaeda and What It Means To Be Modern* (London: Faber and Faber, 2003) p.2. It is also implicit in David C. Rapoport's analysis, discussed below.
4. David C. Rapoport, 'The Four Waves of Modern Terrorism', in Audrey Cronin and James Ludes (eds), *Attacking Terrorism: Elements of a Grand Strategy* (Washington, DC: Georgetown University Press, 2004) pp.46-73. Where no other source is given, my version of Rapoport's analysis derives from his 'Generations and Waves: The Keys to Understanding Rebel Terror Movements', paper delivered at a seminar on global affairs held at the Burkle Center for International Studies, UCLA, 7 Nov. 2003. An earlier version of this paper was published in *Current History*, Dec. 2001, pp.419-25.
5. His waves are in the middle of the ocean, not crashing onto a beach. 'Cycle' was used in Rapoport's 'Fear and Trembling: Terrorism in Three Religious Traditions', *American Political Science Review* 78 (1984) p.672, and 'wave' adopted for 'Generations and Waves'.
6. Rapoport refers to the 'Golden Age of Assassination' in 'Generations and Waves'.
7. Details are given below. Although not usually included in this list, the Shah of Persia might also be added.
8. The earliest instance of this wave, however, was in Ireland after the First World War.
9. Rapoport in fact says about forty years, recognizing that some waves may be shorter.
10. This is a misleading term, since the technique has almost nothing to do with suicide in its central meaning of the hopeless surrender of life to defeat. Again, however, the use of any other term would appear irritatingly pedantic.
11. Rapoport, 'Fear and Trembling' p.672.
12. For the third wave, Rapoport points to Vietnam. I would prefer the 'events' of 1968 in Paris and Czechoslovakia. Vietnam was more significant in America than in Europe, and third-wave groups were more active in Europe than America. The third wave gathered force very quickly, and the crucial years were clearly 1968-69. Both were during the Vietnam era, but 1968 was important in European history for two other reasons: the student uprisings in France, and the Soviet invasion of Czechoslovakia. Before 1968, angry young West European intellectuals often turned to Soviet Communism, and although Soviet Communism sponsored second wave terrorism outside Europe, it rarely sponsored terrorism in Western Europe. The Soviet Union was thus in a sense protecting Western Europe from its own dissidents. After 1968, dissident Europeans turned away from Soviet Communism to other ways of rejecting authority. This probably has more to do with third wave terrorism than Vietnam did. Certainly, as David C. Rapoport points

out, third-wave terrorists refer to Vietnam and not to Czechoslovakia. Czechoslovakia explains reorientation away from Soviet models, including Marxism-Leninism; Vietnam provided an alternative justification to Marxism-Leninism for condemning the Western status quo.

13. Of course, the Muslim Brotherhood engaged in what is often seen as religious terrorism in Egypt in the 1940s. This might however be reclassified as second-wave, anticolonial activity.
14. One objection to my selection of 1967 as the key political event for the start of the fourth wave is that this wave did not really become visible until the 1980s. This objection might be answered by pointing to the delay of forty years, to which Rapoport admits, between the political event at the start of the second (anti-colonial) wave—President Wilson's fourteen points—and that wave's crest. Nationalism existed before the second wave became visible; the resurgence of Islam, similarly, existed before 1979.
15. Found, for example, in Ranstorp, 'Terrorism in the Name of Religion'.
16. Rapoport, 'Fear and Trembling' p.664.
17. Pre-Khomeini Shi'ism, with its instance on the necessary illegitimacy of any government pending the return of the Imam Mahdi, might be considered an exception to this.
18. This argument is advanced in L. Carl Brown, *Religion and State: The Muslim Approach to Politics* (New York: Columbia University Press, 2000) pp.43-51.
19. There is, of course, no real 'church' in Islam, but there are established bodies of authoritative texts, and (until very recently) a defined body of religious experts associated with them. 'Church' can thus be used as shorthand for 'textual and institutional structures of religious authority'. See Mark Sedgwick, 'Is There a Church in Islam?' *ISIM Newsletter,* no. 13 (Dec. 2003) pp.40-1.
20. Those political groups that did explicitly deny the authority of religious norms were radical leftists of the early twentieth century, and suffered for this to the extent that even Moscow-aligned Communist parties in the Arab world subsequently steered clear mentioning religion.
21. Rapoport, 'Fear and Trembling'.
22. Rapoport recognizes, however, that all waves involve nationalism and ethnicity, and so is close to making this distinction. He also emphasizes that religious terrors is not necessarily indiscriminate.
23. Rapoport, 'Fear and Trembling' p.660.
24. Hoffman, 'Old Madness' p.15.
25. Audrey Kurth Cronin, 'Behind the Curve: Globalization and International Terrorism', *International Security* 273 (Winter 2002/03) p.41.
26. Hoffman, 'Old Madness' p.12, and Cronin, 'Behind the Curve' p.30.
27. Cronin, 'Behind the Curve' p.41.
28. Rapoport, 'Fear and Trembling' p.660. Rapoport does not suggest an answer to this question.
29. An offshoot of the 'sevener' Shi'ism of the Fatimids, itself an offshoot of the mainstream 'twelver' Shi'ism familiar in contemporary Iran and Iraq, which is itself seen by Sunnis (though not by the Shi'a themselves) as an offshoot of mainstream, Sunni Islam.
30. Some scholars argued that Soviet objectives during the Cold War were different in kind from American ones, notably Henry Kissinger in passing in *A World Restored: Metternich, Castlereagh and the Problems of Peace,* 1812-22 (Boston: Houghton Mifflin, 1957). This difference was more evident to participants such as Kissinger than to later historians. To respond, as I do, that both Soviet and American objectives were equally political does not need to imply any moral equivalence between the two sides.
31. Rapoport, 'Fear and Trembling' p.672.
32. As has been said, these are the establishment of one or more states ruled by its own favored version of Islam, in which al-Qaeda differs little from the Assassins. Like many similar groups, al-Qaeda has not been explicit about the precise nature of its vision of utopia. This is partly because revolutionary groups commonly worry more about the means to power than about the details of what they might do once in power, and partly because a religiously defined utopia can be designed only with great difficulty. It is also because Muslims see Islam as a single, unchanging and final truth (unlike scholars from outside, who insist on identifying historical development, continuity and change, and multiple perspectives). The nature of the perfect Islamic state is thus in theory well-known and beyond debate. Again, it is outsiders who insist on multiple possibilities.

33. The organizational nature of al-Qaeda is not widely understood, but there is growing recognition (implicit in the *9/11 Commission Report*) that it is closer to a network than a monolithic organization under strong central command. For an excellent description, see Benjamin Orbach, 'Usama bin Laden and al-Qa'ida: Origins and Doctrines', *Middle East Review of International Affairs* 54 (Dec. 2001) pp.58–61. Another excellent work (that unfortunately could not be consulted before this article went to press) is Marc Sageman, *Understanding Terror Networks* (Philadelphia: University of Pennsylvania Press, 2004).
34. Al-Qaeda was formed in Peshawar and Afghanistan, areas on which scholars have done little work. There are hundreds of journalistic accounts of al-Qaeda's emergence, of which the best is probably Ahmed Rashid's *Taliban: The Story of the Afghan Warlords* (London: Pan, 2001), but only one scholar got anywhere near them—Larry Goodson, author of *Afghanistan's Endless War: State Failure, Regional Politics, and the Rise of the Taliban* (Seattle, WA: University of Washington Press, 2001). Middle East scholars who do not specialize in such matters have also generally kept away from security issues and terrorism.
35. Al-Zawahiri, in *Al-Mujahidun* (1998), quoted in Lawrence Wright, 'The Man Behind Bin Laden: How an Egyptian Doctor became a Master of Terror', New Yorker 16 Sept. 2002.
36. This conclusion is based on countless informal discussions over several years with many Muslims in Egypt and other Arab countries.
37. These views are not often spoken aloud, and are even more rarely put in writing, but careful if unscientific research confirms their currency, though it cannot indicate the extent of their spread. Such views are found in the history of all three monotheistic religions—unsurprisingly, since they share much the same eschatology—but are probably more frequent and widespread in Islam than in Christianity or Judaism.
38. This sequence starts with al-Zawahiri's jihad group, which probably killed the speaker of the Egyptian parliament in 1990, and used a motorcycle suicide bomb against the Egyptian minister of the interior in 1993. In 1995, it used a motorized suicide bomb against the Egyptian embassy in Islamabad. In the same year it was probably al-Qaeda that bombed a Saudi military communications facility containing US soldiers in Riyadh, and in 1998 al-Qaeda carried out the well-planned simultaneous bombing of the US embassies in Kenya and Tanzania, causing massive casualties.
39. There were of course other attacks, but the Marine barracks bombing was the decisive event.
40. This is the title of Robert B. Asprey's massive work on the subject, *War in the Shadows: The Guerrilla in History* (New York: William Morrow, 1994).
41. Walter Laqueur, *Guerrilla: A Historical and Critical Study* (Boston: Little, Brown, 1976) p.3.
42. His *Strategamata* was read with appreciation by European military theorists during the eighteenth century. Laqueur, *Guerrilla,* p.101.
43. This was also emphasized, for example, by Johann von Ewald in his *Abhandlung von dem Dienst der Leichten Truppen* (Schleswig, 1796). Laqueur, *Guerrilla* p.106.
44. Laqueur, *Guerrilla* p.140.
45. Different people were thinking along much the same lines. An alternative candidate as originator of the phrase is Johannes Most, certainly the inventor of the letter-bomb. Most was a German anarchist who moved to the United States, where he published *The Science of Revolutionary Warfare: A Handbook of Instruction Regarding the Use of Nitroglycerine, Dynamite, Gun-Cotton, Fulminating Mercury, Bombs, Arsons, Poisons, etc.* (New York, 1885.) Laqueur, *Guerrilla* p.147. Most's book is still in print (and editions may be purchased from specialized websites in the United States).
46. Hippolyte Havel, Errico Malatesta: *The Biography of an Anarchist. A Condensed Sketch of Malatesta, from the Book Written by Max Nettlau* (New York: Jewish Anarchist Federation, 1924). Text available online at *Anarchy Archives: An Online Research Center on the History and Theory of Anarchism,* http://dwardmac.pitzer.edu/anarchist archives/ malatesta/nettlau/nettlauonmalatesta.html (Accessed 16 July 2003).
47. Havel, *Errico Malatesta.*
48. John Simkin, 'Anarchism', online at Spartacus Schoolnet, http://www.spartacus.schoolnet.co.uk/USAanarchist.htm (Accessed 19 July 2003).

49. Gerald Brenan, 'El terrorismo en la España del siglo XIX', (2002), online at *Historia del Anarquismo,* http://ateneovirtual.alasbarricadas.org/historia/index.php?page = El + terrorismo (Accessed 17 July 2003).
50. Simkin, 'Anarchism;' 'Propaganda by Deed', *Workers Solidarity* 55 (Oct. 1998); and similar reference sources.
51. 'Propaganda by Deed', *Workers Solidarity* 55 (Oct. 1998).
52. Laqueur, *Guerrilla,* pp.144, 173-5.
53. Laqueur, *Guerrilla* pp.179-81. There were, of course, other factors.
54. David C. Rapoport, 'Messianic Sanctions for Terror', *Comparative Politics* 20 (1988) p.196. Rapoport does not use the phrase 'shock and awe'.
55. Rapoport, 'Messianic Sanctions for Terror' p.196.
56. He would have approved of its tactical success, at least. I have no idea what Malatesta's actual views on the Arabs and Islam were, though there were various links in the nineteenth century between European anarchists and early Arab and Islamic nationalists. Islam was widely seen in such circles as a progressive—because anti-imperialist—force. Some time around 1878, Malatesta was in Egypt, but Havel (in *Errico Malatesta*) admits ignorance of what he did there. He probably concentrated on the Italian and Greek communities, which seem to have been those most receptive to political radicalism.
57. There is some disagreement as to whether the United States is a direct target of al-Qaeda or an indirect one, with most opinion tending toward the second view—that the United States is incidental to the real struggle, which is against the established regimes in the Middle East. See, for example, Gray, *Al-Qaeda* p.75, and Fawaz A. Gerges, 'Eavesdropping on Osama bin Laden', *Columbia International Affairs Online* October 2001, http://www.ciaonet.org/cbr/cbr00/video/cbr_v/cbr_v_2b.html. See also Feher, 'Robert Fisk's Newspapers', though Feher perhaps puts his argument too strongly. In one sense, it hardly matters; in the political analysis of people such as Bin Laden, the Zionists, Israel, Accessed April 2004. America and regimes 'friendly' to America are all equally 'oppressors of the Muslims'.
58. While public opinion in areas such as Europe generally made a clear distinction between Afghanistan and Iraq, Arab public opinion on the whole did not. These comments and similar comments below are based on discussions with various Arabs in Egypt during the period in question, and on the Arab media and Egyptian mosque sermons (*khutbas*). The majority Arab view included the conviction that 9/11 was not the responsibility of Arabs anyhow. There were several hypotheses regarding alternative actors; what matters is not how plausible these were, but how widely they were accepted. A straw poll of university students in Cairo on 11 September 2002 suggested that less than ten per cent were inclined to accept that Arabs had been behind the events of the previous year.
59. To some extent, these are valid questions, but they fall outside the scope of this article.
60. Indeed, Khalid Shaykh Muhammad told his interrogators that the World Trade Center was chosen as a target as a way of attacking the US economy. *9/11 Commission Report: Final Report of the National Commission on Terrorist Attacks Upon the United States* (Washington, DC: Government Printing Office, 2004) p.153. Such a motivation would fit with the 'second plausible explanation' considered above, that the perpetrators of 9/11 were 'simply not thinking very hard.' It hardly seems likely, however, that the name 'world trade center' could be taken quite so literally. Of course, 9/11 did indeed have an adverse impact on the U.S. economy, but Khalid Shaykh Muhammad would have to have been an unusually smart market analyst to have anticipated its actual impact on the Dow Jones index.
61. 'The New Powder Keg in the Middle East: Mujahid Usamah Bin Ladin Talks Exclusively to 'Nida'ul Islam'. Nida'ul Islam 15 (Oct.-Nov. 1996), http://www.fas.org/irp/world/para/docs/LADIN.htm. (Accessed 17 Sept. 2001). I have edited Nida'ul Islam's translation to remove stylistic peculiarities. The quotation may be from Bin Laden as claimed, or may perhaps have been invented by *Nida'ul Islam*; even in that case, it still establishes familiarity with Malatesta-type theories among some of Bin Laden's followers.
62. Except, perhaps, by Herzl and his followers—but that is a complex argument.
63. Sageman even suggests that certain experiences in the West are among of the key factors in explaining their participation in al-Qaeda. Sageman, *Understanding Terror Networks.*

64. *9/11 Commission Report* p.146.
65. In this context, 'Sharia' has almost lost its original meaning of canon law and instead denotes a form of political ideology.
66. Jonathan Fighel, 'Sheikh Abdullah Azzam: Bin Laden's Spiritual Mentor' (27 Sept. 2001) online at the Institute for Counter-Terrorism, Herlzliya, http://www.ict.org.il/articles/articledet.cfm?articleid = 388. Accessed April 2004. Azzam ran the Office of Services (Maktab al-khidamat), a name ironically reminiscent of the prototype of the CIA (the Office of Strategic Services), the focus of Arab assistance to the Afghan insurgency. Ahmed Rashid, *Taliban: The Story of the Afghan Warlords* (London: Pan, 2001) pp.131-32.
67. *9/11 Commission Report* p.146.
68. Those who knew Bin Laden as a young man did not regard him as particularly clever. Anonymous informants, Cairo, 2002.
69. See, for example, Soeid, 'Taking Stock: An Interview with George Habash', *Journal of Palestine Studies* 281 (Autumn 1998) p.90. It is unlikely, however, that Malatesta-type ideas actually reached al-Qaeda or Khalid Shaykh Muhammad through Habbash and Azzam, since Habash's own explanation of the PFLP's terrorism concentrates on generating publicity rather than on fomenting insurrection. Soeid, 'Taking Stock' p.93.
70. A friend from student days describes passionate discussions with al-Zawahiri about the nature of Arab, Muslim, and Egyptian identity. The friend in question was then a leading member of the Muslim Brothers, but has since passed through Communism to the academic study of psychology. Interview with anonymous informant, Cairo, April 2004.
71. Wright, 'The Man Behind Bin Laden'.
72. *9/11 Commission Report* p.147.
73. *9/11 Commission Report* p.68.
74. Rapoport makes a similar point in a different context in 'Fear and Trembling,' p.673.
75. Usamah Bin Ladin and others, World Islamic Front Statement, 23 Feb. 1998, http://www.fas.org/irp/world/para/docs/980223-fatwa.htm (Accessed 17 Sept. 2001).
76. Martin Kramer, *Arab Awakening and Islamic Revival: The Politics of Ideas in the Middle East* (New Brunswick, NJ: Transaction Publishers, 1996) pp.231-43 and 539-56, http://www.geocities.com/martinkramerorg/Calculus.htm and http://www.geocities.com/martinkramerorg/Sacrifice.htm (Accessed 4 April 2004).
77. 'Notes Found After the Hijackings', *New York Times* 29 Oct. 2001 p.B3. Comparison with photocopies of the Arabic text posted by the FBI confirm the accuracy of the *Times*'s translation.
78. Juan Cole, 'Al-Qaeda's Doomsday Document and Psychological Manipulation', paper presented at a conference on 'Genocide and Terrorism: Probing the Mind of the Perpetrator', Yale Center of Genocide Studies, New Haven, 9 April 2003, http://www.juancole.com/essays/qaeda.htm (Accessed 19 Jan. 2004).
79. Various informants, Cairo, Sept. 2001.
80. Stepniak, in *Underground Russia,* quoted in Rapoport, 'Generations and Waves'.
81. Cronin, 'Behind the Curve' p.41.
82. Hoffman, 'Old Madness' p.15.
83. Cronin, 'Behind the Curve', p.41.
84. Hoffman, 'Old Madness' p.15. See also Cronin, 'Behind the Curve' p.41, for a similar view.
85. Octavio Paz, 'El pachuco y otros extremos', in *El laberinto de la soledad* (Mexico, DF: Cuadernos Americanos, 1950) p.21.
86. Cronin, 'Behind the Curve', p.41.
87. Hoffman, 'Old Madness' p.15.
88. Cronin, 'Behind the Curve' p.56.
89. During the Cold War, for example, the United States made relatively less use of military means than did the USSR, and was much more imaginative in the use of alternative means.
90. It is generally agreed that the factors contributing to the success of any guerrilla campaign include a base, money, and outside support. Given this, military and diplomatic action aimed at denying al-Qaeda bases, money and outside support makes complete sense. It is also, of course, the sort of action that a powerful sovereign state can take most easily. The logic of military action in Iraq is a different question.

91. *9/11 Commission Report* pp.364 and 375-77.
92. Nicolas Marmie, 'Hundreds of Thousands March against Terror after Deadly Suicide Bombings', AP despatch from Morocco, 25 May 2003.
93. 'Moroccans Turn Out Against Terrorism', Reuters despatch from Casablanca, 25 May 2003.
94. It is not clear to what extent, if any, al-Qaeda has alienated potential supporters in other parts of the Muslim world. Unfortunately for US policymakers, Morocco may be something of an exception.

Quintan Wiktorowicz, 2005

A Genealogy of Radical Islam

A genealogy of the radical ideas that underline al-Qaeda's justification for violence shows that the development of jihadi thought over the past several decades is characterized by the erosion of critical constraints used to limit warfare and violence in classical Islam. This erosion is illustrated by the evolution of jihadi arguments related to apostasy and waging jihad at home, global jihad, civilian targeting, and suicide bombings.

Introduction

Al Qaeda and the radical fundamentalists that constitute the new "global jihadi movement" are not theological outliers. They are part of a broader community of Islamists known as "Salafis" (commonly called "Wahhabis").[1] The term "salafi" is used to denote those who follow the example of the companions (*salaf*) of the Prophet Mohammed. Salafis believe that because the companions learned about Islam directly from the Prophet, they commanded a pure understanding of the faith. Subsequent practices, in contrast, were sullied by religious innovations that infected the Muslim community over time. As a result, Muslims must purify the religion by strictly following the Qur'an, the Sunna (path or traditions of the Prophet Mohammed), and the consensus of the companions. Every behavior must be sanctioned by these religious sources.

Although there is consensus among Salafis about this understanding of Islam, there are disagreements over the use of violence. The jihadi faction believes that violence can be used to establish Islamic states and confront the United States and its allies. Nonviolent Salafis, on the other hand, emphatically reject the use of violence and instead emphasize propagation and advice (usually private) to incumbent rulers in the Muslim world.[2] These two groups demarcate the most important fissures within the Salafi community, although there are individuals and movements that do not fall neatly into either, including influential figures like Mohammed Sorour (now in London), Safar al-Hawali, and Salman al-Auda.

Understanding the genealogy of the radical jihadis necessitates identifying the key points of divergence within the Salafi community. Given a common understanding about following the strict model of the Prophet and his companions, what are the major points of disagreement? This article identifies four major points of contention among Salafis: (1) whether Muslims can call leaders apostates and wage jihad against them; (2) the nature of a "defensive" and global jihad; (3) the permissibility of targeting civilians; and (4) the legitimacy of suicide bombings (what radicals call "martyrdom operations"). How and why did the radicals diverge from the majority of Salafis on these issues? Who supported the divergent ideological trends, and how have these trends evolved over time?

The answers to these questions lie, to a large extent, in the inherently subjective process of religious interpretation whereby immutable religious texts and principles are applied to new circumstances and issues. The Qur'an and the Sunna of the Prophet Mohammed outline numerous rules about politics, economics, society, and individual behavior, but they do not directly respond to many questions relevant to the modern period. As a result, Salafis (and other Muslims) ask themselves what the Prophet would do if he were alive today. Given the way he lived his life and the principles he followed, how would he respond to the issues facing contemporary society? It is a process of extrapolation based on independent judgment (*ijtihad*) and reasoning by analogy (*qiyas*). So, for example, what would the Prophet say about the use of weapons of mass destruction? Clearly neither the Qur'an nor the Sunna speaks directly to this issue. Some radicals, however, argue that there is evidence that the Prophet would have supported the use of weapons of mass destruction if he were alive today. Specifically, they cite the siege of Ta'if in which the Prophet authorized the use of a catapult against a walled city where enemy fighters mixed with civilians, what jihadis call the "weapon of mass destruction of his day."[3] This process of reasoning invariably leads to differences of opinion about how the Prophet would respond to current issues.

The subjective nature of this process is nicely captured by a member of the Shura Council and Military Wing of the Gamiyya Islamiyya in Egypt during a group interview in June 2002 in which leaders explained why they abandoned the violent struggle initiated by the movement during the earlier 1990s:

> Shari'ah [the straight path of Islam, Islamic law] cannot be separated from reality. You must read both the reality and the relevant text before applying the right verses to the appropriate reality. Mistakes stem from the fact that the right text is sometimes applied on irrelevant reality.[4]

The leaders cited the decision by certain members of the movement to seize property belonging to Coptic Christians as an example. One responded that, "The person who did this used to apply certain texts to the wrong reality. The Islamic ruling on seizing loot belonging to the infidels applies to wars against the infidels, such as the war against the Jews in 1973 because it was a clear war. As for applying this principle to fellow citizens who are a part of this country's fabric, it is wrong."[5]

In tracing the evolution of jihadi thought over the past few decades, it appears that many of the shifts and changes are the result of new understandings about context rather than new readings of the religious texts and concomitant principles. Jihadis continue to use the same texts, quotes, and religious evidence as other Salafis, but they have developed new understandings about context and concepts such as "belief," "defense against aggression," and "civilians." The evolution of jihadi thought is less about changing principles embedded in the religious texts than the ways in which these principles are operative in the contemporary period.

This is not to argue that theology is completely irrelevant. Certainly, individual thinkers like Taqi al-Din Ibn Taymiyya (1263–1328), Muhammad bin Abdul Wahhab (1703–1792), Mawlana Abul A'la Mawdudi (1903–1979), and Sayyid Qutb (1906–1966) offered new understandings of the religious texts that challenged dominant interpretations, but subsequent thinkers, for the most part, merely adapted these understandings to new issues, often stretching them to their logical conclusion in a way that increased the scope of permissible violence.

Charges of Apostasy (*Takfir*) and Waging Jihad at Home

The vast majority of Muslims are conservative in their approach to declaring someone an apostate, a process known as takfir. The seriousness of the endeavor is underscored by a number of Qur'anic cautionary notes and stories about the Prophet. A few examples include:

> If a Muslim calls another *kafir* [unbeliever], then if he is a *kafir* let it be so; otherwise, he [the caller] is himself a *kafir*. (saying of the Prophet from Abu Dawud, *Book of Sunna*, edition published by Quran Mahal, Karachi, vol. iii, p. 484)

> No man accuses another man of being a sinner, or of being a *kafir*, but it reflects back on him if the other is not as he called him. (saying of the Prophet from Bukhari, *Book of Ethics*; Book 78, ch. 44)

> Withhold [your tongues] from those who say "There is no god but Allah"— do not call them *kafir*. Whoever calls a reciter of "There is no god but Allah" as a *kafir*, is nearer to being a *kafir* himself. (reported from Ibn Umar)[6]

Most Muslims believe that, as the Prophet said, "whoever accuses a believer of disbelief, it is as if he killed him."[7] Therefore, so long as a leader has a "mustard seed of faith" and implements the prayer, he is still considered a Muslim. (Throughout this article, the pronoun "he" is used because this is the jihadi standard. It must be recognized, however, that it encompasses both males and females.) From this perspective, a leader only becomes an apostate if he willingly implements non-Islamic law, understands that it does not represent Islam, and announces that it is superior to Islam. Otherwise, the leader could be ignorant, coerced, or driven by self-interest, failings that signify sinfulness, not apostasy. This is the line of argument represented by the Salafi mainstream.[8]

This reading of apostasy requires absolute proof of intentions, something that is nearly impossible unless the ruler publicly announces his disbelief. Nonviolent Salafis have, in fact, created a complex decision-making tree for excommunication that makes it extremely difficult to declare someone an apostate. They may charge a person with committing an act of apostasy, but unless that individual willingly proclaims that the act is Islamic, after clear evidence to the contrary, or announces that it is superior to Islam, he remains a Muslim. The culprit may go to Hell if he does not repent before dying, but that is for God to decide.

The nonviolent Salafis also believe it is forbidden to fight against rulers. Most cite the well-accepted prohibition against killing other Muslims, as outlined in Qur'an 4:92: "It is not for a believer to kill a believer unless (it be) by mistake."

The current jihadi argument about apostasy developed out of Egyptian and Saudi intellectual streams. The Egyptian lineage has its roots in British-controlled India. Conservative Indian Muslims were concerned that many Hindu converts to Islam were retaining earlier cultural practices and that Shi'ism and the British were undermining the purity of Sunni Islam. Hardliners reacted by drawing a sharp distinction between "true believers" and the infidels, which included Muslims who deviated from a rigid interpretation of Islam (apostates). Radical Sunni groups supporting this Manichean perspective emerged in Northern India during the 1820s and 1830s, including a movement led by Sayyid Ahmad Rai-Barelvi.[9] The conservative bent to these groups prompted the British to denote them as "Wahhabis" after the puritanical sect found on the Arabian Peninsula.

These conservatives were the intellectual predecessors to Mawlana Abul A'la Mawdudi, who in the 1930s seemed to give a "modernist cast to Sayyid Ahmad Rai-Barelvi's approach."[10] Whereas Rai-Barlevi and others rejected anything Western as antithetical to Islam, Mawdudi sought to appropriate Western technology, science, and other aspects of modernity while returning to the fundamentals of Islam. For modernists, the positive aspects of the West could be used to strengthen the Muslim community against Western imperialism. At the same time, despite this difference with earlier conservatives, Mawdudi adopted the strict distinction between belief and disbelief developed by Rai-Barelvi and his ilk.

Mawdudi's work drew extensively from Taqi al-Din Ibn Taymiyya, the best known medieval Salafi scholar, particularly his writings on the sovereignty of God.[11] One of Ibn Taymiyya's most important contributions to Salafi thought is his elaboration of the concept of *tawhid*—the unity of God. He divided the unity of God into two categories: the unity of lordship and the unity of worship. The former refers to belief in God as the sole sovereign and creator of the universe. All Muslims readily accept this. The second is affirmation of God as the only object of worship and obedience. Ibn Taymiyya reasoned that this latter component of divine unity necessitates following God's laws. The use of human-made laws is tantamount to obeying or worshipping other than God and thus apostasy. Mawdudi adopted this position and drew a sharp bifurcation between the "party of God" and the "party of Satan," which included Muslims who adhered to human-made law.

In making this argument, Mawdudi introduced his concept of "the modern jahiliyya" (circa 1939). The term "jahiliyya" refers to the "period of ignorance" (or period of paganism) preceding the advent of Islam. He argued that the deviations of self-proclaimed Muslims, the influence of imperialist powers, and the use of non-Islamic laws were akin to this earlier period of ignorance. For Mawdudi, true Muslims must struggle against this ignorance, just as the Prophet and his companions struggled against the paganism of the dominant Quraysh tribe in Mecca. In 1941, he formed the Jamaat-i-Islami as the spearhead of this struggle, a vanguard viewed as necessary to promote God's sovereignty on Earth.[12]

Mawdudi's importance for the Egyptian stream is his impact on Sayyid Qutb, often seen as the godfather of revolutionary Sunni Islam (he was executed by Nasser in 1966).[13] Qutb read Mawdudi's most influential works, including *Jihad in Islam, Islam and Jahiliyya,* and *Principles of Islamic Government,* which were translated into Arabic beginning in the 1950s. A more direct connection existed through one of Mawdudi's most important protégés, Abdul Hasan Ali Nadvi, who was a central figure in transmitting his mentor's theories to the Arab world. In 1950, Nadvi wrote *What Did the World Lose Due to the Decline of Islam?*, a book published in Arabic that expounded on Mawdudi's theory of modern jahiliyya. When he first traveled to the Middle East in 1951, Nadvi met with Qutb, who had already read his book. Both Mawdudi and Nadvi are quoted at length in Qutb's *In the Shade of the Qu'ran,* published in 1953.[14]

In *In the Shade of the Qu'ran,* Qutb outlines his view of the modern jahiliyya, which provides the cornerstone for declaring rulers apostates and waging jihad.

> Jahiliyya (barbarity) signifies the domination (hakamiyya) of man over man, or rather the subservience to man rather than to Allah. It denotes rejection of the divinity of God and the adulation of mortals. In this sense, jahiliyya is not just a specific historical period (referring to the era preceding the advent of Islam), but a state of affairs. Such a state of human affairs existed in the past, exists today, and may exist in the future, taking the

> form of jahiliyya, that mirror-image and sword enemy of Islam. In any time and place human beings face that clear-cut choice: either to observe the Law of Allah in its entirety, or to apply laws laid down by man of one sort or another. In the latter case, they are in a state of jahiliyya. Man is at the crossroads and that is the choice: Islam or jahiliyya. Modern-style jahiliyya in the industrialized societies of Europe and America is essentially similar to the old-time jahiliyya in pagan and nomadic Arabia. For in both systems, man is under the dominion of man rather than Allah.[15]

Qutb brought together Mawdudi's "modern jahiliyya" and Ibn Taymiyya's argument that the unity of God requires that Muslims follow divine law, creating a synthesis that reinforced the stark distinction between the Party of God and the Party of Satan: all those who do not put faith into action through an Islamic legal system and strictly obey the commands of God are part of the modern jahiliyya and no longer Muslims. In the Middle Eastern context, this meant apostasy because most members of the "jahiliyya community" were born Muslims.

Qutb's solution to the modern jahiliyya, however, was a stark departure from Mawdudi, who sought to work within the system. Whereas Mawdudi formed a political party and social movement to promote reform, Qutb advocated jihad to establish an Islamic state. In doing so, he argued against well-established Islamic legal opinions that jihad was primarily a struggle against the soul (*jihad al-nafs*) or a defensive war to protect the Muslim community. In a kind of Islamic liberation theology, he argued that force was necessary to remove the chains of oppression so that Islamic truth could predominate. Even more importantly, because the rulers in the Muslim world used non-Islamic legal codes, they were part of the modern jahiliyya and therefore not real Muslims. As infidels, they could be fought and removed from power, because the primary objective of Muslims is to establish God's rule on earth (divine *hukm*).

Qutb's argument found its most infamous manifestation in Mohammed al-Faraj's *The Neglected Duty*.[16] Faraj was a member of Islamic Jihad and used the book as a kind of internal discussion paper to explain and defend the group's ideology.[17] The book uses several lines of argument that have become staples of jihadi discourse. First, Faraj draws on Ibn Taymiyya to argue for the centrality of jihad in faith. He uses an assortment of quotes and hadiths (stories about the Prophet) in an effort to demonstrate that "jihad is second only to belief" in Islam. This is used to elevate the importance of jihad as a "pillar of Islam," a mandatory requirement to be a Muslim. Faraj argues that jihad has become "the neglected duty" (a phrase adopted by today's jihadis), something that must be resurrected as a central pillar of the faith.

Second, he reiterates Qutb's argument that rulers who do not implement Islamic law are unbelievers and must be removed from power. This is based on a Qur'anic verse consistently cited by Al Qaeda: "Whoever does not rule by what God hath sent down—they are unbelievers" (Qur'an 5:48). In making this argument, Faraj turns to Ibn Taymiyya's fatwa against the Mongols (or Tatars). As they conquered Muslim territory, the Mongols converted to Islam, thus raising questions about whether combat against them was a legitimate jihad. Ibn Taymiyya responded by arguing that someone who professes to be a Muslim is no longer a believer if he fails to uphold Islamic law or breaks any number of major injunctions concerning society and behavior. As Johannes Jansen notes, "The list of injunctions he draws is quite long; and it is not altogether clear how many nonapplied injunctions bring the ruler (or the individual believer) to the point of no return. When does he become an apostate to be combated?"[18] For the jihadis, the rationale was clear: the Mongols continued to implement the Yasa code of Genghis Khan and were therefore no longer Muslim because they did not adhere to the unity of worship. Jihadis viewed (and continue to view) this as analogous to contemporary states where rulers have adopted Western legal codes rather than Islamic law alone.

Qutb's influence on Faraj and other Egyptian jihadis is unquestionable. He inspired an assortment of radical groups, including The Islamic Liberation Organization, Takfir wal Hijra (Excommunication and Flight), Salvation from Hell, the Gamiyya Islamiyya (Islamic Group), and Islamic Jihad. He also had an important impact on two Egyptian thinkers who have been critical for the international jihadi movement. The first is Omar Abdul Rahman, the former mufti of Islamic Jihad and the Gamiyya Islamiyya who is currently serving a life sentence for conspiracy to commit terrorism in the United States. As a graduate from al-Azhar University, Rahman had substantial cachet among the radicals inspired by Qutb. Because most of his pronouncements were oral (he is blind), there is little textual data about his views. He did, however, fervidly support Qutb's emphasis on the necessity of God's governance on earth and the use of jihad to remove apostate rulers. Rahman also argued that, "the enemy who is at the forefront of the work against Islam is America and the allies."[19] For many jihadis, Rahman replaced Abdullah Azzam, one of Al Qaeda's founders, as the theological leader of the global jihad after the latter was assassinated in 1989. His incarceration, of course, has diminished this role.

Qutb also dramatically impacted Ayman Zawhiri, Al Qaeda's second in command. In his *Knights under the Prophet's Banner,* Zawahiri calls Qutb "the most prominent theoretician of the fundamentalist movements."[20] For Zawahiri, Qutb's greatest contribution seems to have been that,

> He affirmed that the issue of unification [tawhid] in Islam is important and that the battle between Islam and its enemies is primarily an ideological one over the issue of unification. It is also a battle over to whom authority and power should belong—to God's course and the shari'ah, to man-made laws and material principles, or to those who claim to be intermediaries between the Creator and mankind. ... This affirmation greatly helped the Islamic movement to know and define its enemies.
>
> Sayyid Qutub's [sic] call for loyalty to God's oneness and to acknowledge God's sole authority and sovereignty was the spark that ignited the Islamic revolution against the enemies of Islam at home and abroad. The bloody chapters of this revolution continue to unfold day after day.[21]

Zawahiri adopted both Qutb's Manichean view of the world and his unwavering desire to establish an Islamic state at any cost, using violence if necessary. This dichotomous struggle for God's sovereignty on earth eliminates the middle ground and sets the stage for a millennial, eschatological battle between good and evil.

Qutb's arguments inform jihadis in other countries as well. Many of his disciples fled Egypt during the massive crackdown by Nasser in the 1960s and moved to Saudi Arabia, where at least a few prominent thinkers took positions as university professors. Sayyid Qutb's brother, Mohammed, is perhaps the best example. In 1964, he published *The Jahiliyya of the Twentieth Century*, which rearticulated Sayyid's arguments (radicals often cite his *Islam: The Misunderstood Religion* as influential as well).[22] Not only did Mohammed Qutb teach Osama bin Laden at university, but he taught some future Islamist dis-

Table 1

The ten voiders according to Ibn Wahhab
(i.e., automatic apostasy)

1) Polytheism (associating others with God in worship)
2) Using mediators for God (for example, praying to saints)
3) Doubting that non-Muslims are disbelievers
4) Judging by non-Islamic laws and believing these are superior to divine law
5) Hating anything the Prophet Mohammed practiced
6) Mocking Islam or the Prophet Mohammed
7) Using or supporting magic
8) Supporting or helping non-believers against Muslims
9) Believing that someone has the right to stop practicing Islam
10) Turning away from Islam by not studying or practicing it

sidents as well, including Safar al-Hawali. The Saudi government tolerated (perhaps even supported) the spread of Qutb's ideology because it coincided with their antipathy toward Nasser and foreign policy objectives vis-à-vis Egypt. Although it is tempting to place all the blame on Sayyid Qutb for the radicalization of Islamism, the Saudis developed their own jihadi intellectual stream through Ibn Wahhab, who remains extremely influential. The Saudi jihadis recognize Qutb as a good Muslim who did good work, but they do not rely on him to the same extent as the Egyptian groups, instead using Ibn Wahhab as their direct pipeline to Ibn Taymiyya,[23] although there is some evidence that Taymiyya was less of an influence on Ibn Wahhab than is conventionally thought.[24]

Ibn Wahhab's most relevant work for the radicals is a small book titled *The Ten Voiders [or Nullifiers] of Islam* (see Table 1), which outlines ten things that automatically expel someone from the religion.[25] Three are of particular importance for the jihadis. First, a Muslim becomes a disbeliever if he associates someone or something in worshipping God. During his life, Ibn Wahhab was combating some Islamic practices he viewed as deviant polytheism, such as Sufism. Given the jihadis' emphasis on Ibn Taymiyya's argument about the unity of worship, this "voider" is also used to condemn any ruler who uses non-Islamic law.

Second, any Muslim who judges by "other than what God revealed" and believes this is superior to divine law is an apostate. For nonviolent Salafis, the two parts of this "voider" are critical: to be an apostate a ruler must not only implement non-Islamic law but also believe he is using legal means that are better than Islam. Unless the leader flagrantly admits that he has rejected Islam or believes in the supremacy of human-made law (extremely unlikely), he remains a Muslim.[26]

Jihadis, on the other hand, argue that actions are grounds for apostasy. For radicals, there are certain things about Islam that are "known by necessity," such as the ten voiders (some radicals use a much longer list). As a result, if a leader violates one of these, it is evidence of apostasy because he willingly flouts God's will. Like Qutb and the Egyptian radicals, the Saudi jihadis root this argument in Ibn Taymiyya's perspective on the unity of God: it requires both belief in the Creator as well as action (obeying and worshipping God).

Third, supporting or helping nonbelievers against Muslims is apostasy. This one, above all others, seems to have become the central "evidence" used by Al Qaeda to charge regimes in the Muslim world with apostasy. The movement and its supporters continually refer to the same Qur'anic verse: "O you who believe! Take not the Jews and Christians for your friends and protectors [*awliya'*]; they are but friends and protectors to each other" (Qur'an 5:51). It is important to note that there is an important grammatical ambiguity in this verse: it uses the term "wali" (pl. *awliya'*), which is an old Arabic technical term for patron, although in contemporary usage it has developed a broader connotation.[27] The jihadis use an expansive definition of *wali* to include virtually any relationship with non-Muslims.

The jihadis cite, in particular, the Saudi regime's decision to allow American troops in the kingdom to fight Iraq in 1990–1991. This was seen as taking nonbelievers as friends and helping them in a war against other Muslims (though Al Qaeda would never view Saddam Hussein as a Muslim). Bin Laden makes direct reference to this in his 1996 "Declaration of War": "The regime betrayed the Ummah [Muslim community] and joined the Kufr [unbelievers], assisting and helping them against the Muslims. It is well known that this is one of the ten 'voiders' of Islam, deeds of de-Islamisation" (his use of the term "voider" comes from Ibn Wahhab).[28]

The terms "helping" and "supporting" are inherently subjective, and Al Qaeda uses this to create an expansive understanding that includes any kind of support for the United States in its "war on terrorism." Even a word of support is considered apostasy. Take the following statement from a bin Laden tape that emerged in February 2003 as the United States was positioning to invade Iraq:

> We also point out that whosoever supported the United States, including the hypocrites of Iraq or the rulers of Arab countries, those who approved their actions and followed them in this crusade war by fighting with them or providing bases and administrative support, or any form of support, even by words, to kill the Muslims in Iraq, should know that they are apostates and outside the community of Muslims. It is permissible to spill their blood and take their property. God says, "O ye who believe! Take not the Jews and the Christians for your friends and protectors: they are but friends and protectors to each other."[29]

Although it is difficult to verify, it seems that the radicalization of the Saudi Salafis comes from three sources, in addition to Ibn Wahhab himself. First, there were always some radical elements among the Saudi Salafis, what Guido Steinberg refers to as the "radical wing" of the Wahhabiyya. These elements have existed since at least the 1920s and joined the Ikhwan revolts in 1928–1929. Second, Qutb's influence was felt through his books as well as Egyptians working and teaching in Saudi Arabia after the Nasser crackdown against Islamists.[30] Third, there was a radicalization process as a result of the war against the Soviets in Afghanistan. The conflict brought together Egyptians, Saudis, and other nationalities in a conflict zone where they learned about Islam in a context of violence. This period also witnessed the influence of more radical elements coming out of the Deobandi madrasa system in Pakistan. This provided greater opportunity for exposure to the jihadi elements from Egypt and elsewhere, which likely shifted the ideology of some of the Saudi fighters. Prior to that experience, Saudi Salafis were, for the most part, pro-regime, often ferociously so because the regime supported Salafism and helped export it as part of the kingdom's foreign policy. It took Afghanistan to significantly shake that support (exacerbated in the immediate aftermath by the stationing of American troops in Saudi Arabia).

Global Jihad

In Islam, there are two types of external jihad: offensive and defensive. In Islamic jurisprudence, the offensive jihad functions to promote the spread of Islam, enlightenment, and civility to the *dar al-harb* (domain of war). In most contemporary interpretations, the offensive jihad can only be waged under the leadership of the caliph (successor to the Prophet), and it is tempered by truces and various reciprocal agreements between the Islamic state and non-Muslim governments, such as guaranteed freedom of worship for Muslim minorities. Today, very few Islamists focus on this form of jihad.

The defensive jihad (*jihad al-dafa'a*), however, is a widely accepted concept that is analogous to international norms of self-defense and Judeo-Christian just war theory.[31] According to most Islamic scholars, when an outside force invades Muslim territory it is incumbent on all Muslims to wage jihad to protect the faith and the faithful. Mutual protection is seen as a religious obligation intended to ensure the survival of the global Muslim community. At the root of defensive jihad is a theological emphasis on justness, as embodied in chapter 6, verse 151 of the Qur'an: "Do not slay the soul sanctified by God except for just cause." Defending the faith-based community against external aggression is considered a just cause *par excellence*.

Although Muslim scholars almost uniformly agree that a defensive jihad is an obligation for Muslims, the issue remained relatively dormant until the Soviet invasion of Afghanistan in 1979. At the time, the majority of scholars had accepted the argument that jihad should focus on the struggle of the soul and inner purification, what has been dubbed "the greater jihad."[32] For the jihadis, the most important objective was to challenge this perspective and inspire participation in the war against the Soviets on behalf of Muslim brothers and sisters in Afghanistan. As a result, much of the writing at this time included extensive exhortations to jihad that outlined both the duty and glory of participation.

In making this argument, jihadis relied extensively on Ibn Taymiyya, whose contribution to the ideology of jihad has more to do with the religious and moral elements of jihad rather than legalistic issues related to just war or rules of engagement in combat.[33] In his writings, he argued that, "The command to participate in jihad and the mention of its merits occur innumerable times in the Koran and Sunna. Therefore it is the best voluntary [religious] act that man can perform. All scholars agree that it is better than the hajj (greater pilgrimage) and the *'umra* (lesser pilgrimage) [performed at a time other than the Hajj], than voluntary salat [prayer] and voluntary fasting, as the Koran and Sunna indicate. The Prophet, Peace be upon him, has said: "'*The head of the affair is Islam, its central pillar is the salat and its summit is the jihad.' And he has said: 'In Paradise there are a hundred grades with intervals as wide as the distance between the sky and earth. All these God prepared for those who take part in jihad*'."[34] [original italics]

Jihadis also drew extensively from the work of Ibn Nuhaas al-Demyati (d. 1412). In *Advice to Those Who Abstain from Fighting in the Way of Allah,* Ibn Nuhaas methodically addresses the various concerns of those who resist participating in jihad.[35] He touches on fears of death; concern for children, spouses, relatives, friends, social status, and lineage; love for material things; and desire to improve oneself before participating in battle. For each of these, Ibn Nuhaas quotes the Qur'an and Sunna of the Prophet to argue that this life means nothing when compared with the hereafter.

Abdullah Azzam is the most important figure to resurrect active participation in defensive jihad in the contemporary period. Following in the tradition of Ibn Taymiyya and Ibn Nuhaas, parts of his writings are intended to inspire participation. In his *Join the Caravan*, he opens by arguing that, "Anybody who looks into the state of the Muslims today will find that their greatest misfortune is their abandonment of Jihad (due to love of this world and abhorrence of death)."[36] To muster support, Azzam turns to Qur'anic verses consistently cited by Al Qaeda today, such as, "Proscribed for you is fighting, though it be hateful to you. Yet it may happen that you will hate a thing which is better for you; and it may happen that you will love a thing which is worse for you. God knows and you know not" (Qur'an 2:216).

He also makes a more legalistic argument to demonstrate that jihad is an undeniable duty. Azzam uses Ibn Taymiyya's distinction between collective and individual duties (*fard kifayah* and *fard 'ayn*) in Islam. Collective duties are obligations that can be fulfilled by a group of Muslims on behalf of the entire Muslim community. Individual duties are those that each and every Muslim must fulfill to avoid falling into sin. In the context of jihad, Ibn Taymiyya argued that, "jihad is obligatory if it is carried out on our initiative and also if it is waged as defense. If we take the initiative, it is a collective duty [which means that] if it is fulfilled by a sufficient number [of Muslims], the obligation lapses for all others and the merit goes to those who have fulfilled it. ... But if the enemy wants to attack the Muslims, than repelling him becomes a[n] [individual] duty for all those under attack and for the others in order to help him."[37]

Azzam adopted Ibn Taymiyya's reasoning and argued that if a group of Muslims trying to fulfill a duty to repel aggressors fails to do so alone, it becomes an individual obligation for those nearest the conflict zone:

> Ibn 'Abidin, the Hanafi scholar says, "(Jihad is) fard 'ayn [an individual obligation] when the enemy has attacked any of the Islamic heartland, at which point it becomes fard 'ayn on those close to the enemy. ... As for those beyond them, at some distance from the enemy, it is fard kifayah [a collective duty] for them unless they are needed. The need arises when those close to the enemy fail to counter the enemy, or if they do not fail but are negligent and fail to perform jihad. In that case it becomes obligatory on those around them—fard 'ayn, just like prayer and fasting, and they may not abandon it. (The circle of people on whom jihad is fard 'ayn expands) until in this way, it becomes compulsory on the entire people of Islam, of the West and the East.[38] (original sentence structure from translation)

According to Azzam, the Afghans could not fulfill the obligation without help from other Muslims: "the jihad is in need of men and the inhabitants of Afghanistan have not met the requirement which is to expel the Disbelievers from Afghanistan. In this case, the communal obligation (fard kifayah) is overturned. It becomes individually obligatory (fard 'ayn) in Afghanistan, and remains so until enough Mujahideen [holy warriors] have gathered to expel the communists in which case it again becomes fard kifayah."[39]

Azzam also argues that this obligation is eternal. In making this claim, he is clearly influenced by Sayyid Qutb and quotes the following passage from Qutb's writing:

> If Jihad had been a transitory phenomenon in the life of the Muslim Ummah, all these sections of the Qur'anic text would not be flooded with this type of verse! Likewise, so much of the sunnah [sic] of the Messenger of Allah (may Allah bless him and grant him peace), would not be occupied with such matters. ... If Jihad were a passing phenome-

> non of Islam, the Messenger of Allah (may Allah bless him and grant him peace) would not have said the following words to every Muslim until the Day of Judgment, "Whoever dies neither having fought (in Jihad), nor having made up his mind to do so, dies on a branch of hypocrisy."[40]

So, Azzam concludes, the jihad in Afghanistan is an eternal individual obligation. Under these circumstances, it is elevated to the status of the five pillars of Islam, necessary to be a Muslim. Azzam, like Al Qaeda later, uses a quote from Ibn Taymiyya to emphasize the importance of the defensive jihad as a religious obligation: "As for the occupying enemy who is spoiling the religion and the world, there is nothing more compulsory after faith (iman) than repelling him."[41] Building on this, Azzam argues that, "everyone not performing jihad today is forsaking a duty, just like the one who eats during the days of Ramadan without excuse, or the rich person who withholds the Zakat [religiously obligated charity] from his wealth." This means that, "The obligation of jihad today remains fard 'ayn until the liberation of the last piece of land which was in the hands of Muslims but has been occupied by the Disbelievers" (such as Spain, for example). This argument sets the stage for what Olivier Roy has termed "the nomadic jihad," an eternal struggle to "defend" Muslims from the disbelievers.[42]

The influence on Al Qaeda's current thinking is unmistakable. This is not surprising given that Azzam helped found Al Qaeda and provided the underlying rationale for the movement in an April 1988 article titled "The Solid Base" (al-Qa'ida al-Bulba), published in *al-Jihad*. Various Al Qaeda statements extend Azzam's argument about the obligations of the nomadic jihad to justify attacks against the United States. To apply this argument, however, the jihadis have to demonstrate that the Americans are occupying Muslim land. For bin Laden, this rationale became clear in 1990 after King Fahd ignored his offer to use Afghan war veterans to repel Saddam and instead authorized the presence of American troops in Saudi Arabia. In a 1998 fatwa, bin Laden and several other jihadis argued that, "for over seven years the United States has been occupying the lands of Islam in the holiest of places, the Arabian Peninsula, plundering its riches, dictating to its rulers, humiliating its people, terrorizing its neighbors, and turning its bases in the Peninsula into a spearhead through which to fight the neighboring Muslim peoples. If some people have formerly debated the fact of the occupation, all the people of the Peninsula have now acknowledged it."[43]

In this argument, the jihadis received support from less radical Islamists like Safar al-Hawali and Salman al-Auda, who opposed the American presence. In his 1996 "Declaration of War," for example, bin Laden explicitly references Hawali: "The imprisoned Sheikh Safar al-Hawali, may Allah hasten his release, wrote a book of seventy pages; in it he presented evidence and proof that the presence of the Americans in the Arab Peninsula is a preplanned military occupation."[44]

Bin Laden and Al Qaeda also found comfort with the oppositional Islamists who signed the Memorandum of Advice in July 1992, which represented an unprecedented public critique of the Saudi regime's domestic and foreign policies.[45] Although many of these oppositional clerics do not support Al Qaeda's tactics and use of violence, their critique of the regime and overall opposition to the U.S. presence in the kingdom provided the fodder bin Laden needed to frame America as an occupying force supported by an un-Islamic regime, thereby justifying a defensive jihad.

The critical need for a defensive posture to legitimize jihad is apparent in Al Qaeda's penchant for framing all its actions as defensive. In a 1998 interview, bin Laden argued that,

"We are carrying out the mission of the Prophet Muhammad (peace be upon him). The mission is to spread the word of God, not to indulge in massacring people. We ourselves are the target of killings, destruction, and atrocities. We are only defending ourselves. This is a defensive jihad. We want to defend our people and our land. That is why we say, if we don't get security, the Americans, too, would not get security. This is the simple formula that even an American child can understand. Live and let live."[46]

For most jihadis, this "defensive argument" was absolutely necessary to legitimate 11 September in particular. For example, immediately after the 11 September attacks, Abu Hamza al-Misri, a radical Al Qaeda supporter in London, argued that it "was done in self defense. If they did it for that reason then they are justified." He added that, "If you ask how could it be self defense in doing this in America, it is as much as it was in self defense in Hiroshima."[47]

Killing Civilians[48]

The Qur'an and Sunna of the Prophet Mohammed are replete with enjoinments against killing civilians. Nonviolent Salafis and other Muslims repeatedly emphasize the following pieces of religious evidence to argue for a prohibition against targeting noncombatants:

> We decreed for the Children of Israel that whosoever kills a human being for other than manslaughter or corruption in the earth, it shall be as if he had killed all mankind, and whoso saves the life of one, it shall be as if he had saved the life of all mankind. (Quran 5:32).
>
> And fight in God's cause against those who wage war against you, but do not transgress, for God loves not the transgressors. (Qur'an 2:190).
>
> Set out for jihad in the name of Allah and for the sake of Allah. Do not lay hands on the old verging on death, on women, children and babes. Do not steal anything from the booty and collect together all that falls to your lot in the battlefield and do good, for Allah loves the virtuous and the pious. (Sunna of the Prophet Mohammed)
>
> Stop, O people, that I may give you ten rules for your guidance in the battlefield. Do not commit treachery or deviate from the right path. You must not mutilate dead bodies. Neither kill a child, nor a woman, nor an aged man. Bring no harm to the trees, nor burn them with fire, especially those which are fruitful. Slay not any of the enemy's flock, save for your food. You are likely to pass by people who have devoted their lives to monastic services; leave them alone. (Instructions given by Abu Bakr, the first caliph or successor to the Prophet Muhammed, to a Muslim army setting out to battle against the Byzantine Empire in Syria)

Although nonviolent Salafis view this kind of religious evidence as a prohibition against *purposely* targeting civilians, they do recognize the possibility of civilian casualties in the course of warfare, considered an acceptable consequence in a legitimate jihad. Islamic fighters must do everything they can to limit noncombatant casualties, but "collateral damage" (to use Western terminology) is often inevitable. This is particularly the case where the enemy uses human shields. Under these circumstances, the Islamic fighters are permitted to attack, and the responsibility for noncombatant deaths lies with the enemy.

From this perspective, only combatants can be targeted. This includes not only soldiers, political leaders responsible for waging war, and intelligence officers, but support staff outside the military and political structure as well, such as advisors who help plan the war. Although they may not be directly involved in actual fighting and combat, support personnel are considered part of the war effort, thereby making them legitimate targets.

The move toward civilian targeting seems to be a recent development with little precedent. Neither Sayyid Qutb nor Ibn Wahhab argued that civilians could be targeted during combat and war, and there was little discussion about the subject until the 1990s. As a result, Al Qaeda has reached directly back to the example of the Prophet and classical and medieval scholars such as Ibn Taymiyya, Ibn Kathir, Ibn al-Qayyim, Shawkani, Ibn al-Qasim, and Ibn Qudamah. Given the vast religious evidence from the Qur'an and Sunna emphasizing the sanctity of life and limiting attacks against noncombatants, Al Qaeda could hardly argue against noncombatant immunity. But it has broken new ground over the past decade or so to develop an expanded understanding about permissible targets in war.

The jihadi debate about civilian targeting began in the mid-1990s in response to the Algerian civil war, which erupted after the regime cancelled Parliamentary elections in January 1992 as it became clear that the Islamic Salvation Front would dominate the new government.[49] Following the coup, Islamist rebels limited attacks to government officials, military personnel, and the police. The scope and tenor of the conflict, however, escalated dramatically in 1993 with the emergence of the Armed Islamic Group (Groupes Islamiques Armé or GIA). Initially, the GIA launched broader attacks against the security services and assassinated junior ministers and members of the National Consultative Council (formed by President Mohammed Boudiaf to provide a democratic façade following the coup).

During this period, there is some evidence that bin Laden and Al Qaeda provided limited support to the GIA through Qamareddin Kharban, the leader of the "Algerian Afghans" (Algerians who had fought in Afghanistan against the Soviets). This included financial support; Al Qaeda fighters sent to Algeria; and theological cover through Al Qaeda-linked scholars like Abu Qatada, who also helped publish and distribute the GIA's *al-Ansar* bulletin (in conjunction with Abu Musab) in London.[50]

This growing relationship changed dramatically in 1996 when Antar Zouabri became the emir of the GIA. He initiated his new leadership position by issuing a fatwa charging the entire society with apostasy and authorizing attacks against any Algerian who refused to join or aid the GIA (including other armed Islamist groups). In this manner, Zouabri took Qutb's Manichean view of the world to an extreme: you are either with the GIA and thus Islamic truth or against it and thus God. The position was summed up in a GIA communiqué posted in an Algiers suburb in 1997: "There is no neutrality in this war we are waging. With the exception of those who are with us, all others are apostates and deserve to die."[51]

The fatwa shifted GIA operations away from the state and toward softer targets in society, eventually leading to widespread civilian massacres. Whereas civilians comprised only 10% of the casualties in 1992, by 1997 this figure rose to 84%.[52] Thousands were massacred. Ordinary citizens were maimed, decapitated, and burned alive. According to GIA chief Abou el-Moudhir, all of these people "have become the enemies of our fighters, from the youngest of their children to the oldest of their elderly."[53] Although there is some evidence of possible regime complicity in a few attacks, the GIA claimed responsibility for most of them.

The underlying justification for the massacres portended the later Al Qaeda justification for 11 September and purposeful civilian targeting: individuals who support the government act as surrogates and representatives of the enemy; they are thus legitimate targets. Take the GIA's rationale for attacking journalists and editors:

> The rotten apostate regime did not stop using the mercenary media to cover its crimes and rationalize its aggression. This has turned all written, seen, and heard media outlets into a tool of aggression spreading lies and rumors. It would have been an obligation for these writers to stand with their nation in these hard times and embrace the blessed jihad, but instead they have turned their pens into swords defending the low lives of apostasy and treason. Based on that, mujahidin consider every reporter and journalist working for radio and television as no different than regime apostates. GIA calls on every reporter working there to immediately stop work, otherwise the group will continue hitting hard those who do not comply. Whoever fights us with the pen will be fought with the sword.[54]

In other words, "civilian" journalists and editors were no longer noncombatants because they served the interest of the government.

The same kind of reasoning was used to attack teachers and school children: by attending government-controlled schools, they signaled support for the regime. In a statement published in the Arabic daily *al-Hayat*, the GIA warned that those who "continue their studies are helping the tyrant to ensure stability and thereby are not accomplishing the jihad." They are considered heretics and deserve death.[55]

More broadly, the GIA argued that any Algerian who did not support the GIA was tacitly supporting the regime, thereby removing their noncombatant immunity. The menu of legitimate targets was thus expanded to include almost the entire society.

The massacres sparked a debate within international jihadi circles. Supporters were frustrated by the GIA's apparent unwillingness to elaborate on the religious justification for their attacks. Some supporters initially denied GIA involvement, dismissing such claims as government propaganda (Abu Hamza al-Misri is a case in point, although he eventually withdrew his support for the movement in 1997). But when it became clear that Algerian jihadis were involved, there was widespread condemnation and opposition from the international jihadi network. Abu Qatada, considered the GIA's mufti, withdrew his support as a direct response to the massacres.[56] Allegedly dismayed by the un-Islamic nature of the massacres, bin Laden provided support for the rival GSPC (Groupe Salafiste pour la Predication et le Combat, Salafi Group for Combat and Propagation) led by former GIA emir Hassan Hattab. Zouabri became increasingly isolated and the GIA disintegrated into rival factions. He was eventually killed in February 2002.[57]

The primary concern for bin Laden and the international jihadis seems to have been that the targets were Muslims rather than infidels. According to Islamic law, Muslims cannot kill other Muslims, except under very stringent conditions (such as banditry, but even then there are restrictions). The idea of using *takfir* against such a broad portion of the population was rejected by the international jihadis. For Al Qaeda, killing apostate government officials is one thing; attacking ordinary Muslim citizens is entirely different because they have been led astray by the regime and its battalion of state clerics, who purposely obfuscate and hide Islamic truth from the people. The massacres also threatened Al Qaeda's strategy to win the hearts and minds of Muslims in its battle against the United States and its "puppets."[58]

Emerging from the debate about civilian targeting in Algeria, Al Qaeda began sharpening its position in the late 1990s with support from a consortium of contemporary scholars. The movement uniformly rejected targeting Muslim civilians, unless they assisted the infidel (in which case they were no longer Muslims in any event). It also displayed great sensitivity

Table 2

Conditions for killing civilians according to Al Qaeda
(only one condition is necessary)

1)	The enemy has purposefully killed Muslim civilians*
2)	Civilians have assisted the enemy in "deed, word, or mind"*
3)	Islamic fighters cannot distinguish between combatants and non-combatants
4)	There is a need to burn enemy strongholds or fields where there are civilians
5)	Heavy weaponry needs to be used
6)	The enemy uses civilians as human shields
7)	The enemy violates a treaty with the Muslims and civilians must be killed as a lesson

*These are the most often cited conditions.

to concerns that Muslims could be caught in the crossfire, arguing that Muslims should not mix with non-Muslims and should stay away from potential targets. Those who are killed inadvertently are considered martyrs for the cause, and blood money should be paid to the families. This argument about blood payment appears to have come from Ayman Zawhiri, who offered this solution after members of Islamic Jihad inadvertently killed a young child during an attack against Prime Minister Atif Sidqi's motorcade in Egypt in 1993.[59] This was also the solution offered for Muslims killed in the 11 September attacks.[60]

The jihadis predominantly use two lines of argument to justify targeting non-Muslim civilians (see also Table 2). First, they use a "doctrine of proportional response." Although accepting the general prohibition against killing noncombatants, the jihadis consistently draw on Ibn al-Qayyim, al-Shawkani, al-Qurtubi, Ibn Taymiyya, and others to argue that when the infidel kills Muslim civilians it becomes permissible to attack their civilians in kind. This is supported by Qur'an 2:194: "And one who attacks you, attack him in like manner as he attacked you." In his *Shadow of the Lances,* Al Qaeda spokesman Suleiman Abu Gheith argues that, "Anyone who peruses these sources reaches a single conclusion: The sages have agreed that reciprocal punishment to which the verses refer is not limited to a specific instance. It is a valid rule for punishments for infidels, for the licentious Muslims, and for oppressors."[61] In other words, if the enemy uses tactics that are prohibited according to Islam, these tactics become legal for Muslims.

To make the doctrine of proportional response operable against Americans, the jihadis have to demonstrate that the United States is purposely targeting Muslim civilians. It does so by citing a number of conflicts involving the United States in which civilians have been killed, including Afghanistan and Iraq, among others. Without actually demonstrating intent, which is critical for the use of the proportionality doctrine, the radicals conclude that the United States has strategically killed Muslims to terrorize the Islamic nation (umma). It makes this argument with particular emphasis on the Palestinian territories (and unwavering American support for Israel), in effect tapping into the widespread sense of despair felt by millions of Muslims exposed to the images of children and other civilians killed during confrontations with Israeli soldiers. In the justification for 11 September, Al Qaeda argues that,

> There currently exists an extermination effort against the Islamic peoples that has America's blessing, not just by virtue of its effective cooperation, but by America's activity.

> The best witness to this is what is happening with the full knowledge of the world in the Palestinian cities of Jenin, Nablus, Ramallah, and elsewhere. Every day, all can follow the atrocious slaughter going on there with American support that is aimed at children, women, and the elderly. Are Muslims not permitted to respond in the same way and kill those among the Americans who are like the Muslims they are killing? Certainly! By Allah, it is truly a right for Muslims.[62]

For Al Qaeda, the evidence points to a clear conclusion:

> It is allowed for Muslims to kill protected ones among unbelievers as an act of reciprocity. If the unbelievers have targeted Muslim women, children, and elderly, it is permissible for Muslims to respond in kind and kill those similar to those whom the unbelievers killed.[63]

For Suleiman Abu Gheith, the sheer volume of Muslims killed by the United States means that Muslims have the right to kill four million Americans in order to reach parity.[64]

Al Qaeda's use of the doctrine of proportional response hinges on its interpretation of U.S. intentions: are American troops purposely targeting civilians? If the answer is yes, even nonviolent Salafis would agree that it is permissible to target American civilians. If the answer is no, then Muslims are limited by religious edicts against killing women, children, the elderly and other noncombatants. Bombarded by images of young, stone-throwing boys shot by Israeli soldiers, most Muslims accept the argument that Israel purposely targets civilians. Increasingly, many have also come to believe that the United States is doing the same. Some argue, for example, that U.S. technology is so effective that the only way civilians can be killed is if American troops target them. Al Qaeda thus plays into widespread frustration and apprehension about American military power and the "collateral damage" of war.

The second major line of argument builds on Ibn Taymiyya, who argued that, "Since lawful warfare is essentially jihad and since its aim is that the religion is God's entirely and God's word is uppermost, therefore, according to all Muslims, those who stand in the way of this aim must be fought. As for those who cannot offer resistance or cannot fight, such as women, children, monks, old people, the blind, the handicapped and their likes, they shall not be killed, unless they actually fight with words [e.g., propaganda] and acts [e.g., spying or otherwise assisting in the warfare]."[65] This defines enemy populations in terms of their capacity to fight, in effect introducing subjectivity into the definition of "civilian."

The jihadis argue that anyone who assists the enemy in any way loses the protection of noncombatant status: "It is allowed for Muslims to kill protected ones among unbelievers on the condition that the protected ones have assisted in combat, whether in deed, word, mind, or any other form of assistance, according to the prophetic command." Perhaps the most oft-cited piece of evidence for this line of argument is a story about Duraid Ibn al-Simma, a well-known Arab poet who strongly opposed Mohammed and the message of Islam. According to tradition, he was brought to the battlefield to advise the Hawazin troops about battle procedures in a conflict against the Muslims. As a very old man, he posed no physical threat to the Muslim forces, but the intelligence he provided to the enemy made him a target and led to his death in battle.[66]

Although even nonviolent Salafis agree that individuals who directly assist combat through advice in war planning or other supportive functions are legitimate targets, Al Qaeda uses the subjectivity inherent in the "capacity to fight" threshold to dramatically broaden the menu of legitimate targets. Anyone the movement itself deems as supporting the "war against Islam" is fair game, including NGOs, journalists, academics, government consultants, and businesses.

The most important new line of thinking, without precedent in Islamic law, is the jihadi argument about personal and individual culpability in a democracy. This argument is best represented in a fatwa about 11 September issued by Hammoud al-Uqla al-Shuaybi, considered the godfather of the Saudi jihadis. In the fatwa, al-Uqla argues that:

> [W]e should know that whatever decision the non-Muslim state, America, takes—especially critical decisions which involve war—it is taken based on opinion poll and/or voting within the House of Representatives and Senate, which represent directly, the exact opinion of the people they represent—the people of America—through their representatives in the Parliament [Congress]. Based on this, any American who voted for war is like a fighter, or at least a supporter.[67]

In addition to citing Ibn Taymiyya's stance vis-à-vis the capacity of the enemy population to fight, al-Uqla also cites another ruling in which Ibn Taymiyya argued that Christians could be fought because "they assisted the enemies of the Muslims against them, and helped them with their wealth and weapons, despite the fact that they did not fight us." Al-Uqla's perspective has influenced some of his more radical jihadi students, including Ali bin Khudayr al-Khudayr, Nasir Hamad al-Fahd, and Suleiman Alwan. Alwan and al-Khudayr issued fatwas after 11 September saying that anyone who assisted the United States was an apostate. Al-Fahd issued a fatwa supporting the use of weapons of mass destruction.

This kind of argument is replicated in several Al Qaeda publications. In its justification for September 11, the movement reasons that because a democratically elected government reflects the will of the people, a war against Islam of this magnitude must have popular support. Using the term "public opinion" (*al-ra'y al-'amm*) to represent the will of the people in a democracy, Al Qaeda argues that,

> It is stupidity for a Muslim to think that the Crusader-Zionist public opinion which backs its government was waiting for some action from Muslims in order to support the Crusader war against Islam and thereby enkindle a spirit of hostility against Islam and Muslims. The Crusader-Zionist public opinion has expended all it has in order to stand behind the nations of the cross, executing their war against Islam and Muslims from the beginning of the colonization of Islamic countries until the present day. If the successive Crusader-Zionist governments had not received support from their people, their war against Islam and Muslims would not have taken such an obvious and conspicuous form. It is something that would not attain legitimacy except by the voices of the people.[68]

Abd al Aziz bin Saleh al-Jarbu, author of *Basing the Religious Legitimacy of Destroying America,* recounts a story in which the Prophet ordered his followers to kill a woman because she sang songs to inspire the enemy warriors. "If this was the decree against anyone who sang songs of vituperation against the Messenger," he reasoned, "then it is all the more a decree against those who to this added participating in a vote approving massacres of Muslims and against those who spread shame and prostitution to Islam and the Muslims."[69]

Obviously Ibn Taymiyya did not discuss the culpability of individuals in a democracy because this was not a medieval or classical issue. The jihadis have transmogrified his line of argument and a well-established principle in Islamic jurisprudence that those who assist in combat, even if they are not soldiers, are legitimate targets. By declaring all Americans personally responsible simply because they live in a democracy, Al Qaeda has manipulated the subjective nature of defining "the capacity to fight" to justify widescale attacks on non-combatants.

Although GIA emir Zouabri was never considered a theological luminary and had little direct influence on theological debates about civilian targeting, his rationale for the massacres in Algeria runs throughout Al Qaeda's justification for 11 September. In both cases, the definition of "civilian" was stretched to include broad swathes of the population. So whereas Al Qaeda may have objected to killing Muslim civilians in Algeria, its logic for killing non-Muslim civilians mirrors Zouabri's reasoning.

Suicide Bombings

Like civilian targeting, the issue of suicide bombings or "martyrdom operations" is relatively recent. The use of suicide bombings by Muslims began in Lebanon and was popularized by Hizballah. Tactically speaking, this influenced Palestinian groups. Theologically speaking, however, it is unlikely that Hizballah directly influenced Al Qaeda and the Sunni jihadis because its arguments derived from Shi'ite traditions of martyrdom (and it focused on military and political targets). The real debate about the religious permissibility of these kinds of operations among Salafis, in fact, did not emerge until the mid-1990s and was a response to its widespread usage by Hamas and other Palestinian factions.

What is interesting about the current jihadi arguments about suicide bombings is how little attention seems to be given to constructing a theological argument justifying such attacks. Instead, the vast majority of materials focus on extolling the virtues of martyrdom. Abdullah Azzam's *Virtues of Martyrdom in the Path of Allah* is a classic example.[70] In it, he elaborates twenty-seven points of evidence about the benefits of martyrdom. Most writings argue that the martyr has a seat in Paradise, avoids the torture of the grave, marries seventy black eyed virgins, and can advocate on behalf of seventy relatives so that they too might reach Paradise. Scholars from all ideological persuasions agree about the virtues of martyrdom.

Since the 1990s, Al Qaeda and the jihadis have been forced to address two central questions. First, are martyrdom operations suicide? This is critical because Islam explicitly prohibits suicide. Some of the more senior Salafi clerics in Saudi Arabia have argued that these attacks are prohibited. Muhammad Bin Salih Bin Uthaymin (d. 2000), for example, argues that, "as for what some people do regarding activities of suicide, tying explosives to themselves and then approaching disbelievers and detonating amongst them, then this is a case of suicide. ... So whoever commits suicide then he will be considered eternally to Hell-Fire, remaining there forever."[71] In making this condemnation, the focus is on the *act* itself: consciously killing oneself.

The jihadis, however, focus on the *intent* of the perpetrator. Although he is not as radical as Al Qaeda, Yusuf al-Qaradawi outlines the basic reasoning:

> He who commits suicide kills himself for his own benefit, while he who commits martyrdom sacrifices himself for the sake of his religion and his nation. While someone who commits suicide has lost hope with himself and with the spirit of Allah, the *Mujahid* [holy warrior] is full of hope with regard to Allah's spirit and mercy. He fights his enemy

> and the enemy of Allah with this new weapon, which destiny has put in the hands of the weak, so that they would fight against the evil of the strong and arrogant. The *Mujahid* becomes a "human bomb" that blows up at a specific place and time, in the midst of the enemies of Allah and the homeland, leaving them helpless in the face of the brave *Shahid* [martyr] who ... sold his soul to Allah, and sought the *Shahada* [Martyrdom] for the sake of Allah.[72]

Here Al Qaeda shares its view of suicide bombings as legitimate martyrdom operations with less radical, conservative Sunnis. This includes not only figures like al-Qaradawi, but also Mohammed Sayyed Tantawi, the Sheikh of al-Azhar in Egypt.[73] The jihadis thus find ample support among Muslims for the *tactic* itself.

The second question is related to targeting. Can Islamic fighters kill civilians in "martyrdom operations"? Much of the jihadi argument in answering this question is based on its justification for killing civilians in general, outlined in the previous section of this article: it challenges mainstream definitions of "innocent civilians" to include anyone who assists the enemy in "word, deed, or mind," an extremely expansive category. Its reliance on this line of reasoning stems from widespread opposition to killing civilians, even in suicide bombings. Although someone like Tantawi may support suicide bombings in principle, he and others object to killing civilians in the process. Even Muhammed al-Maqdisi, an extreme jihadi Salafi in Jordan, has cautioned against civilian targeting, although noting that in some contexts the Islamic fighters may not be able to distinguish between combatants and noncombatants.[74] From this perspective, collateral damage is permissible but should be avoided where possible.

It is because of the general consensus that Muslims cannot purposely target civilians that Al Qaeda and others must emphasize that alleged "civilians" are not really noncombatants. In the context of Israel, for example, al-Qaradawi and the jihadis frame Israel as a militarized country. Because there is mandatory military service for men and women (and reserve service after that), all men and women become legitimate targets in martyrdom operations. Some more radical elements argue that because children will one day grow up and serve in the Israeli army, they too are legitimate targets. Regardless of the nuances, Al Qaeda is careful to frame the targets of the attacks as combatants through deeds, words, and thoughts.

Conclusion and Future Prospects

The development of jihadi thought is characterized by the erosion of critical constraints used to limit warfare and violence in classical Islam. Whereas most Islamic scholars throughout history have defined apostates as those who clearly leave the faith by declaring themselves non-Muslims or rejecting key tenets of Islam (prayer, the prophethood of Mohammed, monotheism, etc.), jihadis claim that any leader who does not implement and follow Islamic law (as they understand it) is an apostate. Whereas most scholars reject violent uprisings to remove rulers so long as they allow the prayer and have "a mustard seed of faith," jihadis believe it is a divine duty to wage jihad against rulers who refuse to implement the radicals' interpretation of Islamic law. Whereas there is a general acceptance throughout Islamic history that civilians should not be targeted in war, Al Qaeda has defined the term "civilian" in such a way as to make everyone living in a Western democracy subject to attack (reinforced by a doctrine of proportional response that requires Muslims to kill millions of Americans). And although there is broad support for the use of suicide bombings, Al Qaeda has expanded its use to encompass attacks on ordinary civilians in Western countries rather than just military or political targets.

This trajectory indicates that the jihadis will attack increasingly wider categories of people. This is already being witnessed with regard to the Shi'ite community in Pakistan and Saudi Arabia (and to some extent Iraq because of Zarqawi's intention to seed discord between Sunnis and Shi'ites). A number of radicals declared their intention to kill Shi'ites in the early 1990s, and this has become an increasingly common position.[75] More attacks might also be expected against others in the Sunni community, in addition to state officials and government personnel.

However it plays out, the historical development of jihadi thought has been one of increasingly expansive violence, not one of limitations. In the end, this may erode popular support for Al Qaeda, as increased violence did to the GIA in Algeria, but in the meantime more groups of people will likely find themselves on the jihadi list of legitimate targets. Given the jihadi argument about proportional response and intentions to acquire weapons of mass destruction, attacks may become increasingly deadly as well.

Notes

1. Those typically called "Wahhabis" reject the term because it suggests that they follow Ibn Wahhab, a person, rather than God. This, for conservative Muslims, would be tantamount to apostasy. They instead use the term "Salafi." For more on Salafis, see Quintan Wiktorowicz, *The Management of Islamic Activism: Salafis, the Muslim Brotherhood, and State Power in Jordan* (Albany: State University of New York Press, 2001), chapter four; Marc Sageman, *Understanding Terror Networks* (Philadelphia: University of Pennsylvania Press, 2004).
2. See Quintan Wiktorowicz, "The New Global Threat: Transnational Salafis and Jihad," *Middle East Policy* 8(4) (December 2001), pp. 18-38; Michael Doran, "Somebody Else's Civil War," *Foreign Affairs* 81(1) (January/February 2002), pp. 22-42.
3. For the first fatwa on weapons of mass destruction, see the analysis of Sheikh Naser bin Hamad al-Fahd's fatwa, issued on 21 May 2003, by Reuven Paz, "YES to WMD: The First Islamist Fatwah on the Use of Weapons of Mass Destruction," *Prism Special Dispatches* 1(1) (May 2003), available at (http://www.e-prism.org/images/PRISM%20Special%20dispatch%20no%201.doc).
4. *Al-Musawwar,* 21 June 2002, pp. 4-22, in FBIS-NES-2002-0625.
5. Ibid.
6. From quotes provided at (http://tariq.bitshop.com/misconceptions/fatwas/prohibition.htm). These are the standard kinds of evidence used by nonviolent Salafis.
7. *Sahih Bukhari* 8, p. 73; 8, p. 126.
8. For the mainstream Salafi perspective on these issues and others (translated into English), see various publications at (www.salafipublications.com). The website is well known among Salafis as supporting the Saudi religious establishment, which is tied to the Saudi regime.
9. Email from Juan Cole, 25 March 2003.
10. Ibid.
11. For Mawdudi's perspective, see Charles J. Adams, "Mawdudi and the Islamic State," in *Voices of Resurgent Islam,* edited by John L. Esposito (Oxford: Oxford University Press, 1983), pp. 99-133; and Seyyed Vali Reza Nasr, *Mawdudi & the Making of Islamic Revivalism* (Oxford: Oxford University Press, 1995). Mawdudi's most important works are readily available online. For example, see (http://www.masmn.org/Books/).
12. For more on the Jamaat-i-Islami, see Seyyed Vali Nasr, *The Vanguard of the Islamic Revolution: The Jama'at-I Islami of Pakistan* (Berkeley: University of California Press, 1994).
13. For Sayyid Qutb's ideology, see Yvonne Y. Haddad, "Sayyid Qutb: Ideologue of Islamic Revival," in *Voices of Resurgent Islam,* edited by John L. Esposito (Oxford: Oxford University

Press, 1983), pp. 67-98; Ahmad S. Moussalli, *Radical Islamic Fundamentalism: The Ideological and Political Discourse of Sayyid Qutb* (Syracuse: Syracuse University Press, 1994); Ibrahim M. Abu-Rabi, *Intellectual Origins of Islamic Resurgence in the Modern Arab World* (Albany: State University Of New York Press, 1995); and William E. Shepard, *Sayyid Qutb and Islamic Activism: A Translation and Critical Analysis of Social Justice in Islam* (London: Brill, 1996). For his influence on radical jihadis in particular, see Emmanuel Sivan, *Radical Islam: Medieval Theology and Modern Politics* (New Haven: Yale University Press, 1985), Gilles Kepel, *Muslim Extremism in Egypt: The Prophet and Pharaoh*, trans. Jon Rothschild (Berkeley: University of California Press, 1993); Sageman, *Understanding Terror Networks,* chapter one.

14. Sivan, *Radical Islam,* p. 28.
15. As quoted in Sivan, *Radical Islam,* pp. 23-24.
16. Faraj's tract is translated in Johannes J.G. Jansen, *The Neglected Duty: The Creed of Sadat's Assassins and Islamic Resurgence in the Middle East* (New York: MacMillian Publishing Company, 1986). Also, see Kepel, *Muslim Extremism,* chapter seven.
17. Jansen, *The Neglected Duty,* p. 6.
18. Ibid., p. 97.
19. As quoted in Malika Zeghal, "Religion and Politics in Egypt: The Ulema of al-Azhar, Radical Islam, and the State (1952-1994)," *International Journal of Middle East Studies* 31(3) (August 1999), p. 395.
20. From *al-Sharq al-Awsat* published extracts of Ayman Zawahiri's *Knights under the Prophet's Banner,* FBIS-NES-2002-108, available at (www.fas.org/irp/world/para/ayman_bk.html). Qutb's influence on Zawahiri is corroborated in Montasser al-Zayyat, *The Road to Al Qaeda: The Story of Bin Laden's Right-Hand Man,* trans. Ahmed Fekry, edited by Sara Nimis (London: Pluto Press, 2004). Al-Zayyat has acted as the lawyer for a number of radical jihadis in Egypt and is well placed in the jihadi community, although many now view him as a security agent because of his central role in developing a nonviolent ideology among jihadis.
21. From *al-Sharq al-Awsat* published extracts of Ayman Zawahiri's *Knights under the Prophet's Banner,* FBIS-NES-2002-108, available at (www.fas.org/irp/world/para/ayman_bk.html).
22. *Islam: The Misunderstood Religion* is published by New Era publications and is available at (www.barnesandnoble.com).
23. Michael Doran made this observation in an e-mail. For more on Ibn Wahhab's ideology and influence, see Natana J. DeLong-Bas, *Wahhabi Islam: From Revival and Reform to Global Jihad* (Oxford: Oxford University Press, 2004).
24. DeLong-Bas, *Wahhabi Islam.*
25. See (http://www.islambasics.com/view.php?bkID=64).
26. See various publications on the topic at www.salafipublications.com
27. E-mail from Juan Cole, 12 February 2003.
28. The "Declaration" is available at (http://www.pbs.org/newshour/terrorism/international/fatwa_1996.html).
29. Originally played on *al-Jazeera.* Translated transcript available at (http://news.bbc.co.uk/2/hi/middle_east/2751019.stm).
30. E-mail from Guido Steinberg, 25 March 2003. Also, for those who read German, see Guido Steinberg, *Religion und Staat in Saudi-Arabien. Die Wahhabitischen Gelehrten 1902-1953* (Würzburg: Ergon, 2002).
31. See, for example, John Kelsay and James Turner Johnson, eds., *Just War and Jihad: Historical and Theoretical Perspectives on War and Peace in Western and Islamic Traditions* (New York: Greenwood Press, 1991); and James Turner Johnson, *The Holy War Idea in Western and Islamic Traditions* (University Park, PA: The Pennsylvania State University Press, 1997).
32. Jihadis believe that the story about the Prophet's reference to the "greater jihad" was fabricated.
33. Rudolph Peters, *Jihad in Classical and Modern Islam* (Princeton: Markus Wiener Publishers, 1996), chapter five.
34. Peters, *Jihad,* p. 47.
35. Available at (http://www.islamworld.net/advice_jihad.html).

36. Online version available at (http://www.religioscope.com/info/doc/jihad/azzam_caravan_1_foreword.htm).
37. Peters, *Jihad,* pp. 52-53.
38. Online version available at (http://www.religioscope.com/info/doc/jihad/azzam_caravan_4_part2.htm).
39. Online version available at (http://www.religioscope.com/info/doc/jihad/azzam_caravan_5_part3.htm).
40. Online version available at (http://www.religioscope.com/info/doc/jihad/azzam_caravan_3_part1.htm).
41. Ibid.
42. Olivier Roy, "The Radicalization of Sunni Conservative Fundamentalism," *ISIM Newsletter* No. 2, March 1999. Available online at (http://www.isim.nl/files/newsl_2.pdf).
43. The fatwa is available at (http://www.fas.org/irp/world/para/docs/980223-fatwa.htm).
44. Online version at (http://www.pbs.org/newshour/terrorism/international/fatwa_1996.html).
45. See Mamoun Fandy, *Saudi Arabia and the Politics of Dissent* (New York: Palgrave, 1999); and Gwenn Okruhlik, "Making Conversation Permissible: Islamism and Reform in Saudi Arabia," in *Islamic Activism: A Social Movement Theory Approach,* edited by Quintan Wiktorowicz (Bloomington: Indiana University Press, 2004).
46. As quoted in John Esposito, *Unholy War: Terror in the Name of Islam* (Oxford: Oxford University Press, 2002), p. 24.
47. *London Press Association,* 14 September 2001, FBIS-WEU_2001-0914.
48. For a more elaborate discussion of this, see Quintan Wiktorowicz and John Kaltner, "Killing in the Name of Islam: Al Qaeda's Justification for September 11," *Middle East Policy* 10(2) (Summer 2003), pp. 76-92. The article is available at (http://www.mepc.org/public_asp/journal_vol10/0306_wiktorowiczkaltner.asp).
49. For the ideological struggle in the conflict, see Mohammed Hafez, "Armed Islamist Movements and Political Violence in Algeria," *Middle East Journal* 54(4) (Autumn 2000), pp. 572-592; idem., *Why Muslims Rebel: Repression and Resistance in the Islamic World* (Boulder: Lynne Rienner, 2003), chapter five.
50. Quintan Wiktorowicz, "The GIA and GSPC in Algeria," In *In the Service of Al Qaeda: Radical Islamic Movements*, edited by Magnus Ranstorp (New York: Hurst Publishers and New York University Press, forthcoming).
51. AFP, 21 January 1997, in FBIS-NES-97-013.
52. Calculated by the author using the *Middle East Journal* "Chronology of Events."
53. AFP, 7 August 1997.
54. Armed Islamic Group communiqué issued 16 January 1995.
55. AFP, 6 August 1994, in *Joint Publications Research Service*-TOT-94-034-L.
56. Interview by author with one of Abu Qatada's associates in Jordan, 1997.
57. Wiktorowicz, "The GIA and GSPC."
58. This strategy was discussed by Zawahiri in *Knights under the Prophet's Banner,* FBISNES-2002-108, available at www.fas.org/irp/world/para/ayman_bk.html).
59. Ibid.
60. Translation and original Arabic available at (http://www.mepc.org/public_asp/journal_vol10/0306_wiktorowiczkaltner.asp).
61. MEMRI, "'Why We Fight America': Al-Qa'ida Spokesman Explains September 11 and Declares Intentions to Kill 4 Million Americans with Weapons of Mass Destruction," *Special Dispatch Series—No. 388*, 12 June 2002. Available at (http://www.memri.org/bin/articles.cgi?Page=subjects&Area=jihad&ID=SP38802).
62. Available at (http://www.mepc.org/public_asp/journal_vol10/0306_wiktorowiczkaltner.asp).
63. Available at (http://www.mepc.org/public_asp/journal_vol10/0306_wiktorowiczkaltner.asp).
64. MEMRI, "Why We Fight America."
65. Peters, *Jihad,* p. 49.
66. Wiktorowicz and Kaltner, "Killing in the Name of Islam," p. 88.
67. An English translation of the fatwa was posted at (www.azzam.com) after 11 September. The fatwa was dismissed by reformist Salafis in Saudi Arabia. The Council of Ulema argued that

the statement was "not worth adhering to." The council also contested al-Uqla's authority to issue fatwas. See (www.fatwa-online.com/news/0011017_1.htm).

68. Translation and original Arabic available at (http://www.mepc.org/public_asp/journal_vol10/0306_wiktorowiczkaltner.asp).
69. Yigal Carmon, "Contemporary Islamist Ideology Permitting Genocidal Murder," paper presented at the Stockholm International Forum on Preventing Genocide," MEMRI *Special Report*—No. 25, 27 January 2004, available at (http://www.memri.org/bin/articles.cgi?Page=subjects&Area=jihad&ID=SR2501).
70. Available at (http://www.islamicawakening.org/viewarticle.php?articleID=1012&).
71. Available at (www.fatwa-online.com/fataawa/worship/jihaad/jih004/0010915_1.htm). See (www.fatwa-online.com) for additional fatwas along these lines.
72. As quoted in MEMRI, "Debating the Religious, Political and Moral Legitimacy of Suicide Bombings Part 1: The Debate over Religious Legitimacy," *Inquiry and Analysis Series—No. 53,* 2 May 2001. Available at (http://www.memri.org/bin/articles.cgi?Page=subjects&Area=jihad&ID=IA5301).
73. Ibid.
74. Interview with Nida'ul Islam magazine, issue 22, February–March 1998, available at (http://www.islam.org.au/articles/22/maqdisy.htm).
75. See Michael Doran, "The Saudi Paradox," *Foreign Affairs* 83(1) (January/February 2004). Available online at (http://www.foreignaffairs.org/20040101faessay83105/michael-scott-doran/thesaudi-paradox.html).

Chapter 5

Weapons of Mass Destruction

The threat of weapons of mass destruction (WMDs) is a complex issue—not just in the discussion of how to detect, deter, and defend against their use, but also in the complicated difference between the devices, technology, and processes needed to obtain and use these weapons. The authors in this chapter look at the likelihood of terrorists to make use of these weapons and the issues surrounding the policy option of securing the weapons.

Richard K. Betts article, "The New Threat of Mass Destruction," discusses three critical points in this seminal article. First, he says that "[weapons of mass destruction] no longer represent the technological frontier of warfare. Increasingly, they will be weapons of the weak-states or groups that militarily are at best second-class." He goes on to say that biological weapons are now the largest concern followed by nuclear weapons and then chemical weapons. Second, security principles developed during the Cold War such as deterrence are not the "mainstays" they once were. Third, new responses must be developed to deal with the threat. Finally, he argues convincingly that the security interests of protecting America will likely come into conflict with other security interests such as promotion of democracy abroad. He writes, "American activism to guarantee international stability is, paradoxically, the prime source of American vulnerability."

Adam Dolnik challenges the often-cited assertion that religious terrorist groups are more likely to use chemical, biological, radiological, or nuclear weapons than secular terrorists. His work re-evaluates this assertion by looking at an alternative interpretation of the trends in terrorism, one that does not distinguish secular from religious terrorists. Equally important, Dolnik outlines an alternative approach to threat assessment by "defining specific motivational, behavioral and organizational characteristics that a terrorist group will need to satisfy" to conduct a mass-fatality attack using WMDs. The identification of likely attributes of the "superterrorists" with regard to ideological, organizational, and behavioral traits is an important addition to the study of terrorism.

According to Richard Pilch, most analysis of the bioterrorist threat predates September 11, 2001 and does not offer a comprehensive analysis of the current threat in the United States. Pilch updates the threat analysis through an uncomplicated model that offers the possibility for a very nuanced analysis of the threat. He gives special consideration to the capabilities of groups, often the most exaggerated element in threat analysis, and reviews the major technical hurdles involved in the acquisition, production, and dissemination of a biological agent. Pilch presents the reader with an oft-discussed scenario involving the aerial dissemination of anthrax using a crop duster as an example. His conclusion is that while the threat for any given individual is small, the government must consider the worst-case scenario.

"Security Strategy in the Gray Zone" by Michael Eastman and Robert Brown assess three potential strategies for keeping WMDs out of terrorists' hands: deterrence, prevention, and preemption. After analyzing the strengths and weaknesses of each, the authors conclude that "preventing" hostile states from acquiring WMDs in the first place is the "best of three bad options" for safeguarding the nation against WMD terrorist attacks.

In perhaps the most frightening essay in this volume, John Ellis presents the future of biological warfare—genomic terrorism. Ellis describes genetically altered weapons that are engineered to strike, selectively killing one race and not another. While to many this may sound like science fiction, the future is already upon us. Today, much of the food we eat is genetically modified, and before its demise, the Soviet Union developed a vaccine-resistant form of smallpox. This type of genetic engineering, when combined with the complete sequencing of the human genome, creates a power that, as Ellis terms it, is unprecedented.

Richard K. Betts

The New Threat of Mass Destruction

What if McVeigh had used Anthrax?

During the Cold War, weapons of mass destruction were the centerpiece of foreign policy. Nuclear arms hovered in the background of every major issue in East-West competition and alliance relations. The highest priorities of U.S. policy could almost all be linked in some way to the danger of World War III and the fear of millions of casualties in the American homeland.

Since the Cold War, other matters have displaced strategic concerns on the foreign policy agenda, and that agenda itself is now barely on the public's radar screen. Apart from defense policy professionals, few Americans still lose sleep over weapons of mass destruction (WMD). After all, what do normal people feel is the main relief provided by the end of the Cold War? It is that the danger of nuclear war is off their backs.

Yet today, WMD present more and different things to worry about than during the Cold War. For one, nuclear arms are no longer the only concern, as chemical and biological weapons have come to the fore. For another, there is less danger of complete annihilation, but more danger of mass destruction. Since the Cold War is over and American and Russian nuclear inventories are much smaller, there is less chance of an apocalyptic exchange of many thousands of weapons. But the probability that some smaller number of WMD will be used is growing. Many of the standard strategies and ideas for coping with WMD threats are no longer as relevant as they were when Moscow was the main adversary. But new thinking has not yet congealed in as clear a form as the Cold War concepts of nuclear deterrence theory.

The new dangers have not been ignored inside the Beltway. "Counterproliferation" has become a cottage industry in the Pentagon and the intelligence community, and many worthwhile initiatives to cope with threats are under way. Some of the most important implications of the new era, however, have not yet registered on the public agenda. This in turn limits the inclination of politicians to push some appropriate programs. Even the defense establishment has directed its attention mainly toward countering threats WMD pose to U.S. military forces operating abroad rather than to the more worrisome danger that mass destruction will occur in the United States, killing large numbers of civilians.

The points to keep in mind about the new world of mass destruction are the following. First, the roles such weapons play in international conflict are changing. They no longer represent the technological frontier of warfare. Increasingly, they will be weapons of the weak-states or groups that militarily are at best second-class. The importance of the different types among them has also shifted. Biological weapons should now be the most serious concern, with nuclear weapons second and chemicals a distant third.

Second, the mainstays of Cold War security policy—deterrence and arms control—are not what they used to be. Some new threats may not be deterrable, and the role of arms control in dealing with WMD has been marginalized. In a few instances, continuing devotion to deterrence and arms control may have side effects that offset the benefits.

Third, some of the responses most likely to cope with the threats in novel ways will not find a warm welcome. The response that should now be the highest priority is one long ignored, opposed, or ridiculed: a serious civil defense program to blunt the effects of WMD if they are unleashed within the United States. Some of the most effective measures to prevent attacks within the United States may also challenge traditional civil liberties if pursued to the maximum. And the most troubling conclusion for foreign policy as a whole is that reducing the odds of attacks in the United States might require pulling back from involvement in some foreign conflicts. American activism to guarantee international stability is, paradoxically, the prime source of American vulnerability.

This was partly true in the Cold War, when the main danger that nuclear weapons might detonate on U.S. soil sprang from strategic engagement in Europe, Asia, and the Middle East to deter attacks on U.S. allies. But engagement then assumed a direct link between regional stability and U.S. survival. The connection is less evident today, when there is no globally threatening superpower or transnational ideology to be contained—only an array of serious but entirely local disruptions. Today, as the only nation acting to police areas outside its own region, the United States makes itself a target for states or groups whose aspirations are frustrated by U.S. power.

From Modern to Primitive

WHEN NUCLEAR weapons were born, they represented the most advanced military applications of science, technology, and engineering. None but the great powers could hope to obtain them. By now, however, nuclear arms have been around for more than half a century, and chemical and biological weapons even longer. They are not just getting old. In the strategic terms most relevant to American security, they have become primitive. Once the military cutting edge of the strong, they have become the only hope for so-called rogue states or terrorists who want to contest American power. Why? Because the United States has developed overwhelming superiority in conventional military force—something it never thought it had against the Soviet Union.

The Persian Gulf War of 1991 demonstrated the American advantage in a manner that stunned many abroad. Although the U.S. defense budget has plunged, other countries are not closing the gap. U.S. military spending remains more than triple that of any potentially hostile power and higher than the combined defense budgets of Russia, China, Iran, Iraq, North Korea, and Cuba.

More to the point, there is no evidence that those countries' level of military professionalism is rising at a rate that would make them competitive even if they were to spend far more on their forces. Rolling along in what some see as a revolution in military affairs, American forces continue to make unmatched use of state-of-the-art weapons, surveillance and information systems, and the organizational and doctrinal flexibility for managing the integration of these complex innovations into "systems of systems" that is the key to modern military effectiveness. More than ever in military history, brains are brawn. Even if hostile countries somehow catch up in an arms race, their military organizations and cultures are unlikely to catch up in the competence race for management, technology assimilation, and combat command skills.

If it is infeasible for hostile states to counter the United States in conventional combat, it is even more daunting for smaller groups such as terrorists. If the United States is lucky, the various violent groups with grievances against the American government and society will continue to think up schemes using conventional explosives. Few terrorist groups have shown an interest in inflicting true mass destruction. Bombings or hostage seizures have generally threatened no more than a few hundred lives. Let us hope that this limitation has been due to a powerful underlying reason, rather than a simple lack of capability, and that the few exceptions do not become more typical.

There is no sure reason to bet on such restraint. Indeed, some have tried to use WMD, only to see them fizzle. The Japanese Aum Shinrikyo cult released sarin nerve gas in Tokyo in 1995 but killed only a few people, and some analysts believe that those who attacked the World Trade Center in 1993 laced their bomb with cyanide, which burned up in the explosion (this was not confirmed, but a large amount of cyanide was found in the perpetrators' possession). Eventually such a group will prove less incompetent. If terrorists decide that they want to stun American policymakers by inflicting enormous damage, WMD become more attractive at the same time that they are becoming more accessible.

Finally, unchallenged military superiority has shifted the attention of the U.S. military establishment away from WMD. During the Cold War, nuclear weapons were the bedrock of American war capabilities. They were the linchpin of defense debate, procurement programs, and arms control because the United States faced another superpower—one that conventional wisdom feared could best it in conventional warfare. Today, no one cares about the MX missile or B-1 bomber, and hardly anyone really cares about the Strategic Arms Reduction Treaty. In a manner that could only have seemed ludicrous during the Cold War, proponents now rationalize the $2 billion B-2 as a weapon for conventional war. Hardly anyone in the Pentagon is still interested in how the United States could use WMD for its own strategic purposes.

What military planners are interested in is how to keep adversaries from using WMD as an "asymmetric" means to counter U.S. conventional power, and how to protect U.S. ground and naval forces abroad from WMD attacks. This concern is all well and good, but it abets a drift of attention away from the main danger. The primary risk is not that enemies might lob some nuclear or chemical weapons at U.S. armored battalions or ships, awful as that would be. Rather, it is that they might attempt to punish the United States by triggering catastrophes in American cities.

Choose your weapons well

UNTIL THE past decade, the issue was nuclear arms, period. Chemical weapons received some attention from specialists, but never made the priority list of presidents and cabinets. Biological weapons were almost forgotten after they were banned by the 1972 Biological Weapons Convention. Chemical and biological arms have received more attention in the 1990s. The issues posed by the trio lumped under the umbrella of mass destruction differ, however. Most significantly, biological weapons have received less attention than the others but probably represent the greatest danger.

Chemical weapons have been noticed more in the past decade, especially since they were used by Iraq against Iranian troops in the 1980-88 Iran-Iraq War and against Kurdish civilians in 1988. Chemicals are far more widely available than nuclear weapons because the technology required to produce them is far simpler, and large numbers of countries have undertaken chemical weapons programs. But chemical weapons are not really in the same class as other weapons of mass destruction, in the sense of ability to inflict a huge number of single strike. For the tens of thousands of biggest strategic bombing raids of World War II, it would be difficult logistically and operationally to deliver chemical weapons in necessary quantities over wide areas.

Nevertheless, much attention and effort have been lavished on a campaign to eradicate chemical weapons. This may be a good thing, but the side effects are not entirely benign. For one, banning chemicals means that for deterrence, nuclear weapons become even more important than they used to be. That is because a treaty cannot assuredly prevent hostile nations from deploying chemical weapons, while the United States has forsworn the option to retaliate in kind.

In the past, the United States had a no-first-use policy for chemical weapons but reserved the right to strike back with them if an enemy used them first. The 1993 Chemical Weapons Convention (CWC), which entered into force last April, requires the United States to destroy its stockpile, thus ending this option. The United States did the same with biological arms long ago, during the Nixon administration. Eliminating its own chemical and biological weapons practically precludes a no-first-use policy for nuclear weapons, since they become the only WMD available for retaliation.

Would the United States follow through and use nuclear weapons against a country or group that had killed several thousand Americans with deadly chemicals? It is hard to imagine breaking the post-Nagasaki taboo in that situation. But schemes for conventional military retaliation would not suffice without detracting from the force of American deterrent threats. There would be a risk for the United States in setting a precedent that someone could use WMD against Americans without suffering similar destruction in return. Limiting the range of deterrent alternatives available to U.S. strategy will not necessarily cause deterrence to fail, but it will certainly not strengthen it.

The ostensible benefit of the CWC is that it will make chemical arms harder to acquire and every bit as illegal and stigmatized as biological weapons have been for a quarter-century. If it has that benefit, what effect will the ban have on the choices of countries or groups who want some kind of WMD in any case, whether for purposes of deterrence, aggression, or revenge? At the margin, the ban will reduce the disincentives to acquiring biological weapons, since they will be no less illegal, no harder to obtain or conceal, and far more damaging than chemical weapons. If major reductions in the chemical threat produce even minor increases in the biological threat, it will be a bad trade.

One simple fact should worry Americans more about biological than about nuclear or chemical arms: unlike either of the other two, biological weapons combine maximum destructiveness and easy availability. Nuclear arms have great killing capacity but are hard to get; chemical weapons are easy to get but lack such killing capacity; biological agents have both qualities. A 1993 study by the Office of Technology Assessment concluded that a single airplane delivering 100 kilograms of anthrax spores—a dormant phase of a bacillus that multiplies rapidly in the body, producing toxins and rapid hemorrhaging by aerosol on a clear, calm night over the Washington, D.C., area could kill between one million and three million people, 300 times as many fatalities as if the plane had delivered sarin gas in amounts ten times larger.[1]

Like chemical weapons but unlike nuclear weapons, biologicals are relatively easy to make. Innovations in biotechnology have obviated many of the old problems in handling and preserving biological agents, and many have been freely available for scientific research. Nuclear weapons are not likely to be the WMD of choice for non-state terrorist groups. They require huge investments and targetable infrastructure, and are subject to credible threats by the United States. An aggrieved group that decides it wants to kill huge numbers of Americans will find the mission easier to accomplish with anthrax than with a nuclear explosion.

Inside the Pentagon, concern about biological weapons has picked up tremendously in the past couple of years, but there is little serious attention to the problem elsewhere. This could be a good thing if nothing much can be done, since publicity might only give enemies ideas. But it is a bad thing if it impedes efforts to take steps—such as civil defense—that could blunt nuclear, chemical, or biological attacks.

Deterrence and arms control in decline

AN OLD vocabulary still dominates policy discussion of WMD. Rhetoric in the defense establishment falls back on the all-purpose strategic buzzword of the Cold War: deterrence. But deterrence now covers fewer of the threats the United States faces than it did during the Cold War.

The logic of deterrence is clearest when the issue is preventing unprovoked and unambiguous aggression, when the aggressor recognizes that it is the aggressor rather than the defender. Deterrence is less reliable when both sides in a conflict see each other as the aggressor. When the United States intervenes in messy Third World conflicts, the latter is often true. In such cases, the side that the United States wants to deter may see itself as trying to deter the United States. Such situations are ripe for miscalculation.

For the country that used to be the object of U.S. deterrence—Russia—the strategic burden has been reversed. Based on assumptions of Soviet conventional military superiority, U.S. strategy used to rely on the threat to escalate—to be the first to use nuclear weapons during a war—to deter attack by Soviet armored divisions. Today the tables have turned. There is no Warsaw Pact, Russia has half or less of the military potential of the Soviet Union, and its current conventional forces are in disarray, while NATO is expanding eastward. It is now Moscow that has the incentive to compensate for conventional weakness by placing heavier reliance on nuclear capabilities. The Russians adopted a nuclear no-first-use policy in the early 1980s, but renounced it after their precipitous post-Cold War decline.

Today Russia needs to be reassured, not deterred. The main danger from Russian WMD is leakage from vast stockpiles to anti-American groups elsewhere—the "loose nukes" problem. So long as the United States has no intention of attacking the Russians, their greater reliance on nuclear forces is not a problem. If the United States has an interest in reducing nuclear stockpiles, however, it is. The traditional American approach—thinking in terms of its own deterrence strategies—provides no guidance. Indeed, noises some Americans still make about deterring the Russians compound the problem by reinforcing Moscow's alarm.

Similarly, U.S. conventional military superiority gives China an incentive to consider more reliance on an escalation strategy. The Chinese have a long-standing no-first-use policy but adopted it when their strategic doctrine was that of "people's war," which relied on mass mobilization and low-tech weaponry. Faith in that doctrine was severely shaken by the American performance in the Persian Gulf War. Again, the United States might assume that there is no problem as long as Beijing only wants to deter and the United States does not want to attack. But how do these assumptions relate to the prospect of a war over Taiwan? That is a conflict that no one wants but that can hardly be ruled out in light of evolving tensions. If the United States decides openly to deter Beijing from attacking Taiwan, the old lore from the Cold War may be relevant. But if Washington continues to leave policy ambiguous, who will know who is deterring whom? Ambiguity is a recipe for confusion and miscalculation in a time of crisis. For all the upsurge of attention in the national security establishment to the prospect of conflict with China, there has been remarkably little discussion of the role of nuclear weapons in a Sino-American collision.

The main problem for deterrence, however, is that it still relies on the corpus of theory that undergirded Cold War policy, dominated by reliance on the threat of second-strike retaliation. But retaliation requires knowledge of who has launched an attack and the address at which they reside. These requirements are not a problem when the threat comes from a government, but they are if the enemy is anonymous. Today some groups may wish to punish the United States without taking credit for the action—a mass killing equivalent to the 1988 bombing of Pan Am Flight 103 over Lockerbie, Scotland. Moreover, the options the defense establishment favors have shifted over entirely from deterrence to preemption. The majority of those who dealt with nuclear weapons policy during the Cold War adamantly opposed developing first-strike options. Today, scarcely anyone looks to that old logic when thinking about rogues or terrorists, and most hope to be able to mount a disarming action against any group with WMD.

Finally, eliminating chemical weapons trims some options for deterrence. Arms control restrictions on the instruments that can be used for deterrent threats are not necessarily the wrong policy, but they do work against maximizing deterrence. Overall, however, the problem with arms control is not that it does too much but that it now does relatively little.

From the Limited Test Ban negotiations in the 1960s through the Strategic Arms Limitation Talks, Strategic Arms Reduction Talks, and Intermediate-range Nuclear Forces negotiations in the 1970s and 1980s, arms control treaties were central to managing WMD threats. Debates about whether particular agreements with Moscow were in the United States' interest were bitter because everyone believed that the results mattered. Today there is no consensus that treaties regulating armaments matter much. Among national security experts, the corps that pays close attention to START and Conventional Forces in Europe negotiations has shrunk. With the exception of the Chemical Weapons Convention, efforts to control WMD by treaty have become small potatoes. The biggest recent news in arms control has not been any negotiation to regulate WMD, but a campaign to ban land mines.

The United States' Cold War partner in arms control, Russia, has disarmed a great deal voluntarily. But despite standard rhetoric, the United States has not placed a high priority on convincing Moscow to divest itself of more of its nuclear weapons; the Clinton administration has chosen to promote NATO expansion, which pushes the Russians in the opposite direction.

The 1968 Nuclear Nonproliferation Treaty remains a hallowed institution, but it has nowhere new to go. It will not convert the problem countries that want to obtain WMD—unless, like Iraq and North Korea in the 1980s, they sign and accept the legal obligation and then simply cheat. The NPT regime will continue to impede access to fissile materials on the open market, but it will not do so in novel or more effective ways. And it does not address the problem of Russian "loose nukes" any better than the Russian and American governments do on their own.

Civil Defense

DESPITE ALL the new limitations, deterrence remains an important aspect of strategy. There is not much the United States needs to do to keep up its deterrence capability, however, given the thousands of nuclear weapons and the conventional military superiority it has. Where capabilities are grossly underdeveloped, however, is the area of responses for coping should deterrence fail.

Enthusiasts for defensive capability, mostly proponents of the Strategic Defense Initiative from the Reagan years, remain fixated on the least relevant form of it: high-tech active defenses to intercept ballistic missiles. There is still scant interest in what should now be the first priority: civil defense preparations to cope with uses of WMD within the United States. Active defenses against missiles would be expensive investments that might or might not work against a threat the United States probably will not face for years, but would do nothing against the threat it already faces. Civil defense measures are extremely cheap and could prove far more effective than they would have against a large-scale Soviet attack.

During the Cold War, debate about antimissile defense concerned whether it was technologically feasible or cost-effective and whether it would threaten the Soviets and ignite a spiraling arms race between offensive and defensive weapons. One need not refight the battles over SDI to see that the relevance to current WMD threats is tenuous. Iraq, Iran, or North Korea will not be able to deploy intercontinental missiles for years. Nor, if they are strategically cunning, should they want to. For the limited number of nuclear warheads these countries are likely to have, and especially for biological weapons, other means of delivery are more easily available. Alternatives to ballistic missiles include aircraft, ship-launched cruise missiles, and unconventional means, such as smuggling, at which the intelligence agencies of these countries have excelled. Non-state perpetrators like those who bombed the World Trade Center will choose clandestine means of necessity.

A ballistic missile defense system, whether it costs more or less than the $60 billion the Congressional Budget Office recently estimated would be required for one limited option, will not counter these modes of attack. Indeed, if a larger part of the worry about WMD these days is about their use by terrorist states or groups, the odds are higher that sometime, somewhere in the country, some of these weapons will go off, despite the best efforts to stop them. If that happens, the United States should have in place whatever measures can mitigate the consequences.

By the later phases of the Cold War it was hard to get people interested in civil defense against an all-out Soviet attack that could detonate thousands of high-yield nuclear weapons in U.S. population centers. To many, the lives that would have been saved seemed less salient than the many millions that would still have been lost. It should be easier to see the value of civil defense, however, in the context of more limited attacks, perhaps with only a few low-yield weapons. A host of minor measures can increase protection or recovery from biological, nuclear, or chemical effects. Examples are stockpiling or distribution of protective masks; equipment and training for decontamination; standby programs for mass vaccinations and emergency treatment with antibiotics; wider and deeper planning of emergency response procedures; and public education about hasty sheltering and emergency actions to reduce individual vulnerability.

Such programs would not make absorbing a WMD attack tolerable. But inadequacy is no excuse for neglecting actions that could reduce death and suffering, even if the difference in casualties is small. Civil defenses are especially worthwhile considering that they are extraordinarily cheap compared with regular military programs or active defense systems. Yet until recently, only half a billion dollars—less than two-tenths of one percent of the defense budget and less than $2 a head for every American—went to chemical and biological defense, while nearly $4 billion was spent annually on ballistic missile defense.[2] Why haven't policymakers attended to first things first—cheap programs that can cushion the effects of a disaster—before undertaking expensive programs that provide no assurance they will be able to prevent it?

One problem is conceptual inertia. The Cold War accustomed strategists to worrying about an enemy with thousands of WMD, rather than foes with a handful. For decades the question of strategic defense was also posed as a debate between those who saw no alternative to relying on deterrence and those who hoped that an astrodome over the United States could replace deterrence with invulnerability. None of these hoary fixations address the most probable WMD threats in the post-Cold War world.

Opposition to Cold War civil defense programs underlies psychological aversion to them now. Opponents used to argue that civil defense was a dangerous illusion because it could do nothing significant to reduce the horror of an attack that would obliterate hundreds of cities, because it would promote a false sense of security, and because it could even be destabilizing and provoke attack in a crisis. Whether or not such arguments were valid then, they are not now. But both then and now, there has been a powerful reason that civil defense efforts have been unpopular: they alarm people. They remind them that their vulnerability to mass destruction is not a bad dream, not something that strategic schemes for deterrence, preemption, or interception are sure to solve.

Civil defense can limit damage but not minimize it. For example, some opponents may be able to develop biological agents that circumvent available vaccines and antibiotics. (Those with marginal technical capabilities, however, might be stopped by blocking the easier options.) Which is worse—the limitations of defenses, or having to answer for failure to try? The moment that WMD are used somewhere in a manner that produces tens of thousands of fatalities, there will be hysterical outbursts of all sorts. One of them will surely be, "Why didn't the government prepare us for this?" It is not in the long-term interest of political leaders to indulge popular aversion. If public resistance under current circumstances prevents widespread distribution, stockpiling, and instruction in the use of defensive equipment or medical services, the least that should be done is to optimize plans and preparations to rapidly implement such activities when the first crisis ignites demand.

As threats of terrorism using WMD are taken more seriously, interest will grow in preemptive defense measures—the most obvious of which is intensified intelligence collection. Where this involves targeting groups within the United States that might seem to be potential breeding grounds for terrorists (for example, supporters of Palestinian militants, home-grown militias or cults, or radicals with ties to Iran, Iraq, or Libya), controversies will arise over constitutional limits on invasion of privacy or search and seizure. So long as the WMD danger remains hypothetical, such controversies will not be easily resolved. They have not come to the fore so far because U.S. law enforcement has been unbelievably lucky in apprehending terrorists. The group arrested in 1993 for planning to bomb the Lincoln Tunnel happened to be infiltrated by an informer, and Timothy McVeigh happened to be picked up in 1995 for driving without a license plate. Those who fear compromising civil liberties with permissive standards for government snooping should consider what is likely to happen once such luck runs out and it proves impossible to identify perpetrators. Suppose a secretive radical Islamic group launches a biological attack, kills 100,000 people, and announces that it will do the same thing again if its terms are not met. (The probability of such a scenario may not be high, but it can no longer be consigned to science fiction.) In that case, it is hardly unthinkable that a panicked legal system would roll over and treat Arab-Americans as it did the Japanese-Americans who were herded into concentration camps after Pearl Harbor. Stretching limits on domestic surveillance to reduce the chances of facing such choices could be the lesser evil.

Is retreat the best defense?

No PROGRAMS aimed at controlling adversaries' capabilities can eliminate the dangers. One risk is that in the more fluid politics of the post-Cold War world, the United States could stumble into an unanticipated crisis with Russia or China. There are no well-established rules of the game to brake a spiraling conflict over the Baltic states or Taiwan, as there were in the superpower competition after the Cuban missile crisis. The second danger is that some angry group that blames the United States for its problems may decide to coerce Americans, or simply exact vengeance, by inflicting devastation on them where they live.

If steps to deal with the problem in terms of capabilities are limited, can anything be done to address intentions—the incentives of any foreign power or group to lash out at the United States? There are few answers to this question that do not compromise the fundamental strategic activism and internationalist thrust of U.S. foreign policy over the past half-century. That is because the best way to keep people from believing that the United States is responsible for their problems is to avoid involvement in their conflicts.

Ever since the Munich agreement and Pearl Harbor, with only a brief interruption during the decade after the Tet offensive, there has been a consensus that if Americans did not draw their defense perimeter far forward and confront foreign troubles in their early stages, those troubles would come to them at home. But because the United States is now the only superpower and weapons of mass destruction have become more accessible, American intervention in troubled areas is not so much a way to fend off such threats as it is what stirs them up.

Will U.S. involvement in unstable situations around the former U.S.S.R. head off conflict with Moscow or generate it? Will making NATO bigger and moving it to Russia's doorstep deter Russian pressure on Ukraine and the Baltics or provoke it? With Russia and China, there is less chance that either will set out to conquer Europe or Asia than that they will try to restore old sovereignties and security zones by reincorporating new states of the former Soviet Union or the province of Taiwan. None of this means that NATO expansion or support for Taiwan's autonomy will cause nuclear war. It does mean that to whatever extent American activism increases those countries' incentives to rely on WMD while intensifying political friction between them and Washington, it is counterproductive.

The other main danger is the ire of smaller states or religious and cultural groups that see the United States as an evil force blocking their legitimate aspirations. It is hardly likely that Middle Eastern radicals would be hatching schemes like the destruction of the World Trade Center if the United States had not been identified for so long as the mainstay of Israel, the shah of Iran, and conservative Arab regimes and the source of a cultural assault on Islam. Cold War triumph magnified the problem. U.S. military and cultural hegemony—the basic threats to radicals seeking to challenge the status quo—are directly linked to the imputation of American responsibility for maintaining world order. Playing Globocop feeds the urge of aggrieved groups to strike back.

Is this a brief for isolationism? No. It is too late to turn off foreign resentments by retreating, even if that were an acceptable course. Alienated groups and governments would not stop blaming Washington for their problems. In addition, there is more to foreign policy than dampening incentives to hurt the United States. It is not automatically sensible to stop pursuing other interests for the sake of uncertain reductions in a threat of uncertain probability. Security is not all of a piece, and survival is only part of security.

But it is no longer prudent to assume that important security interests complement each other as they did during the Cold War. The interest at the very core—protecting the American homeland from attack—may now often be in conflict with security more broadly conceived and with the interests that mandate promoting American political values, economic interdependence, social Westernization, and stability in regions beyond Western Europe and the Americas. The United States should not give up all its broader political interests, but it should tread cautiously in areas—especially the Middle East—where broader interests grate against the core imperative of preventing mass destruction within America's borders.

Richard K. Betts is Director of National Security Studies at the Council on Foreign Relations and Professor of Political Science and Director of the Institute for War and Peace Studies at Columbia University.

Notes

1. U.S. Congress, Office of Technology Assessment, *Proliferation of Weapons of Mass Destruction: Assessing the Risks,* Washington: Government Printing Office, 1993, p. 54.
2. John F. Sopko, "The Changing Proliferation Threat," *Foreign Policy,* Spring 1997, pp. 3-20.

Adam Dolnik, 2003

All God's Poisons: Re-Evaluating the Threat of Religious Terrorism with Respect to Non-Conventional Weapons

Introduction

Over the course of the past several years, the possibility of the use of chemical, biological, radiological, and nuclear (CBRN) weapons by non-state actors has been a topic of extensive academic and public debate. Originally, the discussion concentrated primarily on capabilities, where the ease of acquisition of CBRN materials following the breakup of the Soviet Union, as well as more widespread availability of information needed for the production and weaponization of such agents, were the main sources of concern. More recently, the debate was brought to a more realistic level through the acknowledgment of technical hurdles associated with the successful delivery of CBRN agents, as well as the possible motivational constraints involved in the decision of terrorist groups to use such weapons. Another shift in the debate was represented by the claim that the rise of religious terrorism had eroded these constraints. According to this argument, religious terrorists whose operations have been observed to be responsible for the vast majority of all casualties in terrorist attacks worldwide are believed to be unconstrained by political considerations, as their only constituency is God. Further, the ability of religious terrorists to dehumanize their enemies indiscriminately is allegedly strengthened by the perceived divine sanction of their actions.[1] Based on this logic, the assertion that religious terrorist groups are more likely to use CBRN weapons than their secular counterparts has become one of the few widely accepted paradigms of terrorism studies. Unfortunately, this logical yet somewhat inaccurate conventional wisdom is often applied mechanically, without further inquiry into the nature of the given organization's belief system. As a result, many of today's simplified threat assessments are based solely on the frequency of the use of the word "God" in a given organization's statements, and consequently do not adequately reflect the CBRN threat level posed by the respective group.

This study will re-evaluate the above-stated conventional wisdom by providing alternative interpretation of the trends in terrorism and by putting to test several commonly cited assertions about the characteristics that allegedly set aside religious terrorism from other forms of the phenomenon. In addition this paper will attempt to outline an alternative approach to threat assessment by defining specific motivational, behavioral and organizational characteristics that a terrorist group will need to satisfy in order to perpetrate a successful mass-fatality CBRN attack in the future. Understanding the nature of this threat is critical, as it is impossible to prepare adequately for such an event in isolation from assessing the likely perpetrators of such an event.

The first part of the paper discusses the contemporary debate about the motivational aspects of religious terrorism. In the second part, shortcomings with regards to terrorism statistics are pointed out, and alternative interpretations of commonly cited characteristics of "religious terrorists" are presented as well. The third part then focuses on identifying likely characteristics of potential "superterrorists" with respect to their ideological, organizational, and behavioral traits. This section also incorporates a threat assessment for the future based on patterns in terrorist innovation and compares the advantages and disadvantages of CBRN terrorism in light of conventional terrorist tactics. An overall evaluation of the threat of mass-casualty CBRN terrorism for the future is presented in the conclusion.

Part I

Traditional vs. "New" Terrorism

One of the two critical components of the contemporary debate about the likelihood of mass-casualty CBRN terrorism is the motivation to inflict indiscriminate mass casualties. But despite the fact that terrorism does typically involve killing and destruction, most terrorists practice a level of restraint on their activities. Traditionally, terrorists have not necessarily been interested in killing a lot of people, but rather in spreading fear among the general population by killing only the necessary few. In this respect, perhaps the best definition of terrorism is the ancient Chinese proverb "kill one, frighten ten thousand," or alternatively, renowned terrorism scholar Brian Jenkins' observation that "terrorists want a lot of people watching, not a lot of people dead."[2] Possibly for this particular reason, terrorists have traditionally not been interested in CBRN weapons because such weapons were deemed too large-scale to serve any purpose useful to the terrorists. Massive destruction is likely to be counterproductive for terrorists who typically strive to attract popular support in order to force a political change, such as creation of a homeland or implementation of social justice norms within the targeted state. Mass killing would likely hinder such support, rather than attract it. Moreover, a large-scale attack might also strengthen the affected government's resolve to track down and punish the terrorists, and may thus jeopardize the group's very existence.

While this traditional interpretation of terrorism has been the consensus for decades, many authors have observed that over the past 20 years, the phenomenon has experienced disturbing new trends. These indicate the rise of violent activities motivated by a religious imperative, as opposed to the still lethal but arguably more comprehensible motives of ethnic nationalism and revolutionary ideologies. Some authors have claimed that religious terrorists are not constrained by the traditional political concerns, such as popular image or the reaction of the constituency or the targeted state. Rather, since they base their justifications for using violence on the sanction of a supernatural authority whose will is absolute, the "new" terrorists are less rational, and therefore more prone to indiscriminate mass-casualty violence.[3]

Let us now look at more closely at this conventional argument as it has been developed by some of the most influential terrorism scholars.

The Conventional Argument

The conventional argument, which in many ways was pioneered by Bruce Hoffman, relies in many of its arguments on the trends in international terrorism. Over the last 20 years, the statistical data drawn from the RAND–St Andrews Chronology of International Terrorist Incidents demonstrates an alarming trend: a continual decrease in terrorist incidents, which is however accompanied by a larger number of overall casualties in those fewer incidents. This seems to confirm the hypothesis previously pronounced by various scholars that terrorist attacks are becoming increasingly lethal. Besides this overarching trend based on the average number of deaths per attack, the mode of individual terrorist incidents also seems to confirm this trend: while only 17 percent of terrorist attacks in the 1970s, and just 19 percent of attacks in the 1980s killed anyone, at least one fatality occurred in 29 percent of terrorist incidents in 1995.[4]

Another trend observed by Hoffman is the increasing proliferation of terrorist organizations motivated primarily by religion, which he documents by several striking statistics. For instance, Hoffman claims that "none of the eleven identifiable international terrorist groups in 1968 could be classified as religious: that is, having aims and motivations reflecting a predominant religious character or influence. Not until the 1980s did the first religious terrorist groups begin to emerge.... By 1995, 26 of the 56 active international terrorist organizations were religious in character."[5] The religions that are most commonly associated with the rise of religious terrorism are the Shi'ia branch of Islam in the 80s represented mainly by the Lebanese Amal and Hizballah, followed by the rise of Sunni violence in the 90s signified by the actions of the Palestinian Hamas and Palestinian Islamic Jihad (PIJ), al-Qaida, the Algerian Armed Islamic Group (GIA) and others; Jewish terrorism characterized by the activities of the Gush Emunim, Kach, Kahane Chai; Sikh terrorism most commonly associated with the Dal Khalsa, Babbar Khalsa and the Khalistan Commando Force; Christian terrorism of the various American militia movements, Christian paramilitary groups and anti-abortion activists; and various sects and cults, most notably the Japanese Aum Shinrikyo.[6]

The main contribution of Bruce Hoffman's work has been the linking of these two aforementioned trends into a directional causal relationship: Hoffman identified the rise of religious motivation among terrorist groups as the primary cause of the higher number of casualties per attack in the modern era:

> "Among the various factors that account for terrorism's increasing lethality (including the terrorist's perennial quest for attention; the increased prevalence of state sponsorship and the greater resources accorded by terrorists; developments in terrorist weaponry, which is getting smaller, more easy to conceal and more powerful; and the increasing sophistication of professional terrorism), the most significant is perhaps the dramatic proliferation of terrorist groups motivated by a religious imperative."[7]

Hoffman documents his assertion by statistical data for 1995, claiming that "although religious terrorists committed only 25 per cent of the recorded international terrorist incidents in 1995, they were responsible for 58 percent of the total number of fatalities recorded that year. Looking at the data from another perspective, those attacks that caused the greatest numbers of deaths in 1995 (8 or more fatalities) were all perpetrated by religious terrorists."[8] Hoffman also offers a concrete example in the record of terrorist acts by Shi'ia

Islamic organizations. "Although these groups have committed only eight percent of all terrorist incidents since 1982, they were nonetheless responsible for 30 percent of the total number of persons killed in terrorist acts throughout the world."[9] This statistic according to Hoffman "reinforces the casual link between terrorism by a religious imperative and the higher levels of lethality compared to secular terrorist organizations."[10] Such revelations, of course, trigger the immediate question of why that seems to be the case. Hoffman offers a sound explanation:

> "The fact that for the religious terrorist violence inevitably assumes a transcendent purpose and therefore becomes a sacramental and divine duty arguably results in a significant loosening of the constraints on the commission of mass murder. Religion, moreover, functions as a legitimizing force, sanctioning if not encouraging wide scale violence against an almost open-ended category of opponents. Thus religious terrorist violence becomes almost an end in itself—a morally justified, divinely instigated expedient toward the attainment of the terrorists' ultimate ends. This is a direct reflection of the fact that the terrorists motivated by a religious imperative do not seek to appeal to any constituency but themselves and the changes they seek are not for any utilitarian purpose, but are only to benefit themselves. The religious terrorist, moreover, sees himself as an outsider from the society that he both abhors and rejects and this sense of alienation enables him to contemplate—and undertake—far more destructive and bloodier types of terrorist operations than his secular counterpart."[11]

Consequently, if we should expect a mass casualty CBRN terrorist attack in the future, it is the religious terrorist that is most likely to perpetrate such an act.

As one can see form the previous quote, an integral part of the conventional argument concerns the core characteristics of religious terrorists, which allegedly set them aside from their secular counterparts. Most authors confirm that drawing the line between religious and secular terrorists is challenging, as many secular organizations also have a strong religious component, and many religious terrorists in addition possess goals that are of a political nature. This distinction becomes even more blurred in the case of Islamic fundamentalism, as Islam draws no distinction between religion and politics.[12] Still, some terrorism scholars have attempted to define the core characteristics of religious terrorists, pointing mainly to the radically different value systems of religious terrorists, the different mechanisms of legitimization and justification, concepts of morality, mechanisms of victim dehumanization and an overall world view. According to Hoffman, for instance, the aims of "religious political" terrorists are defined as the attainment of the greatest possible benefits for themselves and for their co-religionists only, as opposed to the indiscriminately utilitarian goals of secular terrorists.[13] This allegedly further widens the gap between ends and means; "where the secular terrorist sees violence primarily as a means to an end, the religious terrorist tends to view violence as an end in itsself."[14] Another implication defined by Hoffman is that religious and secular terrorists also differ significantly in their constituencies:

> "Whereas secular terrorists attempt to appeal to a constituency variously composed of actual and potential sympathizers, members of communities they purport to "defend," of the aggrieved people they claim to speak for; religious terrorists are at once activists and constituents engaged in what they regard as a "total war." They execute their terrorist

> acts for no audience but themselves. Thus, the restraints on violence that are imposed on secular terrorists by the desire to appeal to a tacitly supportive or uncommitted constituency are not relevant to the religious terrorists. Moreover, this absence of a constituency in the secular terrorist sense leads to a sanctioning of almost limitless violence against a virtually open-ended category of targets—that is, anyone who is not a member of the terrorist's religion or religious sect."[15]

Additional characteristics have been identified by Mark Jurgensmeyer, who characterizes religiously motivated struggles primarily as those involving images of divine warfare.[16] Such images represent what Jurgensmeyer calls a "cosmic struggle" which is played out in history as a war between good and evil, order and chaos.[17] Religious terrorists identify with such a struggle and project its images onto the present situation, which they seek to address. Such heavily mythologized conflict between the believers and their enemies then becomes absolute.

According to Jurgensmeyer, another distinct characteristic of religious terrorists is their dominant reliance on the concept of martyrdom. In the context of a cosmic war, he argues, martyrdom is not only regarded as a testimony of one's commitment, it is also a performance of the most fundamental religious act found in virtually every religious tradition in the world: the act of sacrifice.[18] The word has its roots in the Latin verb "*sacrificium*" which translates as "to make holy." The images of sacrifice thus transform destruction performed within the religious context into something positive, making killing not only permissible but even mandatory.[19]

Another interesting characteristic of religious terrorists defined by Jurgensmeyer is the intangibility of their goals. Terrorist acts are often "devices for symbolic empowerment in wars that cannot be won and for goals that cannot be achieved. The very absence of thought about what the activists would do if they were victorious is sufficient indication that they do not expect to be, and perhaps do not want to be."[20] This presumably makes the political calculus in their violent actions much less relevant, resulting in much more irrational acts of violence.

According to Jurgensmeyer, yet another core characteristic of religious terrorism is the absoluteness of the authority that is used to justify the acts of violence. Under normal circumstances, only the state has the recognized right to take life—for purposes either of military defense, police protection or punishment.[21] "Those who desire to attain moral sanction for their violent acts and who do not have the approval of an officially recognized government, find it helpful to have access to a higher source: the meta-morality that religion provides, which serves to break the state's monopoly on morally sanctioned killing."[22]

Part II

Let us now look at some of the difficulties with the conventional interpretation of the trends in terrorism, and the shortcomings in the definition of the characteristics of religious terrorists presented above.

Trends in Terrorism: The Problems of Statistics

The first major difficulty is the limited representativeness of the cited data. Even though various open source databases of terrorist incidents may seem to suggest that the number of overall terrorist attacks seems to be decreasing, one should be careful not to reach the conclusion that terrorist have attacked with a lesser frequency too quickly, as some shortcomings associated with the process of open source data collection are inevitably present. For instance, certain types of spectacular events such as terrorist attacks tend to draw immediate media attention and are thus initially widely reported. Once such events become a common occurrence, however, the media starts paying significantly lesser attention to them. It is therefore not unfeasible, that once *individual* terrorist attacks have become deadlier and more spectacular, the world media gradually abandoned reporting the small scale attacks with explosive or incendiary devices that were so popular in the 60s and 70s. For this reason, it is quite possible that the frequency of such small scale terrorist attacks has not actually diminished but is only ignored by the media and consequently is no longer reflected in open source databases. This can then result in the perception of a decreasing terrorist activity and an increasing casualty-per-attack ratio. On the other hand, it is also possible that terrorists have in fact gradually abandoned small scale attacks due to the media's disinterest in reporting such events, and in that case the original hypothesis would be correct.

Another similar problem of the cited data is represented by the geographically uneven coverage of events by the international media—terrorist activity in countries of a greater international importance is simply reported on a much greater scale and in much greater detail than incidents in the internationally neglected parts of the world. Consider for instance the enormous differences in the media reporting of terrorist violence in Israel and Algeria. While detailed data on every single individual that was killed or injured in an act of terrorism in Israel is easily obtainable due to the heavy presence of news agencies in that country, the only obtainable data about the number of casualties in the Algerian conflict are guesstimates with a confidence interval in the range of tens of thousands. This is caused not only by the general perception of Algeria's international insignificance, but also by the fact that journalists are not welcomed in the country, neither by the terrorists nor by the government. The key implication of such a disproportion in reporting is that since terrorist violence in Algeria is of a much larger scale than it is in Israel, database records in terms of overall numbers of terrorist attacks and fatalities worldwide are very likely to be heavily skewed.

Yet another difficulty of a quantitative interpretation of the statistical data on terrorism is constituted by the practical obstacles in database maintenance faced by individual database managers. If for instance, the intensity of a certain terrorist campaign escalates profoundly at a given moment, it becomes nearly impossible to record every single incident. This is caused not only by the fact that the overall escalation of a given conflict results into a lesser media coverage of individual events, but also by the practical considerations involved in database maintenance, such as the number of resources and staff members available for data collection and entry. For this reason, most databases of terrorist incidents have incorporated all sorts of creative loopholes into their criteria, so that certain incidents can be omitted if the given armed conflict erupts into an uncontrollable and reciprocal clash between the terrorists and the their opponents. So when, for instance, the terrorist campaign of the Maoist rebels in Nepal escalated and turned into a civil war in 2002, most database managers chose to exclude the terrorist incidents perpetrated within this conflict from their collection. Similar examples can be given with regard to many other escalating conflicts, including the wars in Chechnya, Afghanistan, Colombia, etc. Another technique that has been used by some databases of terrorist incidents has been to collapse several attacks into a single database entry, which is a more honest approach, but which inevitably skews the statistics as well. Such, for instance, was the case of the multiple bombing campaigns perpetrated by Corsican separatists in the 1980s, which no existing open source database reported on individual basis, but rather compiled them together into single entries.

Yet another important aspect that one should bear in mind is the fact that the most of the statistics used to support the conventional argument presented above have originated in the RAND–St Andrews Chronology of International Terrorist Incidents, a database that is quite narrow in scope as it monitors only terrorist incidents that are *international* in nature, defined as "incidents in which terrorists go abroad to strike their targets, select domestic targets associated with a foreign state, or create an international incident by attacking airline passengers, personnel or equipment."[23] The main point to make here is that even though they usually attract much more media coverage, international terrorist incidents are significantly less frequent than domestic incidents. As a result, the commonly cited data that indicates the rise of religious terrorism is only applicable to international terrorism, a relatively small pool that is not necessarily representative of the trends in terrorism in general. So in the end, the correct interpretation of the statistics cited by Hoffman and others seems to document only an increasing *internationalization* of religious terrorism, and not necessarily a global *rise* of the phenomenon. And even though Hoffman's hypothesis is most likely correct, the cited data is limited only to a numerically less prevalent form of the terrorism phenomenon, and should be understood as such.

While I have brought into question the validity of the claims of decrease in the number of attacks over time and the rise of religion as a dominant motivation for terrorist activity, the hypothesis of ever-increasing number of fatalities seems rather convincing. And while this hypothesis is again supported on the basis of data which reflects only the trends in international terrorism, qualitative analysis of all terrorist attacks seems to provide additional support for this claim: while the deadliest incidents prior to the 1980s involved "only" dozens of fatalities, in the 80s and 90s the most lethal attacks were counted in the hundreds, and in the new millennium the plateau has reached into the thousands for the first time in history.

The Historical Record from Another Perspective

Let us now test the conventional hypothesis by looking at some additional qualitative data. The information presented in this section draws on multiple sources, mainly on the detailed chronologies of terrorist attacks compiled since 1968 by Edward F. Mickolus and his colleagues, the Weapons of Mass Destruction Terrorism and the Hydra databases compiled by the Monterey Institute of International Studies' Center for Nonproliferation Studies, and various other chronologies and listings available in the open source literature.

With regard to the hypothesis about religious terrorists being more lethal than their secular counterparts, perhaps the most surprising statistic will be the motivational distribution of perpetrators of the deadliest tactic that has historically been used by terrorists—the downing of civil airliners, either by detonating explosive devices on board, shooting them down with surface-to-air (SAM) missiles, rocket propelled grenades (RPG), or hijacking the planes and crashing them into buildings. Out of some 130 historical attacks or attempts to bring down airplanes in flight, *only 10* were perpetrated by organizations which can safely be labeled as religious in nature. This statistic is in strong opposition to the claim that religious terrorists are psychologically closer to acts of indiscriminate mass-casualty violence than other terrorist organizations.

There are several other striking statistics. Out of the 14 historical terrorist incidents that resulted in the death of more then 100 people, only 4 are attributable to organizations whose primary motivation is of a religious nature. Another interesting statistic concerns the use of suicide bombings, another widely destructive tactic: of the 30 single most deadly terrorist incidents carried out to date since 1990, 18 utilized suicide bombers.[24] Even though suicide bombings are in popular perception frequently associated with religious fanaticism, only one third of over 400 suicide bombings to date were perpetrated by organizations of a religious character. And finally, out of the 74 vehicular bombings that have killed 25 or more people, religious terrorists were again responsible for only one third of incidents.

As is apparent from these numbers, the deadliest forms of conventional terrorism have not been associated with an overarching presence of religious terrorists. Let us now take a closer look at the trends in non-conventional terrorism. Out of 90 Type I[25] uses of a CBRN agent recorded in the Monterey Institute's WMD Terrorism database,[26] only some 34 involved religious groups, with 12 attacks conducted by Aum Shinrikyo alone. With respect to fatalities resulting from these CBRN attacks, the numbers seem to confirm the hypothesis that religious groups are significantly more lethal than their secular counterparts: out of 1311 people listed in the database as killed in incidents involving CBRN, 1121 are associated with attacks perpetrated by religious groups. Upon taking a closer look however, we can see that this statistic is again not nearly as alarming as it may look: all of the 1121 fatalities occurred in the total of only five cases. The vast majority of the fatalities were the 778 members of the Movement for the Restoration of the Ten Commandments of God, which perished in the fire that consumed the cult shrine in Kanungu, Uganda, in March 2000. Later it was discovered that the majority of the people who died in what originally appeared to be a mass suicide were poisoned by an undisclosed substance.[27] Another 304 fatalities were attributed to the events of February 2000 in Kaduna, Nigeria, where the Hausa military youths violently attacked and killed Christian demonstrators who were protesting a government plan to implement the *sharia*. The victims were decapitated, mutilated, burned, and in some cases killed by arrows covered in poison.[28] The final 39 fatalities are people who died in a combination of several incidents perpetrated by Aum Shinrikyo in Japan: seven people were killed in the 1994 sarin attack near the mountain resort town of Matsumoto,[29] a total of 20 others were killed prior to 1994 in several assassinations of the cult's dissenters using VX nerve agent,[30] and 12 more people died in the notorious Tokyo subway sarin attack in 1995.

As we can see from this overview, the causes of the majority of the deaths in the first two instances are unknown, and it is therefore difficult to accept 1121 as the number of people killed by religious terrorists with CBRN. For this reason, it remains the case that none of the empirical data presented in this section seems to confirm the hypothesis that religious terrorists are significantly more lethal and therefore more susceptible to the use of CBRN weapons than their secular counterparts.

Linking Religious Motives and Escalation of Terrorist Violence

Let us now attempt to deconstruct the hypothesis regarding the casual relationship between the rise of religion as a primary motive for terrorists and the ever increasing deadliness of terrorist attacks, into individual components. Hoffman cites a number of reasons for why terrorism has become increasingly deadly, including the terrorists' constant quest for attention, the increased prevalence of state sponsorship, developments in terrorist weaponry, and the increasing sophistication of professional terrorism, but he considers proliferation of terrorist groups motivated by a religious imperative to be the single most important one.[31] Hoffman's list is quite comprehensive, but it should be emphasized that other important reasons exist as well. One is the terrorists' natural tendency to "out-do" their previous attacks, stimulated by the perception that if the present level of violence has thus far failed to succeed in forcing a radical change of the *status quo*, the campaign needs to intensified. Another reason is the fact that no matter how horrific a terrorist campaign might be, the intended audiences become desensitized to the current level of violence over time, forcing the terrorists to escalate in order to maintain or heighten the atmosphere of panic and fear among the general population, and to stay in the spotlight. An escalation in terrorist violence is also sometimes stimulated by the actions of other organizations, with which the given group competes for power or popularity. For instance, the decision of the secular Al Aksa Martyrs Brigades to engage in suicide bombings for the first time was clearly motivated by the growing power and popularity of the Hamas, a phenomenon that has often been attributed to the organization's use of suicide bombings as a tool for disrupting the peace process. Interestingly, following their first suicide bombing in January 2002, the Al Aksa Martyrs Brigades have begun to utilize this tactic with a greater frequency than any other Palestinian organization.

Another reason for the gradual escalation of overall terrorist violence over time has been the formation of new groups. Upon emergence, new violent organizations usually do not undergo the full process of radicalization, but rather pick up at the level of violence where other organizations active in the same struggle have left off. Alternatively, many existing organizations can give birth to new formations through the process of splintering, which usually results in the new entity being more radical and more violent than the core group. For instance, Ahmed Jibril's Popular Front for the Liberation of Palestine–General Command (PFLP-GC) resorted to several extraordinarily deadly bombings of commercial airliners in midcourse flight after its breakup with George Habash's Popular Front for the Liberation of Palestine (PFLP), in order to attain the image of a powerful new player in the Palestinian liberation movement.

The key point to make here is that the escalation of terrorist violence over time is a natural phenomenon, which occurs regardless of the transformation in ideological motives. Motivational factors, of course, do play a role, but they are not the main driving force behind the ever-escalating nature of terrorism—this function is generally fulfilled more significantly by the general dynamics that were defined by Hoffman and expanded upon here.

Terrorism and Religion

Earlier in this paper, the statistics that allegedly document the substitution of secular ideologies by divinely sanctioned violence have been questioned. One thing that remains true, however, is that over the last 20 years religious images have indeed become more prevalent in the rhetoric of today's terrorists. This turn to religion as the main ideological support basis for terrorism did not occur in a vacuum. It has been motivated by a number of factors, among them the lack of progress in regards to the widening gap between the West and the rest, inability of secular organizations to resolve core communal problems as well as larger issues such as the Israeli Palestinian conflict, and the overall breakdown of secular ideologies such as Marxism and purely secular nationalism.[32] The single most important factor for the rise of religion as a dominant motive has been the end of the Cold War, which signified the utter historical failure of communist ideologies, as well as the end of the bipolar world order. These events have not only diminished the attractiveness of ideological compliance with one of the two world power centers in order to attract state assistance, they also triggered immense fear of "one-worldism" symbolized by the emergence of the unipolar world order, which was perceived by radical members of various cultures as a threat to their identity and survival.[33] In the absence of alternatives among secular ideologies, many extremists shifted to religion as the main ideological foundation of their activities. This shift in ideological support mechanisms, however, does not necessarily mean that that the nature of core terrorist motivations and beliefs has changed, or that religion became the *primary* motivating factor for acts of violence. As previously noted by Walter Laqueur, terrorist belief systems may differ significantly based on history, culture or the influence of charismatic leaders. But the ideological content is only secondary to "burning passion," which serves as the primary driving force behind terrorist activity.[34] Or to use a psychologist's perspective:

> "Religion is first and foremost a fantasy system invented to merge with omnipotent forces that protect communities and individuals from death and predation, the terror of the unknown, and the viciousness of nature.... Religion may or may not teach violence, but what is responsible for the violence is the vengeful fantasy itself, which either utilizes, twists, or invents a divine sanction (religious precedent) to justify what is *psychologically* motivating the fantasy."[35]

In other words, religion did in the last 20 years become a more prominent factor as the supporting philosophical basis for many terrorist organizations, but the underlying motives in the belief systems of the majority of today's terrorists have *NOT* changed. Even the religious fanatic sees his violent activity as an essentially altruistic act of self-defense. It is still the perception of humiliation, victimization and injustice that drives the so-called "religious terrorist," rather than a perceived universal command from God. The use of holy rhetoric by most groups commonly labeled "religious" serves much more as a uniting and morale-boosting tool than as a universal justification for acts of unrestrained violence. That is not to say that for many terrorists, religion does not represent a tremendous legitimizing force and that it does not inspire the perception of enormous gratification and empowerment. But the terrorists are still primarily motivated by a grievance that is very real—even though just like most ordinary people, they also look for support of their arguments wherever they can. Religion then represents only one of the possible sources of support. At the same time Jurgensmeyer is probably correct when he claims that "those who are engaged in (acts of violence) would be offended if we concluded that their actions were purely for social and political gain. They argue that they act out of religious conviction, and surely they are to some degree right."[36] But this is not in any way contradictory to what has just been mentioned. Virtually *any* terrorist would be offended by the suggestion that he or she is motivated by political gain, as terrorists in general tend to see themselves and their actions as essentially altruistic, risking their lives for the benefit of future generations. The option of pointing to something greater then themselves not only gives the terrorists a legitimizing force but also provides support for their claims of altruism and self-sacrifice.

Now the key question arises: is it useful or even possible to make a distinction between religious and secular terrorists? Despite the problems of such a categorization, the answer is still yes, but is crucial to make this distinction at the level of *primary* rather than supporting motivations. In most cases, the perpetrators of terrorist violence will have multiple motives, and it will therefore be essential to identify the most dominant one. For example, Aum Shinrikyo's participation in elections does not make their primary motivation political, just as Hamas' constant praise of Allah does not make the primary motive a religious one. We should be careful to not fall into the trap of rhetorical nuances. In many cultures the word "God" figures very strongly in the language and in cultural and political traditions, which can sometimes be misleading. For instance, to an outsider phrases like "In God We Trust" printed on the American currency or the use of the popular slogan "God Bless America" by the American president could easily create the false impression that the United States is essentially a theocratic state. Another factor besides language that has the capacity to mislead us in terms of labeling a terrorist organization as religious is government propaganda. Virtually all states that are victims of a terrorist campaign insist on projecting their opponents as religious fanatics. This is quite understandable, as such labeling can have a de-legitimizing effect on the terrorists' cause—someone who sees himself as fighting on God's orders is popularly perceived as an irrational zealot, with whom no compromise is deemed possible. Rather, this "worshiper of evil" is seen as an exceptionally dangerous creature which uses claims of a just grievance only as a misleading cover, and who can only be stopped by merciless elimination. Israel and to a lesser extent Russia and India are examples of countries that have used such a strategy with some level of success. But while this strategy of promoting the opponent's image as one of an irrational religious fanatic may in some cases be politically successful, it caries the danger of failing to address the actual real-life grievances, which in turn can eventually result in increased support for the terrorists.

In conclusion, many factors contribute to the fact that today's distinctions between secular and religious terrorists are dubious at best. Let us now take a closer look at the some of the shortcomings in the definition of individual characteristics of religious terrorists as they have been defined by Hoffman and Jurgensmeyer.

Nature and Characteristics of Religious Terrorists

Jurgensmeyer in his book "Terror in the Mind of God" provides an excellent analysis of the characteristics of religious terrorists. The difficulty is, however, that nearly all of these characteristics apply to the vast majority of terrorist organizations regardless of the ideological foundations of their belief systems.[37] For instance, Jurgensmeyer describes in great detail the creation of martyrs and their role in religiously motivated violence. He also contends that by giving up their lives, martyrs not only demonstrate their commitment, but they also engage in sacrifice—the most fundamental form of religiosity.[38] But the key to emphasize here is that *all* violent campaigns find it useful to create and glorify martyrs. An act of self-sacrifice in the name of the organization's cause, whether religious or secular, is a uniting factor. Overt praise of the martyr's accomplishment by prominent members of the group can also increase the self-sense of group prestige and can inspire future volunteers. The willingness to die for a cause is sometimes also used as evidence of superiority of the groups' members over their adversaries, who are portrayed as pleasure-seekers and who in spite of their military dominance are essentially weak.[39] The resulting perception among the group is that due to superior determination, their final victory is inevitable.[40]

Another allegedly distinct characteristic of religiously motivated struggles are the aforementioned images of divine warfare, which are equated to the present struggle and are consistently used to create a sense of historical purpose and urgency.[41] This, however, is again a characteristic that is psychologically natural to all ethnic, cultural, or national communities, and is consistently used by all violent movements. Jurgensmeyer's "cosmic struggles" in essence are what psychiatrist Vamik Volkan calls the "chosen traumas": "heavily mythologized historical sufferings that bring with them powerful experiences of loss and feelings of humiliation, vengeance and hatred that trigger a variety of unconscious defense mechanisms that attempt to reverse these experiences and feelings."[42] Such defense mechanisms serve as a powerful dehumanization tool for killing, regardless of ideological context—the new enemies of current conflicts are psychologically transformed into extensions of the old enemy from a historical event.[43] Whether they are the Crusades for the Muslims, the Holocaust for the Jews, the Black September for the Palestinians, the Battle of Karbala for the Shi'ias, the Bloody Sunday for Irish Catholics, the battles of Mahabharata and Ramayana for the Hindus, Operation Blue Star for the Sikhs, the Vietnam war or 9-11 for the Americans, the Wounded Knee Massacre for the Lakota Indians, deportation from Turkey for the Armenians, or the Battle of Stalingrad for the Russians, all of these events can become the mythological "chosen traumas" or "images of cosmic warfare," which will help to dehumanize the enemy in future conflicts. Religious groups are in this respect no different from secular entities.

As we can see from these examples, religious terrorists are essentially very similar to their secular counterparts: they are narrow-minded individuals who fail to see alternative perspectives on the issues on behalf of which they fight for. This is not only a natural, but also an absolutely necessary characteristic for any terrorist—one has to believe in the absolute nature of the cause in order to kill in its name. And while it is true that some organizations are more discriminate and restrained in their violent actions then others, *any* ideology used to support a terrorist campaign becomes in essence a religion—an absolute "perception that there is a tension between reality as it appears and as it really is (or has been or will be)" to use Jurgensmeyer's own definition.[44] Any terrorist is motivated by feelings of frustration and humiliation, any terrorist sees his use of violence as a defensive war, any terrorist fights in the name of the absolute good. As psychologist Ernest Becker has stated long ago, "the most violence perpetrated in history has been to *eradicate* evil."[45] In addition, any perpetrator of a terrorist act empathizes with his or her own victimization and protests against cruelty toward their own people, but at the same time demonstrates minimum empathy for those who he or she kills. Any perpetrator of such an act feels empowered by the execution of "just" violence in the name of a great cause. For all of the above stated reasons, Jurgensmeyer's characterizations are excellent descriptions of the characteristics of terrorists in general, but fail to provide a useful tool for identifying the dreaded religious terrorists.

In contrast, Hoffman's analysis of the distinct features of religious terrorists is much more specific, but in the end also suffers from different weakness—virtually none of the existing terrorist organizations of today fit Hoffman's description. For instance, the number of groups that execute their terrorist acts for "no audience but themselves or God" is rather limited. In fact, most of the existing religious terrorist organizations complement their violence with realistic alternatives to secular rule, by backing their "military" activities with social, medical, and other communal services. As a result, many religious terrorist organizations have over time developed impressive constituencies.[46] Thus, Hoffman's argument that "the restraints on violence that are imposed on secular terrorists by the desire to appeal to a tacitly supportive or uncommitted constituency are not relevant to the religious terrorists"[47] is hardly valid. Furthermore, religious organizations that "unlike secular terrorists who see violence as a means to an end, tend to view violence as an end in itself" are also quite scarce. Even though many terrorist groups today carry out acts of violence that are motivated by revenge, the altruistic component of such violence even when accompanied by religious rhetoric cannot be overemphasized. And while it is true that the goals of some religious terrorists tend to be less clearly defined and seem much less tangible, most organizations commonly labeled as religious nevertheless have a clear strategic calculation behind them and seek to benefit a specific group of people. Even Hoffmann more or less confirms this claim by stating that the aims of "religious political" terrorists are defined as "the attainment of the greatest possible benefits for themselves and for their co-religionists only, as opposed to the indiscriminately utilitarian goals of secular terrorists."[48] This observation again shows the complexity of defining the distinct features of religious terrorists. Are not all ethnically or nationalistically based secular organizations also restricted in their violent actions to the attainment of the greatest possible benefits to members of their own ethnic or national community only?[49] And does not, on the other hand, the religiously motivated Algerian Armed Islamic Group (GIA), indiscriminately kill their co-religionists in some of the most brutal ways imaginable?

As hopefully became apparent throughout the course of this paper, the commonly defined characteristics of the "new terrorists" as religious fanatics who do not seek to benefit a constituency and whose violent actions are not a means to an end but rather a self-serving end in itself, and who are therefore unrestrained in their violence and thus are more likely to perpetrate acts of mass destruction, do not apply to the absolute majority of today's terrorists. Implicitly, many of the organizations that are included in the statistics that show the rise of indiscriminate, divinely sanctioned violence do not belong into this narrowly defined category, rendering the alarmist interpretation of such statistics much less useful than generally believed. For the above-stated reasons, the unfortunate common practice of basing the assessment of future non-conventional terrorists solely on the frequency of the use of the word "God" in a given organization's statements does not adequately reflect the CBRN threat level posed by the respective group. Instead, a more productive approach may be to focus on the individual characteristics of potential mass-casualty terrorists in order to assess the threat. The final part of this paper will focus on identifying some of these characteristics, and will also incorporate an overall threat assessment with regards to the likelihood of a mass-fatality CBRN terrorist attack occurring in the near future.

Part III

Motivational Characteristics of Future "Superterrorists"

As mentioned above, successful mass-casualty non-conventional terrorists will have to possess the capability to acquire and deliver biological agents, as well as the motivation to kill thousands of people indiscriminately. Contrary to popular belief, however, only organizations possessing a rather unique combination of very specific characteristics are likely to satisfy the requirements for mass-casualty non-conventional terrorism.[50] Of greatest concern on the motivational level are cult-like groups that are completely isolated from the mainstream society and are driven by an apocalyptic ideology that could be described as destroying the world to save it. Religious and other cult-like organizations that share the worldview that our planet could use a radical makeover are not in short supply. Fortunately, most such organizations have yet to resort to outward violence. If such a turn of events were to occur, however, the potential ability of apocalyptic organizations to justify killing people as actually benefiting them by sending them to a better place than this world makes such groups particularly dangerous. As in most terrorist attacks, the use of violence in this scenario would again be perceived by the terrorists as altruistic, with the critical difference that the constituency in this case would be the victims themselves. In such cases, the victims would not necessarily be seen as an enemy whom one kills in hate or for symbolic value, but rather poor human beings that are going to be saved by being killed. Under such circumstances, killing thousands of people indiscriminately would be psychologically much easier than doing so as a part of a political strategy or revenge. For instance, the *Thuggees*, an Indian cult of Kali worshippers that according to some claims killed over a million people in acts of sacrificial violence between the 7th and mid-19th century,[51] displayed some of these motivational elements. According to David Rapoport, the *Thuggees* believed that if they do not shed blood, their victims will go to paradise, and allegedly for this reason, the cult used strangulation as its main operational method. And while many historians question even the sole existence of the *Thuggees* claiming that they were a myth that was developed by the British during their colonial rule of India, if this group actually existed and if the numbers are correct, the *Thuggees* are the deadliest terrorist group in history. With the possible exception of the Algerian GIA, their average killing rate of 1,200 people per year remains unchallenged to this day despite great advances in weapons technology.[52]

The *Thuggees* are just one example in history that demonstrates the dangers of "altruistic" desires of terrorist organizations to bring about the Armageddon. Aum Shinrikyo's Shoko Asahara, for instance, also advocated the moral acceptance of mercy killing and argued for the "right of the guru and of spiritually advanced practitioners to kill those who otherwise would fall into hells."[53] And while it would be difficult to claim that an act of mass-fatality CBRN terrorism will never occur in the absence of such an ideology, it is clear that similar belief systems should be a warning sign in this regard. Another key point to emphasize is that a terrorist group does not necessarily have to be religious in nature in order to reach an apocalyptic stage. Fundamentalist environmental or animal rights groups, as well as ethnic-based violent movements might under certain circumstances also reach this stage.

Another element also likely to be present among superterrorists is a strong sense of paranoia among the group's members. Not only will a paranoid worldview enhance the polarization of the terrorists' perception of the world into an "us versus them" mode, it will also consequently increase the ability to victimize the organization's non-members indiscriminately. The greater the presence of paranoia in the group's perception, the greater is also the sense of urgency among the group's members to unite into one cohesive unit and to eliminate dissenters. This is especially critical as the utility of mass-casualty violence tends to be a topic of disagreement among most terrorist groups, possibly creating undesirable schisms within the organization. If the given group can completely eliminate dissent, the restraining nature of a debate about the utility of using weapons of mass destruction will be lost.

Another important characteristic of future CBRN terrorists will be the expressive value attached to a particular mode of attack, in this case perhaps the desire to kill without shedding blood, or a divine fascination with poisons and plagues as God's tools. An example of this is the frequent reference to biblical plagues commonly used by various radical Christian groups, or the strange fascination of Shoko Asahara who wrote poems about sarin. Alternatively, environmentalist cults may interpret diseases as "natural" tools used by Mother Nature to eliminate the human race that has through technological advances and an inconsiderate use of natural resources caused a natural imbalance, which can only be restored by an elimination of the world's most destructive species.

Another important element likely to be present is the terrorists' self-perception of grandiosity and ideological uniqueness. And while it is true that most terrorist organizations believe in their exceptionality, which helps to explain why most armed struggles usually involve not one but several concurring terrorist organizations with virtually identical goals, few groups define their individuality based on such narrow distinctions as weapons selection. The most significant differences among terrorist groups with a common cause and enemy exist mainly in the realm of overall strategy of using violence as a part of the revolutionary process, leader personalities and ambitions, allegiance toward a particular state or non-state sponsor, the appropriateness in terms of intensity of individual acts of violence, legitimacy of targeting civilians, and other similar factors. Future superterrorists, however, are likely to attach extreme importance to the use of chemical or biological agents as a distinct feature of the group. If organizations that possess the above characteristic are in addition led by an uncontested charismatic leader who is violence-prone, and who has the ability to convince his followers that his instructions are direct orders from a supernatural authority, the deadly combination of motivational attributes needed to indiscriminately kill masses of people with biological weapons will likely be established.

Organization and Capability

At the organizational level, the group is likely to be structured as a very tight hierarchical formation or as a number of small independent cells, in order to prevent infiltration and obviation of their grandiose plans. Further, powerful mechanisms of social control such as heavy indoctrination, complete isolation and intimidation will probably be in place in order to prevent internal defections that could also jeopardize attack preparations. With respect to capabilities, a successful terrorist group will need significant financial, logistical and human resources, given the difficulty of weaponizing CBRN agents in a way that they can produce mass-fatalities. Very few groups possess such resources, even though the assistance of state sponsors has the potential of significantly altering this situation. Alternatively, unemployed scientists from state-level CBRN programs could be recruited into the group using incentives such as money, opportunity to conduct high-level research, or the "scientifically cosmic" nature of the given organization's ideology.

Desire and Ability to Innovate

Another important attribute of future "superterrorists" is the desire and ability to innovate, both on technological and tactical level, in order to attain the ability to successfully attack with CBRN weapons. Most terrorist groups to date, however, have been rather conservative, usually innovating only when forced to do so by anti-terrorist countermeasures, such as barometric pressure chambers, metal detectors, x-rays, and vapor detectors at airports. As a result, most of the innovation that has taken place in terrorist campaigns took the form of advancing the methods of weapon concealment, as opposed to adopting new types of weaponry per se.[54] This is quite logical, considering that one of the terrorists' greatest fears is failure—an attack that fails wastes resources and leaves clues, but most importantly, it can have a negative effect on the outward image of the organization and on the self-esteem of the group's members. Most organizations will therefore stick to the methods that have proven to be successful in the past, unless such means become ineffective because of the defensive countermeasures put in place by the adversary, or unless some other factors create the perception of a need for a tactical or technological shift. Especially religious terrorists have not been particularly inventive when it comes to using new types of weaponry.[55]

On the tactical level, terrorist innovation has historically had a more or less cyclical, multiplying character, utilizing proven traditional tactics in a combined and synchronized fashion. An example of this phenomenon is the increasingly frequent use of secondary explosive devices, which are designed to target first responders or bystanders that gather around to watch the impact of the primary explosion. This method has proven to be very effective in reaching a high body count in many terrorist bombings.

Overall, the successful progression to CBRN weapons requires a much more significant level of innovation than the vast majority of terrorist groups have demonstrated so far. In order to undergo such a long and demanding process, an organization will have to possess a combination of several important attributes.[56] First, the decision to innovate requires a high level of technological awareness, something that most organizations that are completely isolated from the rest of the world may find difficult to maintain. Next, the group has to be open to new ideas, so that the organization's members are not afraid to put forward their proposals for adopting new methods. Most cult-like organizations that fulfill the motivational "superterrorist" characteristics identified earlier do not possess this attribute—their members are highly controlled, dissent is not tolerated, and individuality is suppressed. In order for such groups to pursue innovative means, it will be critical to have a leader who is fascinated with biological weapons or the process of innovation itself. Such an inclination on the part of the leader is likely going to be heavily reflected in the group's ideology as well. Highly innovative organizations will also have to demonstrate a positive attitude toward risk-taking, with respect to both the risk of failure and the physical risks associated with handling lethal CBRN agents.

Once the group makes the decision to innovate, other important factors influencing the successful adoption of new technology will emerge. Most importantly, it will be the nature of the technology and the difficulties associated with its acquisition and successful use. Agents that can be delivered via direct personal contact will be much easier to apply than pathogens or toxins that require aerosolization. Assistance of a state sponsor can be a valuable asset when attempting to adopt high-level technology, and organizations that have received such assistance have historically been significantly more deadly than the groups that receive no such support.[57] However, as mentioned above, states have traditionally stayed away from providing high-level technology to proxies, who can never be fully controlled and whose affection toward the sponsoring state may only be short-lived. Further, it is even less likely that any state, no matter how "rogue," would give lethal CBRN agents to an untested, highly volatile, and completely indiscriminate apocalyptic cult, whose ideological foundation does not even remotely resemble that of the state. Consequently, most organizations that satisfy the aforementioned motivational characteristics of potential mass-casualty bioterrorists cannot hope for state support and are left to their own abilities.

Besides financial or material resources, an organization will need personnel with the necessary expertise and the ample time to devote their full attention to acquiring and weaponizing CBRN agents. Organizations whose members are only part-time terrorists and hold daily jobs, or groups that are involved in reciprocal battles in the field, can hardly devote a significant number of their human resources to this type of activity. At the same time, groups that perpetrate terrorist operations infrequently and thus do have the time to devote to discovering new technologies are likely to have difficulties with learning to use such technology effectively, precisely because of the absence of experience resulting from the infrequent nature of their attacks.[58]

Conclusion

The trends in terrorism are ominous. The rising frequency of spectacular and highly lethal attacks along with the existence of global terrorist networks seems to confirm the hypothesis that the ever-escalating nature of terrorism is likely to yield a mass-casualty nonconventional terrorist incident at some point in the future. Advances in communications and weapons technologies, as well as the questionable security of the CBRN facilities in the former Soviet Union also seemingly provide the "new," more violent and reckless terrorists with the tools necessary to perpetrate such an attack.

However, the technological hurdles of perpetrating a mass-fatality CBRN incident are still significant and cannot be overlooked. Even Aum Shinrikyo, the infamous Japanese cult which possessed an estimated $1 billion in assets, some 20 university-trained microbiologists working in top-notch research facilities, and the freedom to conduct unlimited experiments, completely failed in all 10 attempts to attack with anthrax and botulinum toxin.[59] The conditions and resources that were available to Aum Shinrikyo are unparalleled by even the deadliest terrorist organizations today, including al-Qaida.

Moreover, most organizations do not start out directly with weapons of mass destruction; low to medium-level violence which will help the terrorists to get used to the idea of killing indiscriminately is likely to precede an escalation to mass-fatality attacks. It is therefore highly unlikely that organizations possessing both the motivational and the capability characteristics described in this chapter will be able to stay off the radar screen of intelligence agencies for long. At the same time, it should be noted that the low-level violent activity practiced by cult-like organizations may not be immediately obvious, as it is likely to take the form of violence within the group, designed to eliminate dissent. Nevertheless, even though terrorist organizations usually follow an escalatory pattern of violence, most organizations simply do not last long enough to progress all the way to non-conventional weapons—it is estimated that only one out of ten groups survive the first year of operation, and only half of the groups that do make it through the first year survive a decade.[60] In addition, the organizations that do manage to survive for a long enough period to be able to attain the capability to attack with biological weapons, over time usually develop support networks and constituencies, which by giving the given organization something at stake usually serve to create or reinforce rational strategic calculation among the group's leadership. This means that even organizations that rise to the spotlight by perpetrating exceptionally unrestrained high-fatality attacks are usually forced to adjust their strategies and to scale down the level of violence over time, in order to maintain the popular support that has, sometimes unwittingly, been accumulated. In the absence of such an adjustment, the given organization's credibility as an alternative to the existing world order will fade, lessening the chances of the group's long-term survival.[61]

On a final note, even the groups that do overcome all of the motivational constraints against indiscriminate mass-fatality violence have yet to exploit the full killing potential of their current conventional capabilities. If the desire is indeed to kill as many people as possible, why not just attack more often, at more locations, and on a greater scale with weapons that are available and have proven to be effective? Why invest a massive amount of precious resources into a new technology that only few if any know how to use and that could potentially end up killing the perpetrators themselves—all without any guarantee of success? Why risk a negative public reaction and a possibly devastating retaliation likely to be associated with the use of non-conventional weapons? Most of today's terrorist organizations have probably faced such questions at some point and have either decided that non-conventional weapons are not worth pursuing, or have made limited and unsuccessful attempts to explore this avenue. The groups that have decided or will in the future decide that such weapons are an attractive option are likely to possess a mix of unique and fortunately also quite rare characteristics. They are likely to be apocalyptic cults with violence-prone charismatic leaders who are fascinated with diseases and poisons and are not afraid to fail or the get killed in their attempts to pursue such technology. The greatest overall danger is posed by religious cults combining such apocalyptic visions with outward-oriented violence and suicidal tendencies. However, most suicide cults tend to direct their violence only inward, committing collective suicide without attacking others.[62] Apocalyptic cults that do kill non-members, on the other hand, surprisingly tend to be oriented toward survival.[63]

Also, the groups that are particularly dangerous with respect to their motivation to inflict mass casualties may be in a more difficult position to breach the technological hurdles of a biological weapons attack. Acquiring the necessary financial, logistical and human resources is challenging for isolated cults with an obscure ideology. In essence, the more extreme the organization, the less likely it is to attract mass support. For extremely radical groups, attracting state-level assistance and finding a safe haven in which they can conduct their research and low-level violent activities while remaining undetected by intelligence agencies may be particularly difficult. Moreover, the total suppression of individuality in such cults and their isolation from mainstream society does not provide for the organizational dynamics that would be favorable for successful adoption of new technology.

As a result, the same inverse relationship between the motivation to produce mass-fatalities and the ability to do so that was described by Post on the individual level seems to apply to organized formations as well.[64] For this reason, the likelihood of a successful mass-casualty "superterrorist" attack remains low. That being said, many conventional terrorist organizations must have inevitably noticed the enormous fear of chemical, biological and nuclear weapons among the general public, and some are certainly likely to attempt to exploit this fear to their advantage. Such attempts are likely to take the form of threats and expressed desire to use such weapons, attacks involving a small amount of crudely delivered chemical or pathogen, or the inclusion of some chemical, biological or radiological agent in a conventional bomb. Such attempts, however, should be understood as psychological operations that are aimed at creating disproportionate fear, but do not necessarily represent a terrifying shift to catastrophic terrorism.

Adam Dolnik is a research associate at the center for Nonproliferation Studies in Monterey, California. He is associated with the Weapons of Mass Destruction Terrorism Project in the Chemical and Biological Weapons Nonproliferation Program. He conducts research on terrorist motivations and justifications for the use of violence and other terrorist strategies. He has previously worked with the UN Terrorism Prevention Branch in Vienna, Austria.

Notes

1. Bruce Hoffman, *Inside Terrorism* (New York: Orion Publishing Co. 1998), p. 201.
2. Brian Michael Jenkins, "Will Terrorists Go Nuclear?" RAND Paper P-5541 (1975), p. 4.
3. Bruce Hoffman, *Inside Terrorism* (New York: Orion Publishing Co. 1998), p. 205.
4. Bruce Hoffman, *Inside Terrorism* (New York: Orion Publishing Co. 1998), p. 201.
5. Bruce Hoffman, *Inside Terrorism* (New York: Orion Publishing Co. 1998), p. 90–92.
6. Bruce Hoffman, "Holy Terror": The Implications of Terrorism Motivated by a Religious Imperative, RAND 1993, p. 5–6.
7. Bruce Hoffman, *Inside Terrorism* (New York: Orion Publishing Co. 1998), p. 201.
8. Bruce Hoffman, *Inside Terrorism* (New York: Orion Publishing Co. 1998), p. 201.
9. Bruce Hoffman, "Holy Terror": The Implications of Terrorism Motivated by a Religious Imperative, RAND 1993, p. 5.
10. Bruce Hoffman, "Holy Terror": The Implications of Terrorism Motivated by a Religious Imperative, RAND 1993, p. 5.
11. Bruce Hoffman, "Holy Terror": The Implications of Terrorism Motivated by a Religious Imperative, RAND 1993, p. 12.
12. Magnus Ranstorp, Terrorism in the Name of Religion. *Journal of International Affairs*, Summer 1996 Vol. 50, Num. 1.
13. Bruce Hoffman, "Holy Terror": The Implications of Terrorism Motivated by a Religious Imperative, RAND 1993, p. 3.
14. Bruce Hoffman, "Holy Terror": The Implications of Terrorism Motivated by a Religious Imperative, RAND 1993, p. 3.
15. Bruce Hoffman, "Holy Terror": The Implications of Terrorism Motivated by a Religious Imperative, RAND 1993, p. 3.
16. Mark Jurgensmeyer, *Terror in the Mind of God* (Los Angeles: University of California Press, 2000), p. 146.
17. Mark Jurgensmeyer, "The Logic of Religious Violence" in David C. Rapoport: *Inside Terrorist Organizations* (London: Frank Cass, 2001), p. 185–190.
18. Mark Jurgensmeyer, *Terror in the Mind of God* (Los Angeles: University of California Press, 2000), p. 167.

19. Mark Jurgensmeyer, "The Logic of Religious Violence" in David C. Rapoport: *Inside Terrorist Organizations* (London: Frank Cass, 2001), p. 185–190.
20. Mark Jurgensmeyer, *Terror in the Mind of God* (Los Angeles: University of California Press, 2000), p. 214.
21. Mark Jurgensmeyer, "The Logic of Religious Violence" in David C. Rapoport: *Inside Terrorist Organizations* (London: Frank Cass, 2001), p. 182.
22. Mark Jurgensmeyer, "The Logic of Religious Violence" in David C. Rapoport: *Inside Terrorist Organizations* (London: Frank Cass, 2001), p. 183.
23. The database description can be found at www.mipt.org/randterrorismdb.asp.
24. Adam Dolnik, "Die and Let Die: Exploring Links between Suicide Terrorism and Terrorist Use of Chemical, Biological, Radiological, and Nuclear Weapons." *Studies in Conflict and Terrorism*, Vol. 26, No.1, pp. 17–35.
25. Incidents perpetrated by organizations or individuals motivated on ideological or religious grounds.
26. Further information about the database is available at: http://www.cns.miis.edu/dbinfo/about.htm#wmd.
27. Anna Borzello, "New Cult Graves Point to Murder," *Daily Mail and Guardian* (27 March 2000); Internet, available from http://www.mg.co.za/mg/news/, accessed on 5/22/00.
28. "Tears, Blood, as Kaduna Boils," *Post Express Wired* (29 February 2000); Internet, available from www.postexpresswired.com, accessed on 2/29/00.
29. "Asahara Ordered 1994 Sarin Attack, Aum Biologist Says," *Japan Economic Newswire* (14 January 1999).
30. "Aum 'Minister' Admits Using Toxic Chemical to Kill Cultists," *Asahi News Service* (27 June 1995).
31. Bruce Hoffman, *Inside Terrorism* (New York: Orion Publishing Co., 1998), p. 201.
32. Walter Laqueur, *The New Terrorism* (New York: Oxford University Press, 1999), p. 128.
33. Magnus Ranstorp, Terrorism in the Name of Religion. *Journal of International Affairs*, Summer 1996, Vol. 50, Num. 1. p. 18.
34. Walter Laqueur, *The New Terrorism* (New York: Oxford University Press, 1999), p. 230.
35. Jerry S. Piven, "On the Psychosis (Religion) of Terrorists," In Chris E. Stout, *Psychology of Terrorism*, Preager Publishers 2002, p. 121.
36. Mark Jurgensmeyer, "The Logic of Religious Violence" in David C. Rapoport: *Inside Terrorist Organizations* (London: Frank Cass, 2001), p. 185.
37. Further, the majority of the case studies used by Jurgensmeyer to demonstrate the logic of religious violence concern movements that cannot be accurately described as religious in nature.
38. Mark Jurgensmeyer, *Terror in the Mind of God* (Los Angeles: University of California Press, 2000), p. 167.
39. Reuven Paz, 'The Islamic Legitimacy of Suicide Terrorism,' *Countering Suicide Terrorism* (Herzliya: International Policy Institute for Counter-Terrorism, 2000), p. 93.
40. Adam Dolnik, "Die and Let Die: Exploring Links between Suicide Terrorism and Terrorist Use of Chemical, Biological, Radiological, and Nuclear Weapons." *Studies in Conflict and Terrorism*, Vol. 26, No.1, pp. 17–35.
41. Mark Jurgensmeyer, *Terror in the Mind of God* (Los Angeles: University of California Press, 2000), p. 146.
42. Vamik Volkan, *Blood Lines: From Ethnic Pride to Ethnic Terrorism* (New York: Farrar, Straus and Giroux, 1997), p. 82.
43. Vamik Volkan, *Blood Lines: From Ethnic Pride to Ethnic Terrorism* (New York: Farrar, Straus and Giroux, 1997), p. 46.
44. Mark Jurgensmeyer, "The Logic of Religious Violence" in David C. Rapoport: *Inside Terrorist Organizations* (London: Frank Cass, 2001), p. 178.
45. Cited in Jerry S. Piven, "On the Psychosis (Religion) of Terrorists," In Chris E. Stout, *Psychology of Terrorism*, Preager Publishers, 2002, p. 127.
46. Magnus Ranstorp, Terrorism in the Name of Religion. *Journal of International Affairs*, Summer 1996, Vol. 50, Num.1, p. 36.

47. Bruce Hoffman, "Holy Terror": The Implications of Terrorism Motivated by a Religious Imperative, RAND 1993, p. 3.

48. Bruce Hoffman, "Holy Terror": The Implications of Terrorism Motivated by a Religious Imperative, RAND 1993, p. 3.

49. Daniel Byman, The Logic of Ethnic Terrorism, *Studies in Conflict and Terrorism,* Vol.21, Number 2, 1998, p. 151.

50. Stern, Jessica: *Ultimate Terrorists* (London: Harvard University Press 1999), p. 70.

51. Bruce Hoffman, *Inside Terrorism* (New York: Orion Publishing Co. 1998), p. 89.

52. Even though the exact numbers are unknown, only the Groupe Islamique Arme (GIA) of Algeria can challenge the *Thuggees* in terms of killing intensity. Interestingly, the GIA also relies on very primitive weapons in its campaign.

53. Mark Jurgensmeyer, *Terror in the Mind of God* (Los Angeles: University of California Press, 2000), p. 114.

54. Hoffman, Bruce, "Terrorist Targeting: Tactics, Trends, and Potentialities," in Paul Wilkinson ed. *Technology and Terrorism* (Frank Cass: London, 1993), p. 12.

55. Magnus Ranstorp, Terrorism in the Name of Religion. *Journal of International Affairs*, Summer 1996, Vol. 50, Num. 1.

56. Jackson, Brian: "Technology Acquisition by Terrorist Groups: Threat Assessment Informed by Lessons from Private Sector Technology Adoption," Studies in *Conflict & Terrorism*: 24 (2001), p. 189–213.

57. According to some experts, organizations that enjoy the support of a state sponsor have been on average eight times more deadly than groups that receive no such support. (Bruce Hoffman, quoted in Brian Jackson, "Technology Acquisition by Terrorist Groups: Threat Assessment Informed by Lessons from Private Sector Technology Adoption," *Studies in Conflict & Terrorism*: 24, 2001, p. 199.)

58. Jackson, Brian: "Technology Acquisition by Terrorist Groups: Threat Assessment Informed by Lessons from Private Sector Technology Adoption," Studies in *Conflict & Terrorism*: 24 (2001), p. 189–213.

59. Center for Nonproliferation Studies: *Chronology of Aum Shinrikyo's CBW Activities* (March 2001), Internet, available at http://cns.miis.edu/pubs/reports/aum_chrn.htm. (Accessed on 12/12/02)

60. Rapoport quoted in Hoffman, Bruce: *Inside Terrorism* (New York: Orion Publishing Co. 1998), p. 89.

61. The Lebanese Hizballah is a good example of such a transformation.

62. For example 914 members of the People's Temple committed mass suicide in 1978 in Jonestown, Guyana; 39 members of Heaven's Gate committed a similar act in 1997 in Rancho Santa Fe, California.

63. The author is aware of two exceptions: the Zealots who committed mass suicide in the 1st century BC, and the Concerned Christians, a Colorado cult that allegedly planed to perpetrate attacks in Israel in 1999 and whose members reportedly also had plans to commit mass suicide.

64. Post has argued that individuals who want to kill a lot of people indiscriminately are likely to suffer from significant psychological idiosyncrasies. For individuals suffering from such idiosyncrasies it is nearly impossible to function in groups. But one does need to operate in groups in order to be successful in producing a grandiose mass-casualty attack. (Jerrold Post, "Psychological and Motivational Factors in Terrorist Decision-Making: Implications for CBW Terrorism," in Jonathan Tucker ed. *Toxic Terror* (London: MIT Press, 2000), 271–289.

Richard F. Pilch, 2002

The Bioterrorist Threat in the United States*

Only a year ago, the United States was still reeling from the effects of September 11th and the subsequent distribution of "anthrax letters" through the mail.[1] *Yet assessments of the bioterrorist threat generally predate these landmark events and do not offer a comprehensive analysis of the current threat level in the United States. Thus, an updated assessment of the current bioterrorist threat is presented, using the following formula for analysis: THREAT = Vulnerability × Capability × Intent. Special consideration is given to the capability aspect of the threat, with review of the major technical hurdles involved in the acquisition, production, and delivery of a prospective biological warfare agent. A scenario addressing the use of a crop-duster for the aerosol dissemination of* Bacillus anthracis *spores is provided as an example. The author concludes that while the bioterrorist threat for any given individual is very small, from a policy-making standpoint a worst-case scenario must be considered. Most likely, both "high probability, low impact" and "low probability, high impact" biological attacks will be attempted over the next decade. Because vulnerabilities are established and intent and organizational capability have both been demonstrated, whether a terrorist group or individual can overcome the technical hurdles outlined may ultimately determine whether such an attack is successful.*

Introduction

Shortly after last fall's September 11th attack, a series of stories surfaced that Mohammed Atta, the leader of the attack and presumably the pilot of American Airlines flight 11—the Boeing 767 that struck the north tower of the World Trade Center—had demonstrated a persistent interest in crop-dusters over the previous year.[2] This information came prior to the subsequent anthrax mail attacks, but the fear persisted that Atta's terrorist group had somehow acquired a biological warfare (BW) agent and had been seeking a means to deliver it over an unsuspecting population.

Arguably the most curious evidence of Atta's interest was provided by Ms. Johnell Bryant, a U.S. Department of Agriculture (USDA) loan officer from Florida City, Florida, who saw Atta's picture on television after the attack and recognized him from an encounter she'd had in early 2000, some months before Atta and another member of his group began

*The author would like to thank Dr. Raymond A. Zilinskas for his extensive support and guidance throughout the writing of this paper.

taking flying lessons in the nearby town of Venice.[3] According to Bryant's account, Atta had come to her office requesting a $650,000 loan to "finance a twin-engine six passenger aircraft."[4] He had claimed to be an engineer and said he "wanted to [remove the seats and] build a chemical tank that would fit inside the aircraft and take up every available square inch [inside] except for where the pilot would be sitting," essentially converting a passenger plane into a modified crop-duster.

Bryant denied Atta the loan, but not because of his unusual request. Instead, she rejected him because he was not a U.S. citizen, at which point he asked her, in her words, "What would prevent him from going behind [her] desk and cutting [her] throat and making off with the millions of dollars in [the] safe?"

At this point during the encounter, Atta apparently noticed an enlarged aerial photograph of Washington, DC, hanging on Bryant's wall. The single photograph contained numerous targets of symbolic, political, and military significance, namely the structures on Independence Mall—the White House, Capitol Building, Washington Monument, and Lincoln Memorial—and the Pentagon. Atta was very interested in this photograph and offered twice to pay cash for it on the spot, but Bryant informed him that it was not for sale. He then asked her, again in her words, "How would America like it if another country destroyed that city and some of the monuments in it like the cities in his country [have] been destroyed?"

Atta was a citizen of Saudi Arabia but was Egyptian by birth. Thus, when he said "my country," perhaps he was referring to a pan-Arab entity and was hinting at the possibility of retribution for U.S. bombing in Iraq. Alternatively, he may have been referring to the November 17, 1997, terrorist attack at the Hatshepsut Temple in the Valley of the Kings near Luxor, Egypt, in which members of al-Gama'a al-Islamiyya ("the Islamic Group") shot and killed 58 foreign tourists and four Egyptians and wounded 26 others, and was suggesting that the same fate could befall similar American monuments. Al-Gama'a is among the three major Egyptian-led terrorist groups, and one of its leaders, Sheikh Omar Abdel Rahman, is currently imprisoned in the U.S. serving a life sentence for his role in the first World Trade Center bombing in 1993.

The world now knows that Atta was a part of the loose network of terrorist cells of al-Qa'ida. Apart from their Islamic fundamentalist ideology—and presumably a love for Usama bin Ladin, whom Atta had claimed "would someday be known as the world's greatest leader," according to Bryant—a common element among al-Qa'ida operatives is their training. In the al-Qa'ida training manual there is no mention of crop-dusters, nor is there discussion of chemical or biological attacks.[5] However, the extraction process of the toxins ricin and abrin for assassination purposes is described in some detail, as is the production of botulinum toxin (although never named specifically, the preparation and effects of botulinum toxin are covered in a segment entitled "Poisoning from Eating Spoiled Food"). Toxins are chemicals of biological origin, and ricin in particular, which is derived from castor beans of the abundant *Ricinus communis* plant widely used in the production of castor oil, is relatively easy to acquire.[6] Approximately one million tons of castor beans are processed for this purpose each year, yielding a waste product that is 5 percent ricin by weight.[7]

According to a series of August 2002 news reports, the Kurdish group Ansar al-Islam, which has known ties to al-Qa'ida, tested ricin on animals and possibly even a man in Northern Iraq.[8] Ricin acts on a cellular level with lethal effect such that in mouse assays, the injection of 24 micrograms of the toxin per kilogram of body weight was found to be enough to cause death (the equivalent inhalational dose was found to be only 3 to 5 micrograms per kilogram).[9] This representative lethality in extremely low doses, combined with the fact that they degrade very rapidly in situ, makes toxins difficult to detect upon autopsy and thus especially suitable as instruments of murder or assassination.

Despite the absence of explicitly relevant information in the training manual, a number of clues exist that suggest a push by al-Qa'ida in the crop-duster direction. First, it has been learned that Atta had visited Belle Glade Municipal Airport in South Florida, which at the time was home to 8 crop-dusters, at least twice to ask questions about the aircraft,[10] mainly how to start them, how far they could fly, and what load they carried in terms of both fuel and pesticide.[11] Other groups of "Middle Eastern" men had reportedly come and gone frequently during the months preceding the September 11 attack as well, asking similar questions, attempting to take photographs and video of the cockpit (and exterior), and asking to sit in the plane. These groups, which usually consisted of 2 to 3 men, had visited the airport nearly every weekend for six or eight weeks prior to September 11th, including the weekend before the attack.[12]

Second, a search of the residence of Zacarias Moussaoui, who most security analysts believe would have been the 20th hijacker, led to the discovery of operational manuals for crop-dusting equipment.[13] Moussaoui was arrested on immigration charges on August 17, 2001, approximately three weeks before the September 11th attack, after drawing suspicion from a flight school instructor (Moussaoui had asked the instructor how to steer a commercial jetliner in mid-air but stated that he didn't need to know how to take off or land).[14] Apparently, the search also revealed that Moussaoui had downloaded information on aerosol dispersal from the Internet.

Third, Essam al-Ridi, an Egyptian-born citizen of the United States who testified as a federal witness in the trial of four men accused in the 1998 U.S. Embassy bombings in Kenya and Tanzania, has claimed that Bin Ladin himself once asked him to look into starting a crop-dusting business.[15]

Fourth, al-Qa'ida operative Ahmad Rassam, arrested in 2001 for plotting to bomb Los Angeles International Airport, testified that Bin Ladin has displayed a personal interest in dispersing biological agents from low-flying aircraft.[16]

Fifth, Abdul Hakin Murad—currently serving life in prison for his involvement in a plot to bomb 12 U.S. jetliners[17] planned by Ramzi Yousef, the man behind the first World Trade Center bombing in 1993 and who has established links with al-Qa'ida—has described plots involving the use of crop-dusters to distribute biological and chemical weapons over U.S. cities.[18]

And sixth, Johnell Bryant, the USDA loan officer, has passed a polygraph, which lends substantial credibility to her account.[19]

When compiled, this information led to a Federal Bureau of Investigation (FBI) warning about the possibility of crop-duster use by terrorists and the grounding of the approximately 5,000 crop-dusters in the U.S. on at least two separate occasions, and also raised the question of how great the threat really was, and still is, with this type of aircraft and with biological agents in general.[20]

Threat Assessment Defined

The formula for a threat assessment is Threat = Vulnerability × Capability × Intent, with threat being the probability that an adversary will inflict injury or damage. Vulnerability is the extent to which a potential target is open to attack. Capability is whether a given adversary has the technical and also the organizational ability to carry out an attack. With respect to biological weapons, the technical aspect of this component of the threat assessment consists of three major hurdles upon BW agent selection: acquisition of a pathogenic strain, production, and effective delivery. Intent is whether an adversary would actually be likely to carry out an attack. Generally speaking, this component of the assessment requires that a distinction be made between desired acquisition for deterrence, prestige, or other motivations unrelated to imminent use, and desired use in place of or in conjunction with conventional weapons or other weapons of mass destruction (WMD), namely chemical weapons (CW) and radiological and nuclear weapons.[21]

In comparison, a risk assessment follows the formula Risk = Hazard × Exposure, where risk is the magnitude and likelihood of adverse effect, hazard is the harm the agent will cause, and exposure is what population will be exposed to the agent, at what concentration, and for how long. Studies have been done that show that the risk of bioterrorism cannot be accurately assessed due to the imprecision inherent to such an undertaking.[22] Thus, using the above crop-duster scenario as a guide, the author will instead analyze the three dimensions of the threat assessment, paying specific attention to any recent changes that have taken place within each, in order to determine the current level of the bioterrorist threat in the United States.[23]

First, the vulnerability of the U.S. as a nation will be established in general terms. A discussion of capabilities will follow, addressing the following points: what agents warrant the most concern and why; who is in possession of or has access to seed cultures of pathogenic strains; and who can mass-produce and deliver them, and in what situations. Finally, the author will examine terrorist motivations in an attempt to elucidate who would actually use these agents if they could. The author will conclude with recommendations for addressing the current threat, as determined by the threat assessment.

I. Vulnerability

Vulnerability studies are most effective when addressing specific targets, for example the New York City subway system or the Capitol building, as opposed to the United States as a whole. In nonspecific terms, however, it can be stated with some certainty that this nation is in fact vulnerable on a number of levels.[24]

With open borders to goods and people and unregulated interstate movement, the transport of key personnel, equipment and pathogens is possible both into and within the country, despite the concerted efforts of officials and others in the wake of September 11th to tighten physical security along our borders and nationwide. Add to this the fact that the U.S. public health system has essentially been a victim of its own successes. For example, advances in infectious disease management, particularly heralded by the advent of new and improved antibiotics, led to the steadily improving general health of civilians of the middle and upper socioeconomic strata over the past few decades. Neglect in the form of budget cuts followed, leaving the nation largely unguarded against both emerging natural biological threats and deliberate advances (again, in spite of government efforts and great strides in the public health sector to address this problem post-9/11). Along these lines, emergency physicians, nurses, and technicians, as well as family practitioners and other members of the medical community who effectively represent the first line of defense against a biological attack, have virtually no practical experience in the recognition and management of those diseases most likely to be encountered in such an attack and at present have not been extensively trained to overcome this shortfall. And critical targeting information, for example the schematics of symbolic structures in the US, is available both in the open literature and over the Internet, making a potential terrorist's task that much easier.[25]

The hypothetical crop-duster scenario serves to illustrate these points. At that time, Washington DC would have been essentially defenseless against such a threat. While flight restrictions did exist over the metropolitan area (more on this later), crop-dusters are designed to fly low to the ground, below radar coverage of the Federal Aviation Administration (FAA).[26] Thus, it would have been feasible for an aircraft to take off from a remote location and proceed below radar coverage to the target area regardless of any restrictions, or even if radar identification had been made as it was on September 11th. Also, aerial photographs and maps, along with meteorological information vital for the delivery of a BW agent, were (and still are) commonly available in the public domain. And the civilian population was vulnerable: front-line physicians weren't aware of the presenting symptoms caused by the classical biological agents that would most likely be used in an attack, procedures for the rapid mobilization of national pharmaceutical stockpiles were untested, and the public wasn't psychologically ready.

The psychological component of bioterrorism is not to be underestimated because in any attack, biological or otherwise, mass hysteria has the potential to do far more damage than the agent itself. As just one example of this, the emergency department of Tel Aviv's Beilinson Medical Center reported that in 1991, during a stretch of a little over a month in which 39 modified Iraqi SCUD missiles reached Israeli terrain and 23 missile alerts were issued in Tel Aviv, the vast majority of patients who presented to the emergency department suffered from either acute psychological (anxiety) reaction or false atropine injection.[27] Appropriately, the ability to generate public panic has been specified by the Strategic Planning Workgroup of the Centers for Disease Control and Prevention (CDC) as one necessary criterion in order for a prospective agent to be considered a "high priority" threat to national security, as delineated by the workgroup's Category A listing of critical biological agents.[28]

In sum, the recently-released National Strategy for Homeland Security perhaps best states the inherent vulnerability of the US: "[o]ne fact dominates all homeland security threat assessments: terrorists are strategic actors. They choose their targets deliberately based on the weaknesses they observe in our defenses and our preparedness.... Our society presents an almost infinite array of potential targets that can be attacked through a variety of methods."[29]

II. Capability

Conceding that the United States is in fact vulnerable as a nation, the next question is whether a terrorist organization possesses the technical and organizational ability to conduct an attack. In order to attain a technical capability, four steps must be taken: an appropriate agent must be selected, a pathogenic strain of that agent must be acquired, the strain must be used to produce a sufficient amount of the agent in question, and the agent must be effectively delivered.

In terms of the hypothetical crop-duster scenario, before addressing these four points it first must be established that the interest expressed by Atta's group had in fact been with the dissemination of a BW agent in mind. It is important to point out that quite possibly Atta had been considering the crop-duster for something other than the dispersal of a BW agent.

The delivery of a CW agent may have been intended, for example the nerve agent sarin, which killed 12, injured over 1000, and led to the flooding of hospitals and emergency departments (again illustrating the significance of mass hysteria) in the 1995 Tokyo subway attack carried out by the doomsday cult Aum Shinrikyo ("Supreme Truth").[30] A 300-gallon crop-duster hopper tank, the smallest size available, would still be large enough to hold more than a ton of sarin, which according to Pentagon calculations is enough to kill 10,000 people.[31] In 1952, the U.S. BW program compared the effects of sarin with botulinum toxin, an apparent staple of today's suspected BW programs (as discussed below), and found that while botulinum toxin was more toxic upon inhalation, sarin was the more efficient agent in terms of its ability to both withstand the physical stressors of dispersal and create a lethal effect with minimal exposure.[32] Chemical agents are generally easier to produce than biological agents, and precursors for classical CW agents like hydrogen cyanide, which could be used for crude reparations such as those demonstrated in the al-Qa'ida videos discovered during the summer of 2002, are widely available.[33] When so-called toxic warfare is considered, which encompasses the use as a weapon of readily and legally accessible industrial chemicals and waste, this availability increases exponentially.[34] Chemical agents have the drawback of being highly susceptible to the effects of the wind, however, and the universal drawbacks to crop-duster use discussed below apply as well.

Another possibility is that Atta had planned to use the plane as a gasoline bomb, much like the airliners in the September 11th attack (airliners use a kerosene-based jet fuel, but the effect witnessed on 9/11 is essentially analogous to what would be expected with the same amount of gasoline). An Air Tractor 502–A, the prototypical aerial applicator worldwide, holds about 1,900 liters of liquid agent for dispersal and 800 liters of fuel.[35] Thus, if the hopper tank were filled with fuel as well, that plus the fuel in the tank would create a devastating explosion upon impact.[36] This possibility is particularly noteworthy because in light of 9/11 there was, at least prior to the anthrax letters, some renewed doubt as to whether terrorists were preparing to "cross the threshold" to WMD or whether the trend toward the use of conventional weapons—in line with what had previously been the most costly terrorist attack on U.S. soil in terms of human life, the Oklahoma City Bombing of 1995—would continue.

But assuming that the intention had been to employ a biological agent, a post-September 11th report by Dr. Christos Tsonas, an ER physician at Holy Cross Hospital in Fort Lauderdale, Florida, might offer a clue as to what agent Atta's group had intended to use.[37] Tsonas had seen two men in June, about three months before the attack, both of whom had identified themselves as pilots. One of these men presented with a lesion on his leg which he claimed had appeared after bumping into a suitcase two months earlier. The affected area, a well-demarcated dark lesion just less than an inch wide with raised red borders, did not appear to be a bruise, however.

The physician removed the dry scab, cleaned the wound, prescribed the antibiotic Keflex, and discharged the patient. At the time, he had viewed the bump explanation with some skepticism because both the timing and appearance of the lesion were unusual for a healthy young man with no diabetes or other illnesses that might predispose him to such a lesion. However, other potential diagnoses, such as a spider bite, were deemed equally unlikely. The diagnosis provided by Tsonas has not been reported in the open literature, but the patient's condition may have simply been listed as "cellulitis," a nonspecific and catch-all term for the inflammation of connective tissue, often of bacteriological origin.

After 9/11, the prescribed antibiotic was found among the personal belongings of hijacker Ahmed Alhaznawi of United Airlines Flight 93, which crashed in Pennsylvania. The man with him that day in the ER is believed to have been hijacker Ziad al-Jarrah, the suspected pilot of Flight 93. Apparently, the hijackers were well-dressed and had used their own names during their visit to the ER.

FBI officials showed Tsonas pictures of these two men, and he made positive identification. The FBI then gave Tsonas a copy of his own chart, and upon reviewing the case he offered that the lesion had been consistent with cutaneous anthrax. This was after the anthrax mail attacks had begun, the first letter of which had been to American Media Corporation in nearby Boca Raton, and Tsonas had been studying up on the disease. A subsequent review by experts from the Johns Hopkins Center for Civilian Biodefense Strategies verified Tsonas' impression, concluding that a diagnosis of cutaneous anthrax was "the most probable and coherent interpretation of the data available."[38]

In a separate report, a Delray Beach, Florida pharmacist claimed that Atta and another hijacker, Marwan al-Shehhi, had asked him for something to treat infections on Atta's hands.[39] Other circumstantial links between the hijackers and the anthrax mail attacks exist as well, including the close proximity of American Media to the hijackers' places of residence and the fact that Atta had rented his apartment from a woman whose husband was employed by the company. Anthrax, the disease resulting from *Bacillus anthracis* infection, occurs in three forms: cutaneous, gastrointestinal, and inhalational. While the major concern from a BW standpoint is the inhalational form of the disease, skin infections might offer a clue that the agent had been handled.

Ultimately, the FBI searched the cars, apartments and possessions of all of the known hijackers with negative results.[40] If some of the hijackers had been exposed to anthrax, it seems likely that the FBI would have found something; it also seems likely that any data points discussed here are an entirely separate debate from the anthrax letters. Regardless, these interesting coincidences—and more importantly the mail attacks themselves—offer a direction in terms of what might be the BW agent of choice in the terrorism sphere.

Agent Selection

The world seems on the surface to be filled with potential BW agents, but the truth is that many can be ruled out based on (1) access, and (2) infectiousness and pathogenicity.[41] The NATO Handbook on the Medical Aspects of NBC Defensive Operations lists 39 potential BW agents, but of these only a small number can be cultivated and dispersed effectively.[42] Thus, accessible and dangerous agents can be further limited to those that can be effectively produced and delivered. Other considerations include hardiness (environmental stability), resistance (e.g., to host immune defenses), senescence (aging characteristics), viability by aerosol, whether the agent is susceptible to current detection methods, availability of prophylactic and therapeutic measures, and contagiousness (the ability to spread from human to human, which may be seen as a desirable or undesirable trait).

In 1994, a Russian panel of BW experts listed in ranking order 11 agents "very likely to be used" in an attack based on the stringent evaluation of 10 criteria for efficient and effective BW use (see Figure 1.).[43] This list may also effectively represent what is available on the international market as a result of the Soviet Union's collapse, because most of the agents listed are known to have been weaponized, or suitably developed for use in a weapons system, by the former Soviet Union, with typhus and influenza being the only exceptions (typhus, however, is known to have been researched by the Soviets).[44]

Figure 1.

Agents most likely to be used in a BW attack according to the Criterion Rating

1. Variola major (smallpox)
2. *Bacillus anthracis* (anthrax)
3. *Yersinia pestis* (plague)
4. Botulinum toxin (botulism)
5. *Francisella tularensis* (tularemia)
6. *Burkholderia mallei* (glanders)
7. *Rickettsia typhi* (typhus)
8. *Coxiella burnetii* (Q fever)
9. Venezuelan Equine Encephalitis (VEE)
10. Marburg virus
11. Influenza virus

More recently in the year 2000, the Centers for Disease Control and Prevention's (CDC) Strategic Planning Workgroup devised a list of three categories of critical biological agents based in part on intelligence on the credibility of the threat each one poses, as determined by its toxicity, ease of production and delivery, and transmissibility, as well as the potential public health impact of its use.[45] This last consideration includes the effects of social disruption and panic, emphasizing yet again the mass hysteria effect discussed above. Threat Categories are denoted as A, B, and C, with Category "A" Agents deemed to be the greatest threat (see Figure 2.).

Figure 2.

Category "A" agents as listed by the CDC

1. Variola major
2. *Bacillus anthracis*
3. *Yersinia pestis*
4. Botulinum toxin
5. *Francisella tularensis*
6. Filoviruses and Arenaviruses

These agents generally line up with the top of the Russian list, with the hemorrhagic fever viruses (number 6) appearing as a unique entity most likely due to the potential impact associated with their use rather than the likelihood of it. The Russian list's parallel entry is number 10, "Marburg virus," a filovirus known to have been weaponized by the former Soviet Union.[46] The Soviets are also known to have researched Ebola virus, as well as Bolivian and Argentinean hemorrhagic fevers and Lassa fever.[47]

Of the seven state sponsors of terrorism, as designated by the U.S. State Department, at least five are suspected of having active BW programs: Iran, Iraq, Libya, North Korea, and Syria.[48] It has also been suggested that Cuba and Sudan, which round out the State Department's list, possess at least some capability in this area.[49] So-called failed states such as Afghanistan and Chechnya are also important to consider in the context of terrorism sponsorship as well as BW development, as experiences in these locations have shown. Discussion here will be limited to the five designated state sponsors listed above, however, with the goal being to gain some insight into what agents might be available through what state programs and to what terrorist groups.

For the record, it must first be stated that there is no evidence to date that any state has supplied BW capabilities to a terrorist organization. Regardless, it seems wise to prepare for this eventuality, and a superficial analysis of the biological agents thought to have been developed by these states of concern therefore appears to be in order.[50] It is believed that Iran has produced anthrax and botulinum toxin, as well as foot and mouth disease (a potentially devastating anti-livestock agent) and trichothecene mycotoxins (produced by fungi mainly of the *Fusarium* sp. and implicated in the alleged "yellow rain" attacks in Southeast Asia during the 1970s and early 1980s).[51] Following the Gulf War, it was revealed that Iraq had weaponized anthrax and botulinum toxin, along with ricin, aflatoxin (a hepatotoxic carcinogen produced by fungi of the genus *Aspergillus*), and wheat cover smut (an anti-plant agent).[52] Iraq had also researched camelpox and possibly plague—both of which will be discussed below—brucellosis, enterovirus 70 (a.k.a. hemorrhagic conjunctivitis), rotavirus, *Clostridium perfringens*, and trichothecene mycotoxins.[53] The current state of Iraq's BW program is unknown. Also unknown is what agents have been developed by Libya.[54] North Korea is thought to have worked with smallpox, anthrax, plague, and botulinum toxin, as well as typhus (number seven of the Russian expert list), yellow fever, typhoid, cholera, and tuberculosis.[55] And Syria is believed to have developed anthrax, botulinum toxin, and ricin.[56] A trend emerges from the above outline, namely that anthrax appears to be a primary component of every BW program, as does botulinum toxin.

Focusing on Iraq's list—derived from both the fourth Full, Final, and Complete Disclosure of the Iraqi National Biological Program compiled through 1996 for the United Nation's Special Committee (UNSCOM) as part of UN Security Council Resolution 687, the conditional cease-fire agreement that effectively ended the Gulf War, as well as from other governmental and nongovernmental evaluations—four agents that topped both the Russian expert list and the CDC list are prominent in this compendium as well: *Bacillus anthracis*, botulinum toxin, camelpox virus, and *Yersinia pestis*, the causative agent of bubonic and pneumonic plague.[57] Three of the four are classical BW agents, but why camelpox?

In terms of estimating the potential threat of Iraq's BW program, the camelpox virus has to be seen as representing smallpox, or Variola major. Both camelpox and smallpox are orthopoxviruses, a family of 11 closely-related DNA viruses. The central region of the orthopox family's genome is usually conserved from species to species because it houses genes essential for replication, while the outer ends, which contain variable instructions for host targeting, infectiousness, and resistance, tend to vary. The outer regions of the camelpox and smallpox virus genomes, however, are remarkably similar.[58] This close resemblance suggests to some that the Iraqis may have intended to develop an "ethnic weapon" from camelpox as a result of the selective pressures of mass production or even genetic engineering that in theory would affect populations not routinely exposed to camels more than the populations of Iraq, where the disease is endemic and where inhabitants presumably have developed or could easily develop antibodies to the virus. Others theorize that camelpox could be used to fill the evolutionary niche vacated by smallpox.[59] The main theory, however, is that in light of this close resemblance camelpox was used as a simulant for smallpox, offering the Iraqis a model for everything from the formulation, production, and delivery of the virus to the manipulation of its genome.

There are multiple points corroborating this final idea, all of which are circumstantial.[60] In 1994, UNSCOM inspectors discovered a large freeze-dryer, used to make biological products stable over long periods of time (and also to convert wet agents to dry form, a process discussed in some detail below), labeled with the Arabic word for "smallpox." The discovery was made at the maintenance shop of the State Establishment for Medical Appliances on the outskirts of Baghdad. Iraqi officials ensured the inspectors that the freeze-dryer was used for lyophilization of vaccinia, the smallpox vaccine virus, and not smallpox itself, an explanation which was accepted at the time but later called into question when after close to 4 years of steadfast denial Iraq finally admitted to the existence of an extensive BW program. That same year, the Defense Intelligence Agency reported that according to an unidentified scientist of the former Soviet BW program, Russia had provided both Iraq and North Korea with smallpox technology in the early 1990s. In the wake of Iraq's disclosure, the state relinquished a number of documents related to BW, among which were at least 3 papers on smallpox. Later, another document was recovered listing smallpox as one of the diseases against which Iraqi troops were being vaccinated in 1997. This information correlated with a 1991 report issued by the Armed Forces Medical Intelligence Center that the bloodwork of 8 out of 69 Iraqi enemy prisoners of war (EPWs) had revealed neutralizing antibodies against smallpox, indicating that they may have been vaccinated against the disease (these same blood samples had revealed protective antibodies against anthrax as well). This information, along with whatever intelligence had been amassed in the classified realm, led the CIA in 1998 to inform White House officials that Iraq had most likely been in possession of the smallpox virus, and that stockpiles of this agent had probably been effectively hidden from UNSCOM inspectors throughout the nineties.

If, for argument's sake, camelpox is taken to represent smallpox in the Iraqi arsenal, the core list of biological agents becomes *B. anthracis*, Variola major, botulinum toxin, and *Y. pestis*. It should be noted that this list reflects North Korea's suspected arsenal as well. Although any one of a number of agents could potentially be used for illicit purposes, the agents on the Russian expert list, narrowed down first to the CDC list and then further to these four agents, appear to be the most serious threats as far as impact is concerned. These are low probability but high impact threats, and because of the potentially devastating effects of their use, as well as limited time and resources, these threats presently warrant the focus of U.S. preparatory efforts despite the fact that other agents may still be used in lower impact scenarios, as discussed below.[61]

The spores of *B. anthracis* answer to a large degree the question "why anthrax?" All known past military BW programs have investigated anthrax spores in a weapons capacity, and most security analysts consider anthrax to be the major bioterrorist threat agent, mainly because these spores are not only deadly but also very hardy in the environment.[62] They do not desiccate (dehydrate) and are partially resistant to UV light, both of which are important characteristics in terms of effective dissemination.[63] An inhaled dose of 5 to 10 thousand spores is usually enough to cause infection, though the anthrax letter attacks suggest that this number may be much lower with respect to elderly or immunocompromised victims. There are approximately 5×10^{10} spores per gram in a dry, weapons-grade formulation of this agent. Therefore, one gram of weaponized spores is theoretically capable of generating 5×10^6 casualties if evenly dispersed over a densely populated city. In reality, a substantial portion of the payload would not reach the target population, but even if only 1 in 10,000 spores were to do so, an efficiency rate of 0.01%, given appropriate atmospheric conditions the release of one kilogram of anthrax spores over a large population could theoretically cause 500,000 casualties. Mortality for untreated inhalational anthrax is estimated to be about 80 percent, though it must be noted that the anthrax letters led to a mortality rate that was only half of that number,[64] presumably due to heightened awareness and rapid diagnosis and treatment of the disease following identification of the index case.

The smallpox virus would be very difficult for terrorists to acquire, but due to its contagiousness, disfiguring nature and estimated 30 percent lethality among unvaccinated individuals it has become the representative nightmare scenario as far as biological weapons are concerned. Unlike anthrax, *Y. pestis* and the other bacterial agents considered potential BW threats don't produce spores and thus require adequate formulation to prevent rapid die-off upon release, even under favorable meteorological conditions.[65] The pre-1969 U.S. biological weapons program demonstrated that effectively producing and dispensing *Y. pestis* is extremely challenging.[66] Similarly, scientists of the U.S. program learned that botulinum toxin is a very difficult substance to implement in any type of large-scale battlefield scenario because, like most toxins, its protein nature hinders stabilization and effective dissemination via aerosol. However, it is important to note that botulinum toxin, the most toxic substance known to science and more than 100 times more toxic than the nerve agent VX, was the agent of choice in Iraq's arsenal: as far as is known, the Iraqis deployed far more SCUD missiles and artillery shells armed with botulinum toxin than with any other agent, including anthrax spores.[67]

The other end of the spectrum, the "high probability, low impact" agents, generally consists of food- and waterborne pathogens such as *Salmonella*, *Shigella*, and *Vibrio* species, *Listeria monocytogenes*, and *Bacillus cereus*. The toxin SEB (staphylococcal enterotoxin B) might be added to this group for simplification. These agents are for the most part easy to acquire, particularly because they are often available in unprotected hospital labs. They are also cheap and easy to produce and use, and such use would conceivably equate to a public reaction equivalent to the anthrax letter attacks despite their generally non-lethal quality. There is a historical precedent for the illicit use of this type of agent. In 1984, the religious cult the Rajneeshees used a crude preparation of *Salmonella typhimurium* to contaminate a number of restaurant salad bars in the Dalles, Oregon, with the ultimate goal of swaying a local election.[68] This was the first known bioterrorist attack in the United States, and resulted in 751 illnesses but no deaths.[69] A similar agent, *Shigella dysenteriae* type 2, was used in 1996 to contaminate a number of muffins that were then placed in the employees' cafeteria of St. Paul Medical Center in Dallas, Texas. Hospital workers subsequently received an email saying to help themselves to the muffins, which many did, resulting in 12 illnesses and 4 hospitalizations.[70] 2 years later, Diane Thompson, a former employee of the hospital's laboratory, admitted to stealing and using a stock culture of *Shigella* for this and was sentenced to 20 years in prison.

A comparison of these 2 cases manifests the need to distinguish between *bioterrorism* and *biocriminality*. For the purposes of this assessment, bioterrorism will be defined as "the use of pathogens or toxins against human, animal, or plant populations by a terrorist group to achieve political, social, or religious aims."[71] The Rajneeshee incident is a good example.[72] Biocriminality, as was seen in the Diane Thompson case, will be defined as "the use of pathogens or toxins by an individual or group to attack human, animal, or plant populations for reasons of greed, blackmail, revenge, or other apolitical objectives."[73] It should be noted that it is often challenging to make this distinction.

The high probability, low impact agents serve as a reminder that the deadliest weapons are not necessarily the ones most likely to be used. What is the desired effect? What agents have been successfully used in the past to generate this effect? And what agents are the most accessible?

Acquisition

Agent acquisition is the first step toward establishing a capability, and as such presents a significant technical hurdle that must be overcome in order for an attack to be possible. While many potential sources for pathogens and toxins exist, some knowledge of and familiarity with a given agent is generally required in order to successfully procure it. Some locations where prospective BW agents may be available are (1) the environment, including soil, buried animals, and infected animals and humans; (2) U.S. culture collections, for example the American Type Culture Collection (ATCC); (3) foreign culture collections; (4) BW facilities of the former Soviet Union; (5) incubators and private culture collections housed in hospital microbiology laboratories, commercial medical laboratories, and academic laboratories; (6) military laboratories; and (7) vendors (see Figure 3.).

Figure 3.

Examples of BW agent acquisition by terrorist groups[74]

Rajneeshees:	purchased "bactrol disks," used in quality control and which contain *S. tphimurium*, from a medical supply company through a legitimate medical laboratory
Aum Shinrikyo:	obtained *C. botulinum* spores from soil, *B. anthracis* from a Japanese lab, and attempted to secure Ebola from victims of an outbreak in Zaire

Acquiring pathogens from the environment is a possibility, but attempts to do so would likely be ineffective unless the perpetrator possessed a firm understanding of certain epidemiological and microbiological techniques. Techniques described in the open literature could be employed to recover *B. anthracis* spores, for example, from the soil, where they exist in nature.[75] The monitoring of online surveillance sites such as ProMED for evidence of animal and human outbreaks could offer some direction to the search, as the soil in areas where anthrax is endemic is likely to contain an increased concentration of spores.[76] It is important to note, however, that a soil sample contains millions of microorganisms representing literally hundreds to thousands of different species.[77] Therefore, isolating the desired spores, if they are in fact present to begin with, requires a number of fairly technical steps.[78] *C. botulinum* spores also exist in the soil, but the same drawback applies.

Buried animals are another potential source of pathogens in the environment. In most industrialized countries, however, animals that succumb to anthrax, for example, are incinerated.[79] In other countries, if the number of dead animals overruns the capacity for incineration these cadavers may be buried in mass graves, but the locations of these graves are for the most part unpublicized such that only a few local inhabitants and officials know exactly where they might be found.[80] Presumably, an outsider asking questions about or digging in the vicinity of one of these graves would raise some suspicion, but if by chance he or she were able to dig up the site without being discovered the probability of collecting a sample containing viable organisms would still be quite low, because most pathogens are germinating cells and thus die soon after the host itself dies.[81] Even anthrax spores would be difficult to recover because the vegetative cells that cause death would be rapidly killed by resultant putrefaction and acidification, in most cases before spores could be formed.[82]

Briefly, it can be added that some perpetrators might travel to hot areas and pose as health care workers in order to gain access to certain agents. The precedent for this is what is believed to have been an unsuccessful attempt by members of Aum Shinrikyo to acquire Ebola virus from the blood of victims in Africa.[83]

The American Type Culture Collection (ATCC) and other U.S. culture collections contain seed stocks of a number of dangerous agents. In the mid-1980s, the Iraqi government purchased multiple strains from the ATCC which were subsequently developed into BW, an exchange which ultimately led to increased restrictions on the selling of pathogens from these collections. Then in 1996, trained microbiologist and anti-government Christian Patriot Larry Wayne Harris acquired three vials of freeze-dried *Y. pestis* from the ATCC as well, resulting in new legislation enacted by the U.S. Congress that made the transfer of certain pathogens across state borders without CDC clearance a criminal offense.[84] These two steps have made it more difficult, but not impossible, to attain pathogens from U.S. culture collections without proper credentials. Further, even if the system were to be subverted from within, for example by an employee of one of the organizations listed with the CDC, this action would now leave a substantial paper trail that would presumably lead to the rapid identification of the perpetrator (and that might therefore serve as a deterrent to acquisition in this fashion as well). The major weakness of the present system is that it does not regulate secondary shipment, such that if someone were to request a subculture from a colleague or acquaintance the transfer would probably go unnoticed.

In addition to the U.S. collections, there are approximately 1200 culture collections throughout the world, for example the Persian Culture Collection in Tehran, Iran. Very little open source information is available on the security of these facilities or the precautions they take to screen purchasers (if in fact they take any precautions at all).

Facilities of the former Soviet Union such as those that were once a part of Biopreparat, a network of approximately 50 pharmaceutical complexes secretly engaged in the development and production of biological weapons during the Cold War, may still house a number of already weaponized biological agents. The majority of these facilities have poor security, and most scientists working at them are poorly paid. Thus, a terrorist group might try to break in and steal certain cultures or attempt to bribe a scientist already on the inside to commit the act on its behalf. In April 1999, Agence France Presse reported that the terrorist group Islamic Jihad had obtained biological and chemical weapons from one of these facilities, and although this report has never been verified it serves to illustrate the potential for such acquisition.[85] More recently, a man was arrested in November 2002 after entering the Scientific Center of Quarantine and Zoonotic Infections, a former Soviet BW research facility in Almaty, Kazakhstan; allegedly, the man intended to steal vials and cultures of pathogens from the Center.[86]

Hospital microbiology laboratories are often unlocked and unguarded, as are the incubators inside these laboratories. Lab request forms identify each sample that passes through the laboratory in terms of its source, the organism recovered, and the antibiotic sensitivities of that organism, offering a potential roadmap to those in search of more dangerous or resistant pathogens. Further, most clinical microbiologists maintain private culture collections in unlocked cupboards or freezers. Hospital labs are not only accessible to staff, such as Diane Thompson of the *Shigella* incident, but ostensibly to outsiders as well, especially if the outsiders are disguised as hospital staff and act familiar with the setting. Academic laboratories at university hospitals are particularly noteworthy because their research is often highlighted on university websites and brochures, such that a terrorist group could potentially locate a specific pathogen based on knowledge of a given facility's work. However, the majority of these labs are protected by coded entry systems. While outsider access is generally limited by tight physical security, commercial clinical laboratories or reference laboratories containing a wide array of pathogens could potentially be targeted from within. As a final point, facilities within the pharmaceutical industry—for example Allergan, which is known to work with and produce botulinum toxin—could theoretically be targeted as well.

Military laboratories are generally considered in the context of state sponsorship, i.e., a state allowing a terrorist organization access to the pathogens in its lab. In addition, military laboratories in the U.S. might be considered potential sources of BW agents. For example, multiple specimens of anthrax spores, Ebola virus and other pathogens have over the past decade been reported missing from the U.S. Army Medical Research Institute of Infectious Diseases (USAMRIID), which took over facilities at Fort Detrick after the U.S. offensive BW program was abandoned under President Richard Nixon, a fact that suggests at least some level of vulnerability at this type of site.[87]

Vendor sources of potential BW agents can be legitimate, for example agricultural or chemical supply companies, or what would generally be considered illegitimate (albeit legal in many cases). As an example of the latter, in 1994 and 1995 four members of the anti-government group the Minnesota Patriots Council were convicted under the United States' 1989 Biological Weapons Anti-Terrorism Act for conspiring to kill law enforcement officials using ricin.[88] Years previously, these men had responded to a March 1991 advertisement in the right-wing *CBA Bulletin* for a "Silent Tool of Justice… Castor Beans… Silent Death… Including instructions for extracting the deadly poison 'Ricin' from Castor Beans."[89] Such extraction, which requires chemicals generally available in the average grocery store, was achieved by these individuals despite a lack of education and expertise: FBI analysis of the group's recovered stockpile revealed 0.7 grams of powdered ricin of 5 percent strength, estimated by USAMRIID to theoretically contain 129 lethal doses if evenly and effectively distributed.[90]

Given these and other potential sources, where might a supply of anthrax spores have come from in the hypothetical Atta case? An environmental source is possible but does not appear likely given the operational constraints of the group (see the discussion of organizational capability below). Acquisition from a potential state sponsor is supported by circumstantial evidence at best. Czech intelligence reports that Atta met with a senior Iraqi operative in Prague have gone unconfirmed by the CIA, FBI, and British Intelligence,[91] and reports of training links between Iraq and al-Qa'ida—mainly from a defector who served in Saddam Hussein's Fedayeen, one of Iraq's most brutal militias—are uniformly devoid of information pertaining to the transfer of agents or other sensitive materials.[92] As for al-Qa'ida itself, there is evidence of what had been a limited infrastructure for the development of BW agents in Afghanistan prior to U.S. military operations in the region.[93] In March 2002, it was learned that U.S. troops had discovered a laboratory under construction in southern Afghanistan intended for the production of *B. anthracis* and other deadly agents, a conclusion deduced from documents and equipment found at the site (although no traces of any agents themselves were found).[94] That same month, it was reported that trace amounts of both anthrax spores and ricin were found at 5 or 6 of the approximately 110 sites searched throughout Afghanistan, but that the amounts recovered were so small that they may have existed naturally in the environment and regardless were not significant enough to make any accurate determinations.[95] As a final point, it should be noted that outside Afghanistan, for example among the individual terrorist cells, the extent of al-Qa'ida's capability is unknown.[96]

Production

Assuming Atta's group were somehow able to acquire a *B. anthracis* seed stock, the next question is whether it could have successfully produced a substantial amount of spores.[97]

The initial consideration is acquiring the expertise, whether from imported, hired, or homegrown scientists, to carry out such a task. The major concern with respect to imported or hired scientific expertise, dubbed "brain drain," is the former Soviet BW program once again, which employed approximately 65,000 scientists.[98] For example, a December 1998 report by the *New York Times* stated that Iran had recruited at least five Russian BW experts by offering them $5000 a month for their services (versus their regular salary of $100 a month).[99] South Africa's apartheid-era BW program, Project Coast, also trained a number of scientists and therefore must be considered a potential source of brain drain as well. It has been reported for example that Wouter Basson, the program's alleged ringleader, made 5 trips to Libya for unknown reasons after Coast was dissolved in the 1990s.[100] While these examples illustrate the potential transfer of knowledge to states and not necessarily terrorist organizations, the concept is the same.

It should be remembered that these scientists might be pursued simply as consultants. For example, it has been reported that on at least one occasion during a trip to Russia, Aum Shinrikyo chief engineer Kyohide Hayakawa attempted to contact former Biopreparat deputy Anatony Vorobyov in order to learn the technological secrets of the former Soviet BW program.[101] Theoretically, this approach could also be carried out over the Internet, enabling a given terrorist group to benefit from a scientist's technical know-how without physically recruiting him or her, but there is no evidence for or against such distant collaboration at present. Information on how to grow many of the bacterial and viral pathogens on the CDC list—as well as information on aerosolized microbes, dispersal systems, and so on—is widely available in the public domain.[102] And over the past few decades, the number of trained microbiologists has been steadily increasing worldwide, making this information particularly useful to an ever growing number of individuals able and possibly willing to misuse it.

The equipment required to produce biological weapons is widely available on the open market because of its dual-use nature, meaning that the same materials and thus knowledge required for the peaceful development and production of commercial products like food additives, pesticides, pharmaceuticals, and vaccines can be diverted toward the production of biological weapons with relative ease. For example, the large-scale production of the biopesticide *Bacillus thuringiensis* reflects in striking detail the manufacture of *Bacillus anthracis* as a weapon in terms of both equipment and methodology. Dual-use equipment is notoriously difficult to identify and track, and such varied techniques as those used to produce live vaccines, single-celled protein, and even beer can be applied to BW production.

Equipment doesn't necessarily have to be acquired in order to produce BW, however, as illustrated by the late 1971 and 1972 group RISE (an acronym for the Reconstruction—the meaning of the "I" remains uncertain—of Society Extermination).[103] Formed by teenagers Allen Schwandner and Steven Pera (along with five other friends), RISE apparently sought, at least initially, to wipe out all of mankind with the exception of its own members and a few friends.[104] Pera, a laboratory assistant in a Chicago hospital at the time, used the hospital's equipment to successfully grow small amounts of *C. botulinum*, *Neisseria meningitidis*, *Salmonella typhi*, *Shigella sonnei*, and *Corynebacterium diphtheriae* for this purpose (note the prominence of high probability, low impact agents in Pera's collection).[105] The group was discovered shortly thereafter, before any further preparations could be made and before any specific attack was planned.

The primary concern in terms of production is the successful manufacture of an aerosolizable agent that can be delivered in 1 to 5 micron size particles.[106] This is the desired range because particles of this size are readily absorbed in the lungs upon inhalation, but it should be added that larger particles up to 20 microns in size may embed in the upper respiratory tract with significant effect as well. Because biological weapons are not volatile like chemical weapons, the endpoint of production is either a wet or dry agent. As a rule, the preparation of a dry agent, like the anthrax spores used in the mail attacks, requires more elaborate equipment than that of a wet agent.

Some viruses are sufficiently hardy to be used in either wet or dry preparations, especially smallpox, but again the acquisition of a seed stock is a nearly insurmountable obstacle to acquiring a capability with this particular agent. Bacteria are generally easier to produce than viruses because viruses are most often grown in either fertilized eggs or cell culture in order to provide the host machinery they require for replication.[107] At least one alternative to these technically demanding production techniques does exist, however, that is far more basic and would allow for the propagation of a virus with very little technical expertise.

As far as bacterial production is concerned, if a virulent strain of *B. anthracis* were acquired, it could probably then be cultured and propagated fairly easily in a home laboratory because it grows well in commonly available nutrient media at an achievable temperature. Although it is technically more demanding to convert these germinating cells to spores, information on how to do so is available in the open literature. A culture medium inoculated with a seed culture of *B. anthracis* or another bacterium and allowed to ferment properly would, upon separation of the biomass by centrifugation, yield a cloudy solution containing approximately 10^8 to 10^{10} spores per milliliter. This solution would have to be used fairly quickly: for example, *Y. pestis* would probably survive only about 2 weeks at room temperature or 6 weeks at 4 degrees Celsius, while *B. anthracis* might survive a month.[108]

A large financial investment is not required to accomplish such a task. A 2-liter batch fermenter costs approximately $1400, while a 2-liter continuous fermenter, which yields almost ten times as much product per volume of culture as a batch fermenter, can currently be purchased on the open market for approximately $5500.[109] For less than $10,000 then, a scientist or group could in fact establish an effective production capability. In order to gain insight into the feasibility of such efforts, in the late 1990s the CIA built a much larger capacity fermenter for approximately $1 million with parts purchased from hardware stores and other suppliers in the public domain.[110] Due to the lack of signatures associated with BW development, this project remained hidden from both the media and the public until the CIA chose to disclose it, illustrating the ease with which a group might keep such an endeavor secret.

The major technical hurdle to aerosol delivery of a basic wet preparation is overcoming the rapid clogging of disseminating nozzles upon initiation of dispersal. Further, the bulk of agent successfully extruded before clogging forms heavy particles that fall innocuously to the ground. Regardless, this approach can in theory generate mass casualties. It should be added that a very low tech approach precluding the need for a fermenter also exists that might offer a terrorist a proportionally lower chance of success, but a chance nonetheless.

The initial wet preparation can be taken a step further in two separate ways. It can either be suspended in a "formulation" of adjuvants, preservatives, and other chemicals, or dried and then milled to attain the proper-sized particles. Either of these processes demands much more technical ability but yields a far better agent in terms of ease of dissemination and overall effect. The resulting agent can also be stored for much longer periods of time in either case. Dry agents can be taken an additional step further and specially formulated as well, as was the case in the anthrax letters, to prevent clumping due to electrostatic forces. This clumping results in large particles that are either blocked by the mucociliary response of the respiratory tract or fall harmlessly to the ground.

After the Gulf War, it was learned that the Iraqi program, which had been operating for at least 5 years and was very well-funded, had only deployed BW arms in wet formulations despite the possession of dryers and grinders.[111] This effectively illustrates the extent of the leap in going from wet to dry. It must be recognized, however, that years of trial-and-error time toward accomplishing this feat have since passed, and in that time an abundance of information has emerged in the public domain that would prove useful in such an undertaking. Moreover, it has now been demonstrated to the world that this technical hurdle can be overcome.

The anthrax letters of 2001 proved that the technical demands of dry preparation, formulation, and aerosol dissemination can be met, conceivably outside the construct of a state-level program. Regardless of who or what group was responsible, these technical hurdles appear to be eroding. In addition, the letters demonstrated the extensive impact that even a limited threat can have: at the outset of the research process for this writing, the price tag on 23 CDC-confirmed cases and 5 deaths was approximately $6 billion. This profound impact may lead to what's known as a demonstrator effect, i.e., an increased prevalence of copycat letters. Such has indeed been the case, as illustrated by the increased number of hoaxes witnessed in the wake of the mail attacks: while over 400 anthrax threats were documented from March of 1998 to September 11, 2001, more than 1500 threats or hoaxes were recorded from September 11th through mid-2002.[112] While these hoaxes were in many cases handled routinely or even dismissed altogether prior to the events of last fall, such a lax response is no longer possible. Thus, hoaxes now categorically serve as a significant drain on public health resources, an effect compounded by the economic and psychological consequences of these false alarms. Perhaps more importantly, the demonstrator effect is not necessarily limited to hoaxes. Determined individuals or groups who have witnessed the success of the letters could conceivably be motivated to redouble their efforts with the newfound confidence that what was once though nearly impossible can in fact be done.

Delivery

Mode of delivery is generally based on whether the agent is contagious, like the smallpox virus or *Y. pestis*, or noncontagious, like *B. anthracis* or botulinum toxin. As a general rule, contagious agents require a comparatively low tech delivery system that begins with the deliberate infection of a small group or individual, whether that group or individual is unaware of it or is knowingly infected as a so-called smallpox "suicide bomber" would presumably be. This group or individual then serves as a delivery device, spreading the disease by secondary transmission. Such an approach eliminates the need for mass production of the contagious agent (only a small amount is needed to initiate the chain of events potentially leading to an epidemic), specific formulation, or the design of an effective dissemination device. It should be noted, however, that the use of more sophisticated delivery methods for contagious agents cannot be ruled out, as suggested by both the aerosol testing of smallpox and the deployment of ICBMs containing smallpox as [their] payload by the former Soviet Union. Other possible means for spreading a contagious agent, such as the exploitation of zoonotic transmission or the contamination of illicit drugs, exist as well.

The threat of a smallpox suicide bomber has been the focal point of numerous media reports over the past year. A focused assessment has yet to be presented, however, to offer the public some perspective on the potential for success with this type of attack. Without vaccination the human body is susceptible to smallpox, indicating an underlying vulnerability of the U.S. and world population to this virus. However, even if intent—in other words whether what is known about conventional suicide bombers would translate to this type of event—is conceded, there is still a capability issue that must be addressed in order to gain an accurate understanding of this threat.[113] Indeed, if the agent were somehow to be acquired, initiating an epidemic would nevertheless be more complicated than simply injecting it, waiting for a rash, and going to a public place. This is similar to variolation, the immunization technique employed against smallpox before Dr. Edward Jenner developed his breakthrough vaccine from cowpox in 1796 (this cowpox vaccine is the predecessor to the vaccinia vaccine used today).[114] Although a potential suicide bomber might develop fulminating smallpox from such an injection, he or she would be more likely to develop a mild infection with or without a rash that in most cases would not lead to shedding of the virus and secondary spread.[115] There is a historical precedent suggesting the possibility of success with this approach, however: a Revolutionary War siege of Quebec City by Benedict Arnold's Continental Army was halted when smallpox, reportedly introduced into the American ranks by civilians deliberately variolated by the British, broke out among nearly half of Arnold's men.[116] Regardless, the overall likelihood of success with this type of attack is believed to be quite low, especially when the difficulty of acquisition is taken into account.

Non-contagious agents can be delivered using methods ranging from injection to the contamination of food or water to airborne dissemination. Delivery via injection was seen in the 1978 assassination of Bulgarian dissident Georgii Markov with a steel pellet filled with ricin. The pellet was covertly delivered by a Bulgarian secret service agent through the tip of a pneumatic umbrella as Markov was waiting for a bus on Waterloo Bridge in London. A fragmentary bomb with laced shrapnel offers an alternative means for this type of delivery. Such bombs were developed, for example, by scientists of Japan's World War II era BW program "Unit 731," using *Clostridium perfringens*, the causative agent of gas gangrene. More recently, penetrating bone fragments from a suicide bomber in Israel infected a victim with hepatitis B.[117] Although it is highly unlikely that this transmission was deliberate, the event shows that explosive dissemination of an infectious agent in this way is in fact possible.

Contamination of a targeted water supply is very challenging in a number of respects. A given water supply can in the simplest terms be divided into two systems, the pretreatment system and the post-treatment system. The pretreatment portion is almost always a closed system that carries water from its source (for example, a reservoir, Lake Michigan, or the Potomac River) through multiple filters designed to remove particles as small as 0.03 microns in size to a treatment plant, where it is then chlorinated and often treated with ozone as well.[118] The vulnerability comes in the post-treatment area, where contamination can occur via access to storage towers or reservoirs or alternatively via back pressure, in which a vacuum pump is used at a remote faucet or water fountain to force an agent back into the water supply.[119] There remains a very large dilutional effect as well as residual chlorination in the post-treatment system, however, likely minimizing the chance of success with this type of attack.[120] Food and beverage industries are also minimally vulnerable: a terrorist operative covertly placed inside a production or distribution facility could conceivably mount a successful attack from within that with the aid of a given company's own distribution system would then reach a wide target population.

Except for a few very rare exceptions, aerosolized biological agents have to be inhaled to be effective, unlike classical chemical weapons like mustard gas and nerve agents (sarin and VX, for example) that can be absorbed through the skin.[121] Thus, the aerosol dissemination of a BW agent almost always targets the human respiratory system, necessitating (as stated previously) the distribution of proper-sized particles in order for successful absorption and effect. Three general approaches exist for this type of delivery: point source, multiple point source and line source delivery.

Point source delivery traditionally employs a munition—for example an artillery shell, bomb, or rocket (but possibly something as simple as a glass flask containing a biological agent that could be smashed to create a dispersive effect)—that delivers its payload as a stationary source. Impact or detonation causes a burster charge within the munition to explode and the payload to be released. The wind then directs the payload's spread over (or away from) a target population. Point source delivery is considered highly inefficient because approximately 95 to 99 percent of the agent is destroyed in the blast, and much of what survives is driven into the ground or broken down into very small particles that either disperse too widely or are inhaled and exhaled right back out again.

Other theoretically more efficient methods for point source attacks do exist, however, that are considered to be more likely to be seen in a terrorism scenario. An example is the attack of a building's air handling system in which the nozzle of a spraying device is placed into the air intake duct and flow initiated, allowing fans within the air handling system to circulate the agent throughout the building. It should be emphasized that some question remains as to whether the filtration devices inside these systems might offer some protection in the event of an attack, as well as whether anthrax spores in particular might stick to the walls inside the system. Of note, the anthrax letters served as munitions for point source dispersal, and when delivered simultaneously for multiple point source dispersal as well (see below).

Aum Shinrikyo carried out several unsuccessful biological attacks using the point source approach.[122] On two separate occasions, cult members used a sprayer system to release wet anthrax into a giant fan situated atop an eight story building. Apparently, the attempts were made with an avirulent strain of the pathogen used in animal prophylaxis against anthrax and were therefore ineffective.[123]

Multiple point source dispersal is fairly self-explanatory. The classic example is what would be seen in a bombardment. Another approach is the implementation of multiple dispersal devices coordinated by timing mechanisms, a technique also employed by Aum in an unsuccessful attempt to deliver botulinum toxin among a localized target population.[124] Cult members positioned three briefcases equipped with small tanks, vents, and battery-powered fans in a Tokyo subway station, but upon activation the released contents had no effect because an Aum member had sabotaged the operation by filling the tanks with water. Regardless, it appears that Aum was never able to acquire a toxigenic strain of *C. botulinum*, suggesting that even if the operator had loaded what he or she believed to be botulinum toxin into the tanks the attack would nevertheless have been ineffective. It is widely held that this failed attack directly led to the group's decision to use sarin (and to deliver it in a relatively unsophisticated way) in the successful Tokyo subway attack, which took place only five days later.

Line source distribution removes the static element of the dispersal system, such that a moving delivery device releases a flow of agent over an extended period of time. Aum attempted this type of dispersal on multiple occasions as well, again unsuccessfully.[125] As just one example, cult members drove a truck equipped with a custom-made spraying device around the Imperial Palace and Tokyo Tower, intent on distributing a wet anthrax solution. They again used a non-pathogenic strain for this, however, and in any event the nozzle on the truck had apparently clogged prior to the operation and was thus nonfunctional at the time of intended release.

In general, Aum's biological effort can be summarized by its unsuccessful nature. Although a relatively sophisticated operation powered by physicians and scientists with substantial finances and equipment at their fingertips, the program's advance was persistently stalled by the inability of its members to overcome two specific hurdles: acquisition of a pathogenic strain and effective delivery.[126] This experience provides support for the notion that mounting a successful biological attack is not as simple as knowing the information, having the resources, and wanting to do it. It should be remembered, however, that a rumored attack or an attack with an avirulent strain can still lead to significant panic and quickly drain resources vital to the nation's healthcare system and economy. It is also important to remember that the bulk of Aum's biological pursuits occurred approximately 10 years ago. Since that time, the availability of mass casualty agents has increased, as has the number of microbiologists capable of producing such agents; access to Soviet agents and expertise has improved, as has that to the scientists of current and deceased state level programs such as the Iraqi program and Project Coast; information has become more readily available as a result of the Internet; technical hurdles have been steadily eroding, as demonstrated by the anthrax letters; genetic engineering has gained prominence, and so on. And perhaps most importantly, it must be remembered that Aum unequivocally demonstrated that groups do exist that are willing to use these agents, as discussed below.

The classic line source dispersal device is a crop-duster, ideally flown crosswind upwind of a target such that the stream of released agent is carried over the target area.[127] The spraying mechanism of a crop-duster, like that of other agriculture and painting equipment, consists of a hopper tank, a source of compressed air, one or multiple feeding tubes from the hopper tank, and nozzles for expulsion.[128] The compressed air propels material from the hopper tank through the tube or tubes and out the nozzles, which break up the dispersed agent unevenly to produce a wide range of particle sizes. Some of these are 1 to 5 microns, and are thus readily absorbed in the lungs. Most, however, are either too large and fall to the ground or get trapped by mucociliary defenses of the upper respiratory system, or too small and float away or get breathed in and out. The average particle size produced by a crop-duster is approximately 100 microns (a size that causes the particles to descend to the ground, as intended).

Special nozzles with small orifices can be attached to deliver a more uniform size in the desired range. Pressure must be increased accordingly to adequately force the material through these smaller outputs, but as far as crop-dusters are concerned this does not present an insurmountable challenge: most crop-dusters are capable of delivering 40 pounds-per-square-inch of pressure already, which can be enough to overcome wall tension without alteration. Nozzle adjustment, on the other hand, demands a great leap in terms of technical capability, and effectively eliminates the possibility of a "grab-and-go" scenario in which a crop-duster is commandeered at an airfield and used immediately without modification. Regarding the hypothetical crop-duster scenario, this discussion might offer some insight into why Atta had perhaps planned to build the dispersal system himself: if his intention had been to dispense a biological agent, he conceivably could have been aware of the need to incorporate a proper nozzle size.

Even if a group or individual were to successfully modify the aircraft, because a given biological preparation contains protein it would clog the altered nozzles fairly quickly upon initiation of dispersal. This is particularly true if a wet agent were used, as was the case in the Aum Shinrikyo attack described above. In addition, the propulsion of a given preparation through any type of sprayer creates a shearing effect that can kill 95 percent or more of the agent. Because crop-duster hopper tanks hold from approximately 1100 to 3000 liters of solution, however, the five percent that does survive might still be enough to have a devastating effect if a substantial amount of the total potential payload is released before the nozzles clog.

The challenges inherent to any type of wet aerosol delivery are significant but not insurmountable, as illustrated by the fact that both the former U.S. and former Soviet Union's BW programs were able to develop reliable methods for wet agent dispersal. Further, UNSCOM inspections revealed that sprayers and holding tanks had been installed on a number of Iraqi military aircraft and land vehicles. It was subsequently learned that in 1990, the Iraqis had modified a Mig-21 so that it could be a remotely piloted, equipped it with a 2200 liter belly tank from a Mirage F1 fighter plane, put in a spray mechanism, and field tested it with the anthrax simulant *Bacillus subtilis var. niger* (BG) in January 1991.[129] Although the results of the test are unknown, the delivery system nevertheless represents a significant advance in Iraq's technical capability. Of course, these accomplishments were fueled by the virtually limitless funding of dedicated state BW programs, and therefore do not reflect the capabilities of most if not all terrorist organizations at this time.

With respect to the use of a crop-duster as a dissemination device, handling the plane itself is considered the final hurdle to acquiring technical capability. Loading the hopper tank is challenging; taking off requires considerable skill on the part of the pilot; and once airborne, the plane is very difficult to fly, especially with a full load at a low altitude. This might explain why Atta had planned to modify a twin-engine passenger plane instead.

The Hypothetical Attack

Hurdles aside, the potential for the equipment and know-how to fall into the wrong hands is real. Thus, it may prove useful to contemplate what might have happened had Atta's group overcome the technical barriers of acquisition, production and formulation, as well as the barriers to crop-duster use, and carried out an attack on the Washington, DC area.

In a 1950 U.S. Army simulation, BG was dispersed and its spread monitored to assess the potential impact of a comparable release of anthrax spores.[130] Of note, the test employed off-the-shelf technology that has improved tremendously in the last half-century. Despite this limitation, a 2-mile dissemination line yielded a highly infectious area approximately 6 miles in length, with simulant traveling a maximum distance of 23 miles. In all, the release covered approximately 100 square miles, with an infectious area large enough to cover the entire metropolitan DC area.

The simulation began at 5 PM and lasted only 29 minutes. Test conditions included a relative humidity of 100 percent and a 5 mile-per-hour (mph) wind. The agent was released from the deck of a boat, so no data was generated supporting a certain altitude as the most effective for the release of BG (data which would be useful in the crop-duster scenario). However, field tests have shown that 1 to 5 micron particles sprayed by aircraft traveling at an altitude of over a few hundred meters quickly dissipate and thus have virtually no effect, demonstrating the need for a low altitude release in order to achieve the goal of the mission. As mentioned, flying at a low altitude also helps avoid radar detection.

Two atmospheric conditions are desirable in the planning of a biological attack: a 3 to 6 mph wind is considered optimal, as is the presence of an inversion layer, which occurs when a relatively low-lying blanket of warmer air holds a layer of cool air in place below it. This cool air in turn holds the aerosol cloud close to the ground and thus the target population. Inversion layers usually occur a few hours before sunrise, at a time when there is no ultraviolet (UV) light from the sun. UV light kills most pathogens, and also causes atmospheric turbulence that can break up an aerosol cloud. For all of these reasons, the pre-dawn hours are generally considered the most opportune time for an attack. For these same reasons, the pre-dawn hours are the normal spraying time of crop-dusters in the agricultural industry (except in desert areas where spraying often takes place at night), meaning that a crop-duster taking off or flying before sunrise is unlikely to draw suspicion. It should be noted that the simulation, although it had the right wind, did not take place in the presence of an inversion layer or in the absence of sunlight and was still very effective. It is also important to note that *B. anthracis* spores remain stable for several hours in an atmosphere devoid of sunlight, and a considerable amount of time when exposed to UV light as well.

As a basic rule, the higher the temperature and the lower the relative humidity, the faster the desiccation (i.e., dehydration) of an aerosolized agent. Therefore, the 100 percent humidity at the time of the simulation may have allowed for improved dispersal, although it must be conceded that anthrax spores are by nature resistant to desiccation (which, as mentioned, is one of the reasons why they make such a good weapon). Other factors like pollution fall outside the scope of this discussion, but it should be remembered that such less obvious considerations play a role as well.

Had Atta known what time of day was best to go, with what humidity and what wind, he could have monitored the National Weather Service or other sites and waited for the desirable conditions to be present.[131] A 1993 Office of Technology Assessment (OTA) study estimated that the release of 100 kilograms of anthrax spores upwind of the Washington, DC area in such conditions could result in between 130,000 and 3 million deaths, a lethality matching or exceeding that of a hydrogen bomb.[132] Although HEPA (High Efficiency Particulate Air) filters—which advertise a 99.97 percent filtration rate of particles 0.3 microns in size (indicating even better filtration of particles both larger and smaller than 0.3 microns)—and other barriers would limit the impact of this release inside certain buildings, most interior areas would be vulnerable to penetration of the spores via open windows or air intake ducts, meaning that those individuals outside in the hours following the attack would not be the only ones at risk of infection.[133]

The repercussions of such an attack, if successful, would ultimately be profound. Thus, this hypothetical scenario serves as an effective illustration of the inverse relationship between probability and impact, a relationship characteristic of those biological threats most commonly feared by security analysts and civilians alike.

Organizational Capability

While it will only receive very brief mention here, organizational capability is in fact a critical component of every step in the capability progression, from acquisition to production to delivery. Essentially, this is the ability of a group to avoid being penetrated by informers or being discovered in any way. Both Aum Shinrikyo and the Rajneeshees possessed this capability, and thus their attacks were not discovered until long after they had actually taken place. Given Atta's behavior in the USDA office, it might seem that his group would not have had the organizational capability to elude discovery prior to any kind of attack, but on September 11th that certainly was not the case… which leads to intent.

III. Intent

Even if the technical and organizational capability is there, in order for a threat to be considered real there must be intent. Who might actually want biological weapons and why, and who would use them if they could? To address this complex question, it proves useful to first consider four broad categories—among which significant crossover exists—of terrorists or criminals who might try to acquire a BW capability: state-sponsored terrorist groups; large terrorist or criminal groups; small terrorist or criminal groups; and the lone operator.

State-sponsored terrorist groups such the Palestinian groups HAMAS and Islamic Jihad top the list because these groups potentially have access to state BW programs and their agents. Representatives of these groups have at times publicly expressed an interest in BW. For example, Nassar Asad Al-Tamimi, a leader of Palestinian Islamic Jihad, stated in April 1998 that "Jihad has at last discovered how to win the holy war—lethal germs."[134] It is difficult to assess whether agent possession in such a case would serve only as a deterrent or whether use would follow. Because most state-sponsored groups are in some way political entities enmeshed in their respective societies, many analysts believe that such use would be counterproductive to the perpetrator's cause.

The second category consists of large terrorist or criminal groups with substantial resources, namely major drug cartels (or gangs) such as those in Afghanistan and Colombia, large independent terrorist groups like al-Qa'ida or the IRA and religious cults like Aum Shinrikyo, and multinational corporations. Drug cartels already possess well-equipped and well-staffed chemical laboratories that could be redirected to produce biological agents with relative ease, the likelihood of which will assuredly increase should the United Nations Drug Control Program (UNDCP) ever choose to use those fungal agents it has specifically developed to kill opium poppies (certain strains of *Pleospora papaveracea*, for example) on the crops of these cartels.[135] Large terrorist groups and religious cults have access to the funding and manpower necessary to establish a BW capability.[136] And multinational corporations, although not perceived as a present threat, do possess extensive dual-use equipment along with educated scientists and staff that could conceivably be misappropriated to produce BW if a pathogenic strain were acquired. Possible goals in this case might be to eliminate a particular competitor or to increase demand for one of its own products. No such action has ever been reported.

If smaller groups such as domestic militias or criminal organizations were to pursue a BW capability, they would presumably be limited in a number of respects. Expertise and equipment would most likely be of local origin and agents locally acquired, for example from unprotected hospital laboratories. Thus, the predominant threat with respect to these groups is a high probability, low impact threat, as demonstrated by the Rajneeshee attack of 1984. The Minnesota Patriots Council did manage to acquire a lethal agent in ricin, but this does not necessary reflect a large potential for lethal capability among these smaller groups, as ricin in particular is an unusual entity in that castor beans are easy to obtain and the subsequent extraction process is very straightforward. Upon acquisition of a BW capability, potential targets for these agents include the federal or state government and specific nations, races, or populations.

The final category is the lone operator, which essentially represents the disgruntled scientist and which some security analysts still believe to be the greatest domestic threat in the U.S. at this time despite the events surrounding 9/11.[137] Examples include Larry Wayne Harris, who acquired *Y. pestis* from the ATCC, and Diane Thompson, who poisoned the muffins in Texas. If a lone operator were to establish a BW capability, this would not only bring about the potential for subsequent use but also might serve in a capacity similar to the demonstrator effect described above, indirectly providing terrorist organizations with knowledge or ideas beneficial to their own pursuits. For example, had a terrorist group learned that Larry Wayne Harris successfully acquired *Y. pestis* from the ATCC before more stringent regulations were enacted, it could have tried the same approach.[138]

Over the past few decades, the potential for establishing a BW capability has been steadily increasing. Knowledge has become more available, and agents more accessible. Yet for a substantial portion of that time, terrorist motivations to acquire such a capability remained relatively low. In the year 1995, however, certain events led many security analysts to doubt whether the trend would continue: the Oklahoma City Bombing, Aum Shinrikyo's Tokyo subway attack, the disclosure of South Africa's former BW program Project Coast, and verification by the Iraqi government that it had built an extensive BW program of its own (this all only a short time after the dissolution of the Soviet Union and the containment problems that followed). These isolated incidents were essentially viewed by the international community as pieces of the same puzzle, and the term "new terrorism" was born.

The term has since been transformed to represent the present phase of a dynamic threat. Loosely-linked transnational terrorist networks motivated primarily by religious ideologies have replaced the more "traditional" terrorists motivated primarily by politics, and these new organizations do not appear to be bound by the same constraints as their predecessors. New terrorism, as it is now commonly understood, is therefore considered to be much more in line with the intent to pursue and actually use a biological weapon.

Historically, eight characteristics have suggested a propensity for such intent (see Figure 4.). Do these qualities and motivational factors translate to the so-called new terrorist? Evidence appears to be mounting that the answer will be yes. Al-Qa'ida, for example, has demonstrated each of these attributes. More data is warranted, however, before this can be stated with any degree of conviction.

Figure 4.

Attributes associated with CW and BW terrorism in the past[139]

1. Paranoia and grandiosity
2. Lack of political constituency
3. Closed cult or splinter group (or loner)
4. Charismatic, violence-prone leader
5. Apocalyptic ideology
6. Escalatory pattern of violence[140]
7. Technical and tactical innovation
8. Fascination with poisons or plagues

In the final analysis, the willingness of Mohammad Atta and his group to indiscriminately inflict mass casualties, coupled with the organizational and technical ability to do so, suggests to some an escalating trend toward the inevitable use of WMD. Others in the security community question this interpretation, citing the need for a better understanding of a given group's individual goals before such a determination can be made. While it is of course possible to have a best guess with respect to this issue, there is always some underlying level of uncertainty. Thus, from a policy-making standpoint intent must be assumed.

Conclusion: Threat = Capability?

From the above threat assessment, a number of important conclusions can be drawn. First, open societies, the U.S. in particular, are inherently vulnerable to a biological attack. Second, there has been a sharp increase in threats and hoaxes in the past year plus, largely as a result of the anthrax letters. Third, the organizational capability necessary to carry out a biological attack has been demonstrated, both by the anthrax mail attacks and the coordinated attacks of September 11th. Fourth, because intent cannot be uniformly determined with a high degree of accuracy (despite the delivery of the anthrax letters last fall), this intent must be assumed by policymakers tasked with establishing an appropriate level of preparedness and adequate response capability. Fifth, while high probability, low impact threats offer the greatest likelihood of success, in view of limited resources and a pressing timeline it is prudent at this juncture to direct preparedness efforts toward the management of the "low probability, high impact" threats such as anthrax and smallpox, the effective delivery of which could not only devastate a population and trigger large-scale economic fallout but also scar the collective consciousness of humanity for untold generations to come.[141] And finally, these conclusions suggest that whether an individual or group can overcome the technical hurdles of acquisition, production, and delivery will determine whether an attack is ultimately carried out, and if so whether that attack will be successful.

But that doesn't mean that the world is helpless. The potential threat can be addressed, and defensive measures can be taken. These measures exist on three levels: immediate steps, middle range goals that are feasible with effort, and long term goals that require substantial attention. Essentially, these three levels reflect the three components of the threat assessment.

Immediate measures tend to address vulnerabilities. A primary objective in this respect is the enhancement of physical security around potential targets. Another is the improved surveillance, detection and reporting of infectious diseases in the public health sector, a critical task in that it improves the ability of a nation such as the U.S. and the international community at large to identify and manage not only deliberate outbreaks orchestrated by terrorists or states but also the natural outbreaks of emerging and re-emerging diseases. In terms of worldwide impact, natural disease remains the much greater threat when all is said and done, and this type of "dual-use" preparedness and response capability would therefore be highly beneficial to humanity regardless of what malign human intention does or does not lie in wait in the coming years. Public health infrastructure, including finances and resources, must also be augmented to allow for this rapid recognition and response, and front-line physicians must be educated on the classical presentations of the major biological threat agents. Furthermore, measures for effective consequence management must be established, such as the stockpiling of antibiotics and vaccines and the development of adequate response protocols to be implemented in the event of an attack. This requires a conscious effort to bridge the gap between local and federal entities so that (1) supplies are not only acquired and maintained but can also be implemented effectively on a local level should the need arise; (2) mass medical care can be appropriately conducted without overwhelming the relevant infrastructure; and (3) mass fatality management can be arranged. Fortunately, involved parties across the U.S. and around the world are already taking steps to ensure that the majority of these immediate objectives have been met.

In addition to vulnerabilities, middle range goals often address capabilities as well. Of particular importance are the securing of Soviet stockpiles and containment of the "brain drain" phenomenon, for example by providing knowledgeable scientists with constructive research alternatives to those opportunities available within the BW sphere (and often involving terrorist groups or states of proliferation concern). The establishment of an effective intelligence network is another key to curtailing the efforts of both states and terrorist organizations to acquire a BW capability. Building upon earlier objectives, diagnostic methods and materials should be improved to augment existing approaches to the rapid analysis and identification of biological agents, and an increased number of Biosafety Level 4 (BL4) facilities should be made available to perform such work. The scientific community must assume a leadership role in addressing the concern of important and legitimate but potentially dual-use research, and further in limiting access to potential pathogens by providing guidelines for safe storage, shipping, and use of these agents. And international control regimes such as the Biological Weapons Convention (BWC) must be implemented to hinder the production, stockpiling, and use of biological weapons and to further inhibit the proliferation of these weapons to terrorists and non-state actors not bound by the Convention.

Long term objectives mainly involve research. For example, further improvements not only upon existent treatment modalities (e.g., the development of vaccines with improved efficacy and reduced side effects) but also upon detection and identification techniques would serve to greatly improve consequence management in the future. Research is also necessary to better understand the probable threat agents in terms of their fundamental pathogenic mechanisms, as well as the human immune response to these mechanisms. And the investigation of environmental safety and decontamination measures would certainly prove beneficial in the long run. But the notion of intent should be addressed as well, with the goal of generating a mutual understanding of conflicting belief systems and ideologies that might provide new means to conflict resolution in the future.

In closing, the crop-duster scenario serves to illustrate how at least one of the above recommendations might be—and in fact has been—implemented. The initial hope of course is that civilians are now aware of this type of threat, and that this awareness will promote the active reporting of suspicious activities with respect to these aircraft, whether witnessed in and around airfields, observed in pilot training classes, or even acknowledged in chat rooms on the Internet. But should this fail, the FAA currently maintains what is essentially a no fly zone 15 nautical miles in diameter over metropolitan Washington, DC.[142] Regardless of whether this is being enforced to prevent a biological attack or simply another suicide hijacking, it is worth noting that the border of the restricted area is just far enough removed to prevent the effective aerosol dispersal of a given agent over the heart of the city.

Richard F. Pilch serves as scientist-in-residence at the Center for Nonproliferation Studies (Monterey, California). Dr. Pilch, M.D., is working on a joint program to clarify the role of toxins in international law. He also maintains interests in the medical and healthcare aspects of chemical, biological, and radiological threats, and in the monitoring of biotechnological advances for possible offensive or defensive application in a weapons of mass destruction context.

Notes

1. The term "anthrax letters" is technically inaccurate but is nevertheless commonly used to describe the fall 2001 letters containing *Bacillus anthracis* spores. The term will be used as such throughout this paper for the sake of simplicity.
2. While the term "crop-duster" is commonly used by the lay public, "aerial applicator" is the proper name for these aircraft in the agricultural industry. For the sake of simplicity, however, the lay term will be used in this analysis.
3. "USDA official: Atta tried to get loan to buy airplane," Associated Press, June 8, 2002; "Testimony Huffman Aviation by CEO President Rudi Dekkers," March 19, 2002, www.house.gov/judiciary/dekkers031902.htm. As uncovered and widely reported in the aftermath of 9/11, Atta's cell had largely operated out of South Florida, in locations ranging from Vero Beach to Coral Springs, etc. See, for example: "Evidence trails lead to Florida," *BBC News Online*, September 13, 2001.
4. Twin-engine aircraft can generally be divided into two categories, props and jets. An example of a twin-engine, six passenger prop plane is the Beechcraft 300. Examples of twin-engine civilian jets include the Learjet 20/30/55; Cessna Citation 500, 550, and 560; Hawkers 700 and 800; and Raytheon Premier. Captain Lansing R. Pilch, United States Air Force, personal communication with author, August 2002.
5. *Al-Qa'ida Training Manual*, available online at www.fas.org/irp/world/para/manualpart1.html.
6. Because toxins are chemicals of biological origin, many analysts believe that they should only be considered in the context of chemical weapons (CW), despite the fact that toxin production resembles BW production much more closely than CW production. As a further illustration of this gray area, toxins fall under the purview of both the Biological and Toxins Weapons Convention (BWC) and Chemical Weapons Convention (CWC). For the purposes of this paper, toxins will considered BW agents and thus included in the discussion of the bioterrorist threat.
7. See, for example, www.hort.purdue.edu/newcrop/proceedings1996/v3-342.html.
8. David S. Cloud, "Kurdish Militants Conducted Tests With Deadly Toxin Ricin," *Wall Street Journal*, August 20, 2002; John McWethy, "Bush Cancels Iraqi Strike," *ABCNews.com*, August 20, 2002.
9. Franz, D. and Jaax, N., "Ricin Toxin," in Zajtchuk, R. ed., *Textbook of Military Medicine: Medical Aspects of Chemical and Biological Waifare* (Office of the Surgeon General, Department of the Army, United States of America), p. 633.
10. Once in a green van with two men and once alone in a Cessna.
11. See, for example, Brinkley-Rogers, P., et al., "FAA Grounding Order Raises Bioterrorism Suspicions," *Pittsburg Post-Gazette*, September 24, 2001; Blum, J. and Eggen, D., "Crop-Dusters Thought to Interest Suspects," *Washington Post*, September 24, 2001.
12. Brinkley-Rogers et al., "FAA Grounding Order Raises Bioterrorism Suspicions," September 24, 2001.
13. The most complete article on Moussaoui to date is Downey, S., "Who is Zacarius Moussaoui?" *MSNBCNews.com*, December 26, 2002. See also Calabresi, M. and Donnelly, S., "Cropduster Manual Discovered," *Time.com*, September 22, 2001.
14. Initially, FBI headquarters determined that there wasn't enough evidence… to search Moussaoui's residence. After September 11th, however, a complete search was authorized that revealed, in addition to the findings described, a German phone number linked to al-Qa'ida.

15. Brinkley-Rogers et al., "FAA Grounding Order Raises Bioterrorism Suspicions," September 24, 2001.
16. "Bin Laden's Biological Threat," BBC, October 28, 2001.
17. This plan became known as "48 hours of terror."
18. Abuza, Z., *Tentacles of Terror: Al Qaeda's Southeast Asian Network*, Lynne Rienner Publishers (forthcoming in March 2003).
19. "USDA official: Atta tried to get loan to buy airplane," June 8, 2002.
20. Transcript, *ABC World News Tonight*, ABC TV, September 21, 2001. The number of crop dusters in the U.S. has alternatively been reported as 4000; see Blum and Eggen, "Crop-Dusters Thought to Interest Suspects," September 24, 2001.
21. WMD is a categorical term used to describe the large-scale use of CBRN—chemical, biological, radiological, and nuclear—weapons. Technically, chemical and biological weapons are classified separately as mass casualty weapons (MCW) because they do not cause the physical damage implied by the term "destruction," but for the purposes of this paper WMD will be the representative acronym for the full range of CBRN weapons.
22. Homsy, R. and Zilinskas, R., Draft Report on the "Bioterrorist Threat Assessment and Risk Management Workshop," held at the Monterey Institute of International Studies, November 12–13, 2001.
23. It is important to point out that agricultural bioterrorism, which includes the targeting of both crops and livestock, is an integral component of the bioterrorist threat, as is the use of anti-machinery agents and even the dispersal of persistent agents such as anthrax spores as tactical or strategic environmental contaminants, for example to disable a specific highway or airport. For the purposes of this discussion, however, only bioterrorism against living, human targets will be considered.
24. The following review of U.S. vulnerabilities draws extensively from Pate, J., "Anthrax and Mass-Casualty Terrorism: What Is the Bioterrorist Threat After September 11?" *U.S. Foreign Policy Agenda*, November 14, 2001.
25. See, for example, the "Architecture, Design, and Engineering Drawings" available from the Prints and Photographs Online Catalog at http://memory.loc.gov/pp/pphome.html.
26. Class G airspace is uncontrolled airspace from ground level to 700 feet. Planes traveling in this airspace are essentially free from scrutiny. However, should a plane enter restricted airspace, for example around an airport (class B, C, and D), it would be monitored. Thus, for an operation to remain covert a plane would have to take off from a remote location, for example a field or private air strip, and avoid all classes of controlled airspace (anything other than class G). Captain Lansing R. Pilch, United States Air Force, personal communication with author, December 2002.
27. Information on all patients who presented with injuries or complaints directly related to the attacks within an eight hour period of each nationwide alert was collected, with the following results: a total of 103 patients presented with symptoms, 70 of whom suffered from acute psychological reaction, 19 from false atropine injection, 9 from physical injuries resulting from the explosion, 4 from (mild) smoke inhalation, and 1 from myocardial infarction. Rotenberg Z. et al., "Israeli ED experience during the Gulf War," *American Journal of Emergency Medicine*, 1994; 12:188–189.
28. Rotz, L., et al., "Public Health Assessment of Potential Biological Terrorism Agents," *Emerging Infectious Diseases*, Vol. 8, No. 2, February 2002.
29. *National Strategy for Homeland Security*, Office of Homeland Security, July 2002, pg. 7.
30. "Chronology of Aum Shinrikyo's CBW Activities," Monterey Institute of International Studies, 2001; available online at: http://cns.miis.edu/pubs/reports/aum_chrn.htm.
31. A discussion of crop-duster components can be found below. Generally speaking, the hopper tank is the compartment that holds the pesticide or agent for dispersal. Its capacity ranges from 300 to 800 gallons (1,100 plus to 3,000 plus liters). For a discussion of crop-duster dispersal of chemical (and biological) weapons, see the Henry L. Stimson Center webpage: http://www.stimson.org/cbw/?sn=CB2001121259.
32. "Military Utility of Agent X," CMLWG-ORG/TS-006 (19 Feb 52).
33. Miller, J., "Qaeda Videos Seem to Show Chemical Tests," *New York Times*, August 19, 2002.

34. Karasik, T., "Toxic Warfare," *RAND*, 2002; available online at: http://www.rand.org/publications/MR/MR1572/MR1572.pdf.
35. See, for example, http://www.airtractor.com/models/502/AT502B.html. The standard hopper tank for this make and model crop-duster is 500 gallons, while its standard fuel tank is 216 gallons.
36. On a per weight basis, gasoline mixed with air produces 15 times the energy of TNT (based on a conversion rate of 1 gram of gasoline plus air = 10 kilocalories, versus one gram of TNT = 0.65 kilocalories). TNT isn't used so much because of its energy as it is for the power that accompanies the rapid delivery of this energy, which amounts to a significant destructive force. Muller, R., "Cropduster Terrorism," *Technology Review*, March 11, 2002.
37. Broad, W. and Johnston, D., "Report Linking Anthrax and Hijackers Is Investigated," *New York Times*, March 23, 2002.
38. *Ibid.*
39. See, for example, Brennan, P., "FBI Rejects Link Between Anthrax, 9/11 Terrorists," *NewsMax.com*, August 16, 2002.
40. Broad and Johnston, "Report Linking Anthrax and Hijackers Is Investigated," March 23, 2002.
41. Infectiousness for a microbe or virus is often described in terms of its ID50, or the amount of agent required to cause infection in fifty percent of those exposed. The lower the number, the more infectious the agent. "Pathogenicity" then describes the ability to cause disease once infection has occurred. For toxins, the term ED5O is used rather than 1D50 (effective dose as opposed to infectious dose, because toxins do not cause infection), and "toxicity" rather than pathogenicity.
42. *NATO Handbook on the Medical Aspects of NBC Defensive Operations* (Washington, D.C.: Departments of the Army, the Navy, and the Air Force, 1996).
43. Vorobjev, A., "'Criterion Rating' as a measure of probable use of Bioagents as Biological Weapons," presented to the Working Group on Biological Weapons Control of the Committee on International Security and Arms Control, National Academy of Sciences, Washington DC, 1994. The criteria used were as follows: 1. Human sensitivity to microbe; 2. ID50 by aerosol; 3. Contagiousness (Index); 4. Possible routes of infectivity (aerosol, oral, parenteral); 5. Stability in environment; 6. Character of disease (severity, lethality, duration); 7. Feasibility of mass production (cultivation, physical-chemical forms, stability on storage. aerosolization); 8. Feasibility of rapid diagnosis; 9. Available prophylaxis; 10. Available treatment. Those agents rated with a score greater than or equal to 15 were considered "very likely to be used."
44. "Chemical and Biological Weapons: Possessions and Programs Past and Present," published online by the Monterey Institute of International Studies, http://cns.miis.edu/research/cbw/possess.htm.
45. The following characteristics were taken into account when classifying agents: "(1) public health impact based on illness and death; (2) delivery potential to large populations based on stability of the agent, ability to mass produce and distribute a virulent agent, and potential for person-to-person transmission of the agent; (3) public perception as related to public fear and potential civil disruption; and (4) special public health preparedness needs based on stockpile requirements, enhanced surveillance, or diagnostic needs." Rotz, L., et al., "Public Health Assessment of Potential Biological Terrorism Agents," February 2002.
46. "Chemical and Biological Weapons: Possessions and Programs Past and Present," http://cns.miis.edu/research/cbw/possess.htm.
47. *Ibid.* Argentinean hemorrhagic fever is also known as Junin.
48. *Patterns of Global Terrorism—2000*, Office of the Coordinator for Counterterrorism, U.S. Department of State, April 30, 2001; Committee on Armed Services, House of Representatives, "Special Inquiry into the Chemical and Biological Threat," Countering the Chemical and Biological Weapons Threat in the Post-Soviet World (Washington, D.C.: U.S. Government Printing Office, 23 Feb 1993), Report to the Congress, as cited in Zajtchuk, R. ed., *Textbook of Military Medicine: Medical Aspects of Chemical and Biological Warfare*, pg. 456.
49. Most often cited in this respect is Cuba's well-developed pharmaceutical industry and thus abundance of dual-use equipment, and reports that Usama bin Ladin had expressed an interest in developing BW agents in Sudan. See, for example, Hays, D., "Don't Trust Castro—Verify,"

Los Angeles Times, July 21, 2002; Emerson, S., "Trying Usama bin Ladin in Abstentia," *The Middle East Quarterly*, Vol. 8, No. 2, Spring 2001.

50. For the purpose of simplification, in the following discussion disease names will be used to represent the causative agent of the disease; for example, "anthrax" represents *B. anthracis* spores or bacteria.
51. See, for example, Carus, W., "Iran and Weapons of Mass Destruction," *MERIA* 4 (3), September 2000.
52. Zilinskas, R., "Iraq's Biological Weapons: Past as Future?" *Journal of the American Medical Association*, Vol. 278, No. 5, August 6, 1997.
53. *Ibid.*
54. See, for example, http://www.nti.org/e_research/el_libya_1.html.
55. North Korea Advisory Group, Report to the Speaker, U.S. House of Representatives, November 1999.
56. See, for example, http://www.nti.org/e_research/e1_syria_1.html.
57. Sources including *Y. pestis* in the list of pathogens developed by Iran are limited. See, for example, Bowman, S., "Iraqi Chemical and Biological Weapons," Congressional Research Service, Library of Congress, February 17, 1998.
58. Gubser, C. and Smith, G.L., "The Sequence of Camelpox Virus Shows It Is Most Closely Related to Variola Virus, the Cause of Smallpox," *Journal of General Virology*. 83, 855–872 (2002).
59. As an example, Lev Sandakhchiev, head of Russia's Vector Laboratory (State Research Center for Virology and Biotechnology), has voiced this opinion in the past.
60. For information on circumstantial links between Iraq with the smallpox virus, see Milloy, S., "Small Pox Threat Exaggerated, Part II," *Foxnews.com*, October 10, 2002; Broad, W., "White House Debate on Smallpox Slows Plan for Wide Vaccination," *New York Times*, October 13, 2002; Gellman, B., "4 Nations Thought to Possess Smallpox," *Washingtonpost.com*, November 5, 2002.
61. Henderson, D.A., "The Looming Threat of Bioterrorism," *Science*, Vol. 283, pp. 1279–1282, 1999.
62. Inglesby, T., et al., "Anthrax as a Biological Weapon," *Journal of the American Medical Association*, Vol. 281, No. 18, May 12, 1999.
63. Acquisition, production, and dissemination will be discussed in detail below.
64. Only 5 of the 11 inhalational anthrax cases following exposure to the anthrax-laden letters resulted in death, a mortality rate of 45%.
65. The concept of formulation is discussed in detail below, as are the effects of various meteorological factors on a BW attack.
66. Zilinskas, R. and Carus, W., "Possible Terrorist Use of Modern Biotechnology Techniques," *Chemical and Biological Defense Information Analysis Center*, April 2002.
67. Zilinskas, "Iraq's Biological Weapons: Past as Future?" August 6, 1997. The deployed missiles were modified SCUDs called al-Husseins, which had been adjusted in order to double their range.
68. Specifically, cult members contaminated coffee creamers and salad dressing containers at multiple restaurants in the area.
69. See Carus. W., "The Rajneeshees (1984)," in Tucker, J. ed., *Toxic Terror: Assessing Terrorist Use of Chemical and Biological Weapons* (Cambridge: MIT Press, 2000), pp. 115–137.
70. Zilinskas and Carus, "Possible Terrorist Use of Modern Biotechnology Techniques," April 2002.
71. *Ibid.*
72. However, it should be noted that according to some definitions the Rajneeshee incident does not qualify as terrorism per se. For example, Hoffman's definition of terrorism as "the deliberate creation and exploitation of fear through violence or the threat of violence in the pursuit of change" touches upon the notion that terrorism "is meant to instill fear within, and thereby intimidate, a wider 'target audience.'" Hoffman, B. *Inside Terrorism* (New York, Columbia University Press, 1998), pp. 43–44. The Rajneeshees never intended to affect anyone other than

those individuals directly exposed to the agent, and thus did not desire what Hoffman describes as "far-reaching psychological effects beyond the immediate victims." *Ibid.*, pg. 44.

73. Zilinskas and Carus, "Possible Terrorist Use of Modern Biotechnology Techniques," April 2002.
74. Carus, "The Rajneeshees (1984)," pp. 115–137, and Kaplan, D., "Aum Shinrikyo (1995)," pp. 207–226, both in Tucker, ed., *Toxic Terror: Assessing Terrorist Use of Chemical and Biological Weapons* (2000).
75. Zilinskas and Carus, "Possible Terrorist Use of Modern Biotechnology Techniques," April 2002.
76. See http://www.promedmail.org/pls/askus/f?p=2400:1000.
77. Zilinskas and Carus, "Possible Terrorist Use of Modern Biotechnology Techniques," April 2002.
78. *Ibid.*
79. *Ibid.* Examples of countries that incinerate infected animals in this manner are Australia, Canada, and the US.
80. *Ibid.*
81. *Ibid.*
82. *Ibid.*
83. "Chronology of Aum Shinrikyo's CBW Activities;" http://cns.miis.edu/pubs/reports/aum_chrn.htm.
84. Stern, J., "Larry Wayne Harris (1998)," in Tucker, ed., *Toxic Terror: Assessing Terrorist Use of Chemical and Biological Weapons* (2000), pp. 227–246.
85. Zilinskas and Carus, "Possible Terrorist Use of Modern Biotechnology Techniques," April 2002.
86. See, for example, "Concern over Kazakhstan bio-theft bid," *CNN.com*, November 6, 2002.
87. "Report: Specimens disappeared from Army lab," T*he Hartford Courant*, January 21, 2002.
88. Tucker, J. and Pate, J., "The Minnesota Patriots Council (1991)," in Tucker, ed., *Toxic Terror: Assessing Terrorist Use of Chemical and Biological Weapons* (2000), pp. 159–183.
89. *Ibid.*
90. *Ibid.* Another example of vendor acquisition is the purchase of "virus kits" over the Internet. These kits, such as the UK company Sigma-Genosys's Ebola kit, contain DNA strands and the genetic sequence of the virus in question so that the consumer can conceivably assemble the virus himself. Walsh, G. and Robbins, T., "UK Company Offers Ebola Virus 'Kit' for Sale Over Internet," *London Sunday Times*, August 4, 2002.
91. See, for example. Evans, M., "Whitehall Dossier Says Saddam Plans Biological Weapons for Palestinians," *London Sunday Times*, August 3, 2002.
92. This defector alleges that Iraq's military intelligence organization, Unit 999, offered six month training sessions to outsiders, such as members of Mojahedin-e Khalq (an Iranian opposition movement), the Kurdistan Workers Party (PKK, a group of Kurdish rebels based in Turkey), and al-Qa'ida. He claims to have met al-Qa'ida members at Salman Pak, a large BW and military facility southeast of Baghdad where three months of this training was performed. According to the defector, training was specifically directed toward U.S. targets and included such concepts as how to attack a water supply and how to target a building's ventilation system. "Iraq: Defectors Describe Camp Where Weapons Were Made," *Global Security Newswire*, November 8, 2001; Roberts, G., "Militia Defector Claims Baghdad Trained Al-Qaeda Fighters in Chemical Warfare," *London Sunday Times*, July 14, 2002.
93. Johnston, D. and Risen, J., "U.S. Concludes Al Qaeda Lacked a Chemical or Biological Stockpile," *New York Times,* March 20, 2002.
94. Gordon, M., "U.S. Says It Found Qaeda Lab Being Built to Produce Anthrax," *New York Times*, March 23, 2002; Zakaria, T., "US: Al Qaeda Tried for Bio Weapons in Afghanistan," *Yahoo! News*, July 17, 2002; Miller, J., "Lab Suggests Qaeda Planned to Build Arms, Officials Say," *New York Times*, September 14, 2002.
95. Air Force General Richard Meyers, Chairman of the Joint Chiefs of Staff, quoted March 25, 2002. See Weisman, J., "Possible Anthrax Lab Unearthed," *USA Today*, March 26, 2002;

Kelley, M., "Traces of Anthrax Found at Suspected al-Qaida Site," Associated Press, March 26, 2002.

96. Other related claims concerning al-Qa'ida's BW potential with respect to Afghanistan are as follows: In 1997, Usama bin Ladin reportedly ordered his followers to initiate a concerted campaign focusing on the acquisition for chemical and biological weapons; According to CNN, a coalition intelligence agency reported that enough equipment to establish 3 new laboratories capable of producing biological or chemical weapons was purchased by unidentified parties in 1999 and shipped from the Ukraine to Afghanistan; the same intelligence agency reported that in 2002 the Wafa Humanitarian Organization, the assets of which were frozen by the U.S. after it was identified as having terrorist links in the wake of 9/11, purchased roughly the same amount of similar equipment that was then shipped from the United Arab Emirates to Afghanistan, bringing the total to 6 possible labs altogether; A new CD-ROM version of al-Qa'ida's Encyclopedia of Afghan Resistance reportedly contains substantial, technically accurate descriptions of BW production and delivery (although apparently no information related to anthrax in this respect); And on July 10, 2002, U.S. forces detained a suspected BW smuggler in the Afghan village of Hesarak. Testing of the materials in his possession revealed trace amounts of ricin, but testing in the U.S. did not confirm this result. See, for example, Boettcher, M., "Evidence suggests al Qaeda pursuit of biological, chemical weapons," *CNN.com*, November 14, 2001; "Al-Qaeda: U.S. Forces Suspect, But Clear Detainee of CW Possession," *Global Security Newswire*, July 19, 2002.
97. It should be noted that a deliverable amount of agent, as opposed to just a seed culture, could conceivably be provided by a state sponsor, thus eliminating the need for an extensive production capability. In addition, contagious agents such as smallpox do not necessarily require any additional production measures upon acquisition of a pathogenic strain, as discussed in the analysis of delivery mechanisms below. It should be noted that the handling of contagious agents, whether bacteria or viruses, requires a high level of expertise because of demanding isolation techniques.
98. Tucker, J. and Vogel, K., "Preventing the Proliferation of Chemical and Biological Weapons Materials and Know-How," *Nonproliferation Review*, Spring 2000, pp. 88–96.
99. *Ibid.*
100. See, for example, "'Dr. Death' and His Accomplice," *CBSNews.com*, November 4, 2002.
101. Zilinskas. and Carus, "Possible Terrorist Use of Modern Biotechnology Techniques," April 2002.
102. In addition, certain manuals sold at gun shows across the U.S. and books available at popular retail and online shopping venues describe BW production in thorough, although not always technically accurate, detail. Zilinskas, R., "Open publication as sources of biological and chemical terrorism: Defining the problem and applying remedies," in *Implications of 9/11 on National Security and the Path Forward to Peace*, Conference Proceedings of the Twelfth Annual Arms Control Conference, held April 18–20, 2002 (Albuquerque: Sandia National Laboratories), pp. 144–160.
103. Carus, W., "R.I.S.E. (1972)," in Tucker, ed., T*oxic Terror: Assessing Terrorist Use of Chemical and Biological Weapons* (2000), pp. 55–70.
104. *Ibid.*
105. *Ibid.*
106. As will be discussed, injected or ingested agents need not fit these criteria.
107. Viruses are also generally considered to be more hazardous than bacteria because while bacterial infections can often be treated with antibiotics (especially when identified in a timely fashion), most viral diseases have no specific treatment.
108. Zilinskas and Carus, "Possible Terrorist Use of Modern Biotechnology Techniques," April 2002.
109. *Ibid.* The continuous fermenter achieves its higher yield due to both a shorter turnaround time and the indefinite maintenance of the cultured agent in a phase of exponential growth. U.S. Congress, Office of Technology Assessment, *Technologies Underlying Weapons of Mass Destruction, OTA-BP-ISC-115* (Washington, DC: U.S. Government Printing Office, December 1993), pg. 88.

110. Miller, J., et al., "U.S. Germ Warfare Research Pushes Treaty Limits," *New York Times*, September 4, 2001.
111. Zilinskas, R., "Iraq's Biological Weapons: Past as Future?" August 6, 1997.
112. Snyder, L. and Pate, J., "Tracking Anthrax Hoaxes and Attacks," published online by the Monterey Institute of International Studies, May 20, 2002; http://cns.miis.edu/pubs/week/020520.htm.
113. For example, a key component of the suicide bombing tactic is the promise of a quick and honorable death. Dolnik, A., "Die and Let Die: Exploring Links between Suicide Terrorism and Terrorist Use of Chemical, Biological, Radiological, and Nuclear Weapons," *Studies in Conflict and Terrorism* (forthcoming in March 2003).
114. The process of variolation, which consisted of inoculating unexposed individuals—through incisions in their skin—with scabs or pus from mildly infected smallpox patients, began sometime before 1000 B.C. This transdermal approach effectively reduced the fatality rate of subsequent infections from 30 percent to approximately 1 percent. Tucker, J., *Scourge: The Once and Future Threat of Smallpox* (New York: Atlantic Monthly Press, 2001), pg. 15.
115. It should be noted, however, that if the virus were successfully injected intravenously rather than simply into the skin these expectations would conceivably differ.
116. Tucker, J., *Scourge: The Once and Future Threat of Smallpox* (New York: Atlantic Monthly Press, 2001), pg. 21.
117. Braverman, I., et al., "A Novel Mode of Infection with Hepatitis B: Penetrating Bone Fragments Due to the Explosion of a Suicide Bomber," *Israeli Medical Association Journal*, Vol. 4: 528–529. July 2002.
118. Zilinskas and Carus, "Possible Terrorist Use of Modern Biotechnology Techniques," April 2002.
119. *Ibid.* Hearings Before the Select Committee to Study Governmental Operations With Respect to Intelligence Activities of the United States Senate, *Unauthorized Storage of Toxic Agents* (Washington, DC: U.S. Government Printing Office, 1976), pg. 113.
120. Other methods of attacking a water supply exist as well, for example disabling water treatment mechanisms by interrupting the flow of disinfectants and thus allowing nature to take over and contaminate the supply. *Ibid.*; Croddy, E., *Chemical and Biological Warfare: A Comprehensive Survey for the Concerned Citizen* (New York: Copernicus Books, 2001), pg. 81.
121. Agents with skin effects include the trichothecene mycotoxins, along with a limited number of other toxins not generally considered in the context of BW. It is important to keep in mind, however, that anthrax spores can cause cutaneous infection as well.
122. "Chronology of Aum Shinrikyo's CBW Activities"; http://cns.miis.edu/pubs/reports/aum_chrn.htm.
123. Keim, P., et al., "Molecular Investigation of the Aum Shinrikyo anthrax release in Kameido, Japan," *Journal of Clinical Microbiology*, 39 (12), December 2001, pp. 4566–7.
124. "Chronology of Aum Shinrikyo's CBW Activities;" http://cns.miis.edu/pubs/reports/au_chrn.htm.
125. *Ibid.*
126. The group apparently had some difficulty with production as well. For example, a number of cult members, including leader Shoko Asahara himself, reportedly fell ill after attempting to prepare *Coxiella burnetii*, the causative agent of the incapacitating illness Q fever. Kaplan, "Aum Shinrikyo (1995)," in Tucker, ed., *Toxic Terror: Assessing Terrorist Use of Chemical and Biological Weapons* (2000), pg 7.
127. The goal with this approach, and generally with the use of any type of spray device, is to generate an aerosol cloud of the necessary particle size range of 1 to 5 microns in a high enough concentration to cover a broad area.
128. Zilinskas and Carus, "Possible Terrorist Use of Modern Biotechnology Techniques," April 2002.
129. Zilinskas, R., "Iraq's Biological Weapons: Past as Future?" August 6, 1997. The system was tested with water on three other occasions around that time, twice in December 1990 and once in January 1991. Director of Central Intelligence, *Iraq's Weapons of Mass Destruction*

Programs, October 2002; available online at http://www.cia.gov/cia/publications/iraq_wmd/Iraq_Oct_2002.htm.

130. Fothergill, L., "Biological Warfare and Its Defense," *Armed Forces Ghemical Journal*, 12 (5), Sept/Oct 1958.
131. As an example of an alternative source for this information, airports broadcast wind direction, speed, cloud cover, and temperature every three hours in accordance with World Meteorological Organization guidelines.
132. U.S. Congress, Office of Technology Assessment, *Proliferation of Weapons of Mass Destruction, OTA-ISC-559* (Washington, DC: U.S. Government Printing Office, 1993), pp. 53–55, as cited in Inglesby et al., "Anthrax as a Biological Weapon," May 12, 1999.
133. HEPA filtration data drawn from "Holmes HEPA Air Purifier Owner's Guide," info hot-line: 1-800-5-Holmes; see also, www.totalaircare.co.nz/abouthep.htm.
134. Carus, W., "Bioterrorism and Biocrimes: The Illicit Use of Biological Agents in the 20th Century," Center for Counterproliferation Research, National Defense University, August 1998. Similarly, al-Qa'ida spokesman Suleiman Abu Gheith, on June 12, 2002, stated, "We have the right to kill four million Americans—two million of them children—and to exile twice as many and wound and cripple hundreds of thousands. Furthermore, it is our right to fight them with chemical and biological weapons."
135. Stone, R., "Experts Call Fungus Threat Poppycock," *Science*, 290:246, 2000.
136. Cameron, G., "Multi-track Microproliferation: Lessons from Aum Shinrikyo and Al Qaida," *Studies in Conflict and Terrorism*, 22:277–309, 1999.
137. At least prior to 9/11, government officials had expressed this belief as well. For example, FBI and Department of Justice (DOJ) officials quoted in a 1998 article stated that lone operators are "considered the most dangerous domestic terrorists." Suro, R., "Terrorism's New Profile: the Lone Wolf," *Washington Post*, July 22, 1998.
138. Zilinskas and Carus, "Possible Terrorist Use of Modern Biotechnology Techniques," April 2002.
139. Tucker, ed., *Toxic Terror: Assessing Terrorist Use of Chemical and Biological Weapons* (2000), pp. 255–266.
140. A notable exception is the Rajneeshees, whose attack with *S. typhimurium* was the group's first move toward "violence" of any kind.
141. Henderson, "Looming Threat of Bioterrorism," 1999.
142. 15 nautical miles translates to 17.262 miles (1 nautical mile equals 1.1508 miles), giving the restricted area a radius of 8.631 miles.

Michael R. Eastman and Robert B. Brown, 2003

Security Strategy in the Gray Zone

Alternatives for Preventing WMD Handoff to Non-State Actors

Over the past several years, national awareness of and sensitivity to the dangers posed by the shadowy networks of international terror have increased significantly. When combined with the potentially catastrophic consequences of future terrorist attacks conducted not with passenger planes but weapons of mass destruction, the need for comprehensive security strategies that address this threat has never been more pressing. Serious academic and policy work in this area has produced a fair amount of consensus on the merits of deterrence as a strategy to prevent a WMD attack from a rational adversary, as well as the need to resort to preemption when dealing with both irrational opponents and non-state actors with few if any values to hold hostage. However, neither of these security strategies is necessarily appropriate for what we believe to be an understudied aspect of the threat: How to prevent the proliferation of weapons of mass destruction from states to non-state actors. This article assesses three potential strategies directed at the link between a proliferating state and the terrorist end user. Upon examination of the assumptions, strengths and weaknesses of each, we conclude that preventing potentially hostile states from acquiring mature WMD production capabilities is the best of three bad options for safeguarding the public well-being and national interests of the United States.

President Bush, in the 2002 *National Security Strategy*, highlights the threat posed by weapons of mass destruction (WMD) in the hands of radical groups as "the gravest danger our Nation faces…"[1] This emphasis is similarly reflected in the companion document, the *National Strategy to Combat Weapons of Mass Destruction*.[2] However, both strategic blueprints suffer from a common shortcoming. They do not directly confront the critical link between states that might have the capability, intent, and incentive to hand off WMD and terrorists groups with the global reach to employ them against the United States. Despite acknowledging that current approaches to counter-proliferation have not proven foolproof, attention in these strategic blueprints quickly shifts to two propositions that enjoy general

The views expressed in this paper are those of the authors and do not necessarily reflect the official policy or position of the United States Military Academy, the Department of the Army, the Department of Defense, or the U.S. government.

consensus. The first is that America's long-standing reliance on deterrence, based on our substantial nuclear arsenal, continues to present sufficient threats to discourage a WMD strike by a rational state actor. The second is that non-state actors, and religiously motivated terrorist groups in particular, are increasingly undeterrable and must instead be dealt with preemptively.[3]

While we do not disagree with either of these propositions, it is not immediately apparent that either is necessarily appropriate when applied toward the issue of WMD transfer from states to non-state actors. WMD counterproliferation lingers in what we have termed the gray zone between states and non-state actors, where the requirements for both deterrence and preemption confront significant, and often unexplored, difficulties.

This paper is organized in three stages. We first examine the unique challenges posed by WMD handoff between hostile states and non-state actors. Particular emphasis is placed on disrupting the connections between potential state proliferators of WMD and non-state end users. This is based on our belief that, absent the independent ability of terrorist groups to manufacture effective nuclear, biological, chemical or radiological weapons capable of inflicting mass casualties, it is the link between producer and consumer that has not received sufficient attention. After bounding the problem and defining key terms, we then examine three distinct strategic options available to the U.S. national leadership as it evaluates ways to best secure vital American interests at home and abroad. Although current administration policy combines elements of deterrence, preemption and prevention, we choose to examine the theoretical foundations and practical limitations of each strategic option in isolation, hoping to clearly identify the strengths and weaknesses of each. Finally, we compare WMD counterproliferation strategies built on these respective options and highlight key operational requirements and difficulties.

There are fundamental differences between deterrence, preemption and prevention. By identifying the strengths and weaknesses of each we can determine the alternative that is most likely to stop terrorist groups from acquiring WMD. Our conclusion is that a preventive strategy, despite the clear negative consequences it implies for international cooperation and American military overextension, is the only option that promises to halt the transfer of WMD from hostile proliferators to terrorist organizations at a level of risk tolerable to this country.

WMD Handoff—Issues and Challenges

The emergence of Al Qaeda as a major terrorist threat marks a turning point in Western societies' struggles against terrorism. Prior to September 11, most observers discounted the likelihood that terrorists would employ weapons of mass destruction for a variety of reasons: difficulty of acquisition, likelihood of detection and apprehension, and the desire to make a political statement rather than inflict maximum casualties.[4] However, terrorist acts throughout the last decade have shown a troubling trend toward greater violence and destruction, often for its own sake, rather than to achieve a political end. As Al Qaeda's suicide hijackers clearly demonstrated, terrorists and other non-state actors will resort to any means available to inflict harm on the United States and its interests. Therefore, it is no longer reasonable to assume that terrorists will not resort to weapons of mass destruction if the opportunity presents itself. Given this new environment, the United States cannot discount the possibility that terrorists will use weapons of mass destruction.

Serious discussion of the issue, however, first requires setting limits on the threat. Much of the confusion associated with the discussion of counterproliferation strategies results from the application of the term WMD to a wide assortment of loosely related items, from nuclear weapons on one extreme to hijacked commercial airliners on the other. While perhaps useful from a political standpoint, undisciplined usage clouds an already complex issue. While we reluctantly adopt the term WMD for this paper, it is used in a narrowly defined sense to refer to a class of weapons that meets several criteria. First, weapons of mass destruction must actually be independently capable of inflicting significant numbers of casualties under reasonable conditions. An attack on the scale of the World Trade Center is a useful measure as a lower bound. This requirement recognizes that most any well-planned attack can inflict large numbers of deaths in a short period of time, but only under rather unlikely circumstances. Employment of a true weapon of mass destruction directly results in thousands of casualties, ruling out nearly all chemical attacks and the vast majority of biological strikes as well.

Second, the time between a WMD attack and the infliction of casualties is extremely short. There is a necessary distinction between campaigns of terror and the true weapon of mass destruction. This physical quality is most easily satisfied with the detonation of nuclear and radiological weapons. Biological weapons that are highly contagious and rapidly spread would clear this hurdle, as would lethal chemicals capable of efficient, widespread dissemination. However, lesser attacks that could be reasonably contained, such as the anthrax letters of a year ago, would not be considered using this definition.

Finally, genuine weapons of mass destruction create damage of an almost unknowable and uncontrollable quantity. For nuclear and radiological weapons, it is the lasting effects of radioactive contamination that distinguish such bombs from a like quantity of conventional explosives. The threat from weaponized smallpox or a similarly virulent biological agent rests not only in the immediate casualties it would inflict, but the sheer uncertainty implied by its release into a population. How, if at all, can the spread of a contagion be restricted to the target state? It is this final characteristic that makes this class of weapons unconventional in the most basic sense.

Taken together, these qualifiers rule out a large number of weapons normally considered under the rubric of WMD, to include those weapons non-state actors are perhaps most capable of acquiring or producing independently. Terrorists are certainly capable of acquiring or developing chemical and biological agents to inflict widespread damage. In two well-known cases, the Rajneesh cult used *Salmonella* bacteria in Oregon in 1984 and Aum Shinrikyo used sarin nerve agent in Japan in 1995. Although both of these incidents were limited in their scope and resulted in only a handful of deaths, these attacks demonstrated that well-organized and well-financed terror groups have the capability to develop or acquire biological and chemical weapons. We also know that Al Qaeda had crude labs in Afghanistan that experimented with anthrax and chemical agents. But the failure of even the sophisticated and well-funded Al Qaeda to develop weaponized biological and chemical agents capable of being delivered in large quantities is instructive. Despite a strong desire to acquire them, safe haven from which they could operate at will, substantial financial backing, and an extremely sophisticated organization, Al Qaeda was unable to develop such agents on their own. Therefore, we make the distinction between unconventional weapons in the general sense and weapons that have been refined so that they truly have the ability to inflict mass destruction. Fortunately, weapons that are truly capable of inflicting mass destruction remain beyond the grasp of most states, much less terrorist non-state actors.[5] It is therefore on the proliferating states themselves that we focus our attention.

Deterrence—A Classic Response

The manipulation of incentives remains a cornerstone of our security policy, and one that has been successful across many issues of critical importance. In the area of nuclear strategy, for example, the threat of annihilation by secure second strike produced a wary stability between the United States and the Soviet Union for the duration of the Cold War. Applied to WMD handoff, a deterrent strategy is built around a promise of overwhelming retaliation against any adversary who transfers such weapons to non-state actors. Faced with a credible threat of overwhelming punishment, it is hoped that potential proliferators will conclude that it is not in their best interests to transfer WMD to non-state users. The costs simply exceed the benefits. What follows is an overview of the theoretical foundations of a deterrent strategy, along with a brief sketch of how it might be applied to WMD handoff.

The work of Thomas Schelling remains the basis for much of our understanding of deterrence, particularly as it applies to nuclear weapons.[6] In general terms, a deterrent strategy works by threatening the use of force to persuade an adversary not to act in certain ways.[7] An opponent must weigh the possible gains to be had by acting against the costs that the threat, if delivered, would impose. Because such a strategy leaves the initiative to the opponent, proving success is often elusive. However, deterrence is presumed to work when an adversary does not behave in ways that are proscribed. We simply assume that his behavior was modified by the imposition of the threat. Whether or not the Soviets ever truly intended to launch a nuclear attack on this country, for example, we conclude that our ability to strike back was sufficient disincentive to prevent them from acting.

When deterrence fails, lack of success is usually attributed to a lack of credibility on the part of the threatening state. The adversary has either judged the threatened punishment as insufficiently costly, unlikely to be imposed, or some combination of the two.[8] In short, deterrent strategies hinge on credibility as determined from the perspective of the target state. The initiator must seem to possess both the capability and the intent to inflict the threatened punishment, and the adversary must conclude that the risks of acting outweigh the benefits.

Deterrence remains a useful component of our national security strategy. For example, it is generally assumed that any nuclear attack on this country or its allies by a state would meet with an overwhelming response in kind, and this creates enormous disincentives for an enemy contemplating a WMD attack.[9] The issue, however, is whether or not this same strategy will deter states from proliferating weapons to terrorist groups that do not fear retribution. A number of prominent scholars have argued that deterrence does work and assume that the nuclear deterrent threat extends to the case of WMD proliferation. Ken Waltz, for example, believes that the mere suspicion of an Iraqi WMD transfer to a terrorist group would, in the aftermath of an attack, be sufficient to incur a retaliatory nuclear strike from the United States.[10] In similar fashion, John Mearsheimer and Stephen Walt contend that "Saddam could never be sure that we would not incinerate him anyway if we merely suspected that he had made it possible for anyone to strike the United States with nuclear weapons."[11] They then conclude that the risks of an American response are sufficient to convince states not to proliferate.

There are a number of questionable assumptions in this position. First, there is some ambiguity concerning whether or not a nuclear retaliatory strike would be visited upon any state responsible for providing weapons to a non-state actor. Nor is it clear that every WMD attack merits nuclear retaliation. Nonetheless, in the aftermath of a WMD strike on the United States, the desire for punishment would be quite strong. Non-state actors lack tangible assets that might be struck in such a response. The only viable candidates for retaliation after a non-state WMD attack are the countries responsible for providing the weapons and technology needed to carry out the attack. Just as in the current *War on Terrorism*, deterrence holds state sponsors accountable for the actions of any terrorist groups they have empowered through proliferation. It is therefore the risk tolerance of the proliferating state that lies at the core of a deterrent strategy.

Without ruling out conventional responses altogether, the threat of total regime destruction through a nuclear response does pose the greatest conceivable disincentive for a state contemplating WMD handoff. If this level of punishment fails to deter the targeted behavior, then it seems reasonable to assume that lesser included conventional responses would be equally ineffective. Furthermore, because a deterrent strategy presumes that the adversary has a mature WMD program, American threats of conventional punishment are less than credible, if not self-deterred altogether, by our potential fear of escalation. Adversaries need look no further than our recent dealings with North Korea to draw this conclusion, accurate or not. This combination of factors supports the position that our nuclear deterrent would be extended to include WMD transfer.

Relying on a deterrent strategy for WMD handoff produces a straightforward declaratory policy. The United States promises regime destruction for any state that transfers weapons of mass destruction to non-state actors. Successful application of this strategy hinges on two basic conditions. First, the United States must have the ability to monitor WMD transactions and demonstrate to potential adversaries that any attempt to sell or hand off WMD will not go undetected. If a proliferating state thinks it will not get caught, then concerns about potential punishment can be brushed off. Second, efforts should be taken to make the threatened response credible. Proliferators must believe that there is a reasonable chance that the United States has both the capability and the will to impose the promised penalties. If both conditions are met, then a deterrent strategy stands a reasonable chance of success.

Preemption—Just-in-Time Disruption

The 2002 National Security Strategy acknowledges that no state "need suffer an attack before they can lawfully take action to defend themselves against forces that present an imminent threat of attack."[12] Unlike deterrence, a preemptive strategy relies not on the threat of force, but its actual use against an enemy that has demonstrated the intent and the capability to carry out an attack. It is a strategy of striking first, where the initiative is taken by the intended victim. In a general sense, preemptive strategies are "designed to forestall the mobilization and deployment of the adversary's existing military forces."[13] More specifically, rather than relying on the risk tolerance of the aggressor, preemption removes an opponent's ability to strike just before he attacks.

Against terrorists, for example, there is a strong case to be made that preemption is the only appropriate strategy. Non-state actors pose unique challenges for deterrence. They possess no territory or population that may be targeted. They own nothing of sufficient value that may be held hostage. As noted historian John Gaddis and others have argued quite convincingly, there is no effective way to deter someone willing to commit suicide to achieve their aims.[14] Using a similar rationale, the Bush administration has clearly incorporated elements of preemption into the National Security Strategy, vowing to strike first against terrorist organizations rather than retaliate against them in the aftermath of an attack.[15] However, much like deterrence, there is no reason to assume that preemption is an effective way to approach the specific threat of WMD proliferation without first examining the strategy's theoretical and operational requirements.

In the context of WMD handoff, preemption is narrowly bounded to address only the physical transfer of weapons, technology, and expertise from states to non-state actors. It implies no first strike against states that merely develop WMD programs; in fact, a preemptive approach to counterproliferation accepts that states will acquire weapons of mass destruction and requires that the United States maintain a robust nuclear deterrent as a disincentive for their use. What preemption in the gray zone does promise, however, is the use of force justified by the imminent act of proliferation. It is a strategy based on disrupting WMD transactions at the point of exchange, of removing the capability of non-state actors to strike by preventing them from acquiring the means themselves.[16]

Launching a preemptive attack against a likely proliferator requires gathering evidence of two theoretical prerequisites: capability and intent. Potential target states must possess the ability to produce and distribute weapons and/or enabling materials to non-state actors. These may range from transportable nuclear devices and fissile material on one extreme to small vials of biological cultures on the other.[17] Second, the United States must discern the proliferator's intent to conduct the prohibited transfer. As previously stated, malicious intent on the part of the terrorist organization is presumed. However, this is secondary to this approach as striking terrorists already in possession of WMD is both stated policy and an obvious indication that the counterproliferation has already failed. In order to justify preemption, however, the intent of the proliferation to carry out a transfer to a non-state actor must also be determined prior to the act itself.

A preemptive strategy to counter WMD handoff focuses on the potential contacts and transfer options available to states willing to provide weapons and the terrorist organizations trying to acquire them. On the supply side of this relationship, preemption requires intense monitoring of all states that have acquired or are in the process of developing WMD production capabilities. While the bulk of this intelligence effort could be directed at states hostile to the United States, even allies would be subject to intense monitoring in the area of dual-use technologies, unguarded military facilities, and even the flow of trained researchers and weapons experts. Production and movement of weapons and enabling components by land, sea and air would be tracked.

Similar energy would be directed toward terrorist organizations themselves. In addition to ongoing intelligence work aimed at locating and dismantling the command nodes of these shadowy networks, emphasis would be placed on identifying and monitoring individuals in close contact with potential proliferators. Evidence of such ties is a necessary step toward proving the intent to hand off weapons on the part of the state actor. The intent to proliferate would be further reinforced by indications that prohibited weapons or materials were being covertly moved toward a range of viable transfer nodes, ranging from commercial shipping ports to private airfields.

Although it poses significant operational challenges, a preemptive counterproliferation strategy is theoretically viable. Given the generally accepted belief that terrorists would not acquire WMD without the intent to use them, evidence of dealings between states that possess such weapons and terrorist organizations could justify a preemptive strike. Assuming the United States can muster the immense intelligence and analysis assets needed to monitor potential proliferation across the spectrum of transfer modes available to states, and couple it with a military strike complex capable of rapidly interdicting WMD handoff immediately before it occurs, preemption remains a viable policy option.

Prevention—You Can't Transfer What You Don't Have

In contrast to preemption, a preventive strategy seeks to remove the chance that a potentially hostile state may transfer WMD by stripping it of a mature weapons development capability altogether. The concept of prevention is hardly a newcomer to international politics or military affairs. As a motivation for war, states have launched preventive strikes "in an attempt to block or retard the rise of a challenger while that opportunity is still available."[18] Such wars generally assume a hostile intent on the part of an adversary who is in the process of increasing its military capabilities. In practice, they are undertaken to address a threat while the balance of power favors the initiating state, or at the very least at a time and place of the preventer's choosing. Applied more narrowly to the case of WMD counterproliferation, prevention requires that the United States simply presume that mature WMD programs in certain states pose an intolerable proliferation risk. Whether this is due to hostile intent or lack of positive control within the target state is theoretically immaterial. Rather than ceding initiative to a proliferation threat or awaiting definitive evidence of a desire to transfer WMD to a non-state actor, the United States would initiate a range of preventive actions, up to and including the use of force, to stop the acquisition of a mature WMD program.

The causal logic underpinning a preventive strategy is undeniably straightforward. States that are not permitted to develop WMD do not pose a proliferation risk. Take away the weapons themselves, and neither friends with loose arsenals nor enemies with hostile intentions pose a proliferation risk. As Lawrence Freedman has recently written, "prevention provides a means of confronting factors that are likely to contribute to the development of a threat before it has a chance to become imminent."[19] Rather than attempting to discern the intention to proliferate, prevention requires the United States to seek evidence of the intent to develop WMD capabilities. This knowledge alone then justifies a range of passive and active preventive measures designed to counter the acquisition of mature WMD production capabilities.

While significant, the operational prerequisites for a preventive strategy are also less demanding than the two previous options. First, our more restrictive definition of WMD precludes a wide range of weapons currently implied by the term as it is commonly used. It is evident that certain chemical and biological weapons, such as sarin and *E. coli*, can be manufactured by relatively unsophisticated actors. However, weapons meeting more stringent requirements require the collocation of significant assets, assets only available to state actors.[20] It is these that a preventive strategy would target. Furthermore, even though the assets required to monitor potential WMD development around the globe are significant, they are less extensive than those needed to track the transfer of weapons and their component parts through the myriad of private and commercial venues open to a determined proliferator. In fact, the intelligence framework for a strategy of prevention closely resembles the assets currently dedicated to monitoring potential adversaries.

Current passive mechanisms of prevention fall under the rubric of existing non-proliferation regimes such as the Non-Proliferation Treaty and the Nunn-Lugar Co-operative Threat Reduction Program.[21] These programs have met with limited success minimizing the number of nuclear-capable states through both diplomatic pressure to discourage non-nuclear nations from developing WMD capability, and economic assistance to help nuclear-capable nations secure their existing stocks of weapons, raw materials, and technology. However, existing regimes cannot be considered comprehensive tools for a prevention strategy, as they require full cooperation of the states of concern; they have no active components to address states unwilling to comply, or more problematic, states that publicly endorse diplomatic measures and accept inducements, but secretly continue weapons development. The recent failure of the 1994 Framework Agreement between the United States and North Korea illustrates the limited utility of diplomatic measures to constrain a state determined to develop nuclear weapons.

A robust prevention strategy requires mechanisms to address both cooperative and uncooperative potential proliferators. Programs like CTR have continued utility in helping control the unwitting transfer of weapons from generally cooperative states like Russia and Ukraine to less cooperative states like Iran and Syria, and provide viable policy alternatives where the diffusion of responsibility makes deterrence completely ineffective as a strategy. The critical dilemma is how to develop active programs that adequately deal with uncooperative nations that seek WMD, and are potential proliferators.

In general, the quiver of active mechanisms includes diplomatic sanction, economic sanction, and military intervention. It can be assumed that diplomatic sanction has little utility in coercing an uncooperative state. Economic sanctions have some utility, but are problematic in several respects. First, they require near complete international cooperation to be effective—a rare circumstance in international politics. Even a few sympathetic nations can significantly undermine their effectiveness, and the shortages caused by embargoes create huge financial incentives to defect. Even if states cooperate, the ability of multinational corporations to use middlemen, cutouts, and brokers to evade sanctions makes monitoring compliance nearly impossible. Similarly, when applied to authoritarian states, sanctions tend to impact civilian populations significantly more than they alter the policies of their leaders. Iraq's capacity to evade the coercive effects of sanctions—while tolerating their humanitarian consequences—highlights the difficulty of economic coercion.[22] In the end, the most effective mechanism of active prevention remains military action.

The Best of Three Bad Options

Comparison of these three alternate strategies in isolation makes clear that each has both advantages and disadvantages. What remains is a side-by-side comparison to determine which option, if any, has a reasonable probability of successfully achieving the objective of stopping the handoff of WMD. Our focus remains strictly limited to the question of how best to prevent WMD from falling into the hands of groups that would employ them. There is no question that these strategies have significant international and domestic ramifications. In fact, much of the debate over the merits of preemption and prevention resides in the ripples these strategies create for international organizations.[23] However, emphasizing the second order effects of a strategy before asking the fundamental question: "Will it work?" is a bit like putting the proverbial cart before the horse. By highlighting the narrow operational difficulties associated with each strategy, we will demonstrate that only prevention offers a reasonable probability of achieving stated goals. Whether or not it is a politically viable strategic option is of secondary interest to this study.

Regardless of the strategic option under examination, the operational challenges associated with tracking WMD transfer are significant. Given the range of options available to a determined proliferator, one accepts a high level of risk in assuming that even the United States, with its sophisticated global intelligence apparatus, can confidently detect WMD transfers.[24] Our experiences with similar efforts, such as interdicting drug trafficking and stopping illegal immigration, have shown that a determined adversary can evade even our best efforts an alarming portion of the time.[25] Unfortunately, when even low success rates are extended to WMD handoff, where only one failure could result in catastrophic damage, these risks exceed acceptable levels.

While the intelligence requirements for a preventive strategy are significant, they are less than those required of the previous two strategies. A mature WMD production base requires infrastructure, raw materials, and highly specialized scientists operating clandestinely for an extended period of time. Once assembled, the location of such assets is difficult, though not impossible, to disguise.[26] Successful proliferation, however, requires only a working device and a covert way to transfer it from buyer to seller. The more likely case is a weapon assembled from dual-use components acquired from multiple sources through several, intentionally disguised transport means. In relative terms, the intelligence required for both deterrence and preemption dwarfs that needed for a policy of prevention.

A deterrent strategy for the problem of WMD handoff must satisfy two additional conditions. First, potential proliferators must believe that the chance they can evade responsibility for a handoff is prohibitively low. If states think they can transfer WMD and escape detection, then a strategy to deter such acts based on the threat of retribution founders at the outset. Second, proliferators must perceive that the deterrent threat is credible. It must promise to impose severe costs on a proliferator that outweigh any potential gains to be had through WMD handoff. States must also believe that the United States is willing and able to follow through with the threatened response.

There are significant problems with the credibility of any threat the United States might make to deter the handoff of WMD, distinct from the myriad ways states would seek to conduct such transactions covertly and escape punishment altogether. The credibility of a deterrent threat is greatest when "we get ourselves into a position where we cannot fail to react as we said we would… or where we would be obliged by some overwhelming cost of not reacting in the manner we had declared."[27] In the context of WMD handoff, this is cause for concern. The combination of an intelligent adversary determined to avoid detection and a deliberate strategy to diffuse responsibility make it extremely difficult to pin responsibility for proliferation on any one state. In light of this, there is some question in our mind whether potential proliferators would believe that the United States could actually carry out its deterrent threat and punish WMD handoff with nuclear attack.

Several prominent political scientists argued against a preemptive war in Iraq, advocating just such a deterrent policy. A central pillar in their position was the belief that a rogue leader such as Saddam Hussein would never risk the handoff of WMD to terrorist groups for fear of facing nuclear incineration even if it was "merely suspected that he had made it possible for anyone to strike the United States with nuclear weapons."[28] However, this greatly oversimplifies the situation that would confront the president in the face of evidence of a WMD handoff. As we have indicated, the transfer of WMD can take several forms. Critical components of a weapon can be sold off a piece at a time, through one or several front companies. Responsibility for proliferation might be traced to rogue elements within a military, as is speculated in the case of the former Soviet Republics, or to high-tech firms operating within the sovereign territories of multiple states. Assembly of a crude WMD device may involve the transfer of materials and technology from multiple sources, none of which in isolation could provide a functioning weapon. Even in the absence of collaboration, it seems reasonable to assume that non-state actors intent on acquiring WMD might be forced to work through multiple sources. This diffusion of responsibility cuts against the utility of deterrence by removing the target of any threat.

Furthermore, the logic of nuclear deterrence works by holding the core values of an adversary hostage. Deterrence prevents a nuclear first strike because any potential opponent understands that their most prized possessions, whether in the form of territory, military forces, or population, will be destroyed the instant that such an attack is launched. Such calculations cannot be assumed to apply in the case of WMD proliferation. There are many reasons why a president might not be able to muster domestic support for a strike against the population of a proliferator. Unlike a nuclear first strike, the time between a WMD handoff and use of the weapon could be considerable. The parties responsible for the transfer may not be operating with consent of their people, if they even remain in power when the time comes for American retribution.

In each of these cases, there is a diffusion of responsibility for the WMD handoff that makes any retaliation, much less a nuclear response, extremely challenging. Who exactly will be punished for the handoff? The difficulty associated with making that determination can hardly be lost on the potential proliferators of WMD. As such, it creates a second source of risk for a strategy based on deterrence. When combined with the operational challenges of tracking WMD handoffs, it is not altogether unreasonable to assume that risk-acceptant states might see a reasonable probability of success in transferring WMD and then avoiding punishment. Proponents of deterrence assume that in the aftermath of a WMD use against this country, the government will respond swiftly and surely against the state that provided such weapons to the terrorist attacker. They do not contemplate the case where there is not one smoking gun, but many. Nor do they acknowledge that the guns are purposely hidden from view.

A preemptive strategy of counterproliferation suffers from its own operational and theoretical challenges. As previously stated, preemption requires intelligence on the WMD capability of the potential proliferators, and operational knowledge of impending transfers to a third party actor. Relying on "just-in-time" interdiction creates a two-fold hurdle for the preempting nation, and the costs of failure are potentially catastrophic in two distinct ways.

First, preemption requires a clear knowledge of the location, types, and quantities of weapons every potential proliferator possesses—a similar challenge faced by a deterrent strategy. Absent this level of detail, the ability to identify the covert movement of weapons—a signal of impending handoff—becomes unlikely. Adding complexity to the intelligence problem, preemption requires more than simple knowledge of weapons transfers—a sufficient condition for deterrence. It requires detailed, *actionable* intelligence of precisely where weapons are stored, how they are transported, and to whom they are to be delivered. The "smoking gun" demanded by the recent coalition intervention in Iraq pales before the requirements of a true preemptive strike. Second, even if a preempting nation can successfully track weapons and detect a potential transfer, the preemptor now faces the prospect of military action against a WMD-capable adversary. This raises the stakes of preemption considerably, approaching the quandary faced by the Superpowers during the Cold War: a preemptive strike will result in a second strike by the aggrieved party. Against a WMD-capable opponent, preemption not only demands the ability to prevent a single imminent transfer, it likely requires the capability for a comprehensive first strike against an aggressor's *entire* arsenal—a significantly taller order.

Failing to detect a transfer in timely fashion could result in a potentially devastating attack. But even if the intelligence operates perfectly, a tactical failure in a preemptive attack would likely result in the very event preemption is designed to stop—a WMD attack against the United States or an ally. Facing the difficulty of a successful first strike against a nuclear-capable adversary, the preemptor is easily deterred.

As a policy, prevention relies on the standard realist premise that intentions are generally unknowable, and frequently changing: it is dangerous to presume that the future good will or stability of governments can be sufficiently anticipated to warrant tacit acceptance of WMD development. While nuclear weapons cannot be returned to Pandora's Box, it is still good policy to constrain their dissemination to the extent possible. Accordingly, a preventive strategy would discourage *any* further proliferation of WMD capability—particularly nuclear weapons. The tools of prevention should vary, however, based on the relationship with the potential proliferators in question. States can be generally categorized according to three groups—each demanding a different preventive strategy.

The first group involves generally friendly states that seek to develop WMD. It is quite feasible that states allied with the United States could decide that a nuclear capability is in their best interest. Given that U.S. intentions and future security guarantees are likewise unknowable, stable governments with a strong recent history of popular consent and the rule of law could still perceive a need for an independent nuclear deterrent. Japan is such a potential future nuclear power. They certainly have the technical capability to develop nuclear weapons, and have regional rivalry with a current nuclear power in China, and an emerging one in North Korea. In these cases, passive preventive measures are appropriate to discourage the further proliferation of WMD capability. However, regardless of the good will or stability of the state in question, determined diplomatic opposition for any new entrant into the nuclear club should be constant—even for nations friendly to the United States. When the concerns of these threatened states are legitimate, the United States must offer credible security guarantees—both conventional and nuclear deterrent. Financial and economic incentives are similarly suitable when confidence exists in the states involved have sufficient economic and political transparency to verify compliance with agreements. When coupled with peer-to-peer military cooperation and integration, diplomatic measures such as international treaties have significant utility in these cases.

The second group involves generally friendly states that either currently possess WMD capability, or that develop it despite passive measures to prevent it. These states similarly warrant passive measures to prevent handoff of weapons to third party actors. In these cases, the United States should pursue bilateral or international monitoring of WMD programs to verify appropriate security of sensitive technology and weapons components, and proper accountability of existing arsenals. However, a sound prevention strategy should not merely accept the status quo of gradual proliferation. Continued diplomatic and financial incentives such as an expanded Cooperative Threat Reduction program should encourage these WMD-capable states to reduce their arsenals or eliminate them altogether.

The third group involves nations with a recognized hostility to the United States, its interests or its allies. Examples include the states recognized as known supporters of terrorism. Additionally, this list should include states that lack sufficient institutional stability to preserve the rule of law or adequately control their borders, resources, and weapons. These states demand active measures to prevent their development of WMD. As previously discussed, these measures can range in severity from political and economic sanctions, to military blockade and intervention.

After careful consideration of the risks and probabilities of success for each of these three strategic alternatives, we arrive at a rather unsettling conclusion. In most cases, rational decision-making is rightly centered on the most likely outcome instead of the most dangerous. However, as we have attempted to demonstrate, WMD handoff confronts the United States with a unique set of challenges. The costs of failing to sever the link between proliferating states and non-state actors determined to inflict mass casualties are potentially catastrophic. Both deterrence and preemption are hampered by enormous intelligence challenges, leave the initiative to potential adversaries, and rest on a causal logic that involves accepting dangerous levels of risk. Only a strategy of prevention provides something approaching certainty: adversaries cannot transfer items that they don't have.

This is not blind advocacy for a far-reaching military policy of preventive strikes. Simply declaring that potential adversaries bent on acquiring weapons of mass destruction face possible preventive attack from the United States on the grounds that they could hand off WMD to terrorist organizations may serve to strengthen international regulatory bodies and put teeth into existing treaty obligations. When coupled with a broader policy of security agreements and economic incentives, the mere declaration of a preventive policy may be sufficient to deter WMD handoff.[29] However, the sheer gravity of the threat posed by weapons of mass destruction in the hands of terrorists demands closer evaluation of the theoretical underpinnings and operational requirements of our current counterproliferation policy. While all three strategic options are theoretically sound, they differ greatly in terms of risks incurred and requirements for success. In our view, while prevention incurs the greatest costs in terms of international cooperation, it alone offers a reasonable chance of halting the proliferation of weapons of mass destruction from hostile states to terrorist organizations determined to acquire them.

Michael R. Eastman is assistant professor and course director of National Security Studies at the United States Military Academy at West Point. He is a doctoral candidate in political science from the Massachusetts Institute of Technology.

Robert B. Brown is assistant professor and course director of public policy at the United States Military Academy at West Point. He holds a Master of Public Affairs degree from the LBJ School of Public Affairs at the University of Texas, Austin.

Works Cited

Ackerman, Gary and Laura Snyder. "Would They If They Could?" *Bulletin of the Atomic Scientists* (May/June 2002): 1–9.

Albright, David and Khidzhir Hamza. "Iraq's Reconstitution of its Nuclear Weapons Program." *Arms Control Today* (October 1998).

Art, Robert. "A Defensible Defense: America's Grand Strategy After the Cold War." *International Security* 15 (Spring 1991): 3–43.

Betts, Richard. "Fixing Intelligence." *Foreign Affairs* (Jan/Feb 2002): 43-59.

Bush, George W. *National Strategy to Combat Weapons of Mass Destruction*. Washington, D.C.: December 2002.

_____. *The National Security Strategy of the United States of America*. Washington, D.C.: 17 September 2002.

Cirincione, John. "The International Non-Proliferation Regime." The Carnegie Non-Proliferation Project (2000): 283–290.

Cronin, Audrey. "Behind the Curve: Globalization and International Terrorism." *International Security* (Winter 2002): 30–58.

Downs, George. "The Rational Deterrence Debate." *World Politics* (January 1989): 225–237.

Freedman, Lawrence. "Prevention, Not Preemption." *The Washington Quarterly* (April 2003): 104–114.

Gaddis, John Lewis. "A Grand Strategy." *Foreign Policy* (November-December 2002): 50–57.

Hagerty, Dean. *The Consequences of Nuclear Proliferation*. Cambridge: The MIT Press, 1998.

Hoffman, Bruce. "Viewpoint: Terrorism and WMD: Some Preliminary Hypotheses." *The Nonproliferation Review* (Spring-Summer 1997): 45–53.

Huth, Paul and Bruce Russett. "What Makes Deterrence Work?" *World Politics* (July 1987): 496–527.

Lee, Rensselaer. "Nuclear Smuggling from the Former Soviet Union: Threats and Responses." *Foreign Policy Research Institute* (27 April 2001).

Levy, Jack. "Declining Power and the Preventive Motivation for War." *World Politics* 40 (October 1987): 82–107.

_____. "The Causes of War: A Review of Theories and Evidence." in *Behavior, Society and Nuclear War*. Ed. Paul Tetlock et al. New York: Oxford University Press, 1989. 209-333.

Mearsheimer, John. *Conventional Deterrence*. Ithaca: Cornell University Press, 1983.

Mearsheimer, John and Stephen Walt. "Can Saddam Be Contained? History Says Yes." *New York Times*. 12 November 2002.

_____ "Keeping Saddam in a Box." *New York Times*. February 2003.

McNair Paper Number 41. *Radical Responses to Radical Regimes: Evaluating Preemptive Counter-Proliferation*. May 1995

O'Hanlon, Michael, Susan Rice and James Steinberg. *The New National Security Strategy and Preemption*. Brookings Institution Policy Brief #113. January 2003.

Perkovich, George. "Bush's Nuclear Revolution." *Foreign Affairs* 81 (March/April 2003): 2–9.

Perry, William. "The Next Attack." *Foreign Affairs* (Nov/Dec 2001): 31–45.

Pollack, Kenneth. "Next Stop Baghdad?" *Foreign Affairs* 82 (March/April 2002): 32–47.

Potter, William and Leonard Specter. "The Real Sum of All Fears." *Los Angeles Times*. 11 June 2002.

Schelling, Thomas. *Arms and Influence*. New Haven, Connecticut: Yale University Press, 1966.

Sheridan, Ralph. "The Challenge of WMD Detection in Cargo." Seaport Security Conference. 11 June 2002.

Stern, Jessica. "Dreaded Risks and the Control of Biological Weapons." *International Security* (Winter 2002): 89–123.

Worley, D. Robert. "Waging Ancient War: The Preemptive Use of Force." *Strategic Studies Institute Special Report*. U.S. Army War College. 8 November 2001.

Zanders, Jean Pascal. "Assessing the Risk of Chemical and Biological Weapons Proliferation to Terrorists." *The Nonproliferation Review* (Fall 1999):17–34.

Notes

1. George W. Bush, *The National Security Strategy of the United States of America*, 17 September 2002.
2. George W. Bush, *National Strategy to Combat Weapons of Mass Destruction*, December 2002.
3. See Bruce Hoffman, "Terrorism and WMD: Some Preliminary Hypotheses," *The Nonproliferation Review* (Spring-Summer 1997): 45–53.
4. See, for example Thomas Schelling, "Thinking About Nuclear Terrorism." *International Security*. Robert Art also finds fears of nuclear terrorism overstated due to a belief that terrorists, in order to achieve their political objectives, would need to identify themselves and then risk falling prey to retaliation. This overlooks a shift in modern terrorism to the desire to inflict mass casualties as an end in and of itself or as part of a larger religious struggle. See Robert Art, "A Defensible Defense: America's Grand Strategy After the Cold War," *International Security* 15 (Spring 1991): 27.
5. Matthew Bunn, Anthony Wier, and John Holdren, *Controlling Nuclear Warheads and Materials*, Project on Managing the Atom (Cambridge: Harvard University, 2003): 11.
6. Thomas Schelling, *Arms and Influence* (New Haven: Yale University Press, 1966).
7. Ibid, 33–36.
8. Paul Huth and Bruce Russett, "What Makes Deterrence Work?" *World Politics* (July 1987): 497.
9. For a strong argument on the relevance of a deterrent strategy against WMD use by states, see Devin Hagerty, *The Consequences of Nuclear Proliferation* (Cambridge: The MIT Press, 1998).
10. Kenneth Waltz, "Spread of Nuclear Weapons Nothing to Fear, says Waltz." Accessed from http://www.columbia.edu/cu/news/media/03/kennethWaltz/index.html, available 4 March 2003.
11. John Mearsheimer and Stephen Walt, "Can Saddam Be Contained? History Says Yes," *Los Angeles Times*, 12 November 2002.
12. Bush, *National Security Strategy of the United States of America*, 5.
13. Jack Levy, "Declining Power and the Preventive Motivation for War," *World Politics* 40 (October 1987): 91.
14. John Lewis Gaddis, "A Grand Strategy of Transformation," *Foreign Policy* (November-December 2000): 51.
15. Michael O'Hanlon, Susan Rice and James Steinberg, "The New National Security Strategy and Preemption," Policy Brief #113, Brookings Institution (January 2003).
16. D. Robert Worley, "Waging Ancient War: The Preemptive Use of Force," *Strategic Studies Institute Special Report*, U.S. Army War College, 8 November 2001: 17.
17. There are significant challenges associated with dual-use technologies, and these will be addressed in some detail. That states can sell certain classes of WMD components and enablers to non-state actors and claim innocent motives is a significant problem. However, this is partially overcome if the organizational ties of the customer are known, as even the legitimate business interests of terrorist organizations are still tainted by their larger objectives.
18. Jack Levy, "The Causes of War: A Review of Theories and Evidence," in *Behavior, Society, and Nuclear War*, ed. Phillip Tetlock, et al., (New York: Oxford University Press, 1989): 253.
19. Larwrence Freedman, "Prevention, Not Preemption," *The Washington Quarterly* 26 (Spring 2003): 106.
20. Jessica Stern, "Dreaded Risks and the Control of Biological Weapons," *International Security* (Winter 2002): 96. While Stern argues that the production of biological weapons is extremely difficult to detect, particularly as most components are dual-use, she agrees that the infrastructure required for fissile material processing is detectable at long distances using chem-

ical sensors. Our contention is that weaponized biological weapons require a comparable infrastructure. Weapons developed in a home brewery, for instance, are simply not sufficiently hardy and virulent to survive and inflict mass casualties in all but the most unusual circumstances.

21. John Cirincione, "The International Non-Proliferation Regime," in *Repairing the Regime*, The Carnegie Non-Proliferation Project (2000): 283–290.
22. For a detailed critique of the effectiveness of economic sanctions, see Robert A. Pape, "Why Economic Sanctions Do Not Work," *International Security* (Fall 97): 90.
23. For example, see George Perkovich, "Bush's Nuclear Revolution: A Regime Change in Nonproliferation," *Foreign Affairs* 82 (March/April 2003): 2–9.
24. Ralph Sheridan, "The Challenge of WMD Detection in Cargo," Seaport Security Conference, 11 June 2002.
25. Even with dedicated efforts to interdict fast-boat drug smuggling, for example, success rates of 10 percent are cited by the U.S. Coast Guard. See *Statement of Rear Admiral Ernest Riutta, USCG, on Anti-Narcotics Efforts in the Western Hemisphere Before the Subcommittee on the Western Hemisphere, Committee on International Relations, U.S. House of Representatives*, 3 March 1999. The possibility of proliferators adopting these and other tactics to effect the clandestine transfer of WMD does not seem unreasonable.
26. For example, the difficulties the CIA had determining the location and scope of the Soviet Union's biological warfare program are well documented. See William Broad, "The Impossible Task for America's Spies," *New York Times*, 11 May 2003.
27. Schelling, 43.
28. John Mearsheimer and Stephen Walt, "Can Saddam Be Contained? History Says Yes," *Los Angeles Times*, 12 November 2002.
29. For one example of such a comprehensive proposal, minus the emphasis on prevention, see Richard Garwin, "The Technology of Megaterror," *Technology Review* (September 2002).

John Ellis, 2003

Terrorism in the Genomic Age

Two stories were published with little fanfare in the spring of 2003. One, a Reuters dispatch, began as follows: "Scientists have completed the finished sequence of the human genome, or genetic blueprint of life, which holds the keys to transforming medicine and understanding disease. Less than three years after finishing the working draft of the three billion letters that make up human DNA and two years earlier than expected, an international consortium of scientists said on Monday (4/13/2003) the set of instructions on how humans develop and function is done."[1]

The other story, which appeared in the British weekly *The Economist*, reported that after intensive debate, The Institute for Genomic Research (TIGR) had decided to publish the anthrax genome on its website. The Bush Administration had contracted TIGR to produce a finished sequence of the anthrax genome as part of its overall effort to better understand the dimensions of the bio-terror threat. The Administration argued that publishing the anthrax genome might be detrimental to the national security interests of the United States. TIGR argued that publishing scientific research made for better scientific research.[2]

Neither story attracted much media attention, but both stories were emblematic of a profound shift in human affairs. One might call it the dawning of the Genomic Age. As Juan Enriquez, director of the Life Sciences Project at the Harvard Business School wrote in 1998, genomic science promises to "tell us about the past, who evolved from whom, and how." More important, when combined with nanotechnologies, genomic science gives mankind unprecedented power. "By understanding and being able to recreate and modify the instructions that make life, humans will soon be able to directly and deliberately influence their own evolution and that of other species."[3]

Enriquez and others have written at length on how genomics is altering and will eventually transform the global economy. Whole categories of business—including agriculture, pharmaceuticals, petrochemicals and energy—are already reconfiguring themselves to adapt to genomic science and what it implies. The immediate consequence has been a rush of corporate consolidation; a pooling of resources to help fund genomic research. It is likely that by the end of 2010, as few as seven companies will control virtually all of the value-added of agriculture; which is to say that they will own the patents to genetically modified seed that will grow into food that will be more pest-resistant, more nutritious and may well have pharmaceutical benefits as well. It is equally likely that by the end of 2010, as few as seven companies will control much of the value-added of the pharmaceutical business. And with each passing decade of this century, the difference between economic success and economic stagnation will be determined by who possesses genomic knowledge and who does not.[4]

The speed with which genomic knowledge is advancing is breath-taking. It cost a consortium of private interests, the United States and the United Kingdom roughly $5 billion over 13 years to undertake The Human Genome Project, which in the year 2000 produced the first draft of the human genome. It might have taken that consortium forty years, had not the Celera Corporation, under the direction of Dr. Craig Venter, greatly accelerated the process. But once accelerated, it is now moving at breakneck speed. A company in Cambridge, Massachusetts, called U.S. Genomics believes that it will be able to produce a complete genomic sequence of a new-born baby, stamped onto a compact disk, within two days of that child's birth, at a cost of $1000.00 per fully sequenced genome. Mom goes in, has a baby, and two days later walks out with a $1000 CD that will inform that child's medical care for the rest of his or her life. U.S. Genomics expects to be able to do this before the end of this decade.[5]

Vast (and cheap) computing power enables and turbo-charges this extraordinary advance of genomic knowledge. Countries around the world are beginning to grasp the revolutionary implications and are acting accordingly. Singapore has what might be called a genomic industrial policy. Australia has the same thing. And China, fearing it might fall behind not only the United States but its much smaller neighbors, has decided to build an entire city devoted to genomic research and development. The city is known as Genome City, and its construction is perhaps the highest priority of the Chinese government and its military. Work on the project goes 24 hours a day, 7 days a week. When it is all done, Genome City will employ and house over 50,000 people. Construction should be completed by the end of 2004.[6]

Changing the instruction sets that control the evolution of all living things will eventually be the most important business in the world. Changing the instruction sets that control the evolution of pathogens was the most secret business of two countries in the last two decades of the 20th Century. In the former Soviet Union, in direct violation of the 1972 Biological Weapons Convention, a huge team of Soviet scientists working at a facility known as the Biopreparat developed genetically altered anthrax, smallpox and plague. Working under the guidance of the Soviet military, the Biopreparat employed over 30,000 people and produced a vast arsenal of weaponized chemical and biological agents. The head of the Biopreparat, Dr. Ken Alibek, detailed the breadth and scope of the undertaking in a book[7] after he defected to the United States.

It is a terrifying book, not least because Alibek maintains that at least some of the work that was done at the Biopreparat facility carries on to this day. But it is especially terrifying for what it implies. All research into chemical and biological warfare, into virus and pathogen, is essentially "dual use." One must develop the weapon to develop the vaccine or antidote. As research and development of weaponized biological and chemical agents advances, the likelihood of a stable biological or chemical weapon increases. And as the research advances, the possibility of targeting these weapons becomes very real indeed.

The ability to target biological and chemical weapons was the focus of South Africa's top secret chemical and biological program known as Project Coast. Project Coast was created by the then white-minority government in the late 1980s. The idea was to develop a biological or chemical weapon that would kill blacks but not whites, in the event that revolutionary fervor amongst the vast black majority endangered the white population. Project Coast worked on other "ideas," such as anti-fertility drugs that would slow black population growth. But the "big idea," if one can call it that, was to find the genetic key that would enable one ethnic group to exterminate another ethnic group without putting itself at risk.[8]

Just as pharmaceuticals might be targeted at individuals, based on genetic makeup, bioweaponeers in both the Soviet Union and South Africa were exploring the possibility of targeting specific ethnic groups with biological agents. This possibility was given new momentum, in a back-handed way, in 1995, when the Aum Shinrikyo cult attacked the Tokyo subway system with Sarin gas. The attack killed 12 people and injured more than 5000 others.[9]

In his Harvard Business School case study, Juan Enriquez described what didn't happen and why: "One of the mysteries was why more people were not hurt (in the Tokyo subway attack). The crowded subway should have acted as a giant aerosol can and infected many more people. Part of the answer is that the technology used by the cult was second rate. Another part of the puzzle may be that 25% of Asians and 10% of Caucasians have an enzyme called paraoxonase in their blood that allows them to break down Sarin and other pollutants ten times faster than most people."[10]

The key finding, clearly, was that some people would die and some would not in a Sarin gas attack, depending in part on whether they did or did not have the paraoxonase enzyme. Thankfully, some of those who were inside the Tokyo subway system on that fateful day in March of 1995, did have the enzyme and so were injured but not killed in the attack. But for bioweaponeers, the larger point was that biological and chemical agents could indeed be targeted, albeit crudely, by ethnic type.

Ken Alibek and others believe that after the break-up of the Soviet Union, a not insignificant number of the scientists affiliated with the Biopreparat program were, in baseball terminology, picked up on waivers by rogue states, including Iran, Iraq and North Korea. Western intelligence agencies believe that prior to the U.S. invasion of Iraq, the regime of Saddam Hussein was especially active in the development of weaponized chemical and biological agents. It was largely for this reason that President Clinton authorized the U.S. missile attacks on Iraq in 1998 and that President Bush followed up with a full-scale invasion in 2003.[11]

Militarily, it makes sense for economically backward or stagnant states to invest heavily in bioweapons. As Enriquez points out in his HBS case study, "a UN study (conducted in 1969) estimated that the cost of using biological weapons against civilians was 1/2000 that of conventional weapons and 1/800 the cost of using nuclear weapons." As a simple of matter of return on investment, developing bioweapons offer the cheapest path to deadly peril.[12]

This is especially true now that secondary and tertiary states can access genomic information that is routinely published as a matter of scientific protocol. If they need to see a complete sequence of the anthrax genome, as noted at the start of this essay, they need only have scientists acting as cut-outs visit the website of The Institute for Genomic Research. A few such scientists thus piggy-back on the combined enterprise of the wealthiest nations on earth to extract exactly the information necessary to produce more deadly (which is to say, vaccine resistant) anthrax spores. Weaponize those spores, whether in an aerosoal can or in a warhead of some kind, and suddenly a secondary or tertiary state possesses a strategic weapon of frightening lethality.

Perhaps more frightening is the distinct possibility that a secondary or tertiary state would not want to be held accountable for the development and deployment of such a weapon and so, instead of using it, sells it to a terrorist organization that shares a common enemy (more than likely, that enemy would be the United States, the United Kingdom,

Russia or China). If an anthrax aerosol bomb is released in the New York City subway system, it would be difficult if not impossible to determine who put it there. Two years after the anthrax mailings nearly paralyzed Washington, DC, the FBI and the CIA still do not know (definitively) who was responsible. Militarily, the United States (or Russia or China) would not know what to do in response to a biological attack on one of its cities, at a time when political pressure to do *something* would be at its zenith.

It is exactly this possibility that drove the Bush Administration to adopt its policy of pre-emptive action. In his speech to the graduating class of 2002 at West Point, President Bush shifted the national security policy of the United States from containment to preemption to put secondary and tertiary states on notice that if they were caught trafficking in the business of weaponizing chemical and biological agents (and/or nuclear/radiological devices), they would be subject to the full force of U.S. military power.[13] The policy of preemption has sparked considerable controversy in the United States, but it addresses the new reality of warfare. Weaponized chemical and biological agents are inherently de-stabilizing and wreak havoc on conventional military strategy and tactics. Unconventional policies are necessary to confront a thoroughly unconventional threat.

In the near term, there are two key groups whose financial wherewithal and global reach make it possible if not likely that they will use genomic knowledge for destructive and destabilizing purposes. First among these are the drug cartels. The Columbian cartels alone oversee a cash flow business of roughly $25 billion, according to DEA and independent estimates. The margins on cocaine and heroin production and distribution are well into the 70% range. This gives the cartels extraordinary financial leverage. (Obviously, the $25 billion figure is an guesstimate. The U.S. Drug Enforcement Agency and other law enforcement/intelligence services don't have a complete audit of the Cartel cash machine.[14]

That leverage, when applied to genomic drug research, enables them to not only research and develop ever more potent (and addictive) narcotics, but to research and develop next generations of drugs like Ecstasy, Viagra and methamphetamine. It is important to remember that Ecstasy was a legal drug for a number of years before Congress finally passed legislation banning its sale and use. As genomic knowledge advances, the ability to build Ecstasy-like chemical compounds (that produce a much stronger high, but more benign "hangover") will advance with it.

The rewards for building such a drug will be even more enormous than the present returns on the sale of heroin and cocaine. Scientists could stand to make tens of millions of dollars for developing a drug that produces Ecstasy-like euphoria, Viagra-like sexual enhancement and methamphetamine-like alertness. It's even possible that passing a law to outlaw such a drug would not pass, if enough people could be convinced that the after-effects were negligible. Whatever happens, it is certain that the drug environment into which the present generation of children (the so-called "echo boom" generation, which is the largest generational cohort in American history) will be loaded with chemical compounds and narcotic substances of unprecedented potency and/or addictiveness. And that the major financial beneficiaries will be the already cash-heavy cartels of Columbia and Mexico.

The second group with the financial wherewithal and global reach who can be expected to seize upon genomic knowledge for destructive and destabilizing purpose are, of course, terrorist organizations, the leading edge of which (at least for the moment) is Osama bin Laden's Al Qaeda.[15] General Wayne Downing (USA-Rtd), who served as the director of President George W. Bush's Global War on Terror (and who was largely responsible for authoring the U.S. Strategy for Fighting Global Terrorism, told the *Washington Post* at the end of 2002 that the thing that leaped off the pages and discs of the recovered (from Afghanistan) Al Qaeda documents and C-drives was Al Qaeda's zeal for either building or acquiring weapons of mass destruction.[16]

It is very difficult for an organization like Al Qaeda to build a nuclear weapon. It requires the indulgence of a host state and considerable scientific sophistication. It is considerably less difficult for an organization like Al Qaeda to build a radiological weapon, but it is much more difficult without a stable and secure "host." Least difficult is the acquisition or purchase of genetically-altered biological weapons. The price tag is very high, but the black market for such products exists. And again, as genomic knowledge advances, the cost of relatively crude genetically-altered biological and chemical weaponry will decline accordingly.[17]

What distinguishes Al Qaeda and other elements of radical Islam (from, say, nation-states like North Korea or Iran) is their willingness to use such weapons. What makes that willingness even more terrifying is that they have already shown that they can deliver such weapons through the use of what might be called "human missiles." The media call them suicide bombers. They're not. They're delivery mechanisms for strategic weapons.

The willingness of Islamic and Palestinian "terrorists" to use themselves as detonation devices makes problematic even the most basic tactics of "homeland defense." A terrorist willing to die of genetically-altered and vaccine-resistant smallpox can kill literally hundreds of thousands of people. If he or she kills hundreds of thousands of people in lower Manhattan, then the global financial markets have a seizure. If the global financial markets have a seizure, the global economy goes into a tailspin. The attacks on the twin towers of the World Trade Center cost New York City roughly $83 billion, according to a study conducted by the city's leading management consulting firms.[18] A genetically-altered smallpox attack would probably cause the City's finances to collapse altogether. And that would be the least of such an attack's consequences.

Aside from the specific threat posed by drug cartels and terrorist organizations armed with destabilizing and destructive genomic knowledge, there is another, perhaps larger, issue raised by the Age of Genomics. That issue is the separation between those who have genomic knowledge and those who don't. Countries like the United States and China that will be at the forefront of molecular biology, nanotechnologies, next generation information technology and pervasive computing will be on the winning side of what one might call the genomic/digital divide. On the other side will be a host of Islamic and African countries that will be literally unable to compete in or contribute to (except as laborers) the global economy. They will be genomic losers. One side will be able to cure cancer. The other side will beg for the medicial expertise. One side will be able to feed its population a hundred times over. The other side will experience horrific famine. One side will enjoy extraordinary wealth. The other will experience abject poverty. The seeds of resentment sown, when added to an already enraged movement of radical Islamists, will likely prove to be a highly volatile mix.

The underlying reality of modern life in most Islamic nations today is relentlessly grim. Life expectancy is short, illiteracy is high, famine is common, economic stagnation and deprivation is the norm. Governments, many of which have enjoyed long-standing support of the U.S. and its western allies, are notoriously corrupt and frequently barbaric in their abuses of human rights. For large numbers of Muslims, especially Shia Muslims, the inability to attain a better life for themselves or their children has caused them to embrace a much more virulent theocratic ideology. And in so doing, they effectively disconnect from the economically developed world. They have no stake in its success and find only solace and sweet revenge in its destruction. Genomics accentuates this separation to the ultimate degree; on one side are people capable of manipulating the evolution of all living things, on the other are people who have no power at all. Except, of course, the power to create and replicate catastrophic events.[19]

So what does all this suggest, in terms of policy?

First, it is of paramount concern that the United States and its allies do everything possible to enforce strict protocols and conventions with regards to the use of biological and chemical weapons. Any country that indulges in this kind of research, development or deployment must be subject to the harshest possible sanctions, including the possibility of armed intervention.

Second, it is critical that the United States and its allies do everything it can to enhance its capability of responding to bioterrorism. A recent study by the Partnership for Public Service found, according to a *New York Times* report, that "the (U.S.) government is likely to be overwhelmed in the event of a bioterrorism attack because of serious shortages in skilled medical and scientific personnel." Even if one allows considerable leeway for hyperbole (when was the last time a public service advocacy group thought the government was doing a bang-up job?), the fact remains that the anthrax mail attacks in the fall of 2001 did indeed reveal an almost woeful lack of preparedness for biological attack. While U.S. government preparedness has substantially improved since them, the shortage of skilled personnel remains a source of real worry in the event of another attack.[20]

Third, it is critical that molecular biologists and genomic scientists engage in a Manhattan Project–effort to create new scientific protocols that will specifically address the national security issues raised by genomic research and development. Since Hiroshima and Nagasaki, physicists have engaged with the government to control and contain the spread of nuclear weapons. As Henry Kelly, president of the Federation of American Scientists, recently argued in the *New York Times*, the time has come for genomic scientists and molecular biologists to do the same thing.[21]

Fourth and perhaps finally, genomic research must advance. As Henry Kelly wrote in the *New York Times*, "the difference between a lab for producing lifesaving vaccines and one capable of making deadly toxins is largely one of intent." The more genomic knowledge we have, the more ways we will have to combat pathogens, either through vaccine or antidote, the less likely it is that a genetically-altered pathogen will yield a catastrophic result. Our intent must be to act in the best interests of mankind. We must grow the food, fight the disease, enrich and elongate life. The Genomic Age will largely be defined on how well we measure up.[22]

John Ellis is a business and communications consultant based in New York. He is also a columnist for Tech Central Station, a Web site that focuses on technology and media, and a contributor to the op-ed page of the *Wall Street Journal.* Over the course of his writing career, Mr. Ellis has been a columnist for the *Boston Globe* (where he was nominated for a Pulitzer Prize in 1999), *Fast Company* magazine, *Inside* magazine and Inside.com.

Notes

1. http://www.msnbc.com/news/800806.asp?0cv=11A00.
2. http://www.economist.com/displaystory.cfm?story_id=1748489.
3. *Gene Research, the Mapping of Life and the Global Economy* is a Harvard Business School Case Study, N9-599-016, written by Juan Enriquez and is available at www.hbsp.harvard.edu.
4. For more on how genomics is transforming agriculture and pharmaceuticals, see http://harvardbusinessonline.hbsp.harvard.edu/b01/en/common/item_detail.jhtml?id=R00203.
5. The exact cost of the Human Genome Project is, at some level, unknowable, since knowledge begets knowledge and the cost of academic research is fungible. The U.S. government contributions are detailed at http://www.ornl.gov/TechResources/Human_Genome/project/budget.html. The ballpark number of $5 billion includes the contributions of the United Kingdom and private charitable trusts. For more on Eugene Chan and his work at U.S. Genomics, visit http://www.cio.com/archive/010103/37.html. The specifics about stamping out a CD of an infant's genome were taken from notes at the Genomic Sequencing and Analysis Conference in Boston, Massachusetts, in September of 2002. The author attended the conference.
6. This information was gleaned from interviews with Juan Enriquez of the Harvard Business School, who was given a tour of Genome City by Chinese Government Officials.
7. *Biohazard: The Chilling True Story of the Largest Covert Biological Weapons Program in the World—Told from the Inside by the Man Who Ran It.*
8. See the *Washington Post*, April 20 and 21, 2003.
9. http://www.cdc.gov/ncidod/EID/vol5no4/olson.htm.
10. Enriquez, HBS Case Study N9-599-016.
11. See *The Demon in the Freezer*, by Richard Preston as well as *Biohazard*, by Ken Alibek.
12. Enriquez, HBS Case Study N9-599-016.
13. http://www.jinsa.org/articles/print.html?documentid=1492 .
14. For a good overview of the drug threat, see http://www.usdoj.gov/dea/pubs/intel/02046/02046.html.
15. See *Inside Al Qaeda*, by Rohan Gunaratna.
16. http://usembassy.state.gov/mumbai/wwwfns.pdf for National Strategy for Combating Terrorism. For Downing comments, see *Washington Post*, December 24, 2002.
17. *Washington Post*, April 20–21, 2003.
18. http://www.nycp.org/impactstudy/release.htm.
19. See the annual *Economist* survey of 2002 for updated statistics of relative wealth and poverty; http://www.theworldin.com/ .
20. *New York Times*, July 5, 2003.
21. *New York Times* op-ed, July 2, 2003.
22. *New York Times* op-ed, July 2, 2003.

Chapter 6

The Threat of Other Forms of Terrorism

In this chapter, the contributors explore other threats of terrorism: ways in which terrorist groups could expand their power and their powers of destruction. The potential for connections between transnational criminal organizations and terrorist organizations presents policy makers with even more challenges in countering terrorist plots.

According to Barry R. McCaffrey and John A. Basso, the September 11 attacks demonstrated the power produced by the collision of three explosive trends: the United States as a sole superpower in the post–cold war era, and the one clear oppressor left to blame for the woes of underdeveloped peoples; a funding vacuum left after the end of the cold war, which led insurgent and terrorist organizations to turn to criminal activity to gain funds; and terrorists' perceived need for massive loss of life, to gain the attention of the media and the world. "Money is a natural centrifugal force," say McCaffrey and Basso in their exploration of this second trend.

Suicide bombers have been termed "the ultimate smart bomb." The foremost authority on the issue, Bruce Hoffman, provides a rare insight into this very dangerous and potentially imminent threat to the United States. In the past few years, the world has seen this tactic used in Israel, Saudi Arabia, Indonesia, and most recently in London, to name but a few. The threat of suicide bombers is front and center for individuals at all levels of government—from city police and fire departments to the Department of Homeland Security. Ultimately "suicide terrorism is embraced as a psychological weapon designed to induce paralysis in one's opponent," explains Hoffman. One question often asked is when will such a threat come to the United States or other Western democracies? Hoffman's answer is that the United States has already experienced such events and not just the attacks of September 11. Through examination of Palestinian suicide bombers, Hoffman offers the reader insight as to what other countries might be able to expect and the challenges faced in defending against such attacks.

Ami Pedahzur, a leading authority on suicide terrorism, presents a three-part model in this short comment paper that not only presents the reader with a new approach to the issues of suicide terrorism but the framework is useful for students and scholars alike to deconstruct other terrorist phenomena. The relationship between elite decision making, individual motivations of perpetrators, and organizational processes are equally useful for understanding other spheres of terrorism behavior and operations.

One of the more interesting issues that Ami Pedahzur raises in his piece is that of the organizational processes that are used for recruitment and indoctrination. Madeleine Gruen, a counterterrorism specialist and an expert on radicalization on the Internet, discusses the ways in which organizations use the Internet for recruitment and radicalization of target populations. In her article, she explores why the Internet has become such an important medium for groups in the post–9/11 environment. Perhaps most interesting is how well the terrorists understand popular culture and the importance of framing their message in ways that appeal to an increasingly wider range of recruits. Through the use of hip-hop, games, and dynamic Web sites, terrorists make new inroads to populations that previously would have been difficult to reach.

Chris Dishman expands the discussion begun in the McCaffrey and Basso article. Dishman examines the shift from a vertical to a horizontal organizational structure of criminal organizations and concludes that this changing structure creates new and important opportunities for terrorist organizations. Whereas criminal organizations once had very strict command-and-control hierarchies, the newer more loosely organized groups afford more opportunity for individual members to collaborate with terrorist organizations. The implications of this trend are many and will increasingly complicate the counterterror efforts.

Barry R. McCaffrey, General, USA (Retired)
John A. Basso, Major, USA, 2003

Narcotics, Terrorism, and International Crime: The Convergence Phenomenon

Introduction

The recent acceleration of America's unipolar role, when linked to greater interaction between terrorist organizations and transnational criminal organizations (TCOs), increases the possibility of another attack against the United States and the likelihood that terrorist groups will be able to gain the resources necessary for even more devastating attacks. Future terrorist mega-events may well include the use of chemical, biological, radiological, and nuclear (CBRN) material. It is the American government's role to defuse this terrorist explosion before it goes off. The wire that needs to be snipped can be found in the link between terrorist and criminal organizations.

Significance

The introduction of CBRN material to the terrorist-criminal equation underscores why it is so important to comprehend the links between terrorist organizations and transnational criminal organizations (TCOs). If scholars are correct in the conclusion that criminal organizations are increasingly linked to each other and form a global criminal network, then a terrorist who taps into this network will gain extraordinary reach.[1] For instance, a terrorist group may acquire the capability to access not only drug production revenue in Latin America, but also highly enriched uranium (HEU) or plutonium through the Russian Mafia. Additionally, tapping into this network facilitates contact with other terrorist organizations, each of which may provide other valuable services, such as a transportation network. Understanding the convergence of terrorist organizations and TCOs will be one of the keys to the future security of American citizens. To help advance this knowledge we elaborate on three emerging environmental trends that set the conditions for 9/11, and we identify the conditions that foster connections between terrorist organizations and criminal organizations. We then use representative examples to show how these connections are made and,

The views expressed in this paper are those of the authors and do not necessarily reflect the official policy or position of the United States Military Academy, the Department of the Army, the Department of Defense, or the U.S. government.

importantly, how they may be broken. We conclude by using this insight to develop policy recommendations on how best to respond to these dangerous trends.

Strategic Environment

The United States as Target

History has shown that a clear way to gain the support of a constituency is to blame its problems on someone other than itself. In the post–Cold War era, the United States, as the only remaining superpower, became the natural target for blame. Osama bin Laden made that clear in a 1997 interview with CNN's Peter Arnett: "The collapse of the Soviet Union made the U.S. more haughty and arrogant and it has started to look at itself as a master of this world and established what it calls the New World Order."[2] Additionally, as Yossef Bodansky (director of the Congressional Task Force on Terrorism and Unconventional Warfare) reported, bin Laden places the blame for the Saudi financial crisis, increased Saudi taxes, and the deteriorating Saudi education system on the United States.[3]

CIA counterterrorism expert Paul Pillar points out that the proportion of attacks on U.S. interests have risen from 31 percent in the 1980s to 37 percent in the 1990s.[4] The role of America as a primary target will continue based on widespread perceptions of the United States as carrying out unilateral policy and maintaining close ties to Israel, as well as the consistent global poverty coupled with self-evident U.S. massive material wealth. Additionally, those terrorist groups that do not wish to attack the United States directly, such as the IRA, may well try to influence their target by gaining U.S. support. Even attacks not carried out directly against American citizens seek to influence U.S. policy.

Changes to Funding Sources

Money is a natural centrifugal force. Terrorists are necessarily pulled toward it. Criminals have always sought it. Money, and the means of gaining it, brings these two very different lethal organizations together. This magnetic attraction was born of post–Cold War conditions. Money has always been a concern for insurgent groups. War requires weapons. However, since the end of Cold War superpower state sponsorship, ideological insurgents have had to look for alternative ways to raise funds. And these insurgents have had to often turn to terrorism because the states they rebel against have become too strong militarily to allow any reasonable chance at success in conventional civil war. Even some of the modern extremist terrorist groups that never benefited from Cold War funding have moved toward criminal-based funding. The ability to use the chaos wrought by terrorism and insurgency to produce coca or opium and then move narcotics through the soft borders created by the collapse of the USSR is tempting. Likewise, kidnapping of foreign company employees and extortion have grown in prevalence. These groups are drawn together because of their complimentary capabilities. Terrorists can create chaotic circumstances that allow for illicit activities. Criminal organizations have preestablished networks to move and sell narcotics and launder money. The result is that some terrorists and criminal organizations converge and become partners working together to gain revenue. Additionally, some terrorist organizations transform themselves to be able to conduct criminal activities in-house so that they can generate their own revenue. In either case, these terrorist groups become part of a network of criminal organizations, which are considered to be possible sources for CBRN material.

Increased Scope of Attacks

Terrorist organizations now perceive the need for massive loss of life to capture global attention. This perception evolved as 24-hour news media bombarded consumers with an enormous number of stories each week. Insurgents and terrorists learned quickly: To be heard, be loud. Just how loud has evolved over the last 30 years. Black September surprised the world with their 1972 attack on the Israeli Olympic team. Twelve innocent people died. Islamic Jihad stunned the world in 1983 with their attack on the Marine barracks in Beirut. 241 U.S. Marines died. Aum Shinrikyo raised world terror to new levels with their 1995 Tokyo subway attack; 12 Japanese died and over 3,000 were hospitalized from exposure to sarin gas. Al-Qaeda's staggering 1998 East Africa U.S. embassy bombings killed 264 and wounded over 5,000 people. The magnitude of the 9/11 attack was not an aberration. While there are some exceptions, generally terrorists are trying to increase the scope of their carnage in each successive campaign of attacks.[5] This observation holds true not just for extremist terrorist groups but also for ethno-nationalist groups.[6] Terrorists believe that gaining international attention is vital to their cause. In the mind of a terrorist, to get the world's attention—to win—dramatic bloodshed is necessary.[7] Massive bloodshed, though, is not easy to achieve. As the world wakes up to the threat of terrorism, it will be even more difficult to successfully plan, resource, and execute dramatically successful attacks. Success will require flexibility, particularly in acquiring resources for these terrorist operations. Both single spectacular attacks and sustained operations may require large amounts of cash. Shoestring budgets are unlikely to suffice. And, as the previous section outlined, the financial tactics of terrorist groups like Abu Sayyaf, the FARC, and al-Qaeda have evolved as rapidly as the scope of attacks seen in Munich, Beirut, and Tokyo. It has been widely reported that each of these groups has to some degree pursued criminal activities to fund its ultimate goals. In order to craft effective counterterrorism strategy, we must understand how and why terrorist groups collaborate with criminal organizations.

Hypothesis

Previous Work

Some very impressive scholarly work has been done outlining the factors that influence insurgent group behavior.[8] Insurgent groups differ from terrorist groups. Specifically, we define terrorist groups as those who have crossed a line and chosen to target innocent civilians for psychological impact. Once this line is crossed, they are more willing to expand their range of funding sources and the nature of their attacks. The new breed of extremist terror groups significantly differ in their aims from ethno-nationalist groups and in their use of terror as not just an isolated tactic, but as an all-encompassing strategy to gain the change they seek.[9] Nonetheless, there are enough similarities between typical rebel groups and terrorists to warrant an analysis of the burgeoning literature on the incidence of civil war. Paul Collier, director of the Development Research Group of the World Bank, has examined civil wars since 1965 to determine if evidence exists to support the popular perception that rebels begin civil wars to rid their state of an unjust regime, or if instead rebels simply aspire to criminal wealth. Since asking rebels their rationale would inevitably lead to a narrative focused on issues of grievance, Collier instead measures motivation through causal factors that he broadly groups as consistent with greed or grievance. His results overwhelmingly indicate that economic agendas have a greater role in the incidence and continuation of civil war than does grievance.[10]

Terrorism scholar Chris Dishman superbly extends this type of analysis to the relationship between terrorist groups and organized crime.[11] Based on his conclusion that the costs of collaboration outweigh the benefits, Dishman finds that cooperation between the two groups may occur, but it will be short-lived. He further argues that terrorist organizations and criminal organizations will continue to shy away from collaborative arrangements, because their aims and motivations are different than those of their potential collaborators. In general, he believes that these different groups will instead choose to remain on an authentic political or criminal course.[12] Dishman supports this hypothesis by using case studies to outline out how terrorist groups and organized crime have used violence in the past. The terrorist and criminal groups he studies draw and maintain a clear distinction between violence used to advance profit aims and violence used for political reasons. He demonstrates, however, that criminal motives and the lure of profit will transform the aims of some terrorist leaders. This transformation toward profit-making blurs the distinction between violence used to advance political aims and that used to increase revenue. In particular, Dishman warns, "Terrorists and guerrilla groups who view their cause as futile, might turn their formidable assets towards crime—all the while under a bogus political banner." While Dishman's work is excellent, some might suggest that it is far too general and relies too heavily on cases that existed in a world that did not have such open borders and information technologies for coordinating activities on a global basis. By failing to distinguish between insurgent groups and terrorists or between different types of terrorist groups, and by failing to recognize that historical cases miss the complexity of the modern relationship between organized crime and terrorists, we believe that Dishman has missed the meaningful convergence relationships between these dangerous organizations. Instead, Dishman believes that terrorist organizations simply undergo transformation, a conclusion that some experts believe is incorrect.

Typology and Hypothesis

To understand why the terrorist groups most likely to strike the United States are likely to converge into partnerships with criminal organizations, we must analyze their motivations. As the United States prosecutes a broad war on terror, we must sort out which terrorist groups will transform themselves to take on the capabilities of a profit-driven criminal group, and which terrorists groups will remain true to their ideological cause. The vital first step in crafting policy options to defeat these groups will be understanding their vulnerabilities. Three general outcomes exist for terrorist organizations in their dealings with criminal organizations. Terrorist organizations may converge, meaning form a partnership with criminal organizations; terrorist groups may transform themselves into quasi-criminal organizations; or they may maintain themselves as pure terrorist organizations.

Terrorist groups will approach the decision of what type of partnership to pursue based on two independent variables. First, terrorist groups must identify whether they

Figure 1

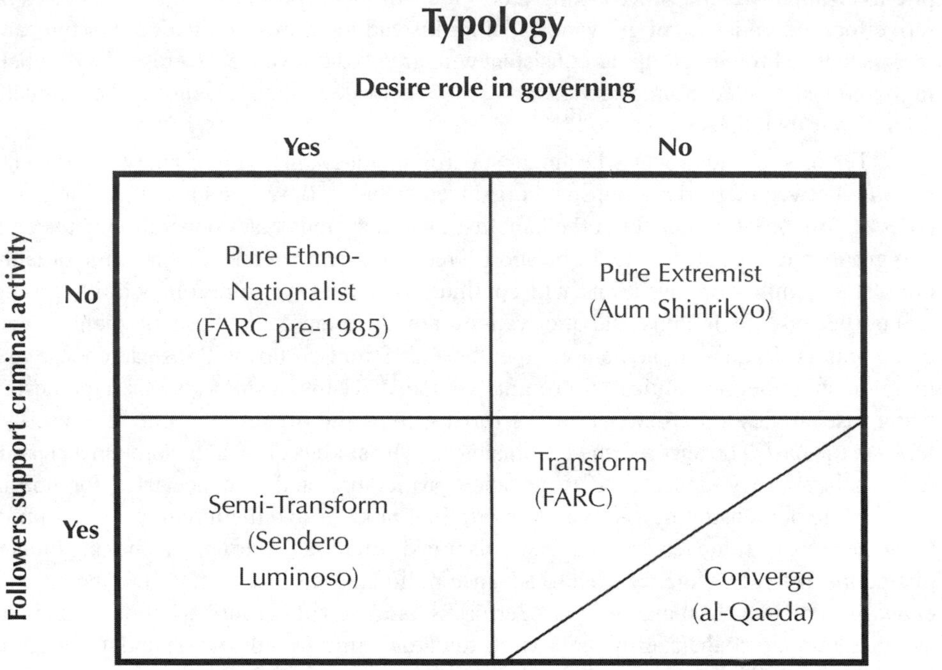
Typology
Desire role in governing
Yes
No
Followers support criminal activity
No
Yes
Pure Ethno-Nationalist (FARC pre-1985)
Pure Extremist (Aum Shinrikyo)
Semi-Transform (Sendero Luminoso)
Transform (FARC)
Converge (al-Qaeda)

intend to seek a future legitimate governance role. While terrorist actions will always have some political aspect to them (or they would not meet RAND terrorism expert Bruce Hoffman's regularly cited definition of terrorism), the political action may have little to do with gaining a governing role in a state.[13] In fact, we suggest that a sea change in terrorism has taken place. Many new groups are extremist in nature instead of ethno-nationalist and will generally not seek a role in state governance. Second, all terrorist groups must determine whether their followers will continue to support them if they pursue criminal activities to gain revenue or resources for future terror attacks. Wesleyan professor and terrorism expert Martha Crenshaw has outlined the rational calculations terrorists make in deciding whether to act. We believe they make this same calculation regarding funding. Terrorists must determine if their actions will cause a loss of popular support from their followers.[14] If so, their ability to interact with criminal organizations is constrained. These two variables, desire to govern and support for criminal activity, interact to determine in large part which path terrorist groups take regarding cooperation with criminal organizations.

Clear logic underlies each part of the typology. For instance, Sendero Luminoso (The Shining Path) participated in criminal activities that its followers supported, but only in an effort to fund Abimael Guzman's bizarre Maoist vision. Sendero never lost its desire to govern. On the other hand, we would suggest that the FARC, after determining that it could not play an active role in the Colombian state, fully transformed itself and turned its focus almost exclusively to profit via criminal activity. In doing so, the FARC lost all but the most determined of its ideological followers. While these two cases briefly illustrate the interaction of the key independent variables, a deeper examination of the convergence case is warranted given the clear danger to U.S. citizens.

We suggest that a vital part of the typology is the differentiation between modern extremist terrorist organizations and those that are of the traditional ethno-nationalist type. We need to determine the ultimate motivation of the group. In our judgment, extremist groups do not seek an active role in governing a state. Moreover, the ideal they seek to achieve so overshadows the distortions to that ideal that their followers see criminal activity as a minor irritant. For example, Shoko Asahara's followers in the millenarian cult Aum Shinrikyo have been accurately described as extremely well educated. Yet, as Walter Laqueur of the Center for Strategic and International Studies perceptively points out, these same followers not only supported the smuggling of weapons from Russia, they also managed to make the cruel and bizarre mental leap that releasing sarin gas on innocent Japanese citizens in the Tokyo subway would aid in preventing an American WMD attack on Japan.[15]

These groups always believe that the ends justify the means. Osama bin Laden implicitly made this point in a 1998 interview with ABC News, during which he altered his previous sentiment that only U.S. military personnel and facilities were targets of his terror campaign and added American civilians to his target list. As experts have pointed out, this escalation was made, "despite the fact that the Koran itself is explicit about the protections offered to civilians."[16] We suggest that the ramifications are clear. If the ends justify any means for some terrorist organizations, then collaboration with criminal organizations will be likely. This partnership is particularly probable if those criminal organizations can provide both revenue and a capability that the terrorist organization does not possess. As our typology indicates in the lower right corner of the box in figure 1, in the future we can expect to see convergence between criminal groups and so-called extremist terrorist groups like al-Qaeda. Extremist groups generally have no genuine desire to govern and their followers are not averse to these groups' criminal connections.

Given al-Qaeda's alleged business structure, which Peter Bergen expertly outlines in *Holy War, Inc.*, this focus on capabilities should not surprise us. Seeking out a partner to gain a capability that you lack has long been the model in the business world, and now we are seeing terrorist groups sophisticated enough to organize as businesses. The frightening part of these capability-based partnerships is that some criminal organizations may have more to exchange than a narcotics distribution network and the cash to fund terrorist operations and training. Some of these TCOs, particularly those that operate in the former Soviet Union and in Pakistan, may also have the capability to acquire CBRN material. Some observers have questioned whether these criminal groups would have the motivation to pursue such transactions, particularly given the assumption that collaboration with terrorists would naturally lead to greater law enforcement attention.

Observers who make this case about criminal organizations are trapped in the same thinking that led to faulty logic regarding whether terrorists would converge with TCOs. We believe that transnational criminal organizations are businesses. Just as businesses seek partners to gain the capabilities they lack, so too will TCOs seek partners. As we have already seen in Colombia, Afghanistan, and Burma, terrorist groups will bring narcotics production and some distribution capacity to the bargaining table. Terrorist groups are particularly well suited to the task of narcotics production since the chaotic environment they create will lead to lawlessness and the ability to conduct illicit business. Effective monopolies create barriers to entry by other firms through legal restrictions, like patents and copyrights, or through exorbitant start-up costs as seen in the jumbo-jet industry. Terrorist groups involved in drug production gain a monopoly on the control of land for the growing of coca or opium. They maintain a barrier to entry through violence. The behavior and values of both the criminal organizations and their terrorist partners becomes congruent.

A second potential argument that might cause criminal organizations to avoid partnering with terrorist groups is the question of scope of violence. Terrorists, even those seeking a legitimate role in a state, are willing to cross lines that many citizens see as sacrosanct. They will carry out kidnapping and murder for instance, and see these terrible acts as legitimate in order to further their cause. Criminal organizations, or at the very least some of their operatives, will also not be queasy about the mass casualty situations that they would create through the sale of CBRN material to terrorists. Crossing this criminal line would not be difficult since both parties will likely feel that the target—the United States—deserves what it gets. It is no secret that some of the poorly paid Russian, Pakistani, North Korean, or Iranian military who may have access to CBRN material maintain strong feelings of animosity toward America.[17] Valentin Tikhonov frighteningly points out in a Carnegie Endowment for International Peace report that given the lack of accountability of tactical nuclear weapons, not to mention weapons grade nuclear material, as well as biological, chemical, and radiological material, the ability of soldiers and scientists to covertly sell this material seems unquestioned.[18] Both sides of the marriage—extremist terrorist organizations and transnational criminal organizations—will see benefits in converging into such a lethal partnership. Arguments that this relationship will be short-lived are moot. It only takes one such criminal-terrorist partnership to realize our greatest fear: terrorists armed with nuclear, chemical, or biological weapons.

Case Studies—Testing the Hypothesis

To flesh out this argument more thoroughly, we believe it is beneficial to examine representative cases of transformed and converged terrorist groups and to outline the evolution of a criminal organization, in order to see characteristics evident in each case. We do not illustrate a pure terrorist group case; each of the groups we examine began as a pure case and eventually changed with its environment. It is useful to see which independent variables mutated over time leading these groups from a pure state to a transformed or converged state. Our purpose is to gain predictive capability for future instances and devise strategies to attack the exposed flank of terrorist organizations. We realize that our examination is only an initial overview and that it ultimately deserves more detailed case study analysis. However, it is clear that the differences in the cases we cite hinge to a certain extent on whether terrorists use terror, as a tactic, as has been prevalent with traditional ethno-nationalist terrorist groups, or if they use terror as a fundamental strategy, as we have witnessed in contemporary terrorist organizations. Additionally, we should note that a comprehensive study should examine a number of factors that help steer a terrorist group's decision on whether to partner with criminal organizations. A vital element included in these factors is having the geography that supports criminal trafficking.

FARC—Transformation

Colombia's vicious rebellion is more than 50 years old.[19] The murderous conflict has cost the country over 200,000 lives. Although insurgent activity has ebbed and flowed over the years, the explosive growth of narco-insurgent financing through cocaine and heroin criminal activity has dramatically strengthened the fighting capacity of Colombia's terrorist groups. They have been ultimately transformed into terrorist organizations that use massive violence against the state to cement their capacity to maintain narcotics profits. This dramatic change from a Marxist revolutionary political organization to a transformed terrorist organization occurred as a response to political failure. Colombia's main rebel group, the Revolutionary Armed Forces of Colombia (FARC), failed in its attempt to gain a voice in Colombian governance via politics.

The FARC attempted to enter mainstream Colombian politics in the mid-1980s by establishing the Patriotic Union party. Threatened by its electoral successes, large landowners used paramilitary units, often with the support of Colombia's armed forces, to carry out a methodical campaign of murder against Patriotic Union officials.[20] These paramilitary units later combined to form the United Self-Defense Forces of Colombia (AUC). The introduction of this other armed force, the paramilitary AUC, now estimated at 4,000 to 5,000 strong, marked a critical intensification in Colombian violence. The FARC responded to this threat by increasing its military capacity. However, it had to seek alternate funding sources, primarily narcotics, to gain this increased capability for violence. While the AUC's use of assassinations hurt the FARC's political ambitions, ultimately, it was its immersion in narcotics activities that eliminated all of the FARC's political legitimacy. Additionally, the FARC's great success in gaining drug money—the State Department's 2002 International Narcotics Control Strategy Report (INCSR) says that Colombia's rebel groups now control much of the country's narcotics production and distribution capacity—has in the eyes of many observers completely transformed it from its Marxist past.[21] With around $500 million in profits from processing and shipping cocaine, "FARC rebels are so involved in the drug business that [a senior Colombian military leader] bluntly calls them 'a cartel'."[22] In other words, the FARC no longer appears to seek any significant role in the governance of Colombia, and it has a group of followers who will ruthlessly support all types of criminal activity from narcotics and kidnapping to outright extortion of the oil and gas industry. These narco-insurgents who fight under the guise of political grievance will back any criminal actions by the leaders of the FARC. They recognize that these terrorist attacks maintain the chaotic environment that creates the conditions for continued narcotics profits.

PKK—Ethno-Nationalist Converged

Abdullah Ocalan formed the Kurdistan Workers Party (PKK) in 1978. The PKK professed Marxist ideology at its inception; however, by the 1990s it advocated nationalism over communism. To that nationalist end, the PKK began including Islam in its literature in 1989. In 1984 the PKK made its critical strategic change—the adoption of violent terrorist tactics. Between 1984 and 1994, 128 teachers were killed as the PKK attacked the educational institutions that it saw as representative of the Turkish state. As the PKK enlarged its campaign of violence from May 1993 to October 1994, 1,600 total deaths were attributed to the group. In response to this increased violence, the Turkish military was given free rein to defeat the terrorists, and by the spring of 1994, the PKK's impact in Turkey had dramatically decreased.[23] However, the PKK's level of involvement in criminal activity to generate the resources needed to continue its war against Turkey did not diminish.

The U.S. State Department indicated in 1992 that the PKK was involved in the acquisition, importation, and distribution of drugs in Europe. Presumably this move toward illicit activities was driven by the need for funds required to support its desperate struggle against Turkey's escalated anti-terror offense. Yet, after the Turkish Armed Forces stunningly defeated the PKK, by 1994 few Turkish Kurds supported the terrorists' violent tactics. However, they continued to pursue drug trafficking, even reportedly partnering with the Medellin cartel by 1995. Interestingly, although the PKK did not gain internal legitimacy from its own followers, it did gain external recognition. The wife of French president Mitterand even penned a letter of support to "President Ocalan" in 1998.[24] Nonetheless, when Ocalan was captured in Nairobi, Kenya, in 1999, the final end of the PKK seemed near. It is curious to note that some elements of the PKK have maintained a discourse that indicates that even now they want some role in governance. Indeed, by February of 2002, the PKK was again threatening to resume its war as the defenders of Kurd cultural autonomy.[25] Regardless of the outcome of its continued political signals, the PKK seems to have effectively converged with criminal organizations. A political group that began as a pure ethnonationalist terrorist group now has all of the characteristics of a partner of criminal organizations. The 1998 State Department INCSR alleges that the PKK used narcotics trafficking to finance its terror operations. However, the capture of Ocalan and the inevitable drop in funding from Kurds living abroad makes it more likely that the PKK is now using terrorism to support its bottom line.

Al-Qaeda—Extremist Converged

Afghanistan under Taliban rule became the world's leading opium and processed heroin producer. Despite Mullah Omar's ban on poppy cultivation as a first grudging response to world pressure in July 2000, trafficking of Afghan heroin continued through the use of massive stockpiles. It seems almost certain that al-Qaeda used their controlling link to the Taliban to profit from narcotics trafficking.[26] In 1998, before the Taliban's prohibition on production, the Italian government had established a link between the financing of Islamic fundamentalist groups and drug trafficking.[27] This conclusion certainly matches logic: The Taliban was said to have levied a 20 percent tax on drug runners, and it is clear that Taliban ties to al-Qaeda were very close and indeed had elements of a subordinate relationship. Moreover, after bin Laden's international bank accounts were frozen, it was clear that he would have had little problem justifying the use of drug money to finance his operations.[28] Bin Laden's closest followers also would have had few problems with this financing method, particularly when the narcotics were being trafficked to Westerners. In fact, fatwas from extremist Islamic leaders allow these highly irregular, seemingly un-Islamic actions because they add to the destruction of Western society.

Finally, there is evidence that bin Laden has spent in excess of $3 million dollars trying to purchase a nuclear device from the former Soviet Union. Given his close relationship with the Chechens, it seems likely that the Chechen Mafia facilitated these efforts. It is also probable that he would have approached the Russian Mafia, as evidence indicates that they have the capacity to acquire CBRN material.[29]

Russian Mafia

The increase in globalization in the 1990s rewarded businesses that took advantage of trends in deregulation by delocalizing and organizing transnational enterprises. Organized crime followed this lead by discarding its traditional pyramid-shaped structure in favor of less visible criminal networks.[30] Russian organized crime reportedly consists of some 110 transnational criminal groups allegedly operating in 40 different countries. The 70,000 members of this extended crime family are believed to control an estimated 50 percent of the Russian economy. There is some evidence of formal agreements linking the Russian Mafia to Colombian narcotics traffickers.[31] There is very little evidence linking the Russian Mafia to terrorist groups. Nonetheless, given the global nature of its business, and the active role the Russian Mafia takes in narcotics trafficking across the porous borders of the former Soviet Union, it seems likely that connections have been made with terrorist groups who participate in narcotics trafficking. As the State Department reports, heroin in Russia is primarily imported by Afghans, Tajiks, and other Central Asians across the southern border with Kazakstan, and then distributed by Russian criminal organizations.

In other words, nationality matters little. Capabilities determine business partnerships. For example, circumstantial evidence exists that links the Russian Mafia to terrorists in an arms-for-cash (or narcotics) transaction. Between 1992 and 1994, the Russian Army lost 14,400 assault rifles and machine guns and 17 shoulder-fired anti-tank weapons.[32] There is little doubt that a profit-driven organization like the Russian Mafia would be willing to take the next step and trade CBRN material for revenue. This transaction is particularly likely in a financial environment in which deregulation has made the control and monitoring of payments virtually impossible. Evidence suggests that $300 to $500 billion of crime proceeds are transferred undetected through the world's financial markets each year.[33] The threat of a nuclear armed al-Qaeda is monumental, and it is unquestionably worth asking: Will a profit-driven organization that will have eventually squeezed every possible corrupt dime out of the Russian state apparatus then turn to an even more profitable transaction if its chances of being caught are minimal?

Conclusion and Recommendations

Case Findings

We believe there is a broad trend that suggests terrorist groups transformed themselves or converged with criminal organizations when they saw diminished chances of defeating government forces or when their funding apparatus collapsed. From the perspective of criminal organizations, there are clear costs to collaboration: The discovery of a criminal-terrorist link would bring unwanted response from national and international law enforcement agencies. But, if it is possible to conceal the link to terrorist organizations, these partnerships could prove to be very valuable. We also suggest that the increasing technical ease of laundering funds in the information age global economy makes discovery unlikely for sophisticated money launderers. In the specific case of al-Qaeda, effective law enforcement against illegal contributions via the money laundering rules put in place post-9/11 might produce the unintended consequence of pushing al-Qaeda away from Saudi contributors and toward more extensive partnerships with criminal organizations.[34] If we do not see this reaction by al-Qaeda, we could certainly see the same outcome by other terrorist organizations that will follow bin Laden's operational lead. As Harvard terrorism expert Jessica Stern points out, terrorists tend to copy each other.[35] This type of convergence from a group with the capabilities of al-Qaeda signals the dangers of the fourth trend—the emergence of CBRN weapons. The possession of CBRN weapons combined with the other three trends would return us to the horror we first saw at the birth of nuclear weapons in 1945. Our current policy must identify effective and rational strategic alternatives for our long-term campaign against terror.

Recommendations

Many would argue that the past 15 years have been marked by a lack of adequate leadership and sensible policy judgments by our democracy's political, economic, media, and military elites in the struggle against global terror. Our leadership was collectively incompetent in the face of growing mountains of evidence indicating that our nation was increasingly at risk of catastrophic losses from terrorist attacks on our citizens, our armed forces, and our economic and political interests. The United States did make multiple calls on the global community to create a new international consensus. Still, we never defined the reward and punishment coefficients that would apply to coerce positive responses in the international community.[36] These failures are not excusable. However, our mind-numbing inactivity occurred during an era when terrorism was not at the forefront of the collective American conscience. To persist in our previous mistakes would be criminal given the clear evidence of convergence between criminal organizations and terrorist groups and the potentially deadly CBRN threat that goes along with this partnership. The global community must use the information gathered through the analysis of this convergence trend to forestall or prevent future attacks by applying the information to the four critical areas outlined below.

1. **Common Conceptual Framework:** Our counterterrorism effort lacks a conceptual framework and the leadership necessary to effectively combat this global problem.[37] We cannot hope to tackle this problem piecemeal. Instead, we must construct a broad strategy that examines our intelligence requirements, includes our foreign policy actions writ large, and imaginatively considers the vulnerabilities and weaknesses of terrorist groups. We must analyze each of the specific weapons we hold for severing the bond between terrorists and criminal organizations—and between separate terrorist groups—in a growing global network. Identifying whether terrorist groups will remain pure, transform themselves, or converge with criminal organizations is a critical part of pinpointing those weaknesses.
2. **Intelligence:** The different relationships that convergence and transformation breed denote distinct weaknesses inherent in terrorist groups. With these weaknesses in mind, convergence and transformation trends point our intelligence community toward making three necessary structural changes. First, the Central Intelligence Agency and the Defense Intelligence Agency need to embark on a 10-year crash program to rebuild a global human intelligence capability adequate to warn the United States and our allies of the new national security nexus of threats posed by terrorism, drugs, and international criminal organizations. Additionally, these agencies must pursue an ethnically diverse group of intelligence operatives. America is the melting pot, and

we need to take advantage of this national strength. This crash program will not come without costs—Congress must fund this initiative. Second, the administration must construct a common organizational scheme that allows for intelligence sharing between these agencies and the FBI. Most importantly, we must construct a single integrating mechanism focused exclusively on counterterror intelligence analysis. America's intelligence community must allocate assets not only to intelligence collection but also, more critically, to intelligence analysis. We are suffering from information overload. We need sophisticated analysts to digest this raw data and find the operationally useful insights. The convergence and transformation trends are an excellent place to begin this analysis. These trends underscore the need to bridge the gap between the CIA and the FBI and our other intelligence bodies. Lastly, the United States must lead the way in creating international mechanisms to coordinate and link national law enforcement and intelligence capabilities in close partnership with global finance and treasury officials.[38]

3. **Legitimacy:** Al-Qaeda and other terrorist groups expose themselves to counterattack by partnering with criminal organizations, particularly when they use narcotics trafficking as a revenue source. Al-Qaeda has survived this weakness because it had a higher calling—a Jihad against the West—on which to focus its constituents. To take advantage of this vulnerability, the international community needs to fashion a Jihad against narcotics trafficking that includes antidrug education by Muslim clerics in the Muslim world. This psyops strategy—linking al-Qaeda to the very narcotics that have been ruled as unholy by Islamic clerics—could potentially weaken some of al-Qaeda's legitimacy with the young men who in their most impressionable years are shaped by extremist education. Perceived religious legitimacy acts as a catalyst for the young people who choose to martyr themselves for this cause. Any step taken to reduce it is worthwhile.

   The difference between a converged terrorist group that still has legitimacy with a broad array of followers and a transformed terrorist group that no longer has broad legitimacy helps define primary steps against these distinct terrorist organizations. For example, al-Qaeda has a legitimacy anchored by anti-Western feelings, so we must also be careful with our military operations in the Arab world. Each person who dies as part of a Western military campaign may add to al-Qaeda's legitimacy and add to the creation of other martyrs, whereas attacking al-Qaeda's legitimacy would weaken the group without the negative side effects. On the other hand, a strategy attacking the legitimacy of the FARC would not significantly affect its followers. A transformed terrorist organization like the FARC, which has substituted the power of criminal gain for ideological purity, has followers that are unaffected by the obvious criminal nature of the group. In the case of these transformed groups, we need to focus our campaign on crippling them by attacking their means of producing terror, including their narcotics revenue source and the narco-insurgents who defend their drug production facilities.[39] These attacks will not add to the FARC's supporters as they might if carried out against al-Qaeda.

4. **Tailored Response:** The United States should also develop new operational response packages created from all the tools of international power including diplomacy, economic aid, and preemptive offensive action. There are enough similarities between the types of terrorist organizations, represented on one hand by al-Qaeda and

on the other by the FARC, to guide the analysis that will allow us to defeat them. Determining whether we expect these terrorist groups to stay pure, to transform themselves to gain criminal capabilities, or to partner with criminal organizations is a good place to start in crafting our mix of responses.

a. **Aid:** The United States must develop the political will to devote significant levels of foreign aid—on the order of $5 billion per year—as a central element of our foreign policy.[40] We cannot continue to prosecute the war on terror as an independent part of our foreign policy, which relies primarily on military action. Counterterrorism operations must be broad in scope. Directed U.S. economic aid can help a fledgling democracy strengthen its institutions of government. Directed aid can also help reduce gross extremes in income disparity and poverty, and aid can create educational opportunities by providing alternative schools to compete with fanatical madrassas.

b. **Preemptive Offensive Action:** Understanding the differences between terrorist and criminal groups that have remained pure, transformed, or converged will help identify the constraints on preemptive offensive action. We must consider the long-term impact of offensive action based on the strength of each of these groups' followings. We must not be paralyzed by the notion of preemption and direct offensive action against the terrorists and their supporters. Terrorist groups that maintain devoted followers can still be aggressively attacked if we more effectively share our proof of terrorist involvement with Arab media outlets and international organizations. And our actions and information-sharing would be less constrained when dealing with those terrorist groups that have completely transformed to criminal organizations. In most cases, these criminal-terrorist groups simply seek to make a profit. They use terrorism to maintain a chaotic state that allows for illicit activity. These groups have few supporters outside of their organization. It is not normally necessary to constrain our actions based on the unintended production of more terrorists. As an example, the United States may consider expanding its Plan Colombia campaign to directly include the FARC. We may also develop a far more aggressive campaign against the Abu Sayyaf Group, which, because of its ties with the Philippines Triad and with Cebu-based smugglers, has lost legitimacy in the eyes of traditional Moro leaders.[41]

In addition to U.S. targeting of terrorists, we must focus on transnational criminal organizations and place them at risk if we have proof that they are linked with terrorists. Foreign nations, even those whose economic, military, and political capabilities we value or fear, must also recognize that we will punish them for any support of terror organizations or the criminal groups partnered with them.[42] We must also be willing to reward those who cooperate. A global campaign requires carrots and sticks. The United States finds itself in the unique position to be able to effectively use both. Our recommendations, which are focused on unraveling the next terrorist plot—not the last one—will sharpen the effectiveness of our counterterrorist policy.

Barry R. McCaffrey, a U.S. Army General who is now retired from active duty, is the Olin Distinguished Professor of National Security Studies at the United States Military Academy, West Point, and president of a consulting firm specializing in international security issues. General McCaffrey stepped down as the director of the White House Office of National Drug Control Policy in January 2001. He is also a national security and terrorism analyst for NBC News.

John A. Basso is a Major in the U.S. Army and an instructor in economics at the U.S. Military Academy, West Point.

Endnotes

1. Alison Jamieson, "Transnational Organized Crime: A European Perspective," in *Studies in Conflict & Terrorism*, Vol. 24, 2001, p. 379.
2. Peter Bergen, *Holy War, Inc.: Inside the Secret World of Osama Bin Laden*, New York: Free Press, 2001, p. 20.
3. Yossef Bodansky, *Bin Laden: The Man Who Declared War on America*, New York: Random House, 2001, pp. 190–191.
4. Paul R. Pillar, *Terrorism and U.S. Foreign Policy*, Washington, D.C.: Brookings Institution Press, 2001, pp. 57, 233.
5. Jessica Stern, *The Ultimate Terrorists*, Cambridge: Harvard University Press, 1999, p. 6. Stern points out that 4,798 deaths were attributed to terrorists in the 1970s, whereas between 1990 and 1996, 51,797 deaths were attributed to terrorists.
6. The FARC admit to firing a homemade mortar on 1 May 2002 that killed 117 Colombians seeking protection in a church in the northwest Colombian village of Bojaya. Palestinian suicide bombers have killed over 400 Israelis in the last 18 months of the second intifada.
7. Stern, p. 35.
8. Among the excellent pieces on insurgent groups and civil wars are: I. William Zartman, "The Unfinished Agenda," in Roy Licklider, ed., *Stopping the Killing: How Civil Wars End*, (NYU, 1993) pp. 20–34. Michael E. Brown, ed., *The International Dimensions of Internal Conflict*, (MIT, 1996). Robert Harrison Wagner, "The Causes of Peace," in Roy Licklider, ed., *Stopping the Killing: How Civil Wars End*, (NYU, 1993) pp. 235–268. Mats Berdal and David Malone, eds., *Greed and Grievance: Economic Agendas in Civil Wars*, Boulder: Lynn Rienner, 2000.
9. Presentation by Bruce Hoffman, West Point, N.Y., 16 April 2002.
10. Paul Collier, "Doing Well Out of War: An Economic Perspective," in *Greed and Grievance: Economic Agendas in Civil Wars*, Boulder: Lynn Rienner, 2000, p. 96.
11. Chris Dishman, "Terrorism, Crime, and Transformation," in *Studies in Conflict and Terrorism*, Jan. 2001, Vol. 24, pp. 43–59.
12. Ibid, p. 44.
13. Bruce Hoffman, *Inside Terrorism*, New York: Columbia University Press, 1998, p. 43. Hoffman's definition of terrorism: it is political in aims and motives; it is violent or threatens; it is designed to have far-reaching psychological repercussions; it is conducted by an organization or cell and perpetrated by a nonstate entity or subnational group.
14. Martha Crenshaw, "The Logic of Terrorism: Terrorist Behavior as a Product of Strategic Choice," in Walter Reich, ed., *Origins of Terrorism*, Washington, D.C.: Woodrow Wilson Center Press, 1990, p. 17.
15. Walter Laqueur, *The New Terrorism: Fanaticism and the Arms of Mass Destruction*, Oxford: Oxford University Press, 1999, p. 242.
16. Bergen, p. 20.
17. Bill Keller lays out this argument for both Pakistan and Russia in, "Nuclear Nightmare," in the *New York Times Magazine*, 26 May 2002.

18. Valentin Tikhonov, *Russia's Nuclear and Missile Complex: The Human Factor in Proliferation*, Washington, D.C.: Carnegie Endowment for International Peace, 2001.
19. Most date the guerrilla groups back to *la violencia*'s start in 1948. Some, however, date the rebellion's beginning to 1965, the year *la violencia* ended.
20. Michael Shifter, "Colombia on the Brink; There Goes the Neighborhood," *Foreign Affairs*, July-August 1999, p.2.
21. State Department, *2002 Colombia INCSR*.
22. Linda Robinson, "In for a Dime, In for a Dollar?," *U.S. News and World Report*, 4 October 1999, p.32.
23. Cindy Jebb, *The Fight for Legitimacy: Liberal Democracy versus Terrorism*," The Center for Naval Warfare Studies, June 2001, Newport: U.S. Naval War College, pp. 80–81.
24. Ibid, p. 90.
25. "Europe: A Turn for the Worse; Turkey and its Kurds," The Economist, 2 Feb. 2002.
26. State Department, *2002 Afghanistan INCSR*.
27. Jamieson, p. 383.
28. Ibid.
29. Bodansky, p. 328.
30. Jamieson, p. 378.
31. Ibid.
32. Chris Smith, "Light Weapons—The Forgotten Dimension of the International Arms Trade," in *Brassey's Defence Yearbook*, 1994 (London: Centre for Defence Studies). The authors thank Cadet Adam Scher, U.S. Military Academy, Class of 2004, for his research assistance on the Russian Mafia.
33. Jamieson, p. 379.
34. "Terrorist Finance: Follow the Money," in *The Economist*, 1 June 2002, p. 67.
35. Stern, p. 74.
36. Some of these comments previously printed in the October 2001 issue of *Armed Forces Journal International*. Reprinted with the editor's permission from "Challenges to U.S. National Security—Dealing with Madness," by General Barry R. McCaffrey, USA (Ret).
37. Ibid.
38. Elements of this recommendation previously printed in February 2002 issue of *Armed Forces Journal International*. Reprinted with the editor's permission from "Challenges to U.S. National Security—Afghanistan: Denying a Sanctuary to Terror," by General Barry R. McCaffrey, USA (Ret).
39. The State Department's *2002 Colombia INCSR* reports that JTFS UH-1N helicopters "were struck 50 times by small arms fire from narcoterrorists attempting to disrupt counternarcotics operations."
40. Elements of this recommendation previously printed in February 2002 issue of *Armed Forces Journal International*. Reprinted with the editor's permission from "Challenges to U.S. National Security—Afghanistan: Denying a Sanctuary to Terror," by General Barry R. McCaffrey, USA (Ret).
41. Military sources in the Philippines confirm open source documents like "Abu Sayyaf Financiers and Couriers Nabbed," in the *Philippine Daily Inquirer*, 3 July 2001, that indicate clear evidence of ties between Abu Sayyaf and criminal organizations and the ramifications of these ties on ASG legitimacy.
42. McCaffrey, "Afghanistan: Denying a Sanctuary to Terror."

Bruce Hoffman, 2003

The Logic of Suicide Terrorism

First you feel nervous about riding the bus. Then you wonder about going to a mall. Then you think twice about sitting for long at your favorite café. Then nowhere seems safe. Terrorist groups have a strategy—to shrink to nothing the areas in which people move freely—and suicide bombers, inexpensive and reliably lethal, are their latest weapons. Israel has learned to recognize and disrupt the steps on the path to suicide attacks. We must learn too.

Nearly everywhere in the world it is taken for granted that one can simply push open the door to a restaurant, café, or bar, sit down, and order a meal or a drink. In Israel the process of entering such a place is more complicated. One often encounters an armed guard who, in addition to asking prospective patrons whether they themselves are armed, may quickly pat them down, feeling for the telltale bulge of a belt or a vest containing explosives. Establishments that cannot afford a guard or are unwilling to pass on the cost of one to customers simply keep their doors locked, responding to knocks with a quick glance through the glass and an instant judgment as to whether this or that person can safely be admitted. What would have been unimaginable a year ago is now not only routine but reassuring. It has become the price of a redefined normality.

In the United States in the twenty months since 9/11 we, too, have had to become accustomed to an array of new, often previously inconceivable security measures—in airports and other transportation hubs, hotels and office buildings, sports stadiums and concert halls. Although some are more noticeable and perhaps more inconvenient than others, the fact remains that they have redefined our own sense of normality. They are accepted because we feel more vulnerable than before. With every new threat to international security we become more willing to live with stringent precautions and reflexive, almost unconscious wariness. With every new threat, that is, our everyday life becomes more like Israel's.

The situation in Israel, where last year's intensified suicide-bombing campaign changed the national mood and people's personal politics, is not analogous to that in the United States today. But the organization and the operations of the suicide bombers are neither limited to Israel and its conflict with the Palestinians nor unique to its geostrategic position. The fundamental characteristics of suicide bombing, and its strong attraction for the terrorist organizations behind it, are universal: Suicide bombings are inexpensive and effective. They are less complicated and compromising than other kinds of terrorist operations. They guarantee media coverage. The suicide terrorist is the ultimate smart bomb. Perhaps most important, coldly efficient bombings tear at the fabric of trust that holds societies together. All these reasons doubtless account for the spread of suicide terrorism from the Middle East to Sri Lanka and Turkey, Argentina and Chechnya, Russia and Algeria—and to the United States.

To understand the power that suicide terrorism can have over a populace—and what a populace can do to counter it—one naturally goes to the society that has been most deeply affected. As a researcher who has studied the strategies of terrorism for more than twenty-five years, I recently visited Israel to review the steps the military, the police, and the intelligence and security services have taken against a threat more pervasive and personal than ever before.

I was looking at x-rays with Dr. Shmuel Shapira in his office at Jerusalem's Hadassah Hospital. "This is not a place to have a wristwatch," he said as he described the injuries of a young girl who'd been on her way to school one morning last November when a suicide terrorist detonated a bomb on her bus. Eleven of her fellow passengers were killed, and more than fifty others wounded. The blast was so powerful that the hands and case of the bomber's wristwatch had turned into lethal projectiles, lodging in the girl's neck and ripping a major artery. The presence of such foreign objects in the bodies of his patients no longer surprises Shapira. "We have cases with a nail in the neck, or nuts and bolts in the thigh..., a ball bearing in the skull," he said.

Such are the weapons of war in Israel today: nuts and bolts, screws and ball bearings, any metal shards or odd bits of broken machinery that can be packed together with homemade explosive and then strapped to the body of a terrorist dispatched to any place where people gather—bus, train, restaurant, café, supermarket, shopping mall, street corner, promenade. These attacks probably cost no more than $150 to mount, and they need no escape plan—often the most difficult aspect of a terrorist operation. And they are reliably deadly. According to data from the Rand Corporation's chronology of international terrorism incidents, suicide attacks on average kill four times as many people as other terrorist acts. Perhaps it is not surprising, then, that this means of terror has become increasingly popular. The tactic first emerged in Lebanon, in 1983; a decade later it came to Israel, and it has been a regular security problem ever since. Fully two thirds of all such incidents in Israel have occurred in the past two and a half years—that is, since the start of the second intifada, in September of 2000. Indeed, suicide bombers are responsible for almost half of the approximately 750 deaths in terrorist attacks since then.

Last December, I walked through Jerusalem with two police officers, one of them a senior operational commander, who were showing me the sites of suicide bombings in recent years. They described the first major suicide-terrorist attack in the city, which occurred in February of 1996, early on a Sunday morning—the beginning of the Israeli work week. The driver of the No. 18 Egged bus was hurrying across a busy intersection at Sarei Yisrael Street as a yellow light turned red. The bus was about halfway through when an explosion transformed it into an inferno of twisted metal, pulverized glass, and burning flesh. A traffic camera designed to catch drivers running stop lights captured the scene on film. Twenty-five people were killed, including two U.S. citizens, and eighty were wounded.

The early years of suicide terrorism were a simpler time, the officers explained. Suicide bombers were—at least in theory—easier to spot then. They tended to carry their bombs in nylon backpacks or duffel bags rather than in belts or vests concealed beneath their clothing, as they do now. They were also typically male, aged seventeen to twenty-three, and unmarried. Armed with these data, the authorities could simply deny work permits to Palestinians most likely to be suicide bombers, thus restricting their ability to cross the Green Line (Israel's pre-1967 border) into Israel proper from the West Bank or the Gaza Strip.

Today, though, suicide bombers are middle-aged and young, married and unmarried, and some of them have children. Some of them, too, are women, and word has it that even children are being trained for martyrdom. "There is no clear profile anymore—not for terrorists and especially not for suicide bombers," an exasperated senior officer in the Israel Defense Forces told me last year. Sometimes the bombers disguise themselves: male *shaheed* (Arabic for "martyrs") have worn green IDF fatigues; have dressed as *haredim* (ultra-Orthodox Jews), complete with yarmulkes and tzitzit, the fringes that devout Jews display as part of their everyday clothing; or have donned long-haired wigs in an effort to look like hip Israelis rather than threatening Arabs. A few women have tried to camouflage bombs by strapping them to their stomachs to fake pregnancy. And contrary to popular belief, the bombers are not drawn exclusively from the ranks of the poor but have included two sons of millionaires. (Most of the September 11 terrorists came from comfortable middle- to upper-middle-class families and were well educated.) The Israeli journalist Ronni Shaked, an expert on the Palestinian terrorist group Hamas, who writes for *Yedioth Ahronoth*, an Israeli daily, has debunked the myth that it is only people with no means of improving their lot in life who turn to suicide terrorism. "All leaders of Hamas," he told me, "are university graduates, some with master's degrees. This is a movement not of poor, miserable people but of highly educated people who are using [the image of] poverty to make the movement more powerful."

Buses remain among the bombers' preferred targets. Winter and summer are the better seasons for bombing buses in Jerusalem, because the closed windows (for heat or air-conditioning) intensify the force of the blast, maximizing the bombs' killing potential. As a hail of shrapnel pierces flesh and breaks bones, the shock wave tears lungs and crushes other internal organs. When the bus's fuel tank explodes, a fireball causes burns, and smoke inhalation causes respiratory damage. All this is a significant return on a relatively modest investment. Two or three kilograms of explosive on a bus can kill as many people as twenty to thirty kilograms left on a street or in a mall or a restaurant. But as security on buses has improved, and passengers have become more alert, the bombers have been forced to seek other targets.

The terrorists are lethally flexible and inventive. A person wearing a bomb is far more dangerous and far more difficult to defend against than a timed device left to explode in a marketplace. This human weapons system can effect last-minute changes based on the ease of approach, the paucity or density of people, and the security measures in evidence. On a Thursday afternoon in March of last year a reportedly smiling, self-satisfied bomber strolled down King George Street, in the heart of Jerusalem, looking for just the right target. He found it in a crowd of shoppers gathered in front of the trendy Aroma Café, near the corner of Agrippas Street. In a fusillade of nails and other bits of metal two victims were killed and fifty-six wounded. Similarly, in April of last year a female suicide bomber tried to enter the Mahane Yehuda open-air market—the fourth woman to make such an attempt in four months—but was deterred by a strong police presence. So she simply walked up to a bus stop packed with shoppers hurrying home before the Sabbath and detonated her explosives, killing six and wounding seventy-three.

Suicide bombing initially seemed the desperate act of lone individuals, but it is not undertaken alone. Invariably, a terrorist organization such as Hamas (the Islamic Resistance Movement), the Palestine Islamic Jihad (PIJ), or the al Aqsa Martyrs Brigade has recruited the bomber, conducted reconnaissance, prepared the explosive device, and identified a target—explaining that if it turns out to be guarded or protected, any crowded place nearby will do. "We hardly ever find that the suicide bomber came by himself," a police officer explained to me. "There is always a handler." In fact, in some cases a handler has used a cell phone or other device to trigger the blast from a distance. A policeman told me, "There was one event where a suicide bomber had been told all he had to do was to carry the bomb and plant explosives in a certain place. But the bomb was remote-control detonated."

The organizations behind the Palestinians' suicide terrorism have numerous components. Quartermasters obtain the explosives and the other materials (nuts, bolts, nails, and the like) that are combined to make a bomb. Now that bomb-making methods have been so widely disseminated throughout the West Bank and Gaza, a merely competent technician, rather than the skilled engineer once required, can build a bomb. Explosive material is packed into pockets sewn into a canvas or denim belt or vest and hooked up to a detonator—usually involving a simple hand-operated plunger.

Before the operation is to be launched, "minders" sequester the bomber in a safe house, isolating him or her from family and friends—from all contact with the outside world—during the final preparations for martyrdom. A film crew makes a martyrdom video, as much to help ensure that the bomber can't back out as for propaganda and recruitment purposes. Reconnaissance teams have already either scouted the target or received detailed information about it, which they pass on to the bomber's handlers. The job of the handlers, who are highly skilled at avoiding Israeli army checkpoints or police patrols, is to deliver the bomber as close to the target as possible.

I talked to a senior police-operations commander in his office at the Russian Compound, the nerve center of law enforcement for Jerusalem since the time when first the Turks and then the British ruled this part of the world. It was easy to imagine, amid the graceful arches and the traditional Jerusalem stone, an era when Jerusalem's law-enforcement officers wore tarbooshes and pressed blue tunics with Sam Browne belts rather than the bland polyester uniforms and blue baseball-style caps of today. Although policing this multi-faith, historically beleaguered city has doubtless always involved difficult challenges, none can compare with the current situation. "This year there were very many events," my host explained, using the bland generic noun that signifies terrorist attacks or attempted attacks. "In previous years we considered ten events as normal; now we are already at forty-three." He sighed. There were still three weeks to go before the end of the year. Nineteen of these events had been suicide bombings. In the calculus of terrorism, it doesn't get much better. "How easy it has become for a person to wake up in the morning and go off and commit suicide," he observed. Once there were only "bags on buses, not vests or belts" to contend with, the policeman said. "Everything is open now. The purpose is to prove that the police can do whatever they want but it won't help."

This, of course, is the age-old strategy of terrorists everywhere—to undermine public confidence in the ability of the authorities to protect and defend citizens, thereby creating a climate of fear and intimidation amenable to terrorist exploitation. In Jerusalem, and in Israel as a whole, this strategy has not succeeded. But it has fundamentally changed daily behavior patterns—the first step toward crushing morale and breaking the will to resist.

The terrorists appear to be deliberately homing in on the few remaining places where Israelis thought they could socialize in peace. An unprecedented string of attacks in the first four months of last year illustrated this careful strategy, beginning at bus stops and malls and moving into more private realms, such as corner supermarkets and local coffee bars. In March, for example, no one paid much attention to a young man dressed like an ultra-Orthodox Jew who was standing near some parked cars as guests left a bar mitzvah celebration at a social hall in the ultra-Orthodox Jerusalem neighborhood of Beit Yisrael. Then he blew himself up, killing nine people, eight of them children, and wounding fifty-nine. The tight-knit religious community had felt that it was protected by God, pointing to the miraculous lack of injury a year before when a booby-trapped car blew up in front of the same hall. Using a strategy al Qaeda has made familiar, the terrorists revisited the site.

Less than a month after the Beit Yisrael attack the suicide bombers and their leaders drove home the point that Israelis cannot feel safe anywhere by going to the one large Israeli city that had felt immune from the suspicion and antipathy prevalent elsewhere—Haifa, with its successful mixture of Jews, Christian and Muslim Arabs, and followers of the Bahai faith. The University of Haifa has long had the highest proportion of Arab students of any Israeli university. The nearby Matza restaurant, owned by Jews but run by an Israeli Arab family from Galilee, seemed to embody the unusually cordial relations that exist among the city's diverse communities. Matza was popular with Jews and Arabs alike, and the presence of its Arab staff and patrons provided a feeling of safety from attack. That feeling was shattered at two-thirty on a quiet Sunday afternoon, when a suicide bomber killed fifteen people and wounded nearly fifty.

As we had tea late one afternoon in the regal though almost preternaturally quiet surroundings of Jerusalem's King David Hotel, Benny Morris, a professor of history at Ben Gurion University, explained, "The Palestinians say they have found a strategic weapon, and suicide bombing is it. This hotel is empty. The streets are empty. They have effectively terrorized Israeli society. My wife won't use a bus anymore, only a taxi." It is undeniable that daily life in Jerusalem, and throughout Israel, has changed as a result of last year's wave of suicide bombings. Even the police have been affected. "I'm worried," one officer told me in an aside—whether in confidence or in embarrassment, I couldn't tell—as we walked past Zion Square, near where some bombs had exploded. "I tell you this as a police officer. I don't come to Jerusalem with my children anymore. I'd give back the settlements. I'd give over my bank account to live in peace."

By any measure 2002 was an astonishing year for Israel in terms of suicide bombings. An average of five attacks a month were made, nearly double the number during the first fifteen months of the second intifada—and that number was itself more than ten times the monthly average since 1993. Indeed, according to a database maintained by the National Security Studies Center, at Haifa University, there were nearly as many suicide attacks in Israel last year (fifty-nine) as there had been in the previous eight years combined (sixty-two). In Jerusalem alone there were nine suicide attacks during the first four months of 2002, killing thirty-three and injuring 464. "It was horrendous," a young professional woman living in the city told me. "No one went out for coffee. No one went out to restaurants. We went as a group of people to one another's houses only."

Again, terrorism is meant to produce psychological effects that reach far beyond the immediate victims of the attack. "The Scuds of Saddam [in 1991] never caused as much psychological damage as the suicide bombers have," says Ami Pedahzur, a professor of political science at Haifa University and an expert on political extremism and violence who manages the National Security Studies Center's terrorism database. As the French philosopher Gaston Bouthoul argued three decades ago in a theoretical treatise on the subject, the "anonymous, unidentifiable threat creates huge anxiety, and the terrorist tries to spread fear by contagion, to immobilise and subjugate those living under this threat." This is precisely what the Palestinian terrorist groups are trying to achieve. "The Israelis... will fall to their knees," Sheikh Ahmad Yassin, the spiritual leader of Hamas, said in 2001. "You can sense the fear in Israel already; they are worried about where and when the next attacks will come. Ultimately, Hamas will win." The strategy of suicide terrorists is to make people paranoid and xenophobic, fearful of venturing beyond their homes even to a convenience store. Terrorists hope to compel the enemy society's acquiescence, if not outright surrender, to their demands. This is what al Qaeda hoped to achieve on 9/11 in one stunning blow—and what the Palestinians seek as well, on a more sustained, if piecemeal, basis.

After decades of struggle the Palestinians are convinced that they have finally discovered Israel's Achilles' heel. Ismail Haniya, another Hamas leader, was quoted in March of last year in *The Washington Post* as saying that Jews "love life more than any other people, and they prefer not to die." In contrast, suicide terrorists are often said to have gone to their deaths smiling. An Israeli policeman told me, "A suicide bomber goes on a bus and finds himself face-to-face with victims and he smiles and he activates the bomb—but we learned that only by asking people afterwards who survived." This is what is known in the Shia Islamic tradition as the *bassamat al-farah*, or "smile of joy"—prompted by one's impending martyrdom. It is just as prevalent among Sunni terrorists. (Indeed, the last will and testament of Mohammed Atta, the ringleader of the September 11 hijackers, and his "primer" for martyrs, *The Sky Smiles, My Young Son*, clearly evidence a belief in the joy of death.)

This perceived weakness of an ostensibly powerful society has given rise to what is known in the Middle East as the "spider-web theory," which originated within Hizbollah, the Lebanese Shia organization, following a struggle that ultimately compelled the Israel Defense Forces to withdraw from southern Lebanon in May of 2000. The term is said to have been coined by Hizbollah's secretary general, Sheikh Hassan Nasrallah, who described Israel as a still formidable military power whose civil society had become materialistic and lazy, its citizens self-satisfied, comfortable, and pampered to the point where they had gone soft. IDF Chief of Staff Moshe "Boogie" Ya'alon paraphrased Nasrallah for the Israeli public in an interview published in the newspaper *Ha'aretz* last August.

> The Israeli army is strong, Israel has technological superiority and is said to have strategic capabilities, but its citizens are unwilling any longer to sacrifice lives in order to defend their national interests and national goals. Therefore, Israel is a spider-web society: it looks strong from the outside, but touch it and it will fall apart.

Al Qaeda, of course, has made a similar assessment of America's vulnerability.

A society facing such a determined foe can respond. Israel, with its necessarily advanced military and intelligence capacities, was able in the first four months of last year to meet the most concerted effort to date by Palestinian terrorists to test the resolve of its government and the mettle of its citizens. Twelve Israelis were killed in terrorist attacks in January, twenty-six in February, 108 in March, and forty-one in April. The population of the United States is roughly forty-seven times that of Israel, meaning that the American equivalent of the March figure would have exceeded 5,000—another 9/11, but with more than 2,000 additional deaths. After April of 2002, however, a period of relative quiet settled over Israel. The number of suicide attacks, according to the National Security Studies Center, declined from sixteen in March to six in April, six in May, five in June, and six in July before falling still further to two in August and similarly small numbers for the remainder of the year. "We wouldn't want it to be perceived [by the Israeli population] that we have no military answers," a senior IDF planner told me. The military answer was Operation Defensive Shield, which began in March and involved both the IDF's huge deployment of personnel to the West Bank and its continuing presence in all the major Palestinian population centers that Israel regards as wellsprings of the suicide campaign. This presence has involved aggressive military operations to pre-empt suicide bombing, along with curfews and other restrictions on the movement of residents.

The success of the IDF's strategy is utterly dependent on regularly acquiring intelligence and rapidly disseminating it to operational units that can take appropriate action. Thus the IDF must continue to occupy the West Bank's major population centers, so that Israeli intelligence agents can stay in close—and relatively safe—proximity to their information sources, and troops can act immediately either to round up suspects or to rescue the agent should an operation go awry. "Military pressure facilitates arrests, because you're there," one knowledgeable observer explained to me. "Not only do you know the area, but you have [covert] spotters deployed, and the whole area is under curfew anyway, so it is difficult for terrorists to move about and hide without being noticed, and more difficult for them to get out. The IDF presence facilitates intelligence gathering, and the troops can also conduct massive sweeps, house to house and block to block, pick up people, and interrogate them."

The IDF units in West Bank cities and towns can amass detailed knowledge of a community, identifying terrorists and their sympathizers, tracking their movements and daily routines, and observing the people with whom they associate. Agents from Shabak, Israel's General Security Service (also known as the Shin Bet), work alongside these units, participating in operations and often assigning missions. "The moment someone from Shabak comes with us, everything changes," a young soldier in an elite reconnaissance unit told me over coffee and cake in his mother's apartment. "The Shabak guy talks in Arabic to [the suspect] without an accent, or appears as an Arab guy himself. Shabak already knows everything about them, and that is such a shock to them. So they are afraid, and they will tell Shabak everything." The success of Defensive Shield and the subsequent Operation Determined Way depends on this synchronization of intelligence and operations. A junior officer well acquainted with this environment says, "Whoever has better intelligence is the winner."

The strategy—at least in the short run—is working. The dramatic decline in the number of suicide operations since last spring is proof enough. "Tactically, we are doing everything we can," a senior officer involved in the framing of this policy told me, "and we have managed to prevent eighty percent of all attempts." Another officer said, "We are now bringing the war to them. We do it so that we fight the war in *their* homes rather than in *our* homes. We try to make certain that we fight on their ground, where we can have the maximum advantage." The goal of the IDF, though, is not simply to fight in a manner that plays to its strength; the goal is to actively shrink the time and space in which the suicide bombers and their operational commanders, logisticians, and handlers function—to stop them before they can cross the Green Line, by threatening their personal safety and putting them on the defensive.

Citizens in Israel, as in America, have a fundamental expectation that their government and its military and security forces will protect and defend them. Soldiers are expected to die, if necessary, in order to discharge this responsibility. As one senior IDF commander put it, "It is better for the IDF to bear the brunt of these attacks than Israeli civilians. The IDF is better prepared, protected, educated." Thus security in Israel means to the IDF an almost indefinite deployment in the West Bank—a state of ongoing low-level war. For Palestinian civilians it means no respite from roadblocks and identity checks, cordon-and-search operations, lightning snatch-and-grabs, bombing raids, helicopter strikes, ground attacks, and other countermeasures that have turned densely populated civilian areas into war zones.

Many Israelis do not relish involvement in this protracted war of attrition, but even more of them accept that there is no alternative. "Israel's ability to stand fast indefinitely is a tremendous advantage," says Dan Schueftan, an Israeli strategist and military thinker who teaches at Haifa University, "since the suicide bombers believe that time is on their side. It imposes a strain on the army, yes, but this is what the army is for." Indeed, no Israeli with whom I spoke on this visit doubted that the IDF's continued heavy presence in the West Bank was directly responsible for the drop in the number of suicide bombings. And I encountered very few who favored withdrawing the IDF from the West Bank. This view cut across ideological and demographic lines. As we dined one evening at Matza, which has been rebuilt, a centrist graduate student at Haifa University named Uzi Nisim told me that Palestinian terrorists "will have the power to hit us, to hurt us, once [the IDF] withdraws from Jenin and elsewhere on the West Bank." Ami Pedahzur, of Haifa University, who is a leftist, agreed. He said, "There is widespread recognition in Israel that this is the only way to stop terrorism." I later heard the same thing from a South African couple, relatively new immigrants to Israel who are active in a variety of human-rights endeavors. "Just the other day," the husband told me, "even my wife said, 'Thank God we have Sharon. Otherwise I wouldn't feel safe going out.'"

Nevertheless, few Israelis believe that the current situation will lead to any improvement in Israeli-Palestinian relations over the long run. Dennis Zinn, the defense correspondent for Israel's Channel 1, told me, "Yes, there is a drop-off [in suicide bombings]. When you have bombs coming down on your heads, you can't carry out planning and suicide attacks. But that doesn't take away their motivation. It only increases it."

Given the relative ease and the strategic and tactical attraction of suicide bombing, it is perhaps no wonder that after a five-day visit to Israel last fall, Louis Anemone, the security chief of the New York Metropolitan Transit Authority, concluded that New Yorkers—and, by implication, other Americans—face the same threat. "This stuff is going to be imported over here," he declared—a prediction that Vice President Dick Cheney and FBI Director Robert Mueller had already made. In March, Secretary of Homeland Security Tom Ridge also referred to the threat, saying in an interview with Fox News that we have to "prepare for the inevitability" of suicide bombings in the United States. Anemone even argued that "today's terrorists appear to be using Israel as a testing ground to prepare for a sustained attack against the U.S." In fact, Palestinians had tried a suicide attack in New York four years before 9/11, their plans to bomb a Brooklyn subway station were foiled only because an informant told the police. When they were arrested, the terrorists were probably less than a day away from attacking: according to law-enforcement authorities, five bombs had been primed. "I wouldn't call them sophisticated," Howard Safir, the commissioner of police at the time, commented, "but they certainly were very dangerous." That suicide bombers don't need to be sophisticated is precisely what makes them so dangerous. All that's required is a willingness to kill and a willingness to die.

According to the Rand Corporation's chronology of worldwide terrorism, which begins in 1968 (the year acknowledged as marking the advent of modern international terrorism, whereby terrorists attack other countries or foreign targets in their own country), nearly two thirds of the 144 suicide bombings recorded have occurred in the past two years. No society, least of all the United States, can regard itself as immune from this threat. Israeli Foreign Minister Benjamin Netanyahu emphasized this point when he addressed the U.S. Congress nine days after 9/11. So did Dan Schueftan, the Israeli strategist, when I asked him if he thought suicide terrorism would come to America in a form similar to that seen in Israel this past year. He said, "It is an interesting comment that the terrorists make: we will finish defeating the Jews because they love life so much. Their goal is to bring misery and grief to people who have an arrogance of power. Who has this? The United States and Israel. Europe will suffer too. I don't think that it will happen in the U.S. on the magnitude we have seen it here, but I have no doubt that it will occur. We had the same discussion back in 1968, when El Al aircraft were hijacked and people said this is your problem, not ours."

The United States, of course, is not Israel. However much we may want to harden our hearts and our targets, the challenge goes far beyond fortifying a single national airline or corralling the enemy into a territory ringed by walls and barbed-wire fences that can be intensively monitored by our armed forces. But we can take precautions based on Israel's experience, and be confident that we are substantially reducing the threat of suicide terrorism here.

The police, the military, and intelligence agencies can take steps that work from the outside in, beginning far in time and distance from a potential attack and ending at the moment and the site of an actual attack. Although the importance of these steps is widely recognized, they have been implemented only unevenly across the United States.

- Understand the terrorists' operational environment. Know their *modus operandi* and targeting patterns. Suicide bombers are rarely lone outlaws; they are preceded by long logistical trails. Focus not just on suspected bombers but on the infrastructure required to launch and sustain suicide-bombing campaigns. This is the essential spadework. It will be for naught, however, if concerted efforts are not made to circulate this information quickly and systematically among federal, state, and local authorities.

- Develop strong, confidence-building ties with the communities from which terrorists are most likely to come, and mount communications campaigns to eradicate support from these communities. The most effective and useful intelligence comes from places where terrorists conceal themselves and seek to establish and hide their infrastructure. Law-enforcement officers should actively encourage and cultivate cooperation in a nonthreatening way.
- Encourage businesses from which terrorists can obtain bomb-making components to alert authorities if they notice large purchases of, for example, ammonium nitrate fertilizer; pipes, batteries, and wires; or chemicals commonly used to fabricate explosives. Information about customers who simply inquire about any of these materials can also be extremely useful to the police.
- Force terrorists to pay more attention to their own organizational security than to planning and carrying out attacks. The greatest benefit is in disrupting pre-attack operations. Given the highly fluid, international threat the United States faces, counterterrorism units, dedicated to identifying and targeting the intelligence-gathering and reconnaissance activities of terrorist organizations, should be established here within existing law-enforcement agencies. These units should be especially aware of places where organizations frequently recruit new members and the bombers themselves, such as community centers, social clubs, schools, and religious institutions.
- Make sure ordinary materials don't become shrapnel. Some steps to build up physical defenses were taken after 9/11—reinforcing park benches, erecting Jersey barriers around vulnerable buildings, and the like. More are needed, such as ensuring that windows on buses and subway cars are shatterproof, and that seats and other accoutrements are not easily dislodged or splintered. Israel has had to learn to examine every element of its public infrastructure. Israeli buses and bus shelters are austere for a reason.
- Teach law-enforcement personnel what to do at the moment of an attack or an attempt. Prevention comes first from the cop on the beat, who will be forced to make instant life-and-death decisions affecting those nearby. Rigorous training is needed for identifying a potential suicide bomber, confronting a suspect, and responding and securing the area around the attack site in the event of an explosion. Is the officer authorized to take action on sighting a suspected bomber, or must a supervisor or special unit be called first? Policies and procedures must be established. In the aftermath of a blast the police must determine whether emergency medical crews and firefighters may enter the site; concerns about a follow-up attack can dictate that first responders be held back until the area is secured. The ability to make such lightning determinations requires training—and, tragically, experience. We can learn from foreign countries with long experience of suicide bombings, such as Israel and Sri Lanka, and also from our own responses in the past to other types of terrorist attacks.

America's enemies are marshaling their resources to continue the struggle that crystallized on 9/11. Exactly what shape that struggle will take remains to be seen. But a recruitment video reportedly circulated by al Qaeda as recently as spring of last year may provide some important clues. The seven-minute tape, seized from an al Qaeda member by U.S. authorities, extols the virtues of martyrdom and solicits recruits to Osama bin Laden's cause. It depicts scenes of *jihadists* in combat, followed by the successive images of twenty-seven martyrs with their names, where they were from, and where they died. Twelve of the martyrs are featured in a concluding segment with voice-over that says, "They rejoice in the bounty provided by Allah. And with regard to those left behind who have not yet joined them in their bliss, the martyrs glory in the fact that on them is no fear, nor have they cause to grieve." The video closes with a message of greeting from the Black Banner Center for Islamic Information.

The greatest military onslaught in history against a terrorist group crushed the infrastructure of al Qaeda in Afghanistan, depriving it of training camps, operational bases, and command-and-control headquarters; killing and wounding many of its leaders and fighters; and dispersing the survivors. Yet this group still actively seeks to rally its forces and attract recruits. Ayman Zawahiri, bin Laden's chief lieutenant, laid out a list of terrorist principles in his book, *Knights Under the Prophet's Banner* (2001), prominent among them the need for al Qaeda to "move the battle to the enemy's ground to burn the hands of those who ignite fire in our countries." He also mentioned "the need to concentrate on the method of martyrdom operations as the most successful way of inflicting damage against the opponent and the least costly to the mujahideen in terms of casualties." That martyrdom is highlighted in the recruitment video strongly suggests that suicide attacks will continue to be a primary instrument in al Qaeda's war against—and perhaps in—the United States. Suleiman Abu Gheith, al Qaeda's chief spokesman, has said as much. In rhetoric disturbingly reminiscent of the way that Palestinian terrorists describe their inevitable triumph over Israel, Abu Gheith declared, "Those youths that destroyed Americans with their planes, they did a good deed. There are thousands more young followers who look forward to death like Americans look forward to living."

Bruce Hoffman is an authoritative analyst of terrorism and a recipient of the U.S. Intelligence Community Seal Medallion, the highest level of commendation given to a nongovernment employee. He is currently the director of the Washington, D.C., office of the RAND Corporation, where he heads the terrorism research unit, and he regularly advises both governments and businesses throughout the world. This reading is a chapter from his book *Inside Terrorism*.

Ami Pedahzur, 2004

Toward an Analytical Model of Suicide Terrorism—A Comment

In this comment, I offer an alternative model for describing and explaining suicide terrorism. The model offers three stages: a) decision making among elites of terrorist organizations, b) individual motivations of the perpetrators and c) the organisational process of recruitment, socialization, and launching of the terrorist.

This is an impressive and interesting article, written by two scholars who have an outstanding understanding of the field of suicide terrorism. The article covers most of the academic literature on the topic and offers an exceptional summary of recent studies. I was also impressed by the professionalism and academic integrity of the writers, while describing the different methodological problems involved in studying this issue, and the limitations which these problems imposed on their study.

In general, I agree with many of the arguments raised in the article. However, I would like to offer a slightly different approach to the study of this important phenomenon. Throughout the article the authors mention the salient questions which preoccupy all of us while studying suicide terrorism, such as what are the root causes of this phenomenon and what fostered its rapid expansion. The question which they put in the heart of the current article is: What motivates suicide terrorists?

In my opinion, all these questions, including the ones that emphasize the individual motivations of the terrorists, call for a broad theoretical endeavour and a comparative analysis of the different manifestations of suicide terrorism in different parts of the world over the last three decades. The authors, however, chose a less ambitious path. Instead of a theory they offer a typology and instead of a comparative study they offer an in-depth look into the case of Palestinian suicide bombers. I must note though that in some parts of the article they do refer the reader to case studies outside the Palestinian scene. Moreover, despite their focus on the typology they do try to offer explanations concerning the causes that lead the different types of suicide bombers to perpetrate this act.

While trying to think of the causes that led the authors to limit their research to a typology it became clear to me that this might have been a result of their decision to stick to the academic tradition of the first wave of studies in the field, those who put the terrorists in the spotlight. The majority of the studies of the second wave shifted the attention from the perpetrator to the leadership of the terrorist organization, as well as to the political and social conditions that allowed the phenomenon of suicide terrorism to take root in different countries. I strongly believe that this focus is more beneficial when trying to attain better understanding of the phenomenon.

To go beyond the limitations of the typology and the relatively narrow scope of the Palestinian case I will offer in the next few paragraphs a tri-stage model, which I believe has both the capacity to describe and explain the process that begins with a rational strategic decision-making among the organizations' elites, and concludes in the explosion of the suicide terrorist. Unlike the current article, this model assumes a more macro approach, yet it does not neglect the individual level of analysis.

Before presenting the model, I should indicate some of its limitations. First, despite my attempt to offer a model which would be applicable to as many cases as possible the current model is mainly relevant to societies and communities which suffered from repression and were involved in a long lasting struggle (for example: Shi'is in Lebanon, Palestinians, Tamils, Kurds, Chechens, etc.). Thus, the model excludes some of the Al-Qaeda suicide terrorists and, most prominently, the hijackers of 11 September. Second, the rapid expansion of suicide terrorism over the last few years and, especially, the events in Chechnya and Iraq, have not yet been documented in a way which would enable academic analysis. This may require some adaptation and modification of the model in the future.

Third, my attempt to divide the process into three stages is mostly for illustrative purposes. Stages one and two will probably take place concurrently. Fourth, while in stages one and two I refer to independent and dependent variables, stage three is still descriptive. Fifth, due to the short nature of the current comment I can only portray its general ideas and not discuss it at length or offer examples to support it (Figure 1).

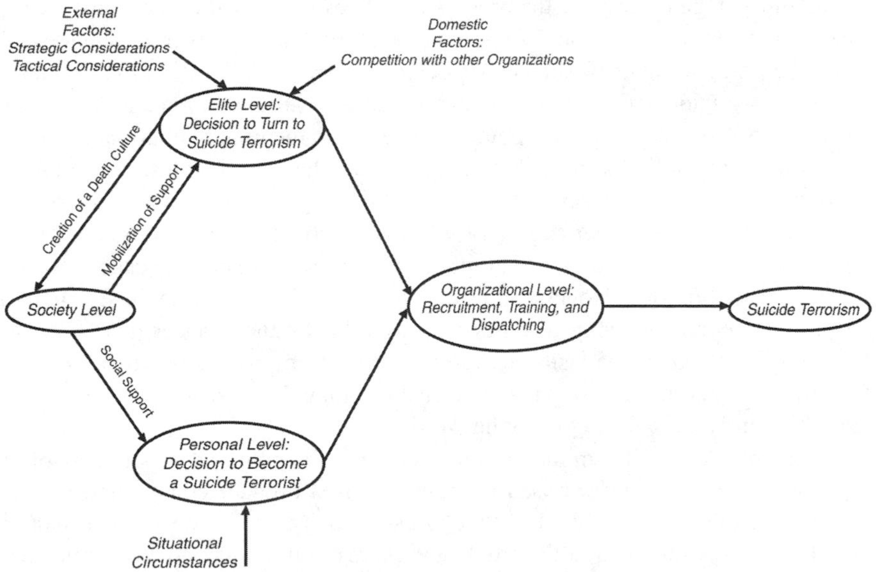

Figure 1. A model for describing and explaining suicide terrorism.

In the first stage, there is the rational process where leaders of the organization, in view of considerations related to the struggle with a stronger enemy,[1] but also in view of internal political considerations,[2] reach a conclusion that suicide terrorism is the most effective way of furthering their goals at a certain point in time. Nevertheless, the decision to mobilize suicide bombers cannot be implemented without a social environment that approves of this type of method of operation, for a terrorist organization acts on behalf of a social category and strives to advance its interests. The elite of the terrorist organization will do anything necessary to convince its constituency that suicide terrorism is a valuable tactic.[3] The best way to do so is by endorsing the "culture of death." The use of religious or nationalistic rhetoric can make martyrdom appear as the right thing for this particular society at this point.

If this social group, or part of it, embraces the "culture of death" and concurs with the organization's decision to deploy suicide bombers, then this support will most likely maximize the benefits of this strategy. To the extent that this social group, on the other hand, will have reservations regarding the use of suicide militants, the organization will be left without much of an option but to engage in alternative methods of action.

The second stage, after the organizational elite has decided on this mode of action, calls for the recruitment of suicide potentials. In contrast to research that is widely covered in the article and which focuses on the psychological problems of the individual which are liable to cause him or her to commit such an act, I believe that the person who chooses this act is mostly motivated by reasons anchored in personal experiences he/she has been exposed to, or is a result of certain feelings evoked by events undergone by the group to which he or she belongs and with whom he or she feels a deep sense of identification. This aspect, as well, cannot be analyzed in isolation from the broader context, namely, the social endorsement of the commitment of such an act. The social environment to which the individual belongs, whether it is a community or a more restricted organizational framework that insists on the idea of suicide, would significantly facilitate his or her enlistment to the mission.

The third stage consists of the process that takes place within the framework of the organization: it starts off with the definition of the individual as a potential suicide and concludes at the point when he or she is considered a "live bomb." After the candidate is recruited for the suicide action, he or she undergoes a process of training. Along with the necessity of operative training, the organization takes on the no less important challenge of training him/her mentally for the task. Despite the fact that, in many instances, this part involves only a short period of training, it still must be long enough to assess the personality of the candidate and his or her degree of willingness to perform the mission. There also must be time to remove any doubts that might be welling up inside the candidate. The objective is to bring him or her to a mental state which enables him or her to set out upon the operation fully reconciled with the purpose, thus reducing the chances that he or she will have a change of heart at the last minute. The preparation process is critical as far as the organization is concerned and organizations in the main will not spare efforts in persuading the candidate and strengthening his or her spirit.

I think that despite its limitations, this model has the potential to put many of the important arguments which were raised in the article in a broader context and help testing comparatively. I am aware of the fact that by using such a model we neglect many of the nuances that were mentioned in the article and seems to me interesting and relevant. Yet, to take one step further towards a theoretical understanding of the phenomenon I think that paying such a price might be beneficial.

Dr. Ami Pedahzur is a senior lecturer of government and political theory and the deputy chair of the National Security Studies Center at the University of Haifa. His books include *The Israeli Response to Jewish Extremism and Violence—Defending Democracy* (Manchester University Press, 2002) and *Political Parties and Terrorist Groups* (with Leonard Weinberg) (Routledge, 2003). He recently completed a book manuscript entitled *Suicide Terrorism* (Cambridge: Polity Press, forthcoming). He is the 2004-2005 Donald D. Harrington Fellow at the University of Texas at Austin.

Notes

1. Robert A. Pape. "The Strategic Logic of Suicide Terrorism." *American Political Science Review* 97/3. (2003). pp. 343–361.
2. Mia M. Bloom. "Palestinian Suicide Bombing: Public Support, Market Share and Outbidding." *Political Science Quarterly* 119/1. (2004). pp. 61–88.
3. For example: Christoph Reuter, *My Life Is a Weapon: A Modern History of Suicide Bombing* (Princeton: Princeton University Press, 2004).

Madeleine Gruen, 2005

Terrorist Indoctrination and Radicalization on the Internet

The Internet is an indispensable component of the American lifestyle. Seventy percent of young adults and more than 80 percent of teens in the United States are online.[1] They use the Internet to conduct research for school, to communicate with others who share common interests, and to maintain relationships with friends and family. The information they find on the Net shapes their political and social opinions and guides their decision making. Without access, the daily lives of young Americans would be compromised.

The Internet is also indispensable to political and militant Islamist groups, who rely on it to support and sustain core components of operations. Their mastery of the medium has made it possible for them to expand their sphere of influence to include Western populations, taking advantage of the fact that so many of their targets for recruitment are online. Terrorist and extremist groups have been met by little to no resistance in cyberspace, and have therefore been able to create a presence for themselves in nearly every chat room and message board their young target would likely visit. Their tactics for online recruitment, indoctrination, and fundraising have become so creative, it will be difficult for Western authorities to identify their presence, much less eliminate it.

To attack the United States on its own soil continues to be a primary objective of the al-Qaeda (AQ) network.[2] Because of increased border security, it has become more challenging for the AQ network to get operatives into the United States. As a result, the Internet has become more important than ever to Salafi jihadi groups because it gives them the ability to influence and incite individuals within adversarial populations from a remote vantage point, without the need for face-to-face interaction. The terrorists' success rests on their ability to lure potential sympathizers to general-interest Web sites, and then to draw them in further through a network of chat groups, forums, listservs, and Web sites that they have produced themselves. Ultimately, their target subject's thoughts and actions will be guided by radical ideology.

This chapter focuses on the ways in which Islamists recruit and indoctrinate young Muslims in the West by taking advantage of their interest in popular culture and their lack of access to proper Islamic education. Their system will be described in three phases:

- the exploration phase, in which terrorist and extremists locate potential sympathizers online,
- the indoctrination phase, when the subject is persuaded to embrace jihadist ideology, and
- the radicalization phase in which subjects become so committed to militant Islam that they are willing to directly support and/or participate in terror operations.

The primary target for Islamist recruitment in the West are Muslims between the approximate ages of 18 and 25, which happens to be the largest online demographic, numbering 10.5 million in the United States alone.[3] On average, these young adults spend approximately 32 hours a month surfing the Web, which is about 17 percent longer than any other age group.[4] Most of that time is spent visiting music Web sites, chatting with friends via e-mail and Instant Messenger, playing computer games, and doing research for school papers. Although not every young Muslim will be vulnerable to indoctrination and radicalization online, a few will be, which makes the terrorist effort to reach targets by this method worthwhile.

Phase I: Exploration: Initiating Contact Between Radicalizing Agents and Targets

Who are the targets for terrorist recruitment? Who are the radicalizing agents? How do they find one another in the vastness of cyberspace? Some Internet surfers have already been partially indoctrinated to radical ideology in the physical world, and will intentionally seek out radical material online. Islamists online have set traps for those who are vulnerable but who have not yet been exposed. The traps are intended to slowly expose the targets to militant ideology in a subtle progression that will not scare the target away.

The Pyramid of Terror

Every recruit to a terrorist organization starts out as a citizen of the general population. Then one day there is an event, a circumstance, or interaction that serves as a catalyst to compel him or her to shift from law-abiding citizen to adherent of a militant movement. The individual's transition may occur quickly, or it may occur in phases in a process sometimes referred to as "the pyramid of terrorism." [5]

In the first transition, a member of the general population becomes a sympathizer—his perceptions about terrorist-group objectives and their means of achieving those objectives soften. In the next transition, the subject becomes a supporter who will provide assistance to a known terrorist organization. Assistance is defined as giving direct or indirect financial backing or supplying arms, false documentation, training, safe houses, communication equipment, or other logistical support.[6] Once he has become a supporter, it is only a small step to take the pledge of loyalty to a terrorist organization. By taking this final step, he has indicated his willingness to participate in attack operations. Terrorist groups have developed a multifaceted Internet presence designed to manage a target through each tier of the pyramid.

The Actors

Those at risk for radicalization online are the same as those who are at risk in the physical world. They include first- and second-generation immigrants living in immigrant communities or those who have not assimilated into the native population, converts to Islam who do not live near a facility that provides proper Islamic instruction, and those who do not have or are not welcome into a local peer group. Such vulnerable individuals venture into cyberspace to find what is lacking for them in the physical world. Radicalizing agents position themselves to provide whatever the potential recruit is in search of when they venture online.

Political and militant Islamist groups use the Internet for functions that include:

Operations planning: Terrorists use the internet to organize and manage operations. In the past, operatives had to meet in person, which left them vulnerable to surveillance. Yael Shahar, who tracks cyber-terror at the International Policy Institute for Counter-Terrorism at the Interdisciplinary Center of Herzliya, notes that the Internet allows terrorists to spread out geographically while continuing to maintain a coherent ideology. In essence, a structure that once depended on a hierarchical chain of command has now evolved into a leaderless resistance. Infiltrating a group without a hierarchy is more difficult. Ultimately, the virtual terror network is more efficient than one run exclusively in the physical world.

Fund-raising: Through the use of Web-only front, cover, and support cyber businesses and charities accessing funds is easy and hard to detect. Terrorists are able to raise small sums of cash that are quickly laundered and put directly into operations.

Influence and psychological warfare: The Internet is a reliable media through which terrorists can broadcast their violent acts without concern about censorship or negative editorial comment. In addition, terrorist groups are also known to post deceptive messages designed to distract their adversaries or to force their adversaries to reveal their capabilities. Along those lines, terrorist groups post denials of their involvement in particular attacks in an effort to postpone or avoid retaliation. Because of their well-established presence and their skill in utilizing propaganda techniques, terrorists have been able to portray themselves as a force to be reckoned with, perhaps giving the impression that they are larger, more capable, and better able to launch large-scale attacks.

Development of a world-wide movement: The Internet is used to spread ideology and the message of group objectives to vulnerable populations around the globe. Many experts concur that AQ's online presence has become more potent and pertinent than its actual physical presence because of the Internet. This is because they have successfully been able to spread their ideology globally via the Internet, helping them to achieve their goal of establishing a worldwide *Ummah* and also giving them the ability to communicate their objectives clearly to adversarial populations and to potential sympathizers within adversarial populations.

Some radicalizing agents are official representatives of jihadi groups, or they may be individuals who have been radicalized by jihadist ideology who then proliferate the ideology on the Web. The radicalizing agents cruise cyberspace, lingering on general-interest chat forums, chat rooms, or e-mail listservs, such as those geared toward young Muslims. These places include sites pertaining to religion, music, gaming, social issues, or school studies. In the physical world, a successful radicalizing agent is charismatic. He appears knowledgeable, well-spoken, and a bit intimidating. In the cyber world, the successful radicalizing agent will be able to express himself easily, intelligently, authoritatively, and persuasively in writing. He has been trained to be reasonable when challenged about ideology; however, he is strong against those who challenge his authority over the group. His ability to write well and maintain control over others suggests that leadership roles in cyberspace are assumed by those who are educated.

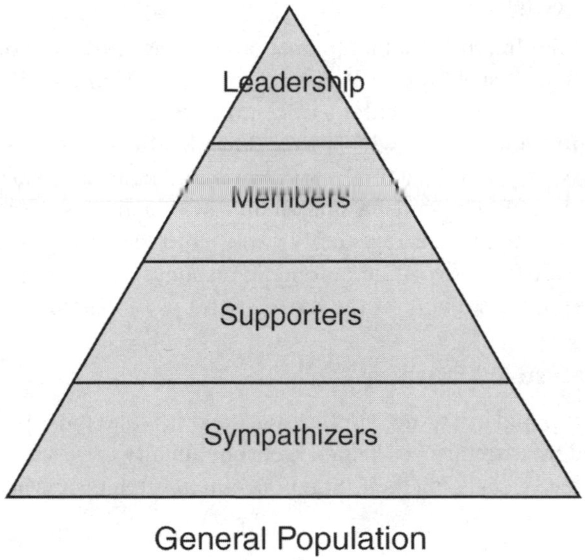

All components of an online indoctrination campaign are based on the elements of a propaganda campaign.[7] These elements include:

- "Name-calling," which links a person or group to a negative name or symbol.
- "Glittering generalities" are words associated with virtuous ideas based on deep-set experience. Buzz words used as glittering generalities will differ according to the culture on which they are being imposed.
- "Transfer" is the association of an idea with a symbol. This concept can either be positive or negative depending on the symbol to which the concept is transferred.
- "Testimonials" are used to convince an individual or population of an idea by having that idea endorsed by someone respected by the community. Conversely, an idea that may otherwise be accepted by an individual or population can be made dubious by associating it with someone who is loathed or not respected.
- "Plain folks" are testimonials from people who appear to be peers.
- "Bandwagon" takes advantage of a person's instinct to follow the crowd. The propagandist directs his campaign at those who are already held together by common ties, whether nationality, religion, or hatred of a common enemy.
- "Card-stacking," in which lies, deception, censorship, fact-dogging, and distortion are used to win support for the propagandists' cause.
- "Fear" is used as a weapon to manipulate populations into following the directives of the propagandist on the threat that if his wishes are not supported, then the population will be victim of their greatest fears. The propagandist also wants to instill fear of dissent through intimidation. The subject's desire to conform to the group prevents him from offering a dissenting opinion.

How elements of a propaganda campaign are employed online will be clarified in each of the subsequent sections of this chapter.

Phase II: Indoctrination

Indoctrination via the Internet is a methodical process that calls for constant attention to the target using the full spectrum of Web applications—from e-mail to audio to visual stimulus—in order to trigger particular associations. Every message sent to the target is meant to inspire trust and respect, which, over time, conditions the target to accept whatever the radicalizing agent tells them. Every Web site the target is steered toward is rich with images of glorious mujahideen and of fellow Muslims suffering as a result of Western aggression. Targets are repeatedly exposed to terrorist group emblems on the sites, which will eventually evoke an automatic response in the target—a feeling of familiarity and pride in the strength of the terrorist groups to vanquish U.S. tyranny.

E-mail and Instant Messenger

E-mail is the most popular internet application,[8] and it is the most practical and convenient method used by extremists to keep targets continually exposed to radical ideology. The process of directly engaging their target via e-mail often occurs according to the following process:[9]

- The target finds chat boards or e-mail groups on the Internet devoted to general discussions with Islamic themes. They usually start with message boards on popular sites that are the first to pop-up on search engines. Such boards are impersonal and are not geared toward a particular demographic.
- Web addresses for new sites and chat boards are posted on the popular boards. Through exploration, the target will find chat boards and e-mail groups populated by his peer demographic.
- The target becomes known to the radicalizing agent as he starts to post to the board. If his posts indicate that he is vulnerable to radicalization—perhaps by expressing frustration with U.S. foreign policy—he will be sent a private e-mail to join another chat group. The second group is smaller than the first, usually with not more than 10 members, and it is private so that it includes only invited participants.
- In order to keep this new group together, the extremists keep the discussions lively. The topics of discussion are initiated by the group moderator, and in some cases one or two others who are partnered with the moderator. These individuals present themselves as social and approachable. Many groups train their recruiters to come across as "calm, competent, and logically minded,"[10] and initiate discussions that cover social issues in order to inspire friendly dialog.
- The skilled radicalizing agent knows his recruitment target; he will be able to use his vernacular, like what he likes, and be whatever his target needs, whether it be a religious instructor or a best friend.
- As members of the group become familiar with one another and have developed trust, either the moderator or another member of the group introduces political topics. The topics are laced with radical ideology. Eventually, entire leaflets downloaded from political Islamist Web sites are posted to the forum.
- Because the topic of conversation is controlled by a moderator who determines which messages get posted and which do not, the dialog eventually becomes entirely devoted to political Islam.
- By the final stage, participants of the chat group have ostensibly built a relationship with the others in the group. They respect the opinions of their peers, and as they

see the others transition from moderate to radical, it will seem socially acceptable for the target to express the same opinions.

In addition to e-mail, radicalizing agents are making use of Instant Messenger (IM) to keep in constant contact with their targets. IM is a popular application with younger Internet users because it allows them to chat with their friends in real time. The application grew from 39 million users in 2000 to 52 million by the summer of 2002.[11] In 2003, the number of people who visited chat rooms and online discussions increased by yet another 21 percent. In 2005, at any hour of the day, there are hundreds of thousands of people worldwide logged onto IM systems. IM systems, such as Yahoo! Messenger or AOL Instant Messenger, turn on automatically as soon as the user logs on. Thus, the radicalizing agents who have been added to the targets' "Buddy List" can immediately engage their target before he or she has had the opportunity to surf around and possibly discover a new community whose worldview is inconsistent with the jihadist worldview.

With such services as PalTalk, the IM concept has broadened to serve entire communities, making it possible for users around the world to enter "rooms" devoted to such discussion topics as world affairs or religion. Users can either communicate by writing messages that are read by others as soon as they are typed, or by using an audio feature that enables them to hear each others' voices, similar to a conference call. Islamist ideologues use PalTalk, and other similar services, to communicate directly with supporters in a private environment where there is no record of what was said. Prior to 9/11, radical clerics like London's Omar Bakri Mohammad and Abu Hamza al-Masri, used the pulpit at Finsbury Park Mosque to incite their followers to become mujahideen and suicide bombers. After 9/11, these radical clerics were forced to become more covert because of increased law enforcement scrutiny. With PalTalk, radical clerics are once again able to incite their supporters without restriction.

In spring 2005, sixteen-year-old Tashnuba Hayder was deported from Queens, New York, to Dhaka, Bangladesh, a country she had not lived in since she was five.[12] Her deportation came about as a result of accusations made by federal law enforcement that she was a would-be suicide bomber. In fact, Tashnuba had been indoctrinated to radical Islam through her online engagement with Al Muhajiroun (ALM), [13] an extremist group based in the UK. ALM leader Omar Bakri Mohammed broadcast his sermons nightly on the Internet through PalTalk. His sermons often encouraged suicide bombings and called for his followers to join AQ.[14] Tashnuba went to a mosque far from her home in Queens that was attended by political Islamists sympathetic to Bakri and AQ. The longer Tashnuba listened to these sermons and interacted with other followers of Bakri Mohammed, the more convinced she became that she wanted to become a martyr. Although Tashnuba did not reach the planning stages, law enforcement officials were convinced that she would have committed an attack on U.S. soil if requested to do so and given the assistance with the explosives.

In this case, a young woman was indoctrinated to radical extremist ideology through a combination of face-to-face interaction with peers at the mosque and through non-physical interaction with an extremist ideologue on PalTalk. PalTalk gave Tashnuba the opportunity to interact with the charismatic leadership of a radical Islamist group, who was located in another country. Hearing his voice in a real-time format was enough to incite a shift in her level of commitment to the global jihad.

Terrorist and Extremist Groups Breed Cottage Industry via the Internet: The example of Hizb ut-Tahrir:

Once radicalization has occurred online, it spreads exponentially. Ideas are carried from one group to another. The core ideological concepts may have originated from multiple sources. Thus, someone who has been radicalized via the Internet may identify with Wahhabist, Salafist, and Takfiri concepts. Others may have been exposed to only one ideology. Extremist groups like Hizb ut-Tahrir (HT) have been exploiting the internet for years and have saturated thousands of chat boards and chat groups. HT is a large political Islamist movement with a world-wide presence. Although it is non-violent, HT is anti-Semitic, is anti-American, and endorses violence by other groups against Westerners. In the physical world, the leadership of HT requires intensive, regimented study before a recruit can call him or herself a member. However, with its corpus of literature with its appealing Utopian/Marxist themes so readily available online, it is possible for anyone to claim himself an HT adherent even though he might not be officially recognized by the group as a member.

Radicalized individuals who identify themselves as members of HT proliferate group ideology through personal Web pages, chat boards, and Yahoo! chat groups. Thus, HT is able to spread its message through sanctioned methods and through a cottage industry.

Why is it a threat when a non-violent extremist group like HT breeds a cottage industry?

1. Ideology takes on a life of its own. Because there is no authority to supervise the radicalization process, non-violent aspects of ideology may not be emphasized and the group, or individuals in the group, will become more militant.
2. The exposure to ideology may be effective in inspiring individuals to become a legitimate member of HT. Thus, a fully sanctioned cell is generated in the city that had no group presence previously, and the extremist ideology will be spread by the cell to a whole new population.
3. Salafist ideology intends to inspire young Muslims to isolate themselves from mainstream society, thereby possibly fostering a sense of marginalization that would make them vulnerable targets for recruitment by more militant groups.

Religion and Political Islam:

One in every four Americans has searched the Web for information on religion. That is more than have used an online dating service, gambled online, or done online banking.[15] Eighty one percent of religion surfers describe themselves as very devout, compared to 61 percent of the general population who describe themselves as such.[16]

It is possible to share experiences with others online in the same way experiences are shared in the physical world, which are the foundations of friendships. Communal worship, for example, creates a bond between parishioners whose ties may be based on common faith, social standing, and values. For some, worship in cyberspace can be as fulfilling as attending a brick-and-mortar church or mosque.

In May 2004, the Methodist Church in the United Kingdom launched the first 3D cyber church, which they called the "Church of Fools."[17] Parishioners selected an avatar, or cartoon representation of themselves, that enabled them to "enter" the 3D cyber church to attend services, "see" and interact with other parishioners, and wander around the church.

The Church of Fools Web site features a chat room, where the faithful worldwide can talk with others 24 hours a day, 7 days a week. Informal interviews with chat room participants[18] indicate that many have substituted a physical church with the Church of Fools. Church of Fools parishioners also express that, while not exactly the same, cyber worship does furnish the same sort of fulfillment as a brick-and-mortar church in terms of making interpersonal connections and getting inspiration from the sermons. Many users have been visiting the church since its inception and spend three or more hours per day in its chat room. Although they are from different parts of the world, their online discussions reflect the same sort of personal knowledge of one another that would be expected among a group of friends in the physical world.

The Church of Fools shows that relationships can be built online when they are based on common cultural ties or shared interests. The fact that churchgoers can also see a physical representation of themselves and other parishioners may also contribute to their strong sense of community and friendship.

These same qualities found in Church of Fools are applied by extremists seeking to exploit a Muslim's desire to find communities of their peers online. What may appear to be a nurturing community where everyone shares common beliefs, may in fact be an artificial environment contrived by Islamists seeking to exploit people's natural "bandwagon" tendencies. There are countless sites devoted to news and religious discussions from an Islamic perspective. While many of these sites are legitimate, many others are "honey pot" sites planted by radical Islamists to influence readers and chat forum participants or to divert targets for recruitment from material that contradicts the Islamist worldview. To a layperson, a "honey pot" looks the same as a legitimate site and can be stumbled upon easily by someone looking for a legitimate news source or for religious guidance. One such example is http://www.islam-online.net, which appears legitimate or benign at first glance, but deeper examination reveals that it is replete with radical ideology.

The thread below[19] is standard of the discussions found on http://www.islam-online.net and other sites of its genre:

> *Subject: What Stand Should Muslims in America Take?*
> *From: KMohammed Date: December 12, 2001*
>
> *Waa'ssalam ulaikum I am not sure what to think as we are watching Americans drop bombs on our Muslim brothers. On one hand, we are Muslims and we need to take a stand against the murder of other Muslims in Afghanistan. On the other hand, we are American Muslims and we were attacked by Osama bin Laden, and we are taught that the killing of innocents is wrong. Any thoughts will be appreciated.*
>
> *Subject: Re: What Stand Should Muslims in America Take?*
> *From: Hamza Date: December 13*
>
> *First of all I am against the term "American Muslims." That is part of the mental game that our politicians and our media try to play with us. Being a Muslim, regardless of what country we are in, our position should always be clear, that is we always stand with the poor Muslims who are getting 'murderd' [sic] by bombs made by your tax money and mine.*

But aren't we Americans and shouldn't we support our country? Once again we should be supporting only just causes and we should be REMINDED that our obedience is to ALLAH first, and that we should always stand with the Muslims in TRUTH

Subject: What Stand Should Muslims in America Take

From: Abu Bakar

Date: December 13, 2001

It seems like you are speaking as if there is concrete evidence against Usama. There isn't any evidence linking him to what happened on the 11th. If there is one that isn't fabricated the world haven't [sic] seen it yet.

KMohammed you should join us in protesting against Americas [sic] aggression towards the Muslims. Muslims don't really care if Americans are happy with us or not. We are Americans too and it does not mean that we have to conform to what our gov. [sic] is doing and shape our view or opinion simply because we are Americans or we want to please Americans, we have the right to differ in views and opinions as Americans.

As Americans we support the fight against terrorists. But not the political agenda which seems to be targeting developing Muslim countries simply by saying they are terrorists and destroying them before they get to a stage strong enough to where they could implement true Islamic laws not the man-made ones. True justice, and peace. Some of the reasons for targeting Afghanistan seem to be to prevent an Islamic State from developing.

May God help all of us see the truth and guide us in that truth.

In this exchange, the person seeking advice was told to be mistrustful of the American government—that the government's true motives in Afghanistan were not to avenge September 11 but to ensure the weakness of Muslim countries. The last message also introduces the concept of the Islamic State, also known as the *Khalifate,* the establishment of which is a primary objective of AQ and other jihadi Salafist groups. The rejection of Western-imposed nationalism is a reoccurring theme on Islamist Web sites and chat forums.

To add credibility to an online discussion, fataawa by Islamic clerics and scholars are posted. The following is an excerpt from an essay by Sabeel Ahmed[20] on ways to spread Islam in secondary schools and colleges in North America, which was posted to a Muslim youth e-mail group. [21] The message appeared to have been posted by a third party, which is a common tactic used by extremists to elevate the status of the scholar in the eyes of the reader, which may also serve the purpose of facilitating the claim that the message was not actually written by the scholar, in the event that his words are used against him.

As a group, the Muslim students should try to contribute an article on Islam in each issue of its paper. The school may not allow you to preach in the school paper, but Al-Hamdullah there are way to circumvent this problem. When your Islamic group holds any Islamic event like lectures, religious/cultural events etc, submit an article about this event as a 'news' article. Thus you are still exposing an aspect of Islam without coming forth as a preacher. Second way to circumvent the problem is to write articles about Islamic holidays e.g. the two EIDs and again submit them as 'news' articles. It also helps to have a good rapport with the editor and the writing staff of the paper. Invite them to your iftar parties, gatherings, lectures etc.

Here, Ahmed advices young Muslims to be deceptive in their dealings with school newspapers in order to preach Islam, which he acknowledges some schools will find problematic. He positions himself as a greater authority than school administrators, telling students that spreading Islam is more important that obeying school rules. Ahmed, and other clerics and scholars who post regularly to Muslim youth message groups, will ultimately assume a position of control over young Muslims who will seek their advice.

Games

Most Americans under the age of 30 were raised on interactive video and computer games, and more than half of all adults in the United States play games online. [22] In early 2002, the racist right began to take advantage of their recruitment population's interest in computer games by producing their own games that promoted racial hatred, such as "Nigger Hunt," "Border Patrol," and "Kill 'Em All." Beginning in 2003, the militant Islamist group Hizbollah followed the trends established by white supremacists by launching "Special Force," a game that gives players a simulated experience of military operations against Israeli soldiers in battles re-created from actual encounters in the south of Lebanon, "real battles that humiliated the Zionist enemy, giving it a lesson …". [23] Hizbollah's intentions with the game were to reverse the scenarios depicted in American computer games, in which the Americans are the heroes and Arabs are the enemies. Hizbollah believes that resistance to the Israelis occurs not only through military operations but through the media as well. They hope that the game will introduce Israeli resistance to a new generation and that it will offer "a mental and personal training for those who play it, allowing them to feel that they are in the shoes of the resistance fighters." [24] Hizbollah has made it clear that the game is not intended to entertain, but to train children physically and mentally for military confrontation with their Israeli enemies.

Games marketed as "educational" may also be used to introduce Americanized Muslims to radical Islamist concepts. At first glance, "Islamic Fun" [25] appears to be a CD-ROM of innocent games for children between 5 and 7 years old to learn about Shi'a Islam. Children navigate cartoon bears, kittens, and rabbits through such tasks as retrieving a ball or catching fish by giving correct answers to questions about Islam. The games, titled "Tree Hop," "Two Bunny Race," and "Meow Tiles," feature a brightly colored interface and Disneyesque cartoon characters. However, the last game on the CD-ROM is called "The Resistance." It is a first-person shooter game, the objective of which is to destroy Israeli tanks that have invaded the players' territory. As the Israeli tank appears on the screen, a question box with a choice of three possible answers to the question appears as well. When the player selects the correct answer, then he or she wins ammunition to fire at the Israelis.

Games with violent themes are intended to dehumanize the victim and diminish the act of killing. Despite many instances of legislators and concerned railing against the violence in computer games, there has been limited success in banning or setting limitations on them in the United States. Games with violent themes elicit violent tendencies. Extremist groups seeking to incite a lone actor residing in an adversarial country to attack a target may use computer games that can be downloaded on the Internet as a component of their campaign to stimulate action. Certain components of games targeting different cultures with various beliefs and values can be modified to optimize the usability within each culture.[26] Thus, one game that supports a particular ideology can be effective in multiple cultures by changing component qualities in order to make them socially and culturally consistent within each target population.

Hip-hop and Hip-hop culture

There are rappers who happen to be Muslim, and then there are Islamists who happen to be rappers. The former have been a fixture on the hip-hop music scene for decades, topping the sales charts, making money, and inspiring fashion trends. Political Islamists have been trying to exploit the popularity of rap music with their target recruitment demographic since shortly after 9/11, despite the fact that most Salafists believe that listening to music is *haram* (prohibited by Shariah law).

In 2002, American adherents of Hizb ut-Tahrir (HT) started hip-hop bands in California and Wisconsin as part of their strategy to recruit and indoctrinate their target demographic: college-age Muslims. Their strategy was twofold: (1) At the invitation of the Muslim Students Association, the band would give concerts at regional colleges, thereby giving them access to educated Muslims. (2) They would use their web sites and chat groups as a way of keeping their targets exposed to HT ideology. Their web sites were comparable to that of record company–backed bands, with slick animation and options to download songs and lyrics, all of which were steeped in Salafist ideology and themes of rising up against the government to replace it with an Islamic regime.

STARING INTO KAFIR'S EYES[27]

How many more
of our sisters do they have to rape!
How many more
of our brothers must they slaughter by hate!
Don't you know we have suffered too long without an Islamic State!
How much more can you take?

Here, listeners are told about the problems caused by non-Muslims in the Muslim world, which will continue until the establishment of a Muslim state.

In "Sleeping Giant," listeners are exposed to the idea that not everyone who calls themselves a Muslim should actually be considered one. The song suggests that the true Muslims (adherents of HT and other Salafist groups) should rise up against the oppression of false Islamic regimes.

SLEEPING GIANT[28]

Governments who claim
They implementing Islam
like who??!
Like Taliban, Iran and Sudan.
All 52
So called Muslim nations
Oppressing the masses
in the name of Islam
They are digging our graves
while we are asleep
over a billion

But ooh so weak
We need to rise up
And get back on our feet

Fans of the music could also join one of several Yahoo! chat groups sponsored by the bands, one of which had more than 2,000 members by the end of 2003.[29] However, the fan base strayed when the HT bands stopped turning out new releases and when more talented Islamist rap groups emerged.

The newer Islamist hip-hop bands have replicated the qualities that make mainstream artists successful—the music itself is more "authentic" sounding, and the artists imitate the mannerisms, dress, and language of mainstream rappers. Several of the bands sell the urban-style clothing popular with hip-hop fans over their Web sites. Most fans are unaware of the band's affiliations with political Islamist organizations, but like the rebellious look of hats and T-shirts with the words "mujahideen" and "jihad" written on them. One post to the Muslimsinhiphop Yahoo! chat group[30] suggested that these articles of clothing could be "placed" on MTV, similar to the way beverage companies place their products on television and in films.

Islamist rap artists have integrated themselves with other Muslim hip-hop artists, taking advantage of the expansive network of web sites and concert promoters in that niche of the industry. The only way to identify which artists are the extremists is either by coming into direct contact with them or by reading the lyrics, which are posted to their web sites.

Phase III: Radicalization

Imam Samudra, field commander for the Jamaah Islamiya October 2002 attack in Bali that killed more than 200 and wounded hundreds more, circulated his radical views over the Internet. Once fully radicalized, Samudra used the Internet to "call fellow Muslims...by summoning them to jihad....The means which I use to call fellow Muslims to jihad is through the chatting channel on the Internet, by sending out URLs for websites I know."[31]

Although evidence, such as the case of Imam Samudra, shows that jihadis have confidence in the Internet as a viable means to recruit and indoctrinate, there are not enough cases to prove that exposure to radical rhetoric on the Internet alone is enough to push an indoctrinated individual to the point where they will commit themselves to participating in an armed attack. However, there is enough evidence to show that exposure to radical ideology on the Internet compounded by exposure to radicalizing agents in the physical world has been an effective combination, as in the case of Tashnuba Hayder.

The Internet for the Radicalized

The final tier of terrorist cyber presence includes Web sites, chat rooms and chat groups, audio and video broadcasts, and message boards for individuals who have been completely indoctrinated to Islamist ideology and for whom there is no more need to continue with the cycle of convincing them to the extremist viewpoint. The messages are more blatant calls to jihad, solicitation for funds to arm mujahideen against the United States and its allies, calls to conduct attacks against Americans and Europeans in their homelands, and detailed instructions on how to construct improvised explosive devices. Once a target has been introduced to the universe of Islamist extremism online, it is easy to find sites for the converted. While most are in Arabic, Urdu, and Indonesian languages, there are a growing number that appear in English, French,

German, and Dutch, signifying the rise of radical Islam in Western countries and the growing efforts by Islamists to reach these populations online.

Many in the terrorists' cyber audience have made the move to travel to Iraq to join the insurgency as a result of the daily Internet broadcasts, delivered in news-style format, that report attacks against and by U.S. and allied forces. Despite having been hit hard by U.S. forces, the Iraqi insurgency managed to grow from approximately 5,000 fighters to approximately 20,000 by February 2005.[32] U.S. forces are caught in a catch-22 because their battle against the insurgency is what fuels it, and the ongoing Internet broadcasts from the front lines will not ease the problem.

The glorification of suicide attacks is also part of the insurgent's campaign to recruit more fighters. Their paeans to martyrs and the videos they broadcast on their Web sites of the devastation caused by the bombers not only contributes to rallying their own constituency, but also enhances their psychological warfare efforts against their adversaries. In order for terrorism to be effective, the terrorists must have an audience for their acts.[33] They have an eager audience of Westerners who have an appetite for the gory media transmitted by terrorists. According to Dan Klinker, who is the Web master for Orgrish.com,[34] with every new beheading video released by the terrorists and posted for Western audiences on Orgrish, they have approximately 50,000 to 60,000 visitors per hour. [35]

Some terrorist sites do not celebrate their violent activities. Instead, regardless of the terrorist or extremist group's agenda, motives, or location, most sites emphasize two issues: the restrictions placed on freedom of expression and the plight of comrades who have become their enemies' prisoners. These issues resonate powerfully with their own supporters and are also calculated to elicit sympathy from Western audiences, playing on the fact that they cherish freedom of expression and frown upon measures to silence political opposition.[36] Their propaganda also intends to plant the seed that Western governments are not being forthright with their citizenry about casualties or the intensity of fighting. In their rhetoric, terrorist groups explain their actions by stating that there is no choice for them to retaliate against the great Satan with violence. They are small and weak, being attacked by the strong.[37]

Because of the difficulty in tracking individuals over the Net, participants on the most radical chat forums are free to use the strongest of rhetoric—stirring feelings of hatred in other participants.

Conclusion

Islamists have already mastered their use of the Internet to reach, indoctrinate, and recruit vulnerable individuals from within adversarial populations. The medium has given them a way to cloak their appearance so that they can appear to their target as rappers, game developers, or simply sympathetic friends. Because their tactics are constantly changing and improving, it is important for future counterterrorism professionals to be able to anticipate the extremists' next move so that they can be prepared to mitigate the potency of the terrorists' newest online strategy. For this reason, it is also important for counterterrorism professionals to know the enemy's ideology well enough to identify it even when the terrorists do not identify themselves by their official name in an online environment. This is how to prove the presence of terrorists online, rather than mistaking extremist rhetoric for free speech or innocent venting.

Even if the individual posting extremist ideology is not an official member of a jihadist group, it is more than likely that he is circulating material or concepts planted on the Web by a recognized terror group.

The key to the terrorists' success online is that they have been able to operate unchallenged, and they have been excellent students of Western culture, vernacular, and sentiments. It will behoove Western counterterrorism specialists to understand their capabilities, motivations, and mindset in order to beat them on the cyber battlefield.

Notes

1. Lee Rainie, et al., "Internet: The Mainstreaming of Online Life, Pew Internet & American Life Project," March 2005, http://www.pewinternet.org.
2. A February 2005 intercepted message from Osama bin Laden to Abu Musab al-Zarqawi urged Zarqawi to expand his operations to include an attack on the U.S. homeland.
3. Mary Madden, "America's Online Pursuits: The Changing Picture of Who's Online and What They Do," Pew Internet and American Life, December 22, 2003, http://www.pewinternet.org.
4. Ibid.
5. Clark R. McCauley, "The Psychology of Terrorism," *Social Science Research Council* http://www.ssrc.org.
6. United States Code: Title 18: Section 2339B, "Providing Support or Resources to Designated Foreign Terrorist Organizations."
7. Institute for Propaganda Analysis, *Propaganda Analysis,* New York, Columbia University Press, 1938.
8. Lee Rainie, et al., "Internet: The Mainstreaming of Online Life, Pew Internet & American Life Project," March 2005, http://www.pewinternet.org.
9. This scenario is based on 4 years of research by Madeleine Gruen on the ways in which terrorists recruit, indoctrinate, and raise funds over the Internet. Part of her study includes the direct interaction with radicalizing agents via the Internet.
10. International Crisis Group, "Implications of the Afghanistan Campaign," January 30, 2002.
11. Mary Madden, "America's Online Pursuits: The Changing Picture of Who's Online and What They Do," Pew Internet and American Life, December 22, 2003, http://www.pewinternet.org.
12. Nina Bernstein, "Bitterness and Exile for Queens Girl in Terror Case," *New York Times,* June 17, 2005.
13. Al Muhajiroun began as a more overtly radical breakaway of Hizb ut-Tahrir. Members of Al Muhajiroun have participated in terrorist attacks and plots. Omar Bakri Mohammed announced that Al Muhajiroun was no more in October 2004; however, the former members have established new groups that continue to take their orders from Omar Bakri Mohammed.
14. "UK Cleric's Hate Message Finds Place in Website," Hindustantimes.com, June 18, 2005.
15. Elena Larsen, "CyberFaith: How Americans Pursue Religion Online, Pew Internet and American Life," 2001, http://www.pewinternet.org.
16. Ibid.
17. http://www.churchoffools.com
18. Gruen interview with members of Church of Fools chat room, 5/31/05–6/3/05, http://www.churchoffools.com.
19. The thread is an actual discussion that took place on http://www.Islam-online.net. Last accessed on 6/23/05.
20. Sabeel Ahmed's authority on Islam is dubious. He claims to have been the student of Ahmed Deedat, whose scholarship centered on discrediting Christianity and Judaism.
21. Posted to Muslim Youth Club on Yahoo! Groups on July 4, 2005 by "son of Islam." The essay, titled "Conveying Islam in Schools and Colleges," was written in 1998.
22. Peter Cohen, "New Survey Shows Gaming Enjoys Broad Appeal," http://www.macworld.com, May 16, 2005.
23. http://www.specialforce.net
24. Ibid.

25. "Islamic Fun" is available from the Innovative Mind's Web site http://www.inminds.co.uk.
26. Lucy A. Joyner and Jim TerKeurst, "Accounting for User Needs and Motivations in Game Design," *Usability News,* September 2003, http://www.inter-disciplinary.net.
27. Lyrics to "Staring Into Kafir's Eyes" can still be found on several Web sites, including http://www.soldiersofallah.com/kafirseye.doc.
28. "Sleeping Giant" can be downloaded at http://www.afghanhits.com.
29. This was the Soldiers of Allah Yahoo! chat group, which discontinued in early 2004.
30. Posting to Muslimsinhiphop Yahoo chat group by Muhammad-Khalil ibn Abdullah, June 7, 2005.
31. Maria A. Ressa, *Seeds of Terror,* New York: Free Press, 2003, page 184.
32. Michael O'Hanlon and James Steinberg, "Time to Announce a Timetable," *Washington Post,* February 2, 2005.
33. Brigitte L. Nacos, *Mass-Mediated Terrorism: The Central Role of the Media in Terrorism and Counterterrorism,* Lanham, MD: Rowman & Littlefield Publishers. Inc., 2002, pages 65-70.
34. Orgrish.com is a Web site that features uncensored events including beheading videos, execution footage, accident videos, and graphic images from Iraq.
35. Ibid.
36. Gabriel Weimann, "www.terror.net: How Modern Terrorism Uses the Internet," United States Institute of Peace, Special Report 116, March 2004, http://www.usip.org.
37. Ibid.

Chris Dishman, 2005

The Leaderless Nexus: When Crime and Terror Converge

This article argues that the breakdown of hierarchical structures in illicit organizations is creating new opportunities for criminals and terrorists to collaborate. The rise of networked organizations has given greater independence to criminals and terrorists who previously answered to a clear chain of command. These members are now willing to engage in operations that before had been off-limits because the leadership believed the activity would hurt the organization's broader mandate. The result is that a "leaderless nexus" is beginning to emerge between criminals and terrorists. The phenomenon has far-reaching and dangerous implications for U.S. security, and should be thoughtfully considered as lawmakers debate homeland security reform.

International law enforcement pressure is forcing criminal and terrorist organizations to decentralize their organizational structures. Mexican law enforcement efforts are causing drug cartels in Mexico to break into smaller units. Many of the leaders who constituted Al Qaeda's command and control leadership are under arrest or dead, forcing bin Laden to play a more inspirational role, no longer micromanaging attacks as he did for the 11 September spectacular. Even groups that still maintain some hierarchical structure, like the terrorist group Hezbollah, have little control over their extensive networks.

The "flattening" of these groups is creating new and dangerous opportunities for collaboration between criminals and terrorists. The actions of criminal underlings or terrorist operatives are not as constrained because criminal or terrorist "headquarters" are no longer able to micromanage employees. Lower to mid-level criminals and terrorists are taking advantage of their independence to form synergistic ties between the two groups. Some political militant groups have also introduced financial incentive systems to recruit and retain militants. Because members join to make money, they will quickly set ideological goals to the side if it affects profits.

Criminals and terrorists have collaborated on some level for centuries. As many observers point out, the two groups work toward nefarious ends in the same underground community. This cooperation, however, was usually restricted to lower level criminals and terrorists and even then only for short durations. A Don, Colombian cartel boss, or Snakehead would not put his organization in bed with a terrorist group— not because of higher moral values—but because it was bad for business; cooperation with political radicals would turn unwanted attention onto his group. In the last two decades, however, these bosses have been forced to decentralize their organizations, and the managerial role of the leader has been replaced by a networked organization. In short, Don Corleone can no longer order his *mafiosi* to stay away from drug trafficking.

Nowhere is this dynamic more apparent than in the financing of terrorist and criminal cells that are forced to generate funds independently without assistance from leadership. International money laundering crackdowns are making it more difficult for terrorist financiers to quickly and continually send money to their operatives. Low- to mid-level terrorist and criminal actors are forced to find their funding sources, fraudulent documents, transportation, and safe houses. Mid to lower-level criminals—who have quickly risen to greater levels of prominence in decentralized structures—have few qualms working with terrorists, in spite of the fact their ultimate boss would certainly disapprove of such an arrangement. The result is that a *leaderless nexus* has emerged between criminals and terrorists; a phenomenon with far-reaching implications that should be a major concern for law enforcement and intelligence.

The Rise of Networks in Corporations, Transnational Criminal Organizations (TCOs), and Terrorist Groups

Early in the twentieth century, industrialists like Henry Ford brought hierarchies to new heights. Hierarchies enabled businesses to mass produce and mass distribute goods and services. Companies were large, maintained tight control over their operations, provided clear roles for each worker, and asked workers to perform specialized tasks.[1]

The dawn of the Information Age, which brought a different set of factors for corporate success, quickly strained the rigid hierarchical organization. Speed, flexibility, integration, and innovation became ingredients for success in the modern era. In a hierarchy, boundaries exist between managers and the rank and file (ceilings and floors) and "walls" divide each function or specialization within the company.[2] Information is compartmented within the upper levels of the organization while the workers perform specialized tasks or functions.

Profits plummeted when hierarchical corporations could not adjust to the demands of the Information Age. Some companies realized that the hierarchy was impeding their success and radically changed their organizational structure to adapt to the new environment.[3] General Electric (GE), for example, implemented a "Workout" program that created permeable boundaries and shifted resources to support its processes versus functions. Workers learned new capabilities and assumed new responsibilities. Information was no longer compartmented and senior managers shared the company's goals and objectives with the rank and file.

The Information Age has not just had severe implications in the business sector, but also for terrorism and organized crime. In the last 20 years, criminal and terrorist organizations have undergone their own versions of GE's "Workout" program. Terrorist and criminal organizations began to transform their own hierarchical structures into networks. Some, like Al Qaeda, expanded the size and importance of networks already imbedded in their traditional hierarchical organizations, whereas others evolved from a networked group into a more complex horizontal design. Unlike the business community, low profits did not drive these organizations to seek change; law enforcement and intelligence, which began to successfully root out subversive organizations, forced illegal armed groups to find new ways to evade authority and become more resilient. Criminals and terrorists needed to ensure that their organization would not collapse if the main leader or leaders were arrested or killed.

John Arquilla and David Ronfeldt, pioneers in the discussion of network design, describe networks as the organizational cornerstone of a new mode of conflict.[4] Networks contain dispersed nodes—either cells or individuals—internetted together by similar beliefs, ideology, doctrine, and goals. There is no central command, headquarters, or single leader. Cells communicate horizontally and rely extensively on technology to facilitate the heavy communication necessary for networks to carry out operations or tasks. Participants in a network can range from the ultra-committed, to individuals who participate for only short periods.

Modern religious terrorist organizations, more so than criminal ones, have aggressively adopted networked structures in the face of intense counterterror actions. Domestic terrorist groups aiming to overthrow closed-political regimes learned quickly that a network provides resilience. Islamist groups in Egypt, for example, have been forced to radically change their organizational structure to be resilient in the face of suffocating counterterror operations.[5] Since 11 September, pressure against international terror organizations like Al Qaeda has also forced those groups to rely more on networks to organize, prepare for, and carry out attacks.

Terrorists have not always used networks extensively. Marxist terrorist groups, for example, were organized along hierarchical lines.[6] Many of these groups were state sponsored, which necessitated a tight line of control from the state liaison to the group's leader. The state needed a single person or group of persons to interface and give assurances about operations and goals. Any rogue actions by the terrorists could undermine the state's larger political objectives.

A networked organization can still contain hierarchical components. A command cadre, for example, can be imbedded within one node of the organization. There could also be an overarching hierarchy that only uses a network for tactical operations. Terrorist organizations that emerged in the 1980s and 1990s adopted this mix of network and hierarchy. Hezbollah, which emerged in earnest in 1982, is a purposeful blend of hierarchy and network.[7] While the hierarchy enables Hezbollah to control parts of Lebanon and participate in state politics, the network gives Hezbollah financial, religious, social, and military support inside and outside of the country. The network is comprised of Hezbollah followers guided by religious clerics on important political, social, or military subjects. As Hezbollah has no "membership," its leaders rely on the clerics and their own following to influence others to work toward the organization's interests. Hezbollah's hierarchy, in contrast, has formal and direct links between its organs. Its structure includes the highest authority, the decision-making *shoura* (council), which is made up of seven special committees: ideological, financial, military, political, judicial, informational, and social affairs. The committee's members are elected every two years and it is headed by the Secretary General. Hezbollah also contains other hierarchical elements including a Politburo and an Executive *shoura* that is responsible for implementing the high council's decisions. The Deputy Secretary General of Hezbollah outlined the decision to pursue a mixed structure: "We concluded at the end (of organizational discussions) that we needed a structural organization which was in some respects rigid enough to be able to prevent infiltration by the enemy and at the same time flexible enough to embrace the maximum sector of people without having to go through a long bureaucratic process of red tape."[8]

Another organization that maintained a mix of network and hierarchy was the Shining Path, a Maoist guerrilla group in Peru that aimed to overthrow the government with a People's Revolution. Before its dismantlement, the Shining Path's hierarchy consisted of a National Directorate, a Central Committee, and several regional commands.[9] Unlike Hezbollah, however, the hierarchy was not a collective body where everyone was given an equal vote. In fact, the hierarchy was designed to implement the decisions of one person,

Abimael Guzman, who alone decided the group's strategy, objectives, and aims. The "rank and file" members comprised the network of the organization. They were organized into cells that had little contact with the hierarchy. The network allowed the Shining Path to operate over a vast geographic area because the widespread rank and file could make decisions without guidance from the command cadre.

Like modern terrorists, law enforcement crackdowns on transnational criminal organizations (TCOs) have forced criminals to expand their use of networks. Networks facilitate illegal commerce and help TCOs avoid and respond to law enforcement. Drug trafficking organizations in Mexico, in particular, have been forced to decentralize as law enforcement continues to decapitate the leadership of their organizations.[10] Mexican authorities have arrested key members of 3 different cartels within a 14-month period.[11] Mexico's senior counter drug official noted that a result of the spate of drug arrests is that drug leaders are realizing that their organization will become disorganized and chaotic if its hierarchy is decapitated.[12] Cells begin to act independently without regard for the organization in order to make money. Leaders understand that this disarrayed organization is even more susceptible to continuing law enforcement pressure.[13] According to the official, one cartel has organized into a "horizontally-structured business council" to sustain its operations in face of intense law enforcement pressure.[14]

Members of drug trafficking organizations (DTOs), including Mexican drug trafficking organizations, are being pushed further from their traditional center of gravity, with the leadership forced to maintain distance from the members in order to evade law enforcement. Criminal expert Phil Williams notes that many criminal organizations still use some form of hierarchical design, only incorporating or expanding networks where needed. Williams outlines a framework for a networked criminal organization: a core, composed of tight-knit leadership and a periphery consisting of expendable, networked criminals.[15] This organizational mutation is probably only temporary—a transition point from a traditional hierarchical criminal group to a fully networked organization. The vulnerability of a core, even within a networked organization, will probably compel criminal leaders to further flatten their organizational structures.

The Role of a Terrorist Leader in Different Organizational Structures

Marsha Crenshaw, an authority on terrorist organizations, believes that one of the most important jobs of a terrorist leader is preventing the defection of persons to the aboveground world or to another radical organization by creating an attractive incentive structure.

> Leaders ensure organizational maintenance by offering varied incentives to followers, not all of which involve the pursuit of the group's stated political purposes. Leaders seek to prevent both defection and dissent by developing intense loyalties among group members. …Leaders maintain their position by supplying various tangible and intangible incentives to members, rewards that may enhance or diminish the pursuit of the organization's public ends.[16]

The creation of an incentive structure, as highlighted by Crenshaw, was an important characteristic of a leader managing an illicit hierarchy. Now, many terrorists groups have transformed into networked organizations, radically changing the role of the leader. At a minimum, a network has no single leader or command cadre that manages and oversees the organization. Sometimes there are no leaders at all, or leaders might be imbedded in various network nodes, or cells, but without authority over the broader organization (see Figure 1).

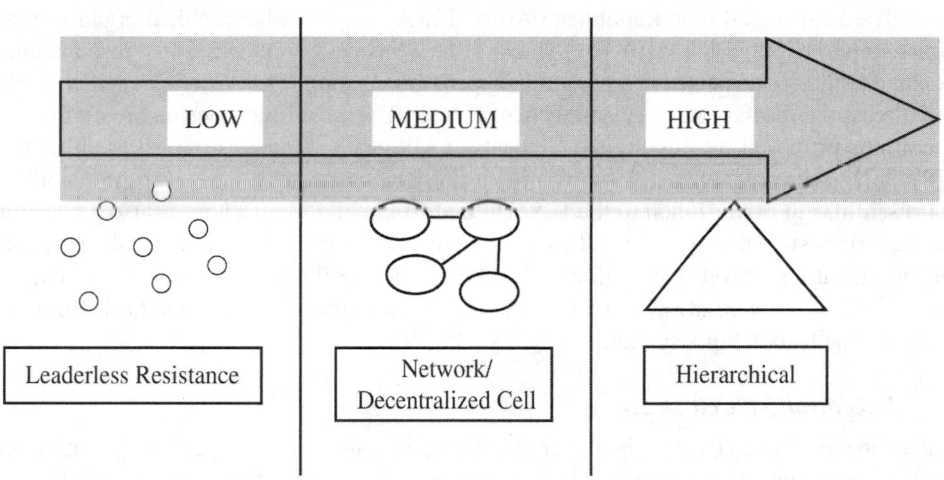

Figure 1. The degree of a leader's control in different forms of terrorist and criminal organizations. In a hierarchy, the leader controls almost all aspects of the organization, including recruitment, promotion, delegation of authority, and the planning of major events (i.e., Terrorist attack or criminal undertaking). In a decentralized cell structure, there is no single leader or command element that controls all the various nodes in the network. Cell leaders guide the activities of individual cells. In a leaderless resistance movement, the leader's role is restricted to providing inspiration to its members (or potential members) to undertake tasks on behalf of the group.

One of the advantages of a network is that there is no leader who assumes so much responsibility that his or her arrest or death derails the organization's mission and capability. The use of networks is almost a natural evolution in response to a law enforcement strategy designed to decapitate the leadership of criminal or terrorist organizations—a hierarchy attacking a hierarchy. In addition to networks, there is another type of organization with no leader—leaderless resistance. This form of organization has no network, no leaders, and cannot be described as "flat" because it only consists of single individuals or very small groups who are not tied to any other organizations—vertically or horizontally.

The role of leaders in these types of organizations merits some discussion.

Hierarchical

In a hierarchical organization, the leader plays a direct role managing the activities of the organization. The leader acts as a Chief Executive Officer, delegating authority to subordinates and maintaining clear chains of command. The hierarchical organization is structured to facilitate top-to-bottom guidance. Ideas are rarely presented from the bottom-up, but even if they are, the group's leaders retain veto power over the idea. The leaders rely on subordinates with different areas of responsibility (i.e., security, financial, recruitment, etc.) to carry out their direction. Hierarchical leaders can be micro-managers; they will punish a low-level subordinate for a mistake, or direct a small activity or operation. Most importantly, however, the leader ensures the organization's operations ultimately support its goals and objectives. In sum, a hierarchy creates a cohesive monolithic unit that acts within well-defined parameters.

The Provisional Irish Republican Army (PIRA), a typical hierarchical organization, offers some insights. The PIRA is organized like a business, with positions, responsibilities, and authority dispersed in a pyramid-shaped organization. The Army Council controls and directs the military strategy and tactics of the PIRA, including ordering or vetoing the operations proposed by subordinate elements.[17] Military guidance is passed to either the PIRA's Northern or Southern Command—military elements with areas of responsibility, not dissimilar in organization to the U.S. Unified Command Plan. There is also a General Headquarters staff that oversees all PIRA activities through its ten departments. Overall, the organization proved very effective (although not resilient), because as one expert notes,[18] disputes were always ruled on by higher authorities ensuring a cohesive unit to carry out the leadership's guidance.

Decentralized Cell Structure

A decentralized cell structure is one characteristic of a networked organization, although not a defining trait. Understanding the leader's role in this form of organization—which is usually prominent in some form of a network—provides insights into the evolving role of leaders within a network.

Arquilla and Ronfeldt describe the structure and role of leaders in one form of network:

> The network as a whole (but not necessarily each node) has little to no hierarchy; there may be multiple leaders. Decision making and operations are decentralized, allowing for local initiative and autonomy. Thus the design may look acephalous (headless) at times, and polycephalous (Hydraheaded) at other times, though not all nodes may be "created equal." In other words, it is a heterarchy, or what may be better termed a panarchy.[19]

As Arquilla and Ronfeldt note, the major difference in leadership in a decentralized cell structure versus a hierarchy is that a cell structure can have multiple leaders—a panarchy—whose functions and responsibilities change depending on circumstances. The leader is usually the person with the most experience in the cell, and its members naturally defer to this veteran. Within the cell, the leader ensures tasks are carried out appropriately without attracting law enforcement attention. The cell leader is also responsible for external relations, although contact is usually kept to a minimum and the cell retains extensive independence. Along these lines, Marc Sageman, whose examination of Al Qaeda focuses on social networks, believes that hub leaders are dynamic, outgoing personalities with extensive social reach. These persons are able to attract recruits and can help guide them to the training necessary to participate in jihad.[20]

The absence of the top-down guidance existing in a hierarchical organization makes it imperative for the nodes in the network to communicate on a regular basis to ensure that each is operating within the context of a larger plan. He or she is also the ideological or doctrinal espouser and watchdog—ensuring that everyone maintains the ideological fervor necessary for the success of the cell and its broader networked organization. This is perhaps the most important responsibility, because the broader networked organization, of which the cell is a part, will only be successful if cell members retain similar goals, aims, and beliefs.[21]

Leaderless Resistance

A third type of organization has been coined by experts as "leaderless resistance." Jeffrey Kaplan defines leaderless resistance as:

> . . . A lone wolf operation in which an individual, or a very small, highly cohesive group, engage in acts of anti-state violence independent of any movement, leader, or network of support.[22]

In a leaderless organization, there are no leaders—only perpetrators—involved in an attack. Ideologues goal or motivate the radical masses into conducting attacks. As terrorism expert Jessica Stern notes, "inspirational leaders" encourage their followers to attack targets but the leaders do not provide funding, direct orders, or any other form of tangible support. Anti-abortionists, for example, will raise money for jailed militants, but never participate in any pre-attack measures.[23]

The White Aryan Nation (WAR) urged followers to conduct violent attacks after Proposition 187, which would bar illegal immigrants from receiving government services in California, was stopped by a Federal court. The leader stated that "Today, California ceased to exist as an Aryan-dominated state. W.A.R. releases all associates from any constraints, real or imagined, in confronting the problem in any way you see fit."[24]

Leaderless resistance was popularized by the right-wing preacher and radical Louis Beam. Right wing groups such as the Phineas Priesthood and the White Aryan Resistance embraced Beam's vision by ensuring that no formal organization existed in their movements. There is no hierarchy or chain of command between the group's activists and its leadership. Activists do not rely on support from other cells so there is very little—if any—communication between operatives or their cells. Each operative is self-sufficient; they will choose the site of an attack and plan the attack on their own. Interestingly, left wing groups also adopted Beam's vision of a leaderless organization. The radical environmental group, the Earth Liberations Front (ELF) encourages its followers to create their own cell rather than joining an existing cell because efforts to locate an existing cell could compromise the organization.[25] ELF's cells are independent and autonomous, and members do not know the identities of members in a different cell; the cells are "linked" together by a shared ideology.[26]

Al Qaeda Is Forced to Decentralize

Al Qaeda is the most salient example of a terrorist organization that has been forced to decentralize. Since 11 September Al Qaeda has lost roughly 70 percent of its leadership, which comprised the heart of Al Qaeda's command cadre. Experts have given different names to this centralized element, including the Al Qaeda hard core, Al Qaeda hierarchy, Al Qaeda's professional cadre, or Al Qaeda's central staff. This centralized element, created in 1998, coordinates and oversees the functions and tasks of Al Qaeda, including preparing for and executing terrorist attacks.[27]

Terrorist expert Peter Bergin believes Al Qaeda's centralized structure functions like a corporation, where bin Laden, acting as director, formulates policies in consultation with his top advisors.[28] These policies are implemented by a series of subordinate "committees," the most senior of which is the *shura majlis*, or "Advisory Council," which is attended by Al Qaeda's most veteran leaders and reports directly to bin Laden.[29] Under this council are at least four committees, including a military; finance and business; fatwa and Islamic study; and media and publicity committee.[30] Committee members can serve on more than one committee and sometimes individuals work directly for bin Laden on special assignments.[31] Committee membership is based on family, nationality, and friendship. In this regard, Al Qaeda's command element resembles the mafia: merit and performance play little role in success in the hierarchy.[32]

Bin Laden utilizes this structure to carry out spectacular mass attacks. The military committee, for example, plans and executes attacks for Al Qaeda, conducts surveillance, gathers intelligence, and trains members in military tactics.[33] The head of Al Qaeda's military committee prior to 11 September, Khalid Sheikh Muhammad, conceived and helped plan the plot to crash airliners into symbolic U.S. targets.[34] Bin Laden operates both within and outside this structure. For the most important terrorist attacks, bin Laden dealt directly with those executing the plot. The National Commission on Terrorist Attacks revealed, for example, that bin Laden played a very "hands-on" role in planning the 11 September attacks: he handpicked the operatives that participated in the operation; he cancelled a planned operation to crash airliners in Southeast Asia; he personally interceded to keep an operative in the plot who Muhammad wanted removed; and rejected several shura members' recommendations to abort the attacks.[35] Although the degree of bin Laden's involvement, as revealed by the Commission, could be overstated, it's clear that at a minimum he was heavily involved in operational decision making.

The loss of Al Qaeda's Afghanistan haven, and the death or arrest of many of its senior leaders, has forced Al Qaeda to decentralize. Because communication links between Al Qaeda's centralized command and its operatives have been disrupted, bin Laden and his central staff now play a less direct role in planning attacks.[36] Al Qaeda's operational commanders and cell leaders exert more authority and make decisions that used to be under bin Laden's purview.[37] Although it's unclear to what extent the committees are still functioning, bin Laden's essential need for secrecy since 11 September suggests that at a minimum, the committees are not operating as efficiently as before. According to J. Cofer Black, the State Department's Counterterrorism Coordinator, some terrorist cells have delayed attacks because of communication mix-ups between the group and Al Qaeda's leadership. Black cites the attack on the Muhaya housing compound in Riyadh as an example of the lack of clear direction Al Qaeda is providing to its network. The attack resulted in the deaths of many Muslims during Ramadan and as Cofer dryly noted, "was a public relations disaster"—the attack awoke the dormant Saudi counterterrorism apparatus that began to flush out Al Qaeda cells.[38] Additionally, the international financial crackdown on Al Qaeda's finances has probably hurt the finance committee's ability to fund operations worldwide.

The Negative Results of Decentralization: Criminal, Terrorist Boundaries Less Clear

Al Qaeda provides a sharp illustration of a terrorist group forced to decentralize. Many other criminal and terrorist organizations also use networks to plan terrorist attacks or run illicit rackets. In the case of Al Qaeda, decentralization has probably hurt the organization's ability to carry out spectacular terrorist attacks. Nevertheless, the proliferation of international criminal and terrorist networks like Al Qaeda pose new threats to stability. Because networks marginalize or eliminate the command cadre, cells and nodes now have expanded roles and responsibilities. These lower to mid-level members define the organization, its actions, its direction and its goals. The activities of these operatives, who are the critical pillars of terrorist and criminal organizations, are no longer constrained by a leader or elder. This freedom allows individuals or small cells to pursue multiple nefarious ends, even at the expense of broader organizational goals. Although political[39] and financial aims are two distinct, usually incompatible ends, lower and midlevel operators do not wrestle with such academic distinctions. A criminal seeks to keep the status quo, stay out of the lime-

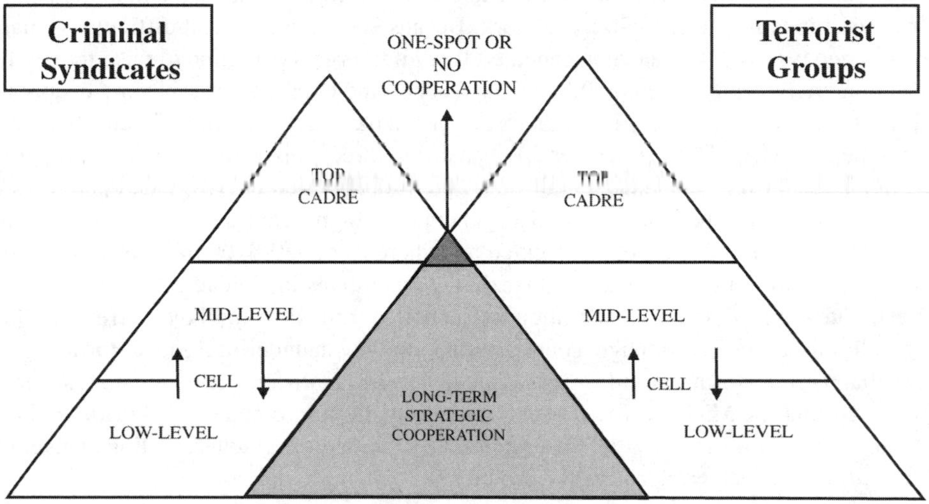

Figure 2. Graphic depiction of a new dynamic where low- to mid-level criminals and terrorists create strategic alliances with each other. These lower to mid-level members are the pillars of decentralized criminal and terrorist organizations, and cooperation between the two will lead to new challenges for law enforcement authorities.

light, not commit collateral violence, and make money. A terrorist in contrast seeks attention, wants to commit collateral violence, and wants to alter the status quo. Lower to mid-level cell leaders are not concerned with incompatible goals, however, and without oversight will pursue personal and organizational agendas.

Historically, the distinction between a criminal and a terrorist has not always been clear. Many terrorists use crime to generate revenue to support their ultimate political goal, whereas some criminals use illicit funds to support radical political causes. Even prior to 11 September, Al Qaeda directed its cells to be financially self-sufficient.[40] Some criminals use terrorism (as a violent tactic) against authorities if a large-scale crackdown on their organization occurs. Nevertheless, within hierarchical organizations there is still some degree of leadership control that could bring the organization back on course should the organization's goals begin to stray from the original cause.[41] An organization that is completely decentralized, or contains a large decentralized component, is usually unwilling or unable to control the activities of its members. This dynamic is most applicable to criminal syndicates, where the transition from hierarchy to a decentralized network has sometimes created an "every cell for itself" atmosphere. Cash-strapped cells are now willing to conduct any crime in order to stay afloat.[42] These crimes could include operations previously "out of bounds" for most transnational organized criminal groups, including smuggling weapons of mass destruction, creating fraudulent documents for terrorists, or smuggling terrorist personnel. These cells are also no longer constrained by a leadership that prohibited interaction with terrorists because of the unwanted law enforcement attention such activities would bring.[43]

In addition to being unable to control its members, a decentralized network is unable to provide continuous financial assistance to its nodes. The need for secrecy and resiliency between nodes in the network means that money is not often passed between nodes or amassed in a single node in the network. There is no "terrorist bank" that a member can go to request funds in a decentralized network. Because of these financial difficulties, many terrorist nodes have taken an unprecedented foray into organized crime to raise money for their financially depleted cell or hub. Al Qaeda cells and hubs, for example, are deeply involved with drug trafficking in Afghanistan and have purchased illegitimate diamonds from rebels in Africa.[44] In December 2003 coalition forces seized three vessels smuggling heroin and hashish in the Persian Gulf that were probably tied to Al Qaeda operatives.[45] Far-flung Hezbollah networks have also generated a significant amount of money. According to one official, Hezbollah received anywhere from \$50-\$100 million from the tri-border region in South America. Two Hezbollah operatives in Cuidad del Este, Paraguay are estimated to have moved \$50 million to Hezbollah from 1995 until their arrest in 2001. The cell raised money through counterfeiting, money laundering, and extortion.[46] A Hezbollah cell in North Carolina took advantage of the tax difference on cigarettes sold in North Carolina and Michigan to net over \$7.9 million. Law enforcement authorities believe that terrorist groups in the United States continue to smuggle cigarettes, netting an average of \$2 million on each truckload of the product.[47]

Dangerous Dynamics Emerge

Two phenomenon result from the increasing authority of low- to mid-level criminal and terrorist leaders and their need to survive in a decentralized environment. First, these leaders will increasingly seek to collaborate with criminal or terrorist counterparts outside of the organization for extended periods of time. These new cadre of leaders will be more likely to create strategic alliances with other terrorist or criminal subversives. Second, the decentralized organization will internally transform so that both criminals and terrorists are critical ingredients in the organization's structure.

External Convergence

Past criminal/terrorist alliances were usually short-term relationships that existed on a case by case basis only. These were "one spot" arrangements, where terrorists or criminals would collaborate for only short periods of time.[48] Terrorists might provide bomb-making skills to a criminal group for a set fee, but the relationship would end after the training was over. In 1993, for example, some reports alleged that Pablo Escobar hired National Liberation Army (ELN) guerrillas to plant car bombs because Escobar's organization could not carry out such attacks.[49] One-spot arrangements can also include single transactions between criminal and terrorist groups. In one example, four members of the United Self-Defense Groups of Colombia were arrested in Houston, Texas when they tried to exchange \$25 million of cocaine and cash for shoulder-fired anti-aircraft missiles and other weapons.[50]

From now on, criminal and terrorist cell or hub leaders will build long-term alliances with their criminal or terrorist counterpart, allowing each group to benefit from the other's knowledge and experience. In January 2002, members of a Hezbollah drug ring were arrested in "Operation Mountain Express" by U.S. and Canadian authorities. The Hezbollah ring was smuggling pseudoephedrine, a precursor chemical for methamphetamines, from Canada to Mexican criminal gangs in the Midwest. The Hezbollah operatives had established a long-standing criminal alliance with the Mexican drug dealers from which they netted at least millions of dollars that were laundered to terrorists in the Middle East.[51] Although this Hezbollah group laundered the proceeds to a Middle Eastern terrorist group, the cell could have also kept the money to sustain the cell and possibly prepare for an attack. In this respect, long-term alliances radically improve the effectiveness of each cell or small group. Terrorists will be able to raise more money from criminal actions. Ramzi Yousef, mastermind of the 1993 bombing of the World Trade Center, wanted to build a bigger bomb to topple one tower into the other, but he could not because he lacked the necessary funding.[52]

"External" alliances could become internal as the outside party becomes integrated into the network. A decentralized network facilitates these relationships by allowing cells or individuals to participate in the network in any capacity. As Williams states, "networks can be highly structured and enduring in nature or they can be loose, fluid, or amorphous in character, with members coming and going according to particular needs, opportunities and demands. Some individuals or even small organizations will drift in and out of networks when it is convenient for them to do so."[53] Businessmen and criminals who benefit from a guerrilla war economy would probably be folded into a network because their financial security is directly tied to the ongoing war and the guerrilla rebellion.

Hybrid Organizations

A second and equally important dynamic is the "hybridization" of criminal or terrorist networks. A model example of a functioning network would consist of cells and members with similar ideologies, motives, and views of success or failure. When cells or nodes begin to pursue their own agendas, the like-minded identity that binds the network together dissolves and a hybrid organization emerges. The new hybrid organization is dominated by persons in cells, fronts, or other organizational components that retain multiple motives and desired end-states. Some Islamic militants, for example, are heavily involved in drug trafficking and reap major profits from the illegal activity. These militants justify drug trafficking because they believe their enemies suffer from drug consumption. In their view, they receive a dual benefit from the crime: they generate profits and hurt their enemies. These profits can be used to support the cell's activities, be invested in personal bank accounts, or given to friends and families. Hezbollah, for example, which has been involved in drug trafficking in Lebanon, views drug trafficking as another weapon to use against its enemies. One Hezbollah *fatwa* (religious edict) stated that "We are making these drugs for Satan America and the Jews. If we cannot kill them with guns, so we will kill them with drugs."[54] In more recent illustration, law enforcement officials investigating the Madrid bombings noted that one of the suspect bombers "justified drug trafficking if it was for Islam … he saw it as part of jihad."[55]

Identifying a hybrid is difficult. Cells within hybrid organizations are chameleons — criminal by day, terrorist by night. A sleeper cell may not look like a sleeper cell at all; its activities focused on organized crime: extortion, counterfeiting, drug trafficking, and so on. Authorities investigating the Madrid train bombings stated that one of the suspect's drug trafficking activities masked his involvement in terrorism; authorities never considered him part of a terrorist plot.[56] Identifying a hybrid is also challenging because it has no hierarchy from which an analyst can determine aims, goals, and degree of control.

Hybrid organizations form synergistic ties internally to build criminal or terrorist expertise (see Figure 2). Cell leaders collaborate with other cells or nodes to maximize criminal gains or prepare for violent attacks. One result is that terrorist cells increase their financial intake by participating in sophisticated organized criminal rings. The examples shown earlier

(Al Qaeda and Hezbollah) illustrate the millions of dollars that can be generated from organized crime. As noted earlier, emerging information about the Madrid bombings shows that many of the plotters were heavily involved in drug trafficking. Jamal Ahmidan, one of the cell's ringleaders, allegedly traded hashish for 220 pounds of dynamite used in the attack. He also brought in six drug traffickers who participated in the plot.[57] The result of this criminal, terrorist synergy was a devastating blast that killed 191 people.

Enforcement Implications

The breakdown of hierarchical organizations poses a unique challenge for law enforcement and intelligence. Law enforcement's successful strategy of arresting high value targets has forced criminal and terrorist leaders to be less involved in the day to day direction of the organization. The result is a growing independence, sophistication, and number of small cells or criminal gangs that multiplies the number of targets law enforcement must pursue. Decentralized organizations leave few evidentiary trails between the leadership and its cells, and between the cells themselves. Many cell leaders cannot identify other cell members or their support personnel. In Colombia, for example, a senior law enforcement official noted that Colombian traffickers now operate in small, autonomous cells that make it more difficult for law enforcement to discover them.[58] Gathering information about a hierarchical organization was easier because law enforcement agents only needed to recruit one well-placed informant to break up the entire organization.[59]

The combustible mix of lower and mid-level profit-minded criminals and terrorists makes it difficult to delineate between the two. As a result, law enforcement agents working criminal cases could provide critical information on a terrorist cell or plot. Terrorists have traditionally used a criminal support structure in their operations, but now longer term relationships are being established between terrorist cells and criminal organizations. Terrorist cells could in fact become fully involved in profit-driven activities.

Since 11 September, many experts, think tanks, and commissions have debated the need to create a domestic counterterrorism intelligence service separate from the FBI. The 9-11 Commission, which is sure to make heavy recommendations for U.S. intelligence, has already hinted at the possibility of recommending the creation of a domestic intelligence service. Many proposals have emerged, some of which are tweaks of Britain's internal security service, MI5. Two proposals have received the most attention:

- *John Deutch's Proposal.* He proposed the creation of a domestic intelligence service under the Director of Central Intelligence, making the DCI responsible for both the foreign and domestic collection of terrorist threats. This is organizationally different than Britain's MI5 as Deutch's proposal places the service under the Director of Central Intelligence, versus Britain's Home Secretary—which is the closest equivalent of the Department of Homeland Security.
- *Gilmore Commission.* The Gilmore commission recommended the creation of a stand-alone agency to analyze domestic and foreign collected information on foreign terrorist groups. The agency would have the more muscular collection powers established under the post-11 September Foreign Intelligence Surveillance Act (FISA) regulations. It would be the primary coordinating point for sharing information with state and local officials, but would not collect or analyze information on national domestic terrorist groups.

Each proposal contains different components. Some place the new organization under the Director for Central Intelligence; others make it a stand-alone agency, and others not mentioned here recommend that the agency stay within the Department of Justice or the FBI. The common thread between all recommendations is that they separate the investigation of profit-driven crimes from terrorism investigations. At first glance, such a separation seems warranted. For years terrorism has been considered a law enforcement phenomenon, an issue that did not deserve the attention of other higher priority national security interests.

The problem, however, is that separating criminal from terrorist investigations could hinder, rather than help, identify and arrest terrorists. As this article has noted, it is increasingly difficult to label a terrorist a terrorist and a criminal a criminal. Many terrorists and guerrilla movements are engaged in organized crime, and many profit-minded criminals no longer have inhibitions about working with terrorists. Thus a criminal lead could very well trace back to a terrorist. The creation of a terrorism-only agency would create an institutional barrier between the criminal and terrorism analysts.

Conclusion

The transformation of terrorists and criminal organizations from hierarchy to network has dangerous and largely unnoticed implications. With the emergence of decentralized organizations, a centuries-old dynamic between hierarchical terrorist and criminal organizations has begun to change. Criminals and terrorists now have few reservations about cooperating with each other. Many will create long-term strategic alliances to harness each other's expertise—making their groups more dangerous and elusive than ever.

Notes

1. Ron Ashkenas, Dave Ulrich, Todd Jick, and Steve Kerr, *The Boundaryless Organization: Breaking the Chains of Organizational Structure* (Jossey-Bass, San Francisco, 2002).
2. Ibid.
3. Horizontal organization experts, however, still stress that some amount of hierarchy is necessary to guide and orchestrate the horizontal organizations. Ibid.
4. There are many works that provided the basis for this analysis. See John Arquilla and Theodore Karasik, "Chechnya: A Glimpse of Future Conflict," *Studies in Conflict & Terrorism,* 22, pp. 207-229 (1999). "Networks and Netwars," edited by John Arquilla and David Ronfeldt, RAND Report (2001). "In Athena's Camp: Preparing for Conflict in the Information Age," edited by John Arquilla and David Ronfeldt, RAND report (1997). "Networks, Netwar, and Information-Age Terrorism," John Arquilla, David Ronfeldt, and Michele Zanini, *Countering the New Terrorism* (Washington, DC: RAND, 1999).
5. Other paths were also chosen. Some organizations like Islamic Jihad chose to leave Egypt, while others, like the Muslim Brotherhood, gave up violence to pursue a political path.
6. Michele Zanini and Sean J. A. Edwards, "The Networking of Terror in the Information Age," in *Networks and Netwars*," edited by John Arquilla and David Ronfeldt, RAND Report (2001).
7. Magnus Ranstorp, "Hizbollah's Command Leadership: It's Structure, Decision-Making and Relationship with Iranian Clergy and Institutions," *Terrorism and Political Violence* (Autumn 1994) and from Hala Jaber, "Hezbollah: Born with a Vengeance" (New York: Columbia Press, 1997), pp. 63-66.
8. Hala Jaber, *Hezbollah: Born with a Vengeance* (New York: Columbia Press, 1997), p. 64.
9. Gordon McCormick, "The Shining Path and Peruvian Terrorism," *Inside Terrorist Organizations,* edited by David Rapaport. Also see Gordon McCormick, "The Shining Path and the Future of Peru," RAND report (March 1990).

10. The same dynamic exists in Colombia. See Joseph Contreras and Steven Ambrus, "The DEA's Nightmare: Colombian Targets Get Smart, Techno-Hip and Phenomenally Successful," *Newsweek,* 21 February 2000. Also see Jeremy McDermott and Oscar Becerra, "Mexican Drug Trade Faces Fragmentation," *Jane's Intelligence Review* (May 2003).
11. Ibid.
12. *Tijuana La Frontera,* UEDO Director Says Mexican Drug Cartels Operate Like Companies, 1 July 2003.
13. Ibid.
14. Ibid.
15. Phil Williams, "Transnational Criminal Networks," *Networks and Netwars*, edited by John Arquilla and David Ronfeldt, RAND Report (2001).
16. Marsha Crenshaw, "Theories of Terrorism: Instrumental and Organizational Approaches," *Inside Terrorist Organizations,* edited by David Rapaport, p. 14.
17. John Horgan and Max Taylor, "The Provisional Irish Republican Army: Command and Functional Structure," *Terrorism and Political Violence,* 9(3) (Autumn 1997), pp. 1-32.
18. Ibid., p. 3.
19. The network form described in this section is an "all-channel network." See John Arquilla and David Ronfeldt "The Advent of Netwar: Analytic Background," *Studies in Conflict and Terrorism,* 2(1999), p. 193.
20. See Marc Sageman, *Understanding Terror Networks* (Philadelphia: University of Pennsylvania Press, 2004), pp. 70-71.
21. Jeremy Pressman, "Leaderless Resistance: The Next Threat?" *Current History* (December 2003).
22. Jeffrey Kaplan, "Leaderless Resistance," *Terrorism and Political Violence* (Autumn 1997), p. 43.
23. Jessica Stern, *Terror in the Name of God: Why Religious Militants Kill* (New York: Harper Collins, 2003), pp. 148, 165.
24. Jo Thomas, "New Face of Terror Crimes: 'Lone Wolf' Weaned on Hate," *New York Times* (16 August 1999).
25. Stefan Leader and Peter Probst, "The Earth Liberation Front and Environmental Terrorism," *Terrorism and Political Violence* (Winter 2003).
26. Ibid.
27. "Overview of the Enemy," The National Commission on Terrorist Attacks Upon the United States, Staff Statement No. 15. Rohan Gunaratna, *Inside Al Qaeda* (New York: Berkeley Books, 2002), p. 76.
28. Peter Bergin, *Holy War, Inc.* (New York: Simon and Schuster, 2002), p. 31.
29. Rohan Gunaratna, *Inside Al Qaeda* (New York: Berkeley Books, 2002), p. 77.
30. A recent report by the National Commission on Terrorist Attacks cites two other committees: A foreign purchase committee and security committee. Rohan Gunaratna, *Inside Al Qaeda* (New York: Berkeley Books, 2002), p. 77. U.S.A. v. Usama bin Laden, 98 Cr. 1023 (SDNY) Indictment. Bergin, *Holy War, Inc*. (New York: Simon and Schuster, 2002), p. 31.
31. Rohan Gunaratna, *Inside Al Qaeda,* p. 77.
32. Rohan Gunaratna, *Inside Al Qaeda,* p. 76. U.S.A. v. Usama bin Laden, 98 Cr. 1023 (SDNY) Indictment.
33. Rohan Gunaratna, *Inside Al Qaeda* (New York, Berkeley Books, 2002), p. 77. U.S.A. v. Usama bin Laden, 98 Cr. 1023 (SDNY) Indictment.
34. "Outline of the 9/11 plot," The National Commission on Terrorist Attacks Upon the United States, Staff Statement No. 16.
35. "Overview of the Enemy," The National Commission on Terrorist Attacks Upon the United States, Staff Statement No. 16.

36. Testimony to the House Committee on International Relations, J. Cofer Black, "Al- Qaida: The Threat to the United States and Its Allies," 1 April 2004.
37. It is important to note that it's unclear to what extent Al Qaeda's centralized element still exists and functions. Rohan Gunaratana believes the four committees still existed after the U.S. invasion of Afghanistan. See Rohan Gunaratna, *Inside Al Qaeda,* p. 78. Also see "Overview of the Enemy."
38. Testimony to the House Committee on International Relations, J. Cofer Black.
39. The word "political" will be used loosely in this article. The purpose of "political" is to differentiate it from the financial goals of an organized crime group. As defined here, the word will encompass a wide range of motivations including irredentism, desire to overthrow a government, sectarian violence, and the host of religious motivations including establishment of an Islamic caliphate, pushing the United States out of the Middle East, overthrowing Western-minded Middle Eastern government, etc.
40. Mark Basile, "Going to the Source: Why Al Qaeda's Financial Network Is Likely to Withstand the Current War on Terrorist Financing," *Studies in Conflict & Terrorism,* 2004.
41. Some leaders might not be interested in steering the organization back to its original cause in which case the organization's ends and objectives have transformed. See Chris Dishman, "Terrorism, Crime, and Transformation," *Studies in Conflict & Terrorism,* 24, pp. 43-58 (January 2001).
42. *Tijuana La Frontera,* UEDO Director Says Mexican Drug Cartels Operate Like Companies.
43. Chris Dishman, "Terrorism, Crime and Transformation," *Studies in Conflict & Terrorism* (January 2001).
44. Rachel Ehrenfield, *Funding Evil—How Terrorism Is Financed and How to Stop It* (Chicago: Bonus Books, 2003), pp. 33-71. Al Qaeda reportedly taxes Afghanistan poppy growers and heroin refiners; launders money for the Taliban; purchases poppy crops directly; and distributes refined heroin throughout the Balkans to Europe. Al Qaeda cells also laundered over $20 million by purchasing illegitimate diamonds from Liberia and Revolutionary United Front rebels.
45. Series of CNN wire reports describe the boat seizures: 29 December 2003. "U.S. holds al Qaeda drug suspects: Navy intercepts hauls of hashish, heroin and methamphetamines," 20 December 2003, "U.S. seizes drugs on boats in Persian Gulf," 2 January 2004, "More drugs seized in Gulf-U.S."
46. Rachel Ehrenfield, *Funding Evil—How Terrorism Is Financed and How to Stop It* (Chicago: Bonus Books, 2003), pp. 147-149.
47. Sari Horwit, "Cigarette smuggling linked to terrorism." *Washington Post,* 8 June 2004 (New York: St. Martins Press), p. 53.
48. Prepared testimony of Dr. Phil Williams before the House International Relations Committee, 31 January 1996.
49. Patrick Clawson and Rensselear Lee, The Andean Cocaine Industry, p. 53.
50. "Narco-Terrorism: International Drug Trafficking And Terrorism—A Dangerous Mix," United States Senate, Committee on the Judiciary, Opening Statement of Senator Orrin G. Hatch, Tuesday, 20 May 2003. Available at (http://frwebgate.access.gpo.gov/cgibin/useftp.cgi?IPaddress=162.140.64.88&filename=90052.wais&directory=/diskb/wais/data/108_senate_hearings).
51. See Ehrenfeld, *Funding Evil,* pp. 11-12. "Drug Money For Hezbollah?," CBSNEWS.COM, Washington, D.C., 1 September 2002. Also see DEA transcript release, "More Than 100 Arrested In Nationwide Methamphetamine Investigation," available at (http://www.usdoj.gov/dea/major/ me3.html).
52. Members of the cash-strapped cell were discovered when they attempted to get back their deposit on the rental van. Cited in Testimony of Matthew A. Levitt Senior Fellow in Terrorism Studies, The Washington Institute for Near East Policy Before the United States Subcommittee on International Trade and Finance, Committee on Banking, Housing, and

Urban Affairs "Charitable And Humanitarian Organizations in the Network of International Terrorist Financing," 1 August 2002.

53. Williams, "Transnational Criminal Networks," p. 70.
54. Fatwa quoted in Rachel Ehrenfeld, *Funding Evil,* pp. 143-145.
55. Sebastian Rotella, "The World; Jihad's Unlikely Alliance; Muslim extremists who attacked Madrid funded the plot by selling drugs, investigators say," *Los Angeles Times,* 23 May 2004.
56. Ibid.
57. One of the Madrid suspect bombers was also an informant for authorities investigating a drug gang. See Rotella, "The World; Jihad's Unlikely Alliance."
58. See Douglas Farah, "Colombian Drug Cartels Exploit Tech Advantage," *Washington Post,* 15 November 1999.
59. See Joseph Contreras and Steven Ambrus, "The DEA's Nightmare: Colombian Targets Get Smart, Techno-Hip and Phenomenally Successful," *Newsweek,* 21 February 21, 2000.

Part II

Countering the Terrorist Threat

Chapter 7

The Challenges of Terrorism to a Free Society

In Chapter 7, the authors explore the tragedies of September 11 as a cornerstone—on how the events of a single day can focus new light on America's stature in the world, and how the tragedies that occurred in the space of a few hours have caused a deep ripple effect in the nation's government and its policy-making efforts.

Richard K. Betts maps out the landscape, explaining why terror can be an effective means against a nation as powerful as the United States, why such tactics have an impact despite a significant power imbalance. "American global privacy is one of the causes of this war," he writes. It is not just the way the United States and its moves are perceived by certain parties around the world: "Remaking the world in the Western image is what Americans assume to be just, natural, and desirable, indeed in only a matter of time. But that presumption is precisely what energizes many terrorists' hatred," writes Betts, but is also the perception here at home. Betts discusses the tactics and countermeasures of this situation, when "intense political grievance and gross imbalance of power" become an explosive equation for terror.

At a time when nations are under the threat of terrorist actions, timely intelligence collection is central to any successful counterterrorism strategy. Bruce Hoffman examines the more difficult questions that Western democracies are grappling with in regard to limits of interrogations. "The struggles against Osama bin Laden and his minions will rely on good intelligence," writes Hoffman, but the experiences of other countries, fighting similar conflicts against similar enemies, suggest that "Americans still do not appreciate the enormously difficult—and morally complex—problem that the imperative to gather 'good intelligence' entails." Hoffman cites scenarios, both fictional and real, about those who have been responsible for information gathering in times of crises and the unsavory but perhaps necessary measures they have taken. They act in times when extraordinary circumstances create extraordinary pressure to deliver results.

The relationship between terrorists and the traditional media has always been one of much controversy. Two schools of thought have emerged on this issue. The first theory addresses the idea that terrorist organizations seek to achieve widespread media coverage that, in turn, will further intimidate the public and influence policy makers. The second theory challenges the centrality of media to terrorists' strategy. Boaz Ganor explores the tension between these two theories through an examination of the terrorist events in Israel. This article presents difficult questions to policy makers with regard to the role of the media and media coverage of terrorist incidents.

An equally significant challenge to the issues of the press and free speech are the issues surrounding terrorist financing. As discussed in earlier articles, money is a centrifugal force for terrorists. Without it, they cannot sustain their operations let alone expand to new fronts, recruit new members, or purchase new weapons. Mark Basile outlines how al Qaeda has managed to build a network of financiers who have skillfully hidden al Qaeda's assets and who have also "learned to effectively leverage the global financial system of capital markets." Basile argues that as a result of these extensive measures, al Qaeda's financial system is not only healthy but that it may be likely to withstand the international efforts to date.

Richard K. Betts, 2002

The Soft Underbelly of American Primacy: Tactical Advantages of Terror

In given conditions, action and reaction can be ridiculously out of proportion.... One can obtain results monstrously in excess of the effort.... Let's consider this auto smash-up.... The driver lost control at high speed while swiping at a wasp which had flown in through a window and was buzzing around his face.... The weight of a wasp is under half an ounce. Compared with a human being, the wasp's size is minute, its strength negligible. Its sole armament is a tiny syringe holding a drop of irritant, formic acid.... Nevertheless, that wasp killed four big men and converted a large, powerful car into a heap of scrap.

—Eric Frank Russell[1]

To grasp some implications of the new first priority in U.S. foreign policy, it is necessary to understand the connections among three things: the imbalance of power between terrorist groups and counterterrorist governments; the reasons that groups choose terror tactics; and the operational advantage of attack over defense in the interactions of terrorists and their opponents. On September 11, 2001, Americans were reminded that the overweening power that they had taken for granted over the past dozen years is not the same as omnipotence. What is less obvious but equally important is that the power is itself part of the cause of terrorist enmity and even a source of U.S. vulnerability.

There is no consensus on a definition of "terrorism," mainly because the term is so intensely pejorative.[2] When defined in terms of tactics, consistency falters, because most people can think of some "good" political cause that has used the tactics and whose purposes excuse them or at least warrant the group's designation as freedom fighters rather than terrorists. Israelis who call the Khobar Towers bombers of 1996 terrorists might reject that characterization for the Irgun, which did the same thing to the King David Hotel in 1946, or some Irish Americans would bridle at equating IRA bombings in Britain with Tamil Tiger bombings in Sri Lanka. Anticommunists labeled the Vietcong terrorists (because they engaged in combat out of uniform and assassinated local officials), but opponents of the Saigon government did not. Nevertheless, a functional definition is more sensible than one conditioned on the identity of the perpetrators. For this article, terrorism refers to the illegitimate, deliberate killing of civilians for purposes of punishment or coercion. This holds in abeyance the questions of whether deliberate killing of civilians can ever be legitimate or killing soldiers can be terrorism.

In any case, for all but the rare nihilistic psychopath, terror is a means, not an end in itself. Terror tactics are usually meant to serve a strategy of coercion.[3] They are a use of force designed to further some substantive aim. This is not always evident in the heat of rage felt by the victims of terror. Normal people find it hard to see instrumental reasoning behind an atrocity, especially when recognizing the political motives behind terrorism might seem to make its illegitimacy less extreme. Stripped of rhetoric, however, a war against terrorism must mean a war against political groups who choose terror as a tactic.

American global primacy is one of the causes of this war. It animates both the terrorists' purposes and their choice of tactics. To groups like al Qaeda, the United States is the enemy because American military power dominates their world, supports corrupt governments in their countries, and backs Israelis against Muslims; American cultural power insults their religion and pollutes their societies; and American economic power makes all these intrusions and desecrations possible. Japan, in contrast, is not high on al Qaeda's list of targets, because Japan's economic power does not make it a political, military, and cultural behemoth that penetrates their societies.

Political and cultural power makes the United States a target for those who blame it for their problems. At the same time, American economic and military power prevents them from resisting or retaliating against the United States on its own terms. To smite the only superpower requires unconventional modes of force and tactics that make the combat cost exchange ratio favorable to the attacker. This offers hope to the weak that they can work their will despite their overall deficit in power.

Primacy on the Cheap

The United States has enjoyed military and political primacy (or hegemony, unipolarity, or whatever term best connotes international dominance) for barely a dozen years. Those who focus on the economic dimension of international relations spoke of American hegemony much earlier, but observers of the strategic landscape never did. For those who focus on national security, the world before 1945 was multipolar, and the world of the cold war was bipolar. After 1945 the United States had exerted hegemony within the First World and for a while over the international economy. The strategic competition against the Second World, however, was seen as a titanic struggle between equal politicomilitary coalitions and a close-run thing until very near the end. Only the collapse of the Soviet pole, which coincided fortuitously with renewed relative strength of the American economy, marked the real arrival of U.S. global dominance.

The novelty of complete primacy may account for the thoughtless, indeed innocently arrogant way in which many Americans took its benefits for granted. Most who gave any thought to foreign policy came implicitly to regard the entire world after 1989 as they had regarded Western Europe and Japan during the past half-century: partners in principle but vassals in practice. The United States would lead the civilized community of nations in the expansion and consolidation of a liberal world order. Overwhelming military dominance was assumed to be secure and important across most of the domestic political spectrum.

Liberal multilateralists conflated U.S. primacy with political globalization, indeed, conflated ideological American nationalism with internationalist altruism.[4] They assumed that U.S. military power should be used to stabilize benighted countries and police international violence, albeit preferably camouflaged under the banner of institutions such as the

United Nations, or at least NATO. They rejected the idea that illiberal impulses or movements represented more than a retreating challenge to the West's mission and its capacity to extend its values worldwide.

Conservative unilateralists assumed that unrivaled power relieved the United States of the need to cater to the demands of others. When America acted strategically abroad, others would have to join on its terms or be left out of the action. The United States should choose battles, avoid entanglements in incompetent polities, and let unfortunates stew in their own juice. For both multilateralists and nationalists, the issue was whether the United States would decide to make an effort for world welfare, not whether a strategic challenge could threaten its truly vital interests. (Colloquial depreciation of the adjective notwithstanding, literally vital U.S. interests are those necessary to life.)

For many, primacy was confused with invulnerability. American experts warned regularly of the danger of catastrophic terrorism—and Osama bin Ladin explicitly declared war on the United States in his *fatwa* of February 1998. But the warnings did not register seriously in the consciousness of most people. Even some national security experts felt stunned when the attacks occurred on September 11. Before then, the American military wanted nothing to do with the mission of "homeland defense," cited the Posse Comitatus act to suggest that military operations within U.S. borders would be improper, and argued that homeland defense should be the responsibility of civilian agencies or the National Guard. The services preferred to define the active forces' mission as fighting and winning the nation's wars—as if wars were naturally something that happened abroad—and homeland defense involved no more than law enforcement, managing relief operations in natural disasters, or intercepting ballistic missiles outside U.S. airspace. Only in America could the nation's armed forces think of direct defense of national territory as a distraction.

Being Number One seemed cheap. The United States could cut the military burden on the economy by half after the cold war (from 6 percent to 3 percent of GNP) yet still spend almost five times more than the combined military budgets of all potential enemy states. And this did not count the contributions of rich U.S. allies.[5] Of course the margin in dollar terms does not translate into a comparable quantitative margin in manpower or equipment, but that does not mean that a purchasing power parity estimate would reduce the implied gap in combat capability. The overwhelming qualitative superiority of U.S. conventional forces cuts in the other direction. Washington was also able to plan, organize, and fight a major war in 1991 at negligible cost in blood or treasure. Financially, nearly 90 percent of the bills for the war against Iraq were paid by allies. With fewer than 200 American battle deaths, the cost in blood was far lower than almost anyone had imagined it could be. Less than a decade later, Washington waged another war, over Kosovo, that cost no U.S. combat casualties at all.

In the one case where costs in casualties exceeded the apparent interests at stake—Somalia in 1993—Washington quickly stood down from the fight. This became the reference point for vulnerability: the failure of an operation that was small, far from home, and elective. Where material interests required strategic engagement, as in the oil-rich Persian Gulf, U.S. strategy could avoid costs by exploiting its huge advantage in conventional capability. Where conventional dominance proved less exploitable, as in Somalia, material interests did not require strategic engagement. Where the United States could not operate militarily with impunity, it could choose not to operate.

Finally, power made it possible to let moral interests override material interests where some Americans felt an intense moral concern, even if in doing so they claimed, dubiously, that the moral and material stakes coincided. To some extent this happened in Kosovo, although the decision to launch that war apparently flowed from overoptimism about how quickly a little bombing would lead Belgrade to capitulate. Most notably, it happened in the Arab-Israeli conflict. For more than three decades after the 1967 Six Day War, the United States supported Israel diplomatically, economically, and militarily against the Arabs, despite the fact that doing so put it on the side of a tiny country of a few million people with no oil, against more than ten times as many Arabs who controlled over a third of the world's oil reserves.

This policy was not just an effect of primacy, since the U.S.–Israel alignment began in the cold war. The salience of the moral motive was indicated by the fact that U.S. policy proceeded despite the fact that it helped give Moscow a purchase in major Arab capitals such as Cairo, Damascus, and Baghdad. Luckily for the United States, however, the largest amounts of oil remained under the control of the conservative Arab states of the Gulf. In this sense the hegemony of the United States within the anticommunist world helped account for the policy. That margin of power also relieved Washington of the need to make hard choices about disciplining its client. For decades the United States opposed Israeli settlement of the West Bank, terming the settlements illegal; yet in all that time the United States never demanded that Israel refrain from colonizing the West Bank as a condition for receiving U.S. economic and military aid.[6] Washington continued to bankroll Israel at a higher per capita rate than any other country in the world, a level that has been indispensable to Israel, providing aid over the years that now totals well over $100 billion in today's dollars.[7] Although this policy enraged some Arabs and irritated the rest, U.S. power was great enough that such international political costs did not outweigh the domestic political costs of insisting on Israeli compliance with U.S. policy.

Of course, far more than subsidizing Israeli occupation of Palestinian land was involved in the enmity of Islamist terrorists toward the United States. Many of the other explanations, however, presuppose U.S. global primacy. When American power becomes the arbiter of conflicts around the world, it makes itself the target for groups who come out on the short end of those conflicts.

Primacy and Asymmetric Warfare

The irrational evil of terrorism seems most obvious to the powerful. They are accustomed to getting their way with conventional applications of force and are not as accustomed as the powerless to thinking of terror as the only form of force that might make their enemies do their will. This is why terrorism is the premier form of "asymmetric warfare," the Pentagon buzzword for the type of threats likely to confront the United States in the post–cold war world.[8] Murderous tactics may become instrumentally appealing by default—when one party in a conflict lacks other military options.

Resort to terror is not necessarily limited to those facing far more powerful enemies. It can happen in a conventional war between great powers that becomes a total war, when the process of escalation pits whole societies against each other and shears away civilized restraints. That is something seldom seen, and last seen over a half-century ago. One does not need to accept the tendentious position that allied strategic bombing in World War II constituted terrorism to recognize that the British and Americans did systematically assault the urban population centers of Germany and Japan. They did so in large part because precision bombing of industrial facilities proved ineffective.[9] During the early phase of the cold war, in turn, U.S. nuclear strategy relied on plans to counter Soviet conventional attack on Western Europe with a comprehensive nuclear attack on communist countries that would have killed hundreds of millions. In the 1950s, Strategic Air Command targeteers even went out of their way to plan "bonus" damage by moving aim points for military targets so that blasts would destroy adjacent towns as well.[10] In both World War II and planning for World War III, the rationale was less to kill civilians per se than to wreck the enemy economies—although that was also one of Osama bin Laden's rationales for the attacks on the World Trade Center.[11] In short, the instrumental appeal of strategic attacks on noncombatants may be easier to understand when one considers that states with legitimate purposes have sometimes resorted to such a strategy. Such a double standard, relaxing prohibitions against targeting noncombatants for the side with legitimate purposes (one's own side), occurs most readily when the enemy is at least a peer competitor threatening vital interests. When one's own primacy is taken for granted, it is easier to revert to a single standard that puts all deliberate attacks against civilians beyond the pale.

In contrast to World War II, most wars are limited—or at least limited for the stronger side when power is grossly imbalanced. In such cases, using terror to coerce is likely to seem the only potentially effective use of force for the weaker side, which faces a choice between surrender or savagery. Radical Muslim zealots cannot expel American power with conventional military means, so they substitute clandestine means of delivery against military targets (such as the Khobar Towers barracks in Saudi Arabia) or high-profile political targets (embassies in Kenya and Tanzania). More than once the line has been attributed to terrorists, "If you will let us lease one of your B-52s, we will use that instead of a truck bomb." The hijacking and conversion of U.S. airliners into kamikazes was the most dramatic means of asymmetric attack.

Kamikaze hijacking also reflects an impressive capacity for strategic judo, the turning of the West's strength against itself.[12] The flip-side of a primacy that diffuses its power throughout the world is that advanced elements of that power become more accessible to its enemies. Nineteen men from technologically backward societies did not have to rely on home-grown instruments to devastate the Pentagon and World Trade Center. They used computers and modern financial procedures with facility, and they forcibly appropriated the aviation technology of the West and used it as a weapon. They not only rebelled against the "soft power" of the United States, they trumped it by hijacking the country's hard power.[13] They also exploited the characteristics of U.S. society associated with soft power—the liberalism, openness, and respect for privacy that allowed them to go freely about the business of preparing the attacks without observation by the state security apparatus. When soft power met the clash of civilizations, it proved too soft.

Strategic judo is also apparent in the way in which U.S. retaliation may compromise its own purpose. The counteroffensive after September 11 was necessary, if only to demonstrate to marginally motivated terrorists that they could not hope to strike the United States for free. The war in Afghanistan, however, does contribute to polarization in the Muslim world and to mobilization of potential terrorist recruits. U.S. leaders can say that they are not waging a war against Islam until they are blue in the face, but this will not convince Muslims who already distrust the United States. Success in deposing the Taliban may help U.S. policy by encouraging a bandwagon effect that rallies governments and moderates among the Muslim populace, but there will probably be as many who see the U.S. retaliation as confirming al Qaeda's diagnosis of American evil. Victory in Afghanistan and follow-up operations to prevent al Qaeda from relocating bases of operation to other countries will hurt that organization's capacity to act. The number of young zealots willing to emulate the "martyrdom operation" of the nineteen on September 11, however, is not likely to decline.

Advantage of Attack

The academic field of security studies has some reason to be embarrassed after September 11. Having focused primarily on great powers and interstate conflict, literature on terrorism was comparatively sparse; most of the good books were by policy analysts rather than theorists.[14] Indeed, science fiction has etched out the operational logic of terrorism as well as political science. Eric Frank Russell's 1957 novel, from which the epigraph to this article comes, vividly illustrates both the strategic aspirations of terrorists and the offense-dominant character of their tactics. It describes the dispatch of a single agent to one of many planets in the Sirian enemy's empire to stir up fear, confusion, and panic through a series of small covert activities with tremendous ripple effects. Matched with deceptions to make the disruptions appear to be part of a campaign by a big phantom rebel organization, the agent's modest actions divert large numbers of enemy policy and military personnel, cause economic dislocations and social unrest, and soften the planet up for invasion. Wasp agents are infiltrated into numerous planets, multiplying the effects. As the agent's handlers tell him, "The pot is coming slowly but surely to the boil. Their fleets are being widely dispersed, there are vast troop movements from their overcrowded home-system to the outer planets of their empire. They're gradually being chivvied into a fix. They can't hold what they've got without spreading all over it. The wider they spread the thinner they get. The thinner they get, the easier it is to bite lumps out of them."[15]

Fortunately al Qaeda and its ilk are not as wildly effective as Russell's wasp. By degree, however, the phenomenon is quite similar. Comparatively limited initiatives prompt tremendous and costly defensive reactions. On September 11 a small number of men killed 3,000 people and destroyed a huge portion of prime commercial real estate, part of the military's national nerve center, and four expensive aircraft. The ripple effects, however, multiplied those costs. A major part of the U.S. economy—air travel—shut down completely for days after September 11. Increased security measures dramatically increased the overall costs of the air travel system thereafter. Normal law enforcement activities of the Federal Bureau of Investigation were radically curtailed as legions of agents were transferred to counterterror tasks. Anxiety about the vulnerability of nuclear power plants, major bridges and tunnels, embassies abroad, and other high-value targets prompted plans for big investments in fortification of a wide array of facilities. A retaliatory war in Afghanistan ran at a cost of a couple billion dollars a month beyond the regular defense budget for months. In one study, the attacks on the World Trade Center and the Pentagon were estimated to cost the U.S. economy 1.8 million jobs.[16]

Or consider the results of a handful of 34-cent letters containing anthrax, probably sent by a single person. Besides killing several people, they contaminated a large portion of the postal system, paralyzed some mail delivery for long periods, provoked plans for huge expenditures on prophylactic irradiation equipment, shut down much of Capitol Hill for weeks, put thousands of people on a sixty-day regimen of strong antibiotics (potentially eroding the medical effectiveness of such antibiotics in future emergencies), and overloaded police and public health inspectors with false alarms. The September 11 attacks and the October anthrax attacks together probably cost the perpetrators less than a million dollars. If the cost of rebuilding and of defensive investments in reaction came to no more than $100 billion, the cost-exchange ratio would still be astronomically in favor of the attack over the defense.

Analysts in strategic studies did not fall down on the job completely before September 11. At least two old bodies of work help to illuminate the problem. One is the literature on guerrilla warfare and counterinsurgency, particularly prominent in the 1960s, and the other is the offense-defense theory that burgeoned in the 1980s. Both apply well to understanding patterns of engagement between terrorists and counterterrorists. Some of the axioms derived from the empirical cases in the counterinsurgency literature apply directly, and offense-defense theory applies indirectly.

Apart from the victims of guerrillas, few still identify irregular paramilitary warfare with terrorism (because the latter is illegitimate), but the two activities do overlap a great deal in their operational characteristics. Revolutionary or resistance movements in the preconventional phase of operations usually mix small-unit raids on isolated outposts of the government or occupying force with detonations and assassinations in urban areas to instill fear and discredit government power. The tactical logic of guerrilla operations resembles that in terrorist attacks: the weaker rebels use stealth and the cover of civilian society to concentrate their striking power against one among many of the stronger enemy's dispersed assets; they strike quickly and eliminate the target before the defender can move forces from other areas to respond; they melt back into civilian society to avoid detection and reconcentrate against another target. The government or occupier has far superior strength in terms of conventional military power, but cannot counterconcentrate in time because it has to defend all points, while the insurgent attacker can pick its targets at will.[17] The contest between insurgents and counterinsurgents is "tripartite," polarizing political alignments and gaining the support of *attentistes* or those in the middle. In today's principle counterterror campaign, one might say that the yet-unmobilized Muslim elites and masses of the Third World—those who were not already actively committed either to supporting Islamist radicalism or to combating it—are the target group in the middle. As Samuel Huntington noted, "a revolutionary war is a war of attrition."[18] As I believe Stanley Hoffman once said, in rebellions the insurgents win as long as they do not lose, and the government loses as long as it does not win. If al Qaeda-like groups can stay in the field indefinitely, they win.

Offense-defense theory applied nuclear deterrence concepts to assessing the stability of conventional military confrontations and focused on what conditions tended to give the attack or the defense the advantage in war.[19] There were many problems in the specification and application of the theory having to do with unsettled conceptualization of the offense-defense balance, problematic standards for measuring it, and inconsistent applications to different levels of warfare and diplomacy.[20] Offense-defense theory, which flourished when driven by the urge to find ways to stabilize the NATO-Warsaw Pact balance in Europe, has had little to say directly about unconventional war or terrorism. It actually applies more clearly, however, to this lower level of strategic competition (as well as to the higher level of nuclear war) than to the middle level of conventional military power. This is because the exchange ratio between opposing conventional forces of roughly similar size is very difficult to estimate, given the complex composition of modern military forces and uncertainty about their qualitative comparisons; but the exchange ratio in both nuclear and guerrilla combat is quite lopsided in favor of the attacker. Counterinsurgency folklore held that the government defenders need something on the order of a ten-to-one advantage over the guerrillas if they were to drive them from the field.

There has been much confusion about exactly how to define the offense-defense balance, but the essential idea is that some combinations of military technology, organization, and doctrine are proportionally more advantageous to the attack or to the defense when the two clash. "Proportionally" means that available instruments and circumstances of engagement give either the attack or the defense more bang for the buck, more efficient power out of the same level of resources. The notion of an offense-defense balance as something conceptually distinct from the balance of power means, however, that it cannot be identified with which side wins a battle or a war. Indeed, the offense-defense balance can favor the defense, while the attacker still wins, because its overall margin of superiority in power was too great, despite the defense's more efficient use of power. (I am told that the Finns had a saying in the Winter War of 1939–40: "One Finn is worth ten Russians, but what happens when the eleventh Russian comes?") Thus, to say that the offense-defense balance favors the offensive terrorists today against the defensive counterterrorists does not mean that the terrorists will prevail. It does mean that terrorists can fight far above their weight, that in most instances each competent terrorist will have much greater individual impact than each good counterterrorist, that each dollar invested in a terrorist plot will have a bigger payoff than each dollar expended on counterterrorism, and that only small numbers of competent terrorists need survive and operate to keep the threat to American society uncomfortably high.

In the competition between terrorists on the attack and Americans on the defense, the disadvantage of the defense is evident in the number of high-value potential targets that need protection. The United States has "almost 600,000 bridges, 170,000 water systems, more than 2,800 power plants (104 of them nuclear), 190,000 miles of interstate pipelines for natural gas, 463 skyscrapers… nearly 20,000 miles of border, airports, stadiums, train tracks."[21] All these usually represented American strength; after September 11 they also represent vulnerability:

> Suddenly guards were being posted at water reservoirs, outside power plants, and at bridges and tunnels. Maps of oil and gas lines were removed from the Internet. In Boston, a ship carrying liquefied natural gas, an important source of fuel for heating New England homes, was forbidden from entering the harbor because local fire officials feared that if it were targeted by a terrorist the resulting explosion could lay low much of the city's densely populated waterfront. An attack by a knife-wielding lunatic on the driver of a Florida-bound Greyhound bus led to the immediate cessation of that national bus service.… Agricultural crop-dusting planes were grounded out of a concern that they could be used to spread chemical or biological agents.[22]

Truly energetic defense measures do not only cost money in personnel and equipment for fortification, inspection, and enforcement; they may require repealing some of the very underpinnings of civilian economic efficiency associated with globalization. "The competitiveness of the U.S. economy and the quality of life of the American people rest on critical infrastructure that has become increasingly more concentrated, more interconnected, and more sophisticated. Almost entirely privately owned and operated, there is very little redundancy in this system."[23] This concentration increases the potential price of vulnerability to single attacks. Tighter inspection of cargoes coming across the Canadian border, for example, wrecks the "just-in-time" parts supply system of Michigan auto manufacturers. Companies that have invested in technology and infrastructure premised on unimpeded movement "may see their expected savings and efficiencies go up in smoke. Outsourcing contracts will have to be revisited and inventories will have to be rebuilt."[24] How many safety measures will suffice in improving airline security without making flying so inconvenient that the air travel industry never recovers as a profit-making enterprise? A few more shoe-bomb incidents, and Thomas Friedman's proposal to start an airline called "Naked Air—where the only thing you wear is a seat belt" becomes almost as plausible as it is ridiculous.[25]

The offense-dominant character of terrorism is implicit in mass detentions of Arab young men after September 11, and proposals for military tribunals that would compromise normal due process and weaken standard criminal justice presumptions in favor of the accused. The traditional liberal axiom that it is better to let a hundred guilty people go free than to convict one innocent reflects confidence in the strength of society's defenses—confidence that whatever additional crimes may be committed by the guilty who go free will not grossly outweigh the injustice done to innocents convicted, that one criminal who slips through the net will not go on to kill hundreds or thousands of innocents. Fear of terrorists plotting mass murder reversed that presumption and makes unjust incarceration of some innocents appear like unintended but expected collateral damage in wartime combat.

Offense-defense theory helps to visualize the problem. It does not help to provide attractive solutions, as its proponents believed it did during the cold war. Then offense-defense theory was popular because it seemed to offer a way to stabilize the East-West military confrontation. Mutual deterrence from the superpowers' confidence in their counteroffensive capability could substitute for defense at the nuclear level, and both sides' confidence in their conventional defenses could dampen either one's incentives to attack at that level. Little of this applies to counterterrorism. Both deterrence and defense are weaker strategies against terrorists than they were against communists.

Deterrence is still relevant for dealing with state terrorism; Saddam Hussein or Kim Jong-Il may hold back from striking the United States for fear of retaliation. Deterrence offers less confidence for preventing state sponsorship of terrorism; it did not stop the Taliban from hosting Osama bin Laden. It offers even less for holding at bay transnational groups like al Qaeda, which may lack a return address against which retaliation can be visited, or whose millennialist aims and religious convictions make them unafraid of retaliation. Defense, in turn, is better than a losing game only because the inadequacy of deterrence leaves no alternative.[26] Large investments in defense will produce appreciable reductions in vulnerability, but will not minimize vulnerability.

Deterrence and defense overlap in practice. The U.S. counteroffensive in Afghanistan constitutes retaliation, punishing the Taliban for shielding al Qaeda and sending a warning to other potential state sponsors. It is also active defense, whittling down the ranks of potential perpetrators by killing and capturing members of the Islamist international brigades committed to jihad against the United States. At this writing, the retaliatory function has been performed more effectively than the defensive, as the Taliban regime has been destroyed, but significant numbers of Arab Afghans and al Qaeda members appear to have escaped, perhaps to plot another day.

Given the limited efficacy of deterrence for modern counterterrorism, it remains an open question how much of a strategic success we should judge the impressive victory in Afghanistan to be. Major investments in passive defenses (airline security, border inspections, surveillance and searches for better intelligence, fortification of embassies, and so forth) are necessary, but will reduce vulnerability at a cost substantially greater than the costs that competent terrorist organizations will have to bear to probe and occasionally circumvent them. The cost-exchange ratio for direct defense is probably worse than the legendary 10:1 ratio for successful counterinsurgency, and certainly worse than the more than 3:1 ratio that Robert McNamara's analysts calculated for the advantage of offensive missile investments over antiballistic missile systems—an advantage that many then and since have thought warranted accepting a situation of mutual vulnerability to assured destruction.[27]

The less prepared we are to undertake appropriate programs and the more false starts and confusions that are likely, the worse the cost-exchange ratio will be in the short term. The public health system, law enforcement organizations, and state and local bureaucrats are still feeling their way on what, how, and in which sequence to boost efforts. The U.S. military will also have to overcome the natural and powerful effects of inertia and attachments to old self-conceptions and preferred programs and modes of operation. Impulses to repackage old priorities in the rhetoric of new needs will further dilute effectiveness of countermeasures.

Nevertheless, given low confidence that deterrence can prevent terrorist attacks, major improvements in defenses make sense.[28] This is especially true because the resource base from which the United States can draw is vastly larger than that available to transnational terrorists. Al Qaeda may be rich, but it does not have the treasury of a great power. Primacy has a soft underbelly, but it is far better to have primacy than to face it. Even at an unfavorable cost-exchange ratio, a number of defensive measures are a sensible investment, but only because our overwhelming advantage in resources means that we are not constrained to focus solely on the most efficient countermeasures.

At the same time, as long as terrorist groups remain potent and active, a serious war plan must exploit efficient strategies as well. Given the offense-dominant nature of terrorist operations, this means emphasis on counteroffensive operations. When terrorists or their support structures can be found and fixed, preemptive and preventive attacks will accomplish more against them, dollar for dollar, than the investment in passive defenses. Which is the more efficient use of resources: to kill or capture a cell of terrorists who might otherwise choose at any time to strike whichever set of targets on our side is unguarded, or to try to guard all potential targets? Here the dangers are that counteroffensive operations could prove counterproductive. This could easily happen if they degenerate into brutalities and breaches of laws of war that make counterterrorism begin to appear morally equivalent to its target, sapping political support and driving the uncommitted to the other side in the process of polarization that war makes inevitable. Whether counteroffensive operations gain more in eliminating perpetrators than they lose in alienating and mobilizing "swing voters" in the world of Muslim opinion depends on how successful the operations are in neutralizing significant numbers of the organizers of terrorist groups, as opposed to foot soldiers, and in doing so with minimal collateral damage.

Primacy and Policy

September 11 reminded those Americans with a rosy view that not all the world sees U.S. primacy as benign, that primacy does not guarantee security, and that security may now entail some retreats from the economic globalization that some had identified with American leadership. Primacy has two edges—dominance and provocation. Americans can enjoy the dominance but must recognize the risks it evokes. For terrorists who want to bring the United States down, U.S. strategic primacy is a formidable challenge, but one that can be overcome. On balance, Americans have overestimated the benefits of primacy, and terrorists have underestimated them.

For those who see a connection between American interventionism, cultural expansiveness, and support of Israel on one hand, and the rage of groups that turn to terrorism on the other, primacy may seem more trouble than it's worth, and the need to revise policies may seem more pressing. But most Americans have so far preferred the complacent and gluttonous form of primacy to the ascetic, blithely accepting steadily growing dependence on Persian Gulf oil that could be limited by compromises in lifestyle and unconventional energy policies. There have been no groundswells to get rid of SUVs, support the Palestinians, or refrain from promoting Western standards of democracy and human rights in societies where some elements see them as aggression.

There is little evidence that any appreciable number of Americans, elite or mass, see our primacy as provoking terrorism. Rather, most see it as a condition we can choose at will to exploit or not. So U.S. foreign policy has exercised primacy in a muscular way in byways of the post-cold war world when intervention seemed cheap, but not when doing good deeds threatened to be costly. Power has allowed Washington to play simultaneously the roles of mediator and partisan supporter in the Arab-Israeli conflict. For a dozen years nothing, with the near exception of the Kosovo War, suggested that primacy could not get us out of whatever problems it generated.

How far the United States goes to adapt to the second edge of primacy probably depends on whether stunning damage is inflicted by terrorists again, or September 11 gradually fades into history. If al Qaeda and its ilk are crippled, and some years pass without more catastrophic attacks on U.S. home territory, scar tissue will harden on the soft underbelly, and the positive view of primacy will be reinforced. If the war against terrorism falters, however, and the exercise of power fails to prevent more big incidents, the consensus will crack. Then more extreme policy options will get more attention. Retrenchment and retreat will look more appealing to some, who may believe the words of Sheik Salman al-Awdah, a dissident Saudi religious scholar, who said, "If America just let well enough alone, and got out of their obligations overseas... no one would bother them."[29]

More likely, however, would be a more violent reaction. There is no reason to assume that terrorist enemies would let America off the hook if it retreated and would not remain as implacable as ever. Facing inability to suppress the threat through normal combat, covert action, and diplomatic pressure, many Americans would consider escalation to more ferocious strategies. In recent decades, the march of liberal legalism has delegitimized tactics and brutalities that once were accepted, but this delegitimation has occurred only in the context of fundamental security and dominance of the Western powers, not in a situation where they felt under supreme threat. In a situation of that sort, it is foolhardy to assume that American strategy would never turn to tactics like those used against Japanese and German civilians, or by the civilized French in the *sale guerre* in Algeria, or by the Russians in Chechnya in hopes of effectively eradicating terrorists despite astronomical damage to the civilian societies within which they lurk.

This possibility would highlight how terrorists have underestimated American primacy. There is much evidence that even in the age of unipolarity, opponents have mistakenly seen the United States as a paper tiger. For some reason—perhaps wishfully selective perception—they tend to see retreats from Vietnam, Beirut, and Somalia as typical weakness of American will, instead of considering decisive exercises of power in Panama, Kuwait, Kosovo, and now, Afghanistan.[30] As Osama bin Laden said in 1997, the United States left Somalia "after claiming that they were the largest power on earth. They left after some resistance from powerless, poor, unarmed people whose only weapon is the belief in Allah.... The Americans ran away."[31]

This apparently common view among those with an interest in pinning America's ears back ignores the difference between elective uses of force and desperate ones. The United States retreated where it ran into trouble helping others, not where it was saving itself. Unlike interventions of the 1990s in Africa, the Balkans, or Haiti, counterterrorism is not charity. With vital material interests involved, primacy unleashed may prove fearsomely potent.

Most likely America will see neither absolute victory nor abject failure in the war against terror. Then how long will a campaign of attrition last and stay popular? If the United States wants a strategy to cut the roots of terrorism, rather than just the branches, will American power be used effectively against the roots? Perhaps, but probably not. This depends of course on which of many possible root causes are at issue. Ironically, one problem is that American primacy itself is one of those roots.

A common assertion is that Third World poverty generates terrorism. While this must certainly be a contributing cause in many cases, there is little evidence that it is either a necessary or sufficient condition. Fundamentalist madrassas might not be full to overflowing if young Muslims had ample opportunities to make money, but the fifteen Saudis who hijacked the flights on September 11 were from one of the most affluent of Muslim countries. No U.S. policy could ever hope to make most incubators of terrorism less poor than Saudi Arabia. Iran, the biggest state sponsor of anti-American terrorism, is also better off than most Muslim countries. Poverty is endemic in the Third World, but terrorism is not.

Even if endemic poverty were the cause, the solution would not be obvious. Globalization generates stratification, creating winners and losers, as efficient societies with capitalist cultures move ahead and others fall behind, or as elite enclaves in some societies prosper while the masses stagnate. Moreover, even vastly increased U.S. development assistance would be spread thin if all poor countries are assumed to be incubators of terrorism. And what are the odds that U.S. intervention with economic aid would significantly reduce poverty? Successes in prompting dramatic economic development by outside assistance in the Third World have occurred, but they are the exception more than the rule.

The most virulent anti-American terrorist threats, however, do not emerge randomly in poor societies. They grow out of a few regions and are concentrated overwhelmingly in a few religiously motivated groups. These reflect political causes—ideological, nationalist, or transnational cultural impulses to militant mobilization—more than economic causes. Economic development in an area where the political and religious impulses remain unresolved could serve to improve the resource base for terrorism rather than undercut it.

A strategy of terrorism is most likely to flow from the coincidence of two conditions: intense political grievance and gross imbalance of power. Either one without the other is likely to produce either peace or conventional war. Peace is probable if power is imbalanced but grievance is modest; the weaker party is likely to live with the grievance. In that situation, conventional use of force appears to offer no hope of victory, while the righteous indignation is not great enough to overcome normal inhibitions against murderous tactics. Conventional war is probable if grievance is intense but power is more evenly balanced, since successful use of respectable forms of force appears possible.[32] Under American primacy, candidates for terrorism suffer from grossly inferior power by definition. This should focus attention on the political causes of their grievance.

How are political root causes addressed? At other times in history we have succeeded in fostering congenial revolutions—especially in the end of the cold war, as the collapse of the Second World heralded an End of History of sorts.[33] The problem now, however, is the rebellion of anti-Western zealots against the secularist end of history. Remaking the world in the Western image is what Americans assume to be just, natural, and desirable, indeed only a matter of time. But that presumption is precisely what energizes many terrorists' hatred. Secular Western liberalism is not their salvation, but their scourge. Primacy could, paradoxically, remain both the solution and the problem for a long time.*

*The author thanks Robert Jervis for comments on the first draft.

Richard K. Betts is a specialist on national security policy and military strategy. He is the director of the Institute of War and Peace Studies at Columbia University and was a senior fellow and research associate at the Brookings Institution in Washington, D.C. Betts has served on the National Commission on Terrorism and the U.S. Senate Select Committee on Intelligence. He is author, editor, and coauthor of several books on the subject, including *The Irony of Vietnam: The System Worked* (1979), which won the Woodrow Wilson Prize.

Notes

1. William Wolf in Eric Frank Russell, *Wasp* (London: Victor Gollancz, 2000, originally published 1957), 7.
2. "The word has become a political label rather than an analytical concept." Martha Crenshaw, *Terrorism and International Cooperation* (New York: Institute for East-West Security Studies, 1989), 5.
3. For a survey of types, see Christopher C. Harmon, "Five Strategies of Terrorism," *Small Wars and Insurgencies* 12 (Autumn 2001).
4. Rationalization of national power as altruism resembles the thinking about benign Pax Britannica in the Crowe Memorandum: "... the national policy of the insular and naval State is so directed as to harmonize with the general desires and ideals common to all mankind, and more particularly... is closely identified with the primary and vital interests of a majority, or as many as possible, of the other nations.... England, more than any other non-insular Power, has a direct and positive interest in the maintenance of the independence of nations, and therefore must be the natural enemy of any country threatening the independence of others, and the natural

protector of the weaker communities." Eyre Crowe, "Memorandum on the Present State of British Relations with France and Germany," 1 January 1907, in G. P. Gooch and Harold Temperley, eds., *British Documents on the Origins of the War, 1898–1914*, vol. 3: *The Testing of the Entente, 1904–6* (London: His Majesty's Stationery Office, 1928), 402–403.

5. At the end of the twentieth century, the combined military budgets of China, Russia, Iraq, Yugoslavia (Serbia), North Korea, Iran, Libya, Cuba, Afghanistan, and Sudan added up to no more than $60 billion. *The Military Balance*, 1999–2000 (London: International Institute for Strategic Studies, 1999), 102, 112, 132, 133, 159, 186, 275.
6. Washington certainly did exert pressure on Israel at some times. The administration of Bush the Elder, for example, threatened to withhold loans for housing construction, but this was a marginal portion of total U.S. aid. There was never a threat to cut off the basic annual maintenance payment of several billion dollars to which Israel became accustomed decades ago.
7. The United States has also given aid to friendly Arab governments—huge amounts to Egypt and some to Jordan. This does not counterbalance the aid to Israel, however, in terms of effects on opinions of strongly anti-Israeli Arabs. Islamists see the regimes in Cairo and Amman as American toadies, complicit in betrayal of the Palestinians.
8. Theoretically, this was anticipated by Samuel P. Huntington in his 1962 analysis of the differences between symmetrical intergovernmental war and asymmetrical antigovernmental war. "Patterns of Violence in World Politics" in Huntington, ed., *Changing Patterns of Military Politics* (New York: Free Press of Glencoe, 1962), 19–21). Some of Huntington's analysis of insurrectionary warfare within states applies as well to transnational terrorism.
9. The Royal Air Force gave up on precision bombing early and focused deliberately on night bombing of German cities, while the Americans continued to try precision daylight bombing. Firestorms in Hamburg, Darmstadt, and Dresden, and less incendiary attacks on other cities, killed several hundred thousand German civilians. Over Japan, the United States quickly gave up attempts at precision bombing when weather made it impractical and deliberately resorted to an incendiary campaign that burned most Japanese cities to the ground and killed at least 300,000 civilians (and perhaps more than half a million) well before the nuclear attacks on Hiroshima and Nagasaki, which killed another 200,000. Michael S. Sherry, *The Rise of American Air Power: The Creation of Armageddon* (New Haven: Yale University Press, 1987), 260, 413–43.
10. The threat of deliberate nuclear escalation remained the bedrock of NATO doctrine throughout the cold war, but after the Kennedy administration, the flexible response doctrine made it conditional and included options for nuclear first-use that did not involve deliberate targeting of population centers. In the Eisenhower administration, however, all-out attack on the Soviet bloc's cities was integral to plans for defense of Western Europe against Soviet armored divisions.
11. In a videotape months after the attacks, bin Laden said, "These blessed strikes showed clearly that this arrogant power, America, rests on a powerful but precarious economy, which rapidly crumbled… the global economy based on usury, which America uses along with its military might to impose infidelity and humiliation on oppressed people, can easily crumble.… Hit the economy, which is the basis of military might. If their economy is finished, they will become too busy to enslave oppressed people.… America is in decline; the economic drain is continuing but more strikes are required and the youths must strike the key sectors of the American economy." Videotape excerpts quoted in "Bin Laden's Words: 'America Is in Decline,' the Leader of Al Qaeda Says," *New York Times*, 28 December 2001.
12. This is similar to the concept of political judo discussed in Samuel L. Popkin, "Pacification: Politics and the Village," *Asian Survey* 10 (August 1970); and Popkin, "Internal Conflicts—South Vietnam" in Kenneth N. Waltz and Steven Spiegel, eds., *Conflict in World Politics* (Cambridge, MA: Winthrop, 1971).
13. Soft power is "indirect or cooptive" and "can rest on the attraction of one's ideas or on the ability to set the political agenda in a way that shapes the preferences that others express." It "tends to be associated with intangible power resources such as culture, ideology, and institutions." Joseph S. Nye, Jr., "The Changing Nature of World Power," *Political Science Quarterly*, 105

(Summer 1990): 181. See also Nye, *Bound to Lead: The Changing Nature of American Power* (New York: Basic Books, 1990).

14. For example, Bruce Hoffmann, *Inside Terrorism* (New York: Columbia University Press, 1998); Paul R. Pillar, *Terrorism and American Foreign Policy* (Washington, DC: Brookings Institution Press, 2001); Richard A. Falkenrath, Robert D. Newman, and Bradley S. Thayer, *America's Achilles' Heel: Nuclear, Biological, and Chemical Terrorism and Covert Attack* (Cambridge: MIT Press, 1998).
15. Russell, *Wasp*, 64. The ripple effects include aspects of strategic judo. Creating a phony rebel organization leads the enemy security apparatus to turn on its own people. "If some Sirians could be given the full-time job of hunting down and garroting other Sirians, and if other Sirians could be given the full-time job of dodging or shooting down the garroters, then a distant and different life form would be saved a few unpleasant chores.... Doubtless the military would provide a personal bodyguard for every big wheel on Jaimec; that alone would pin down a regiment." Ibid., 26, 103.
16. Study by the Milken Institute discussed in "The Economics: Attacks May Cost 1.8 Million Jobs," *New York Times*, 13 January 2002.
17. Mao Tse-Tung's classic tracts are canonical background. For example, "Problems of Strategy in China's Revolutionary War" (especially chap. 5) in *Selected Works of Mao Tse-Tung* (Beijing: Foreign Languages Press, 1967), vol. i, and "Problems of Strategy in Guerrilla War Against Japan," in *Selected Works*, vol. ii (1967). Much of the Western analytical literature grew out of British experience in the Malayan Emergency and France's role in Indochina and Algeria. For example, Franklin Mark Osanka, ed., *Modern Guerrilla Warfare* (New York: Free Press, 1962); Gerard Chaliand, ed., *Guerrilla Strategies: An Historical Anthology from the Long March to Afghanistan* (Berkeley: University of California Press, 1982); Roger Triniquier, *Modern Warfare: A French View of Counterinsurgency*, Daniel Lee, trans. (New York: Praeger, 1964); David Galula, *Counterinsurgency Warfare: Theory and Practice* (New York: Praeger, 1964); Sir Robert Thompson, *Defeating Communist Insurgency* (New York: Praeger, 1966); Richard L. Clutterbuck, *The Long Long War: Counterinsurgency in Malaya and Vietnam* (New York: Praeger, 1966); George Armstrong Kelly, *Lost Soldiers: The French Army and Empire in Crisis, 1947–1962* (Cambridge: MIT Press, 1965), chaps. 5–7, 9–10; W. P. Davison, *Some Observations on Viet Cong Operations in the Villages* (Santa Monica, CA: RAND Corporation, 1968). See also Douglas S. Blaufarb, *The Counter-Insurgency Era: U.S. Doctrine and Performance, 1950 to the Present* (New York: Free Press, 1977); D. Michael Shafer, *Deadly Paradigms: The Failure of U.S. Counterinsurgency Policy* (Princeton: Princeton University Press, 1988); Timothy J. Lomperis, *From People's War to People's Rule: Insurgency, Intervention, and the Lessons of Vietnam* (Chapel Hill: University of North Carolina Press, 1996).
18. Huntington, "Patterns of Violence in World Politics," 20–27.
19. George Quester, *Offense and Defense in the International System*, 2nd ed. (New Brunswick, NJ: Transaction Books, 1988); Robert Jervis, "Cooperation Under the Security Dilemma," *World Politics* 30 (January 1978); Jack L. Snyder, *The Ideology of the Offensive: Military Decision Making and the Disasters of 1914* (Ithaca, NY: Cornell University Press, 1984); Stephen Van Evera, *Causes of War: Power and the Roots of Conflict* (Ithaca, NY: Cornell University Press, 1999), chaps. 6–8; Charles L. Glaser and Chaim Kaufmann, "What Is the Offense-Defense Balance and Can We Measure It?" *International Security* 22 (Spring 1998).
20. For critiques, see Jack S. Levy, "The Offensive/Defensive Balance of Military Technology," *International Studies Quarterly* 28 (June 1984); Scott D. Sagan, "1914 Revisited," *International Security* 11 (Fall 1986); Jonathan Shimshoni, "Technology, Military Advantage, and World War I: A Case for Military Entrepreneurship," *International Security* 15 (Winter 1990/91); Richard K. Betts, "Must War Find a Way?" *International Security* 24 (Fall 1999); Betts, "Conventional Deterrence: Predictive Uncertainty and Policy Confidence," *World Politics* 37 (January 1985).
21. Jerry Schwartz, Associated Press dispatch, 6 October 2001, quoted in Brian Reich, "Strength in the Face of Terror: A Comparison of United States and International Efforts to Provide Homeland Security" (unpublished paper, Columbia University, December 2001), 5.

22. Stephen E. Flynn, "The Unguarded Homeland" in James F. Hoge, Jr. and Gideon Rose, eds., *How Did This Happen? Terrorism and the New War* (New York: PublicAffairs, 2001), 185.
23. Ibid., 185–186.
24. Ibid., 193–194.
25. Thomas L. Friedman, "Naked Air," *New York Times*, 26 December 2001.
26. See Steven Simon and Daniel Benjamin, "America and the New Terrorism," *Survival* 42 (Spring 2000); 59, 66–69, 74.
27. Estimates in the 1960s indicated that even combining ABM systems with counterforce strikes and fallout shelters, the United States would have to counter each Soviet dollar spent on ICBMs with three U.S. dollars to protect 70 percent of the industry, assuming highly ABMs (.8 kill probability). To protect up to 80 percent of the population, far higher ratios would be necessary. Fred Kaplan, *The Wizards of Armageddon* (New York: Simon and Schuster, 1983), 321–324.
28. For an appropriate list of recommendations see *Countering the Changing Threat of International Terrorism*, Report of the National Commission on Terrorism, Pursuant to Public Law 277, 105th Congress (Washington, DC, June 2000). This report holds up very well in light of September 11.
29. Quoted in Douglas Jehl, "After Prison, a Saudi Sheik Tempers His Words," *New York Times*, 27 December 2001.
30. See data in the study by Barry M. Blechman and Tamara Cofman Wittes, "Defining Moment: The Threat and Use of Force in American Foreign Policy," *Political Science Quarterly* 114 (Spring 1999).
31. Quoted in Simon and Benjamin, "America and the New Terrorism," 69.
32. On why power imbalance is conducive to peace and parity to war, see Geoffrey Blainey, *The Causes of War*, 3rd. ed. (New York: Free Press, 1988), chap. 8.
33. Francis Fukuyama's thesis was widely misunderstood and caricatured. He noted that the Third World remained mired in history and that some developments could lead to restarting history. For the First World, the defeated Second World, and even some parts of the Third World, however, the triumph of Western liberalism could reasonably be seen by those who believe in its worth (as should Americans) as the final stage of evolution through fundamentally different forms of political and economic organization of societies. See Fukuyama, "The End of History?" *National Interest* no. 16 (Summer 1989); and Fukuyama, *The End of History and the Last Man* (New York: Free Press, 1992).

Bruce Hoffman, 2002

A Nasty Business

Intelligence is capital," Colonel Yves Godard liked to say. And Godard undeniably knew what he was talking about. He had fought both as a guerrilla in the French Resistance during World War II and against guerrillas in Indochina, as the commander of a covert special operations unit. As the chief of staff of the elite 10th Para Division, Godard was one of the architects of the French counterterrorist strategy that won the Battle of Algiers, in 1957. To him, information was the sine qua non for victory. It had to be zealously collected, meticulously analyzed, rapidly disseminated, and efficaciously acted on. Without it no antiterrorist operation could succeed. As the United States prosecutes its global war against terrorism, Godard's dictum has acquired new relevance. Indeed, as is now constantly said, success in the struggle against Osama bin Laden and his minions will depend on good intelligence. But the experiences of other countries, fighting similar conflicts against similar enemies, suggest that Americans still do not appreciate the enormously difficult—and morally complex—problem that the imperative to gather "good intelligence" entails.

The challenge that security forces and militaries the world over have faced in countering terrorism is how to obtain information about an enigmatic enemy who fights unconventionally and operates in a highly amenable environment where he typically is indistinguishable from the civilian populace. The differences between police officers and soldiers in training and approach, coupled with the fact that most military forces are generally uncomfortable with, and inadequately prepared for, counterterrorist operations, strengthens this challenge. Military forces in such unfamiliar settings must learn to acquire intelligence by methods markedly different from those to which they are accustomed. The most "actionable," and therefore effective, information in this environment is discerned not from orders of battle, visual satellite transmissions of opposing force positions, or intercepted signals but from human intelligence gathered mostly from the indigenous population. The police, specifically trained to interact with the public, typically have better access than the military to what are called human intelligence sources. Indeed, good police work depends on informers, undercover agents, and the apprehension and interrogation of terrorists and suspected terrorists, who provide the additional information critical to destroying terrorist organizations. Many today who argue reflexively and sanctimoniously that the United States should not "over-react" by over-militarizing the "war" against terrorism assert that such a conflict should be largely a police, not a military, endeavor. Although true, this line of argument usually overlooks the uncomfortable fact that, historically, "good" police work against terrorists has of necessity involved nasty and brutish means. Rarely have the importance of intelligence and the unpleasant ways in which it must often be obtained been better or more clearly elucidated than in the 1966 movie *The Battle of Algiers*. In an early scene in the film the main protagonist, the French paratroop commander, Lieutenant

Colonel Mathieu (who is actually a composite of Yves Godard and two other senior French army officers who fought in the Battle of Algiers), explains to his men that the "military aspect is secondary." He says, "More immediate is the police work involved. I know you don't like hearing that, but it indicates exactly the kind of job we have to do."

I have long told soldiers, spies, and students to watch *The Battle of Algiers* if they want to understand how to fight terrorism. Indeed, the movie was required viewing for the graduate course I taught for five years on terrorism and the liberal state, which considered the difficulties democracies face in countering terrorism. The seminar at which the movie was shown regularly provoked the most intense and passionate discussions of the semester. To anyone who has seen *The Battle of Algiers*, this is not surprising. The late Pauline Kael, doyenne of American film critics, seemed still enraptured seven years after its original release when she described *The Battle of Algiers* in a 900-word review as "an epic in the form of a 'created documentary'"; "the one great revolutionary 'sell' of modern times"; and the "most impassioned, most astute call to revolution ever." The best reviews, however, have come from terrorists—members of the IRA; the Tamil Tigers, in Sri Lanka; and 1960s African-American revolutionaries—who have assiduously studied it. At a time when the U.S. Army has enlisted Hollywood screenwriters to help plot scenarios of future terrorist attacks, learning about the difficulties of fighting terrorism from a movie that terrorists themselves have studied doesn't seem far-fetched.

In fact, the film represents the apotheosis of cinema verite. That it has a verisimilitude unique among onscreen portrayals of terrorism is a tribute to its director, Gillo Pontecorvo, and its cast—many of whose members reprised the real-life roles they had played actually fighting for the liberation of their country, a decade before. Pontecorvo, too, had personal experience with the kinds of situations he filmed: during World War II he had commanded a partisan brigade in Milan. Indeed, the Italian filmmaker was so concerned about not giving audiences a false impression of authenticity that he inserted a clarification in the movie's opening frames: "This dramatic re-enactment of The Battle of Algiers contains NOT ONE FOOT of Newsreel or Documentary Film." The movie accordingly possesses an uncommon gravitas that immediately draws viewers into the story. Like many of the best films, it is about a search—in this case for the intelligence on which French paratroops deployed in Algiers depended to defeat and destroy the terrorists of the National Liberation Front (FLN). "To know them means we can eliminate them," Mathieu explains to his men in the scene referred to above. "For this we need information. The method: interrogation." In Mathieu's universe there is no question of ends not justifying means: the Paras need intelligence, and they will obtain it however they can. "To succumb to humane considerations," he concludes, "only leads to hopeless chaos."

The events depicted on celluloid closely parallel those of history. In 1957 the city of Algiers was the center of a life-and-death struggle between the FLN and the French authorities. On one side were the terrorists, embodied both on screen and in real life in Ali La Pointe, a petty thief turned terrorist cell leader; on the other stood the army, specifically the elite 10th Para Division, under General Jacques Massu, another commander on whom the Mathieu composite was based. Veterans of the war to preserve France's control of Indochina, Massu and his senior officers—Godard included—prided themselves on having acquired a thorough understanding of terrorism and revolutionary warfare, and how to counter both. Victory, they were convinced, would depend on the acquisition of intelligence. Their method was to build a meticulously detailed picture of the FLN's apparatus in

Algiers which would help the French home in on the terrorist campaign's masterminds Ali La Pointe and his bin Laden, Saadi Yacef (who played himself in the film). This approach, which is explicated in one of the film's most riveting scenes, resulted in what the Francophile British historian Alistair Horne, in his masterpiece on the conflict, *A Savage War of Peace*, called a "complex organigramme [that] began to take shape on a large blackboard, a kind of skeleton pyramid in which, as each fresh piece of information came from the interrogation centres, another [terrorist] name (and not always necessarily the right name) would be entered." That this system proved tactically effective there is no doubt. The problem was that it thoroughly depended on, and therefore actively encouraged, widespread human-rights abuses, including torture.

Massu and his men—like their celluloid counterparts—were not particularly concerned about this. They justified their means of obtaining intelligence with utilitarian, cost-benefit arguments. Extraordinary measures were legitimized by extraordinary circumstances. The exculpatory philosophy embraced by the French Paras is best summed up by Massu's uncompromising belief that "the innocent [that is, the next victims of terrorist attacks] deserve more protection than the guilty." The approach, however, at least strategically, was counterproductive. Its sheer brutality alienated the native Algerian Muslim community. Hitherto mostly passive or apathetic, that community was now driven into the arms of the FLN, swelling the organization's ranks and increasing its popular support. Public opinion in France was similarly outraged, weakening support for the continuing struggle and creating profound fissures in French civil-military relations. The army's achievement in the city was therefore bought at the cost of eventual political defeat. Five years after victory in Algiers the French withdrew from Algeria and granted the country its independence. But Massu remained forever unrepentant: he insisted that the ends justified the means used to destroy the FLN's urban insurrection. The battle was won, lives were saved, and the indiscriminate bombing campaign that had terrorized the city was ended. To Massu, that was all that mattered. To his mind, respect for the rule of law and the niceties of legal procedure were irrelevant given the crisis situation enveloping Algeria in 1957. As anachronistic as France's attempt to hold on to this last vestige of its colonial past may now appear, its jettisoning of such long-standing and cherished notions as habeas corpus and due process, enshrined in the ethos of the liberal state, underscores how the intelligence requirements of counterterrorism can suddenly take precedence over democratic ideals.

Although it is tempting to dismiss the French army's resort to torture in Algeria as the desperate excess of a moribund colonial power, the fundamental message that only information can effectively counter terrorism is timeless. Equally disturbing and instructive, however, are the lengths to which security and military forces need often resort to get that information. I learned this some years ago, on a research trip to Sri Lanka. The setting—a swank oceanfront hotel in Colombo, a refreshingly cool breeze coming off the ocean, a magnificent sunset on the horizon—could not have been further removed from the carnage and destruction that have afflicted that island country for the past eighteen years and have claimed the lives of more than 60,000 people. Arrayed against the democratically elected Sri Lankan government and its armed forces is perhaps the most ruthlessly efficient terrorist organization-cum-insurgent force in the world today: the Liberation Tigers of Tamil Eelam, known also by the acronym LTTE or simply as the Tamil Tigers. The Tigers are unique in the annals of terrorism and arguably eclipse even bin Laden's al Qaeda in professionalism, capability, and determination. They are believed to be the first nonstate group in history to stage a chemical-weapons attack when they deployed poison gas in a 1990 assault on a Sri Lankan military base—some five years before the nerve-gas attack on the Tokyo subway by the apocalyptic Japanese religious cult Aum Shinrikyo. Of greater relevance, perhaps, is the fact that at least a decade before the seaborne attack on the U.S.S. *Cole*, in Aden harbor, the LTTE's special suicide maritime unit, the Sea Tigers, had perfected the same tactics against the Sri Lankan navy. Moreover, the Tamil Tigers are believed to have developed their own embryonic air capability—designed to carry out attacks similar to those of September 11 (though with much smaller, noncommercial aircraft). The most feared Tiger unit, however, is the Black Tigers—the suicide cadre composed of the group's best-trained, most battle-hardened, and most zealous fighters. A partial list of their operations includes the assassination of the former Indian Prime Minister Rajiv Gandhi at a campaign stop in the Indian state of Tamil Nadu, in 1991; the assassination of Sri Lankan President Ranasinghe Premadasa, in 1993; the assassination of the presidential candidate Gamini Dissanayake, which also claimed the lives of fifty-four bystanders and injured about one hundred more, in 1994; the suicide truck bombing of the Central Bank of Sri Lanka, in 1996, which killed eighty-six people and wounded 1,400 others; and the attempt on the life of the current President of Sri Lanka, Chandrika Kumaratunga, in December of 1999. The powerful and much venerated leader of the LTTE is Velupillai Prabhakaran, who, like bin Laden, exercises a charismatic influence over his fighters. *The Battle of Algiers* is said to be one of Prabhakaran's favorite films.

I sat in that swank hotel drinking tea with a much decorated, battle-hardened Sri Lankan army officer charged with fighting the LTTE and protecting the lives of Colombo's citizens. I cannot use his real name, so I will call him Thomas. However, I had been told before our meeting, by the mutual friend—a former Sri Lankan intelligence officer who had also long fought the LTTE—who introduced us (and was present at our meeting), that Thomas had another name, one better known to his friends and enemies alike: Terminator. My friend explained how Thomas had acquired his sobriquet; it actually owed less to Arnold Schwarzenegger than to the merciless way in which he discharged his duties as an intelligence officer. This became clear to me during our conversation. "By going through the process of laws," Thomas patiently explained, as a parent or a teacher might speak to a bright yet uncomprehending child, "you cannot fight terrorism." Terrorism, he believed, could be fought only by thoroughly "terrorizing" the terrorists—that is, inflicting on them the same pain that they inflict on the innocent. Thomas had little confidence that I understood what he was saying. I was an academic, he said, with no actual experience of the life-and-death choices and the immense responsibility borne by those charged with protecting society from attack. Accordingly, he would give me an example of the split-second decisions he was called on to make. At the time, Colombo was on "code red" emergency status, because of intelligence that the LTTE was planning to embark on a campaign of bombing public gathering places and other civilian targets. Thomas's unit had apprehended three terrorists who, it suspected, had recently planted somewhere in the city a bomb that was then ticking away, the minutes counting down to catastrophe. The three men were brought before Thomas. He asked them where the bomb was. The terrorists—highly dedicated and steeled to resist interrogation—remained silent. Thomas asked the question again, advising them that if they did not tell him what he wanted to know, he would kill them. They were unmoved. So Thomas took his pistol from his gun belt, pointed it at the forehead of one of them, and shot him dead. The other two, he said, talked immediately; the bomb, which had been placed in a crowded railway station and set to explode during the evening rush hour, was found and defused, and countless lives were saved. On other occasions, Thomas said, similarly recalcitrant terrorists were brought before him. It was not surprising, he said, that they initially refused to talk; they were schooled to withstand harsh questioning and coercive pressure. No matter: a few drops of gasoline flicked into a plastic bag that is then placed over a terrorist's head and cinched tight around his neck with a web belt very quickly prompts a full explanation of the details of any planned attack.

I was looking pale and feeling a bit shaken as waiters in starched white jackets smartly cleared the china teapot and cups from the table, and Thomas rose to bid us goodbye and return to his work. He hadn't exulted in his explanations or revealed any joy or even a hint of pleasure in what he had to do. He had spoken throughout in a measured, somber, even reverential tone. He did not appear to be a sadist, or even manifestly homicidal. (And not a year has passed since our meeting when Thomas has failed to send me an unusually kind Christmas card.) In his view, as in Massu's, the innocent had more rights than the guilty. He, too, believed that extraordinary circumstances required extraordinary measures. Thomas didn't think I understood—or, more to the point, thought I never could understand. I am not fighting on the front lines of this battle; I don't have the responsibility for protecting society that he does. He was right: I couldn't possibly understand. But since September 11, and especially every morning after I read the "Portraits of Grief" page in *The New York Times*, I am constantly reminded of Thomas—of the difficulties of fighting terrorism and of the challenges of protecting not only the innocent but an entire society and way of life. I am never bidden to condone, much less advocate, torture. But as I look at the snapshots and the lives of the victims recounted each day, and think how it will take almost a year to profile the approximately 5,000 people who perished on September 11, I recall the ruthless enemy that America faces, and I wonder about the lengths to which we may yet have to go to vanquish him.

The moral question of lengths and the broader issue of ends versus means are, of course, neither new nor unique to rearguard colonial conflicts of the 1950s or to the unrelenting carnage that has more recently been inflicted on a beautiful tropical island in the Indian Ocean. They are arguably no different from the stark choices that eventually confront any society threatened by an enveloping violence unlike anything it has seen before. For a brief period in the early and middle 1970s Britain, for example, had something of this experience—which may be why, among other reasons, Prime Minister Tony Blair and his country today stand as America's staunchest ally. The sectarian terrorist violence in Northern Ireland was at its height and had for the first time spilled into England in a particularly vicious and indiscriminate way. The views of a British army intelligence officer at the time, quoted by the journalist Desmond Hamill in his book *Pig in the Middle* (1985), reflect those of Thomas and Massu.

> Naturally one worries—after all, one is inflicting pain and discomfort and indignity on other human beings… [but] society has got to find a way of protecting itself… and it can only do so if it has good information. If you have a close-knit society which doesn't give information then you've got to find ways of getting it. Now the softies of the world complain—but there is an awful lot of double talk about it. If there is to be discomfort and horror inflicted on a few, is this not preferred to the danger and horror being inflicted on perhaps a million people?

It is a question that even now, after September 11, many Americans would answer in the negative. But under extreme conditions and in desperate circumstances that, too, could dramatically change—much as everything else has so profoundly changed for us all since that morning. I recently discussed precisely this issue over the telephone with the same Sri Lankan friend who introduced me to Thomas years ago. I have never quite shaken my disquiet over my encounter with Thomas and over the issues he raised—issues that have now acquired an unsettling relevance. My friend sought to lend some perspective from his country's long experience in fighting terrorism. "There are not good people and bad people," he told me, "only good circumstances and bad circumstances. Sometimes in bad circumstances good people have to do bad things. I have done bad things, but these were in bad circumstances. I have no doubt that this was the right thing to do." In the quest for timely, "actionable" intelligence will the United States, too, have to do bad things—by resorting to measures that we would never have contemplated in a less exigent situation?

An international expert on terrorism and political violence, **Bruce Hoffman** is the RAND Corporation's vice president of external affairs and director of its Washington, D.C., office. He is well known for *Inside Terrorism* (1998), which has been translated into foreign language editions in nine countries, and was the founding director of the Center for the Study of Terrorism and Political Violence at the University of St. Andrews in Scotland. In 1998, Hoffman was awarded the Santiago Grisolía Prize and the accompanying chair in violence studies by the Queen Sofia Center for the Study of Violence (Valencia, Spain). Even before the terrorist attacks on September 11, he was consulting with governments and businesses on terrorism and political violence.

Boaz Ganor, 2005

Dilemmas Concerning Media Coverage of Terrorist Attacks

Terrorist and guerrilla organizations throughout the world differ from one another in their methods, their aims, the weaponry at their disposal, the extent of outside help they receive, and so on. Therefore, scholars are at odds regarding the very existence of a collective strategy among terrorist organizations.

One school of thought asserts that terrorist organizations operate according to a multi-phase rational strategy, which begins with perpetrating a terrorist attack aimed at achieving widespread media coverage. The media coverage is supposed to intimidate the public, and in this way influence the political perspectives and attitudes of the citizens. The anxiety felt by the nation's citizens will be translated into public pressure on decision makers to accede to terrorists' demands and make decisions that coincide with the interests of the terrorist organizations. This theory perceives the media and public opinion as central elements in the terrorist organizations' attack policy. Another school of thought is doubtful as to the central importance of the media in the terrorists' operational strategy and the extent to which public opinion can influence the attitudes of decision makers, especially on matters of security and foreign affairs.

According to the first school of thought, the written and electronic media play a major role in modern democratic society, among other things, as an agent that mediates between the public and its leadership, and has an impact on shaping public opinion and government decisions. Given the media's importance in modern society, it is a major element in the strategy used by terrorist and guerrilla organizations. This was expressed by Carlos Marighella, who noted that the rescue of prisoners, executions, kidnappings, sabotage, terrorism, and the war of nerves—all these are acts of armed propaganda, carried out solely for propaganda effect.

Terrorist attacks, then, are aimed at achieving maximum coverage in the written and electronic press. Terrorist organizations, aware of the media's importance as a tool for broadcasting their message, do their utmost to attract media attention. As part of this, they act to increase the number of victims in terrorist attacks and escalate the nature of these acts, using means that are increasingly ruthless or terrifying.

Weimann outlines the advantages that terrorists gain from media coverage of terrorist attacks: generating public interest in the terrorists' activities and enhancing their influence; attributing a positive spin to the restrictive acts of the terrorist organizations and shaping their image; portraying terrorists as the weak side in the conflict and promoting support for their motives; providing important information regarding counter-terrorism activities, etc. Crenshaw notes that the history of terrorism reveals a series of developments whereby terrorists deliberately choose targets that had previously been considered taboo or locations where violence is unexpected, and the innovation is then disseminated via the international media. Post mentions the fact that terrorists have succeeded in gaining a virtual monopoly over the weapon of the television camera, and in manipulating their target audience through the media. According to Post, terrorist organizations have demonstrated the power and importance of the media and have used this means to highlight the legitimacy of their goals.

This theory postulates that the relationship between terrorist organizations and the media is one of mutual profit. On the one hand, terrorists gain a great deal from the media coverage they receive. The media serve as a stage from which the terrorists broadcast their messages to various target audiences, earning support for the terrorist organization and its actions among its supporters and enhancing its scope and capability far beyond its actual power. Media coverage also helps in gathering vital intelligence information for planning attacks and assessing the offensive intentions of the other side; for imitating successful attacks perpetrated by other organizations; and securing international legitimacy for the terrorist organization while damaging the international image and status of the nation coping with terrorism. On the other hand, terrorists give the media newsworthy and interesting information—drama that involves human lives; a basis for political commentary; human-interest stories on the victims and their families, as well as the terrorists involved in the attack, background coverage, and more. In general, terrorism offers the media gripping stories with an interesting plot, and as a result, they also get higher ratings. Terrorist organizations do not have to do very much in order to attract media attention. It is given to them all too easily, among other things, because of the competition between the different media channels and the desire for financial profit.

Violent incidents (especially terrorist attacks) "sell newspapers" and interest the public. Schmid and De Graff argue that one cannot ignore the fact that the media operate on considerations of profits, which are based on advertising revenue. This revenue depends on the number of television viewers and radio listeners, and newspaper sales. Terrorist acts attract the public's interest, and thus increase sales figures.

As a result of the importance of the media aspect of any terrorism strategy, news coverage may have an impact on the different components of an attack: the target (depending on the symbolism of the target, its security sensitivity, the degree to which it is well-populated, its location, etc.), the duration, the timing, the method chosen. Hoffman stresses, therefore, that modern media play a key role in terrorist activity. Moreover, when the media prepare for coverage and the attack does not take place, it is sometimes forced to justify the money spent by bringing background coverage with a "human interest angle." Thus, there is a distorted focus on the human aspect instead of the overall picture, and the large networks, in fact, become agents that influence the shaping of policy rather than agents that merely report.

Most of the public in the United States identified during the 1980s with the arguments heard against the media regarding their coverage of terrorist attacks. In a public opinion poll conducted by ABC and *The Washington Post* in January 1986, most of the American public (76 percent of those surveyed) felt that the terrorists' success was dependent upon the publicity they received in the media, and that the media sometimes exaggerated terrorist attacks and played into the terrorists' hands by giving them the coverage they were seeking. It was proposed that such television coverage be made illegal, empowering the police to prevent television coverage when necessary. Nonetheless, most respondents felt that media coverage of terrorism serves the public interest, and most believed that television should continue covering terrorist acts even if this led to additional attacks. The vast majority felt that terrorism existed both with television and without it.

This double standard in the public's feelings about the media coverage of terrorist attacks is reflected in academic studies as well. In contrast with the accepted approach regarding the reciprocal relationship between the media and terrorist organizations, another approach was put forth claiming that terrorist organizations do not consider media coverage of their acts to such a large extent, and they certainly do not plan their strategies according to the media. Supporters of this approach rely, *inter alia*, on statements made by terrorist leaders who minimize the media's importance, and at times even attack the media. Moreover, those who side with this theory emphasize that the ability of the terrorist organizations to influence decision makers on political matters by exerting pressure and intimidating the public is not high, and is actually doubtful.

Crenshaw notes in this context that studies conducted with regard to the IRA and the ETA have shown that these organizations find no benefit in media coverage. In reality, they perceive the media as being hostile, prejudiced, and subjective. From their point of view, news reports broadcast through the media are part of the policies of the nations to which they are opposed. Representatives of these organizations claimed the line characterizing the media was one that supported the status quo while exaggerating their reports of the violence so as to damage the organizations' image in the eyes of the public, while at the same time ignoring their non-violent activity. Furthermore, coverage of terrorist attacks usually paints terrorists in a very negative light, which casts doubt on the claim that limiting media coverage reduces the number of attacks.

Hoffman highlights the fact that media coverage sometimes plays a positive role in coping with terrorism. This was the case, for example, when the Unabomber was exposed in the United States following his demand that his ideological manifesto be published in the daily press. The same holds true for the American media's near-obsession with the hostages of the TWA flight hijacked in 1985 which, according to the families of the hostages, kept the issue at the top of the agenda of American decision makers and ultimately led to the release of the hostages. In addition, we must consider the fact that avoiding media coverage of terrorist attacks, or reducing its scope, is liable to cause an escalation in the number of attacks and their nature by the terrorist organizations, in an effort to force the media to cover these acts regardless. And if this were not enough, there is the fear that avoiding media coverage would lead to rumors and that the lack of reliable and up-to-date information would cause widespread, and unnecessary, panic.

Those supporting this theory claim that not only do the media not serve the true goals of the terrorist organization, but even if terrorism also influences the political attitudes of the public through media coverage, it is not at all clear whether public opinion ultimately has any effect on decision makers and their political attitudes. This is because alongside the influence of public opinion, decision makers are exposed to additional—and, at times, contradictory—influences from other sources. Furthermore, even if media coverage of terrorist attacks has an effect on the public and that is indeed translated as pressure on decision makers, it isn't at all clear that this is the influence that terrorist organizations actually hoped for. Quite the reverse, media coverage is likely to arouse public protests that would increase the resources allocated to fight terrorism. Wilensky believes that terrorism does not achieve its goals by employing fear and threats. He claims, on the contrary, that terrorism hardens the population's attitude and leads to counter-terrorism measures. Laquer states that society is willing to suffer terrorism as long as it remains a nuisance. But when a feeling of insecurity begins to spread and when terrorism becomes a genuine danger, people no longer denounce the government for ignoring human rights in order to fight it. Quite the contrary, in such a situation there is increased demand to use more aggressive counter-terrorism measures, without consideration of human rights.

Gur notes that waves of terrorist attacks in Western Europe were accompanied by a rise in public support for taking serious steps against terrorist organizations. According to Gur, waves of terrorism is democratic societies often sow the seeds of its own demise because such violence jeopardized support for the terrorists, and security forces can then gather intelligence information about them more easily. Hoffman, who bases himself on a study conducted at the RAND Institute in 1989, stresses that in spite of the comprehensive coverage of terrorist attacks by the American media during the five years preceding the study, no support or sympathy was generated among the American public for the attitudes and motives of the terrorists. Gur and Hoffman naturally refer to internal terrorism (which takes place within the nation itself), and their study doesn't necessarily relate to international terrorism (which involves at least two nations), or terrorism that has been "imported" into a country.

Perhaps Abu Iyad, Yasser Arafat's former deputy, can actually bridge the gap between the two opposing theories regarding the question of whether media coverage of terrorist attacks and their influence on public opinion serves the interests of the terrorist organizations or not. In this context, Abu Iyad stated (referring to the attack at the Munich Olympics in September 1972) that one of the goals of the attack was: "To exploit the unusual concentration of media coverage in Munich to give our struggle an international resonance—*positive or negative, it didn't matter!* . . . In essence, Abu Iyad stresses that in terms of the organization perpetrating the attack, the type of criticism the act evokes is unimportant so long as it succeeds in drawing the public's attention to the problem of the Palestinian people. In other words, it isn't important what the world says about you, the main thing is that they talk about you and are aware of your problems and demands. Hoffman continues this line of thought when he states that the success in achieving the impact you desire is usually measured by terrorists in terms of the amount of publicity and attention garnered, and not in terms of the type of publicity, and whether it is positive or negative.

The Media as Part of the Strategy of Terrorism

The media plays a key role in the strategy of terrorism. Damage from a terrorist attack is usually limited to the scene of the attack itself, but the act also aims to influence a target audience that goes way beyond the victims themselves. The way to reach target audiences and to broadcast the messages the terrorist organization wants to transmit is through the media. Thus, the media serve as a vital means for transmitting messages simultaneously to three different target audiences (see Figure 1). For the native population from which the organization originates and activists within the organization itself, the media transmit messages of power; the ability to achieve their strategic goals in spite of their technology inferiority, fewer numbers, and lack of resources; a call to support the organization and join its ranks; and above all—to raise the morale of this target audience. A completely opposite message is broadcast concomitantly to another of the organization's target audiences—the population targeted with terrorism. A terrorist attack is supposed to transmit to this target audience the feeling that they are vulnerable as individuals anywhere and anytime, and

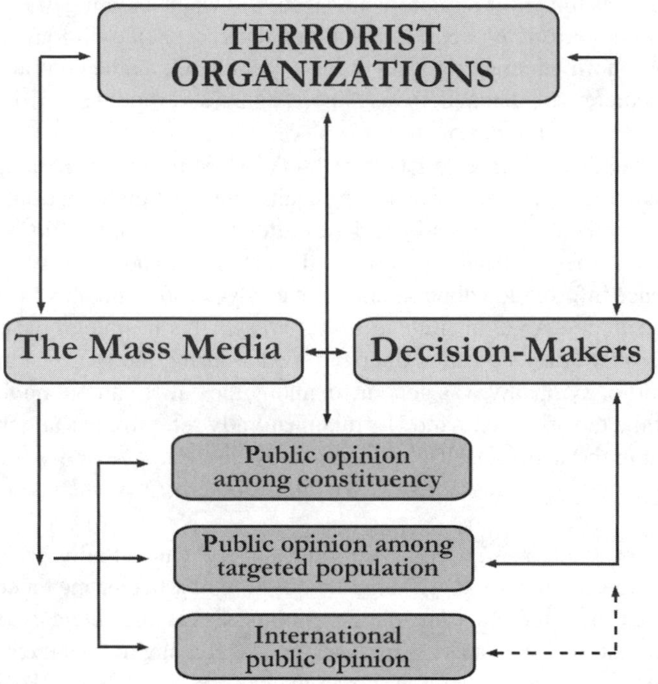

Figure 1. The strategy of modern terrorism

therefore their military-economic strength cannot guarantee their lives, their well-being, their health or their property. The message being sent to this audience is usually accompanied by a series of concrete demands, whether political or operational, acquiescence to which would allegedly ensure the end of the attacks and the restoration of peace. With regard to this target audience, the goal of the terrorist organization is to demoralize them and compromise their ability to cope with terrorism. The third message transmitted by the media is geared towards international public opinion, that same audience that is not involved in the conflict and observes events from the sidelines. The terrorist organization uses the attack to focus this audience's attention on the conflict in which it is embroiled, the arguments presented by the terrorists and their representatives around the world, and the suffering of the terrorist organization's native population.

Thus, the media serve as a magnifying glass that can intensify the impact of the attack and turn terrorism into an effective tool. Without the media aspect, terrorism remains one more cause of death, one of many, and not necessarily the most important or most dangerous one. Weimann compares the domain of terrorism to a stage. Indeed, almost all of the components found in a theatrical show can be found in a terrorist show, including: a producer—the initiator of the attack; a director—the organizer of the attack; a casting director—who locates and recruits the terrorists for the mission; an audience—the different types of target audiences who observe the attack; the setting—the backdrop chosen to perpetrate the attack; a plot—the story behind the attack, the background and events; a message—the various messages broadcast to the different types of audiences; actors—the terrorists, the victims, and other involved. But beyond all of this, there is the stage. The stage in a theater is usually raised in order to enable a larger and wider audience to observe what is taking place and absorb the message. The stage of terrorism is the media, which serve the terrorist organization in precisely the same way.

The Journalist's Dilemma

In an attempt to justify and explain the way in which the media cover terrorist acts, the media usually cite two main arguments. One is that the media play a major role in the democratic way of government—guaranteeing the "public's right to know." This value necessitates, they believe, media coverage of terrorist attacks without censorship, restrictions, or moral or other types of obstacles. Even if the media act as an essential stage for terrorist organizations and indirectly assists them, their central role in a democracy requires journalists to behave as they do. The other argument, which is held by many in the media, is that in this modern age the main factor that determines the scope of media coverage and its nature is ratings. So long as the public is interested in watching the atrocities of terrorism, there will always be someone to supply this need and therefore, it is impossible to restrict or change the nature of the media's coverage.

These two statements call for thorough study and examination. On the face of it, the equation that "blood equals ratings" appears correct, but only up to a certain limit. When the public is exposed to images that are particularly harsh—close-ups of body parts, for example, or repeated broadcasts of the death and destruction at the scene of an attack, at least some prefer to turn off the television, switch to another channel, or do something else. This can be concluded, for example, from the severe criticism aimed at the media by the public in Israel during the 1990s, concerning the unlimited and unrestrained media coverage from the scenes of terrorist acts, particularly suicide bombings. Such disapproval was expressed in television interviews, calls from radio listeners, review articles in the press, and at times, even from direct contact by citizens to the different media outlets. This criticism ultimately led to positive changes in the nature of Israeli television coverage from the end of 2000 (with the beginning of a wave of terrorist activity and intensive violence by the Palestinians, which became known as "the Al Aksa intifada").

The public's demand that reporters cover terrorist attacks in a sober and responsible manner challenges journalists with a very serious dilemma—the journalist's dilemma. This dilemma has two aspects: On one level, the reporter must find the proper balance of his professional obligation as a journalist to cover the events as they happen with the need to respond to the legitimate demands of those in his country who receive this information. On another level, he must find a balance between contingencies derived from competition among the many channels and media outlets, and his civic duty not to become a pawn in the hands of the terrorist organizations and assist them, even indirectly, in achieving their short-term and long-term objectives. The call for the media to perform their civic duty is reflected in statements made by Weimann, who declared that along with the public's right to receive precise, genuine, and up-to-date information as far as possible, that is, the public's "right to know," the public also has a "right not to know," that is, the victim's right to privacy; the right of the public not to be exposed to the personal and intimate details of the terror victims through media coverage that infringes upon their dignity; the right of the public to uphold the state's security secrets that preserve their safety, etc. The journalist's need to cope with these two types of obligations was illustrated most vividly following the terrorist attacks in the United States on September 11, 2001. Television camera crews who covered the horrors of the attack decided at that time to stick small American flags on their cameras, or to cover the live broadcasting vans of the various television networks with American flags or photographs of the missing. Such acts illustrate more than anything else the awareness and responsiveness by American journalists of their two parallel obligations—their professional obligation and their civic duty.

In 1997, the International Policy Institute for Counter-Terrorism at the Herzliya Interdisciplinary Center held a professional conference, called "The Shefayim Conference," which was attended by Israeli media personnel (journalists and editors), and counter-terrorism experts to discuss the media coverage of terrorist attacks in Israel. The goal was to try and find a proper balance between these two obligations. . . . Among recommendations made by conference participants were two main proposals: to avoid close-up images of terrorist victims, and to limit as much as possible the repeated broadcasting of images of death and destruction from the scene of the attack. These two recommendations actually enable journalists to maintain the delicate balance between the journalist's professional obligation and his civic duty. On the one hand, acceptance of these recommendations will help protect the public's right to receive information, since media coverage of the attacks in real time will not be halted. But, on the other hand, without close-up photos of the horrors of the attack, the media will not encourage anxiety and fear and, thus, will not be used as a pawn by the terrorists. Avoiding frequent broadcasts from the scene of the attack will limit the damage to the people's morale from terrorist attacks, and on the other hand, will reduce television viewers' tendency to stop watching or switch to another channel.

The Live Broadcast Dilemma

Among all the different types of media, it would appear that television has the greatest influence on public morale. The terrible images broadcast from the scene of an attack into every home in the targeted nation, and the entire world, serves the propaganda and fear-provoking goals of the terrorist organization more than any other outlet.

Israel's experience during the mid-1990s with regard to television coverage of terrorist attacks is instructive regarding the problem of live coverage at the scene of an attack. The paradox is that through the use of live close-up footage the viewer is exposed, at times, to more horrible scenes than those to which the people at the scene itself are witness. People at the scene are busy carrying out their specific tasks—security, reporting, rescue, recovery—and they are neither interested nor able to actually focus on the particularly horrible images from the scene such as body parts strewn around the ground or other grisly sights. In contrast with these, when a television cameraman arrives on the scene of the attack who is unaware of the conflict between his professional obligation and his civic duty, he naturally wanders around the scene in search of the most shocking images.

From this perspective, Israel has seen an improvement in its media coverage since the early 2000s. From time to time, if television cameras begin to focus on particularly harsh images during the course of a live broadcast from the scene of an attack, the live broadcast is sometimes suspended and the newscaster or a studio commentator appears on the screen until the camera is no longer focused on the difficult scene. These were correct editing decisions as a result of public criticism.

In this context one must, of course, be careful not to throw the baby out with the bath water. The warranted criticism of the nature of the media coverage must not detract from the importance of media coverage in general, and live broadcasts in particular, when it comes to terrorists attacks. If there is anything more dangerous than irresponsible coverage of terrorist attacks, it is a lack of any coverage. Lack of coverage in real time could lead to the spreading of rumors that are unfounded, and their effect on public morale is liable to be even more damaging and destructive.

To summarize this dilemma, the advantages of live broadcasts of terrorist attacks outweigh the disadvantages, even when the correspondent is unaware of his civic responsibility. When covering terrorist attacks it is possible, and certainly necessary, to employ editorial considerations in real time, to avoid camera close-ups of dead bodies and the wounded, to avoid broadcasting expressions of panic and extreme fear, and to photograph from somewhere slightly removed from the center of the attack. . . .

Boaz Ganor is the deputy dean of the Lauder School of Government and is one of the founders of the International Institute for Counterterrorism (ICT) at the Interdisciplinary Center Herzliya, where he serves as its director. Boaz Ganor is the author of numerous articles on counter-terrorism and *The Counter-Terrorism Puzzle: A Guide for Decision Makers*.

Mark Basile, 2004

Going to the Source: Why Al Qaeda's Financial Network Is Likely to Withstand the Current War on Terrorist Financing

On 24 September 2001, President Bush announced the first stage of the War on Terrorism with an attack against the terrorist financial infrastructure. Since then, the impact of this attack on Al Qaeda's ability to operate has been minimal, for three reasons. First, Al Qaeda has built a strong network of financiers and operatives who are both frugally minded and business savvy. *As a result, terrorist finances are often hidden in legitimate and illegitimate businesses and disguised as commodities and cash. Second,* Al Qaeda has learned to effectively leverage the global financial system of capital markets. *Small financial transfers, underregulated Islamic banking networks and informal transfer systems throughout the world make it almost impossible to stop Al Qaeda from moving money. Third,* Al Qaeda has built a significant base of Islamic charities in Saudi Arabia with international divisions that have not been scrutinized or controlled by the regime. *As a result, Al Qaeda's sophisticated financial network may be able to sustain international efforts to disrupt it. Financial regulations imposed to reduce terrorist financing must be applied more broadly and be supported by significant resources. An improvement in the war on terrorist financing requires better international coordination, more effective use of financial regulations, and regulating the Saudi Arabian charity structure.*

The war on terrorist financing is currently ill-equipped to starve Al Qaeda of its funding. Al Qaeda is an effective organization that has taken advantage of the weaknesses in global financial markets to develop a network of financing options that cannot be easily overcome. This article will examine the mechanisms that enable Al Qaeda to continue to raise and disperse funds for future operations, and policy options to improve the ability of regulators to reduce Al Qaeda's financial strength.

Al Qaeda's strengths include its network structure and doctrine, which leverages wealthy donors and charities for funding, as well as training operatives to develop self-funding strategies. Al Qaeda's strength is a global financial system of licit and illicit companies, private investors, government sponsors, and religious "charities" that fund Al Qaeda operations.

Al Qaeda always benefits from numerous financial channels, away from government regulation and control. U.S. domestic regulations will have an impact on Al Qaeda finances in the United States, but applying these regulations to international markets and foreign banking systems is problematic. In addition, Al Qaeda always has a fallback financial system to rely on, including the underregulated Islamic banking system and the international hawala transfer system. The hawala system is Al Qaeda's most effective means of money movement through cash smuggling.[1]

Al Qaeda benefits from weak U.S. foreign policy and coalition building with allies, such as Saudi Arabia, who are unwilling to effectively implement stringent regulations to stem terrorist funding. Al Qaeda benefits from the weak financial regulations of failed states and weak regulation of charities throughout the Middle East to fund its organization. As such, the United States must make a significant foreign policy push for banking oversight and regulation in the Middle East and a local government crackdown on the unregulated charity structure in Saudi Arabia. The United States must use diplomatic and economic tools to push developing countries toward higher standards of regulation in order to cut off Al Qaeda sources of funding.

Al Qaeda's financial structure is well equipped to last in a long war on terrorist financing against the United States and its allies. Most of the evidence underlying this author's arguments is based on academic research, public trials, and Congressional testimony from authorities on Al Qaeda, terrorist financing, and financial regulation. The primary evidence on Al Qaeda that supports many of these findings is based on interviews with Al Qaeda detainees and documents found in Al Qaeda facilities; evidence that may be fabricated because Al Qaeda operatives are taught the tools of denial and deception when conducting operations. Therefore, there is always a possibility, especially before the war on terrorism has come to a conclusion and more evidence is available, that the information provided by detained Al Qaeda operatives and confiscated Al Qaeda paperwork is misleading or incomplete.

The Background of Al Qaeda's Financial Network

> It is neither a single group nor a coalition of groups: it comprises a core base or bases in Afghanistan, satellite terrorist cells worldwide, a conglomerate of Islamist political parties, and other largely independent terrorist groups that it draws on for offensive actions and other responsibilities.[2]

Unlike the leaders of other terrorist organizations, Osama Bin Laden did not rise to power primarily as a religious authority, military hero, or political figure. He was a wealthy financier from a wealthy Saudi family with close ties to the United States. Although his personal fortune is estimated to be between $30 and $200 million, it is quite clear that his organization, Al Qaeda, does not rest on his financial coattails. Rather, Al Qaeda operates a significant financial network, approximated at over $300 million in value, dispersing between $30 and $40 million per year.[3] This network has grown from its origins as the financing arm of the Mujahideen in Afghanistan to a decentralized network of financial capabilities that leverages a limited set of funding channels to fund its organization.

Al Qaeda uses limited funding channels very effectively. In its *Guidance for Financial Institutions in Detecting Terrorist Financing,* the Financial Action Task Force (FATF) on Money Laundering claims that terrorists raise funds from two sources: states and "revenue-generating" activities including fraud, narcotics trafficking, kidnapping, and extortion in addition to running legitimate businesses.[4] Al Qaeda is notable for primarily using fraud and legitimate businesses to support a network, rather than engaging in the full spectrum of "revenue-generating" activities.

The decentralized nature of Al Qaeda makes the overall financial structure very self-sufficient and potentially regenerative. The leadership structure comprises four committees, each reporting to a council of leadership members, the *majlis al-shura*,[5] which, in turn, reports directly to the Emir-General of Al Qaeda. The committee structure includes military, business, religious, and media arms. The business and finance committee, a group of professional bankers, accountants, and financiers,[6] is responsible for setting up and running the financial network that sustains Al Qaeda, from providing logistics for operational cells and bases, to sourcing funds from charities and other sources. It runs a number of illegitimate and legitimate businesses as part of its network. Diamond trading, import-export, manufacturing, transport, and financial services are businesses that Al Qaeda owns and uses. Until recently, the financial arm was run by one of bin Laden's close associates, Mustafa Ahmed al-Hawsawi, who was recently captured. Although the capture of Hawsawi was a good step in the war on terrorist financing, it also showed how Al Qaeda can adapt: Hawsawi was presumably replaced as early as October 2002 by an Egyptian named Abdullah Ahmed Abdullah.[7]

Al Qaeda keeps the funding for its operational cells unconnected from the network of sources from which it raises funds. Al Qaeda requires terrorist cells to be self-managed and often self-sufficient when it comes to finances. Separately, Al Qaeda relies on its businesses and charities to send funding to Al Qaeda's central base of financial operations. In this manner, Al Qaeda runs its sources of funding separately from the funding needs of terrorist cells.[8] This keeps Al Qaeda's financial sources as discreet as possible while allowing operational cells to deploy without ever giving away information on Al Qaeda's underlying financial network.

A Flexible, Extensive, and Deep Financial Network

Al Qaeda's financial capabilities benefit from a network of wealthy supporters, a number of legitimate and illegitimate businesses, and a consistent source of funding from Islamic charities. Moreover, Al Qaeda compounds this financial base of strength with an operational doctrine that teaches deception and denial, frugal financial behavior, and self-sustaining financing tools to its operatives. Al Qaeda's financial network is strong and adaptive, built on a base of networked financiers and operationally strong terrorists. Its means for sourcing funds, managing or hiding funds, and dispersing funds are numerous and complex. To date, each Al Qaeda cell that has conducted a successful operation has received or raised funds from a different channel. The flexibility of Al Qaeda's financial network relies on three strengths of its network: the operational doctrine, the extensive financial network of financiers and businesses, and the consistent source of funding from Islamic charities.

Operational Doctrine

Al Qaeda's operational doctrine breeds frugal financial practices and a self-sustaining attitude in the field. Parts of Al Qaeda's doctrine are exposed in the military training manual of Al Qaeda, *Declaration of Jihad against the Country's Tyrants,* which instructs its operatives in the tools of deception and denial.[9] In the section on financial security precautions, the commander of the cell is instructed to divide finances into funds to be invested for financial return and funds to be saved for operations. In general, these funds must be dispersed, occasionally left with non-members of the cell, and the locations of the funds are not to be divulged to cell soldiers,[10] thus reducing the chances that a captured cell will divulge the source of its financing. The cell commander is given responsibility for the effective allocation, use, and occasionally raising of cell funds.

Al Qaeda operatives are also taught to use credit card fraud, document forgery, and other criminal scams to support their objectives. This self sufficiency hurt the early cells of Al Qaeda, notably the first World Trade Center bombing cell in 1993. In the early part of the 1990s, Al Qaeda either did not have the necessary resources, or at least chose not to use them for its operational cells. Ramzi Yousef, the mastermind and commander of the first World Trade Center bombing was financed by donations from a Holy Water company in the Middle East.[11] Yet the limited nature of Yousef's funding not only caused him to build a bomb that was too small, but also forced one of his operatives, Mohammed Salameh, to foolishly try to retrieve the deposit on the rental truck used to hold the bomb.[12]

Although Al Qaeda's doctrine is frugal in spirit, it is intelligent in its funding allocations. In the days before 11 September 2001, Al Qaeda operatives returned unused funds from their cell in the form of wire transfers for over $20,000 dollars to Al Qaeda leaders in the Middle East. At the same time, the operational commanders did not spare any expense in buying business-class seats so that the hijackers were in the optimal position to take over the cabin.[13]

Businesses and Financiers

Al Qaeda's financial strength is also based on its ability to raise funds from legitimate and illegitimate business and from its network of financiers. In the time since September 11, many Al Qaeda legitimate businesses and financiers have been exposed. However, Al Qaeda is still able to operate businesses in states that are failing around the world such as diamond trafficking in Africa and honey trading out of Yemen, and many financiers still exist that have not been exposed.

The United States shut down a number of Al Qaeda's businesses in the war in Afghanistan, but Al Qaeda continues to run businesses in developing parts of the world. One such business is the diamond business, which Al Qaeda runs in Liberia and Burkina Faso, two countries involved in the illicit diamond trade. Al Qaeda diamond trafficking, which has gone undisturbed since 1998 when it was established in the $20 million industry in West Africa, represents an illegitimate business that Al Qaeda has significantly profited from by working with a number of local companies.[14] In addition to illicit diamond trading, Al Qaeda engages in legitimate business, such as honey trading. Although some claim that this business is a cover for smuggling of money, weapons, and drugs,[15] the business may also be legitimate because the honey trade in the Middle East is important to the culture, religion, and trade. Regardless of how Al Qaeda uses the business, its ability to successfully run overt businesses in honey and covert businesses in gems illustrates a complexity in Al Qaeda's financial network.

The 19 hijackers on 11 September 2001 used less than $500,000[16] from 20 key financiers to fund the hijacking of 4 American commercial jetliners. This $500,000 was transferred to the hijackers in a large number of small installments over time, through different financial channels, indirectly passed to the terrorists from the Middle East, through Germany, the United Arab Emirates (UAE), and Malaysia.[17] The source of these funds was unclear to U.S. authorities until a recent document, recovered from the Arlington, Texas headquarters of Benevolence International Foundation (BIF), listed 20 top Al Qaeda financiers, known as the Golden Chain.[18] In the United States Court case against the President of BIF, Ennam Arnaout, it was suggested that this list of 20 financiers helped provide the funding for the 9/11 cell. More importantly, if true, these 20 individuals highlight the deep pockets of Al Qaeda financiers.

Islamic Charities

The third contributor to Al Qaeda's financial resilience is income from charities. Since September 11, the U.S. arms of a number of Islamic charities that funded Al Qaeda have been shut down and their assets have been frozen. Many of these charities were run by Al Qaeda operatives, such as Ennam Arnaout, who was sentenced to 11 years in prison for money-laundering rather than terrorism. Of course, while charities on U.S. soil are governed by American regulations, Middle East-based charities are not constrained by U.S. law. These charities not only represent a seemingly uncontrollable source of funding, they are also a stable source of funding.

Zakat, or alms giving, is one of the five pillars of Islam, a religious duty for all Muslims. As such, Islamic charities through the Middle East and the rest of the world have a consistent source of funding from religious Muslims. Although the vast majority of charities are legitimate enterprises, funding community development in Islamic communities, a number also have close ties to terrorist groups. Additionally, a number of terrorist organizations, such as Hamas and Hezbollah, include charity and nongovernmental organizations (NGOs) as an overt part of their organizational structure, which raises questions of whether charitable funds are channeled to charitable purposes or terrorism. In the case of Al Qaeda, charities and NGOs act primarily under cover in their financing of terrorism, rather than funding any charitable purposes Al Qaeda may have. Many of these charities were not specifically created to fully fund Al Qaeda, but have since become supportive of its cause.

Many of the charities that support Al Qaeda financially have done so since the Soviet Afghan war. Three of the charities that have come to the attention of the U.S. Justice Department are the Muslim World League (MWL), Benevolence International Foundation, and Qatar Charitable Society (QCS).[19] Even though there were public suggestions that these charities funded Al Qaeda as early as 1993, it was not until a year after 9/11 that the Treasury Department froze the assets of the first two charities.[20] Each of these charities has existed for many years; in the case of the Muslim World League, since 1962.

The case against Ennam Arnaout and his Islamic charity, BIF, uncovered the illegal and yet virtually undetectable ability of Al Qaeda to pull funds from its charities. Funds would be allocated, and accounted for, by the charity for community development and charitable activities. Once the full amount was pulled out for the charitable project, a small percentage (around 10%) of the cash was skimmed off the top and physically passed to an Al Qaeda operative who deposited this clean money into Al Qaeda accounts in the Middle East or dispersed it to operational cells in other parts where Al Qaeda operates, such as Bosnia.[21]

The problem with MWL, BIF, and any Islamic charity that supports Al Qaeda is twofold. First, because their objectives are typically noble and many of their activities may be justifiable, shutting them down may create serious problems for local beneficiaries and have negative impacts on humanitarian needs that the charity is funding. Second, there are typically other illegitimate charities that will accept the cash when charities like MWL and BIF are closed down. While religious Muslims are called to give to charities, with the belief that their money is being used toward an ethical cause, the cash flow out of charities is very loosely regulated and easy to move to terrorist organizations, often without the donor's knowledge or consent. This is especially beneficial to Al Qaeda because the money that is received from charities is clean money, and unlike illicit financing sources, does not need to be laundered.

Al Qaeda has a flexible, extensive, and deep financial network. Its flexibility lies in its doctrinal ability to self-fund operations and save money by the frugal behavior of its operatives. Glimpses of the extensive nature of the network are evident by the deep pockets of financiers and the diversity of legitimate and illegitimate businesses on which Al Qaeda has relied. Finally, Al Qaeda has its hands in the pockets of unknowing Muslims, who, in fulfilling their religious duty to give alms to charities are unknowingly funding terrorist operations.

Al Qaeda's Financial Channels

> Al Qaeda has three financial systems organized by bankers who are as "aware of the cracks inside the Western Financial System as they are aware of lines on their own hands."
>
> —Osama bin Laden in an interview in a Pakistani newspaper[22]

Presumably, the three primary financial systems that Osama Bin Laden divulged include the formal international banking system, the Islamic Banking financial system, and the underground hawala system. Al Qaeda uses these three financial systems, each under varying degrees of regulation, to channel its funds around the world. More recently, Al Qaeda has also used a fourth financial channel in physical movement of cash, diamonds, and precious metals in suitcases in order to evade government oversight.[23]

International Banking System

Al Qaeda's financial network reaches around the world. Although U.S. regulations and legislation have allowed the government to freeze terrorist assets in U.S. jurisdictions, it has limited abilities outside of the U.S. financial system. Al Qaeda's only limitation, in the wake of U.S. regulations and legislation, is a greater difficulty of moving money into the United States. There are two primary reasons that regulations in the international environment are not a long-term solution to winning the war on terrorist financing. The first is that the legal and regulatory structures of foreign financial markets are different and financial transfers regulations between these markets are not yet designed to identify terrorist funds. The second is that Al Qaeda has a global financial system of non-U.S. based regulated and unregulated banks, including the Islamic banking system, through which it can still transfer, store, and invest its funds.

The global financial system was not created to stop the war on terrorist financing. After Bretton Woods, central bank control of international finance decreased, as global currencies floated on international capital markets and investors put their money in places with strong economic activity. In the last 30 years, regulation of global capital markets has decreased as many countries have been gaining access to markets in New York, London, Tokyo, and Hong Kong. The goal of investing in these markets is to gain access to cheaper sources of financing and more stable rates of return. Countries that integrate into capital markets accordingly reduce their cost of capital. Tighter integration also requires faster transactions and allocation of funds, a benefit that increased regulation reduces.

In the developing world, central banks often still control foreign financial transactions. In general, economists believe that when central banks allow their currency to be traded and transacted freely, local investors will choose to invest internationally and repatriate gains into local markets. This type of laissez-faire attitude suggests that access to international markets will cause efficiencies that will force developing countries to develop their own internal financial and banking oversight to protect their new sources of funds. Unfortunately, reducing central bank control in developing countries may also allow terrorists to easily access global financial markets and rely on commercial banking systems with limited oversight.

Islamic Banking

In addition to benefiting from weak banking oversight in the developing world and the unlikely direction of reduced capital market integration, Al Qaeda also takes advantage of a financial structure close to home: the Islamic banking network. This global financial network has strong relationships through the third world, notable tax havens, and most importantly most of the developed world, including the United Kingdom and United States. The Islamic banking system is legitimate and operates under *sharia*, Islamic law, which prohibits bankers or customers from earning interest on funds. The profits that banks do earn (not specifically called "interest") are used for internal bank projects or are given to charities. Because of *sharia*, Islamic banks typically have excess cash (the interest) that must be allocated.[24] Reputable Islamic banks typically have Sharia Boards[25] who act as a religious and accounting standards committee, making decisions about what financial instruments their bank is able to use under Islamic law.[26] Unfortunately, even with Sharia Boards (who have had their share of scandals[27]), Islamic banks are known for lacking regulatory oversight, and the unclear guidelines for the use of interest make Islamic banks a possible source of funding for Al Qaeda.

Al Qaeda is no different from other terrorist organizations, arms smugglers, and drug traffickers in its use of Islamic banks. As the leading financial institutions of areas of the world rich with oil and natural resources, Islamic banks are the primary channel for investment and transactions into the Middle East and many other parts of the developing world. Therefore, they are networked into sophisticated capital markets around the world. Al Qaeda uses front companies to funnel its finances through this system. For example, the Advice and Reformation Committee, a presumed front for Al Qaeda, received funds in a Barclay's account from correspondent Islamic banks in Sudan, Dubai, and the UAE. The funds in the Barclay's account were then forwarded to operational cells in Western Europe by the signatory on the account, a presumed Al Qaeda associate.[28] To bin Laden's advantage, the correspondent nature of Islamic banks to Western banks allows for transfers that receive less scrutiny. This advantage is also detrimental to international efforts to curb the transfers as international trade relies on banking ties between the Middle East and the Western banks. Condemning the correspondent nature of this banking relationship may hurt the movement of terrorist funds, but it will also significantly impact the ability of large corporations to invest in the region and therefore is likely infeasible.

Hawalas

The hawala system, in the United States and globally, is used by legitimate persons and terrorists to move money around the world without the detection of the global banking system.[29] Similar to the Islamic Banking system, it is governed by Sharia law, but accounts are not kept, nor are financial instruments provided.[30] The legitimate hawala network has not yet been regulated, which makes it an opportune channel for Al Qaeda to use in transferring funds, not only internationally, but into the United States.

Hawala, the Arabic word for "transfer,"[31] refers to an informal global network of individuals who transact cash for their clients, similar to a wiring service. In a hawala, no money transfers are made between traders. Instead, a phone call or fax is sent from one hawaladar to another hawaladar, instructing the latter to dispense cash to the intended recipient. This cash transaction itself is not accounted for, as the hawaladars only hold balances against each other that will eventually be settled through a single wire transfer, movement of precious stones, or other means.[32] The hawala system is an ancient one that is particularly important in parts of the world with weak banking infrastructure and few bank accounts, such as the developing world.

Although Congress tried to regulate the hawala system in the United States in 1994, proposed legislation did not pass. Although the USA Patriot Act requires hawala registration in the United States, strict enforcement may be a difficult task. Executive Order 13224 closed down the Somalia Al Barakaat hawala office in the United States soon after the attacks of September 11. Unfortunately, such enforcement against one of the financial channels of 9/11 is reactive and provides little improvement in proactively preventing terrorist funds from moving through hawalas. Furthermore, even if the United States could put regulations on U.S.-based hawalas, it would be unable to have any affect on the international network of traders. Nevertheless, one of the Treasury Departments' annual money laundering priorities is to "concentrate on informal value transfer systems, such as hawalas, as a means of moving money."[33] Unfortunately, the hawala network can also be used as a money-laundering apparatus, where dirty funds are given to a trader on the inbound side of a transaction and clean funds are dispersed on the outbound side of the transaction.

Financial Regulations Used Against Terrorist Financing

> We will starve terrorists of funding, turn them against each other, rout them out of their safe hiding places, and bring them to justice.
>
> —President George W. Bush, 24 September 2001[34]

The United States has attempted to curb the funding capabilities of Al Qaeda and other terrorist organizations by passing strict money-laundering laws, ensuring tighter regulation of less structured transactions and by giving closer scrutiny to the financial network that Al Qaeda uses to fund operations. Executive Order 13224, the International Emergency Economic Powers Act (IEEPA), and the USA PATRIOT of 2001 (the Patriot Act) have all addressed the issue of terrorist financing. Although results have been significant on U.S. soil, and to a certain extent, European soil, these American regulations have had limited success in constraining Al Qaeda's international network. If the goal was to prevent Al Qaeda financing from entering the U.S. capital markets, then many of the regulations might be considered successful and appropriate. But, as President Bush said on his passage of Executive Order 13224, the war on terrorist financing must "starve" the terrorists and "route them out of their safe hiding places." In this area of regulation, the war on terrorist financing may only achieve success in blocking funds in the United States.

Although U.S. regulations have frozen terrorist assets in U.S. jurisdiction, these regulations will have limited success outside of the U.S. financial system. Eighteen months after the war on terrorist financing was announced,[35] its success must be judged at two levels: blocking Al Qaeda funds in U.S. jurisdictions and blocking Al Qaeda funds in non-U.S. jurisdictions. By 10 June 2002, $112 million had been seized from all terrorist organizations (including Al Qaeda), $34.3 million blocked domestically, and $77.8 million internationally.[36] Unfortunately, the specific magnitude of this action on Al Qaeda is impossible to judge without knowing how much of the funds specified were Al Qaeda's and how big Al Qaeda's financial network was originally.

Not withstanding Executive Order 13224, the IEEPA, improvements in the Financial Crimes Enforcement Network (FinCEN), and new attention to anti-money laundering laws, the UN member nations and some foreign bodies believe that the overall war on Al Qaeda financing has waned in its second year. In a report of the Monitoring Group on Al Qaeda, the United Nations suggested that only $10 million in funds has been blocked since the original $112 million, and that Al Qaeda still raises over $46 million a year from financiers in North Africa, the Middle East, Europe, and Asia.[37] The report also suggests that these funds are often transferred from accounts in developed markets, but once Al Qaeda receives funds it often converts the assets into untraceable gold, precious metals, and gems.

American regulatory action against Al Qaeda finances is effective within the financial system that the government controls. When President Bush signed Executive Order 12334, and invoked the IEEPA, funds in U.S. banks that were linked with terrorist groups or activities were frozen and people under U.S. jurisdiction were prevented from doing business with terrorist organizations and individuals.

The Patriot Act and the National Money Laundering Strategies have realigned the administrative focus on tighter money-laundering reporting requirements. The 2002 National Money Laundering Strategy in particular made "effectiveness of efforts to combat terrorist financing" and "dismantling terrorist financial networks" its top two goals.[38] These actions are a direct turnaround in policy as of the attacks of 9/11. Before the attacks, Treasury Secretary Paul O'Neill and the Bush Administration opposed any and all new upgrades to money-laundering legislation.[39]

The Financial Crimes Enforcement Network (FinCEN) is one of the most practical groups for fighting terrorist financing, especially when the funds come from "clean" sources and are transacted through "non-traditional" systems.[40] FinCEN and banking agencies have put some regulatory pressure on the business community to report possible terrorist financing activities, in the form of Suspicious Activity Reports (SARs). Unfortunately, SARs have a $5,000 threshold, and Al Qaeda can easily transfer smaller sums of money to avoid suspicion, as they did to discretely fund the 9/11 cell.

Although domestic legislation has improved U.S. ability to fight terrorist financing on U.S. soil, organizational barriers have limited the government's success. Tracking terrorist finances is a joint effort between the CIA, FBI, Treasury Department, Justice Department, and elements of the Department of Homeland Security. Most of the asset freezing is done by the Justice Department and the Treasury Department, and yet the Foreign Terrorist Asset Tracking Center, intended to be the lead organization on terrorist financing is housed within the CIA, which has limited overt diplomatic powers. Although the CIA's involvement is important in tracking foreign assets and catching terrorists, the war of terrorist financing requires diplomatic and legal actions that domestic law enforcement and international diplomatic efforts must coordinate. Unfortunately, Treasury is prevented from taking the lead on terrorist financing, even though it must enforce such regulations. This could cause timing problems if Treasury were unable to quickly shut down terrorist bank accounts in U.S. banks.

The U.S. government should be hesitant to apply strenuous regulations to global capital markets, such as New York, because the regulations themselves may hurt the liquid nature of its international transactions. However, freezing U.S.-based bank accounts is one action the Treasury can take without adverse effects on capital markets, although freezing Middle East bank accounts may lead to a significant decrease in Middle Eastern investment accounts in U.S.-controlled banks. Controlling foreign import and export financial flows will also significantly hurt global capital markets in developing countries. More generally, free market principles are often not compatible with the regulatory mechanisms that are intended to protect them from terrorist abuse.

Central bank control of foreign transactions is generally not a favorable long-term economic condition for developing countries. However, such countries also have loosely regulated banking systems that are ideal for Al Qaeda. An appropriate solution requires international private industry participation. Large international companies, especially those involved in developing markets, rely on access to global capital markets. These companies, typically of American or European origin, are often important to the developing economic prosperity. A war on terrorist financing and improvements in developing market banking regulation must put these new companies in a leadership role. Given their U.S. or EU origins, large international companies are often subject to their own country's financial jurisdiction. Therefore, stringent accounting regulations may transcend to developing markets through international investment, rather than local government enforcement. This transfer of regulatory ideals may enable developing markets to continue to grow legitimately rather than turning into financial havens for terrorists. However, the onus of such regulatory change is on the international companies, whose ethical standards are often called into question in the international arena.

Global markets and foreign financial systems are simply not built for scrupulous regulations that can catch terrorist financing. Therefore, shutting down links in Al Qaeda's financial web, outside of developed financial markets like the United States, will be very challenging. Even other developed markets like Europe either suffer from limited financial institutional capabilities (supported by the low volume of Suspicious Activity Reports[41]) or legal systems with "stringent evidentiary standards" to block terrorist assets.[42] Regardless of the problem, international markets do not operate in the same way that the American formal financial system operates. As a result, U.S.-based terrorist financing initiatives will not apply effectively when enforced in other countries. Moreover, limiting liquidity between international capital markets will only increase the cost of capital in such markets, causing economic losses and general discontent for upstanding global investors.

Within the current actions on its war on terrorist financing, the United States has limited regulatory power to impact Al Qaeda's financial network outside of the United States. Even if increasing regulatory constraints from Executive Order 13224, IEEPA, and the Patriot Act create a more vigil environment within U.S. jurisdictions, the United States faces an uphill battle in enforcing regulatory actions in foreign markets. The formal financial system has not benefited in the past from regulatory controls and is unlikely to withstand long periods of slower international transfers. Foreign banking and financial systems are not equipped to build the regulatory environments that are required to fight an effective war on terrorist financing. And, even if regulatory actions were somewhat effective against terrorist transactions domestically and internationally, Al Qaeda has access to a well-established, global, unregulated hawala system. This system is strongly networked with hawaladars in the United States and Europe as well as in the failing states of the developing world, where Al Qaeda recruits, trains, and builds capabilities.

Current U.S. financial regulations used to target terrorist financing are incompatible with the international financial system and foreign banking systems. Unfortunately, even if international systems could follow the U.S. lead and develop self-regulating capabilities that were agreeable across nations, Al Qaeda could still easily transfer funds through the global Islamic banking network and correspondent banks or the unregulated hawala system.

Recommendations for Diplomatic Action in the War on Terrorist Financing

> We will direct every resource at our command to win the war against terrorists, every means of diplomacy, every tool of intelligence, every instrument of law enforcement, every financial influence.
>
> —-President George W. Bush, 24 September 2001

The United States has, to date, failed to strike the heart of Al Qaeda's financial structure: its charities and financier network in the Middle East. Not only has the United States failed to use every diplomatic tool, but it has also failed to use every financial and economic tool at its disposal. Although U.S. efforts domestically to track down and freeze Al Qaeda finances have had some success with the use of the Patriot Act, Executive Order 13224, and the IEEPA, the United States is not using all of the tools at its disposal to eliminate Al Qaeda's international financial base. First, it seems that the Bush administration is hesitant to take further diplomatic and regulatory action in the international community. U.S. work with international bodies such as the Financial Action Task Force (FATF) and the United Nations Counter-Terrorism Committee has not gone far enough. Second, the U.S. has not used all of its tools to impose change in unregulated offshore markets and underregulated markets that are known for terrorist financing. Third, and most important, the United States has begun to lose the diplomatic battle to fight financial networks in the Middle East. More specifically, the United States must put significant diplomatic and economic pressure on Saudi Arabia to stem charity flows to Al Qaeda, the single largest source of Al Qaeda funding.[43]

Working with the International Community

The United States must work closely with international bodies that are able to bridge the differences in financial structures between the United States and foreign allies. An independent task force of the Council on Foreign Relations recommended that the United States create a new international organization dedicated solely to curbing terrorist financing. Their rationale was that such an organization would "drive other countries—whose efforts are woefully inadequate—to greater effectiveness and cooperation."[44] Unfortunately, the United States has begun to lose international allies recently over its policies in Iraq, and gaining credibility and support for a U.S.-led organization could be very difficult. An alternative to this suggestion is the empowerment of the existing FATF, an international body representing 29 governments, established by the G-7 in 1989. The FATF published a report in April 2002 to help financial institutions in detecting terrorist financing.[45] The FATF was also instrumental in "naming and shaming" international money-laundering havens, publishing best practices for regulating charities and suggestions to "bring the hawala system out from the shadows."[46] Given these recent actions and leadership role on key terrorist financing issues, the United States must leverage the international success of the FATF and push them toward an implementation approach of their guidelines. However, the FATF has until now remained a standards body, with limited enforcement power and resources. The organization should change to certify international financial regulators that can be assigned to international banking communities.

Al Qaeda benefits from its ability to wait out political pressures in the international community. In the war on terrorism financing, the gap in European and U.S. relations is widening at the same time as the United States and the United Nations disagree on the effectiveness of the war on terrorist financing. The difference in financial systems is not the only barrier in U.S.-EU relations. As a report by the Watson Institute at Brown University suggests, the EU is significantly ill-equipped to detect and track terrorist transactions. The report states that whereas the U.S. Treasury Office of Foreign Assets Control (OFAC) has more than 100 staff "working full time on implementation of financial sanctions, the Bank of England had a staff of about seven, the French Ministry of Finance has two people working part-time, the German Bundesbank had one, and the European Commission in Brussels had only one person and a half-time assistant."[47] At the same time, a recent report by the United Nations Counter-Terrorism Committee suggested that the war on terrorist financing has had limited results. Rather than collaborate with the United Nations on such measurements, the United States has failed to provide complete information on suspected Al Qaeda members.[48] In summary, the United States must look to the international community and its allies for more support and in return must share intelligence and resources to track Al Qaeda finances and operatives.

Using All of the Financial Tools in the Toolbox

> We put the world's financial institutions on notice: if you do business with terrorists, if you support them or sponsor them, you will not do business with the United States of America.[49]
>
> —President George W. Bush

Under the "special measures" section of the Patriot Act, and sections of the IEEPA, the United States has the ability to cut off foreign countries from U.S. capital markets. This tool is currently being used in a threatening way to force a number of countries to improve their regulatory environment. The "special measures" section has also been evoked by the Secretary of the Treasury against Nauru and until recently Ukraine to cut off their access to American capital markets. Unfortunately, neither of these countries is a source of terrorist finances, although certainly their money-laundering credentials are extensive.[50] Of the current list of countries under scrutiny by the Treasury's Foreign Asset Control Office,[51] certain key Middle East countries are missing, including Egypt, the United Arab Emirates, and Saudi Arabia, whereas poorer states such as Iran and Libya are listed.

According to Lee Wolosky, Chairman of the National Commission on Terrorist Attacks Upon the United States, "Al Qaeda has been particularly attracted to operating in under-regulated jurisdictions, places with limited bank supervision, no anti-money laundering laws, ineffective enforcement institutions, and a culture of no-questions-asked bank secrecy."[52] While foreign investors have a number of choices outside of U.S. capital markets, invoking the "special measures" provision against offshore, unregulated markets in the Cayman Islands and other financial havens would send a clear sign to financial markets on the legitimacy of such offshore markets. In order to push the international community to regulate itself, the United States must deny certain countries and territories access to its capital markets. To flush Al Qaeda funds out of these underregulated markets, the United States must use all of the tools at its disposal, specifically listing countries that are not implementing appropriate levels of terrorist financing regulations.

Saudi Arabian Charities

The diplomatic relationship between the Saudi Royal Family and the U.S. administration has been historically strong, although Islamic extremism in Saudi Arabia and popular anti-American sentiment jeopardizes the strength of the Saudi Royal Family's regime. As the wealthiest state in the Middle East, the home of Osama bin Laden, his Golden Chain, and most of his prominent charities, Saudi Arabia is the source of Al Qaeda's funding that must be addressed directly and continuously.

"Charitable and humanitarian organizations have long been a preferred venue for terrorist financing, with or without the knowledge of the organizations or their donors."[53] Al Qaeda is no exception to this rule. Since 9/11, U.S. and allied authorities have discovered a number of charities that were financing Al Qaeda's operations. However, with the exception of U.S.-based charities, the United States has been powerless within its own right to shut down many of these charities in territories outside of U.S. and NATO command and has had to rely on international cooperation. If the United States is going to have a significant impact on the financial network of Al Qaeda, it must direct efforts at the source of Al Qaeda's finances—Islamic charities in Saudi Arabia. This requires consistent and devoted diplomatic efforts with Saudi Arabia to include FATF inspectors and set up internationally monitored Financial Intelligence Units (FIUs) through the Egmont Group.

Al Qaeda's charity structure is critical to its long-term funding needs. In the Middle East, zakat requires all Muslims to give 2.5% of their income to charitable organizations. Without regulation, Muslims can justify giving such alms to any charitable organizations. The Saudi government recently passed new regulations governing private fundraising and is now encouraging that funds be donated only through established groups operating under the direct patronage of the royal family. Unfortunately, some of these approved groups feature prominently on U.S. terrorist lists.[54] And even if the Saudis shut down these approved groups, "encouraging" Saudis to use established groups is not incentive enough for those that oppose the Saudi Royal Family and the United States. While it is unlikely the Muslims will accept the regulating of zakat without significant public resistance, the Saudi regime must regulate the charity structure itself, while ensuring that innocent Saudis are still encouraged to fulfill their religious duty. New legislation in August 2003 increased penalties for terror financing to up to 15 years in jail and significant fines.[55] However, these penalties are unlikely stringent enough for the Saudi Arabian Monetary Agency to enforce.

The Saudi Royal Family must also seek out those Saudis that are intentionally funding Al Qaeda with law enforcement efforts and a FIU. Unfortunately, "one Saudi official stated that a Saudi organization created to crack down on charities that fund terrorism has been ineffective because its personnel do not want to uncover high-ranking Saudis actively financing such charities."[56] In this case, executive leadership and support is required on both sides of the U.S.-Saudi relationship. If high-ranking Saudis are connected to charities that fund Al Qaeda, the United States must push to have these charities closed and the high-ranking Saudis removed from power and prosecuted. Regardless of its relationship with Saudi Arabia, the United States must also freeze the assets of charities and, when possible, expose guilty Saudi leadership. Although uncovering highlevel scandals within the Saudi government may be somewhat destabilizing in the short term, it is a better long-run alternative than continuing to fund a terrorist organization that is against both the United States and Saudi Arabia.

The United States has known for some time about the Saudi charities that fund and support Al Qaeda. In 1998, Mercy International Relief Organization smuggled weapons into Kenya from Somalia for Al Qaeda,[57] and recent discoveries have shown that Benevolence International Foundation raised funds in America for support of Al Qaeda operatives in Bosnia.[58] Regardless of whether a Saudi charity is smuggling weapons or smuggling money, the Saudi government, with the strong support and enforcement of U.S. diplomatic action must shut these charities down. This is not an action that has been successful under current U.S.-Saudi diplomatic relations. Regardless of close historic ties between the United States and Saudi Arabia, the United States must address Saudi charities, with or without Saudi government support. In the absence of rigid Saudi support, the United States may take a number of financial actions. Such actions may include stringent actions such as adding Saudi Arabia to the list of IEEPA culprits or less stringent action such as limiting foreign direct investment into Saudi Arabia. While the later policy may create dissent in the U.S. business community, it will also force U.S. businesses to put pressure on the Saudi regime.

The United States and Saudi Arabia share many interests in the war against terrorism. President Bush must abide by his words on 7 November 2001: "if you do business with terrorists, if you support them or sponsor them, you will not do business with the United States of America." The United States must use all its diplomatic and economic tools to address the largest source of Al Qaeda's fundraising: charities and financiers in Saudi Arabia.

U.S. diplomacy cannot be underrated in the war on terrorist financing. Al Qaeda's financial pockets are deep outside of the United States, and therefore, the United States must take decisive action with allies in Europe and the Middle East to stop funding to Al Qaeda. In addition, the United States must diplomatically provide options to help countries regulate their financial systems and defend them against Al Qaeda abuses. In situations where countries are unwilling to take decisive and immediate action, at the strategic and tactical level, the United States must leverage economic tools to persuade foreign countries to comply.

Conclusion and Suggestions for Further Research

The war on terrorist financing may be purging terrorist funds from U.S. and European bank accounts, but it is not attacking the source of Al Qaeda's financial network. Al Qaeda's flexibility and financial doctrine make cutting of funds very difficult. This difficulty is compounded by the inability of U.S. regulations to have a significant effect outside of U.S. markets. Therefore, the United States must build more aggressive international coalitions and use all of its regulatory tools to stem the flow of financing to Al Qaeda. This starts with two actions: empowering and backing the FATF to impose terrorist financing regulations internationally and taking decisive action on Saudi Arabia's financial network of charities.

Given the complexity of the international financial system and the numerous foreign banking systems that connect to it, the United States must support an international organization in the global war on terrorist financing. This organization must be responsible for oversight of illegal international transactions, enforcing a progressive schedule of banking oversight in developing countries (working with organizations like the IMF and OECD) and exposing illegal terrorist financial havens around the world. Such an organization requires the full support and financial backing of the U.S. coalition on the war on terrorism.

Unfortunately, taking the war on terrorist financing to Saudi Arabia poses a significant change in U.S. foreign policy. Saudi Arabia's inability to control the financial flows to terrorist groups poses a problem to U.S. national security that must be directly addressed. While U.S. regulators in the Saudi banking system will not be well received, the United States must nonetheless require the Saudi government to invite international banking inspectors in to regulate their financial systems. It is not enough for the Saudi government to request that Muslims give zakat through government charities, it must also regulate and oversee the charity structure.

Although charity oversight will certainly cut off many sources of Al Qaeda's financing, there will always be financiers who are willing to fund Al Qaeda in cash. Whereas tighter regulation and banking oversight will fix structural problems, no regulations will prevent the basic smuggling of cash and the existence of financiers sympathetic to Al Qaeda's cause. Therefore, the United States must continue to support the fighting of financial networks as part of the larger war on terrorism with military, political, and social capabilities.

Terrorist financial sources have evolved significantly from the days of state-based terrorist financing. In this relatively new field of research, Al Qaeda represents just one example of how non-state actors fund global operations. As such, there are a number of further research topics on fighting terrorist financing and fighting Al Qaeda's network structure. The United States has only started to uncover the network of financiers behind Al Qaeda and other international terrorist organizations such as Hezbollah, a topic that will grow as more evidence is uncovered. While terrorist financing continues to evolve, so does the international financial system, as regulations change and markets increase their level of integration. Limited research has looked at how the international financial systems are inefficient in their tracking of terrorist financing. In addition, balancing the development of economic prosperity with preventing terrorist abuses of the system is a topic that development and security organizations must continue to study. Looking in particular at Al Qaeda, further research should look at preemptive tools to identify economically strong non-state actors that threaten U.S. national security. While there were many signs of the attacks on 9/11, in hindsight, the financial trail of Al Qaeda was one indication of the nature of their threat on U.S. soil that might have been exposed yet failed to translate into financial regulation against the channels that funded the World Trade Center attack in 1993.

The war on Al Qaeda's financial network is certainly not over. Al Qaeda is able to leverage a number of financial systems to hide funds from U.S. and allied governments as well as leverage an underregulated base of Islamic charities for funding. A decisive victory in the war on terrorist financing requires a more aggressive U.S. foreign policy on issues of finance. While U.S. political and military policy has directly targeted threats to national security, the United States has not adequately addressed the financial networks that support international terrorist groups like Al Qaeda.

Notes

1. Congress. Senate. Committee on Banking, Housing, and Urban Affairs, Subcommittee on International Trade and Finance, *Hawala and Underground Terrorist Financing Mechanisms: Hearing before the Subcommittee on International Trade and Finance.* 107th Congress., 1st sess., 14 November 2001.
2. Rohan Gunartna, *Inside Al Qaeda: Global Network of Terror* (New York: Columbia University Press, 2002), p. 54.
3. R. T. Naylor, *Wages of Crime: Black Markets, Illegal Finance, and the Underworld Economy* (Ithaca: Cornell University Press, 2002), p. 288.
4. Financial Action Task Force on Money Laundering, "Guidance for Financial Institutions in Detecting Terrorist Financing," April 2002; available at (http://www.fatf-gafi.org/TerFinance_en.htm).
5. Gunaratna, *Inside Al Qaeda,* 57.
6. Ibid., p. 61.
7. Susan Schmidt and Douglas Farah, "Al Qaeda's New Leaders; Six Militants Emerge from Ranks to Fill Void," *The Washington Post,* 29 October 2002, p. A01.
8. "Government's Evidentiary Proffer Supporting the Admissibility of Co-Conspirator Statements," *United States of America v. Ennam Arnaout.* United States District Court Northern District of Illinois, Eastern Division. Case # 02 CR 892. 31 January 2003.
9. "Declaration of Jihad Against the Country's Tyrants, Military Series," recovered by Manchester Police from home of Nazihal Wadih Raghie, 10 May 2000, p. 66. www.usdoj.gov/ag/trainingmanuel.htm.
10. Ibid., p. 22
11. Mark Hubard, "Bankrolling bin Laden," *The Financial Times,* 20 November 2001, p. 10.
12. Gunaratna, *Inside Al Qaeda,* 64.
13. Ibid., p. 65.
14. Douglas Farah, "Report Says Africans Harbored Al Qaeda; Terror Assets Hidden in Gem-Buying Spree," *The Washington Post,* 29 December 2002, p. A01.
15. Judith Miller and Jeff Gerth, "Trade in Honey is Said to Provide Money and Cover for Bin Laden," *The New York Times,* 11 October 2001, p. A01.
16. Council on Foreign Relations, "Terrorism Q&A," available at (http://www.terrorismanswers.com/responses/money.htm).
17. Gunaratna, *Inside Al Qaeda,* 104.
18. "Government's Evidentiary Proffer Supporting the Admissibility of Co-Conspirator Statements," p. 30.
19. U.S. Congress. House. Committee on Financial Services, Subcommittee on Oversight and Investigations, *Progress since 9/11: The Effectiveness of U.S. Anti-Terrorist Financing Efforts,* 108th Cong. 1st sess., 11 March 2003.
20. Office of Public Affairs, United States Treasury Department, "Treasury Department Statement on the Designation of Wa'el Hamza Julidan." 6 September 2002. Document #PO-3397.
21. "Government's Evidentiary Proffer Supporting the Admissibility of Co-Conspirator Statements," pp. 65-74.
22. Congress. Senate. Committee on Banking, Housing, and Urban Affairs, Subcommitee on International Trade and Finance, *Hawala and Underground Terrorist Financing Mechanisms: Hearing before the Subcommittee on International Trade and Finance.* 107th Cong., 1st sess., 14 November 2001.
23. U.S. General Accounting Office, *Terrorist Financing: U.S. Agencies Should Systematically Assess Terrorists' Use of Alternative Financing Mechanisms*, United States General Accounting Office, November 2003, GAO-04-163, p. 19.
24. Ibrahim Warde, *Islamic Finance in the Global Economy* (Edinburgh: Edinburgh University Press, 2000), p. 144.
25. Reputable Islamic banks typically are part of the International Association of Islamic Banks (IAIB)
26. Warde, *Islamic Finance in the Global Economy,* p. 227.
27. Ibid., p. 227.
28. Loretta Napoleoni, *Modern Jihad: Tracing the Dollars behind the Terror Networks* (Sterling, VA: Pluto Press, 2003), p. 126.
29. Warde, *Islamic Finance in the Global Economy,* p. 227.
30. Napoleoni, *Modern Jihad,* p. 125

31. Hawala is also translated as "trust," but according to Ibrahim Warde, an Islamic banking scholar, the word actually means "transfer" in Arabic.
32. U.S. General Accounting Office, *Terrorist Financing,* p. 18.
33. National Money Laundering Strategy, July 2002, p. 21.
34. Fact Sheet on Terrorist Financing Executive Order, 24 September 2001, available at (http://www.whitehouse.gov/news/releases/2001/09/print/20010924-2.htm).
35. President George W. Bush announced the war on terrorist financing with the passage of Executive Order 13224 on 24 September 2001.
36. National Money Laundering Strategy, July 2002, p. 18.
37. Colum Lynch, "War on Al Qaeda Funds Stalled; Network 'Fit and Well,' Ready to Strike, Draft of U.N. Report Says," *The Washington Post,* 29 August 2002, p. A01.
38. National Money Laundering Strategy, July 2002, p. iii.
39. Ibrahim Warde, "The War on Terrorist Financing," Lecture at the Fletcher School of Law and Diplomacy, Tufts University, 7 April 2003.
40. In the National Money Laundering Strategy, The Department of Treasury and Department of Justice define "Non-traditional" systems as a family of monetary remittance systems that provide for the transfer of value outside of the regulated financial industry. National Money Laundering Strategy, July 2002, p. 21.
41. Maurice R. Greenberg (Chair), "Terrorist Financing: Report of an Independent Task Force Sponsored by the Council on Foreign Relations," *Council on Foreign Relations,* New York, October 2002, p. 21.
42. Ibid.
43. U.S. Congress. House. Committee on Financial Services, Subcommittee on Oversight and Investigations, *Progress since 9/11.*
44. Greenberg, "Terrorist Financing," p. 5.
45. Financial Action Task Force on Money Laundering, "Guidance for Financial Institutions in Detecting Terrorist Financing," April 2002; available at (http://www.fatf-gafi.org/TerFinance_en.htm).
46. Lee Wolosky, *Public Hearing on the National Commission on Terrorist Attacks Upon the United States,* 1 April 2003 available at (http://www.9-11commission.gov/hearings/hearing1/witness_wolosky.htm).
47. Greenberg, "Terrorist Financing," p. 22.
48. Lynch, "War on Al Qaeda Funds Stalled," p. A01.
49. Remarks of President George W. Bush, 7 November 2001.
50. Wolosky, *Public Hearing on the National Commission on Terrorist Attacks Upon the United States.*
51. A list of countries currently under scrutiny can be found at (http://www.ustreas.gov/ offices/enforcement/ofac/sanctions/index.htm).
52. Wolosky, *Public Hearing on the National Commission on Terrorist Attacks Upon the United States.*
53. Matthew Levitt, *The Network of Terrorist Financing,* Washington Institute, 15 August 2002, available at (http://www.washingtoninstitute.org/media/levitt/levitt080102.htm).
54. Ibid.
55. Royal Embassy of Saudi Arabia, *Initiatives and Actions Taken by the Kingdom of Saudi Arabia in the War on Terrorism,* Royal Embassy of Saudi Arabia, Washington, DC, September 2003, available at (http://www.saudiembassy.net), p. 9.
56. Levitt, *The Network of Terrorist Financing.*
57. Levitt, *The Network of Terrorist Financing.*
58. "Government's Evidentiary Proffer Supporting the Admissibility of Co-Conspirator Statements," pp. 65-74.

Chapter 8

Strategies and Approaches for Combating Terrorism

General Wayne A. Downing (retired) argues that the only way to defeat the terrorists is through a multinational and multilateral approach. In his article, he states that "the United States has unsought opportunities to shape the future. The task is great: conduct a worldwide global war on terrorism with complex, diverse campaigns with old allies and new friends. We must seize opportunities to do things better, with ingenuity, innovation and the strength of the American people. Our actions will likely set the conditions for the remainder of the twenty-first century." He argues that we must focus our national strategy so that we can better combat the threats at hand, especially given the complicating factors such as the Iraq war, globalization, and continued U.S. presence around the world.

Brigadier General Russell Howard (ret.) argues that the Bush administration—or any administration—has no choice but to have a preemptive military doctrine when addressing terrorists who are transnational, non-state actors who possess weapons of mass destruction. According to Howard, Westphalian rules don't apply when dealing with transnational, non-state actors. The normal means of influence in dealing with states—diplomatic, economic, and military—are not applicable when dealing with al Qaeda or any other terrorist group that owes no allegiance to a state.

Barry Posen advocates for a grand strategy to combat terrorism. "The United States faces a long war against a small, elusive, and dangerous foe," he writes. Posen defines the adversary, maps the goals and structure and depth of their motives: "It seeks to expel the most powerful state in history from a part of the world that has been central to U.S. foreign policy ... and it intends to do so without a standing military.... It will seek to kill Americans so long as the United States does not give in to its demands," says Posen. The author advocates for a long-term, comprehensive strategy in dealing with the group. The effort he outlines will require discipline and determination and significant change in our national security strategy.

Paul Pillar delves into these issues even deeper with an article addressing counterterrorism in a post–al Qaeda environment. He, like others in this volume, describes the current al Qaeda threat as less of an organization and more of an ideological threat. This shift from organization to ideology presents distinctly different problems than the United States and other Western democracies have faced thus far in the conflict against terrorism. Governments like to fight against defined enemies, be they other states or non-state actors. In 2005, though, the threat from al Qaeda is compounded by the lack of organizational structure, hierarchy, or defined network.

This chapter concludes with an article by Steven Simon and Jeff Martini that explores the most critical issue raised in this volume—the need to deny al Qaeda its appeal. Without the development of a comprehensive strategy to accomplish this critical goal through the reordering of the U.S. national security norms, the al Qaeda derivative organizations will continue to regenerate and continue to attack U.S. interests.

General (Retired) Wayne A. Downing, 2005

The Global War on Terrorism: Re-Focusing the National Strategy

In mid-2003, I contributed a chapter to *Defeating Terrorism* with a title similar to this chapter: "The Global War on Terrorism: Focusing the National Strategy."[1] In that chapter, I sought to describe the new realities of terrorism and the U.S. strategy for the so-called global war on terrorism as conceived in America in the year following 9/11.[2] I also summarized the challenges of the future, concluding:

> [O]ur successes have led the enemy to shift attacks to other geographic regions against softer targets which have killed and injured Americans and our friends. The war in Iraq did not eliminate the threat. In fact, it may have energized and coalesced our enemies. More terrorist attacks at home and abroad are likely and [weapons of mass destruction] will be employed if available. Time does not appear to be on our side. As the scope and intensity of the conflict increases, it is clear that the U.S. must drive a wedge between the extremists and the rest of the Islamic world before Osama bin Laden and company persuade Muslims that the U.S. is the common enemy and to join the fight. The failure to stabilize both Afghanistan and Iraq undermines the perception of U.S. power and resolve.[3]

Four years have passed since 9/11, and 2 years have gone by since I wrote the above-quoted passage. Yet the challenges identified therein still exist, while challenges not fully appreciated in 2003 have become known. Indeed, the ongoing worldwide struggle against terrorists and their support structure has provided the U.S. extensive knowledge about the enemy and its intentions, as well as insights into America's own strengths and weaknesses. This knowledge and these insights must be used to update the National Strategy for Combating Terrorism, which is the focus of this chapter.

The chapter is organized in two general sections. The first part identifies the primary insights America has gained over the past 4 years in terms of both the threats encompassed by global terrorism and the appropriate methods for combating those threats. The remainder of the chapter then employs these insights in recommending a series of actions that the United States must take to reinvigorate and refocus international and national efforts to combat the insidious threats facing the United States today.[4]

Part One: Insights and Lessons Since 9/11

The True Threat: Sunni Salafist Islam

The most significant insight gained since 9/11 is that the people who attacked the United States on 9/11 and their supporters are more than terrorists; they are revolutionaries who use terrorism among other tactics to conduct a worldwide insurgency. The purpose of this insurgency is political: to transform the entire Islamic world into a group of fundamentalist Islamic states in the mold of the ninth-and tenth-century caliphates, or —in twenty-first-century terminology—Taliban-like governments.[5] The groups executing the politically motivated insurgency fall under the banner of Salafist extremists, a term describing those who justify holy war (Jihad) and appeal to other Muslims through ancient interpretations of the Koran and the life and writings of the Prophet, Mohammed.

In order to create their envisioned new world order, Sunni Salafist groups —including al Qaeda —must actively oppose the United States and our allies (broadly, "the West"), as we are the stabilizing anchor of the world they intend to change, and the principal supporters of the regimes they aim to depose.[6] More specifically, the goals of al Qaeda and other semi-autonomous Sunni Salafist franchises include:

- the elimination of U.S./Western presence in the Arabian Gulf and access to its oil;
- the lessening—and eventual elimination—of American and Western influence in the Islamic world;
- the promotion of conflict between Islam and the West; and the destabilization—and ultimate toppling of—corrupt and apostate Islamic regimes.[7]

The U.S. Interagency Process Is Broken and Must Be Fixed

A second major insight is that there are significant weaknesses in the interagency system responsible for coordinating the efforts of the vast American federal bureaucracy. In the context of the so-called war on terror, this process has almost been moribund at times due to a lack of interagency consensus and direction. A primary source of the dysfunction is that the methods and goals of the U.S. Department of Defense have largely dominated the interagency system at the expense of the other departments. At the same time, the State Department has been uncharacteristically passive in regard to the nation's efforts to combat terrorism (although this may be changing under the leadership of the new secretary of state, Condoleezza Rice). The result is that the vast potential of the United States to effectively counter the threats posed by global terrorism has not been realized.

The National Strategy: A Progress Report

In addition to the insights identified above, the experience of the past 4 years has provided important intelligence on the effectiveness of the U.S. National Strategy for Combating Terrorism ("National Strategy") developed by the Bush administration following 9/11. The goals of the National Strategy are organized around the "4-D strategy": to defend, defeat, deny, and diminish global terrorism (Figure 1). The nation's progress in achieving these goals has received mixed reviews to-date.

We have been fairly successful in accomplishing the first goal of the 4-D National Strategy: defending U.S. citizens and interests at home and abroad. However, the U.S. homeland is definitely not secure—a fact aptly demonstrated when focus turned to security in the nation's public transportation system following the recent attacks in London on 7/7.

The United States has also had fair success in goal two of the National Strategy: defeating and destroying terrorist organizations. In close cooperation with select allies, the United States has rooted out numerous insurgent cells overseas, and thus far countered the proliferation of dangerous weapons.[8] Importantly, the aim to defeat terrorist organizations has received broad international support. After 9/11, NATO

Figure 1: Fundamental Goals of the 4 D's

- Defend U.S. citizens and interests at home and abroad
- Defeat/destroy terrorist organizations
- Deny sanctuary and support to terrorist organizations
- Dimish the underlying causes

Source: *National Strategy for Combating Terrorism,* February 2003

invoked Article V of the collective defense organization's treaty, which states, in part, "an armed attack against one or more [NATO members] shall be considered an attack against them all." Non-NATO member Australia invoked Article IV of the ANZUS treaty among Australia, New Zealand, and the United States., with similar implications. Over 37 nations have provided military, law enforcement, intelligence, or humanitarian support in America's declared global war on terror.[9]

As a result of this broad support and cooperation toward defeating terrorism, many highly successful (and often unpublicized) operations have taken place overseas, conducted by friendly host-nation police, military, and intelligence organizations supported by small teams of Americans. Few of these operations, except the most newsworthy, have been revealed.[10] Yet, the operations have succeeded in decimating the original al Qaeda by eliminating 70 percent of the organization's initial leadership, and killing, arresting, and/or incarcerating thousands of al Qaeda members, including, most recently, its third-ranking leader, Abu Faraj al-Libbi.[11] Another undeniable success of the global effort to defeat terrorism was the outing of the Taliban from Afghanistan under Operation Enduring Freedom, which helped secure an elected Afghani government that has made great progress toward stable, democratic rule and the establishment of law and order.

The bad news is that the Sunni Salafist insurgents have proven to be remarkably resilient. New groups have emerged, and a message of universal Jihad against the West has been effectively trumpeted by ingenious use of the Internet and other means of mass communication.

The third goal of combating terrorism, as stated in the National Strategy, is to deny terrorist groups sanctuary and support from other nations. As the National Strategy makes clear, the United States "has a long memory and is committed to holding terrorists and those who harbor them accountable for past crimes."[12] Yet while the United States has partially achieved this goal, future efforts will demand a higher level of allied cooperation and renewed commitment from those countries helping us in the past. For example, eliminating sanctuary and support will require the establishment of an international standard of accountability based on current international counterterrorism conventions and protocols, UN Security Council Resolution 1373, and the recognition and enforcement of international rights to collective and self-defense. An effective denial of support also requires combined intelligence and coordinated law enforcement efforts, sanctions against nations that sponsor terrorism, assistance to nations that lack national security resources, and/or the will to oppose the terrorists. Indeed, the experience of Afghanistan under the Taliban clearly established that we can no longer ignore these so-called uncontrolled areas in Muslim Africa, Southeast Asia, and Central Asia because they can become insurgent base areas.

Obviously, support from the host countries is critical to the defeat and deny goals of the National Strategy, but this help has not been consistent. For the first six to nine months after 9/11, the United States enjoyed a high level of international empathy and support from many nations, especially in Europe. Unfortunately, the broad commitment expressed by other nations in the aftermath of the 2001 tragedy has since deteriorated significantly, due in part to an international perception that the United States is waging an unilateral struggle without regard to the sensibilities and prerogatives of other nation states. The 2003 invasion of Iraq and subsequent occupation of the country have exacerbated international discontent with United States policies, particularly in the Islamic world. The United States must do much more to foster greater international support and understanding for its goals.

The United States has made little, if any, progress in achieving its fourth goal: diminishing the causes of terrorism. In fact, perhaps the opposite has occurred. Since 9/11, groups opposed to what they view as unwarranted American action, and simultaneously sympathetic to al Qaeda's ideology, have developed worldwide. A Spanish counterterrorism official explained the phenomenon as follows:

> Al Qaeda has four different networks . . . [F]irst, there is the original network, the one that committed 9/11, which uses its own resources and people it has recruited and trained. Then, there is the ad-hoc terrorist network, consisting of franchise organizations that Al Qaeda created—often to replace ones that weren't bloody enough—in countries such as the Philippines, Jordan, and Algeria. A third network is "more subtle, a strategic union of like-minded companies." The final network, to which the U.S. should pay the closest attention, is the network of "imitators, emulators, who are ideologically aligned with Al Qaeda but are less tied to it financially."[13]

The latter type of network operates not only in the Islamic world and places such as Iraq, where the establishment of law and order is still in progress, but also in the West, where permissive human civil rights laws impede local law enforcement and intelligence agencies' actions against the insurgents.

The noble and daring effort to establish a democratic state in Iraq has created great challenges and opportunities in terms of diminishing terrorist activity. The prime challenge created by the U.S. efforts in Iraq, as summarized by CIA Director Porter Goss, is that Iraq is now a magnet for Jihadists.[14] The former head of the CIA bin Laden unit, Michael Scheuer, is even more forceful in identifying this challenge, saying"[t]here's no bigger gift we could have given to Osama bin Laden than the invasion of Iraq."[15] At the same time, the director of Georgetown's Security Studies Program and Center for Peace and Security Studies, Daniel Byman, explains, the United States and its allies have "failed to capture al-Qaeda's recuperative capacity, its relationships with other groups, and its broader appeal in the Muslim world."[16]

Yet, while still a serious challenge to the United States and its coalition partners, Iraq also presents an opportunity for the very reason that the struggle in that country is a matter of life and death for the Salafists. An Islamic democracy—specifically, a Shia Islamic democracy—is an apostasy to these radicals that they cannot accept; a state that they cannot accept. Accordingly, they will fight to the death. If the United States and its coalition allies can assist the duly elected Iraqi government in providing the security necessary to allow the political, economic, and social processes of the new State to take place, it will be a strategic victory of the first magnitude and a resounding defeat for the insurgents.

Part Two: Re-focus the National Strategy

The remainder of this chapter sets forth a series of actions the United States should take to re-focus the National Strategy as a result of the lessons learned over the past 4 years. These changes are necessary if the United States and its allies are to be successful in this long-term conflict.

Acknowledge That the United States and the World Face a Global Insurgency, not a Global Outbreak of Terrorism

The most fundamental change required to make the National Strategy successful is that the United States must recognize and articulate the true nature of this conflict. We are not engaged in a "global war on terrorism"; the United States and the world are challenged by a worldwide insurgency. Terrorism is a tactic used by the Salafist insurgents to attain their strategic goals, which are political in nature. To concentrate only on the tactics—as opposed to the strategic goals—will lead to series of local engagements that may well lose the war.[17]

The U.S. government must therefore redefine the struggle not as a "global war on terrorism," but as a global counterinsurgency campaign.[18] This campaign must not just eliminate insurgents, but must also achieve other, subtler and more difficult, goals.[19] These aims include driving a wedge between the Salafist extremist groups and their potential supporters. In addition, we must connect not only target populations to their legitimate governments, but the rest of the world to collective counterinsurgency objectives that support the emergence of democratic, stable governments in the Islamic world and peaceful, integrated Muslim expatriate communities living in the West.[20]

The United States will have to be very skillful as it describes the nature of the insurgency to avoid the potential appearance of appearing anti-Islam and inadvertently facilitating one of al Qaeda's aims, a war between Islam and the West. Public diplomacy will be critical in informing the world of the true nature and danger of the threat.

The National Strategy will itself need clarification to further the proper understanding—both within the United States and abroad—of this struggle. At present, the National Strategy identifies the intent of the United States in this conflict as follows (Figure 2):

> The intent of our national strategy is to stop terrorist attacks against the United States, its citizens, its interests, and our friends and allies around the world and ultimately to create an international environment inhospitable to terrorists and all those who support them.[21]

This statement and the goals—the 4 Ds, discussed earlier—must reflect our newly discovered understanding of the Sunni Salafist insurgent enemy. Substituting "insurgent" for "terrorist" and "global counterinsurgency campaign" for "global war on terrorism" in the strategy will not be enough. The execution of the strategy must follow through and pursue all of the 4 Ds simultaneously with emphasis on "diminish" and special attention to the political, economic, and social dimensions of the worldwide counterinsurgency campaign. The U.S. military will not win this war alone.

Figure 2: Intent of the Global War on Terrorism

- Stop terrorist attacks against the United States, our interests, friends, and allies around the world
- Ultimately, create an international environment that is inhospitable to terrorists and those who support them

Fix the U.S. Interagency System: It Does not Work!

The power of the U.S. federal government is immense. There is practically no single task it cannot accomplish. The challenge, therefore, is to get all the diverse elements of the federal government to work in concert to achieve national goals. This is difficult because the government is constituted by a large and complex bureaucracy. While not intrinsically evil, bureaucracies can become dysfunctional when departments work for their own departmental goals (and jealously guard their departmental rice bowls) at the expense of identified national objectives.

Unfortunately, internal government competition hamstrings the current struggle against the Salafist insurgents. Immediately following 9/11, there was a rare period of cooperation and sacrifice among various relevant U.S. agencies, especially at the working level in Washington and in the field. This period did not last long. Within nine months, familiar squabbles between competing government factions began anew. In some cases, the personalities of key cabinet officials and their personal desires to dominate the interagency process exacerbated long-standing issues. Meanwhile, Congress—especially those members and committees involved in authorizations and appropriations—did little to help resolve these competitions. To the contrary, some in the Congress, operating behind the scenes through their oversight roles, protected their own committee turf by supporting certain Executive Branch entities at the expense of others.

It is clear that the United States must ameliorate this internal competition and focus the federal government on the task at hand. The National Strategy, the 9/11 Commission Report, and the Robb/Silberman Report each discusses the necessity of applying all elements of national power in a harmonious and coherent manner.[22] Obviously, this goal cannot be realized if one element of the U.S. government expects to dominate the others. For example, the military, a blunt instrument, is not the long-term answer to countering the Islamist insurgency. Counterinsurgency campaigns are by essence political struggles and necessitate the application of all elements of national power—especially diplomacy and information, along with intelligence, law enforcement, and financial/economic power and policies.[23] Cooperation with other governments will be crucial, as the United States cannot do this unilaterally. This means the State Department must play a crucial and key role.

The United States must continue to use the military decisively into the near future, but not as the lead element in the global counterinsurgency campaign. The front line in this conflict consists of U.S. diplomats, intelligence operatives, information specialists, and law enforcement agents working in close coordination with U.S. allies overseas. The

U.S. military can play a key role in training and advising host countries' security forces and in denying sanctuaries when political measures fail. The military can also reinforce host nation security forces when invited and, in rare cases, intervene directly to support U.S. agencies when required. For example, special operations forces can conduct surgical raids, especially in uncontrolled regions, to capture or kill high-value targets and destroy training camps and base areas.

It is clear that reforms are needed to enable these diverse elements of the United States to work together for the common good.[24] Many actions are underway toward achieving such reform—some more successful than others. Reorganization, or "moving the deck chairs," is one approach popular inside the Beltway. The creation of the Department of Homeland Security and the recent appointment of a Director of National Intelligence are monumental undertakings and will take years to realize. The White House has just recently announced a series of reforms and initiatives in response to the Weapons of Mass Destruction ("WMD") Report. The problem with all of these important changes is that they appear uncoordinated among the various relevant arms of the federal government. In sum, there is no systemic government approach to the challenge of creating a systematic government approach to the global insurgency.

Some are now calling for the Congress to create such a master plan and streamline the entire federal government with legislation akin to the 1986 Goldwater-Nichols legislation used to reform the U.S. Department of Defense. Of course, Goldwater-Nichols did not just happen; it took several years to debate and craft this fundamental change to the Defense Department. This country is at war, and time may not be available to enact such legislation. An alternative approach would be for the Bush administration to take the initiative by exercising the powers of the Executive Branch rather than waiting for legislation. This was the approach taken by President Truman in enacting the 1947 National Security Act, which effected major reforms reflecting the lessons learned from WW II. The President could create an empowered National Security Council Staff or some other interagency task force with operational (as opposed to merely coordination) responsibilities for hands-on management of this struggle. In order for this approach to be effective, the newly empowered body—which could perhaps be led by the vice president—must have direct access to the president.[25] Ignoring the current situation and allowing this interagency "gridlock" to persist could well turn out to be a "war loser."

Win the War of Ideas

To date, U.S. public diplomacy efforts to combat insurgents overseas have been generally unsuccessful.[26] The initial wave of support enjoyed by the U.S. following the 9/11 attacks was by no means universal. From September 14 to 17, 2001, Gallup surveyed individuals in 14 foreign countries on whether they thought that the United States should attack the country (or countries) serving as a base for the 9/11 terrorists "once the identity of the terrorists is known." According to the poll's results, "well over half of the respondents in almost all the countries supported extradition and trial for suspected terrorists," but "only Israel and India supported a military attack."[27] Since the beginning of the current war in Iraq, support for U.S. policy abroad has eroded even further. America is failing to get its message across, nowhere more so than in the Islamic world and on the Arab street. "The facts," states one writer, "sad but stubborn, are that hatred of the United States in the Muslim world is greater today than ever before, and shows no sign of diminishing; and that Washington's efforts to counter it have had little success."[28] Muslims on the whole perceive actions taken by the United States in the conduct of the global counterinsurgency campaign as anti-Islamic, and that perception fuels the Jihad by creating sympathy and recruits.

U.S. foreign policy angers many Muslim populations.[29] Surveys conducted by the University of Jordan's Center for Strategic Studies in Jordan, Syria, Lebanon, Egypt, and the Palestinian territories show that it is U.S. regional policies—not a clash of values, religion, or the "al Jazeera factor"—that influence anti-American attitudes in the Middle East. According to a Pew Center survey, since the Iraq war, "many Muslims, even in countries with reasonably good relations with the United States, such as Nigeria, Indonesia and Pakistan, fear that the United States may attack them."[30] Al Qaeda clearly focuses on this source of discontent. According to Michael Scheuer, Osama bin Laden has "turned Clausewitz on his head." "The biggest fear Al Qaeda has, besides fighting a superpower," he says, "is that that superpower will somehow change some of the policies that have been in place for the last 20 years."[31]

Recognizing that the foreign audience differs vastly from the audience at home, the United States must transmit believable, persuasive, and explicit messages beyond the current themes of "freedom is on the march," and we are opposed by "freedom-haters" and "evil-doers." The United States and our allies must convince the Islamic people (and the world) that we support political reform and the reduction of poverty while promoting human rights and education. The United States must assist host countries to regain the moral high ground from the Islamists, discredit their tactics, and persuade the majority Islamic-fence sitters to oppose the Islamist agenda.

There are overlapping mutual interests between the Islamic democracies and the United States. Many Islamic governments recognize that there is no fundamental dichotomy between democracy and Islam. Bangladesh, Kuwait, Jordan, Turkey, Pakistan, Malaysia, Egypt, Indonesia, Tunisia, Algeria, and Nigeria all identify themselves as "democratic" political systems as opposed to "Islamic."[32] These democratic states are, as we have seen, unacceptable to the Salafists who have declared democracy an apostasy that must be ruthlessly exterminated.[33] This dichotomy must be exploited by American diplomacy.

Scientific and technological collaboration represents another potential area of mutual agreement since these elements of "progress" enjoy unprecedented acceptance among Muslims abroad. According to one study, "in the Islamic world, widespread hostility to the West results partly from the perception that people there are disconnected from progress that is being made elsewhere, and from a sense of dependence on foreign, more prosperous countries."[34] A 2004 Arab American Institute/Zogby International survey found that 90 percent of those surveyed in Morocco, 83 percent in Jordan, 52 percent in Lebanon, and 84 percent in the United Arab Emirates view U.S. science and technology favorably. According to the same study, these countries have a profoundly unfavorable view towards U.S. terrorism policy—13 percent, 21 percent, 10 percent, and 9 percent, respectively.[35] Because 40 percent of the populations in the countries surveyed connected science and technology with their attitudes toward the United States., one may reasonably assume that a strong effort to emphasize U.S.-Muslim scientific cooperation on the basis of equals would positively impact the perception of the United States on the Muslim street.[36]

Using themes like scientific cooperation with Islamic states depends on a coordinated campaign of public diplomacy. This campaign has yet to take shape. The White

House established the Office of Global Communications (OGC) in January 2003. To date, the OGC has not developed an overarching strategy, nor has it produced the guidance necessary to "promote the effective coordination of U.S. public diplomacy efforts."[37] The National Security Council's Strategic Communications Policy Coordinating Committee (established in September 2002) failed to gain consensus on a national communications strategy and was disbanded in 2003. Other efforts, such as the Muslim World Outreach Policy Coordinating Committee (tasked by the National Security Council to develop "strategic and tactical plans to help guide and coordinate U.S. communications with Muslims around the world") remain underway, yet have thus far proved unsuccessful.[38]

According to the U.S. Government Accountability Office (GAO), "the absence of a national strategy complicates the task of conveying consistent messages and thus achieving mutually reinforcing benefits." Because no strategy has come down from the U.S. Executive Branch, messages to the Muslim world lack consistency and are prone to misinterpretation, lessening the "efficiency and effectiveness of government wide public diplomacy efforts."[39] State Department and USAID officials interviewed by the U.S. GAO echo the findings of the Defense Science Board, which issued a report stating that the OCG has "evolved into a second-tier organization devoted principally to tactical public affairs coordination."[40] Instead of formulating a strategy, looking at methods of message delivery, ensuring message consistency, and coordinating teams of communicators, OCG prepares "message briefs" and "holds conference calls."[41]

There have been some successes. The American-funded Al Iraqiya network shows a popular prime-time show called "Terrorism in the Grip of Justice." On air for less than a year but already a major hit throughout Iraq, the show attempts to counter the vision of the fierce, brave, and pure insurgent fighter as promoted by Salafist propaganda videos and Web sites by showing imagery of captured insurgents. As vividly described by the journalist Peter Maass:

> [T]he insurgents, or suspected insurgents . . . come off as cowardly lowlifes who kill for money rather than patriotism or Allah. They tremble on camera, stumble over their words, and look at the ground as they confess to everything from contract murders to sodomy. The program's clear message is that there is now a force more powerful than the insurgency: the Iraqi government. . . .[42]

While extending American values and ideals through "muppet diplomacy" has its place in the war of ideas, shows like "Terrorism in the Grip of Justice" put an indigenous face on global counterinsurgency efforts, serving to more strongly connect potentially disenfranchised citizens with their governments while discrediting extremism.

Clearly, making progress in the war of ideas entails influencing education at the earliest level. In Uganda, the U.S. embassy built three Islamic elementary schools, and in the primarily Muslim countries in the Horn of Africa, the U.S. military builds public schools and strengthens local infrastructure in areas where intelligence has uncovered proposed religious schools. In Pakistan, where 500,000 people attend *madrassahs*, USAID very quietly funds and trains madrassah teachers in science, math, civics, and health. In math and science, where Arab countries lag behind the rest of the world, the United States could contribute significant resources to help reduce the hegemony of religion-based curricula, without appearing to wield political influence.[43]

The United Nations Development Programme (UNDP) *Arab Human Development Report 2004* gives the following insight into the role played by education in Arab societies:

> Once children enter school, they find an educational institution, curricula, teaching and evaluation methods which tend to rely on dictation and instill submissiveness. This learning environment does not permit free dialogue and active exploration and consequently does not open up the doors to freedom of thought and criticism. On the contrary, it weakens the capacity to hold opposing viewpoints and to think outside the box. Its societal function is the reproduction of control in Arab societies.[44]

The president's new undersecretary for public diplomacy and public affairs, long time presidential adviser Karen Hughes, must reform the Executive Branch's programs.[45] As suggested by Bruce Hoffman, the United States must better exploit existing media outlets in the Arab world, such as Al-Jazeera and Al-Arabiya, to "directly challenge and counter the misperceptions that they foster."[46] Overall, to incorporate the war of ideas fully into the global counterinsurgency campaign, the Executive Branch must develop a coordinated strategic information strategy prioritizing education and media aimed specifically to discredit extremism, preferably using Arab media outlets, avoiding over -U.S. sponsorship as appropriate.[47] The United States must also develop a sophisticated campaign unique to each country and region. Using U.S. domestic arguments has not only been unsuccessful overseas, in many cases it has further alienated and incensed foreigners, especially in third world countries.

Stay the Course in Iraq

The Salafists realize that the stakes in Iraq are enormous and accordingly have made this new state a key battleground in their global insurgency campaign. The elections in January were a strategic victory for the Iraqi people and the U.S. and coalition partners. In spite of dire warnings from Salafist insurgents and predictions of widespread bloodshed, on January 30, 2005, 58 percent of the Iraqi population went to the polls in a relatively peaceful election. Despite the Sunni boycott, the elections produced a government representative of 80 percent of the population. More broadly, the Iraq election underscored President Bush's resolve to "seek and support the growth of democratic movements and institutions in every nation and culture, with the ultimate goal of ending tyranny in [the] world."[48] Bolstered by the fact that no freely elected government has been deposed by insurgents in modern time, the U.S. and its allies must now provide the requisite level of security for the political, economic, and social development of a stable and democratic Iraq. Training, equipping, and standing by the Iraqi Security Forces are the keys to security, but the military alone will not defeat the insurgency. The politicians must draft an inclusive constitution and sell it to the Iraqi people while improving their lives and protecting their rights.

The Iraqi insurgency continues to gain strength, making it more difficult for the elected interim government to write the new constitution and continue the electoral processes resulting in the much-awaited elections in early 2006.[49] The insurgency has also slowed much-needed economic reform and initiatives as well as social programs designed to create a functioning stable state post–Saddam Hussein. There are other long-term effects. A 2004 CIA study states, "Iraq and other possible conflicts in the future could provide recruitment, training grounds, technical skills, and language proficiency for a new class of terrorists who are 'professionalized' and for whom political violence becomes an end in itself."[50]

Sunni Salafist hatred of the Shia further intensifies the conflict, driving it toward the brink of civil war. In December 2004, Salafist insurgents specifically targeted the Shiite Imam Ali and Imam Hussein shrines in Najaf and Karbala, respectively, undoubtedly hoping to incite sectarian violence and derail the electoral process, which the majority Shiites were expected to win.[51] The Sunnis, who in large part boycotted the elections, have been given seats in the new government and on the committee drafting the new constitution. Communal tensions among the Sunni groups are exacerbated by widespread distrust among Shiites and Kurds, many of whom view all Sunnis as affiliated with the insurgents. Coalition forces and Iraqi police regularly target Sunnis in the crackdown on the insurgency, yet the insurgents themselves attack would-be Sunni middlemen for attempting to negotiate with the government.[52] The United States is taking stronger efforts to identify Sunni moderates and convince them that they have a stake in the new government. According to one U.S. official with extensive regional experience, "we need people who can go out to places like Tikrit and Ramadi, and persuade them that violence is not the answer."[53]

Intensifying training of Iraqi Army and police forces while taking meaningful steps to accommodate moderate and cooperative Sunni leaders will improve the security necessary for the United States and its allies to accelerate development and infrastructure-building projects. Counterinsurgency campaigns are by their nature long-term affairs lasting for decades, but this one must be successful.[54]

Inhibit Insurgent Access to Nuclear Weapons and Nuclear Materials

Based on interviews with key incarcerated al Qaeda leaders and information from captured computers, manuals, writings, and manuscripts, we know that al Qaeda is fascinated with weapons of mass destruction, including nuclear weapons, improvised nuclear devices,[55] and radiological dispersal devices.[56] Al Qaeda and the Salafist franchises make no distinction between weapons of mass destruction and other, less lethal, weapons. Moral reservations on mass casualties, the availability of conventional weapons, lack of precedent, and risk aversion do not constrain Salafist use of WMD.[57]

The Salafists could gain access to these weapons in several ways. For example, they could steal one. Despite the excellent mutual cooperation engendered by the Cooperative Threat Reduction (CTR) program, there are still great concerns about warhead and weapons-grade material security in the former Soviet Union. They might also obtain the weapons from a nuclear power like Pakistan; a distinct possibly if Musharraf were overthrown and a Salafist regime emerged.

The Salafists have another option: They could make a warhead from stolen weapons-grade nuclear material or weapons-usable material obtained from waste by-products of spent nuclear fuel from civilian nuclear power reactors.[58] A homemade "nuke" is a viable option for the Salafists because they could outsource the job. There are very capable Islamic nuclear engineers to include the Pakistanis. In fact, AQ Khan, the father of the Pakistani nuclear program, and a known proliferator, has disturbing ties to bin Laden and al Qaeda leadership.[59]

In order to prevent the insurgents from acquiring nuclear weapons, the United States should seek to further improve the safeguards on nuclear weapon and weapons-grade material storage sites, both at home and abroad. Of equal importance is gaining control of the weapons-usable material obtained from nuclear power plants.

The CTR program described above has successfully secured hundreds of tons of nuclear weapons–building material and nuclear weapons. It must be continued and expanded. Significant amounts of weapons-grade plutonium and highly enriched uranium reportedly remain in old Soviet military storage facilities throughout the region, many of which are very poorly guarded.[60] Enhanced coordination with Russia, Ukraine, Belarus, and Kazakhstan is required. Moreover, by transforming the CTR program from an assistance-based program to a genuine partnership with robust standards of accountability, in which Russia's experts would fully participate, we can accelerate Russian nuclear facility security upgrades.[61] In addition, both the United States and Russia must fully capitalize on the opportunities to incorporate securing nuclear arms into the ongoing Nuclear Nonproliferation Treaty additional protocol negotiations.[62]

The next step is to establish strict international controls on nuclear waste from commercial power plants to discourage the acquisition of weapons-usable material. There are over 400 civilian nuclear power plants in 31 countries spread around the world.[63] Several of these countries, including Russia and Ukraine, have security problems, and none of the countries is immune to a sophisticated pilferage or actual raid to gain materials. All 31 countries are essential partners in this effort to account for and control nuclear waste.

The decentralization of counterproliferation programs and the complex web of interagency responsibility have not been conducive to the development of an overarching set of counterproliferation strategic priorities. To its credit, the United States will most likely meet its commitment as a key member of the Global Partnership against the Spread of Weapons and Materials of Mass Destruction to invest $10 billion.[64] As part of the ongoing Global Partnership negotiations, the United States should encourage governments possessing weapons-grade or industrial nuclear materials to appoint counterproliferation officials solely responsible for controlling WMD and fissile materials.[65]

Executing the National Strategy

The National Strategy is designed to ultimately reduce the geographic reach of the insurgents and reduce their lethality (Figure 3). Operating through a global community of shared interest, assisting with political, economic, and social programs to address the root causes of the insurgency, and pursuing mutually beneficial campaigns to kill or capture the insurgents will reduce the magnitude of insurgent activities and shrink Salafist operations from the global to the regional, then to the state, and ultimately to the local level. The imperatives discussed earlier will keep nuclear weapons materials out of the hands of the terrorists, precluding future devastating attacks against the United States or another country.

Once the insurgent threat is confined to the local level, it becomes a police problem, not a national security issue. Strong local police operating in an efficient and honest judicial system is probably the most effective defense against insurgent groups. Because intensive, sustained police action is unmatched in disrupting and halting insurgent violence, United States aid to the host country's judicial system to include the police and prosecutors must be steady, consistent, and encourage federal, state, and local *law enforcement* elements to work in concert to detect the threat, share information, and act decisively.

When the global reach of the Salafist franchises has been curtailed and their capability to commit violence is reduced (forced into the lower-left quadrant of Figure 3), the host countries cannot ease the pressure. Recent experience with the Abu Sayyaf Group

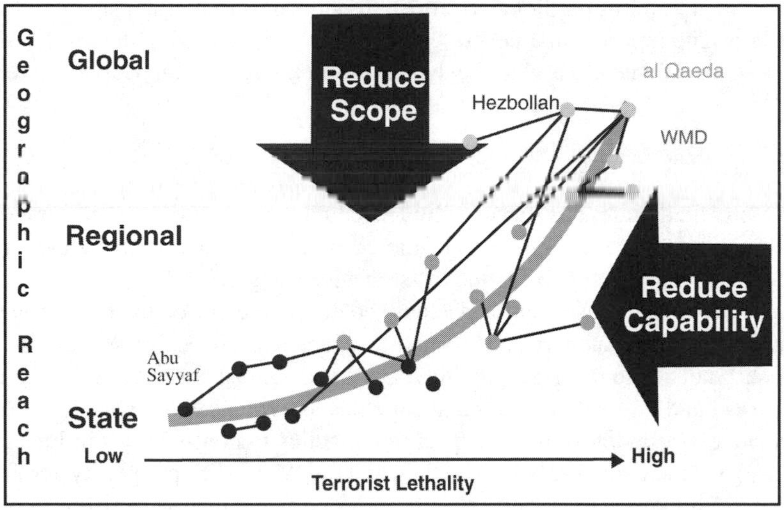

Figure 3: Executing the Strategy

(ASG) in the southern Philippines serves as a cautionary tale of how independent, networked insurgent groups can quickly reconstitute following a setback. The ASG's leader, Abu Sabaya, and other key leaders were killed in June 2002 as a result of a prolonged and combined Filipino/U.S. operation in Zamboanga Province. The Philippine government declared the group mortally wounded, and U.S. support paused. But, in the absence of continued government pressure, the ASG recovered and continues to kill Americans and Filipinos and take hostages. The United States and its allies cannot afford to take pressure off these types of groups.

The United States must retain the will to stay the course for as long as it takes to reduce the threat of Salafist insurgents. The National Strategy recognizes that this is a long-term struggle:

> [W]e will be resolute. Others might flag in the face of the inevitable ebb and flow of the campaign against terrorism. But the American people will not. We understand that we cannot choose to disengage from the world, because in this globalized era, the world will engage us regardless.[66]

Because this is a prolonged American "test of will" like the cold war that will span many presidencies, it will be very unfortunate if U.S. counterinsurgency efforts become a domestic political issue. If the current bickering and charges continue and escalate, it could have the detrimental effect of eroding America's patience and resolve, ultimately causing a premature withdrawal from key battleground states. Both political parties must act responsibly and conduct the debate in a bipartisan manner for the good of the country and the world.

The American people need to perceive some measure of progress in the struggle. To ensure the strategy's longevity, robustness, and nonpartisanship, performance metrics appropriate to counterinsurgency must be created, distributed, and emphasized in policy discussions. The decision by the State Department to stop publishing terrorism statistics as part of its annual Patterns of Global Terrorism report sends the wrong signal to the American people.[67] The report with a new title and format and measuring the results of the National Strategy would be a useful tool to better inform the American people and retain their support.[68]

Recap

Thus far, the United States has successfully prevented further attacks on the homeland, and has killed and captured large numbers of the enemy. Some analysts have even predicted that the Salafists may already be losing the strategic struggle.[69]

The United States has assembled a loose coalition to carry on the long-term struggle, but more international support and commitment are needed. Early success has led the enemy to shift attacks to other geographic regions and against softer targets, in attacks that continue to kill and injure Americans and our allies as evidenced by the July 7, 2005 coordinated attacks in London. We can expect these tactics to continue as bin Laden and the Salafists try to expand the war between Islam and the West. U.S. popularity abroad is at an all-time low, and many new recruits have been added to the insurgent's rolls as a result of perceived U.S. insensitivity and unilateralism. The stakes in Iraq are immense as the threat of a democratic state has energized and focused the extremists. Survival of a democratic Iraq will be a terrible blow to the Salafist insurgency and a major victory for the U.S. global counterinsurgency campaign. Additional terrorist attacks at home and abroad are likely, and nuclear weapons will assuredly be employed by the insurgents if they become available. Again, as I cautioned in 2003, time does not appear to be on our side. The United States and its allies must conduct coordinated diplomatic, social, economic, intelligence, information, and military campaigns to assist beleaguered nations. Key battleground states like Afghanistan, Pakistan, Saudi Arabia, Egypt, and countries in the Horn and central Africa must be encouraged to reach out to the disenfranchised citizens that bin Laden and his cohorts recruit. Salafist ideology will never be completely eradicated, but it is possible to contain and limit the extremists.

Every nation in the world will feel the impact if Osama bin Laden and his fellow Salafists are victorious in this struggle. The creation of Salafist states and regions will have a devastating impact on the world order as we know it today. It is in every country's best interests to work together to combat this Salafist insurgency and benefit from a safer world. This will require statecraft of the highest order.

General Wayne A. Downing, U.S. Army (Retired) is a highly decorated combat veteran who retired after a 34-year career in the U.S. Army. While on active duty, he served in a variety of command assignments in infantry, armored, special operations, and joint units, culminating in his appointment as the commander-in-chief of the U.S. Special Operations Command. Following retirement, General Downing was appointed by the president to assess the 1996 terrorist attack on the U.S. base at Khobar Towers in Saudi Arabia. From 1999 to 2000, General Downing also served as a member of the congressionally mandated National Commission on Terrorism (the Bremer Commission), charged with examining the terrorist threat to the United States, evaluating America's laws, policies, and practices for preventing and punishing terrorism directed at U.S. citizens, and recommending corrective actions.

In 2001, General Downing served the White House as national director and deputy national security advisor for combating terrorism. As the president's principal advisor on matters related to combating terrorism, he was responsible for the close coordination among the military, diplomatic, intelligence, law enforcement, and financial operations of our war on terror, and for developing and executing a strategy that integrates all elements of national power.

In 2003, General Downing was appointed as the distinguished chair of the Combating Terrorism Center at West Point, where he teaches the Terrorism Studies seminar. As the distinguished chair, he directs the Center's research activities and work supporting the Department of Defense and other agencies' efforts in combating terrorism.

General Downing graduated from the U.S. Military Academy at West Point with a B.S. degree in 1962 and has a M.B.A. from Tulane University.

Notes

1. Downing, Wayne A., *Defeating Terrorism,* McGraw Hill, 2004, "The Global War on Terrorism: Focusing the National Strategy," pp. 146-57.
2. After 9/11, I returned to government service as the national director and deputy national security advisor for combating terrorism, responsible for closely coordinating the military, diplomatic, intelligence, law enforcement, and financial operations of our war on terror, and for developing and executing a strategy that integrated all elements of national power.
3. Downing, *op cit*, p. 156.
4. This chapter borrows some material from another book chapter in draft, "Recasting the National Strategy for Combating Terrorism," written by this author and Jason M. Pogacnik for the Maxwell School of Citizenship and Public Affairs, Syracuse University Bantle Chair Symposium, "The Global War on Terrorism," Round 2.
5. CRS Report for Congress, Al Qaeda: Statements and Evolving Ideology, CRS-3.
6. *Ibid,* CRS-4, 160. Additionally, some scholars compare counterinsurgency techniques to counterterrorism policy and find the former more useful when considering the specific threat posed by Salafist organizations such as al Qaeda. Counterinsurgency is an even more useful way to frame the issue when the struggle occurs in areas where the rule of law has yet to be established, or exists in only a weak form—such as in Iraq.
7. *See* Mariam Fam, "Al-Qaeda No. 2 Decries U.S. Idea of Reform: On New Video, Zawahiri Says Jihad Is Only Way to Achieve Change," *Washington Post,* June 18, 2005. A posting by Global Islamic Media on qal3ah.net read as follows: "Do not find it strange if after a while, a year or so, you will hear about secret negotiations by one country and representatives of Al Qaeda. . . .The organization has come to represent the Islamic ummah and speaks in its name. It appears that we are returning to the days of the caliphate." Cited in Lawrence Wright, "The Terror Web: Were the Madrid Bombings Part of a New, Far-Reaching Jihad Being Plotted on the Internet?" *The New Yorker*, Aug. 2, 2004, 17. *See also* General Intelligence and Security Service, Dutch Ministry of the Interior and Kingdom Relations, "From Dawa to Jihad: The Various Threats from Radical Islam to the Democratic Legal Order," Dec. 19, 2004, retrieved from http://www.fas.org/irp/world/netherlands/dawa.pdf, May 2005; Marc Sageman, *Understanding Terrorist Networks,* University of Pennsylvania Press, 2004, pp. 17–24.
8. Consider the following statistics: Number of Taliban-style states created since 9/11: 0; number of countries that have recognized al Qaeda: 0; number of nations that have adopted "state-sponsored" terrorism as an official policy: 0; number of states that have voluntarily given up weapons of mass destruction programs since 9/11: 1; number of transnational nuclear smuggling networks broken up since 9/11: 1; number of Middle Eastern states that have moved closer to democracy: 5. James Carafano, "Terrorism by the Numbers," Heritage Foundation Commentary, May 4, 2005, retrieved from http://www.heritage.org/Press/Commentary/ed050405c.cfm, May 2005.

9. Jim Garamone, "International Coalition Against Terror Grows," *American Forces Press Service,* May 23, 2002.
10. Significant operations include the apprehension of Khalid Sheikh Mohammed in Rawalpindi, Pakistan, in cooperation with the Pakistani Police and Intelligence Services in March 2003 after a month-long pursuit throughout Pakistan. In another success, Thai security forces, with the invaluable assistance of American intelligence agents, in August 2003 captured Hambali, the main Jemaah Islamiyah (JI) strategist and al Qaeda liaison, in Ayutthaya, Thailand (50 miles north of Bangkok).
11. al-Libbi, a Libyan, is also implicated in two assassination attempts on President Musharraf of Pakistan. See, for example, Kamran Khan and John Lancaster, "Top Al Qaeda Figure Is Held in Pakistan," *Washington Post*, May 5, 2005, A1.
12. *National Strategy for Combating Terrorism,* February 2003, 17.
13. Quoted in Lawrence Wright, "The Terror Web: Were the Madrid Bombings Part of a New, Far-Reaching Jihad Being Plotted on the Internet?" *The New Yorke*r, Aug. 2, 2004, 6–7.
14. Cited in Peter Katel, "Exporting Democracy: Will President Bush's Efforts Succeed?," *CQ Researcher,* April 2005, 269–292.
15. Daniel L. Byman, Michael Scheuer, Anatol Lieven and W. Patrick Lang, "Iraq, Afghanistan, and the War on 'Terror,'" *Middle East Policy*, (Spring 2005), 4.
16. Daniel L. Byman, "Al Qaeda as an Adversary; Do We Understand Our Enemy?" *World Politics,* (Oct. 2003), pp. 139, 158.
17. Scholars recognize that the use of terrorism itself is a tactical-level activity, secondary in the minds of those who use such tools. *See, e.g.,* Charles Knight & Melissa Murphy, *International Security* 28, 2 (2003) 192–98.
18. The U.S. Executive Branch is slowly beginning to examine such a reformulation. A new National Security Policy Directive is expected to broadly outline new roles of the major agencies, including putting the State Department in charge of "counter-ideology" while leaving the Defense Department responsible for destroying terrorist networks themselves. See Jim Hoagland, "A Shifting Focus on Terrorism," *Washington Post,* Apr. 24, 2005, B7.
19. Susan B. Glasser, "Review May Shift Terror Policies: U.S. Is Expected to Look beyond Al-Qaeda," Washington Post, May 29, 2005.
20. AIVD Report Rekrutering in Nederland voor de Jihad, van incident tot trend (recruitment for the Jihad in the Netherlands, from incident to trend) 2002.
21. National Strategy, p. 11.
22. *See,* among many others, *The 9/11 Commission Report,* 363–364; National Strategy for Combating Terrorism, *Rethinking the Interagency System,* Michael Donley, Hicks and Associates, Inc.; Address to a Joint Session of Congress and the American People, delivered by President Bush, the White House Office of the Press Secretary, September 20, 2001.
23. Dana Priest, "Help from France Key in Covert Operations: Paris's 'Alliance Base' Targets Terrorists," Washington Post, July 3, 2005.
24. *Rethinking the Interagency System,* Michael Donley, Hicks & Associates, Inc., March 2005. This is an excellent 17-page summary of the options available to reform the interagency system.
25. This obvious solution will be considered dangerous by many in the Executive Branch. One aftermath of the 1980s Iran Contra affair is a strong reluctance for the White House and the president to be associated with operational activities because of the possible domestic "blow-back" when policies fail or problems occur. The counterargument is that the nation is involved in a war that requires extraordinary measures. The nation expects a president to take active charge and manage the affairs of State. It's hard to imagine Roosevelt or Truman in WW II being reluctant to exercise these powers in a direct and forceful manner.
26. Public diplomacy refers to government-sponsored programs intended to inform or influence public opinion in other countries; its chief instruments are publications, motion pictures, cultural exchanges, radio, and television. U.S. Department of State, Dictionary of

International Relations Terms, 1987, p. 85. Public diplomacy seeks to promote the national interest and the national security of the United States through understanding, informing, and influencing foreign publics and broadening dialogue between American citizens and institutions and their counterparts abroad. USAID definition.

27. Nations polled were Israel, India, United States, Korea, France, Czech Republic, Italy, South Africa, United Kingdom (excluding N. Ireland), Germany, Bosnia, Columbia, Pakistan, Greece and Mexico. The two nations with less than a majority supporting trial and extradition, Israel and India, overwhelmingly supported an attack (77 percent and 72 percent, respectively). *See* Peter Ford, "Why Do They Hate Us?" *Christian Science Monitor,* Sept. 27, 2001.
28. Derk Kinnane, "Winning Over the Muslim Mind," *The National Interest,* (Spring 2004), 93. The sentiment expressed here has been widely echoed by scholars and practitioners alike. For example, in June 2004, the Diplomats and Military Commanders for Change, a "collection of 27 distinguished diplomats, flag officers, and other senior officials," stated publicly, "Muslim youth are turning to anti-American terrorism. Never in the two and a quarter centuries of our history has the United States been so isolated among the nations, so broadly feared and distrusted." Cited in Augustus Richard Norton, "The United States in the Middle East: Grand Plans, Grand Ayatollahs, and Dark Alleys," in Louis J Cantori and Augustus Richard Norton, eds., "Evaluating the Bush Menu for Change in the Middle East," *Middle East Policy,* No. 1 (Spring 2005), 101–102.
29. B. Raman, "Counterterrorism Revisited," *Asia Times Online*, 8 March 2005. See also the World Values Surveys, retrieved from http://www.worldvaluessurvey.org/statistics/index.html, May 2005, and cited in United National Development Programme, "Arab Human Development Report 2004: Towards Freedom in the Arab World," New York, NY: United Nations Publications, 2005, 68. See also Pew study cited in Muqtedar Khan, "Prospects for Muslim Democracy: The Role of U.S. Policy," *Middle East Policy,* Fall 2003, retrieved from http://www.brookings.edu/views/articles/khan20031001.pdf, April 7, 2005, in which people in all countries surveyed (except the United States) thought the United States was too pro-Israel. Even in Israel, "47% felt that the United States was not balanced, while only 38% felt that the United States had a fair approach to the conflict." In addition, many Muslims interpret U.S. offers of aid to other countries as evidence of imperialist designs, while not offering aid is certain proof that the United States does not care. See Michael Mousseau, "Market Civilization and Its Clash with Terror," *International Security,* vol. 27, no. 3 (2002/03) 5–29, 23.
30. Khan, 7, citing Pew survey retrieved from http://people-press.org/reports/display.php3?ReportID=185.
31. Byman, *et al.,* 5.
32. Khan, 12. See also Dutch General Intelligence and Security Service, 22, which concludes "by and large, Islam and democracy are not incompatible, citing the correlation between old Islamic sources such as "Shura" (providing for social consultation) and "Bajat" (a kind of social contract), and democratic principles.
33. Sageman, *op cit,* 73.
34. Michael A. Levi & Michael B. D'Arcey, "Untapped Potential: U.S. Science and Technology Cooperation with the Islamic World," *Brookings Institutional Analysis Paper,* No. 8 (March 2005), 3, retrieved from http://www.brookings.edu/fp/saban/analysis/darcy20050419.pdf, April 2005.
35. Zogby International, "Impressions of America 2004," Washington, DC: Zogby International, 2004, 3, retrieved from http://www.aaiusa.org/PDF/Impressions_of_America04.pdf, April 2005.
36. Levi & D'Arcey, 10. The authors recommend: (1) prioritizing technology over research and development because it is tied more directly to economic and social development, (2) paying attention to the political structure of scientific interactions—i.e., whether initiatives cover a wide or narrow area, (3) leveraging the Islamic scientific community living and working abroad, (4) actively promoting and publicizing scientific collaborations and accomplishments as part of a

comprehensive public diplomacy campaign, (5) not overstating the political and diplomatic benefits of scientific cooperation, and (6) creating an integrated arms control and nonproliferation strategy. *See* Levi & D'Arcey, Executive Summary, VI-VII. *See also,* Zogby, 3.

37. United States Government Accountability Office, GAO-05-323, "U.S. Public Diplomacy: Interagency Coordination Efforts Hampered by the Lack of a National Communication Strategy," Washington, DC: Government Printing Office, April 2005, retrieved from http://www.gao.gov/new.items/d05323.pdf, 3.
38. Ibid.
39. Ibid, 11.
40. *Report of the Defense Science Board Task Force on Strategic Communication,* Washington, D.C., September 2004, cited in *Ibid,* 12.
41. U.S. GAO, 12.
42. Peter Maass, "The Way of the Commandos," *New York Times Magazine,* May 1, 2005, 38.
43. According to the 2003 Trends in International Mathematics and Science Study (TIMSS 2003), the average eighth-grade student in Jordan, Bahrain, Tunisia, Syria, Palestine, Lebanon, Egypt, Morocco, and Yemen scored a 392 and 416 in mathematics and science, respectively, compared to international averages of 476 and 474. See TIMSS 2003, cited in *Ibid,* 36.
44. UNDP, 17.
45. The under secretary for public diplomacy and public affairs helps ensure that public diplomacy (engaging, informing, and influencing key international audiences) is practiced in harmony with public affairs (outreach to Americans) and traditional diplomacy.
46. Hoffman, "The Changing Face," 557.
47. Pervez Hoodbhoy, "Can Pakistan Work?" *Foreign Affairs,* vol. 83, Issue 6 (November/December 2004). The new center could operate as part of a proposed, larger "Trust for Democracy in the Middle East," comprised predominantly of NGOs, but supported by the U.S. and European governments. *See* Everts, 684. One unfortunate example of blowback is Pakistan, where USAID funds were used to publish a book—still widely available in Pakistan and Afghanistan—that told children to "pluck out the eyes of their enemies and cut off their legs."
48. Cited in Peter Katel, "Exporting Democracy: Will President Bush's Efforts Succeed?" *CQ Researcher* (Apr. 2005), 269–292, 271.
49. Richard A. Oppel, Jr., "A New Political Setback for Iraq's Cabinet," *New York Times*, May 9, 2005, A1.
50. Katel, 278.
51. *See,* e.g., John F. Burns, "At Least 64 Dead as Rebels Strike in 3 Iraqi Cities," *New York Times,* Dec. 20, 2004, A6.
52. Robert F. Worth, "For Some in Iraq's Sunni Minority, a Growing Sense of Alienation," *New York Times*, May 8, 2005, A1.
53. *Ibid.*
54. Eliot Cohen, "A Hawk Questions Himself as His Son Goes to War." *Washington Post,* July 10, 2005, B01.
55. Improvised nuclear devices are defined by the Department of Defense as devices incorporating radioactive materials designed to result in the dispersal of radioactive material or in the formation of nuclear-yield reaction. Such devices may be fabricated in a completely improvised manner or may be an improvised modification to a U.S. or foreign nuclear weapon.
56. Radiological dispersal devices, also known as "dirty bombs," consist of radioactive material combined with conventional explosives. They are designed to use explosive force to disperse the radioactive material over a large area, such as multiple city blocks. Around the world, there are many sources of radioactive material that are not secure or not accounted for. Rogue nations and/or terrorist groups can obtain these materials for dirty bombs. These explosive weapons may initially kill a few people in the immediate area of the blast but are used primarily to produce psychological rather than physical harm by inducing panic and

terror in the target population. Their use would also result in costly clean-up for decontamination. OSHA Definition.

57. Richard A. Falkenrath, "Confronting Nuclear, Biological and Chemical Terrorism," *Survival,* Vol. 40, No. 3 (Autumn 1998), pp. 43-65, 28.
58. Weapons-grade material is typically defined as uranium enriched to about 90 percent or greater uranium-235 or uranium-233, or plutonium containing about 90 percent or greater plutonium-239. Weapons-usable nuclear material is defined as uranium enriched to 20 percent or greater in the uranium-235 or uranium-233 isotopes (highly enriched uranium, HEU) and any plutonium containing less than 80 percent of the isotope plutonium-238. A 10 kt gun-type fission weapon would cause between half a million and 2 million immediate deaths if detonated in lower Manhattan, not to mention a huge impact on the American economy and infrastructure. See William C. Potter, Charles D. Ferguson, and Leonard S. Spector, "The Four Faces of Nuclear Terror and the Need for a Prioritized Response," *Foreign Affairs* (May/June 2004), and Ashton B. Carter, "How to Counter WMD," *Foreign Affairs,* (September/October 2004), pp. 72–85, 76. See also the arguments made by Joseph Cirincione, director of the Non-Proliferation Project at the Carnegie Endowment for International Peace and author of *Deadly Arsenals: Tracking Weapons of Mass Destruction,* Washington, DC: Carnegie Endowment, 2002.
59. Seymour M. Hersh, "The Deal," *The New Yorker,* Mar. 8, 2004.
60. For example, 20,000 kg reportedly are loosely secured in civilian research facilities.
61. U.S. DOD CTR Web site, http://www.defenselink.mil/pubs/ctr/.
62. I base these recommendations on Matthew Bunn, John P. Holdren, & Anthony Wier. "Securing Nuclear Weapons and Materials: Seven Steps for Immediate Action." Project on Managing the Atom, Belfer Center for Science and International Affairs, John F. Kennedy School of Government, Harvard University, May 2002, Executive Summary. *See also* Joby Warrick, "An Easier, but Less Deadly, Recipe for Terror," *Washington Post,* Dec. 31, 2004, A1.
63. IAEA PRIS database, June 2005.
64. For further reference on this G8 initiative, see the U.S. State Department Bureau of Nonproliferation Global Partnership homepage, at http://www.state.gov/t/np/c12743.htm.
65. France, Germany, the UK, and Belgium, among other Western countries, are all key players in these initiatives.
66. *National Strategy,* 29–30.
67. For a good description of the arguments on both sides, *see* Susan B. Glassner, "Global Terrorism Statistics Debated; New Report Leaves Some Wondering How to Measure the Number of Attacks," *Washington Post,* May 1, 2005, A23.
68. Possible titles include "Patterns of Global Extremism" or "Patterns of Salafist Insurgencies."
69. Gilles Kepel makes the argument that the Salafists are already losing. In a discussion of Kepel's book, *The War for Muslim Minds,* David Ignatius writes: "the Taliban regime in Afghanistan has been toppled; the fence-sitting semi-Islamist regime in Saudi Arabia has taken sides more strongly with the West; Islamists in Sudan and Libya are in retreat; and the plight of the Palestinians has never been more dire. And Baghdad, the traditional seat of the Muslim caliphs, is under foreign occupation. Not what you would call a successful jihad." As another example, Kepel argues that the August 2004 capture in Iraq of two French journalists, whom the insurgents said they would release when the French government reversed its ban on headscarves in public schools, provoked Muslim outrage directed at the insurgents themselves—not the French government. See David Ignatius, "Are the Terrorists Failing?" *Washington Post,* Sept. 28, 2004, A27. For laudatory commentary connecting the global war on terrorism to Syria's actions, see, e.g., Peter Brookes. "Syria, W's Next Win?" Heritage Foundation Commentary, February 28, 2005, retrieved from http://www.heritage.org/Press/Commentary/ed022805b.cfm, May 2005.

Brigadier General Russell D. Howard (Ret.), 2005

Preemptive Military Doctrine: No Other Choice

Emphasis on the preemptive uses of force is a response to the terrorist attacks of September 11, 2001, which brought home the necessity to address potentially catastrophic threats before the United States is attacked.[1] The first manifestation of this more forceful security doctrine was President George W. Bush's seminal September 20, 2001, address to a joint session of Congress in which he vowed to hold responsible both those who perpetuate attacks against the United States and those who harbor them.[2] The preemption concept was more clearly articulated in a speech delivered June 1, 2002, to graduating cadets at the U.S. Military Academy at West Point, in which the president asserted his administration's intention to carry out preemptive military attacks if necessary to protect American lives.[3]

In its implications, the West Point speech signaled a historic shift from long-accepted Cold War applications of the use of force. "For much of the last century," the president said, "America's defense relied on the Cold War doctrines of deterrence and containment. In some cases, those strategies still apply." However, he contended, "new threats also require new thinking."

> Deterrence—the promise of massive retaliation against nations—means nothing against shadowy terrorist networks with no nation or citizens to defend. Containment is not possible when unbalanced dictators with weapons of mass destruction can deliver those weapons on missiles or secretly provide them to terrorist allies.[4]

This paper endorses the president's assertion that a preemptive strategy is necessary in a post–Cold War security environment, when America's most dangerous adversaries are transnational, non-state actors who have access to weapons of mass destruction (WMDs) and intend to use them.

During the Cold War, most international terrorism was related one way or another to an East versus West, left-versus-right confrontation—a small but dangerous sideshow to the greater, bi-polar, Cold War drama. Terrorism in this era was almost always the province of groups of militants that had the backing of political forces and states hostile to the United States. What is new today is the emergence of terrorism that is not ideological in a traditional political sense. Instead, it is inspired by religious extremists and ethnic separatists. These may be individuals, like the Unabomber, or similarly minded people working in cells, small groups, or larger coalitions.[5] They do not answer completely to any government, they operate across national borders, and they have access to funding and advanced technology.[6]

The new terrorist groups are not bound by the same constraints or motivated by the same goals as nation-states. They are not amenable to traditional diplomacy or military deterrence because there is no state to negotiate with or to retaliate against. And they are not so concerned about limiting casualties. Under the old rules, "terrorists wanted a lot of people watching, not a lot of people dead."[7] They did not want large body counts; particularly, they wanted converts and a seat at the table. Today's terrorists are less concerned about converts; and rather than wanting a seat at the table, "they want to destroy the table and everyone sitting at it."[8] Religious terrorists, al Qaeda in particular, want casualties—lots of them.[9]

Today's terrorism is not ideological like Communism or capitalism, with values that can be debated in the classroom or voted on at the polls. Rather, it is an adaptation of an ancient tactic and instrument of conflict. The major difference between modern terrorism and its ancient roots is that the "new terrorism" is better financed and has a global reach that it owes to globalization and the information revolution. The new terrorism can ride the back of the Web, using advanced communications systems to move vast sums from anyplace to anywhere else. And for $28.50, any Internet surfer can purchase *Bacteriological Warfare: A Major Threat to North America,* which explains how to grow deadly bacteria that could be used in a WMD.

Terrorists and WMD

The prospect of terrorists using WMD (nuclear, radiological, biological, or chemical weapons) to attack the United States is the main reason the president has little choice but to add "preemption" to his menu of potential military options. About this, the president has been very clear:

> When the spread of chemical and biological and nuclear weapons—along with ballistic missile technology—occurs, even weak states and small groups could attain a catastrophic power to strike great nations. Our enemies have declared this very intention, and have been caught seeking these terrible weapons. They want the capability to blackmail us, or to harm us, or to harm our friends—and we will oppose them with all our power.[10]

Indeed, al Qaeda has threatened the United States with WMD. Recent discoveries in Afghanistan have confirmed that al Qaeda and other terrorist groups are actively seeking the ability to use biological agents against United States and its allies. [11] According to David Kay, this should not be a surprise:

> Only a blind, deaf and dumb terrorist group could have survived the last five years and not been exposed at least to the possibility of the use of WMD, while the more discerning terrorists would have found some tactically brilliant possibilities already laid out on the public record.[12]

Steven Miller, director of the International Security Program at Harvard's Kennedy School, agrees that policymakers should be concerned about terrorists' access to nuclear weapons. According to Miller, "opportunities for well-organized and well-financed terrorists to infiltrate a Russian nuclear storage facility are greater than ever."[13] Miller believes there have been more than two-dozen thefts of weapons-usable materials in the former Soviet Union in recent years. Though several suspects have been arrested in undercover sting operations, others may have gotten away.[14] In 1994, Miller points out, "350 grams of plutonium were smuggled on board a Lufthansa flight from Moscow to Munich. Fortunately, SWAT teams confiscated the material as soon as it arrived."[15]

Given the known goals of terrorists, the United States can no longer rely solely on a reactive, crisis-response military posture, as it has in the past. Our inability to deter a potential attacker, the immediacy of today's threats, and the catastrophic consequences of a WMD attack do not permit that option. The United States simply cannot allow its enemies to strike first with nuclear, radiological, biological, or chemical weapons.[16]

Arms Control Protocols and Westphalian Rules No Longer Apply

The U.S.' inability to negotiate with non-state actors and its over-reliance on treaties and conventions limit the usefulness of diplomacy in reducing the likelihood of chemical, biological, radiological, and nuclear attacks. For example, it is stated U.S. policy not to negotiate with terrorists.[17] The rationale behind this policy is clear: Giving in to terrorist demands will prompt more terrorist activity. This is especially true in hostage situations, because negotiations with terrorists could potentially force the United States to risk having to meet certain demands for ransom or safe passage.

However, it would be very beneficial to have a mechanism—presumably secret—that could enable an opportunity to dialogue with terrorists. This would be especially important in regard to transnational, non-state actors who have no formal diplomatic voice. The manner in which this dialogue might take place would depend on the situation. Discussions could be held in secret or through surrogates. Preferably, a dialogue—not necessarily negotiations—with terrorists could be established before an attack that might prevent it from happening, thus avoiding the necessity of preemption. In any case, opening a dialogue is important if for no other reason than that understanding what is really on a terrorist's mind has intelligence value. Even more important, having a terrorist understand what is on our mind may well have deterrent value.

Nuclear arms control and reduction treaties promulgated during the Cold War were, and still are, valuable assets for preventing conflict. They provided baseline agreements that fostered cooperation between the powers and led to greater transparency and confidence-building measures that still exist today. Unfortunately, treaties meant to control and reduce the number of chemical and biological weapons have not been as effective.

The Chemical Weapons Convention (CWC) entered into force on April 29, 1997. It has been signed by 120 states and bans chemical weapons production and storage as well as use. The strength of the convention is that it calls for unprecedented and highly intrusive inspections, including routine and challenge inspection mechanisms. The weakness of the convention is that several countries that pose concerns about chemical proliferation have not joined the CWC regime. These include Iraq, Libya, North Korea, and Syria.[18]

Biological weapons are also prohibited by a treaty, the Biological and Toxin Weapons Convention (BWC), which entered into force in 1975 and now comprises some 140 members. The strength of the BWC is that it bans an entire class of weapons, prohibiting the development, production, stockpiling, or acquisition of biological agents or toxins of any type or quantity that do not have protective, medical, or other peaceful purposes. "However, the major shortfall of the BWC is its lack of any on-site verification mechanism."[19]

The chemical warfare and biological warfare conventions and nuclear arms control and reduction treaties only affect state behavior. They have no impact on the behavior of transnational and other non-state actors that might possess and use chemical, biological, or nuclear weapons, or on those rogue states that are not signatories to the conventions.

The major problems the United States has in addressing international WMD threats are outdated military doctrine and the traditional way the United States employs military force. The traditional uses of military force are defense, deterrence, compellence, and presence. Defense against terrorist use of WMD is extremely difficult, especially in a democracy. Without compromising civil liberties in draconian ways—a goal of terrorists—no defense regime could come close to guaranteeing security against a terrorist intent on attacking the United States with WMD. As Secretary of Defense Donald Rumsfeld reflected in a speech at the National Defense University in January 2002: "It is not possible to defend against every conceivable kind of attack in every conceivable location at every minute of the day or night. The best, and in some cases, the only defense is a good offense."

Deterrence against non-governmental actors is also extremely difficult. Where exactly do you retaliate against Osama bin Laden if he launches a biological attack?

> Deterrence generally does not work against terrorists. Stateless and usually spread over wide regions or even among continents, terrorists do not present a viable target for retaliation. The death and destruction that can be visited upon a terrorist organization in a retaliatory attack is greatly exceeded by the damage even a small terrorist cell can inflict on civilian society.[20]

Presence would certainly help get U.S. forces to a crisis area more rapidly, but U.S. military presence overseas is declining, as is the number of military personnel in the United States who can be deployed. Therefore, compelling adversaries to stop what they are doing or planning to do, by using military force against them, has more utility in the post–Cold War world.

Historically, the United States has employed its military to compel enemies to change their behavior after a crisis has occurred. In fact, the National Security Act of 1947 and its subsequent amendments have structured the U.S. security apparatus to react to crises, not prevent them. However, given the nature of the post–Cold War WMD threats, ways must be found to compel adversaries to change their behavior before they attack and crisis occurs. This is preemption.

Preemption—Not Fighting Fair?

Preemption has long been an important and widely accepted U.S. security policy option.[21] However, the preemptive use of military force is a difficult concept for many Americans to accept. It defies American's sense of fairness and proportionality as well as the rules of warfare, as Brad Roberts points out:

> Moral philosophy establishes that wars of self-defense are just, whereas wars of aggression are not. But there has long been a healthy debate about precisely what constitutes a war of self-defense. A mid-sixteenth-century scholar of just war wrote, "There is a single and only just cause for commencing a war … namely, wrong received." In our day Michael Walzer has argued, "Nothing but aggression can justify war. … There must actually have been a wrong, and it must actually have been received (or its receipt must be, as it were, only minutes away)."[22]

However, this view has not been held by all. Hugo Grotius wrote in 1625, "The first just cause of war … is an injury, which even though not actually committed, threatens our persons or our property."[23] Grotius emphasized that to safeguard against wars of aggression, it was essential to be certain about the enemy's intent to attack.

In 1914, Elihu Root said that international law did not require the aggrieved state to wait before using force in self-defense "until it is too late to protect itself."[24] Interestingly, in *Just Wars,* Michael Walzer seems to contradict his earlier statements by arguing that "states can rightfully defend themselves against violence that is imminent but not actual."

Roberts contends, rightly I think, that there can be "no blanket reply to the question, is there a moral case for preemption. Some acts of preemption will be deemed just, others unjust." In the case of preemption against WMD threats, Roberts further argues that the strongest moral case for U.S. preemption exists under the following conditions:

> (1) an aggressor has actually threatened to use his WMD weapons, has taken steps to ready the means to do so, and has specifically threatened the United States (including its territory, citizens, or military forces); (2) those WMD weapons have been built in violation of international law; (3) the aggressor's threatened actions invoke larger questions about the credibility of security guarantees or the balance of power within a region; (4) the president has secured the approval of the U.S. Congress; and (5) the United States has secured the backing of the U.N. Security Council and any relevant regional organization. The prudential tests of last resort, proportionality, and reasonable chance of success must also be met.[25]

I agree with the first four of Robert's conditions but not with the last. The backing of the UN and regional organizations would certainly strengthen the moral argument for preemption but may be impossible to obtain, given China's reluctance to violate sovereignty under any circumstances and Russia's recurring post-Kosovo habit of siding with rogue states like Iraq and Iran. Moreover, the United States must never forgo the option to act unilaterally.

Domestic Political Support

The commonly held view that the U.S. public disapproves of preemption is simply mistaken. A good example is the 1998 bombing of a Sudanese chemical plant that was suspected of having ties to Osama bin Laden. Even when it was revealed that the plant was probably making nothing sinister, public opinion in the United States was still strongly in favor of the attacks.[26] In fact, two-thirds of Americans approved the military strike, while only 19 percent were opposed.[27]

More recent data show that Congress is in favor of preemption under certain conditions, particularly when conducted against non-state actors intent on harming the United States. Dr. Scott Silverstone, a professor and researcher at the U.S. Military Academy, has categorized data from congressional hearings, memos, media articles, and personal statements showing that members of the Senate and House are nearly unanimous in their support for preemption as a strategy. In fact, Silverstone's data show that 90 percent of the Senate favored a preemption strategy against non-state actors. The figure in the House was 81 percent. Interestingly, not one elected official in the House or Senate explicitly rejected the notion of preemptive warfare directed against non-state actors.[28]

Preemption and International Law

"Under the regime of customary international law that developed long before the UN Charter was adopted, it was generally accepted that preemptive force was permissible in self-defense."[29] If a state could demonstrate necessity—that another state was about to engage in an imminent armed attack—and act proportionately, preemptive self-defense was acceptable and legal.[30] Today, given the stealthy nature of terrorist groups' activities, it is unlikely that specific attacks can be identified in advance. "So these groups' past practices and explicit statements provide an adequate substitute for the doctrine's requirement for imminent threat."[31]

In the post–UN Charter world, Article 2(4) stipulated that states were to refrain in their international relations from the threat or use of force against another state unless—as stipulated in Article 39—the Security Council authorizes the use of force against offending states because of a threat to peace, breach of the peace, or an act of aggression. However, Article 51 confirms that the Charter will not impair the inherent right of individual or collective self-defense if an armed attack occurs against a UN member.[32]

Two interpretations of Article 51 create friction in the willingness of the international body to accept the preemptive use of force as an acceptable national strategy. Restrictionists interpret Article 51 to mean that a state can only respond if attacked, while counter-restrictionists believe states can use anticipatory self-defense, for much the same reason preemptive self-defense was acceptable prior to the UN Charter.

My view is that neither "customary" nor "post–UN Charter" international law addresses the issue of preemptive self-defense against transnational, non-state actors with access to WMDs who are intent on committing acts of terrorism. Therefore, preemption as defined by President Bush is as valid as any other interpretation of "preemptive self-defense."

Conclusion

I was on the dais at West Point when President Bush gave his "preemption speech" and was taken with one of his statements, which I paraphrase here. He told the audience: "The gravest danger to freedom lies at the perilous crossroads of radicalism and technology. When the spread of chemical and biological and nuclear weapons, along with ballistic missile technology… occurs, even weak states and small groups could attain a catastrophic power to strike great nations." He went on: "Our enemies have declared this very intention, and have been caught seeking these terrible weapons. They want the capability to blackmail us, or to harm us, or to harm our friends—and we will oppose them with all our power."

In my view, "opposing them with all our power" must include the "preemptive use of force" to defeat terrorists before they can inflict pain on the United States. Traditional applications of American power—economic, political, diplomatic, and military used to leverage and influence states in the past are not effective against non-state actors. Who do you sanction or embargo? With whom do you negotiate? How do you defend against or deter Osama bin Laden? You don't. The only effective way to influence the bin Ladens of the world is to preempt them before they can act.

Notes

1. Michael E. O'Hanlon, Susan Rice, and James B. Steinberg (December 2002), "The New National Security Strategy and Preemption," *Brookings Policy Brief #113,* p. 1.
2. Ibid.
3. President George W. Bush (June 1, 2002), West Point, New York.
4. Ibid.
5. Stephen A. Cambone (1996), *A New Structure for National Security Policy Planning* (Washington D.C.: Government Printing Office), p. 43.

6. Gideon Rose (March–April 1999), "It Could Happen Here—Facing the New Terrorism," *Foreign Affairs,* p. 1.
7. Frequently quoted remark made by Brian Jenkins in 1974.
8. Quote attributed to James Woolsey, 1994.
9. Bruce Hoffman (1998), *Inside Terrorism* (New York: Columbia University Press), p. 205.
10. George W. Bush, June 1, 2002.
11. Judith Miller (September 14, 2002), "Lab Suggests Qaeda Planned to Build Arms, Officials Say," *New York Times,* p. 1.
12. David Kay (2001), "WMD Terrorism: Hype or Reality." In James M. Smith and William C. Thomas, eds., *The Terrorism Threat and United States Government Response: Operational and Organizational Factors* (United States Air Force Academy: INSS Book Series), p. 12.
13. Doug Gavel (Autumn 2002), "Can Nuclear Weapons Be Put Beyond the Reach of Terrorists," *Kennedy School of Government Bulletin,* p. 43.
14. Ibid., p. 45.
15. Ibid., p. 48.
16. See the National Security Strategy of the United States.
17. Stansfield Turner (1991), *Terrorism and Democracy* (Boston: Houghton Mifflin Company), p. xii. Actually, Admiral Turner makes the argument that the United States will negotiate with terrorists. See chapter 26, *We Will Make Deals.*
18. "Weapons of Mass Destruction" (1999), *Great Decisions,* p. 51.
19. Ibid., p. 52.
20. James Wirtz and James A. Russell (Spring 2003), "U.S. Policy on Preventive War and Preemption," *The Nonproliferation Review,* vol. 10, no. 1, p. 116.
21. O'Hanlon, et al., p. 4.
22. Brad Roberts (March 1998), "NBC-Armed Rogues: Is there a Moral Case for Preemption?" In Elliott Abrams, ed., *Close Calls: Intervention, Terrorism, Missile Defense, and 'Just War' Today* (EPPC), p. 11.
23. Hugo Grotius, *The Law of War and Peace,* book 2, chapter 1, section 2.
24. Elihu Root (1914), "The Real Monroe Doctrine," *American Journal of International Law,* vol. 35, p. 427.
25. Roberts, p. 13.
26. "Excerpts: United States Editorials Assess Impact of Anti-Terrorist Strikes" (June 14, 2000), *USIS Washington File,* p. 1-6, http://www.fas.org/man/dod-101/ops/docs/98082307_tpo.html.
27. John Diamond (August 21, 1998), "US Strikes Tougher Stance Against Terrorism," *Cnews,* http://www.canoe.ca/CNEWSStrikeAtTerrorism/aug20_us.html.
28. Multiple conversations with Dr. Scott Silverstone.
29. Anthony Clark Arend (Spring 2003), "International Law and Preemptive Use of Military Force," *Washington Quarterly,* p. 90.
30. Ibid., p. 91
31. O'Hanlon, p. 5.
32. Ibid.

Barry R. Posen, 2001

The Struggle Against Terrorism: Grand Strategy, Strategy, and Tactics

Three to four thousand people, nearly all American citizens, perished in the aircraft hijackings and attacks on the World Trade Center and the Pentagon on September 11, 2001.[1] They were murdered for political reasons by a loosely integrated foreign terrorist political organization called al-Qaeda. Below I ask four questions related to these attacks: First, what is the nature of the threat posed by al-Qaeda? Second, what is an appropriate strategy for dealing with it? Third, how might the U.S. defense establishment have to change to fight this adversary? And fourth, what does the struggle against al-Qaeda mean for overall U.S. foreign policy?

The Adversary

Al-Qaeda is a network of like-minded individuals, apparently all Muslim but of many different nationalities, that links together groups in as many as sixty countries. Osama bin Laden, a wealthy Saudi who took part in the Afghan rebellion against the Soviet occupation (1979–89), developed this network. He inspires, finances, organizes, and trains many of its members. He seems to be in direct command of some but not all of them. Bin Laden and his associates share a fundamentalist interpretation of Islam, which they have opportunistically twisted into a political ideology of violent struggle. He and his principles enjoy some popular support in the Islamic world, though it is difficult to gauge its depth and breadth. Al-Qaeda wants the United States, indeed the West more generally, out of the Persian Gulf and the Middle East. In bin Laden's view, the United States helps to keep Muslim peoples in poverty and imposes upon them a Western culture deeply offensive to traditional Islam. He blames the United States for the continued suffering of the people of Iraq and for the Israeli occupation of the West Bank and the Gaza Strip. For him, Israel is a foreign element in the Middle East and should be destroyed. The U.S. military presence in Saudi Arabia is a desecration of the Islamic holy places and must end.[2] Once the United States exits the region, al-Qaeda hopes to overthrow the governments of Saudi Arabia and Egypt and replace them with fundamentalist, Taliban-like regimes. It is no wonder that the Saudi regime considered bin Laden so dangerous that it stripped him of his citizenship in 1994.

Al-Qaeda is an ambitious, ruthless, and technically proficient organization. The stark evidence is at hand. It has attacked the United States before, but not with such striking results.[3] For the September 11 attack, at least nineteen men, supported by perhaps a dozen others, plotted for years an action that at least some of them knew would result in their deaths. Each member of the conspiracy had numerous opportunities to defect. The terrorists piloting the four passenger jets understood the level of destruction they would exact. They carefully studied airport security and found the airports that seemed most vulnerable. Several of these men appear to have trained for years in U.S. flight schools to learn enough to pilot an aircraft into a building. The cockpits of the 757 and 767 are quite similar, which does not seem coincidental; a single experienced pilot could tutor all of the hijackers on the fine points of operating the aircraft. Between the two aircraft types, the conspirators could choose from a wide selection of flights. The 767s, the aircraft with the most fuel and hence the greatest destructive potential, were directed at the biggest target, the World Trade Center. The proximity of the departure airports to the targets permitted tactical "surprise." All four planes had small passenger complements relative to their capacity; this hardly seems coincidental given the hijackers' plan to take the aircraft with box-cutters. The hijackings of all four airliners were carefully synchronized. If this had been a Western commando raid, it would be considered nothing short of brilliant. Given the demonstrated motivation and organizational and technical skills of its members, al-Qaeda will likely attempt further large-scale attacks on the United States or its citizens and soldiers abroad, or both.

Al-Qaeda benefited from the direct support of Afghanistan, which had been governed in recent years by the fundamentalist Taliban religio-political movement. The Taliban ruled Afghanistan as a kind of crude police state. Not only was bin Laden protected by the regime, but his money and his forces were a pillar of its power. The Taliban had been asked before by the United States to expel bin Laden but always demurred. This base proved to be of great utility to bin Laden and to al-Qaeda. Individuals came from around the world to receive training in terrorist techniques and tactics.[4] Afghanistan is a large country, with rugged terrain and long and lawless borders, far from any Western base; it is hard to monitor, let alone attack—in other words, a perfect hideout. Without this bastion, bin Laden would probably have been on the run much of the time. Al-Qaeda also seems to have benefited from the tacit support of some other governments; persistent reports suggest that wealthy individuals in several Gulf states have contributed to the organization, with the knowledge though not the active cooperation of their governments. Saudi Arabia is often mentioned by name.[5]

As has often been pointed out, the United States and most developed, democratic countries are extremely vulnerable to terrorist attacks. These are open societies that have not policed their borders successfully. Drugs and illegal immigrants move into the United States with ease; cash, guns, and stolen cars move out. Dangerous activities occur in modern society every day. Aircraft take off and land; hazardous materials—flammable, explosive, or poisonous—move by truck, train, and ship. And in the United States, those with money and some patience can obtain explosives, firearms, and quantities of ammunition. Prosaic means can be employed against everyday targets to produce catastrophic results. One must nevertheless also be concerned about chemical, biological, or nuclear attacks. The ability to make chemical agents and biological poisons is more widespread than ever, though turning the basic ingredients into useful weapons and delivering them effectively on a large scale has thus far not proven easy for small clandestine groups.[6] Nuclear weapons are more difficult to obtain, but fears remain that some of the very large number manufactured during the Cold War, or some of those built by new nuclear states, could fall into the wrong hands. Alternatively, primitive nuclear weapons designs are widely available; getting the fissionable material to make a nuclear bomb is still difficult, but not all of this material is as secure as it should be. Thus the possibility of a major terrorist attack with biological, chemical, or nuclear weapons cannot be ruled out.

Most terrorists do not exploit the vulnerabilities of advanced industrial societies; law enforcement helps to make it difficult, though obviously not impossible. More important, most terrorist organizations do not wish to make the United States an implacable enemy. Many have limited political objectives, which the United States can hinder or help. Al-Qaeda clearly has more ambitious objectives than most terrorist organizations; it seeks to expel the most powerful state in history from a part of the world that has been central to U.S. foreign policy for more than half a century, and it intends to do so without a large standing military. Hence al-Qaeda has opted for large-scale murder to achieve its objectives, and it will seek to kill Americans so long as the United States does not give in to its demands.

What Is to Be Done?

Like any war, or even any large civil project, the war against al-Qaeda and other terrorist groups bent on mass destruction requires a strategy. A strategy lays out an interlinked chain of problems that must be solved to address the ultimate problem, the defeat of the adversary. Although the United States and its allies may never fully destroy al-Qaeda, or aligned organizations, or new organizations that emulate them, the antiterror coalition that the United States has built can aspire to reduce the terrorists to desperate groups of exhausted stragglers, with few resources and little hope of success. A strategy sets priorities and focuses available resources—money, time, political capital, and military power—on the main effort. Strategies have both a military and a diplomatic dimension. Within the military dimension, states may choose among offensive, defensive, and punitive operations. In this war, diplomacy will loom larger than military operations, and within the military dimension, defensive activities will loom larger than offensive and punitive ones. That said, without a militarily offensive component, this war cannot be won. Finally, this is a war of attrition, not a blitzkrieg. Al-Qaeda cannot be rounded up in a night's work. If the United States wishes to pursue a major effort against al-Qaeda, its supporters, and any future imitators, it must be prepared to accept significant costs and risks over an extended period. There will likely be an exchange of blows, in the United States and abroad. This war is necessary because bin Laden and others like him will continue to attack the United States so long as it asserts its power and influence in other parts of the world.

Sound strategy requires the establishment of priorities because resources are scarce. Resources must be ruthlessly concentrated against the main threat. There are two primary adversaries in this fight against terrorism: the extended al-Qaeda organization and the states that support it. Al-Qaeda is the principal terrorist organization that has attempted to engage in mass destruction attacks on the United States.[7] It has shown itself to be more capable and more politically ambitious than most. It is the imminent threat. Other terrorist organizations, however, must be kept under surveillance and attacked preemptively if they seem ready to strike the United States or its allies in mass attacks, or if they appear intent on aligning themselves with al-Qaeda.

Allies are essential for success in the war on terrorism, which helps to explain the determination of President George W. Bush and his administration to build a broad coalition. Bin Laden had training camps and bases in Afghanistan, but in other countries al-Qaeda's presence has been more shadowy. Wherever this organization takes root, it must be fought. But it will not always be necessary or possible for the United States to do the fighting. Allied military and police forces are more appropriate instruments to apprehend terrorists operating within their national borders than are U.S. forces. They have information that the United States may not have, and they know the territory and people better. The odds of finding the adversary and avoiding collateral damage increase to the extent that the "host" nation-state does the hard work. Moreover, host states can deal better politically with any collateral damage—that is, accidental destruction of civilian life and property. Much of the war will look a lot like conventional law enforcement by the governments of cooperative countries. Efforts must also be made to weaken terrorist organizations by attacking their infrastructure; both cooperative and clandestine methods can be used to deny these groups access to funds and matériel.

As noted earlier, al-Qaeda has found tacit and active support from nation-states. In the case of partial or tacit support, it may be assumed that there is some disagreement within the political leadership of the country in question about the wisdom of such a policy. The objective is to induce these states to change their practices through persuasion, bribery, or nonviolent coercion. Again, diplomacy looms large in this struggle. Nevertheless, the United States must be prepared to bypass national governments should they fail to cooperate. Given the utter ruthlessness of al-Qaeda, the United States cannot afford to allow it a sanctuary anywhere. From time to time, U.S. forces may simply need to attack al-Qaeda cells directly. This may be a job for special operations forces who would try to avoid contact with national armed forces. In any case, to deter national armed forces from getting in the way, or to foil them if they try, the United States must maintain a strong conventional military capability. Occasionally, it may be necessary to engage in conventional wars with such countries.

Some regimes may choose to support bin Laden's cause, like the Taliban did in Afghanistan. Where a regime has close relations with the terrorists, it is reasonable to treat the host nation as an ally of al-Qaeda and an enemy of the United States. The United States must be prepared to wage war against such states to destroy terrorist groups themselves, to prevent their reconstitution by eliminating the regimes that support them, and to deter other nation-states from supporting terrorism. The United States must make it clear that direct support of terrorists who try to kill large numbers of Americans is tantamount to participation in the attack. If a nation-state had directed a conventional weapon of war at the World Trade Center, U.S. forces would have retaliated immediately. Particularly in the age of weapons of mass destruction, the United States cannot allow any state to participate in catastrophic attacks on its homeland with impunity. More intensive defensive precautions can reduce but not eliminate U.S. vulnerability to mass destruction attacks, so deterrence must be the first line of defense. For these reasons, the Taliban regime in Afghanistan had to be destroyed.

Initially, the Bush administration hesitated to embrace the objective of ousting the Taliban regime.[8] The administration was more interested in bin Laden and al-Qaeda than in their hosts, and in his speech of September 20, President Bush gave the Taliban an opportunity to "hand over the terrorists" *or* "share their fate."[9] Even after the first five days of air strikes, in his press conference of October 11, President Bush gave the Taliban a "second chance" to turn over bin Laden and evict his organization from Afghanistan.[10] Given the difficulty of finding these terrorists, as well as the political complexities of waging war in Afghanistan, this was a reasonable offer, though in my judgment a harmful one from the point of view of deterrence of future attacks. Once the Taliban declined the opportunity to cooperate, the United States had no choice but to wage war on them to the extent that was militarily and politically practical, with the objective of driving them from power.[11]

Tactics: Forces and Methods

Any military campaign has defensive and offensive aspects. Because of its geographical position and great military potential, the United States is accustomed to being on the offensive, but in this campaign the defensive must assume equal or greater importance. Considerable time will be required to develop enough political and military pressure on al-Qaeda to suppress its ability to conduct operations. That organization will probably have the opportunity to attack the United States or its friends again. The United States must thus do all it can defensively to reduce the probability of additional attacks on the U.S. homeland, and to limit the damage should such attacks occur. The United States has been taught a costly but valuable lesson about the vulnerability of modern society to terrorism. Thus, even after al-Qaeda is destroyed, the United States will need to maintain its defenses. This means new vigilance in the most fragile corners of the transportation, energy, power, and communication systems and closer attention to the security of government buildings.

The mobilization of thousands of National Guardsmen and reservists after September 11 had the immediate purpose of enhancing U.S. territorial defenses—including more attentive airspace management, port surveillance, and airport security. This is only the beginning. A new or reoriented joint, multiservice command, staffed by active-duty regulars and reservists and dedicated exclusively to territorial defense, should be created to oversee this enduring mission.[12] Many additional military man-hours will likely be required on a sustained basis for territorial defense. Elements of the active armed forces, the Coast Guard, and the National Guard and Reserves may require redirection or expansion, or possibly both. The United States may need to ask its weekend warriors to serve more weekends, and indeed more weeks, each year.

Enhanced intelligence capabilities are necessary for both defense and offense. Students of terrorism and its close cousin, insurgency, invariably stress the critical importance of intelligence.[13] Intelligence must be gathered on terrorist groups overseas. Such intelligence will come not only from U.S. technical surveillance methods and spies but also from the daily hard work of national police forces abroad. The critical importance of intelligence is one of the main reasons why the United States needs the support of allies. U.S. law enforcement agencies will also have to redouble their efforts. Intelligence provides the data necessary for preventive and preemptive attacks by the national military or police forces of the countries in which the terrorist groups have taken refuge, or by U.S. forces. Even tardy warning of terrorist attacks as they get under way may provide a useful and life-saving margin of time. Intelligence from abroad must also be blended with intelligence gathered at home.

More sustained attention is necessary to the organization of the U.S. counterterrorism intelligence effort. Historically, the following has proven of great utility in all kinds of military endeavors: the staffing of a dedicated intelligence center with full-time, long-serving professionals with a deep knowledge of the adversary; the timely collection of intelligence from multiple sources in that center; the analysis of that data for specific information as well as patterns that reveal the adversary's presence or intentions; and the transmission of that data to those who can best use it for offensive or defensive purposes.[14] Anecdotal information suggests that the United States suffered shortcomings in this regard; data may have been present that could have permitted the early detection of the September 11 plot, but it was not fully exploited.[15] Formally, the Central Intelligence Agency's Counterterrorist Center (CTC) is responsible for "coordinating the counterterrorist efforts of the Intelligence Community," including "exploiting all source intelligence."[16] Nevertheless, this intelligence effort has been the subject of persistent criticism, in particular for weaknesses in interagency cooperation; failure to concentrate all potentially useful information in one place, especially information gathered by law enforcement agencies in the United States; and untimely analysis.[17] The CTC's mandate needs to be strengthened so that all useful information gathered by any intelligence or law enforcement agency is concentrated for analysis. The CTC will also require more money and staff.

Offensive action and offensive military capabilities are necessary components of a successful counterterror strategy. Offensive action is required to destroy regimes that align with terrorists; offensive capabilities allow the United States to threaten credibly other regimes that might consider supporting terrorists. Offensive action against terrorists is needed to eliminate them as threats. But even unsuccessful offensive actions, which force terrorist units or terrorist cells to stay perpetually on the move to avoid destruction, will help to reduce their capability. Constant surveillance makes it difficult for them to plan and organize. Constant pursuit makes it dangerous for them to rest. The threat of offensive action is critical to exhausting the terrorists, whether they are with units in the field in Afghanistan or hiding out in cities and empty quarters across the world. This threat will be credible only if the United States launches an offensive operation from time to time, large or small. Offensive action is also necessary to support U.S. diplomacy. Thus far, U.S. diplomats have stressed the concerns of existing and prospective allies that the United States might overreact with excessive and indiscriminate violence. It is disturbing that they believe that U.S. decisionmakers could be so stupid and brutal, but it is a good thing that they understand the deep emotion that drives U.S. purpose. The United States must threaten offensive war so that these allies understand the seriousness of U.S. intent. The more cooperation the United States gets from allies on the intelligence and policing front, the less necessary it becomes for the United States to behave unilaterally, militarily, and with the attendant risks of collateral damage and escalation. If the United States does not act militarily from time to time, this risk will lose its force as an incentive for U.S. allies. Periodically taking the offensive is also necessary to maintain morale at home. Given that al-Qaeda will continue to try to hit the United States and its friends, the public will probably want to see the United States "bring justice to our enemies."[18]

To take the offensive, the United States will need to exploit perishable intelligence on the existence and location of terrorist cells. Flexible, fast, and relatively discriminate forces are essential. The American people and the leaders of the American military must be prepared to accept the risk of significant U.S. casualties in small, hard-hitting raids. Even when other nations cooperate by providing intelligence, and would be willing to arrest or destroy terrorists in their midst, they may lack the capability and need augmentation from the United States. In any event, political decisionmakers in the United States and abroad who approve strikes on the basis of this information will have to come to terms with the risks to innocent civilians. Occasions will surely arise when there are trade-offs between effectiveness against the adversary and casualties to U.S. and allied forces, or to innocents caught in the crossfire. It will occasionally be necessary to err on the side of effectiveness. This is a tragic fact of war that will stress the persuasive skills of U.S. diplomats, as it did in the first weeks of the air campaign against Afghanistan.

The United States has large special operations forces well suited to the counterterror mission: small groups of highly trained individual fighters from all the services, supported by an array of specially designed and expertly piloted helicopters, aircraft, and small watercraft. (They also include experts at training and advising foreign soldiers.) These forces may be more effective and cause less collateral damage than cruise missiles or precision guided bombs in certain situations. In the past, U.S. decisionmakers have been reluctant to employ these forces because their missions involve a significant risk to the troops. Given the seriousness of the new war and the apparent commitment of the American people, such concerns are likely to diminish. These forces may require additional mobility assets—planes, helicopters, and other more exotic equipment. It may also be reasonable to expand the special operations forces by reorienting some active units such as the 82d Airborne Division and the 101st Air Assault (Helicopter) Division to this mission. The U.S. Marine Corps also deploys many units that could prove useful to the counterterror mission. Three separate reinforced battalions of marines are generally deployed afloat, on special assault ships loaded with helicopters and hovercraft, around the world at any one time. Though the marines judge these forces to be "special operations capable," it would be sensible to stress even further their special operations mission. Moreover, given that most U.S. Navy carrier air wings do not currently fill the hangar space available on existing carriers, it is reasonable to put a company of army or marine special operations troops and their associated helicopters on each one.[19] To permit speedy action, emergency basing and overflight rights around the world must be obtained in advance—yet another task for diplomacy.

The military will also need to augment its ability to gather tactical intelligence to support operations under way. Often the United States will have only a rough idea of where terrorist training camps, quasi regular units, or clandestine units are hiding. An enhanced ability to focus intelligence assets on key objectives is of great importance. Insofar as the adversary operates in small groups without much heavy equipment, the task will be difficult. For the last decade, the United States has experimented with unmanned aircraft, "intelligence drones." It needs to buy more drones, and soon. These devices have been used profitably to police Bosnia and Kosovo. They also played a role in the Kosovo war. Unlike satellites, intelligence drones are extremely flexible; they can focus on a small piece of terrain and remain overhead for several hours at a time. They are just machines, and by current standards not very expensive ones; the American people will not mind losing one every now and then to obtain critical information.[20]

Above all, the "war" against terrorism will require patience and sustained national will. It will take time for the United States and its allies build up a full intelligence picture of the adversary and enhance existing worldwide intelligence capabilities to better detect these elusive foes. As the United States pursues terrorist groups, they will fight back. They will resist locally when U.S. and other forces try to apprehend or destroy them. More important, the terrorists will try to mount additional attacks against the United States, against U.S. installations abroad, and against U.S. allies. Terrorists will attempt this anyway, but in seeking to destroy them, the United States may cause them to accelerate their attacks.

The U.S. security establishment will need to be innovative and adaptive, just as the adversary has proven to be.[21] The American people cannot go into this fight without understanding that they may suffer more pain before the problem recedes.

Finally, American leaders will have to fight political and bureaucratic inertia at home and abroad. Prior to September 11, the United States had a counterterror "administered policy." Administered policies prevail in democracies, where the political leadership regularly trades off initiatives that might be highly effective in one policy area against their costs measured in terms of other agendas, values, and policies. Bureaucracies struggle to maintain their autonomy and often fail to cooperate to achieve stated purposes. Change, when it comes, is incremental. Before September 11 the counterterror effort was like any other administered policy; although it enjoyed higher priority and more resources than it once did, it still competed for political, financial, and human resources on a relatively level playing field with many other policies. That approach was entirely reasonable to me, but has been proven wrong. War is different; in war other policies assume significantly lower priority. Because terrorists are elusive, it will be difficult to sustain the kind of focus that war requires. Failure to sustain that focus will allow al-Qaeda to remain quiet, lick any wounds it sustains in the first flush of U.S. anger and coalition solidarity, rebuild its cadres, and then strike again—harder and more effectively than before. While life must go on, a return to treating counterterrorism as an administered policy must await significant evidence of real success in destroying the al-Qaeda organization.

The Diplomacy of a Counterterror War and the Implications for U.S. Grand Strategy

Both enthusiastic allies and quiet back-channel assistance from around the world will be central to a successful counterterror campaign, but allies are not always easy to find. The United States has been spoiled by its Cold War success. Threatened neighbors of the Soviet Union quickly sought alignment with the United States. During Operation Desert Shield, Arab states in the way of Saddam Hussein's legions did not require much persuading to join the U.S. coalition; those farther away needed subsidies just to show up. The war against terrorism is more difficult. The major al-Qaeda terrorist action has been directed against the United States, though attacks both at home and abroad have caught many foreign nationals in the crossfire. States that have been the victims of tenuously related or unrelated terrorist groups have proven responsive to U.S. requests for help (e.g., Russia, India, and Israel). The United States also needs the assistance of states whose leaders believe that (1) they are not terrorist targets, (2) they can easily redirect terror toward others, or (3) their own citizens may sympathize with al-Qaeda.

The United States needs friends, and thus must prioritize among its many foreign policy and defense policy initiatives, because these initiatives have frequently antagonized other governments and peoples. All the governments whose help is required, whether they are democratic or not, must deal with their own publics. Therefore the United States must find ways to explain to their people why cooperation against these terrorists is in their interest. The United States clearly cannot afford to make every state in the world prosperous and happy. It cannot afford to end every conflict in favor of any ally the United States needs. Sometimes the United States will want the help of both parties to a regional conflict, and cannot reward one party at the expense of another. And it cannot afford to peremptorily abandon long-standing allies in a heartbeat. Such actions have their own costs and risks. But the United States must be much more disciplined in its choices, and much more attuned to the views of others, if it is to sustain this coalition over the long term.[22]

In the years since the Cold War ended, the United States has been immensely powerful, and relatively capricious. It has often acted against the interests of others in pursuit of modest gains, as it did in the case of NATO expansion, the Kosovo war, and the Bush administration's early insistence that national missile defenses would be built with or without Russian cooperation. All these policies had alternatives that could have achieved many of the goals of their U.S. advocates while leaving Russia and others less displeased. Similarly the United States has often failed to act out of fear of incurring modest costs: It has applied insufficient pressure on Israel to suppress its settlement policy in the West Bank and Gaza; has shown little creativity in trying to end the politically damaging low-grade war and leaky economic embargo of Iraq; and made no effort to help others inhibit the course of the Rwanda genocide. The American media have been content to cover international politics episodically and often superficially. The U.S. foreign and security policy record is not one of unalloyed failure.[23] It is, however, a record of indiscipline in which calculations of short-term domestic political gains or losses often dominated decisionmaking.

The post–Cold War world of easy preeminence, controlled low-cost wars, budgetary plenty, and choices avoided is over. In the past I argued that the United States failed to settle on a grand strategy to guide its international behavior after the demise of the Soviet Union.[24] Democrats and Republicans could agree on only one thing: The United States should remain the most powerful state in the world. Beyond that, a good many Democrats wanted to use this power to pursue liberal purposes: improving international organizations and institutions, strengthening international treaties, increasing the power of international law, and spreading democracy. Republicans seem to have wanted to use this power to consolidate U.S. superiority and to create still more power. Russia was viewed as perpetually on the verge of backsliding toward Soviet-style imperialism, and China was feared as a budding peer competitor; both needed containment. Neither political party energetically discussed its preferred policies with the American people. Neither was willing to ask the American people for serious sacrifices to pursue its preferred objectives, and neither had to do so. Sacrifice is now necessary if the United States is to sustain an activist foreign policy, and thus the reasons to pursue such a policy must be explained to and accepted by the American people. Otherwise, if the war on terrorism proves to be not only long but more costly than Americans hope, the temptation to retreat from the world stage will be strong.

Although the outlines are not clear, advocates of alternative U.S. grand strategies during the last decade now seem inclined to superimpose these strategies on the campaign against terror. Advocates of greater restraint in U.S. foreign policy, often unfairly dubbed "neo-isolationists," argue that the United States must retaliate strongly for the September 11 attacks if it is to deter future attacks. But they are uninterested in what comes after, because they believe that the United States should do less in the world. If the United States is less involved, it will be less of a target. If it is less often a target, it needs less assistance to defend itself and its interests. This approach to terror is internally consistent, but it definitely does not defend an active U.S. world role.

Liberal internationalists seem much more interested in the process by which the campaign against terrorism is conducted. The United Nations must be involved at every step. Resort to law must take precedence over tactical advantage. Terrorists must be treated like criminals, not enemies: Police should apprehend them; courts should try them. Military action should occur seldom if at all, and it should always be precise. A state that sponsors terrorism, such as Afghanistan, should be diplomatically isolated, condemned at the UN, subjected to an arms embargo, and economically sanctioned in any way that does not harm the general populace. The United States should join the international criminal court, and as a token of its good intentions sign most of the treaties it has eschewed. This approach preserves a world role for the United States but, given the determination of the adversary and the foibles of other countries, seems doomed to failure.

Primacists have also tried to direct this campaign. Perhaps the strangest advice is rumored to have come from Paul Wolfowitz, the U.S. deputy secretary of defense. He seems to believe that the time is ripe to deal with all of the United States' enemies and problems in the Middle East and Persian Gulf and further consolidate an already dominant U.S. power position. Wolfowitz is reported to have recommended action against Iraq, Syria, and Hezbollah bases in Lebanon.[25] Violent regimes and movements they are, and no strangers to terrorism, but none of them seems to be connected to al-Qaeda and its maximalist objectives and methods. Were this to change, Wolfowitz's inclinations would make more sense. But going after all of them now looks too much like a script written by al-Qaeda propagandists; such attacks would surely cause states whose cooperation the United States needs to see the campaign as anti-Arab and anti-Islam, and sit this war out. Such a multifront attack might produce the very rebellions in Saudi Arabia, the other Gulf states, and Egypt that the United States hopes to prevent. This proposed four-front war is especially odd given that the Bush administration campaigned on the proposition that the U.S. military was incapable of dealing with two nearly simultaneous major regional wars.

One grand strategy advocated over the last decade is broadly consistent with the requirements of an extended counterterror war. That strategy, termed "selective engagement," argues that the United States has an interest in stable, peaceful, and relatively open political and economic relations in the part of the world that contains important concentrations of economic and military resources: Eurasia. This is an interest that others share. In this strategy, U.S. power is meant to reassure the vulnerable and deter the ambitious. This is a big project that requires a careful setting of priorities. Yet its objectives are limited: The project seeks neither power for its own sake, nor the wholesale reform of other states' domestic constitutions, nor a transformation of international politics. The U.S. position in the Persian Gulf and the Middle East is a central element of this strategy. Al-Qaeda aims to challenge this position. Its leaders believe that if the United States left the region, they could take power in the Gulf and in Egypt. Were this to happen, one can easily imagine several possible dangers: a war between Iraq and Saudi Arabia as Saddam Hussein tries to strangle the fundamentalist Islamic baby in the cradle before its strangles him; war with Iran over security, religious, and nationalist issues; or war with Israel. Given the extreme destructiveness of the 1980–88 Iraq-Iran War (500,000 dead), which saw the use of chemical weapons and rocket attacks on cities—as well as the continued presence of chemical, biological, and nuclear weapons, and rocket delivery systems in the area—any of these possible wars could prove devastating for those in the region and harmful to those farther away. Moreover, any one of them would surely affect the production, distribution, and price of oil—still important to the global economy. Their political, military, and economic ripple effects would likely be felt globally, affecting other political relationships. The grand strategy of selective engagement does necessitate the campaign against al-Qaeda. The requirements of that campaign have already forced the Bush administration to act in ways that are more consistent with the strategy of selective engagement than they are with primacy.

The United States faces a long war against a small, elusive, and dangerous foe. That struggle must be pursued with discipline and determination if it is to be successful. The United States requires a strategy to guide its efforts, including the allocation of resources. That strategy must set priorities, because resources are scarce and this war will prove expensive. Significant changes in the U.S. national security establishment, including intelligence collection and analysis, military organization and equipment, and emergency preparedness, will prove essential. Finally, if the United States is to sustain both public and international support for the war on terrorism, it will need to resolve long-delayed questions about its future foreign and security policy through an extended discussion involving policymakers, policy analysts, and the American people.

Barry R. Posen is a professor of political science in the Security Studies Program at the Massachusetts Institute of Technology. His first book, *Sources of Military Doctrine: France, Britain and Germany Between the World Wars* (1986), won the American Political Science Association's Woodrow Wilson Foundation Book Award and Ohio State University's Edward J. Furniss Jr., Book Award. He has been an international affairs fellow with the Rockefeller Foundation and with the Council on Foreign Relations and is also the author of *Inadvertent Escalation: Conventional War and Nuclear Risks* (1992).

Notes

1. It is impossible at this time to offer a more precise figure. See Eric Lipton, "Numbers Vary in Tallies of the Victims," *New York Times*, October 25, 2001, pp. B1, B10.
2. United Kingdom, Foreign and Commonwealth Office (FCO), *Responsibility for the Terrorist Atrocities in the United States, 11 September 2001*, pp. 4–5, http://www/fco.gov.uk/news/keythemepages.asp. See also Kenneth Katzman, *Terrorism: Near Eastern Groups and State Sponsors, 2001*, Congressional Research Service, report for Congress, September 10, 2001, pp. 2, 9.
3. FCO, *Responsibility for the Terrorist Atrocities in the United States*, pp. 6–10, links al-Qaeda to the fight against U.S. special operations forces in Somalia in October 1993, to the bombing of the U.S. embassies in Kenya and Tanzania in August 1998, and to the attack on the USS *Cole* in October 2000, as well as to several thwarted operations. See also Katzman, *Terrorism*, pp. 10–11, which also links bin Ladin indirectly to the February 1993 World Trade Center bombing.
4. Ali A. Jalali, "Afghanistan: The Anatomy of an Ongoing Conflict," *Parameters*, Vol. 31, No. 1 (Spring 2001), p. 5, http://carlisle-www.army.mil/usawc/Parameters/o1spring;jalali.htm.
5. "Saudi Arabia: The Double-Act Wears Thin," *Economist*, September 29, 2001, pp. 22–23.
6. As of this writing, the anthrax poisonings in the United States do not contradict this statement. Until we know more, all we can conclude is that small amounts of lethal anthrax can be obtained and, through the mail, can hurt or kill small numbers of people.
7. The February 1993 bombing of the World Trade Center is not directly attributed to al-Qaeda, but Ramzi Yusef, convicted of masterminding that crime, reportedly collaborated with al-Qaeda to organize several unsuccessful terrorist efforts in Asia. Katzman, *Terrorism*, p. 10.
8. Indeed, as of late October 2001, both the U.S. Department of State and the U.K. Foreign and Commonwealth Office used elliptical language to discuss coalition war aims in Afghanistan.

Secretary of State Colin Powell could only bring himself to say, "There is, however, no place in a new Afghan government for the current leaders of the Taliban regime." See "Campaign against Terrorism," prepared statement for the House International Relations Committee, U.S. Department of State, October 24, 2001, p. 2, http://www.state.gov/secretary/rm/2001. The United Kingdom's statement of war aims suggests that "we require sufficient change in the leadership to ensure that Afghanistan's links to international terrorism are broken." Foreign and Commonwealth Office, "Defeating International Terrorism: Campaign Objectives," p. 1, http://www.fco.gov.uk/news/keythemehome.asp.

9. See "The President's Address," *Washington Post*, September 21, 2001, p. A24.
10. Patrick E. Tyler and Elisabeth Bumiller, " 'Just Bring Him In,' President Hints He Will Halt War If bin Laden Is Handed Over," *New York Times*, October 12, 2001, pp. A1, B5.
11. U.S. leaders wisely exercised some restraint; they did not put large ground forces into the country, who would have provided numerous targets for Afghan riflemen and the appearance of a mission of conquest. Nor did they use firepower indiscriminately, and by large-scale killing of Afghan civilians create the appearance of making war on all Muslims.
12. U.S. Department of Defense, *Quadrennial Defense Review Report*, September 30, 2001, p. 19, states that "DOD will review the establishment of a new unified combatant commander to help address complex inter-agency issues and provide a single military commander to focus military support." This is too tentative.
13. "Nearly all of the threatened or their experts agree that the key to an effective response to terrorism is good intelligence and that such intelligence is difficult to acquire." J. Bowyer Bell, *A Time of Terror: How Democratic Societies Respond to Revolutionary Violence* (New York: Basic Books, 1978), p. 134. Douglas S. Blaufarb draws similar lessons from the U.S. counterinsurgency effort in Vietnam: "Small, lightly armed units, pinpointed operations assisted by 'hunter-killer' squads, imaginative psychological warfare operations—and all of this based upon coordinated collection and exploitation of intelligence—should be the main reliance of the military side of the effort. The police, if they have or can be brought to develop the capability, should play a major role in the intelligence effort and in other programs requiring frequent contact with the public." Blaufarb, *The Counterinsurgency Era: U.S. Doctrine and Performance, 1950 to the Present* (New York: Free Press, 1977), p. 308.
14. The clearest historically grounded exposition of this argument is to be found in Patrick Beesly, *Very Special Intelligence* (New York: Ballantine, 1977), pp. 1–24, which details the formation of the Royal Navy's Operational Intelligence Center, to exploit all source intelligence for the antisubmarine warfare campaign early in World War II.
15. James Risen, "In Hindsight, C.I.A. Sees Flaws That Hindered Efforts on Terror," *New York Times*, October 7, 2001, pp. A1, B2. "In hindsight, it is becoming clear that the C.I.A., F.B.I. and other agencies had significant fragments of information that, under ideal circumstances, could have provided some warning if they had all been pieced together and shared rapidly."
16. "The War on Terrorism," DCI Counterterrorist Center, http://www.cia.gov/terrorism.ctc.html.
17. The National Commission on Terrorism, Ambassador L. Paul Bremer III, Maurice Sonnenberg, Richard K. Betts, Wayne A. Downing, Jane Harman, Fred C. Iklé, Juliette N. Kayyem, John F. Lewis, Jr., Gardner Peckham, and R. James Woolsey, *Countering the Changing Threat of International Terrorism,* report of the National Commission on Terrorism (Washington, D.C., June 5, 2000), http://www.fas.org/irp/threat/commission.htm; and James Kitfield, "CIA, FBI, and Pentagon Team to Fight Terrorism," September 18, 2000, GOVEXEC.com, http://www.govexec.com/dailyfed/0900/091900nt.htm.
18. This sentiment was expressed by President Bush in his address to a joint session of Congress on September 20, 2001: "Whether we bring our enemies to justice or bring justice to our enemies, justice will be done." See "The President's Address."
19. If U.S. Army special operations units are to be permanently deployed at sea, they will need to purchase new "marinized" versions of their current helicopters that are better able to fit below decks, communicate with navy vessels and aircraft, and withstand the corrosive effects of salt air.
20. The U.S. Air Force RQ-1A Predator costs about $8 million apiece. This is the price for a small production run; production on a larger scale would reduce the unit cost. The air force currently

has only thirteen Predators. Ted Nicholas and Rita Rossi, *Military Cost Handbook*, 22d ed. (Fountain Valley, Calif.: Data Search Associates, 2001), p. 4–2. See also Craig Hoyle, "U.S. Build-Up Highlights UAV shortage," *Jane's Defence Weekly*, October 10, 2001, p. 5.

21. For example, the Bush administration has appointed Governor Tom Ridge head of the new Office of Homeland Security to coordinate the activities of all the disparate governmental organizations that contribute to territorial defense; he controls nothing. It may instead prove necessary to organize a new Department of Territorial Security, to consolidate control over some or all of the following: air surveillance and defense units, the Coast Guard, the Border Patrol, counterterror elements of the FBI; and federal-level emergency medical response, humanitarian relief, and damage-repair capabilities.
22. Examples of the kinds of diplomatic choices that the United States faces abound. Russia can control its own nuclear materials and weapons and provide intelligence; Russia has been unhappy with NATO expansion and the Bush administration's national missile defense program. Saudi Arabia and the Gulf states have great air bases, all used by the United States during the Gulf War. These bases would prove useful if the counterterror campaign expands to Iraq. These countries find U.S. tolerance of Israeli settlement policies on the West Bank and Gaza to be a significant irritant. Though the UN oil-for-food program has enabled Iraq to feed and care for its people—and Saddam Hussein deserves the blame for their current misery—the continuation of Gulf War sanctions and the regular bombing of Iraq by U.S. and British warplanes help Saddam portray Iraq as the aggrieved party in the Arab world. Pakistan, a former close supporter of the Taliban, was alienated by the United States' cavalier treatment after the end of the Soviet occupation of Afghanistan. Pakistan was also, until recently, under economic sanctions enacted to show U.S. displeasure with its May 1998 nuclear weapons tests. Pakistan may have the most political influence over Pashtun tribes in Afghanistan whose cooperation will be needed to bring a stable government to that country.
23. Russia did not collapse; the nuclear weapons of the Soviet Union were gathered up and consolidated in Russia for safekeeping; the Balkan wars ended; and the great and middle powers of the world have not yet fallen into any new cold wars with one another. U.S. foreign policymakers get much of the credit.
24. Barry R. Posen and Andrew L. Ross, "Competing Visions for U.S. Grand Strategy," *International Security*, Vol. 21, No. 3 (Winter 1996/97), pp. 5–53.
25. Steven Mufson and Thomas E. Ricks, "Debate over Targets Highlights Difficulty of War on Terrorism," *Washington Post*, September 21, 2001, p. A25. The article depicts a policy fight between Secretary of State Colin Powell, the principal advocate of a policy focused on al-Qaeda, and Deputy Secretary of Defense Wolfowitz, "pushing for a broader range of targets, including Iraq."

Paul R. Pillar, 2004

Counterterrorism after Al Qaeda

The fight against Osama bin Laden's Al Qaeda, the principal terrorist menace to U.S. interests since the mid-1990s, has come a long way. The disciplined, centralized organization that carried out the September 11 attacks is no more. Most of the group's senior and midlevel leaders are either incarcerated or dead, while the majority of those still at large are on the run and focused at least as much on survival as on offensive operations. Bin Laden and his senior deputy, Ayman al-Zawahiri, have survived to this point but have been kept on the run and in hiding, impairing their command and control of what remains of the organization. Al Qaeda still has the capacity to inflict lethal damage, but the key challenges for current counterterrorism efforts are not as much Al Qaeda as what will follow Al Qaeda.

This emerging primary terrorist threat has much in common with Al Qaeda in that it involves the same global network of mostly Sunni Islamic extremists of which bin Laden has been the best known voice. "Al Qaeda" is often broadly applied to the entire terrorist network that threatens U.S. interests although, in fact, the network extends beyond members of this particular organization. The roots of this brand of extremism, if not its most visible advocates and centralized structure, remain very much alive and in some cases are growing deeper. They include the closed economic and political systems in much of the Muslim world that deny many young adults the opportunity to build better lives for themselves and, often, the political representation to voice their grievances peacefully over the lack of such opportunity. Among other lasting causal factors behind the rise of Islamist terrorism are the paucity of credible alternatives to militant Islam as vehicles of opposition to the established order as well as widespread opposition toward U.S. policies within and toward the Muslim world, especially the U.S. position on the Israeli-Palestinian conflict and, more recently, the invasion and occupation of Iraq. In short, even with Al Qaeda waning, the larger terrorist threat from radical Islamists is not.

That radical Islamist threat will come from an eclectic array of groups, cells, and individuals. Those fragments of Al Qaeda that continue to carry on bin Laden's malevolent cause and operate under local leaders as central direction weakens will remain part of the mix. Also increasingly part of the greater terrorist network are like-minded but nameless groups associated with Al Qaeda, such as the Middle Eastern organization headed by Abu Musab al-Zarqawi, and regionally based groups with established identities such as the Iraq-centered Ansar al-Islam and the Southeast Asian Jemaah Islamiya. Many of these groups have local objectives but share the transnational anti-Americanism of the larger network. Finally, individuals best labeled simply as jihadists, who carry no group membership card but move through and draw support from the global network of like-minded radical Islamists, are also part of the picture. From their ranks, some will likely emerge with the leadership skills needed to organize operational cells and conduct terrorist attacks.

In a word, the transformation of the terrorist threat from the Al Qaeda of September 11, 2001, to the mixture described above is one of decentralization. The initiative, direction, and support for anti-U.S. terrorism will come from more, and more widely scattered, locations than it did before. Although the breaking up of Al Qaeda lessens but does not eliminate the risks posed by particularly large, well-organized, and well-financed terrorist operations, the decentralization of the threat poses offsetting problems for collecting and analyzing related intelligence, enlisting foreign support to counter it, and sustaining the United States' own commitment to combat it while avoiding further damage to U.S. relations with the Muslim world. For these reasons, the counterterrorism challenges after the defeat of Al Qaeda may very well be even more complex than they were before.

Uncertain Targets for Intelligence

The small, secretive nature of terrorist plots and the indeterminate nature of the target—likely to become an even greater problem as the Islamic terrorist threat further decentralizes—have always made terrorism a particularly difficult target subject. The mission of intelligence in counterterrorism is not only to monitor known terrorists and terrorist groups but also to uncover any individuals or groups who might conduct a terrorist attack against the United States and its interests. The greater the number of independent actors and centers of terrorist planning and operations, the more difficult that mission becomes. Exhortations to the intelligence community to penetrate terrorist groups are useless if the groups that need to be penetrated have not even been identified.

The U.S. intelligence community's experience a decade ago may help it adjust to the transformation currently underway. Prior to the 1993 World Trade Center (WTC) bombing, the terrorist threat against the United States was thought of chiefly in terms of known, named, discrete groups such as the Lebanese Hizballah. The principal analytical challenges involved identifying the structure and strength of each group as well as making sense of the pseudonymous "claim names" commonly used to assume responsibility for attacks. The 1993 WTC bombing and the subsequent rolled-up plot to bomb several other New York City landmarks introduced the concept of ad hoc terrorists: nameless cells of radicals who come together for the sole purpose of carrying out a specific attack.

The term "ad hoc" was subsequently discarded as too casual and as not reflecting the links to the wider network that intelligence work through the mid-1990s gradually uncovered. Even with those links, however, the New York plots were examples of a decentralized threat in that they were evidently initiated locally. As demonstrated by the shoestring budget on which the 1993 WTC bombers operated, the plots were not directed and financed by bin Laden from a lair in Sudan or South Asia but rather by the operation's ringleader, Ramzi Yousef, and his still unknown financial patrons. Now, in 2004, with Al Qaeda having risen and mostly fallen, the threats that U.S. intelligence must monitor in the current decade have in a sense returned to what existed in the early 1990s; only now the threat has many more moving parts, more geographically disparate operations, and more ideological momentum.

Much, though not all, of the intelligence community's counterterrorism efforts over the past several years can be applied to the increasingly decentralized threat the world now faces. Even the intelligence work narrowly focused on Al Qaeda has unearthed many leads and links, involving anything from telephone calls to shared apartments, that are useful in uncovering other possible centers of terrorist planning and operations. These links are central to intelligence counterterrorism efforts because linkages with known terrorists can uncover other individuals who may be terrorists themselves. Most successful U.S. efforts to disrupt terrorist organizations in the past, including the capture of most of the Al Qaeda leadership since September 11, 2001, have resulted from such link analysis.

The danger now lies in the fact that the looser the operational connections become and the less Islamist terrorism is instigated by a single figure, the harder it will be to uncover exploitable links and the more likely that the instigators of future terrorist attacks will escape the notice of U.S. intelligence. In a more decentralized network, these individuals will go unnoticed not because data on analysts' screens are misinterpreted but because they will never appear on those screens in the first place.

The September 11 plot helps to illustrate the point. Retrospective inquiries have given a great deal of attention to the tardiness in placing two of the hijackers, Khalid al-Mihdhar and Nawaf al-Hazmi, on U.S. government watch lists. Had these individuals been identified, they might have been prevented from entering the United States and launching the attack. Ironically, less attention has been paid to what made al-Mihdhar and al-Hazmi candidates for a watch list in the first place: their participation in a meeting with an Al Qaeda operative in Kuala Lumpur. U.S. intelligence acquired information about the meeting by piecing together Al Qaeda's activities in the Far East and by developing rosters of Al Qaeda intermediaries whose activities could be tracked to gain information that would provide new leads. Although skillful and creative intelligence work, it relied on linkages to a known terrorist group, Al Qaeda—linkages that existed because bin Laden and senior Al Qaeda leadership in South Asia ultimately directed and financed the terrorist operation in question. A decentralized version of the threat will not necessarily leave such a trail.

Muhammad Atta and some of the other September 11 hijackers were never even considered candidates for the watch lists because intelligence reporting had not previously associated them with known terrorists. In fact, one of Al Qaeda's criteria for selecting the hijackers almost certainly was that they were relatively clean, in that they did not have any such associations. In a more decentralized future network, such connections are even less likely.

Yet, even a decentralized terrorist threat has some linkages that can be exploited, and this will be key to intelligence community counterterrorist efforts from here on out. Within the networks of Sunni Islamic extremists, almost everyone can be linked at least indirectly, such as through their past common experiences in camps in Afghanistan, to almost everyone else. The overwhelming majority of these linkages, however, consists of only casual contacts and do not involve preparations for terrorist operations directed against the United States, as the meeting in Kuala Lumpur evidently did. No intelligence service has the resources to monitor all of these contacts, to compile the life history of every extremist who has the potential to become a terrorist, or to construct comprehensive sociograms of the radical Islamist scene. Detecting the perpetrators of the next terrorist attack against the United States will therefore have to go beyond link analysis and increasingly rely on other techniques for picking terrorists out of a crowd.

Mining of financial, travel, and other data on personal actions and circumstances other than mere association with questionable individuals and groups[1] is one such technique. The potential for such data mining goes well beyond current usage. Yet, data mining for counterterrorism purposes will always require a major investment in obtaining and manipulating the data in return for only a modest narrowing of the search for terrorists. Numerous practical difficulties in gaining access to personal information, significant privacy issues, and the lack of a reliable algorithm for processing the data all inhibit the effectiveness of this technique. The September 11 attacks, however, significantly lowered the threshold for all investments in counterterrorist operations, including data mining, making this technique worth trying even if it appears no more cost effective than it did before September 11, 2001. The Transportation Security Administration already uses profiling to screen air passengers, the intelligence community might reasonably extend this technique to include profiling of foreigners to identify possible terrorists even before they buy an airplane ticket.

It is the U.S. population and the U.S. government, not the intelligence community, that will have to make the most important adjustment concerning intelligence operations. The reality is that they will have to lower their expectations of just how much of the burden of stopping terrorists that intelligence can carry. An increasingly decentralized terrorist threat and indeterminate intelligence target will mean that an even greater number of terrorists and terrorist plots may escape the notice of intelligence services altogether. The transformation in the threat itself coupled with the inherent limits of intelligence operations implies that more of the counterterrorist burden will have to be borne by other policy instruments, from initiatives to address the reasons individuals gravitate toward terrorism in the first place to physical security measures to defeat attempted attacks.

Fragile International Cooperation

The willingness of governments worldwide to join the campaign against terrorism has increased significantly over the last two decades—a welcome change from earlier days when many regimes, through their representatives at the United Nations General Assembly and elsewhere, were more apt to condone terrorism than to condemn it because of their support for "national liberation movements." The September 11 attacks further strengthened an apparent global antiterrorism consensus. This apparent collective commitment to counterterrorism should not be taken for granted. Despite many governments' declarations that they stand with the United States in combating terrorism, each decision by a foreign government on whether to cooperate with the United States reflects calculations about the threat that nation faces from particular terrorist groups, its relations with the United States, any incentives Washington offers for its cooperation, domestic opinion, and the potential effect of enhanced counterterrorist measures on its domestic interests. Such calculations can change, and the perceived net advantage of cooperating may be slim. In short, global cooperation against terrorism is already fragile.

Much of foreign governments' willingness to help has depended on Al Qaeda's record and menacing capabilities. The sheer enormity of the September 11 attacks and the unprecedented impact they had on the U.S. government's priorities and policies have accounted for much of the increased willingness among foreign governments to assist in efforts to combat terrorism. The threat Al Qaeda has posed to some of the governments themselves, particularly the Saudi regime, also has helped the United States gain cooperation. The bombings in Riyadh in May and November 2003 were wake-up calls that partly nullified the numerous reasons for the Saudis' sluggishness in cracking down on Islamic extremists in their midst. Most of the victims of the November bombing were Arabs of modest means; this sloppy targeting undoubtedly cost Al Qaeda some of its support in the kingdom.

Foreign cooperation will become more problematic as the issue moves beyond Al Qaeda. How will governments respond to a U.S. appeal to move against groups that have never inflicted comparable horrors on the United States or on any other nation or against groups that do not conspicuously pose the kind of threat that Al Qaeda has posed to Saudi Arabia? How can regimes be motivated to tackle Islamic groups that may represent an emerging terrorist threat but have not yet resorted to terrorism, such as the Central Asian–based Hizb al-Tahrir? Without the special glue that the attacks of September 11 provide against a centralized and directed Al Qaeda, many of the past reasons for foot-dragging in counterterrorist efforts are likely to reassert themselves. These reasons include the sympathy that governments or their populations feel for many of the anti-Western or anti-imperialist themes in whose name terrorists claim to act, an aversion to doing Washington's bidding against interests closer to home, and a general reluctance to rock local boats.

Problems that the United States has already encountered in dealing with Lebanese Hizballah[2] illustrate some of the difficulties in more generally enlisting foreign help against terrorist groups—even highly capable groups—other than Al Qaeda. Deputy Secretary of State Richard Armitage once called Hizballah the "A-team" of international terrorism;[3] the group's 1983 bombing of U.S. Marine barracks in Beirut is second only to the events of September 11, 2001, in the number of American deaths attributable to a terrorist attack. Hizballah's terrorist apparatus, led by its longtime chief Imad Mughniyah, remains formidable today. The dominant view of Hizballah in Lebanon and elsewhere in the Middle East, however, is that the group is a legitimate participant in Lebanese politics: the group holds seats in Parliament and provides social services within the country. Despite the events two decades ago in Lebanon, including other bombings and a series of kidnappings of Westerners, Hizballah's accepted political status has prevented U.S. officials from effectively appealing for cooperation against Hizballah in the way that the September 11 attacks have allowed them to appeal for cooperation against Al Qaeda. Notwithstanding the major potential terrorist threat it poses, Hizballah has not been clearly implicated in any attack on Americans since the bombing of Khobar Towers eight years ago.

An underlying limitation to foreign willingness to cooperate with the United States on antiterrorist efforts is the skepticism among foreign publics and even elites that the most powerful nation on the planet needs to be preoccupied with small bands of radicals. Even the depth of the trauma that the September 11 attacks caused the American public does not seem to be fully appreciated in many areas overseas, particularly in the Middle East. In addition, the skepticism is likely to be much greater when the U.S. preoccupation is no longer with the group that carried out the September 11 attacks.

Any reduced foreign support for the campaign against terrorism will not be clear or sudden. Certainly, no foreign government will declare that it now supports the terrorists. Instead, foreign governments may be a little slower to act, a little less forthcoming with information, or slightly more apt to cite domestic impediments to cooperation. Whether counterterrorism cooperation weakens, therefore, will rest largely on whether and how Washington responds to the concerns and needs of its foreign partners. As antiterrorist cooperation becomes increasingly more difficult to obtain and more vulnerable to frictions over other issues, sustaining such cooperation will require increased sensitivity to foreign interests.

Muslims' Suspicions

Skepticism and distrust among Muslims across the world about U.S. counterterrorist efforts have impeded international cooperation and may become an even bigger problem in the post–Al Qaeda era. With the perpetrators of the September 11 attacks disabled and Muslims—especially Muslims claiming to act in the name of their religion—still dominating international terrorism, Muslims will still dominate Washington's counterterrorist target list. This fact will continue to encourage questions about whether the so-called U.S. war on terrorism is really a war on Islam. Many Muslims will ask whether a sustained counterterrorist campaign has less to do with fighting terrorism than with maintaining the political status quo in countries with pro-U.S. regimes. Other Muslims will see the campaign as many already see it: as part of a religiously based war between the Muslim world and a Judeo-Christian West.

The "war on terrorism" terminology exacerbates this problem, partly because a war is most clearly understood as a war against somebody rather than a metaphorical war against a tactic. The fact that counterterrorist operations have been aimed primarily at a particular group, Al Qaeda, has minimized this problem thus far. The less the fight is conducted against a single named foe, the greater the problem of misinterpreting the term "war." The problem has been exacerbated by extension of the "war on terrorism" label to the invasion and occupation of Iraq. Even though much of the violence that has plagued Iraq since the operation began is unmistakably attributable to terrorism, the U.S. government undertook the military operation in Iraq primarily for reasons other than counterterrorism, feeding Muslim misperceptions and fears that the United States also has ulterior motives every other time it talks about fighting terrorism.

Such perceptions among Muslims will strengthen the roots of the very Islamist terrorism that already poses the principal threat to U.S. interests. They will encourage a sense that the Muslim world as a whole is in a struggle with the Judeo-Christian West and foster a view of the United States as the chief adversary of Muslims worldwide. Given the fact that Islamist extremism is likely to continue to be the driving force behind significant terrorist threats to U.S. interests, fighting terrorism without the effort being perceived simply as a war against Muslims may be a challenge that can only be lessened and not altogether avoided. President George W. Bush and senior U.S. officials have been careful to disavow any antipathy toward Muslims, which has helped to a certain extent. Most Muslims' attitudes will be shaped more by deeds than by words, however, which means that U.S. policies toward Iraq and the Arab-Israeli conflict in particular will be especially influential.

Maintaining the Commitment

The greatest future challenge to the U.S. counterterrorist efforts that may emerge with a more decentralized terrorist threat is the ability to sustain the country's own determination to fight it. The American public has shown that its commitment to counterterrorism can be just as fickle as that of foreign publics. Over the past quarter century, the U.S. population and government has given variable attention, priority, and resources to U.S. counterterrorist programs, with interest and efforts spiking in the aftermath of a major terrorist incident and declining as time passes without an attack.

Important to keep in mind about the strong U.S. attention to counterterrorism during the last three years is that it took a disaster of the dimensions of September 11, 2001, to generate. Although intended to topple the twin towers and kill thousands, the 1993 WTC bombing sparked nothing near a similar amount of attention. Bin Laden and the prowess his group demonstrated with overseas attacks garnered full appreciation among U.S. government specialists of Al Qaeda's intentions and capabilities by at least the late 1990s but still remained comparably unnoticed by the greater U.S. public and government. U.S. citizens and their elected leaders and representatives respond far more readily to dramatic events in their midst than to warnings and analysis about threatening events yet to occur. The further the events of September 11 fade into the past, the more difficult it will be to keep Americans focused on the danger posed by terrorism, especially that posed by terrorists other than the perpetrators of the WTC and Pentagon attacks.

The U.S. response to the March 2004 bombing of commuter trains in Madrid suggests how difficult it is to energize or reenergize Americans about counterterrorism. (Early investigation of the attack indicated that it was also a good example of the decentralized Islamist terrorist threat, being the work of Muslim radicals with only loose associations with Al Qaeda.) Commentary in the United States focused less on the continued potency of the global terrorist threat than on inter-allied differences over the Iraq war, with charges of "appeasement" leveled against Spanish voters for ousting the governing party in an election held three days after the attack. For most Americans, the difference between terrorism inside the United States and terrorism against even a close ally is huge, with only the former capable of boosting their commitment to counterterrorism.

Here again, the "war on terrorism" metaphor appears problematic. Americans tend to think in non-Clausewitzian terms, in which war and peace are markedly different and clearly separated states of being. War entails special sacrifices and rules that the United States does not want to endure in peacetime. Peace means demobilization, relaxation of the nation's guard, and a return to nonmartial pursuits. In U.S. history, in particular, peace has usually meant either victory or withdrawal and a rejection of the reasons for having gone to war in the first place, such as with the Vietnam War. Americans are not accustomed to the concept of a war that is necessary and waged with good reason but offers no prospect of ending with a clear peace and especially a clear victory.[4]

U.S. leaders have conveyed some of the right cautions to the public. Secretary of Defense Donald Rumsfeld correctly observed that the war on terrorism will not end with a surrender on the deck of the USS *Missouri*.[5]Attitudes in the United States, however, probably will be shaped less by such words of caution than by the historical conception of war and peace. Moreover, not having a clear end is not the same as having no end—and the latter is, for practical purposes, what the United States faces in countering terrorism during the years ahead.

In fact, an end, whether clear or not so clear, will be even more elusive in the fight against terrorism than it was during the Cold War. Though the Cold War did not conclude with the signing of any surrender agreement on a battleship, its end was nonetheless fairly distinct, highlighted by the dismantling of the Berlin Wall in November 1989 and the dissolution of the Soviet Union in December 1991. It also entailed an indisputable victory for the West, achieved with the collapse of a single arch foe. Success in counterterrorism offers no such prospect.

The sense of being at war has been sustained thus far not only by war on terrorism rhetoric but also by certain practices that resemble those used in real shooting wars of the past, such as indefinite detention of prisoners without recourse to civilian courts. Although quite useful in mustering support for the invasion, the application of the "war on terrorism" label to the campaign in Iraq will compound the difficulty in sustaining domestic public support for counterterrorism in the post–Al Qaeda era. Even if the reconstruction and democratization of Iraq go well, the fact that this campaign will not bring an end to anti-U.S. terrorist attacks elsewhere might lead many in the United States to question whether the sacrifices made in the name of fighting terrorists had been worthwhile. With so much attention having been paid to state sponsorship of terrorists, and to one (now eliminated) state sponsor in particular, further appeals to make still more sacrifices to defeat disparate and often nameless groups are apt to confuse many U.S. citizens.

More specifically, an unfavorable outcome in Iraq would mean that the Bush administration could face an increase in skepticism about the credibility of warnings concerning threats to U.S. security, including terrorist threats. Meanwhile, the existence of a specific, recognizable, hated terrorist enemy has helped the U.S. population retain its focus. As long as Al Qaeda exists, even in its current, severely weakened form, it will serve that function. Yet, when will Al Qaeda be perceived as having ceased to exist? The group's demise will be nowhere near as clear as, say, the fall of a government.

For the U.S. public, the signal that terrorism has been eliminated as a threat is likely to be the death or capture of bin Laden. Americans tend to personalize their conflicts by concentrating their animosity on a single despised leader, a role that Adolf Hitler and Saddam Hussein played at different times in history. This personalized perspective often leads to an overestimation of the effect of taking out the hated leader, as if the conflict were a game of chess in which checkmate of the king ends the contest. The euphoria following Saddam's capture in December 2003 is an example. Bin Laden, although on the run since 2001, probably has played a role in Al Qaeda's operations almost as limited and indirect as Saddam's influence was on the Iraqi insurgency during his eight months in hiding. Yet, this is where any similarities with Iraq ends. The elimination of bin Laden, if followed by several months without another major Al Qaeda operation against the United States, would lead many in the United States to believe that the time had come to declare victory in the war on terrorism and move on to other concerns. Meanwhile, bin Laden's death would not end or even cripple the radical Islamist movement. Fragments of the organization are likely to spread, subdivide, and inject themselves into other parts of the worldwide Islamist network, like a metastasizing cancer that lives on with sometimes lethal effects even after the original tumor has been excised.

Context and Consequences

Any erosion in the U.S. commitment to counterterrorism that may occur in the years ahead will depend not only on popular perceptions (or misperceptions) of the terrorist threat but also on the broader policy environment in which national security decisions are made. Available resources constitute part of that environment. The resources devoted to counterterrorist operations may decline not because of a specific decision to reduce them but because any further reductions in spending for national security would reduce funds available for counterterrorism. Recent surges in both defense spending and budget deficits make some such reductions likely during the next several years. Departmental comptrollers seeking to spread the pain of those budget cuts will inflict pain on counterterrorist programs along with everything else.

Controversies over privacy and civil liberties constitute another part of the policy environment. The United States has already experienced a backlash against some provisions of the principal post–September 11 counterterrorist legislation, the USA PATRIOT Act. In the wake of the attacks, the U.S. government's investigative powers expanded in some ways that would have been unthinkable earlier. As the clear danger represented by Al Qaeda appears to recede, pressures to roll back those powers will increase.

Any diminution, for whatever combination of reasons, of the priority the United States gives to counterterrorist operations will have consequences that go well beyond specific counterterrorist programs. At home, the impact would be seen in everything from reduced vigilance by baggage screeners to less tolerance by citizens for the daily inconveniences brought about by stricter security measures. Abroad, a weaker commitment to counterterrorism on the part of the U.S. public would make it more difficult for U.S. diplomats to insist on cooperation from foreign governments.

How long any reduction of the U.S. commitment to counterterrorism lasts depends on how much time passes before the next major terrorist attack against U.S. interests, especially the next such attack on U.S. soil. Time, as always, is more on the side of the terrorist, whose patience and historical sense is greater than that of the average American. Americans' perception of the threat almost certainly will decline more rapidly than the threat itself.

The United States thus faces during the next several years an unfortunate combination of a possibly premature celebration along with a continuing and complicating terrorist threat. The counterterrorist successes against Al Qaeda thus far have been impressive and important, and the capture or death of bin Laden will unleash a popular reaction that probably will be nothing short of ecstatic. That joy could be a harmful diversion, however, from attention that will be needed more than ever in the face of remaining problems: difficulty in cementing the counterterrorist cooperation of foreign partners, antagonism and alienation within the Muslim world that breeds more terrorists, and added complexity for intelligence services charged with tracking the threat.

The chief counterterrorist problem confronting U.S. leaders in the years ahead will be a variation on an old challenge: sustaining a national commitment to fighting terrorism even in the absence of a well-defined and clearly perceived danger. The demise of Al Qaeda will make the need for that commitment less apparent to most U.S. citizens, even though the danger will persist in a different form. Political leaders will bear the heavy burden of instilling that commitment, and they will have to do so with analysis, education, and their powers of persuasion, not just with symbols and war cries. No doubt, that will be a very difficult task.

Paul R. Pillar is a former deputy chief of the Central Intelligence Agency's Counterterrorist Center and author of *Terrorism and U.S. Foreign Policy*.

Notes

1. Paul R. Pillar, "Statement to Joint Inquiry of the Senate Select Committee on Intelligence and the House Permanent Select Committee on Intelligence," Washington, D.C., October 8, 2002, www.cia.gov/nic/testimony_8oct2002.html (accessed March 20, 2004).
2. See Daniel Byman, "Should Hizballah Be Next?" *Foreign Affairs* 82, no. 6 (November/December 2003): 54–66.
3. Office of International Information Programs, U.S. Department of State, "Conditions Underlying Conflict Must Be Addressed, Armitage Says," September 5, 2002, http://usinfo.state.gov/topical/pol/terror/02090504.htm (accessed March 20, 2004) (speech and question and answer session with Deputy Secretary of State Richard Armitage at the U.S. Institute of Peace, Washington, D.C., September 5, 2002).
4. One of the more thoughtful statements that looks to a "victory" against terrorism is found in Gabriel Schoenfeld, "Could September 11 Have Been Averted?" *Commentary* 112, no. 5 (December 2001): 21–29. See also *Commentary* 113, no. 2 (February 2002): 12–16 (subsequent correspondence about Schoenfeld's article).
5. Donald Rumsfeld, interview, *Face the Nation*, CBS, September 23, 2001.

Steven Simon and Jeff Martini, 2004/2005

Terrorism: Denying Al Qaeda Its Popular Support

A consensus among states is emerging, undoubtedly hastened by the September 11 attacks, that terrorism is of universal concern and in direct violation of the principles of the international community. This agreement contrasts markedly with the deep division on the issue immediately following the process of decolonization in the mid–twentieth century. At that time, many newly independent states were reticent to cede the authority over coercive means wholly to state actors, thereby denying legitimacy to future freedom fighters. Today, however, the number of states that have rejected the legitimacy of terrorism has reached critical mass, with holdouts increasingly forced to capitulate (Libya) or to be dealt with as rogue nations (Sudan).[1]

A convergence in strategic interests has certainly helped to bridge this divide between the West and the developing world. Significantly, many of the newly independent states of the 1950s and 1960s now face terrorism problems of their own. The governments of still other states seem to manipulate the global war on terrorism to provide the necessary pretext for cracking down on long-standing domestic opposition movements. The decreasing likelihood of states debating the merits of terrorism, however, is also at least partly attributable to efforts to propagate international norms.

Studies of terrorism frequently address the concept of target audiences, groups generally defined as those whom terrorists seek to intimidate or influence through violence. However, it is also important to understand terrorists' other target audience—the aggrieved populations that they purport to represent. This latter group, not to be confused with terrorists' actual cadres, extends to a broader, less radicalized population that has the power to confer a degree of legitimacy on the terrorists simply by responding positively to their tactics. In the case of Al Qaeda, this group consists of diffuse or very loosely aligned supporters who welcome the news of a new terrorist attack or do not make an effort to distance themselves from Al Qaeda's claim to represent their cause. Denying terrorists the support of these constituents is a crucial component in the war on terrorism and requires approaches that go beyond the standard strategies employed in the current campaign. Marshaling international norms to stigmatize terrorism further stands as one such initiative that would deny terrorists the approval of these populations, pushing the terrorists' tactics farther toward the margins.

What's in a Norm?

Norms are generally defined as "a standard of appropriate behavior for actors with a given identity."[2] A "standard" is thus meant to imply a behavioral regularity.[3] "Appropriate," on the other hand, alludes to a subjective understanding of what is "proper," or how one "ought" to behave.[4] Simply put, from the perspective of norm proponents, there are no such things as bad norms.[5] Moreover, in the context of the war on terrorism, norms are not simply abstract moral guidelines, but powerful ordering principles with very practical implications.

In the life cycle of norms, norm entrepreneurs[6] play a crucial role as catalysts in the earliest stages of development. They are the community leaders who through persuasion, mobilization, and activism begin to create the initial momentum that, if sustained, can lead to general acceptance and eventually institutionalization of these ideas.[7] Operationalizing the norm, however, requires the constructive engagement of holdouts that continue to reject its relevance. Appeals can be tailored either to the universality of the concept or to its compatibility with the violators' own value system if it too obligates the prescribed behavior. In effect, norm entrepreneurs provide the information and publicity that can be leveraged to convince or shame norm violators into compliance.

The Helsinki Process is a good example of an initiative designed to provoke this type of cognitive dissonance. These negotiations between the West and the Soviet bloc, which were eventually codified in a series of principles that committed the signatories to mutual respect of territorial sovereignty and basic human rights, drew attention to the incompatibility between the former Soviet Union's self-professed commitment to the rights of individuals and individuals' obligations to the party as well as the state under Communist rule.[8] Although the Helsinki Final Act of August 1975 did not establish any real enforcement body, the agreement provided a foundation for future negotiation and, importantly, a convenient platform for the West to promote its own view of the respective obligations of individuals and society, an area in which the West had a clear stake in resolving in favor of personal liberties.[9]

Defining Standards of Behavior

The establishment of legal codes defining states' rights and restraints regarding the use of force is a crucial first step in creating the conditions for accountability. Subsequently, rewarding compliant behavior and sanctioning noncompliant behavior creates the necessary incentives to spread the norm through a process of socialization.

The Geneva conventions are probably the most notable instance of an effort to codify limits on states' use of force. Although their precise application is sometimes disputed, the conventions provide a powerful reference for the treatment of noncombatants in wartime. In addition, the international community has endorsed a number of terrorism-specific initiatives such as the Hague Convention for the Unlawful Seizure of Aircraft (1970); the Convention Against the Taking of Hostages (1979); and, more recently, UN Security Council Resolution 1373 (2001), which criminalizes a host of activities that have been used to support or provide a haven for terrorist organizations. The acceptance and eventual internalization of an emerging norm demands passage of a series of litmus tests, most critically the norm's durability in the face of challenges.[10] The first step, however, must be the clear communication of a standard or expectation of behavior. The aforementioned agreements help to provide this framework.

In effect, terrorists disregard two fundamental prohibitions. First, violence is not a legitimate means of solving political disputes, particularly when the aggressors are nonstate actors. This transcends Max Weber's well-known formulation that states have a monopoly over the legitimate use of force. A critical legitimizing condition when considering the use of force is that the agent in question is a sovereign power. Even in the language of those who assert Muslims' fundamental right to physical jihad, historical precedents suggest that resort to force requires authorization from some higher authority, particularly when the battle is for the expansion of Islam rather than the collective defense of the *ummah*.

The second norm essential to delegitimizing the strategy of terrorism is the belief that noncombatants are entitled to immunity and should not be subject to attack. Although terrorists often attempt to circumscribe this restraint by stressing their adversaries' own record of civilian casualties, the fact that this argument is made at all is a tacit recognition of the relevance of proportionality.

Importantly, these two norms are more than just theoretical constructs; their practical implications have long been debated both in Western and Islamic traditions. The Western discourses of *jus in bello* (what type of force is justified) and *jus ad bellum* (when force is justified) have led to the development of formal and informal codes regulating belligerents' responsibilities and obligations in wartime. Although the specific manifestations of these traditions have, of course, varied according to the particular historical context, general trends can be identified. Whether one speaks of the Hebraic, Roman, early Christian, or Germanic conceptions of war, each included provisions outlining justifications for war as well as treatments of the distinction between combatant and noncombatant.[11] Gradually, these notions have coalesced, developing into a Western consensus prohibiting tactics that are indiscriminate or disproportionate in scope and limiting the use of force to instances of self-defense.[12] Thus, although these rules are still contravened, their *de jure* acceptance does provide states with important normative referents that help order expectations and behavior.

Similarly, Arab culture and Islamic thought have a parallel tradition of theorizing on the definition of just war. Islamic interpretations also vary widely depending on the particular temporal, social, and political context. The Koran may be ubiquitous in the Muslim world, but its precise application and the interpretation of it and other essential texts differ considerably.[13] Nevertheless, overriding themes emerge regulating force based on obligations both to God and to fellow man, Muslim or otherwise. Fred Donner, a scholar of the Islamic tradition, notes "examples of injunctions against killing women, children, and other noncombatants; similarly, [juristic literature] bars attacks on the enemy without first inviting them to embrace Islam, discusses the problem of 'double effect' (e.g., unintended deaths of noncombatants during a nighttime assault), and so on."[14] Stepping back from the polarizing and largely misunderstood concept of jihad, a great deal of common ground actually exists on the restrictions applied to the use of force. What remains is the search for a mechanism to institutionalize these restrictions at the state and community level that would significantly help to undermine popular support for terrorist organizations.

Enforcing Compliance

Once they are defined and recognized, the second step is to enforce adherence to a norm. The U.S. decision to publish its list of active state sponsors of terrorism—and in the process shame nations such as Cuba, Libya, Iran, Sudan, and Syria, all of which have been suspected of aiding terrorist organizations or being slow to recognize the emerging norm against terrorism—is one example of how Washington seeks to enforce the international norm against terrorism. The Financial Aid Task Force (FATF), which publishes a list of

"Non-Cooperative Countries and Territories," uses a similar strategy in the fight against money laundering and terrorist financiers. Punishing states with military action or economic sanctions, such as the sanctions regime against Libya imposed in the wake of the bombing of Pan Am Flight 103, the cruise missile strikes against Sudan and Afghanistan in 1998 in the aftermath of Al Qaeda's attacks on the U.S. embassies in Nairobi and Dar es Salaam, and the present Syria Accountability Act predicated in part on Damascus' continued support of terrorist organizations, stands as an even more coercive approach. In short, the United States has long appealed to norms to build coalitions against terrorism.

Norm adherence should not be confused with or even imply voluntary agreement absent coercion. For example, compellance, or "acquiescence through fear,"[15] is one of several means to secure adherence to a norm. What matters most is the expectation that actors comply with a code of behavior. At least initially, their rationale for compliance may be and often is self-interest or fear, but their adherence reinforces the pressure on others to follow suit. Over time, habitual compliance lends the norm a "taken-for granted quality,"[16] relieving norm proponents from the need to police its enforcement. A good example is the norm that developed against the slave trade, a case in which Britain, throughout the nineteenth century, employed its naval resources and credible threats of force to ensure the success of its antislavery campaign.[17] Other norms even compel states to use force, such as the emerging norm for states to intervene in the case of genocide or other humanitarian disasters.[18] In short, the propagation of a norm is not an abstract exercise in consensus building; it often involves a good bit of arm twisting, and depending on the nature of the enforcement regime, the emerging norms may come with sharp teeth.

Deepening the Norm against Terrorism

To enforce the norm against state-supported terrorism, a top-down approach has largely been successful, with fewer states (with some notable exceptions, including Syria and Iran) now willing openly to flaunt the prohibitions against supporting terrorist organizations. To what extent these norms have diffused to the general population, however, is an open question. It is also a critical one, in that today's most dangerous terrorist threat, Al Qaeda and its affiliate groups, has attained a surprisingly wide base of support throughout the Muslim world. Indeed, a study by the Pew Research Institute in June 2003 found that "solid majorities in the Palestinian Authority, Indonesia, and Jordan—and nearly half of those in Morocco and Pakistan—say they have some confidence in Osama bin Laden 'to do the right thing regarding world affairs.'"[19]

The creation of norms goes to the heart of this issue and stands as one means of addressing the gulf between the values to which states and their respective populations subscribe. Can the emerging consensus from the topdown effort spread to Muslim populations more generally, or must a second initiative be undertaken to coalesce support for restraints on violence at a grassroots level? In what ways would such a bottom-up approach differ from the experience of state-driven initiatives?

The Top-Down Agenda

The international community undoubtedly should continue its efforts to delegitimize state-supported terrorism. Both UN Security Council Resolution 1373 and the FATF Eight Special Recommendations, which criminalizes the financial support of terrorist organizations, stand as important recent initiatives. Additionally, the international community should push to elicit unequivocal denunciations of terrorism from regional bodies such as the Arab League and the Organization of Islamic Conference. Both of these organizations have ratified antiterrorism conventions, but in an attempt to satisfy the international community without delegitimizing the Palestinian struggle in the process, they define terrorism in such a way as to render their commitment less forceful. One caveat in the Arab Convention for the Suppression of Terrorism, for example, states, "All cases of struggle by whatever means, including armed struggle, against foreign occupation and aggression for liberation and self-determination, in accordance with the principles of international law, shall not be regarded as a [terrorist] offence. This provision shall not apply to any act prejudicing the territorial integrity of any Arab State."[20] Thus according to this provision, liberation movements, unless they threaten a member state of the Arab League, may be exempt from the terrorist label.

Work also must be done to reinforce and broaden prohibitions against the funding of terrorist organizations, particularly those with multiple personalities such as the military, political, and social welfare wings of Hamas. Increasingly, terrorist groups are compartmentalizing their operations in order to bypass existing regulations. This not only serves to reopen avenues to outside funding but also provides a convenient veneer of legitimacy for the terrorists. Whether or not these groups do good social work is in many ways beside the point.[21] Their ties to terrorism and the benefit this relationship bestows on the parent organization is the critical question. For example, that Hamas provides much needed social services in Gaza is not disputed. The possible diversion of financing meant for these humanitarian projects to terrorist operations, however, is problematic. Indeed, the social welfare arm of Hamas has legitimized the less noble tactics of the organization, allowing Hamas to promote itself as something other than a strictly terrorist organization. Not until September of last year did the European Union finally accede to U.S. pressure to cut off funding to affiliate groups of Hamas. The difficulty in reaching consensus on this issue points to the need to define support for terrorism more broadly.

Additionally, the definition of state culpability must be expanded to include other indirect support to terrorists, such as willful neglect in securing borders or a failure to crack down on activities such as the narcotics trade that may facilitate terrorist activities by providing access to hard currency, transnational networks, etc. Thus far, the propagation of norms has appropriately focused on direct support for terrorists, but holding states accountable to some minimum level of effort in deterring terrorists from using their territory as a base of operations or policing criminal networks that have natural linkages with terrorist organizations is a logical next step. In sum, to sustain momentum, the international community should raise the bar to reflect an expectation that states not just passively accept their obligations to refrain from supporting terrorist organizations, but also proactively take steps to eliminate them.

Finally, the depoliticization of efforts to strengthen international norms is necessary to create objective metrics for judging state commitments to the war on terrorism as well as an effective enforcement regime. Rather than the current sliding scale that defines state support of terrorism differently based on political considerations, standards should be harmonized. Whether the case in question is Pakistan's support for Kashmiri groups or Iran's arming of Hizballah, inconsistently applying standards does not aid efforts to eliminate terrorism. Similarly, although defining terrorism is notoriously difficult, terrorist organizations should be classified based on the tactics they use rather than a quid pro quo whereby, for example, states make their cooperation in the global war on terrorism contingent upon defining bothersome opposition movements in their own country as terrorist organizations.

Developing Norms from the Bottom Up

Although state-driven initiatives have made and continue to make significant progress, such initiatives must be complimented by a parallel bottom-up approach to deny terrorist groups access to their bases of popular support. Top-down initiatives are limited because state diplomacy is often at odds with the value systems of a state's citizenry. This is particularly true in the Middle East, where few regimes can be described as being truly representative. Moreover, a number of states have charted a decidedly pro-Western course (Egypt, Jordan, Morocco, Turkey) while significant segments of their populations hold very different political and cultural sensibilities.

Secondly, although states have crucial roles to play in regulating the use of force, terrorism is fundamentally a subnational phenomenon. As such, its elimination will require changing perceptions at the community level. To expect state-driven initiatives alone to be commensurate with the task is to assume complete state sovereignty as well as states' unhindered ability to project their authority. This is not always the case, and thus states alone are inadequate to the task; self-policing at the community level is required to deny terrorists the room to operate. Moreover, only refusal by the aggrieved populations that terrorists purport to defend to implicitly justify the violence committed on their behalf—by remaining silent or, worse, acting as the terrorists' cheering section—can weaken terrorists' populist cover.

What makes these bottom-up efforts so difficult is the fundamental difference in their implementation from the state-driven initiatives that have dominated previous efforts. Namely, although a process of coercion, whereby the strong can compel weak states to submit to their will, can expedite the propagation of norms in the international system, norm creation at the subnational level will require either appealing to the community's self-interest or to the inherent legitimacy of the norms themselves.[22] Diffuse ideological support for terrorists is simply not subject to the logic of conventional power politics. Therefore, U.S. efforts must rely primarily on persuasion to stigmatize the use of terrorist tactics.

Practical Steps Forward at the Grassroots Level

What then can the United States do to expedite the emergence of norms against violence at the community level? Acknowledging that change is difficult to institute from the top down, the United States should find creative means to support the efforts of local norm entrepreneurs. That said, providing this support is much more complicated than simply identifying members of a society that are sympathetic to the notion that violence is not the preferred means of settling disputes. The (negative) net effect of U.S. backing for Mahmoud Abbas during his brief tenure as the Palestinian prime minister in the summer of 2003 illustrates the potential pitfalls of overtly supporting a norm entrepreneur. The Bush administration's vocal support of Abbas simply undermined his domestic support. In the future, the United States should support norm entrepreneurs in a way that enables their work without also leading to their labeling as a U.S. proxy.

Fortunately, more subtle ways do exist to support norm entrepreneurs without engendering this backlash. However, such efforts will require time and patience. Contributing to the development of local institutions that promote norm convergence with Western values is one method that allows local norm entrepreneurs to receive support while remaining an arms length from its source. U.S./EU support for Birzeit University in Palestine, an institution that is both independent and (relatively) liberal, is an example of this approach. Bringing scholars and students to the West is another potential means to generate the conditions under which norm entrepreneurs may grow as intellectuals and activists. The resulting epistemic communities, or associations based on shared academic training, represent one type of norm entrepreneurship that has had significant success in advancing value-based agendas. Notable examples include loose organizations of natural scientists—coalitions whose members have very different cultural backgrounds but similar professional training—that have succeeded in mobilizing the international community to rethink state obligations toward the environment.[23]

The United States also needs to improve its public diplomacy, specifically by communicating the compatibility of U.S. policy and values with the aspirations of those living in the Muslim world. This does not imply a foreign policy driven by global opinion, but the United States should clearly explain the rationale behind its decisions, which in turn should be carried out in a manner that demonstrates respect for the sensibilities and cultural sensitivities of others. Absent this effort, Muslim audiences have no compelling alternative to the tortured logic of Al Qaeda.[24] Better communication will require significant investment in the U.S. capacity to reach audiences in the Middle East, either via mass media or through a buttressed and better-trained Foreign Service.[25] The goal of such a process would not be to indoctrinate but rather to engage dissenters and provoke introspection among those prone to supporting terrorism framed as resistance.

Change often does come from the bottom up, and overwhelming military force is not always the most effective means of communication. Important historical precedents exist of introspection catalyzing dramatic shifts in thinking as well as policy. The Soviet Union's liberalization and South Africa's rejection of apartheid are two notable examples. Neither took place within a strategic vacuum, but both changes in posture reflected internal unease with the unifying logic of the regime.[26] Another example is the U.S. drive in the 1970s to rein in the CIA and to prohibit assassination as a foreign policy tool. At that time, spreading awareness that the CIA had plotted the murder of a number of foreign leaders under the administrations of Dwight D. Eisenhower, John F. Kennedy, Lyndon B. Johnson, and Richard M. Nixon provoked concerns that the United States was forfeiting any claims to moral leadership.[27] The investigating Church Committee's public admonishment was intended in part to recapture some credibility in the international community and to foster a norm against assassination internationally.

Today, Executive Order (EO) 12333, a successor to earlier efforts undertaken during the Ford administration, embodies the code against assassination, with every administration since confirming its expression of self-restraint. Although the order is consistent with the stipulations of the Hague Convention IV (1907), of which the United States is a party, EO 12333 goes a step further in specifying the restrictions as well as including a prohibition against indirect participation in an assassination plot.[28] This unilateral expression of U.S. willingness to sanction its own breaches and excesses is the same process of self-reflection that the United States should be promoting elsewhere. Today, the prisoner abuse scandal in

Abu Ghraib calls for an even more robust effort at self-policing to salvage some of the credibility that the United States has lost from this episode. The blatant disregard for human rights not only invites backlash, but also cripples U.S. ability to exert moral influence and promote a broader norm against the use of unregulated violence.

Finally, a corresponding effort must be made to address the material conditions under which terrorists prey on the frustrations of the disenfranchised. Any attempt to win hearts and minds that simply skirts around root causes dooms itself to failure. Poverty, lack of social mobility, a poor educational infrastructure, and the denial of basic human rights all contribute to the hopelessness that terrorists exploit. Unfortunately, these conditions are widespread in the developing world and, even with enhanced commitment to development initiatives, these issues will persist far into the future. Progress in addressing root causes will help pave the way for broader acceptance of norms against terrorism at the subnational level. The slow and incremental nature of that progress should not deter the West from dramatically increasing its investment and commitment to addressing root causes.

The Feedback Loop: Norms Are Working

In general, the compulsion of norm-breakers to offer ex post facto justifications of their actions provides evidence that a threshold has been crossed and, moreover, that the boundary is becoming more well defined.[29] A useful example of this is the U.S. need to rationalize its continued use of antipersonnel landmines in the Korean Demilitarized Zone. In this case, the norm has not yet reached a point where the United States has been forced to cease employing these devices, but it does carry enough weight to compel the United States to explain its position and to adhere to certain limitations, thus signaling a shift in thinking on this issue.[30]

In the case of terrorism specifically, recent messages attributed to Al Qaeda suggest a consensus growing within the Muslim world against the targeting of noncombatants. Following the bombings in Casablanca, Riyadh, and Istanbul in 2003, operations that amounted essentially to Muslim-on-Muslim violence, Al Qaeda made repeated attempts to justify the indiscriminate nature of their attacks explicitly. For example, on November 17, 2003, members of Al Qaeda sent the following message to the Arabic daily *Al Quds Al Arabi*:

> Some claim that we consider most Muslims as non-believers and sanction killing them. How do we go everywhere to protect them and then sanction shedding their blood? This cannot be accepted by sound reason, let alone a Muslim who knows the rulings of God. We have repeatedly warned Muslims against approaching the places of infidels, and we now renew the warning. Moreover, it is impermissible, according to Shari'a … to mix with those infidels, neither in their homes nor in work places, until they stop their crusading war against Islam and Muslims.[31]

Similarly, attackers described the Muhaya residential compound bombed in Riyadh as "teeming with Arab translators for the U.S. intelligence services."[32] These determined efforts to revise the nature of targets are not insignificant; the attackers' evident compulsion to redefine the identity of those killed indicates fear over the implication of killing civilians. In short, Al Qaeda's statements suggest that disregard for the sanctity of noncombatants is no longer without political cost among their constituencies. The norm is spreading.

The Place for Norms in U.S. Strategy

Promoting respect for the rule of law, both domestically and at the international level, is in the U.S. national interest. Because the United States carries enormous normative weight in the international system, its values exert disproportionate influence in the development of international norms.[33] Free trade is one example of this dynamic whereby the United States and other leading economies have used their leverage to lobby for a more uniform international trade regime and, on the strength of this effort, have created an expectation reducing barriers to trade and reinforcing their own self interest. Thus, norms are not so much about imposing restraints on dominant states as subjecting the entire state system to the rules by which dominant states would prefer to play.[34] Moreover, in the specific case of restricting the use of violence, creating some semblance of order benefits the entire international community in that it allows states to pursue other national interests beyond narrow security concerns.

In effect, norms mitigate the need for states to operate assuming the worst of others. Whether or not other states behave as the United States would like, the predictability of their behavior is quite helpful. Subscription to or rejection of a norm stands as an important means for state actors to signal their intentions, reducing the considerable transaction costs of this uncertainty. In this sense, order has intrinsic benefits for all states. Although other methods, including the projection of overwhelming force, can also foster this type of environment, international norms offer a more efficient, cost-effective approach.

Finally, the propagation of norms as a method of combating terrorism need not come at the exclusion of other complimentary approaches. Ideational change is necessarily a long, slow process, and the propagation of norms is unlikely to make the world dramatically safer in the near term. On the other hand, the current mix of preemptive force, counterterrorism, and homeland security strategies are a quick fix. They will not serve as sustainable, long-term solutions without a parallel commitment to strengthening and broadening coalitions against terrorism. Norms have the potential to hold these coalitions together, absent the U.S. ability to affect conformity through coercion.

History is replete with examples of norms developing to limit the use of force. Whether we are speaking of outlawing the assassination of world leaders, prohibiting the use of chemical weapons, or exempting medical personnel from being targeted in wartime, ideas and values have played a key role in limiting the circumstances when violence may be employed legitimately. In all these examples, however, the critical actors were states and the benchmark for compliance was state behavior. With respect to terrorism, the case must be made to publics directly. In short, delegitimizing terrorism requires establishing consensus both at the community and national levels.

The United States and the international community can help to build these norms not with patronizing platitudes, but by patiently articulating a compelling alternative to the logic of terrorism. Notable examples exist of aggrieved populations that chose to reject violence, be it the antiapartheid struggle or the majority of black Americans during the civil rights movement. In each instance, indigenous norm entrepreneurs overcame significant resistance to their causes to effect ideational and structural change. Corollaries exist in the Arab World; the West must find a way to support their efforts.

Steven Simon is a senior analyst at the RAND Corporation in Washington, D.C. Jeff Martini is a research assistant at RAND.

Notes

1. Ilias Bantekas, "The International Law of Terrorist Financing," *American Journal of International Law* 97, no. 2 (April 2003): 318.
2. Martha Finnemore, *National Interests in International Society* (Ithaca: Cornell University Press, 1996), p. 22; Peter Katzenstein, ed., *The Culture of National Security* (New York: Columbia University Press, 1996), p. 5.
3. Christopher Gelpi, "Crime and Punishment: The Role of Norms in Crisis Bargaining," *American Political Science Review* 91, no. 2 (June 1997): 340.
4. Ibid.
5. Martha Finnemore and Kathryn Sikkink, "International Norm Dynamics and Political Change," *International Organization* 52, no. 4 (Autumn 1998): 892.
6. Finnemore and Sikkink employ the term "norm entrepreneur" while others prefer "transnational moral entrepreneur." For the latter usage, see Ethan Nadelmann, "Global Prohibition Regimes: The Evolution of Norms in International Society," *International Organization* 44, no. 4 (Autumn 1990): 485.
7. Finnemore and Sikkink, "International Norm Dynamics and Political Change," p. 904.
8. Geoffrey Edwards, "Human Rights and Basket III Issues: Areas of Change and Continuity," *International Affairs* 61, no. 4 (Autumn 1985): 632.
9. Ibid.
10. Jeffrey Legro identifies durability, specificity, and concordance as the three benchmarks of a norm's robustness. Jeffrey Legro, "Which Norms Matter? Revisiting the 'Failure' of Internationalism," *International Organization* 51, no. 1 (Winter 1997): 34.
11. James Turner Johnson, "Historical Roots and Sources of the Just War Tradition in Western Culture," in *Just War and Jihad*, eds. John Kelsay and James Turner Johnson (Westport, Conn.: Greenwood Publishing Group, 1991), pp. 7–12; Michael Walzer, *Just and Unjust Wars: A Moral Argument With Historical Illustrations* (New York: Basic Books, 1977).
12. Johnson, "Historical Roots and Sources of the Just War Tradition in Western Culture," p. 15.
13. These would of course include the Sunna and the Hadith.
14. Fred Donner, "Sources of Islamic Conceptions of War," in *Just War and Jihad*, eds. John Kelsay and James Turner Johnson (Westport, Conn.: Greenwood Publishing Group, 1991), pp. 31–33.
15. Ian Hurd describes "compellance" in this fashion: "Coercion refers to a relation of asymmetrical physical power among agents, where this asymmetry is applied to changing the behavior of the weaker agent. The operative mechanism is fear or simple 'compellance'; fear produces acquiescence." Ian Hurd, "Legitimacy and Authority in International Politics," *International Organization* 53, no. 2 (Spring 1999): 383. See Thomas Schelling, *Arms and Influence* (New Haven, Conn.: Yale University Press, 1966).
16. Finnemore and Sikkink, "International Norm Dynamics and Political Change," p. 895.
17. Nadelmann, "Global Prohibition Regimes," p. 492.
18. See Martha Finnemore, *The Purpose of Intervention* (Cornell: Cornell University Press, 2003).
19. Pew Global Attitudes Project, "Views of a Changing World," June 2003, p. 3.
20. "The Arab Convention for the Suppression of Terrorism," April 1998, http://www.albab. com/arab/docs/league/terrorism98.htm (accessed September 17, 2004).
21. For a more in-depth discussion, see International Crisis Group, "Islamic Social Welfare Activism in the Occupied Palestinian Territories: A Legitimate Target?" *Middle East Report*, no. 13 (April 2, 2003), pp. 18–20.
22. Hurd, "Legitimacy and Authority in International Politics," p. 383.
23. Peter Haas, "Introduction: Epistemic Communities and International Policy Coordination," *International Organization* 52, no. 1 (Winter 1992): 5.

24. Edward P. Djerejian et al., "Changing Minds Winning Peace," *Report of the Advisory Group on Public Diplomacy for the Arab and Muslim World*, October 1, 2003, p. 8.
25. Ibid.
26. For the role of ideas in the Soviet transformation, see Janice Gross Stein, "Political Learning by Doing: Gorbachev as Uncommitted Thinker and Motivated Learner," *International Organization* 48, no. 2 (Spring 1994): 155–163.
27. Daniel Schorr, "Stop Winking at the Ban," *Christian Science Monitor*, September 21, 2001; Thomas Ward, "Norms and International Security: The Case of International Assassination," *International Security* 25, no. 1 (Summer 2000).
28. Elizabeth B. Bazen, "Assassination Ban and E.O. 12333: A Brief Summary," *CRS Report for Congress*, RS21037, January 4, 2002, http://www.fas.org/irp/crs/RS21037.pdf (accessed October 9, 2004).
29. Finnemore and Sikkink, "International Norm Dynamics and Political Change," p. 892.
30. Ibid.
31. Abu Hafs Al Masri Brigades, "A Statement From the Jihad Rule About the Islamic Iron Hammer Operation," November 15, 2003, http://www.homelandsecurityus.com/Turkey.htm (accessed October 9, 2004).
32. Ibid.
33. Nadelmann, "Global Prohibition Regimes," pp. 484–485.
34. A more detailed discussion on this phenomenon can be found in Hedley Bull, *The Anarchical Society* (New York: Columbia University Press, 1977).

Chapter 9

Organizing to Fight Terrorism

The effort of building the proper governmental structures and organizations for fighting terrorism goes beyond the development of a comprehensive strategy. Executing the right strategy requires the right structure with the will to do what is necessary—morally and ethically—in this conflict.

Martha Crenshaw explores how American counterterrorism policy is formed and discusses the fact that these policies are not simply a response to the threat of terrorism but that the policies also reflect the domestic political process. The stakeholders in a given counterterrorism policy are wide-ranging. The Executive Branch, Congress, and interest groups such as the victims' families play important roles in the formal and informal policy-development process. The history of specific policy decisions is presented as an illustration of the complexity of the policy-formulation process among actors with competing interests and diffuse authority. The author concludes that it is unlikely that the process will change and unlikely that counterterrorism policy will be based solely on an objective appraisal of the threat of terrorism without being filtered through the political lens.

According to military expert Rob de Wijk, the events of September 11 "clarified the urgent need to refocus and restructure the way the United States and its allies think about and plan for a military campaign." This effort will require a new approach and new assets: developing irregular forces that are well-practiced in guerrilla tactics and asymmetrical retaliation; strengthening both special operations forces and human intelligence capabilities; abandoning some beliefs about traditional warfare; and sharpening the skills of coercive diplomacy, when dealing with states. Finally, de Wijk delves into the cultural aspect of this new war, of which a central component is "the campaign to win the support of the populace of the opponent. In other words, the United States and its allies must also wage a battle for the hearts and minds of the people ... in the Islamic world."

Finally, Richard Shultz describes the processes and decisions that went into not deploying our special operations forces against terrorists prior to 9/11. This article is not only a poignant reminder of how bureaucratic inertia can affect the execution of military strategy or a historical examination of past events but is also an important statement about how we must think about the future—about how the will to win must be present across all instruments of national power.

Martha Crenshaw, 2001

Counterterrorism Policy and the Political Process

American counterterrorism policy is not just a response to the threat of terrorism, whether at home or abroad, but a reflection of the domestic political process. Perceptions of the threat of terrorism and determination and implementation of policy occur in the context of a policy debate involving government institutions, the media, interest groups, and the elite and mass publics. The issue of terrorism tends to appear prominently on the national policy agenda as a result of highly visible and symbolic attacks on Americans or American property. However, the threat is interpreted through a political lens created by the diffused structure of power within the American government.[1]

In general, focusing events, such as crises or disasters, trigger attention to a problem by attracting the attention of the news media and the public.[2] Such sudden and harmful events, rare by definition, come to the notice of the mass public and policy elites simultaneously. In the case of terrorism, focusing events frequently come in clusters, so that it is often difficult to trace a specific policy response to a single event. The reaction to the Oklahoma City bombing, for example, is linked to perceptions of the 1993 World Trade Center bombing and the 1995 Aum Shinrikyo sarin gas attack on the Tokyo subways. Under the Reagan administration, the 1986 military strike against Libya was a response not just to the La Belle disco bombing in Berlin but to earlier attacks such as the TWA and Achille Lauro hijackings and the shooting attacks at the Rome and Vienna airports in 1985. Thus, sequences of events rather than single disasters typically serve as policy catalysts.

As Robert Johnson has emphasized, in the United States threatening events are filtered through a political process that is characterized by lack of consensus among political elites.[3] The decision-making process is disaggregated and pluralistic, and power is diffused. Because not all issues can be dealt with simultaneously, political elites—the president, different agencies within the executive branch, Congress, the media, interest groups, and "experts" in academia and the consulting world—compete to set the national policy agenda. They compete to select certain problems for attention, interpret their meaning and significance, conceive of solutions, put them into practice, and evaluate their outcomes. Despite the secrecy inherent in formulating and implementing policy toward terrorism, issues are developed, interests formed, and policies legitimized through public debates.[4] Decision makers with different identities and preferences define and represent problems, or frame issues, in order to gain public support for their positions. Furthermore, the selection and implementation of policy depend on the particularistic interests of the actors or coalitions that assume the initiative as much as consistent policy doctrine or strategy based on a broad national consensus about what can and ought to be done. Lack of coordination and fragmentation of effort are often the result.

The Politics of the Executive Branch

The political process within the executive branch is characterized by progressive expansion of the number of agencies involved; overlapping lines of authority among them; expansion of jurisdictions to encompass new issues; parochialism; and competition. No agency in the executive branch of the government wants an issue on the agenda unless it has an efficient and acceptable solution for it. Thus, public policy problems such as terrorism are typically linked to proposed solutions that are in turn linked to specific institutions within the government. How an issue is defined will typically determine which government institution has jurisdiction over it and can thus take charge of policy solutions, often with corresponding budget increases. (Spending on antiterrorism programs jumped from $61.7 million to $205.3 million in the fiscal 1999 appropriations.[5] Overall spending on terrorism is generally estimated at $7 billion per year.)

As the definition of the threat of terrorism changes, so too does jurisdiction. If the image of an issue can be changed, then its institutional venue may change accordingly. Issues can be partitioned among agencies, or different institutions can have more or less authority at various stages or sequences of a decision. For example, if terrorism is defined as a crime, it is a problem for the Department of Justice and the nation's law enforcement agencies such as the Federal Bureau of Investigation (FBI). However, if it is defined as warfare or as a threat to national security, responsibility shifts accordingly. The Central Intelligence Agency (CIA) and the military become central to the process. Nevertheless, the FBI did not lose its role. In 1986, major legislation established extraterritorial jurisdiction for crimes committed against Americans abroad, which has led to prosecutions in the World Trade Center bombing and East Africa bombing cases, along with others. Definition of the threat of terrorism as "bioterrorism" in the 1990s brought a host of new agencies into the jurisdictional competition, including Health and Human Services (HHS) and its Centers for Disease Control. Previously, when the threat of "super terrorism" was interpreted as the danger of the acquisition of nuclear materials, the Department of Energy assumed a key role. In the 1990s, as the threat of terrorism came to be seen as a threat to the "homeland," not only did local and state governments enter the picture but the military was called on to provide "homeland defense." The Defense Authorization Act for Fiscal Year 1997 called on the Department of Defense (DOD) to train local "first responders" and to establish response teams to assist civilian authorities should there be a terrorist incident involving weapons of mass destruction (WMD).[6] The result was Joint Task Force Civil Support, established in 1999.[7]

Responsibility for dealing with terrorism is widely distributed, and lines of jurisdiction tend to be blurred and overlapping, with no clear institutional monopoly of the issue. The U.S. government tried to deal with this problem by establishing the "lead agency" concept. The Department of State is the lead agency for responding to international terrorism, while the FBI is the lead agency for domestic terrorism.[8] Nevertheless, the White House National Security Council (NSC) and the Department of State have traditionally competed for institutional control of the issue of international terrorism, and the FBI and the State Department sometimes clash. For example, Secretary of State Cyrus Vance resigned after his advice against a hostage rescue mission in Iran was overruled by the president and the NSC under National Security Adviser Zbigniew Brzezinski. Former Director of the Central

Intelligence Agency Stansfield Turner described the relationship between the NSC and executive branch agencies as it affected the rescue decision:

> The National Security Adviser and his staff often are frustrated because they have no direct authority to carry out the President's decisions. That's the task of the bureaucracy, which frequently resists outside direction, even from the President. Bureaucrats are even more likely to resist what they suspect are directives from the National Security Council staff. A result of these tensions is that the staff of the NSC often attempts to sidestep the bureaucracy and do as much as possible on its own.[9]

Turner and the CIA also resisted the NSC's proposals for covert operations against Iran, seeing the dispute as a case of "the professionalism of the experts keeping the political leadership from undertaking ventures that would be embarrassingly unsuccessful."[10]

Rivalries between the NSC and other executive branch agencies also emerged under the Clinton administration. In April 1998, as a result of having read the Richard Preston novel, *The Cobra Event*, the president held a meeting with a group of scientists and Cabinet members to discuss the threat of bioterrorism. The briefing impressed Clinton so much that he asked the experts to brief senior officials in DOD and HHS. On May 6 they delivered a follow-up report, calling for the stockpiling of vaccines (an idea that was soon dropped). *The Washington Post* reported with regard to the stockpiling proposal that "Some administration officials outside the White House expressed surprise at how fast the president and his National Security Council staff had moved on the initiative..., noting with some concern that it had not gone through the customary deliberative planning process."[11] Critics noted that not all scientific experts were disinterested; some stood to gain financially if the government invested large sums in developing technology against bioterrorism.

In the investigation of the October 2000 bombing of the destroyer U.S.S. *Cole* the State Department was said to be less than enthusiastic about the FBI's hard-line approach to Yemeni authorities.[12] While the FBI appealed to the president to demand that Yemen accept a central FBI role, the State Department countered by warning that the pressure would likely backfire.

Clinton's move to establish the position of a national coordinator for counterterrorism policy on the NSC staff also provoked opposition from within the executive branch. *The New York Times* reported that Clinton's May 1998 initiative "had provoked a bitter fight within the Administration, with the Departments of Defense and Justice opposing a key provision that critics feared would have created a terrorism czar within the White House."[13] As a result, Clinton created a national coordinator with limited staff and no direct budget authority. *The Washington Post* reported, "It is not clear how much real authority [Richard] Clarke will have.... The Defense Department successfully fought off proposals to give this coordinator a large staff and independent budget similar to those of the drug policy coordinator.... Clarke's appears to be essentially a staff job, reporting to National Security Adviser Samuel R. "Sandy" Berger."[14]

Moreover, agencies may reject jurisdiction and try to exclude issues from the agenda, especially if they think that they do not have a solution or that the new task is not appropriate to their mission or routine. The DOD, for example, appears divided and ambivalent about its new role in homeland defense. As early as July 1995, some Pentagon officials were calling for an expanded military role in counterterrorism, but this view did not appear to reflect an internal consensus. In a speech to the Council on Foreign Relations in New York in September 1998, Secretary of Defense William Cohen prominently mentioned terrorism.[15] His description of the military mission, however, was vague; he said that the administration hoped to consolidate the task of coordination into one lead federal agency, and that DOD would provide "active support" for that agency's operation. Falkenrath et al. argued that the DOD is not "fully committed to this mission."[16] The military see "homeland defense" as law enforcement, which the military supports only if ordered and when possible. Essentially, in their view, it is a diversion and misuse of defense dollars, and they would prefer that the entire domestic preparedness program be shifted to the Federal Emergency Management Agency (FEMA). The military's reluctance is confirmed by John Hillen, who sees DOD as dominated by interservice rivalries rather than leadership from the president or the secretary of defense: "Today the services are interested in neither the White House's new wars (peacekeeping, terrorism, organized crime, and the like) nor the Joint Staff's futuristic technological blueprint. . . ."[17] The military really wants to fight wars that are like those of the past, only with upgraded equipment on all sides. In January 1999, press reports announcing Cohen's decision to seek presidential approval for a permanent DOD task force, with a senior officer, to plan for a chemical or biological attack on the U.S. quoted Deputy Defense Secretary John Hamre as saying "Frankly, we're not seeking this job."[18]

Similarly, FEMA did not want to take charge of the domestic preparedness program.[19] FEMA officials opted out on budgetary grounds, fearing that the program would be inadequately funded, and thus be a drain on already scarce resources, and that the agency would then be criticized for ineffective implementation of the program. Since they could not afford the solution, they did not want to take on the problem.

In 1998, the decision to retaliate against the Sudan and Afghanistan also revealed disarray within the executive branch, a state of confusion and contentiousness that threatened to eclipse terrorism as the issue at the forefront of public debate.[20] The FBI and the CIA were accused of failing to share complete information on threats in East Africa with the State Department.[21] Disagreement surfaced between Washington and bureaucracies in the field. The ambassador in Kenya in December 1997, and again in April and May 1998, asked unsuccessfully for support from the State Department Bureau of Diplomatic Security for the construction of a new and less vulnerable building. The decision to retaliate was controversial. Some analysts in the CIA and the State Department Bureau of Intelligence and Research remained unconvinced of the reliability of the evidence linking Osama bin Ladin's network to the pharmaceuticals plant in Khartoum and informed the news media of their doubts after the cruise missile strikes. The FBI and the Defense Intelligence Agency were excluded from the decision. Apparently Chairman of the Joint Chiefs of Staff General Shelton objected to the original targeting plan and succeeded in reducing the number of targets.

Congressional Politics

Congress frequently plays a critical role in shaping the counterterrorism policy agenda, without the constraint of necessarily having to present an integrated solution to the problem. Although the president typically has the most power to set the agenda, he depends on Congress to appropriate funds for the measures he proposes, and Congress can block issues or push forward others that the president has not chosen. Furthermore, executive branch agencies usually have their own channels of communication and influence with congressional committees. Congressional staffers and career bureaucrats often have extensive back-channel contacts. Individuals move back and forth between positions in Congress and in the executive branch. Thus, even if the president wants to keep an issue off the agenda or to minimize a problem, he may have to confront it because congressional actions have captured media and public attention. Confrontation is especially likely when the government is divided along partisan lines. The president cannot afford to appear to ignore a potential threat of terrorism, even if restraint might be the most appropriate and effective response. In the 1990s, the president and Congress often seemed to be engaged in a highly partisan politics of anticipatory blame avoidance.

Examples of congressional influence on critical policy decisions include President Reagan's decision to withdraw American troops from Lebanon in the aftermath of the 1983 bombing of the Marine barracks. Reagan was apparently dissuaded by congressional and military opposition encountered in the context of an upcoming campaign for reelection.[22] Initially Reagan resisted the idea of withdrawal, although the House Committee on Armed Services urged him to reconsider his policy and issued its own report critical of security at the Marine barracks. Reagan withheld the release of the DOD's Long Commission report for several days in order to limit the damage he feared it would create as a rallying point for opposition in Congress. Congressional responses from both Republicans and Democrats to Reagan's press conferences and speeches were lukewarm at best. Although the movement to reassess policy was largely bipartisan, House Speaker O'Neill assumed a prominent role in the debate, organizing the passage of resolutions calling for an end to the military presence in Lebanon, and Democratic presidential candidate Walter Mondale seized on withdrawal as a campaign issue. The State Department and the National Security Adviser opposed withdrawal, but DOD and the Joint Chiefs favored it. In early January, Reagan sent his national security adviser, secretary of defense, and the chairman of the Joint Chiefs of Staff to speak with leading House Republicans. Nevertheless, Minority Whip Trent Lott stated publicly that the Republicans had told them that they wanted the Marines out by March 1985. Still, in his State of the Union address in January 1984, Reagan persisted: "We must have the courage to give peace a chance. And we must not be driven from our objectives for peace in Lebanon by state-sponsored terrorism."[23] Within two weeks of the State of the Union address, Reagan announced the withdrawal.

An earlier instance of congressional influence over policy occurred during the Ford administration. Secretary of State Kissinger ordered the recall of the ambassador to Tanzania, Beverly Carter, when he learned that Carter had played an active role in facilitating negotiations for the release of American students held hostage in Zaire. Kissinger took strong exception to this violation of the official policy of no concessions and reportedly intended to end Carter's State Department career, although Carter had expected to be appointed ambassador to Denmark. However, when the Congressional Black Caucus intervened on Carter's behalf, generating negative publicity for the State Department, Kissinger relented.[24] It was also helpful to Carter's defense that he was a former journalist.

In the 1990s, as Richard Falkenrath points out, one source of the difficulties of the domestic preparedness program was "its origin in a series of discrete, uncoordinated legislative appropriations and administrative actions," the result of ad hoc initiatives rather than strategic concept.[25] In 1996, for example, Congress began "earmarking" specific counterterrorism projects, such as providing $10 million for counterterrorism technologies for the National Institute of Justice in the Fiscal Year 1997 Department of Justice budget. The FBI counterterrorism budget was also dramatically increased, largely as a result of the Oklahoma City bombing. Congress also instructed the Departments of Justice and Defense to prepare long-term plans for counterterrorism, and established an independent National Commission on Terrorism to investigate government policy. Lawmakers are also concerned about lack of congressional oversight of administration efforts.

Outside the Government

Actors outside the government also try to shape the public policy agenda. Interest groups and communities of "experts," sometimes associated with professional consulting firms, or think tanks, seek access to decision makers in order to promote favored issues. They often accumulate the scientific or technical information about the problem that then causes decision makers to recognize it. They can promote a specific conception of an issue, such as the idea of a new, more lethal and irresponsible terrorism in the 1990s.[26] They contribute the "talking heads" who appear regularly on television news programs such as CNN. They may also be influential in shaping policy solutions because of their expertise.

Among interest groups, in the area of terrorism, business interests may oppose economic sanctions against state sponsors. Interest groups devoted to protecting civil liberties are likely to oppose measures that restrict individual freedoms, such as expanding the power of the FBI or the use of passenger profiling at airports. The American Civil Liberties Union, for example, has frequently opposed legislative initiatives such as assigning responsibility for domestic preparedness to the military. Along with conservative Republicans, civil liberties interest groups blocked the wiretapping provisions of the 1996 bill.

The families of victims of terrorism, as well as victims themselves, such as the former hostages in Lebanon, have mobilized to influence policy. They have lobbied the State Department as well as the White House and Congress, and gone to the courts to press their claims against Iran and Libya. For example, the Victims of Pan Am Flight 103 organization established a political action committee, a legal committee, an investigation committee, and a press committee. They lobbied the State Department, published a newsletter, picketed Pan Am offices, and met with the president and Congress.[27] They were instrumental in the creation of a presidential Commission on Aviation Security and Terrorism to investigate the bombing. They played an influential role in the 1996 Iran-Libya Sanctions Act of 1996.[28] Their intervention led to major changes in airline procedures for handling disasters.

During the Iran hostage crisis, the families of the victims formed the Family Liaison Action Group, which, according to Gary Sick, "played a crucial role in public and government perceptions throughout the crisis."[29] Sick adds that President Carter promised the families that he would take no action that would endanger the lives of the hostages, although Brzezinski was pressing for a decisive response that would protect national honor.

The early development of counterterrorism policy was influenced by interactions between individual government agencies and specific interest groups. The debate over the Airport Security Act of 1973 shows how insider–outsider coalitions form.[30] The government players included Congress, the Departments of Transportation, State, and Justice, and the Federal Aviation Administration (FAA). The outside actors were the Air Line Pilots Association (ALPA), the Air Transport Association of America (ATAA), and the Airport

Operators Council International (AOCI). In the jurisdictional dispute between Justice and the FAA, the ATAA and AOCI preferred the FAA, while ALPA preferred Justice. In fact, Justice did not want jurisdiction. While the interest groups wanted the federal government to take responsibility for airport security measures, the Department of Transportation and the FAA wished to rely on local law enforcement.

All of these actors use the news media to articulate and disseminate their views not only to the public but to other elites. Government officials (or former officials) are the main source of information for reporters, as well as for Congress, sometimes openly and sometimes through strategic leaks. Leaks to the press can be a way of conducting internal battles as much as informing the public. The media's attraction to drama and spectacular events also makes it hard for the government to ignore an issue when policymakers assume that public opinion will track media attention. But the news media do not set the agenda, according to John Kingdon: "The media's tendency to give prominence to the most newsworthy or dramatic story actually diminishes their impact on governmental policy agendas because such stories tend to come toward the end of a policy-making process, rather than at the beginning."[31] The media tend to be responsive to issues already on the agenda, to accelerate or magnify them, rather than initiate attention. They report on what the government is doing or not doing.

Jeffrey D. Simon agrees.[32] He argues that the media image of crisis is due to the way presidents and their aides handle events; the press depends almost exclusively on authoritative official sources. Government officials set the tone through background briefings and off the record interviews as well as public speeches and press conferences. Presidents, not reporters, make hostage seizures into personal dramas. On the other hand, Brigitte Nacos argues that government policy is exceptionally sensitive to the news media and to public opinion, especially during hostage crises.[33] Yet the tone of general mass media coverage of U.S. counterterrorism policy is positive.[34]

Conclusions

It is unlikely that the politics of the domestic policy process will change. Thus, expectations for the future should be grounded in the assumption that the trends described in this article will continue. Terrorist attacks, especially spectacular incidents causing large numbers of casualties or targeting important national symbols, will contribute to putting the issue on the national policy agenda. They focus public attention on the threat of terrorism. However, policy will be developed within a general framework of diffusion of power. Multiple actors, inside and outside government, will compete to set the agenda and to determine policy through public debate, conducted largely in the news media. Each actor, whether an executive branch agency, Congress, or an interest group, wants to forge a national consensus behind its particular preference. Due to pressures from Congress, the president will not be able to set the agenda for counterterrorism policy with as much freedom as he can in other policy areas. Where the president dominates is in the rare use of military force, but these decisions may also be controversial within the executive branch. Implementation of policy decisions will also be affected by controversy, due to rivalries among agencies with operational responsibilities. Thus it will be difficult for any administration to develop a consistent policy based on an objective appraisal of the threat of terrorism to American national interests.

Martha Crenshaw is John E. Andrus professor of government at Wesleyan University, where she has taught international politics since 1974. She is the editor, with John Pimlott, of the *International Encyclopedia of Terrorism* and the author of countless articles and texts on the subject of political terrorism. Crenshaw currently serves on a task force concerning foreign policy toward the Islamic world at the Brookings Institution.

Notes

1. Despite its significance, little systematic attention has been paid to the politics of the counterterrorism policy process. William Farrell's early book, *The U.S. Government Response to Terrorism: In Search of an Effective Strategy* (Boulder, CO: Westview Press, 1982), analyzed the organizations behind counterterrorism policy. David Tucker, *Skirmished at the Edge of Empire: The United States and International Terrorism* (Westport, CT: Praeger, 1997), is also relevant, particularly Chapter 4 (pp. 109–132). Paul Pillar's *Terrorism and U.S. Foreign Policy* will also help fill this gap (Washington, DC: Brookings, 2001).
2. Thomas A Birkland, *After Disaster: Agenda Setting, Public Policy, and Focusing Events* (Washington, DC: Georgetown University Press, 1997).
3. Robert H. Johnson, *Improbable Dangers: U.S. Conceptions of Threat in the Cold War and After* (New York: St. Martin's, 1997), Chapter 2, "American Politics, Psychology, and the Exaggeration of Threat," pp. 31–48.
4. The classic work is John W. Kingdon, *Agendas, Alternatives, and Public Policies*, 2nd ed. (New York: Harper Collins, 1995). See also Frank R. Baumgartner and Bryan D. Jones, Agendas and Instability in American Politics (Chicago: University of Chicago Press, 1993) and Deborah A. Stone, *Policy Paradox: The Art of Political Decision Making* (New York: W. W. Norton, 1997).
5. See *Congressional Quarterly Weekly Report*, 16 January 1999, p. 151.
6. See Richard A. Falkenrath, "Problems of Preparedness: U.S. Readiness for a Domestic Terrorist Attack," *International Security* 25(4) (Spring 2001), pp. 147–186. See also Martha Crenshaw, "Threat Perception in Democracies: 'WMD' Terrorism in the U.S. Policy Debate," presented to the 22nd Annual Scientific Meeting of the International Society for Political Psychology, Amsterdam, 18–21 July 1999.
7. It has 82 members and an annual budget of $8.7 million, and is expected to increase to 121 people by 2003. It is based in Virginia, as part of the U.S. Joint Forces Command. In the event of a request from local or state government authorities, it would probably take direction from FEMA. See James Dao, "Looking Ahead to the Winter Olympics, a Terrorist Response Team Trains," *The New York Times*, 11 April 2001.
8. However, the Federal Emergency Management Agency (FEMA) has jurisdiction over "consequence management," which is in effect disaster response policy in the event of a domestic attack, especially one involving mass casualties.
9. In *Terrorism & Democracy* (Boston: Houghton Mifflin, 1991), p. 39.
10. Ibid., p. 81. Brzezinski set up an NSC committee to oversee covert actions because the CIA estimated that prospects for success were low. The CIA then vetoed the list of operations the NSC suggested, but Brzezinski was reluctant to take the dispute to the president.
11. 21 May 1998, p. A1.
12. See John F. Burns, "U.S. Aides Say the Yemenis Seem to Hinder Cole Inquiry," *The New York Times*, 1 November 2000.
13. 26 April 1998.
14. 23 May 1998, p. A3.
15. For the text of the speech, see http://www.defenselink.mil/news/Sep1998.
16. Richard A. Falkenrath, Robert D. Newman, and Bradley A. Thayer, *America's Achilles Heel: Nuclear, Biological, and Chemical Terrorism and Covert Attack* (Cambridge, MA: MIT Press,

1998), p. 263. See also Falkenrath, "Problems of Preparedness," p. 162, who says that the military see this role as a distraction from their core mission.

17. "Defense's Death Spiral," *Foreign Affairs* 78(4) (July-August 1999), p. 4.
18. *The New York Times*, 28 January 1999; also *The Hartford Courant*, with *Washington Post* byline, 1 February 1999.
19. See Falkenrath, "Problems of Preparedness," p. 163.
20. On this subject, see James Risen, "To Bomb Sudan Plant, or Not: A Year Later, Debates Rankle," *The New York Times*, 27 October 1999, and Seymour Hersh, "The Missiles of August," *The New Yorker*, 12 October 1998, pp. 34–41.
21. See Report of the Accountability Review Boards: Bombings of the U.S. Embassies in Nairobi, Kenya and Dar Es Salaam, Tanzania on August 7, 1998, 11 January 1999. Available at (http://www/zgram.net/embassybombing.htm). See further details from the classified report in James Risen and Benjamin Weiser, "Before Bombings, Omens and Fears," *The New York Times*, 9 January 1999. According to this account, the Kenyan authorities arrested a group of suspects but the CIA station chief declined to interview them.
22. This section relies on research assistance by Karen Millard. See press reports such as Lou Cannon, "Political Pressure for Marine Pullout Likely to Increase," *Washington Post*, 29 December 1983; Martin Tolchin, "House Leaders Urge New Study of Beirut Policy," *The New York Times*, 3 January 1984; and John Goshko and Margaret Shapiro, "Shultz Asks for Support on Lebanon; Holds Hill Parleys as Pressure for Withdrawal Grows," *The Washington Post*, 27 January 1984.
23. See text in *The Washington Post*, 26 January 1984, p. A16.
24. See *The New York Times*, 14, 18, and 20 August 1975. Kate Whitman assisted with the research of this case.
25. Falkenrath, "Problems of Preparedness," p. 149.
26. For example, Ian O. Lesser et al., *Countering the New Terrorism* (Santa Monica, CA: Rand Corporation, 1999). The study was commissioned by the Air Force.
27. See Steven Emerson and Brian Duffy, *The Fall of Pan Am 103: Inside the Lockerbie Investigation* (New York: G. P. Putnams' Sons, 1990), especially pp. 221–225.
28. See Gideon Rose's account of the politics of the legislative process in his chapter on Libya in Richard N. Haass, ed., *Economic Sanctions and American Diplomacy* (New York: Council on Foreign Relations, 1998), pp. 129–156, especially pp. 142–144. See also Patrick Clawson's chapter on Iran, pp. 85–106.
29. See his chapter, "Taking vows: The domestication of policy-making in hostage incidents," in *Origins of Terrorism*, edited by Walter Reich (Washington, DC: Woodrow Wilson Center and Cambridge University Press, 1990), pp. 238–239.
30. Joel Rothman assisted with research on this debate. See U.S. Senate, Committee on Commerce, Subcommittee on Aviation, *The Anti-Hijacking Act of 1971*. Hearings. 92nd Cong., 2d sess., 1972.
31. Kingdon, *Agendas, Alternatives, and Public Policies*, p. 59.
32. *The Terrorist Trap: America's Experience with Terrorism* (Bloomington: Indiana University Press, 1994), especially Chapter 7, "Media Players," pp. 261–308.
33. *Terrorism and the Media* (New York: Columbia University Press, 1994).
34. Measured by references to international terrorism in the *Readers' Guide to Periodical Literature 1968–1998*. Database available upon request.

Rob de Wijk, 2001

The Limits of Military Power

Defense planning had only fleetingly dealt with the threat of apocalyptic terrorism prior to September 11. If the hastily revised U.S. quadrennial defense guidelines give any insight, the basis of defense planning will now shift from a threat-based model, analyzing whom the adversary might be, to capability-based planning, which focuses more on how an adversary might fight. Adopting this model is a great step forward, but the review itself offers little insight into the question of how an adversary might actually fight and what forces are needed to fight and win future wars.[1] The events of September 11 clarified the urgent need to refocus and restructure the way the United States and its allies think about and plan for a military campaign.

- The West's armed forces are fundamentally flawed. Conceptually, the focus is still on conventional warfare, but the new wars will be unconventional.
- Contemporary concepts, such as limited collateral damage and proportionality, have little value when preparing for the new wars.
- How concepts such as coercive diplomacy and coercion can be used effectively is unclear.

In sum, the United States and its allies face significant practical as well as conceptual challenges. The September 11 attacks demonstrated that terrorism no longer can be considered a tactical or local challenge, requiring cooperation between the national intelligence services and the police. The new terrorism is a strategic or international challenge, requiring international cooperation between intelligence services and armed forces. Meeting the challenge requires a new approach as well as new assets.

'Savage Warfare'

Western armed forces demonstrated their superiority clearly during the Persian Gulf War in 1991 when, after the extensive use of airpower, U.S. ground forces gained a decisive victory over Iraq within 100 hours. In contrast to conventional warfare, which relies on technological capabilities—manned arms and standoff weaponry—to engage the enemy, terrorists fight unconventionally. Technology plays a supporting role at best, for personal protection, communications, and targeting. In the final analysis, however, successes depend on old-fashioned fighting skills and the use of knives or small-caliber arms in search-and-destroy operations. In conventional warfare, armies take and hold ground, air forces conduct strategic bombing operations and engage the enemy, and navies support land forces by conducting offshore attacks and cutting off lines of supply. This method of operation is the Western way of waging war. The new wars on terrorism, however, will have to deal with irregular forces that practice guerrilla tactics, instill panic, and retaliate asymmetrically—when, where, and how they choose.

Actually, referring to the military campaign now under way as the "new" war demonstrates little understanding of the history of warfare. In 1898, in *Lockhart's Advance through Tirah*, Capt. L. J. Shadwell wrote about "savage warfare" (that is, non-European warfare) "that differs from that of civilized people." Some areas in the world have not changed much since Shadwell's time.

> A frontier tribesman can live for days on the grain he carries with him, and other savages on a few dates; consequently no necessity exists for them to cover a line of communications. So nimble of foot, too, are they in their grass shoes, and so conversant with every goat-track in their mountains that they can retreat in any direction. This extraordinary mobility enables them to attack from any direction quite unexpectedly, and to disperse and disappear as rapidly as they came. For this reason, the rear of a European force is as much exposed to attack as its front or flanks.[2]

In Afghanistan today, the biggest change is that army boots or Nikes have replaced grass shoes. Furthermore, local fighters possess limited numbers of modern weapons systems, such as Stinger antiaircraft missiles, which were acquired during the 1980s when the United States considered Afghans to be freedom fighters who needed support in their struggle against Soviet occupation. The basic Afghani weapons platform is the pickup truck, which carries fighters armed with guns; in mountainous regions, the mule is still the most important mode of transportation.

In most Western countries, irregular warfare has always been considered "savage warfare," for which there is no preparation. Historically, the British and the Dutch, in particular, fought insurgents quite successfully in their colonies. With the loss of Indonesia in the 1950s, the Dutch lost not only all their experience in waging this kind of war but also their mental preparedness for such action.

The Dutch army is now preparing a new field manual on counterinsurgency and counterterrorism. In drafting the manual, the army's staff utilized the old manuals that General Johannes van Heutsz used during the early twentieth century when he was combating insurgents and terrorists in what is now the Republic of Indonesia. Van Heutsz also reorganized his conventional ground forces to confront the insurgents, creating small units of a dozen armed men to carry out search-and-destroy missions. This military action led to an episode that the Dutch do not want to repeat. Today, that army's counterinsurgency operations could be perceived as war crimes. Because no distinction could be made between combatants and noncombatants, the Dutch burnt down entire villages in order to eliminate fighters' bases. For this reason, U.S. Secretary of Defense Donald Rumsfeld argued that direct attacks on terrorists are useless; forces are required to "drain the swamp they live in."[3]

In addition to consulting van Heutsz's tactics, the Dutch used the British counterinsurgency manual, which is still considered the most detailed manual for this type of warfare. Of the former colonial powers, only the British have not given up their military skills; at the same time, British forces have maintained the mental preparedness needed to carry out counterinsurgency operations.

The West needs special forces to confront irregular fighters such as terrorists, and these forces are not available in large quantities. A distinction should be made between special operations forces (SOF), which are used for covert or clandestine action, and specialized forces, which carry out specialized overt missions. The most famous of all SOF, Great Britain's Special Air Service (SAS), conceived by Captain David Stirling, has existed since 1941. Most SOF—such as Australia's Special Air Service Regiment; Holland's Bijzondere Bijstands Eenheid (BBE); France's new joint Commandement des Operation Speciale (COS) units; Germany's Grenzschutsgruppe (GSG)-9; Israel's Sayeret Matkal/Unit 269, and the U.S. Army 1st Special Forces Operational Detachment, Delta Force, and Naval Special Warfare Development Group—were established in the 1970s as a direct response to terrorist incidents.

When radical supporters of Iran's revolution captured 53 staff members and guards at the U.S. embassy in Tehran in November 1979, however, the United States still had no standing counterterrorist task force. As a result, a rescue team had to be assembled from scratch, and it took six months of preparation before the rescue operation could be launched. Charged with rescuing the hostages was the newly created Delta Force, with the support of U.S. Navy and Air Force airlifts. The tragic end of this attempt is well known. Technical problems and tactical failures caused the operation's abortion, and it ended in disaster in April 1980. Nevertheless, after this failed rescue operation, U.S. SOF received more funding and better equipment and training. Consequently, SOF became an important foreign policy tool for U.S. policymakers.[4]

SOF specialize in clandestinely rescuing hostages. SOF's military tasks focus on infiltrations into enemy territory to carry out sabotage as well as search-and-destroy and rescue missions and forward air control. Western militaries have extremely limited true SOF capabilities, probably no more than 3,000–5,000 troops for all of NATO.

In addition, Western governments have specialized forces that carry out overt actions. The United States has approximately 45,000 such troops; its NATO allies have 20,000–30,000. The U.S. Army Ranger battalions, which specialize in seizing airfields, are among the better known of these units; another is the 82nd Airborne Division, the world's largest parachute force. These forces seize key targets and prepare the ground for the general-purpose forces that follow.

Nevertheless, new concepts such as swarming, netwar, and counternetwar also need to be developed. Deployed SOF and specialized forces must disperse and form a network that covers large areas. These forces must make use of advanced communications, including uplinks and downlinks with unmanned and manned aircraft and satellites to enable quick-response strikes against high-value targets. For the military, netwar requires a different mindset because, unlike traditional formations, it has less hierarchy and less emphasis on combined arms operations.

Even though NATO countries have more than three million individuals in their collective armed services, only a very small portion of them are SOF or specialized armed forces—too few to engage in sustained combat operations. Clearly, it is too late to increase this capability for the campaign in Afghanistan and other countries hosting terrorists. Even if a decision were made to create more of these units, only a small number of young people would be willing or able to join these forces; according to some estimates, less than 10 percent make it through the grueling selection process.

The status of the West's human intelligence (HUMINT) capabilities is similar. For data collection, the intelligence communities of the United States and its NATO allies focus primarily on satellite imagery, signals intelligence, and electronic intelligence. Satellite imagery guides both SOF and HUMINT to targets. Although satellite imagery obtains important strategic information, SOF and HUMINT are the best way to obtain tactical information on the ground, especially because terrorist groups make only limited use of cellular telephones and satellite communications. Since the U.S. Cruise missile attacks on his training camps in August 1998, Osama bin Laden no longer uses his satellite telephone, which had made him easy to detect. Instead, he issues "mission orders," instructing his lieutenants orally, in writing, or on videotape that television stations broadcast widely. Consequently, the United States and its allies have no choice but to infiltrate his network.

Tapping into this network is an enormous task, however, because the al Qaeda organization has bases and cells in 50–60 countries, including the United States and most European nations, where so-called sleeper agents live. The individuals who carried out the attacks on the World Trade Center and the Pentagon had been ordinary residents in the United States and other Western countries. Therefore, agents from Islamic states' intelligence communities must infiltrate networks and cells both inside and outside the Islamic world, while Western governments must at the same time recruit agents in the Islamic communities in their own countries. Consequently, effective use of HUMINT requires intensive cooperation among intelligence services worldwide.

Without sufficient HUMINT capabilities, as well as SOF and specialized forces that can effectively address unexpected threats and unconventional warfare—the only option open to the West's opponents—the United States and its allies will find the campaign on terrorism almost impossible. In its most basic form, asymmetrical warfare utilizes one side's comparative advantage against its enemy's relative weakness. Successful asymmetrical warfare exploits vulnerabilities—which are easy to determine—by using weapons and tactics in ways that are unplanned or unexpected. The weakness of Western societies is perceived as their desire to reduce collateral damage by emphasizing technological solutions, the need to maintain coalitions, and the need to adhere to the international rule of law. Moreover, Western industrialized societies are economically and socially vulnerable. Thus, dealing with these new threats requires groups of well-trained, well-equipped, and highly motivated individuals who can infiltrate and destroy terrorist networks.

At the tactical level, the opponent conducting asymmetrical warfare tries to change the course of action in order to prevent the achievement of political objectives. These tactics—including guerrilla warfare, hit-and-run attacks, sabotage, terrorism, and the capture of soldiers who are then shown on television—will confront allied ground forces in Afghanistan and other places that harbor terrorist training camps and headquarters.

At the strategic level, the opponent using asymmetrical tactics exploits the fears of the civilian population, thereby undermining the government, compromising its alliances, and affecting its economy. The September 11 attacks were only partly successful on this score. The fear of further attacks has led to uncertainty about the future among the populations of most Western nations and as a result their economies have fallen into recession. On the other hand, the attackers very likely miscalculated not only the resolve of the leadership and population of the United States but also most of the world's willingness to form and maintain coalitions to fight terrorism.

Direct military action against insurgents and terrorists requires both SOF and HUMINT gathering. Both assets are scarce, however, and not available in the quantities necessary to fight and win sustained wars. Moreover, deploying SOF is extremely risky, and effective engagement requires skills and techniques that come very close to war crimes. Therefore, the United States and its allies need to develop a new defense-planning concept.

The Limited Value of Contemporary Western Concepts

For historical and cultural reasons, the armed forces of Western countries have been disinclined to prepare for military action that was considered uncivilized. As a consequence, policymakers, the military, and the public are psychologically ill-prepared for this war. They have become used to concepts such as limited collateral damage, proportionality of response, and the absence of body bags. The current situation, however, calls for a willingness to abandon these ideas, at least partially, a sacrifice that may be difficult for some individuals and nations to make.

During his visit to Pakistan on October 5, British Prime Minister Tony Blair called for "proportionate strikes… [that should] not be directed against the Afghan people." These concepts have little value when carrying out military operations against insurgents and terrorists for a number of reasons.

- *Collateral damage*. Because asymmetrical fighters do not usually wear uniforms, combatants are indistinguishable from civilians. These fighters depend on the local civilian population for logistics and shelter in rural areas, and in urban areas the population is used as a shield. Moreover, because the Afghan population is loyal to tribes and clans, differentiating between combatants and noncombatants is almost impossible. Thus, the concept of limited collateral damage is almost useless in unconventional warfare, in which civilian casualties cannot be avoided.
- *Proportionality of response*. Proportionality refers to the size and character of the attack and the interests at stake. On September 11, the terrorists turned airliners into weapons of mass destruction. Indeed, for two conventional bombs to cause the death of more than 5,000 civilians is nearly impossible. Additionally, the United States must now defend its national security, leadership, and credibility. If one takes the concept of proportionality literally, retaliation with a few low-yield nuclear weapons would certainly be justifiable, because only nuclear weapons could cause the same amount of damage as the September 11 attacks. Keeping the fragile coalition with Islamic countries together requires less than a proportional response, however, rendering nuclear weapons a non-option.
- *Absence of body bags*. Because vital interests of the United States and its allies are at stake, the concept of an absence of body bags carries little value either. Both Blair and President George W. Bush have the popular political support to withstand the inevitable heavy human losses. General Joseph Ralston, NATO's supreme allied commander, warned, "We cannot be in the mindset of a zero-casualty operation."[5] Whether most European allies are also willing to pay this high price is doubtful. Initially, the Belgian and Dutch governments saw invoking Article 5 of the NATO treaty as a symbolic measure and a demonstration of transatlantic solidarity. Other governments agreed so that they would be consulted on U.S. decisions and have some influence on U.S. decisionmaking. Except for the United Kingdom, few European NATO allies acknowledged that the decision to invoke Article 5 implies sending their own troops to Southwest Asia.

Thus, combating insurgents and terrorists requires mental firmness, a quality evident in the United States and the United Kingdom today but uncertain in other allies. The traditional concepts of proportionality and limited collateral damage, however, do not have much value under the present circumstances.

Coercion and Coercive Diplomacy

Another obstacle to using military means effectively to combat the new threats that terrorism poses is the limited insight that academics, and therefore policymakers, offer into the theories of coercion and coercive diplomacy, as well as governments' lack of experience using them to achieve the desired outcome. Coercion is defined as the deliberate and purposeful use of economic and military power to influence the choices of one's adversaries; coercive diplomacy focuses on the latent use of the instruments of power to influence those choices. The studies on which these theories are based, however, do not have much relevance for policymakers today. The terrorist attacks on the United States demonstrate the need for policymakers and the military to reevaluate the concepts that underlie their approaches to balancing political ends and military means.

Most theories of coercion find their origin in the Cold War period, but preoccupation with deterrence has distorted the concept. Deterrence as a concept is useless for today's challenges because the world cannot deter individuals such as bin Laden and his lieutenants. Deterrence also does not work for failed states, many of which provide sanctuaries for insurgents and terrorists. Because negotiating with failed states and terrorists is impossible, both coercive diplomacy and coercion are meaningless. The only solution in those cases is direct action with SOF support, backed up by airpower.

The United States can only use coercive diplomacy and coercion against functioning states that actively support or shelter terrorists. For that reason, Vice President Dick Cheney's warning that the "full wrath" of the United States would be brought down against nations sheltering attackers is an indication of the administration's emerging strategy for combating terrorism.

The problem is the West's lack of experience with this approach. Many cases of coercion and coercive diplomacy have failed. For example, the Gulf War was an unprecedented success, but attempts to coerce Saddam Hussein to comply with United Nations (UN) resolutions during the 1990s failed. The humanitarian intervention in Somalia during the early 1990s resulted in failure. The success of Operation Allied Force in the war in Kosovo was limited because it took 78 days to convince Serbian president Slobodan Milosevic to accept a diplomatic solution based on the Rambouillet agreements signed in early 1999.

Existing theories are based primarily on studies that Thomas Schelling, Alexander George, and Robert Pape conducted,[6] yet even these "classics" do not apply to the circumstances that the West faces today. Schelling distinguishes between "brute force" and "compellence." Brute force is aimed at forcing a military solution; compellence is aimed at using the threat of force to influence an actor's choice.[7] According to Schelling, armed conflict can only be averted when the opponent refrains from taking action. This situation requires a deadline because, without a clear ultimatum, threats are hollow.[8] Accordingly, the United States gave Afghanistan's Taliban regime a deadline, which it rejected, to surrender bin Laden and his lieutenants.

For Schelling, coercive diplomacy involves not only undoing a particular action but also threatening the opponent with the use of force, which can bring about complete surrender. The crux of Schelling's approach is "risk strategy": by threatening the civilian population and presenting the prospect of terror, the actor expects the opponent's behavior to change. This notion made sense during the Cold War, when Schelling's book—in which he sought alternatives to the concept of deterrence—was published in 1966. A risk strategy is meaningless in the war against terrorism, however, because the coercers—the United States and its allies—must clearly indicate that the war is not against the Afghan people, but against terrorists and the regime supporting them. Thus there are no civilian populations (such as the Soviet people in the Cold War) to threaten in the effective use of coercion. Worse, excessive military force could split the fragile Islamic alliance that is cooperating with the United States in the war against terrorism. In other words, coercion might not only be ineffective, it might also backfire. For that reason, humanitarian aid for the civilian population accompanied the initial attacks on Afghanistan in early October 2001.

George's study of coercive diplomacy first appeared in 1971; a new edition was published in 1994, in which George tested his theory on more recent cases. George distinguishes between defensive "coercive diplomacy" and offensive "military strategy." Coercive diplomacy consists of using diplomatic means, reinforced with instruments of power. Coercion, in the form of threats or military interventions, must force an adversary to cease unacceptable activities.

George's main argument is that coercion and diplomacy go hand in hand with rewards for the opponent when complying with demands.[9] In the case of the Taliban, Bush and Blair have stated there is no room for compromise and that no rewards will be given for handing bin Laden over. Consequently, the Taliban had no incentive not to fight for its survival, forcing the United States and its allies to confront the prospect of a prolonged struggle and also undermining the fragile coalition forged between Western and Islamic states.

Schelling's and George's theories focus primarily on the latent use of instruments of power, whereas Pape's theory concerns their actual use. Pape posits that coercion is effective when it aims at the benefit side of the cost-benefit calculation that every actor makes. To be effective, the opposing side must consider the cost of surrendering to the demands of the intervening states to be lower than the cost of resistance. Pape argues that this outcome is possible when the actor withholds military success from the opponent, while offering a reward after the demands have been met. Both the Taliban as well as the U.S. and British governments have vital interests at stake; therefore, the Taliban's will to defend and the West's will to coerce are at maximum levels. Consequently, both sides are willing to pay a high price, and neither will give up easily.

Regarding military strategy, Pape focuses on strategic bombing, which can be decisive only in long wars of attrition. The overall superiority of materiel determines the success of this approach, which was Russia's strategy in Chechnya during the strategic bombing campaign in Grozny, a strategy most Western governments severely condemned as inhuman. Nevertheless, a military coalition may have no option but to use elements of an attrition strategy. Given the unavailability of other assets, the destruction of some training camps and underground facilities may require the use of low-yield tactical nuclear weapons or fuel-air explosives. Moreover, some U.S. strategists are reportedly beginning to consider using the threat of a limited nuclear strike as a method of deterring potential adversaries that support terrorist organizations from using chemical and biological weapons or of destroying the storage site of these weapons.[10] Thus, the use of nuclear weapons might actually be militarily useful in the war against terrorism, but potentially grave consequences—such as fracturing the coalition—prevent policymakers from using them.

Pape argues that deposing political regimes is not feasible "because leaders are hard to kill, governments are harder to overthrow, and even if the target government can be overthrown, the coercer can rarely guarantee that its replacement will be more forthcoming."[11] In other words, Blair's warning to the Taliban "to surrender terrorists or to surrender power"[12] does not have many successful historical precedents. The removal of Panama's President Manuel Noriega from power in 1989 is one of the few successful examples.

Pape concluded that the use of airpower can be successful when it denies the opponent the use of military capabilities. This approach requires a strategy of denial—that is, the destruction of key military targets, including headquarters and command and control centers, logistics, and staging areas. In the case of unconventional warfare, however, the number of high-value targets is extremely limited; therefore, there is little to bomb. Consequently, the only strategy that can be successful is a military strategy of control, which requires search-and-destroy missions using land forces such as SOF reinforced by specialized forces and airpower, but as argued earlier, the United States and its allies have very limited capabilities in these areas.

These studies are useful as a starting point for further academic research, but their work has limited utility for contemporary policymaking. Consequently, the September 11 incidents have prompted both policymakers and the military to rethink their basic concepts and to seek another approach to the old challenge of balancing political objectives and military means. For example, a mechanism of second-order change could be developed, aimed at mobilizing neighboring states against a target state. The Islamic Republic of Iran, which is strongly opposed to the Taliban regime, could play a crucial role by putting pressure on Afghanistan. Pressure from Iran would have the added advantage of involving an Islamic country and thus strengthening the coalition. Thus, reexamining old concepts and traditional approaches are essential to employing military means successfully in the campaign on terrorism.

The Battle for Hearts and Minds

A significant component of the new war—one that has been historically successful for both allies and adversaries of the United States—is the campaign to win the support of the populace of the opponent. In other words, the United States and its allies must also wage a battle for the hearts and minds of the people, in this case, in the Islamic world. This effort—using several approaches, including humanitarian aid and propaganda—must be made along with diplomatic measures and military operations. The humanitarian aid that accompanies the bombs being dropped in Afghanistan in the current fight demonstrates that the United States recognizes the importance of this campaign.

Israel serves as an example of the difficulties that a nation confronts in a war against terrorists and of the way the battle to win the hearts and minds of the population can accompany military measures. Terror persists in Israel, despite the fact that the country has military assets that are important for waging this type of war, including defense forces and intelligence services that are among the best in the world, policymakers and a public who are willing to take risks and to accept casualties, and widespread public support for the military even if mistakes are made. Yet the country cannot prevent or deter terrorist acts or attacks with rockets from southern Lebanon. Israel's experience shows that armed forces—trained, structured, and equipped for conventional war—are incapable of dealing with insurgents. Israel had no choice but to develop new tactics, employ different weapons systems, and use small task forces to carry out small-scale operations; but even this shift in modus operandi has not guaranteed success.

Bin Laden, who is accused of being the force behind the September 11 attacks, fights a battle similar to the Intifada but on a global scale. His objective seems to be to unite the Islamic world under a political-religious figure, or caliph, by removing pro-Western regimes, the state of Israel, and the U.S. presence from the Islamic world.

Israel's experience also shows that, at best, governments can only manage the problem of terrorism. Its solution requires offensive military action, heavy security measures to prevent radical elements from carrying out their attacks, and the building of coalitions with moderate political figures. Israel's experience with gaining the support of the civilian population is important. For example, when the security zone in southern Lebanon still existed, Israel carried out a counterinsurgency campaign within it while providing aid to the Lebanese population therein, including projects to rebuild infrastructure and programs to provide health care. On the other side of the coin, radical movements such as Hamas use nongovernmental organizations extensively for these purposes.

Bin Laden is popular because of his "good works" in the Islamic world, especially in Pakistan and Afghanistan. Indeed, in most Islamic countries, radical groups of fundamentalists have developed a social and cultural infrastructure to build an Islamic civil society and fill a vacuum that their countries' governments have neglected. For example, during the 1990s in Egypt, Jordan, the West Bank and Gaza, Afghanistan, and Pakistan, radical movements provided health care, education, and welfare for those nations' poor. After the 1992 earthquake in Cairo, these organizations were on the streets within hours, whereas the Egyptian government's relief efforts lagged behind. In fact, Qur'an study centers have become the single most important source for recruiting new members for the radical movements.

These types of campaigns waged by radical Islamic movements have very successfully undermined the legitimacy of governments and gained the support of the local civilian population. Consequently, the diplomatic and military actions of the United States and its allies should go hand in hand with a campaign for the hearts and minds in order to win the support of the Islamic world's population. In addition to food rations, U.S. aircraft have dropped leaflets and small transistor radios to enable the Afghans to receive Washington's message. Nevertheless, even a dual strategy of humanitarian aid and military intervention does not guarantee success. Other factors must be taken into account.

Clashing Civilizations

The major obstacle to success in the campaign against terrorism is not military, political, or diplomatic, but cultural. Because of strong anti-Western sentiments in the Islamic world, a coalition to counter terrorism is fragile by nature but critical to the success of military measures. The geostrategic changes that occurred in the 1990s have contributed to anti-Western feelings in large parts of the world. First, the West "won" the Cold War, with the United States remaining the sole superpower; and in international relations the "hegemon" is always met with distrust. Second, in 1998 the differences between the United States and non-Western nations countries became clearer as a result of a new version of interventionism.

The year 1998 seems to be a turning point in recent history. Events that took place in 1998 and 1999 indicated that the U.S. approach had once and for all shifted to a narrower and more selective foreign and national security policy of unilateralism and preservation of the nation's dominant position in the world. A number of events contributed to this image:

- In response to the bombings of the U.S. embassies in Kenya and Tanzania, the United States intervened unilaterally—and without a UN Security Council mandate—in Sudan and Afghanistan in August 1998. The U.S. goal was to strike a blow against bin Laden's alleged terrorist network.
- In December that same year, Operation Desert Fox took place, in which the United States and the United Kingdom carried out bombing raids against Iraq. The military action was meant as retribution for Saddam Hussein's obstruction of the UN Special Commission's inspections of Iraq's development of weapons of mass destruction. In 1999 and 2000, the bombings continued, albeit with limited intensity.
- In 1998, the U.S. government decided to increase its defense budget (which had undergone a period of decline) by 5.6 percent, a development that some nations viewed with apprehension.[13]
- In March 1999, Operation Allied Force—led by the United States and without a mandate by the UN Security Council—intervened in Kosovo to force Milosevic to end his terror against the Albanian Kosovars and to find a solution to the situation in Kosovo.
- In July 1999, the United States presented its national missile defense initiative, designed to protect the country against limited attacks by rogue states using ballistic missiles. This development demanded a review of the 1972 Anti-Ballistic Missile Treaty. With the U.S. Senate's refusal to ratify the Comprehensive Test Ban Treaty, a general prohibition on conducting nuclear tests was dropped.

As a result of these events, many non-Western countries began to perceive the United States as a superpower that wants to change the status quo and create a "new world order" according to its own views. Because of the fundamental difference between Western and non-Western ideas, Russia, China, and Islamic countries distrust interventions that are based on normative principles, such as democracy and humanitarianism. According to Chinese commentators, for example, interventions by the United States indicate that the West can impose its liberal values on the rest of the world without fear of confrontation with Russia.[14]

Only Western governments appeal to normative principles as a reason for intervention. The notion that these principles are universal and that sovereignty is secondary to human interest won ground in the 1990s. The concepts of democracy, respect for human rights, the free-market economy, pluralism, the rule of law, and social modernization are deeply rooted in Western culture and are the product of a civilization that developed over centuries. Universal pretensions and a feeling of superiority are not alien to Western culture.

In 1860 Isaac Taylor wrote about the "ultimate civilization." He dealt with the moral supremacy of Western civilization and considered other civilizations barbaric because they held polygamy, prostitution, slavery, and torture to be legal. After the fall of the Berlin Wall in 1989, many came to the conclusion that Western values, particularly democracy, had triumphed. In 1992 Francis Fukuyama even referred to the end of history, because liberal democracies had prevailed and the collapse of dictatorships was supposedly inevitable.[15] In September 2001, Italian prime minister Silvio Berlusconi praised Western civilization as superior to that of the Islamic world and urged Europe to "reconstitute itself on the basis of its Christian roots." In a briefing to journalists, he talked about the "superiority of our civilization, which consists of a value system that has given people widespread prosperity in those countries that embrace it and [that] guarantees respect and religion."[16] Other Western politicians and the Islamic world did not appreciate Berlusconi's frankness.

Beginning in 1990, Western countries believed that they had the evidence for their claim to universal acceptance of their principles because a steadily growing group of countries, including Russia, claimed that they had embraced Western values. Similar declarations by non-Western governments ultimately mean little. First, these governments can pay lip service for purely opportunistic reasons that may relate to other issues of importance to them, such as trade policy. Second, declarations of acceptance of these principles do not necessarily indicate that governments actually embrace them. Their unwillingness to accept the consequences of noncompliance with these principles at times or, in certain situations, their willingness to set aside sovereignty—for example, in the event of a humanitarian disaster—belie these claims. This notion is particularly true for countries, such as Russia and China, that have rebellious minorities, leading to internal unrest, and aspirations to remain great powers.

The British-Canadian scholar and journalist Michael Ignatieff appropriately posed the following question: Whose universal values are actually involved? He pointed out that the outlooks of Western countries, Islamic countries, and authoritarian regimes in East Asia have fundamental differences.[17] In Asia, authoritarian state and family structures dominate for the most part, and democracy and individual rights are secondary. In general, Islamic countries reject the Western concept of the separation of church and state. Apart from Ignatieff's observation, however, the claim of universal acceptance of Western values constitutes a threat in the eyes of many non-Western countries, if acceptance is accompanied by dismissal of the cornerstones of international law, such as sovereignty and noninterference in domestic affairs. These countries perceive even humanitarian interventions as a new form of imperialism that should not be endorsed without question.

The war against terrorism is a golden opportunity for Western nations to enter a new era of cooperation with Russia and China, which are equally concerned about terrorism. Indeed, bin Laden and the Islamic insurgents in Chechnya are linked. Furthermore, the Islamic insurgency in Xinjiang in eastern China has a connection with the Taliban regime and, most probably, bin Laden as well.

The biggest challenge, however, is the resurgence of Islam, which is a mainstream movement and not at all extremist. This resurgence is a product of modernity and of Muslims' attempt to deal with it by rejecting Western culture and influence, committing to Islam as the guide to life in the modern world. Fundamentalism, commonly misperceived as political Islam, is only one aspect of this resurgence, which began in the 1970s when Islamic symbols, beliefs, practices, and institutions won more support throughout the Islamic world. As a product of modernity, the core constituency of Islamic resurgence consists of middle-class students and intellectuals. Even the fundamentalists who carried out the September 11 attacks were well-educated, middle-class men.

Because the resurgence of Islam is fundamentally an anti-Western movement, building coalitions incorporating Islamic nations in the battle against terrorism is not easy. The coalition that was built in the aftermath of the September 11 attacks was primarily based on attitudes against bin Laden, who seeks to establish an undivided *umma* (community of believers) under a political-religious leader—thereby presenting a challenge to most regimes in the Islamic world. Nevertheless, most regimes and large parts of their populations share some of bin Laden's anti-Western sentiments. Consequently, the coalition is fragile and, at best, willing to give only passive support. Thus, many Islamic people will consider a military campaign that is carried out by Western forces as, to use bin Laden's words, "a Zionist Crusade." Unfortunately, a controversial 1996 assertion that conflicts between cultures will dominate future international relations remains germane in the new millennium.[18]

The war on terrorism could improve the West's relations with China and Russia, but, if handled unwisely, it could also lead to a confrontation with the Islamic world. The United States' nightmare scenario is that friendly regimes in the Islamic world will fall and anti-Western regimes willing to play the oil card and support terrorists will emerge. Thus, the immediate consequence of the war on terrorism could be both ineffectiveness and a struggle for energy resources so vital to the Western world.

Limiting Expectations

As the war against terrorism shifts into full gear, the United States and its allies must meet significant practical and conceptual challenges if the campaign is to be successful. A war against terrorists or insurgents can be manageable, at best, if certain approaches are adopted. In principle, the following options, which are not all mutually exclusive, are available to the United States and its allies, depending on the target of the campaign:

- Pursue a military strategy of control in failed states that terrorists use as sanctuaries. Control involves search-and-destroy missions by SOF, supported by specialized forces and airpower. This option requires the United States and its allies to expand the number of SOF and specialized forces significantly.
- Adopt a strategy of coercive diplomacy or coercion against unfriendly regimes to pressure these regimes to end their support of terrorist movements. If they do not comply with these demands, these regimes should be removed from power, which is easier said than done. This strategy requires new thinking about the optimum way to coerce regimes.
- Use HUMINT gathering methods extensively to infiltrate the terrorists' networks in friendly countries and then destroy the terrorist bases from within. This option also requires the United States and its allies to expand their HUMINT capabilities substantially and to embark on even closer cooperation with intelligence services in other countries.
- Wage a campaign to win the hearts and minds of the Islamic people. This option would enable the United States and its allies to gain the support of the populace and thereby drive a wedge between the population and the terrorists or insurgents.

Nevertheless, even if these options are adopted and prove successful at least in the short term, an overriding issue must be addressed in order to achieve long-term success. The primary obstacle to success in the war against terrorism is a cultural one. To some degree, the battle is a clash of civilizations. Political Islam is fundamentally anti-Western, thus the prospect for success is limited. Using military means may exacerbate the potential that this campaign will be cast as a clash of civilizations, ultimately making the problem of terrorism even worse.

Rob de Wijk is an expert on military aspects of security issues at the Clingendael Institute for International Relations (The Netherlands). He also is a professor of international relations at the Royal Military Academy and professor of strategic studies at Leiden University. A former head of the Defence Concepts Division of the Netherlands Ministry of Defence, he is also co-author of *NATO on the Brink of the New Millennium: The Battle for Consensus* (1998).

Notes

1. U.S. Department of Defense, *Quadrennial Defense Review Report*, September 30, 2001.
2. L. J. Shadwell, *Lockhart's Advance through Tirah* (London: W. Thacker & Co., 1898), pp. 100–105.
3. "Rumsfeld," *International Herald Tribune*, September 19, 2001, p. 6.
4. S. L. Marquis, *Unconventional Warfare: Rebuilding U.S. Special Operations Forces* (Washington, D.C.: Brookings Institution, 1997), p. 2.
5. "Rumsfeld," p. 6.
6. See Thomas A. Schelling, *Arms and Influence* (New Haven: Yale University Press, 1966); Alexander L. George and W. E. Simons, eds., *The Limits of Coercive Diplomacy* (Boulder, Colo.: Westview Press, 1994); Robert A. Pape, *Bombing to Win: Air Power and Coercion in War* (Ithaca, N.Y.: Cornell University Press, 1996). See also Lawrence Freedman, *Strategic Coercion* (Oxford: Oxford University Press, 1998); Colin S. Gray, *Modern Strategy* (Oxford: Oxford University Press, 1999); Richard N. Haass, *Intervention: The Use of American Military Force in the Post–Cold War World* (Washington, D.C.: Carnegie Endowment for International Peace, 1994); Michael O'Hanlon, *Saving Lives with Force: Military Criteria for Humanitarian Intervention* (Washington, D.C.: Brookings Institution, 1997); and B. R. Pirnie and W. E. Simons, *Soldiers for Peace* (Santa Monica, Calif.: RAND, 1996).
7. Schelling, *Arms and Influence*, pp. 2–3.
8. Ibid., pp. 69–91; see also Thomas Schelling, *The Strategy of Conflict* (New York and London: Oxford University Press, 1965).
9. George and Simons, *Limits of Coercive Diplomacy*, p. 7.
10. "U.S. Strategists Begin to Favor Threat to Use Nuclear Weapons," *International Herald Tribune*, October 6–7, 2001, p. 4.
11. Pape, *Bombing to Win*, p. 316.
12. Prime Minister Tony Blair, speech to the Labor Party Conference, London, October 2, 2001.
13. International Institute for Strategic Studies, "U.S. Military Spending," *Strategic Comments* 6, no. 4 (May 2000).
14. J. Teufel Dreyer, *The PLA and the Kosovo Conflict* (Carlisle, Penn.: U.S. Army War College, May 2000), p. 3.
15. F. Fukuyama, *The End of History and the Last Man* (New York: Free Press, 1992).
16. "Berlusconi Vaunts West's Superiority," *International Herald Tribune*, September 27, 2001.
17. M. Ignatieff, *Whose Universal Values? The Crisis in Human Rights* (The Hague: Paemium Ersmianum, 1999).
18. Samuel P. Huntington, *The Clash of Civilizations and the Remaking of World Order* (New York: Simon & Schuster, 1996).

Richard H. Shultz, Jr., 2004

Showstoppers: Nine Reasons Why We Never Sent Our Special Operations Forces after al Qaeda before 9/11

Since 9/11, Secretary of Defense Donald Rumsfeld has repeatedly declared that the United States is in a new kind of war, one requiring new military forces to hunt down and capture or kill terrorists. In fact, for some years, the Department of Defense has gone to the trouble of selecting and training an array of Special Operations Forces, whose forte is precisely this. One president after another has invested resources to hone lethal "special mission units" for offensive—that is, preemptive—counterterrorism strikes, with the result that these units are the best of their kind in the world. While their activities are highly classified, two of them—the Army's Delta Force and the Navy's SEAL Team 6—have become the stuff of novels and movies.

Prior to 9/11, these units *were never used even once* to hunt down terrorists who had taken American lives. Putting the units to their intended use proved impossible—even after al Qaeda bombed the World Trade Center in 1993, bombed two American embassies in East Africa in 1998, and nearly sank the USS *Cole* in Yemen in 2000. As a result of these and other attacks, operations were planned to capture or kill the ultimate perpetrators, Osama bin Laden and his top lieutenants, but each time the missions were blocked. A plethora of self-imposed constraints—I call them showstoppers—kept the counterterrorism units on the shelf.

I first began to learn of this in the summer of 2001, after George W. Bush's election brought a changing of the guard to the Department of Joining the new team as principal deputy assistant secretary of defense for special operations and low-intensity conflict was Bob Andrews, an old hand at the black arts of unconventional warfare. During Vietnam, Andrews had served in a top-secret Special Forces outfit codenamed the Studies and Observations Group that had carried out America's largest and most complex covert paramilitary operation in the Cold War. Afterwards, Andrews had joined the CIA, then moved to Congress as a staffer, then to the defense industry.

I'd first met him while I was writing a book about the secret war against Hanoi, and we hit it off. He returned to the Pentagon with the new administration, and in June 2001 he called and asked me to be his consultant. I agreed, and subsequently proposed looking into counterterrorism policy. Specifically, I wondered why had we created these superbly trained Special Operations Forces to fight terrorists, but had never used them for their primary mission. What had kept them out of action?

Andrews was intrigued and asked me to prepare a proposal. I was putting the finishing touches on it on the morning of September 11, when al Qaeda struck. With that blow, the issue of America's offensive counterterrorist capabilities was thrust to center stage.

By early November, I had the go-ahead for the study. Our question had acquired urgency. Why, even as al Qaeda attacked and killed Americans at home and abroad, were our elite counterterrorism units not used to hit back and prevent further attacks? That was, after all, their very purpose, laid out in the official document "*Special Operations in Peace and War*" (1996). To find the answer, I interviewed civilian and military officials, serving and retired, at the center of U.S. counterterrorism policy and operational planning in the late 1980s and 1990s.

They included senior members of the National Security Council's Counterterrorism and Security Group, the interagency focal point for counterterrorism policy. In the Pentagon, I interviewed the top leaders of the offices with counterterrorism responsibility, as well as second-tier professionals, and their military counterparts in the Joint Staff. Finally, the U.S. Special Operations Command, headquartered in Tampa, Florida, is responsible for planning and carrying out counterterrorism strikes, and I interviewed senior commanders who served there during the 1990s.

Some were willing to speak on the record. Others requested anonymity, which I honored, in order to put before the top leadership of the Pentagon the detailed report from which this article is drawn. My findings were conveyed to the highest levels of the Department of Defense in January 2003.

Among those interviewed, few were in a better position to illuminate the conundrum than General Pete Schoomaker. An original member of the Delta Force, he had commanded the Delta Force in 1991-92, then led the Special Operations Command in the late 1990s. "Counterterrorism, by Defense Department definition, is offensive," Schoomaker told me during a discussion we had over two days in the summer of 2002. "But Special Operations was never given the mission. It was very, very frustrating. It was like having a brand-new Ferrari in the garage, and nobody wants to race it because you might dent the fender."

As terrorist attacks escalated in the 1990s, White House rhetoric intensified. President Clinton met each successive outrage with a vow to punish the perpetrators. After the Cole bombing in 2000, for example, he pledged to "find out who is responsible and hold them accountable." And to prove he was serious, he issued an increasingly tough series of Presidential Decision Directives. The United States would "deter and preempt … individuals who perpetrate or plan to perpetrate such acts," said Directive 39, in June 1995. Offensive measures would be used against foreign terrorists posing a threat to America, said Directive 62, in May 1998. Joint Staff contingency plans were revised to provide for offensive and preemptive options. And after al Qaeda's bombings of the U.S. embassies in Kenya and Tanzania, President Clinton signed a secret "finding" authorizing lethal covert operations against bin Laden.

These initiatives led to the planning of several operations. Their details rest in the classified records of the National Security Council's Counterterrorism and Security Group. Its former coordinator, Dick Clarke, described them as providing the White House with "more aggressive options," to be carried out by Special Operations Forces (or SOF, a category that includes the Green Berets, the Rangers, psychological operations, civilian affairs, the SEALS, special helicopter units, and special mission units like the Delta Force and SEAL Team 6).

Several plans have been identified in newspaper accounts since 9/11. For example, "snatch operations" in Afghanistan were planned to seize bin Laden and his senior lieutenants. After the 1998 embassy bombings, options for killing bin Laden were entertained, including a gunship assault on his compound in Afghanistan.

SOF assaults on al Qaeda's Afghan training camps were also planned. An official very close to Clinton said that the president believed the image of American commandos jumping out of helicopters and killing terrorists would send a strong message. He "saw these camps as conveyor belts pushing radical Islamists through," the official said, "that either went into the war against the Northern Alliance [an Afghan force fighting the Taliban in northern Afghanistan] or became sleeper cells in Germany, Spain, Britain, Italy, and here. We wanted to close these camps down. We had to make it unattractive to go to these camps. And blowing them up, by God, would make them unattractive."

And preemptive strikes against al Qaeda cells outside Afghanistan were planned, in North Africa and the Arabian Gulf. Then in May 1999, the White House decided to press the Taliban to end its support of bin Laden. The Counterterrorism and Security Group recommended supporting the Northern Alliance.

These examples, among others, depict an increasingly aggressive, lethal, and preemptive counterterrorist policy. But *not one* of these operations—all authorized by President Clinton—was ever executed. General Schoomaker's explanation is devastating. "The presidential directives that were issued," he said, "and the subsequent findings and authorities, in my view, were done to check off boxes. The president signed things that everybody involved knew full well were never going to happen. You're checking off boxes, and have all this activity going on, but the fact is that there's very low probability of it ever coming to fruition. ..." And he added: "The military, by the way, didn't want to touch it. There was great reluctance in the Pentagon."

From my interviews, I distilled nine mutually reinforcing, self-imposed constraints that kept the special mission units sidelined, even as al Qaeda struck at American targets around the globe and trumpeted its intention to do more of the same. These showstoppers formed an impenetrable phalanx ensuring that all high-level policy discussions, tough new presidential directives, revised contingency plans, and actual dress rehearsals for missions would come to nothing.

1. Terrorism as Crime

During the second half of the 1980s, terrorism came to be defined by the U.S. government as a crime, and terrorists as criminals to be prosecuted. The Reagan administration, which in its first term said that it would meet terrorism with "swift and effective retribution," ended its second term, in the political and legal aftermath of Iran-contra, by adopting a counterterrorism policy that was the antithesis of that.

Patterns of Global Terrorism, a report issued by the State Department every year since 1989, sets forth guidance about responding to terrorism. Year after year prior to 9/11, a key passage said it was U.S. policy to "treat terrorists as criminals, pursue them aggressively, and apply the rule of law." Even now, when President Bush has defined the situation as a war on terrorism, "*Patterns of Global Terrorism*" says U.S. policy is to "bring terrorists to justice for their crimes."

Criminalization had a profound impact on the Pentagon, said General Schoomaker. It came to see terrorism as "not up to the standard of our definition of war, and therefore not worthy of our attention." In other words, militaries fight other militaries. "And because it's not war," he added, "and we don't act like we're at war, many of the Defense Department's tools are off the table." The Pentagon's senior leadership made little if any effort to argue against designating terrorism as a crime, Schoomaker added derisively.

"If you declare terrorism a criminal activity, you take from Defense any statutory authority to be the leader in responding," a long-serving department official agreed. Whenever the White House proposed using SOF against terrorists, it found itself facing "a band of lawyers at Justice defending their turf." They would assert, said this old hand at special operations, that the Pentagon lacked authority to use force—and "lawyers in the Defense Department would concur. They argued that we have no statutory authority because this is essentially a criminal matter."

In effect, the central tool for combating terrorism would not be military force. Extradition was the instrument of choice. This reduced the Pentagon's role to providing transportation for the Justice Department.

To be sure, Justice had its successes. With the help of the Pakistani government, it brought back Mir Amal Kansi, the gunman who opened fire outside CIA headquarters in 1993; with the help of the governments of the Philippines and Kenya, it brought several of the terrorists responsible for the first World Trade Center bombing and the attacks on the U.S. embassies in East Africa back to stand trial. But those were lesser al Qaeda operatives. Against the group's organizational infrastructure and leadership, there were no such successes. Law enforcement had neither the access nor the capability to go after those targets.

2. Not a Clear and Present Danger or War

Since terrorism had been classified as crime, few Pentagon officials were willing to call it a clear and present danger to the United States—much less grounds for war. Any attempt to describe terrorism in those terms ran into a stone wall.

For instance, on June 25, 1996, a truck bomb killed 19 Americans and wounded another 250 at the U.S. military's Khobar Towers housing facility near Dhahran, Saudi Arabia. In the aftermath, a tough-minded subordinate of Allen Holmes, then the assistant secretary of defense for special operations and low-intensity conflict, asserted that the Defense Department needed a more aggressive counterterrorism policy to attack those responsible for these increasingly lethal terrorist attacks. Holmes told him, "Write it down, and we'll push it."

The aide laid out a strategy that pulled no punches. Khobar Towers, the World Trade Center bombing, and other attacks were acts of war, he wrote, and should be treated as such. He called for "retaliatory and preemptive military strikes against the terrorist leadership and infrastructure responsible, and even against states assisting them." In his strategy, he assigned a central role for this to SOF.

Holmes ran the proposal up the flagpole. A meeting to review it was held in the office of the undersecretary of defense for policy. As the hard-charging aide explained his recommendations, a senior policy official blurted out: "Are you out of your mind? You're telling me that our Middle East policy is not important and that it's more important to go clean out terrorists? Don't you understand what's going on in terms of our Middle East policy? You're talking about going after terrorists backed by Iran? You just don't understand." And that was that.

In the wake of Khobar Towers, Secretary of Defense William Perry asked retired General Wayne Downing to head a task force to assess what had happened. Formerly the head of the U.S. Special Operations Command, Downing had been in counterterrorism a long time. He was more than willing to pull the trigger and cajole policymakers into giving him the authority to do so. Interviewed in 2002 during a year-long stint as President Bush's deputy national security adviser for combating terrorism, he reflected on his report: "I emphasized that people are at war with us, and using terrorism as an asymmetrical weapon with which to attack us because they can't in a direct or conventional manner." It was war, he told the department's senior leadership; they needed to wake up to that fact. But his plea fell on deaf ears. He lamented, "No one wanted to address terrorism as war."

Even after bin Laden declared war on America in a 1998 *fatwa*, and bombed U.S. embassies to show his followers that he meant business in exhorting them to "abide by Allah's order by killing Americans . . . anywhere, anytime, and wherever possible," the Pentagon still resisted calling terrorism war. It wasn't alone. A CIA assessment of the *fatwa* acknowledged that if a *government* had issued such a decree, one would have had to consider it a declaration of war, but in al Qaeda's case it was only propaganda.

During the late 1990s, the State Department coordinator for counterterrorism was Mike Sheehan. A retired Special Forces officer who had learned unconventional warfare in El Salvador in the late 1980s, he was considered one of the most hawkish Clinton officials, pushing for the use of force against the Taliban and al Qaeda. His mantra was "drain the Afghan swamp of terrorists."

I visited Sheehan at his office at the U.N. building in New York, where he had become assistant secretary-general for peacekeeping. He recounted how aggressive counterterrorism proposals were received in the Defense Department: "The Pentagon wanted to fight and win the nation's wars, as Colin Powell used to say. But those were wars against the armies of other nations—not against diffuse transnational terrorist threats. So terrorism was seen as a distraction that was the CIA's job, even though DOD personnel were being hit by terrorists. The Pentagon way to treat terrorism against Pentagon assets abroad was to cast it as a force protection issue."

"Force protection" is Pentagon lingo for stronger barriers to shield troops from Khobar Towers-type attacks. Even the attack on the USS *Cole* did not change that outlook. As far as causing anyone to consider offensive measures against those responsible, "the *Cole* lasted only for a week, two weeks," Sheehan lamented. "It took a 757 crashing into the Pentagon for them to get it." Shaking his head, he added: "The near sinking of a billion-dollar warship was not enough. Folding up a barracks full of their troops in Saudi Arabia was not enough. Folding up two American embassies was not enough."

Of course, Washington continued to try to arrest those who had carried out these acts. But the places where terrorists trained and planned—Afghanistan, Lebanon, Sudan, Yemen—remained off-limits. Those were not areas where the Defense Department intended to fight. A very senior SOF officer who had served on the Joint Staff in the 1990s told me that more than once he heard terrorist strikes characterized as "a small price to pay for being a superpower."

3. The Somalia Syndrome

In the first year of his presidency, Bill Clinton suffered a foreign policy debacle. The "Fire Fight from Hell," *Newsweek* called it. The *Los Angeles Times* described it as culminating in "dozens of cheering, dancing Somalis dragging the body of a U.S. soldier through the city's streets." Those reports followed the 16-hour shootout portrayed in the movie "*Black Hawk Down*," pitting SOF units against Somali warriors in the urban jungle of Mogadishu on October 3-4, 1993. The American objective had been capturing Mohammed Aidid, a warlord who was interfering with the U.N.'s humanitarian mission. The new administration had expected a quick surgical operation.

The failure caused disquieting questions and bad memories. How could this happen? What had gone wrong? Some Clinton officials recalled that the last time the Democrats had held the White House, similar forces had failed in their attempt to rescue American hostages in Tehran ("Desert One"), a catastrophe instrumental in President Carter's 1980 reelection defeat.

Some senior generals had expressed doubts about the Mogadishu operation, yet as it had morphed from a peacekeeping mission into a manhunt for Aidid, the new national security team had failed to grasp the implications. The Mogadishu disaster spooked the Clinton administration as well as the brass, and confirmed the Joint Chiefs in the view that SOF should never be entrusted with independent operations.

After Mogadishu, one Pentagon officer explained, there was "reluctance to even discuss pro-active measures associated with countering the terrorist threat through SOF operations. The Joint Staff was very happy for the administration to take a law enforcement view. They didn't want to put special ops troops on the ground. They hadn't wanted to go into Somalia to begin with. The Joint Staff was the biggest foot-dragger on all of this counterterrorism business."

Another officer added that Somalia heightened a wariness, in some cases outright disdain, for SOF in the senior ranks. On the Joint Staff, the generals ranged from those who "did not have a great deal of respect" for SOF, to those who actually "hated what it represented, … hated the independent thought process, . . . hated the fact that the SOF guys on the Joint Staff would challenge things, would question things."

During Desert Storm, for example, General Norman Schwarzkopf was reluctant to include SOF in his war plan. He did so only grudgingly, and kept SOF on a short leash, wrote the commander of all Special Operations Forces at the time, General Carl Stiner, in his book *Shadow Warriors*. But SOF performed well in Desert Storm, and afterwards Schwarzkopf acknowledged their accomplishments. In 1993, Mogadishu turned back the clock.

4. No Legal Authority

August 1998 was a watershed for the White House. The embassy bombings led to the reexamination of preemptive military options. President Clinton proposed using elite SOF counterterrorism units to attack bin Laden, his lieutenants, and al Qaeda's infrastructure.

Also considered was unconventional warfare, a core SOF mission very different from counterterrorism. The Special Operations Command's *Special Operations in Peace and War* defines unconventional warfare as "military and paramilitary operations conducted by indigenous or surrogate forces who are organized, trained, equipped, and directed by an external source." For the White House, this meant assisting movements like the Northern Alliance in Afghanistan.

Both the Special Operations Command's counterterrorism units and Special Forces training for and executing unconventional warfare operate clandestinely. That is what their doctrine specifies. But because such operations are secret, the question arose in the 1990s whether the department had the legal authority to execute them.

This may seem baffling. If these missions are specified in the military doctrine of the Special Operations Command, and actual units train for them, isn't it obvious that the Department of Defense must have the authority to execute them? Perhaps, yet many in government emphatically deny it.

A gap exists, they believe, between DOD's *capability* for clandestine operations and its *authority* under the United States Code. In the 1990s, some Pentagon lawyers and some in the intelligence community argued that Title 10 of the U.S. Code, which covers the armed forces, did not give Defense the legal authority for such missions, Title 50, which spells out the legal strictures for covert operations, gave this power exclusively to the CIA.

Title 50 defines covert action as "an activity of the United States Government to influence political, economic, or military conditions abroad, where it is intended that the role of the United States Government will not be apparent or acknowledged publicly." Covert action and deniability go hand in hand. If a story about a covert action hits the newspapers, the president must be able to avow that the United States is not mixed up in it.

But is it the case that *only* the CIA has this authority? Title 50, Chapter 15, Section 413b of the U.S. Code stipulates: "The President may not authorize the conduct of a covert action by departments, agencies, or entities of the United States Government unless the President determines such an action is necessary to support identifiable foreign policy objectives of the United States and is important to the national security of the United States, which determination shall be set forth in a finding that shall meet each of the following conditions." The key condition is: "Each finding shall specify each department, agency, or entity of the United States Government authorized to fund or otherwise participate in any significant way in such action." Title 50 leaves the choice of agency to the president and does not exclude the Pentagon.

At the heart of this debate, said a former senior Defense official, was "institutional culture and affiliation." The department took the position that it lacked the authority because it did not *want* the authority—or the mission. He told me, "All of its instincts push it in that direction."

One senior member of the National Security Council's counterterrorism group recalled encountering this attitude during deliberations over counterterrorism operations and clandestine support for the Northern Alliance. To the Joint Staff, neither was "in their minds a military mission. It was a covert action. The uniformed military was adamant that they would not do covert action." And, he added, if you presented them with "a legal opinion that says 'You're wrong,' then they would say, 'Well, we're not going to do it anyway. It's a matter of policy that we don't.'"

The authority argument was a "cop-out," said a retired officer who served in the Pentagon from 1994 to 2000. Sure enough, the Defense Department could have bypassed Title 50 by employing SOF on a *clandestine* basis. While both clandestine and covert missions are secret, only the latter require that the U.S. role not be "acknowledged publicly," which is Title 50's key requirement. Using SOF to preempt terrorists or support resistance movements clandestinely in peacetime is within the scope of Title 10, as long as the U.S. government does not deny involvement when the mission is over.

But this interpretation of Title 10 was considered beyond the pale in the 1990s. The Pentagon did not want the authority to strike terrorists secretly or to employ Special Forces against states that aided and sheltered them.

5. Risk Aversion

The mainstream military often dismisses special operations as too risky. To employ SOF requires open-minded political and military leadership willing to balance risks against potential gains. Supple judgment was in short supply in the Pentagon in the 1990s.

Walter Slocombe served as Clinton's undersecretary of defense for policy, and took part in all counterterrorism policy discussions in the Department of Defense. "We certainly looked at lots of options which involved the possible use of SOF," he stressed. But in the end they were never selected because they seemed too hard to pull off, he acknowledged. Options that put people on the ground to go after bin Laden were "much too hard." It was much easier and much less risky to fire off cruise missiles.

During Clinton's first term, someone would always find something wrong with a proposed operation, lamented General Downing. The attitude was: "Don't let these SOF guys go through the door because they're dangerous. … They are going to do something to embarrass the country." Downing recalls that during his years in command, he "sat through the preparation of maybe 20 operations where we had targeted people who had killed Americans. Terrorists who had done bad things to this country, and needed either to be killed or apprehended and brought back here, and we couldn't pull the trigger." It was too risky for the Pentagon's taste.

The other side of the risk-aversion coin is policymakers' demand for fail-safe options. A general who served in the Special Operations Command in the 1990s encountered "tremendous pressure to do something," he said, but at the same time, the requirement was for "perfect operations, no casualties, no failure." There were some "great opportunities" to strike at al Qaeda, "but you couldn't take any risk in doing so. You couldn't have a POW, you couldn't lose a man. You couldn't have anybody hurt." It was Catch-22. There were frequent "spin-ups" for SOF missions, but "in the end, the senior political and military leadership wouldn't let you go do it."

In the mid-1990s, and again at the end of the decade, the Clinton administration flirted with supporting the Iraqi resistance and then the Northern Alliance. An officer who served on the Joint Staff recounted how the senior military leadership put the kibosh on these potentially bold moves.

The CIA ran the Iraqi operation. But its unconventional warfare capabilities were paltry, and it turned to the military for help, requesting that SOF personnel be seconded to bolster the effort. The Joint Staff and its chairman wanted nothing to do with it, he said. "The guidance I got from the chairman's director of operations was that we weren't going to support this, and do everything you can to stall or keep it in the planning mode, don't let it get to the point where we're briefing this at the National Security Council or on the Hill."

Later, the National Security Council's counterterrorism group proposed supporting the Northern Alliance. They pushed the proposal up to the "principals" level. But attached to it was a "non-concurrence" by the Joint Staff, opposing it as too complex and risky. That was the kiss of death.

None of this was new to the Joint Staff officer, who had been in special operations for a long time. "Risk aversion emerges as senior officers move into higher positions," he explained. "It's a very common thing for these guys to become non-risk takers. They get caught up in interagency politics and the bureaucratic process, and get risk-averse."

A member of the counterterrorism group in the late 1990s noted that General Hugh Shelton, a former commander of the Special Operations Command, considered the use of SOF for counterterrorism less than anyone when he was chairman of the Joint Chiefs. The official said Shelton directed the Joint Staff "not to plan certain operations, I'm sure you've heard this from others." In fact, I had. "It got to the point," he said, where "the uniforms had become the suits, they were more the bureaucrats than the civilians."

6. Pariah Cowboys

When events finally impelled the Clinton administration to take a hard look at offensive operations, the push to pursue them came from the civilians of the National Security Council's Counterterrorism and Security Group.

One of the hardest of the hard-liners was the group's chief, Dick Clarke. For nearly a decade, this career civil servant began and ended his work day with the burgeoning terrorist threat to America. He knew in detail the danger the bin Ladens of the world posed, and it worried him greatly. Defensive measures were just not enough. "Clarke's philosophy was to go get the terrorists," one former senior Pentagon special operations official told me, "Go get them anywhere you can."

Asked if that meant using SOF, he replied: "Oh yeah. In fact, many of the options were with special mission units." But "Dick Clarke was attempting to take on a Pentagon hierarchy that wasn't of the same philosophical mindset."

Clarke was not alone. Mike Sheehan also pushed for assisting the Northern Alliance and striking al Qaeda with SOF. Such measures worried the senior brass, who proceeded to weaken those officials by treating them as pariahs. That meant portraying them as cowboys, who proposed reckless military operations that would get American soldiers killed.

Sheehan explained: Suppose one civilian starts beating the drum for special operations. The establishment "systematically starts to undermine you. They would say, 'He's a rogue, he's uncooperative, he's out of control, he's stupid, he makes bad choices.' It's very damaging. … You get to the point where you don't even raise issues like that. If someone did, like me or Clarke, we were labeled cowboys, way outside our area of competence."

Several officials who served on the Joint Staff and in the Pentagon's special operations office remembered the senior brass characterizing Clarke in such terms. "Anything Dick Clarke suggested, the Joint Staff was going to be negative about," said one. Some generals had been vitriolic, calling Clarke "a madman, out of control, power hungry, wanted to be a hero, all that kind of stuff." In fact, one of these former officials emphasized, "when we would carry back from the counterterrorism group one of those SOF counterterrorism proposals, our job was to figure out not how to execute it, but how we were going to say no."

By turning Clarke into a pariah, the Pentagon brass discredited precisely the options that might have spared us the tragedy of September 11, 2001. And when Clarke fought back at being branded "wild" and "irresponsible," they added "abrasive" and "intolerant" to the counts against him.

7. Intimidation of Civilians

Another way the brass stymied hard-line proposals from civilian policymakers was by highlighting their own military credentials and others' lack of them. One former defense official recounted a briefing on counterterrorism options given the secretary of defense by senior civilians and military officers. "The civilian, a political appointee with no military experience, says, 'As your policy adviser, let me tell you what you need to do militarily in this situation.' The chairman sits there, calmly listening. Then it's his turn. He begins by framing his sophisticated PowerPoint briefing in terms of the 'experience factor,' his own judgment, and those of four-star associates. The 'experience factor' infuses the presentation. Implicitly, it raises a question intended to discredit the civilian: 'What makes you qualified? What makes you think that your opinion is more important than mine when you don't have the experience I have?' 'Mr. Secretary,' concludes the chairman, 'this is my best military advice.'" In such situations, the official said, civilians were often dissuaded from taking on the generals.

Wayne Downing, the former special operations commander, had plenty of experience providing such briefings. "Occasionally you would get a civilian champion," he said, who would speak up enthusiastically in favor of the mission being presented. "And then the chairman or the vice chairman would say, 'I don't think this is a good idea. Our best military judgment is that you not do this.' That champion is not going any further."

During the 1990s, the "best military advice," when it came to counterterrorism, was always wary of the use of force. Both risk-aversion and a deep-seated distrust of SOF traceable all the way back to World War II informed the military counsel offered to top decision makers. Almost all those I consulted confirmed this, and many, including General Stiner, have described it in print.

When President Clinton began asking about special operations, one former senior official recounted, "those options were discussed, but never got anywhere. The Joint Staff would say, 'That's cowboy Hollywood stuff.' The president was intimidated because these guys come in with all those medals, [and] the White House took the 'stay away from SOF options' advice of the generals."

Another former official during both Clinton terms described several instances where "best military advice" blocked SOF options under White House review. "The Pentagon resisted using Special Forces. Clinton raised it several times with [Joint Chiefs chairmen] Shalikashvili and Shelton. They recommended against it, and never really came up with a do-able plan."

Occasionally, policymakers kept pushing. When support for the Northern Alliance was on the table after the embassy bombings in Africa, the senior military leadership "refused to consider it," a former counterterrorism group member told me. "They said it was an intelligence operation, not a military mission."

The counterterrorism group at the National Security Council pushed the proposal anyway, but the Joint Staff strongly demurred and would not support it. They argued that supporting the Northern Alliance would entangle the United States in a quagmire. That was the end of the line. Let's suppose, said the former counterterrorism group member, that the president had ordered a covert strike "despite the chairman going on record as opposing it. Now, if the president orders such an operation against the best military advice of his chief military adviser, and it gets screwed up, they will blame the president who has no military experience, who was allegedly a draft dodger." The Northern Alliance was left to wither on the vine.

8. Big Footprints

The original concept for SOF counterterrorism units was that they would be unconventional, small, flexible, adaptive, and stealthy, suited to discreet and discriminate use, say those "present at the creation" following the Desert One disaster. Force packages were to be streamlined for surgical operations. The "footprint" of any operation was to be small, even invisible.

By the 1990s, this had dropped by the wayside. One former official recalled that when strikes against al Qaeda cells were proposed, "the Joint Staff and the chairman would come back and say, 'We highly recommend against doing it. But if ordered to do it, this is how we would do it.' And usually it involved the 82nd and 101st Airborne Divisions. The footprint was ridiculous." In each instance the civilian policymakers backed off.

To some extent, SOF planners themselves have been guilty of this. "Mission-creep," one official called it. Since you can't "totally suppress an environment with 15 guys and three helicopters," force packages became "five or six hundred guys, AC-130 gunships, a 900-man quick-reaction force ready to assist if you get in trouble, and F-14s circling over the Persian Gulf." The policymakers were thinking small, surgical, and stealthy, so they'd take one "look at it and say that's too big."

One original Delta Force member traced this problem back to Desert One. "We took some bad lessons from that," he said. "… One was that we needed more. That maybe it would have been successful if we'd had more helicopters. That more is better. And now we add too many bells and whistles. We make our footprint too large. We price ourselves out of the market."

It's a way of dealing with the military's aversion to risk. "One way we tend to think we mitigate risk," he said, "is by adding more capabilities for this contingency and that contingency." Asked if this thinking had found its way into the Special Operations Command, he replied, "Yes. Absolutely."

9. No Actionable Intelligence

A top official in the Office of the Under Secretary of Defense for Policy in the 1990s described the intelligence deficit with respect to targeting Osama bin Laden: "If you get intelligence, it's by definition very perishable. He moves all the time and he undoubtedly puts out false stories about where he's moving," making it extremely difficult "to get somebody from anyplace outside of Afghanistan into Afghanistan in time. The biggest problem was always intelligence."

But if the target had been broadened to al Qaeda's infrastructure, the intelligence requirements would have been less demanding, noted Dick Clarke. "There was plenty of intelligence. We had incredibly good intelligence about where bin Laden's facilities were. While we might never have been able to say at any given moment where he was, we knew half a dozen places that he moved among. So there was ample opportunity to use Special Forces."

In effect, to turn the need for "actionable intelligence" into a showstopper, all you have to do is define the target narrowly. That makes the intelligence requirements nearly impossible to satisfy. Broaden the picture, and the challenge of actionable intelligence became more manageable.

Special Operators are actually the first to seek good intelligence. But according to an officer on the Joint Staff at the time, "no actions [were] taken to pre-position or deploy the kinds of people that could have addressed those intelligence shortfalls"—people who could have provided the operational-level intelligence needed for SOF to deploy rapidly against fleeting targets in the safe havens where terrorists nest.

What was essential for counterterrorism operations was to establish intelligence networks in places harboring targets. This "operational preparation of the battlespace" is accomplished by infiltrating special operators who pass for locals. Their job includes recruiting indigenous elements who can help SOF units enter an area of interest, and organize, train, and equip local resistance and surrogate forces to assist them.

But no such preparation took place in the 1990s in terrorist havens like Afghanistan, Yemen, Lebanon, and Sudan. Operating in those lands "would have taken official approval that prior to 9/11 would have never been given to us," one knowledgeable individual explained. "Prior to 9/11 there was no willingness to put Department of Defense personnel in such places. No such request would have been authorized."

Why? Because it's dicey, was the bottom line for a former senior Clinton appointee at the Pentagon. Asked if there were proposals at his level for it, he said: "Not that I remember," adding, "I can understand why. It raises a lot of questions. Without saying you shouldn't do it, it is one of those things that is going to cause concern. ... You're talking not just about recruiting individuals to be sent, but recruiting whole organizations, and you think about it in the context of Somalia. I'm sure that would have raised a lot of questions. I can see why people would have been reluctant."

During clinton's second term, then, the possibility of hunting down the terrorists did receive ample attention at the top echelons of government. But somewhere between inception and execution, the SOF options were always scuttled as too problematic.

War and tragedy have a way of breaking old attitudes. September 11, 2001, should have caused a sea change in SOF's role in fighting terrorism. To some extent, it has. Consider the stellar contribution of Special Operations Forces to the campaign in Afghanistan in 2001-02. In the early planning stages, SOF was only ancillary to the war plan; but by the end of October 2001, it had moved to center stage. It played a decisive role in toppling the Taliban and routing al Qaeda.

Since then, SOF have deployed to places like Yemen and the Philippines to train local militaries to fight al Qaeda and its affiliates. And last year, Secretary Rumsfeld ordered the Special Operations Command to track down and destroy al Qaeda around the globe. In effect, he ordered a global manhunt to prevent future 9/11s, including attacks with weapons of mass destruction.

In the war against terrorism, a global SOF campaign against al Qaeda is indispensable. Happily, our special counterterrorism units are tailor-made for this. And now that the United States is at war, it should be possible to overcome the showstoppers that blocked the "peacetime" use of those forces through the 1990s.

It should be—but will it? The answer is mixed. Some showstoppers have been neutralized. While law enforcement still has a role to play, we are clearly fighting a war, in which the Department of Defense and the armed forces take the lead. Thus, there should be far less latitude for turning advocates of tough counterterrorism missions into pariahs. September 11 and the president's response to it changed the terms of the policy discussion.

Yet the other showstoppers have not ceased to matter. Competing power centers continue to jockey for influence over counterterrorism policy. In a war in which the CIA may feel it has both a role to play and lost ground to regain, the Title 10/Title 50 debate and arguments over actionable intelligence are likely to persist. In our democratic society, fear of another Somalia remains. And the conventional military's mistrust of SOF has not evaporated.

Once again, a civilian is pushing for greater use of Special Operations Forces. Secretary of Defense Rumsfeld wants the Special Operations Command, for the first time in its history, to play the role of a "supported command," instead of supporting the geographic commands, as it has in the past. Neither those commands nor their friends on the Joint Staff are likely to welcome a reversal of the relationship in order to facilitate SOF missions. "Who's in command here?" could become a new wartime showstopper. Some in SOF believe it already has.

Once again, the problem involves institutions, organizational cultures, and entrenched ways of thinking. "Rumsfeld might think we're at war with terrorism," observed one former general, "but I'll bet he also thinks he is at war within the Pentagon. … The real war's happening right there in his building. It's a war of the culture. He can't go to war because he can't get his organization up for it."

Donald Rumsfeld may believe that Special Operations Forces should be in the forefront of the global war on terrorism. But for that to happen, he will have to breach what remains of the phalanx of resistance that blocked the offensive use of special mission units for over a decade—and he'll have to overcome the new showstoppers as well.

For now, it appears that the most powerful defense secretary ever has failed in his attempt to do this. In a disquieting October 16, 2003, memo to the Pentagon elite in the war on terror—General Dick Meyers, Joint Chiefs chairman; Deputy Defense Secretary Paul Wolfowitz; General Pete Pace, vice chairman of the Joint Chiefs; and Doug Feith, undersecretary of defense for policy—Rumsfeld laments that progress has been slow and the Defense Department has not "yet made truly bold moves" in fighting al Qaeda. And he wonders whether his department "is changing fast enough to deal with the new 21st century security environment."

It's a good question. As al Qaeda regroups and deploys to new battlefields in Iraq and elsewhere, our special mission units—the Delta boys, the SEALs, and the rest—remain on the shelf. It's time to take them off.

Richard H. Shultz Jr. is director of international security studies at the Fletcher School, Tufts University, and director of research at the Consortium for the Study of Intelligence in Washington, D.C.

Appendix A

Background Information on Designated Foreign Terrorist Organizations

The following descriptive list constitutes the 33 terrorist groups that currently are designated by the Secretary of State as Foreign Terrorist Organizations (FTOs), pursuant to section 219 of the Immigration and Nationality Act, as amended by the Antiterrorism and Effective Death Penalty Act of 1996. The designations carry legal consequences:

- It is unlawful to provide funds or other material support to a designated FTO.
- Representatives and certain members of a designated FTO can be denied visas or excluded from the United States.
- U.S. financial institutions must block funds of designated FTOs and their agents and must report the blockage to the U.S. Department of the Treasury.

Abu Nidal Organization (ANO)

a.k.a. Fatah Revolutionary Council, Arab Revolutionary Brigades, Black September, and Revolutionary Organization of Socialist Muslims

Description

International terrorist organization led by Sabri al-Banna. Split from PLO in 1974. Made up of various functional committees, including political, military, and financial.

Activities

Has carried out terrorist attacks in 20 countries, killing or injuring almost 900 persons. Targets include the United States, the United Kingdom, France, Israel, moderate Palestinians, the PLO [Palestine Liberation Organization], and various Arab countries. Major attacks included the Rome and Vienna airports in December 1985, the Neve Shalom synagogue in Istanbul and the Pan Am Flight 73 hijacking in Karachi in September 1986, and the City of Poros day-excursion ship attack in Greece in July 1988. Suspected of assassinating PLO deputy chief Abu Iyad and PLO security chief Abu Hul in Tunis in January 1991. ANO assassinated a Jordanian diplomat in Lebanon in January 1994 and has been linked to the killing of the PLO representative there. Has not attacked Western targets since the late 1980s.

Strength

Few hundred plus limited overseas support structure.

Location/Area of Operation

Al-Banna relocated to Iraq in December 1998, where the group maintains a presence. Has an operational presence in Lebanon including in several Palestinian refugee camps. Financial problems and internal disorganization have reduced the group's activities and capabilities. Authorities shut down the ANO's operations in Libya and Egypt in 1999. Has demonstrated ability to operate over wide area, including the Middle East, Asia, and Europe.

External Aid

Has received considerable support, including safe haven, training, logistic assistance, and financial aid from Iraq, Libya, and Syria (until 1987), in addition to close support for selected operations.

Abu Sayyaf Group (ASG)

Description

The ASG is the most violent of the Islamic separatist groups operating in the southern Philippines. Some ASG leaders have studied or worked in the Middle East and allegedly fought in Afghanistan during the Soviet war. The group split from the Moro National Liberation Front in the early 1990s under the leadership of Abdurajak Abubakar Janjalani, who was killed in a clash with Philippine police on 18 December 1998. His younger brother, Khadaffy Janjalani, has replaced him as the nominal leader of the group, which is composed of several semi-autonomous factions.

Activities

Engages in kidnappings for ransom, bombings, assassinations, and extortion. Although from time to time it claims that its motivation is to promote an independent Islamic state in western Mindanao and the Sulu Archipelago, areas in the southern Philippines heavily populated by Muslims, the ASG now appears to use terror mainly for financial profit. The group's first large-scale action was a raid on the town of Ipil in Mindanao in April 1995. In April of 2000, an ASG faction kidnapped 21 persons, including 10 foreign tourists, from a resort in Malaysia. Separately in 2000, the group abducted several foreign journalists, 3 Malaysians, and a U.S. citizen. On 27 May 2001, the ASG kidnapped three U.S. citizens and 17 Filipinos from a tourist resort in Palawan, Philippines. Several of the hostages, including one U.S. citizen, were murdered.

Strength

Believed to have a few hundred core fighters, but at least 1,000 individuals motivated by the prospect of receiving ransom payments for foreign hostages allegedly joined the group in 2000–2001.

Location/Area of Operation

The ASG was founded in Basilan Province, and mainly operates there and in the neighboring provinces of Sulu and Tawi-Tawi in the Sulu Archipelago. It also operates in the Zamboanga peninsula, and members occasionally travel to Manila and other parts of the country. The group expanded its operations in Malaysia in 2000 when it abducted foreigners from a tourist resort.

External Aid

Largely self-financing through ransom and extortion; may receive support from Islamic extremists in the Middle East and South Asia. Libya publicly paid millions of dollars for the release of the foreign hostages seized from Malaysia in 2000.

Al-Aqsa Martyrs Brigade

Description

The al-Aqsa Martyrs Brigade comprises an unknown number of small cells of Fatah-affiliated activists that emerged at the outset of the current *intifadah* to attack Israeli targets. It aims to drive the Israeli military and settlers from the West Bank, Gaza Strip, and Jerusalem and to establish a Palestinian state.

Activities

Al-Aqsa Martyrs Brigade has carried out shootings and suicide operations against Israeli military personnel and civilians and has killed Palestinians who it believed were collaborating with Israel. At least five U.S. citizens, four of them dual Israeli-U.S. citizens, were killed in these attacks. The group probably did not attack them because of their U.S. citizenship. In January 2002, the group claimed responsibility for the first suicide bombing carried out by a female.

Strength

Unknown.

Location/Area of Operation

Al-Aqsa operates mainly in the West Bank and has claimed attacks inside Israel and the Gaza Strip.

External Aid

Unknown.

Armed Islamic Group (GIA)

Description

An Islamic extremist group, the GIA aims to overthrow the secular Algerian regime and replace it with an Islamic state. The GIA began its violent activity in 1992 after Algiers voided the victory of the Islamic Salvation Front (FIS)—the largest Islamic opposition party—in the first round of legislative elections in December 1991.

Activities

Frequent attacks against civilians and government workers. Between 1992 and 1998 the GIA conducted a terrorist campaign of civilian massacres, sometimes wiping out entire villages in its area of operation. Since announcing its campaign against foreigners living in Algeria in 1993, the GIA has killed more than 100 expatriate men and women—mostly Europeans—in the country. The group uses assassinations and bombings, including car bombs, and it is known to favor kidnapping victims and slitting their throats. The GIA hijacked an Air France flight to Algiers in December 1994. In late 1999 a French court convicted several GIA members for conducting a series of bombings in France in 1995.

Strength

Precise numbers unknown; probably around 200.

Location/Area of Operation

Algeria

External Aid

Algerian expatriates, some of whom reside in Western Europe, provide some financial and logistic support. In addition, the Algerian Government has accused Iran and Sudan of supporting Algerian extremists.

'Asbat al-Ansar

Description

'Asbat al-Ansar—the Partisans' League—is a Lebanon-based, Sunni extremist group, composed primarily of Palestinians, which is associated with Usama bin Laden. The group follows an extremist interpretation of Islam that justifies violence against civilian targets to achieve political ends. Some of those goals include overthrowing the Lebanese Government and thwarting perceived anti-Islamic influences in the country.

Activities

'Asbat al-ansar has carried out several terrorist attacks in Lebanon since it first emerged in the early 1990s. The group carried out assassinations of Lebanese religious leaders and bombed several nightclubs, theaters, and liquor stores in the mid-1990s. The group raised its operational profile in 2000 with two dramatic attacks against Lebanese and international targets. The group was involved in clashes in northern Lebanon in late December 1999 and carried out a rocket-propelled grenade attack on the Russian Embassy in Beirut in January 2000.

Strength

The group commands about 300 fighters in Lebanon.

Location/Area of Operation

The group's primary base of operations is the 'Ayn al-Hilwah Palestinian refugee camp near Sidon in southern Lebanon.

External Aid

Probably receives money through international Sunni extremist networks and Bin Laden's al-Qaida network.

Aum Supreme Truth (Aum)

a.k.a. Aum Shinrikyo, Aleph

Description

A cult established in 1987 by Shoko Asahara, the Aum aimed to take over Japan and then the world. Approved as a religious entity in 1989 under Japanese law, the group ran candidates in a Japanese parliamentary election in 1990. Over time the cult began to emphasize the imminence of the end of the world and stated that the United States would initiate Armageddon by starting World War III with Japan. The Japanese Government revoked its recognition of the Aum as a religious organization in October

1995, but in 1997 a government panel decided not to invoke the Anti-Subversive Law against the group, which would have outlawed the cult. A 1999 law gave the Japanese Government authorization to continue police surveillance of the group due to concerns that Aum might launch future terrorist attacks. Under the leadership of Fumihiro Joyu the Aum changed its name to Aleph in January 2000 and claimed to have rejected the violent and apocalyptic teachings of its founder. (Joyu took formal control of the organization early in 2002 and remains its leader).

Activities

On 20 March 1995, Aum members simultaneously released the chemical nerve agent sarin on several Tokyo subway trains, killing 12 persons and injuring up to 6,000. The group was responsible for other mysterious chemical accidents in Japan in 1994. Its efforts to conduct attacks using biological agents have been unsuccessful. Japanese police arrested Asahara in May 1995, and he remained on trial facing charges in 13 crimes, including 7 counts of murder, at the end of 2001. Legal analysts say it will take several more years to conclude the trial. Since 1997 the cult [has] continued to recruit new members, engage in commercial enterprise, and acquire property, although it scaled back these activities significantly in 2001 in response to public outcry. The cult maintains an Internet home page. In July 2001, Russian authorities arrested a group of Russian Aum followers who had planned to set off bombs near the Imperial Palace in Tokyo as part of an operation to free Asahara from jail and then smuggle him to Russia.

Strength

The Aum's current membership is estimated at 1,500 to 2,000 persons. At the time of the Tokyo subway attack, the group claimed to have 9,000 members in Japan and up to 40,000 worldwide.

Location/Area of Operation

The Aum's principal membership is located only in Japan, but a residual branch comprising an unknown number of followers has surfaced in Russia.

External Aid

None.

Basque Fatherland and Liberty (ETA)

a.k.a. Euzkadi Ta Askatasuna

Description

Founded in 1959 with the aim of establishing an independent homeland based on Marxist principles in the northern Spanish Provinces of Vizcaya, Guipuzcoa, Alava, and Navarra, and the southwestern French Departments of Labourd, Basse-Navarra, and Soule.

Activities

Primarily involved in bombings and assassinations of Spanish Government officials, security and military forces, politicians, and judicial figures. ETA finances its activities through kidnappings, robberies, and extortion. The group has killed more than 800 persons and injured hundreds of others since it began lethal attacks in the early 1960s. In November 1999, ETA broke its "unilateral and indefinite" cease-fire and began an assassination and bombing campaign that has killed 38 individuals and wounded scores more by the end of 2001.

Strength

Unknown; may have hundreds of members, plus supporters.

Location/Area of Operation

Operates primarily in the Basque autonomous regions of northern Spain and southwestern France, but also has bombed Spanish and French interests elsewhere.

External Aid

Has received training at various times in the past in Libya, Lebanon, and Nicaragua. Some ETA members allegedly have received sanctuary in Cuba while others reside in South America.

Al-Gama'a al-Islamiyya (Islamic Group, IG)

Description

Egypt's largest militant group, active since the late 1970s, appears to be loosely organized. Has an external wing with supporters in several countries worldwide. The group issued a cease-fire in March 1999, but its spiritual leader, Shaykh Umar Abd al-Rahman, sentenced to life in prison in January 1996 for his involvement in the 1993 World Trade Center bombing and incarcerated in the United States, rescinded his support for the cease-fire in June 2000. The Gama'a has not conducted an attack inside Egypt since August 1998. Senior member signed Usama Bin Laden's *fatwa* in February 1998 calling for attacks against U.S.. Unofficially split in two factions; one that supports the cease-fire led by Mustafa Hamza, and one led by Rifa'i Taha Musa, calling for a return to armed operations. Taha Musa in early 2001 published a book in which he attempted to justify terrorist attacks that would cause mass casualties. Musa disappeared several months thereafter, and there are conflicting reports as to his current whereabouts. Primary goal is to overthrow the Egyptian Government and replace it with an Islamic state, but disaffected IG members, such as those potentially inspired by Taha Musa or Abd al-Rahman, may be interested in carrying out attacks against U.S. and Israeli interests.

Activities

Group conducted armed attacks against Egyptian security and other government officials, Coptic Christians, and Egyptian opponents of Islamic extremism before the cease-fire. From 1993 until the cease-fire, al-Gama'a launched attacks on tourists in Egypt, most notably the attack in November 1997 at Luxor that killed 58 foreign tourists. Also claimed responsibility for the attempt in June 1995 to assassinate Egyptian President Hosni Mubarak in Addis Ababa, Ethiopia. The Gama'a has never specifically attacked a U.S. citizen or facility but has threatened U.S. interests.

Strength

Unknown. At its peak the IG probably commanded several thousand hard-core members and a like number of sympathizers. The 1999 cease-fire and security crackdowns following the attack in Luxor in 1997, and more recently security efforts following September 11, probably have resulted in a substantial decrease in the group's numbers.

Location/Area of Operation

Operates mainly in the al-Minya, Asyu't, Qina, and Sohaj Governorates of southern Egypt. Also appears to have support in Cairo, Alexandria, and other urban locations, particularly among unemployed graduates and students. Has a worldwide presence, including the United Kingdom, Afghanistan, Yemen, and Austria.

External Aid

Unknown. The Egyptian Government believes that Iran, Bin Laden, and Afghan militant groups support the organization. Also may obtain some funding through various Islamic nongovernmental organizations.

HAMAS (Islamic Resistance Movement)

Description

Formed in late 1987 as an outgrowth of the Palestinian branch of the Muslim Brotherhood. Various HAMAS elements have used both political and violent means, including terrorism, to pursue the goal of establishing an Islamic Palestinian state in place of Israel. Loosely structured, with some elements working clandestinely and others working openly through mosques and social service institutions to recruit members, raise money, organize activities, and distribute propaganda. HAMAS's strength is concentrated in the Gaza Strip and a few areas of the West Bank. Also has engaged in political activity, such as running candidates in West Bank Chamber of Commerce elections.

Activities

HAMAS activists, especially those in the Izz el-Din al-Qassam Brigades, have conducted many attacks—including large-scale suicide bombings—against Israeli civilian and military targets. In the early 1990s, they also targeted Fatah rivals and began a practice of targeting suspected Palestinian collaborators, which continues. Increased operational activity in 2001 during the *intifadah*, claiming numerous attacks against Israeli interests. Group has not targeted U.S. interests and continues to confine its attacks to Israelis inside Israel and the territories.

Strength

Unknown number of hard-core members; tens of thousands of supporters and sympathizers.

Location/Area of Operation

Primarily the West Bank, Gaza Strip, and Israel. In August 1999, Jordanian authorities closed the group's Political Bureau offices in Amman, arrested its leaders, and prohibited the group from operating on Jordanian territory. HAMAS leaders also present in other parts of the Middle East, including Syria, Lebanon, and Iran.

External Aid

Receives funding from Palestinian expatriates, Iran, and private benefactors in Saudi Arabia and other moderate Arab states. Some fund-raising and propaganda activity takes place in Western Europe and North America.

Harakat ul-Mujahidin (HUM) (Movement of Holy Warriors)

Description

The HUM is an Islamic militant group based in Pakistan that operates primarily in Kashmir. It is politically aligned with the radical political party, Jamiat-i Ulema-i Islam Fazlur Rehman faction (JUI-F). Long-time leader of the group, Fazlur Rehman Khalil, in mid-February 2000 stepped down as HUM emir, turning the reins over to the popular Kashmiri commander and his second-in-command, Farooq Kashmiri. Khalil, who has been linked to Bin Laden and signed his fatwa in February 1998 calling for attacks on U.S. and Western interests, assumed the position of HUM Secretary General. HUM operated terrorist training camps in eastern Afghanistan until Coalition airstrikes destroyed them during fall 2001.

Activities

Has conducted a number of operations against Indian troops and civilian targets in Kashmir. Linked to the Kashmiri militant group al-Faran that kidnapped five Western tourists in Kashmir in July 1995; one was killed in August 1995 and the other four reportedly were killed in December of the same year. The HUM is responsible for the hijacking of an Indian airliner on 24 December 1999, which resulted in the release of Masood Azhar—an important leader in the former Harakat ul-Ansar imprisoned by the Indians in 1994—and Ahmad Omar Sheikh, who was arrested for the abduction/murder in January–February 2002 of U.S. journalist Daniel Pearl.

Strength

Has several thousand armed supporters located in Azad Kashmir, Pakistan, and India's southern Kashmir and Doda regions. Supporters are mostly Pakistanis and Kashmiris and also include Afghans and Arab veterans of the Afghan war. Uses light and heavy machine-guns, assault rifles, mortars, explosives, and rockets. HUM lost a significant share of its membership in defections to the Jaish-e-Mohammed (JEM) in 2000.

Location/Area of Operation

Based in Muzaffarabad, Rawalpindi, and several other towns in Pakistan, but members conduct insurgent and terrorist activities primarily in Kashmir. The HUM trained its militants in Afghanistan and Pakistan.

External Aid

Collects donations from Saudi Arabia and other Gulf and Islamic states and from Pakistanis and Kashmiris. The HUM's financial collection methods also include soliciting donations from magazine ads and pamphlets. The sources and amount of HUM's military funding are unknown. In anticipation of asset seizures by the Pakistani Government, the HUM withdrew funds from bank accounts and invested in legal businesses, such as commodity trading, real estate, and production of consumer goods. Its fundraising in Pakistan has been constrained since the government clampdown on extremist groups and freezing of terrorist assets.

Hizballah (Party of God)

a.k.a. Islamic Jihad, Revolutionary Justice Organization, Organization of the Oppressed on Earth, and Islamic Jihad for the Liberation of Palestine

Description

Formed in 1982 in response to the Israeli invasion of Lebanon, this Lebanon-based radical Shi'a group takes its ideological inspiration from the Iranian revolution and the teachings of the Ayatollah Khomeini. The Majlis al-Shura, or Consultative Council, is the group's highest governing body and is led by Secretary General Hassan Nasrallah. Hizballah formally advocates ultimate establishment of Islamic rule in Lebanon and liberating all occupied Arab lands, including Jerusalem. It has expressed as a goal the elimination of Israel. Has expressed its unwillingness to work within the confines of Lebanon's established political system; however, this stance changed with the party's decision in 1992 to participate in parliamentary elections. Although closely allied with and often directed by Iran, the group may have conducted operations that were not approved by Tehran. While Hizballah does not share the Syrian regime's secular orientation, the group has been a strong tactical ally in helping Syria advance its political objectives in the region.

Activities

Known or suspected to have been involved in numerous anti-U.S. terrorist attacks, including the suicide truck bombings of the U.S. Embassy in Beirut April 1983, and U.S. Marine barracks in Beirut in October 1983, and the U.S. Embassy annex in Beirut in September 1984. Three members of Hizballah, 'Imad Mughniyah, Hasan Izz-al-Din, and Ali Atwa, are on the FBI's list of 22 Most Wanted Terrorists for the hijacking in 1985 of TWA Flight 847 during which a U.S. Navy diver was murdered. Elements of the group were responsible for the kidnapping and detention of U.S. and other Western hostages in Lebanon. The group also attacked the Israeli Embassy in Argentina in 1992 and is a suspect in the 1994 bombing of the Israeli cultural center in Buenos Aires. In fall 2000, it captured three Israeli soldiers in the Shabaa Farms and kidnapped an Israeli noncombatant whom it may have lured to Lebanon under false pretenses.

Strength

Several thousand supporters and a few hundred terrorist operatives.

Location/Area of Operation

Operates in the Bekaa Valley, Hermil, the southern suburbs of Beirut, and southern Lebanon. Has established cells in Europe, Africa, South America, North America, and Asia.

External Aid

Receives substantial amounts of financial, training, weapons, explosives, political, diplomatic, and organizational aid from Iran and received diplomatic, political, and logistical support from Syria.

Islamic Movement of Uzbekistan (IMU)

Description

Coalition of Islamic militants from Uzbekistan and other Central Asian states opposed to Uzbekistani President Islom Karimov's secular regime. Before the counterterrorism coalition began operations in Afghanistan in October, the IMU's primary goal was the establishment of an Islamic state in Uzbekistan. If IMU political and ideological leader Tohir Yoldashev survives the counterterrorism campaign and can regroup the organization, however, he might widen the IMU's targets to include all those he perceives as fighting Islam. The group's propaganda has always included anti-Western and anti-Israeli rhetoric.

Activities

The IMU primarily targeted Uzbekistani interests before October 2001 and is believed to have been responsible for five car bombs in Tashkent in February 1999. Militants also took foreigners hostage in 1999 and 2000, including four U.S. citizens who were mountain climbing in August 2000, and four Japanese geologists and eight Krygyzstani soldiers in August 1999. Since October, the Coalition has captured, killed, and dispersed many of the militants who remained in Afghanistan to fight with the Taliban and al-Qaida, severely degrading the IMU's ability to attack Uzbekistani or Coalition interests in the near term. IMU military leader Juma Namangani apparently was killed during an air strike in November. At year's end, Yoldashev remained at large.

Strength

Militants probably number under 2,000.

Location/Area of Operation

Militants are scattered throughout South Asia and Tajikistan. Area of operations includes Afghanistan, Iran, Kyrgyzstan, Pakistan, Tajikistan, and Uzbekistan.

External Aid

Support from other Islamic extremist groups and patrons in the Middle East and Central and South Asia. IMU leadership broadcasts statements over Iranian radio.

Jaish-e-Mohammed (JEM) (Army of Mohammed)

Description

The Jaish-e-Mohammed (JEM) is an Islamic extremist group based in Pakistan that was formed by Masood Azhar upon his release from prison in India in early 2000. The group's aim is to unite Kashmir with Pakistan. It is politically aligned with the radical political party, Jamiat-i Ulema-i Islam Fazlur Rehman faction (JUI-F). The United States announced the addition of JEM to the U.S. Treasury Department's Office of Foreign Asset Control's (OFAC) list—which includes organizations that are believed to support terrorist groups and have assets in U.S. jurisdiction that can be frozen or controlled—in October and the Foreign Terrorist Organization list in December. The group was banned and its assets were frozen by the Pakistani Government in January 2002.

Activities

The JEM's leader, Masood Azhar, was released from Indian imprisonment in December 1999 in exchange for 155 hijacked Indian Airline hostages. The 1994 HUA kidnappings by Omar Sheikh of U.S. and British nationals in New Delhi and the July 1995 HUA/AI Faran kidnappings of Westerners in Kashmir were two of several previous HUA efforts to free Azhar. The JEM on 1 October 2001 claimed responsibility for a suicide attack on the Jammu and Kashmir legislative assembly building in Srinagar that killed at least 31 persons, but later denied the claim. The Indian Government has publicly implicated the JEM, along with Lashkar-e-Tayyiba for the 13 December attack on the Indian Parliament that killed 9 and injured 18.

Strength

Has several hundred armed supporters located in Azad Kashmir, Pakistan, and in India's southern Kashmir and Doda regions, including a large cadre of former HUM members. Supporters are mostly Pakistanis and Kashmiris and also include Afghans and Arab veterans of the Afghan war. Uses light and heavy machine-guns, assault rifles, mortars, improvised explosive devices, and rocket grenades.

Location/Area of Operation

Based in Peshawar and Muzaffarabad, but members conduct terrorist activities primarily in Kashmir. The JEM maintained training camps in Afghanistan until the fall of 2001.

External Aid

Most of the JEM's cadre and material resources have been drawn from the militant groups Harakat ul-Jihad al-Islami (HUJI) and the Harakat ul-Mujahedin (HUM). The JEM had close ties to Afghan Arabs and the Taliban. Usama Bin Laden is suspected of giving funding to the JEM. The JEM also collects funds through donation requests in magazines and pamphlets. In anticipation of asset seizures by the Pakistani Government, the JEM withdrew funds from bank accounts and invested in legal businesses, such as commodity trading, real estate, and production of consumer goods.

Al-Jihad

a.k.a. Egyptian Islamic Jihad, Jihad Group, Islamic Jihad

Description

Egyptian Islamic extremist group active since the late 1970s. Merged with bin Laden's al-Qaida organization in June 2001, but may retain some capability to conduct independent operations. Continues to suffer setbacks worldwide, especially after 11 September attacks. Primary goals are to overthrow the Egyptian Government and replace it with an Islamic state and attack U.S. and Israeli interests in Egypt and abroad.

Activities

Specializes in armed attacks against high-level Egyptian Government personnel, including cabinet ministers, and car-bombings against official U.S. and Egyptian facilities. The original Jihad was responsible for the assassination in 1981 of Egyptian President Anwar Sadat. Claimed responsibility for the attempted assassinations of Interior Minister Hassan al-Alfi in August 1993 and Prime Minister Atef Sedky in November 1993. Has not conducted an attack inside Egypt since 1993 and has never targeted foreign tourists there. Responsible for Egyptian Embassy bombing in Islamabad in 1995; in 1998 attack against U.S. Embassy in Albania was thwarted.

Strength

Unknown, but probably has several hundred hard-core members.

Location/Area of Operation

Operates in the Cairo area, but most of its network is outside Egypt, including Yemen, Afghanistan, Pakistan, Lebanon, and the United Kingdom, and its activities have been centered outside Egypt for several years.

External Aid

Unknown. The Egyptian Government claims that Iran supports the Jihad. Its merger with al-Qaida also boosts Bin Laden's support for the group. Also may obtain some funding through various Islamic nongovernmental organizations, cover businesses, and criminal acts.

Kahane Chai (Kach)

Description

Stated goal is to restore the biblical state of Israel. Kach (founded by radical Israeli-American rabbi Meir Kahane) and its offshoot Kahane Chai, which means "Kahane Lives," (founded by Meir Kahane's son Binyamin following his father's assassination in the United States) were declared to be terrorist organizations in March 1994 by the Israeli Cabinet under the 1948 Terrorism Law. This followed the groups' statements in support of Dr. Baruch Goldstein's attack in February 1994 on the al-lbrahimi Mosque—Goldstein was affiliated with Kach—and their verbal attacks on the Israeli Government. Palestinian gunmen killed Binyamin Kahane and his wife in a drive-by shooting in December 2000 in the West Bank.

Activities

Organizes protests against the Israeli Government. Harasses and threatens Palestinians in Hebron and the West Bank. Has threatened to attack Arabs, Palestinians, and Israeli Government officials. Has vowed revenge for the death of Binyamin Kahane and his wife.

Strength

Unknown.

Location/Area of Operation

Israel and West Bank settlements, particularly Qiryat Arba' in Hebron.

External Aid

Receives support from sympathizers in the United States and Europe.

Kurdistan Workers' Party (PKK)

Description

Founded in 1974 as a Marxist-Leninist insurgent group primarily composed of Turkish Kurds. The group's goal has been to establish an independent Kurdish state in southeastern Turkey, where the population is predominantly Kurdish. In the early 1990s, the PKK moved beyond rural-based insurgent activities to include urban terrorism. Turkish authorities captured Chairman Abdullah Ocalan in Kenya in early 1999; the Turkish State Security Court subsequently sentenced him to death. In August 1999, Ocalan announced a "peace initiative," ordering members to refrain from violence and requesting dialogue with Ankara on Kurdish issues. At a PKK Congress in January

2000, members supported Ocalan's initiative and claimed the group now would use only political means to achieve its new goal, improved rights for Kurds in Turkey.

Activities

Primary targets have been Turkish Government security forces in Turkey. Conducted attacks on Turkish diplomatic and commercial facilities in dozens of West European cities in 1993 and again in spring 1995. In an attempt to damage Turkey's tourist industry, the PKK bombed tourist sites and hotels and kidnapped foreign tourists in the early to mid-1990s.

Strength

Approximately 4,000 to 5,000, most of whom currently are located in northern Iraq. Has thousands of sympathizers in Turkey and Europe.

Location/Area of Operation

Operates in Turkey, Europe, and the Middle East.

External Aid

Has received safe haven and modest aid from Syria, Iraq, and Iran. Damascus generally upheld its September 2000 antiterror agreement with Ankara, pledging not to support the PKK.

Lashkar-e-Tayyiba (LT) (Army of the Righteous)

Description

The LT is the armed wing of the Pakistan-based religious organization, Markaz-ud-Dawa-wal-Irshad (MDI)—a Sunni anti-U.S. missionary organization formed in 1989. The LT is led by Abdul Wahid Kashmiri and is one of the three largest and best-trained groups fighting in Kashmir against India; it is not connected to a political party. The United States in October announced the addition of the LT to the U.S. Treasury Department's Office of Foreign Asset Control's (OFAC) list—which includes organizations that are believed to support terrorist groups and have assets in U.S. jurisdiction that can be frozen or controlled. The group was banned and its assets were frozen by the Pakistani Government in January 2002.

Activities

The LT has conducted a number of operations against Indian troops and civilian targets in Kashmir since 1993. The LT claimed responsibility for numerous attacks in 2001, including a January attack on Srinagar airport that killed five Indians along with six militants; an attack on a police station in Srinagar that killed at least eight officers and wounded several others; and an attack in April against Indian border security forces that left at least four dead. The Indian Government publicly implicated the LT along with JEM for the 13 December attack on the Indian Parliament building.

Strength

Has several members in Azad Kashmir, Pakistan, and in India's southern Kashmir and Doda regions. Almost all LT cadres are non-Kashmiris, mostly Pakistanis from madrassas across the country and Afghan veterans of the Afghan wars. Uses assault rifles, light and heavy machine-guns, mortars, explosives, and rocket propelled grenades.

Location/Area of Operation

Has been based in Muridke (near Lahore) and Muzaffarabad. The LT trains its militants in mobile training camps across Pakistan-administered Kashmir and had trained in Afghanistan until fall of 2001.

External Aid

Collects donations from the Pakistani community in the Persian Gulf and United Kingdom, Islamic NGOs [nongovernmental organizations], and Pakistani and Kashmiri businessmen. The LT also maintains a website (under the name of its parent organization Jamaat ud-Daawa), through which it solicits funds and provides information on the group's activities. The amount of LT funding is unknown. The LT maintains ties to religious/military groups around the world, ranging from the Philippines to the Middle East and Chechnya through the MDI fraternal network. In anticipation of asset seizures by the Pakistani Government, the LT withdrew funds from bank accounts and invested in legal businesses, such as commodity trading, real estate, and production of consumer goods.

Liberation Tigers of Tamil Eelam (LTTE)

Other known front organizations: World Tamil Association (WTA), World Tamil Movement (WTM), the Federation of Associations of Canadian Tamils (FACT), the Ellalan Force, and the Sangilian Force.

Description

Founded in 1976, the LTTE is the most powerful Tamil group in Sri Lanka and uses overt and illegal methods to raise funds, acquire weapons, and publicize its cause of establishing an independent Tamil state. The LTTE began its armed conflict with the Sri Lankan Government in 1983 and relies on a guerrilla strategy that includes the use of terrorist tactics.

Activities

The Tigers have integrated a battlefield insurgent strategy with a terrorist program that targets not only key personnel in the countryside but also senior Sri Lankan political and military leaders in Colombo and other urban centers. The Tigers are most notorious for their cadre of suicide bombers, the Black Tigers. Political assassinations and bombings are commonplace. The LTTE has refrained from targeting foreign diplomatic and commercial establishments.

Strength

Exact strength is unknown, but the LTTE is estimated to have 8,000 to 10,000 armed combatants in Sri Lanka, with a core of trained fighters of approximately 3,000 to 6,000. The LTTE also has a significant overseas support structure for fund-raising, weapons procurement, and propaganda activities.

Location/Area of Operations

The Tigers control most of the northern and eastern coastal areas of Sri Lanka but have conducted operations throughout the island. Headquartered in northern Sri Lanka, LTTE leader Velupillai Prabhakaran has established an extensive network of checkpoints and informants to keep track of any outsiders who enter the group's area of control.

External Aid

The LTTE's overt organizations support Tamil separatism by lobbying foreign governments and the United Nations. The LTTE also uses its international contacts to procure weapons, communications, and any other equipment and supplies it needs. The LTTE exploits large Tamil communities in North America, Europe, and Asia to obtain funds and supplies for its fighters in Sri Lanka often through false claims or even extortion.

Mujahedin-e Khalq Organization (MEK or MKO)

a.k.a. The National Liberation Army of Iran (NLA, the militant wing of the MEK), the People's Mujahidin of Iran (PMOI), National Council of Resistance (NCR), Muslim Iranian Student's Society (front organization used to garner financial support)

Description

The MEK philosophy mixes Marxism and Islam. Formed in the 1960s, the organization was expelled from Iran after the Islamic Revolution in 1979, and its primary support now comes from the Iraqi regime of Saddam Hussein. Its history is studded with anti-Western attacks as well as terrorist attacks on the interests of the clerical regime in Iran and abroad. The MEK now advocates a secular Iranian regime.

Activities

Worldwide campaign against the Iranian Government stresses propaganda and occasionally uses terrorist violence. During the 1970s the MEK killed several U.S. military personnel and U.S. civilians working on defense projects in Tehran. It supported the takeover in 1979 of the U.S. Embassy in Tehran. In 1981 the MEK planted bombs in the head office of the Islamic Republic Party and the Premier's office, killing some 70 high-ranking Iranian officials, including chief Justice Ayatollah Mohammad Beheshti, President Mohammad-Ali Rajaei, and Premier Mohammad-Javad Bahonar. In 1991, it assisted the government of Iraq in suppressing the Shia and Kurdish uprisings in northern and southern Iraq. In April 1992, it conducted attacks on Iranian Embassies in 13 different countries, demonstrating the group's ability to mount large-scale operations overseas. In recent years the MEK has targeted key military officers and assassinated the deputy chief of the Armed Forces General Staff in April 1999. In April 2000, the MEK attempted to assassinate the commander of the Nasr Headquarters—the interagency board responsible for coordinating policies on Iraq. The normal pace of anti-Iranian operations increased during the "Operation Great Bahman" in February 2000, when the group launched a dozen attacks against Iran. In 2000 and 2001, the MEK was involved regularly in mortar attacks and hit-and-run raids on Iranian military and law enforcement units and government buildings near the Iran-Iraq border. Since the end of the Iran-Iraq War the tactics along the border have garnered few military gains and have become commonplace. MEK insurgent activities in Tehran constitute the biggest security concern for the Iranian leadership. In February 2000, for example, the MEK attacked the leadership complex in Tehran that houses the offices of the Supreme Leader and President.

Strength

Several thousand fighters located on bases scattered throughout Iraq and armed with tanks, infantry fighting vehicles, and artillery. The MEK also has an overseas support structure. Most of the fighters are organized in the MEK's National Liberation Army (NLA).

Location/Area of Operation

In the 1980s the MEK's leaders were forced by Iranian security forces to flee to France. Since resettling in Iraq in 1987, the group has conducted internal security operations in support of the Government of Iraq. In the mid-1980s the group did not mount terrorist operations in Iran at a level similar to its activities in the 1970s, but by the 1990s the MEK had claimed credit for an increasing number of operations in Iran.

External Aid

Beyond support from Iraq, the MEK uses front organizations to solicit contributions from expatriate Iranian communities.

National Liberation Army (ELN)—Colombia

Description

Marxist insurgent group formed in 1965 by urban intellectuals inspired by Fidel Castro and Che Guevara. Began a dialogue with Colombian officials in 1999 following a campaign of mass kidnappings—each involving at least one U.S. citizen—to demonstrate its strength and continuing viability, and force the Pastrana administration to negotiate. Peace talks between Bogotá and the ELN, started in 1999, continued sporadically through 2001 until Bogotá broke them off in August, but resumed in Havana, Cuba, by year's end.

Activities

Kidnapping, hijacking, bombing, extortion, and guerrilla war. Modest conventional military capability. Annually conducts hundreds of kidnappings for ransom, often targeting foreign employees of large corporations, especially in the petroleum industry. Frequently assaults energy infrastructure and has inflicted major damage on pipelines and the electric distribution network.

Strength

Approximately 3,000–5,000 armed combatants and an unknown number of active supporters.

Location/Area of Operation

Mostly in rural and mountainous areas of north, northeast, and southwest Colombia, and Venezuela border regions.

External Aid

Cuba provides some medical care and political consultation.

The Palestine Islamic Jihad (PIJ)

Description

Originated among militant Palestinians in the Gaza Strip during the 1970s. PIJ-Shiqaqi faction, currently led by Ramadan Shallah in Damascus, is most active. Committed to the creation of an Islamic Palestinian state and the destruction of Israel through holy war. Also opposes moderate Arab governments that it believes have been tainted by Western secularism.

Activities

PIJ activists have conducted many attacks, including large-scale suicide bombings against Israeli civilian and military targets. The group increased its operational activity in 2001 during the *Intifadah* [Palestinian uprising], claiming numerous attacks against Israeli interests. The group has not targeted U.S. interests and continues to confine its attacks to Israelis inside Israel and the territories.

Strength

Unknown.

Location/Area of Operation

Primarily Israel, the West Bank, and Gaza Strip, and other parts of the Middle East, including Lebanon and Syria, where the leadership is based.

External Aid

Receives financial assistance from Iran and limited logistic support assistance from Syria.

Palestine Liberation Front (PLF)

Description

Broke away from the PFLP-GC in mid-1970s. Later split again into pro-PLO, pro-Syrian, and pro-Libyan factions. Pro-PLO faction led by Muhammad Abbas (Abu Abbas), who became member of PLO Executive Committee in 1984 but left it in 1991.

Activities

The Abu Abbas–led faction is known for aerial attacks against Israel. Abbas's group also was responsible for the attack in 1985 on the cruise ship Achille Lauro and the murder of U.S. citizen Leon Klinghoffer. A warrant for Abu Abbas's arrest is outstanding in Italy.

Strength

Unknown.

Location/Area of Operation

PLO faction based in Tunisia until *Achille Lauro* attack. Now based in Iraq.

External Aid

Receives support mainly from Iran. Has received support from Libya in the past.

Popular Front for the Liberation of Palestine (PFLP)

Description

Marxist-Leninist group founded in 1967 by George Habash as a member of the PLO. Joined the Alliance of Palestinian Forces (APF) to oppose the Declaration of Principles signed in 1993 and suspended participation in the PLO. Broke away from the APF, along with the DFLP, in 1996 over ideological differences. Took part in meetings with Arafat's Fatah party and PLO representatives in 1999 to discuss national unity and the reinvigoration of the PLO but continues to oppose current negotiations with Israel.

Activities

Committed numerous international terrorist attacks during the 1970s. Since 1978 has conducted attacks against Israeli or moderate Arab targets, including killing a settler and her son in December 1996. Stepped up operational activity in 2001, highlighted by the shooting death of Israeli Tourism Minister in October to retaliation for Israel's killing of PFLP leader in August.

Strength

Some 800.

Location/Area of Operation

Syria, Lebanon, Israel, West Bank, and Gaza.

External Aid

Receives safe haven and some logistical assistance from Syria.

Popular Front for the Liberation of Palestine—General Command (PFLP-GC)

Description

Split from the PFLP in 1968, claiming it wanted to focus more on fighting and less on politics. Opposed to Arafat's PLO. Led by Ahmad Jabril, a former captain in the Syrian Army. Closely tied to both Syria and Iran.

Activities

Carried out dozens of attacks in Europe and the Middle East during 1970s–80s. Known for cross-border terrorist attacks into Israel using unusual means, such as hot-air balloons and motorized hang gliders. Primary focus now on guerrilla operations in southern Lebanon, small-scale attacks in Israel, West Bank, and Gaza.

Strength

Several hundred.

Location/Area of Operation

Headquarters in Damascus with bases in Lebanon.

External Aid

Receives support from Syria and financial support from Iran.

Al-Qaida

Description

Established by Usama Bin Laden in the late 1980s to bring together Arabs who fought in Afghanistan against the Soviet Union. Helped finance, recruit, transport, and train Sunni Islamic extremists for the Afghan resistance. Current goal is to establish a pan-Islamic Caliphate throughout the world by working with allied Islamic extremist groups to overthrow regimes it deems "non-Islamic" and expelling Westerners and non-Muslims from Muslim countries. Issued statement under banner of "The World Islamic Front for Jihad Against the Jews and Crusaders" in February 1998, saying it was the duty of all Muslims to kill U.S. citizens—civilian or military—and their allies everywhere. Merged with Egyptian Islamic Jihad (Al-Jihad) in June 2001.

Activities

On 11 September 2001, 19 al-Qaida suicide attackers hijacked and crashed four U.S. commercial jets, two into the World Trade Center in New York City, one into the Pentagon near Washington, DC, and a fourth into a field in Shanksville, Pennsylvania, leaving about 3,000 individuals dead or missing. Directed the 12 October 2000 attack on the USS *Cole* in the port of Aden, Yemen, killing 17 U.S. Navy members, and injuring another 39. Conducted the bombings in August 1998 of the U.S. Embassies in Nairobi, Kenya, and Dar es Salaam, Tanzania, that killed at least 301 individuals and injured more than 5,000 others. Claims to have shot down U.S. helicopters and killed U.S. servicemen in Somalia in 1993 and to have conducted three bombings that targeted U.S. troops in Aden, Yemen, in December 1992.

Al-Qaida is linked to the following plans that were not carried out: to assassinate Pope John Paul II during his visit to Manila in late 1994, to kill President Clinton during a visit to the Philippines in early 1995, the midair bombing of a dozen U.S. trans-Pacific flights in 1995, and to set off a bomb at Los Angeles International Airport in 1999. Also plotted to carry out terrorist operations against U.S. and Israeli tourists visiting Jordan for millennial celebrations in late 1999. (Jordanian authorities thwarted the planned attacks and put 28 suspects on trial.) In December 2001, suspected al-Qaida associate Richard Colvin Reid attempted to ignite a shoe bomb on a transatlantic flight from Paris to Miami.

Strength

Al-Qaida may have several thousand members and associates. Also serves as a focal point or umbrella organization for a worldwide network that includes many Sunni Islamic extremist groups, some members of al-Gama'a al-Islamiyya, the Islamic Movement of Uzbekistan, and the Harakat ul-Mujahidin.

Location/Area of Operation

Al-Qaida has cells worldwide and is reinforced by its ties to Sunni extremist networks. Coalition attacks on Afghanistan since October 2001 have dismantled the Taliban—al-Qaida's protectors—and led to the capture, death, or dispersal of al-Qaida operatives. Some al-Qaida members at large probably will attempt to carry out future attacks against U.S. interests.

External Aid

Bin Laden, member of a billionaire family that owns the Bin Laden Group construction empire, is said to have inherited tens of millions of dollars that he uses to help finance the group. Al-Qaida also maintains moneymaking front businesses, solicits donations from like-minded supporters, and illicitly siphons funds from donations to Muslim charitable organizations. U.S. efforts to block al-Qaida funding has hampered al-Qaida's ability to obtain money.

Real IRA (RIRA)

a.k.a. True IRA

Description

Formed in early 1998 as clandestine armed wing of the 32-County Sovereignty Movement, a "political pressure group" dedicated to removing British forces from Northern Ireland and unifying Ireland. The 32-County Sovereignty Movement opposed Sinn Fein's adoption in September 1997 of the Mitchell principles of democracy and nonviolence and opposed the amendment in December 1999 of Articles 2 and 3 of the Irish Constitution, which laid claim to Northern Ireland. Michael "Mickey" McKevitt, who left the IRA to protest its cease-fire, leads the group; Bernadette Sands-McKevitt, his wife, is a founder-member of the 32-County Sovereignty Movement, the political wing of the RIRA.

Activities

Bombings, assassinations, and robberies. Many Real IRA members are former IRA members who left that organization following the IRA cease-fire and bring to RIRA a wealth of experience in terrorist tactics and bombmaking. Targets include British military and police in Northern Ireland and Northern Ireland Protestant communities. RIRA is linked to and understood to be responsible for the car bomb attack in Omagh, Northern Ireland, on 15 August, 1998 that killed 29 and injured 220 persons. The group began to observe a cease-fire following Omagh but in 2000 and 2001 resumed attacks in Northern Ireland and on the UK mainland against targets such as M16 headquarters and the BBC.

Strength

100–200 activists plus possible limited support from IRA hard-liners dissatisfied with IRA cease-fire and other republican sympathizers. British and Irish authorities arrested at least 40 members in the spring and summer of 2001, including leader McKevitt, who is currently in prison in the Irish Republic awaiting trial for being a member of a terrorist organization and directing terrorist attacks.

Location/Area of Operation

Northern Ireland, Irish Republic, Great Britain.

External Aid

Suspected of receiving funds from sympathizers in the United States and of attempting to buy weapons from U.S. gun dealers. RIRA also is reported to have purchased sophisticated weapons from the Balkans. Three Irish nationals associated with RIRA were extradited from Slovenia to the UK and are awaiting trial on weapons procurement charges.

Revolutionary Armed Forces of Colombia (FARC)

Description

Established in 1964 as the military wing of the Colombian Communist Party, the FARC is Colombia's oldest, largest, most capable, and best-equipped Marxist insurgency. The FARC is governed by a secretariat, led by septuagenarian Manuel Marulanda, a.k.a. "Tirofijo," and six others, including senior military commander Jorge Briceno, a.k.a. "Mono Jojoy." Organized along military lines and includes several urban fronts. In 2001, the group continued a slow-moving peace negotiation process with the Pastrana Administration that has gained the group several concessions, including a demilitarized zone used as a venue for negotiations.

Activities

Bombings, murder, kidnapping, extortion, hijacking, as well as guerilla and conventional military action against Colombian political, military, and economic targets. In March 1999 the FARC executed three U.S. Indian rights activists on Venezuelan territory after it kidnapped them in Colombia. Foreign citizens often are targets of FARC kidnapping for ransom. Has well-documented ties to narcotics traffickers, principally through the provision of armed protection.

Strength

Approximately 9,000–12,000 armed combatants and an unknown number of supporters, mostly in rural areas.

Location/Area of Operation

Colombia with some activities—extortion, kidnapping, logistics, and R&R—in Venezuela, Panama, and Ecuador.

External Aid

Cuba provides some medical care and political consultation.

Revolutionary Nuclei

a.k.a. Revolutionary Cells

Description

Revolutionary Nuclei (RN) emerged from a broad range of antiestablishment and anti-U.S./NATO/EU leftist groups active in Greece between 1995 and 1998. The group is believed to be the successor to or offshoot of Greece's most prolific terrorist group, Revolutionary People's Struggle (ELA), which has not claimed an attack since January 1995. Indeed, RN appeared to fill the void left by ELA, particularly as lesser groups faded from the scene. RN's few communiqués show strong similarities in rhetoric, tone, and theme to ELA proclamations. RN has not claimed an attack since November 2000.

Activities

Beginning operations in January 1995, the group has claimed responsibility for some two dozen arson attacks and explosive low-level bombings targeting a range of U.S., Greek, and other European targets in Greece. In its most infamous and lethal attack to date, the group claimed responsibility for a bomb it detonated at the Intercontinental Hotel in April 1999 that resulted in the death of a Greek woman and injured a Greek man. Its modus operandi includes warning calls of impending attacks, attacks targeting property [and] individuals; use of rudimentary timing devices; and strikes during the late evening-early morning hours. RN last attacked U.S. interests in Greece in November 2000 with two separate bombings against the Athens offices of Citigroup and the studio of a Greek/American sculptor. The group also detonated an explosive device outside the Athens offices of Texaco in December 1999. Greek targets have included court and other government office buildings, private vehicles, and the offices of Greek firms involved in NATO-related defense contracts in Greece. Similarly, the group has attacked European interests in Athens, including Barclays Bank in December 1998 and November 2000.

Strength

Group membership is believed to be small, probably drawing from the Greek militant leftist or anarchist milieu.

Location/Area of Operation

Primary area of operation is in the Athens metropolitan area.

External Aid

Unknown, but believed to be self-sustaining.

Revolutionary Organization 17 November (17 November)

Description

Radical leftist group established in 1975 and named for the student uprising in Greece in November 1973 that protested the military regime. Anti-Greek establishment, anti-U.S., anti-Turkey, anti-NATO, and committed to the ouster of U.S. bases, removal of Turkish military presence from Cyprus, and severing of Greece's ties to NATO and the European Union (EU).

Activities

Initial attacks were assassinations of senior U.S. officials and Greek public figures. Added bombings in 1980s. Since 1990 has expanded targets to include EU facilities and foreign firms investing in Greece and has added improvised rocket attacks to its methods. Most recent attack claimed was the murder in June 2000 of British Defense Attaché Stephen Saunders.

Strength

Unknown, but presumed to be small.

Location/Area of Operation

Athens, Greece.

Revolutionary People's Liberation Party/Front (DHKP/C)

a.k.a. Devrimci So, Revolutionary Left, Dev Sol

Description

Originally formed in 1978 as Devrimci Sol, or Dev Sol, a splinter faction of the Turkish People's Liberation Party/Front. Renamed in 1994 after factional infighting, it espouses a Marxist ideology and is virulently anti-U.S. and anti-NATO [North Atlantic Treaty Organization]. Finances its activities chiefly through armed robberies and extortion.

Activities

Since the late 1980s has concentrated attacks against current and retired Turkish security and military officials. Began a new campaign against foreign interests in 1990. Assassinated two U.S. military contractors and wounded a U.S. Air Force officer to protest the Gulf War. Launched rockets at U.S. Consulate in Istanbul in 1992. Assassinated prominent Turkish businessman and two others in early 1996, its first significant terrorist act as DHKP/C. Turkish authorities thwarted DHKP/C attempt in June 1999 to fire light antitank weapon at U.S. Consulate in Istanbul. Conducted its first suicide bombings, targeting Turkish police, in January and September 2001. Series of safehouse raids and arrests by Turkish police over last three years have weakened group significantly.

Strength

Unknown.

Location/Area of Operation

Conducts attacks in Turkey, primarily in Istanbul. Raises funds in Western Europe.

External Aid

Unknown.

The Salafist Group for Call and Combat (GSPC)

Description

The Salafist Group for Call and Combat (GSPC) splinter faction that began in 1996 has eclipsed the GIA since approximately 1998, and currently is assessed to be the most effective remaining armed group inside Algeria. In contrast to the GIA, the GSPC has gained popular support through its pledge to avoid civilian attacks inside Algeria (although, in fact, civilians have been attacked). Its adherents abroad appear to have largely co-opted the external networks of the GIA, active particularly throughout Europe, Africa, and the Middle East.

Activities

The GSPC continues to conduct operations aimed at government and military targets, primarily in rural areas. Such operations include false roadblocks and attacks against convoys transporting military, police, or other government personnel. According to press reporting, some GSPC members in Europe maintain contacts with other North African extremists sympathetic to al-Qaida, a number of whom were implicated in terrorist plots during 2001.

Strength

Unknown; probably several hundred to several thousand inside Algeria.

Location/Area of Operation

Algeria.

External Aid

Algerian expatriates and GSPC members abroad, many residing in Western Europe, provide financial and logistics support. In addition, the Algerian Government has accused Iran and Sudan of supporting Algerian extremists in years past.

Sendero Luminoso (Shining Path, or SL)

Description

Former university professor Abimael Guzman formed Sendero Luminoso in the late 1960s, and his teachings created the foundation of SL's militant Maoist doctrine. In the 1980s SL became one of the most ruthless terrorist groups in the Western Hemisphere; approximately 30,000 persons have died since Shining Path took up arms in 1980. Its stated goal is to destroy existing Peruvian institutions and replace them with a communist peasant revolutionary regime. It also opposes any influence by foreign governments, as well as by other Latin American guerrilla groups, especially the Tupac Amaru Revolutionary Movement (MRTA).

In 2001, the Peruvian National Police thwarted an SL attack against "an American objective," possibly the U.S. Embassy, when they arrested two Lima SL cell members. Additionally, Government authorities continued to arrest and prosecute active SL members, including, Ruller Mazombite, a.k.a. "Camarada Cayo," chief of the protection team of SL leader Macario Ala, a.k.a. "Artemio," and Evorcio Ascencios, a.k.a. "Camarada Canale," logistics chief of the Huallaga Regional Committee. Counterterrorist operations targeted pockets of terrorist activity in the Upper Huallaga River Valley and the Apurimac/Ene River Valley, where SL columns continued to conduct periodic attacks.

Activities

Conducted indiscriminate bombing campaigns and selective assassinations. Detonated explosives at diplomatic missions of several countries in Peru in 1990, including an attempt to car bomb the U.S. Embassy in December. Peruvian authorities continued operations against the SL in 2001 in the countryside, where the SL conducted periodic raids on villages.

Strength

Membership is unknown but estimated to be 200 armed militants. SL's strength has been vastly diminished by arrests and desertions.

Location/Area of Operation

Peru, with most activity in rural areas.

External Aid

None.

United Self-Defense Forces/Group of Colombia (AUC—Autodefensas Unidas de Colombia)

Description

The AUC—commonly referred to as the paramilitaries—is an umbrella organization formed in April 1997 to consolidate most local and regional paramilitary groups each with the mission to protect economic interests and combat insurgents locally. The AUC—supported by economic elites, drug traffickers, and local communities lacking effective government security—claims its primary objective is to protect its sponsors from insurgents. The AUC now asserts itself as a regional and national counterinsurgent force. It is adequately equipped and armed and reportedly pays its members a monthly salary. AUC political leader Carlos Castaño has claimed 70 percent of the AUC's operational costs are financed with drug-related earnings, the rest from "donations" from its sponsors.

Activities

AUC operations vary from assassinating suspected insurgent supporters to engaging guerrilla combat units. Colombian National Combat operations generally consist of raids and ambushes directed against suspected insurgents. The AUC generally avoids engagements with government security forces and actions against U.S. personnel or interests.

Strength

Estimated 6,000 to 8,150, including former military and insurgent personnel.

Location/Area of Operation

AUC forces are strongest in the northwest in Antioquia, Córdoba, Sucre, and Bolivar Departments. Since 1999, the group demonstrated a growing presence in other northern and southwestern departments. Clashes between the AUC and the FARC insurgents in Putumayo in 2000 demonstrated the range of the AUC to contest insurgents throughout Colombia.

External Aid

None.

Appendix B

Chronology of Significant Terrorist Incidents, 2002–2004

Note: The incidents listed have met the US Government's Incident Review Panel criteria. An International Terrorist Incident is judged significant if it results in loss of life or serious injury to persons, abduction or kidnapping of persons, major property damage, and/or is an act or attempted act that could reasonably be expected to create the conditions noted.

2002

January

12 Venezuela

In El Amparo, armed militants kidnapped two persons, an Italian and Venezuelan citizen. On 17 May, a rebel defecting from the Revolutionary Armed Forces of Colombia (FARC) released the two hostages.

15 West Bank

In Bayt Sahur, militants attacked a vehicle carrying two passengers, killing one person, who was a US-Israeli citizen, and wounding the other. The Al-Aqsa Martyrs Battalion claimed responsibility.

22 India

In Kolkata (Calcutta), armed militants attacked the US Consulate, killing five Indian security forces and injuring 13 others. The Harakat ul-Jihad-I-Islami and the Asif Raza Commandoes claimed responsibility.

India

In Jammu, Kashmir, a bomb exploded in a crowded retail district, killing one person and injuring nine others. No one claimed responsibility.

23 Pakistan

lIn Karachi, armed militants kidnapped and killed a US journalist working for the *Wal Street Journal* newspaper. No one claimed responsibility.

24 Algeria
In Larbaa-Tablat Road, militants set up an illegal roadblock, killing three persons, including one Syrian. No one claimed responsibility.

31 Philippines
Two hikers on the slopes of the Pinatubo volcano were attacked by militants. One of the hikers, a US citizen, was killed.

February

9 France
In Saint-Jean-De-Luz, unidentified persons threw gasoline bombs at a police headquarters, causing material damage to police barracks and three parked vehicles but resulting in no injuries. No one claimed responsibility, but authorities suspect radical groups associated with the Basque Fatherland and Liberty.

16 West Bank
In Karnei Shomron, a suicide bomber attacked a pizzeria in an outdoor food court, killing four persons, two of whom were US citizens, and wounding 27 others including two US citizens. The Popular Front for the Liberation of Palestine (PFLP) claimed responsibility.

28 Colombia
In Antioquia, an Italian tourist was kidnapped at a checkpoint armed rebels had illegally set up. On 17 March in San Francisco, the rebels released the Italian tourist.

Jordan
In Amman, a bomb placed in a car was detonated by a timing device, killing an Egyptian and an Iraqi laborer who worked in a nearby food shop. The car belonged to the wife of the head of the Jordanian Anti-Terrorism Unit and was parked near their home. No one claimed responsibility.

March

7 West Bank
In Ariel, a suicide bomber entered a large supermarket collocated with a hotel and detonated the explosive device he was wearing, wounding 10 persons including a US citizen, according to media and US Embassy reporting. The PFLP claimed responsibility.

9 Israel
In Jerusalem, a suicide bomber entered a restaurant/cafe detonating the explosive device he was wearing, killing 11 persons and wounding 52 others including a US citizen, according to media and US Embassy reporting. The Al-Aqsa Martyrs Brigade claimed responsibility.

14 Colombia
In Cali, two US citizens were shot and killed by motorcycle-riding gunmen. The two US citizens were brothers who arrived in town the day before to negotiate the release of their father who had been taken captive by the FARC. No one claimed responsibility.

17 Pakistan

In Islamabad, during a Protestant service, several grenades were thrown inside a church used by diplomatic and local personnel, killing five persons—including two US citizens and 46 others, according to press reports. The Lashkar-e-Tayyiba probably is responsible.

18 Georgia

In Abkhazia, Georgian guerrillas kidnapped four Russian peacekeepers to negotiate an exchange for two Georgian gunmen who were being held by Russian authorities. On 21 March, the four Russian peacekeepers and their weapons were released in exchange for the two Georgian gunmen. Georgian guerrillas claimed responsibility.

20 Peru

In Lima, a vehicle bomb exploded at a shopping center some 50 meters from the US Embassy, killing nine persons, injuring 32 others, and causing major damage. Authorities suspect the Maoist Shining Path rebels and/or the Tupac Amaru Revolutionary Movement. The dead included two police officers and a teenager but no US citizens. The attack occurred three days before the US President's planned visit to Peru.

21 Israel

In Jerusalem, a suicide bomber detonated the explosive device he was wearing, killing three persons and wounding 86 others, including two US citizens, according to US Consulate and media reporting. The Palestinian Islamic Jihad claimed responsibility.

22 India

In Shopiyan, Kashmir, militants threw several grenades into a busy market at midmorning, injuring 35 persons. No one claimed responsibility.

India

In Anantnag, Kashmir, militants tossed several grenades at a busy bus stand, injuring 17 persons. No one claimed responsibility.

India

In Rajouri, Kashmir, a bomb exploded in a sweet shop, injuring five persons. No one claimed responsibility.

22 Uganda

In Kalosaric, gunmen stopped a vehicle traveling on the Moroto-Kotido Road, killing three persons—an Irish Catholic priest, his driver, and his cook. Karamojong gunmen are probably responsible.

23 India

In Kadal, Kashmir, a grenade hurled at a police installation missed its target and landed in a group of civilians, killing two persons and injuring 20 others, including nine policemen. No one claimed responsibility.

26 Senegal

In Kafountine, Casamance Province, rebels attacked the coastal resort, killing five persons and wounding four others including a French citizen. The Casamance Movement of Democratic Forces is probably responsible.

West Bank

In Hebron, gunmen stopped and fired on a vehicle owned and operated by the Temporary Presence in Hebron (TIPH), killing two persons—a Turkish Army officer and a Swiss office worker—and wounding a Turkish Army officer, according to media and government reports. No one claimed responsibility. The Palestinian Authorities and the Israeli Army accuse each other of the incident.

27 Israel

In Netanya, a suicide bomber entered the crowded restaurant of a hotel and detonated the explosive device he was wearing, killing 22 persons including one US citizen and wounding 140 others. The Islamic Resistance Movement (HAMAS) claimed responsibility.

30 India

In Jammu, Kashmir, a bomb exploded at a Hindu temple, killing 10 persons, according to press reports. The Islamic Front has claimed responsibility.

31 West Bank

In Efrat, a suicide bomber standing next to an ambulance station detonated the explosive device he was wearing, injuring four persons including one US citizen, according to press and US Consulate reporting. The Al-Aqsa Martyrs Brigades claimed responsibility.

April

1 Nigeria

In Niger Delta, 10 oil workers contracted to the Royal Shell Oil Group were kidnapped by militant youths, according to press reports. Six of the hostages were foreign nationals, including one US citizen, one Filipino, and four Ghanaians.

10 India

In Gando, Kashmir, armed militants killed five persons and injured four others in their residence. No one claimed responsibility.

11 Tunisia

In Djerba, a suicide bomber crashed and detonated a propane gas truck into the fence of a historic synagogue, killing 16 persons including 11 German citizens, one French citizen, and three Tunisians and injuring 26 German citizens. The Islamic Army for the Liberation of the Holy Sites claimed responsibility.

12 Israel

In Jerusalem, a suicide bomber detonated the explosive vest she was wearing, killing six persons, including two Chinese citizens, and wounding 90 others. The Al-Aqsa Martyrs Brigade claimed responsibility.

14 India

In Pulwama, Kashmir, a grenade fired at a police vehicle missed its target, landing in a crowded bus stop, killing one person and injuring 13 others. No one claimed responsibility.

16 India

In Balhama-Rafiabad, armed militants killed five persons and injured two others. The Ikhwan are probably responsible.

26 India

In Gharat, Kashmir, a bomb planted under a bus was detonated by remote control, killing one person and injuring 21 others—nine security personnel and 12 civilians. No one claimed responsibility.

28 Colombia

In Bogota, according to US Embassy reporting, a car packed with 88 pounds of explosives was discovered adjacent to the World Business Port commercial building that houses the US Agency for International Development (USAID) and other international organizations. A policeman identified the vehicle as suspicious and called the bomb squad who disarmed the device. No one claimed responsibility.

May

4 Istanbul

In Istanbul, an armed gunman entered a large tourist hotel and took several Turkish nationals and one Bulgarian hostage, according to press and US Embassy reporting. About an hour later, all the hostages were released unharmed, and the gunman surrendered. No group claimed responsibility.

7 Colombia

In Quebradas, a section of the Cano Limon-Covenas pipeline was bombed, killing two persons, wounding four others, and causing millions of dollars in property damage. The FARC or National Liberation Army (ELN) is probably responsible.

8 Pakistan

In Karachi, a vehicle parked next to a Navy shuttle bus exploded, killing 10 French nationals and two Pakistanis and wounding 19 others—11 French nationals and eight Pakistanis—-shattering windows in nearby buildings and leaving a large crater in the road, according to press reports. Al-Qaida is probably responsible.

9 Lebanon

In Tripoli, a bomb placed beside a US fast food restaurant—Kentucky Fried Chicken (KFC)—detonated, wounding an employee, according to press reports. No one claimed responsibility.

9 Russia

In Kapiisk, Dagestan, militants detonated a remote-controlled bomb in the bushes as the May Day Parade was passing by on Main Street, killing 42 persons, including 14 soldiers, and wounding 150 others, including 50 soldiers, according to press reports. Islamist militants linked to al-Qaida are probably responsible.

9 Thailand
In Tachilek, a bomb exploded at a hotel, killing one Burmese national and injuring three others. No one claimed responsibility.

10 United Kingdom
In London, a timer-detonated bomb exploded at the Armenian Embassy. No casualties were reported, and no one claimed responsibility.

14 India
In Kaluchak, Jammu, militants fired on a passenger bus, killing seven persons, then entered a military housing complex killing three soldiers, four soldiers' wives, and three children. The Al-Mansooran and Jamiat ul-Mujahedin claimed responsibility.

17 India
In Srinagar, Kashmir, a bomb exploded outside the high-security civil secretariat area, injuring six persons. No one claimed responsibility.

In Jammu, Kashmir, a bomb exploded at a fire services headquarters, killing two persons and injuring 16 others. No one claimed responsibility.

21 Colombia
In Srinagar, armed gunmen killed a senior Hurriyat conference leader, according to press reports. No one claimed responsibility.

30 India
In Kashmir, armed militants shot and injured a subeditor of a local English language newspaper, *Kashmir Images*. No one claimed responsibility.

June

1 India
In Kulgam, Kashmir, a grenade thrown into a crowd killed one person and injured seven others. No one claimed responsibility.

1 India
In Srinagar, armed militants threw a grenade into a paramilitary foot patrol, killing one person and injuring 13 others. No one claimed responsibility.

1 India
In Anantnag, armed militants threw a grenade into a police station, injuring 18 persons. No one claimed responsibility.

7 India
In Pindi, armed militants killed one person, injured three others, and damaged several houses. No one claimed responsibility.

Philippine military units on a rescue mission engaged terrorists from the ASG in a firefight that took the life of US citizen Martin Burnham, who had been held hostage along with his wife, for more than a year. She was wounded and freed.

9 India
In Rajouri, Kashmir, armed militants wounded six persons including three security personnel and damaged a television tower building. No one claimed responsibility.

14 Pakistan
In Karachi, a vehicle bomb exploded on the main road near the US Consulate and Marriott Hotel, killing 11 persons, injuring 51 others, including a US and a Japanese citizen, and damaging nearby buildings. Al Qaida or Al-Qa'nun is possibly responsible.

19 Israel
In Jerusalem, a suicide bomber jumped out of a car, ran into the concrete shelter at a bus stop, and detonated the explosive device he was wearing, killing six persons and wounding 43 others, including two US citizens. The Al-Aqsa Martyrs Brigades claimed responsibility.

20 Pakistan
In Neelum Valley, armed militants fired on a passenger bus sending it over a cliff, killing the driver and nine passengers and injuring 12 others. No one claimed responsibility.

21 Spain
In Fuengirola, a vehicle bomb exploded in a parking lot adjacent to a beach hotel/ apartment building injuring six persons, including four Britons, one Moroccan, and one Spaniard. The Basque Fatherland and Liberty is probably responsible.

24 India
In Kupwara, Kashmir, a bomb exploded at the State Law and Parliamentary Minister's residence, injuring five police officers guarding the home. No one claimed responsibility.

30 India
In Nishat, Kashmir, armed militants killed a National Conference leader. No one claimed responsibility.

July

5 Algeria
In Larbaa, rebels detonated a homemade bomb in the downtown area, killing 35 persons, including two Nigerian citizens, and wounding 80 others. The Armed Islamic Group is possibly responsible.

8 India
In Indh, Kashmir, a bomb exploded near a water tank, killing three persons. No one claimed responsibility.

13 India
In Jammu, armed militants attacked a village, killing 27 persons. The Lashkar-e-Tayyiba is probably responsible.

13 Pakistan
In Mansehra, a grenade thrown into a group of European tourists visiting at an archeological site exploded, injuring 12 persons—seven Germans, one Austrian, one Slovak, and three Pakistanis. No one claimed responsibility.

17 India
In Anantnag, Kashmir, a bomb exploded in a government building, killing three persons and injuring nine others. No one claimed responsibility.

17 Israel
In Tel Aviv, two suicide bombers carried out an attack simultaneously near the old bus station, killing five persons, including one Romanian and two Chinese, and wounding 38 others, including one Romanian. The Islamic Jihad claimed responsibility.

22 India
In Sumber, Kashmir, armed militants killed three persons, all members of the Village Defense Committee. No one claimed responsibility.

24 India
In Rajouri, Kashmir, a grenade exploded in a crowded marketplace, killing one person and injuring 27 others. No one claimed responsibility.

25 India
In Batmaloo, Kashmir, militants threw a grenade into a crowded marketplace, injuring 15 persons. No one claimed responsibility.

31 West Bank
In Jerusalem, a bomb hidden in a bag that was placed on a table in the Frank Sinatra International Student Center, Hebrew University, detonated, killing nine persons including five US citizens and four Israeli citizens and wounding approximately 87 others including four US citizens, two Japanese citizens, and three South Korean citizens, according to media reports. The Islamic Resistance Movement (HAMAS) claimed responsibility.

August

4 Israel
In Safed, a suicide bomber boarded a bus and detonated the explosive device he was wearing, killing nine persons, including two Philippine citizens, and injuring 50 others, including an unspecified number of military personnel returning from leave. HAMAS claimed responsibility.

5 India
In Malik, Kashmir, a grenade was thrown into a crowded marketplace injuring 10 persons. No one claimed responsibility.

5 Pakistan
In Murree, gunmen attacked a Christian School attended by 146 children of missionaries from around the world, killing six persons—two security guards, a cook, a carpenter, a

receptionist, and a private citizen—and injuring a Filipino citizen visiting her son. A group called al-Intigami al-Pakistani claimed responsibility.

6 Colombia
In Cuanata, a bomb exploded on a segment of the Canadian-owned Ocensa oil pipeline, causing oil spillage and environmental damage. The explosion forced the suspension of crude oil transport to the Port of Covenas. The FARC is responsible.

6 India
In Pahalgam, Kashmir, armed militants threw several grenades and then fired into a group of Hindu pilgrims, killing nine persons and injuring 32 others. The Lashkar-e-Tayyiba claimed responsibility.

13 India
In Anantnag, Kashmir, a bomb exploded at a bus stop, killing one person and injuring 21 others. No one claimed responsibility.

20 Germany
In Berlin, militants occupied the Iraqi Embassy, taking hostage six Iraqi nationals and injuring two persons. German police ended the five-hour siege and arrested the five militants. The Democratic Iraqi Opposition is responsible.

25 Afghanistan
In Kabul, a bomb exploded outside the United Nations main guesthouse, injuring two persons. There were 50 persons living at the guesthouse. No one claimed responsibility.

28 Ecuador
In Guayaquil, a pamphlet bomb exploded at a McDonald's restaurant, injuring three persons and causing major property damage. The Revolutionary Armed Forces of Ecuador is responsible.

31 India
In Mahore, armed militants entered the private residence of a Revenue Department official who had been deployed on election duty, killing three persons. No one claimed responsibility.

September

3 India
In Langet, Kashmir, armed militants attacked a political rally, killing three persons and injuring four others. No one claimed responsibility.

3 India
In Kishtwar, Kashmir, a bomb exploded near the downtown area, injuring 19 persons. The Hizb ul-Mujahedin is possibly responsible.

6 Macedonia
In Skopje, a bomb exploded in a restaurant, injuring two persons including one Turkish citizen. No one claimed responsibility.

8 India
In Dodasanpal, Kashmir, armed militants killed five persons and injured one other. No one claimed responsibility.

11 India
In Dhamhal Hanjipora, Kashmir, militants hurled a grenade at the private residence of the Minister of Tourism, injuring four persons inside. No one claimed responsibility

11 India
In Tikipora, Kashmir, armed militants killed the Law Minister and six security guards escorting him while he was out campaigning. Three different groups claimed responsibility: Lashkar-e-Tayyiba, Jamiat ul-Mujahedin, and Hizb ul-Mujahedin.

15 India
In Dhamhal Hanjipora, Kashmir, armed militants fired on then threw an improvised explosive device at the motorcade carrying the Minister of Tourism, killing a police officer and injuring two others. The Minister of Tourism escaped unharmed. No one claimed responsibility.

17 India
In Srinagar, Kashmir, armed militants shot and injured the leading editor of the *Urdu Daily Srinagar Times* at his private residence. No one claimed responsibility.

17 India
In Srinagar, militants lobbed a grenade at the office of a local political party, injuring a security guard. No one claimed responsibility.

18 West Bank
In Yahad, gunmen ambushed and overturned a vehicle on the Mevo Dotan-Hermesh Road, killing one person, an Israeli, and wounding a Romanian worker. The Al-Aqsa Martyrs Brigades claimed responsibility.

19 Israel
In Tel Aviv, a suicide bomber boarded a bus and detonated the explosive device concealed in his backpack, killing five Israelis and one UK citizen and wounding 52 others, according to media and US Embassy reporting. HAMAS claimed responsibility.

20 India
In Jammu, Kashmir, armed militants killed a senior National Conference Party worker in his home. No one claimed responsibility.

20 India
In Srinagar, Kashmir, armed militants opposed to Indian held elections, killed a political activist of the ruling National Conference Party. A National Conference leader stated that the Hizb ul-Mujahedin may be responsible.

22 India
In Shopian, Kashmir, armed militants threw grenades and then fired at the residence of the ruling National Conference legislator who was in residence at the time but was unharmed in the attack. No one claimed responsibility.

22 India
In Bandgam, Kashmir, armed militants shot and killed the Ruling Block president. No one claimed responsibility.

23 India
In Bijbiara, Kashmir, militants hurled a grenade at a vehicle belonging to the Jammu and Kashmir's Peoples Democratic Party. The grenade missed its target and exploded on the roadside, injuring eight persons. No one claimed responsibility.

23 India
In Sangam, Kashmir, armed militants attempted to hurl a grenade at a political rally, but it missed the intended victims, exploded near a group of private citizens and injured eight persons. No one claimed responsibility.

23 India
In Srinagar, Kashmir, militants hurled a grenade at an army vehicle but missed its target and exploded in a crowded marketplace, injuring 12 persons and two police officers. No one claimed responsibility.

27 India
In Pulwama, Kashmir, a grenade exploded on the road, injuring 17 persons and five soldiers. The attack came right before India's scheduled elections.

28 India
In Devsar, Kashmir, a landmine exploded under a vehicle carrying a National Congress Party member and three other persons. The explosion killed the three passengers and injured the National Congress Party member. No one claimed responsibility.

29 India
In Tral, Kashmir, militants threw a grenade at a bus station, killing one person and injuring 12 others, according to press reports. No one claimed responsibility.

29 India
In Ganderbal, Kashmir, armed militants killed a political activist belonging to the ruling National Conference Party. No one claimed responsibility.

30 India
In Manda Chowk, Kashmir, a timed device exploded on a bus carrying Hindu pilgrims, killing one person and injuring 18 others. No one claimed responsibility.

October

1 India
In Kathu, Kashmir, militants hijacked a minivan, driving it into a utility pole near an open-air vegetable market. The gunmen fired grenades at the minivan, killing all nine passengers. The Al-Arifeen, an offshoot group of the Lashkar-e-Tayyiba, claimed responsibility.

2 India
In Haihama, Kashmir, armed militants killed three political activists working with India's ruling National Conference Party. The Al-Arifeen, an offshoot group of the Lashkar-e-Tayyaiba, claimed responsibility.

6 Yemen
In al Dhubbah, a small boat carrying a large amount of explosives rammed the hull of the French oil tanker Limburg as it was anchored approximately 5 miles from port. The attack killed one person and wounded four others. Al-Qaida is probably responsible.

8 India
In Doda, Kashmir, armed militants hurled grenades and then fired into a polling station, causing no injuries. No one claimed responsibility.

8 India
In Kashmir, militants attempted to throw a grenade at a security patrol, but the grenade missed the target and exploded in a crowded marketplace, injuring 14 persons. No one claimed responsibility.

8 Kuwait
On Failaka Island, gunmen attacked US soldiers while they were conducting a non-live-fire exercise, killing one US Marine and wounding one other. Al-Qaida claimed responsibility.

12 Indonesia
In Manado, a bomb exploded near the Philippine Consulate, damaging the front gate and breaking several windows. No one claimed responsibility.

12 Indonesia
In Bali, a car bomb exploded outside the Sari Club Discotheque on Legian Street, a busy tourist area filled with nightclubs, cafes, and bars, killing at least 187 international tourists and injuring about 300 others. The resulting fire also destroyed the nearby Padi Club and Panin Bank and other buildings and cars. Al-Qaida claimed responsibility for this attack.

20 India
In Onagam, armed militants killed three persons and injured two others near a mosque. No one claimed responsibility.

23 Russia
In Moscow, 50 armed Chechen rebels took control of the Palace of Culture Theater to demand an end to the war in Chechnya. The theater was rigged with landmines and explosive devices to control hostages and promote leverage with Russian authorities. The rebels held more than 800 hostages including foreign nationals from the United Kingdom, France, Belarus, Germany, Azerbaijan, Georgia, Bulgaria, Netherlands, Ukraine, Israel, Austria, United States, and two permanent residents of the United States. During the three-day siege, rebels killed one Russian police officer and five Russian hostages.

On 26 October, the third day of the siege, Russian Special Forces administered the anesthetic gas fentanyl through the ventilation system. Commandos stormed the theater and killed all of the Chechen rebels after a brief gun battle. In the rescue attempt, 124 hostages died including citizens from Russia (115), United States (1), Azerbaijan (1), Netherlands (1), Ukraine (2), Armenia (1), Austria (1), Kazakhstan (1), and Belarus (1). Chechen rebels led by Movsar Barayev claimed responsibility.

25 Russia

In Moscow, an explosive device described as a shrapnel-filled artillery shell equivalent to five kilograms of TNT exploded in an automobile parked in a McDonald's parking lot, killing one person and injuring eight others. The explosion caused major damage to the restaurant. The explosive device was similar to the type commonly used in Chechnya. Russian authorities arrested a Chechen male in connection with the explosion. No one claimed responsibility.

28 Jordan

In Amman, press reports stated that gunmen shot and killed a US diplomat, the senior administrator at the US Agency for International Development (USAID). The Honest People of Jordan claimed responsibility.

November

18 Turkey

In Istanbul, an Israeli Arab attempted to hijack El Al Flight 581, 15 minutes before landing. The passenger ran toward the cockpit, attacked the stewardess with a penknife, and demanded that she open the cockpit door. Security guards simultaneously overpowered the man and took him into custody. Shin Bet stated that his actions were nationalistically motivated. No one claimed responsibility.

21 Israel

In Jerusalem, a suicide bomber entered a bus on Mexico Street near Kiryat Menachem and detonated the explosive device he was wearing, killing 11 persons including a Romanian citizen and wounding 50 others, according to media and US Consulate reports. HAMAS claimed responsibility.

21 Kuwait

In Kuwait City, a Kuwaiti police officer stopped and shot two US soldiers driving a rental car, wounding both, according to media and US Embassy reports. The military personnel were both in uniform and armed but did not return fire. No group claimed responsibility.

21 Lebanon

In Sidon, a gunman shot and killed a US citizen who was an office manager/nurse for a church-run health facility, according to media and US Embassy reports. The female victim, married to a citizen of the United Kingdom, was shot as she entered the facility. An Asbat al-Ansar–linked extremist is probably responsible.

24 India

In Jammu, Kashmir, armed militants attacked the Reghunath and Shiv temples, killing 13 persons and wounding 50 others. The Lashkar-e-Tayyiba claimed responsibility for this attack.

28 Kenya

In Mombasa, a vehicle containing three suicide bombers drove into the front of the Paradise Hotel and exploded, killing 15 persons including three Israelis and 12 Kenyans and wounding 40 others including 18 Israelis and 22 Kenyans. Al-Qaida, the Government of Universal Palestine in Exile, and the Army of Palestine claimed responsibility. Al-Ittihad al-Islami (AIAI) is probably linked to the attack.

28 Kenya

In Mombasa, two SA-7 Strela anti-aircraft missiles were launched but missed downing a Arkia Boeing 757 taking off from Mombasa enroute to Israel. The aircraft carried 261 passengers and continued its flight. Al-Qaida, the Government of Universal Palestine in Exile, and the Army of Palestine claimed responsibility. AIAI is probably linked to the attack according to reports.

30 India

In Awantipora, Kashmir, a grenade exploded, injuring four persons. No one claimed responsibility.

30 India

In Srinagar, Kashmir, a bomb exploded near a police vehicle, injuring seven persons. No one claimed responsibility.

30 India

In Srinagar, Kashmir, a bomb exploded near a police vehicle, injuring seven persons. No one claimed responsibility.

December

4 India

In Srinagar, Kashmir, authorities safely defused a bomb found at a bus station. No one claimed responsibility.

5 Pakistan

In Karachi, a bomb exploded at the Macedonia Consulate destroying the consulate building. When the authorities searched through the debris, they found three local workers with their throats slit. No one claimed responsibility.

6 India

In Rajpora Chowk, Kashmir, militants threw a grenade toward a vehicle carrying several military officers, but it missed its mark and landed near a group of private citizens, injuring eight persons. No one claimed responsibility.

6 India

In Damhal Hanjipora, Kashmir, militants threw a grenade and fired shots at the private residence of a former minister. The Lashkar-e-Tayyiba probably is responsible.

6 India

In Pulwama, Kashmir, armed militants killed the brother of the recently slain Law Minister outside his private residence. The militants threw a grenade then fired shots at him. The Lashkar-e-Tayyiba claimed responsibility in a communique to a local television station.

6 India

In Bombay, a bomb exploded at a local McDonald's restaurant located in a busy rail station mall, injuring 23 persons. The bomb consisted of gunpowder, nails, and iron balls and followed a bomb attack on 6 December at a McDonald's outlet in the Indonesian city of Makassar. No one claimed responsibility.

6 Indonesia

In Makassar, a bomb exploded in a McDonald's restaurant, killing three persons, injuring 11 others, and causing major damage to the restaurant. No one claimed responsibility though police are focusing on a hardline Islamic group, Laskar Jundullah.

18 India

In Yaripora, Kashmir, militants lobbed a hand grenade at a parked military vehicle, but it missed its target and landed near a group of private citizens, injuring 15 persons, three military personnel, and causing major damage to the military vehicle. No one claimed responsibility.

20 India

In Kashmir, armed militants killed a newly elected state legislator. No one claimed responsibility.

24 Pakistan

In Islamabad, authorities safely dismantled several grenades and about 30 rounds of ammunition, which had been placed in a bag near a church where local and Western worshippers were to gather for Christmas services. An anonymous phone call to the local authorities had warned that a bomb had been placed near the church. No one claimed responsibility.

26 Philippines

In Zamboanga del Norte, armed militants ambushed a bus carrying Filipino workers employed by a local Canadian mining company, killing 13 persons and injuring 10 others. Police said that the Moro Islamic Liberation Front (MILF) had been extorting money from the workers' employer, the Calgary-based mining firm Toronto Ventures Inc. Pacific. The Catholic charity Caritas-Philippines said that the Canadian mining company has been harassing tribesmen opposed to mining operations on their ancestral lands. Authorities have accused the MILF of carrying out the attack.

27 Chechnya

In Grozny, suicide bombers drove two trucks packed with explosives to the headquarters of Chechnya's pro-Moscow government building and detonated them, killing 72 persons and wounding 210 others. Chechen officials believe the explosives had the force of one ton of TNT and left a 20-foot-wide crater. The explosions destroyed the government building and caused extensive damage to surrounding government facilities. The Kavkaz Center, which operates a Chechen Web site, reported that Chechen shaheeds (martyrs) were responsible.

30 Yemen

In Jibla, a gunman entered a Baptist missionary hospital, killing three persons and wounding one other, all US citizens. The gunman is believed to have acted alone. He admitted, however, to being affiliated with the Islah Party and coordinated the attack with Ali al-Jarala who had killed Yemeni Socialist Party leader Jarala Omar.

2003

January

5 Israel

In Tel Aviv, two suicide bombers attacked simultaneously, according to media reports. Victims included 23 killed (15 Israelis, two Romanian citizens, one citizen from Ghana, one Bulgarian citizen, three Chinese citizens, and one Ukrainian citizen) and 107 wounded (nationalities not specified). The attack took place in the vicinity of the old central bus station, where foreign national workers live. The detonations took place within seconds of each other and were approximately 600 feet apart—one in a pedestrian mall and one in front of a bus stop. The al-Aqsa Martyrs Brigade is considered responsible.

5 Pakistan

In Peshawar, two gunmen fired on the residence of an Afghan diplomat, injuring a guard, according to press reports. The diplomat was not in residence at the time of the incident. No one claimed responsibility.

5 India

In Kulgam, Kashmir, a grenade exploded at a bus station, wounding 40 (36 private citizens and four security personnel), according to press reports. No one claimed responsibility.

14 Panama

In Darien, rebels kidnapped three U.S. citizens, including a reporter, and released them ten days later, according to press reports. Media reports state the United Self-Defense Forces of Colombia are probably responsible.

17 West Bank

In Givat Harina, two gunmen killed one person and wounded three others, all Israelis, according to press reports. The Islamic Resistance Movement (HAMAS) claimed responsibility.

21 Kuwait

In Kuwait City, a gunman ambushed a vehicle at an intersection where the car had halted for a stoplight. Victims included one U.S. citizen killed and one U.S. citizen wounded, according to media reports. The victims were civilian contractors working for the U.S. military. The incident took place close to Camp Doha, an installation housing approximately 17,000 U.S. troops.

21 Colombia
In Tame, rebels kidnapped two journalists working for the *Los Angeles Times* newspaper. One was a British reporter and the other a U.S. photographer. The National Liberation Army (ELN) is considered responsible. On 1 February 2003, the two journalists were released unharmed.

23/24 Kuwait
A Kuwaiti was apprehended attempting to cross the border from Kuwait to Saudi Arabia. The 20-year-old Kuwaiti civil servant, Sami al-Mutayri, confessed to the 21 January attack and stated that he embraces al-Qaida ideology and implements Osama Bin Ladin's instructions, although there is no evidence of an organizational link. The assailant acted alone but had assistance in planning the ambush. No group claimed responsibility.

27 Afghanistan
In Nangarhar, armed militants attacked a convoy, killing two security officers escorting several United Nations vehicles, according to press reports. No one claimed responsibility.

31 India
In Srinagar, Kashmir, India, armed militants shot and killed a local journalist in his office, according to press reports. No one claimed responsibility.

February

5 Saudi Arabia
In Riyadh, three gunmen fired five shots at the vehicle of a United Kingdom citizen as he was traveling from work to home, according to television reports. The victim, a British Airways employee, received only superficial wounds from broken glass. No one claimed responsibility.

7 Saudi Arabia
In Riyadh, eight gunmen fired on police, killing one Kuwaiti and wounding three others, including two policemen.

13 Colombia
Five crew members (four U.S. citizen-U.S. Government defense contractors and one Columbian citizen) survived an airplane crash, although two were injured. They were subsequently captured by militants. A Colombian service member and a U.S. citizen were later shot and killed by the militants, according to press reports. The Revolutionary Armed Forces of Colombia (FARC) claim they are holding captive the three missing U.S. persons. As of 18 June 2004, the three were still being held by the FARC.

20 India
In Varmul, a landmine planted near a busy marketplace exploded, killing six and wounding three, according to press reports. No one claimed responsibility.

20 Saudi Arabia
In Riyadh, a gunman ambushed a car at a stoplight, killing one—a United Kingdom citizen employed by British Aerospace Engineering (BAE), according to press reports. The

gunman, arrested by Saudi police, is a Yemen-born naturalized Saudi. No group claimed responsibility.

20 Algeria

The Swiss Embassy in Algeria reported four Swiss citizens were missing while touring the Sahara Desert in a small group without a guide, according to press reports. The tourists were later confirmed kidnapped by the Salafist Group for Call and Combat (GSPC).

From mid-February to mid-May, there were eight separate incidents of the kidnapping of European tourists by the GSPC. The 32 hostages from the various incidents were later intermingled. Algerian Special Forces rescued 17 hostages on 13 May 2003. One hostage, a German woman, died 28 July of heatstroke while in captivity. On 18 August, the remaining 14 hostages were released in northern Mali. Press reports claimed a ransom of 4.6 million euros was paid to the GSPC in return for the hostages' freedom.

22 Algeria

The German Embassy in Algeria reported four German citizens were missing while touring the Sahara desert in a small group without a guide, according to press reports. The tourists were later confirmed kidnapped by terrorist members of the Salafist Group for Call and Combat (GSPC).

From mid-February to mid-May, there were eight separate incidents of the kidnapping of European tourists by the GSPC. The 32 hostages from the various incidents were later intermingled. Algerian Special Forces rescued 17 hostages on 13 May 2003. One hostage, a German woman, died 28 July of heatstroke while in captivity. On 18 August, the remaining 14 hostages were released in northern Mali. Press reports claimed a ransom of 4.6 million euros was paid to the GSPC in return for the hostages' freedom

25 Venezuela

In Caracas, two bombs exploded within minutes of each other, wounding four (one Colombian and three Venezuelans). The blasts also damaged the Spanish and Colombian Embassies and other buildings nearby. No one claimed responsibility.

25 Saudi Arabia

In al-Dammam, an incendiary bomb was thrown at a McDonald's restaurant, according to press reports. Two people in a car approached the business, and the passenger got out and hurled the canister. When the bomb failed to explode, the perpetrator unsuccessfully attempted to ignite the device, and then fled in the vehicle. Employees called authorities, and after an investigation, police arrested a person whose clothes contained the same substance as that found in the bomb. The suspect was later identified by witnesses. No group claimed responsibility.

March

2 Venezuela

In Maracaibo, at around 5:00 AM, a car bomb exploded. The blast damaged surrounding buildings, including a local office of the U.S. oil company Chevron Texaco, according to press reports. The car bomb was composed of explosives similar to the substance used in the bombings at the Spanish and Colombian Embassies the previous week. The explosion occurred directly outside the home of controversial cattle livestock producer, Antonio Melian. Mr. Melian is a leading activist in Zulia State, and he has been the center of opposition-government debate following the two-month nationwide labor-management work stoppage, which failed in its aim to bring down the Chavez Frias government. No one claimed responsibility.

4 Philippines

In Davao, Philippines, a bomb hidden in a backpack exploded in a crowded airline terminal, killing 21 (one U.S. citizen) and wounding 149 (including three U.S. citizens), according to press reports.

5 Israel

In Haifa, a suicide bomber detonated an explosive device aboard a bus on Moriya Boulevard in the Karmel neighborhood. Victims included 15 killed (including one U.S. citizen) and 40 wounded, according to media reports. HAMAS claimed responsibility.

7 West Bank

In Qiryat Arba, two gunmen disguised as Orthodox Jewish students infiltrated and attacked the settlement, killing three (two U.S. citizens) and wounding eight, according to media reports. HAMAS claimed responsibility.

9 India

In Doda District, Kashmir, armed militants kidnapped and killed a private citizen, according to press reports. No one claimed responsibility.

11 India

In Rajouri, Kashmir, a bomb exploded in a candy store, killing two and wounding nine, according to press reports. No group has claimed responsibility.

13 India

In Rajouri, Kashmir, at 11:10 AM a bomb exploded on a bus parked at a terminal, killing four, according to press reports. No one claimed responsibility.

16 India

In Indh, Kashmir, armed militants attacked a police installation, killing 11 (nine police officers and two civilians) and wounding nine (eight police officers and one civilian), according to press reports. No one claimed responsibility.

20 Lebanon

In Sidon, an explosive device consisting of approximately 2 kilograms of TNT exploded, killing two persons and wounding nine others. The bomb was placed on the first-floor stairs of an apartment building where the likely target, a Dutch woman, lived with her Lebanese husband. Three apartments were damaged and a number of cars set ablaze from the explosion. No one claimed responsibility.

22 Greece
In Koropi, a makeshift incendiary device exploded in an ATM outside a Citibank branch. The explosion and subsequent fire caused severe damage to the ATM. No one claimed responsibility.

22 Iraq
In Sayed Sadiq, a taxi raced up alongside an Australian journalist and exploded, killing one (an Australian journalist/cameraman) and wounding ten (an Australian on assignment for Australian Broadcasting Corporation and nine others). Ansar al-Islam is believed to be responsible.

24 India
In Nadi Marg, Kashmir, armed militants dressed in military uniforms entered and attacked a village. Victims included 11 men, 11 women, and two small boys who were lined up and shot and killed by the gunmen, according to press reports. No group claimed responsibility.

25–26 Italy
In Vicenza, extremists firebombed three cars belonging to U.S. service members. The Anti-Imperialist Territorial Nuclei, an extremist group believed to be close to the new Red Brigades, has claimed responsibility for the attacks.

25 Serbia
In Pristina, four bomb attacks were carried out on the same day against the UN Interim Administration Mission in Kosovo (UNMIK) police stations. UNMIK police suspect the founder and commander of a local mujahidin unit was responsible for this attack.

26 India
In Narwal, Kashmir, a bomb placed inside the engine of an empty oil tanker parked outside a fuel storage area exploded and caught fire, killing one and wounding six, according to press reports. No one claimed responsibility.

26 Chile
In Santiago, around 11:00 PM, anti-war protesters exploded a small bomb at a branch of the U.S.-based BancBoston. The bomb smashed windows, destroyed an ATM, and caused minor damage to two adjacent stores. No one has claimed responsibility.

28 Afghanistan
In Tirin Kot, armed militants shot and killed a Salvadoran Red Cross worker, according to press reports. The victim was traveling with Afghan colleagues to check on water supplies when his group was captured. The leader of the militants was instructed via telephone to kill the only Westerner in the captured group. No one claimed responsibility.

28 Italy
In Rome, extremists firebombed a Ford and Jaguar dealership, two brands taken as symbols of the Anglo-American coalition that is fighting in Iraq. Approximately a dozen Fords were burned and another ten damaged. A five-pointed star, a symbol of the Red Brigades, was found at the site; however, the Red Brigades are not known to plan firebomb attacks. No one claimed responsibility.

29 Greece

In Athens, at approximately 1:20 AM, an unknown assailant threw a hand grenade at a McDonald's restaurant, causing significant property damage. No one claimed responsibility.

30 India

In Poonch, Kashmir, a bomb exploded in a field during a cricket match, killing one and wounding two, according to press reports. No one claimed responsibility.

31 Cuba

In Havana, a man armed with two grenades hijacked a domestic airliner with 46 passengers and crew aboard in an attempt to reach the United States. After making an emergency landing at a Havana airport due to insufficient fuel, the plane was kept all night on the runway.

On the next day, 1 April 2003, more than 20 passengers left the aircraft, apparently unharmed. With at least 25 passengers on board, the hijacked plane then departed the Havana airport and safely landed in Key West, Florida.

April

2 Philippines

In Davao, a bomb exploded on a crowded passenger wharf. There were 16 killed and 55 wounded, according to press reports. This attack is believed to have been carried out by two Indonesian members of Jemaah Islamiyah, a regional terrorist group with links to al-Qaida. Two individuals were later arrested. Ismael Acmad, also known as Toto, was identified as the alleged planner. Tahome Urong, also known as Sermin Tohami, was identified as an alleged accomplice. They reportedly belong to the Special Operations Group of the Moro Islamic Liberation Front (MILF). The two men told investigators they were also involved in the Davao Airport bombing and were given funds to carry out these attacks by Jemaah Islamiyah.

The ammonium nitrate explosive used in the wharf attack is similar to that purchased by a Jemaah Islamiyah operative, Fathur Rohman Ghozi, and seized by police in January 2002 shortly after Ghozi's arrest by Philippine police. Several Indonesian members of Jemaah Islamiyah have been spotted in terrorist training camps on the southern island of Mindanao.

3 Turkey

In Istanbul, at around 12:50 AM, a bomb went off near the British Consulate General. The blast caused considerable damage to the Consulate and blew out windows of an adjacent hotel, leaving one Turkish hotel guest with minor cuts.

Turkish police believe the bomb was a resonant device (sound bomb) of relatively crude construction. The terrorist group MLK-P (Marxist-Leninist Communist Party) is suspected to be responsible, although no one has claimed responsibility for the attack.

3 Algeria

In the Sahara Desert, eight Austrian tourists were kidnapped by terrorists while traveling in that region, according to press reports. The Salafist Group for Call and Combat (GSPC) is considered responsible for the abduction.

From mid-February to mid-May, there were eight separate incidents of the kidnapping of European tourists by the GSPC. The 32 hostages from the various incidents were later intermingled. Algerian Special Forces rescued 17 hostages on 13 May 2003. One hostage, a German woman, died 28 July of heatstroke while in captivity. On 18 August, the remaining 14 hostages were released in northern Mali. Press reports claimed a ransom of 4.6 million euros was paid to the GSPC in return for the hostages' freedom.

4 Algeria

In the Sahara Desert, terrorists kidnapped 11 German tourists traveling in small groups without guides, bringing the total number of Germans abducted (up to this point) to 15. The Salafist Group for Call and Combat (GSPC) is considered responsible.

From mid-February to mid-May, there were eight separate incidents of the kidnapping of European tourists by the GSPC. The 32 hostages from the various incidents were later intermingled. Algerian Special Forces rescued 17 hostages on 13 May 2003. One hostage, a German woman, died 28 July of heatstroke while in captivity. On 18 August, the remaining 14 hostages were released in northern Mali. Press reports claimed a ransom of 4.6 million euros was paid to the GSPC in return for the hostages' freedom.

5 Lebanon

In Dowra, at 4:40 PM, 500 grams of TNT placed in the men's room trash receptacle of a McDonald's restaurant exploded, according to media and U.S. Embassy reports. Victims included ten wounded. The restaurant also sustained considerable damage. Five to ten seconds later, a minor explosion took place in a vehicle adjacent to the building. The explosion was a partial detonation of a three-stage improvised explosive device (IED) that consisted of three timers, 50 kilograms of TNT, an unidentified quantity of C-4, and three gas-filled containers. No one claimed responsibility.

8 Jordan

In Amman, Jordan, at 10:45 PM, three militants fired a shot at a U.S. official outside his hotel, when he stepped out to make a call, according to press reports. The sole victim was lightly wounded. No one claimed responsibility.

8 Algeria

In the Sahara Desert, one Swede and one Dutch citizen were kidnapped, according to press reports. The Salafist Group for Call and Combat (GSPC) is considered responsible for kidnapping the two tourists.

From mid-February to mid-May, there were eight separate incidents of the kidnapping of European tourists by the GSPC. The 32 hostages from the various incidents were later intermingled. Algerian Special Forces rescued 17 hostages on 13 May 2003. One hostage, a German woman, died 28 July of heatstroke while in captivity. On 18 August, the remaining 14 hostages were released in northern Mali. Press reports claimed a ransom of 4.6 million euros was paid to the GSPC in return for the hostages' freedom.

11 Algeria

The Austrian Foreign Ministry reported two mountaineers disappeared while in the Sahara Desert, Algeria, bringing the total number of Austrian tourists recently abducted in that area to ten, according to press reports. The Salafist Group for Call and Combat (GSPC) is considered responsible for kidnapping the two tourists.

From mid-February to mid-May, there were eight separate incidents of the kidnapping of European tourists by the GSPC. The 32 hostages from the various incidents were later intermingled. Algerian Special Forces rescued 17 hostages on 13 May 2003. One hostage, a German woman, died 28 July of heatstroke while in captivity. On 18 August, the remaining 14 hostages were released in northern Mali. Press reports claimed a ransom of 4.6 million euros was paid to the GSPC in return for the hostages' freedom.

12 India

In Anantnag, Kashmir, militants threw a grenade into a bus station, killing one and wounding 20, according to press reports. No one claimed responsibility.

In Anantnag, Kashmir, militants threw a grenade at an army patrol, wounding 23 (two soldiers and 21 civilian bystanders), according to press reports. No one claimed responsibility.

12 India

In Kulgam, Kashmir, militants threw a grenade at a police patrol, but missed, wounding two civilian bystanders, according to press reports. No one claimed responsibility.

12 Venezuela

In Caracas, at 2:40 AM, a bomb made of C-4 exploded in the Organization of American States (OAS) office. No one was injured, but the basement was significantly damaged. No one claimed responsibility.

13 Pakistan

Near Chaman, armed militants shot relatives of the Governor of Kandahar, Afghanistan, while they and the Governor were traveling by car to a local bazaar, killing two and wounding one, according to press reports. One attacker was later caught by authorities.

14 France

In Sergy, militants set fire to a car parked outside the rear entrance of a McDonald's restaurant. The blaze partially destroyed the restaurant. No one claimed responsibility.

15 Turkey

In Istanbul, extremists bombed a McDonald's restaurant. A wall partially collapsed, injuring a pedestrian. The Revolutionary People's Liberation Party/Front (DHKP/C) claimed responsibility.

15 Turkey

In Istanbul, extremists bombed a second McDonald's restaurant. No injuries were reported. The Revolutionary People's Liberation Front (DHKP/C) claimed responsibility.

15 Gaza Strip
At the Karni (Qarni) border crossing, a gunman, hiding in the inspection booths, killed two persons and wounded six others, all Israelis, according to media reports. HAMAS claimed responsibility.

16 Afghanistan
In Jalalabad, a bomb destroyed the UNICEF building, according to press reports. No one claimed responsibility.

22 India
In Gulshanpora Batagund, Kashmir, a bomb exploded in a dairy yard, killing six and wounding 12, according to press reports. No one claimed responsibility.

24 Israel
In Kefar Saba, a suicide bomber blew himself up at the entrance to a busy train station, killing a security guard, who was a dual citizen of Israel and Russia, and wounding 11, according to press reports. The Al-Aqsa Martyrs Brigade claimed responsibility.

25 India
In Patan, Kashmir, India, a bomb exploded on the lawn of a courthouse, killing three and wounding 34, according to press reports. No one claimed responsibility.

26 India
In Kashmir, a landmine exploded near a site being inspected by the Finance Minister, injuring 11. The Finance Minister was not injured, according to press reports. No one claimed responsibility.

30 Israel
In Tel Aviv, suicide bombers attacked a pub, Mike's Place, popular with foreigners, just a few hundred yards from the U.S. Embassy. One of the bombers detonated his device, killing three Israeli citizens and wounding 64 others, including one U.S. citizen, according to press reports. The second bomber fled the scene after his bomb failed to detonate. His body was later found washed up on a Tel Aviv beach. HAMAS and Al-Aqsa Martyrs Brigade have claimed responsibility.

May

5 India
In Doda, Kashmir, at 11:00 AM, a bomb exploded at a bus stand. Victims included one killed and 25 injured, according to press reports. No one claimed responsibility.

5 India
In Duderhama, Kashmir, militants threw a grenade at a National Conference leader's car, injuring the leader who was inside, according to press reports. No one claimed responsibility.

9 Israel
In Sederot, six rockets fired on a kibbutz settlement injured two persons, according to press reports. HAMAS claimed responsibility.

12 Saudi Arabia

In Riyadh, at about 11:15 PM, suicide bombers driving booby-trapped cars filled with explosives drove into the guarded Jedawal compound, which housed international workers, killing four Saudi citizens, according to press reports. Al-Qaida is considered responsible.

12 Saudi Arabia

In Riyadh, suicide bombers driving booby-trapped cars filled with explosives drove into the Al-Hamra complex, killing 11 (one U.S. citizen, two Jordanian citizens, four Saudi citizens, two Filipino citizens, one Lebanese citizen, and one Swiss citizen) and wounding 194, according to press reports. Al-Qaida is considered responsible for this attack.

12 Saudi Arabia

In Riyadh, suicide bombers driving booby-trapped cars filled with explosives drove into the guarded Vinnell housing complex, killing 15 (eight U.S. citizens and seven Saudi citizens) and wounding 22 (including six U.S. citizens), according to press reports. Al-Qaida is considered responsible.

12 Algeria

According to press reports of 12 May 2003, terrorists had kidnapped a German tourist in the Sahara, bringing the total number of German tourists kidnapped recently to 16. The kidnapping possibly took place in April or early May timeframe. The Salafist Group for Call and Combat (GSPC) is considered responsible for the abduction.

From mid-February to mid-May, there were eight separate incidents of the kidnapping of European tourists by the GSPC. The 32 hostages from the various incidents were later intermingled. Algerian Special Forces rescued 17 hostages on May 13, 2003. One hostage, a German woman, died July 28 of heatstroke while in captivity. On 18 August, the remaining 14 hostages were released in northern Mali. Press reports claimed a ransom of 4.6 million euros was paid to the GSPC in return for the hostages' freedom.

16 Morocco

In Casablanca, five near-simultaneous bomb attacks occurred at or near a restaurant, hotel, Jewish cemetery, Jewish Community Center, and the Belgian Consulate, killing 33 (including three Spaniards and one Italian) and wounding 101, according to press reports. The group Salafiya Jihadiya with possible links to al-Qaida, is considered responsible.

19 Israel

In French Hill Intersection, Northern Jerusalem, at about 6:00 AM, a suicide bomber dressed as an Orthodox Jew and wearing a prayer shawl boarded a commuter bus and detonated the bombs he had attached to himself. Victims included seven killed and 26 wounded (one U.S. citizen), according to press reports. HAMAS claimed responsibility for this attack.

19 India

In Srinagar, Kashmir, India, two bombs exploded at Kashmir's busiest bus terminal, wounding 14, according to press reports. No one claimed responsibility.

19 India

In Rajouri, Kashmir, armed militants fired into a private residence, killing six, according to press reports. No one claimed responsibility.

23 Gaza Strip

In Netzarim, an anti-tank missile fired at an Israeli bus injuring nine passengers, according to press reports. HAMAS claimed responsibility.

24 Afghanistan

In Haska Meyna, a remote-controlled land mine exploded under a vehicle. Three NGO workers were injured, according to press reports. No one claimed responsibility.

27 Colombia

In Guamalito, guerillas attacked a section of the Cano Limon-Covenas oil pipeline, spilling nearly 7,000 barrels of crude oil and leaving about 4,700 families without drinking water, according to press reports.

This pipeline is jointly owned by Ecopetrol of Colombia and a consortium of U.S. and West European companies. No group claimed responsibility, although both the Revolutionary Armed Forces of Colombia and the National Liberation Army (ELN) guerillas have previously attacked this pipeline.

June

1 India

In Jammu, Kashmir, militants set fire to a private residence and exchanged gunfire with police while fleeing the scene, killing two civilians and wounding two others in the crossfire, according to press reports. The militants escaped. No one claimed responsibility.

4 Belgium

In Brussels, letters containing the nerve agent adamsite were sent to the U.S., British, and Saudi Embassies as well as the office of Prime Minister Guy Verhofstadt, the Court of Brussels, a Belgian ministry, the Oostende Airport, and the Antwerp Port Authority, according to press reports.

Victims included ten people who were hospitalized. At least two postal workers and five policemen were hospitalized with skin irritation, eye irritation, and breathing difficulty. In Oostende, three persons exposed to the tainted letter at the airport authority were taken to a hospital for further observation.

Belgian police investigated a 45-year-old Iraqi political refugee who had repeatedly expressed opposition to the war in Iraq. In searching the suspect's residence on 5 June, police confiscated a document that resembled a chemical formula and a plastic bag containing powder. The next day anti-terrorism investigators opened the plastic bag, releasing some of the powder and suffered skin irritation, eye irritation, and difficulty breathing. The Iraqi was charged that day with premeditated assault.

7 Afghanistan

In Kabul, a taxi rigged with explosives rammed into a bus carrying German peacekeepers of the International Security Assistance Force (ISAF) heading to the airport for their return home. Five were killed and 29 wounded, according to press reports. The U.S.-funded police school, which stands about 300 feet from the explosion, was damaged. No one claimed responsibility, but al-Qaida is suspected.

8 Somalia

In Mogadishu, an armed militia group fired several times on a car carrying an American freelance journalist, his driver, and his interpreter. The journalist was slightly wounded, according to press reports. No one claimed responsibility.

9 Peru

In Lima, approximately 60 Shining Path terrorists kidnapped 71 workers employed by Techint Group, an Argentine company helping to build a natural gas pipeline in southeastern Peru. The kidnapped group consisted of 64 Peruvians, four Colombians, two Argentines, and one Chilean. All of the hostages were freed on 11 June 2003 through a successful rescue operation by Peruvian authorities. The terrorists, however, managed to escape.

11 Turkey

In Adana, a man threw two hand grenades into the garden of the U.S. Consulate, allegedly in retaliation for a recent assassination attempt by Israel on a leader of HAMAS. One of the grenades did not explode and was later securely detonated by the police. No one was injured, according to press reports.

11 Israel

Near Jerusalem, a suicide bomber who was a member of HAMAS boarded a bus and exploded a bomb near Klal Center on Jaffa Road, killing 17 (including two U.S. citizens) and wounding 99 (including one U.S citizen).

11 Greece

In Thessaloniki, unidentified attackers entered the front lobby of the U.S.-owned Citibank branch and doused the ATM in a flammable liquid. They then placed a gas canister in the ATM machine and set it on fire. The resulting explosion destroyed the machine and caused extensive damage to the lobby and office equipment, according to press reports.

17 Italy

In Rome, a bomb exploded in front of the Cervantes Spanish School (Liceo Cervantes), damaging the school and a few cars within a 20-meter radius. Authorities believe that the device contained approximately 500 grams of chlorite and nitrate-based explosives.

According to the Carabinieri, the roof of the school is the terrace of the Spanish Ambassador's residence. Although no one claimed responsibility for the attack, according to press reports, investigators believe that whoever placed the device had experience with explosives and was most likely connected to an Italian anarchist group that aligns itself with the ETA Basque terrorist group. Similar devices have been used in past attacks against Spanish targets and have been ultimately linked to Italian anarchists that support the ETA.

17 India

In Khiram, Kashmir, armed militants entered a private residence and killed the son of a Muslim politician, according to press reports. No one claimed responsibility.

17 India

In Shopian, Kashmir, a bomb exploded outside a store, wounding five persons, according to press reports. No one claimed responsibility.

18 France

In Yvelines, militants from the Corsican National Liberation Front (FLNC) detonated explosive charges during the early morning hours, seriously damaging two French villas and a British housing company, according to press reports. The houses were unoccupied, and nobody was injured in the attack.

20 India

In Srinagar, Kashmir, a bomb exploded at a crowded market, according to press reports, wounding 16. No one claimed responsibility.

20 India

In Charar-i-Sharif, Kashmir, militants hurled a grenade at a police station, wounding two officers, according to press reports. No one claimed responsibility.

20 West Bank

One was killed (a U.S. citizen) and three wounded in a shooting attack near the settlement of Ofra. HAMAS claimed responsibility.

23 India

In Pulwama, Kashmir, militants threw a grenade at a military vehicle, but missed the intended target, killing two and wounding 48 (all civilian bystanders), according to press reports. No one claimed responsibility.

26 Kenya

In Mandera, armed militants attacked aid workers using hand grenades, killing one and seriously wounding four (including a doctor from the Netherlands working with the organization Doctors Without Frontiers), according to press reports. No one claimed responsibility.

28 Gaza Strip

In Bayt Lahiyah, several bombs exploded near a U.S. Embassy car, according to press reports. The bombs were aimed at a diplomatic-plated vehicle belonging to the U.S. Consulate.

30 Israel

In Yabed, a truck came under fire. Victims included one killed (a Bulgarian construction worker), according to press reports. The al-Aqsa Martyrs Brigade claimed responsibility.

July

3 Iraq
In Baghdad, militants killed a British journalist outside the Iraq National Museum, according to press reports. No one claimed responsibility.

3 Colombia
In Caldono, armed militants kidnapped five people, including a Swiss citizen working for the non-governmental organization (NGO), Hands of Colombia Foundation, according to press reports. The Revolutionary Armed Forces of Colombia claimed responsibility.

4 India
In Larnu, Kashmir, militants opened fire and threw several grenades into a meeting between a rural development minister of Jammu Kashmir and health officials, killing two (a school teacher and a private citizen) and wounding 20 (including the two government officials, and two police officers), according to press reports. No one claimed responsibility.

9 India
In Aram Mohalla Shopian, Kashmir, militants threw a grenade toward a security patrol party. The grenade missed the intended target and exploded on the roadside, injuring three persons, according to press reports. No one claimed responsibility.

14 Afghanistan
In Jalalabad, in the early morning hours, a bomb exploded near the offices of the United Nations Human Rights Commission (UNHCR) causing major damage to both buildings, according to press reports. No one claimed responsibility.

21 India
In Jammu, Kashmir, two grenades exploded at a crowded community kitchen, killing seven and wounding 42, according to press reports. No one claimed responsibility.

23 India
In Katra, a bomb exploded near a Hindu temple, killing six persons and doing extensive damage to the temple, according to press reports. Lashkar-e-Tayyiba and the Students Islamic Movement of India are suspected.

August

2 Iraq
In Baghdad, a vehicle bomb exploded in front of the Jordanian Embassy, killing 19, wounding 50, and damaging the outside facade of the Embassy, according to press reports. No one claimed responsibility.

4 India
In Mahore Tehsil, Kashmir, armed militants shot and killed an educator attending a marriage function, according to press reports. No one claimed responsibility.

5 Indonesia
In Jakarta, Indonesia, a car bomb exploded in the front of the Marriott Hotel during lunchtime rush hour, killing 12 and wounding 149 (including two U.S. citizens), according to press reports. The adjoining office block was set on fire, with several cars burned in the hotel's front driveway, and windows in the hotel shattered to the height of 21 stories. Al-Qaida claimed responsibility.

5 Iraq
In Tikrit, an improvised explosive device detonated beneath a U.S. vehicle, killing one person, according to press reports. The U.S. citizen was a contractor with the firm Kellogg Brown and Root, a subsidiary of Halliburton. His vehicle was under military escort when the explosion occurred. No group has claimed responsibility.

5 India
in Katjidhok, Kashmir, armed militants shot and killed one person, according to press reports. No one claimed responsibility.

10 Eritrea
In Adobha, armed militants attacked a vehicle carrying Eritrean passengers working for the U.S. charity Mercy Corps, killing two and wounding one, according to press reports. No one claimed responsibility, though Eritrean authorities blamed Eritrean Islamic Jihad.

12 Israel
In Ariel, a suicide bomber at the entrance of a shopping mall detonated explosives, killing two and injuring ten, according to press reports. HAMAS claimed responsibility.

13 India
In Bandipora, Kashmir, a bomb attached to a bicycle exploded outside the State Bank of India, injuring 31, according to press reports. No one claimed responsibility.

15 India
In Pakherpora, Kashmir, a grenade thrown at a police patrol missed its target, exploding instead in a crowd of people standing nearby, injuring 18, according to press reports. No one claimed responsibility.

19 Israel
In Jerusalem, shortly after 9:00 pm, a suicide bomber riding on a bus detonated explosives attached to him, killing 20 (five U.S. citizens) and wounding 140, according to press report. HAMAS claimed responsibility.

19 Iraq
In Baghdad, a truck driving into the driveway of the Canal Hotel housing the headquarters of the United Nations was stopped by a security guard, then moved a few feet and exploded, killing 23 (three U.S. citizens and the UN Secretary General's Special Representative in Iraq) and wounding 100. It also badly damaged several stories of the Canal Hotel and other buildings almost a mile away, according to press reports. The arrested suspects stated the bomb was meant to go off in the hotel lobby, beneath a scheduled meeting of U.S. officials on the second floor.

25 India

In Mumbai, two bombs detonated near the Mumba Devi temple and the Gateway of India Historical monument, killing 40 and wounding 120, according to press reports. The Mumbai police commissioner reportedly suspects Lashkar-e-Tayyiba, but no group has claimed responsibility.

September

6 India

In Srinagar, Kashmir, a bomb exploded in a busy marketplace, killing six and wounding 37 (including an Indian army officer), according to press reports. Police believe the intended target of the blast was the army officer. No one claimed responsibility.

8 Spain

In Madrid, authorities safely defused a parcel bomb hidden in a book that was sent to the Greek Consulate, according to press reports. Authorities suspect an anarchist group is responsible.

9 Afghanistan

Near Moqor, armed militants killed four Danish members working for the Danish Committee for Aid to Afghan Refugees (DACAAR), a non-governmental organization (NGO) assisting local Afghanis on an irrigation project, according to press reports. The Taliban are probably responsible.

9 India

In Sopat, Kashmir, armed militants shot at a former State Forest minister, injuring him slightly and killing one security officer, according to press reports. No one claimed responsibility.

9 Israel

In Jerusalem, a suicide bomber blew himself up at the Café Hillel, killing seven (two U.S. citizens) and wounding 47, according to press reports. No one claimed responsibility.

11 India

In Srinagar, Kashmir, a grenade was thrown at a military bunker house, missing its target, killing one private citizen and injuring 14 others standing nearby, according to press reports. No one claimed responsibility.

14 Colombia

In Tayrona National Park, armed militants attacked several cabins in the national park, kidnapping eight foreign nationals (four Israelis, two Britons, one German, and one Spaniard), according to press reports. On 25 September 2003, one of the two kidnapped Britons escaped safely from the kidnappers. On 24 November 2003, the German and Spanish nationals were released. The National Liberation Army (ELN) has claimed responsibility for this attack.

15 Somalia
In the Gedo region of southwestern Somalia, a Kenyan aid worker was murdered by suspected Islamic militants, according to press reports. No one claimed responsibility.

19 Afghanistan
In Ghazni, four rockets were fired at a facility housing Turkish road workers and equipment, causing no injuries or damage, according to press reports. The Taliban are probably responsible.

22 Iraq
In Baghdad, a vehicle bomb exploded near the United Nations headquarters, killing a guard and injuring 18 others, according to press reports. No damage was done to the UN headquarters. No one claimed responsibility.

25 Iraq
In Baghdad, a bomb exploded at the news bureau of the U.S. NBC broadcast network, killing one person and injuring another, according to press reports. No one claimed responsibility.

30 India
In Gagran, Kashmir, a grenade thrown at a police patrol exploded, injuring six police officers and 14 civilians, according to press reports. No one claimed responsibility.

October

4 Israel
In Haifa, a suicide bomber blew himself up at the Maxim Restaurant, killing 20 persons and injuring 60 others, including a U.S. citizen. The Palestinian Islamic Jihad (PIJ) claimed responsibility.

5 Malaysia
In Sabah, armed militants kidnapped six persons from a resort area. One escaped, but on 29 October 2003, in Languyan, Philippines, the remaining five hostages (three Indonesians and two Filipinos) were found executed, according to press reports. No one claimed responsibility. The Abu Sayyaf Group is suspected of the kidnappings and executions.

5 Somalia
In Borama, armed militants shot and killed an elderly Italian nun, according to press reports. Two suspects were subsequently arrested.

9 Iraq
In Baghdad, armed militants shot and killed a Spanish military attaché at his private residence, according to press reports. No one claimed responsibility.

12 Iraq
In Baghdad, a vehicle bomb exploded near the Baghdad Hotel housing U.S. and Iraqi officials, killing eight persons and wounding 45 others, according to press reports. No one claimed responsibility.

14 Iraq
In Baghdad, a suicide car bomb detonated near the Turkish Embassy, wounding one Turkish and one Iraqi employee, according to press reports. No one claimed responsibility.

15 Gaza Strip
A U.S. Embassy Tel Aviv motorcade was struck by an apparent roadside charge, according to press reports. The blast destroyed the second car in the convoy, killing three and wounding one (all U.S. citizens). The victims were working for a contracting firm providing security for the United States in Israel and the Middle East. The Popular Resistance Committee initially claimed responsibility but later said it was not responsible.

15 India
In Lolab, Kashmir, rebels triggered a landmine in a forested area. Victims included nine wounded, according to press reports. No one claimed responsibility.

20 India
In Battamaloo, Kashmir, a grenade hurled at a police security patrol missed its target and exploded at a busy bus stop. Victims included one killed and 53 wounded, according to press reports. No one claimed responsibility.

20 India
In Anantnag, Kashmir, a grenade thrown at a security patrol missed its target and exploded in a busy market. Victims included one killed and seven wounded, according to press reports. No one claimed responsibility.

20 Somalia
In northern Somalia, two British teachers were shot and killed inside their residence on an SOS Children's Villages compound, according to press reports. Somaliland authorities, who suspected the involvement of Islamist militants, arrested several persons by year's end.

20 India
In Doda, Kashmir, armed militants shot and killed two persons, according to press reports. No one claimed responsibility.

26 Iraq
In Baghdad, rockets were fired at the al-Rashid Hotel, which was housing U.S. and Coalition personnel. One person was killed (a U.S. military officer) and 15 were wounded (including a U.S. citizen Department of State employee assigned to the Coalition Provisional Authority). The blast also damaged the hotel, according to press reports. No one claimed responsibility.

26 India
In Bijbehara, Kashmir, a grenade thrown at a military convoy missed its target and exploded on the road, injuring 14 persons (including one police officer and a worker in the office of the Indo-Tibetan border police), according to press reports. No one claimed responsibility.

26 India
In Samba, Kashmir, a bomb exploded in the toilet of a coach car, causing no injuries but derailing five cars, according to press reports. No one claimed responsibility.

26 India
In Gagal, Kashmir, armed militants dressed in army uniforms hijacked a car, killing two of the occupants and injuring four others, according to press reports. No one claimed responsibility.

27 Iraq
In Baghdad, a car bomb exploded inside the compound of the headquarters of the International Committee of the Red Cross (ICRC), killing 12 persons and injuring 22 others, according to press reports. No one claimed responsibility.

27 Afghanistan
In Shkin, armed militants ambushed and killed two U.S. government contract workers, according to press reports. No one claimed responsibility.

28 India
In Lal Chowk, Kashmir, a bomb exploded at the customer billing counter in a busy telegraph office building, injuring 36 persons, according to press reports. No one claimed responsibility.

29 India
In Anantnag, Kashmir, a grenade thrown at a police patrol missed its target and exploded in a busy market, injuring 13 persons, according to press reports. No one claimed responsibility.

30 Afghanistan
Between Moqor and Ghazni districts, armed militants kidnapped a Turkish engineer and his driver, threatening to kill them unless the Afghan government released six of its leaders, according to press reports. Following negotiations with the kidnappers, both were subsequently released. The Taliban are suspected.

November

8 Saudi Arabia
In Riyadh, a bomb attack on a residential compound killed 17 foreigners, mostly from Arab states, and injured 122 others, according to press reports. No one claimed responsibility.

10 Iraq
In Samarra, a remote-controlled bomb was detonated against a convoy, injuring three Fijians working for a British security firm, according to press reports. No one claimed responsibility.

11 Greece
In Athens, authorities neutralized an explosive device that was detected outside an Athens Citibank branch. An unidentified person phoned an Athens newspaper and announced that a bomb was going to explode at the bank, according to press reports. The Organization Khristos Kassimis was probably responsible.

11 Afghanistan
In Kandahar, a vehicle bomb exploded outside the office of the United Nations Assistance Mission in Afghanistan (UNAMA), killing one person, injuring one other, and causing

major damage to the building, according to press reports. The Taliban or al-Qaida may have been responsible.

12 Iraq
In al-Nasiriyah, two vehicles approached the Italian Carabinieri Corps' MSU (multinational specialized unit) command post. A white car with four persons inside preceded another, heavier vehicle carrying explosives. When the first vehicle passed in front of the Carabinieri base, diversionary shots were fired from the lead vehicle, while the second truck reached the target and exploded, resulting in the death of 19 Italians and 13 Iraqi civilians, according to media reports. At least 80 others were wounded in the attack. Abu-Muhammad Ablay later claimed responsibility on behalf of al-Qaida in an e-mail to the Saudi weekly *al-Majallah*.

14 India
In Pulwama, Kashmir, militants opened fire on a Christian school and on a bus from the same school, causing no injuries, according to press reports. No one claimed responsibility.

15 India
In Pulwama, Kashmir, a grenade thrown by militants at a Christian missionary school landed on the lawn and exploded, injuring nine (including two employees of the school and a police guard), according to press reports. No one has claimed responsibility.

15 Turkey
In Istanbul, a vehicle bomb exploded at the Beth Israel synagogue, killing four and wounding 60, according to press reports. Turkish authorities believe the same group is also responsible for the other incidents on November 15 and 20 in Istanbul. Turkish authorities have arrested some of the persons believed responsible for these attacks. Others remain at large.

15 Turkey
In Istanbul, a vehicle bomb exploded at the Neve Shalom synagogue, killing 16 and wounding 240, according to press reports. Many of the casualties were passersby. Turkish authorities believe the same group is also responsible for the other incidents on November 15 and 20 in Istanbul. Turkish authorities have arrested some of the persons believed responsible for these attacks. Others remain at large.

15 Colombia
In Bogota, two fragmentation grenades exploded in two crowded bars, the Bogota Beer Company and Palos De Moguer Bar, killing one person and injuring 72 others (including three U.S. citizens), according to press reports. The Revolutionary Armed Forces of Colombia (FARC) is suspected.

16 Afghanistan
In Ghazni, armed militants riding on a motorcycle shot and killed a French national working for the United Nations High Commissioner for Refugees and wounded her driver while they were driving through a local bazaar, according to press reports. No one claimed responsibility.

19 Israel
In Arava, a terrorist at the Arava border terminal shot and killed one and wounded four South American tourists, apparently from Ecuador. The terrorist was killed by authorities, according to press reports.

20 Turkey
In Istanbul, a vehicle loaded with explosives exploded in front of the British Consulate, killing 30 people, including the Consul General, and wounding 450 others, according to press reports. Turkish authorities believe the same group is also responsible for the other incidents on November 15 and 20 in Istanbul. Turkish authorities have arrested some of the persons believed responsible for these attacks. Others remain at large.

20 Turkey
In Istanbul, a vehicle bomb detonated outside the HSBC bank, killing 11 people, wounding 105 others, and causing significant damage to the building, according to press reports. Turkish authorities believe the same group is also responsible for the other incidents on November 15 and 20 in Istanbul. Turkish authorities have arrested some of the persons believed responsible for these attacks. Others remain at large.

21 Iraq
In Baghdad, at 7:20 AM, at least six rockets were fired at hotels where Western journalists and Coalition contractors were staying. The rockets hit the Palestine Hotel, heavily damaging at least five floors and slightly damaging the 16th and 18th floors of the Sheraton Hotel located next door. A U.S. contractor was wounded, according to press reports. A makeshift multiple rocket launcher with 30 unfired rockets in its tubes was found later close to the Italian Embassy. No group claimed responsibility.

22 Iraq
Over Baghdad, the wing of a DHL parcel service cargo plane caught on fire when it was struck by a SAM-7, man-portable surface-to-air missile, according to press reports. The plane managed to land safely. No one claimed responsibility.

23 Afghanistan
In Kabul, a rocket was fired at the Intercontinental Hotel, which was crowded with guests, including foreign diplomats, journalists, and UN aid workers. The attack caused no injuries and only minor damage, according to press reports. Though there was no claim of responsibility, authorities suspected remnants of Taliban and al-Qaida for the attack.

27 Algeria
In Messad, a well-known poet and member of the extended Royal Saudi family was killed and four others were injured in an apparent terrorist attack, according to press reports. No one claimed responsibility, but authorities suspected the Salafist Group for Call and Combat (GSPC) was responsible.

30 Iraq
In Tikrit, militants shot and killed two Japanese diplomats, according to press reports. An organization, believed to have been al-Qaida, said in statements issued in mid-October and mid-November that Japan and other countries helping the U.S. would be targeted.

30 Iraq

Near the city of Tikrit, armed militants shot and killed two South Koreans and wounded two others while they were riding in a car belonging to the former Iraqi president Saddam Hussein. The Koreans were working for South Korea's OMU Electric Company, which has a subcontract to a U.S. company building a power transmission line in Iraq. No one claimed responsibility.

December

2 India

In Kashmir, 18 policemen were injured when militants threw a grenade at the District police headquarters, according to press reports. No one claimed responsibility.

3 Afghanistan

In Kandahar, two Americans were injured when an attacker threw a grenade at their vehicle, according to press reports. No one claimed responsibility.

10 India

In Kashmir, one policeman and one civilian were killed and six others were wounded when two suspected terrorists threw grenades and opened fire at a bus stop, according to press reports. No one claimed responsibility.

12 Iraq

In Beyci, an armed group targeting a restaurant killed two Turkish truck drivers in an attack, according to press reports. No one claimed responsibility.

19 Iraq

Eyewitnesses said that three gunmen in a car opened fire on a UN building. There were no casualties, and no one claimed responsibility.

29 Iraq

In Baghdad, unidentified gunmen opened fire on a vehicle killing two Iraqi sentries and a British engineer in the Mahmudia neighborhood. No one claimed responsibility.

30 India

In Kashmir, a woman and 33 soldiers were injured and four were killed in an explosion targeting a bus carrying Indian troops. Hizbul-Mujahedin claimed responsibility.

31 Iraq

In Baghdad, a car bomb exploded outside Nabil Restaurant, killing eight people and wounding 35 others. According to press reports, the wounded included three *Los Angeles Times* reporters (all U.S. citizens) and three local employees. No one claimed responsibility.

2004

All data below comes directly from the National Counterterrorism Center's report entitled, "A Chronology of Significant Terrorist Incidents for 2004." Prior to 2004, the U.S. State Department established the criteria that defined "significant terrorist incidents" and compiled the annual statistics. With the establishment of the National Counterterrorism Center in 2004, this responsibility for this statutory reporting requirement was transferred from the State Department. Additionally, the criteria for inclusion of terrorist incidents were dramatically changed in 2004, resulting in a much greater number of terrorist incidents being included in the final report. The data below represent only a small sample of the 92-page report. The exclusion of any one incident should not be construed as a statement that that particular incident is not significant.

January

2 Colombia

Between Puerto Colon and San Miguel, 11 bombs exploded at different points along the Trans-Andean Pipeline, suspending Colombia's exports of petroleum. No group claimed responsibility, although local police blamed the Revolutionary Armed Forces of Colombia (FARC).

2 India

In Kashmir, at about 6:30 PM, two armed militants opened fire at a Jammu railway station, killing four Indian security personnel and wounding 17 civilians. This attack occurred one day before the Indian prime minister was to make his first visit to Pakistan in four years. No group claimed responsibility.

5 United Kingdom

In Manchester, England, anarchists sent a letter bomb to the office of Gary Titley, leader of the Labor Party's members of the European Parliament. The device burst into flames when Titley's secretary opened the package, and a fire spread throughout the office. There were no reported injuries. This was the sixth bomb sent from Italy to European Union officials throughout Western Europe. A group calling itself the Informal Anarchic Federation claimed responsibility.

14 Gaza Strip

A female Palestinian suicide bomber blew herself up at a major border crossing point between Israel and the Gaza Strip, killing four Israelis and wounding 10 others. HAMAS and the Al-Aqsa Martyrs Brigade claimed joint responsibility.

28 Iraq

In Baghdad, a car bomb exploded, killing four civilians, including one South African, and wounding 17 others, including four South Africans. The blast also caused damage to the Shahine Hotel and destroyed a police station. No group claimed responsibility.

29 Israel
In Jerusalem, a suicide bomber destroyed a bus near the Prime Minister's residence, killing 11 civilians, including one Ethiopian, and injuring 30 civilians. The Al-Aqsa Martyrs Brigade and HAMAS claimed joint responsibility.

February

1 Iraq
In Irbil, suicide bombers launched simultaneous attacks on the offices of the Kurdistan Democratic Party and the Patriotic Union on Kurdistan, killing 109 people and wounding 200 others. Among the dead were the region's deputy prime minister and a Turkish businessman. Ansar al-Sunna claimed responsibility.

6 Russia
In Moscow, at about 8:40 AM, a suicide bomber attacked a subway car that had just departed Avtozavodskaya Station, killing 41 people (2 Armenian, 1 Moldovan) and injuring 230 others. No group claimed responsibility, but it is widely believed that the Karachayev Djamaat was responsible.

20 Greece
In Thessaloniki, at 3:20 AM, a gas canister bomb exploded under a British diplomatic vehicle, causing a small fire that damaged the vehicle and another car parked nearby. A group calling itself the Indomitable Marxists claimed responsibility.

22 Israel
In Jerusalem, two Palestinian suicide bombers blew themselves up on a crowded bus, killing eight people and wounding 62 others. The Al-Aqsa Martyrs Brigade claimed responsibility.

March

2 Iraq
In Karbala, suicide bombers set off explosives as Shia Muslims were celebrating the Shia religious holiday, Ashura, killing 106 civilians, including 49 Iranians, and wounding 233 others. No group claimed responsibility, although Iraqi officials believe al Qa'ida terrorists were responsible for this attack and a near-simultaneous bombing in Baghdad. U.S. officials, however, point to Abu Mus'ab al-Zarqawi's Jama'at al-Tawhid wa'al-Jihad group.

2 Iraq
In Baghdad, three suicide bombers set off explosives at a shrine as Shia Muslims celebrated the Shia religious holiday, Ashura, killing 65 worshipers and wounding 320 others. No group claimed responsibility, but Iraqi officials believe al-Qa'ida terrorists were responsible for this attack and a near-simultaneous bombing in Karbala. U.S. officials, however, point to Abu Mus'ab al-Zarqawi's Jama'at al-Tawhid wa'al-Jihad group.

11 Spain
In Madrid, during the morning, 10 bombs exploded on the city's commuter transit system, killing 191 people and wounding approximately 1,900 others. The bombs, hidden in backpacks, were placed in stations and on trains along a single rail line. By the end of March, Spanish authorities had arrested over 20 people in connection with the attacks. On 3 April 2004, a key figure in the attacks blew himself up, along with six other suspects, in his apartment after police surrounded the building. The Abu Hafs al-Masri Brigades, on behalf of al-Qa'ida, and several other groups claimed responsibility, but Spanish authorities are investigating an al-Qa'ida affiliated network with transnational ties to Pakistan, Spain, Morocco, Algeria, Tunisia, and Syria, and possible links to the September 11, 2001 attacks in the United States.

14 Israel
In Ashdod Port, two suicide bombers launched near-simultaneous attacks inside a workshop and outside the port, killing 10 and wounding 18 others. HAMAS and the Al-Aqsa Martyrs Brigade claimed joint responsibility.

17 Iraq
In Baghdad, a car bomb exploded at the Mount Lebanon Hotel (Jabal Libnan Hotel), killing seven civilians, including one Briton, and wounding 35 others. The attack also caused significant damage to the hotel and surrounding homes, offices, shops, and cars. Although the hotel was known to be frequented by Westerners, U.S. officials believe that the hotel may not have been the target of the attack. No group claimed responsibility, although it is widely believed that either Abu Mus'ab al-Zarqawi's Jama'at al-Tawid wa'al-Jihad, al-Qa'ida, or Ansar al-Islam was responsible for the attack.

31 Iraq
In Fallujah, unidentified assailants ambushed a contractor convoy, killing four U.S. civilian contractors and setting them ablaze. The burned bodies of the four Americans were mutilated and dragged through the streets, and at least two bodies were hanged from a bridge over the Euphrates River. The contractors, employed by Blackwater Security Consulting of North Carolina, were providing security for food-delivery trucks headed to a U.S. military base at the time of the attack. The Brigades of Martyr Ahmed Yassim claimed responsibility.

April

9 Iraq
In Baghdad, militants kidnapped and later killed a U.S. businessman. An Islamist Web site broadcast a video, which showed the victim's decapitation and ended with the appearance of Abu Musab al-Zarqawi's signature and date 11 May 2004. Abu Mus'ab al-Zarqawi's Jama'at al-Tawhid wa'al-Jihad claimed responsibility.

21 Saudi Arabia
In Riyadh, a car bomb exploded at the Public Security Department, killing 5 people, including one Syrian child and wounding 148 other civilians. No group claimed responsibility, although it is widely believed that al-Qa'ida was responsible.

May

1 Saudi Arabia

In Yanbu, four gunmen attacked the offices of ABB Lummus, killing six civilians (2 American, 2 British, 1 Australian, 1 Italian) and wounding 19 policemen. The gunmen then attacked a Holiday Inn, a McDonald's restaurant, and various shops before throwing a pipe bomb at the International School in Yanbu. Al-Qa'ida claimed responsibility.

30 Saudi Arabia

In Al-Kobar, militants attacked two oil industry compounds, housing offices, and employee apartments, killing 22 civilians (1 American, 8 Indian, 3 Filipino, 2 Sri Lankan, 1 Swedish, 1 Italian, 1 British, 1 Egyptian, 1 South African) and wounding 25 Saudi civilians. Al-Qa'ida claimed responsibility.

June

4 Russia

In Samara, at about 1:50 PM, a bomb exploded at a busy section of a market near a rail line, killing at least 11 civilians (2 Armenians, 3 Vietnamese), and injuring 71 others. No group claimed responsibility, but officials detained Chechen separatists from Kazakhstan on 10 June 2004 in connection with the incident.

12 Saudi Arabia

In Riyadh, three militants shot and killed an American citizen, working for Advanced Electronics Company, as he parked his car in front of his villa. Al-Qa'ida claimed responsibility.

12 Saudi Arabia

In the evening, in Riyadh, attackers abducted an American contractor. On 19 June 2004, an Islamist Web site posted pictures of the victim's decapitated body, which was later found on a street in eastern Riyadh. The al-Qa'ida organization in the Arabian Peninsula claimed responsibility.

14 Iraq

In Al-Tahrir Square, near Al-Sa'dun Street, Baghdad, at 8:15 AM, a suicide car bomber detonated his explosives next to a convoy of General Electric contractors, killing 13 people (2 British; 1 French; 1 American; 1 Filipino) and wounding 60 others, including two Sudanese. Abu Mus'ab al-Zarqawi's Jama'at al-Tawid wa'al-Jihad claimed responsibility.

16 Afghanistan

Near Kunduz City, Kunduz Province, at about 9:35 A Man improvised explosive device exploded near a vehicle belonging to the German-run Provincial Reconstruction Team, killing four Afghans and wounding one other. No group claimed responsibility, but it is widely believed that al-Qa'ida was responsible.

17 Iraq

Unidentified assailants kidnapped a South Korean contractor and beheaded him on 22 June 2004. Abu Mus'ab al-Zarqawi's Jama'at al-Tawid wa'al-Jihad claimed responsibility.

20 Pakistan
In Chaman, Baluchistan Province, at about 10:15 PM, assailants destroyed an oil tanker belonging to Shell Pakistan Limited, a majority-owned subsidiary of Royal Dutch Shell, wounding three civilians and destroying two other tanker trucks parked in the area. The Taliban claimed responsibility.

July

4 Iraq
Unidentified assailants kidnapped a Filipino truck driver. The victim was later released on 22 July 2004, when President Gloria Arroyo started to pull Filipino troops out of Iraq. The Khaled Ibn al-Walid Brigade claimed responsibility.

30 Uzbekistan
In Tashkent, Uzbekistan, between 4:42 PM and 5:00 PM, a suicide bomber detonated his explosives at the U.S. Embassy, killing two Uzbek guards. The incident occurred a few days after Uzbek prosecutors began their case against 15 suspects accused of aiding and/or conducting a series of bomb attacks and shootings in late March. The Islamic Jihad Group of Uzbekistan claimed responsibility.

August

2 Iraq
Unidentified assailants kidnapped three Turkish truck drivers and later released footage of one being shot and killed. The other two Turkish truck drivers had been released by 4 August 2004 when their employers agreed to stop shipping goods into Iraq for the U.S. military. Abu Mus'ab al-Zarqawi's Jama'at al-Tawid wa'al-Jihad claimed responsibility.

10 Iraq
Unknown assailants kidnapped and decapitated an Egyptian national. Abu Mus'ab al-Zarqawi's Jama'at al-Tawid wa'al-Jihad claimed responsibility.

14 Iraq
In Mosul, armed assailants kidnapped two Turkish truck drivers. Police later discovered the bodies of the two victims and one unidentified man. Abu Mus'ab al-Zarqawi's Jama'at al-Tawid wa'al-Jihad claimed responsibility.

20 Iraq
Between Baghdad and Najaf, militants attacked a vehicle carrying an Italian journalist and killing his driver. On 26 August 2004, the journalist was executed. A group calling itself the Islamic Army in Iraq, the 1920 Brigade claimed responsibility.

21 Spain
In San Xenxo, a small bomb in a glass-recycling container exploded near a resort, injuring four people, including two Portuguese citizens. This was one of two attacks reported in northern Spain on this day, although this was the only attack to impact international assets. The Basque Fatherland and Liberty (ETA) claimed responsibility.

24 Russia
At 11:56 PM, a suicide bomber aboard a Sibir Airlines Tu-134 airplane traveling from Domodedovo airport in Moscow to Volgograd, detonated an explosive device in the lavatory, causing the plane to crash in the Tula region, near the village of Buchalki, Russia, killing 44 people, including one Israeli civilian. The Islambouli Brigades and the Riyad us-Saliehyn Martyrs' Brigade both claimed responsibility.

29 Afghanistan
In the Shari-i-Naw area of Kabul, an improvised explosive device exploded in front of a DynCorp facility, killing ten people (3 American, 3 Nepalese, 4 Afghan) and wounding 22 others (1 American, 2 Nepalese, 19 Afghan). The blast also destroyed several vehicles in the surrounding area and caused unspecified damage to the building. The Taliban claimed responsibility.

31 Russia
In Moscow, at night, a female suicide bomber blew herself up at the Rizhskaya subway stop, killing nine civilians and wounding more than fifty others, including a Georgian citizen. The Islambouli Brigades claimed responsibility.

September

1 Russia
In North Ossetia, Beslan, at 10:20 AM, 32 armed men and women seized School Number 1 on the first day of school taking over 1,300 people hostage for two days with little or no food or water. On 3 September 2004, an explosion inside the gymnasium where hostages were held sparked a fierce gun battle between the hostage takers and security forces. According to official figures, 331 people were killed, 172 of them children, though many believe the actual number of deaths was higher. More than 600 were injured. The Riyad us-Saliheyn Martyrs' Brigade claimed responsibility.

9 Indonesia
In Jakarta, Indonesia, at 10:15 AM, armed militants detonated a car bomb outside the Australian Embassy, killing 10 people, including nine Indonesians and wounding 182 others (4 Chinese, 1 Australian child). The car was packed with nearly 200 kilograms of explosives and caused significant damage to the embassy and nearby buildings. On 5 November 2004, Indonesian authorities captured four Jemaah Islamiya (JI) members in connection with the attack. JI claimed responsibility.

13 Iraq
Armed men loyal to Abu Mus'ab Al-Zarqawi abducted and beheaded a Turkish truck driver. The video of his death was broadcast on Abu Mus'ab Al-Zarqawi's Jama'at al-Tawhid wa'al-Jihad group's Web site.

15 Saudi Arabia
In Riyadh, two gunmen shot and killed a British contractor, who had been working for the Marconi Communications firm, in a shopping center parking lot. The al-Qa'ida Organization in the Arabian Peninsula claimed responsibility.

16 Iraq
In Mansour District, Baghdad, unknown assailants abducted two Americans and one British citizen. On 20 September 2004, the assailants beheaded the other American. The Briton was killed on 7 October 2004. Abu Mus'ab Al-Zarqawi's Jama'at al-Tawhid wa'al-Jihad claimed responsibility.

17 Venezuela
In Apure State, unidentified armed militants launched an attack along the Venezuela-Colombia border, killing five soldiers and one state oil company employee and wounding one soldier and one civilian. No group claimed responsibility, but Venezuelan authorities suspect either Colombian left-wing guerrillas or the United Self-Defense Forces of Colombia (AUC).

18 Iraq
In Yusufiye, unknown assailants kidnapped 10 Turkish construction employees from Visnan. In September 2004, the company began freezing operations in hope of saving the workers. On 10 October, the assailants released the 10 Turkish hostages. The Safist Brigades of Abu Bakr al-Siddiq claimed responsibility.

20 Afghanistan
In the province of Zabul, a group of men that included two Pakistanis and an Arab beheaded three Afghan soldiers who had been traveling out of uniform from the Naubahar District to the provincial capital of Qalat. The Taliban Jaish-e-Muslimeen claimed responsibility.

October

2 Iraq
Assailants released footage showing the executions of one Turkish and one Iraqi civilian. A group calling itself the Salafist Brigades of Abu Bakr al-Siddiq claimed responsibility.

7 Egypt
At the Moon Island and Baddiyah campsites, Ras al-Shitan, near Nuweiba, two car bombs exploded, killing two Israelis and wounding 12 other people, including seven Egyptians. This incident was part of a series of attacks that occurred on this day. Egyptian security service officials claimed that two Egyptians carried out the attacks and were still at large. Authorities arrested five other Egyptian citizens on 26 October 2004 in connection with the attacks. The Battalions of the Martyr Abdullah Azzam, Al-Qa'ida in the Levant and Egypt claimed responsibility.

7 Egypt
In Taba, Islamic assailants drove a car bomb into the lobby of the Hilton Hotel, detonating the explosives and killing 34 people (13 Israeli, 10 Egyptian, 2 Italian, 1 Russian, 1 American) and wounding 159 others (8 Russian, 2 Briton, 2 American). The hotel sustained major damage, including 10 collapsed floors. This incident was part of a series of attacks that occurred on this day. Egyptian authorities identified two militants, a Palestinian and an Egyptian, as the two perpetrators. On 26 October, authorities arrested five other Egyptian citizens in connection with the attacks. Tawhid Islamic Brigades; Jamaah al-Islamiya

organization (JI); and the Battalions of the Martyr Abdullah Azzam, Al-Qa'ida in the Levant and Egypt all claimed responsibility.

8 France
In Paris, at about 4:00 AM, a bomb exploded at the Indonesian Embassy, injuring 10 people and shattering windows in the embassy and nearby buildings. A group calling itself the French Armed Islamic Front claimed responsibility.

8 Iraq
Near Bayji, unknown assailants attacked a civilian fuel convoy with rocket-propelled grenades and automatic firearms, injuring one Turkish driver and destroying a fuel tanker. The attackers also kidnapped one other Turkish driver, who was later beheaded on 11 October 2004. Ansar al-Sunna claimed responsibility.

14 Iraq
In Baghdad, two bombs exploded at an outdoor shopping area and in a café in the Green Zone, killing four U.S. citizens and wounding 18 other people. Abu Mus'ab Al-Zarqawi's Jama'at al-Tawhid wa'al-Jihad claimed responsibility.

24 Iraq
In Baghdad, unknown assailants kidnapped a Japanese civilian. Authorities found the victim's beheaded body on 31 October 2004. Abu Mus'ab Al-Zarqawi's Tanzim Qa'idat al-Jihad fi Bilad al-Rafidayn (QJBR) (al-Qa'ida in Iraq) claimed responsibility.

28 Pakistan
In Islamabad, at about 9:25 PM, a bomb exploded at the Marriott Hotel, injuring eight people (1 American diplomat, 3 Italian, 4 Pakistani). The hotel lobby also suffered minor damage from the blast. Al-Qa'ida claimed responsibility.

30 Iraq
In Baghdad, unidentified attackers detonated a car bomb outside of the Dubai-based al-Arabiya television station, killing five civilians, wounding 14 others, and collapsing the first floor of the building. A group calling itself the Islamic Army in Iraq, the 1920 Revolution Brigades claimed responsibility.

November

1 Israel
At the Carmel Market in Tel Aviv, a suicide bomber detonated an explosive device, killing three civilians and injuring 30 others. The Popular Front for Liberation of Palestine (PFLP) claimed responsibility.

December

6 Saudi Arabia
In Jeddah, five attackers broke through the gate of the U.S. Consulate, threw explosives, and fired automatic weapons, killing five people (1 Filipino, 1 Sudanese, 1 Yemeni, 1 In-

dian, 1 Sri Lanken) and injuring nine others, including two Saudi Arabian National Guardsmen at the gate. The al-Qa'ida Organization in the Arabian Peninsula claimed responsibility.

12 Gaza Strip
Near Rafah, on the Gaza-Egypt border, attackers detonated half a ton of explosives in a tunnel under an Israeli checkpoint, killing five Israeli Defense Forces troops and wounding another six. The Fatah Hawsk and HAMAS claimed joint responsibility.

Acknowledgments

Foreword Copyright © 2002 by Barry R. McCaffrey.

Part I Defining the Threat

Chapter 1

Bruce Hoffman, INSIDE TERRORISM, 1998, pp. 13-44. Copyright © 1998 by Columbia University Press. Reprinted by permission.

Paul R. Pillar, TERRORISM AND U.S. FOREIGN POLICY, 2001, pp. 12-40, 237-240. Copyright © 2001 by Brookings Institution Press. Reprinted by permission.

Eqbal Amhad and David Barsamian, TERRORISM: THEIRS & OURS, 2001, pp. 7-9, 11-26. Copyright © 2001 by Seven Stories Press. Reprinted by permission.

Chapter 2

Martha Crenshaw, ORIGINS OF TERRORISM: PSYCHOLOGIES, IDEOLOGIES, THEOLOGIES, STATES OF MIND, Walter Reich, ed., 1998, pp. 7-24. Copyright © 1998 by Johns Hopkins University Press. Reprinted by permission.

Audrey Kurth Cronin, International Terrorism, vol. 27, no.3, Winter 2002/03, pp. 30-58. Copyright © 2002 by the President and Fellows of Harvard College and the Massachusetts Institute of Technology. Reprinted by permission.

Chapter 3

John Arguilla, David Ronfeldt, and Michele Zanini, COUNTERING THE NEW TERRORISM, 1999, pp. 39-72, 80-81. Copyright © 1999 by Rand Corporation, Santa Monica, CA. Reprinted by permission.

Rohan Guaranta, The Washington Quarterly, vol. 73, no. 3, Summer 2004, pp. 91-100. Copyright © 2004 by MIT Press Journals. Reprinted by permission.

Matthew Levitt, SAIS Review, vol. XXIV, no. 1, Winter-Spring 2004. Copyright © 2004 by Washington Institute. Reprinted by permission.

Chapter 4

Magnus Ranstorp, Journal of International Affairs, vol. 50, no. 1, Summer 1996, pp. 41-62. Copyright © 1996 by Journal of International Affairs. Reprinted by permission.

Mark Juergensmeyer, INSIDE TERRORIST ORGANIZATIONS, David C. Rapoport, ed., 1998, pp. 172-193. Copyright © 1998 by Taylor & Francis, Ltd. Reprinted by permission.

Mark Sedwick, Terrorism and Political Violence, vol. 16, no. 4, Winter 2004, pp. 795-817. Copyright © 2004 by Taylor & Francis - Philadelphia. Reprinted by permission.

Quintan Wiktorowicz, STUDIES IN CONFLICT & TERRORISM, 2005, pp. 75-97. Copyright © 2005 by Taylor & Francis Journals. Reprinted by permission.

Chapter 5

Richard K. Betts, Foreign Affairs, vol. 77, issue 1, January/February 1998. Copyright © 1998 by Foreign Affairs. Reprinted by permission.

Adam Dolnik, Montery Institute International Studies Report Prepared for the Defense Threat Reduction Agency, 2003. Copyright © 2003 by Adam Dolnik. Reprinted by permission.

Richard Pilch, THE BIOTERRORIST THREAT IN THE UNITED STATES, 2003. Copyright © 2003 by Richard Pilch. Reprinted by permission.

Chapter 6

Bruce Hoffman, Atlantic Monthly, vol. 291, no. 5, June 2003. Copyright © 2003 by Bruce Hoffman. Reprinted by permission.

Ami Pedahzur, Terrorism and Political Violence, vol. 16, no. 4, Winter 2004, pp. 841-844. Copyright © 2004 by Taylor & Francis Journals. Reprinted by permission.

Chris Dishman, STUDIES IN CONFLICT & TERRORISM, 2005, pp. 237-252. Copyright © 2005 by Taylor & Francis Journals. Reprinted by permission.

Part II Countering the Terrorist Threat

Chapter 7

Richard K. Betts, Political Science Quarterly, vol. 117, no. 1, 2002, pp. 19-36. Copyright © 2002 by The Academy of Political Science. Reprinted by permission.

Bruce Hoffman, Atlantic Monthly, vol. 289, no. 1, January 2002. Copyright © 2002 by Bruce Hoffman. Reprinted by permission.

Boaz Ganor, THE COUNTER-TERRORISM PUZZLE, A GUIDE FOR DECISION MAKERS, 2005, pp. 229-249. Copyright © 2005 by Transaction Publishers. Reprinted by permission.

Mark Basile, Studies in Conflict and Terrorism, vol. 27, 2004, pp. 169-185. Copyright © 2004 by Taylor & Francis - Philadelphia. Reprinted by permission.

Chapter 8

Barry R. Posen, International Security, Vol. 26, Issue 3, Winter 2001, pp. 39-55. Copyright © 2001 by the President and Fellows of Harvard College and the Massachusetts Institute of Technology. Reprinted by permission.

Paul Pillar, Washington Quarterly, summer 2004. Copyright © 2004 by the Center for Strategic and International Studies (CSIS) and the Massachusetts Institute of Technology. Reprinted by permission.

Steve Simon, The Washington Quarterly, Winter 2004-05, pp. 131-145. Copyright © 2004 by MIT Press Journals. Reprinted by permission.

Chapter 9

Martha Crenshaw, Studies in Conflict & Terrorism, vol. 24, 2001. Copyright © 2001 by Taylor & Francis - Philadelphia. Reprinted by permission.

Rob de Wijk, The Washington Quarterly, vol. 25, no. 1, Winter 2002, pp. 75-92. Copyright © 2001 by the Center for Strategic and International Studies (CSIS) and the Massachusetts Institute of Technology. Reprinted by permission. Reprinted by permission.

Richard H. Shultz Jr., Weekly Standard, January 26, 2004, pp. 25-33. Copyright © 2004 by Weekly Standard. Reprinted by permission.